A STUDY OF CRISIS

A STUDY OF CRISIS

MICHAEL BRECHER
AND
JONATHAN WILKENFELD

Ann Arbor
THE UNIVERSITY OF MICHIGAN PRESS

Copyright © by the University of Michigan 1997
All rights reserved
Published in the United States of America by
The University of Michigan Press
Manufactured in the United States of America
⊗ Printed on acid-free paper

2000   1999   1998   1997   4   3   2   1

A CIP catalog record for this book is available from the British Library.

Library of Congress Cataloging-in-Publication Data

Brecher, Michael.
     A study of crisis / Michael Brecher and Jonathan Wilkenfeld.
        p.   cm.
     Includes bibliographical references (p.   ) and index.
     ISBN 0-472-10806-9 (hardcover)
     1. World politics—20th century.   I. Wilkenfeld, Jonathan.   II. Title.
D443.B7135   1997
909.82—dc21   97-6067
                                                                           CIP

To Eva and Judy

For infinite encouragement, support, and patience through the years.

Contents

Figures

Tables

Preface and Acknowledgments

This book is the culmination of two decades of research on crisis, conflict, and war. At first, we planned a straightforward updating and revision of *Crises in the Twentieth Century* (1988).* But as so often happens, a continuing quest for knowledge, newly discovered sources, and suggestions by colleagues led us far afield. Many changes were introduced in scope, structure, and focus so that the initial version was transformed into a veritable new book.

First, the time span has been extended: whereas our earlier work covered the period 1929–79, this volume begins with cases in late 1918 and reaches to the end of 1994. The number of cases has grown substantially: from 278 to 412 international crises and from 627 to 895 foreign policy crises for individual states. Moreover, some cases were merged and others split, in light of new material.

There are changes, too, in the data set. New variables were constructed to tap hitherto-neglected dimensions (e.g., ethnicity). And many of the key variables (e.g., value threat, form of outcome) were checked and recoded as part of an ongoing attempt to achieve maximal clarity, rigor, and salience in the overall objectives of the inquiry.

Another basic change relates to the framework. While the earlier version examined crises at both the international (system) and state (actor) levels, this book applies the "Unified Model of Crisis," as set out in Michael Brecher's *Crises in World Politics: Theory and Reality* (1993). Thus Part I presents an integrated framework for the two levels of analysis. Part II specifies the combined methodology. And Part III offers comparable summaries of the cases, interweaving the flow of events from a system perspective and the behavior of the principal actors, along with the roles of the involved major power(s) and international organization(s).

Noteworthy, too, is the enlarged conceptual and substantive scope of this book. While crisis remains the primary focus, much greater attention is given to protracted conflicts. This is evident in the presentation of the cases in a format designed to make a large body of knowledge more user friendly and more relevant. All crises are classified into two types, instead of being presented in a simple chronological sequence: those that form part of a protracted conflict (PC)—60 percent of the cases—and those that are unrelated to a PC. The former are grouped into 31 protracted conflicts, some that have ended (e.g., East/West),

---

*For the full citation of all works noted in this book, see References and Sources, pp. 887–974.

others that are still unresolved (e.g., India/Pakistan). A brief background to a PC is followed by a summary of each case, in chronological sequence, providing a broader conflict perspective for the unfolding of related crises between the same adversaries. The other 40 percent of the crises are grouped by region (Africa, Americas, Asia, Europe, and Middle East) and are presented chronologically. A multiple cross-reference system in Part III and the Master Table (Table III.1), which contains information about the key dimensions of each of the 412 cases, will, hopefully, ease the reader's task.

This book also attempts to break fresh ground in the analysis of crisis, conflict, and war (Part IV). The innovation takes the form of an intensive inquiry into seven enduring topics/themes: polarity; geography; ethnicity; democracy; protracted conflict; violence; and third-party intervention—their roles and effects on the configuration of crises and conflicts. Most of these distinct analytical "cuts" are guided by models from which hypotheses are derived and tested against the voluminous evidence generated by the ICB (International Crisis Behavior) Project. The objectives of these analyses are twofold: theory construction, through a systematic and rigorous search for patterns of turmoil in the twentieth century; and an indirect contribution to world order, through the generation of knowledge to be communicated to policymakers and the attentive public alike about this pervasive phenomenon in the global system.

From the beginning of this long voyage of discovery we were convinced that no single path to knowledge is flawless or even adequate. Competing claims to the "correct" method always struck us as arrogant and counterproductive. We recognize that deductive logic is capable of generating models and hypotheses to guide systematic inquiry. We also believe that generalizations can be derived from inductive research, both from comparative case studies, usually a small N, and from aggregate data analysis through large N studies. In short, we try to demonstrate the merit and validity of multiple paths to knowledge.

One final reflection, on the structure of the conflict domain, is in order. When this inquiry began, in 1975, the state was still the hegemonic actor in the global system. Since then, the state-centric or Westphalian model of world politics has been increasingly challenged as no longer an accurate representation of reality (e.g., Keohane and Nye 1977; Rosenau 1990). Certainly, a plethora of nonstate actors have acquired high visibility—transnational, international, nongovernmental, intergovernmental, subnational. And nationalism, in the guise of ethnicity, has reemerged as a powerful force, especially in the domain of crisis, conflict, and war. We have taken note of this important development, both in the data set and in our analyses (e.g., the specification of nonstate actors as triggering entities, the section in Part IV on "Ethnicity").

At the same time, interstate turmoil has continued unabated in the post–Cold War years: from 1990 to 1994 there were 21 full-scale international crises (see the Master Table of ICB Crises, Table III.1). The most violent were the Gulf crisis-war of 1990–91 and the interstate and intrastate conflict that wreaked havoc in former Yugoslavia from 1991 to 1995. Moreover, other high-profile, non-violent crises in unresolved protracted conflicts contained a potential for grave regional and global instability, notably the Kashmir III–India/Pakistan Nuclear crisis of 1990 and the North Korea Nuclear Crisis in 1993–94. And in 1995-early 1996 there have been eight more international crises, of which one, between the People's Republic of China (PRC) and Taiwan, indicated that their protracted conflict continues to pose a threat to stability in East and Southeast Asia, with a potential fallout far beyond those regions.

In terms of the structure of the global system, it is noteworthy that, despite the assault on the state-centric paradigm, dozens of nationalities/ethnic groups continue to seek self-determination, more precisely, the right to create an independent state, with all of the rights to statehood that the global system confers on its members. In sum, while the state is no longer the virtually exclusive actor in terms of crisis, conflict, and war, it remains, in our judgment, the most important actor in world politics, certainly in the military-security and political-diplomatic issue-areas. Nor is this likely to change significantly in the coming decades.

Many scholars gave generously of their time and their knowledge as regional specialists, with much benefit to the ICB enterprise: Douglas Anglin, Alexandre de Barros, Luigi Bonanate, Thomas Bruneau, Naomi Ghazan, Karen Dawisha, Richard H. Dekmejian, Jorge I. Dominguez, Alan Dowty, Benjamin Geist, Galia Golan, Kjell Goldmann, Ehud Harari, Karl Jackson, Ellis Joffe, Nelson Kasfir, Paul Kattenburg, Edy Kaufman, Jacob Landau, Guy Pauker, Leo Rose, Martin Rudner, Amnon Sella, Yaacov Shimoni, Saadia Touval, Yaacov Y. I. Vertzberger, Robert Vogel, and George T. C. Yu.

In the preparation of this book, we have incurred many other debts. One is to a group of dedicated coders who, working under stress, meticulously gathered the data relating to the cases from 1918 to 1928, and from 1980 to 1994: Tod Hoffman, Eric Laferriere, Michael Lebrun, Ronit Lupu, Iris Margulies, Meirav Mishali, Mark Peranson, Joel Schleicher, Noam Shultz, Michael Vasko, and Sarah Vertzberger.

Another debt is to colleagues who read with care and made helpful comments on parts of a very large manuscript: Hemda Ben Yehuda-Agid, Mark A. Boyer, J. Joseph Hewitt, Patrick James, and two anonymous readers for the University of Michigan Press.

Ben Yehuda-Agid and Hewitt deserve special recognition for invaluable assistance on many aspects of this work: the former supervised the coding in Jerusalem, helped in the task of recoding key variables, and contributed thoughtful ideas on the structure of the book; the latter generated the data on power and power discrepancy for the cases in the 1920s, 1980s, and 1990s, helped to prepare the massive Master Table (Table III.1), and coauthored an earlier version of the "Democracy" section in Part IV.

Two institutions provided generous funding for the myriad of tasks associated with this book: the Social Sciences and Humanities Research Council of Canada, through a research grant to Michael Brecher, 1993–96, and the National Science Foundation, through research grants to Jonathan Wilkenfeld. The University of Maryland Computer Science Center provided extensive support throughout this project, and the General Research Board of the Graduate School provided key research support. Finally, Brecher is grateful for a one-term annual leave from McGill University, and Wilkenfeld is grateful for a one-semester leave from his duties as department chair in fall 1995 and for the support of the University of Maryland Institute for Advanced Computer Studies, where he was able to work in comparative peace during that period.

We are also indebted to several persons for their valuable technical services: Sarah Lemann and Cissy Abell for outstanding work on preparing the manuscript; Andrea Olson for rigorous copyediting; Glenda Pringle for the comprehensive name and subject indexes; and Charles T. Myers of the University of Michigan Press for supervising the splendid production of the work.

Michael Brecher   Jonathan Wilkenfeld
McGill University   University of Maryland

PART I. FRAMEWORK

Prologue

As the twentieth century draws to a close, it is timely to look back on an epoch of pervasive turmoil—two world wars, the end of the colonial era, and a large number of crises and conflicts. Notwithstanding the "long peace" between the two superpowers,[1] the post–World War II international system has been characterized by persistent violence in many regions.

The most frequent type of hostile interaction in global politics during the past century has been *interstate military-security crises,* the main focus of this volume.[2] Like its predecessors (Brecher and Wilkenfeld 1988, 1989; Wilkenfeld and Brecher 1988), this book builds upon insightful studies of great power images and behavior in one global crisis—1914;[3] the conflicts over Berlin and the Taiwan Strait;[4] decision making by the United States in several high-profile crises;[5] one type of crisis management—the practice of deterrence—by the same superpower;[6] and evidence of the promising state of the art.[7]

In the mid-1970s, however, there was still little systematic knowledge about crisis perceptions and the decision-making style of the USSR;[8] the myriad of twentieth-century crises in regions other than Europe;[9] crises experienced by weak states;[10] the role of alliance partners in crisis management; the immediate triggers of crises; crisis outcomes; and the consequences of crises for the power, status, behavior, and subsequent perceptions of participant states. Nor was there systematic work on protracted conflicts (enduring rivalries) or a widely shared theory of crisis.[11]

It was an awareness of these lacunae that led to the initiation of the International Crisis Behavior (ICB) Project in 1975. Underlying the project are three assumptions: first, that the destabilizing effects of crises, as of conflicts and wars, are dangerous to global security; second, that understanding the causes, evolution, actor behavior, outcomes, and consequences of crises is possible by systematic investigation; and third, that knowledge can facilitate the effective management of crises so as to minimize their adverse effects on world order.

The aim of the ICB Project is to shed light on a pervasive phenomenon of world politics. There are four specific objectives: the accumulation and dissemination of knowledge about interstate crises and protracted conflicts; the generation and testing of hypotheses about the effects of crisis-induced stress on coping and choice by decision makers; the discovery of patterns in key crisis dimensions—onset, actor behavior and crisis management, superpower activity, involvement by international organizations, and outcome; and the application of the lessons of history to the advancement of international peace and world order.

To attain these ends we undertook an inquiry into the sources, processes, and outcomes of all military-security crises since the end of World War I, within and outside protracted conflicts,[12] and across all continents, cultures, and political and economic systems in the contemporary era.[13] Its methods are both qualitative and quantitative: in-depth studies of perceptions and decisions by a single state; and studies in breadth of the 412 crises that plagued the international system from the end of World War I to the present, involving the participation of 895 individual states as crisis actors.

This book is both theory directed and policy directed. Its rationale goes beyond the goal of lessening the probability of violence. Many crises do not involve violence (see Part III and the Master Table [Table III.1]). In fact, one significant question is why some do—and some do not—escalate to military hostilities (see Part IV). Another relates to the types of situational change that lead to more intense violence. Some changes are induced or are accompanied by violence; others are not. Thus the focus of our research on crises and conflicts is not exclusively or primarily on violence. Rather, it is *change* in the international system, with crisis and protracted conflict serving as the analytical keys.

The links between crisis, conflict, and change are threefold. Crisis and conflict erupt from change in the environment. Crisis and conflict generate change in state behavior. And crisis and conflict often lead to change in an international system. These links draw attention to both system and actor levels of analysis (see the next section).

In the realm of theory, the data on crises and conflicts facilitate the testing of hypotheses and thereby contribute to the framing of generalizations about world politics. There are also policy benefits from a large-scale study: improved crisis management, control over escalation, and reliable crisis anticipation. If the data support propositions regarding crises and state behavior, we will acquire a reliable basis for projecting the profile of future crises. Moreover, an understanding of behavior under crisis-induced stress can assist in reducing the likelihood of resort to violence in crisis management.

Concepts

Our first task was to frame definitions of crisis at both micro- (actor) and macro- (system) levels that are valid and comprehensive. It was recognized that the definitions must differentiate the two levels of analysis, yet relate them to each other.

Foreign Policy Crisis

A *foreign policy crisis,* that is, a crisis for an individual state, is a situation with three necessary and sufficient conditions deriving from a change in the state's internal or external environment. All three are perceptions held by the highest level decision makers of the state actor concerned: a *threat to one or more basic values,* along with an awareness of *finite time for response* to the value threat, and a *heightened probability of involvement in military hostilities.*[14]

This view of crisis, which guided the aggregate and in-depth case studies at the actor level, concentrates on the perceptions and behavior of a single state.[15] Interaction among states, too, is explored, for crisis decisions are usually made in response to threatening physical and/or verbal acts by another state. Moreover, the catalyst to a foreign policy crisis may be a destabilizing event in the international system. Nevertheless, the state remains the central object of inquiry into foreign policy crises: how its decision makers perceive change; and how they choose in conditions of complexity and uncertainty and in the context of perceived escalating or de-escalating threat, time pressure, and probability of war.

Our definition builds upon a view of crisis for a state enunciated by Hermann (1969b:414): "A crisis is a situation that (1) threatens high-priority goals of the decision-making unit, (2) restricts the amount of time available for response before the decision is transformed, and (3) surprises the members of the decision-making unit by its occurrence. . . . Underlying the proposed definition is the hypothesis that if all three traits are present then the decision process will be substantially different than if only one or two of the characteristics appear."[16]

The definition of foreign policy crisis presented here differs from that of Hermann on five points: (1) the omission of "surprise" as a necessary condition; (2) the replacement of "short" time by "finite" time for response; (3) the recognition that a crisis may originate in the internal, as well as the external, environment of the crisis actor; (4) the concept of "basic values," rather than "high-priority goals," as the object of perceived threat; and (5) the addition of "higher-than-normal probability of involvement in military hostilities" (hereafter, war).

The most important change is the addition of heightened probability of war as a necessary condition of crisis.[17] This probability can range from virtually nil to near certainty. For a crisis to erupt, however, perception of war likelihood *need not be high.* Rather, it *must be qualitatively higher than the norm* in the specific adversarial relationship. This applies both to states for which the "normal" expectation of war is "high" and to those for which it is "low."

In sum, it is an *upward change* in perceived probability, from a "high" or "low" norm, that is necessary to trigger a foreign policy crisis. The term "heightened" is preferred to "high" because it encompasses all types of upward change, from "very low" to "low," "low" to "high," and "high" to "very high." What is crucial to the explanation of crisis outbreak is a *change in,* not the *level of,* probability. Finally, the probability of war clearly implies a perceived threat to values and time pressure, but the reverse does not always obtain. Thus, while the presence of all three perceptions is necessary, probability of war is the pivotal perceptual condition for the *eruption* of a foreign policy military-security crisis.[18]

The role of perceived probability of war is also evident in the Snyder-Diesing definition of crisis (1977:7): "The centerpiece of [the] definition is 'the perception of a dangerously high probability of war' by the governments involved. Just how high the perceived probability must be to qualify as a crisis is impossible to specify. . . . [It] must at least be high enough to evoke feelings of fear and tension to an uncomfortable degree." (See also Snyder 1972:217.)

While perceived probability of war is common to the Snyder-Diesing and Brecher-Wilkenfeld definitions of crisis, there are important differences. For Snyder-Diesing, crisis is an *interaction process;* we focus on both the *perceptions* and *behavior* of one state, a foreign policy crisis, and *disruptive interaction,* an international crisis. Second, they ignore the time component, though we share their view that crises need not be short; some last months, even a year or more. Third, our view of the violence condition is much broader, not solely *war* likelihood, but the perception of likely involvement in any *military hostilities.* And finally, for Snyder-Diesing (1977:7), "the term *probability of war* excludes war itself from the concept 'crisis' . . . ," whereas we have developed the concept of *intra-war crisis* (see the next section).

There are several spillover effects among the three elements of a foreign policy crisis. First, the more active and stronger the threat and the more basic the value(s) threatened, the higher will be the perceived probability of war. That, in turn, will lead to more intense stress. Second, the more active, the stronger, and the more basic the threatened value(s), the more limited will be the perceived time for response. Third, the more acute the time pressure, the higher will be the perceived probability of war and the more intense the perception of threat. The reverse relationship also holds: the higher the perceived probability of war, the more basic and intense will be the perceived value threat and the more limited will be the perceived time for response.

The linkages among the three components of a foreign policy crisis determine the extent of *stress* experienced by decision makers.[19] Stress begins with a higher-than-normal perception of value threat (pre-crisis period). It escalates with more intense threat and the addition of time pressure and anticipated military hostilities (crisis period). It ends with de-escalation toward "normal," that is, non-crisis, perceptions of threat, time pressure, and war likelihood (end-crisis period). (This process is elaborated in the Part I section, "Phases and Periods: The Unified Model.")

International Crisis

There are two defining conditions of an *international crisis:* (1) a change in type and/or an increase in intensity of *disruptive,* that is, hostile verbal or physical, *interactions* between two or more states, with a heightened probability of *military hostilities;* that, in turn, (2) destabilizes their relationship and *challenges* the *structure* of an international system—global, dominant, or subsystem. In terms of formal logic, these are **necessary and sufficient** conditions: that is, a crisis follows whenever they occur, and whenever a crisis erupts it must be preceded by them (X always leads to Y; and Y is always preceded by X). The likelihood that these conditions will exist is illuminated by system, interactor, actor, and situational attributes (e.g., structure and level, conflict setting and capability, regime type and territory, trigger and violence). As such, these are **enabling** variables, the **most likely** conditions in which an international crisis will erupt, escalate, de-escalate, or affect the adversaries and/or the system(s) of which they are members (Brecher 1993:29–42).[20]

An international crisis begins with a disruptive act or event, a *breakpoint (trigger),* that creates a foreign policy crisis for one or more states; for example, the Soviet-supported attempt by Iran's Tudeh party on 23 August 1945 to take over the Azerbaijan capital of Tabriz, the beginning of the Azerbaijan crisis; the crossing of the Thag La Ridge in the North East Frontier Agency by Chinese forces on 8 September 1962, setting in motion the China/India Border crisis-war; and the dispatch of Egypt's 4th Armored Division into Sinai on 17 May 1967, along with its overflight of Israel's nuclear center at Dimona the same day, leading to the June Six Day War.

An international crisis ends with an act or event that denotes a qualitative reduction in conflictual activity. In the cases noted earlier, crisis termination was marked by the following: the withdrawal of Soviet troops from Iran on 9 May 1946; the unilateral declaration of a cease-fire by China on 1 December 1962; and the end of the Six Day War on 11 June 1967.[21]

Crisis, Protracted Conflict, War

International crisis and international conflict are closely related but not synonymous. The focus of crisis is usually a single issue: a territorial dispute, an economic boycott, a threat to a political regime, etc. By contrast, *protracted conflict* has been defined as "hostile interactions which extend over long periods of time with sporadic outbreaks of open warfare fluctuating in frequency and intensity. . . . the stakes are very high. . . . they [protracted conflicts] linger on in time. . . . [They] are not specific events . . . , they are processes" (Azar et al., 1978:50).

All protracted conflicts are lengthy, some of them several decades or more. All have fluctuated in intensity: many have moved from war to partial accommodation and back to violence (e.g., India/Pakistan since 1947); others have been characterized by continuous war, but of varying severity (Vietnam 1964–75). All have aroused intense animosities, with spillover to a broad spectrum of issues. And conflict termination has yet to occur in many of them.

Even when an international crisis is very long, it can be distinguished from an international conflict, as with the Kashmir war in 1947–48, which was one of nine international crises during the India/Pakistan protracted conflict over many issues, tangible and intangible, since the end of British rule over the subcontinent.

Using a modified version of the Azar et al. definition—deleting violence as a necessary condition, because it did not accord with reality (Brecher 1984)—we have uncovered 31 protracted conflicts since the end of World War I: for example, at the global level, East/West; and, at the regional level, Ethiopia/Somalia (Africa), Ecuador/Peru (Americas), China/Japan (Asia), France/Germany (Europe), and Iraq/Iran (Middle East), among others. Many international crises in the twentieth century erupted within a protracted conflict (PC). Others occurred outside that setting; that is, they emerged in an environment without the prior condition of prolonged dispute over one or more issues and without the spillover effects of cumulative crises between the same adversaries. Operationally, for a conflict to qualify as a PC, there must be at least three international crises between the same pair of adversaries over one or more recurring issues during a period of at least five years.

This distinction in conflict setting provides the conceptual basis for the presentation of the 412 cases in Part III and for the guiding questions in the analysis of protracted conflicts and crises in Part IV. Are there differences in the configuration of crises that occur within and outside protracted conflicts and, if so, what are they? Specifically, how does the attribute of protractedness affect the crisis dimensions from onset to termination?[22]

Conceptually and empirically, crisis is also closely linked to *war.* Most international crises erupt in a nonwar setting. Some do not escalate to war (e.g., Berlin Blockade, 1948–49). Others begin in a nonwar setting and escalate to war later (Entry into World War II, 1939). And still others occur during a war, such as defeat in a major battle (Stalingrad in 1942–43) or the dropping of atomic bombs on Japan in 1945. These *intra-war crises* (IWCs) profoundly affected the decisions of German and Japanese leaders during World War II.

All of these types of international crisis manifest its necessary conditions, namely, a basic change in disruptive interactions and a likely outbreak of military hostilities (or an adverse change in the military balance), which undermine the relationship between the adversaries and pose a challenge to system stability. Moreover, the effects of the intra-war crises cited here were more significant than most non-IWCs for state behavior and the evolution of world politics. In sum, a crisis can erupt, persist, and end without violence, let alone war. Perceptions of harm and stress do not require war. Nor do they vanish with war. Rather, the occurrence of war at any point in the evolution of a crisis intensifies disruptive interaction, along with perceived harm and stress.

Since war does not eliminate or replace crisis, intra-war crises were integrated into the overall set of international crises from 1918 to 1994. At the same time, IWCs have one distinctive attribute, a war setting. Of the 412 international crises that comprise the ICB data set, 76 (18 percent) were IWCs. Thus they can

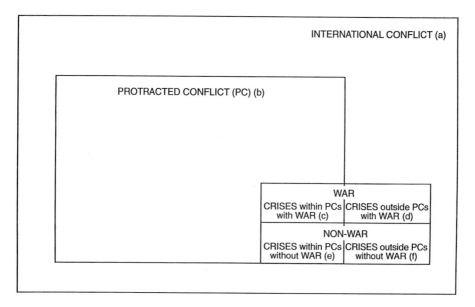

Figure I.1.   Conflict, Crisis, War

be separated from the nonwar cases and analyzed as a distinct subset of crises, as can other segments of a multifaceted data set: the geographic dimension of crises; a specific time/polarity frame, for example, crises in the post–World War II bipolar system; subsystem crises; superpower cases; etc. (In Part IV of this volume we will analyze several such subsets of ICB data.)

To conclude the discussion of core concepts, the relationships among crisis, protracted conflict, and war are presented in Figure I.1.

As evident, not all crises escalate to war. Some crises occur within, others outside, protracted conflicts. Some crises within and some outside protracted conflicts are accompanied by war. In the most general sense, all types of inter-state turmoil are encompassed in international conflict. In terms of conflict space, protracted conflict is the broadest phenomenon, followed by crisis and war. In fact, war is a subset of crises; that is, all wars result from crises, but not all crises lead to war.[23]

Actor-System Linkages

There are several levels of analysis in all branches of knowledge. Every level is capable of illuminating part of the whole, but no more. The challenge is to link the findings in order to comprehend as much as possible of knowledge in any field.[24] It is in this spirit that we approach the task of linking the actor or unit (micro-) and system (macro-) levels of crisis analysis.

At the unit level there are crisis actors, that is, states whose foreign pol-

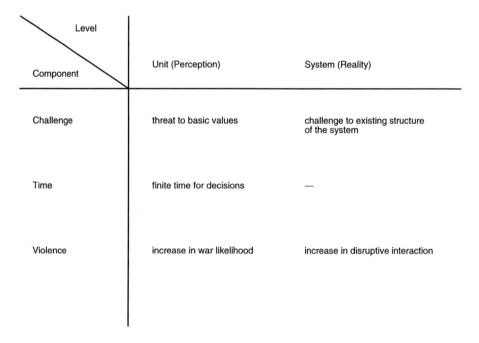

Level Component	Unit (Perception)	System (Reality)
Challenge	threat to basic values	challenge to existing structure of the system
Time	finite time for decisions	—
Violence	increase in war likelihood	increase in disruptive interaction

Figure I.2.   Unit- and System-Level Crisis Components

icy/national security decision makers perceive the three conditions of crisis. For threat at the unit level the system counterpart is challenge to the structure. Threat to basic values, such as existence, influence, territorial integrity, political regime survival, and economic welfare, guides decisions and actions of states. At the system level, stability is the core value. Threat at the actor level denotes (subjective) perceptions by decision makers. Challenge at the system level means an (objective) possibility of disruptive change in the structure. A challenge to the structure may or may not materialize, just as a threat to one or more basic values may or may not be realized (see Figure I.2).

In the 1948–49 Berlin Blockade crisis, the threat to Soviet and Western influence in Germany and, more generally, in Europe generated a sharp increase in conflictual interaction. This posed a challenge to the existing structure of the system, both to the number of Germanys and to the degree of polarization around the superpowers as a result of the crisis.

The link between unit- and system-level concepts of crisis can be further illustrated by two different cases: when a crisis is identical in time for all the actors; and when their foreign policy crises overlap but are not identical in time. Establishing this link requires the clarification of static and dynamic concepts at both levels. The former are trigger and termination at the unit level, breakpoint and endpoint at the system level. The dynamic concepts are escalation and de-escalation, distortion and accommodation (see Figure I.3).

Nature of Concept \ Level	Unit	System
Static	trigger/termination	breakpoint/endpoint
Dynamic	escalation/de-escalation	distortion/accommodation

At the unit level, a *trigger* is defined as the catalyst to a foreign policy crisis. In the Berlin Blockade case, the trigger to the Soviet Union's crisis was the publication by the Western powers on 7 June 1948 of the recommendation at their March London Conference to integrate the three Western zones of occupation into West Germany; the trigger for the U.S., the U.K., and France was the Soviet decision on 24 June to block all Western transportation into and out of Berlin. Viewed in terms of a dynamic process, a trigger denotes *escalation* in perceived threat, time pressure, and the likelihood of war.

Crisis *termination* at the actor level takes the form of exit points: it occurs when decision makers' perceptions of threat, time pressure, and war likelihood decline to the level that existed prior to the trigger. In the Berlin case, the termination date for each of the Four Powers was 12 May 1949, when an agreement regarding West and East Germany as separate political entities was signed. Thus, while the triggers did not coincide, the exit points, that is, termination dates, did. In dynamic terms, crisis termination for each actor marks the final *de-escalation* in perceived threat, time pressure, and war likelihood.

Parallel notions exist at the macrolevel—breakpoint and endpoint as counterparts of trigger and termination. A *breakpoint* is a systemic disturbance created by the entry of an actor into a crisis. An international crisis, as noted, erupts with an initial breakpoint event, such as the Western powers' challenge to Moscow on 7 June 1948 regarding the integration of their zones of occupation. In dynamic terms, this change denoted *distortion* in East/West interaction. Similarly, *endpoint* refers to a qualitative reduction in conflictual activity, such as the Four Power agreement on 12 May 1949 about the future of Germany and the lifting of

Distortion may be gradual or rapid; so too with accommodation. In general, international crises are characterized by gradual distortion, that is, several escalation points (entry points) over time, and rapid accommodation, one or few exit points. The reason is that an international crisis is usually a process in which actors cumulatively challenge one another. The result is that escalation points tend to differ in time, and, therefore, distortion is gradual. Accommodation, however, usually requires agreement. Thus actors tend to exit from an international crisis at the same time. Conceptually, termination of a foreign policy crisis for the last participant and the end of the international crisis are identical in time.

Trigger/breakpoint and termination/endpoint also indicate the entry into, or departure from, an international crisis. Each escalation point denotes an increase in conflictual interaction whereas exit points signal withdrawal of crisis actors and, therefore, accommodation. Linking the unit upward to the system level of analysis, the effects of trigger/termination on breakpoint/endpoint are immediate and direct; that is, a trigger at the actor level always denotes an escalation point at the system level and thus a further distortion in international interaction. In the Berlin case, both 7 June and 24 June 1948, triggers for the Soviet Union and the Western powers, respectively, were also escalation points in the international crisis. However, when international crisis is linked downward to actors, the effects of exit points on de-escalation are immediate and direct for some but may be delayed and indirect for others; that is, not all system-level changes affect all units (actors) simultaneously and equally. The Berlin Blockade crisis provides an example of direct and immediate effects: the last exit point—by all four actors— on 12 May 1949 denoted final de-escalation for the Four Powers and the end of the crisis.

In sum, an international crisis requires behavioral change by at least two adversarial actors leading to more intense conflictual interaction. Although a crisis is catalyzed by a behavioral act or an event, this act or event, the trigger to an actor-level crisis, can always be traced to its perceptual origin. Here lies the conceptual and empirical link between the two levels of crisis.

Phases and Periods: The Unified Model

Having defined the links between the two levels, we now specify them in more formal terms, via the Unified Model of Crisis (Unified Model, UMC). The Unified Model is a heuristic device to explain interstate crisis as a whole. The

PHASE	ONSET	ESCALATION	DE-ESCALATION	IMPACT
Interaction	incipient distortion	peak distortion	accommodation	non-crisis interaction
PERIOD	PRE-CRISIS	CRISIS	END-CRISIS	POST-CRISIS
Perception	higher-than-normal Value Threat (increasing stress)	acute Threat + finite Time Pressure + heightened Probability of War (maximal stress)	declining Threat, Time Pressure, Probability of War (decreasing stress)	below-crisis level of Threat, Time, War (non-crisis stress)

Figure I.4.   Toward a Unified Model of Crisis: Phases and Periods

theory of interstate crisis, as represented by the Unified Model, integrates the two levels. Separately, each captures a segment of complex reality. Together, they illuminate more of the whole. Specifically, cause-effect relationships at the international level require the analysis of images and behavior at the state level.

The Unified Model of Crisis is based upon the concept of four interrelated phases/periods: onset/pre-crisis, escalation/crisis, de-escalation/end-crisis, and impact/post-crisis. What do the phases and periods mean? How do they differ from each other? And what is the nature of their relationship?

The phases and periods of crisis, along with the linkages at international and state levels, are presented in Figure I.4.[26]

As evident, each phase of an international crisis has its counterpart at the state level, a period in a foreign policy crisis. The essential traits of the former are interaction and distortion, of the latter, perception and stress. In terms of sequence, phases and periods are inextricably linked in time; that is, escalation must be preceded by onset, the crisis period follows the pre-crisis period, etc. However, phases and periods may diverge in another sense; that is, the corresponding phase and period do not necessarily begin or end at the identical time.

Phase-change from onset to escalation, for example, occurs when at least one crisis actor experiences a change from pre-crisis to crisis period; but not all actors need undergo that change simultaneously. In fact, the evidence indicates that, in most interstate crises, actors made the "step-level" jump from pre-crisis to crisis period at different points in time, in response to different triggers to escalation.

A notable example was the Cuban Missile crisis: the U.S.'s crisis period and, with it, the escalation phase were triggered on 16 October 1962, when the CIA presented to President Kennedy photographic evidence of the presence of Soviet offensive missiles in Cuba. However, the USSR and Cuba continued to perceive low threat, no time pressure, and no or low probability of war until six days later. The catalyst for their step-level change from pre-crisis to crisis period was the official announcement of a U.S. "quarantine" against all ships en route to Cuba. The crisis period for both the U.S. and the USSR, and the escalation phase of the Cuban Missile crisis, came to an end with their semiformal agreement on 28 October; and, with it, the international crisis entered its de-escalation phase. However, Cuba, the third crisis actor, continued at the high stress level of the crisis period until 20 November when it yielded to joint superpower and UN pressure and agreed to the removal of the Soviet IL-28 bombers from the island. With that act, marking Cuba's exit from the crisis, the Cuban Missile crisis ended for all three actors; that is, de-escalation gave way to stable equilibrium between the two superpowers.

What we seek to explain about each of the four phases can be stated in dichotomous terms: for onset, the eruption or noneruption of a crisis; for escalation, whether or not it leads to military hostilities; for de-escalation, whether or not it terminates in some form of voluntary agreement, formal, semiformal, or tacit; and for impact, the reduction or increase in tension between the adversaries, and change or no change—in one or more state actors and/or their regimes, the balance of power, the alliance configuration, and the rules of behavior—in the relevant international system. In short, we seek to uncover the conditions in which an interstate crisis is most likely to break out, to escalate, to wind down, and to effect change.

Onset identifies the initial phase of an international crisis. Conceptually, it begins with the *pre-crisis period* of the first actor, in which the non-crisis norm of no (or low) perceived value threat gives way to low (or higher, that is, increasing) threat from an adversary and, with it, low (or higher, that is, increasing) stress. Onset/pre-crisis does not refer to *any* hostile interaction or threat perception, for conflict and stress are pervasive in a global system of fragmented authority and unequal distribution of power and resources. Rather, it is characterized by a change in the intensity of disruption between two or more states and in threat perception by at least one of them, for example, a statement by A threatening to attack B unless it complies with some demand from A.

Operationally, onset is indicated by the *outbreak* of a crisis, that is, the eruption of higher-than-normal disruptive interaction. The onset of an international crisis requires at least two adversaries, one or both of which perceive higher-than-normal value threat and respond in a manner that generates heightened disruption. As such, an interstate crisis erupts as a foreign policy crisis for a state through one of three kinds of trigger: a hostile act by state A, a disruptive event, or an environmental change. The catalyst may be internal or external.[27] In order for B to experience a crisis, however, the catalyst must be perceived by B's decision makers as a source of higher-than-normal value threat. That perception, in turn, generates modest stress, indicating the beginning of B's pre-crisis period. However, the change is not yet an international crisis. Thus the outbreak of a foreign policy crisis is a prerequisite to, but not synonymous with, the onset phase.

Whether or not B's pre-crisis period will set an international crisis in motion depends on its decision makers' (henceforth B's) perception and response. If B ignores A's trigger or the adverse event or change as posing a marginal or transitory threat—and does nothing—B's incipient foreign policy crisis will be aborted, and an international crisis will not ensue.[28] More often than not, B will perceive a trigger as seriously threatening and will respond, in accordance with the dictates of a universally shared security dilemma (Herz 1950) that arises from the underlying anarchy of the interstate system (Carr 1939; Morgenthau 1948; Waltz 1979; Gilpin 1981; Mearsheimer 1990). B's preliminary response may be a verbal, political, economic, non-violent military, or violent act; or it may take the form of a multiple response. Whatever B's response, other than "do nothing" or compliance, it will generate a reciprocal perception of threat by A's decision makers and, with it, A's pre-crisis period. If A responds, more-than-normal hostile interaction between A and B would follow. That, in turn, would transform a pre-crisis period into the onset phase of an international crisis, characterized by incipient distortion. Considerable time—days or weeks—may elapse between pre-crisis and hostile interaction (e.g., the pre-crisis period for Kuwait started on 17 July 1990 as a result of Saddam Hussein's verbal threat; but hostile interaction—the outbreak of the Gulf international crisis—began on 1 August with Iraq's military invasion and conquest of Kuwait).

A pattern of behavior is associated with the onset phase. In response to a perceived opportunity or a perceived threat from an external or internal source, A triggers a perception of low value threat by B, generating low stress. B's decision makers cope with modest threat and stress through several crisis management mechanisms, notably a preliminary probe of each other's intention, capability, and resolve, to test what Ellsberg termed their "critical risk" (Snyder and Diesing 1977:50, 198–207). The parties may negotiate, formally or informally. They may accept mediation by an international organization or a mutually trusted state. They will try to enlist support from one or more major powers[29]—economic aid, diplomatic pressure on the adversary, and/or pledges of military assistance. Where alliance commitments exist, these will be invoked. In their absence a crisis actor may attempt to forge a coalition. It may seek legitimacy for its intended course of action by attempting to enlist the involvement of the global and/or regional organizations, usually in the form of statements or resolutions supporting its cause.

For the same reasons—low value threat, unawareness of time constraint, and the perception of war as unlikely—decision makers will rely on bureaucrats to process information, essentially as in a non-crisis period.[30] Consultation and decision making, too, are likely to follow the non-crisis norm. Because the cost of erroneous decisions is small in the onset phase/pre-crisis period, decision makers often will not seek fresh options on how to respond to the challenge. Alternatives will be assessed by the non-crisis decisional forum. Choice takes the form of one or more decisions designed to meet the perceived threat. Time is irrelevant. And military hostilities are viewed as remote. In general, the decision-making process will be unhurried and largely free from stress. The same coping pattern characterizes state A, once it responds to B's trigger.[31]

The key to the first phase-change, from onset to escalation, is a new constellation of system, interactor, and/or actor attributes that generates for at least one of the adversaries an image of more acute value threat, along with an awareness of time pressure and an expectation of war before the disruptive challenge is overcome. For example, in the Berlin Blockade crisis, the severance by the Soviet Military Command of all land communications between West Berlin and the three Western occupation zones in Germany on 24 June 1948 transformed the low-intensity pattern of East/West hostile interaction and generated a high risk of force. With that type of fundamental change, one or more actors—in the Berlin case, all three Western powers—experience a higher level of stress, denoting a change from pre-crisis to the crisis period. And the international crisis experiences a step-level jump, that is, from onset to escalation. The *escalation* phase and *crisis* period mark peak distortion and maximal stress, respectively. Escalation may be characterized by a change from *no violence* to *violence;* or the entire crisis may be non-violent (e.g., Berlin Blockade, 1948–49). As in the onset phase, hostile interaction is not constant; that is, there may be *escalation points* within the escalation phase. If non-violence prevails, a military buildup may occur through sharp increases (e.g., Prague Spring, 1968). If hostilities have begun, the buildup will become more intense (e.g., China/India Border, 1962). In short, stress and disruptive interaction, while higher than in pre-crisis/onset, may fluctuate as well during the crisis period and escalation phase.[32]

Escalation begins with a process replicating the move from pre-crisis period to onset phase. The catalyst may be a verbal, political, economic, non-violent military, or violent act. Or it may be a disruptive event or environmental change. The target may comply with the initiator's demand, in which case the crisis will terminate abruptly in victory/defeat. This is a rare response because of *raison d'état.* More likely, the target will perceive the trigger to escalation as communicating a step-level change in hostility and respond accordingly. The combination of A's trigger and B's response, or vice versa, completes the initial jump from onset/pre-crisis to escalation/crisis.

The Unified Model postulates a different pattern of *coping* in the crisis period. The number of important decisions is likely to be larger than in the pre-crisis period, due to higher stakes, emergent time salience, and greater expectation of war. Actors will continue to seek to uncover each other's intention, capability, and resolve, that is, to assess their critical risk. But the emphasis will shift: to the adversary's disposition to use violence or diplomacy (or both); to relative military capability; and to the likelihood that the adversary will stand fast, rather than compromise or yield. More important, the search for options will be much more intense because of the higher stress.

Crisis management will be more elaborate generally. Actors will search more intensely for information and process it quickly, at the highest level. Senior decision makers will become more directly involved. They will broaden the scope of consultation and possibly include competing elites in order to enhance national unity (e.g., Israel in the October–Yom Kippur crisis-war, 1973–74). They may create an ad hoc decisional forum in order to expedite the decision-making process. And because basic values are under threat, they will embark upon a more careful search for, and consideration of, alternatives to manage the crisis. Time becomes highly salient; thus decision makers will be more concerned with the present than the long-term future. Military hostilities will be viewed as increasingly probable. Stress will be high. Choice is more likely to be novel, to deal with a more serious threat. Crisis actors will also seek support from one or more major powers, other states, and international organizations (e.g., Zambia, in Rhodesia UDI, 1965–66). Moreover, because the stakes are higher and the risks greater, actors are more likely to adopt a strategy of coercive diplomacy as the basis for crisis bargaining.

What produces the next phase-change in an interstate crisis? According to the Unified Model, as long as behavior by the adversaries sustains the high level of mistrust, hostility, disruptive interaction, and stress, or as long as cost-benefit assessments remain unchanged, the escalation phase will persist. However, eventually, an act or event will indicate a willingness to accommodate (e.g., the cessation of hostilities and the second cease-fire between Egypt and Israel on 26 October 1973 marked the start of de-escalation in the October–Yom Kippur crisis-war, 1973–74). This portends another phase-change, from escalation to de-escalation. It is preceded, at the actor level, by a shift from crisis period to end-crisis period, with a lessening of overt hostility.

De-escalation denotes the "winding-down" of a crisis. At the macrolevel it is manifested in a reduction of hostile interactions leading to accommodation and crisis termination (e.g., the Berlin Blockade crisis ended with the Four Power Accord of 5 May 1949, formalized a week later, that removed all restrictions imposed by the USSR on access to West Berlin, in exchange for a meeting of the Council of Foreign Ministers to "consider" the future of Germany). At the actor level, de-escalation is expressed in a decline in perceived threat, time pressure, and war likelihood toward the non-crisis norm. As such, the *end-crisis* period is characterized by decreasing stress for the decision maker(s).

Several scenarios of de-escalation are evident in twentieth-century interstate crises. This phase may begin *force majeure,* that is, when one actor achieves a decisive military victory and imposes the conditions of crisis termination (e.g., the USSR's military occupation, in the 1968 Prague Spring crisis). At the other extreme, de-escalation may occur with a mutual signaling of a wish to terminate a crisis. Such a calculus may occur before military hostilities have erupted (e.g., Berlin Blockade, 1948–49) or during a war (e.g., October–Yom Kippur, 1973–74), with a coincidence of perceptions that continuing the war will increase one's losses, whereas accommodation (cooperation) will increase one's gains. If the adversaries arrive at this assessment simultaneously, phase-change will occur abruptly and is likely to be of brief duration. The awareness that military victory is impossible or too costly relative to the anticipated gains rarely is simultaneous, in which case a bargaining process will ensue. Its duration will depend upon the parties' assumptions concerning the military balance before or during a war.

There are other scenarios for phase-change from escalation to de-escalation. In all of them, at least one crisis actor must perceive a decline in value threat and/or time pressure and/or war likelihood. That perceptual shift marks the beginning of a "crisis downswing" toward the non-crisis norm.

The volume of disruptive interaction is expected to decline in the de-escalation phase, as will the intensity of perceived harm on the part of crisis actors. As a result, the decision makers' stress level will decline. And behavior will be affected. Because of the downward spiral, coping will differ in the end-crisis period. Adversaries will continue to engage in bargaining, with threats, promises, and the inducement of future benefits to accrue from a less harsh outcome. The search for information about the adversary's "critical risk" is now expendable. Information processing is expected to revert to the pre-crisis norm, with bureaucrats playing the main role. Consultation and the decisional forum will likewise revert to the pre-crisis norm. The focus shifts to accommodation; and adversaries seek to involve global/regional IOs in facilitating an agreement.[33]

The end of an interstate crisis does not mark the termination of its role in world politics. Crises have multiple effects—on the actors, on their relations, and on one or more international systems. These are captured by the concept of *impact.* In temporal terms, impact designates the phase after the crisis, that is, its aftermath, the counterpart of *post-crisis* at the actor level of analysis. Moreover, following normal usage, it identifies the consequences of a crisis. Impact means the extent of change in both adversarial relations and the core elements of a system. The focus, in this domain, is the "fallout" or legacy of crises.

Impact differs from the other three phases in several respects. Its time frame is arbitrary. It has no coping dimension. It is less precise than the other phases; that is, the empirical traces of impact/post-crisis are more difficult to discover than the evidence of a crisis proper. Nevertheless, its boundaries and content can be measured in terms of the extent of change in: actors/regimes, power distribution, alliance configuration, and in rules of the game, formally or informally.

In sum, the impact phase is an integral part of crisis viewed holistically. Moreover, it provides the dynamic link between a specific, time- and space-bound disruption, an interstate crisis, and global politics writ large. Without impact, the dynamism of the Unified Model of Crisis is confined to the perception-decision-behavior-interaction flow from phase to phase and period to period, within an interstate crisis, per se. Impact traces the feedback from a crisis to the system, interactor, and actor attributes of the larger environment from which the crisis originated. As such, it links crises to the array of events, acts, and changes that, together, constitute the flow of world politics.

Research Design

Now that the concepts, system-actor linkages, and phases-periods have been delineated, we present the research design for our inquiry into interstate crises.

The aggregate study has two distinguishing characteristics. It is *cross-national* in scope and *quantitative* in form. Two types of analyses probe the cross-national data set. One explores the distributions of crisis attributes over time, such as triggers/breakpoints, the gravity of value threat, crisis management techniques, the severity and centrality of violence, and crisis outcomes. The other focuses on the international system at the time of a crisis, the extent of major power activity, international organization involvement, and similar systemic variables.

The quantitative form of the aggregate data set permits the use of statistical techniques to test propositions, in an effort to explain various aspects of the phenomenon of crisis. (The methodology used to construct the data set is elaborated in Part II.)

Although the ultimate decision was arrived at in stages, a fundamental determination was made to span the entire twentieth century from the end of World War I onward. Several considerations shaped this choice.

First, a data set encompassing the twentieth century since the end of World War I maximizes the bases for comparison: crises in multipolar, bipolar, polycentric, and unipolar international systems with diverse global and regional organizations. For the period under inquiry, every international crisis falls within one of the following system-periods of polarity: multipolar—1918–39; World War II—1939–45; bipolar—1945–62; polycentric—1963–89; unipolar—1990–94.

Second, by incorporating the 135 new states emerging from the end of the European imperial era, we achieve great variation in such actor attributes as age, size of territory, population, regime type, regime duration, belief system, economic development, and so forth. Third, we can explore the crisis-laden years of Germany's reascent to major power status and the approach of World War II, 1933–39, as well as the profusion of crises in Africa since the mid-1970s. Finally, the reliability of our findings from aggregate data analysis is enhanced by a relatively large number of cases.[34]

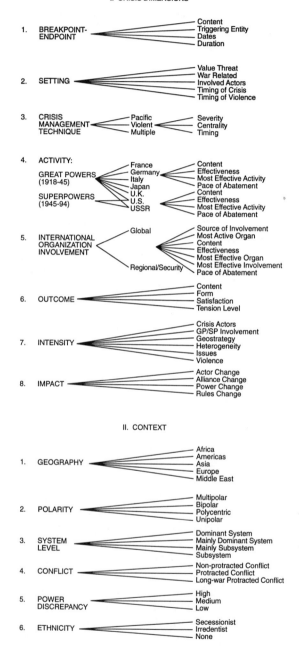

Figure I.5.   Conceptual Map: Macro Level

Data have been collected on four sets of variables, two at the state (micro-) level, two at the international (macro-) level. Data on the first relate to the foreign policy crisis for each crisis actor, that is, every state whose decision makers perceive for themselves the conditions of threat, time, and war likelihood. Data on the second relate to the international crisis as a whole. Guided by a two-level Conceptual Map (see Figures I.5 and I.6) two codebooks were designed to tap the myriad of data. Research on 85 actor-level attributes and on 67 system-level attributes yielded comparable data on 895 foreign policy crises and 412 international crises in the period end of 1918–end of 1994. (The codebooks and data are discussed in Part II.)

All the variables were incorporated into the two-level Conceptual Map (see Figures I.5 and I.6).

At the system (macro-) level, there are eight clusters of Crisis Dimensions: Breakpoint-Endpoint, Setting, Crisis Management Technique, Major Power Activity, International Organization Involvement, Outcome, Intensity, Impact. Each cluster contains one or more specific variables, as indicated in the map. From these variables we inferred a set of macrolevel questions that guided our research. These will now be elucidated.

Breakpoint-Endpoint
Content: What was the specific event(s), act(s), or situational change(s) that catalyzed disruptive interactions by generating the three perceptual conditions of crisis for the first crisis actor in the international crisis?

Triggering entity: Which state(s) or nonstate actor(s) triggered an interstate crisis?

Dates: When did the crisis erupt? When did the international crisis end?

Duration: How long did the international crisis last?

Setting
Value threat: What was the most salient value threatened during the international crisis?

Timing of crisis: Did a crisis occur during a war (IWC), or did it erupt in a nonwar context?

Involved actors: How many states were involved in an international crisis?

Crisis Management Technique (CMT)
Content: What was the primary CMT for the crisis as a whole?

Severity of violence: Did violence occur as a crisis management technique?

Centrality of violence: If violence occurred in crisis management, how central was it to the achievement of foreign policy objectives?

Timing of violence: When did violence occur (if at all)?

Major Power Activity

Content: What was the substance of major power activity in the international crisis?

Effectiveness: How effective was major power activity in preventing hostilities or contributing to crisis termination; or did it escalate the crisis? If positive, which activity was most effective in crisis abatement? Did major power activity affect the rapidity of de-escalation?

International Organization (IO) Involvement[35]

Source: Who initiated intervention by the global or regional organization?

Most active organ: If an international organization was involved in crisis management, which organ was the most active?

Content: What was the most salient IO role in the crisis?

Effectiveness: How effective was IO involvement in abating the crisis; or did it escalate the crisis? What was the most effective type of IO involvement? Did IO involvement affect the rapidity of crisis abatement?[36]

Outcome

Content: What was the outcome of the crisis as a whole?

Form: What was the form of crisis outcome?

Satisfaction: Were the adversaries satisfied or dissatisfied with the crisis outcome?

Effect: Did the crisis outcome lead to more or less tension between the adversaries?

Intensity

How intense was the crisis, in terms of the following indicators.

Number of actors: How many states were direct participants in the crisis?

Major power involvement: What was the extent of major power activity?

Geostrategic salience: How broad was the relevance of the crisis?

Heterogeneity: What was the extent of heterogeneity between the adversaries?

Issues: Which issue(s) and issue-area(s) were the focus of contention in the crisis?

Violence: What was the extent of violence in the crisis?

Impact

What was the impact of the crisis, in terms of the following indicators.

Actor change: What were the effects on the participants?

Alliance change: What were the effects on the pattern of alliances?

Power change: What were the effects on the relative power of the adversaries and on their ranking in the power hierarchy?

Rules change: What were the effects on rules of the game?

(The data on these eight macrolevel Crisis Dimensions can be examined through six Contextual Variables—Geography, Polarity, System Level, Conflict, Power Discrepancy, and Ethnicity [see the "Contextual Variables" section pp. 23–30]).

The second part of our aggregate data analysis was guided by the unit- or actor- (micro-) level Conceptual Map (Figure I.6).

There are five clusters of Crisis Dimensions at the actor level: Trigger, Actor Behavior, Major Power Activity, International Organization Involvement, and Outcome. As with the system level, a set of questions was inferred from the Conceptual Map to guide the actor-level research.

Trigger
Content: What act, event or situational change generated crisis perceptions by decision makers?
Date: What was the date of the crisis trigger?
Triggering entity: Which state(s) or nonstate actor(s) triggered the crisis?
Source: What was the perceived source of threat?

Actor Behavior
Decision making: What was the size of the decision-making group? Was it an institutional or ad hoc unit? What was the highest level of communications with its adversary?
Major response: What was the crisis actor's major response? What was the date of its response? How long was the time span from trigger to response?
Crisis management technique [CMT]: Was the primary CMT peaceful, violent, or a mix?
Violence: If it was violence, how central was it in coping with the crisis? And how severe was the violence?

Major Power Activity
Content: What was the most salient type of activity by the great powers (1918–45) or the two superpowers (1945–94) toward the crisis actor?
Actor perception: How did the crisis actor view major power activity in its crisis?

International Organization (IO) Involvement
Organ: Which IO organ was most actively involved in the crisis?
Content: What was the most salient verbal or physical IO involvement in the crisis?
Actor perception: How did the crisis actor view the IO's involvement?

Outcome
Content: How did a foreign policy crisis end?
Form: What form did the crisis outcome take?

I. CRISIS DIMENSIONS

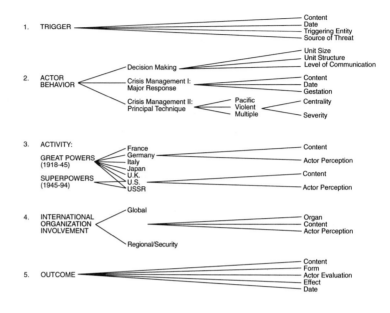

II. CONTEXT

(A) SYSTEM ATTRIBUTES

(B) ACTOR ATTRIBUTES

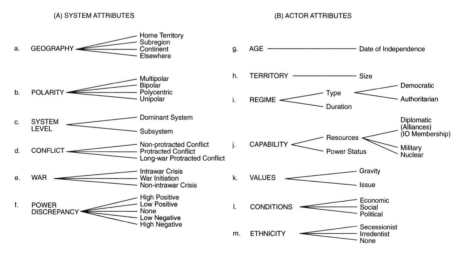

Figure I.6.   Conceptual Map: Micro Level

Actor perception: Was the crisis actor satisfied or dissatisfied with the outcome?

Date: When did the crisis end?[37]

(How the system- and actor-level variables, along with the contextual variables [see the next section], were operationalized for purposes of ICB data accumulation is discussed in Part II, in the "Variables" and "Indices" sections.)

Contextual Variables

The data on twentieth-century crises form the empirical basis of the analyses presented in Part IV of this book. In particular, the evidence is used to test models and hypotheses on enduring facets of crisis, conflict, and war. Moreover, analysis is enriched, we discovered, by the introduction of contextual variables, for patterns are often obscured when a large body of data is aggregated. Thus we added six system-level contextual variables to our inquiry into international crises. For foreign policy crises, the same system-level variables were employed, along with war/nonwar setting, and seven additional actor-level contextual variables. All these are specified in the map. We turn now to their conceptual underpinnings.

The first contextual variable in the analysis of data on crisis is *Geography.* Each international crisis was located in one of 18 subregions: for example, the North Korea nuclear crisis of 1993–94 in East Asia; the Teschen crisis of 1919–20 in Central Europe; the Gulf crisis-war of 1990–91 in the Middle East; the Angola crisis-war of 1975–76 in southern Africa; and the Ecuador/Peru border crisis of 1981 in South America. For purposes of analysis the subregions were collapsed into five regions: Africa, the Americas, Asia, Europe, and the Middle East.

Each crisis actor, too, is placed in a geographic subregion, for example, the U.S. (North America), the USSR (East Europe), and Cuba (Central America) in the Cuban Missile crisis. Moreover, all crises are coded in terms of their proximity/distance from the participants. That distinction provides the rationale for geography as a context of crisis: major powers are likely to behave differently in foreign policy crises "close to home" than elsewhere: for example, the USSR's military intervention, in the 1968 Prague Spring crisis, compared to its military aid to government forces via Cuba in the Angola crisis-war of 1975–76; the U.S.'s political pressure on the U.K., France, and Israel to withdraw from Sinai, in the Suez crisis-war of 1956–57, compared to its threat of direct military intervention, at the risk of superpower nuclear war, in the Cuban Missile crisis. (The link between geography and crisis is analyzed in Part IV of this book.)

Polarity refers to the number of power and decision centers in an international system: a structure may be unipolar, bipolar, or multipolar, the counterparts to monopolistic, duopolistic, and oligopolistic market systems (Keohane and Nye 1977:20). These are structures with one, two, and more than two centers of power and decision, respectively. Hybrid systems, with unequal numbers of power and decision centers, are also possible. The most notable is polycentric.

A *unipolar* structure requires an overwhelming concentration of military capability and political decisions in one entity, a virtual "world state" that would shape the rules of the system, dominate relations among lesser actors, and assert its hegemony at will. There is no historical case of pure unipolarity. The western, international system of antiquity, with Rome at the height of its power and authority, constituted quasi-unipolarity. The Ch'in empire was the unipolar center of China for a very brief period (221–207 B.C.E.). In the contemporary era, both the USSR (in Eastern Europe) and the U.S. (in Latin America) have exhibited subsystemic power unipolarity but with at least one other autonomous decisional center—Tito's Yugoslavia in the former and several in the latter, meaning Argentina, Brazil, Mexico, and, most visibly since 1961, Castro's Cuba. Finally, the post–Cold War global system resembles unipolarity, with the U.S. as the military hegemon.[38]

Bipolarity denotes two centers of military power and political decision in an international system. The poles may be individual actors (e.g., the U.S. and the USSR after World War II).[39] Or they may be coalitions (e.g., the Ch'i- and Ch'u-led alliances during the "Spring and Autumn" period of the Chinese state system, 771–483 B.C.E. [Walker 1953]; the Athens- and Sparta-led blocs in the Greek city-state system from 431 B.C.E. onward [Thucydides 1930]). The two poles or coalitions determine the "essential rules of the system" (Kaplan 1957), the conditions of stability, the limits of independent behavior by bloc members or unaffiliated actors, and the outcomes of major wars. Bipolarity is characterized by tight alliances and greater certainty about the behavior of the "other" power or coalition. This pattern of hostile interaction constrains crisis behavior, notably with regard to the use of violence, and assures bloc support in a crisis, unless core interests of the coalition leader contradict those of the crisis actor.

Multipolarity denotes a diffusion of military power and political decisions among three or more relatively equal units in an international system (e.g., the Greek city-state system prior to the Peloponnesian War; Italy in the fifteenth century [Mattingly 1955]; and most of the Western state system, 1648–1919 [Schuman 1933; Holsti 1991]). The diffusion of power led to flexible alliances and pervasive violence.

The twentieth-century inter–world war period was a multipolar system par excellence, with seven relatively equal great powers: France, Germany, Great Britain, Italy, Japan, the Soviet Union, and the United States. At the subsystem level, the Middle East since 1948 and Southeast Asia after 1949 qualify as multipolar systems. Unlike unipolarity and bipolarity, the inter–world war system was characterized by flexible alliances, multiple centers of power and decision, and uncertainty about behavior by the other great powers in the system. These traits are likely to influence the behavior of crisis actors, for they perceive more opportunities to gain support from one or more great powers. The result is more freedom of choice (and constraints) in crisis management techniques, the resort to violence, etc.

Polycentrism, a novel ICB construct, refers to a hybrid structure—two centers of military power and many centers of political decision. As such, it resembles both bipolarity and multipolarity. This type of structure was present in premodern "international" systems: the Greek city-state system on the eve of the Peloponnesian War, with Athens- and Sparta-led military coalitions, along with a diffusion of decisional authority among the lesser members; the Indian state system of antiquity (Ghoshal 1947; Modelski 1964); and the Ch'i- and Ch'u-led alliances of northern and southern states during the latter phase of the "Spring and Autumn" period of the Chinese state system, 741–483 B.C.E. This duality also existed in early nineteenth-century Europe, with Napoleonic France and the coalition of traditional European powers—England, Austria, Prussia, and Russia —exhibiting power bipolarity but with each state an independent decisional unit. A similar pattern of power bipolarity and multiple decisional centers characterized the period before World War I, with the loose coalition of Triple Alliance and Triple Entente (Rosecrance 1963).

The empirical referent for polycentrism at the global level in the twentieth century is from late 1962 onward. However, polycentrism began to reemerge in the late 1950s. The international system remained essentially bipolar in terms of military capability. At the same time, intrabloc cohesion was seriously undermined by the assertion of independence within the U.S.- and USSR-led coalitions, notably China's withdrawal from the Soviet bloc and France's military dissociation from *NATO,* a process dating from soon after de Gaulle's return to power in 1958. More broadly, the global system experienced a profound structural change created by the vast and sweeping process of decolonization. The global system had moved in the direction of universality and a notable diffusion of decisional authority from the bipolar concentration of decisions organized around U.S.- and USSR-led bloc organizations—*NATO* and *WTO, EEC* and *COMECON,* etc. In short, by 1963, polycentrism had arrived.

While a precise date marking the onset of contemporary polycentrism is uncertain, the change can be identified with the immediate aftermath of the Cuban Missile crisis and the Sino-Indian Border war, both in October–November 1962. In the former, the superpowers withdrew from the brink of nuclear war, dramatizing the constraints on overwhelming military capability; and, in the latter, the deepening Sino-Soviet split became irrevocable. Together they indicated that power bipolarity and decision bipolarity are not synonymous and that other centers of decision in the international system could no longer be controlled by the U.S. and the USSR; that is, bipolarity had given way to polycentrism, the global structure until the end of the Cold War.[40]

To recapitulate the conceptual distinctions and similarities: multipolarity is characterized by wide dispersion among many centers of military power, while polycentrism retains the bipolar concentration of power; both have many centers of political decision. Thus, the difference between the conception of polarity specified here and definitions cited earlier is the addition of polycentrism as a distinctive structural type, a hybrid between bipolarity (dual power concentration) and multipolarity (diffusion of decisional centers). In both conceptual and operational terms, this means a polarity variable with four values—unipolarity, bipolarity, multipolarity, and polycentrism.

One further point to be clarified is the disjuncture between the number of centers of power and decision. It is inconceivable that a state with a noteworthy level of power would fail to function independently in terms of decision; even the choice of isolationism would constitute an individual selection of policy. In sum, every center of power is, ipso facto, a center of decision, but the reverse does not obtain.

The assumption underlying polarity as a contextual variable is that the structure of power and decision in an international system will affect the dimensions of crisis and crisis behavior, from trigger (breakpoint) to outcome, including the propensity to war.[41]

A third macrolevel context is *System Level*. Every crisis can be located in one of four system categories: dominant system, mainly dominant system, subsystem, mainly subsystem. The *dominant system* is identified with interaction among the major powers in world politics. For the inter–world war period, this means the Europe-centered great power complex, with the U.S. and Japan as members. And for 1945–89 it refers to the U.S./USSR interbloc system. The *mainly dominant system* category denotes a situation in which crisis interactions among great powers have spillover effects on one or more subsystems and their state actors (e.g., the Suez Nationalization crisis-war in 1956–57).

The two main attributes of a *subsystem* are geographic proximity and regular interaction among its members. Others cited are intrarelatedness, external recognition as a distinctive region, self-identification, shared bonds, inferior military capability, evidence of integration, etc. (Brecher 1963; Haas 1970:101; Thompson 1973). *Subsystem* crises are those that occur within a subsystem without the direct participation of any major power (e.g., El Salvador and Honduras in the 1969 Football War).[42] There are also *mainly subsystem* crises, in which the key crisis actors are lesser powers with a predominantly regional focus but where there is some spillover to the dominant system, as a result of participation by one or more of the major powers, for example, the Angola crisis-war in 1975–76.

Underlying the choice of system level as a contextual variable is the assumption that crisis actors will behave with greater caution in dominant system and mainly dominant system crises than in crises at the subsystem level because the stakes are higher, the constraints are more visible, and vulnerability to pressure from the major powers is greater.

Some interstate crises, as noted, occur in a setting unburdened by long-term hostility. Others erupt in a context of *protracted conflict*. This distinction provides the rationale for *Conflict Setting* as a contextual variable. More precisely, it is assumed that long-term, multiple-issue hostility affects all the dimensions of an international crisis: type of breakpoint/trigger; value threatened; crisis management, in particular, the role of violence; major power activity and its effects; IO involvement and effectiveness in crisis abatement; and the substance and form of crisis outcome.

Power Discrepancy refers to the capability gap between adversaries. As a contextual variable in the analysis of crisis, it derives from the concept of power relative to a specific international crisis. Capability incorporates several types of resources: human (size of population); economic (a composite of several components, notably gross national product [GNP]); diplomatic (alliance relations with major powers); geographic (size of territory); and military (conventional and nuclear weapons, as well as military expenditure). The extent of power discrepancy in a crisis ranges from none (e.g., Rwanda/Burundi, 1964) to maximal discrepancy when the principal adversaries are a superpower and a small power (Mayaguez, 1975, between the U.S. and Cambodia).

As with other system-level attributes, the rationale for using power discrepancy as a contextual variable is the assumption that differences in capability will affect crisis dimensions after the breakpoint; that is, crisis management behavior of the more—and less—powerful actors; the type and degree of intervention by major powers and international organizations and its effectiveness; and the substance and form of outcome.

Ethnicity, in the context of crisis analysis, refers to the role of ethnic conflict in the hostility between crisis adversaries. Interstate ethnic conflict takes one of two forms: *secessionism*—where an ethnic group aspires and acts to secede from a state in which it is a minority community (e.g., Armenians in the Nagorno-Karabakh conflict between Armenia and Azerbaijan); and *irredentism*—where a state claims part of another state's territory on grounds of ethnic affinity with its population and/or its historical association with the territory (Italy's claim to Trieste in the 1953 crisis with Yugoslavia).

It is assumed that the presence of secessionist or irredentist ethnicity as the driving force in an international crisis will affect many crisis dimensions, notably the following: the greater likelihood of severe violence in the trigger and in the major response by the adversaries; the gravity of value threat—high values, including existence; the substance of outcome—victory/defeat, rather than compromise; and the form of outcome—an imposed agreement or a unilateral act, rather than a voluntary agreement.

Seven actor attributes, too, are applied to the data set in an attempt to explain state behavior in crises and crisis outcomes. These actor-level contextual variables are indicated in the Conceptual Map: Age, Territory, Regime, Capability, Ethnicity, Values, and Social/Economic Conditions.

Members of the global system from 1918 to 1994 vary in *Age:* from European and Asian major powers (e.g., Britain, France, Russia, China, and Japan), whose independence antedates the beginning of the Western state system in 1648, to the vast majority of African states, all but four of which (Egypt, Ethiopia, Liberia, South Africa) became independent from 1957 onward, Eritrea as recently as 1993. Most Latin American states attained sovereignty in the early years of the nineteenth century, almost all Middle East and Southern Asian states in the decade following World War II.

It is assumed that many components of state behavior in crises will vary with age, notably the following: primary crisis management technique, including the intensity of violence; the time span between trigger and major response to the value threat; the level of communication among crisis adversaries; the size and structure of the decision-making unit; the likelihood of an appeal to an international organization for support, etc.

Territory has three dimensions as an actor-level contextual variable: size; number of borders; and contiguity with major powers. Large states, such as the USSR and China, are assumed to have greater flexibility than small states, like Denmark and Israel, in coping with crises, especially violent ones: their primary CMT is likely to be different because of the risk involved (e.g., the USSR's strategy of trading space for time in crisis-wars, compared to Israel's strategic doctrine of interceptive war). Moreover, states that are encircled, such as Austria and Hungary, are likely to experience more constraints in crisis management than states that are distant from the geographic center of the dominant system and/or their subsystem. And states that are contiguous to one or more major powers, such as Belgium and Poland, will be more constrained in coping with crises than states that are distant from the powers (e.g., Indonesia, Peru).

Behavior in interstate crises is also likely to vary with political *Regime,* both type and duration. It is expected that democratic states will respond with less resolve than civil authoritarian regimes (e.g., France and the U.K. in the 1936 Remilitarization of the Rhineland crisis or Munich in 1938, compared to Germany in both cases).[43] There may also be different response patterns among military regimes (e.g., Pakistan in the 1965 Rann of Kutch crisis). Regimes also vary in *Duration,* from long-time parliamentary or presidential regimes (the U.K., the U.S.), to many African states in which regimes change rapidly, sometimes more than once within a year. These and similar expectations underlie the selection of regime as a context for actor-level behavior in crisis.

Capability, as noted in the discussion of power discrepancy, is a multifaceted attribute, comprising human, diplomatic, military, and economic resources. For example, it is expected that state behavior during a crisis will vary with the *alliance* configuration of the adversaries; that is, if an actor perceives reliable support from one or more major powers, it is likely to act with greater resolve than in a situation where it must act alone, especially if the adversary has a great power as a patron (e.g., Israel, in alliance with Britain and France during the Suez crisis of 1956, compared to its "waiting period" alone during most of the May–June 1967 crisis).

The assumed link between military power and crisis behavior is even more pronounced for *nuclear* capability. States with large stockpiles of nuclear weapons (the U.S., the USSR) are likely to be prudent in using violence as a crisis management technique because of the risk of rapid and destructive escalation. States with modest nuclear arsenals, such as France, the U.K., and China, may act with greater confidence in coping with a crisis. Near-nuclear states (e.g., India, Pakistan) may manifest a third pattern of behavior and nonnuclear states, a fourth.

Closely related to capability is *Power Status,* which is determined by a state's military capability in the international system in which its crisis occurs. Power status denotes the scope of its potential impact—superpower, great power, middle power, small power. However, a state may be a small power in the global power hierarchy but a middle power—or even a great power—within its subsystem (e.g., Egypt and Israel were small powers in global terms after 1956 but great powers in the Middle East subsystem).

The choice of power status as a contextual variable is based upon an assumed link between state behavior in a crisis and its perceived capability. Small powers are expected to differ from others in their techniques of crisis management. The time span from trigger to major response will be different for superpowers than for all others. Middle powers are more likely to accept a compromise outcome because of their inability to impose their will on an adversary with the same status.

Another actor-level contextual variable is threatened *Values.* It is assumed that violence will be the most likely primary crisis management technique when a state's existence is threatened. Differences when high, medium, or low values are threatened are likely to be manifested in other facets of behavior as well: in decision making—by large or small, ad hoc or institutional groups; in response time—slowly or quickly or instantaneously; in crisis management technique— pacific or violent and, if the latter, severe or moderate, central or marginal in coping with crises; in reliance on external support by a major power or an international organization, or both; and in crisis outcome—willingness to compromise will be more evident in cases where values other than existence are threatened.

Social and Economic Conditions, too, have been postulated as affecting state behavior in a crisis. Some argue that political leaders beset with internal difficulties tend toward more aggressive external behavior. Others contend that decision makers are less able to deal effectively with external challenges, such as crises, while trying at the same time to maintain their positions in the face of internal dislocation. An overall index of social/economic conditions is imposed as a context in order to test these propositions in a crisis setting.[44]

As with the crisis dimensions, a set of research questions was inferred from the system- and actor-level contextual variables specified in Figures I.5 and I.6.

Geographic location: In which region did the crisis occur—Africa, the Americas, Asia, Europe, the Middle East?

Polarity: What was the structure of the international system in which the crisis erupted—unipolarity, bipolarity, multipolarity, polycentrism?

System level: Did the crisis take place within the dominant system of world politics or a subsystem; or was the context mainly dominant system or mainly subsystem?

Conflict setting: Did the crisis occur outside a protracted conflict, within a protracted conflict, or was it part of a long-war protracted conflict?

Power discrepancy: Was the power discrepancy between the adversaries high, medium, or low?

Ethnicity: Did the crisis adversaries belong to the same or different ethnic group(s)? Was ethnicity the driving force in their hostile interaction? If so, did secessionism or irredentism shape their crisis behavior?

The questions relating to context at the actor level are the same as those at the system level, except for *War:* did the crisis occur during a war or in a nonwar setting, or was the crisis initiated by war? Among the actor attributes employed as intervening variables in this inquiry, one cluster of questions will suffice.

Age: Are young states more inclined than old, established states to do the following: to rely on violence rather than negotiation or mediation to cope with crises; to respond more quickly to a value threat; to decide by small, ad hoc units, rather than larger, institutional forums; and to rely more on major powers and/or international organizations in coping with crises?

Similar questions guide our use of the other actor-level contextual variables: territory (large or small crisis actors); regime type (democratic or authoritarian); regime duration (long or short); capability; power status (major, middle, small powers); ethnicity (secessionist, irredentist, nonethnic); values (high, low); socio/economic conditions (stable or unstable).

The framework for this book has been introduced, along with core concepts, research questions, a model linking the macro- and microlevels of analysis, and the contextual variables to be applied as controls in the analysis of data on crises and conflicts.[45] In Part II, the procedures used in data collection and related methodological issues will be discussed. Part III will present a summary of each of the 412 cases. This is accompanied by a Master Table (Table III.1) containing 11 attributes for each international and foreign policy crisis from the end of 1918 to the end of 1994: its duration, power status, triggering entity, trigger, gravity of threat, crisis management technique, extent of violence, major power activity, IO involvement, content, and form of outcome. Finally, Part IV will analyze enduring themes in the study of world politics. This will focus on the impact of seven basic attributes—polarity, geography, ethnicity, democracy, protracted conflict, violence, and role of major powers and global organizations as third parties—in order to illuminate the lessons of twentieth-century crises and conflicts.

Notes to Part I

1. The most lucid statement of the "long peace" thesis is by Gaddis (1986, 1987, 1991). For a dissenting view, see Brecher and Wilkenfeld (1991).

2. The term, "interstate crisis," as used in this book, applies to any military-security crisis between or among legally sovereign members of the global system. It does not include the following: environmental, political, economic, social, or cultural crises; interethnic disputes within a state; civil strife between nonstate actors; or conflicts between colonial powers and groups aspiring to independence.

3. The Stanford Group's mediated stimulus-response model and their analysis of the crucial link between perceptions and decisions in the crisis leading to World War I (Holsti 1972; Nomikos and North 1976).

4. McClelland's (1964, 1972) examination of quantitative data pertaining to actions and responses by contending parties in two "conflict arenas"—Berlin from 1948 to 1963 and Taiwan from 1950 to 1964.

5. Paige's (1968) "guided reconstruction" of America's response to the outbreak of the Korean War in 1950 and application of Snyder, Bruck, and Sapin's (1962) decision-making framework; and Allison's (1969, 1971) use of three paradigms—rational actor, bureaucratic politics, and organizational process—to explain U.S. behavior in the Cuban Missile crisis.

6. George and Smoke's (1974) "focused comparison" of deterrence in 11 crises for the U.S., from the Berlin Blockade in 1948 to the Missile crisis in 1962.

7. At a more general level, Hermann (1972) presented the collective wisdom of behavioral research into crisis in the late 1960s.

Notable works in the second wave were Snyder and Diesing's (1977) analysis of the bargaining process in 16 international crises, from the Anglo-French dispute over Fashoda in 1898 to the Middle East conflagration in 1973; Azar et al.'s (1978, 1985) concept of protracted conflict; Leng et al.'s (1979, 1982) studies of bargaining in nineteenth- and twentieth-century crises; Stein and Tanter's (1980) analysis of Israel's multiple paths to choice in the 1967 Middle East Crisis; and Lebow's (1981) probe of 26 cases, from Cuba in 1897–98 to the events preceding the 1967 Arab/Israel War, with emphasis on misperceptions, cognitive closure, and crisis management.

The most recent wave of high-quality works on crises include Brams and Kilgour's (1988) game-theoretic studies of bargaining in crises; Leng's (1993) emphasis on the dynamics of bargaining within crises; Mor's (1993) use of game theory to analyze the 1967 Middle East crisis; Morgan's (1994) theory of international crisis; Brams's (1994) theory of moves by crisis actors; and Lebow and Stein's (1994) comparison of U.S. and USSR behavior during the Cuban Missile crisis of 1962 and the October–Yom Kippur crisis-war of 1973–74.

The ICB Project concentrates on interstate crises and on the behavior of states under externally generated stress. In so doing, it continues in the tradition associated with, among others, the scholars noted in the preceding paragraph. At the same time, it analyzes in detail the multiple roles of suprastate actors (League of Nations, United Nations, regional organizations) in crisis management, as well as the (often significant) roles of substate actors (e.g., nationalist movements, ethnic and tribal groups in Africa) as triggering entities, stimuli to state behavior, etc. Moreover, the activity of nonstate actors is discussed in the summaries of the 412 international crises in Part III.

8. For attempts to overcome this lacuna see Adomeit (1982); K. Dawisha (1984); George (1983); Horelick (1964); Kaplan (1981); Triska and Finley (1968); Valenta (1979); and Wilkenfeld and Brecher (1982).

9. There were a few exceptions: George (1991); Stremlau (1977); and Whiting (1960).

10. This is indirectly explored in Paul (1994); and Singer (1972).

11. For surveys of the theoretically oriented literature on crisis see Brecher (1993); M. Haas (1986); Holsti (1989); Hopple and Rossa (1981); and Tanter (1979).

12. In earlier works (Brecher and Wilkenfeld 1988; Wilkenfeld and Brecher 1988) we described and analyzed 278 international crises comprising 627 foreign policy crises from 1929 to 1979, the initial time frame. We also compared the configuration of crises within and outside 24 protracted conflicts from 1929 to 1979 (Brecher and Wilkenfeld 1989:chaps. 10, 11). Since then the ICB data set has been expanded by 50 percent in both the number of cases and time span. Protracted conflicts, too, have grown—to 31, from 1918 to 1994. (The concept of protracted conflict is discussed later in this Part and in Part IV.)

13. One of the major constraints on research into crises in world politics prior to ICB was the paucity of reliable data about their range, volume, and content in any historical era or geographic region. This was partly overcome by some inventories of related phenomena—conflicts, military engagements, deadly quarrels, and wars: Deitchman (1964); Greaves (1962); K. J. Holsti (1966); Kende (1971); Leiss and Bloomfield (1967); Haas et al. (1972); Richardson (1960); Singer and Small (1972); Wood (1968); Wright (1942, 1965). For the types of disruptive interactions addressed, the years covered, and the number of cases in these and other compendia on interstate turmoil, see Table II.1.

14. For an elaboration of this definition see Brecher (1979a).

15. The ICB case studies published thus far are Brecher (1979b); Brecher with Geist (1980); A. I. Dawisha (1980); Shlaim (1983); Dowty (1984); Dawisha (1984); Jukes (1985); Hoffmann (1990); and Anglin (1994).

16. Hermann's definition emerged from Robinson's (1962) conception of international crisis as a decisional situation with three components: "(1) identification of the origin of the event—whether external or internal for the decision-makers; (2) the decision time available for response—whether short, intermediate, or long; and (3) the relative importance of the values at stake to the participants—whether high or low." (The quotation is from Robinson in Sills [1968:3, 511] and is also in Hermann [1972: 23].)

Hermann retained two of Robinson's traits, time and threat, but with significant changes: "restricted" (or short) time only; and threat to "high-priority goals," not values. And he replaced "origin of event" with surprise. The first Hermann formulation is in a paper (1963:61–82). See also his article in Rosenau (1969:409–21). The Hermann version was adopted by many scholars. Holsti, for example, in his major work on the subject (1972:9), wrote: "crisis—defined here as a *situation of unanticipated threat to important values and restricted decision time . . .* " He did not question its validity or utility, though he noted: "there are many usages of the term 'crisis'" (1972:263 n. 3). Nomikos and North, in their detailed narrative of the processes of conflict escalation in 1914 (1976:1), also accepted Hermann's definition. For a suggestive view of the link between time pressure and the initiation of war, see Paul (1995).

17. The term "military hostilities" is much broader than "war." In fact, it encompasses any interstate hostile physical interaction, classified as "minor clashes," "serious clashes," or "full-scale war." However, for stylistic convenience, the terms "war likelihood," "probability of war," "likelihood of (involvement in) military hostilities," and "probability of (involvement in) military hostilities" are used interchangeably throughout this book. They all denote the prospects for any level of military hostilities, from minor clashes to full-scale war.

18. The other definitional changes are elaborated here.

(a) There are high-threat, finite-time, and probability-of-war perceptions by decision makers that do not occasion surprise; that is, they are not unanticipated. For example, the situational change created by East Germany in 1961, triggering the Berlin Wall crisis, did not come as a surprise to U.S. decision makers. But the perceived threat—to Western influence in Europe—catalyzed a crisis atmosphere in Washington, leading to changes in the American behavioral response and decision-making process.

Hermann and others, too, were skeptical about the surprise component (Hermann 1969a:69; 1972:208). The lower frequency of "surprise" and doubt about the adequacy of the overall definition of crisis are also evident in the findings of Brady (1974:58). McCormick (1975:1, 16) questioned whether "surprise" could be operationalized at all. And Hermann (Hermann and Mason 1980:193–94) dropped "surprise" as a necessary condition of crisis.

(b) The lack of universality of the short time condition is demonstrated by the behavior of the three Western powers in the Berlin Deadline crisis of 1958–59. Choice could not be delayed indefinitely: it was not a short time, a week or a month, but six months; there was a realization that a major response to the Soviet announcement on 27 November 1958 setting a six-month deadline for the change in West Berlin's status to a demilitarized "Free City" had to be made within that time frame; in fact, the Western powers responded on 14 December with a communiqué rejecting the Soviet Note; it was formally presented on 30 December. The response could have been earlier—or later; it could not have been after 27 May 1959; the time constraint was finite, not short.

(c) For many states, the change that triggers a foreign policy crisis occurs internally, via verbal or physical challenges to a regime—strikes, demonstrations, riots, assassination, sabotage, and/or attempted *coups d'état*. Thus, on 25 July 1934, Austrian Nazis attacked the Chancellery in Vienna and killed Chancellor Dollfuss, triggering a crisis for Austria, as well as for Czechoslovakia and Italy. Such crisis triggers are frequent in the new states of Africa and Asia, which are deeply penetrated political systems; there, domestic changes, some of which derive from foreign sources, may give rise to an image of external threat, time pressure, and war likelihood, as illustrated in a 1976 coup attempt to overthrow the Numeiri regime in Sudan, triggering a crisis for Sudan vis-à-vis Libya.

(d) "High-priority goals" as the focus of threat, in Hermann's definition of crisis, has been broadened to "basic values." These include "core" values, which are few in number, such as survival of a state and its population, and the avoidance of grave damage through war. A second value dimension is context-specific "high-priority" values that derive from ideological and/or material interests as defined by decision makers at the time of a specific crisis. "Core" values, by contrast, are shared by changing regimes and decision-making groups, as well as by the attentive and mass publics of the state under inquiry. A foreign policy crisis may be said to exist when an external threat is perceived to either "core" or "high-priority" values, though the former alone, and a combination of the two types, will evoke more stress than the latter alone. In any event, it is values, not goals, as Hermann later acknowledged (Hermann and Mason 1980:193–94), that are under threat in a crisis situation.

All five departures from the Hermann definition of crisis—the omission of surprise, finite rather than short time, internal as well as external trigger mechanisms, basic values instead of high-priority goals, and the high probability of war—are strongly supported by empirical evidence.

19. A precise operational definition of the ICB concept of stress levels, which combines type of threat to values and the power of the adversarial actor, is presented in Part II.

20. Definitions of international (or systemic) crisis can be classified into two groups, process and interaction-structure.

Process definitions view an international crisis as a turning point marked by an unusually intense period of conflictual interactions: for McClelland (1968:160–61), a "change of state in the flow of international political actions"; for Azar (1972:184), "Interaction above the . . . upper critical threshold . . . for more than a very short time." Structural-interaction definitions view an international crisis as a situation characterized by basic change in processes that might affect structural variables of a system: for Young (1968:15) "a process of interaction occurring at higher levels of perceived intensity than the ordinary flow of events and characterized by . . . significant implications for the stability of some system or subsystem."

Some definitions of crisis are a mix of unit- and system-level concepts, for example, Wiener and Kahn's (1962) 12 generic dimensions of crisis. They include a turning point in a sequence of events; a new configuration of international politics as a crisis outcome and changes in relations among actors, along with such unit-level indicators as a perceived threat to actor goals; a sense of urgency, stress, and anxiety among decision makers; and increased time pressure.

For a critique of 25 definitions of crisis at both the macro- and microlevels, see M. Haas (1986:25–33). The definition of international crisis presented here is based upon a revised concept of system and system properties. This was elaborated in Brecher and Ben Yehuda (1985).

21. Economic processes can produce changes at the international level that are no less significant, and sometimes more significant, than military-security issues. Although this book focuses on dilemmas of war and peace, some international crises will reflect the prior and cumulative impact of conflicting economic interests, for example, Cod Wars I and II in 1973 and 1975.

22. The concept of protracted conflict elucidated here is similar to that of "enduring international rivalry." An emerging consensus specifies three conditions of an enduring international rivalry: severity—at least five militarized interstate disputes between the same adversaries, each lasting at least one month; durability—25 years from the first to the last dispute within the rivalry; and continuity—a gap of no more than 10 years between two of these disputes. A militarized interstate dispute, the counterpart of the ICB concept of international crisis, has been defined as "a set of interactions between or among states involving threats to use military force, displays of military force, or actual uses of military force" (Gochman and Maoz 1984:587). For analyses of enduring international rivalries, see Geller

and Jones (1991); Goertz and Diehl (1992a, 1993); Huth, Jones, and Maoz (1991); Maoz and Mor (1996).

23. Even in cases of seemingly unprovoked military invasion (e.g., Germany's invasion of Belgium and the Netherlands in World Wars I and II), there was a notable increase in the intensity of hostile verbal and physical interactions, that is, an international crisis that enveloped many states in Europe—the June–July 1914 crisis and the August 1939 crisis. Germany's invasions of the Low Countries flowed from these crises. More generally, all but one of the twentieth century's recorded wars in the Correlates of War project are included in the ICB data set of international crises.

24. McClelland (1955:34; 1958) was perhaps the earliest to specify levels in the study of world politics. Boulding (1956:202, 201) introduced the idea of "system rungs" (levels). The "levels of analysis" problem in world politics was first given explicit formulation by Singer (1961). North (1967:394) emphasized the need to probe—and compare the findings from—the unit and system levels. Deutsch (1974:152–56) set out a 10-level political system, including four levels in international politics. Andriole (1978) argued in favor of five levels of analysis.

25. The duration of an international crisis is measured from the first breakpoint to the endpoint which, in unit-level terms, means from the trigger for the first actor to termination for the last actor. For the initial breakpoint to occur there must be two or more adversarial actors in higher-than-normal conflictual interaction. The adversaries may become crisis actors simultaneously, a rare occurrence, for this requires triggers on the same day, as in the 1965 India/Pakistan crisis over the Rann of Kutch. More often, international crises begin with one crisis actor and one adversary that triggers the crisis; the latter may later become a crisis actor, as with Belgium and the Congo in the 1960 Congo crisis, or it may not.

A variant is one initial crisis actor (the U.S.) and one adversary (the USSR), the initiator, with the latter joined by another (Cuba) in the process of becoming a crisis actor, as in the 1962 Missile crisis. Another variation is one crisis actor at the outset with several adversaries that later become crisis actors simultaneously, as with the USSR and the U.S., the U.K., and France in the 1948–49 Berlin Blockade crisis. As for the winding down of an international crisis, the majority of cases reveal simultaneous termination for all crisis actors. By definition, the international crisis has only one endpoint, the date the last actor exits from the crisis.

26. The outer closed lines in Figure I.4, both vertical and horizontal, indicate that the four phases and four periods are an integrated whole. The broken vertical lines between the four phases and the four periods indicate that, while each phase and each period is distinct, they are closely linked, sequentially, from onset to impact and from pre-crisis to post-crisis. The summary of the phases presented here is based upon the Unified Model of Crisis, elaborated in Brecher (1993:chap. 6).

27. The types and varieties of external and internal triggers are specified later in Part I.

28. There are many such "failed" interstate crises in the twentieth century, for example, Bulgaria/Greece Border Dispute, 1932; Communist Threat to Burma, 1945; Buraimi Oasis, 1955; Hong Kong Riots, 1967; Indonesia/Netherlands Hostages, 1978. See Brecher and Wilkenfeld (1988:32, n. 3) for a list of 65 "failed" cases.

29. The hierarchy of powers comprises the following: superpowers; great powers; medium powers; and small powers. Throughout this book superpowers = the U.S. and the USSR 1945–94; great powers = France, Germany, Italy, Japan, the U.K., the U.S., the USSR 1919–39; and

China (since 1949), France, the U.K. (since 1945). The term "major powers" refers to the superpowers and great powers together, differentiating them from lesser or minor powers.

30. The one exception to this non-crisis norm of information processing is an interstate crisis in which pre-crisis is characterized by very high value threat, despite the absence of perceived heightened probability of war and little, if any, time pressure: in this situation, information processing will resemble that of the crisis period, with direct involvement by senior decision makers, for example, the U.K. in the 1938 Munich crisis.

31. This pattern is derived from the findings on coping with low threat and stress in the pre-crisis period in 10 foreign policy crises, from the U.K. in the Munich crisis of 1938 to Argentina in the Falklands/Malvinas crisis of 1982. See Brecher 1993:77–129.

32. In this context, the difference between *escalation point* and *escalation phase* merits attention. Acts or events such as mobilization of reserves or more extreme language of threat are escalation points, that is, specific markers of more disruptive interaction. But they operate below the new and higher threshold of distortion created by the phase-change from onset to escalation. Escalation points are thus not synonymous with phase-change. That occurs only when an act, event, or environmental change causes a fundamental shift in perceptions of impending harm and in disruptive interaction. Moreover, once the jump to the escalation phase occurs there is no reversion to the lower level of disruptive interaction that characterizes the onset phase. In sum, an escalation point designates a specific increase in disruptive interaction within a phase, while the escalation phase refers to a general pattern of higher distortion. The former constitutes change within existing bounds while the latter creates new boundaries and new upper and lower thresholds of hostile interaction.

33. The distinction between phase-change and point-change applies to de-escalation as well. A de-escalation point designates a specific decrease in disruptive interaction—a conciliatory statement by an adversary, its partial withdrawal of forces or their shift to a defensive posture, a mediatory role by a major power, etc. The de-escalation phase, by contrast, denotes a general pattern of lower distortion. De-escalation points represent changes within the bounds of a downward spiral of hostility as the parties move toward crisis termination. When that point is reached, the de-escalation phase and the international crisis as a whole come to an end. Perceptions of harm revert to the non-crisis norm, as does the intensity of disruptive interaction.

34. The period 1939–45 is similar to the preceding two decades (multipolarity), with many centers of decision. It also resembles the succeeding period (bipolarity), with two coalitions of power in direct confrontation. Thus it was most akin to polycentrism. However, in essence, it stands apart from all of these system types, for it was characterized by extreme interbloc hostility and intrabloc cohesion, in a hegemonic war of the most intense violence; that is, it was a *long-war protracted conflict*. (See the discussion on Contextual Variables for an elaboration of the rationale for the five polarity structures.)

An additional reason for treating World War II as a distinct system is that nearly all international crises during that period were intra-war crises, whose main dimensions—trigger, actor behavior, great power activity, and outcome—were affected by the setting of an intense, long-war protracted conflict.

35. The inclusion of international organization variables is designed to replicate for crisis management the role of the League of Nations, the United Nations, and regional organizations in conflict management, as reported in Haas, Nye, and Butterworth (1972); and E. B. Haas (1983, 1986).

36. The phrasing of the questions regarding major powers and IO effects on crisis abatement

should not be interpreted as bias in favor of the status quo. Stability is preferred only in the Hobbesian sense of the desirability of avoiding interstate *anarchy,* since anarchy generates intolerable costs for all members of an international system.

37. Many variables in the Conceptual Map (Figures I.5 and I.6) have been explored during the past four decades.

Crucial system traits and their impact on state behavior have been analyzed by Azar (1972); Cannizo (1978); Deutsch and Singer (1964); Kaplan (1957); McClelland (1964, 1968, 1972); Rosecrance (1963, 1966); Singer and Small (1968); Waltz (1979); and Young (1967).

Actor attributes—a state's age, territorial size and location, regime, military and economic resources (capability), and domestic conditions—and their effects on foreign policy behavior were probed by, among others, Andriole et al. (1975); East (1973); East and Hermann (1974); Hopple et al. (1977); Rosenau (1966); Rummel (1968, 1969); Ward and Widmaier (1982); and Wilkenfeld et al. (1980).

The decision-making unit—its size, structure, and the rank of participants, their values at stake, information processing, and various effects on decision making and crisis management—have been dissected by Allison (1969, 1971); Brecher et al. (1969, 1980); George (1980); Hermann (1963, 1969); Stein and Tanter (1980); Vertzberger (1984, 1990, 1997); and others.

The crisis dimension of actor behavior was a major focus of the works noted at the beginning of Part I (Allison, Brams, Brams and Kilgour, George and Smoke, Hermann, O. R. Holsti, Lebow, McClelland, Mor, Paige, Snyder and Diesing, and the Stanford Group), as well as Allan (1983); Bueno de Mesquita (1981, 1985); Frei (1982); Goldmann (1983); James (1988); Maoz (1990); Stein and Tanter (1980); among others.

All have contributed insights into one or several aspects of interstate crises. The ICB inquiry encompasses all of these dimensions of crisis and conflict.

38. On the ongoing debate over American "unipolarity" or hegemony, see Keohane (1984); Russett (1985); Strange (1987); Nye (1990, 1993); Layne (1993).

39. Bipolarity, in the sense of two concentrations of *military* power, characterized the global system from 1945 to 1989. However, in the wider structural meaning of hostile centers of power and *decision* the term applies to the period 1945 to late 1962, the Cuban Missile crisis.

Even within that time frame there were distinct phases: *embryonic* bipolarity, from the end of World War II to the summer of 1948, when the power preeminence of the U.S. and the USSR (and the emerging bloc structure) had not yet fully crystallized; *tight* bipolarity, referring to two centers of decision, as well as power, an emergent reality with two "turning point" developments closely related in time—the imposition of a communist regime in Czechoslovakia (February 1948) and the eruption of the Berlin Blockade crisis (June 1948), culminating in the formal creation of *NATO* and the two German states in 1949. The entry of the Soviet Union into the nuclear club in 1949, superimposed upon its conventional military power, marked the advent of bipolarity in the power sense; and *loose* bipolarity was ushered in by the passive cooperation of the superpowers in the Suez crisis (October–November 1956).

After 1962, the marked diffusion of influence and nonmilitary power, highlighted by the increasing prominence of China and France, created a hybrid system of power bipolarity and decision multipolarity, which is designated *polycentrism.* (This is elaborated in the subsequent discussion of polycentrism.)

40. The multidimensional character of polarity has been noted by others. Bueno de Mesquita (1975, 1978) identified three attributes of polarity: the number of poles or clusters of states; their tightness and discreteness; and the degree of inequality in the distribution of power.

Rapkin and Thompson with Christopherson (1979) distinguished between polarity (the distribution of power) and polarization (the tendency for actors to cluster around the system's most powerful states). Wayman (1984) differentiated power polarity (power distribution) from cluster polarity (alliance clustering). Stoll (1984) developed a single indicator that combines elements of polarity (concentration of power) and polarization (the number of poles and their tightness). Hart (1985:31), too, distinguished between polarity—"the number of autonomous centers of power in the international system"—and polarization—"the process by which a power distribution is altered through alignment and coalition formation." And Wallace (1985:97) defined polarization in terms of two key structural attributes of a system: the distribution of military capability and the configuration of military alliances within it. Wayman and Morgan (1990) examined the various multidimensional measures of polarity and found that the degree of convergence among the indicators was very weak. Kegley and Raymond (1992) distinguished between "the propensity of actors to cluster around the most powerful states" (polarization) and the level of fluidity among alliances ("commitment norms") as mediating variables in the polarity/stability relationship.

41. The assumed link between polarity and war has been the basis of an influential debate. Notable contributors are Morgenthau (1948); Kaplan (1957); Deutsch and Singer (1964); Waltz (1964, 1967); Rosecrance (1966); Haas (1970); Singer, Bremer, and Stuckey (1972); Wallace (1973); Bueno de Mesquita (1975, 1978, 1981); Jackson (1977); Rapkin and Thompson with Christopherson (1979); Wayman (1984, 1990); Garnham (1985); Levy (1985); Hart (1985); Thompson (1986, 1988); Domke (1988); Midlarsky (1988, 1989, 1993); Mearsheimer (1990); Hopf (1991); Saperstein (1991); Kegley and Raymond (1992); Wagner (1993); Mansfield (1993); James (1995).

42. The concepts of dominant system and subsystem are elaborated in Brecher and James (1986:Part 1.1).

43. The theory of democratic peace is elaborated and assessed in Part IV.

44. Ethnicity, the last of the actor attributes, was discussed earlier among the macrolevel contextual variables.

45. We recognize that scholars frequently disagree about how best to translate a concept into a precise definition and that some of the concepts as defined in the ICB framework differ from other definitions in the international relations literature, such as foreign policy crisis, international crisis, intra-war crisis, multipolarity, polycentrism, power discrepancy, and power status. The definitions of concepts discussed in Part I seem to us to meet the criteria specified earlier. They are valid. They are analytically comprehensive. They incorporate concepts related to change. And they have operational utility, as will be amply demonstrated in Parts III and IV.

PART II.   METHODOLOGY

Introduction

The aggregate data segment of the International Crisis Behavior Project consists of data on 412 international crises and 895 foreign policy (actor) crises spanning the period 1918–94. Initial planning for this massive data collection began in 1975, with the most intense design work accomplished while Brecher and Wilkenfeld worked together in Jerusalem from 1977 to 1979. The assembly of the ICB data sets proceeded in four stages.

Stage 1: 1978–86   data collected for the 1929–79 period and served as the basis for *Crises in the Twentieth Century,* Vols. I, II (1988)

Stage 2: 1987–88   data collected for the 1980–85 period and, together with Stage 1, served as the basis for *Crisis, Conflict and Instability* (1989)

Stage 3: 1989–91   data collected for the 1918–28 and 1986–88 periods and, together with Stages 1 and 2, served as the basis for *Crises in World Politics* (1993)

Stage 4: 1993–95   data collected for the 1989–94 period and, together with Stages 1, 2, and 3, served as the basis for *A Study of Crisis* (1997).

It is always tempting when reporting on the procedures of a large-scale and long-term project such as ICB to provide a historical account of how methods, definitions, and priorities evolved over the 20 years of the project. While this would make fascinating reading for those of us and our students who over the years have been intricately involved in the endeavor, most readers would find it superfluous to their understanding at best and confusing at worst. Therefore, in the following pages, we will provide a summary of our current procedures, as if they have always, from the beginning in 1975, followed a straight and entirely predetermined path. For the reader who is nevertheless fascinated with the early details of the evolution of the ICB Project, Parts II of Brecher and Wilkenfeld (1988) and Wilkenfeld and Brecher (1988) should be consulted.

For readers familiar with earlier versions of the ICB data sets, a word of caution is in order. Stage 4 was devoted primarily to expanding the data set to include the 1989–94 period. However, we also reopened many previously coded cases and added to the coding in light of new information that had come to light since the original coding was done, some of which dated to the late 1970s. In the course of that process, it became clear that some earlier cases would now need to be dropped from the data set, while still others would be combined and otherwise modified. Furthermore, several key variables, including gravity of threat and form of outcome, were recoded from scratch for the entire 76-year period, because serious shortcomings were identified in their earlier formulations. Finally, several new variables were added to the data set, most notably variables assessing the ethnic content (if any) of a crisis and variables distinguishing major power crisis activity from their activities as third parties. Therefore, the current ICB data set supersedes all earlier releases and should be used exclusively by researchers interested in crises in the twentieth century.

As noted in Part I, ICB has been interested in all phases of an international crisis, from onset, through escalation, to de-escalation and termination and finally to impact. Key dimensions of the situation have been tracked for the international crisis as a whole, as well as for the individual states that became actors in the crisis. This dual focus necessitated the generation and maintenance of two separate data sets which, although closely linked, are used to answer different types of questions pertaining to crisis phenomena. For example, behavioral characteristics such as the choice among various crisis management techniques—from pacific to violent—to achieve foreign policy objectives in crisis are best assessed for the individual actor. Other factors, such as the circumstances under which third parties—superpowers or global organizations—are effective in crisis abatement, are best assessed from the point of view of the international crisis as a whole. Later, we will discuss the groupings of variables that emerged from each of these perspectives.

First, however, it will be useful to provide some information on procedures, including how cases were identified for inclusion (or exclusion), how the set of variables evolved, how coders were trained, and how the data were compiled and readied for analysis, as well as some discussion of the extensive sources consulted in the assembly of the data sets and the statistical procedures employed. We turn now to this task.

ICB Data Collection Procedures

Cases

In Part I we provided the full ICB definitions for international (system-level) and foreign policy (actor-level) crises (see pp. 4–5, 3). Employing these definitions, initial lists of international crises were assembled, relying primarily on the *New York Times* and *Keesing's Contemporary Archives*. These lists were then sent to a large number of area specialists at universities, notably in Israel, Canada, and the United States, and expanded or contracted accordingly. In fact, these area specialists were consulted repeatedly throughout the coding process to assess both the reliability and validity of the coding.[1] This consultation process was particularly delicate, since the term "crisis" has not always been used with great precision in the international relations literature, and we needed to ensure that the specialists were employing the ICB definition as they provided their input to the project. As new official documents, memoirs, histories, and other sources became available over the years, some additional international crises for previously coded periods were identified and incorporated into the data set,[2] while the coding of some previously coded cases was modified based on new information.[3]

Once the list of international crises had been assembled, the states that were to be considered actors in each crisis were identified according to three basic criteria. First, they had to be sovereign states and recognized members of the international system. Second, there had to be persuasive evidence that the decision makers of these states perceived the three conditions of a foreign policy crisis—a threat to basic values, finite time for response, and heightened probability of military hostilities, all resulting from a change in a state's external or internal environment. And third, there had to be a clear indication that the adversary was another sovereign state or, in some cases, an opposing coalition of states.

The requirement of sovereignty for crisis actors and adversaries excluded all crises involving campaigns for independence, even though many had important international ramifications. For example, Algeria's eight-year struggle to achieve independence from France (1954–62) involved several crises for both France and the *FLN*-led nonindependent Algeria. These crises, as well as many others, such as those between Portugal and Mozambique, or India's struggle for independence from Britain, were not included in the final case list because they lacked an adversarial relationship between two or more independent states at the time of the crisis.

Similarly, crises involving terrorist or nationalist groups only were omitted. However, in the crisis over an Air France plane hijacked to Uganda (1976), an adversarial relationship was created between Israel and Uganda when the latter refused to withdraw its support for *PLO* guerrillas, who had triggered the crisis and were holding Israeli citizens hostage in Entebbe. Civil wars that did not include other states as crisis actors, such as Nigeria's internal conflict over Biafra (1967–70), were also excluded. On the other hand, Spain's three-year civil war (1936–39), in which Italy and Germany allied themselves with the Nationalist rebels, appears as four international crises in the ICB data set. So too, does Yemen's five-year civil war (1962–67), in which Saudi Arabia and Egypt allied themselves with Royalist and Republican Yemen. In Greece's long civil war from 1944 to 1949, two international crises were included: the first in 1944, as a crisis for the U.K., when its influence in the area was threatened by a possible communist takeover in Greece; and the second for Greece in 1946, when infiltrators from Yugoslavia, Albania, and Bulgaria threatened severe setbacks to the Greek government's struggle against Greek communist guerrillas. And in Bosnia's lengthy civil war (1992–95) among Croats, Muslims, and Serbs, the patron role of the rump of Yugoslavia for the Bosian Serbs transformed ethnic civil strife into an international crisis.

Strict enforcement of the decision rules resulted in the inclusion of two types of crises that might at first glance appear as anomalies. First, 138 of the 412 ICB crises (33 percent) were single-actor cases. That is, the state that triggered a crisis for another state did not itself become a crisis actor. For example, Libya's expulsion of Tunisians from its territory in 1985 triggered a crisis for Tunisia (but not for Libya); the imposition of a "no-fly zone" over portions of Iraq by the U.S. and its allies in 1992 triggered a crisis for Iraq (but not for the U.S., U.K., France).

A second apparent anomaly was the identification of a small number of cases in which decision makers of a state could experience more than one crisis for their state within the duration of an international crisis. For example, India experienced two foreign policy crises during the Kashmir II crisis of 1965: the first was triggered by Pakistan in August of that year when Pakistani "freedom fighters" began infiltrating into the Vale of Kashmir, lasting until January of 1966; and the second was triggered by China when it issued an ultimatum to the Indian government to dismantle all military bases near the Chinese border, lasting from September 16 through the 21st. Similarly, Israel experienced two foreign policy crises during the October–Yom Kippur War of 1973: the first was triggered on October 5 by the movement of Egyptian forces toward the Suez Canal and a change to offensive posture, lasting until the end of the overall crisis in May 1974; and the second was triggered by Egypt when it successfully crossed the Suez Canal on October 7, lasting until October 14 when Israel won a decisive tank battle. In other words, when crisis perceptions decreased to pre-crisis levels, a state's foreign policy crisis was deemed to have terminated. When fresh perceptions of threat, time, and probability of violence were discovered during an overall international crisis, we considered that the relevant state was experiencing another foreign policy crisis.

It should be clear to the reader that a relatively large number of potential crises were considered and even researched by ICB staff, but ultimately rejected because they did not satisfy one or more of the definitional criteria we established. Some illustrations may serve to further clarify the ICB procedures. Tibet's declaration of independence from Chinese suzerainty in 1949 was never recognized by the international community. Thus, neither China's invasion and annexation of Tibet in 1950–51 nor the flight of the Dalai Lama in 1959 constituted ICB crises as defined by an adversarial relationship between two or more independent state actors. Exceptions to this decision rule were made in one category only—those states whose crises began before formal independence but terminated after its achievement, for example, Indonesia from 1945 to 1949, Bangladesh in 1971, or Angola in 1975.

Other cases appeared on the surface to be extremely serious, such as the crisis between Japan and the Netherlands over Japanese penetration of the Dutch East Indies in 1930, or Togo's 1965 action closing its border with Ghana after accusing the latter of harboring antigovernment guerrillas. But in each of these instances, the former exclusively economic, the latter political-diplomatic, there was an extremely low perceived probability of military hostilities between the adversaries. And some cases were excluded because of the absence of a clear external threat. For example, the serious and violent demonstrations that began in Gdansk in 1970 and that subsequently spread throughout Poland constituted a domestic crisis for the Polish government. The Soviet Union extended political support to the government of Poland but did not become—and was not perceived as likely to become—militarily involved.

Finally, there was no dearth of incidents or crisislike situations within protracted conflicts,[4] where great care had to be exercised in determining cases for inclusion or exclusion. The Arab/Israeli protracted conflict, for example, has witnessed 50 years of hostilities. Thus its "normal" tension level is extremely high. Within that Middle East conflict, "only" 25 cases were included in the ICB data set, from the crisis over the partition of Palestine and Israeli independence 1947–49, to Israel's invasion of Lebanon (Operation Accountability) in 1993 [replicated in Israel's Operation "Grapes of Wrath" in 1996]. Israeli military reprisals constituted a particularly difficult problem as regards case selection. Blechman (1972) lists 101 Israeli reprisal raids into Jordan, Egypt, and Syria between 1949 and 1969. Within this setting of increased violence, infiltration and reprisals were identified as crisis situations for Israel and/or its neighboring Arab states only when evidence was found of state behavior beyond standard operating procedures, that is, decision making at the highest political level, in order to deal with the situation of change within this protracted conflict. Consequently, only four appear in the ICB data set: Hula Drainage 1951 (Israel/Syria); Qibya 1953 and Qalqilya 1956 (Israel/Jordan); and Gaza Raid–Czech. Arms Deal 1955–56 (Israel/Egypt). Similarly, during extended wars the criterion of nonstandard operating procedures was applied. In World War II, for example, the ICB cases include those crises where a state entered into, or exited from, the ongoing war and turning points that strongly influenced the outcome, such as the battles of El Alamein, Stalingrad, or Saipan. Thus, 24 international crises were included as intra-war crises during World War II.

The distributions of international crises from 1918–94 across time, geographic regions, international systems, triggering entities, and crisis proneness of actors are presented in Figure II.1 and Tables II.1–II.4. Taken together, these trends across time, space, and actors provide a first glimpse of patterns of crisis in the twentieth century. Figure II.1 indicates a general increase in the number of international crises per year from multipolarity through polycentrism and a decline during the post–Cold War era. Table II.1 gives evidence of a significant shift in the locus of crises, with Africa in particular evidencing a sharp increase, and a similar decline for Europe. Table II.2 further confirms the propensity for

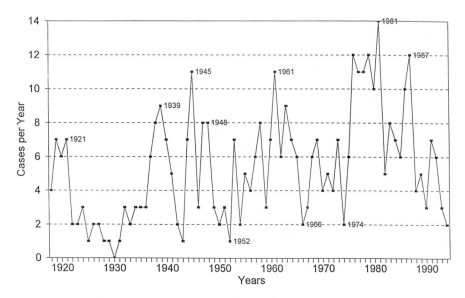

Figure II.1. Distribution of Crises, 1918–94 (N = 412)

certain systems, notably polycentrism, to be particularly crisis prone. These and other implications of the distributions for the international system are discussed in detail in Part IV.

Table II.3 lists the 10 states responsible for triggering the largest number of international crises in the twentieth century—together they account for 30 percent of all crises in the ICB data set. One need only look at the polycentric period to realize that the nature of the international system has changed dramatically— South Africa, Libya, Iraq, and Israel play critical roles in triggering international crises for this system-period. And Table II.4 examines crisis proneness, that is, the states that experienced the largest number of foreign policy crises in this century. Twelve states account for 35 percent of all foreign policy crises. Once again, it is evident that, with the exception of the U.S., which continued to experience crises at an accelerated rate in both polycentrism and the post–Cold War era, the burden of coping with crises in the latter part of the twentieth century has shifted to states such as Libya, Israel, Egypt, and Syria.

For a chronological listing of the entire ICB set of crises and actors, as well as key descriptive variables, see the Master Table (Table III.1), which appears at the end of Part III.

Variables

While the initial set of crises to be included in the ICB Project was being assembled, work was also begun on compiling a list of cross-national variables that would be used in coding the cases. The identification of distinguishing

TABLE II.1.   Regional Location of International Crises, 1918–94

Region	Frequency	Percent
Africa		
North Africa (Egypt, Libya, Tunisia, Algeria, Morocco)	22	5.3
East Africa (Ethiopia, Somalia, Kenya, Tanzania, Uganda, Sudan)	26	6.3
Central Africa (Rwanda, Burundi, Cameroon, Central African Republic, Chad, Niger)	16	3.9
West Africa (from Nigeria through Ghana, Guinea, Mauritania, Senegal)	16	3.9
Southern Africa (Angola, Botswana, Mozambique, Rhodesia/Zimbabwe, South Africa, Zambia)	28	6.8
Americas		
North America (Canada, U.S., Mexico)	0	0.0
Central America (south of Mexico, north of Colombia)	34	8.3
South America (from Colombia to Argentina)	14	3.4
Asia		
East Asia (China, Japan, North and South Korea, Mongolia, Taiwan)	22	5.3
Central Asia/Caucasus (Armenia, Azerbaijan, Georgia)	8	1.9
Southeast Asia (Burma, Laos, Cambodia, North and South Vietnam, Thailand, Malaysia, Singapore, Indonesia, Philippines)	41	10.0
South Asia (India, Pakistan, Bangladesh, Afghanistan, Sri Lanka, Nepal)	19	4.6
Europe		
North Europe (Denmark, Finland, Iceland, Norway, Sweden)	10	2.4
East Europe (Baltic states, Poland, Romania, Bulgaria, Russia/USSR)	26	6.3
Central Europe (Czechoslovakia, Germany, Austria, Hungary, Switzerland)	22	5.3
West Europe (U.K., France, Belgium, Netherlands, Luxembourg)	7	1.7
South Europe (Portugal, Spain, Italy, Greece, Albania, Cyprus)	23	5.6
Middle East		
Middle East (Israel, Jordan, Lebanon, Syria, Turkey, Iraq, Iran, Gulf States, Saudi Arabia, Yemens)	78	18.9
TOTAL	412	100.0

characteristics of crises for a diverse set of actors across a 76-year period entailed certain methodological challenges. The most serious was the inability to develop quantitative indicators for certain kinds of information on a uniform cross-national basis. At the outset of this project we realized that it would make a distinctive contribution to crisis research only if we adopted a creative approach to variable operationalization. While many of our variables can be thought of as "hard"—geographic location, number of actors, extent of violence, global organization involvement—others are "softer" in nature. This latter category includes

TABLE II.2. Location of International Crises in Time and Space[a]

		Africa		Americas		Asia		Europe		Middle East		TOTAL	
Multipolarity	1918-39	2	3%	9	12%	13	17%	39	53%	11	15%	74	18%
World War II	1939-45	2	11%	1	3%	8	25%	17	53%	4	13%	32	8%
Bipolarity	1945-62	10	11%	12	13%	31	35%	17	19%	20	22%	90	22%
Polycentrism	1963-89	88	45%	24	12%	32	16%	13	7%	38	20%	195	47%
Unipolarity	1990-94	6	29%	2	9%	6	29%	2	9%	5	24%	21	5%
TOTAL		108	26%	48	12%	90	22%	88	21%	78	19%	412	100%

[a] In this and all subsequent contingency tables, frequencies and percentages are summed across rows.

TABLE II.3.　Ten Leading Triggering Entities of Crises in the Twentieth Century

	Multipolarity	World War II	Bipolarity	Polycentrism	Unipolarity	TOTAL
USSR	3	6	8	4	1	22
Germany	8	6	0	0	0	14
South Africa	0	0	0	14	0	14
U.S.	0	7	2	5	0	14
Israel	0	0	6	6	0	12
Libya	0	0	0	12	0	12
Japan	8	1	0	0	0	9
Iraq	0	0	0	6	3	9
Pakistan	0	0	4	4	1	9
U.K.	3	2	3	0	0	8

such variables as content and extent of satisfaction about outcome, effectiveness of third parties in crisis abatement, and values threatened. Here we consulted often with regional experts while relying on the coders'—and our—ability to reach conclusions based upon research on the case in question. While readers may differ in interpretation, it is hoped that errors resulting from bias have been kept to a minimum.

The ultimate set of variables, along with elaborate codesheets and code-books containing definitions and instructions, evolved over a period of years and involved extensive pretests and debriefing sessions with groups of coders. In fact, during 1978–79 a seminar for all ICB coders and senior ICB researchers was convened weekly in Jerusalem, and difficulties were jointly discussed and resolved. Many of the definitions for individual variables were sharpened in these sessions. Again, we will present only the final versions of these documents.

Data were collected at the level of the individual crisis actor and the level of

TABLE II.4.　Most Crisis-Prone States in the Twentieth Century (15 or more crises)

	Multipolarity	World War II	Bipolarity	Polycentrism	Unipolarity	TOTAL
U.S.	1	2	22	27	4	56
U.K.	10	12	10	6	1	39
USSR	6	4	14	11	0	35
France	11	4	7	7	2	31
Israel	0	0	7	17	2	26
Egypt	0	0	9	13	2	24
Germany[a]	7	10	4	2	0	23
Libya	0	0	0	18	0	18
Turkey	7	1	4	5	0	17
Greece	5	2	2	6	0	15
Japan	8	7	0	0	0	15
Syria	0	1	3	10	1	15

[a] Includes Federal Republic of Germany and German Democratic Republic.

the international crisis as a whole. This distinction is important to keep in mind, because these two perspectives complement each other in a way that is truly unique to ICB. Some variables, notably those dealing with the perceptions of crisis decision makers, were collected exclusively at the actor level of analysis. Moreover, data on sociopolitical conditions at the time of the crisis, or structure of the decision-making unit involved, were collected solely at the actor level. Data on other variables, such as effectiveness of third parties in crisis abatement and geographic proximity of the crisis actors, were collected exclusively at the level of the international crisis as a whole. And a large set of variables was amenable to measurement at both levels. Thus, crisis trigger identifies both the event that triggered a crisis for an individual state (actor level) and the event that catalyzed the international crisis as a whole (system level). Similarly, gravity of threat can be identified as the gravest threat perceived by the decision makers of a state in crisis, and summarized for the crisis as a whole as the most salient threat experienced by actors in the international crisis.

In the case of the variables for which data are available at both the actor and system levels, a word relating to procedures is in order. In some cases, such as crisis trigger, the system-level variable was coded as the earliest trigger date for any of the actors in the crisis. Similarly, termination date was based on the date when the last crisis actor perceived a decline to pre-crisis levels of threat and potential for military hostilities. In the case of threat, the gravest threat perceived by the key actor was taken to signify threat for the crisis as a whole. This rule was also used for centrality and severity of violence. In the case of some variables, the mix of system-level values had to be examined to determine the overall coding—this was true of outcome variables such as content, form, and satisfaction. Overall, care was taken to capture, in the international system-level variables, the essence of combined coding for the individual states involved in the crisis. Specific details are provided in the ICB codebooks, available with the data sets.

In the following pages, we present all the ICB variables, followed by a brief definition of each. We indicate after each whether it was coded at the actor level (A), international crisis level (C), or both (A&C). Many of the key variables are discussed more extensively in Part IV, where they are employed in the analyses presented there, and this definition will also be indicated in parentheses (Part IV). The order in which variables are presented and discussed follows that employed in the ICB Project codebooks. For full definitions, see the codebook for the ICB Project Datasets, available as Study #9286 from the Interuniversity Consortium for Political and Social Research of the University of Michigan.

Dimensions of Crisis Onset

Crisis Trigger (A&C, Part IV). The specific act, event, or situational change perceived by the decision maker(s) as a threat to basic values, with finite time for response and a heightened probability of military hostilities.

Trigger Date (A&C). The date on which the decision makers perceived the trigger.

Triggering Entity (A&C). The entity—single state, coalition, nonstate actor—that initiated the crisis.

Context of Crisis Onset

Value Threatened (A&C, Part IV). The type of threat perceived by the actor, ranging from threat to existence, of grave damage, to influence, territory, political system, economic threat, or limited threat to population and property.

Decision Maker(s)' Stress (A&C). An index that combines the degree of threat and the power of the threatening actor (see below for discussion of this index).

Crisis Issue (A). The most important initial issue-area of a crisis for an actor: military-security, political-diplomatic, economic-developmental, or cultural-status.

Change in Crisis Issue (A). Major change in the initial issue-area of a crisis.

Source of Threat (A). The entity perceived by the decision makers as the source of threat to values. In most but not all instances, this will be identical to the triggering entity (see above).

Power Status of Source of Threat (A). The threatening entity classified according to small, middle, great, superpower.

Overall Violence (A&C, Part IV). The amount of violence, if any, that occurred during any stage of the crisis?

Intra-War Crisis (A&C, Part IV). Crises in which a situational change during an ongoing war triggered the crisis.

Protracted Conflict (A&C, Part IV). Was the crisis part of a protracted conflict involving the same group of actors?

Protracted Conflict Identification (A&C, Parts III, IV). If the crisis was part of a protracted conflict, which PC was it? For example, East/West, India/Pakistan, etc?

Territorial Conflict (C). Did the crisis involve a conflict over territory?

Ethnicity-Related (C, Part IV). Was ethnicity a factor in the crisis?

Ethnicity-Driven (C, Part IV). Was ethnicity the central factor dividing the adversaries in the crisis?

Crisis Management

Size of Decisional Unit (A). The number of persons who formulated a state's major response to the crisis.

Structure of Decisional Unit (A). The structure (institutional, ad hoc, etc.) that formulated the actor's major response.

Level of Communications (A). The highest ranking person responsible for communications with other actors during the crisis.

Crisis Management 1: Major Response (A&C, Part IV). The major thrust of the actor's response to the crisis trigger.

Date of Major Response (A). The date the major response was implemented.

Gestation 1: Elapsed Time, Trigger to Response (A). Elapsed time in days from trigger to major response.

Crisis Management 2: Principal Technique (CMT) (A&C, Part IV). From pacific techniques such as negotiation and mediation, to nonviolent military, violence, or any multiple thereof involving violence.

Timing of Violence (C). The first occurrence of violence, if any, prior to, at the onset of, or during a crisis.

Centrality of Violence as CMT (A&C, Part IV). The relative importance decision makers attributed to their use of violence, in terms of achieving their crisis goals, ranging from preeminent, important, minor to none.

Severity of Violence (A&C, Part IV). The most severe use of violence in crisis management, from war, serious clashes, minor clashes, to none.

Crisis Termination

Date of Termination (A&C). The date on which a crisis actor's perception of threat, time pressure, and war likelihood declined toward pre-crisis levels.

Gestation 2: Trigger to Termination (A&C). Elapsed time, in days, from trigger to termination.

Gestation 3: Response to Termination (A). Elapsed time, in days, from response to termination.

Substance of Outcome (A&C, Part IV). From the actor's perspective, perception of victory, defeat, stalemate, or compromise; from the perspective of the crisis as a whole, ambiguous outcome (stalemate and/or compromise), definitive outcome (victory and/or defeat).

Form of Outcome (A&C, Part IV). Type of outcome, from agreement, tacit understanding, unilateral act, compliance, to imposed.

Extent of Satisfaction with Outcome (A&C, Part IV). How satisfied was the actor with the outcome (actor level); what was the mix of satisfaction levels for all actors (system level)?

Crisis Legacy (A&C, Part IV). Escalation or reduction of tension, measured by whether or not the same parties became involved in a crisis with each other during the subsequent five years.

Third-Party Crisis Management Activity

Major Powers (Great Powers 1918–45, Superpowers 1945–94)

Activity (A&C, Part IV). The type of major power activity in crisis abatement, if any, including political, economic, covert, semi-military, and military.

Effectiveness (C, Part IV). Measures the major power's contribution to crisis abatement, if any, ranging from most important, important, marginal effect, to escalated the crisis.

Most Effective Activity (C). If activity occurred, which type was most effective?

Impact on Pace of Crisis Abatement (C). Impact of activity, if any, on the rapidity of crisis abatement.

Actor Perception of Favorableness of Major Power Activity (A). Actor perception—favorable, unfavorable, neutral—of third-party activity by the major powers.

Global Organization (GO) Involvement (League of Nations 1920–39, United Nations 1945–94)

Source of GO Involvement (C). If the League of Nations or the United Nations was approached, was the approach by the actor(s), major power(s), other third party(ies), or initiated by the GO itself?

Most Active GO Organ (A&C, Part IV). The most active GO organ in an effort to abate the crisis: Secretary-General, (General) Assembly, (Security) Council, other.

Content of GO Involvement (C, Part IV). Involvement by the most active organ, from discussion without a resolution, through fact-finding, good offices, mediation, call for action, sanctions, to emergency military force.

Effectiveness of GO Involvement (C, Part IV). The GO's contribution to crisis abatement, from single most important, important, or marginal contribution, no effect, to escalation.

Most Effective GO Organ (C). How effective was the organ that made the greatest contribution to crisis abatement?

Most Effective Involvement (C). The activity of the most effective organ.

Impact on Pace of Crisis Abatement (C). The impact, if any, on the rapidity of crisis abatement, from more rapid termination to delay.

Actor Perception of Favorableness of GO Involvement (A). A crisis actor's perception of GO activity or inactivity as favorable, unfavorable, or neutral.

Regional/Security Organization (RSO) Involvement

Source of RSO Involvement (C). If a RSO was approached, which entity made the approach?

Most Active RSO (A&C). Which was most active RSO, including *OAS, OAU, SEATO, NATO, WTO, LAS, CENTO,* other?

Content of RSO Involvement (A&C). See GO Involvement above.

Effectiveness of RSO Involvement (C). See GO Involvement above.

Most Effective RSO (C). Which organization made the greatest contribution to crisis abatement?

Most Effective RSO Involvement (C). See GO Involvement above.

Impact on Pace of Crisis Abatement (C). See GO Involvement above.

Actor Perception of Favorableness of RSO Involvement (A). See GO Involvement above.

Crisis Attributes

Geographic Location of Actor (A). The region in which the crisis actor is located.

Geographic Location of International Crisis (A&C, Part IV). The region in which the crisis occurred.

Geographic Proximity of Crisis (A, Part IV). How proximate was the actor to the crisis, ranging from home territory, same continent, region, remote?

Adversarial Proximity of Crisis Actors (C, Part IV). How close were the principal adversaries to each other, from contiguous, near neighbors, to distant?

Number of Involved Actors (A&C, Part IV). The number of actors perceived as being involved (although not necessarily as actors) in the crisis.

System Polarity (A&C, Part IV). In which system-period does the international crisis fall: multipolarity 1918–39, World War II 1939–45, bipolarity 1945–62, polycentrism 1963–89, post–Cold War unipolar 1990–94?

System Level (A&C). At what system level did the crisis take place, from subsystem, mainly subsystem, mainly dominant, to dominant system?

Power Discrepancy (A&C, Part IV). Measures the capability gap between adversaries, whether individual states or coalitions (see below for discussion of this index).

Number of States in System (A). The number of states in the international system at the time of the crisis.

Age of Actor (A). Ranges from old established states—pre-1648—to new states—post-1957.

Territorial Size (A). Small (less than 50,000 square miles), medium (50,000–500,000 square miles), large (over 500,000 square miles).

Political Regime (A). A distinction between civil or military authoritarian regimes and democratic regimes.

Duration of Political Regime (A). The number of years of continuous existence of a specific political authority within a state.

Alliance with Great Power/Superpower (A). Formal or informal alliance with one of the great powers (1918–45) or a superpower (1945–94).

Membership in the Global Organization (A). Membership in the League, the UN, or neither, at the time of the crisis.

Nuclear Capability (A). Ranging from no nuclear capability to second strike capability at the time of the crisis.

Military Expenditures (A). Military expenditures for the year of the crisis.

Level of Cost of Living (COL) (A). Deviation from the normal level for that actor relative to the trend exhibited during the four years preceding the crisis.

Level of Unemployment (A). See COL above.

Level of Inflation (A). See COL above.

Level of Food Prices (A). See COL above.

Level of Labor Disruptions (A). See COL above.

Level of Consumer Goods Shortages (A). See COL above.

Level of Societal Unrest (A). Significant increases or decreases as evidenced by assassinations, terrorism, general strikes, demonstrations, and riots, up to six months prior to the crisis.

Level of Mass Violence (A). Demonstrated by insurrections, civil war, and revolution within the society of a crisis actor during the six months before the onset of the crisis.

Level of Regime Repression (A). Examples include exile, deportation, purges, harassment of political organizations, martial law, restrictions on the press.

Level of Government Instability (A). Indicated by executive changes and changes in administrative structure.

Source Used for Coding Crisis (A&C). Types of sources used for coding the crisis.

Overall Intensity of Crisis

Number of Crisis Actors (C).

Extent of Involvement by Powers (C). Adversarial behavior of the major powers, from no activity through military activity.

Geostrategic Salience (C). The significance of the location of a crisis in terms of its natural resources, distance from power centers, etc., measured by the number of international systems—global, dominant, subsystem—that were affected by the crisis.

Heterogeneity among Adversarial Actors (C). Measured by the number of attribute differences between the most heterogeneous pair of adversaries in the international crisis—military capability, political regime, economic development, and culture.

Issues (C). Coded according to the principal issue-area and any change during a crisis.

Overall Violence (C). See the preceding "Context of Crisis Onset" section.

Overall Importance of Crisis

Change in Actors (C). Comprises both regime change, whether in orientation or type, and a more basic structural shift, that is, the emergence or disappearance of one or more independent states as a result of the international crisis.

Change in Alliances (C). Shifts in the structure or functioning, or the elimination, of an alliance, from the entry (exit) of one or more actors into (or from) a formal or informal alliance, to an increase or decrease of cohesiveness in an existing alliance, to no change.

Change in Power Balance (C). Change in both the number of power centers and the hierarchy of power.

Change in Rules of the Game (C). In those norms, derived from law, custom, morality, or self-interest, that serve as guidelines for behavior by actors in a system.

Indices

During the course of the 20 years that the International Crisis Behavior Project has devoted to data collection and analysis, a number of indices were developed as a way of addressing particularly complex aspects of the structure of the international system and the actions of states within that system. In the cases of stress and power discrepancy, these indices have been included in the ICB data sets themselves. Others are derived from combinations of existing ICB variables. At the level of the individual crisis actor, ICB has developed indices for power, power discrepancy, economic conditions, and decision maker stress. At the level of the international crisis, ICB indices include power discrepancy, instability, proportion of democratic actors, stress, intensity and importance of crisis. In the following sections, we will briefly discuss these indicators and point the reader to studies in which they have been employed.

Actor-Level Indices

Power

Preoccupation with state power has been central to the study of international relations since the birth of the nation-state. It has been employed to explain differences in state behavior, including whom they choose to go to war with and how successful they are expected to be, what alliances they will form, and what political and developmental strategies they will pursue. In fact, in explaining state behavior, the realist approach to international relations relegates virtually all factors other than power, such as domestic conditions and decision maker attributes, to secondary importance.

The ICB power index is composed of measures of human, territorial, and material resources available to the actor at the time of the crisis. This index comprises six elements and is computed additively once categories have been established: size of population, GNP, territorial size, alliance capability, military expenditures, and nuclear capability.

Studies utilizing the power index are noted in the discussion of Power Discrepancy.

Power Discrepancy

Closely related to the notion of the power of an individual state is a relational concept that assesses the power of a state vis-à-vis its adversary(ies). State behavior is a product of the power that a state possesses at the time of the crisis, as well as how that power stacks up against the potential power which can be marshaled by its conflict partner(s). Once again, the literature of international relations is replete with theories that attempt to explain state behavior based on relations of power polarity or hegemony among state actors.

The ICB power discrepancy (PD) index is based on the power score (see above) of the crisis actor at the onset of a crisis. The power of a crisis actor and the power available to it from tight alliance partners (if any)—immediately prior to the actor's major response—was compared to that of its principal adversary or adversaries—whether or not they were themselves crisis actors—to create the final score. These scores were then grouped into five categories, where positive discrepancy indicates power greater than the adversary and negative discrepancy means power less than the adversary: high positive PD, low positive PD, power parity, low negative PD, and high negative PD.

Studies utilizing the power discrepancy index include Brecher and Wilkenfeld (1989); Wilkenfeld (1991); and Part IV.

Economic Conditions

Many theoretical and empirical studies have taken the position that the conditions within a state significantly affect the type of behavior that a state directs externally. In general terms, it has been argued that states experiencing difficult economic conditions, combined with internal unrest, are more likely than others to engage in aggressive forms of foreign policy behavior in general and conflictual behavior in particular. It is to be expected that state behavior in crisis will also reflect the impact of particularly adverse internal conditions.

The ICB index of economic conditions is composed of six indicators: cost of living, unemployment, inflation, food prices, labor disruption, and consumer goods shortages. If any two of these six variables indicated a significant increase during the six months leading up to the crisis, the economic conditions indicator was coded as deteriorating.

Studies utilizing the economic conditions index include Brecher and Wilkenfeld (1989); Wilkenfeld (1991); Hewitt and Wilkenfeld (1996); and Part IV.

Decision Maker Stress

The ICB definition of a foreign policy crisis includes as one of its core criteria the threat to basic values of the state. And among the dimensions that form the context of the onset of crisis is a variable identifying the type of threat that decision makers perceived.

The ICB index of decision maker stress seeks to combine the type of threat perceived by decision makers with the difference in power status between the actor and its adversary. For example, a territorial threat takes on meaning in terms of the amount of stress that it generates only when account is taken of the relative strength of the adversary. Operationally, stress is computed as follows.

(Stage 1). Values are assigned to the categories of the value threat variable: threat to existence = 10; threat to influence of great power or superpower = 7; threat of grave damage, threat to territory, political threat = 6; economic threat, threat to influence of nongreat power or nonsuperpower = 4; limited threat, other = 1.

(Stage 2). Values are assigned to a new variable called power relations, based on the differences between the power status of the actor and its

adversary—small, middle, great, superpower. A complex set of interrelationships is defined, where, for example, the highest value (10) is assigned to a small power with a superpower adversary, as well as to a case in which the two superpowers are adversaries.

(Stage 3). The indicator of stress is computed for each of the 895 crisis actors in the ICB data set, based on the addition of Stages 1 and 2.

The stress index is utilized in Part IV.

International Crisis-Level Indices

Power Discrepancy
As indicated above, power discrepancy was computed for each crisis actor in relation to its principal adversary(ies) in the crisis. At the international crisis level, the highest positive power discrepancy score for any actor in the crisis is taken as the indicator of power discrepancy for the crisis as a whole. These scores were then collapsed into low, medium, and high power discrepancy for the crisis.

Instability
The ICB Project has undertaken the construction of an index of instability for each of the 412 international crises. This index involves the simultaneous use of several scaled indicators of the seriousness of the crisis and the incorporation of two additional crisis attributes: power status of the actors and duration of the crisis. The inclusion of power status recognizes that the degree of systemic disruption resulting from an international crisis is a function not only of the type of behavior exhibited by the parties to the crisis, but also reflects the power status of these actors; that is, crises with more powerful actors, ipso facto, generate more turmoil than crises with less powerful participants. Furthermore, the inclusion of duration for each actor recognizes that systemic disruption will be more extensive the longer the elapsed time from trigger to termination.

The index of instability is represented by the following equation.

$$I_j = (T_j) \left(\log_{10} \left[\sum_{i=1}^{n} (P_i(D_i)) + 1 \right] \right)$$

where

I_j = instability generated by crisis "j" ($j = 1, \ldots, 412$)

T_j = turmoil associated with crisis "j," composed of intensity of violence, crisis management technique, and trigger

P_i = power status of actor "i" in international crisis "j"

D_i = duration in days as a crisis actor for actor "i" in crisis "j."

The instability generated by an international crisis is a function of its turmoil, the relative power status of its participants, and its duration.

The instability index was employed in Brecher and Wilkenfeld (1989, 1991); and Brecher, James, and Wilkenfeld (1990).

Proportion of Democratic Actors in Crisis

In order to investigate propositions derived from the *theory of democratic peace,* the ICB Project has developed an index of democracy that is sensitive to two aspects: the proportion of democracies within each of the opposing coalitions and the overall proportion of democracies in the crisis. Creation of this index, DEM, is based on the actor-level variable regime and is computed for the international crisis according to the following formula.

$$\text{DEM} = (p_1 + p_2)/2$$

where p_1 is the proportion of democracies in one coalition and p_2 is the proportion in the other. In other words, DEM is the average proportion of democracies in each of the opposing coalitions in the international crisis.

The democracy index is employed in Hewitt and Wilkenfeld (1996); and in Part IV.

Stress

We have already discussed stress from the point of view of its calculation for an individual crisis actor. Stress for the international crisis as a whole is taken as the highest stress level experienced by any of the individual crisis actors.

The stress index is employed in Part IV.

Intensity of International Crisis

As noted earlier, an international crisis is characterized by two necessary and sufficient conditions: (1) an increase in the intensity of disruptive interactions among system actors, with a high probability of military hostilities; and (2) incipient change in one or more structural attributes of an international system, namely, power distribution, actors/regimes, rules, and alliance configuration.

Six ICB variables are used to construct the index of intensity: number of actors, involvement of the powers, geostrategic salience (from subsystem to global system), heterogeneity among the actors (in terms of military capability, economic development, political regime, and culture), issues, and extent of violence (if any) during the crisis.

The intensity index was employed in Brecher and Wilkenfeld (1988, 1989).

Importance of International Crisis

The extent of disequilibrium resulting from an international crisis, that is, its long-term importance, is measured by four indicators of system change: change in power distribution; actors; rules of the game; and alliance configuration. The first two represent structural change, while the latter influence the process of interaction.

The importance index was employed in Brecher and Wilkenfeld (1989).

Coders

The critical task of researching the international crises and collecting data on the variables and indices previously discussed was borne mainly by a dedicated cadre of graduate students from the Hebrew University of Jerusalem and Bar Ilan University in Israel, McGill University in Montreal, and the University of Maryland. Over the years, more than 30 students assisted on various aspects of the project, and several, including Hemda Ben Yehuda-Agid, Mark Boyer, Patrick James, Etel Solingen, Brigid Starkey, and Alice Ackerman, have gone on to professorial positions in universities in the U.S., Canada, and Israel. The history of their training with ICB is described in some detail in Brecher and Wilkenfeld (1988); and Wilkenfeld and Brecher (1988).

In Stage 1, during which data for 51 of the 76 years were collected (see the section on Data Collection above), each international crisis was assigned to a pair of coders, each of whom devoted approximately 25 hours to researching the case, filling out the codesheets, and, for one coder preparing a draft case summary. During Stages 2 through 4, where we had increased confidence in both our training and coding procedures, cases were assigned to single coders and only occasionally to a second coder when a particularly complex crisis was being researched. In all four stages, this process culminated in a lengthy debriefing session with one of the senior ICB researchers. Conflicts between coders were resolved, and in some instances more research was required. For the crises that were coded by two coders working independently, an intercoder reliability score of .85 was obtained, well within the range of acceptability for this type of research. In fact, it was this high intercoder reliability score, coupled with the procedures developed to debrief each case, that led us to conclude that single coders for Stages 2, 3, and 4 could be used with reasonable confidence.

Sources

Several types of sources were used as the basis for the collection of ICB data. As noted, the *New York Times* and *Keesing's Contemporary Archives* were the starting point for purposes of compiling the initial set of cases to be investigated. The National and Hebrew University Library in Jerusalem provided the bulk of the material, supplemented by the libraries at McGill University and the University of Maryland and the Library of Congress in Washington, DC. Additional sources were obtained from Project and private collections. Extensive use was made of newspapers, scholarly articles, historical accounts, memoirs, and official documents. For example, recently declassified Central Intelligence Agency documents covering substantial portions of the early Cold War period were used to update and supplement previously coded cases and periods. For cases where information was abundant, all of the above were consulted to enable the coders to make an informed choice among several alternative codings posed for particularly difficult variables. In most cases, some combination of available source material provided sufficient information for coding. In all cases, coders carefully documented the nature of the sources consulted.

The problem of "Western bias" was dealt with as honestly as possible. It was aggravated by the abundance of source materials in English—a large majority of which was presented by American and British authors with their own prejudices. The ICB Project endeavored to offset this in three ways. First, extensive use was made of regional specialists whose knowledge of the crises under inquiry was broad and detailed. This task was made easier by the authors' association with three different universities. Second, we sought and achieved a diversity of language skills among the coders; students were able to research cases from source materials published in English, French, German, Hebrew, and Spanish. And third, the ICB case list was compared to lists of conflicts, wars, disputes, incidents, armed acts, etc., in the international literature (see Table II.5). Despite these compensatory efforts, much information, particularly for recent crises, as well as for those pertaining to the Soviet bloc, China, and African states, was not as abundant as desired.

Tables II.6 and II.7 present frequency distributions for categories of sources used by the coders. These categories range from the most extensive, designated as "all sources" and including a combination of documents, memoirs, books, articles, and chronologies, to the least extensive—chronologies only. Overall, multiple sources were consulted in 83 percent of all cases. With regard to system-periods (Table II.6), it is generally the case that the earlier the crisis, the more extensive the sources available for consultation. As might be expected, World War II provided the most extensive sources to the coders, while 24 percent of all polycentric crises and 62 percent of the very recent post–Cold War unipolarity cases were coded on the basis of chronologies alone.

In Table II.7, we note that the most extensive sources were available for cases in Asia, Europe, and the Middle East. The African cases, most of which occurred in the most recent periods, show a high reliance on chronologies (30 percent) and very few instances (10 percent) in which a mix of all sources was available.

All sources used to collect data for this volume, across all four stages of the data collection beginning in 1978, are listed in the bibliography. The section called "General Sources" contains 71 items that were widely used. This is followed by 62 "Primary Sources," mostly government, League of Nations, and UN documents. The most extensive section, "Secondary Sources," includes a list of about 1,600 books and articles consulted in the coding of the 412 ICB crises for the twentieth century. Taken together, these three lists provide the complete citations for every reference used to gather data for the 76 years of this

TABLE II.5. Compendia of Conflicts, Crises, Disputes, Wars

Author	Focus	Period	Cases
Axell et al. (1993)	armed conflicts	1989-92	118
	wars	1989-92	78
Blechman and Kaplan (1978)	U.S. use of military force	1946-75	215
Bouthoul and Carrère (1976)	interstate wars	1920-74	31[a]
		(1740-1974	157)
Brecher and Wilkenfeld (1997)	international crises (ICB)	1918-94	412
	foreign policy crises (ICB)	1918-94	895
	protracted conflicts (ICB)	1918-94	31
Butterworth (1976)	interstate security conflicts	1945-74	310
CACI (1978)	international crises for USSR	1946-75	386
Carroll (1968)[b]	wars	1945-68	65
Cusack and Eberwein (1982)	serious international disputes	(1900-76	634)
Deitchman (1964)[b]	military engagements	1945-62	30
Donlean and Grieve (1973)	international disputes	1945-70	50
Eckhart and Azar (1978)	international conflicts (COPDAB)	1945-75	144
Gochman and Maoz (1984)	militarized interstate disputes (COW)	(1816-1976	960)
Greaves (1962)[b]	wars, revolts, coups, crises	1945-62	55
Haas (1983)	international disputes	1945-81	282
Haas (1986)	international disputes	1945-84	319
Haas, Butterworth, Nye (1972)	International disputes	1945-70	146
Heldt and Wallensteen (1993)	armed conflicts	1990-91	107
Holsti (1966)	international conflicts	1919-65	77
Holsti (1991)	wars/major armed interventions	1918-41	30
		1945-89	58
		(1648-1989	177)

TABLE II.5.—*Continued*

Author	Focus	Period	Cases
Kaplan (1981)	Soviet use of military force	1944-79	190
Kellog (n.d.)[b]	wars, coups, crises	1945-64	38
Kende (1971)	local wars	1945-70	95
Kende (1978)	wars	1945-76	120
Leiss and Bloomfield (1967)[b]	local conflicts, limited wars	1945-65	27
Leng and Singer (1988)	militarized interstate crises	(1816-1975	38[c])
Lindgren et al. (1991)	armed conflicts	1989	110
Luard (1987)	principal wars	1917-84	161
	international wars in Europe +	(1648-1984	470)
	civil wars in Europe +		
	international wars elsewhere +		
	wars of national independence +		
	civil wars elsewhere +		
	wars of decolonization		
Maoz (1982)	militarized interstate disputes (COW)	(1815-1976	827)
	serious interstate disputes	1929-76	95[c]
Nordlander et al. (1994)	armed conflicts over government and territory	1993	31
Richardson (1960)[b]	deadly quarrels	1946-54	13
	(armed clashes)	(1819-1949	289)
Singer and Small (1972)	interstate and extra-systemic wars (COW)	1919-65	24
		(1816-1965	93)
Siverson and Tennefoss (1982)	interstate conflicts	1919-65	152
		(1815-1965	256)
Small and Singer (1982)	interstate and extra-systemic wars (COW)	1919-79	47
		(1816-1980	118)
Snyder and Diesing (1977)	international crises	1938-62	8
		(1898-1962	12)
Sorokin (1937)	international wars	(1801-1925	189[d])
Tillema (1991)	wars and military interventions	1945-88	269

(continued)

TABLE II.5.—*Continued*

Author	Focus	Period	Cases
Wainhouse (1966)[b]	global organization peace activity	1946-65	21
Wallensteen et al. (1989)	armed conflicts	1988	111
Wallensteen and Axell (1994)	armed conflicts	1989-93	90
Wilson and Wallensteen (1988)	armed conflicts	1987	36
Wood (1968)[b]	conflicts	1946-67	53
Wright (1942, 1965)[b]	international, civil, colonial and imperial wars	1919-64 (1480-1964	25 291)
Zacher (1979)	international conflicts	1947-77	116

[a] The number of cases specified within parentheses here and elsewhere in Table II.5 refers to a period extending beyond the time frame of the ICB data set, 1918-94.
[b] These 9 lists, conflicts from 1945 to 1968, are contained in SIPRI (1969).
[c] A random sample of cases.
[d] Wars involving one or more of the following European powers: Austria-Hungary, France, Germany, Great Britain, Italy, Russia, Spain.

inquiry. An abbreviated form of these sources is provided at the end of each summary in Part III. When no specific citation is indicated, only general sources were used. Finally, a list of "References" is provided, which includes those works cited in the Preface, Part I (Framework), Part II (Methodology), and Part IV (Analysis).

TABLE II.6. Sources of Data: System-Periods

		All sources		Most sources		Chronologies only		TOTAL	
Multipolarity	1918-39	17	23%	56	76%	1	1%	74	18%
World War II	1939-45	22	69%	10	31%	0	0%	32	8%
Bipolarity	1945-62	37	41%	44	49%	9	10%	90	22%
Polycentrism	1963-89	30	15%	119	61%	46	24%	195	47%
Unipolarity	1990-94	0	0%	8	38%	13	62%	21	5%
TOTAL		106	26%	237	57%	69	17%	412	100%

TABLE II.7. **Sources of Data: Geography**

	All sources		Most sources		Chronologies only		TOTAL	
Africa	11	10%	65	60%	32	30%	108	26%
Americas	9	19%	29	60%	10	21%	48	12%
Asia	38	42%	42	47%	10	11%	90	22%
Europe	26	30%	58	66%	4	4%	88	21%
Middle East	22	28%	43	55%	13	17%	78	19%
TOTAL	106	26%	237	57%	69	17%	412	100%

Summary

Part II provided the reader with information on the selection of cases for inclusion in the International Crisis Behavior data set, discussed the variables used at the international crisis and actor levels of analysis, explained the coding procedures, and indicated the extensive sources consulted in assembling the data sets. These data sets contain a large body of information on crisis phenomena from onset, through escalation, de-escalation, to termination. In Part IV, we will analyze several of the enduring themes in the study of crisis: polarity, geography, ethnicity, regimes, protracted conflict, violence, and third party intervention. Much is left to be explored, and it is our hope that the preceding detailed descriptions of procedures and data will allow other researchers to tap the richness of these data.

Notes to Part II

1. A list of all regional experts consulted appears in the preface to this volume.
2. An example of such a discovery was the case of Able Archer 83. This November 1983 crisis for the USSR was triggered by a large-scale *NATO* war game, stretching from Norway to Turkey and designed to test nuclear release mechanisms in the case of a first

strike against the USSR; the USSR misperceived this as the real thing. Little was known of the gravity of this crisis for the USSR at the time, and only later documents attested to the seriousness of the event, hence its late addition to the ICB data set.

3. The ICB coding of the Berlin Wall crisis of 1961 was revised as a result of the publication by Garthoff of an article in *Foreign Policy* in 1991 entitled "Berlin 1961: The Record Corrected." This article supplied information to the effect that the crisis lasted 11 more days than previously known for both the U.S. and the USSR, after a near-confrontation with tanks at "Check Point Charlie." More generally, the publication of documents from the Soviet and East German archives shed light on an array of cases: some East/West, such as Korean War II; many Soviet-bloc cases, such as East German Uprising 1953, Hungarian Uprising 1956, Poland 1956, Prague Spring 1968. These documents were published by the Woodrow Wilson Center, International Cold War History Project, through their *Bulletin* and *Working Papers*.

4. For a detailed discussion of ICB use of the protracted conflict concept, see Parts I and IV.

Part III. Cases

Introduction

ICB research has uncovered 412 **international crises** and 895 **foreign policy crises** since the end of World War I, that is, eruptions that met the defining conditions of these concepts as specified at the beginning of this book (pp. 4–5, 3). Almost 60 percent of the cases occurred in **protracted conflicts (PC),** the other 40 percent outside this context.

During the period from November 1918 until the end of 1994 we identified 31 protracted conflicts, distributed by region as follows.

Africa
PC Number
1   Angola
2   Chad/Libya
3   Ethiopia/Somalia
4   Rhodesia
5   Western Sahara

Americas
PC Number
6   Costa Rica/Nicaragua
7   Ecuador/Peru
8   Honduras/Nicaragua

Asia
PC Number
9   Afghanistan/Pakistan
10   China/Japan
11   China/Vietnam
12   India/Pakistan
13   Indochina
14   Indonesia
15   Korea

Europe
PC Number
16   Czechoslovakia/Germany
17   Finland/Russia
18   France/Germany

The entire set of international crises will be presented in two clusters: crises that erupted in protracted conflicts (**PC** crises); and **non-PC** crises. Within each cluster they are grouped by **region** and in **alphabetical** and **chronological** sequence. To facilitate reader access to a large body of knowledge, only the names of **PC** crises will be cited in the regional set, with a cross-reference to the protracted conflict where that case is presented in full.

Each **PC** cluster will begin with a general **background** of the conflict under discussion. A case summary begins by providing **background** information, including links to previous crises between the same adversaries, and the setting in which the international crisis under discussion erupted.

A summary then specifies the crisis actors, the first trigger and trigger date, the **triggering entity,** and the **duration** of the international crisis. **Crisis actors** are those states whose decision makers perceive the three defining conditions of a foreign policy crisis: an increase in threat to one or more basic values; an awareness of time constraints on decisions; and heightened probability of involvement in military hostilities at some point during a crisis. **Trigger** refers to the act, event, or situational change that catalyzes a crisis. **Trigger date** designates the day these three perceptions became manifest for the decision makers. **Triggering entity** is the state or nonstate actor that initiates a crisis. **Duration** is measured from the entry of the first participant in an international crisis to the exit of the last participant; in operational terms, from the first crisis actor's trigger date to the last **termination date;** that is, when the crisis perceptions of the last state to leave an international crisis decline to pre-crisis norms.

The case summary then specifies the trigger for other crisis actors, along with the content and date of their **major response,** namely, the act that captures the major thrust of each state's behavior in coping with its crisis. The summary also contains information about the highest **value** perceived to be at risk, from limited military damage, through threat to political regime, territory, or influence, to the gravest value threat, a threat to a state's existence. The **crisis management technique** employed by each state is also noted, with special reference to the intensity and centrality of **violence.** So too is crisis termination, both the **content** and **form** of **outcome,** for each actor and for the international crisis as a whole. **Major power (in)activity** during the course of an international crisis, too, is indicated, as is the extent of **involvement by global and/or regional organizations** to bring about crisis abatement. Finally, attention is drawn to the primary and secondary **sources** of the data assembled for each crisis and for the presentation of the case summary. We begin with PC crises in Africa.

The number assigned to each case—1–412—follows the sequence of trigger dates of the international crises; and it matches the numbering system used in the **Master Table** (Table III.1) at the end of Part III, a schematic presentation of the most salient information about each case. That is, while the summaries of PC cases are organized sequentially within their respective PCs, the entire set of 412 international crises is listed sequentially in the Master Table.

Africa: Protracted Conflicts

Angola

There have been 11 international crises during the protracted conflict (PC) over **Angola** since its inception in 1975, as follows.

Case #260 **War in Angola,** in 1975–76;
   #277 **Shaba I,** in 1977;
   #291 **Cassinga Incident,** in 1978;
   #292 **Shaba II,** in 1978;
   #297 **Angola Invasion Scare,** in 1978;
   #302 **Raids on SWAPO,** in 1979;
   #308 **Raid on Angola,** in 1979;
   #313 **Operation Smokeshell,** in 1980;
   #331 **Operation Protea,** in 1981;
   #347 **Operation Askari,** in 1983–84;
   #380 **South Africa Intervention in Angola,** in 1987–88.

General Background

Angola, a vast territory in southern Africa (1.246 million square kilometers), was first settled by Portugal in 1574. For almost four centuries it was part of Portugal's extensive empire in Africa, comprising two large colonies, Angola and Mozambique, along with Portuguese Guinea, the Cape Verde Islands, and São Tomé. Together, they were several times the area of Portugal itself.

In an atmosphere of emerging "winds of change" in Africa, Angola (and Mozambique) were given limited local autonomy in 1951; and their people were accorded full Portuguese citizenship in 1961.

The struggle for Angola's independence began in the 1950s: the left-wing Popular Movement for the Liberation of Angola *(MPLA),* the victor in the long-drawn-out civil war, was founded in 1956. External pressure on Portugal mounted: in 1964 the UN Committee on Colonialism called for the independence of Angola (and Mozambique); and the Organization of African Unity *(OAU)* imposed a boycott on Portugal. However, Angola (and all its other colonies) remained firmly under Portugal's control until 1974.

Portugal had been ruled as a dictatorship by Antonio de Oliveira Salazar from his election as Premier in July 1932 until he suffered a stroke in 1968; he died in 1970. The Portuguese dictatorship was overthrown on 24 April 1974 in a military coup that brought to power the Portuguese Armed Forces Council, a body favorable to the end of empire. Within months the new regime announced its intention to grant independence to all of Portugal's colonies in Africa.

(260) War in Angola

Zaire, Zambia, South Africa, Angola, Cuba, the Soviet Union, and the United States were direct participants in a crisis from 12 July 1975 until 27 March 1976.

Pre-crisis
The *Alvor* Agreement, signed on 15 January 1975, formally granted independence to Angola, to take effect on 10 November 1975 after elections in October. A transitional government was to be composed of representatives of the following: the *FNLA* (the National Front for the Liberation of Angola), formed in 1957, supported by the U.S. and Zaire, with its power base in the Bakongo tribe of northern Angola; the marxist-oriented *MPLA,* supported by the Soviet Union and Cuba and popular in Angola's coastal urban areas, among intellectuals of the north-central Kimbundu tribe; and *UNITA* (the National Union for the Total Independence of Angola), formed in the mid-1960s, in a split from the *FNLA*—it had a strong popular base among the Ovimbundu tribe in the south and central rural areas and received support from South Africa and Zambia. There was to be a unified security force under a Portuguese high commissioner. The *Alvor* Agreement broke down as early as March 1975, with major fighting between the *FNLA* and the *MPLA* erupting in late April. Portugal declared martial law on 15 May. President Kenyatta of Kenya mediated a cease-fire on 21 June, but it was broken almost immediately.

Crisis
On 12 July 1975 Soviet-backed *MPLA* forces attacked the *FNLA* headquarters in the capital, Luanda, triggering a crisis for Zaire and Zambia when the essential Benguela railroad was closed down. Zaire began sending small-scale commando units into Angola in mid-July to assist the *FNLA*. By that time the Soviet Union had started providing massive aid to the *MPLA,* causing alarm in Zaire, Zambia, and South Africa, as well as in the United States, which had been providing covert aid to both the *FNLA* and the *UNITA* movements.

Zambia responded on 27 July with an appeal to the U.S. for aid. Hydro-electric power projects, built jointly by South Africa and Portugal, were located on the Kunene River bordering South-West Africa (later Namibia). Clashes between *UNITA* and *MPLA* forces began approaching the power projects on 8 August, triggering a crisis for South Africa, which sent small units of troops to the projects on the 11th and 12th. On the 15th the *FNLA* captured the major port of Lobito, triggering a crisis for the *MPLA* (Angola), Cuba, and the Soviet Union. Cuba and the USSR were concerned that South African intervention would result in the defeat of the *MPLA* in the struggle for power and influence in Angola.

Cuba's response, on 20 August, was a decision to increase military aid to the *MPLA* (which was later to be recognized as the government of Angola). More South African troops were sent to the district capital on 21–22 August. On the 21st *UNITA* declared war on the *MPLA*, after concluding an alliance with the *FNLA*. On the 31st the USSR, too, increased its aid to Angola. On 1 September the *MPLA* (Angola) responded with a major offensive that succeeded in reversing its losses, triggering a crisis for the United States. Cuban troops began to arrive on the 3rd. On 11 September Zaire sent two full battalions to strengthen the *FNLA*. President Mobutu approached the U.S. for aid and initiated diplomatic activity with other African states. The U.S. responded on 25 September with an increase of covert aid to Zaire, to be funneled to *UNITA* and the *FNLA*. President Ford requested that Congress increase emergency aid to Zaire.

South Africa's response to the escalating crisis was the dispatch of a strike force into Angola on 23 October 1975 to aid the *FNLA/UNITA* alliance. It was successful in recouping earlier losses. A further escalation for Zaire, Zambia, the U.S., and South Africa was catalyzed by the arrival of a large number of Cuban troops to fight alongside the *MPLA*, together with massive arms supplies to Angola from the Soviet Union. On 10 November the remaining Portuguese personnel were withdrawn from Angola. Both the *MPLA* and the *FNLA/UNITA* declared the independence of Angola. The former was recognized by the USSR, Soviet-bloc members, including Cuba, and some African states. The latter was never officially recognized.

The U.S. crisis ended on 19 December 1975, when Congress refused to grant aid to Zaire or to support the *FNLA/UNITA*. An earlier appeal by Secretary of State Kissinger to the *NATO* Foreign Ministers' Council for support to the *FNLA/UNITA* was also rejected. The crisis for Zambia ended after a *MPLA* victory had become more apparent: on 18 February 1976 Zambia announced that it would recognize the state of Angola but not the *MPLA* government. This was done on 22 February, after negotiations. The crisis for Angola, Cuba, and the USSR ended on 24 February after *UNITA* announced, on the 12th, its decision to retreat and revert to guerrilla warfare, followed by a similar *FNLA* announcement on the 24th. On 28 February Zaire announced its decision to recognize the Angola government, after talks between Mobutu and the *MPLA* head, Neto. South Africa, after extensive negotiations via British Foreign Secretary Callaghan and the Soviet ambassador to London, achieved *MPLA* guarantees for the security of the hydroelectric projects and the safety of the personnel there. On 27 March South Africa announced a complete troop withdrawal from Angola.

There was intense foreign involvement in the Angolan War. Cuba, the Soviet Union, Congo (Brazzaville), and Yugoslavia actively supported the *MPLA*, with Cuban forces directly engaged in combat. The United States, China, North Korea, and Zaire aided the *FNLA;* Zaire, in addition to extensive diplomatic activity, provided military bases on its territory. Zambia supported *UNITA* diplomatically. And Tanzania provided diplomatic support and port facilities for the unloading of Soviet arms for the *MPLA*. There was also diplomatic activity by the Ivory Coast, Kenya, Uganda, and Nigeria.

The *OAU* used several procedures in an attempt to settle the conflict; all were unsuccessful. In January 1975 it supported the *Alvor* Accords. In July it called for a cease-fire and a National Unity Government for Angola. *OAU* conciliation commissions were sent to the area in July and October 1975. On 10–13 January 1976 the *OAU* held an emergency summit meeting on Angola; it broke down on the 13th with members divided evenly vis-à-vis the crisis. By 2 February 1976 a majority of *OAU* members had recognized the *MPLA* government, automatically extending *OAU* recognition. Angola was admitted to the *OAU* on 10 February. By 22 February 70 states, including members of the European Economic Community *(EEC)* (later the European Community *[EC]* and, since 1992, the European Union *[EU]*), had granted recognition.

The UN was less active. The good offices of Secretary-General Waldheim were used to relay *MPLA* guarantees to South Africa. The UN sent an inquiry and conciliation mission to Angola on 14 October 1975. On 10 March 1976 Kenya requested an emergency Security Council session on South Africa's "act of aggression." The Council met from 26 to 31 March; and, despite South Africa's claim that its troops had already left Angola, a resolution was passed condemning South Africa and demanding that it respect the territorial integrity of Angola, as well as that it cease the use of Pretoria-controlled South-West Africa (later, Nambia) for military incursions.

Washington had been supplying aid covertly to the *FNLA* since the Kennedy administration. In January 1975 an interagency National Security Task Force on Angola was formed. In December the State Department instructed the Gulf Oil Company to suspend the payment of $125 million in royalties to the *MPLA*-controlled Angolan finance ministry. During the Angola crisis there were widespread strikes and unemployment in the United States in the aftermath of Vietnam and Watergate. These legacies prompted Congress to decide to withdraw aid to Zaire, thereby extricating the U.S. from a major crisis in southern Africa.

Angola was viewed by both the Soviet Union and Africans as a watershed in American attitudes toward U.S. military intervention in the Third World. The initial Soviet position on Angola was to favor the right of all three rival Angolan movements to participate in the transitional government, but that posture changed early in 1975. Sino/Soviet rivalry was a major factor in Moscow's approach to the Angolan conflict. Soviet MIG-21s, tanks, and missiles were airlifted into Angola for the *MPLA,* and Soviet naval movements took place outside Angolan waters. With Cuban military assistance, Moscow was able to help its local ally, the *MPLA,* to establish itself as Angola's legitimate government.

(The *FNLA* and *UNITA* factions remained in control of large parts of Angola's territory—by 1979 *UNITA* controlled much of the southern third of Angola—and continued to pose a military challenge to *MPLA* and Cuban troops. The *FNLA* ceased to function as a separate force, but the civil war continued for 20 years. There were several abortive or short-lived cease-fire agreements and a comprehensive UN-brokered peace agreement between the *MPLA*-dominated government and *UNITA* in November 1994. However, a stable peace in Angola remains elusive.)

(See *Master Table,* pp. 714–15.)

Sources
ACR 1975, 1976; *ARB* 1975, 1976; Barratt 1976; Bender 1978, 1981; Carter and O'Meara 1977; Davis 1978; Dobrynin 1995; Dominguez 1978; Ebinger 1984; Ford 1979; Garthoff 1985; George 1983; Gonzalez 1980; Grieg 1977; Hodges 1976; Hosmer and Wolfe 1983; Isaacson 1992; Kaplan 1981; Kitchen 1976; Klinghoffer 1980; Larrabee 1976; Legum 1975, 1976, 1981; Legum and Hodges 1976; Lemarchand 1981; Marcum 1976, 1978; Mazrui 1977; Menon 1986; Napper 1983a; Nyerere 1977; Papp 1993; Porter 1984; Stevens 1976; Stockwell 1978; Valenta 1980.*

(277) Shaba I

An invasion of Zaire by Katangan exiles based in Angola brought about a crisis for Zaire and Angola from 8 March to 26 May 1977.

Background
Rebel forces in the Congo (later, Zaire) fled across the border to Angola and Zambia after Colonel Mobutu instigated a successful coup in Zaire in November 1965 (see Case #211—**Congo II,** in 1964, in **Africa: Non-PCs**). In Angola, members of the Congolese National Liberation Front *(FLNC)* were trained and aided by personnel and equipment from the Soviet Union and Cuba. During 1966 and 1967 armed rebels in Angola received assistance from Zaire, while Portugal supported separatist sentiments in Angola. Border incidents intensified as guerrilla movements became stronger. These conflicts continued throughout the Angolan civil war, with Zaire complaining to the UN Security Council on several occasions of rebel incursions from Angolan territory into its southern province of Shaba.

Crisis
On 8 March 1977 Shaba was invaded by Katangan exiles residing in Angola, triggering a crisis for Zaire. A crisis for Angola was triggered the same day when

---

*See Sources for Part III for the full citation of all documents, books, articles, and journals cited at the end of each case summary.

President Mobutu accused Angola, together with Cuba and the USSR, of being involved in an attempt to overthrow his regime. Angola feared an attack on its territory from Zaire and an internationalization of the conflict. Zaire responded with force on the day of the attack but, aware of its inability to repel the invaders alone, sent an appeal for help to African states, Belgium, and the United States. Morocco dispatched 1,500 troops in a French-supplied airlift. Pilots and mechanics were sent from Egypt. Nonlethal aid was supplied by the U.S. Angola responded on 11 March with a statement by the Defense Ministry disclaiming any responsibility for the invasion. On that day the *FLNC* announced in Paris that the goal of the invasion was to overthrow Mobutu's regime.

With the help of Moroccan troops and French advisors the Zairian army was able to stop the advance of the Katangan exiles and, subsequently, to reoccupy all the towns and villages. The Moroccans completed their mission on 22 May and withdrew, as did the Egyptians on the 25th. When the foreign troops left Zaire, Angola's fear of internationalization of the conflict subsided, and its crisis terminated on 25 May. The following day Zairian troops recaptured the last town held by the secessionist rebels in Shaba, ending Zaire's crisis and the Shaba crisis as a whole.

The UN was not involved in this crisis.

(See *Master Table,* pp. 716–17.)

Sources

ACR 1977; ARec 1977; ARB 1977; Bender 1978; Garthoff 1985; Hul 1977; Lellouche and Moisi 1979; LeoGrande 1980; Mangold 1979; Moose 1985; Schatzberg 1989; Vance 1983; Zartman 1989.

Background to Postindependence Angola PC

Almost all of the *Angola protracted conflict* following the War of 1975–76 took the form of South African cross-border raids into Angola. Military hostilities in the area bordering South-West Africa, then still a disputed mandated territory under South Africa's de facto control, were almost continuous since Pretoria's withdrawal from Angola at the end of the latter's civil war in 1975–76 (see Case #260—**War in Angola** above). Initially these hostilities took the form of limited *SADF* (South African Defence Forces) strikes against bases of the South-West African People's Organization *(SWAPO)* and Namibian refugee camps in Angola. When *SWAPO* adopted the tactic of dividing its forces and scattering them in the countryside, South Africa's raids became broader in scope. Economic targets, too, came under attack in an attempt to raise the price for Angola's support of *SWAPO*. Incursions into Angola were launched in May 1978, March 1979, October–November 1979, June–July 1980, August–September 1981, December 1983–February 1984, October 1987–August 1988 (see Cases #291, 302, 308, 313, 331, 347, and 380—below).

(291) Cassinga Incident

Fighting between South African forces and guerrillas based in Angola led to a crisis for South Africa and Angola from 3 to 17 May 1978.

Background
For much of the period since the *SWAPO* guerrilla war against the *SADF* stationed in Namibia began in 1966, its raids had been carried out from neighboring states. Since its civil war in 1975–76 (see Case #260—**War in Angola** above), Angola had become the main staging area for *SWAPO* raids. In the early months of 1978 there was an intensification of *SWAPO* activity. *SADF* losses were reported in periodic clashes in the northern Namibian border region. In February 1978 Angola complained to the UN Secretary-General of South African violations of its territory and airspace.

Crisis
A *SWAPO* attack on the Ruacana hydroelectric power station in Namibia's border area with Angola on 3 May triggered a crisis for South Africa. The South African foreign minister and the army chief of operations reported that a raid of approximately 700 South African troops into Angola, on 4 May, was a response to the upsurge of guerrilla activity and the *SWAPO* raid the day before. That act catalyzed a crisis for Angola.

Angolan sources stated that the *SADF* occupied the town of Cassinga, 230 kilometers north of the border, which South Africa claimed to be *SWAPO*'s main operational base. The town of Chetequera was also attacked. South Africa's raid was the largest since 1975–76, when its forces were involved on the side of *UNITA* in the Angolan civil war. In the operations at Cassinga, which lasted for 12 hours, six South African soldiers and about 1,000 refugees were reportedly killed. In addition to ground forces, aircraft were alleged to have been involved.

Angolan troops met the attacking forces. On 5 May Angola appealed to the United Nations for support. The following day a resolution was passed by the Security Council unanimously condemning South Africa and warning that "more effective measures might be taken." With the resolution, and the end of the raid, the crisis ended for Angola on 6 May. The ambassadors of Canada, France, the U.K., the U.S., and West Germany in South Africa formed a committee, known as the Contact Group, to investigate and propose solutions to the problem. On 17 May, for the first time since the raid, the South African foreign minister met with the Contact Group. This meeting, signaling a major reduction in stress, ended the crisis over Cassinga for South Africa.

U.S. activity was confined to the political realm. On 6 May the United States expressed grave concern and urgently requested that South Africa explain its behavior. The U.S. also participated in the Contact Group. The USSR was a major supplier of arms to Angola through Cuba, as well as arms and advisors to

SWAPO. The *OAU* condemned South Africa on 9 May 1978 and called for the withdrawal of South African troops from Namibia.
(See *Master Table,* pp. 718–19.)

Sources
ACR 1978; *ARB* 1978; *Keesing's* 1978.

(292) Shaba II

A second invasion of Shaba from Angola created a crisis for Zaire, Angola, Belgium, France, and the U.S. from 11 May to 30 July 1978.

Crisis
After a year of reorganizing and strengthening their forces, Katangan rebels invaded Shaba on 11 May 1978, triggering a crisis for Zaire. Zaire accused Angola of harboring the rebels and threatened to retaliate, triggering a crisis for Angola the same day. During the ensuing four days killings occurred on the part of both the rebels and the Zairian army. President Mobutu called for intervention by Belgium, France, Morocco, China, and the U.S. in order to quell the insurgents. In addition, he accused the governments of Algeria, Angola, Cuba, Libya, the Soviet Union, and Zambia of supporting, training, and actively fighting alongside the rebels.

On 14 May a crisis was triggered for Belgium, France, and the U.S. when their governments were informed of a massacre of French and Belgian citizens working in the mines, and of the danger facing the white community in Zaire. The U.S. viewed the events in Zaire as threatening its influence in the international system. On 16 May it responded with a decision to mount an airlift to carry foreign troops to the battleground. The French response, on 17 May, was a decision by President Giscard d'Estaing, together with the foreign and defense ministers and the chief of staff, to dispatch French troops to Zaire. Belgium, too, decided on the 18th to send troops. The foreign troops arrived in Zaire on the 19th, airlifted in American planes. That day, at the UN, Zaire accused Angola of aggression. However, the issue was not brought up for discussion in the Security Council since it was claimed that the dispute was an African matter.

The tide of battle turned with the intervention of foreign forces. Within two days Belgian troops had evacuated those persons who wished to leave the Shaba area. On 22 May the crisis ended for the United States and Belgium as Belgian forces began to withdraw from Shaba. French troops assumed a larger burden of the fighting. They occupied the towns around Kolwezi and cleared the area on 25 May, terminating the crisis for France. An African force, consisting of soldiers from Morocco, Senegal, and Zaire, took over from the French and the Belgian forces on 4 June. On the 10th Angola's major response to the crisis took the form of an announcement by President Neto that the incursion by *FLNC* rebels across

Angola's border would be halted and that any Zairian troops crossing the border into Angola would be disarmed. Angola also denied any Soviet involvement in the invasion. By the end of June all foreign troops had left the conflict area.

Presidents Mobutu and Neto held talks during July ending with the Brazzaville Agreement on 30 July 1978; the latter informally undertook to stop *FLNC* infiltrators from crossing into Zaire.

(See *Master Table* pp. 718–19.)

Sources
See sources for Case #277; and *ACR* 1978; *ARec* 1978; *ARB* 1978.

(297) Angola Invasion Scare

A South African troop buildup precipitated a crisis for Angola from 7 to 14 November 1978.

Pre-crisis
In May 1978 South Africa invaded Angola after a guerrilla attack on the Ruacana hydroelectric power station in Namibia (see Case #291—**Cassinga Incident** above). On 22 October Angolan, *SWAPO,* Cuban, and East German forces launched a major offensive against *UNITA* in the southern and central parts of Angola.

Crisis
On 7 November 1978 Angola's minister of defense stated that intelligence reports had reached him of a major buildup of South African forces along the border with Namibia; further, that South Africa planned a large incursion into Angola. The same day Angola responded with a general mobilization of the Angolan army (about 200,000 men) and a curfew in the five largest urban centers. On 8 November the *SADF* command issued a statement denying any intention of invading Angola. But on the 10th a bomb explosion in Angola's second largest city, Muambo, gave rise to the fear of an imminent South African attack. The next day Angola's President Neto accused South Africa of fighting an undeclared war against Angola and closed its airspace to South African overflights.

South African statements claimed that Angola's perception of war was the result of *UNITA* successes in the 22 October campaign and that Angola wished to detract attention from its domestic problems. The crisis ended with a statement on 14 November by South Africa's Prime Minister Botha, denying any intention to invade Angola.

UN activity took the form of an appeal by the UN Special Committee on Apartheid to all governments on 14 November to help Angola repel South African "aggression." Angola accused the Security Council of ineffective measures to stop the threat of invasion.

There was no U.S. or USSR involvement in this crisis.

(See *Master Table,* pp. 720–21.)

Sources
ACR 1978; *ARB* 1978; *Keesing's* 1978.

(302) Raids on *SWAPO*

South African raids on *SWAPO* bases in Angola caused a crisis for Angola from 6 to 28 March 1979.

Background and Pre-crisis
SWAPO had carried on guerrilla warfare against South African troops in South-West Africa since 1966. In 1978 activity was intensified, and a crisis occurred from 3 to 17 May (see Case #291—**Cassinga Incident** above). In November of that year Angola perceived the possibility of a South African invasion (see Case #297—**Angola Invasion Scare** above). Guerrilla activity against South Africa reached its highest intensity in January 1979.

Crisis
On 6 March air and ground attacks by the *SADF* on *SWAPO* targets in southern Angola triggered a crisis for Angola. The attacks lasted until the 15th, the targets being mainly arms dumps and supplies. Some villages were attacked as well, and minor clashes were reported. Angola accused South Africa of using napalm, but there was no verification of this claim. On 16 March Angola approached the United Nations for help. The Security Council met between 20 and 28 March and passed a resolution on the 28th: it condemned South Africa and demanded an immediate end to provocative acts; it also called for "aid to strengthen the defensive capabilities" of Angola. The resolution ended the crisis for Angola's decision makers.

The United States abstained from the Security Council vote. The U.S. and the USSR were not involved in this crisis.

(Following the crisis, in April, President Neto announced to the Angolan people that he planned to increase the size of the armed forces. In October 1979 South African troops invaded Angola once more [see Case #308 below].)

(See *Master Table*, pp. 720–21.)

Sources
ACR 1979; *AD* 1979; *ARec* 1979; *ARB* 1979.

(308) Raid on Angola

A South African incursion into Angola caused another brief crisis for Angola from 28 October to 2 November 1979.

Background and Pre-crisis
In September 1979 Augustino Neto, who had led Angola to independence and had been its president since 1975, died. A day after his death Angola reported a

South African attack on several economic targets in southern Angola by troops stationed in South-West Africa. Then, on 13 October, reportedly for the first time, Angolan forces crossed into South-West Africa.

Crisis
On 28 October South African troops attacked roads and bridges 190 kilometers inside Angola, in the Sierra da Leba area. Angola responded on the 31st with an appeal to the United Nations. The Angolan ambassador to Belgium and the *MPLA*'s Politburo were especially vocal in their accusations of South African hostile activity.

Angola's crisis ended on 2 November when the Security Council adopted another resolution condemning South Africa and calling for an immediate *SADF* withdrawal. The U.S.'s abstention from the vote was perceived unfavorably by Angola. There was no change in the Angola/South Africa relationship after the crisis ended and no reports of withdrawal by the *SADF* from Angola at the end of the raids. The stalemate continued.

There was no regional organization activity during the crisis, though earlier, on 6–20 July, the *OAU* Council of Ministers, as well as the *OAU* heads of state and government, had met to discuss the ongoing dispute between South Africa and Angola.

Neither the U.S. nor the USSR was involved in this crisis.
(See *Master Table*, pp. 720–21.)

Sources
ACR 1979; *ARec* 1979; *ARB* 1979.

(313) Operation Smokeshell

Angola experienced another crisis with South Africa from 7 June to 2 July 1980.

Crisis
Angola's crisis was triggered on 7 June 1980, when units of the *SADF* penetrated deep into Angola from South-West Africa and carried out large-scale operations in Angola's southern border provinces of Cunene and Cuando-Cubango. Prime Minister Botha of South Africa described the raid as a "shock attack" designed to destroy the operational headquarters of *SWAPO*.

Angola's major response was a request on 26 June for an urgent meeting of the Security Council. The next day it warned the Council that, if Angola's forces were unable to repel the *SADF* in the fierce fighting then raging, it would request outside help, implying Soviet or Moscow-backed Cuban intervention. On 27 June, too, the Security Council passed a resolution condemning South Africa for its raid and called for the withdrawal of *SADF* units from Angola immediately. This had a decisive impact on crisis resolution: on the 30th Pretoria notified the UN that all its forces in Angola had been withdrawn; but this claim was disputed by Angola.

At the beginning of July Angolan troops claimed to have reoccupied several villages and towns. Crisis termination occurred on 2 July: that day the *SADF* flew Western journalists and military attachés to the border zone, where they were briefed on Operation Smokeshell as an incident that had passed into history. *SADF* raids continued, but at a subcrisis level of intensity.

Neither the U.S. nor the USSR was active in this crisis, causing dissatisfaction by Angola. By contrast, as noted, the UN was highly involved. The global organization had been involved in the South-West Africa–Namibia Question since its creation in 1945, as the successor to the League of Nations Mandate over that territory. For years it had tried, without success, to arrange negotiations between South Africa and *SWAPO* to move toward independence for Namibia. The *OAU* reinforced the UN posture during this crisis. On 30 June its Council of Ministers condemned South Africa's intrusion into Angola and called upon the Security Council to impose comprehensive mandatory economic sanctions against the Pretoria regime. These were to come many years later.

(See *Master Table,* pp. 722–23.)

Sources
ACR 1980–81; *AR* 1980; *ARB* 1980; *ARec* 1980; *Keesing's* 1980.

(331) Operation Protea

Angola experienced one of its many crises with the Union of South Africa during the 1970s and 1980s from 23 August to 30 September 1981.

Pre-crisis
There were several *SADF* "hot pursuit" operations into Angola, in May and at the end of July 1981. The most dramatic of these, which escalated to a full-fledged interstate crisis, was Operation Protea.

Crisis
Heavy bombing raids on the Angolan towns of Cahama and Chibemba, deep inside Angola, on 23 August triggered a crisis for Angola. These were followed the next day by a South African invasion consisting of two motorized columns, with 80 vehicles and 32 tanks. The town of Xangongo was reduced to rubble and was occupied on the 25th. Units of the South African Defence Forces extended their operations in several directions, with the aims of cutting off *SWAPO* guerrillas from possible escape to the east and of preventing interference by Angola's armed forces.

Angola's Defense Ministry responded with general mobilization and a threat to deploy 20,000 troops to repel the invaders. Supplementing this with diplomatic pressure, President dos Santos sought the UN Secretary-General's help in repelling the invasion, with a threat to invoke Article 51 of the UN Charter—the right of self-defense, including the use of Cuban troops then in Angola. On the 27th

Angola requested that the UN Security Council demand an immediate withdrawal of South Africa's forces. The next day the commander in chief of the *SADF* announced that his troops were already withdrawing from Angola; but this seemed a diversionary tactic.

The objectives of Operation Protea were to thwart Angola's plans to extend its radar missile air defense system southward, to cover the strategic town of Cunene, and to create a no-man's land along the northern side of the Namibian border in order to act as a buffer against *SWAPO* infiltration into northern Namibia. While *SWAPO* bases were the primary goal, Angolan army headquarters in Xangongo had also been heavily bombed.

On 31 August, in accordance with the Reagan administration's policy of "constructive engagement" with the Union of South Africa's apartheid regime, the U.S. vetoed a Security Council draft resolution that strongly condemned the "racist regime" of South Africa and demanded the immediate and unconditional withdrawal of South African forces from Angola.

On 1 September Angola's ambassador to Portugal renewed the threat to employ Cuban forces against South Africa's invaders.

UN pressure mounted with a resolution by a special session of the General Assembly on 14 September calling upon the Security Council to impose comprehensive mandatory sanctions against South Africa. At the same time South Africa's army commander pronounced Operation Protea a partial success.

Angola's crisis ended on 30 September with its reoccupation of Xangongo and several other towns vacated by the *SADF.*

The superpowers were active politically in this crisis. The U.S., as noted, adhered to "constructive engagement." The USSR called for unqualified condemnation of South Africa's invasion and the imposition of sanctions. So too did the *OAU,* which also urged the expulsion of South Africa from the UN.

(South African forces withdrew; but other incursions into Angola, in the long-term war against SWAPO, continued until Namibia finally achieved its independence in 1990.)

(See *Master Table,* pp. 724–25.)

Sources
ACR 1981–82; *AR* 1981; *ARec* 1981; *ARB* 1981; *Keesing's* 1981.

(347) Operation Askari

Angola experienced another crisis with the Union of South Africa from 6 December 1983 until 16 February 1984.

Crisis
On 6 December 1983 the South Africa Defence Forces launched their most formidable invasion of southern Angola since **Operation Protea** in 1981 (see Case #331 above): they attacked targets more than 150 miles inside Angola. According

to a Pretoria spokesman, the aim of the operation was to disrupt preparations by *SWAPO* guerrillas for their annual incursions into South-West Africa.

Serious clashes continued throughout December around the towns of Cubama, Caiundo, and Cassinga, with the most intense fighting early in January at Curelai, where South African troops clashed not only with *SWAPO,* but also with Angolan and Cuban forces. Angola responded to the crisis with military resistance and with a complaint to the UN Security Council that South Africa had committed aggression against its territory, requesting an emergency session of the Council.

The Council adopted a resolution on 20 December 1983: it censured South Africa for its military operations in Angola and demanded the *SADF*'s unconditional withdrawal from Angola.

The winding down of this international crisis began soon after its eruption. South Africa's Foreign Minister, Pik Botha, put forward proposals for a cease-fire in Angola on 15 December, to take effect at the end of January 1984. President dos Santos responded on 30 December with a conditional acceptance. On 20 January 1984 talks were held in Cape Verde among Angolan, South African, and UN representatives. On 26 January Chester Crocker, the U.S. Assistant Secretary of State for Africa, flew to Cape Town with a "special message" from the Angolan government. On 31 January Prime Minister Botha announced to the South African Parliament that he had ordered a complete *SADF* withdrawal from Angola.

Angola's President dos Santos met with Zambia's President Kaunda on 6 February. Ten days later, on 16 February, Angolan and South African delegations, with Crocker and Kaunda present, reached the "Lusaka Agreement" to establish a joint monitoring commission to supervise the withdrawal of South African troops from Angola which, in return, undertook not to permit *SWAPO* forces to move into Namibia. This marked the end of Angola's crisis and, with it, the end of Operation Askari.

Both of the superpowers were politically active in this crisis. As noted, the U.S. was influential in brokering the Lusaka Agreement between South Africa and Angola. The USSR, on 5 January 1984, called for concerted international action to halt South Africa's "aggression" against Angola. Later that month it warned Pretoria of the logical consequences of its behavior, without specifying any likely Soviet action beyond support for Angola. On 11 January military delegations from Angola, Cuba, and the USSR reached an agreement in Moscow on strengthening Angola's defenses.

(See *Master Table,* pp. 726–27.)

Sources
ACR 1983–84; *AR* 1984; *ARB* 1984; *Keesing's* 1984; *New York Times* 1984.

(380) South Africa Intervention in Angola

Angola and South Africa were embroiled in another of their many cross-border crises from 3 October 1987 to 22 August 1988.

Crisis

A crisis for Angola was triggered by a South Africa Defence Forces attack on *SWAPO* bases in Angolan territory on 3 October 1987. This was one of a number of such intrusions by the *SADF* since 1978, noted above, part of Pretoria's continuing struggle to thwart *SWAPO*'s attempt to create an independent state of Namibia in South African–controlled South-West Africa. For Angola the incursion posed a threat of grave damage. For South Africa, Angola's provision of sanctuary to *SWAPO* forces threatened its control over South-West Africa and, generally, its primacy in the southern African region.

Angola's initial response followed its behavior in earlier intrusions of this kind: it appealed to the UN Security Council. As in the past, the Council unanimously passed a resolution condemning South Africa's "continued and intensified acts of aggression" against Angola and called for the immediate, unconditional withdrawal of its forces from Angola's territory. However, it did not impose economic sanctions on Pretoria.

This routinized Security Council behavior did not, per se, catalyze a crisis for South Africa. The trigger occurred on 10 December, when Angola launched a counterattack against *SADF* units.

Serious clashes between the *SADF* and Angolan forces continued intermittently for months, intertwined with the ongoing civil war in Angola between the *MPLA*-led government and *UNITA*. The latter's leader, Jonas Savimbi, claimed on 12 November that his forces had repulsed a three-month offensive by government forces. In mid-December, the Head of the *SADF,* General Johan Geldenhuys, admitted for the first time that his troops were fighting alongside *UNITA* inside Angola. Government forces had the active backing of 2,000 Soviet military advisors and of a large Cuban contingent in reserve, estimated as 30,000–35,000 troops.

The winding down of this cross-border crisis was a slow process. After lengthy negotiations, Angola and South Africa signed a cease-fire agreement on 22 August 1988, with a mutual commitment to continue talks on the issue of a complete *SADF* withdrawal. This ended the crisis—but not the protracted conflict between Angola and South Africa. (A substantive agreement on withdrawal and disengagement of forces was signed by Angola, Cuba, and South Africa on 22 December 1988.)

The UN role was limited to its routinized condemnation of South Africa's military incursion into Angola. More forceful Security Council action, notably economic sanctions, was prevented by the threat of a U.S. veto. For years the Reagan administration had provided South Africa and *UNITA* with covert aid. Moreover, its policy of "constructive engagement" with Pretoria included preventing any sanctions by the global organization. Complementing this policy, U.S. relations with Angola had steadily deteriorated after July 1985, when the U.S. Congress repealed the Clark Amendment, which had imposed legal restrictions on U.S. assistance to *UNITA*. Export credit funds to Angola were cut off. And pressure was put on U.S. oil firms to cease their operations in oil-rich

Angola, so as to deny funds to the pro-Soviet *MPLA*-led Angolan government. Both the USSR and Cuba, as noted, provided substantial military aid to government forces.

(South Africa Intervention in Angola was the last international crisis of the Angola protracted conflict: the December 1988 accord was fully implemented by Angola, Cuba, and South Africa. And with the active involvement of the U.S., Russia, and South Africa, Namibia's independence became a reality in 1990.

There were several abortive peace agreements over the years, notably the Angola Peace Accords (Bicesse Accords) on 31 May 1991, and the UN-supervised elections in September 1992. The electoral outcome, a decisive *MPLA* victory, was rejected by *UNITA*, and large-scale violence was renewed. However, the 20-year-old civil war, the primary source of the Angola PC and its international crises, appeared to be winding down.

A peace agreement, the Lusaka Protocol, was signed in November 1994 between the *MPLA*-dominated government of Angola and the *UNITA* movement. Their leaders, dos Santos and Savimbi, had a public reconciliation in Lusaka in early May 1995, their first meeting since the ill-fated UN-organized Angola elections in 1992. After further negotiations, Angola's president announced in August 1995 that they had agreed to a merger—and large-scale demobilization—of their armed forces, as well as the formation of a coalition government in which Savimbi would serve as Vice President. But the deadline for the UN-sponsored demobilization, 8 February 1996, passed with little progress in this crucial domain of the Lusaka peace process. Still another agreement between dos Santos and Savimbi was reported at a meeting in Libreville, the capital of Gabon, on 1 March 1996. They reaffirmed their commitment to the Lusaka Accord. The *UNITA* leader pledged the completion of the demobilization of his forces and the creation of an integrated national army, along with the assumption of ministerial posts by *UNITA*, including the vice presidency by Savimbi—as provided in the Accord. However, the internal Angola conflict was not yet fully resolved).

(See *Master Table*, pp. 732–33.)

Sources
ACR 1987, 1988; *AR* 1987, 1988; *ARB* 1987, 1988; Crocker 1992; *Keesing's* 1987, 1988; Papp 1993.

Chad/Libya

The protracted conflict between Chad and Libya generated eight international crises from 1971 to 1987, as follows.

Case #243 **Chad/Libya I,** in 1971–72;
    #288 **Chad/Libya II,** in 1978;
    #290 **Chad/Libya III,** in 1978;
    #304 **Chad/Libya IV,** in 1979;

#321 **Chad/Libya V,** in 1981;
#342 **Chad/Libya VI,** in 1983–84;
#362 **Chad/Libya VII,** in 1986;
#370 **Chad/Libya VIII,** in 1986–87.

The conflict has been dormant since 1994.

General Background

Along with many other French colonies in equatorial Africa, Chad was granted independence in 1960. The new state is landlocked: Libya to the north; Niger and Nigeria to the west; Cameroon to the southwest; the Central African Republic to the south; and Sudan to the northeast, east, and southeast. In terms of conflicts and crises, Chad's most important neighbor is Libya, particularly because of their conflicting claims to the Aozou Strip, 45,000 square miles of northern Chad lying astride the entire Chad/Libya border and reputed to contain uranium and oil deposits.

Chad comprises many ethnic groups, the largest being the Black African and Christian Saras in the south, with many Muslim tribes in the north. Neither the French colonial regime nor the Sara-based Chad government exercised effective control in the north.

Attempts to extend Libya's influence into Chad can be traced to the early years of the twentieth century: first, by the Ottoman rulers of Libya; after 1911, by the new colonial power, Italy; and, after independence in 1951, by the Sanussi monarchy. In 1954, troops of King Idris tried to occupy the Aozou Strip but were repelled by French colonial forces in Chad. And, from 1966 to 1969, the king actively supported a revolt by Muslim rebels in northern Chad, organized as the *Front Liberation Nationale de Tchad (FROLINAT).*

Libya became more deeply involved in the internal affairs of its southern neighbor after the overthrow of King Idris and the assumption of power by Muammar Qaddhafi in 1969. The new Libyan leader did not conceal his country's long-standing claim to a large part of northern Chad—the Aozou Strip. This area had been ceded to Italy, then the colonial ruler of Libya, by France in the 1930s, but the treaty of cession was not ratified by the French National Assembly. Nor did Qaddhafi conceal his goal of hegemony vis-à-vis Chad's political regime.

During the 1970s Libya was a direct participant in four international crises over two enduring Chad-related issues: the struggle for power among Chad's political factions, notably Hissene Habré's *Forces Armées du Nord (FAN)* and Goukouni Oueddei's *Forces Armées Populaires (FAP);* and a conflict over the uranium-rich Aozou Strip. The last of those crises ended on 10 November 1979, when a transitional National Unity Government was formed with Goukouni as President and Habré as Defense Minister.

There were four additional crises over Chad in the 1980s, and the conflict over Aozou continued until 1994 (see Case #370—**Chad/Libya VIII** below).

(243) Chad/Libya I

The first of four Chad/Libya crises in the 1970s lasted from 24 May 1971 to 17 April 1972.

Crisis

In an attempt at Christian-Muslim reconciliation, half of the portfolios in the Chad government were granted to Muslim politicians on 24 May 1971. This act created a crisis for Libya by threatening its future influence in the domestic affairs of its southern neighbor. The pro-Libyan *FROLINAT* rejected the Chad government's offer.

On 27 August Libya responded by backing a coup against President Tombalbaye. Although it failed, the coup attempt triggered a crisis for Chad, which responded the same day by severing diplomatic relations with Libya. The perceived threat to its regime having been overcome, Chad's crisis ended the following day. On 17 September Libya recognized *FROLINAT*'s claim to being the legitimate government of Chad. However, persistent pressure on Libya by France bore fruit: on 17 April 1972 Libya resumed relations with Chad, marking the end of this international crisis.

The UN, the U.S., the USSR, and the *OAU* were not involved in this crisis.

(See *Master Table,* pp. 710–11.)

Sources

ACR 1971, 1972; *AR* 1971, 1972; *ARec* 1971, 1972; *ARB* 1971, 1972; Brownlie 1979; Day 1987; Decalo 1980a, 1980b, 1987; Foltz 1988; Haley 1984; Neuberger 1982; Thompson and Adloff 1981.

(288) Chad/Libya II

Libya's continuing involvement in Chad's internal conflict generated a second crisis for those two states between 22 January and 27 March 1978.

Background

In April 1972 Libya occupied the Aozou Strip. (Later that year, on 28 November, Tombalbaye agreed, under pressure, to the cession of the Strip to Libya, and in December 1972 Chad and Libya signed a Treaty of Friendship.)

Chad President Tombalbayé was overthrown in an army coup on 14 April 1975 and was replaced by Felix Malloum, who pledged national unity by peaceful means. Within the opposition *FROLINAT,* Hissene Habré was ousted from the leadership by Goukouni Oueddei, who led the loosely organized Command Council of the Northern Armies. In April 1976 a Qaddhafi-supported mutiny and planned assassination of President Malloum failed. Throughout 1977 there were continuous pro-Libyan rebel attacks against Chad troops, with Libyan activity reaching its peak in the summer, when *FROLINAT* forces occupied territory south of the Aozou Strip.

Crisis

As in 1971, Libya perceived a threat to its influence in Chad as a result of a domestic Chadian political agreement, on this occasion between Hissene Habré and President Malloum, signed in Khartoum on 22 January 1978 with the help of Sudan's mediation. The agreement provided for a National Unity Government; the establishment of a constituent assembly; an amnesty for all political prisoners; and the reorganization of Chad's armed forces. Libya's major response, on the 29th, was active support for a *FROLINAT* offensive against Faya-Largeau, the administrative center of the province of Borkou-Ennedi-Tibesti, in northern Chad.

This act, in turn, triggered a crisis for Chad. President Malloum responded by severing diplomatic relations with Libya on 6 February. A Chad appeal to the UN Security Council on the 8th to condemn Libya's involvement in the renewed fighting, as well as its occupation of the Aozou Strip, had to be withdrawn and a cease-fire accepted because of the loss of half the Chad army and the fall of Faya-Largeau to *FROLINAT* forces on 19 February. Libya halted the advance of its proxy on the Chad capital because of strong pressure by France, then an important arms supplier to Libya, and partly to avoid a clash with French military forces in Chad.

The crisis ended for Libya on 24 February when, at the first Sebha Conference, attended by Qaddafi, Malloum, Niger's president, and the vice president of Sudan, Chad and Libya agreed to settle their differences in a "new fraternal spirit"; to resume diplomatic relations; to hold a peace conference between the Chad government and *FROLINAT* on 21 March; and to establish a joint military committee to supervise affairs in Chad during the interim period, thereby legitimizing Libyan intervention in Chad.

Chad's crisis and the second Chad/Libya international crisis as a whole ended on 27 March 1978, following a second Sebha Conference and a comprehensive agreement announced in Benghazi that day. Under the Benghazi Accords, Chad agreed to recognize *FROLINAT*. Both agreed to abide by the cease-fire; to allow free movement throughout Chad; and to assist a Libya-Niger military committee in implementing the Accords. Most important, Chad agreed to the termination of foreign (French) military bases and military presence in Chad. However, the Benghazi Accords were short lived, and other Chad/Libya crises were soon to erupt.

The two superpowers, as well as the UN and the *OAU*, were not involved in this crisis.

(See *Master Table,* pp. 718–19.)

Sources

See sources for Case #243; and *ACR* 1978; *AR* 1978; *ARec* 1978; *ARB* 1978; Decalo 1980; Deeb 1991; Kelley 1986; Lemarchand 1985, 1988; Moose 1985.

(290) Chad/Libya III

France, Libya, and Chad were the crisis actors in the third eruption during the protracted **Chad/Libya** conflict from 15 April to 29 August 1978.

Pre-crisis
The Benghazi Accords of 27 March 1978 provided a brief respite in the ongoing struggle between President Malloum's regime and the Libya-backed rebels led by Goukouni Oueddei for control over the territory and government of Chad. The cease-fire, authorized by the Benghazi Accords to take effect on 10 April, broke down almost at once.

Crisis
On 15 April *FROLINAT* forces, led by Goukouni Oueddei, seized Salal and advanced south to within 100 miles of Chad's capital, N'Djamena. This created a crisis for France by threatening its continued influence in equatorial Africa generally and, in particular, its secure access to the uranium resources of neighboring Niger, vital for France's *force de frappe*. France, which, since 1960, had assumed a proprietary right to protect former French colonies—and French interests—in Africa against external threats, responded on the 26th to an appeal by Malloum with an airlift of 1,700 troops, a heavy bombardment of rebel convoys, and the creation of a defense perimeter around the capital, thereby preventing the fall of Malloum's regime.

French intervention in April–May 1978 and its success in halting Goukouni's advance was perceived by Libya in mid-May as a serious threat to its hegemony in Chad. Qaddhafi responded on 22 June with an invasion by 800 Libyan troops, who overran several provinces in northern and central Chad. Libya's escalation of hostilities, in turn, created a crisis for Chad. President Malloum responded on 20 July with an appeal to the *OAU* to denounce Libya's intervention and to press for the withdrawal of Libya's forces from Chad's territory.

While an *OAU* commission was investigating Chad's charges, France and Libya concluded a secret agreement in late July 1978 providing for a de facto partition of Chad at the 16th Parallel into two spheres of influence. The formation of a virtual condominium over Chad ended the crisis for these two actors. Chad's crisis ended on 29 August, when an agreement was reached in Khartoum creating a National Unity Government, with Habré as Prime Minister and Malloum continuing as President and their military forces formally integrated.

The UN, the U.S., and the USSR remained aloof from this crisis.

(See *Master Table,* pp. 718–19.)

Sources
See sources for Cases #243 and 288, and Lellouche and Moisi 1979.

(304) Chad/Libya IV

Another crisis for Libya, Chad, and France in equatorial Africa occurred from 12 April to 10 November 1979.

Pre-crisis
Shortly after the formation of a National Unity Government for Chad on 29 August 1978, fighting erupted once more between government and rebel forces. Rivalries among the latter and mass killings of minority Muslims in the south aggravated the situation. The Malloum-Habré coalition government broke down in February 1979. Thousands of Christian Saras were reported slaughtered in the capital by Habré's followers. By the end of February, *FROLINAT* leader Goukouni's forces entered N'Djamena. And by 11 March, when the first Kano Conference on national Chad reconciliation opened, there were four competing power centers, led by Goukouni, Habré, Asil, and Kamougue. France and Nigeria pressed Goukouni and Habré to share power. And this was done in a new Provisional State Council, Gouvernement de l'Unité Nationale Tchadienne *(GUNT),* formed on 23 March in accordance with an agreement a week earlier. Goukouni became interim Head of State, following Malloum's resignation that day. And in mid-April, after an inconclusive second Kano Conference from 3 to 11 April, Goukouni took over the Interior portfolio, with Habré as Defense Minister. While they had yielded to Libyan and Nigerian pressure at Kano to enlarge *GUNT,* they reneged upon their return to Chad.

Crisis
It was the volte-face by Goukouni and Habré that triggered a crisis for Libya on 12 April 1979, the onset of Chad/Libya IV. While there was some minor Libyan troop activity in the north, beginning on the 13th, and Libyan support for a secessionist movement in southern Chad, its major response did not come until 25 June, following another inconclusive reconciliation conference, at Lagos, Nigeria, on 26–27 May. The four factions represented in the Provisional State Council were absent from Lagos; but dissidents, backed by six of Chad's neighbors (Cameroon, the Central African Republic, Libya, Niger, Nigeria, and Sudan), demanded the formation of a new, enlarged National Unity Government by 25 June. When this call went unheeded, Libya sent 2,500 troops into northern Chad aimed at Faya-Largeau. The Libyan invasion, in turn, triggered a crisis for Chad and France the same day. The former appealed to Paris not to withdraw its forces from Chad. France agreed; and French reconnaissance planes and bombers played a crucial role in the Chad counteroffensive that forced the Libyans to retreat.

A second Lagos Conference, the fourth concerned with Chad in 1979, met in mid-August, with all eleven Chad factions represented, along with all Chad's neighbors and also Benin, Congo, Liberia, and Senegal. The upshot was an agreement providing for the following: a cease-fire, to be monitored by a peace force with contingents from states not bordering on Chad, headed by the *OAU* Secretary-General; demilitarization of N'Djamena; amnesty for all political prisoners; the merger of all factional militias into a national army; and the formation of a broad-based transitional National Unity Government. When that government was established, on 10 November 1979, the crisis ended for all three actors, Chad, France, and Libya. Yet the complex civil and international conflict over Chad continued.

The U.S. and the USSR were not involved in this crisis, the UN marginally so. (See *Master Table*, pp. 720–21.)

Sources
ACR 1979; *AR* 1979; *ARec* 1979; *ARB* 1979.

(321) Chad/Libya V

France and Libya, the two major powers in this PC, experienced a crisis from 6 January to 16 November 1981 over the latter's merger plan with Chad.

Pre-crisis
Fighting between Habré's *Forces Armées du Nord (FAN)* and Goukouni's *Forces Armées Populaires (FAP)* resumed in March 1980. On 6 June the former took control of Faya-Largeau, a strategic town in northern Chad. Goukouni's transitional government responded by signing a Treaty of Friendship with Libya on 15 June. Toward the end of 1980 the balance of political and military power in Chad changed dramatically following a large-scale intervention by Libyan troops in support of forces loyal to Goukouni, who launched an attack on the capital, N'Djamena, on 6 December. On 14–15 December Habré's *FAN* evacuated their positions, and a cease-fire agreement was signed the next day.

France, too, despite a warning to Libya and an expression of "grave concern" on the 13th, decided in principle to withdraw all the forces it had stationed in Chad since independence.

(Tension between France and Libya had become exacerbated by France's military support for Tunisia after an attack on the Tunisian town of Gafsa in January 1980, allegedly with Libyan involvement [see Case #311—**Raid on Gafsa,** in **Africa: Non-PCs**]. France was also concerned about a possible military confrontation with Libyan forces in Chad.)

Crisis
The catalyst to the fifth international crisis in the protracted Chad/Libya conflict was a joint communiqué by Goukouni Oueddei and Qaddhafi in Libya's capital, Tripoli, on 6 January 1981 announcing that they had decided "to work to achieve full unity between the two countries." The merger plan evoked strong adverse reaction in Africa. It also triggered a crisis for France, which responded on the

8th with a sharp condemnation of the merger plan. Libya's leader tried to offset the hostile reception by redefining the goal the following day as "full unity, rather than a merger."

On 11 January, two days after President Giscard offered to increase French garrisons in friendly African states, a fresh contingent of French troops arrived in the capital of the Central African Republic. This triggered a crisis for Libya, which was accentuated on the 15th when France's Mediterranean fleet was placed on alert.

During the following month Libya and France exchanged recriminations and threats: by Libya, to impose an economic boycott including an embargo on oil; by France, to act if Libyan troops in Chad moved to invade another state in Africa. In response to a series of threatening French words and deeds and in another attempt to deflect widespread criticism of the merger plan, Qaddhafi promised on 15 February to withdraw from Chad as soon as its government deemed the presence of Libyan forces no longer necessary. In March and again in May he announced the intention to withdraw the estimated 7,000–12,000 Libyan troops in Chad; but only 200 were evacuated.

Goukouni, along with France and several African states, was dissatisfied. In late April 1981 clashes occurred between Goukouni's forces and those of Libya's ally in Chad, Foreign Minister Ahmad Acyle. The calls for Libya's withdrawal from Chad became increasingly insistent after a series of Libyan air raids on border villages in Sudan, where the FAN was believed to be rearming and regrouping its forces. Moreover, Libya's approval of President Sadat's assassination on 6 October heightened tension with Egypt and other countries that feared further Libyan destabilization attempts in the region: Qaddhafi had already called upon the Touareg, desert nomads, to revolt against Niger and Mali.

Pressure from France and several African states finally led Goukouni to seek the withdrawal of Libyan troops from Chad. This was formally requested on 29–30 October. An airlift of Libyan troops began on 3 November. And by 16 November all Libyan soldiers had departed, marking the end of the crises for Libya and France and the international crisis over the merger plan.

The most highly involved actor in this crisis, other than France and Libya, was Africa's regional organization. Following the announcement of the merger plan an OAU ad hoc committee held an emergency summit meeting in Lomé, Togo, and sharply condemned Libya's military presence in Chad. It rejected the merger scheme and called on Libya to withdraw its forces from Chad so as to enable the OAU to arrange elections in April 1982. This démarche helped to abate the crisis. The superpowers were minimally involved. The U.S., which had been providing military aid to Habré's FAN, issued a statement of support for Sudan, then experiencing border attacks from Libyan forces in Chad. The USSR, long a patron of Qaddhafi's Libya, continued its close military and economic relations but played no role in this crisis per se. The UN Security Council was apprised but did not take any specific measures to abate the crisis.

(See *Master Table*, pp. 722–23.)

Sources
ACR 1981; *AR* 1981; *ARec* 1980–81; *ARB* 1981; Amoo and Zartman 1992; *Keesing's* 1981.

(342) Chad/Libya VI

Chad, France, and Libya were embroiled in another international crisis from 24 June 1983 to 11 December 1984.

Pre-crisis
After a lull in Qaddhafi's involvement in Chad—because of his (failed) attempt to become chairman of the *OAU*—he became more active from late October 1982 onward. He recognized Goukouni's transitional government and supported his forces with arms and equipment in the prolonged civil war for mastery of Chad. He also resumed reconnaissance flights over Chad. Habré accused Qaddhafi of planning to attack the Aozou Strip; the Libyan leader denied the accusation.

In February 1983 talks between Habré and Qaddhafi broke down. In March Habré accused Libya of being directly involved in the Chadian internal struggle for power, following Goukouni's capture of a strategic outpost on the road to Chad's capital. On 17 March Chad asked for an urgent meeting of the UN Security Council to consider Libya's "aggression and occupation" of Chadian territory. On 17 May Chad (Habré) claimed to have repulsed a rebel (Goukouni) attack against the strategic oasis, Faya-Largeau, gateway to control over the northern part of Chad.

Crisis
The persistent low-intensity conflict, interstate (Chad/Libya) and intrastate (Habré/Goukouni), generated another full-scale crisis for Chad on 24 June 1983, when Libya-supported Goukouni forces occupied Faya-Largeau. The same day French Foreign Minister Claude Cheysson warned Libya that France would "not remain indifferent" to Libya's intervention in Chad. Moreover, France (and Zaire) decided to dispatch military aid to the Habré regime, in response to its appeal on 5 July for direct military support. On the 11th Chad accused Libya once more of direct involvement in its internal crisis. The *OAU* discussed the matter on the 15th and called for an immediate cease-fire, the withdrawal of foreign forces from Chad, and the resumption of negotiations between the contending parties within Chad.

Along with its diplomatic efforts to oust Libya, Chad's (Habré's) forces, assisted by weapons from France, Zaire, and the U.S., began a counteroffensive on 9 July. Faya-Largeau was recaptured on 30 July. The next day Libyan MIG fighter-bombers attacked Faya-Largeau, the first undisguised and direct Libyan intervention in Chad's civil war. This act triggered a crisis for France. French President Mitterand responded on 6 August with an order to activate "Operation Manta," designed to oust Libya from Faya-Largeau and, more generally, to weaken its influence in the internal affairs of Chad. Three days later, several hundred French troops were dispatched to Chad's capital from the Central African Republic, triggering a crisis for Libya. Although France—and Libya— wanted to avoid a confrontation between their forces, France threatened Libya on 25 August that it would not accept Libya's control over Faya-Largeau.

Peace talks among all the rival Chad factions, sponsored by the *OAU,* were held in November 1983, but deadlock ensued. In January 1984 the smoldering crisis became more acute when a French plane was shot down by Chad rebel forces. France responded by strengthening its military presence in Chad. On 10 March an Air France plane was damaged at N'Djamena airport.

The "winding down" of Chad/Libya VI was slow to crystallize. On 30 April Qaddafi presented a mutual withdrawal proposal, which was accepted by France. However, it took five months to implement this de facto agreement. On 17 September 1984 Qaddafi and French President Mitterand met and announced that mutual withdrawal of all their forces in Chad would begin on 25 September and be completed by 10 November, the termination date for Chad's and Libya's crisis. France met the withdrawal deadline. However, Qaddafi did not adhere to the agreement fully: France accused him on 5 December of leaving 3,000 troops in northern Chad. By the 11th tension had eased sufficiently so that France's crisis over Chad—and the international crisis of which it was a part—came to an end. Mitterand renewed France's commitment to Chad's independence, while recognizing the de facto partition of Chad at the 16th Parallel into Libyan and French spheres of influence.

The USSR, as usual, provided political support for Libya. The UN role was limited to discussion.

(In addition to its persistent involvement in crises with Chad, Libya was also enmeshed in crises with other African neighbors [see Cases #311—**Raid on Gafsa,** in 1980; #314—**Libyan Threat–Sadat,** in 1980; #318—**Libyan Intervention in The Gambia,** in 1980; and #340—**Libyan Threat to Sudan,** in 1983, in **Africa: Non-PCs**].)

(See *Master Table,* pp. 726–27.)

Sources
ACR 1983–84, 1984–85; *AR* 1983, 1984; *ARec* 1983, 1984; *ARB* 1983, 1984; *Keesing's* 1983, 1984.

(362) Chad/Libya VII

Chad, France, and Libya were enmeshed in another crisis from 10 February to the end of March 1986.

Background
Libyan forces continued to occupy the Aozou Strip after the termination of **Chad/Libya VI.** And the Libyan-backed *GUNT* remained in control of more

than a third of Chad's territory—north of the 16th Parallel. There were frequent reports of Libyan reinforcements in Chad during 1985. In December President Habré of Chad indicated that he expected a fresh Libyan offensive. As often in the past, Mitterand warned Qaddhafi against an invasion.

Crisis
On 10 February 1986 the Libya-backed rebels, the *GUNT,* renewed their attacks on government forces at Oum Chalouba and captured Koro Toro near the 16th Parallel, triggering a crisis for Chad. France, too, perceived a crisis because the 16th Parallel was its "red line" against Libya's proxy, the *GUNT,* and Libyan forces in Chad. The same day Libyan forces reportedly attacked Chadian troops 480 kilometers northeast of the Chadian capital.

On 13 February France's defense minister arrived in N'Djamena for talks with President Habré, who had appealed for direct French military intervention. The next day French forces in the neighboring Central African Republic were put on alert, and French commandos and fighter planes were dispatched to N'Djamena.

Once more Mitterand warned Qaddhafi not to intervene in Chadian internal affairs. And on the 16th French aircraft bombed a rebel airstrip at Qadi-Doum.

Libya denied that its troops took part in the fighting. But on the 17th it responded to the French attack by sending two aircraft to bomb the airport of N'Djamena. However, it also indicated its approval of negotiations with Chad.

Fighting continued until the end of March, when the crisis faded; but the Chad/Libya conflict remained unresolved.

There were many attempts at mediation between President Habré of Chad and *GUNT* leader Goukouni Oueddei: by the *OAU*'s chairman, President Abdou Diouf of Senegal; and by the presidents of Congo, Nigeria, Togo, and Zaire. However, Goukouni demanded an *OAU* condemnation of "French aggression" prior to any direct negotiations with the government. On 29 March Diouf declared that "Habré is the one who wants peace, unity and territorial integrity."

The U.S. State Department announced on 13 March that it would provide Chad with emergency military aid of $10 million. The UN and the USSR were marginally involved.

(See *Master Table,* pp. 730–31.)

Sources
ACR 1986; *AR* 1986; *ARec* 1986; *ARB* 1986; *Keesing's* 1986.

(370) Chad/Libya VIII

Chad and Libya were embroiled in another crisis from 12 December 1986 to 11 September 1987.

Background and Pre-crisis
In the months following the violence of February–March 1986 (**Chad/Libya VII**), Libyan forces remained in northern Chad, supporting the *GUNT,* as in the past. In June Chad complained to the UN Security Council against Libya's continuing occupation of its northern territory.

A crucial change in the balance of internal Chadian forces occurred in August, a split in the *GUNT.* This was followed in October by a new round of fighting—between the forces of former *GUNT* leader Goukhouni and the Libyans. Chad claimed on 10 November that Libyan armed forces had killed hundreds of people in air and ground attacks in the north. On the 15th President Habré of Chad stated that government forces (the *FANT*) were cooperating with Goukouni's forces, now known as the Popular Armed Forces—*FAP.*

Crisis
On 11 December 1986 Libyan troops launched an attack on Goukouni's *FAP* forces in northern Chad and, according to the Chad government, used napalm and poison gas. This triggered a crisis for Chad. The same day a Libyan fighter plane was shot down over northern Chad.

Habré appealed for French, U.S., and Soviet armed intervention. On the 17th French aircraft dropped food, medical supplies, and ammunition to the *FAP* forces. However, the French defense ministry declared the same day that no French soldiers or aircraft would intervene to liberate northern Chad from Libyan occupation: the 1,000 French troops and aircraft in N'Djamena would be used only to defend the capital. On the 18th the U.S. State Department said it was rushing emergency military aid to the Chadian government.

Libya responded by appealing to the Arab League and the *OAU* for help against "a dangerous threat as a result of the U.S.-French military intervention" in the crisis. Chad, by contrast, complained that the *OAU* did not condemn Libya, despite its "inhuman acts." The USSR demanded that all "imperialist interference" in Chad cease.

In late December Chad government troops, now allied with Goukouni's former rebels, succeeded in crossing the 16th Parallel, the informal boundary between Libyan and French spheres of influence in Chad since 1984. Moreover, on 2 January 1987 Chad pressed its attack; and, after heavy fighting it claimed the recapture of the northeast oasis of Fada and the northwest oasis of Zouar. This triggered a crisis for Libya. On the 4th Libyan aircraft bombed civilians in Arada, south of the 16th Parallel. The same day Libya called up all army reservists.

In accord with France's defensive strategy, French forces in Chad established an air defense system to prevent any further Libyan military action south of the 16th Parallel; and French aircraft bombed Libyan radar at the airstrip at Qadi-Doum. France also continued to send military aid to the Chadian government army.

Fighting continued in the north, especially around the area of Zouar, a crucial point in Libya's plan to form a ring around the northern Tibesti region.

In this phase of the fighting, Algeria, Nigeria, and Zaire offered to mediate; and Niger called for an emergency *OAU* meeting to consider the crisis. The *OAU* Secretary-General visited the Chadian and Libyan capitals. Egypt condemned Libya's military intervention in Chad's internal affairs.

Despite the flurry of African mediation diplomacy, both sides continued their military buildup in the north. Low-intensity clashes continued intermittently during the next six months.

In a brief breakthrough, Chad government troops captured the town of Aozou in the disputed Strip on 8 August. On the 29th Libya launched a counter-attack and took back control over Aozou. Libya also continued to bomb Chad, including towns south of the 16th Parallel.

Following the Chadian attack on 8 August, Libya complained to the UN Security Council that Chad had attacked its territory.

Despite repeated requests from Habré, France refused to provide air cover for its exposed towns, other than the capital.

As the fighting escalated, Chadian government forces invaded Libya on 5 September 1987—for the first time—and occupied the important air base of Maaten-es-Sara: it claimed the destruction of 30 combat aircraft and the base itself. France expressed concern at Chad's actions, while the U.S. welcomed the Chadian raid.

Following mediation efforts by the *OAU* Chairman, President Kaunda of Zambia, de-escalation was swift. The crisis came to an end on 11 September, when both sides accepted an *OAU* call for a cease-fire. They also agreed to a meeting of an ad hoc *OAU* committee in Lusaka on 23 September.

(The long-standing territorial dispute between Chad and Libya—Libya first occupied the Aozou Strip in 1973—was submitted by them to the International Court of Justice *[ICJ]* in 1990 for a binding ruling. In a turning-point decision on 3 February 1994 the *ICJ* ruled, by a vote of 16–1, in favor of Chad's claim to the Strip. The Court decided that the international border between Chad and Libya had been formally fixed by a treaty between France, then the colonial power in Chad, and Libya in 1955, which clearly assigned the Aozou Strip to Chad. Libya had also claimed 310,000 square miles of northern Chad and had long occupied it under the terms of a de facto agreement with France that divided Chad at the 16th Parallel into spheres of influence [see Case #290—**Chad/Libya III** above].

Negotiations between Chad and Libya to implement the Court's ruling led to an agreement on the withdrawal of Libyan troops from the Aozou Strip, to begin on 15 April and to be completed on 10 May, and to be monitored by international observers. The Strip was formally transferred by Libya to Chad on 30 May 1994.)

(See *Master Table,* pp. 730–31.)

Sources
ACR 1986, 1987; *AR* 1986, 1987; *ARec* 1986, 1987; *ARB* 1986, 1987; *Keesing's* 1986, 1987.

Ethiopia/Somalia

There were six international crises in the **Ethiopia/Somalia** protracted conflict since its inception in 1960, as follows.

Case #179   **Ethiopia/Somalia,** in 1960–61;
#208   **Ogaden I,** in 1964;
#282   **Ogaden II,** in 1977–78;
#320   **East Africa Confrontation,** in 1980–81;
#338   **Ogaden III,** in 1982;
#373   **Todghere Incident,** in 1987.

The conflict remains unresolved.

General Background

Ethiopia's eastern frontier was established by treaties with Italy and the U.K. at the end of the nineteenth century. The treaties included the ceding to Ethiopia of the Haud territory, which contained a large nomadic Somali population. Italy occupied Ethiopia in 1936 (see Case #47—**Ethiopian War, in Africa: Non-PCs**). Full sovereignty was restored to the Emperor, Haile Selasse, in 1941 after the British liberation of his kingdom during World War II. In 1946 the Ogaden and Haud territories were returned to Ethiopia after five years of British military administration. Italy regained authority over Italian Somaliland.

A 1954 agreement between Britain and Ethiopia confirmed the 1897 annexation of the Haud region by Ethiopia but also granted grazing rights to Somali tribes in that area. On 5 June 1960 Ethiopia announced that the 1954 agreement would become invalid upon Somalia's independence on 3 July. The Somalia government published a manifesto on 30 August calling for a Greater Somalia which would include British- and Italian-held territories of Somalia, as well as parts of Ethiopia and Kenya which were inhabited by Somalis; it also charged that the agreement of 1897 with Ethiopia violated the treaties of protection Britain had concluded with northern Somali tribes in 1885. The All-African People's Solidarity Organization Conference of January 1960 and the Afro-Asian People's Solidarity Organization Conference of April 1960 adopted resolutions supporting Somalia's struggle for independence and unification. Several attempts to reach agreement over the territorial dispute before Somalia's independence in July 1960 failed, and its boundary with Ethiopia was still not demarcated. Although friction between grazing Somali tribes and Ethiopian authorities contributed to the PC, the conflict concerned Somalia's right to self-determination and its ambition for territorial expansion based upon irredentist claims. This was a challenge to Ethiopia's sovereign integrity: Addis Ababa feared that granting privileges to one tribe in its multinational state would open the door for other requests. The prospect of an independent Somalia Republic alarmed Ethiopia.

Somalia, on the other hand, was threatened by disintegration and felt that it was not bound to accept colonial boundaries.

(179) Ethiopia/Somalia

A crisis for Ethiopia began on 26 December 1960 and faded after about a year, with no fixed termination date.

Crisis
On 26 December 1960, 7,000 Somali tribesmen surrounded an Ethiopian police garrison and launched a heavy attack. The Ethiopian response occurred on the 29th when military units, including the air force, invaded Somalia, forcing the tribesmen to retreat. A strong protest was sent from Ethiopia to Somalia. The crisis continued with accusations, violence, and clashes for several months thereafter. During January 1961 Ethiopia bombed Somalia; there were clashes between their forces in Haud; Somalia postponed an oil shipment to Ethiopia; and the leader of the nationalist movement in Somalia warned of an imminent war. On 5 February there was a Somali invasion of Ethiopia with propaganda distributed in the disputed province. The All-African People's Conference of 1961 decided in favor of Ethiopia. In May, at the Monrovia Conference, an appeal was made to both sides to renew their efforts for a settlement. On 25 August talks were held between President Osman of Somalia and Emperor Haile Selassie at the Non-Aligned Conference in Belgrade. On 31 August clashes were reported once again between Somali tribesmen and Ethiopians. And on 27 September there was an official complaint from Somalia that the dispute was not yet solved.

The superpowers maintained a neutral stance in the 1960 crisis. The UN was not involved. And the *OAU* was not yet in existence.

(See *Master Table,* pp. 698–99.)

Sources
AR 1960; Austin 1963; Brown 1961; Castango 1960; Dei-Anang 1975; Farer 1976; Hoskyns 1969; Lewis 1963; Oliver 1972; Spencer 1977; Touval 1963, 1971, 1972; Widstrand 1969.

(208) Ogaden I

The first of several crises between Ethiopia and Somalia over Ogaden in the Horn of Africa lasted from 7 February until 30 March 1964.

Background
These two traditional enemies had contested ownership of the Ogaden Desert long before Somalia became independent in 1960. The root cause was Somalia's deep-rooted disaffection and irredentism regarding the territorial map of East

Africa, with large ethnic Somali populations under foreign control—in Ethiopia, Kenya, Djibouti, and Tanzania.

Since Somalia's independence in 1960 the creation of a "Greater Somalia," to include the then-French colony of Djibouti, the Northern Frontier District of Kenya, and, above all, the Ogaden Desert on its western border with Ethiopia, had been a firm and clearly stated aim of the Somalia government. The water and grazing resources of Ogaden were essential to the nomadic peoples of both countries. Ogaden, the core territorial issue, was a focus of interstate dispute since 1960: Ethiopia controlled it; and Somalia claimed it.

The protracted conflict between Ethiopia and Somalia was enmeshed in the East-West Cold War during the 1960s, 1970s, and 1980s. From 1960 until 1974 Somalia was a military client of the Soviet Union, Ethiopia of the United States.

Pre-crisis
Economic conditions were severe in Somalia preceding the crisis. In November 1963 the Soviet Union concluded a military aid agreement with Somalia. Border clashes occurred in January 1964.

Crisis
A crisis for Ethiopia was triggered on 7 February 1964 when military forces of the Republic of Somalia carried out a large-scale attack on the Ethiopian frontier post at Tog Wajale. Ethiopia responded during the next three days with the following: military resistance at the frontier post; a declaration of a state of emergency in the border region; a call for an immediate meeting of the *OAU;* and a strong protest by Ethiopia's foreign minister to the Soviet chargé d'affaires in Addis Ababa. In addition, Emperor Haile Selassie addressed a message to all African heads of state informing them of the incident. Military clashes reportedly continued until 10 February. The Ethiopian retaliation on the 8th on Somali territory triggered a crisis for Somalia. Its response, on the 9th, was also multiple: resistance to the Ethiopian attack; a declaration of a state of emergency throughout Somalia; an accusation of Ethiopian penetration into Somali territory, presented to Ethiopia's embassy in Mogadishu, and notification of the conflict to the *OAU.*

Somalia perceived the *OAU* members, many of whom experienced border disputes with their neighbors, as insensitive to its territorial claims. Success for Somalia, they feared, would constitute a precedent that would threaten the territorial integrity of other newly independent African states. Somalia looked upon the UN as a more friendly forum for its case. Thus on 10 February it requested a meeting of the Security Council, if the *OAU* failed to end the border dispute. Secretary-General U Thant appealed to the parties to settle the dispute peacefully. A cease-fire was accepted by them on 16 February but did not hold.

The crisis ended on 30 March 1964 with a cease-fire agreement along the original boundary, concluded in Khartoum. A joint border commission was established.

The U.S. was the major source of weapons for Ethiopia, as the USSR was for Somalia.

(Sporadic fighting continued for 10 days after the agreement. The territory in dispute—the Ogaden Desert—was retained by Ethiopia after the crisis ended. The persistent tension escalated to a full-scale crisis on several occasions later, in 1978 and 1980—see below.)

(See *Master Table,* pp. 704–5.)

Sources
ARB 1964; Brownlie 1979; Day 1987; Farer 1979; Hoskyns 1969; Lewis 1963; Mariam 1964; Markakis 1987; Perham 1969; Spiegel and Waltz 1971; Touval 1963, 1972; Widstrand 1969.

(282) Ogaden II

The continuing dispute over the territory of Ogaden generated another crisis between Ethiopia and Somalia from 22 July 1977 to 14 March 1978.

Background
After the overthrow of the Ethiopian monarchy in 1974, the marxist ruling group in Addis Ababa, the *Derge,* turned to Moscow for military support. From 1977 a large contingent of Cuban troops was stationed in Ethiopia to assist the marxist regime against its domestic enemies and Somali irredentism. Somalia responded by realigning with the United States.

The revolution of 1974 that overthrew the monarchy in Ethiopia also generated an upsurge of competing regional nationalisms. Brutal repression was practiced by the Mengistu regime. Ten out of Ethiopia's 14 provinces were in a state of armed insurrection against the central government in Addis Ababa. Its failure to suppress the revolt in Eritrea, along with the hostility of Ethiopia's other neighbors, was perceived in Mogadishu as an opportunity to realize the long-standing Somali goal of liberating Ogaden.

Crisis
On 22 July 1977 the Somalia-backed Western Somalia Liberation Front *(WSLF)* mounted a full-scale attack in the Ogaden region, triggering a crisis for Ethiopia. Within days most of Ogaden was overrun; and Somali troops pushed on to capture a score of Ethiopian posts on the outskirts of the Ogaden Desert. Ethiopia responded on 7 August by severing diplomatic relations with Somalia. Two days later the *OAU*'s mediation committee, created in 1973, reaffirmed the inviolability of borders from the colonial era. By October, 90 percent of the Ogaden had been captured by Somali forces: Somalia was on the threshold of total victory.

At that point the Soviet Union came to the aid of Ethiopia with an airlift of weapons. And after Somalia broke relations with the USSR and Cuba, the Soviets poured air force and army advisors, along with thousands of Cuban troops from Angola, into Ethiopia.

The counteroffensive by Ethiopian and Cuban forces began on 21 January 1978, triggering a crisis for Somalia. Jijiga, which had fallen to the Somalis in September 1977, was retaken in early March 1978; and, despite U.S. military aid, the Somalis were now a broken force. The dramatic Ethiopian breakthrough was masterminded by the Cubans and Soviets. On 9 March Somalia announced its intended withdrawal from the Ogaden region, conceding victory to Ethiopia. The withdrawal was completed on 14 March 1978, terminating the crisis—but not the protracted conflict—for both states.

The U.S. provided Somalia with weapons. The UN was not involved in this crisis.

(See *Master Table,* pp. 716–17.)

Sources
ACR 1978–79; *ARB* 1978; Brind 1983–84; Brownlie 1979; Brzoska and Pearson 1994; Cheg 1979; Day 1987; Farer 1979; Garthoff 1985; Ghardnay 1979; Gorman 1981; Hosmer and Wolfe 1983; Laitin 1979; Legum 1981; Legum and Lee 1979; LeoGrande 1980; Lewis 1980; Lewis 1985a; Makinda 1982; Markakis 1987; Mayall 1978; Napper 1983b; Ottaway 1982; Porter 1984; Schwab 1978; Sheik-Abdi 1977; Spencer 1977; Valenta 1981; Vance 1983; Zartman 1989.

(320) East Africa Confrontation

Somalia, Ethiopia, and Kenya experienced a crisis over territory from 5 December 1980 until 29 June 1981.

Pre-crisis
In 1980 two Somali offensives tried—but failed—to take control of Ogaden.

Crisis
On 5 December 1980 Kenya's President Daniel Arap Moi and Ethiopia's ruler, Mengistu Mariam, called on Somalia to renounce all territorial claims against Ethiopia, Kenya, Djibouti, and Tanzania—and to pay reparations for damage caused to Ethiopia in its full-scale attack on Ogaden in 1977 (see Case #282—**Ogaden II** above). This demand, the culmination of an Ethiopian diplomatic offensive against the U.S.-Somalia military assistance agreement of July 1980, triggered a crisis for Somalia, which perceived it as a declaration of war: it feared having to defend its borders with Ethiopia and Kenya simultaneously.

Somalia responded two days later: a joint declaration by all of its governing institutions—the Supreme Revolutionary Council, the Central Committee of the ruling Somalia Revolutionary Socialist Party, the Council of Ministers, and the People's Assembly—called on the Somali people to defend their national rights.

This was perceived as a declaration of war by Kenya and Ethiopia, triggering crises for them.

Despite the intense hostility and the danger of war—ever-present in the prolonged struggle for control over Ogaden and other Somali-claimed territories, there was no violence during the ensuing months. Crisis termination was signaled by a formal agreement for cooperation between President Barré of Somalia and President Moi of Kenya on 29 June 1981.

The *OAU* reiterated its opposition to Somali territorial claims in August 1980. Neither of the patron states, the U.S. and the USSR, nor the UN, was involved in this crisis.

(See *Master Table,* pp. 722–23.)

Sources
ACR 1980–81; *AR* 1980, 1981; *ARec* 1980, 1981; *ARB* 1980, 1981; *Keesing's* 1980, 1981.

(338) Ogaden III

Somalia and Ethiopia experienced another crisis over the Ogaden Desert from 30 June until August 1982.

Crisis
Another international crisis erupted on 30 June 1982, when Ethiopian troops attacked Somali army units in the Hiran region, thereby threatening to sever communications between the two halves of Somalia. Ethiopia was accused by Mogadishu of "naked aggression." And on 12 July Somalia's President Barré sought *OAU* and UN support against Ethiopia's alleged plans for full-scale war. Two days later Africa's regional organization called upon Ethiopia to desist from destabilizing East Africa.

Somalia responded with an urgent request to the U.S. for assistance. The U.S. began a flow of arms and economic aid in July, in accordance with a 1980 agreement that granted U.S. forces valuable naval and air facilities at the northern Somali port of Berbera. U.S. aid triggered a crisis for Ethiopia, which declared on 26 July that this posed a threat to its territorial integrity. Ethiopia also denied that it had invaded Somalia.

Barré declared a state of emergency in the war zone on 15 September, following Ethiopia's successful incursion 20 miles into Somali territory. However, with no further advances by either party, the crisis faded in August 1982.

The USSR and the UN were not involved in this crisis.

(See *Master Table,* pp. 726–27.)

Sources
ACR 1982–83; *AR* 1982; *ARec* 1982; *ARB* 1982; Day 1987; Markakis 1987; Zartman 1989.

(373) Todghere Incident

Somalia experienced another crisis with Ethiopia from 12 February until early April 1987.

Background
Low-intensity violence between these long-standing adversaries continued unabated through the 1980s, for the most part indirectly: the protagonists acted through ethnic, paramilitary, proxy organizations—the Ethiopian-backed Somali Salvation Democratic Front *(SSDF)* and the Somali National Movement *(SNM)*, against the Somalia-supported Western Somali Liberation Front *(WSLF)*. Somalia persistently claimed jurisdiction over Somalis living in the Ogaden Desert. Ethiopia persistently rejected the Somali claim. Occasionally border incidents escalated to an interstate crisis. One of these occurred in 1987.

Crisis
A crisis for Somalia was triggered on 12 February 1987 when Ethiopia-backed *SNM* irregulars penetrated 20 kilometers beyond the border and attacked six Somali villages in Todghere Province. Somalia repulsed the attack, reportedly within hours, each side suffering about 25 casualties in the incident. On 17 February Ethiopia indirectly acknowledged responsibility by announcing that an official inquiry would be held to determine the cause of the incident. Addis Ababa also reaffirmed its interest in achieving a peace accord with its neighbor. Lesser incidents occurred during the next six weeks. An interim cease-fire agreement was reached in Mogadishu in early April, terminating the crisis.

(A year later, on 3 April 1988, Ethiopia and Somalia agreed to demilitarize their border and to restore diplomatic relations.)

The U.S., the USSR, the UN, and the *OAU* were not involved in this crisis. (See *Master Table,* pp. 732–33.)

Sources
ACR 1987–88; Day 1987; *Keesing's* 1987.

Rhodesia

The protracted conflict between Rhodesia and its neighbors, Botswana, Mozambique, and Zambia, and the concomitant internal racial struggle within Rhodesia lasted from 1965 to 1980. It culminated in the transformation of Rhodesia from a white minority regime to a black majority–ruled state, Zimbabwe, in January 1980. During those 15 years there were 11 international crises, as follows.

Case #218 **Rhodesia's UDI,** in 1965–66;
     #250 **Zambia Raid,** in 1973;

#267 **Operation Thrasher,** in 1976;
#273 **Nagomia Raid,** in 1976;
#276 **Operation Tangent,** in 1976–77;
#278 **Mapai Seizure,** in 1977;
#283 **Rhodesia Raid,** in 1977–78;
#286 **Chimoio-Tembue Raids,** in 1977–78;
#293 **Air Rhodesia Incident,** in 1978;
#300 **Raids on ZIPRA,** in 1979;
#307 **Rhodesia Settlement,** in 1979–80.

General Background

Rhodesia (since 1980, Zimbabwe) is a large landlocked state in southern Africa, with Zambia to the north, Botswana to the west, the Union of South Africa to the south, and Mozambique to the east. It has a land area of 150,660 square miles, with a population of approximately 10 million.

Its historical roots can be traced to the era of European colonization of Africa. In October 1889 a charter was given by the U.K. government to the British South Africa Company, headed by Cecil Rhodes, with virtually unlimited powers and rights over a large area north of the Transvaal region of what became the Union of South Africa and west of Portuguese-controlled Mozambique. A year later, the town of Salisbury (later, Harare) was founded by the company in Mashonaland. In May 1895 the territory was named Rhodesia, in honor of Cecil Rhodes. In August 1911 the northeastern and northwestern parts of Rhodesia were united as Northern Rhodesia (later, Zambia) under the administration of the South Africa Company; the bulk of the territory was henceforth known as Southern Rhodesia.

Attempts to draw Southern Rhodesia into the Union of South Africa failed: a white-only referendum in October 1922 resulted in a large vote against merger. In September 1923 Southern Rhodesia (and, the next year, Northern Rhodesia) became a crown colony, with internal self-rule—limited to white settlers.

There was a short-lived merger of the three British colonies that were carved from the original territory of Rhodesia: in October 1953 Southern Rhodesia (later, Zimbabwe), Northern Rhodesia (later, Zambia), and Nyasaland (later, Malawi) were integrated into the Federation of Rhodesia and Nyasaland; it was dissolved at the beginning of 1964. The dominant politician in the Federation was Roy Welensky, leader of the racially moderate United Federal Party. In December 1962 the extremist white supremacy Rhodesian Front was elected to power in Southern Rhodesia, under the leadership of Winston Field and then, in April 1964, under Ian Smith, the dominant figure in Southern Rhodesia during the entire protracted conflict from 1965 to 1980.

The struggle for black majority rule in Rhodesia began in the late 1950s. Two competing movements and paramilitary organizations emerged from various nationalist groups. One was the Zimbabwe African Peoples Union *(ZAPU)*, headed by Joshua Nkomo; its military wing was the Zimbabwe Peoples Revolutionary Army *(ZIPRA)*, based in Northern Rhodesia (Zambia). The other was the Zimbabwe African National Union *(ZANU)*, headed by Robert Mugabe; its military wing was the Zimbabwe National Liberation Army *(ZANLA)*, based in Mozambique. Together they formed the African National Council, whose office was situated in Botswana. Later they formed the Patriotic Front *(PF)*, which remained a loose political-military coalition of *ZAPU-ZIPRA* and *ZANU-ZANLA* in the struggle against white rule until independence. According to figures published by the Central Statistical Office in Salisbury, Rhodesia, there were, in June 1975, a total of 277,000 "Europeans" in Rhodesia, 6,000,000 "Africans," 10,000 "Asians," and 20,400 "Coloureds."

(218) Rhodesia's UDI

A proclamation of a state of emergency by the white minority regime in Southern Rhodesia precipitated a crisis for Zambia from 5 November 1965 to 27 April 1966.

Pre-crisis
With the dissolution of the Federation on 1 January 1964, competing pressures mounted within Rhodesia. There was growing evidence in 1964 and 1965 that the white regime in Southern Rhodesia planned to issue a Unilateral Declaration of Independence *(UDI)*. At the same time, the African National Council and its key members pressed for black majority rule.

In that atmosphere of increasing conflict, 18 Commonwealth heads of government, meeting in July 1964, unanimously pledged not to recognize a unilateral declaration of independence by Rhodesia. Tension increased when many African leaders were detained in late August. On 27 October British Prime Minister Wilson publicly warned against *UDI* and threatened sanctions. In May 1965 Ian Smith's Rhodesian Front won an overwhelming victory in white-only elections. In early October Prime Minister Smith of Rhodesia, in London, demanded immediate independence.

Zambia, which itself had become independent on 24 October 1964, viewed the possible establishment of a hostile white-ruled state, independent of the U.K., as a threat to its existence: being landlocked, Zambia was totally dependent on Rhodesia for rail routes to ports, sources of coal and oil, and power from the jointly owned hydroelectric stations at the Kariba Dam on the Rhodesia-Zambia border.

Crisis
The trigger to Zambia's gravest foreign policy crisis was Rhodesia's proclamation of a state of emergency on 5 November 1965, granting the white regime in Salisbury sweeping powers. Zambia correctly perceived this to be a prelude to

Rhodesia's declaration of independence. The next day, Zambia issued a final warning to Rhodesia of the consequences of such an act. Rhodesian troops were moved to the Zambian border on 9 November. And on the 11th independence was declared.

Zambia's response, the next day, combined the dispatch of troops to the Zambezi River, a promulgation of emergency regulations, and limited economic sanctions against Rhodesia: Rhodesia's currency and money orders would not be negotiable in Zambia as of 13 November. And on the 17th Zambia's President Kaunda began sustained pressure on the U.K. for an immediate military response or, at least, British guarantees for Zambia's supply of Kariba power. Zambia also pressed for an emergency meeting of the UN Security Council. Despite U.K. objections to intervention by the global organization, the Council did pass several resolutions—on 12 October and 5, 12, and 20 November. The most important, on 12 November, condemned *UDI,* urged nonrecognition by member-states, and appealed to them to refrain from rendering any assistance to Rhodesia.

On 20 November, at an *OAU* meeting in Dar es Salaam, representatives from Egypt, Kenya, Nigeria, Tanzania, and Zambia debated the setting up of a multinational African army; but as a result of Zambia's opposition, no action was taken. After initial British refusal to exert military pressure on Rhodesia, the U.K. finally offered to send ground troops to Zambia for protection against invasion. Zambia, which viewed this suggestion as designed to prevent, rather than prepare for, military action against Rhodesia, refused. On 23 November discussions began on a proposal to station Royal Air Force *(RAF)* units at Zambia's three international airfields, in order to deter a Rhodesian air attack. The following day, Zambian troops were withdrawn from the border, and the U.K. Prime Minister, Harold Wilson, announced that Britain and Zambia had agreed on the provision of *RAF* planes and personnel for Zambia's air defense. By the time the Extraordinary Meeting of the *OAU* Council of Ministers convened, on 3 December, to consider the severance of diplomatic relations with the U.K. by several states, the *RAF* was being installed at Zambia's airfields. On the 28th Zambian ministerial missions visited Washington and Moscow with a view to securing superpower support for a more vigorous response to *UDI* and increased assistance to Zambia. A UN oil embargo on Rhodesia (and therefore, Zambia) led to the mounting of an Anglo-American-Canadian oil airlift to Zambia in early January 1966. The Commonwealth, too, acted in support of Zambia, at its Lagos summit meeting in January 1966: it established a committee to monitor the effect of sanctions; and it urged members to provide aid to Zambia in a Commonwealth-coordinated program.

The success of the Berlin-style (1948–49) airlift to Zambia, and the development of alternative surface supply routes, encouraged Wilson to believe that *UDI* could end "within weeks, not months," providing that Zambia imposed complete sanctions and broke entirely with Rhodesia. Wilson promised massive external support and a tougher British policy on Rhodesia, but these promises were adjusted during February and March 1966. And, finally, London reneged altogether on 27 April, following the British general elections, which returned a commanding majority for Labour. On that day the crisis ended for Zambia: although it felt betrayed by Wilson's announcement of the initiation of "talks about talks" with Rhodesia's Prime Minister Smith, Zambia's existence was no longer in peril.

(The completion of a pipeline from Dar es Salaam on the Indian Ocean, almost three years later, reduced Zambia's dependence on Rhodesia for oil, coal, and electricity.)

(See Master Table, pp. 706–7.)

Sources
AR 1965, 1966; *ARB* 1965, 1966; Anglin 1980, 1994; Good 1973; Hall 1973; Sklar 1974; Wilson 1971.

(250) Zambia Raid

Zambia experienced another crisis with Rhodesia from 19 January to 3 February 1973.

Pre-crisis
On 9 January 1973 the Rhodesian government closed the border with Zambia except for copper exports, which constitute 90 percent of all exports from Zambia. Rhodesia's Prime Minister Ian Smith accused Zambia of harboring terrorists who were allegedly responsible for incidents threatening Rhodesian citizens. Preceding and immediately following the closure there had been several border incidents between the two countries.

Crisis
On 19 January 1973, the government of Zambia perceived that Rhodesia might use an incident in which Zambian troops and police fired on a threatening South African police motorboat on the Zambezi River as an excuse to launch a military attack on Zambia. The same day, in response to this trigger, Defense Minister Grey Zulu declared that Zambian forces had been moved to the border. On 24 January Zambia requested an urgent session of the Security Council and accused Rhodesia, with South African aid, of violating Zambia's sovereignty and territorial integrity. On the 27th President Kaunda sent a letter to Secretary-General Waldheim stating that Zambia would not tolerate violations of its territory by Rhodesia or South Africa. The Security Council met on the 29th (at that time, Rhodesia and South Africa were the targets of UN economic sanctions; and South Africa's formal status at the UN had been reduced). The crisis ended on 3 February, when Rhodesia, satisfied that its objectives had been achieved, reopened the border with Zambia.

Neither the U.S. nor the USSR was involved in this crisis.

(On 10 March, after the termination of the crisis, the Security Council

passed a resolution calling upon Britain to convene a conference to bring about self-determination and independence to Rhodesia and called upon Rhodesia's government to release all political prisoners.)
(See *Master Table,* pp. 712–13.)

Sources
ACR 1973; *AR* 1973; *ARec* 1973; *ARB* 1973.

(267) Operation Thrasher

The first of several international crises arising from the struggle for black majority rule in Rhodesia erupted on 22 February and ended in April 1976. Rhodesia and Mozambique were the crisis actors.

Background
War between Rhodesia and Zambia, Mozambique, and Botswana had been raging since 1976 when Rhodesia set up a War Council to supervise the destruction of guerrilla bases in those countries. Beginning in February 1976 Rhodesian troops and aircraft repeatedly raided across the 1,200-kilometer border with Mozambique in order to harass Zimbabwean guerrillas before they could infiltrate into Rhodesia, and to strike at economic targets in a bid to drive home to the Maputo regime the high cost of its support for the Zimbabwean insurgents.

Pre-crisis
Systematic guerrilla activity against Rhodesia's *UDI* had begun in December 1972 but was restricted to the northeast. When the campaign spread throughout the country in 1976 Rhodesia became involved in a full-scale war. The scale of operations also changed, as large groups of guerrillas entered Rhodesia, operating from Mozambique, Botswana, and Zambia.

The heads of state of the "Front-line States"—Botswana, Mozambique, Tanzania, and Zambia—met in Mozambique on 7 and 8 February 1976. There they reaffirmed the need for an armed struggle to achieve majority rule in Rhodesia. On the 8th Mozambique President Machel threatened to invade Rhodesia. Constitutional talks between Rhodesia's Prime Minister Smith and Nkomo, representing the African National Council, were resumed on 10 February.

Crisis
The first clash between Rhodesian security forces and unidentified guerrillas from across the Mozambique border, a three-hour battle on 22 February 1976, triggered a crisis for Rhodesia. Further guerrilla activity was reported in the Chipinga district, 180 miles south of the northeastern border, on the 24th. Rhodesia responded that day by launching Operation Thrasher, an attack on *ZANLA* bases near its southeastern border with Mozambique, causing the deaths of a number of people and extensive damage, which in turn triggered a crisis for

Mozambique. Machel described the attack as an "act of war" and stated that Mozambique forces had shot down Rhodesian aircraft and helicopters, a claim that was not backed by other sources. The Mozambique response was to meet the Rhodesian forces with violence, an announcement on 3 March that all communications with Rhodesia had been banned, and the imposition of sanctions—including the confiscation of all Rhodesian property and assets in Mozambique in accordance with earlier UN and *OAU* resolutions. On the 8th Mozambique closed its border with Rhodesia, and the country was put on a war footing.

The crisis for Rhodesia faded in March 1976 with a temporary halt in guerrilla activities. The Smith-Nkomo talks ended in deadlock on 19 March with each side blaming the other. The crisis ended in April for Mozambique with a decision to set up a joint institute for the training of defense and police forces with Tanzania and Zambia.

The Security Council met in March and adopted a resolution on the 17th condemning Rhodesia. Mozambique's foreign minister appealed to the Council for $57 million in aid to cover the loss of revenue for Mozambique from the UN imposition of sanctions against Rhodesia. Another Security Council resolution on 6 April strengthened the sanctions. The *OAU* supported UN sanctions and granted military aid to the guerrillas.

The United States' involvement was limited to several statements by Secretary of State Kissinger favorable to Mozambique. The Soviet Union supplied weapons to both of Rhodesia's guerrilla organizations, *ZIPRA* and *ZANLA*.

(See *Master Table,* pp. 714–15.)

Sources
ACR 1976; *AD* 1976; *ARec* 1976; *ARB* 1976; *Keesing's* 1976.

(273) Nagomia Raid

A Rhodesian "hot pursuit" operation precipitated a second crisis for Mozambique on 9 August 1976 ending in November of that year.

Pre-crisis
In March 1976 President Machel had announced the closure of his country's borders with Rhodesia, and Mozambique was put on a war footing (see Case #267—**Operation Thrasher** above). A sharp rise in guerrilla activity had increased Rhodesian hot pursuit operations since Rhodesia's war spread to its eastern border with Mozambique. Early in August guerrilla attacks on Rhodesian security forces occurred at a camp at Ruda.

Crisis
On 9 August 1976 Rhodesian forces raided a guerrilla camp at Nagomia, Mozambique, and triggered a crisis for that state: it was reported that more than 300 Zimbabweans were killed. This dramatic operation, in which, according to

Mozambique sources, approximately 600 were killed, was the largest raid across the border by Rhodesia. Mozambique responded on 11 August with a 30-minute mortar attack by government troops on a white residential suburb in Umtali, Rhodesia, close to the Mozambique border. Mozambique requested an investigation by the UN High Commissioner for Refugees: it subsequently reported that the Pungwe camp on the Nagomia road was a refugee camp containing 8,000 black Rhodesians and that many women and children were among the 500 dead counted by UN officials. Rhodesia, on the other hand, produced captured documents on 29 August to provide evidence that the camp was a military base for several thousand Rhodesian African nationalist guerrillas. Further attacks on Mozambique territory were reported during August.

On 6 September the "Front-Line States" (then Botswana, Mozambique, Tanzania, and Zambia) met in Dar es Salaam to coordinate their defense policies. Secretary of State Kissinger arrived in the area on the 13th, and soon thereafter agreements were concluded for $10 million in U.S. aid to Mozambique. Mozambique's foreign minister addressed the UN General Assembly on 5 October. And at a meeting in November 1976 of the Inter-State Defense Commission, created by the Front-Line States, it was decided to organize joint action for their defense. This ended the crisis for Mozambique.

The USSR, which had been supplying military, medical, and other aid to the guerrillas, published a condemnation of Rhodesia in *Pravda* in August.

(See *Master Table,* pp. 716–17.)

Sources
ACR 1976; *AD* 1976; *ARec* 1976; *ARB* 1976; *Keesing's* 1976.

(276) Operation Tangent

The extension of Rhodesia's military operations against African guerrillas to the border area with Botswana caused a crisis for Botswana from 20 December 1976 to 31 March 1977.

Pre-crisis
In February 1976 Rhodesia had launched **Operation Thrasher** to deal with military incursions by Mozambique-based guerrillas into its territory (see Case #267 above). During that year a number of guerrilla operations were mounted from Botswana staging camps. Rhodesia's security forces dramatically increased their incursions into Botswana, which issued a public accusation on 12 August. In November a villager was killed and several bombs exploded in Francistown at the office of the African National Council *(ANC)*. On 15 December Rhodesian forces raided a village on the border and kidnapped three Botswana citizens. Three days later fire was exchanged between Botswana police and Rhodesian troops. And on the 20th Botswana claimed that its territory had been violated by Rhodesian forces 31 times since the beginning of November 1976.

Crisis

On 20 December 1976 the Rhodesian government announced the creation of a new operational military zone—Operation Tangent—in the northwest and west covering the Botswana border area. This announcement triggered a crisis for Botswana, particularly because it had no army, only a police force. Botswana responded by declaring the 30-kilometer border with Rhodesia a protected area, imposing a curfew, and appealing to the UN Security Council on 21 December. It also set up a Police Mobile Unit to patrol the border and expanded it in January 1977. The Security Council met on 14 January and condemned Rhodesian incursions into Botswana, demanding the cessation of all hostile acts. The Council accepted a Botswana invitation to send a mission to assess its needs and requested the Secretary-General to organize immediately financial and other forms of assistance to Botswana and to report back to the Council not later than 31 March. The UN mission, which visited Botswana in February, reported that there was evidence of Rhodesian incursions and stated that Botswana's difficulties had been increased severely by the influx of refugees. The report recommended a $50 million grant over three years, half to reinforce the Police Mobile Unit and the rest for the care of refugees. The same day, 31 March 1977, Botswana decided to establish an army, terminating its crisis.

The USSR offered economic aid to Botswana. There was no U.S. involvement in this crisis.

(See *Master Table,* pp. 716–17.)

Sources
ACR 1977; *AD* 1977; *ARec* 1977; *ARB* 1977; *Keesing's* 1977.

(278) Mapai Seizure

Rhodesian raids on guerrilla camps inside Mozambique caused a third crisis for that state from 29 May to 30 June 1977.

Crisis
On 29 May 1977 Rhodesia's military command announced that security forces, with air support, had entered southwest Mozambique and had overrun guerrilla bases. The attack triggered a crisis for Mozambique. The same day its minister of defense stated that the Rhodesian military operation had been directed at military installations. On 30 May, after more raids, Mozambique announced a counter-offensive. The following day the crisis escalated when the commander of Rhodesia's armed forces announced that troops had occupied the town of Mapai and were prepared to stay in Mozambique as long as necessary in order to destroy the *ZANLA* guerrillas in the area.

Rhodesia's actions drew strong condemnations from the international community. On 1 June UN Secretary-General Waldheim condemned Rhodesia, as did the U.S. and the U.K. Even South African Prime Minister Vorster issued a statement of concern that the Rhodesian action would lead to increased communist (Cuban) activity in southern Africa.

Rhodesia's troops withdrew from Mapai on 1–2 June, but the tension level remained high. On 18 June Mozambique's President Machel accused Rhodesia of waging open warfare against his country and requested a meeting of the UN Security Council. The Council passed a resolution at the end of June condemning Rhodesia for aggression against Mozambique. The resolution also requested immediate and substantial material assistance to enable Mozambique to strengthen its defense capability in order to safeguard its sovereignty and territorial integrity. This resolution, on 30 June, ended Mozambique's crisis. There was no USSR involvement.

(See *Master Table*, pp. 716–17.)

Sources
ACR 1977; *AD* 1977; *ARec* 1977; *ARB* 1977; *Keesing's* 1977.

(283) Rhodesia Raid

Rhodesian air raids on *ZIPRA* bases in Zambia brought about a crisis for that state from 31 August 1977 until 14 August 1978.

Background
Despite ongoing discussions in search of an acceptable constitutional settlement to the Rhodesian conflict, the situation deteriorated in 1977. In May of that year the British government released information that claimed that Rhodesia's Prime Minister Smith had proposed to take preemptive action against guerrilla attacks on the grounds that a buildup of African forces was taking place on the Zambian side of Rhodesia's border. Zambia was the home base for *ZAPU* and its revolutionary army, *ZIPRA*. On 16 May Zambia's President Kaunda said that a state of war existed with Rhodesia. On 8 July he stated that his country had approached one or two other states, presumably Cuba and Somalia, for aid. Earlier, on 8 June, Rhodesia accused Zambia of a rocket attack and threatened to disconnect Zambia's power from Rhodesia's Kariba hydroelectric station. In August an increasing number of incidents were reported on Rhodesia's borders with Zambia and Botswana. On the 27th it was reported from Zambia that air strikes were feared. In the light of tensions since May and the growing fear in late August, the first incident to take place was likely to trigger a fresh crisis.

Crisis
On 31 August 1977 a crisis was triggered for Zambia when Rhodesian jet bombers strafed the border district of Luanshya causing casualties and damage to property. Kaunda's response, on 3 September, was to impose several days of blackout and curfew in Lusaka, Zambia's capital, and in other cities. On the 7th the blackout and curfew were extended indefinitely when Kaunda invoked full

powers under the state of emergency that had existed since Rhodesia's declaration of independence in 1965 (see Case #218—**Rhodesia's UDI** above). On the 11th the president accused Rhodesia of using napalm, which was denied the following day by the Combined Operational Headquarters in Rhodesia. The curfew was lifted on 20 September.

A period of highly conflictual relations between the two states followed. Escalation occurred on 6 March 1978 when Rhodesian forces entered Zambian territory in force with aircraft, helicopters, and ground troops attacking the Luanshya district in what the Smith regime described as "hot pursuit." A secret meeting between Prime Minister Smith and *ZAPU* leader Nkomo in Lusaka on 14 August 1978 ended Zambia's crisis. The meeting, held under the auspices of President Kaunda, indicated an easing of tension. Smith attempted to bring Nkomo into his domestic support group via changes in the Executive Council of Rhodesia, to include local black representation. The council was set up in March 1978 but had been losing support among Rhodesia's black population.

The UN Security Council met on 15–17 March 1978 and adopted a resolution reaffirming sanctions against Rhodesia, which Zambia had been carrying out fully at great sacrifice. The *OAU* held discussions without passing a resolution. The United States and Britain attempted to seek implementation of the Anglo-American proposals for a constitutional settlement leading to internationally recognized independence for Rhodesia. There was no USSR involvement in this crisis.

(The Zambian railway to Rhodesia was reopened on 6 October 1978.)

(See *Master Table*, pp. 716–17.)

Sources
ACR 1977, 1978; *AD* 1977, 1978; *AR* 1977, 1978; *ARec* 1977, 1978; *ARB* 1977, 1978; *Keesing's* 1977, 1978.

(286) Chimoio-Tembue Raids

Rhodesian attacks on bases of the Zimbabwe African National Liberation Army *(ZANLA)* in Mozambique triggered another crisis for Mozambique from 23 November 1977 to 22 March 1978.

Pre-crisis
After the **Mapai Seizure** of May–June 1977 (see Case #278 above), there was a decline in military activity on the Mozambique border. However, in November 1977 the raids of Rhodesian forces into Mozambique were reported to be the heaviest since the guerrilla war had begun. Serious food shortages prevailed in Mozambique prior to the crisis.

Crisis
On 23–24 November 1977 Rhodesian forces attacked the main operational headquarters of *ZANLA* near Chimoio in Mozambique. This was followed by raids on

a base at Tembue, on 25–26 November. These attacks triggered a crisis for Mozambique. Salisbury announced that 1,200 *ZANLA* "terrorists" had been killed, expressing regret at the possibility of civilian deaths, but emphasizing that Rhodesia was at war and that civilians, particularly women and children, should not be in such camps. On 1 December Prime Minister Smith added that the raids had been essential to stop heavy attacks that had been planned against Rhodesia. *ZANLA* leader Mugabe denied that the Chimoio camp was a guerrilla base. On 23 December 1977 and on 14–15 February 1978, Rhodesia made public documents it claimed to have seized during the raids listing women guerrillas with their weapons, adding there had been armed clashes between rival *ZANLA* and *ZIPRA* (Zimbabwe Peoples Revolutionary Army) units.

President Machel visited Nigeria and Angola for talks between 13 and 17 December; and on the 18th, upon his return to Mozambique, he met with leaders of the "Front-Line States" to discuss joint strategy. At that meeting the presidents of Angola, Mozambique, Tanzania, and Zambia drew up a four-point declaration expressing their support for some aspects of the Anglo-American plan to develop a clear timetable for achieving majority rule in Rhodesia, while reaffirming the unity of their group and its commitment to the Patriotic Front in its "liberation war." Termination of Mozambique's crisis occurred on 22 March when it approved a law for compulsory military service.

The *OAU* Ministerial Committee met in January 1978 to discuss this crisis. The Rhodesian raids were condemned by the U.K. and the U.S. And the UN General Assembly passed a resolution calling for assistance to Mozambique. Several months before these Rhodesian raids, arms to aid the guerrillas had been received in Mozambique from both China and the Soviet Union, though neither was directly involved in the crisis.

(See *Master Table*, pp. 718–19.)

Sources
ACR 1977, 1978; *AD* 1977, 1978; *AR* 1977, 1978; *ARec* 1977, 1978; *ARB* 1977, 1978.

(293) Air Rhodesia Incident

The shooting down of a Rhodesian civilian plane precipitated a crisis for Rhodesia and Zambia from 3 September to 31 October 1978.

Crisis
On 3 September 1978 an Air Rhodesia Viscount civilian plane was shot down unexpectedly by *ZAPU* (Zimbabwe African Peoples Union) guerrillas near Kariba, in Rhodesia's border area with Zambia, triggering a crisis for Rhodesia. Ten survivors were reportedly murdered on the ground after the plane had crashed. The plane was shot down by a heat-seeking SAM-7 missile, the first time such advanced weaponry had been used in the war over Rhodesia. Zambia, anticipat-

ing Rhodesian retaliation, appealed to the U.K. to restrain Rhodesia. The U.S. and Britain urged Prime Minister Smith of Rhodesia not to retaliate. The UN Secretary-General condemned the guerrilla attack. Within Rhodesia, the incident had caused great indignation. Smith announced on 10 September that martial law legislation would be introduced. Four days later Smith rejected the inclusion of *ZAPU* leader Nkomo in any internal settlement and objected to British and American support for the Zimbabwean guerrillas. Zambia complied with a Rhodesian demand to ground all civil aviation.

Smith visited the U.S. on 7 October. On the l0th all racial discrimination in Rhodesia was formally abolished. The same day the Security Council passed a resolution, at India's initiative, condemning the U.S. for allowing Smith's visit. On 19 October Rhodesia launched a major offensive against targets in Zambia, triggering a crisis for the latter. The raid was mainly against *ZAPU* bases, and 300 followers of Nkomo were reportedly killed. Zambia responded with military resistance: minor clashes ensued. President Kaunda declared on 23 October that his country was militarily weaker than Rhodesia and was unable to fight back. Kaunda also had 18 foreigners arrested on suspicion of aiding Rhodesia. Kaunda's statement of weakness ended Zambia's crisis. Rhodesia's crisis ended on 31 October with an extension of martial law to half the country. The crisis ended with no change in the status quo.

The USSR was not involved, the U.S. marginally so.

(See *Master Table*, pp. 718–19.)

Sources
ACR 1978; *AD* 1978; *ARec* 1978; *ARB* 1978; *Keesing's* 1978.

(300) Raids on *ZIPRA*

Rhodesian raids on guerrilla bases in Angola and Zambia occurred during a crisis for these three states from 12 February to 31 May 1979.

Pre-crisis
The transitional Rhodesian government established in April 1978 made little progress toward reaching an understanding with the Patriotic Front, with no cease-fire in sight. By the beginning of 1979 Rhodesia's security forces reportedly totaled 50,000, including a 10,000-man army. In February 1979 guerrilla attacks on power and transport installations in Rhodesia increased.

Crisis
On 12 February 1979 another Air Rhodesia Viscount, on a flight from Kariba to Salisbury, was shot down by a SAM-7 missile, and all 59 passengers and crew were killed (see Case #293 above). In response to the downing of the plane by guerrillas in Zambia, Rhodesian forces attacked Zimbabwe People's Revolutionary Army *(ZIPRA)* bases in Zambia on 23 February. Three days later seven

Rhodesian planes bombed a *ZIPRA* base near Luso in Angola, marking a new phase in the Rhodesian war, with Angolan territory now a target for Rhodesian raids. The attack triggered a crisis for Angola, which responded the following day with a strongly worded statement condemning Rhodesia, as well as South Africa. (The latter was thought to have provided Mirage planes for the attack.) March 1979 was marked by repeated skirmishes on all fronts.

On 13 April Rhodesian commandos again attacked guerrilla bases in Zambia, including *ZAPU* leader Joshua Nkomo's house in Lusaka, as well as other targets in the city and countryside. This triggered a crisis for Zambia, which responded on the 16th with a declaration by President Kaunda of a curfew on parts of the country close to the national railway line. On the 22nd Kaunda announced that Zambia would be receiving new weaponry.

On 10 May 1979 Angola's President Neto met with Kaunda and concluded an agreement declaring that an attack on either party would be considered an attack on both. A Joint Security Force was to be set up to repel Rhodesian or South African incursions into their territories. This pact marked the termination of Angola's crisis, while Zambia's crisis ended two days later with the lifting of the curfew that had been imposed on 16 April. The crisis ended for Rhodesia on 31 May with the change of government: that day Ian Smith handed over the reins of government to Bishop Abel Muzorewa.

The UN Security Council met on 8 March 1979 to discuss the strengthening of sanctions against Rhodesia, while condemning the forthcoming Rhodesian elections as insufficient in the provision for black representation in government.

The Ministerial Council of the *OAU* met between 1 and 3 March and adopted a resolution condemning Rhodesia. The U.S. and the USSR were not involved in this case.

(See *Master Table*, pp. 720–21.)

Sources
ACR 1979; *AD* 1979; *ARec* 1979; *ARB* 1979.

(307) Rhodesia Settlement

Rhodesia, Botswana, Mozambique, and Zambia were enmeshed in the decisive crisis of the protracted conflict over black majority rule in Rhodesia from 15 July 1979 to 4 March 1980.

Background and Pre-crisis
Guerrilla warfare against Rhodesia, as noted, began in 1972 and expanded in scope and intensity in 1976. Operations were carried out from bases in Botswana, Mozambique, and Zambia. On 13 April 1979 Rhodesian forces captured 14 people in Francistown, Botswana, which had been occupied by *ZAPU,* destroying the ferry between Botswana and Zambia, allegedly used for supplies to

ZIPRA. Clashes between Rhodesian and Mozambiquean forces, the latter better equipped than those of Botswana, were frequent in 1979. The attacks were primarily on economic targets. Some of the more serious recorded attacks took place on 9–10 February, on the Mapai-Pafuri road; on 20 February, on the Chimoio guerrilla base; the 14 March bombing of Chokene; and the 18–21 April bombings of Mozambique army positions in the Gaza Province. In Zambia, as well, raids were numerous. Zambia was the target several times in 1979, on 26 June, 1 and 20 July, 23 August, and throughout the month of October.

After the elections in Rhodesia in April 1979 a new government led by Bishop Abel Muzorewa took office on 31 May. Muzorewa quickly made it clear that his government intended to continue the policy of preemptive attacks on guerrilla bases and economic targets in Botswana, Mozambique, and Zambia. The war inside Rhodesia-Zimbabwe escalated quite rapidly, with reports of about 1,000 people being killed each month. The number of guerrillas operating within Rhodesia during July was estimated at about 12,000. Early in July Muzorewa visited the U.S. and U.K. in order to seek recognition for Zimbabwe and to get economic sanctions lifted.

Crisis

A crisis for Rhodesia was triggered internally on 15 July 1979 when a large number of security forces loyal to Ndabamingi Sithole, the leader of the opposition *ZANU* Party (Zimbabwe African National Union), were killed—apparently by regular Rhodesian forces. Internal events, peaking with the massacre, made it clear to Bishop Muzorewa that his regime did not have the ability to cope with the issues at hand. Further, on 18 July the High Court ruled that seven MPs of the Zimbabwe Democratic Party could take their seats in Parliament, thereby causing Muzorewa to lose parliamentary control. On 25 July U.K. Prime Minister Margaret Thatcher announced that recognition of independence and sovereignty would not be forthcoming as long as the government and constitutional structure of Muzorewa's Zimbabwe-Rhodesia remained unchanged.

From 1–8 August the Commonwealth heads of government met in Lusaka, Zambia, and decided on an all-party conference to end the Rhodesian conflict. The conference would be held in London in September. Invitations were sent to the Zimbabwe-Rhodesia government and to members of the Patriotic Front, along with a draft outline for a new constitution for Zimbabwe.

The trigger to Botswana's crisis was an attack by Rhodesian troops and helicopters on *ZIPRA* bases at Francistown on 8 August. The response was immediate—an air attack on the helicopters returning to Rhodesia.

On 15 August Rhodesia responded to its crisis by accepting the invitation issued at the end of the Lusaka Commonwealth Conference: Prime Minister Muzorewa's decision was based upon the need to stop the internal challenges to his regime and to achieve some political stability.

A crisis for Mozambique was triggered on 5 September when important economic targets in the Limpopo Valley were attacked by Rhodesian forces.

Severe damage caused a reduction in the country's capacity to wage war. Mozambique responded the same day with strong resistance by its army. Fighting in the valley continued until 10 September, and attacks on other targets were reported on the 13th, as well as on 27 September to 1 October and on 11–13 and 18–20 October.

During October Muzorewa sent a message to Zambia's president threatening to take nonmilitary measures if Kaunda did nothing to stop *ZIPRA* infiltration into Rhodesia-Zimbabwe. Indeed, this threat was realized on 5 November when trains carrying maize shipments to Zambia were prevented from passing through Rhodesia.

British Foreign Secretary Lord Carrington opened the constitutional conference on Rhodesia at Lancaster House on 10 September. By 15 November some progress had been made at Lancaster House: agreement on transitional arrangements for Rhodesia had been reached; and the British government had proposed the establishment of a Cease-Fire Commission on which military commanders of both sides would be represented.

Despite apparent political progress, Rhodesia expanded its economic pressure on Zambia with a series of major military attacks. A crisis for Zambia was triggered on 17 November when Rhodesian forces attacked a bridge on the main road to Tanzania; Zambian villagers were killed, and another vital bridge linking Zambia to Malawi and Mozambique was blown up. On the 20th Kaunda responded by declaring a full alert, canceling all military leaves, and announcing a call-up of reserves. On 12 December Lord Soames, newly appointed Governor of Rhodesia for the interim period, arrived in Salisbury to oversee the cease-fire, elections, and the transfer of government.

The crises for Botswana and Mozambique ended with a cease-fire on 21 December. Zambia's crisis ended on 31 January 1980 when its border with Zimbabwe was reopened, once the situation had stabilized. And on 4 March 1980, with the election of Robert Mugabe, former leader of the Mozambique-based *ZANU,* as Prime Minister of the new state of Zimbabwe, the crisis terminated for Rhodesia as well.

United Nations activity consisted of a Security Council resolution, passed on 23 November 1979, condemning Rhodesia for its raids into Zambia and calling for full compensation. A condemnation of Rhodesia was also issued by the *OAU.* The United States supported the Lancaster House discussions. The Soviet Union provided military aid and advisors to *ZIPRA.*

(Following the elections in Zimbabwe, internal unrest persisted, especially in Matabeleland—where Joshua Nkomo, former leader of *ZANU/ZIPRA,* enjoyed the total support of his fellow Ndebele tribespeople.)

(See *Master Table,* pp. 720–21.)

Sources
ACR 1979, 1980; *AD* 1979, 1980; *ARec* 1979, 1980; *ARB* 1979, 1980; *Keesing's* 1979, 1980; Parsons 1988; Stedman 1991; Wiseman and Taylor 1981.

Western Sahara

Morocco has been enmeshed in a protracted conflict with the *Polisario* movement, supported by Algeria, over the territory of Western Sahara since 1975. There have been 10 international crises during this conflict, as follows.

Case #261 **Moroccan March,** in 1975–76;
#268 **Nouakchott I,** in 1976;
#280 **Nouakchott II,** in 1977;
#285 **French Hostages in Mauritania,** in 1977;
#299 **Tan Tan,** in 1979;
#305 **Goulimime-Tarfaya Road,** in 1979;
#312 **Operation Iman,** in 1980;
#332 **Galtat Zemmour I,** in 1981;
#375 **Sand Wall,** in 1987;
#390 **Galtat Zemmour II,** in 1989.

Two earlier international crises were geographically related but are not an integral part of the Western Sahara PC, namely, Case #160—**Ifni,** in 1957–58; and #199—**Algeria/Morocco Border,** in 1963 (see *Master Table*).

The protracted conflict over the Western Sahara remains unresolved.

General Background

Spanish (Western) Sahara, a territory bordering Morocco on the northeast and Mauritania on the west and south, had been under Spanish rule since 1884. In 1965 the United Nations passed a resolution calling on Spain to divest itself of authority over Spanish Sahara. Spain's ruler, General Francisco Franco, refused.

The Algerian-backed Popular Front for the Liberation of Saguia el Hamra and Rio de Oro *(Polisario)* was formed in 1968. *Polisario* was originally based in Mauritania, where it received government support. It later moved to Algeria, which became *Polisario*'s faithful ally for 20 years.

The dispute is partly traceable to a long-standing rivalry between Morocco and Algeria for dominance of the *Maghreb,* the Arabic-speaking region of North Africa, stretching from Mauritania to Libya.

(261) Moroccan March

Spain and Morocco, and later, Algeria and Mauritania were the direct participants in a two-stage crisis over Western Sahara that lasted from 16 October 1975 to 14 April 1976.

Pre-crisis

Morocco, interested in its rich phosphate mines, renewed a long-standing claim to Western Sahara in 1974. In August 1974 Spain proclaimed its internal autonomy as the first step toward decolonization. Morocco objected and called for Spain's immediate withdrawal, UN supervision, and the repatriation of some 20,000 refugees then in southern Morocco. In early October Morocco and Mauritania took the question of sovereignty over Western Sahara to the International Court of Justice (*ICJ,* World Court), through the UN Committee on Non-Self-Governing Territories, to determine if Morocco or Mauritania had a legal claim to Western Sahara. Algeria, the most visible advocate of Western Sahara's independence, was concerned about Morocco's expansion, while Libya declared its willingness to fight Spain for the "liberation" of the disputed territory.

A secret agreement between Morocco and Mauritania to divide Western Sahara was reached on 1 October 1975, after a Spanish announcement that a referendum offering the people of that territory the choice between independence and association with Spain would be held during the first half of 1976. Morocco reaffirmed its categorical rejection of any referendum on independence for Western Sahara. On 15 October a UN mission reported sentiment for independence in Western Sahara. On the 16th the World Court ruled that, despite some historical links and legal ties, neither Morocco nor Mauritania had a valid claim to sovereignty over Western Sahara.

Crisis

The same day King Hassan of Morocco declared that he interpreted the *ICJ*'s reference to Saharan "links" to Morocco as validating Moroccan claims to sovereignty over the area and that he intended to lead a march of 350,000 civilians into Western Sahara to hasten its integration into his kingdom. This triggered a crisis for Spain. Fearing a military clash it attempted to stop the proposed march by appealing to the UN Security Council. It also noted that force would be used only against an armed invasion. On 28 October Spain imposed emergency measures in order to prevent hostilities.

An announcement by Spain and Algeria on 2 November that the march would be countered by force triggered a crisis for Morocco. The same day Spain's Acting Head of State, Prince (later, King) Juan Carlos, flew to Sahara. He returned to Spain the next day to hold talks with the Moroccan prime minister. A Moroccan minister was sent to Algeria; and 20,000 Moroccan troops were moved to the Western Sahara border.

Spain's major response to the crisis was to withdraw its forces eight miles from the border on 5 November. The march began on the 6th but was halted by King Hassan on the 10th, a day after Spain agreed to exclude Algeria from negotiations over the future of Western Sahara. An agreement was signed on 14 November 1975 by Mauritania, Morocco, and Spain dividing Western Sahara between the two African claimants but leaving Spain a share in the valuable Bu

Craa phosphate mines. It also provided for Spain's withdrawal from the territory on 28 February 1976. Until then Western Sahara was to be administered jointly by the three countries.

The 14 November agreement terminated Spain's crisis. It also generated a crisis for Algeria, where *Polisario* bases were located. Clashes between troops from Morocco and Mauritania, on the one hand, and *Polisario* guerrillas and regular Algerian troops, on the other, began in December.

A crisis for Mauritania was catalyzed by the first major *Polisario* offensive on 10 December 1975, allegedly aided by Cuban and North Vietnam "volunteers." Mauritania, surprised by the very strong resistance to its occupation of part of Western Sahara, confronted force with force.

A major Algerian attack on Moroccan forces on 27 January 1976 marked the beginning of the second stage of this crisis. Morocco responded with increased efforts to occupy more of the disputed territory. Spain withdrew from Western Sahara two days ahead of schedule, on 26 February. The following day *Polisario* declared the disputed territory's independence as the Saharan Arab Democratic Republic. The SADR, called SAHRAWI, was recognized on 6 March by Algeria, marking the end of its crisis. Other African states and North Korea, too, granted recognition to SAHRAWI. Morocco and Mauritania responded by severing relations with Algeria on the 7th. And on the 14th they signed a convention fixing the borders of the disputed territory between them: Morocco annexed the northern two-thirds of Western Sahara, Mauritania the other third. (Morocco annexed the rest of Western Sahara in 1980 when Mauritania renounced its claim.) This terminated the crisis for Morocco and Mauritania, and the Moroccan March crisis as a whole.

(Clashes continued to the end of April, particularly between Mauritanian and *Polisario* troops. New tensions were to break out once more in June [see Case #268—**Nouakchott I** below].)

The UN played an active role in crisis management. The Security Council, responding to Spain's appeal, met on 20 October 1975 and passed a resolution on the 22nd calling for restraint by all parties. It also requested Secretary-General Waldheim to begin negotiations. These were conducted between 26 and 28 October. The Council convened twice more, on 2 and 8 November. Mediation was also attempted in March and April 1976 by the Secretary-General and his representative, Sweden's Ambassador to the UN, Olof Rydbeck; but the parties refused to compromise.

The United States supplied military aid to Morocco. A visit to the area by the U.S. assistant secretary of state for Africa in early November contributed to the winding down of the first stage of the crisis—the 14 November 1975 agreement. Mediation was also attempted by Egypt and Libya. The *OAU* debated the issue from 26 February to 1 March 1976 and passed a compromise resolution that left to individual members the decision whether or not to recognize the Saharan Arab Democratic Republic. The *OAU* also supported the Arab League's dispatch of its Secretary-General, Mahmoud Riad, to the area but without tangible effect.

Evidence of covert Soviet aid to Algeria and *Polisario* came in the form of the shooting down of a Moroccan plane by a Soviet SAM-3 missile.

(Four years after this crisis, in July 1980, the SADR was admitted to *OAU* membership following recognition by 36 of the 49 member-states.)

(See *Master Table,* pp. 714–15.)

Sources
ACR 1975, 1976; *ARB* 1975, 1976; Brownlie 1979; Brzoska and Pearson 1994; Damis 1983; Day 1987; Fraenkel 1976; Franck 1976; Gretton 1980; Hodges 1983; Lewis 1985b; Marks 1976; Mercer 1976a, 1976b, 1976c; Moose 1985; Ramchadani 1977; Thompson and Adloff 1980; *WA* 1975, 1976; Zartman 1989.

(268) Nouakchott I

A *Polisario* attack on Mauritania's capital caused a one-day crisis for Mauritania on 8 June 1976.

Crisis
On 8 June 1976 a force of 600–700 *Polisario* guerrillas attacked the city of Nouakchott, threatening Mauritania's political regime. The attack took the form of a lightning mortar and machine-gun offensive with several mortar shells falling around the presidential palace of Ould Daddah, causing turmoil and panic in the city. The Mauritanian response came immediately after the firing when troops reportedly crushed the attacking forces, killing *Polisario* leader El-Ouali. The remaining *Polisario* troops withdrew after an hour, thus terminating the crisis on the day of the attack. Nouakchott was attacked a second time in March 1977.

Neither the U.S. or the USSR, nor the UN or the *OAU,* was active in this crisis.

(See *Master Table,* pp. 714–15.)

Sources
See sources for Case #261; and *ACR* 1976; *AD* 1976; *ARec* 1976; *New York Times* 1976; *WA* 1976.

(280) Nouakchott II

A second *Polisario* attack on Mauritania's capital, on 3 July 1977, precipitated another crisis for Mauritania lasting until late that month.

Pre-crisis
During the year after **Nouakchott I,** the Moroccan and Mauritanian armies had undergone major expansion to deal with the increasing frequency and severity of *Polisario* attacks, the former from 60,000 to 90,000, the latter from 3,000 to

12,000. On 13 May 1977 the Moroccan-Mauritanian Supreme Defense Committee was established to deal with the Western Sahara problem. Its first meeting took place in June.

Crisis
Polisario forces, backed by Algeria, attacked the capital of Mauritania on 3 July 1977, triggering a second crisis for Mauritania. *Polisario* claimed to have caused heavy losses and damage; Mauritania reported one civilian and one soldier killed. On 12 July the Mauritanian permanent representative to the UN sent a letter to the president of the Security Council accusing Algeria of responsibility for both the attack on Nouakchott and an assault on the Mauritanian ambassador in Paris, and requested an urgent meeting of the Council. However, no UN activity took place. On 15 July Mauritania responded with a reorganization of key positions in its armed forces. The following day the city of Zouerate was attacked by *Polisario*. And on 18 and 19 July Morocco airlifted 600 troops to Mauritania. Toward the end of July the reorganization of the Mauritanian army had been completed and the threat to the regime was reduced, terminating the crisis for Mauritania.

The *OAU* met between 2 and 5 July in Gabon and arranged for a special meeting on Western Sahara for October 1977. The U.S. and the USSR remained aloof from this crisis.

(See *Master Table,* pp. 716–17.)

Sources
See sources for Cases #261 and 268; and *WA* 1977; Zartman 1989.

(285) French Hostages in Mauritania

As part of the ongoing conflict over Western Sahara, French citizens working in Mauritania were held hostage by *Polisario*. This created a crisis for France and Algeria from 25 October to 23 December 1977.

Pre-crisis
The Mauritanian town of Zouerate was attacked by *Polisario* guerrillas on 1 May and 16 July 1977. Zouerate was an important mining settlement housing a fairly large French community, consisting mainly of engineers and their families. In the May attack two French citizens were killed and six others taken prisoner. France, which had been supplying Morocco and Mauritania with arms and instructors, evacuated 450 women and children and issued a strong protest calling on Algeria to use its good offices to free the hostages. In May Mauritania and France considered reactivating their military defense agreements, which the former had terminated in January 1973. France brought the matter before the UN. However, all attempts to release the prisoners met with little success, due mainly to *Polisario*'s unwillingness to cooperate.

Crisis

The abduction of two French engineers working on the Mauritanian railway 60 kilometers west of Zouerate, on 25 October 1977, triggered a crisis for France. On the 28th eight alleged members of *Polisario* were expelled from France.

France's major response, which was also the trigger to Algeria's crisis, was the placing of French paratroops on alert on 29 October, amid rumors that French troop-carrying aircraft had departed for Senegal. Algeria feared that the French would attack targets on Algerian soil, which housed major *Polisario* bases and training camps. On the 30th Algeria responded with a démarche from Foreign Minister Bouteflika to the ambassadors from the five permanent members of the UN Security Council, drawing their attention to the risks of French intervention in the area and the subsequent danger to international security. On 1–2 November DC-8 and Transall transport planes flew to Dakar with approximately 300 reinforcements for the 1,100 French troops stationed in Cape Vert, Senegal. During the first two weeks in November French instructors were sent to Mauritania to establish communication facilities. From 1 to 7 November a French Foreign Ministry official, Claude Chayets, talked with *Polisario* leaders in Algiers, and from 5 to 6 November a second official visited the Algerian capital. On 7 November the Front Liberation National *(FLN),* Algeria's sole legal political organization, staged a demonstration against French threats of intervention— reportedly one of the largest since Algeria's independence from France in 1962. From 12 to 18 December French Jaguar aircraft strafed *Polisario* columns in Mauritania.

Negotiations with *Polisario* succeeded in freeing the hostages, who were handed over to UN Secretary-General Kurt Waldheim in Algiers on 23 December 1977. This ended the crisis for Algeria and France.

At France's request, the UN General Assembly met on 31 October. The Secretary-General offered his good offices. And a resolution was adopted by the General Assembly on 9 November calling upon all members to respect Western Sahara's right to self-determination. The U.S. was not involved; the USSR, marginally so.

(See *Master Table,* pp. 716–17.)

Sources

See sources for Cases #261 and 268; and *WA* 1977.

(299) Tan Tan

A *Polisario* attack on the Moroccan town of Tan Tan triggered a crisis for Morocco on 28 January 1979. The crisis faded in March of that year.

Pre-crisis

On 10 July 1978 the government of Mauritania, under President Mokhtar Ould Daddah, was overthrown in a bloodless coup led by Lieutenant-Colonel Mustapha Ould Mohammed Salek. *Polisario* immediately announced a unilateral cease-fire in Mauritania and entered into peace talks with that country. Concentration of activities by *Polisario* then moved against Moroccan troops stationed in the northern section of the disputed territory.

By the fall of 1978 *Polisario* raids began to creep closer to southern Morocco, and in September a group of guerrillas carried out a spectacular raid 70 kilometers into Moroccan territory. Morocco appealed to the UN, without success. On 27 December Algerian President Houari Boumedienne died. He had been viewed by *Polisario* as one of its main sponsors and supporters and a source of political, military, and ideological strength. His death gave rise to a series of *Polisario* offensives that were termed "Houari Boumedienne Attacks." In December alone, Morocco reportedly lost 600 troops.

Mauritania's involvement in the Saharan conflict had resulted in serious economic difficulties. With the overthrow of President Ould Daddah, Mauritania began to pull out of the Western Sahara conflict in 1979. On 1 January 1979 Colonel Salek of Mauritania spoke of his support for the right of self-determination for all peoples. Shortly thereafter he announced that he had asked Morocco to withdraw all its forces from Mauritania by March 1979. More serious *Polisario* attacks in Morocco occurred on 16 and 17 January 1979.

Crisis

On 28 January *Polisario* forces attacked Tan Tan, a garrison town, air force base, and convoy assembly point 40 kilometers inside Moroccan territory. Fighting continued for three days as the Moroccan forces in the area resisted and ultimately succeeded in defeating the invaders. King Hassan sent his top military advisor to the area and summoned other military officers to a meeting in Marrakesh. On 2 February Morocco's Foreign Minister, Boucetta, stated, in a message to his Algerian counterpart, Bouteflika, that Morocco did not intend to exercise its "right of pursuit." Morocco's major response, on 8 March, was an announcement by King Hassan that he had decided to establish a Defense Council, comprising two members of each political organization or party, to deal with the Saharan situation which, he said, had reached the "limit of the intolerable." The Moroccan Chamber of Representatives approved the king's decision and adopted a declaration that recommended that the government exercise its right of pursuit and mount retaliatory operations whenever Moroccan territory was the object of military aggression.

The crisis faded sometime in March, with a temporary halt in *Polisario* activities.

Neither the U.S. nor the USSR, nor the UN, was involved in this crisis.

(See *Master Table*, pp. 720–21.)

Sources
ACR 1979; *ARB* 1979; *WA* 1979.

(305) Goulimime-Tarfaya Road

A *Polisario* attack on a strategic road in Morocco led to a crisis for Morocco and Algeria from 1 to 25 June 1979.

Crisis

A large-scale *Polisario* military operation inside Moroccan territory, on the Goulimime-Tarfaya road, triggered a crisis for Morocco on 1 June 1979. The targeting of an important mineral area within Morocco was quite rare. An additional incident took place on 4 June, north of Zag. The Moroccan response was multiple, including violence. Its troops met the *Polisario* guerrillas, losing about 20 soldiers, with a number of others wounded. On 6 June King Hassan announced that he had ordered the Moroccan army, in the future, to exercise its "right of pursuit" whenever lives of Moroccan citizens were endangered; that decision had been taken by the Moroccan Chamber of Representatives in March. The next day Hassan appealed to the *OAU*. Moreover, the ambassadors of the five permanent members of the Security Council were summoned to the Foreign Ministry and told that Morocco would not stand by "with arms folded" against repeated aggression. And on the 15th Morocco requested an urgent meeting of the Security Council.

The right of pursuit claim made by the king on 6 June triggered a crisis for Algeria, which feared Moroccan incursions into its territory. On the 10th Algeria appealed to the incumbent Chairman of the *OAU*, Sudan's President Numeiri. Ambassadors of the permanent members of the Security Council were summoned to Algeria's Foreign Ministry as well.

A major *Polisario* offensive took place at Tan Tan on 13 June. This city had been the victim of an earlier attack in January 1979 (see Case #299 above).

The Security Council discussed the issue from 15 to 25 June; no resolution was passed. On the 25th Morocco requested the indefinite suspension of the UN debate, having perceived the lowering of tensions after the incidents at the beginning of the month. *Polisario* attacks into Morocco had been temporarily stopped; and it did not exercise its right of pursuit into Algeria. Morocco's request ended the crisis, but there was no agreement between the adversaries. The *OAU* "Committee of Wise Men" (Sudan, Mali, Nigeria, Guinea, and the Ivory Coast) met on 23 June to discuss the conflict and set forth recommendations.

There was no superpower involvement during the 1979 crisis. However, *Polisario* was armed with Soviet-made antiaircraft missiles, tanks, and artillery, while the United States supplied King Hassan with large amounts of military equipment, including jet fighters and radar.

(In subsequent years Morocco adopted a strategy of building massive walls of sand across the Sahara Desert, advancing steadily and bringing nearly one-third of the territory of Western Sahara and almost all of its population inside their ramparts. Since 1981 *Polisario* has been unable to breach the advancing walls. Nonetheless, despite military losses, *Polisario* has scored important diplomatic victories: it was admitted into the *OAU* in 1982; and in November 1984 the Sahrawi Arab Democratic Republic was seated as a full-fledged member. In protest, Morocco quit the *OAU*. It was supported by Zaire, which suspended its participation.)

(See *Master Table,* pp. 720–21.)

Sources
ACR 1979; *AD* 1979; *ARec* 1979; *ARB* 1979; *WA* 1979.

(312) Operation Iman

Morocco experienced another crisis with *Polisario* in their long-standing conflict over Western Sahara from 1 March to mid-May 1980.

Pre-crisis
Mauritania withdrew from the southern part of Western Sahara in August 1979: it had received the area in 1976 via an agreement with Morocco as the successors to Spanish Sahara (see Case #261—**Moroccan March** above). In an attempt to fill the vacuum, both Morocco and *Polisario* renewed their spasmodic military operations in various parts of the disputed territory during the succeeding months; but these incidents were routine, not crises.

Crisis
A crisis for Morocco was triggered on 1 March 1980 when *Polisario* forces reportedly defeated units from Morocco's Zegalla column dispatched to clear the area of Oued Draa in the north toward the Western Sahara frontier with Morocco. Serious clashes continued throughout the first two weeks of the month.

On 9 March the Moroccan force began the second part of its mission—to relieve the besieged Moroccan garrison of 4,000 at Zag. The *Polisario* Front claimed a major victory, a turning point in the war, in which they "put out of action" 2,000 Moroccan troops and caused heavy damage to Moroccan equipment. While Morocco denied these claims, it confirmed that serious fighting had taken place. And a call by Morocco's King Hassan to his troops on 14 March "to make the necessary sacrifices . . . for the defence of the territorial integrity of the country" indicates a serious military setback: it appears that Moroccan forces were forced by *Polisario* guerrillas to withdraw to Jbel Ouarkziz.

On 24 March *Polisario* reportedly submitted to the UN, the *OAU,* and the Non-Aligned Movement documents purporting to prove collusion between Morocco and South Africa, which allegedly provided weapons in the campaign to subdue Western Sahara. But the international organizations did not respond.

Fighting broke out in the area again on 6 May after a few weeks of calm. Moroccan forces were more successful in this phase, claiming to have destroyed several "enemy centers" in a "large-scale mopping-up operation" against the "mercenary elements filtering across the Algerian border." Morocco also renewed its criticism of Algeria and Libya for allegedly providing *Polisario* with North Korean military equipment.

Clashes continued on 9 and 10 May and then tapered off.

In the nature of this protracted conflict, incidents continued to erupt, reportedly in early June, on 21 June, on 10 July, and again in July–August. Thus the conflict continued unabated—and is still unresolved. However, the March–May 1980 round of serious clashes related to Morocco's "Operation Iman" wound down by mid-May 1980.

The U.S., the USSR, and the UN were not involved in this crisis. (See *Master Table,* pp. 722–23.)

Sources
Foreign Broadcast Information Service—Daily Report/Middle East and Africa (FBIS-DR/MEA) 1980; *ACR* 1980; *AR* 1980; *ARB* 1980; *Keesing's* 1980; *SWB* 1980; *WA* 1980.

(332) Galtat Zemmour I

Morocco experienced one of many crises over the Western Sahara from 13 October until 9 November 1981.

Pre-crisis
From the outset *Polisario* favored a UN-supervised referendum, including the option of independence. Morocco's King Hassan rejected this idea and pressed for a settlement with Algeria, *Polisario*'s long-standing protector. Algeria insisted that only direct negotiations between the parties could resolve this by-product of colonialism. The UN and the *OAU* shared the Algerian approach to conflict resolution. The Western powers, by contrast, notably the U.S. and France, were primarily concerned about demoralization in the Moroccan army and, therefore, potential instability in a pro-Western North African state.

Early in July 1981 King Hassan offered to hold a referendum in Western Sahara. On the 12th *Polisario* reiterated the need to include the option of independence. An *OAU* implementation committee adopted a compromise resolution on 26 August regarding the modalities of the referendum. Morocco demurred.

Crisis
A crisis for Morocco was triggered on 13 October 1981 by a large-scale *Polisario* attack—3,000 troops, tanks, and armored personnel carriers—on its garrison at Galtat Zemmour, 25 miles from the border with Mauritania. Morocco accused *Polisario* of launching the attack from Mauritania. The latter denied any involvement in the crisis.

The same day King Hassan informed the presidents of France and the U.S., the UN, and the *OAU* of the attack and accused his neighbors—Algeria and Libya—of supporting *Polisario*. On 19 October he assured Mauritania that Morocco would not intrude into its territory; but his field commander acknowledged doing so in "hot pursuit" of the *Polisario* guerrillas who had sought sanctuary in Mauritania after their attack.

During 10 days of fighting the *Polisario* guerrillas shot down three Moroccan planes, allegedly using Soviet-type SAM missiles, and put to flight Moroccan troops at their Galtat Zemmour base and another base to the southwest. The crisis ended by a unilateral act of Morocco: it withdrew from these bases on 7 and 9 November 1981.

Soviet President Brezhnev, on 5 November, denied a Moroccan charge on 26 October that the USSR had provided SAM missiles to *Polisario*. The U.S. adopted a pro-Morocco "neutral" stance: on 23 October its assistant secretary of state for Africa affirmed a U.S. role in resolving the *Polisario*/Morocco conflict because it had relations with all the parties; but in early November a U.S. military delegation visited Morocco and reiterated its support.

(See *Master Table*, pp. 724–25.)

Sources
ACR 1981–82; AR 1981, 1982; ARB 1981, 1982; ARec 1981, 1982; *Keesing's* 1981, 1982; WA 1981, 1982.

(375) Sand Wall

Morocco, along with Mauritania and Algeria, experienced a crisis from 25 February to 4 May 1987 over the "Sand Wall" Morocco constructed across Western Sahara.

Background and Pre-crisis

In February 1976, early in the protracted conflict over Western (former Spanish) Sahara, the *Polisario* Front proclaimed an independent Saharan Arab Democratic Republic (SADR or SAHRAWI) (see Case #261 above). Despite strenuous efforts by Morocco to abort the incipient political entity, the SADR was recognized by many African states and was admitted to the *OAU* as a full member in 1984. This led to Morocco's withdrawal from Africa's regional organization.

As part of its defensive "wall strategy" in the ongoing war against *Polisario,* Morocco began in mid-February 1987 to build a new sand wall, the sixth: it was designed to go further south along the Mauritanian border in order to prevent *Polisario* direct access to the Atlantic Ocean, unless it passed through Mauritanian territory.

Crisis

Heavy fighting broke out in Western Sahara on 25 February 1987 between Morocco's armed forces and the Algerian-backed *Polisario* Front, in the area between Farsia and Mahbes near the Algerian border. That triggered a new crisis for Morocco in the protracted conflict over Western Sahara.

In late February and March both sides claimed victory on the battlefield. Morocco accused *Polisario* of launching an offensive in order to "bring down the defense wall and get a foothold inside the wall enclosure" and claimed success "along the whole defense line," including progress in the building of the sixth defensive wall in Oued Eddahab Province. *Polisario* reported that "hundreds of Moroccan soldiers were put out of action" and claimed failure in Morocco's defensive wall strategy.

On 4 March the SADR ambassador in Algeria announced that an assassination attempt against the President of the SADR, Mohamed Abd-ul Aziz, planned for 27 February, had failed. He accused Morocco's interior minister of being behind the plot. The official Algerian Press Service (APS) condemned Morocco for its trying to "bring about the physical elimination of SAHRAWI leaders." On the 17th Morocco denied any involvement in the assassination attempt.

In mid-April 1987 the new Moroccan sand wall impinged on Mauritania's territorial integrity since *Polisario* forces would be obliged to pass through Mauritania in order to reach the Atlantic Ocean: the Moroccan wall, at one point, was only 400 meters from a key Mauritanian railway line, used to transport iron ore from the mines at Zerouate to Mauritania's commercial capital, Nouadhibou.

This development catalyzed a crisis for Mauritania and, as a spillover effect, for Algeria as well. The likelihood of new clashes on its territory triggered a crisis for Mauritania in mid-April. That threat to Mauritania, in turn, increased the danger of a wider conflict involving Algeria, thus triggering a crisis at the same time for Algeria as well.

On 13 April Mauritania delivered a strong warning to Morocco over the new sand wall close to its border; specifically, that the wall obliged Mauritania to "give priority to ways of defending itself." The Mauritanian statement, however, reaffirmed its neutrality in the war over Western Sahara.

Morocco, through its commander in the southern zone, tried to reassure Mauritania by claiming that there was a no-man's-land between the borders of Morocco and Mauritania and that the latter's railway installations would not be impaired by the wall.

Algeria, too, expressed concern over the "dangerous situation" created by Morocco's new sand wall, blaming Morocco for undermining the stability of the region and for acting against the efforts to solve the conflict. Its foreign ministry issued a statement that declared total support for Mauritania's territorial integrity and for the "security of its towns and economic installations which are now directly exposed to military operations linked to the conflict imposed on the Western Saharan people." On 26 April President Chadli Ben-Jedid of Algeria visited Mauritania and promised support for Mauritania's territorial integrity.

Notwithstanding this verbal tension, the Moroccan/Algerian dimension of this episode in the protracted conflict de-escalated quickly. On 4 May King Hassan of Morocco and President Ben-Jedid of Algeria met on the Algerian-Moroccan border under the auspices of King Fahd of Sa'udi Arabia. The summit was held in order to defuse tension on the border and did not attempt to resolve the whole Western Sahara conflict. They agreed only to continue contacts to "solve the existing problems." Although their summit meeting did not generate a formal agreement or any solution to the conflict, it reduced tension between Morocco and Algeria and terminated the crisis for all three state participants.

Before the meeting *Polisario* expressed doubt about King Fahd's role as a mediator since it perceived Sa'udi Arabia as the major source of financial aid to Morocco; and it demanded a direct dialogue with Morocco. Algeria, as usual, backed *Polisario*'s demand for direct negotiations between Morocco and the SADR. A U.S. State Department spokesman said on the 4th that the U.S. "applauded" the meeting, the first one between Morocco and Algeria since 1983.

The UN and the USSR were not involved in this crisis.

(See *Master Table,* pp. 732–33.)

Sources
ACR 1987–88; *AR* 1987; *ARB* 1987; *ARec* 1987; *WA* 1987.

(390) Galtat Zemmour II

Morocco experienced another crisis with *Polisario* from 7 October to late November 1989.

Background
Although clashes erupted in January and August 1988, there was a marked shift toward diplomacy and accommodation that year. On 30 August Morocco and *Polisario* agreed to a UN-*OAU* peace plan aimed at ending their 13-year-old conflict for control of Western (former Spanish) Sahara. The plan called for a cease-fire and a referendum on self-determination among the people of the territory. This breakthrough was followed by the first meeting between senior officials of the Saharan Arab Democratic Republic (SADR) with King Hassan of Morocco, on 4 January 1989 in Marrakesh.

The embryonic peace process was assisted by another basic change: on 16 May 1988 diplomatic relations between Algeria and Morocco were restored after a break of 12 years. Since Algeria had been the main source of military and political support for *Polisario* since 1975, this, too, augured well for a resolution of the conflict. The process was further reinforced on 17 February 1989 when, at a two-day summit of North African heads of state in Marrakesh, an Arab Maghreb Union *(AMU)* was proclaimed by Algeria, Libya, Mauritania, Morocco, and Tunisia. Moreover, on 14 May the Algerian and Moroccan foreign ministers ratified a long-moribund agreement (signed in 1972) that settled their border dispute (see Case #199—**Algeria/Morocco Border,** in 1963, in **Africa: Non-PCs**). And on 5 August they signed a border and cooperation agreement.

In that atmosphere of peace-seeking, *Polisario* was compelled to restrain its military activity. However, when no significant progress was made in negotiations with Morocco since the meeting of January 1989, *Polisario* reverted to the path of violence. It began with a small-scale attack on 24 September in which four Moroccan soldiers were killed. This was followed by serious clashes in October–November, which threatened the agreements of the preceding year.

Crisis
On 7 October 1989 the *Polisario* Front broke the truce with an attack on Moroccan positions at Galtat Zemmour, its first major offensive since September 1988. This triggered a fresh crisis for Morocco. Another major attack occurred four days later. And despite the reconciliation between Morocco and Algeria in May 1988, Algeria continued to provide diplomatic support to *Polisario*. Thus the renewed fighting also posed a danger to the incipient accommodation between Algeria and Morocco.

Tension rose on the 9th when Morocco threatened military intervention in Mauritania if *Polisario* attacks from its territory continued. Four days later King Hassan declared that the Moroccan people had decided to fight "another 100 years if necessary" to defend its territory and sovereignty.

On 13 October UN Secretary-General Perez de Cuellar issued a report on the Western Sahara conflict, expressing the hope that further meetings between King Hassan and *Polisario* would take place, as the UN-*OAU* peace plan could only succeed if the two sides held direct negotiations.

On 7 November the SADR called for a dialogue with Morocco in order to achieve peace in Western Sahara. However, the next day *Polisario* launched a third massive attack against Moroccan forces at Amgala. And further clashes erupted on the 16th. Serious fighting ended in the second half of November 1989; and the crisis faded.

Because of the scale of *Polisario* attacks, Morocco suspected complicity by the Algerian military. Nonetheless the economic cooperation between Algeria and Morocco was sustained.

Neither the U.S. nor the USSR was involved in this crisis.

(Following a request by the UN Secretary-General, *Polisario* agreed to a truce on 21 February 1990 until the end of March, in order to create a positive atmosphere for UN peace efforts in the region.)

(A UN-brokered cease-fire in 1991 between Morocco and *Polisario* continues to hold with few violations. The agreement created a peacekeeping force, initially with 320 peacekeepers. And the parties agreed to a UN-supervised referendum, with two options for the tiny population of Western Sahara, 72,000 according to the last Spanish census in 1974: they could vote for integration into Morocco or for independence. Scheduled for January 1992, the referendum was repeatedly postponed.)

(See *Master Table*, pp. 734–35.)

Sources
ACR 1988–89; *ARB* 1988, 1989, 1990; *ARec* 1989, 1990; *Keesing's* 1988, 1989, 1990.

Americas: Protracted Conflicts

Costa Rica/Nicaragua

There were three crises in the protracted conflict between Costa Rica and Nicaragua from 1918 to 1955, as follows.

Case #2 **Costa Rican Coup,** in 1918–19;
#126 **Costa Rica/Nicaragua I,** in 1948–49;
#147 **Costa Rica/Nicaragua II,** in 1955.

(2) Costa Rican Coup

A two-stage crisis between Nicaragua and Costa Rica, arising from a military coup in the latter, lasted from 25 May 1918 until 3 September 1919.

Pre-crisis
A military coup led by Federico Tinoco overthrew Costa Rica's president, Alfredo Gonzalez Flores, on 27 January 1917. U.S. policy, nonrecognition, and persistent opposition by supporters of the deposed president across the border in Nicaragua made it increasingly difficult for Tinoco to maintain control in Costa Rica.

Crisis
The movement of 500 Costa Rican troops to the Nicaraguan border on 25 May 1918, amid rumors of an imminent invasion of Costa Rica by pro-Gonzalez forces, triggered a crisis for Nicaragua. President Chamorro responded five days later by seeking U.S. advice and support and, in October, by attempting to forge a pact with Honduras designed to impose sanctions against Costa Rica and to assist Costa Rican rebels. On 4 November U.S. Secretary of State Lansing cautioned the presidents of Nicaragua and Honduras against supporting armed rebellion in Costa Rica. Nicaragua's crisis ended on 15 December 1918 when Chamorro informed its National Congress that Nicaragua was observing strict neutrality vis-à-vis Costa Rica.

Tension between the two Central American neighbors remained high due to continuing rumors of an anti-Tinoco invasion plan by rebel forces in Nicaragua, with aid from Honduras. President Tinoco communicated this perceived threat to the U.S. Consul—and chargé d'affaires—in Costa Rica, Chase, and to the American political leader, William Jennings Bryan, on 25 January 1919. This marked the onset of a crisis for Costa Rica.

Nicaragua accused Costa Rica of dispatching 5,000 troops to its border, a charge denied by Costa Rica's agent in Washington. On 30 April the U.S. minister in Nicaragua backed Nicaragua's charge in a report to Undersecretary of State Polk. Then on 6 May rebel forces under the command of Julio Acosta invaded Costa Rica and proclaimed a provisional government at Peña Blanca. Nicaragua denied Costa Rica's charge of direct involvement in the military hostilities and was backed by the U.S. Minister, Jefferson. But in June Nicaragua, Honduras, and Guatemala recognized the Acosta regime. Despite his military victories, Tinoco fled Costa Rica on 12 August largely as a result of U.S. pressure. A new government formed by an associate of Tinoco collapsed on 3 September 1919, and the international crisis ended in Costa Rica's defeat.

The U.S. was highly involved throughout the crisis, mostly through political pressure on Tinoco to resign, but also more visibly through the landing of U.S. marines in Costa Rica in mid-June 1919, at the insistence of the U.S. consul and against the secretary of state's advice, to protect American citizens in Puerto Limón, Costa Rica. Honduras and Guatemala were also involved actors. (Acosta was elected President of Costa Rica on 9 December 1919, and his regime was accorded U.S. recognition in 1920.)

There was no global organization at the time of this crisis; and the Pan American Union, precursor to the Organization of American States *(OAS)*, was not involved.

(See *Master Table,* pp. 666–67.)

Sources
Foreign Relations of the United States (FRUS) 1917 [pub. 1926], *1918* [1930], *1919* [1934], *1920* [1935]; Bermann 1986; Howland 1929; Munro 1964.

(126) Costa Rica/Nicaragua I

A crisis for Costa Rica took place from 11 December 1948 until 21 February 1949.

Pre-crisis
Civil war broke out in Costa Rica in March 1948. President Picado, who supported former President Calderón, opposed the election in February of Otilio Ulate as President. Ulate fled the country, and Picado was subsequently overthrown. He left Costa Rica for Nicaragua on 20 April. The country was then governed by a 10-man military junta headed by José Figueres.

Crisis
A crisis for Costa Rica was triggered on 11 December 1948 by an invasion of about 1,000 men, primarily Nicaraguan National Guardsmen, and a number of

exiled supporters of Calderón. Costa Rica's response, the same day, was an order for immediate mobilization, the imposition of martial law, and the movement of troops to the frontier with Nicaragua. In addition, Costa Rica appealed to the UN Security Council and the *OAS* and protested to the Nicaraguan government, which denied the charge. Fighting continued until mid-December, when Costa Rican troops recovered the La Cruz area, which had been occupied by the invaders, and forced them back to the Nicaraguan border.

On 14 December the *OAS* appointed and dispatched an inquiry commission to the area of conflict to investigate the facts. The report, on 24 December, stated that the invasion had been led by Costa Rican political exiles and criticized Nicaragua for not having prevented it. A military commission was appointed to supervise activity on the Costa Rican/Nicaraguan border. The crisis ended on 21 February 1949, when the two countries signed a treaty of friendship.

The UN discussed Costa Rica's complaint but left the matter to the *OAS*. The U.S. was marginally involved in this crisis. The USSR was not involved.

(See *Master Table,* pp. 688–89.)

Sources
Ameringer 1978; Bird 1984; Connell-Smith 1966; de Lima 1971; Mecham 1961; Slater 1967; Wainhouse 1966.

(147) Costa Rica/Nicaragua II

Another crisis for these two Central American neighbors lasted from 8 to 20 January 1955.

Crisis
While Nicaragua had a well-trained army of about 7,500 men, Costa Rican defense was entrusted to the National Police Force. On 8 January 1955 Costa Rican President José Figueres received information that Venezuela had sent a fleet of 10 military transports, fully manned, to Nicaragua. Costa Rica appealed to the *OAS,* mobilized volunteer reserve troops, and placed its police on standby alert. Three days later about 500 Costa Rican rebels crossed the frontier from Nicaragua and captured a town 30 miles north of the capital city, San José. Costa Rica proclaimed a state of emergency and broke diplomatic relations with Nicaragua.

The *OAS* Council met in emergency session on 11 January and voted to send a fact-finding mission to Costa Rica. On the 14th the mission reported that there were serious indications that the rebels were being supplied with arms from Nicaragua and that foreign aircraft had flown over Costa Rica, strafing and bombing cities. The Council then called upon Nicaragua to stop the flow of arms to the rebels and voted to send observers to the area. The Council decided further, on 16 January, to grant Costa Rica's request for aircraft. Four F-51 Mustang fighter-planes were delivered from the United States. This triggered a crisis for Nicaragua.

President Somoza responded on the 19th by reinforcing Nicaragua's borders and stepping up military flights. Costa Rican forces drove the rebels from the captured territory and forced them back across the Nicaraguan border.

The crisis ended on 20 January 1955 when the Costa Rican rebels withdrew and both states agreed to an *OAS* plan for demilitarized zones along the border. Whereas Figueres considered the outcome a victory for Costa Rica and credited the *OAS* and the United States, Nicaragua's Somoza was disappointed that the attempt to overthrow Figueres had failed.

The UN and the USSR were not involved in this crisis.

(See *Master Table,* pp. 692–93.)

Sources
See sources for Case #126.

Ecuador/Peru

The long-standing territorial dispute between Ecuador and Peru gave rise to four crises from 1935 to 1991, as follows.

    Case #50   **Ecuador/Peru Border I,** in 1935;
        #86   **Ecuador/Peru Border II,** in 1941–42;
      #322   **Ecuador/Peru Border III,** in 1981;
      #400   **Ecuador/Peru Border IV,** in 1991.

The conflict remains unresolved, with a fresh crisis early in 1995 (see the last paragraph in Case #400 below).

General Background

For a century—since Ecuador became an independent state in 1830—Ecuador and Peru pressed their claims to a large swampy region of 125,000 square miles on the periphery of the Amazon jungle, known as the Cordillera del Condor. Ecuador claimed the area on the basis of territorial adjustments after the end of Spanish colonial rule, for it was denied access to either the Amazon River or the Marañón River.

The Marañón is an area lying between the equator and the Javalry River, and between the Andes and Leticia; but the maps left to Ecuador and Peru by the departing Spanish empire were unclear about the demarcation of frontiers.

During the first hundred years of the dispute the conflict was carried on at three levels—diplomatic, military, and demographic. During that time Peruvian settlers, traders, and soldiers gradually extended the occupation of the Oriente region; the Ecuadorians maintained a few troops in outposts in the region. Some minor clashes occurred, and, in 1910, mediation by the United States, Argentina, and Brazil prevented the outbreak of war. In October 1932 there was a clash at the western end of the frontier.

(50) Ecuador/Peru Border I

The first crisis between Peru and Ecuador over the territory of the Marañón River basin lasted from 1 to 30 November 1935.

Crisis
On 1 November 1935 Ecuadorian cavalry and police invaded the Peruvian province of Tumbes. The following day Peru delivered a protest note to Ecuador. The Peruvian Congress met in secret session on 13 November. Peru's major response, on the 14th, was to send strong reinforcements, including infantry and planes, to its garrison in Tumbes. This triggered a crisis for Ecuador. Further protests were sent by Peru to Ecuador. The crisis terminated on 30 November when the Peruvian foreign minister announced that Ecuador had been invited to submit the question of the disputed territory to arbitration. Ecuador agreed. There was no League of Nations, *OAS,* or U.S. involvement in this crisis.
    (See *Master Table,* pp. 674–75.)

Sources
Bowman 1942; Davis, Finan, and Peck 1977; Ireland 1938; Owens 1964; Veliz 1968; Wood 1966.

(86) Ecuador/Peru Border II

Ecuador and Peru experienced another crisis over the territory of Marañón from 5 July 1941 to 29 January 1942.

Background
The long-standing dispute between Peru and Ecuador remained unresolved after the crisis in 1935. Another border clash, which threatened to escalate to war, occurred in June 1938. Ecuador appealed to several Latin American presidents in October for mediation. In December 1938, at the Eighth Conference of American States, several unofficial attempts were made to achieve a settlement: none was successful. During 1939–40 there were numerous border incidents. Relations between Ecuador and Peru deteriorated, and, toward the end of 1940, there were rumors of Peruvian troop movements in two directions toward Ecuadorian positions in the east and west. Ecuador increased the number of military posts and built roads for greater maneuverability. By December 1940 the danger of war was fully recognized by Ecuador.

Crisis

On 5 July 1941, according to Ecuador's foreign minister, Peruvian agricultural workers, accompanied by civil guards, entered Ecuador and opened fire on an Ecuadorian patrol, triggering a crisis for Ecuador. Fighting spread to several frontier posts and included Peruvian artillery and air attacks. Argentina, Brazil, and the United States proposed a joint effort by all American states to establish peace, but Chile refused to support it. Their plan for each side to withdraw its troops 15 kilometers from the recognized boundary was accepted by the adversaries, whose representatives arrived in Washington on 11 July for separate talks with Under-Secretary of State Sumner Welles—to no effect.

On 23 July, as hostilities were renewed along a 50-kilometer front, Argentina, with U.S. support, renewed its appeal to cease hostilities. Two days later Peru's foreign minister indicated a willingness to accept a cease-fire. Ecuador began to mobilize on the 24th but agreed to a cease-fire on the 26th. Peru demanded that Ecuador annul the mobilization decree as a condition for accepting a cease-fire. After much deliberation Ecuador complied on 31 July. On 2 August the mediating powers proposed a 15-kilometer withdrawal of all troops behind the status quo boundaries of 1936 and the placing of international observers. Ecuador accepted, but Peru did not reply. A cease-fire was implemented in the western zone; but in the Oriente, where there were no observers, Ecuador reported continued Peruvian advances. On 2 October military commanders of Ecuador and Peru agreed to the "Talara Truce" in which a neutral zone was established between the two lines in the provinces of Guayas, El Oro, and Loja. The situation in the Oriente was not affected. And on 4 October the mediators rejected a boundary line that Lima proposed on 13 September, which corresponded to the most advanced Peruvian posts.

The third Conference of Foreign Ministers of the American States began on 15 January 1942 in Rio de Janeiro, where informal negotiations were carried out by the foreign ministers of Ecuador and Peru. Under strong pressure from Argentina, Brazil, Chile, and the U.S., they signed a boundary protocol on 29 January 1942 ending the fighting between them: the agreement allocated 70,000 square miles of the disputed territory to Peru, granted Ecuador navigation rights on the Amazon River, and called for demarcation of the border. The second Marañón crisis was over—but the border conflict continued.

The League of Nations was not involved in this crisis.

(See *Master Table*, pp. 682–83.)

Sources

See sources for Case #50.

(322) Ecuador/Peru Border III

Ecuador and Peru experienced another violent crisis over their long-disputed border from 22 January to 2 April 1981.

Background

As noted, there were several incidents and two international crises over the disputed territory, in 1935 and 1941–42 (see Cases #50 and 86 above). The two disputants had signed the Protocol of Rio de Janeiro on 29 January 1942, which allocated the territory to Peru but gave Ecuador navigation rights on the Amazon River; it also called for demarcation of the border.

Demarcation work was suspended in August 1951, following Peruvian attacks on Ecuadorian posts in the disputed Gualingo area. In 1960 Ecuador declared the Rio Protocol null and void, asserting that it had signed under duress. Border incidents continued, the latest in 1978, a minor clash at a border post near Qualquiza, in Peru.

Crisis

The catalyst was a minor clash on 22 January 1981. Ecuador viewed the trigger as an attack by a Peruvian helicopter on a military outpost near Paquisha. Peru countered that its plane had been fired on by Ecuadorian forces while en route to Peruvian border posts with supplies. On 28 January skirmishes erupted, each side accusing the other of initiating the attacks. Peruvian forces occupied three Ecuadorian border posts. The two disputants closed their border, mobilized their forces, and suspended commercial flights.

At that point in the escalating crisis the *OAS* initiated mediation. On 29 January its Permanent Council called on Ecuador and Peru to accept a commission of inquiry. Ecuador agreed; but Peru balked, contending that the four guarantors of the 1942 Rio Protocol—Argentina, Brazil, Chile, and the U.S.—should be directly involved in any settlement. The *OAS* Council also approved, by a vote of 20–0, an Ecuadorian request for an *OAS* foreign ministers meeting.

The four guarantors of the Rio Protocol met on 31 January and arranged a cease-fire. Hostilities ended on 1 February, and the cease-fire took effect the next day. However, while tension and stress declined, the crisis lingered on. On 20 February a Peruvian helicopter was attacked by Ecuadorian forces. Both states again sealed their borders on the 23rd. The four guarantors once more mediated, with a proposal for mutual withdrawal of troops behind a nine-mile zone. The parties agreed, withdrawing their troops by 17 March. The border was reopened on 2 April, marking the end of this Ecuador/Peru border crisis.

The UN and the USSR were not involved in this crisis.

(See *Master Table,* pp. 724–25.)

Sources

See sources for Case #50; and Avery 1984–85; Child 1985; Day 1987; *Facts on File* 1982; Hopkins 1983; Institute for Study of Conflict 1982; *Keesing's* 1981; Krieg 1987.

(400) Ecuador/Peru Border IV

Ecuador and Peru experienced another crisis over territory from 6 to 15 October 1991.

Background
The most recent flare-up in this protracted conflict over territory occurred near a Peruvian border post on the Corrientes River in January 1984.

Pre-crisis
Tension between the two disputants rose in August 1991. On 30 September, at the UN, Ecuador's President Rodrigo Borja urged that Pope John Paul II be invited to mediate the dispute. (A South American precedent existed—a Vatican-mediated agreement between Argentina and Chile in 1984 that resolved their dispute since the mid-nineteenth century over the ownership of islands in the Beagle Channel [see Cases #287, 295—**Beagle Channel I, II,** in 1977–78, 1978–79, in **Americas: Non-PCs**].) On 2 October Peru's Defense Minister, General Torres, reaffirmed Lima's "trust" in the 1942 Rio Protocol, which had allocated the vast area in dispute to Peru. He also accused Ecuador of establishing a military post on Peruvian territory. The charge was rejected the next day by Ecuador's Defense Minister, Jorge Feliz, in a "we will not yield an inch" statement. This was echoed on the 5th by President Fujimori of Peru.

Crisis
A crisis for Ecuador was triggered by a perceived overflight of its territory on 6 October 1991 on the part of a Peruvian helicopter gunship. Ecuador responded the same day by suspending bilateral talks on the border then under way. This triggered a crisis for Peru. The threat of a serious military confrontation led the other three members of the five-state Andean Pact—Bolivia, Colombia, and Venezuela (along with Ecuador and Peru)—to urge a peaceful solution on the 8th. Ecuador accepted this initiative the next day, but Peru did not, calling, as always, for a solution "within the framework" of the 1942 Rio Protocol, that is, arbitration by its guarantors, Argentina, Brazil, Chile, and the United States. Ecuador rejected the idea.

A meeting between the two foreign ministers on 10 October led to a statement, "we are on the right track." The crisis ended on 15 October, when the two sides withdrew their forces simultaneously from the border.

The UN and the USSR were not involved in this case.

(Another Ecuador/Peru crisis over the small, undemarcated part of their disputed border, approximately 130 square kilometers, occurred in late January and February 1995, with serious clashes and an estimated 80 soldiers killed and 200 wounded. A cease-fire was signed on 1 March; but the parties continued to resist pressure by the four guarantors of the 1942 Rio Protocol to negotiate the substantive issue in dispute. Further—minor—incidents were reported in September 1995.)

(See *Master Table*, pp. 736–37.)

Sources
Foreign Broadcast Information Service—Daily Report/Latin America (FBIS—DR/LAT) 1991; *Keesing's* 1991; *New York Times* 1991.

Honduras/Nicaragua

The protracted conflict between Honduras and Nicaragua includes six crises from 1937 to 1989, as follows.

Case #57   **Postage Stamp Crisis,** in 1937;
#156   **Mocorón Incident,** in 1957;
#326   **Contras I,** in 1981;
#369   **Contras II,** in 1986;
#383   **Contras III,** in 1988;
#389   **Contras IV,** in 1989.

General Background

The boundary between Nicaragua and Honduras had not been settled since 1869: in dispute was a small area north of the Segovia River. In 1906, the king of Spain, acting as the arbitrator, ruled in favor of Honduras. Nicaragua refused to accept this award and continued to claim sovereignty over the disputed area. During the next half century Nicaragua maintained a small military presence between the Segovia and Cruta Rivers, in the southern part of the disputed territory; Honduras controlled the northern part. The last attempt to resolve the dispute was in 1931.

(57) Postage Stamp Crisis

A postage stamp issued by Nicaragua, showing a map of its territory including a large part of southeastern Honduras, created a crisis for both states from mid-August to 10 December 1937.

Crisis

During the second week of August 1937 Nicaragua issued a postage stamp bearing a map of the Republic that included a considerable part of southeastern Honduras, marked as being "territory in dispute." This triggered a crisis for Honduras, which protested this "affront to her sovereignty" on the 25th. On 30 August Honduras responded with a concentration of forces along the Nicaraguan border. The likelihood of military hostilities triggered a crisis for Nicaragua. Its response, on 3 September, was a refusal to withdraw the stamp, declaring it to be the official map of Nicaragua.

Armed hostilities were prevented by the mediation of Costa Rica, Venezuela, and the United States. On 10 December 1937 the two crisis actors signed a Pact of Reciprocal Agreement at San José in Costa Rica, terminating the crisis. (The conflict flared up again in 1957 [see Case #156 below].) This crisis was not brought to the League of Nations or the Pan American Union.
(See *Master Table,* pp. 676–77.)

Sources
Ireland 1938; Mecham 1961.

(156) Mocorón Incident

Another crisis over territory between Nicaragua and Honduras lasted from 26 February until 9 May 1957.

Crisis
A second crisis between these Central American neighbors occurred 20 years after their **Postage Stamp Crisis** (see Case #57 above). Nicaragua perceived a threat on 26 February 1957 when Honduras began to organize the administration of the disputed area, including some sections over which Nicaragua had been exercising de facto control. On 18 April, after Nicaragua had strengthened its military presence in this area, its troops crossed the Coco River and occupied Mocorón, on the Honduran bank of the river. This triggered a crisis for Honduras, which responded by putting its army on alert and issuing orders to clean up the area around Mocorón. On 1 May the Mocorón area was recaptured by Honduran ground and air forces. Nicaragua's President Somoza ordered general mobilization.

The Council of the *OAS* met on 2 May to consider a Honduran charge of Nicaraguan aggression and appointed a five-person investigating committee. By the 5th the OAS committee succeeded in getting both parties to sign a cease-fire agreement. However, fighting—and the crisis—continued until 9 May 1957 when a truce–*cum*–troop withdrawal plan, along with the creation of a military Observer Group along the border, was accepted by both states. The dispute was submitted to the International Court of Justice which, in November 1960, ruled in favor of Honduras.

U.S. activity was channeled through the *OAS*. The UN and the USSR were not involved.

(See *Master Table,* pp. 694–95.)

Sources
Connell-Smith 1966; de Lima 1971; Mecham 1961; Slater 1967; Wainhouse 1966.

(326) Contras I

Honduras and Nicaragua experienced the first of their four crises in the 1980s from 28 April to 13 May 1981.

Background

The last 15 years of the Honduras/Nicaragua protracted conflict were shaped by an internal struggle for power between the Sandinistas and the right-wing contras. This conflict has deep roots in Nicaragua.

The *Frente Sandinista de Liberacion Nacional (FSLN)* (Sandinista National Liberation Front) were the followers of General Agustino Sandino, who led anti-Conservative and anti-American insurrections from 1926 until his death in 1934. The "Sandinistas" triumphed over the dictatorship of Anastasio Somoza (see Case #294—**Nicaraguan Civil War, in Americas: Non-PCs**). On 19 July 1979 they formed a provisional government, the first pro-Soviet regime in the Americas since Castro's triumph in Cuba 20 years earlier.

Almost from the moment the Sandinistas assumed power in Managua, U.S. antagonism led to financial support to the right-wing "National Resistance," better known as the "contras." From 1981 onward the contras launched cross-border raids against the Sandinista regime from sanctuaries in Honduras and Costa Rica, mostly the former. This was to generate interstate crises between Honduras and Nicaragua in 1981, 1986, 1988, and 1989.

Pre-crisis
As soon as the Sandinistas achieved power in Nicaragua (see Case #294—**Nicaraguan Civil War, in 1978-79, in Americas: Non-PCs**), the contras began to mobilize funds and fighters, to organize in sanctuaries in Honduras and Costa Rica, and to induce border incidents between Nicaragua and its neighbors. Typical was the overflight of Honduran territory by Nicaraguan planes on 9 November 1980: Honduras claimed that it shot down two Nicaraguan planes in its Paraiso area; Nicaragua attributed the loss to its planes being "blown over the border by adverse winds."

In early April 1981 the Reagan administration cut off U.S. aid to the new regime in Nicaragua. And in the spring Honduran officers were expressing the view that "war with Nicaragua is unavoidable."

Crisis
A crisis for Honduras was triggered on 28 April 1981 by a Nicaraguan attack on a Honduran border post at Guasale, in search of contras. The same day troops of both states were placed on alert, and the border was closed. This catalyzed a crisis for Nicaragua. For Honduras it was perceived as a threat to territory, for Nicaragua, a threat to its political regime.

Clashes occurred on 3 May at el Tablazo and again on the 5th. On 7 May Nicaragua's defense ministry denounced Honduras for 120 acts of "aggression" and charged that Honduras disregarded five official notes of protest. Nonetheless, the same day a meeting was held between the Honduras President, General Policarpo Paz Garcia, and a senior Nicaraguan government official. After six days of negotiations a joint declaration was issued, emphasizing the willingness of the two adversaries to reduce the tension between them. This ended the low-intensity crisis of 1981.

There was no UN, U.S. or USSR involvement in this crisis.

(Although the contras were not directly involved in this crisis, their presence in the border area of Honduras was perceived by the Sandinista rulers of Nicara-

gua as a constant source of threat; and they were a catalyst to hostile acts by Honduras against Nicaragua [see also Cases #369, 383, 389 below].)
(See *Master Table,* pp. 724–25.)

Sources
ISLA April, May 1981; *Keesing's* 1981; *LACCR* 1981–82; *LAWR* 1981.

(369) Contras II

Honduras and Nicaragua were embroiled in the second of several interstate crises linked to the contras and their anti-Sandinista rebellion from 4 to 12 December 1986.

Pre-crisis
In August 1986 the military regime in Honduras reaffirmed its formal strictures on the training of contras by foreign (U.S.) forces on its territory. However, American pressure during talks in October led to the creation of a U.S.-Honduras joint military commission to coordinate training of the contras and to the first large shipment of U.S. arms in early November.

During October and November fighting between the contras and Sandinista forces escalated near the Honduran border village of Arenales. On 1 November Nicaraguan troops pursued contra rebels, penetrating five kilometers into Honduras. Further incursions into the El Paraiso Department of Honduras were reported in late November. The civil war was about to spill over into an interstate crisis.

Crisis
A crisis for Honduras was triggered by a major Sandinista cross-border military operation against contra bases on 4 December: a Honduran border post at Las Mieles was overrun, three Honduran soldiers were wounded, and two were captured. A Honduran protest was rejected by Nicaragua, which denied its incursion, even though its troops were operating at least five kilometers across the border near the town of Teotecacinte.

Honduras launched a combined political-military response. On 6 December President Azcona del Hoyo requested U.S. military assistance, which was granted by President Reagan immediately. The same day Honduran planes bombed Sandinista troops in the border area, triggering a crisis for Nicaragua, which reported seven soldiers and two civilians killed.

U.S. military involvement in this crisis became more visible on 7–8 December, when American helicopters transported more than 1,000 Honduran soldiers to the border area, 40 kilometers from the fighting. Nicaragua responded on the 9th by appealing to the UN Security Council. At the Council's meeting on the 10th Nicaragua's representative blamed Honduras for rejecting its proposal to dispatch a UN commission of inquiry; and it claimed that Honduras's army launched attacks against Nicaragua "on orders from Washington." The U.S. delegate denied the charge. Honduras made the countercharge of repeated Nicaraguan incursions into its territory.

The fighting ended within several days. There was no formal agreement or tacit understanding between the adversaries. Rather, crisis termination was evident in a confirmation by Honduras on 12 December that it had requested the U.S. to remove contra rebels from its territory.

Although the USSR was a patron of the Sandinista regime in Nicaragua from its inception, Moscow remained aloof from this crisis.

(See *Master Table*, pp. 730–31.)

Sources
Keesing's 1987; *New York Times* December 1986.

(383) Contras III

Honduras and Nicaragua were enmeshed in another crisis generated by the contra rebellion from 6 to 28 March 1988.

Pre-crisis
Peace talks between the Nicaraguan regime and the contra rebels, initiated by President Arias of Costa Rica, led to a cease-fire agreement in March 1987. However, the U.S. Congress's approval of $48 million of nonmilitary aid to the contras on 30–31 March led to a contra violation of the cease-fire.

In August 1987, as a conciliatory gesture, Nicaragua withdrew the complaint it had submitted to the World Court in July 1986 against Honduras and Costa Rica, charging that they were providing the contras with sanctuaries for raids into its territory. The pattern of cross-border raids by the contras, retaliation by Nicaragua, cease-fire agreements, and violations by one or both of the parties continued through the autumn of 1987. Another cease-fire agreement in October broke down amid renewed Nicaraguan charges of CIA-organized air drops of military supplies to the contras in November. And in December the contras intensified their cross-border attacks into Nicaragua.

Crisis
This phase of low-intensity violence culminated in a major Nicaraguan offensive against contra camps in Honduras on 6 March 1988, triggering a crisis for Honduras. President Azcona del Hoyo responded on 15 March with an appeal for U.S. assistance. The next day Nicaragua's President Daniel Ortega denied that an incursion had occurred and invited observers from the UN and the OAS. On the 16th, too, the U.S., patron of the contras and of Honduras, replied to the latter's appeal by ordering the immediate dispatch of 3,200 U.S. troops to Honduras, triggering a crisis for Nicaragua. On the 17th U.S.-supplied Honduran fighter planes bombed Nicaraguan troops operating in the border zone. And Honduras's

president threatened further land attacks if Nicaragua's troops were not withdrawn across the border.

The crisis began to wind down on 17 March, when Nicaragua ended its military incursion. On the 19th Nicaragua renewed its case before the World Court, accusing Honduras of "complicity and active participation . . . in the bombings and acts of aggression, promoted by the U.S. government, against Nicaragua." Crisis termination was signaled on 28 March by the beginning of the withdrawal of U.S. troops from Honduras.

(Three days later, as a quid pro quo, Nicaragua once more suspended its suit against Honduras before the World Court.)

Although the UN and the *OAS* were approached by Nicaragua for observers, none was dispatched. In general, these two international organizations, along with the USSR, were not involved in this Central American crisis.

(See *Master Table,* pp. 732–33.)

Sources
Keesing's 1988; *New York Times* 1988.

(389) Contras IV

The decade-old conflict between Nicaragua and the anti-Sandinista contras generated another crisis for Honduras from 9 September to 7 November 1989.

Pre-crisis
Nicaragua had filed a complaint against both Honduras and Costa Rica with the International Court of Justice (World Court) in 1986, for allowing the contras to launch raids into Nicaragua from their territories. In a turning-point regional development, the heads of all five Central American states—Costa Rica, El Salvador, Guatemala, Honduras, and Nicaragua—met in Tela, Honduras, on 5–7 August 1989 and signed a declaration calling for the "voluntary demobilization, repatriation or relocation" of the contras in Nicaragua or in other countries within three months, beginning in September 1989, under the supervision of an international commission. On 7 August, too, in a bilateral agreement, Honduras agreed to the demobilization of the contras on its territory, in return for Nicaragua's withdrawal of its complaint against Honduras at the World Court.

Crisis
A crisis for Honduras was triggered by a Nicaraguan attack on several Honduran army posts on 9 September 1989. The Honduras Foreign Ministry protested the same day. On the 13th the head of Nicaragua's Military Intelligence responded that contra raids from Honduran bases had increased markedly in the preceding two weeks. (This turned out to be the only violent exchange during the crisis.)

In October, at the 43rd session of the UN General Assembly, the Honduras foreign minister called on the UN Secretary-General to create a multinational UN peacekeeping force to patrol the border with Nicaragua. The latter approved the idea. However, on 1 November President Ortega of Nicaragua declared a formal end to the cease-fire with the contras. This came in the aftermath of a contra attack on 22 October, in which 19 persons were killed. Ortega proposed meetings with contra leaders, the Honduras government, and the UN Demobilization Commission. Honduras responded sharply on 2 November, criticizing Ortega for his cancellation of the cease-fire and rejecting Nicaragua's call for new talks on demobilizing the rebel army, claiming that the peace agreement was sufficient.

The UN Security Council, responding to the Honduras foreign minister's request, adopted a resolution on 7 November that created an Observer Group in Central America to monitor compliance with the Tela Agreement and to patrol the borders between Honduras and Nicaragua. Both the conflicting parties approved the resolution. This ended the crisis for Honduras and the Contras IV international crisis, for the UN Observer Group reduced tension and reduced the likelihood of further violence.

Nicaragua was a pivotally involved actor in this crisis. However, its source of threat was a nonstate actor, the contras, operating from a neighboring state, not Honduras per se: Nicaragua's leaders did not perceive value threat, time pressure, or higher probability of involvement in military hostilities with Honduras in this case.

The U.S. and the USSR were involved in the Nicaragua/contra domestic conflict but not in the interstate conflict between Honduras and Nicaragua.

(Talks between Nicaragua and the contras took place at UN headquarters on 9–10 November under the auspices of the UN-*OAS* International Commission for Support and Verification, with Honduras present as an observer.)

(See *Master Table,* pp. 734–35.)

Sources
Keesing's 1989, 1990; *New York Times* 1989, 1990.

Asia: Protracted Conflicts

Afghanistan/Pakistan

There were three international crises in the protracted conflict between Afghanistan and Pakistan from 1949 to 1961–62, as follows.

Case #129 **Pushtunistan I,** in 1949–50;
#150 **Pushtunistan II,** in 1955;
#182 **Pushtunistan III,** in 1961–62.

General Background

The root of this protracted conflict lies in the ethnic composition of the Afghanistan/Pakistan borderland: the population of southern Afghanistan and British India's (later, Pakistan's) North West Frontier Province *(NWFP)* were—and are—Pushtu-speaking Pathans. Over the centuries these tribespeople maintained their independence from British Indian or Afghan rule; but, in terms of culture and religion, they identified with the Afghan people. And all rulers of Afghanistan pressed their claim to the territory of the *NWFP.*

In 1893 a boundary agreement was negotiated between Sir Mortimer Durand and Afghanistan's ruler, Amir Abdur Rahman. The "Durand Line," which was imposed by superior British power, formally split the Pushtu-speaking tribespeople between two sovereign states, Afghanistan and British India. From the outset there was a disagreement as to the meaning of the Durand Line: Abdur Rahman perceived it as delineating "zones of responsibility"; the British insisted it fixed a permanent international boundary. This combination of shared ethnicity among the people on both sides of the border and disputed interpretation of the Durand Line created a persistent conflict over Pushtunistan between whoever held sway in Kabul and Delhi (and, after 15 August 1947, Islamabad).

In July 1947, before the partition of British India, Afghanistan demanded that the Pushtu-speaking Pathans of the *NWFP* be allowed to choose between independence and integration into Afghanistan. This demand was rejected by the U.K. and, later, Pakistan, as a violation of the Durand Line, the formally recognized international boundary, as incorporated in the still-valid 1921 treaty between Afghanistan and British India.

The crisis in 1949–50 was the first between Afghanistan and Pakistan over the still-unresolved issue of Pushtunistan.

(129) Pushtunistan I

Afghanistan and Pakistan experienced a two-stage crisis over a long-standing border dispute from mid-March 1949 to 5 October 1950.

Crisis

Afghanistan's demand for an independent Pathan state was followed by a propaganda campaign between the two countries in March 1949. The crisis trigger for Afghanistan occurred in mid-March when the Pakistani government arrested infiltrators into its North West Frontier Province *(NWFP)* and initiated efforts toward more effective control of that region, while rejecting any Afghanistan claims to the territory. On 27 March it was reported that Afghanistan had moved two divisions and part of its air force to the Pakistani frontier. On 2 April Afghanistan recalled its diplomatic representatives to Pakistan. Tension between the two countries increased following an incident on 12 June when a Pakistani plane bombed the village of Moghulgai, 2,100 yards from the frontier. After an investigation by a joint Afghanistan-Pakistan commission, Pakistan took responsibility for an unintentional flight and offered to pay compensation, ending Afghanistan's crisis on 31 July 1949.

On 12 August a large group of Afridi Pathans met on the Pakistani side of the Durand Line and established a Pushtunistan Assembly. When Pushtunistan's independence was proclaimed, it was immediately recognized by Afghanistan.

The tension level remained low for several months. The beginning of 1950 signaled the start of new propaganda campaigns between the two countries. The pro-Pushtunistan movement in Afghanistan strengthened during the spring and summer. Tribal unrest was prevalent, and demands for the separation of Pathanistan increased.

The trigger for Pakistan occurred on 30 September 1950, more than a year after the termination of Afghanistan's crisis, when Afghan troops invaded Pakistan. Pakistan responded with troops and aircraft and succeeded in driving the Afghan forces across the border on 5 October 1950, which marked the termination date of Pakistan's crisis.

The U.S., the USSR, and the UN were not involved.

(See *Master Table*, pp. 688–89.)

Sources

Adamec 1974; Burke 1973; Day 1987; Dupree 1961a, 1961b, 1961c, 1980; Feldman 1967; Fletcher 1966; Franck 1952; Fraser-Tyler 1967; Hussain 1966; Qureshi 1966; Razvi 1971; Spain 1963.

(150) Pushtunistan II

High tension between Afghanistan and Pakistan in the border area was further revived from 27 March to November 1955.

Background

This crisis was another stage in the ongoing conflict over Afghanistan's demand for the creation of an independent Pushtu (Pathan) state in territory that, at that time, was under Pakistani control.

Crisis

The crisis began on 27 March when information reached Afghanistan of the Pakistani government's proposal to incorporate the areas of Pushtu-speaking people in the North West Frontier into a unified province of West Pakistan, the "One Unit Scheme." Afghanistan responded with a broadcast by Prime Minister Daoud voicing his government's protest and a formal note protesting the proposed merger. This reached Karachi on 29 March and triggered a crisis for Pakistan. The next day Pakistan's embassy in Kabul was attacked. Pakistan responded on 1 April with a declaration by Prime Minister Mohammed Ali that Pakistan would not tolerate any intervention in its domestic affairs and would not rest until amends were made for the attack on its embassy. Further Pakistani steps were taken on 1 May: the breaking off of diplomatic relations; the closing of the borders; and the termination of economic relations, including the closing down of all Afghan trade agencies in Pakistan. The latter had a severe effect on Afghanistan, which was dependent on Pakistani ports for trade. Afghanistan announced a mobilization and declared a state of emergency. Pakistan dispatched troops to the border. By 9 September the two adversaries reached an agreement whereby Afghanistan promised to make amends for the insult to Pakistan's flag. On 14 October a united West Pakistan was inaugurated, including areas of the North West Frontier Province that bordered Afghanistan. The One Unit Scheme terminated Pakistan's crisis. The diplomatic issue regarding Pakistan's embassy in Afghanistan was solved by a formal reopening in Kabul in November 1955, terminating the crisis for Afghanistan.

(After diplomatic and economic relations were restored the core issue of independence for the Pushtuns was once more brought to the fore. Although the conflict over Pushtunistan continued, the high level of tension was reduced by reciprocal visits of Pakistan's prime minister and Afghanistan's president in August 1956 when both declared their intentions to improve relations.)

The USSR was marginally involved in this crisis. The U.S. and the UN were not involved.

(See *Master Table*, pp. 692–93.)

Sources

See sources for Case #129.

(182) Pushtunistan III

The ongoing territorial conflict between Pakistan and Afghanistan escalated to crisis proportions again from 19 May 1961 to 29 January 1962.

Crisis

Another crisis for Pakistan was generated by reports on 19 May 1961 of a violent infiltration by 1,000 Afghan troops into its territory. Two days later the Pakistan air force bombed areas along the border that it claimed were illegally occupied by Afghan troops. This claim was categorically denied by an Afghanistan embassy spokesman in Karachi. On 23 August 1961, in a note to the Afghanistan government, Pakistan's foreign ministry demanded the closure of Afghan consulates and trade agencies in Pakistan, which it claimed were being used for anti-Pakistani and other subversive activities. This triggered a crisis for Afghanistan. Kabul responded on 30 August that it would consider diplomatic relations as broken unless Pakistan withdrew its demands. Pakistan replied on 2 September by issuing a White Paper claiming that Afghanistan's policy of "expansionism" was the main cause of the hostilities. Diplomatic relations were severed on the 6th.

U.S. and U.K. efforts in October to settle the dispute did not bear fruit immediately. However, on 29 January 1962 President Kennedy's special envoy, L. T. Merchant, succeeded in making possible the delivery of goods from Pakistan to Afghanistan, and the frontier was temporarily reopened, ending the crisis for both actors. During the crisis the Soviet Union supplied economic aid and weapons to Afghanistan. The UN remained aloof from this crisis.

(Diplomatic relations between the adversaries were not reestablished until 24 January 1964.)

(See *Master Table*, pp. 698–99.)

Sources

See sources for Case #129.

China/Japan

China and Japan were engaged in a protracted conflict from 1927 to 1945. During part of that period, 1937–45, they were locked in a full-scale war. And the PC generated five crises, as follows.

> Case #35 **Shantung,** in 1927–29;
> #39 **Mukden Incident,** in 1931–32;
> #40 **Shanghai,** in 1932;
> #43 **Jehol Campaign,** in 1933;
> #56 **Marco Polo Bridge,** in 1937–38.

There were also many crises in the Pacific Theater of World War II in which China and Japan were crisis actors (see **Multiregional PCs: World War II**).

General Background

A weak, disunited China was the object of intense rivalry among the Western imperialist powers and Japan in the late nineteenth century. As part of the struggle for influence and material gain, Germany extracted a 99-year lease over Kiaochow Bay in March 1898, along with mining and railway concessions and a preferential status for German traders and manufacturers throughout Shantung Province.

Seizing the opportunity of the outbreak of World War I, Japan, on 15 August 1914, demanded the transfer of the Kiaochow lease within a month "with a view to eventual restoration of the same to China." After a successful military campaign in Shantung, Japan achieved de facto control by November. On 18 January 1915 Japan issued its "Twenty One Demands" including China's acquiescence in the transfer of the 1898 concessions in Shantung from Germany to Japan. These were incorporated in imposed treaties and exchanges of notes between China and Japan on 25 May 1915.

The Beijing regime persisted in denying the validity of the 1915 "agreements" and in asserting the claim that its declaration of war against Germany on 12 August 1917 had automatically canceled the German lease to Kiaochow, but in vain: the transfer of all German rights in Shantung to Japan was given global legitimacy by its inclusion in the Treaty of Versailles.

Beijing continued to refuse to negotiate with Japan over Shantung until, under U.S. pressure, a compromise agreement was reached near the close of the Washington Conference in 1921–22. Japan was to transfer that part of the Chinese Eastern Railway in Shantung within nine months of the ratification of the agreement. Japanese troops were to withdraw from Tsingtao within 30 days of the transfer of the German-leased territory. Japan retained its economic primacy through a central role in the customs service, along with administrative and political influence in Shantung.

The transfer of the Kiaochow-Tsinan rail line to China took place on 1 January 1923. However, the Japanese military evacuation from Shantung remained in abeyance.

(35) Shantung

China and Japan were enmeshed in a two-stage crisis over the former's northern province of Shantung from 28 May 1927 until 28 March 1929. It was the first military-security crisis in their post–World War I protracted conflict.

Pre-crisis
Nationalist forces under Chiang Kai-shek advanced northward during the spring of 1927. Newly appointed Japanese Prime Minister Tanaka perceived this as a danger to Japan's primary interest in mainland China, namely, the strategic and resource-rich northeast region of Manchuria. Thus on 20 May 1927 Japan's ambassador to China was instructed to offer moral support to Chiang in his attempt to suppress the communists. Moreover, inducements were offered to northern warlord, Chang Tso-lin, to concentrate his forces in Manchuria. Both steps were designed to ensure Japan's control over Manchuria.

Crisis

The potential collapse of Chang Tso-lin's forces led to the dispatch of Japanese troops to Tsinan on 28 May, triggering a crisis for China. The next day the nationalist Nanking regime protested Japan's action as a violation of the Sino/Japanese treaty of 1922 regarding China's sovereignty, triggering a crisis for Japan. Japanese forces landed at the port of Tsingtao on 31 May and began to march on Tsinan. On 1 June the Beijing government added its voice of protest on the same grounds.

A direct military confrontation between Japan and China was averted on this occasion: Japanese troops entered Tsinan on 16 June; and two days later Chiang's forces were defeated by Chang Tso-lin.

The result of Japan's incursion into Shantung was a wave of anti-Japanese sentiment in China including the boycott of Japanese goods. On 13 July the Beijing regime demanded the withdrawal of Japanese forces. On 29 August Tokyo announced its intended evacuation, which occurred on 8 September 1927, ending China's crisis and the first phase of the Shantung crisis.

In late December, following an inconclusive meeting between Chiang and Tanaka, rumors surfaced about a renewed northward offensive by China's nationalists: this alarmed Japanese decision makers, concerned about the implications for their goal of hegemony over Manchuria.

Boycotts of Japanese goods reappeared in China in March 1928. Early in April Chiang did, in fact, renew his advance northward. And on the 17th an antinationalist counterattack by Chang Tso-lin's forces failed. Two days later Japanese troops were dispatched from Tientsin to Tsinan, a response to a perceived escalation of the crisis: they arrived on the 20th. The Beijing regime immediately protested Japan's "show of force," as did the Nanking regime on the 21st. A minor skirmish between Japanese and Chinese troops was reported on the 30th, followed by a more serious confrontation at Tsinan on 3 May. A truce was arranged on the 5th. However, two days later a Japanese ultimatum called for the withdrawal of Chinese forces from Tsinan within 12 hours. When the deadline went unheeded hostilities resumed, and the Chinese were forced to evacuate the city on the 11th.

In the meantime both the Nanking and Beijing governments protested to the League of Nations, alleging a violation of China's territorial integrity and political independence. They offered to accept arbitration or an international inquiry; but the world body took no action.

Tension persisted, exacerbated by Tanaka's memorandum on 16 May asserting that Japan would use force to protect Manchuria from Chiang and Chang Tso-lin. Both Chinese regimes protested once more. Japanese troops remained in Tsinan throughout 1928. Serious negotiations began in October. A formal agreement was signed on 28 March 1929 providing for the withdrawal, once more, of Japanese forces from Tsinan. This ended Japan's crisis and the lengthy crisis over Shantung.

The U.S. alone among the powers with a stake in China was an involved actor: it offered good offices to both China and Japan to help end the fighting. The offer was declined; but the U.S. consul in Tsinan reportedly helped to wind down the hostilities.

(See *Master Table*, pp. 672–73.)

Sources
Foreign Relations of the United States (FRUS) 1927, vol. 2 (1942), *1928,* vol. 2 (1943); Bamba 1972; Beasley 1964; MacNair and Lach 1955; Morton 1980; Toynbee 1929a, 1929b, 1930; Walters 1952.

(39) Mukden Incident

A crisis for both China and Japan began on 18 September 1931 and ended on 18 February 1932.

Pre-crisis
On 5 May 1931 a People's National Convention in Nanking adopted a provisional constitution that confirmed the separation of five branches within the Chinese government. Chinese nationalism had penetrated into China's three northeastern provinces, and authority in all of China was fragmented.

Unrest and dissatisfaction with economic conditions in Japan were marked by 1930: the military, while opposing the alliance between government and business, began to assume control. Strong pressure was brought to bear on the government to act positively in defense of Japanese interests in Manchuria, threatened by the policies of the Chinese nationalists. Manchuria was perceived, in part, as an economic panacea.

Crisis
On the night of 18 September 1931 the Japanese Kwantung Army, engaged in night maneuvers at Mukden, used an explosion on the railway as an excuse for the preconceived seizure, before morning, of the arsenal and of Antung, Yingkow, and Changchun. This triggered a crisis for China and also for the Japanese government—the invasion being an act by the Japanese army without previous sanction by the civil authority, which was not interested at that time in war with China. China had no choice but to withdraw after serious clashes. On 21 September Kirin was seized. The same day, China appealed to the League of Nations and to the U.S. for aid. No serious military response was attempted. On the 24th the Japanese government called for direct Sino/Japanese negotiations, while rejecting involvement by the League. At the same time Japanese military pressure continued, and the northeastern provinces of China were steadily occupied. The Chinese instituted a boycott of Japanese imports into the country.

The crisis ended for Japan and, by *force majeure,* for China on 18 February 1932, when Japan unilaterally declared the independence of Manchuria, now called Manchukuo. (China did not regain Manchuria until the end of World War II.) The League of Nations adopted a resolution on 10 December 1931 to dispatch a fact-finding mission.

(After the end of the crisis the Lytton Commission gently chided Japan: it found that the Japanese action of 18–19 September 1931 was not in self-defense and that the creation of Manchukuo did not flow from a "genuine and spontaneous independence movement." The Commission's criticism of Japan's behavior was adopted by the League Assembly, leading to Japan's notice of withdrawal from the League in February 1933.)

The United States condemned Japan's behavior but confined its action to nonrecognition of Manchukuo. Japan viewed the U.S. with hostility and suspicion, while China was dissatisfied with the paucity of the U.S. response. The USSR proposed a nonaggression pact to Japan. Territory previously recognized by Japan to be in the Soviet sphere of influence was now included in Manchukuo as the new state expanded its borders; but Moscow assumed Chinese rights to the Chinese Eastern Railway, which proved to be a continuing source of friction. The U.K. was modestly involved.

(See *Master Table*, pp. 672–73.)

Sources
Cameron et al. 1952; Carr 1945; Clyde 1958; Eagleton 1957; Grew 1953; Hane 1972; Hull 1948, vol. I; Lee 1973; MacNair and Lach 1955; Morley 1974; Ogata 1964; Schurmann and Schell 1967–74; Thorne 1972; Vinacke 1959; Walters 1952; Zimmern 1936.

(40) Shanghai

A Sino/Japanese crisis over Shanghai occurred from 24 January to 5 May 1932.

Pre-crisis
At the beginning of the 1930s relations between foreigners and local Chinese authorities were fairly amicable in the "treaty port" of Shanghai. When news of the Japanese takeover in Manchuria reached Shanghai, anti-Japanese sentiment increased markedly. The Chinese, in retaliation, had staged a boycott of Japanese goods, and some Japanese residents in Shanghai were molested. During the first three weeks of January 1932 a number of violent incidents took place.

On 18 January some Japanese residents of Shanghai were attacked by Chinese. Five Japanese demands were presented to the Chinese mayor of Greater Shanghai, who claimed he was ready to comply with three of these, dealing directly with the incident, but not with the two involving the anti-Japanese movement. The commander of the Japanese fleet in Chinese waters threatened to take direct action; Japanese naval reinforcements were ordered to Shanghai. Twenty thousand Japanese troops arrived on 24 January 1932.

Crisis

A crisis for China was triggered on 24 January, when the Japanese notified Mayor Wu T'ieh-ch'eng that, if no reply was forthcoming within a reasonable time or if the reply was unsatisfactory, the Japanese government reserved the right to take action by 28 January. The Municipal Council of the International Settlement in Shanghai held a meeting on the 28th and declared a state of emergency. Despite the complete acceptance of all Japanese demands on the 28th, military operations began. This was met with Chinese armed resistance.

A crisis for Japan occurred on 29 January, when Admiral Shiuzawa concluded that the Japanese forces were inadequate to deal with the developing situation. An aerial bombardment of densely populated sections of the city was ordered, and additional troops were requested from Tokyo. This was approved by a cabinet decision on 4 February. Japan's major response, on 18 February, was an ultimatum requiring the Chinese to withdraw all their troops from Shanghai within two days. The Chinese refused. A Japanese attack followed.

Conditions for a cease-fire were initiated by the U.K. and were agreed to by the adversaries on 28 February, but fighting continued until 3 March, when the Chinese withdrew beyond the 20-kilometer limit upon which the Japanese had insisted.

At China's request, a special session of the League Assembly was held on 3 March to consider the Shanghai incident. On the 11th, a resolution was passed that reaffirmed the doctrine of nonrecognition of situations achieved in violation of treaty obligations. The U.S., too, condemned Japan.

It was largely through British mediation that an agreement between China and Japan was negotiated and an armistice signed on 5 May 1932, establishing a demilitarized zone around Shanghai and terminating the economic boycott. This ended the Shanghai crisis.

(See *Master Table,* pp. 672–73.)

Sources

See sources for Case #39.

(43) Jehol Campaign

China's crisis over the province of Jehol lasted from 23 February to 31 May 1933.

Pre-crisis

The creation of the State of Manchukuo by Japan in 1932 (see Case #39— **Mukden Incident** above) included the territory of China's three northeastern provinces, Jehol, and parts of Inner Mongolia. The Japanese-Manchukuon forces had been operating to clear the area of all anti-Japanese and anti-Manchukuo Chinese pockets in Jehol. In order to resist Japanese advances, China resolved to concentrate troops south of the Great Wall at various points in the province of Jehol in December 1932. Despite Japan's repeated warning, three Chinese brigades were moved to Jehol. Japanese forces occupied Shanhaikwan on 3 January 1933 to provide a preliminary base for the expected occupation of Jehol. A state of extreme tension prevailed in China, but the Chinese military remained confident of its ability to halt a Japanese advance in Jehol.

Crisis
On 23 February 1933 the Japanese issued an ultimatum calling for the evacuation of all Chinese troops from Jehol and warning that no guarantees could be given that military hostilities would not spread to North China. That day 30,000 Japanese and 1,000 Manchukuon troops launched an attack on Jehol. The ultimatum was rejected the next day by the Chinese, who moved more troops to the area. Jehol fell on 4 March to the Japanese, and by May they had advanced to within three kilometers of Beijing. On 31 May 1933 the Chinese government signed a truce at Taugku, in accordance with which Chinese forces withdrew west of Beijing and the Japanese undertook to stay north of the Great Wall. This ended the Jehol crisis.

During March 1933 the U.K., France, and the U.S. were informed that China would not negotiate with Japan and that resistance was its legitimate right as a member of the League of Nations. In February recommendations had been submitted by the League, but China felt that they did not go far enough in sanctioning Japan and withdrew its request. The British then refused to mediate. The U.S. was approached in May; President Roosevelt issued a noncommittal statement. Italy strongly condemned Japan. Plans for joint efforts by Italy, the U.S., and the U.K. to end the fighting in northern China never came to fruition.
(See *Master Table,* pp. 672–73.)

Sources
Borg 1964; MacNair and Lach 1955; Thorne 1972; Vinacke 1959.

(56) Marco Polo Bridge

The crisis for China and Japan arising from the Marco Polo Bridge incident began on 8 July 1937 and terminated on 16 January 1938.

Background and Pre-crisis
A civil-military conflict in Japan throughout the 1930s was reflected in its foreign policy behavior. The lines between official government policy and policy emanating from field commanders or other military decision makers were often blurred. Five different Japanese decision-making groups operated simultaneously on matters related to China: the emperor; the civil government; the general staff in Tokyo; the Kwantung Army headquarters in Manchuria; and the local field commanders. Since the **Mukden Incident** of 1931 (see Case #39 above), Japa-

nese forces had strengthened their grip over Manchuria/Manchukuo and over areas in North China. Japanese garrisons, with China's agreement, had been positioned near Beijing and were carrying out maneuvers. The Marco Polo Bridge, near Lukouchiao, served two important railways. On the evening of 7 July 1937 the Japanese were attacked by Chinese troops. The Japanese commander immediately demanded entry into the neighboring town of Wanping to search for one of his soldiers allegedly captured by the Chinese forces. He was refused entry.

Crisis

The trigger for China occurred on 8 July 1937, when a reinforced Japanese army unit attacked Chinese forces. China's response, the next day, was to send additional troops to the area to assist the 29th and 37th Chinese divisions stationed there. When the Japanese authorities received reports of heavy reinforcements moving into the area on 9 July, a crisis was triggered for Japan. Heavy bombardment of Chinese forces ensued. Japan's major response, on the 11th, was to dispatch units of the Kwantung Army, as well as forces stationed in Korea, to the Honan-Hopei border region, into which hostilities had already spread.

Soon after the initial clashes at Lukouchiao in July 1937, China and Japan were fighting a full-scale war. Points of escalation in the crisis coincide with the military campaigns in the Sino/Japanese War. On 13 December 1937 Nanking fell, ending China's crisis but not the prolonged Sino/Japanese conflict; and it was only the first stage of their long war. The crisis ended for Japan on 16 January 1938, when Japan's prime minister stated that Japan would no longer recognize the Chinese government and would now attempt to set up Japanese regimes in different areas of China.

China appealed to the League of Nations on 12 September 1937. There were two Assembly resolutions, on 28 September and 6 October 1937, which condemned Japanese bombing of several cities in China. Unsuccessful attempts to find a solution were made by the following: the U.K., at the Brussels Conference of November 1937; France, with a 14 July 1937 statement in favor of peaceful resolution; Italy, with a similar statement on 21 July; and Germany, through the Trautmann Mission, which began on 28 October 1937. The U.S. was politically involved through the Roosevelt Quarantine Speech on 5 October. The USSR, which had signed a Treaty of Non-Aggression with China, supplied it with military equipment.

(The Sino/Japanese war, enlarged by the participation of the U.S., the U.K., and many other states after the Japanese attack on **Pearl Harbor** in December 1941 [see Case #88, in **Multiregional PCs: World War II**], raged on until the Japanese surrender in 1945.)

(See *Master Table,* pp. 674–75.)

Sources

See sources for Case #39.

China/Vietnam

There were four interstate crises in the **China/Vietnam** protracted conflict from 1978 to 1988, as follows.

Case #298 **Sino/Vietnam War,** in 1978–79;
    #352 **Sino/Vietnam Clashes,** in 1984;
    #371 **Sino/Vietnam Border,** in 1987;
    #384 **Spratly Islands,** in 1988.

There were related cases, notably Case #284—**Vietnam Invasion of Cambodia,** in 1977–79 (see **Indochina PC** below).

General Background

The historic conflict between China and Vietnam was dramatically revived in the late twentieth century after the Vietnam War, which ended in 1975 with the withdrawal of U.S. forces, the integration of North and South Vietnam, and the conquest of Cambodia by the Maoist Khmer Rouge (see **Indochina PC**). From 1975 onward China airlifted military and economic aid to Cambodia, while military equipment was being shipped to Hanoi from the USSR. Beijing's perception of threat from a new arena of Soviet encirclement, part of the Sino/Soviet conflict over borders (see Case #231—**Ussuri River,** in 1969, in **Asia: Non-PCs**), as well as from Vietnam's regional ambitions, increased as border incidents between China and Vietnam escalated. While reluctant to challenge USSR prestige in the area to the point of risking direct Soviet intervention, the People's Republic of China (PRC) was nevertheless determined to resist what it considered to be Soviet-inspired Vietnamese expansionism. In particular, China objected to Vietnam's attempt to gain control over its client, Cambodia. Thus the crisis that generated the **Sino/Vietnam War** became enmeshed with the **Vietnam Invasion of Cambodia** crisis (see Case #284, in **Indochina PC**).

(298) Sino/Vietnam War

A crisis between China (PRC) and Vietnam, which escalated to full-scale war, lasted from 25 December 1978 to 15 March 1979.

Background
China and Vietnam were hostile neighbors for a thousand years. Most of what later became North and South Vietnam—Cochin China (from 1862) and Annam (from 1874)—was controlled by France through the first half of the twentieth century. Although Vietnam declared its independence in September 1945, French domination ended only after its defeat at Dien Bien Phu in May 1954 and the Geneva Agreement on Indochina soon after (see Case #145, in **Indochina PC**).

From that point onward there were several incidents and disputes between China and Vietnam including armed conflict over the Paracel Islands in 1959 and 1974.

Pre-crisis
Tension between China and Vietnam mounted in the summer of 1978. On 29 June Vietnam joined the Soviet bloc's economic community, *COMECON*. On 12 July China tightened border controls in order to stem the influx of refugees, which had reached 169,000 of the Hoa people fleeing Vietnam to China. Moreover, a significant military buildup occurred along the Sino/Vietnam border. The two countries edged toward full-scale war during the summer of 1978, while fighting continued during the autumn, followed by a break during the rainy season. In November Vietnam and the USSR signed a Treaty of Friendship, which pledged Soviet assistance in the event of an attack. And in December the continued drain on Vietnam's resources led to its decisive **Invasion of Cambodia** (see Case #284, in **Indochina PC**).

Crisis
Vietnam's invasion of Cambodia on 25 December 1978 triggered a crisis for China. Its response was a military incursion into Vietnam on 17 February and the occupation of several border villages. This, in turn, triggered a crisis for Vietnam.

Chinese troops met with stronger than anticipated opposition leading to a halt in military operations. They were resumed on the 23rd, after the invasion force had been enlarged to 200,000. Vietnam responded by launching two counterattacks into Chinese territory the same day. Fighting subsided on 5 March. A PRC government statement that day announced that the Chinese troops had attained their goal—"to punish the Vietnamese aggressor"—and would withdraw to Chinese territory; but the image of China's military embarrassment persisted. The same day the government of Vietnam issued a decree proclaiming general mobilization. Chinese troops were withdrawn from Vietnam by 15 March 1979 terminating the crisis for the PRC and Vietnam.

On 17 February, the day of the Chinese incursion, Vietnam urged the UN Secretary-General to take appropriate measures to put an end to China's "aggression" but did not request a formal session of the Security Council. On the 22nd the U.S., the U.K., Norway, and Portugal requested an urgent meeting of the Council to consider the situation in Southeast Asia. The five *ASEAN* countries (Association of Southeast Asian Nations) circulated a draft resolution calling for a halt to all hostilities in Indochina; but, as with the proposed resolution on Vietnam's invasion of Cambodia, it was vetoed by the Soviets.

China's exercise in deterrence had mixed results: it was revealed as unable to prevent the toppling of a regime (in Cambodia) to whose support it was publicly committed; and it failed "to punish" Vietnam. At the same time China emerged in a stronger political position because the USSR abstained from participation in the war. And there was no apparent damage to the normalization of U.S./PRC relations, which had been strengthened in December 1978. (See *Master Table,* pp. 720–21.)

Sources
Burchett 1981; Buszynski 1980; Chang 1986; Chen 1987; Duiker 1986; Duncanson 1979; Elliott 1981; Gilks 1992; Jackson 1979; Jencks 1979, 1985; van der Kroef 1979a, 1979b; Lawson 1984; Leifer 1979; Pike 1979; Ross 1980; Ross 1988; Segal 1985; Tretiak 1979; Yahuda 1979.

(352) Sino/Vietnam Clashes

Vietnam and China were enmeshed in a crisis from 2 April until the second half of June 1984.

Crisis
A crisis for Vietnam was triggered by Chinese long-range shelling from across the border in Yunnan Province and the Guangxi autonomous region, beginning on 2 April 1984. This attack coincided with Vietnam's military offensive near Kampuchea's (Cambodia's) border with Thailand. Two days later Vietnam's foreign minister accused China of a calculated act to put pressure on Vietnam from two sides. China denied the linkage and termed its action a response to Vietnam's "provocations." On 6 April Chinese forces penetrated deep into Vietnam, to a point only 150 kilometers from Hanoi. On the 8th Hanoi Radio acknowledged heavy casualties and accused Beijing of an act of war, reflecting China's expansionist aims. The same day the PRC's foreign minister responded in kind, claiming that Vietnam forces crossed the frontier into Yunnan on 5 April. On the 12th Vietnam dismissed this charge as "nonsense."

During the month of April 1984 both sides claimed that incidents occurred almost daily, with heavy casualties for the other side. A major border clash was reported on 28 April, the probable trigger to China's crisis. Beijing accused Vietnam of invading the Loashan area; Vietnam denied the charge. However, on 3 May a Vietnam defense ministry spokesman told a press conference that Vietnam had succeeded in stopping a Chinese invasion from 28 April to 1 May.

Another serious border clash occurred on 15 May. Again, both sides claimed victory, with heavy casualties suffered by the enemy. Low-intensity violence continued through May and much of June. The crisis faded in the latter part of June.

There was no direct involvement by either superpower in this crisis; but both were exploited by the adversaries. The U.S. president's visit to China from 26 April to 1 May 1984 was noted in a critical vein by Vietnam: on 1 May Hanoi Radio linked the 28 April border clash, the peak of Sino/Vietnamese tension and hostilities, to President Reagan's presence in Beijing. The USSR, too, was involved on the periphery—by its client's adversary: on 8 May China criticized

Moscow for a display of military support for Vietnam, a landing exercise by 400 Soviet sailors on the Vietnamese coast 145 kilometers from Haiphong. Vietnam complained to the UN, but the world body remained aloof.

(See *Master Table,* pp. 728–29.)

Sources
Keesing's 1984.

(371) Sino/Vietnam Border

Vietnam and China were embroiled in another border crisis from 5 to 10 January 1987.

Crisis
The two long-standing adversaries accused each other of initiating the crisis on 5 January 1987 by an attack across their border—in the Vi Xuyen District of Ha Tuyen Province of Vietnam, claimed Hanoi; in Yunnan Province of China, asserted Beijing. For both it was a threat to territorial integrity.

Whichever state set the crisis in motion, the response was identical—a large-scale counterattack across the border. Vietnam claimed that 1,500 Chinese were killed in battles that raged for three days and that the Chinese had penetrated 18 kilometers into Vietnam territory. By the 8th, according to Hanoi, the Chinese advance had been halted, with Chinese forces being compelled to retreat across the border. This marked the end of Vietnam's crisis. China acknowledged that, on 7 January, its "frontier guards" made "counterattacks" against Vietnamese troops—as a response to a Vietnamese attack in the Laoshan area of Yunnan Province. The crisis ended for China on 10 January when it claimed that 500 Vietnamese troops were killed or wounded. China also denied Vietnamese reports that 1,500 Chinese soldiers were killed, although it admitted that there were "considerable losses," due to the inexperience of its soldiers.

While both parties claimed victory, the crisis ended in a stalemate: neither had achieved its main objective—defeating and, if possible, humiliating its longstanding rival for influence in Southeast Asia; neither emerged with enhanced power and influence; and both suffered considerable casualties. In all of these respects, the outcome seemed to replicate their full-scale war from mid-December 1978 to March 1979 (see Case #298 above).

Neither the U.S. or the USSR, nor the UN or any regional organization, was involved in this crisis.

(On 13 January China rejected a Vietnamese proposal for talks on the border confrontation and linked the resolution of their conflict with the withdrawal of Vietnam from Cambodia—which Vietnam had occupied since the beginning of 1979 [see Case #284—**Vietnam Invasion of Cambodia,** in **Indochina PC**].

Although this crisis ended quickly, further border incidents between China and Vietnam occurred during the months of February and March. More important, it was followed a year later by a major Sino/Vietnam crisis over potentially valuable territory and a continuing source of tension [see Case #384—**Spratly Islands** below]. And their protracted conflict remains unresolved.)

(See *Master Table*, pp. 730–31.)

Sources
Foreign Broadcast Information Service—Daily Report/China (FBIS—DR/ China) 1987; *Keesing's* 1987.

(384) Spratly Islands

Vietnam and China were embroiled in a crisis over the Spratly Islands from 14 March until late April 1988.

Background
The Spratlys and the South China Sea generally had long been part of the territorial domain of imperial China. Control by the "Middle Kingdom," however, eroded along with its decline as the regional hegemon during the penetration of European powers into Southeast Asia in the sixteenth century. But the issue of sovereignty over the Spratlys remained dormant until the late nineteenth century.

France emerged as the dominant power in Indochina and the islands of the South China Sea, a status formalized in the France/Annam treaty of 1874. China was compelled to accept France's primacy following the defeat of its navy in the Sino/French war of 1884–85. Extending its influence southward from its Indochina colony, France sent a survey mission to the Spratlys in 1927 and formally annexed the islands in April 1930.

Japan emerged as the next claimant: with most of coastal China under Japan's control early in the Sino/Japanese war (see Case #56—**Marco Polo Bridge**, in 1937–38, in **China/Japan PC**), the Japanese navy occupied the Spratlys in March 1939. The Itu Aba Island within the Spratly archipelago became a submarine base for Japan's invasion of the Philippines in December 1941. And the Spratlys assisted the Japanese conquest of Southeast Asia.

At the end of World War II, (Republican) China reasserted its claim to the Spratlys. So too did France, now restored to control over Indochina. China established a military post on Itu Aba. In October 1950 the newly (formally) independent Vietnam proclaimed possession of France's maritime boundaries in the South China Sea, including the Spratlys. And with the end of French rule in 1956, following its dramatic defeat at Dien Bien Phu two years earlier (see Case #145, in **Indochina PC**), South Vietnam dispatched a military unit to the islands.

The legal status of the Spratlys remains uncertain. The San Francisco Peace Treaty of 1951 ending the Pacific War failed to resolve the dispute. It remained dormant for the next two decades because the two major contenders were preoccupied: mainland China, with the consolidation of communist power; Vietnam, with the long war against the United States.

Competing claims became more visible in the early 1970s. In July 1971, following the firing on a Filipino ship by a Taiwan navy patrol in the waters of the Spratlys, the Philippines claimed ownership of 53 islets in the eastern part of the far-flung Spratly archipelago. The PRC occupied the Paracel Islands in 1974, signaling its intent to reassert China's historic claim to the Spratlys. North Vietnam declared its sovereignty over the Spratlys in April 1975, following its victory in the Vietnam War and the unification of the two Vietnams. Then, in 1978, Malaysia asserted its claim to 10 atolls in the southern part of the Spratlys. In short, by that time there were five claimants to sovereignty over all or part of the Spratlys: China, Taiwan, Vietnam, the Philippines, and Malaysia. The Sultan of Brunei put forward a claim to part of the islands in 1988, adding Indonesia to the disputants.

China served notice of its intent in December 1984 when the PRC's State Council announced the integration of the Paracel and Spratly Islands into the Hainan administrative zone. With the legitimacy of a *UNESCO* decision in March 1987, assigning it the task of setting up observation posts in the Spratlys, Beijing reportedly established 167 posts by the end of that year. On 16 April 1987 the PRC made its intent unequivocal, with a statement that China "reserved the right to recover [the Spratlys] at an appropriate time." And in May–June 1987 it conducted naval exercises near the Spratlys.

Not by accident, China selected Vietnam as the focus of an even more tangible expression of its claim to the Spratlys. Vietnam was an historic enemy-rival of China. It was still a pariah state, the only state in the region that was not a member of *ASEAN* with which China had carefully nurtured an image of a friendly great power and increasingly important trading partner. Vietnam was further weakened by the decline of the Soviet Union, its military and economic patron through the Vietnam War and beyond. And the U.S. had not yet embarked on a policy of reconciliation with Vietnam.

Pre-crisis
PRC forces took possession of two reefs in the Spratlys on 31 January 1988. Near clashes between the navies of China and Vietnam were frequent in January and February. On 24 February Vietnam accused China of violating its sovereignty over the Spratlys and warned of "disastrous consequences." China responded on the 26th, repeating its claims and warning that Vietnam "must take full responsibility for all the consequences" if it "obstructs China's legitimate activities" in the Spratlys.

Crisis
A crisis was triggered for Vietnam and, almost simultaneously, for China on 14 March 1988: a brief (half-hour) naval battle left two Vietnamese ships destroyed, with three Vietnamese soldiers killed and 74 missing. A defeated Vietnam's

proposal on the 24th for negotiations was rejected. Both sides upgraded their forces and deployed troops to several contested islands and reefs during the ensuing weeks. Nonetheless, the crisis began to wind down in April and faded by the end of that month.

Several of the other parties to the dispute over the Spratly Islands were involved actors. The Philippines warned both Vietnam and China on 17 March not to intrude into the area it claimed. An agreement was signed by a Philippines congressional delegation and Vietnam at the beginning of April committing both to non-violent means of settling the dispute. Similarly, China and the visiting president of the Philippines agreed in late April to set their dispute aside. Malaysia and Taiwan adopted a more bellicose response: the former increased its patrols around the islets it claimed and, in August 1988, announced its intention of building a naval base on the north coast of Sabah; the latter reinforced its garrison on Itu Aba Island in March. But all this was posturing designed to buttress claims to part of the Spratlys.

The U.S., the USSR, the UN, and *ASEAN* were not involved in this crisis.

(Physical and verbal expressions of hostility continued through June. Vietnam conducted a large military exercise in May clearly designed to cope with an anticipated battle against the Chinese in the Spratlys. China deployed additional units to Spratly reefs in May; and they held a military exercise in June, reportedly simulating a tactical nuclear attack. Moreover, there were exchanges of undisguised threats by both sides. But, while the conflict continued—and the dispute remains unresolved in the late 1990s—the crisis triggered by the naval battle of 14 March had passed.)

(See *Master Table*, pp. 732–33.)

Sources
Chang 1990; Chen Jie 1994; Varon 1994.

India/Pakistan

There have been nine interstate crises in the **India/Pakistan** protracted conflict from 1947 to 1990, as follows.

Case #118   **Junagadh,** in 1947–48;
#119   **Kashmir I,** in 1947–49;
#124   **Hyderabad,** in 1948;
#135   **Punjab War Scare I,** in 1951;
#214   **Rann of Kutch,** in 1965;
#216   **Kashmir II,** in 1965–66;
#242   **Bangladesh,** in 1971;
#372   **Punjab War Scare II,** in 1987;
#392   **Kashmir III: India/Pakistan Nuclear,** in 1990.

This protracted conflict remains unresolved after half a century.

Background

The roots of the India/Pakistan protracted conflict can be traced to two closely related phenomena. One is *intercommunal* (Hindu/Muslim) and *civilizational* (Hinduism/Islam) strife during the past four centuries. The other is the partition of the subcontinent into two independent states in 1947, the catalyst to half a century of *interstate* conflict.

Before independence the British empire in India comprised two segments: 11 provinces, with increasingly representative governing institutions, each headed by a governor under the authority of the viceroy and governor-general, the British Crown's representative in India; and more than 500 autocratically ruled "princely states," each linked by treaty to the reigning British monarch.

The rulers of almost all the princely states signed an "Instrument of Accession" to India or Pakistan by 15 August 1947, the date of the transfer of power from the U.K. to the new Dominions of India and Pakistan. Although many would have preferred independence, they had no meaningful choice, for they were surrounded by the territory of India or Pakistan; and the ruler and the ruled were from the same community, Hindu or Muslim.

The three exceptions were Junagadh, Jammu and Kashmir (Kashmir), and Hyderabad, in which one or both of these conditions did not obtain. In Junagadh and Hyderabad, a Muslim nawab and a Muslim nizam ruled over a population of whom 75 percent were Hindu. In Kashmir, both conditions were lacking: the state was ruled by a Hindu maharaja, with an overwhelmingly Muslim population; and its territory is contiguous to both India and Pakistan.

These special cases were accentuated by a human tragedy on the grand scale, an unparalleled migration of 15 million people—Hindus and Sikhs fleeing from Pakistan to India and Muslims in the reverse direction. It was estimated that a million people were killed in the riots that accompanied the transfer of population. Thus it was no accident that these three princely states were the focus of the first three international crises in the India/Pakistan protracted conflict.

(118) Junagadh

The crisis between India and Pakistan over Junagadh took place from 17 August 1947 to 24 February 1948.

Crisis
The news of Junagadh's accession to Pakistan on 17 August 1947 triggered a crisis for India. New Delhi responded on 25 October by approving a plan to occupy Mangrol and Babariawad with civil personnel accompanied by a small military force. This triggered a crisis for Pakistan on 1 November 1947. After the nawab left Junagadh, its government formally requested India to assist in the administration. Accordingly, instructions were issued on 9 November to occupy Junagadh, marking the termination of India's crisis.

Pakistan's response on 11 November took the form of a reply by Liaquat Ali Khan to a cable from Nehru requesting a discussion on Junagadh. Pakistan's prime minister contended that, since Junagadh had already acceded to Pakistan, there was no room for discussion and that India's action was a clear violation of Pakistani territory. However, Pakistan was in no position to defend Junagadh because they were not contiguous and Junagadh was 300 miles from the sea. Pakistan's crisis ended on 24 February 1948 when a plebiscite was held in Junagadh, reinforcing India's control over the state.

The U.K. was deeply involved in this crisis. Lord Mountbatten, India's last viceroy and governor-general, held talks in Lahore with Liaquat Ali Khan and received Pakistan's agreement to hold a plebiscite in Junagadh. The U.S., the USSR, and the UN were not involved.

(See *Master Table,* pp. 686–87.)

Sources
See sources for Case #119.

(119) Kashmir I

The first crisis between India and Pakistan over Kashmir lasted from 24 October 1947 to 1 January 1949.

Background and Pre-crisis
In 1847 the British sold the Vale of Kashmir to the *Dogra* ruler of Jammu who, in turn, acknowledged British paramountcy. In 1947 it was run along orthodox Hindu lines. If the disposition of Jammu and Kashmir had been made according to the principles applied to British India, the state—with the possible exception of a Hindu majority area in Jammu, adjacent to the Indian Punjab—would have gone to Pakistan. At that time Kashmir had a Hindu ruler, with an overwhelming Muslim population, approximately 75 percent of more than four million. However, the power of decision rested with the maharaja. Accession to a democratic India had no appeal for him; but the future looked even less promising in a Muslim Pakistan.

The last viceroy of British India visited Kashmir in July 1947 in an effort to convince the maharaja to accede to either India or Pakistan. However, he was suspicious of the British and resisted Mountbatten's pressure to make a definite decision. Hoping to achieve independence, the maharaja arrested most of the state's politicians and tried to arrange "standstill agreements"—status quo arrangements—with both India and Pakistan.

The importance of this territory for Pakistan lay in the fact that the upper regions of four of the rivers upon which Pakistan depended for irrigation—the Indus River and its tributaries—were inside Kashmir or on the border. The location of Kashmir, contiguous to India and Pakistan, Chinese-controlled Tibet, and the Afghanistan-controlled narrow Wakhan corridor leading to the Soviet

Union, endowed it with strategic value. For India, in addition to the strategic dimension, Kashmir, the only Muslim majority state in independent India, was crucial to its claim and goal of being a secular, multireligious, pluralist democracy.

The communal rioting in Punjab spread to Jammu, where Hindu and Sikh refugees attacked Muslims. In September a Muslim revolt against the government of Kashmir erupted in the western part of the state. A provisional *Azad* (Free) Kashmir government was established by the rebels. At this point, with much of the northern and northwestern parts of the subcontinent in near chaos, Muslim tribesmen from the North West Frontier Province of Pakistan invaded Kashmir. Pakistan aided these tribesmen by allowing them to use its territory as a base and enabling them to pass through to Kashmir.

Crisis

The trigger to India's crisis was an invasion of the Kashmir valley by Pakistan-armed and Pakistan-backed Muslim tribesmen from the North West Frontier Province on 24 October 1947. The (Hindu) maharaja of Kashmir immediately appealed to India for help in suppressing the threat to his rule. India responded on the 26th, only after receiving Kashmir's formal accession, by ordering an airlift of troops, equipment, and supplies into the area. This triggered Pakistan's crisis on 27 October.

On 6 February 1948 rebel forces launched an attack on the key junction of Naushara. At that point Pakistani officers realized that the Azad Kashmir forces could not hold the Indian army. They decided to maintain the Pakistani Seventh Division in position behind the front. Pakistan's major response came on 17 March 1948, long after it had become involved in a related crisis over Junagadh: Pakistan launched an unsuccessful attack on Poonch that resulted in an Indian spring offensive. The crisis over Kashmir ended for both India and Pakistan with a UN-mediated cease-fire on 1 January 1949.

India referred the issue to the UN, charging Pakistan with complicity in the tribal invasion: it asked the Security Council to call upon Pakistan to halt its assistance to the Muslim tribesmen fighting in Kashmir. Pakistan charged New Delhi with genocide. Resolutions were adopted on 15 and 17 January 1948 calling upon the parties to refrain from aggression. A UN Commission for India and Pakistan *(UNCIP)* was established to investigate and mediate the dispute. After much delay *UNCIP* submitted a three-part resolution proposing a cease-fire, Indian and Pakistani withdrawals, with India retaining forces in Kashmir to maintain order, and a plebiscite. Pakistan refused. A cease-fire resolution of the Security Council was finally accepted by both parties in December 1948 and took effect on 1 January 1949.

The U.S. and the USSR were not involved in this crisis.

(Since then two-thirds of Jammu and Kashmir has been occupied by India and one-third by Pakistan, with a UN Observer Group to monitor the cease-fire. Almost half a century later, the conflict over Kashmir remains unresolved).

(See *Master Table,* pp. 688–89.)

Sources
Birdwood 1956; Blinkenberg 1972; Brecher 1953; Brines 1968; Choudhury 1968; Das Gupta 1958; Day 1987; Ganguly 1986; Goodspeed 1967; Gupta 1966; Hodson 1985; *Keesing's* 1973; Korbel 1954; Lamb 1966; Menon 1956; Muhammad 1967; Nehru 1956.

(124) Hyderabad

India experienced a crisis over Hyderabad from 21 August to 18 September 1948.

Background and Pre-crisis
Hyderabad was the second largest princely state in the subcontinent, after Jammu and Kashmir. It is located in the geographic center of India and, in 1948, 80 percent of its population was Hindu while most of the political elite were Muslim. The nizam of Hyderabad did not favor accession to distant Pakistan. Nor did predominantly Hindu India attract him. He therefore opted for independence a few days after the British left. The Indian government stated that Hyderabad was far too important to India's territorial integrity and economic needs to be permitted to choose independence.

Throughout late 1947 and early 1948 tension and communal violence mounted. India, insisting that the nizam liberalize his government and curb the violence, organized an economic blockade. The nizam then loaned Pakistan some of his Government of India securities which it began to cash, despite promises not to do so while the Standstill Agreement between Hyderabad and India continued to operate. These developments, coupled with border raids and frequent attacks on trains passing through the state territory, had undermined the Standstill Agreement. Hyderabad raised the question of arbitration on the alleged breaches of the Agreement; but the infringements had become relatively unimportant in the context of the increasing deterioration of law and order within the state.

Crisis
India's crisis over the state of Hyderabad, which had proclaimed its independence, was triggered on 21 August 1948 by Hyderabad's request for UN discussion of India's economic blockade and incidents of violence in the area. India's reply to a grave threat to its territorial integrity came on 9 September after efforts to deploy Indian troops in the state failed. A decision was taken to send troops into Hyderabad to restore law and order: this was implemented on the 15th. The crisis terminated on 18 September 1948 when an Indian military governor was appointed and a military administration was installed in Hyderabad.

On 23 September the nizam sent a cable to the Security Council withdrawing the Hyderabad case from its agenda. Pakistan continued to press for discussion, but it was ultimately dropped. Hyderabad's complaint to the Security Council was included in the Council's provisional agenda. India argued that, because

Hyderabad was not an independent state, it had no right to seek international legal intervention in what was a purely domestic affair. There was no substantive consideration of the question at the UN. Neither the U.S. nor the USSR was involved in this crisis.

(See *Master Table*, pp. 688–89.)

Sources
See sources for Case #119.

(135) Punjab War Scare I

Another crisis for India and Pakistan began on 7 July 1951 and ended the following month.

Pre-crisis
Protests against a number of alleged Pakistani violations of the Kashmir Cease-Fire Agreement of 1 January 1949 (see Case #119 above) were made to the UN Security Council by India in the latter half of June 1951. In a letter on 25 June it was stated that the Indian government saw the incidents as being "very grave," especially when "coupled with the fanatical war propaganda that is daily growing in volume in Pakistan which justify the suspicion that they are part of a planned program calculated to lead, if unchecked, to an outbreak of hostilities between the two countries." The Pakistani minister of Kashmir affairs maintained that there was nothing new or extraordinary in the incidents mentioned by India.

Crisis
India's crisis was triggered on 7 July 1951 when Pakistan moved a brigade to within 15 miles of the Kashmir district of Poonch. These military movements, along with the perception of talk of *jihad* (holy war) and the growing evidence of political instability in Pakistan, led Prime Minister Nehru to respond on 10 July with an order to move Indian troops to the Punjab border and to Jammu and Kashmir. Leaves for Indian army officers were canceled. Nehru's response constituted the trigger to Pakistan's crisis.

Acting upon advice by Pakistan's Chief of Staff, General Ayub Khan, that Pakistan was unprepared for war, Prime Minister Liaquat Ali Khan decided to attempt to manage the crisis through diplomatic channels. His major response, on 15 July, was to inform a press conference that the heavy concentration of Indian troops was within easy striking distance of Pakistan's borders. He requested that Nehru remove the threat and added that Pakistan "would not allow itself to be intimidated or influenced by any threat of force." In addition, on 27 July, four battalions of the Pakistan National Guard were sent to reinforce the Pakistani army on the border. Prolonged correspondence between Nehru and Liaquat Ali Khan took place from 15 July throughout August.

The crisis wound down sometime in August when the withdrawal of forces by both armies began. Violence was not employed by either country.

U.S. activity was limited to an expression of concern. There was no Soviet activity. Dr. Frank Graham, the UN-appointed Representative for India and Pakistan, that is, Kashmir, was in the area from 30 June to the end of July and had discussions with Nehru, Liaquat Ali, and other officials; but his offer of good offices was ineffective in abating the crisis.

(See *Master Table,* pp. 690–91.)

Sources
Ayub Khan 1967; Gopal 1979.

(214) Rann of Kutch
A crisis over territory between India and Pakistan, one of several since 1947, lasted from 8 April until 30 June 1965.

Background
The princely state of Kutch acceded to the Indian Union in 1947; but Pakistan claimed the northern part of the Rann of Kutch as its territory. Incidents occurred in 1956, but Indian control over the disputed territory was quickly restored. In January 1965 Pakistani forces began patrolling in areas claimed by India.

Crisis
Crises were triggered for India and Pakistan on 8 April 1965 when each attacked the other's police post in the disputed territory (the question, who attacked first, remains shrouded in competing reports by the two crisis actors). On the 14th both parties agreed to stop fighting; but intense military hostilities resumed during the last week of April.

The U.K. called for a cease-fire based upon the restoration of positions held by each side as of 1 January 1965. This was followed by intense trilateral negotiations, involving New Delhi, Islamabad, and London, ending in a cease-fire agreement on 11 May. However, the crisis for India and Pakistan did not end until 30 June, when both parties agreed to all the terms of the cease-fire: mutual withdrawal of forces; direct negotiations; and arbitration, if all else failed to settle the dispute.

Moscow expressed the hope that India and Pakistan would exercise restraint and settle the dispute in a manner safeguarding the interests of both states. A U.S. statement deplored the fighting and offered American help in restoring peace to the subcontinent. India charged that Pakistani forces were using American equipment. And U.S.-Indian relations deteriorated. Beijing supported Pakistan throughout the crisis.

(A few months later, India and Pakistan were at war once more [see Case #216 below].)

(On 19 February 1968 the ad hoc Indo-Pakistani Western Boundary Tribunal, established by the U.K.-mediated agreement of 30 June 1965, awarded India 90 percent of the Rann of Kutch and 10 percent [300 square miles] to Pakistan.) (See *Master Table,* pp. 704–5.)

Sources
See sources for Case #216 below.

(216) Kashmir II

The second India/Pakistan crisis over Kashmir—there had been many incidents—lasted from 5 August 1965 to 10 January 1966.

Pre-crisis
In accordance with the Rann of Kutch agreement (see Case #214 above), Pakistan's President, Ayub Khan, ordered the withdrawal of all Pakistani troops from the frontiers with India on 2 July 1965. Shortly thereafter similar instructions were issued to Indian forces.

Crisis
Another 1965 crisis for India was triggered on 5 August when Pakistani "freedom fighters" began infiltrating into the Vale of Kashmir to create a large-scale uprising against Indian control over most of the former princely state. On 25 August India sent several thousand troops across the 1949 Kashmir Cease-Fire Line, capturing most of the areas through which the infiltrators came and triggering a crisis for Pakistan. The latter responded on 1 September by dispatching an armored column across the cease-fire line in southern Kashmir and threatening the vital road linking the capital city of Srinagar with the plains of India. India's major response was to invade West Pakistan on 5 September. On 4 and 6 September, the UN Security Council called for a cease-fire and the withdrawal of armed forces. On the 7th China denounced Indian "aggression" against Pakistan and alleged Indian provocation on the border of Sikkim and Tibet.

An intrawar crisis was triggered for India on 16 September when China issued an ultimatum: unless the Indian government dismantled all military bases near the Chinese border and stopped all intrusions into China, it would have to bear full responsibility for the grave consequences. India responded on the 17th by rejecting Chinese allegations while hinting at a willingness to make minor concessions. Although India reported Chinese troop movements to within 500 meters of Indian positions on the 18th, by 21 September China had withdrawn its ultimatum by an announcement on Beijing Radio that India had complied with the Chinese demands. This diversionary crisis for India was thus resolved on 21 September 1965.

The threat of Chinese intervention stimulated the superpowers to seek a rapid termination of the war between India and Pakistan. New efforts were made through the Security Council. A resolution, to which both parties agreed, was drawn up on 17 September, and the UN Observer Mission, in Kashmir since 1949, was strengthened. Military hostilities subsided by 25 September. However, this did not mark the termination of the crisis, for both armies still faced each other across the Punjab border, each occupied one another's territory, and a series of violations of the cease-fire agreement occurred.

On 17 September Soviet Premier Kosygin proposed a conference in Tashkent between Pakistan's President Ayub Khan and India's Prime Minister Shastri. The conference, held between 4 and 10 January 1966, ended with a declaration affirming the intentions of both parties to restore diplomatic, economic, and trade relations, to withdraw troops to the internationally recognized borders, and to repatriate prisoners of war. The Tashkent Declaration ended the crisis on 10 January 1966.

On 8 September 1965 U.S. Secretary of State Rusk had informed the Senate that the U.S. had suspended military aid to both India and Pakistan and that no new commitments of economic assistance to either party had been made. Since the U.S. was the sole supplier of arms to Pakistan, while India received arms from several sources, notably the USSR, the embargo was especially effective against Pakistan.

UN Secretary-General U Thant visited the area but was unable to persuade either side to take a more flexible position. However, the Security Council resolution of 17 September was agreed to by India on the 20th and by Pakistan on the 22nd.

(See *Master Table*, pp. 704–5.)

Sources
Barnds 1972; Blinkenberg 1972; Brines 1968; Brzoska and Pearson 1994; Burke 1973; Choudhury 1968; Ganguly 1986; Gopal 1967; Kavic 1967; Korbel 1954; Lamb 1966; Thornton 1985.

(242) Bangladesh

The crisis over Bangladesh took place from 25 March to 17 December 1971; Bangladesh, Pakistan, and India were the crisis actors.

Background and Pre-crisis
When the British withdrew from the Indian subcontinent in 1947, West and East Pakistan were separated by 1,000 kilometers of Indian territory. Since 1958 Pakistan was ruled by a military junta led by Ayub Khan and, later, Yahya Khan. The overwhelming victory of the Awami League in the 1970 East Pakistan (East Bengal) elections for representatives to the Pakistan National Assembly placed Pakistan's political structure in jeopardy, especially the supremacy of the military-controlled executive over representative institutions, and West Pakistan's dominance over East Pakistan. Negotiations between the two principal political leaders, West Pakistan's Zulfikar Ali Bhutto and the Awami League's Sheikh

Mujibar Rahman, including an offer of the prime ministership to the latter, failed to break the impasse.

In mid-February 1971 a decision was made by the military rulers in West Pakistan to suppress the growing fervor of East Bengali nationalism. Troops were posted to the East. On 1 March President Yahya Khan postponed the opening of the National Assembly. This was protested by the Awami League, which launched a noncooperation movement on the 6th. A declaration of Bangladesh's independence was scheduled for 6 March; but on that day Yahya Khan announced that the National Assembly would convene on 25 March. While the West Pakistani military buildup in East Pakistan continued, the Awami League took over civil administration of the region.

Crisis
On 25 March a crisis for Bangladesh (still formally known as East Pakistan and East Bengal) was triggered by a West Pakistani army attack on the student dormitories of Dacca University. The response, the following day, was a declaration of independence by East Bengali political leaders. This triggered a crisis for Pakistan, which responded the same day by outlawing the Awami League and suppressing the East Pakistan (East Bengal) revolt with violence. While fighting raged over the spring and summer, an estimated nine million refugees fled from Bangladesh to India, causing severe economic problems there. A number of these refugees were then trained and armed by India to fight the West Pakistanis.

Throughout the autumn of 1971 there were minor clashes between the Indian and Pakistani armies. The situation reached crisis proportions for India when, on 12 October, orders were given to concentrate Pakistani troops on the Indian Punjab border. On 21 November the Indian army crossed into West Pakistan, causing another crisis for Pakistan, already at war with Bangladesh. Pakistan responded on 3 December with an air attack on Indian airfields in Kashmir. Indian forces poised on the East Pakistan border overwhelmed the Pakistani troops in the seceding territory within a fortnight. The war ended on 17 December 1971 with Pakistan's surrender and the emergence of a new sovereign state on the Indian subcontinent.

The UN, approached by Bangladesh in March 1971, declared the problem an internal matter for Pakistan. The Security Council was the most active UN organ; it discussed the situation several times but was unable to pass a resolution, due to a Soviet veto. During the war between Pakistan and India, on 7 December, the General Assembly succeeded in passing a resolution calling for a cease-fire, which, although ignored by India, did have a marginal effect on abating the crisis. On 22 December the Security Council passed a compromise resolution calling for the withdrawal of all armed forces "as soon as practicable."

The most important Soviet activity was the signing of a Treaty of Friendship with India in August 1971, providing active support by a superpower in case of war with Pakistan. The USSR also moved naval vessels in the direction of the Bay of Bengal on 15 December, as a symbol of support for India. And it moved troops closer to the Sino/Soviet border in order to deter Beijing from becoming involved. Besides considerable U.S. political activity, its Seventh Fleet was moved into the Bay of Bengal on 13 December 1971, in support of Pakistan. (See *Master Table*, pp. 710–11.)

Sources
Anderson with Clifford 1973; Ayoob and Subrahmanyam 1972; Ball 1974; Barnds 1972; Blinkenberg 1972; Brzoska and Pearson 1994; Burke 1974; Chopra 1974; Choudhury 1974; Day 1987; Feldman 1975; Gandhi 1972; Ganguly 1986; Garthoff 1985; Hall 1978; Hollen 1980; Isaacson 1992; Jackson 1975; Jain 1974a, 1974b; Keegan 1983; Kissinger 1979; Misra 1973; Nixon 1978; Palit 1972; Rahman 1972; Rizvi 1981; Sen Gupta 1974, 1981; Sisson and Rose 1990.

(372) Punjab War Scare II

India and Pakistan were embroiled in one of the many crises during their protracted conflict from mid-January to 19 February 1987.

Background
Despite periodic attempts to improve relations between India and Pakistan, the dominant traits for almost half a century have been mutual mistrust, hostility, tension, and frequent eruptions of violence. So it was in 1986, when relations worsened because of renewed fighting in Kashmir, a prize territory in dispute since independence (see Cases #119—**Kashmir I**, in 1947–49; #216—**Kashmir II**, in 1965–66; above, and #392—**Kashmir III**, in 1990, below), and because of India's allegation of Pakistan's material assistance to Sikh guerrilla activities aimed at independence in the Indian state of Punjab.

The concerns of both parties began to escalate when the adversary's forces did not return to their bases after substantial military exercises in October–December 1986 along the Indo/Pakistani border. At the beginning of December India and Pakistan increased the number of soldiers concentrated near their border, each side claiming it was part of routine military exercises in the area.

Crisis
In mid-January 1987 Indian reports claimed that Pakistani troops had crossed the Sutlej, one of the five major rivers in the Indus river system, and had massed troops and equipment in Pakistani (West) Punjab. The Pakistani buildup triggered a crisis for India in mid-January.

Tension intensified with reports of a large-scale Indian military exercise code-named "Brass Tacks" in the Rajasthan Desert contiguous to Pakistan. On 20 January Prime Minister Rajiv Gandhi expressed India's "tremendous concern" over the continuing massing of Pakistani troops along the border; but he added that India was always willing to discuss the situation with Pakistan to solve their problems.

India's major response to the crisis, on 23 January, was to place its army and air force on red alert and to move troops closer to the border. An Indian defence ministry spokesman said "India will not be taken by surprise"; and the Indian navy was asked to "keep its eyes open." India's crisis management also took the form of diplomacy: Pakistan's high commissioner to New Delhi was summoned to the Ministry of External Affairs the same day and was asked to convey to Islamabad India's concern over the continuing deployment of Pakistani troops on the border. At the same time India's view of Pakistan's warlike activities was also communicated to the U.S. and Soviet ambassadors and to the members of the UN Security Council, with an expression of India's sincere desire to de-escalate the tension.

India's assertive military and diplomatic response triggered a crisis for Pakistan. Whatever the intention of its military buildup, Pakistan adopted a conciliatory line at once. India's high commissioner (ambassador) to Islamabad was informed on the 23rd of Pakistan's willingness to begin a dialogue in order to wind down the border tension. And the next day Pakistan's high commissioner to Delhi said his country had no aggressive intentions. He described the deployment of Pakistani troops as part of normal military exercises; and he repeated Pakistan's willingness for immediate talks to defuse the tension. This was reciprocated by an Indian defence ministry spokesman, who declared that India's escalatory military moves were only a reaction to the provocative movements of Pakistani forces.

In the frame of diplomatic efforts at accommodation, talks began on 31 January in New Delhi at the level of senior civil servants—the foreign secretary of each state. After five days of negotiations India and Pakistan signed an agreement on 4 February. It provided for a gradual troop withdrawal, sector-by-sector, to end the military confrontation within 15 days. The two countries agreed "not to attack each other" and to avoid provocative actions along the border. India reportedly agreed that its large-scale military exercise in Rajasthan, Brass Tacks, would remain several kilometers from the border with Pakistan. It was also agreed that further talks would be held in Islamabad later.

On 19 February India and Pakistan completed the withdrawal of their troops from the Ravi-Chenab corridor in the Jammu sector along the border. That terminated the crisis for both sides. (The Brass Tacks exercise ended on 25 March.)

Unlike in earlier South Asian crises, neither of the superpowers, nor the U.K., or the UN, was involved in this India/Pakistan crisis: the global organization was highly involved in 1947–49 (see Case #119—**Kashmir I**), among others; the U.K. was active in 1965 (see Case #214—**Rann of Kutch**); the USSR was an active mediator in 1965–66 (see Case #216—**Kashmir II**); and the U.S. was active in 1971 (see Case #242—**Bangladesh**), among others.

The only, low-key, third party involvement was that of Egypt. On 28 January 1987 President Mubarak phoned Prime Minister Gandhi from Kuwait, where he and Pakistan's President, Zia-ul-Haq, were attending a meeting of the Islamic

Conference Organization. Gandhi asked Mubarak to convey a message to Zia, namely, that he was totally opposed to the military buildup, and to inform all heads of state at the conference that India had no hostile intentions against Pakistan.

(See *Master Table,* pp. 730–31.)

Sources
Asian Recorder 1987; Bajpai 1995; *Data India* 1987; *Facts on File* 1987; *Keesing's* 1987.

(392) Kashmir III: India/Pakistan Nuclear Crisis

India and Pakistan were enmeshed in another crisis over Kashmir, compounded by a near-nuclear confrontation, from 14 January until late June 1990.

Background
As noted, the India/Pakistan conflict over Jammu and Kashmir has persisted since the end of British rule on 15 August 1947, with a norm of high tension, a myriad of incidents, and two full-scale interstate crises (see Cases #119 and 216 above). There was also a Kashmir dimension to the crisis over **Bangladesh** (see Case #242 above).

All through the 1980s anti-India forces in the India-occupied part of Kashmir pressed their opposition to continued Indian rule by (often violent) acts of disobedience, including the taking of hostages, foreign and Indian.

Crisis
A fresh Kashmir crisis for India was triggered by a dramatic act of repression: on 13 January 1990 Indian police opened fire and killed 50 proindependence demonstrators in the Vale of Kashmir; and the next day a statement from Pakistan's foreign office expressed "deep concern over the deteriorating situation in Indian-occupied Kashmir." As often in the past, India's external affairs ministry retorted the next day that Pakistan's statement was "an unacceptable interference in India's internal affairs," catalyzing a crisis for Pakistan. Many escalation points were to follow.

The two foreign ministers met in Delhi on 21–23 January, without any breakthrough. On the 30th India's army chief of staff declared that India's troops were prepared to protect Kashmir's borders "at any cost."

From January to April 1990 Indian Kashmir witnessed violent anti-India demonstrations and brutal suppression by an expanded Indian police and military presence: hundreds of Kashmiris were killed. Evidence that Pakistan was providing paramilitary training, weapons, and funds for Kashmiri militants in Pakistani-held Azad Kashmir and was organizing mass demonstrations in Srinagar against Indian rule only served to reinforce a near-universal conviction in India that Pakistan was responsible for the turmoil within Kashmir.

On 6 April the Jammu and Kashmir Liberation Front seized—and killed—three Indian hostages. On the 11th India's Prime Minister V. P. Singh publicly warned his neighbor: "Our message to Pakistan is that you cannot get away with taking Kashmir without a war." And, ominously in that context, he added that Pakistan would not be permitted to achieve nuclear superiority. On 13, 15, and 16 April the USSR, Iran, and the U.S. expressed concern over the escalating tension in the subcontinent. At the same time India rejected a Pakistani proposal for a fresh UN observer role in Kashmir—there had been a small UN Observer Group in the disputed area since 1949.

After a month of relative calm the crisis escalated on 21 May with the killing of Kashmir's leading Muslim cleric, Maulvi Muhammad Farooq, by unidentified gunmen. It escalated further when Indian security forces killed approximately 100 mourners in a vast throng of 100,000 attending the funeral. This incident, in turn, increased mutual suspicion and fear in both India and Pakistan, especially since, in the spring of 1990, both had deployed large numbers of troops in the desert borderlands of Rajasthan (India) and Sind (Pakistan).

This movement of forces on both sides seemed like another tit-for-tat conventional military confrontation that triggered or escalated an international crisis (see Cases #135 and 372—**Punjab War Scare I, II,** in 1951 and 1987, above). However, in the spring of 1990 a large body of U.S.-intelligence–gathered evidence indicated an ominous dual change in South Asia's balance of power: first, that Pakistan now had a few operational nuclear weapons and that orders had been given by Pakistan's Army Chief of Staff, General Beg, to assemble them at Pakistan's nuclear center, Kahuta; and, second, that in order to prevent a repetition of its humiliating defeat by India in the war over Bangladesh in 1971 (see Case #242 above), Pakistani leaders were prepared to respond with a nuclear strike in case of an (anticipated) Indian invasion of Sind that aimed to cut the rump of West Pakistan into two.

President Bush, alarmed by the growing risk of a miscalculated nuclear war in South Asia, sent Deputy Director of the CIA Robert Gates to Islamabad and Delhi on 20–21 May: he warned President Khan and General Beg that Pakistan would suffer a grave defeat in a war with India; and he warned India's Prime Minister Singh and Army Chief, General Sundarji, that Pakistan, in desperation, might resort to a nuclear strike.

Both sides responded to the escalating crisis with important gestures. Pakistan's leaders agreed to close the training camps for Kashmiri militants. And India invited U.S. military attachés in Delhi to go to Kashmir and Rajasthan to see for themselves that an Indian invasion of Pakistan was not imminent. More important, on 3 June Pakistan began to withdrew its troops from the Indian border for use in reasserting law and order in Sind, where ethnic violence had erupted; and India responded by pulling its troops back from their forward deployment. The winding down of the crisis took several weeks. By late June 1990 the most dangerous India/Pakistan "war scare" had ended.

The UN was not involved in this crisis.

(Tension continued for several months. On 13 August, despite bilateral talks on confidence-building measures on 10–11 August, following an earlier round of talks on 18–19 July, Pakistan accused India of attacking a border post. There was an exchange of heavy artillery fire across the 1949 Kashmir cease-fire line on 20–21 August. By October 1990, with the formation of new governments in both states, India/Pakistan tension declined. The new prime ministers met on 22 November at the fifth summit of the South Asian Association for Regional Cooperation *[SAARC]*.)

(See *Master Table,* pp. 734–35.)

Sources
Ballard 1991; Hersh 1993; Hagerty 1995–96; *Keesing's* 1990; Malik 1993; Malik 1990; Zinkin 1987.

Indochina

The protracted conflict in—and over—**Indochina** lasted from 1946 to 1990. During that period there were two long wars: between France and North Vietnam from 1946 to 1954; and between North Vietnam and the United States from 1964 to 1975. There were also lengthy civil wars between North and South Vietnam and in Laos, as well as invasions and occupations of one state by another in Indochina, notably Vietnam's domination of Cambodia from 1979 to 1989.

During this protracted conflict there were 18 international crises before, during, and after the two long wars, as follows.

Case #139 **Invasion of Laos I,** in 1953;
#145 **Dien Bien Phu,** in 1954;
#167 **Cambodia/Thailand,** in 1958–59;
#180 **Pathet Lao Offensive,** in 1961;
#186 **Vietcong Attack,** in 1961;
#193 **Nam Tha,** in 1962;
#210 **Gulf of Tonkin,** in 1964;
#213 **Pleiku,** in 1965;
#225 **Tet Offensive,** in 1968;
#230 **Vietnam Spring Offensive,** in 1969;
#237 **Invasion of Cambodia,** in 1970;
#241 **Invasion of Laos II,** in 1971;
#246 **Vietnam Ports Mining,** in 1972;
#249 **Christmas Bombing,** in 1972–73;
#258 **Final North Vietnam Offensive,** in 1974–75;
#259 **Mayaguez,** in 1975;
#284 **Vietnam Invasion of Cambodia,** in 1977–79;
#388 **Cambodia Peace Conference,** in 1989–90.

In addition, there were several closely related international crises, notably from the China/Vietnam protracted conflict: Cases #298—**Sino/Vietnam War,** in 1978–79; #351—**Vietnam Incursion into Thailand,** in 1984; #352—**Sino/Vietnam Clashes,** in 1984; #353—**Village Border Crisis I,** in 1984; #371—**Sino/Vietnam Border,** in 1987; #381—**Village Border Crisis II,** in 1987–88; and #384—**Spratly Islands,** in 1988 (see *Master Table*).

General Background

The roots of the **Indochina** protracted conflict can be traced to the era of French colonial rule. Most of Indochina was ruled at the beginning of the nineteenth century by the emperor of Annam. The French presence began in 1858 with the occupation of Saigon, the largest city in Cochin China. During the next 25 years France achieved domination by force of arms and imposed agreements with indigenous rulers.

It began with a Treaty of Saigon in 1862 when the emperor yielded to France de facto control of the three eastern provinces of Cochin China. France occupied the three western provinces of Cochin China in 1867 and captured Hanoi in 1873–74. Under the terms of another Treaty of Saigon, in 1874, the emperor accepted French primacy regarding foreign policy and France's possession of Cochin China. The protectorate was extended to Tonkin and Annam in 1883, completing the process of control over all of Vietnam. Cambodia accepted a French protectorate in 1863; and Laos did so in 1893.

During the next half century French control over Indochina was not seriously challenged from within, although a Vietnamese nationalist movement grew in strength from the late 1920s onward.

Early in 1942 Japan seized power from a gravely weakened France, itself under German occupation. France returned to Indochina in 1945, with the help of its wartime allies. By then the Vietnamese nationalist movement had become a formidable political force. On 2 September 1945, the day of Japan's formal surrender at the end of World War II, Ho Chi Minh proclaimed the independence of the Vietnam Republic. France responded in March 1946 by according Vietnam the status of a "free state" in the French Union.

In terms of the protracted conflict, the first turning-point event occurred on 23 November 1946: the French bombarded the northern port of Haiphong, killing 6,000 people. This marked the onset of the protracted conflict and, within it, the France/Vietnam long war. Early in 1950 the USSR and the PRC formally recognized the Ho Chi Minh regime in Vietnam, while the U.S. and the U.K. recognized Vietnam, Cambodia, and Laos as "associated states" within the French Union. In short, the struggle for control of Indochina became enmeshed with the East/West Cold War very early. They remained inextricably linked until both protracted conflicts ended four decades later.

(139) Invasion of Laos I

The crisis began on 24 March 1953 and faded, with no specific termination date. The two actors were France and Laos.

Pre-crisis

The invasion of Laos occurred during the first Indochina long war, which had begun after the restoration of French control following World War II. Within Laos there were communist-oriented guerrilla groups, the Pathet Lao, which cooperated with the Vietminh guerrillas of Vietnam. The northern frontier of Laos was occupied by Vietminh forces in December 1952; and, for the next three months, they massed along the border. By mid-March 1953 their strength had grown to four divisions.

Crisis

The crisis trigger for France can be dated 24 March when the massing of Vietminh troops in Laos reached its peak. The trigger for Laos was the launching of a Vietminh offensive on 5 April. The French responded on 13 April by evacuating the first major town along the Laos border. The same day Laos ordered a general mobilization and appealed to the UN to halt the invasion. On the 27th Prince Souphanouvong declared the formation of a "Free Laotian Government." Vietminh forces surrounded the airfield and the fortified camp on the *Plaine des Jarres* and advanced toward the two Laotian capitals of Vientiane (administrative) and Luang Prabang (royal). French-Laotian troops, supplied by an extensive airlift from Saigon, clashed with the Vietminh at Sam-heva. The widely dispersed Vietminh garrisons began withdrawing to North Vietnam by mid-May, leaving behind Laotian guerrilla forces. The French proceeded to recapture the abandoned position. On 2 June two columns of French-Laotian forces advancing north and south reestablished contact between the provinces of Vientiane and Xiengkhouang. Fighting erupted and subsided and finally led to the Navarre military plan and the Battle of Dien Bien Phu the following year (see Case #145), with no precise termination date for this crisis.

There was no UN or USSR involvement. The only regional organization activity was a communiqué on 25 April by *NATO* citing the invasion of Laos as an example of continuing communist aggression.

(See *Master Table*, pp. 690–91.)

Sources

Buttinger 1967; Goldstein 1973; Gravel 1971, vol. I; Gurtov 1967; Hammer 1966; Lebar 1960; Stevenson 1972.

(145) Dien Bien Phu

The crisis over Dien Bien Phu for France, the U.S., and the U.K. lasted from 13 March to 21 July 1954.

Background and Pre-crisis

France's strategy in the first Indochina War (1946–54) changed in early 1953 when a new commander, Henri Navarre, arrived in its Southeast Asia colony. Laos had been invaded by the communist-led Vietminh (see Case #139—**Invasion of Laos I** above); and the French sought proof of their ability to remain in Indochina before the scheduled May 1954 Geneva Conference on Indochina. The new strategy consisted of regrouping and reinforcing local forces and areas held by the French and opening areas held by the Vietminh. This plan was not successful.

Dien Bien Phu lay in a flat valley surrounded by Vietminh-occupied hills on the entrance road to Laos and at the crossroads of three other roads. Throughout the winter of 1953–54 the French fortified the area. The plan was to draw the Vietminh forces to Dien Bien Phu for a showdown battle. Both forces underestimated the strength of their adversary.

Crisis

On 13 March 1954 the Vietminh launched their first major offensive against Dien Bien Phu, triggering a crisis for France. By 17–18 March the surrounding French defensive positions had been taken. France's major response, on the 20th, was an appeal to its allies for increased aid and the threat of strong military action, to be used as a bargaining chip in an anticipated negotiated settlement. This appeal—the call for direct and immediate U.S. involvement in the war—triggered a crisis for the United States.

French General Ely met with the U.S. Joint Chiefs of Staff on 21 and 24 March and with President Eisenhower on the 22nd. Matters involving the supply of U.S. bombers and ground strategy were discussed. The U.S.'s initial response on 29 March took the form of a speech by Secretary of State Dulles, stressing the vital importance of Indochina to U.S. security; and he proposed that the U.S. and its allies meet the communist threat with undefined "united action." The next day the second Vietminh offensive began.

Strategy discussions were held by the U.S. Joint Chiefs from 29 March to 3 April. A plan, "Operation Vulture," was proposed by Admiral Radford, Chairman of the Joint Chiefs of Staff, for limited tactical nuclear air strikes against Vietminh positions around Dien Bien Phu by the Seventh Fleet then positioned in the Philippines. The U.S. president rejected this proposal. The need to strengthen France's will to fight was emphasized. There was also a plan to dispatch seven armored divisions—contingent upon the U.S. being allowed to train the South Vietnamese forces. This did not appeal to either France or the U.K.

The U.K.'s crisis was triggered on 11 April by Dulles's arrival in London, posing a threat of pressure for direct British participation in the Indochina War. The same day another Vietminh attack brought its forces within a quarter of a mile of the French stronghold, cutting off the use of its airstrip and preventing the evacuation of the wounded, as well as the arrival of supplies. In London Dulles reiterated that his plan for united action was not designed to prejudice the upcoming Geneva talks on Indochina, scheduled to begin on 8 May. On 13 April Dulles and Prime Minister Eden issued a statement referring to a regional collective defense arrangement, under the UN Charter, which would be considered at the Geneva Conference. A similar U.S.-France statement was issued the next day.

On 21 April General Navarre informed Paris that Dien Bien Phu could not hold out unless there were allied air attacks on Vietminh supply routes. Dulles, in Paris for a *NATO* meeting, met with Eden and heard Prime Minister-Foreign Minister Bidault's request for air strikes. The U.S. refused to act without U.K. cooperation, which Eden would not grant. U.S. aid was formally requested by France on 25 April. A plan was formulated by Dulles and the French ambassador to London to push for a U.K. decision.

An emergency British cabinet meeting ended with a decision that the U.K. would not join in any "precipitate military intervention" in Indochina before the Geneva Conference, along with a promise to consider a collective defense scheme in the area after the conference. On 26 April Eisenhower stated that, in view of the absence of a joint Allied response, the U.S. would not send ground forces, and no unilateral action would be taken. The U.K.'s crisis ended on 27 April with a speech by Prime Minister Churchill to the House of Commons announcing the nonintervention decision. Eisenhower made a similar statement on the 29th.

On 7 May Dien Bien Phu fell. The following day a formal cease-fire took effect; and the U.S. crisis ended. The crisis for France persisted until the signing of a bilateral armistice agreement with the Vietminh: a final declaration, on 21 July 1954, provided for the partition of Vietnam into north and south, along with a call for elections and unification two years later.

A regional collective defense arrangement, first considered at the beginning of April 1954, became the basis for the Southeast Asia Treaty Organization *(SEATO)*. The UN was not involved in this intrawar crisis.

(See *Master Table*, pp. 692–93.)

Sources
Foreign Relations of the United States (FRUS) 1952–54, vol. XII; Anderson 1991; Artaud 1990; Billings-Yun 1988; Burke and Greenstein 1989; Davidson 1991; Eisenhower 1963; Ely 1964; Fall 1966; Giap 1962; Gibbons 1986, vol. I; Gravel 1971, vol. I; Hammer 1966; Herring and Immerman 1984; Hoopes 1973; Immerman 1987; Khong 1992; Lacouture and Devillers 1969; Laniel 1957; Navarre 1956; O'Ballance 1964; Radford and Jurika 1980; Randle 1969; Roberts 1954; Steinberg 1996.

(167) Cambodia/Thailand

A crisis for Thailand and Cambodia took place from 24 July 1958 to 6 February 1959.

Background
Relations between these two Southeast Asian states had been tense for centuries; for long periods Thailand occupied Cambodian territory. Ideological differences, mixed border populations, and extreme suspicion on both sides persisted. The temple of Khao Phra Viharrn, a place of worship for the Cambodian Khmer, was accessible only through Thai-held territory, and even then with much difficulty. Prince Sihanouk of Cambodia claimed that the territory surrounding the temple was part of Cambodia, according to a Franco-Siamese (Thai) treaty of 1907, while the Thai foreign minister claimed it belonged to Thailand, according to the geographic principle of "natural watershed."

Crisis
A crisis for Thailand was triggered on 24 July 1958 when diplomatic relations were established between Cambodia and the PRC. Thailand, fearing communist infiltration, declared a state of emergency on the Cambodian border on 8 August. Negotiations followed, with a final Thai offer to allow Cambodian visitors to the site of the temple. Cambodia rejected the offer. When the negotiations broke down, Thailand's response took a military form: on 1 September 10 bridges on the Thai-Cambodian border were blown up in order to prevent infiltration. This triggered a crisis for Cambodia, which feared Thai involvement in its internal affairs and perceived Thai ambitions to rule all Buddhist countries in Indochina once more. On 7 September several thousand Thais marched to the Cambodian embassy in Bangkok. Cambodia's response was a de facto suspension of diplomatic relations on 24 November 1958. The following day Thailand closed the border between the two countries, withdrew its ambassador from Phnom Penh, and suspended air service between the capitals. The United Nations was introduced into the crisis when Cambodians asked Secretary-General Hammarskjöld to appoint a UN mediator. Baron Johan Beck-Friis, a retired Swiss diplomat, mediated between the adversaries, and, on 6 February 1959, a joint communiqué announced the reopening of the frontier and the return of the respective ambassadors to each other's capital.

The US was not involved in this crisis, the USSR marginally so.

(Subsequent events were an appeal to the International Court of Justice in October 1959 by Cambodia and a rejection of its verdict by Thailand.)

(See *Master Table,* pp. 696–97.)

Sources
Armstrong 1964; Ayal 1961; Blanchard 1958; Darling 1960; Insor 1963; Leifer 1961–62, 1962; Silcock 1967; Vella 1955.

(180) Pathet Lao Offensive

The first Pathet Lao crisis for the United States and Thailand began on 9 March and ended on 16 May 1961.

Pre-crisis
From December 1960 supplies and equipment from the Soviet Union had been airlifted to the Pathet Lao. This aid included heavy weapons and combat specialists.

Crisis
A crisis for the United States was triggered on 9 March 1961 when Pathet Lao troops, with Vietminh support, launched a major offensive breaking through the Laotian government defenses in central Laos, severing the key road junction between Vientiane and Luang Prabang. The Laotian troops retreated and, within days, the two cities were threatened by communist and neutralist troops.

President Kennedy felt that, if Laos were to be abandoned, the communists would hold the north-south road along the Mekong lowlands from which stronger pressure would be mounted against South Vietnam, Cambodia, and Thailand. U.S. troops were ordered to be ready to move into Laos. A helicopter air base was established in Thailand. Supplies and ammunition were stocked at forward bases along the Mekong River. And the task force on Okinawa, specially trained for combat in Southeast Asia, was put on alert. In addition, the Seventh Fleet was sent to the Gulf of Siam. On 23 March Kennedy held a televised news conference in which he warned that USSR and North Vietnam support of the Pathet Lao increased the probability of war, and that the shape of the necessary response would be carefully considered by the U.S. and its *SEATO* allies. At the same time Kennedy supported U.K. proposals for a joint U.S.-USSR appeal for a cease-fire followed by an international conference on Laos.

The situation in Laos deteriorated during April. On the 10th the advance of Pathet Lao forces toward the Mekong River threatened to divide Laos, triggering a crisis for Thailand. Thai troops were sent to the areas bordering Laos. On the 20th, when communist forces advanced to within 10 miles of Takhek, the Thai prime minister declared that the Thai army was ready to go into action immediately if Takhek were attacked. On 28 April some token U.S. forces were ordered into Laos, and the (military) advisors serving in Laos were ordered into uniform and sent into battle with the Laotians. Impressed by the persistence of U.S. resolve, the USSR agreed to cosponsor the U.K. proposal on 24 April. On 3 May a cease-fire between the Laotian government and the Pathet Lao went into effect. And on 16 May the Geneva Conference on Laos opened, terminating the crisis for both the U.S. and Thailand.

The *SEATO* Council met on 27 March at the request of the U.S. A communiqué was issued stating that, if peaceful efforts failed, *SEATO* would take appropriate action. Another session was held on 29 April, and a resolution was passed supporting U.S.-USSR proposals for a cease-fire.

The UN was not involved, the USSR marginally so.

(See *Master Table*, pp. 698–99.)

Sources
See sources for Case #193.

(186) Vietcong Attack

A crisis for South Vietnam and the United States took place from 18 September to 15 November 1961.

Pre-crisis
For several years prior to this crisis Vietcong groups, backed by the North Vietnam regime, had been brought together for attacks on civilian and military centers in South Vietnam. By September 1961 these attacks had trebled in number. Vietcong guerrilla forces were situated in the northern marshlands of South Vietnam. When approached by South Vietnam government forces, they disappeared across the border into North Vietnam making their capture extremely difficult.

Crisis
A crisis for South Vietnam and the United States was triggered on 18 September 1961 when Phuoc Vinh, the provincial capital of Phuoc Thanh, only 55 miles from Saigon, was captured and held for a day by the Vietcong. Before government troops arrived, the provincial governor was publicly beheaded, and arms and ammunition were captured and removed. This attack had a shattering effect on the South Vietnam regime, despite the quick success in forcing the Vietcong to retreat. The United States, whose influence in Southeast Asia had been threatened by North Vietnam and, therefore, Soviet gains, was reluctant to increase its commitment to the area.

In view of the dangerously deteriorating security situation South Vietnam President Diem responded on 29 September by requesting a bilateral defense treaty with the United States. On 11 October President Kennedy and his advisors decided to send National Security Advisor Walt Rostow and General Maxwell Taylor to Vietnam to assess the political and military feasibility of U.S. intervention. A state of emergency was proclaimed in South Vietnam on 19 October.

In a report to the U.S. president on 3 November Rostow and Taylor recommended a significant expansion of U.S. aid to South Vietnam, as well as the dispatch of an 8,000-person logistical task force. On 11 November a joint recommendation from the Secretaries of State and Defense (Rusk and McNamara) to the president stated that a decision to commit ground forces in South Vietnam could be deferred. The U.S. major response, on 15 November, was a National Security Council decision for a limited commitment of aid and advisors to South Vietnam—several hundred specialists in guerrilla warfare, logistics, communication, and engineering—to train South Vietnam forces. Aircraft and other special equipment would be sent as well. That decision ended the crisis for the U.S. and South Vietnam.

The Rostow-Taylor trip to South Vietnam was assailed by Moscow and North Vietnam as a prelude to U.S. military intervention in Southeast Asia. On the regional level, *SEATO*'s military advisors met from 3–6 October and issued a communiqué on the 6th to the effect that practical measures were being taken to increase the effectiveness of *SEATO* defenses.

The UN was not involved.

(See *Master Table,* pp. 700–701.)

Sources
See sources for Case #193; and McNamara 1995.

(193) Nam Tha

The duration of this second Pathet Lao crisis for Thailand and the United States was from 6 May to 12 June 1962.

Pre-crisis
Following the cease-fire of May 1961, talks in Geneva began on the problem of Laos. Negotiations proceeded slowly, with such issues as the seating of the Pathet Lao delegation as a full representative and frequent violations of the cease-fire threatening the continuation of the talks in general. The Kennedy/Khrushchev meeting in Vienna on 3–4 June 1961 resulted in a joint statement calling for a neutralized Laos and an effective cease-fire. Difficulties among the three Laotian factions—pro-communist, pro-West, nonaligned—prevented the forming of a coalition government. Negotiations reached a deadlock in early 1962. This was followed by an increased Pathet Lao military presence in the Nam Tha area bordering Thailand. In February Pathet Lao forces, with Vietminh support, began a siege of the capital of Nam Tha. On 13 February Thai troops were deployed to strategic areas near the Laotian border. At a news conference the following day President Kennedy expressed concern about the situation. By the end of April there was no progress in the negotiations, and new fighting had broken out.

Crisis
A crisis for Thailand and the United States was triggered on 6 May 1962 when a heavy Pathet Lao attack was launched against Nam Tha. Laos government forces retreated without resistance across the Mekong River into Thai territory, abandoning northwest Laos to the Pathet Lao and thereby opening the way for them to move to the northern border of Thailand. On 11 May Thailand's Prime Minister Sarit ordered several units of the Thai armed forces to reinforce defenses along the border with Laos. The United States' response, on 12 May, was an order by President Kennedy to send the Seventh Fleet to the Gulf of Siam and to put U.S.

armed forces elsewhere in the Pacific and at home on standby alert. At the request of the Thai government 1,000 U.S. marines, in Thailand for *SEATO* exercises, were moved to the Laotian border on 14 May. On the 15th Kennedy announced that 4,000 more U.S. troops had been ordered into Thailand to protect its territorial integrity. The U.S. deployment put a stop to the Pathet Lao drive, and political pressure was successful in reopening negotiations.

The crisis ended on 12 June 1962 for both actors when the three Laotian princes (Souvanna Phouma, Boum Oum, and Souphanouvong) signed an agreement on their participation in a "Government of National Union," indicating a tacit understanding between Thailand and the U.S., on the one hand, and North Vietnam, on the other.

An emergency meeting of the *SEATO* Council requested that members send token military forces to Thailand on 16 May: all agreed, with the exception of France. The USSR's involvement was political: Ambassador Dobrynin and U.S. Secretary of State Rusk met on 15 May and agreed on the need to maintain the cease-fire and establish a neutral and independent Laos. The USSR condemned the movement of U.S. troops to Thailand as aggression. There was no UN involvement.

(See *Master Table,* pp. 700–701.)

Sources
Adams and McCoy 1970; Bowles 1971; Brandon 1970; Dommen 1971; *Facts on File* 1973–74; Fall 1969; Gibbons 1986, vol. II; Goldstein 1973; Gravel 1971 vol. I; Hall 1978; Herring 1986; Hilsman 1967; Johnson 1971; Kahin and Lewis 1967; Langer and Zasloff 1970; Lee 1970; Lewy 1978; Macmillan 1973; Neuchterlein 1965; Randolph 1986; Schlesinger 1965; Sorensen 1965; Stevenson 1972; Thee 1973; Toye 1968; Young 1991.

(210) Gulf of Tonkin

The first international crisis of the Vietnam War (1964–75) began on 30 July 1964. It ended for the United States on 7 August. North Vietnam's crisis faded in mid-August.

Background
Until the Gulf of Tonkin crisis in 1964 the U.S. presence in Southeast Asia was limited to military and economic aid to Thailand, Cambodia, and South Vietnam. United States policy in Vietnam was based upon the maintenance of a separate state in South Vietnam. Any support to the insurgency in the south by North Vietnam was viewed as external aggression. The U.S. supported the repressive Ngo Dinh Diem regime in Saigon against rebellion, but the growth of insurgency in the south was rapid. Southerners, regrouped in North Vietnam, began to return to join the expanding military strength of the Vietcong. During 1962 the United States undertook a major military buildup in Vietnam: U.S. helicopter crews took

an active part in the war. A Buddhist uprising against the Diem government, accompanied by acts of suicide by Buddhist monks, dramatized the situation and brought about U.S. political pressure against Diem.

Pre-crisis

On 1 November 1963 Diem was murdered, and a Military Revolutionary Council took power under General Duong van Minh. At that time less than half the territory of South Vietnam was under effective Saigon control. President Kennedy's assassination followed shortly thereafter. In the 1964 presidential campaign, Johnson reassured the public that Americans would not be sent to fight in Vietnam. Nevertheless, he would never permit communist expansion there. Across the Pacific, on 25 July 1964, Hanoi Radio charged that Americans had fired on a North Vietnamese fishing craft.

Crisis

On 30 July 1964 South Vietnamese patrol boats, on a U.S.-backed covert 34A mission, attacked two North Vietnamese islands in the Gulf of Tonkin. This triggered a crisis for North Vietnam. It responded by a tit-for-tat attack on 2 August—the U.S. destroyer *Maddox* was attacked by North Vietnamese torpedo boats in the Gulf of Tonkin off North Vietnam, with a second attack on 4 August against two U.S. destroyers. Neither resulted in casualties or damage.

The U.S. response was prompt. Shortly after the second attack President Johnson ordered an air attack against North Vietnamese gunboats and their supporting facilities. And on the 5th he asked the U.S. Congress to pass a resolution to authorize all necessary action to protect U.S. armed forces and to assist nations covered by the *SEATO* treaty. The Gulf of Tonkin Resolution, giving the president broad war powers in defense of U.S. and allied interests in Southeast Asia, was passed on 7 August. This ended the U.S.'s crisis. The bombing of North Vietnam ceased in mid-August; and North Vietnam's crisis faded shortly thereafter.

The United States requested a UN Security Council meeting and called for a session of *SEATO*, as well as informing its *NATO* allies of events through high-level consultations. Nothing concrete emerged from these meetings. No clear agreement between Hanoi and Washington was reached. The outcome of the crisis led to an escalation of tension in the area. The USSR provided political support to Hanoi.

(See *Master Table*, pp. 704–5.)

Sources

See sources for Case #225; and Austin 1971; Gardner 1995; Gelb with Betts 1979; Gibbons 1986, vol. II; Goulden 1969; Gravel 1971, vols. II, III; Halberstam 1972; Herring 1986; Johnson 1971; Kahin 1986; Kahin and Lewis 1967; McNamara 1995; Windchy 1971.

(213) Pleiku

This intrawar crisis for the United States, South Vietnam, and North Vietnam lasted from 7 February to late March 1965.

Pre-crisis
In the six months after the **Gulf of Tonkin** crisis, fighting took place between South and North Vietnam with minimum U.S. participation. In the United States a debate ensued regarding U.S. commitments to the government in Saigon which, on 27 January 1965, had been taken over by a military coup.

Crisis
A crisis for the United States and South Vietnam was triggered on 7 February 1965 when Vietcong guerrillas staged a night raid against U.S. and South Vietnam army barracks at Pleiku, killing eight and wounding 126. The U.S. response was a decision by President Johnson on the 13th, following a meeting of his National Security Council, in favor of measured and limited air action jointly with South Vietnam against selected military targets in North Vietnam. When news of "Operation Rolling Thunder" became public, on 19 February, it triggered an intrawar crisis (IWC) for North Vietnam.

The Pleiku crisis for the U.S. and South Vietnam ended on 2 March, the day the first of the U.S. air strikes began. This action marked a sharp escalation in the evolution of U.S. involvement in the Vietnam War. For North Vietnam the crisis faded later in March. There was no clear outcome: the U.S. was pulled deeper into the morass of Vietnam; the North Vietnamese suffered from—but learned to adapt to—increased U.S. bombing.

There was minimal UN activity: Secretary-General U Thant called for all sides to negotiate, but his efforts were unsuccessful. The USSR extended military aid to North Vietnam.

(See *Master Table,* pp. 704–5.)

Sources
See sources for Case #210; and Gibbons 1989; Khong 1992; Shapley 1993.

(225) Tet Offensive

The Tet crisis for South Vietnam and the United States began on 30 January and ended on 31 March 1968.

Pre-crisis
"Operation Rolling Thunder" marked a basic U.S. policy change aimed at compelling the enemy to negotiate on Washington's terms. By the end of 1966 U.S. military personnel in South Vietnam had increased to 375,000. The escalation of

the air war proceeded steadily. In early 1965, too, the USSR and China began to provide economic assistance and military equipment to Hanoi. The U.S. bombed the Ho Chi Minh Trail and retreating enemy troops in Cambodia. Bombing was stopped briefly on two occasions in an effort to bring about negotiations, but Hanoi's demand to seat the *FLN* (communist-controlled *Front Liberation National*) of South Vietnam at the conference table as a full and equal partner was rejected by the U.S. Raids were resumed with greater U.S. involvement in Vietnam.

In 1967 an important shift in Soviet policy occurred, indicating a desire to end the war. Each side began by softening its position, leading to cautious optimism. In the summer of 1967 a North Vietnamese offensive undermined that appraisal. North Vietnam's attempt to turn the tide of the war and to place Hanoi and the Vietcong in a stronger position for negotiations led to an attack on a U.S. marine outpost near the Demilitarized Zone (DMZ) between the two parts of Vietnam on 21 January 1968. The Vietcong announced a three-day truce from the 27th, but South Vietnam revealed its decision to continue the bombing of the North. During the *Tet* (lunar New Year) holiday the Vietcong launched its biggest offensive.

Crisis
On 30 January 1968 a Vietcong attack on Saigon, Hué, and 36 of the 44 provincial capitals in South Vietnam, along with military installations and district towns, triggered another intrawar crisis for South Vietnam. The South Vietnamese responded on 2 February by urging an extension of U.S. bombing of North Vietnam to cover all military objectives. After heavy fighting the Vietcong were expelled from all the towns into which they had infiltrated.

A state of martial law in the south was declared by President Thieu. In Saigon a 24-hour curfew was imposed so that the South Vietnam army could drive out the Vietcong unhindered by the civilian population. American infantry and tanks were rushed to the city on 1 February, and a U.S. general assumed control of the whole operation. The main Vietcong forces withdrew on 3 February; but on the 18th another attack was launched in and around the capital. Fighting continued until the 24th, when the Vietcong troops were expelled once more. This terminated the Tet crisis for South Vietnam. The U.S. ordered more combat troops into the area.

A pessimistic report on 27 February by the Chairman of the U.S. Joint Chiefs of Staff, General Wheeler, on the situation in Vietnam shocked Washington and triggered a U.S. crisis. President Johnson's major response to the Tet Offensive was an announcement on 31 March that he had ordered a halt to the bombing of North Vietnam and had renewed a U.S. willingness to negotiate. This policy decision ended the U.S. crisis, for it marked the beginning of a fundamental change in Washington's appraisal of the Vietnam War.

The Vietcong was defeated militarily; but it scored a psychological and political victory. Its belief that a massive offensive against the cities and towns would demonstrate the weakness of the government in the South and bring about a general uprising of civilians proved wrong and caused its military defeat; but the battle raised public opposition in the U.S. to a new level of intensity. The president and his advisors were shocked by the suddenness and magnitude of the Tet Offensive; and this crisis proved to be a turning point on the American path to disengagement from Vietnam five years later.

A mediation proposal by the UN Secretary-General during the Tet crisis proved ineffective. The Warsaw Pact condemned South Vietnam and the U.S. Soviet involvement included active military personnel in the antiaircraft operations by the North and the supply of arms to Hanoi.

(See *Master Table,* pp. 706–7.)

Sources
Adams and McCoy 1970; Berman 1989; Brandon 1970; Clifford 1991; Davidson 1991; Dommen 1971; Gelb with Betts 1979; Gravel 1971, vol. IV; Herring 1994; Hoopes 1969; Johnson 1971; Karnow 1984; Kearns 1976; Kolko 1985; Lewy 1978; Maclear 1981; Oberdorfer 1971; Rostow 1972; Rusk 1990; Schandler 1977; Schoenbaum 1988; Steinberg 1996; Wirtz 1993.

(230) Vietnam Spring Offensive

A North Vietnam countrywide offensive against the South led to a crisis for the United States and South Vietnam from 22 February until 8 June 1969.

Pre-crisis
The 1968 **Tet Offensive** broke the stalemate that had existed in the Vietnam War since 1966. Thereafter U.S. policy underwent several changes. President Johnson restricted U.S. bombing to south of the 20th Parallel and offered to begin negotiations with North Vietnam, which responded favorably. Agreement was reached to begin talks in Paris. In October 1968 the U.S. announced that all air, naval, and artillery attacks against North Vietnam would be halted on 1 November. The U.S. also agreed to allow representatives of the (South Vietnam) Vietminh National Liberation Front to participate in the talks, despite South Vietnam objections. Nevertheless, while war raged, all parties maintained inflexible positions at the talks. On 20 January 1969 Richard Nixon was inaugurated as President of the United States.

Crisis
On 22 February 1969 Hanoi launched an offensive into South Vietnam, the day before a scheduled Nixon visit to Europe, triggering a crisis for the U.S. According to Nixon the offensive was a deliberate test, clearly designed to take the measure of the new Nixon administration. On 23 February Nixon ordered the bombing of sanctuaries in Cambodia but canceled the order two days later upon the recommendation of National Security Advisor Kissinger. On 4 March orders

were once more given, only to be retracted on the 7th. Meanwhile U.S. casualties were mounting. Finally, as the North Vietnam attack continued, and U.S. casualties remained intolerably high, Nixon reverted to his earlier decisions; and on 15 March orders were given to bomb Cambodian sanctuaries ("Operation Menu"). These orders were carried out three days later, terminating the U.S. crisis. Thereafter there was a steady decline in U.S. casualties in Vietnam.

The secret bombing of Vietcong sanctuaries in Cambodia put military pressure on the North Vietnamese. Nevertheless, they were still able to launch a major attack throughout South Vietnam on 12 May 1969: it contained the largest number of strikes since the **Tet Offensive.** These attacks catalyzed a crisis for South Vietnam. The crisis was accentuated by Nixon's 14 May speech in which he elaborated an eight-point peace plan for Vietnam that included the setting of a precise timetable for withdrawal and a cease-fire under international supervision.

Saigon's fears about U.S. intentions and a possible change in the military balance, which would threaten South Vietnam's existence, caused President Thieu to object strongly to U.S. proposals for withdrawal from South Vietnam. On 17 May Thieu responded by calling for a meeting with Nixon in order to coordinate a common policy. Nixon and Thieu met on 8 June on Midway Island. Nixon's assurances that day of steadfast U.S. support terminated the crisis for South Vietnam. After the meeting Nixon announced the redeployment of 25,000 U.S. troops from Vietnam. Although Thieu was appeased by U.S. guarantees, he perceived the withdrawal as an irreversible process that would end with the departure of all American forces from Vietnam.

There was no UN or USSR activity, although Secretary-General U Thant issued a statement applauding the peace efforts of both sides.

SEATO and *CENTO* meetings were held in May at which the Vietnam War was reviewed.

(See *Master Table,* pp. 708–9.)

Sources
See sources for Case #237; and *Facts on File* 1973–74.

(237) Invasion of Cambodia

A crisis over Cambodia occurred from 13 March to 22 July 1970. The crisis actors were North Vietnam, Cambodia, South Vietnam, and the United States.

Pre-crisis
Despite Cambodia's declaration of neutrality in the ongoing war in Indochina, eastern Cambodia was being used by the Vietcong *(Front Liberation National* or *FLN)* and North Vietnamese as a base for launching military operations against South Vietnam. From March 1969 the United States had been secretly bombing enemy sanctuaries in Cambodia. As a result, the Vietcong began to move deeper into Cambodia, bringing them into increasing conflict with Cambodian authori-

ties. The situation, coupled with Cambodia's deepening economic crisis, placed ruling Prince Sihanouk in a precarious position. On 8 March and again on the 11th, while Sihanouk was in France for medical treatment, there were violent demonstrations in Phnom Penh demanding the removal of Vietcong and North Vietnamese troops from Cambodia. These demonstrations were denounced by Sihanouk. On 12 March the two houses of the Cambodian parliament met in a joint session and adopted a resolution condemning the presence of the Vietcong and North Vietnamese on Cambodian territory and demanding that the Cambodian army be expanded. On 12 March an announcement was made suspending the trade agreement that allowed the Vietnamese to use Sihanoukville Port and purchase supplies in Cambodia.

Crisis

A crisis for North Vietnam was triggered on 13 March 1970 when the Cambodian foreign ministry sent notes to the Vietcong provisional government and to the North Vietnam government demanding that all Vietcong and North Vietnamese troops be withdrawn from Cambodia within 48 hours. Sihanouk left Paris for meetings in Moscow with President Podgorny and Premier Kosygin in order to get their support in persuading Hanoi and the *FLN* to curb their activities in Cambodia. On 18 March he traveled to Beijing for the same reason. That day the Cambodian National Assembly deposed Prince Sihanouk. The following day it declared a state of emergency, suspending a number of civil liberties. On the 21st Cheng Heng became the new Head of State.

The crisis trigger for Cambodia came on 23 March when Sihanouk issued a proclamation dissolving the new government in Cambodia and announcing his intention of forming a Government of National Union and a National Liberation Army. Mass demonstrations in support of Sihanouk began on 26 March, with the Cambodian armed forces being placed on alert. Vietcong troops moved deeper into Cambodia; and on 31 March North Vietnam responded to the crisis by attacking a Cambodian regiment 100 miles northeast of Phnom Penh and five miles from the frontier, marking the beginning of the combined Vietcong, North Vietnamese, and Sihanoukist invasion of Cambodia. By early April these forces had reached the Svay Rieng province known as "Parrot's Beak," which was surrounded by South Vietnam territory on three sides.

The crisis trigger for South Vietnam occurred on 10 April when Cambodian troops were forced to evacuate border positions in Parrot's Beak. Cambodia's major response to the crisis came on the 14th, when Premier Lon Nol stated that, due to the gravity of the situation, the Cambodian government was prepared to accept foreign aid from all sources. A request was sent to the United States the next day and again on 20 April.

The U.S. crisis began on 21 April when communist forces attacked the town of Takeo, cutting the road connecting it with Phnom Penh. The U.S. response, on the 28th, was a decision by Nixon to send U.S. troops into Cambodia. South Vietnam's response, the next day, was to send troops into Cambodia. U.S. troops remained in Cambodia until 30 June 1970, the termination date for North Vietnam and the United States. The crisis for Cambodia and South Vietnam ended on 22 July with the beginning of South Vietnam's withdrawal from Cambodia.

Although Nixon termed the campaign a complete success, the situation in Cambodia remained more or less the same. South Vietnam obtained a victory in Parrot's Beak, and North Vietnam obtained a strong foothold in Cambodia.

The UN was approached by Cambodia on 30 March. Secretary-General U Thant proposed peace negotiations, but this had no effect on ending the crisis. The USSR continued to provide political support to North Vietnam.

(See *Master Table,* pp. 710–11.)

Sources
Gordon and Young 1970, 1971; Isaacson 1992; Kalb and Kalb 1974; Kissinger 1979; Nixon 1978; Shawcross 1979; Sihanouk 1970; Simon 1974; Steinberg 1996.

(241) Invasion of Laos II

This intrawar crisis lasted from 8 February until 25 March 1971. The two crisis actors were Laos and North Vietnam.

Pre-crisis
A major North Vietnamese offensive was expected in 1972. U.S. and South Vietnamese military planners therefore scheduled an invasion of Laos, in order to cut off the Ho Chi Minh Trail, through which the North Vietnamese transported supplies to their strongholds in South Vietnam and Cambodia. The invasion was to be carried out by South Vietnamese troops with U.S. air support. Although Laos had been neutralized by the Geneva Protocols of 1954 and 1962, there were thousands of North Vietnamese troops operating there, along with the Pathet Lao communist guerrillas. During the crisis Nixon announced that action to cut off the Ho Chi Minh Trail had been under consideration since 1965.

Crisis
The South Vietnam–U.S. invasion of Laos began on 8 February 1971. This triggered a crisis for Laos, whose borders and neutrality had been violated, and for North Vietnam, against which the invasion was directed. The major response by Laos was a declaration of a state of emergency on 12 February. North Vietnam, too, responded that day by beginning the first wave of a counteroffensive. A day earlier the International Control Commission (ICC) had convened at the urgent request of Canada in order to initiate an investigation into the violation of Laotian neutrality by foreign forces. The ICC reached no conclusion.

At that time Paris was hosting talks among the U.S., South Vietnam, and North Vietnam. South Vietnam stated that there could be no negotiations while North Vietnamese troops remained in Laos.

From the beginning to the middle of March South Vietnamese forces launched a drive to move further into Laos. On 7 March Tchepone, a key town in the Trail network, was captured. It was recaptured after a second major counter-offensive was launched by North Vietnamese troops on 12 March. The U.S. began to airlift South Vietnamese troops out of Laos by mid-March. This was completed by 25 March, the termination date for both crisis actors.

Soviet activity was limited to declarations against the U.S. and South Vietnam. The United States gave South Vietnam air support but announced that it would not use any ground forces. It repeatedly denied support to a possible South Vietnam invasion of the North. The only UN activity was an appeal by Secretary-General U Thant for Laos/Pathet Lao negotiations.

(See *Master Table*, pp. 710–11.)

Sources
Goldstein 1973; Kissinger 1979; Nixon 1978; Stevenson 1972.

(246) Vietnam Ports Mining

South Vietnam, the United States, and North Vietnam were the crisis actors in a Vietnam intrawar crisis that lasted from 30 March to 19 July 1972.

Pre-crisis
The period preceding the 1972 Vietnam Ports Mining crisis was marked by periodic escalation in fighting. Announcements of substantial U.S. troop withdrawals undermined the political strength of the U.S. at the Paris Peace Talks, conducted between Henry Kissinger and the North Vietnamese representatives Le Duc Tho and Xuan Thee. This crisis occurred during a U.S. presidential election year. At the same time there were ongoing demonstrations in the United States against the war in Vietnam.

Crisis
North Vietnam launched another spring offensive in South Vietnam on 30 March 1972, triggering a crisis for South Vietnam and the United States. South Vietnam, perceiving a threat of a further loss of territory, responded the same day with defensive fighting. The U.S. immediately renewed B-52 bombing of the Hanoi-Haiphong industrial complex. Despite these bombings, the North Vietnamese undertook further escalation on 24 April by initiating a renewed attack on South Vietnamese troops in the Central Highlands and forcing them to withdraw. The major U.S. response was an order by President Nixon on 8 May to mine all North Vietnamese ports in an effort to prevent military shipments from reaching North Vietnam by sea.

The announcement of the mining and blockade of the ports triggered a crisis for North Vietnam. Its response to the threat of isolation from crucial sources of supplies was a statement at the Paris Peace Talks on 9 May declaring the American act to be the gravest step so far in the escalation of the war, and that North Vietnam would never accept an American ultimatum. At the same time North Vietnamese delegates appealed to all governments and peoples of fraternal socialist countries to persuade the U.S. to negotiate seriously at the Paris talks.

The USSR and China played constructive roles in abating the crisis. Diplomatic talks between the U.S. and the USSR, including a summit meeting held in Moscow in May, resulted in intensive Soviet pressure on North Vietnam.

The crisis ended for all actors on 19 July 1972 with renewed talks in Paris: the negotiations shifted to a serious exchange of views, with a promise of compromise.

In a letter from UN Ambassador George Bush to the president of the Security Council on 8 May 1972, U.S. actions were reported to be measures of collective self-defense. Secretary-General Waldheim held a series of meetings at the Security Council between 8 and 10 May and advocated an active UN role in ending hostilities. However, he received no support. On 19 May the Security Council merely issued a statement calling on all the parties to act with utmost restraint.

(See *Master Table*, pp. 710–11.)

Sources
See sources for Case #225; and Kalb and Kalb 1974; Kissinger 1979, 1994; Nixon 1978.

(249) Christmas Bombing

This intrawar crisis for South Vietnam, the United States, and North Vietnam began on 23 October 1972 and ended on 27 January 1973.

Pre-crisis
The peace talks at Paris broke down once more; and, when a deadlock could no longer be avoided, it was followed by an escalation in hostilities on the battlefield.

Crisis
The crisis trigger for South Vietnam occurred on 23 October 1972 when it learned of agreements reached between the delegates of the United States and North Vietnam at the Paris talks. The response, the next day, was a public refusal to comply with these agreements. Fighting in Vietnam and negotiations in Paris were carried on simultaneously. But on 4 December 1972 North Vietnam rejected all U.S. proposals and withdrew its acceptance of early changes already agreed upon while making new demands. This triggered a crisis for the U.S. Secretary of State Kissinger surmised that North Vietnam was now willing to risk a break in the talks. When additional meetings on 6, 11, and 13 December ended in stale-

mate, the U.S. concluded that Hanoi had in effect made a strategic decision to prolong the war, abort all negotiations, and seek an unconditional victory.

On 14 December the U.S. responded with an order by Nixon to renew the aerial bombing of the Hanoi-Haiphong military complex and the mining of North Vietnamese ports. Massive bombing began on 17 December and triggered a crisis for North Vietnam. It responded on the 26th by signaling a willingness to return to serious negotiations without preconditions. On the 26th the U.S. bombed the Hanoi railway station, killing 283 people and wounding 266. North Vietnam proposed 8 January 1973 for meetings in Paris. The crisis ended for all three actors on 27 January, with the formal signing of the Peace Accords in Paris.

As with so many crises during this protracted conflict, the USSR was marginally involved—politically. Neither the UN nor *SEATO* was involved in this crisis.

(See *Master Table*, pp. 712–13.)

Sources
See sources for Cases #225 and 246; and Isaacson 1992.

(258) Final North Vietnam Offensive

The final crisis for South Vietnam and Cambodia during the long war in Indochina occurred from 14 December 1974 to 30 April 1975.

Background
Civil wars in Cambodia and Vietnam persisted after the United States formally withdrew its forces in 1973. The U.S. continued to supply economic and military aid to the governments of both Cambodia and South Vietnam. Some U.S. advisors stayed in the area. By the end of 1974 forces of the Khmer Rouge in Cambodia and the Vietcong and North Vietnamese army in South Vietnam had increased their activities in preparation for a final offensive.

Crisis
The trigger for South Vietnam occurred on 14 December 1974, with the beginning of the North Vietnam offensive. For Cambodia, the crisis was triggered on 1 January 1975 with the launching of a major Khmer Rouge offensive. Several areas in Cambodia were lost and recaptured as fighting raged between the two sides. On 17 February Cambodia responded with a counteroffensive. The South Vietnamese response was a combination of continued fighting, a request to the U.S. for aid, and a tactical retreat instigated by President Thieu on 11 March. On 17 April the Cambodian capital, Phnom Penh, fell to the rebels, forcing the government to flee and marking the end of Cambodia's last crisis in the Vietnam War. Meanwhile, North Vietnamese troops pressed on with their offensive as the South Vietnam army retreated toward Saigon. Thousands of refugees fled before

the advancing troops, clogging the roads and filling the ports and airports. Saigon fell on 30 April, ending the crisis—and independent existence—for South Vietnam.

U.S. involvement took the form of aid to both governments. Despite special appeals to Congress on 28 January by President Ford and, subsequently, by Secretary of State Kissinger, Congress decided to cut aid to both Cambodia and South Vietnam. Assistance was given to Vietnamese refugees; and by the end of the crisis U.S. activity was limited to evacuating U.S. citizens. UN involvement was confined to calls for a cease-fire and the fact-finding activities of the UN High Commissioner for Refugees.

(See *Master Table*, pp. 712–13.)

Sources
See sources for Cases #225 and 246.

(259) Mayaguez

The Mayaguez episode was a crisis for the United States and Cambodia from 12 to 15 May 1975.

Background
America's prestige was at a low point in the wake of the U.S. withdrawal from Indochina and the collapse of U.S.-supported regimes in Cambodia and Vietnam. In Cambodia the Khmer Rouge had emerged victorious from the civil war. While U.S. relations with China had improved considerably since 1971, relations with the new government of Cambodia were hostile.

Crisis
On 12 May 1975 a U.S.-registered cargo ship, the *Mayaguez*, was seized off Cambodian coastal waters by the Khmer Rouge, triggering a crisis for the United States. The ship was taken into custody, together with its crew, with no word of their fate. Washington looked upon this incident as a challenge to U.S. influence in Southeast Asia. Following demands for the return of the ship and crew, on the 12th, the U.S. threat, on 13 May, to use force if necessary triggered a crisis for Cambodia.

The U.S. decision to use military force was taken on the 14th by President Ford at the fourth and final meeting of the National Security Council on this issue. Cambodia's response, also on the 14th, was a statement accusing the U.S. of interfering in its internal affairs and threatening reprisals. A few minutes after fighting began, the Cambodians released the ship and crew, ending the crisis for the United States. Nevertheless, even after Cambodia's acquiescence, serious clashes took place between Khmer Rouge forces and U.S. marines in the vicinity of Koh Tong, an island thought to be in the area where the *Mayaguez* crew was being held. The U.S. employed massive force, and heavy casualties were reported on both sides.

The crisis for Cambodia ended on 15 May when the U.S. ceased its military operations. UN involvement was minimal: the Secretary-General offered his good offices to settle the dispute, but this had little effect. In addition to the two crisis actors, the PRC became involved when Cambodia requested Beijing to conduct limited negotiations on its behalf. The USSR remained aloof from this crisis.

(See *Master Table*, pp. 712–13.)

Sources
Hearings 1975; Head et al. 1978; Paust 1976; Poole 1976; Simmons 1976.

(284) Vietnam Invasion of Cambodia

A two-stage post–Vietnam War crisis in Indochina occurred from 24 September 1977 to 7 January 1979. The direct participants were Cambodia, Vietnam, and, on the periphery, Thailand.

Background

The deep-rooted conflict between Cambodia and Vietnam derived from many sources: ethnic hatred, traditional hostility, territorial disputes, and ideological differences. In essence, the former was engaged in a persistent struggle to maintain an independent existence against the steady encroachment of the much more powerful Vietnam. In March 1970 Cambodia attempted to expel North Vietnamese and Vietcong military concentrations from its territory (see Case #237—**Invasion of Cambodia** above). Fighting began immediately after the fall of Cambodia's capital, Phnom Penh, to the Cambodian Maoist Khmer Rouge in April 1975 (see Case #258—**Final North Vietnam Offensive** above). From that time onward the tension was exacerbated by disputes over boundaries imposed by the French colonial administration concerning some potentially oil-rich islands in the Gulf of Siam and, more importantly, threats to the survival of the diminishing Cambodian state. The conflict was intensified by the reluctance of North Vietnam's army to withdraw from acknowledged Cambodian territory after 1975.

The persistent border conflict between Cambodia and Vietnam escalated in 1977. In April Cambodian forces staged heavy raids into Vietnam, whose militia guarding the area was forced to withdraw. In May Vietnam unilaterally extended its territorial waters to 12 miles and established a 200-mile "exclusive economic zone" that encompassed islands and archipelagos outside those territorial waters. These acts directly affected islands contested by Vietnam and China (see Case #384—**Spratly Islands,** in 1988, in **China/Vietnam PC**), as well as those in dispute between Vietnam and Cambodia. A treaty of economic and defense cooperation between Vietnam and Laos in August 1977 transformed Laos into a Vietnamese client, another step in Vietnam's efforts to gain control over all of Indochina.

For Vietnam, a serious refugee problem in an economically strategic area, together with Cambodian attacks, exacerbated the tense situation. Cambodia was troubled by the continued presence of Vietnamese troops in the eastern part of its territory. Cambodia charged Vietnam with a plan to reconstitute the *Union Indochinoise* established by France, as well as an attempt to instigate an internal coup in Cambodia against the regime. Vietnam countered by accusing Khmer Rouge leader, Pol Pot, of plans to reconquer Saigon and the Mekong Delta, which had belonged to Cambodia 300 years earlier.

The Thai/Cambodia conflict was less acute than that between Cambodia and Vietnam. Nevertheless, uncertain borders, poor communication between Phnom Penh and its forces in the field, the lack of discipline among the Khmer Rouge troops, provocative Thai military action, smuggling operations, ideological factors, and the presence of an enormous Cambodian refugee camp in Thailand all contributed to poor relations between Cambodia and Thailand.

Crisis
The beginning of a lengthy crisis for Cambodia and Vietnam can be traced to 24 September 1977: Cambodia reported an invasion by several Vietnam divisions supported by hundreds of tanks, artillery pieces, and aircraft; and the same day Vietnam alleged that four divisions of Cambodian forces had launched attacks along the entire border of Tayninh Province where over 1,000 civilians had been killed or wounded. Vietnam's initial response was a punitive assault in December by six divisions 50 miles into Cambodia.

After inflicting a substantial defeat Vietnamese troops pulled back, with some units remaining in Cambodia to support subsequent diplomatic approaches. Cambodia moved 13 of its 17 divisions to hold the border against a renewed Vietnamese invasion. On 13 December Phnom Penh broke off diplomatic relations with Hanoi and quietly abandoned its Moscow embassy as well, thereby emphasizing the link between the Indochina dispute and the Sino/Soviet conflict. Vietnamese diplomats were ordered to leave Cambodia; and air services between the two countries were to be suspended as of 7 January 1978. A Vietnamese offer on 3 January to negotiate was rejected by Cambodia.

There were contradictory reports concerning the fighting in January. Cambodia claimed to have expelled the Vietnamese after a major victory on 6 January, while Vietnam continued to report incursions into its territory. The Vietnamese invasion was suspended in mid-January, and its forces were gradually withdrawn from Cambodia.

From the second half of January until June 1978 Vietnam's forces remained largely on the defensive repelling repeated Cambodian raids across the border. Vietnam's air force began systematic attacks against Cambodia in June 1978. After China cut off all aid to Vietnam the latter joined the Soviet bloc's economic union, *COMECON*, on 29 June. (Six months later it signed a Treaty of Friendship with the Soviet Union.)

In September 1978 the Khmer Rouge launched another series of raids deep into Vietnam, while the latter continued systematic incursions into Cambodia. Cambodia alleged the participation of foreign nationals—Russians and Cubans—as advisors to Vietnam's artillery companies and tank squadrons. By mid-September Vietnam's policy of minimum military reaction changed.

The Thai dimension of this international crisis emerged soon after the end of the first stage of the Cambodia/Vietnam crisis. Despite an agreement on 2 February 1978 to normalize Cambodian/Thai relations, Cambodian troops, often acting in collaboration with Thai communist guerrillas, continued to make frequent raids into Thailand. On the 9th a sharp increase in Cambodia's raids into Thai border villages triggered a crisis for Thailand. Assaults on police posts in the frontier zone and destruction of small nearby population centers took place with no serious obstacles on the part of the Thai army or its border police units. The Thai government, while opting for diplomatic measures to control Cambodia, responded on 10 April with a statement by its prime minister vowing swift and drastic retaliation. With the onset of the second stage of the Cambodia/Vietnam crisis in mid-December and a Cambodian invasion directed at the Vietnamese port of Ha Tien, the scale of incidents in Thailand was reduced, marking the end of its crisis.

The second stage of the crisis between Hanoi and Phnom Penh was initiated by Cambodia's intrusion into Vietnam on 15 December 1978. Vietnam responded with a massive and rapid strike into Cambodia on 25 December escalating the crisis for Cambodia (and the PRC—[see Case #298—**Sino/Vietnam War,** in 1978–79, in **China/Vietnam PC**]). Cambodia responded on the 31st with a request to the UN to condemn Vietnam and to demand that it cease "aggression" and that all Soviet military aid to Vietnam be stopped. The Cambodian foreign minister also requested an urgent meeting of the UN Security Council.

Vietnam's conquest of Cambodia was completed in less than a fortnight. On 7 January 1979 a puppet regime was installed in Phnom Penh terminating the crisis for Vietnam, for Cambodia—by force majeure—and the international crisis as a whole. However, it spilled over to a brief but intense military confrontation between China and Vietnam (see Case #298).

Many states were involved in this complex crisis. China and the USSR urged the parties to resolve their disputes through negotiation. At the same time substantial aid programs—the USSR to Vietnam, the PRC to Cambodia—continued throughout the crisis. North Korea sent pilots to fight alongside Cambodia—and China—in the Sino/Vietnam War. The Soviet bloc and Albania supported Vietnam. Laos, Yugoslavia, and Romania remained neutral. The divisions in the communist world were thus widened, a development for which Moscow denounced Beijing. Indonesia, the Philippines, Malaysia, and Thailand condemned the Vietnam invasion of Cambodia in December 1978 and halted aid to Vietnam, as did Australia, Britain, Denmark, and Japan. The UN Security Council overruled Soviet and Czechoslovak objections and agreed to convene a

formal meeting on 11 January 1979. Soviet proposals were rejected. And Prince
Sihanouk was invited to address the meeting. A draft resolution was submitted on
the 15th but was not adopted because of a Soviet veto.

(The Vietnam invasion of Cambodia succeeded in toppling the Pol Pot
regime but failed to destroy the Khmer Rouge forces, thereby initiating a protracted guerrilla war for a decade. Under massive international pressure and
internal problems Vietnam withdrew from Cambodia in 1989.)

(See *Master Table*, pp. 716–17.)

Sources
Amer 1992; An 1978; Bellows 1979; Bui Dien 1979; Galbraith 1980; Hung
1979; Jackson 1978, 1979; Kallgren 1979; Kershaw 1979; Leighton 1978a,
1978b; Pike 1978; Poole 1978; Sandler 1976; Thien 1978.

(388) Cambodia Peace Conference

Cambodia and Vietnam experienced a shared crisis over the former's political
system from 30 August 1989 to 27 January 1990.

Background and Pre-crisis
At the end of a lengthy, complex post–Vietnam War crisis in Indochina, Vietnam
swept the Khmer Rouge from power in Cambodia in a swift military campaign and,
on 7 January 1979, installed a puppet regime in Phnom Penh (see Case #284—
Vietnam Invasion of Cambodia above). During the next decade Vietnam was the
de facto ruler of Cambodia with 160,000 troops stationed there. All attempts to end
Vietnam's occupation failed. By the late 1980s, however, the declining power and
foreign aid resources of Vietnam's patron, the Soviet Union, along with Vietnam's
growing isolation in Southeast Asia, its internal economic stagnation, and the
cumulative high cost of occupying Cambodia, created a favorable climate for a new
diplomatic effort to resolve the conflict over Cambodia.

France and Australia took the lead in convening an international peace
conference on Cambodia in Paris on 30 July 1989, with many other participants
or observers: Canada, India, Indonesia, Japan, Laos, Malaysia, Thailand, the
U.S., the USSR, Vietnam; and all the major Cambodian factions—the Armed
National Sihanoukistes *(ANS),* led by former ruler Prince Norodom Sihanouk;
the Khmer People's National Liberation Front *(KPNLF),* led by Son Sann, a
former premier under Sihanouk; and the Party of Democratic Kampuchea (the
China-backed Khmer Rouge), comprising the anti-Vietnam Coalition Government of Democratic Kampuchea *(CGDK);* and, on the other side, the Vietnam-
created People's Republic of Kampuchea *(PRK),* led by Premier Hun Sen.

Crisis
Cambodia and its then-patron, Vietnam, perceived a crisis when the Paris conference was suspended on 30 August 1989 because of an irreconcilable disagree-

ment over the place of the Khmer Rouge in a future Cambodian political system: the pro-Vietnam *PRK* regime was unalterably opposed to legitimizing a party responsible for genocide while in power from 1975 to 1979; and Sihanouk insisted on its inclusion, to avert a prolonged civil war. It was widely feared that the diplomatic deadlock would lead to the resumption of hostilities among the contending Cambodian factions. The expected escalation of military hostilities did, in fact, occur, especially because of the uncertainty accompanying Vietnam's withdrawal of its forces from Cambodia: it was publicly pledged on 5 April 1989 and was completed on 30 September, on schedule.

An attempt by Thailand's prime minister to arrange a cease-fire in September failed. However, the idea of an enlarged UN role in the Cambodian peace process, initiated by U.S. Congressman Stephen Solarz, revived the diplomatic effort. It took the form of a three-point peace plan formulated and urged upon all parties by Australia's Foreign Minister, Garth Evans. The plan called for the following: UN verification of Vietnam's complete withdrawal from Cambodia; a cease-fire and termination of external arms aid to all parties; and UN-supervised elections.

The Security Council approved the plan on 16 January 1990. China played a key role in enlisting the support of the three leaders of the anti-Vietnam coalition, Sihanouk, Son Sann, and the Khmer Rouge's Khieu Samphan. And Vietnam ensured the approval of the *PRK* regime—Hun Sen expressed his approval on 27 January. This marked the end of the crisis arising from the Cambodia peace conference.

Cambodia experienced a crisis because the Paris conference and pressure from the international community posed a threat to its political system, specifically, continued rule by the *PRK*. For Vietnam, its future influence in Indochina was at risk. China was actively involved, supplying weapons and diplomatic support to the Khmer Rouge, but it did not perceive a crisis for itself. The U.S. was barely involved, supporting the Australian diplomatic initiative. The USSR continued to provide military and diplomatic support to Vietnam.

(See *Master Table*, pp. 734–35.)

Sources
Keesing's 1989, 1990.

Indonesia

The protracted conflict over Indonesia and the territorial residue of its struggle for independence included seven international crises from 1945 to 1976, as follows.

Case #109 **Indonesia Independence I,** in 1945–47;
 #116 **Indonesia Independence II,** in 1947–48;
 #127 **Indonesia Independence III,** in 1948–49;

#161   **West Irian I,** in 1957– ;
#164   **Abortive Coup–Indonesia,** in 1958;
#187   **West Irian II,** in 1961–62;
#264   **East Timor,** in 1975–76.

General Background

Like India, the Indonesia archipelago was a classic example of Western colonialism in Asia. It began with the Portuguese, who arrived early in the sixteenth century to spread Catholicism and to benefit from the rich trade in spices. They held sway for 70 years from their capture of the Islamic center of Malacca in 1511, but they did not establish political control over Indonesia.

The Dutch arrived at the end of the sixteenth century, primarily for economic motives as well. Their United East India Company took control of the spice trade and successfully resisted the competition of British, Spanish, and other traders. Full-scale Dutch colonial rule over Java, the most populous of Indonesia's islands, dates from 1816, when it reverted to the Netherlands after a brief interregnum of French and then British control, from 1808 to 1816.

Indonesia was the "crown jewel" of the Dutch empire until its occupation by Japan from early 1942 until 15 August 1945. On the 17th Indonesian national leaders proclaimed its independence and established a provisional government of the new Republic.

(109) Indonesia Independence I

The first of three crises over Indonesia's struggle for independence began on 29 September 1945 and terminated on 25 March 1947. The crisis actors were the Netherlands and Indonesia.

Crisis

A crisis for the Netherlands was triggered on 29 September 1945 when the Supreme Allied Commander for Southeast Asia announced that his troops would maintain law and order in the Netherlands East Indies until a lawful government was again functioning, and that Indonesian leader Ahmad Sukarno was to continue to direct civil administration in those areas not occupied by Allied forces. This was regarded by the Netherlands as de facto recognition of the provisional Indonesian government and, therefore, a grave threat to its influence, long sustained by the Dutch empire. The Hague responded on 1 October with an official statement that the Netherlands would neither recognize nor negotiate with Sukarno.

Indonesia's crisis was triggered on 2 October by the arrival of a Dutch administrator and the landing of additional Dutch forces, interpreted by the Indonesians as a Dutch effort to restore colonial rule. Severe fighting ensued between nationalist and Dutch and British forces. On 13 October 1945 Indonesia responded with a declaration of war against the Netherlands and the prohibition of the sale of food to the enemy. The British were accused of promoting the return of the Dutch administration. In late 1946 British forces were withdrawn. The fighting continued, along with prolonged negotiations, until the signing of the Linggadjati Agreement on 25 March 1947, which provided for a transitional regime until 1 January 1949 at which time the Dutch government would transfer authority to an independent Republic of Indonesia. The agreement, which terminated the first international crisis over Indonesia's independence, provided for a truce and stabilization of existing military positions, the establishment of a Truce Supervisory Committee composed of Dutch, British, and Indonesian representatives, and the creation of the United States of Indonesia linked to the Netherlands.

The UN Security Council was involved because of a joint USSR-Ukrainian complaint on the issue of Dutch military intervention. Draft resolutions calling for on-the-spot investigation and limitation—and withdrawal—of British forces were rejected. The U.S. and the USSR were not active in this early post–World War II crisis, except for the latter's verbal support for Indonesia's nationalists at the UN and in general.

(See *Master Table,* pp. 686–87.)

Sources
Agung 1973; Crouch 1978; Dahm 1971; Eagleton 1957; Emerson 1948; Fifield 1958; Gerbrandy 1950; Goodspeed 1967; Kahin 1952; van der Kroef 1951; Reinhardt 1971; Taylor 1960.

(116) Indonesia Independence II

The second crisis over the Netherlands' opposition to Indonesia's declaration of independence occurred between 21 July 1947 and 17 January 1948.

Pre-crisis
The Linggadjati Agreement of 25 March 1947, which called for the transfer of power by the Netherlands to Indonesia on 1 January 1949, was regarded by many Dutch colonials as inadequate in its provisions for the protection of Dutch interests. Indonesians, on the other hand, felt that Prime Minister Sjahrir had gone too far in conceding to Dutch demands; he resigned on 3 July 1947 as internal pressure mounted.

Crisis
Indonesia's second crisis was triggered on 21 July 1947 when the Netherlands, dissatisfied with the deteriorating relations between the two countries, authorized the launching of military action. Indonesia's response, on 22 July, was an appeal to India for aid and foreign intervention. India, and later Australia, brought the issue to the Security Council. Its discussion on 31 July, with the implied danger of international intervention, was the crisis trigger for the Netherlands. That day, the

Dutch representative to the Security Council denied UN jurisdiction over what he termed a police action in an internal Dutch matter. He set forth the Netherlands' conditions for reopening talks. The crisis ended on 17 January 1948 when U.S. activity helped to bring about the Renville Agreement, calling for a truce and adopting the UN Good Offices Committee's recommendation for a plebiscite.

The Security Council adopted two resolutions. In the first, submitted by China and Australia, the Council noted with satisfaction the Dutch government statement affirming its intention to recognize a sovereign, democratic United States of Indonesia in accordance with the provisions of the Linggadjati Agreement. Further, the Council requested that member-states having consular representatives in Batavia (Djakarta, later Jakarta) supervise the carrying out of the cease-fire and report their findings. The second resolution, submitted by the United States, expressed Security Council resolve to render its good offices to the parties in order to assist in the pacific settlement of the dispute through a committee of three members, one each from the disputing parties and the third to be appointed by the first two.

UN intervention clearly implied that the crisis was international, not a matter of Dutch domestic jurisdiction. As such, it was considered a political victory for the Republic of Indonesia, increasing its international prestige. The Renville Agreement included a truce along the Van Mook Line—the position held by the Dutch after 21 July 1947—and a number of political principles. Dutch acceptance suggested the possibility that the Netherlands would not evacuate the territories it administered and that Indonesian guerrilla forces would be removed from these areas. Nevertheless, there was a guarantee that plebiscites would be held in the Dutch-occupied territories in 6–12 months under supervision of the UN Good Offices Committee, which would remain in Indonesia to supervise the implementation of the agreement by both parties. Overall the outcome was a compromise between Indonesia and the Netherlands.

The USSR continued to provide verbal support to Indonesia's nationalists during this crisis.

(See *Master Table,* pp. 686–87.)

Sources
See sources for Case #109; and Miller 1967.

(127) Indonesia Independence III

The last of three interrelated crises between Indonesia and the Netherlands over the former's independence occurred between 19 December 1948 and 27 December 1949.

Pre-crisis
The Linggadjati and Renville Agreements of 25 March 1947 and 17 January 1948 had recognized the de facto authority of the Republic of Indonesia over

Java, Sumatra, and Madura. The Dutch, nevertheless, created autonomous regions and states on those islands, thus violating the agreements. Tension began to mount again in 1948, and negotiations reached a deadlock when the Dutch tried to force a one-sided agreement. It became clear to the Indonesians that the Netherlands would once more attempt to solve the problem unilaterally by force.

Crisis
A crisis for Indonesia was triggered on 19 December 1948 when Dutch forces occupied Djakarta and other cities in Java and Sumatra, while capturing eminent Republican political leaders. The trigger for the Netherlands was a critical report to the Security Council by the Good Offices Committee on 23 December 1948, threatening the Dutch empire in Southeast Asia. Indonesia responded on 25 December by setting up an emergency government in Sumatra and appealing to Prime Minister Nehru of India, who transmitted to the Security Council the resolution adopted by the second New Delhi Conference on Indonesia, with strong recommendations for action. The Netherlands responded on the 27th by rejecting the Security Council's call for an immediate cease-fire and the transfer of sovereignty to Indonesia after free elections. On the 30th it refused to accept the cease-fire and release political prisoners. International pressure—from the second New Delhi Conference, an Arab League resolution calling for a Dutch cease-fire, and intense U.S. pressure—finally convinced the Netherlands to comply. The crisis ended for both actors on 27 December 1949, when Queen Juliana signed a formal act transferring sovereignty over the Dutch East Indies to the Republic of Indonesia.

The Soviet Union supported Indonesia politically throughout its conflict with the Netherlands, 1945–49. The U.S., on the other hand, changed from supporting the Netherlands to pressing them to sign the Renville Agreement, to securing Dutch compliance with UN resolutions by threatening to suspend U.S. aid.

(See *Master Table,* pp. 688–89.)

Sources
See sources for Cases #109 and 116.

(161) West Irian I

The Netherlands experienced a crisis over West Irian (West New Guinea) on 1 December 1957. The crisis faded until it erupted into a new crisis almost four years later.

Background and Pre-crisis
In order to prevent last-minute obstacles to the Dutch-Indonesian agreement of 1949 concerning the transfer of power from the Netherlands to the Republic of Indonesia (see Case #127 above), the issue of West Irian (West New Guinea) had been left open. In November 1957 talks were held between Australian and Dutch

leaders on practical measures for improving their joint administration of West Irian. Indonesia, which had begun a campaign for its liberation, viewed this as an attempt to undermine a peaceful outcome to Indonesia's claim to West New Guinea.

Crisis

A crisis for the Netherlands was triggered on 1 December 1957 when Indonesia's minister of information authorized a general strike by all Indonesian workers employed by Dutch enterprises. This was followed by a ban on all Dutch publications and on *KLM* landings in Indonesia. A large number of Dutch businesses were seized by groups of Indonesian workers and youth. The Dutch response, on 3 December, was a statement by the prime minister pledging the safeguarding of Dutch national interests in Indonesia. On 5 December the Indonesian minister of justice announced that some 50,000 Dutch nationals would be expelled and that all Dutch consulates, with the exception of the one in Djakarta, would be closed. On the 6th the Netherlands government called for an urgent session of the North Atlantic Council, which met but did not issue an official statement. This was followed on 9 December by an Indonesian decree placing all Dutch-owned estates and plantations under the control of the Indonesian government. Another Netherlands attempt to gain international support was made on 23 December with a letter to the UN Secretary-General asking that the situation be brought before the General Assembly and the Security Council. In the meantime two Dutch navy destroyers were dispatched to reinforce troops already in the New Guinea area.

There is no clear termination date. The issue lingered on at below-crisis level until 1961 (see Case #187 below).

The U.S. was marginally involved in this crisis, the USSR not at all.

(See *Master Table,* pp. 694–95.)

Sources
See sources for Cases #109 and 116.

(164) Abortive Coup-Indonesia

An internally generated international crisis for Indonesia took place from 21 February until 20 May 1958.

Background and Pre-crisis
A series of bloodless army coups in regional districts of Indonesia served to undermine the power of the central government in Djakarta. Nationwide martial law was imposed in March 1957. The dispute between the Netherlands and Indonesia over West Irian had not been resolved in UN discussions. An abortive attempt on President Sukarno's life took place on 30 November 1956. On 3 December labor groups began seizing Dutch enterprises in Indonesia: within a fortnight virtually all were under military control. That month 46,000 Dutch

nationals were repatriated. Tension between the president and regional powers was high. By 10 February 1958 opposition in the outer islands had erupted. An ultimatum demanding central government changes was rejected by the Djakarta cabinet the following day. On the 15th a revolutionary state was proclaimed. U.S. sympathies lay with the anti-communist secessionists, and there is evidence that U.S. military aid had arrived in West Sumatra before the ultimatum, along with the presence of U.S. intelligence officers. Sukarno returned to Indonesia on 16 February and called for cabinet deliberations to consider the issue of civil war, compounded by an apparent threat of possible U.S. intervention.

Crisis
The first indication of an Indonesian government perception of a threat of foreign involvement was Sukarno's rejection of rebel demands on 21 February 1958: in his call for measures against the rebels, he cited his conviction that the rebels were acting as instruments of a foreign power, clearly implying the U.S., which wished to force Indonesia to join the Western bloc. Indonesia's major response was a military move against the rebels in central Sumatra on 22 February, with air force bombing and strafing. During the course of the fighting, from 7 to 12 March, government paratroops occupied Pakanbahru, where U.S. personnel were located at oil fields. This step was taken partly out of fear that the U.S. might send in marines. The Seventh Fleet, situated offshore, caused great anxiety in Djakarta, where anti-American sentiments were at a fever pitch. By mid-April two key rebel towns had fallen. After the fall of Padang, the U.S. began an effort to improve relations with Indonesia. U.S. Ambassador Jones's initiatives met with positive Indonesian responses. On 20 May, in the form of an official statement, Secretary of State Dulles formally reiterated the U.S. position of not being involved in what was an internal Indonesian affair. The statement set in motion a chain of events pointing to a rapprochement between the two states and marks the end of Indonesia's crisis.

The USSR provided political support to Indonesia during this crisis. The UN was not involved.

(The rebellion lasted until 4 April 1961. There was guerrilla warfare with several thousand casualties.)

(See *Master Table,* pp. 696–97.)

Sources
Feith 1962; Feith and Lev 1963; Kahin 1963; Kosut 1967; Lev 1966; Mozingo 1976.

(187) West Irian II

Indonesia and the Netherlands experienced a second crisis over this territorial residue of the struggle for independence. It began on 26 September 1961 and ended on 15 August 1962.

Pre-crisis
Following an Indonesian decision to "liberate" West Irian, President Sukarno appealed to the USSR for political and military support, which was granted. A new Dutch plan was designed stressing the idea of self-determination for the Papuans.

Crisis
A crisis for Indonesia began on 26 September 1961 when the Dutch foreign minister submitted a proposal to the UN for the decolonization of West Irian and the transfer of sovereignty to its people, with the UN assuming its administration temporarily. Indonesia, which viewed the proposal as a means of consolidating Dutch administration and thus keeping Indonesia out of West Irian indefinitely, responded on 19 December 1961 by inaugurating a triple command for the "liberation" of New Guinea, along with general mobilization. In order to focus world attention, a small-scale infiltration into West Irian was initiated. This triggered a crisis for the Netherlands.

Active participation by the UN Secretary-General and an announcement by President Kennedy of the U.S.'s intention to seek a solution persuaded the Netherlands to respond on 3 January 1962: it announced its decision of the previous day to drop the demand that Indonesia accept the principle of self-determination for the Papuans as a condition for negotiations.

Once the U.S. had abandoned its neutral position for a policy of active mediation, a solution—by U.S. Ambassador Ellsworth Bunker, acting as the UN Secretary-General's Personal Representative—became possible. According to an agreement signed by Indonesia and the Netherlands on 15 August 1962, the termination date of the crisis, the UN would supervise the evacuation of Dutch military forces and take over administration of the area until it was handed over to Indonesia, not later than 1 May 1963. The USSR supplied arms to Indonesia.

(See *Master Table*, pp. 700–701.)

Sources
Agung 1973; Bone 1962; Crouch 1978; Grant 1964; Henderson 1973; Jones 1971; Kosut 1967; van der Kroef 1963; Leifer 1983; Sundhausen 1982; van der Veur 1964.

(264) East Timor

The disputed territory of East Timor generated a crisis for Indonesia from 28 November 1975 to 17 July 1976.

Background and Pre-crisis
The three most important political parties in Portuguese East Timor were Fretilin, which demanded immediate independence, *UDT*, which favored eventual independence with the continuation of ties to Portugal, and Apodeti, which wanted

integration into Indonesia. After the Portuguese government announced in June 1975 its intention to relinquish control over all overseas territories, the *UDT* held high-level talks with Indonesian officials and announced, on 6 August 1975, that the party had decided to follow a political line acceptable to Indonesia. On 11 August the *UDT* carried out a coup in East Timor and demanded immediate independence from Portugal. Fighting between Fretilin and *UDT* factions broke out immediately. On 27 August the governor of East Timor admitted that the Portuguese authorities had lost control of the situation. The Portuguese administration then abandoned East Timor and retreated to the offshore island of Atauro. Portugal rejected Indonesia's offer to move in and restore order. As fighting intensified in September, an announcement was made by the defense ministry in Jakarta, on 9 September, that Indonesia would refuse to accept any Portuguese move to hand over East Timor to a government dominated by Fretilin, which at that time controlled a major part of the East Timor territory. This was followed by an announcement by the foreign minister that Indonesia had the right to intervene in East Timor if war endangered its territory. Border clashes increased in October and, on the 11th, Fretilin announced that a transitional administration had been established.

Crisis
The crisis trigger for Indonesia was the Fretilin declaration of East Timor's independence on 28 November 1975. Indonesia feared that an independent East Timor would encourage internal secessionist movements in Sumatra, West Irian, and the South Moluccas, as well as aid communist infiltration and influence in the area. On 29 November the pro-Indonesian political parties in East Timor declared it to be a part of Indonesia. That day, too, Portugal rejected all declarations of independence and, on 30 November, formally requested help from the UN to settle the problem. The major Indonesian response, on 7 December, was a large-scale invasion of East Timor. Portugal severed relations with Indonesia and requested a meeting of the Security Council. A second invasion was launched on 25 December, with heavy fighting between Fretilin and Indonesian forces continuing throughout December.

In March 1976 the East Timor Provisional Government announced its intention to integrate the island with Indonesia. This was followed by an Indonesian declaration that its troops would be withdrawn. The integration was approved by the East Timor People's Assembly on 31 May. On 17 July 1976 the crisis for Indonesia ended when President Suharto signed a bill formally incorporating East Timor into Indonesia. At that time the Indonesian forces had achieved control of the entire coastal area but not much of the interior.

The UN General Assembly passed a resolution on 12 December 1975 condemning Indonesian military intervention and calling for the withdrawal of Indonesian forces. The UN Security Council met five times between 15 and 22 December 1975. On the 22nd it passed a resolution calling on Indonesia to withdraw its forces from East Timor without delay and urged that a special representative of the Secretary-General be sent to assess the situation. This was done in late January 1976, but he was unable to establish contact with the Fretilin. On 22 April another resolution with the same content was adopted by the Security Council. None of these resolutions helped to abate the crisis.

The U.S. and the USSR were not involved in this crisis.

(See *Master Table,* pp. 714–15.)

Sources
Kamm 1981; Lawless 1976; Leifer 1976; Nichterlein 1977; Viviani 1976.

Korea

The protracted conflict between North and South Korea, with the U.S. a direct participant most of the time, generated six international crises from 1950 to 1994, as follows.

Case #132   **Korean War I,** in 1950;
 #133   **Korean War II,** in 1950–51;
 #140   **Korean War III,** in 1953;
 #224   **Pueblo,** in 1968;
 #274   **Poplar Tree,** in 1976;
 #408   **North Korea Nuclear Crisis,** in 1993–94.

Other crises, primarily associated with the **East/West** protracted conflict, had a visible **Korea** dimension, notably Case #233—**EC-121 Spy Plane,** in 1969 (see *Master Table*).

The half-century **Korea** PC remains unresolved.

General Background

For much of its history the Korean peninsula was ruled indirectly by the reigning dynasty in China as the suzerain power: the *Khitan* (*Liao* dynasty) in 996; the *Jurchen* (*Chin* dynasty) in 1123; the Mongols in 1259; the *Mings* in 1369; the *Manchus* (*Ch'ing* dynasty) from 1637 until the late nineteenth century.

Under the terms of the Treaty of Shimonoseki that ended the Sino/Japanese War of 1894–95, China recognized the independence of Korea. During the next decade Japan and Russia competed for hegemony over Korea. Russia recognized Japan's primacy in the economic, military, and political affairs of Korea in the Treaty of Portsmouth, following Japan's victory in the Russo/Japanese War, 1904–5. During the next five years Japan's control over Korea increased steadily. And in August 1910 Korea was formally annexed by Japan. From 1910 to 1945 the Korean peninsula was a stringently ruled colony of Japan. After setting up dependent but Korean-led regimes in their respective occupation zones in 1945 following World War II, the United States and the Soviet Union subsequently evacuated South and North Korea.

(132) Korean War I

The first international crisis related to the Korean War began on 25 June and ended on 30 September 1950. There were four crisis actors: South Korea, formally the Republic of Korea (ROK), the United States, the People's Republic of China (PRC), and the Republic of China (ROC or Taiwan).

Pre-crisis
There was constant tension, and minor incidents were reported in 1949. That year, too, General MacArthur, the Supreme Commander of Allied Powers *(SCAP)* and de facto ruler in Japan, and Secretary of State Acheson had defined Korea as beyond the U.S. defense perimeter in East Asia. The Chinese Communist regime was preoccupied with internal reconstruction after the China civil war (see Case #125—**China Civil War,** in 1948–49, in **Multiregional PCs: Taiwan Strait**), and plans were made for a probable invasion of Taiwan in 1950. From September 1949 until June 1950 the South Korean leader, Syngman Rhee, frequently announced a "march-to-the-north" policy, to unify Korea by force. During June 1950 Kim Il-Sung, the leader of North Korea, initiated an all-out campaign for the reunification of Korea.

Crisis
On 25 June 1950 forces of the Democratic People's Republic of Korea (DPRK) (North Korea) invaded the Republic of Korea (ROK) (South Korea) by crossing the 38th Parallel, the de facto border between the two Koreas. This triggered a crisis for South Korea and the United States. Rhee responded the same day with an appeal to the U.S. for military aid. On 27 June President Truman authorized U.S. forces to fight alongside troops of the ROK. He also reacted to the critical situation developing between the two Chinas by ordering the Seventh Fleet to the Taiwan Strait and establishing a naval blockade. This was the trigger for the PRC, whose plans for the invasion of Taiwan were complicated by a possible combined U.S.-Taiwan invasion of the mainland. The PRC response, on 28 June, was contained in a speech by Prime Minister Zhou Enlai accusing the U.S. of aggression. Taiwan, still fearful of a Chinese Communist invasion, as PRC forces were massed along the coast, perceived Zhou's speech as a threat with possible grave consequences and responded the following day with general mobilization.

A U.S.-sponsored resolution at the Security Council was passed on 25 June by a vote of 9 to 0, with Yugoslavia abstaining and the Soviet Union absent—its delegates had walked out of the Council. The resolution condemned the North Korean attack and demanded the immediate cessation of hostilities and the withdrawal of North Korean forces to the 38th Parallel. A second Security Council resolution, on 27 June (7 to 1, with Yugoslavia opposed, India and Egypt abstaining, and the Soviet Union still absent), called on UN members to provide assistance to South Korea. And on 7 July, after U.S. and ROK forces had come under heavy attack and had been driven southward, the Security Council passed a third resolution in the USSR's absence—7 to 0, with India, Egypt, and Yugoslavia abstaining: it urged all members to contribute forces to a UN Unified Command. U.S. General MacArthur was appointed to lead the combined forces.

The PRC crisis faded in July as events in the area merged with the ongoing Korean War. There was no specific United Nations action concerning the PRC/Taiwan crisis.

The Soviet attitude and role are now known. After almost a year of hesitation, according to official USSR documents, Stalin gave Kim Il-Sung a "green light" to launch a full-scale attack on South Korea: first, in a message to the Korean leader on 30 January 1950, via the Soviet embassy in Pyongyang—"tell him that I am ready to help him in this matter [a large matter in regard to South Korea such as he wants to undertake]"; and second, during a meeting with Kim in Moscow in April 1950. Thereafter Soviet military advisors were sent to North Korea to help plan the campaign, along with a large amount of weapons and supplies. The Soviet Union also provided air cover over North Korean cities. Kim Il-Sung also secured the support of Mao Tse-tung at a meeting in Beijing in May.

By 29 September 1950 UN forces had restored control of South Korea to the Rhee government, and the crisis ended for South Korea and the United States. The following day the crisis ended for Taiwan with the reduction of intensity of the conflict.

(See *Master Table,* pp. 690–91.)

Sources
Foreign Relations of the United States (FRUS) 1950, vol. VII; Academy of Sciences of the Democratic People's Republic of Korea 1961; Acheson 1951a, 1951b, 1969, 1971; Bajanov 1995–96; Berger 1957; Bernstein and Matusow 1966; Bullock 1983; Caridi 1968; Chan 1978; Clark 1954; Collins 1969; Cumings 1981, 1990; Cumings and Weathersby 1995–96; Dean 1954; Donovan 1977b; Dupuy and Dupuy 1986; Foot 1985; George and Smoke 1974; Goncharov et al. 1993; Goodrich 1956; Guang 1992, 1994; Gurtov and Hwang 1980; Halle 1967; Hastings 1987; Hoopes 1973; Kalicki 1975; Kennan 1967; Khrushchev 1970; Kim 1991; Kim Il-Sung 1976; Knapp 1967; La Feber 1976; Leckie 1962; Lie 1954; Lowe 1986; McCullough 1992; McLellan 1976; O'Ballance 1969; Oliver 1952; Paige 1968; Rees 1964; Ridgway 1967; Rusk 1990; Schoenbaum 1988; Simmons 1975; Spanier 1959; Stone 1952; Truman 1956; Tsou 1963; U.S. Department of State 1951; Warner 1951; Weathersby 1993a, 1993b, 1995, 1995–96; Yoo 1965; Zagoria and Zagoria 1981; Zimmerman 1981.

(133) Korean War II

A second, closely related international crisis during the Korean War lasted from 30 September 1950 to 10 July 1951. The crisis actors were North Korea, the People's Republic of China, the Soviet Union, the United States, and South Korea.

Pre-crisis

In August 1950 the PRC warned the United Nations that it would retaliate if U.S. or ROK forces crossed the 38th Parallel. On 29 September the UN forces handed control of South Korea back to the civilian government headed by Syngman Rhee.

Crisis

On 30 September the Third Division of the ROK army crossed the 38th Parallel and advanced rapidly, triggering a crisis for North Korea. This threat was accentuated on 1 October by MacArthur's ultimatum to the DPRK demanding unconditional surrender. The same day Kim Il-Sung, the ruler of North Korea, appealed to Beijing for immediate military intervention to save his regime.

These three events triggered a crisis for the PRC, as evident in a secret decision by the Standing Committee of the Chinese Communist Party's Politburo on 2 October to dispatch "Chinese Volunteers" to assist North Korea. The decision was taken under pressure from Stalin—but only after the PRC's leaders perceived a serious threat to the security of China and to the very existence of the DPRK. The crossing of the 38th Parallel by U.S. forces on 7 October escalated the stress level in Beijing—and triggered a crisis for the Soviet Union. Mao issued the formal order to enter the Korean War on the 8th; but the PRC's military intervention, its major response to this crisis, did not occur until 19 October, after lengthy—and disappointing—consultations with Stalin. In response to Mao's telegram on the 2nd, conveying the decision to send "Chinese Volunteers" and warning of possible U.S. military retaliation against the PRC, Stalin initially pledged to dispatch fighters and bombers to North Korea. However, on the 9th, at a meeting with Zhou Enlai in Moscow, just two days after the direct entry of U.S. forces into North Korea, Stalin reneged: the USSR's major response, that day, was to promise military equipment for 20 PRC divisions engaged in the Korean War and to place its forces both in the Soviet Far East and in Manchuria on alert, pending further penetration by U.S. forces in the DPRK, which might bring U.S. troops closer to the Soviet border.

News of the crossing of the Yalu River by thousands of "Chinese Volunteers," initiated in secrecy, reached Washington on 31 October, triggering a crisis for the United States. By late November the Chinese had begun successful major attacks against UN forces. The U.S. response, on 30 November, was a statement by President Truman announcing that the United States was prepared to use whatever weapons it had in its arsenal to defeat the Chinese troops.

PRC and North Korean forces recrossed the 38th Parallel on 26 December 1950. That, along with heavy fighting in Seoul, triggered a crisis for South Korea. On 3 January 1951 UN and South Korean forces abandoned the capital, which was captured the following day. The reversal of the tide of battle terminated the crisis for the Soviet Union. Differences between President Truman and General MacArthur over the expansion of the war led to MacArthur's dismissal in the early spring of 1951. The UN forces recaptured Seoul on 14 March 1951. There was a PRC counterattack in late April, but by June the fighting stabilized around the 38th Parallel. A cease-fire and armistice negotiations began on 10 July 1951, ending the crisis for North and South Korea, the PRC, and the U.S.

The USSR's use of its great power veto had effectively blocked UN Security Council action during this crisis and, therefore, the General Assembly became increasingly involved. On 7 October 1950 the Assembly created the UN Commission for the Unification and Rehabilitation of Korea *(UNCURK)*. When the Security Council was unable to do so, a new resolution, the Uniting for Peace Resolution, was passed on 3 November, granting the General Assembly authority to take action on threats to peace and security when the Security Council was unable to fulfill this responsibility, a crucial element in the UN Charter. In December the Assembly created the UN Korean Reconstruction Agency *(UN-KRA)* and a three-person group on a cease-fire. And on 1 February 1951 a resolution was passed by the General Assembly declaring the PRC to be an aggressor and demanding the withdrawal of its forces from Korea.

(See *Master Table,* pp. 690–91.)

Sources
See sources for Case #132 above; and Appleman 1989; Bernstein 1977; Christensen 1992; Farrar-Hockley 1984; Guang 1995; Hinton 1966; Hunt 1992; Jian 1992, 1994, 1995–96; Lee 1990; Mansourov 1995–96; Panikkar 1955; Pogue 1987; Segal 1985; Spurr 1988; Stueck 1995; Whiting 1960, 1991; Yufan and Zhihai 1990.

(140) Korean War III

The third crisis during the Korean War began on 16 April and ended on 27 July 1953. The crisis actors were the U.S., China, North Korea, and South Korea.

Pre-crisis
In January 1953 Eisenhower succeeded Truman in the White House. Primary U.S. concerns in Korea were the release of the prisoners of war and an end to the stalemate. On 2 February President Eisenhower mentioned the possibility of removing the Seventh Fleet from the Taiwan Strait: it had been serving as an effective barrier to Chinese Nationalist (Taiwan) plans to invade the mainland. In addition, Stalin's death on 5 March left a power vacuum in the USSR, the PRC's

closest ally during this period. Armistice and prisoner of war (POW) negotiations at Panmunjom continued with little progress, as a reported 46,000 PRC and North Korean prisoners in South Korea stated that they did not wish to return to their homelands. While the communist powers demanded their return, the UN sought ways not to force them to do so.

Crisis

On 16 April 1953 the PRC–North Korean forces began a new offensive against UN troops at Pork Chop Hill and Old Baldy. In the setting of the political discussions at Panmunjom and the general lull in the fighting, this new attack catalyzed an intrawar crisis for the United States. Washington responded on 22 May when Secretary of State Dulles threatened the PRC, via India's Prime Minister Nehru, with the possible use of tactical nuclear weapons to break the deadlock in Korea. This triggered a fresh crisis for the PRC and North Korea. Their combined response, on 8 June, was an agreement at Panmunjom for the voluntary repatriation of POWs, which broke the political deadlock. The softening of the communist position, on 8 June, triggered a crisis for South Korea which, fearing a U.S. withdrawal, viewed any agreement on the POW issue as a compromise of its reunification plans for the Korean peninsula. The South Korean response, on 18 June, was the unauthorized release of about 25,000 prisoners of war who had declared their preference not to return to the PRC or North Korea. This act, while angering the U.S., did not succeed in halting the negotiating process. An Armistice Agreement was signed on 27 July 1953 terminating the crisis for all four actors.

The agreement established a demarcation line in Korea, a Demilitarized Zone *(DMZ)*, a Military Armistice Committee *(MAC)* to resolve violations of the agreement, and a commission to supervise troop withdrawals.

The USSR was not involved in this crisis.

(There were many violations of the Armistice Agreement over the years, including an estimated 700 minor armed incidents in the *DMZ*. The most recent occurred in early April 1996, when 300 heavily armed DPRK troops entered the *DMZ* at Panmunjom—the agreement permitted the entry of only 35 lightly armed soldiers from each side. North Korea's motive was unclear but seemed to be aimed at pressure on Washington to negotiate a formal bilateral peace agreement between the U.S. and the DPRK, excluding the ROK [South Korea], to replace the 43-year-old Armistice Agreement. The abortive crisis, which occurred days before elections to South Korea's National Assembly, faded after three days.)

(See *Master Table,* pp. 690–91.)

Sources

See sources for Cases #132 and 133; and Dingman 1988–89; Eisenhower 1963; Foot 1985, 1988–89, 1991; Gordenker 1959; Henderson 1968; Higgins 1970; Murphy 1964.

(224) Pueblo

A crisis for South Korea, the U.S., and North Korea began on 21 January and ended on 23 December 1968.

Background
The U.S. and North Korea were engaged in negotiations at Panmunjom since the end of the Korean War in 1953 but were unsuccessful in areas other than the exchange of prisoners (see Case #140—**Korean War III** above). The U.S.S. *Pueblo* was an electronic surveillance intelligence ship that had been stationed off the coast of North Korea, purportedly on an oceanographic research mission, with orders to stay at least 14 miles off the coast of North Korea. Relations between North Korea and the USSR were strained; and the former wished to assert its influence in East Asia.

Crisis
The Pueblo crisis was closely linked to another intra-Korea crisis, which began on 21 January 1968 when a North Korea commando unit penetrated the Blue House in Seoul in a failed attempt to assassinate South Korea's President, Park Chung Hee. This triggered a security crisis for South Korea. In response to North Korea's commando raid, South Korea sought a security guarantee from the U.S. This was granted de facto in a joint communiqué by Presidents Johnson and Park on 17 April 1968, terminating South Korea's 21 January crisis.

A day after the commando raid, that is, 22 January, a crisis for the U.S. was triggered by seizure of the *Pueblo* by North Korean patrol and torpedo boats. The major response of the U.S. was to call up army and air force reservists on 25 January and to dispatch naval power to the North Korea coast: the U.S. aircraft carrier, *Enterprise,* and its task force were diverted from their course toward the North Vietnam coast and ordered into the Sea of Japan. This U.S. response triggered a crisis for North Korea.

At the Panmunjom Armistice Talks the U.S. demanded the return of the *Pueblo* and its crew. This demand was refused, with North Korea claiming that the *Pueblo* was spying in its territorial waters. The U.S. insisted that the *Pueblo* was 25 miles off the North Korean coast. The Soviets refused a request by the U.S. ambassador in Moscow to use their good offices to bring about the *Pueblo*'s release. An appeal was also made to the Security Council by the U.S. The next day, 26 January, the Soviet Union, which supported North Korea's claim that the *Pueblo* was in its territorial waters, sent a trawler to shadow the *Enterprise.* A second request for USSR intervention to restrain North Korea, made by U.S. Ambassador Thompson, was rejected. Inter alia the incident provided the means for an improvement of relations between the Soviet Union and North Korea.

By 3 February North Korea and the U.S. reached agreement to continue to use the Panmunjom talks as a vehicle for negotiating the end of the Pueblo crisis. The U.S. then withdrew the *Enterprise* and its task force, and the military threat decreased. The admission of spying by the *Pueblo* commander was broadcast by North Korea on 16 February. It was rejected by the U.S. as fabricated.

Negotiations between North Korea and the U.S. over the *Pueblo* continued for 10 months until an imposed agreement was reached on 23 December 1968. The U.S. representative, Major-General Woodward, issued an apology stating that the *Pueblo* had been in North Korean waters and acknowledged that the confessions of its commander and, later, some crew members were genuine. Before signing it, however, Woodward read a public statement disavowing the apology. The crew was returned to South Korea, but the ship was never recovered by the U.S.

The UN was approached by the U.S. but only discussed the issue. The USSR continued to provide military aid to North Korea.

(See *Master Table*, pp. 706–7.)

Sources
Armbrister 1970; Brandt 1969; Bucher 1970; Chung 1978; Druks 1971; Duncan-Jones 1972; Gallery 1970; Johnson 1971; Kim Il-Sung 1976; Koh 1969a, 1969b; Lentner 1969; Murphy 1971; Rusk 1990; Simmons 1976; Zagoria and Zagoria 1981.

(274) Poplar Tree

The United States and North Korea were enmeshed in a crisis in the Demilitarized Zone *(DMZ)* from 17 August to 16 September 1976.

Background
Since the end of the Korean War (1950–53) there had been many incidents and several full-scale crises between North Korea and South Korea and/or the U.S. The most recent were **Pueblo** in 1968 and **EC-121 Spy Plane** in 1969 (see Cases #224, above, and 233, in **Multiregional PCs: East/West**). High tension in and near the *DMZ* was endemic, with a potential for instantaneous military flare-ups. One such outbreak generated a crisis in the summer of 1976.

Pre-crisis
During the first half of August there were several indicators of a North Korean perception of higher-than-normal threat. One was a White Paper issued on the 5th by the Pyongyang regime, which declared that "war may break out at any moment," that is, a U.S.–South Korean invasion of the North. Another was President Kim Il-Sung's cancellation, on the 15th, of his planned trip to Sri Lanka to participate in the conference of the Non-Aligned Movement. But the catalyst was a curious incident.

On 6 August, after notifying North and South Korea of its (the UN Command's) intent to enter the Joint Security Area *(JSA)* of the *DMZ* for construction work, six South Korean workers and four UN (U.S.) guards approached a poplar tree, which had long obscured the view from one UN observation post to another, with the intention of cutting it down. North Korean guards immediately demanded their withdrawal, and they complied. Neither the commander of UN forces nor Washington was yet aware of this episode. It required a more dramatic incident to trigger a full-scale crisis.

Crisis

On 17 August, in a scuffle between forces of the UN Command and the North Korean People's Army, two U.S. soldiers were killed and nine wounded in the *JSA* of the *DMZ:* they were members of a group of 15 who had entered the area to prune the poplar tree. This triggered a crisis for the United States. President Ford was informed immediately. In an initial response the State Department demanded that the Pyongyang regime do the following: accept responsibility for the casualties; pledge that such an incident would not occur again; and punish those who perpetrated the attack. More significantly, two meetings of the crisis management group in the Ford (and Nixon) administrations, the *WSAG* (Washington Special Action Group), on 18 and 19 August, led to a series of visible military measures. These included the dispatch of a squadron of 20 F-111s and a navy task force, including an aircraft carrier, along with a B-52 training mission, to South Korea; and the placing of U.S. forces in South Korea on a higher state of alert—*Defcon* (Defense Condition) 3, the same as in the 1973 October–Yom Kippur crisis-war and only slightly lower than in the Cuban Missile crisis. U.S. decision makers at the highest level (Ford and Secretary of State Kissinger) perceived this incident as a test of their resolve and a challenge to U.S. influence worldwide.

The U.S. military response, though non-violent, triggered a crisis for North Korea on the 19th. Kim Il-Sung responded the same day with an order for a war posture by the Korean People's Army, reserves, and all auxiliary forces. The next day the U.S. president approved General Stilwell's plan to cut down the poplar tree—to demonstrate U.S. resolve—but with strict orders not to use force first. "Operation Paul Bunyan" was implemented on the 21st, with U.S. bombers and fighters flying over South Korean airspace, B-52 strategic bombers flying close to the *DMZ,* and 26 helicopter-gunships protecting the special unit of tree cutters, protected by U.S. and South Korean troops. The operation was completed without violence. It was the most dramatic show of U.S. force in Korea since the Korean War.

The Poplar Tree crisis began to wind down with a rare statement by Kim Il-Sung on 22 August, within hours of the completion of Operation Paul Bunyan. It was conveyed by North Korea's foreign minister to his U.S. counterpart at Panmunjom. "It is regretful that an incident occurred. . . . ; an effort will be made so that such incidents may not recur in the future"; and "Our side will never provoke first." After an initial cool reaction, because it did not meet the three U.S. conditions, the State Department, on 23 August, termed the message "a positive step."

The de-escalation phase had begun. After several meetings within the framework of the Military Armistice Committee *(MAC)* beginning on 25 August, the U.S. and North Korea signed a new *JSA* agreement on 6 September. It took effect on 16 September, marking the end of the most serious international crisis in Korea since the Korean War. The outcome was a compromise, an informal apology by North Korea, with the U.S. desisting from its three-condition ultimatum.

The USSR, on 19 August, called for the withdrawal of U.S. forces from South Korea. North Korea's other ally, the PRC, remained aloof from this crisis. So too did the UN, other than the UN (U.S.) Command in Korea. The conference of Non-Aligned States in Sri Lanka passed a resolution condemning U.S. acts.

(See *Master Table,* pp. 716–17.)

Sources
Head et al. 1978; Kirkbride 1984.

(408) North Korea Nuclear Crisis

North Korea, South Korea, and the United States were enmeshed in a post–Cold War crisis over nuclear proliferation from early March 1993 until 21 October 1994.

Background and Pre-crisis
The Nuclear Non-Proliferation Treaty *(NPT)* formally came into effect in 1970. The Democratic People's Republic of Korea (DPRK, or North Korea) became a signatory in December 1985, part of the price for Soviet assistance in realizing its nuclear reactor program. As such, it undertook not to engage in activities that could lead to the production of nuclear weapons.

Further commitments were undertaken—by both Koreas—in their 1992 Denuclearization Agreement, notably a ban on the production of fissile material and the signing of a Joint Declaration on Denuclearization, an agreement in principle to establish a nuclear-free zone on the Korean peninsula. More tangibly, in the January 1992 *IAEA* Safeguards Agreement, the DPRK undertook to reveal the existence of 13 hitherto-unknown nuclear facilities and to permit regular inspections of North Korea's Yongbyon complex by the International Atomic Energy Agency *(IAEA)*. Notwithstanding these commitments, evidence of an incipient North Korean nuclear bomb program was reported by U.S. intelligence as early as February 1992.

Tension between the International Atomic Energy Agency and North Korea was endemic: the former, acting as the *NPT*'s monitoring body, kept pressing for total access to the latter's nuclear facilities, while North Korea attempted to restrict access.

In February 1993 *IAEA* inspectors, on a routine check, discovered a substantive discrepancy between the amount of weapons-grade plutonium and the amount reported by North Korea to the *IAEA*. This created the setting for an impending crisis.

Crisis

In early March 1993 the *IAEA* sought permission from the DPRK for a "special inspection" of two suspect, that is, hitherto-undeclared, nuclear waste sites. This triggered a crisis for North Korea, which perceived a threat to the "crown jewel" of its national security. It refused the request, claiming that these were restricted military nonnuclear facilities.

More ominously for the DPRK's adversaries, the ROK and its patron, the U.S., North Korea responded by giving public notice on 12 March of its intention to withdraw from the *NPT* regime. The reasons cited were the *IAEA*'s unprecedented pressure to conduct special inspections and the impending annual "Team Spirit" military cooperation exercise by ROK and U.S. forces. Pyongyang's announcement, raising the specter of a full-scale, unmonitored North Korean nuclear weapons program, triggered a crisis for South Korea and the U.S.

South Korea's leaders had perceived a threat of renewed war with the DPRK since the Korean Armistice in 1953. The declaration from Pyongyang sharply accentuated Seoul's perception of the high likelihood of war, initiated by the North's larger and more powerful armed forces. For the U.S., the crisis threatened its primacy in the post–Cold War world order and, specifically, constituted a potentially dangerous precedent of nuclear proliferation by a small, ambitious state. The next day, 13 March, the *IAEA* called upon North Korea to reconsider its announcement.

Further escalation occurred in May–June. On 14 May the DPRK reportedly began removing nuclear fuel rods from its Yongbyon reactor—without the presence of *IAEA* inspectors. On 10 June the *IAEA*'s Board of Governors adopted a sanctions resolution, suspending technical assistance to Pyongyang. North Korea responded on the 13th by formally withdrawing from the *IAEA*. And on 14 June the U.S. called for an international coalition against North Korea's nuclear program, to be implemented through UN-authorized economic sanctions.

In a context of acutely rising tension the DPRK and the U.S. held two rounds of talks in June–July 1993. The first, 2–11 June in New York, achieved a "suspension" of the DPRK's withdrawal from the *NPT*. At the second, 14–19 July in Geneva, the DPRK made a proposal that turned out to be the core of their ultimate accord—a replacement of its more dangerous graphite-moderated nuclear reactors with light-water nuclear reactors. After a lengthy period of deadlock they reached an interim agreement on 25 February 1994: the U.S. and the ROK would not hold the Team Spirit military exercise that year; and North Korea would allow a resumption of *IAEA* inspections.

The crisis escalated once more on 14 March 1994 when *IAEA* inspectors reported the discovery of additional discrepancies in the DPRK's nuclear program; but Pyongyang denied them permission to take samples for further examination. This led to a suspension of bilateral U.S./DPRK talks. On 31 March the

UN Secretary-General called on Pyongyang to allow *IAEA* inspectors to complete their investigation.

On 15 April South Korea made a concession—giving up its demand for North/South Korea talks before additional North Korea/U.S. meetings. The North reciprocated on the 19th by inviting *IAEA* inspectors to be present when nuclear fuel rods were removed from one of its reactors. On 19 May these inspectors reported that there was no evidence of misuse of the extracted nuclear fuel. And in mid-June, at the invitation of North Korea's ruler, Kim Il-Sung, former U.S. President Jimmy Carter went to Pyongyang as a "private" mediator. Carter's statement on 19 June that the crisis was over turned out to be premature; but it provided both a cooling-off period and a necessary face-saver for the adversaries.

Intense North Korea/U.S. negotiations took place very briefly in July 1994. They were interrupted on 8 July by the death of Kim Il-Sung but were resumed from 5 to 12 August and from 20 September to 17 October 1994. The outcome was a four-page "Agreed Framework" and a separate secret document signed on 21 October. The terms revealed a carefully calibrated schedule of mutual concessions.

The DPRK pledged to freeze its nuclear activities within a month and to store, that is, not reprocess, its 8,000 spent fuel rods. Once it received two replacement reactors, by the year 2003, it undertook to dispose of—abroad—its inventory of spent nuclear fuel, the sine qua non of a weapons program. It also promised not to refuel its existing five-megawatt reactor and not to complete the construction of two large reactors, one of 50 megawatts, the other of 200 megawatts, which the *IAEA* and the U.S. feared could generate enough weapons-grade plutonium to produce several—some estimates were as high as 30—nuclear bombs each year. In sum, the DPRK renounced any ambition to become a nuclear power, a goal that it constantly denied during the negotiations.

In return, the U.S. agreed to arrange for an "international consortium" to build two new light-water "proliferation-resistant" nuclear reactors, with a generating capacity of 2,000 megawatts, by the year 2003. These would provide North Korea with ample nuclear energy, with much less risk of extracting plutonium for a weapons program. The reactors were to be financed almost entirely by South Korea and Japan, the two most directly concerned states, and would be built in South Korea. In the interim, as compensation for the DPRK's freezing of its nuclear program, the U.S. would provide, at no cost to the DPRK, all of its heavy oil requirements for heating and electricity until the new reactors were installed: this would reach 500,000 metric tons annually by 1996. Finally, North Korea would not be obliged to open for inspection the two suspect nuclear facilities until a "significant portion" of the light-water project was completed, that is, for five years. The quid pro quo was that the DPRK would not receive the nuclear components to start its light-water reactors until it allowed all nuclear inspections sought by the *IAEA*. In sum, North Korea achieved almost all of its goals, through a comprehensive security, political, and economic package, but it yielded on its nuclear weapons program, a very high value. The U.S. seemed to have succeeded in aborting a nuclear weapons program by what it perceived as a rogue state.

Throughout the nuclear crisis on the Korean peninsula South Korea assumed a very low profile: it did so largely because of U.S. pressure not to compel the DPRK to lose face by negotiating directly with its mortal enemy, whose legitimacy it denied. In this sense the ROK was an observer of the very-high-stakes nuclear poker game between its patron and its feared foe. However, Seoul made known to Washington, frequently, its dissatisfaction with aspects of agreements reached in the bilateral talks.

In June 1993 President Kim Young Sam publicly cautioned the U.S. against acquiescing in the DPRK's efforts to shut the ROK out from any role in implementing an agreement. He also pressed for holding the Team Spirit military exercise in 1994, a point on which the U.S. conceded to the DPRK. He urged the U.S. to deploy Patriot missiles in the ROK, which the U.S. did in January 1994. And he successfully pressed the U.S., through former President Carter, to arrange a meeting with Kim Il-Sung. Only the sudden death of North Korea's leader in July 1994 prevented the realization of a North/South Korea dialogue. Most important, South Korea made known its dissatisfaction with the vagueness surrounding its intended role in the implementation of the 21 October 1994 agreement, especially since it was to bear the overwhelming financial burden, $4 billion. And this spilled over to public criticism of the U.S. by the ROK's president on 7 October 1994 for its "naive and overly flexible" negotiations with a regime on the verge of collapse. In this respect, South Korea ultimately achieved its primary goal during the crisis (see below).

The October 1994 agreement terminated the North Korea Nuclear Crisis—but not the conflict over the DPRK's suspected aspirations to join the nuclear weapons club.

(For eight months after the agreement its implementation foundered on the extremely sensitive issue of who would construct, supply, and install the two light-water nuclear reactors. The U.S. contended that the only possible source was South Korea, especially since it had agreed to bear most of the $4 billion cost, and that North Korean negotiators had accepted this provision. DPRK negotiators denied this contention and adamantly refused to accept reactors from its archenemy, the ROK. The obstacle was overcome through a bilateral agreement reached in Kuala Lumpur, Malaysia, on 12 June 1995: North Korea accepted South Korea's primary role in building, supplying, and installing the two new reactors. The U.S. provided a fig leaf to its adversary: everything to do with the two new reactors was to be implemented through the newly created (9 March 1995) Korean Peninsula Energy Development Organization *[KPEDO]*, comprising South Korea, the U.S., and Japan. The implementation process was set in motion by a supplementary supply contract agreement between North Korea and the *KPEDO* on 15 December 1995, which included "compensation" to the former for dismantling its nuclear reactors.)

Russia played no role in this crisis. China, the DPRK's sole major power ally, offered important political support, notably a threat to veto any UN Security Council economic sanctions resolution; for the rest it was passive throughout. Japan perceived a threat from North Korea's nuclear program along with time pressure. But unlike with South Korea, the crucial "high probability of war" condition was not visible. Japan was highly involved but not a direct crisis actor. It offered financial assistance in the construction of the two new reactors. At the same time, along with China and South Korea, it urged Washington not to impose economic sanctions, which North Korea had repeatedly declared it would treat as an "act of war." The UN was involved indirectly, through its specialized agency, the *IAEA*.

(See *Master Table,* pp. 736–37.)

Sources
Garrett and Glaser 1995; Kim 1995, 1996; Lee and Sohn 1995; Mack 1993; Merrill 1994; *New York Times,* June–November 1994, June 1995; Snyder 1995.

Europe: Protracted Conflicts

Czechoslovakia/Germany

In terms of international crises, the protracted conflict between Czechoslovakia and Germany lasted only a year. The three crises were as follows.

Case #62 **Czechoslovakia's May Crisis,** in 1938;
      #64 **Munich,** in 1938;
      #68 **Czechoslovakia's Annexation,** in 1939.

The conflict, however, lasted from 1919, when German-speaking areas of Sudetenland were allocated to the new Czechoslovak state, through the harsh German occupation of Czechoslovakia from 1939 to 1945, and the expulsion of German-speaking residents of Sudetenland by Czechoslovakia after World War II. The resentment created by these events perpetuated mistrust, tension, and conflict for many decades. They were accentuated by the deep ideological divide between democratic West Germany and communist Czechoslovakia after 1948. Closely related to the Czechoslovakia/Germany crises in 1938–39 was Case #60—**Anschluss**—which, in perspective, revealed much about Nazi Germany's strategy of territorial expansion and the tactics used to achieve that goal.

General Background

All parties in Germany, except the Communists, were dissatisfied with the provisions of the Versailles Treaty in 1919. The most vociferous were the National-Socialists (Nazis) who made the revision of the treaty the centerpiece of their political platform. This was a major electoral plank in the 1933 election that brought Hitler to power. It was also evident in the **Remilitarization of the Rhineland** crisis in 1936 (see Case #51, in **France/Germany PC**). And the broader policy of German expansion, to incorporate into the Third Reich territory with a high concentration of German speakers, found its most dramatic expression in the annexation of Austria in 1938 and, soon after, in the mounting pressure on Czechoslovakia to cede the Sudetenland to Germany.

In sum, Czechoslovakia, along with France, Poland and other states, was to uphold the European status quo as embodied in the Versailles Treaty, while Nazi Germany was determined to change it in its favor. The U.K. and, to a lesser extent, France were amenable to changes provided they were not accompanied by military action, as evident in their acquiescence in Hitler's remilitarization of the Rhineland, the rearming of Germany, and the annexation of Austria, all in defiance of the Versailles Treaty.

(62) Czechoslovakia's May Crisis

The threat of German military hostilities against Czechoslovakia created a crisis for Czechoslovakia, France, the U.K., and Germany from 19 to 23 May 1938.

Pre-crisis
The widespread perception of Hitler's objectives vis-à-vis Czechoslovakia, namely, to annex the German-speaking Sudetenland to the Reich, was reinforced by his speeches. The Sudeten Nazi Party, led by Konrad Henlein, received open support from Germany. Elections in the Sudetenland had been scheduled for 22 May 1938, and there was a heightening of turbulence in the area.

Crisis
A crisis for Czechoslovakia, France, and the U.K. was triggered on 19 May 1938 when intelligence sources reported that Germany was concentrating troops in Saxony, near the Czechoslovak border. These troops were, in fact, carrying out a combined army and air military game near and on the Koenigsbruck military training ground.

Czechoslovakia responded on the 20th by declaring a state of emergency and partial mobilization. Britain's and France's response, on 21 May, took the form of strong warnings to Germany, with a threat of intervention should Germany attack Czechoslovakia. Hitler, who apparently had no intention of invading Czechoslovakia in the immediate future, was surprised by the Czechoslovak response, as well as by that of the other actors, and perceived it as a threat to Germany. The German response was a decision by its War Council to retreat, as the Wehrmacht was not yet ready to meet the British-French-Czechoslovak challenge. On 23 May the Czechoslovak ambassador to Berlin was assured that Nazi Germany had no aggressive intentions toward his country, and the crisis ended for all the participants. The underlying conflict, however, continued unabated and reached a further stage of crisis four months later—the **Munich** crisis (see Case #64 below).

There was no USSR intervention in the May weekend crisis. Nor was its aid solicited by the U.K. and France, despite the fact that the Soviet Union had an alliance with France and Czechoslovakia concerning the latter's independence and territorial integrity. This crisis did not come before the League of Nations.

(See *Master Table,* pp. 676–77.)

Sources
See sources for Case #64.

(64) Munich

The Munich crisis—for Czechoslovakia, France, the U.K., and the USSR—took place from 7 September to early October 1938.

Background
The annexation of Austria by Germany in March 1938 (see Case #60—**Anschluss**, in **Europe: Non-PCs**) created an immediate threat to Czechoslovakia, which feared that its German-speaking areas would be Hitler's next target. Czechoslovakia sought assurances from France and the U.K., which refused to give firm guarantees. In April Anglo-French leaders met in London to seek a solution to the problem. In order to avoid the possibility of war with Hitler the two powers began to press Czechoslovakia to make concessions over Sudetenland. In the third week of May rumors reached Prague that large German military forces were gathering near the frontier in Silesia and northern Austria, possibly in preparation for an operation against Czechoslovakia (see Case #62 above). The activity of the Sudeten German Party *(SdP)*, which was strongly supported by Germany, was intensified. Its leader, Konrad Henlein, presented the party's demands in the Karlsbad Programme on 7 June. In June, July, and August there was an intensification of *SdP* activity. On 18 July the British government decided to send a mediator to Prague and, on 3 August, Lord Runciman arrived. A "Third Plan" was presented by the Czechoslovak government on 24 August, which proposed a compromise between its original proposals over the Sudetenland and the *SdP*'s demands. As tension in the country built up, Runciman came up with a "Fourth Plan" between 3 and 7 September, leaning strongly toward the earlier Sudeten German demands. The Nazi Party Congress convened at Nuremberg on 5 September.

Crisis
On 7 September 1938 tension in Czechoslovakia escalated when 82 members of the Sudeten German Party were detained in Moravska Ostrava for arms smuggling and other offenses against the state. The *SdP*, for its part, charged the Czechoslovak police with violence, and Hitler ordered Henlein to break off all negotiations with Prague. That day, too, the *Times of London* published a leading article supporting the "Fourth Plan" as the solution to the Sudeten problem. The arrests on 7 September, which had effectively laid to rest any hope of reaching a compromise solution through the Runciman Mission, triggered a crisis for Czechoslovakia. This was followed by almost daily demonstrations accompanied by acts of violence by the *SdP*. On the 9th President Beneš addressed his people and attempted to win goodwill for the "Fourth Plan."

On 12 September a crisis was triggered for France and the U.K. when Hitler addressed the Nazi Party Congress and demanded self-determination for the Sudeten Germans. That evening riots began in the Sudeten districts. The French and British responses came the following day: Prime Minister Chamberlain cabled Hitler that he was willing to travel to Germany to seek a solution to the crisis. That day, too, Premier Daladier requested Chamberlain to arrange a Three-Power Conference to allow the transfer of Sudetenland to Germany. Several French economic and financial decrees were prepared, as well, in case of war.

On 15 September Chamberlain met with Hitler at Berchtesgaden. He returned the next day, bringing his colleagues and the French government Hitler's plan for the cession of the Sudeten districts to Germany. Anglo-French discussions began in London on 18 September to work out a proposal that Chamberlain could bring to Hitler at their forthcoming meeting in Godesberg. The Anglo-French Plan, announced on the 19th, called for the immediate transfer to Germany of Sudeten areas with over 50 percent German inhabitants and the acceptance by Czechoslovakia of a neutralized status, which would require the abrogation of its treaties with France and the USSR.

That day a crisis was triggered for the Soviet Union when President Beneš requested USSR affirmation of the Soviet-Czechoslovak Pact. The Soviets responded the same day by affirming the Pact on condition of prior French action. On 20 September Czechoslovakia rejected the Anglo-French Plan. But on the 21st Prague reversed its decision and accepted the Plan, after having been served an ultimatum by both Britain and France.

The Godesberg meeting between Hitler and Chamberlain took place on 22 and 23 September. The German leader increased his demands and issued an ultimatum for the territorial transfer by 1 October, the date originally set by Hitler in April. Beneš ordered general mobilization in Czechoslovakia. On the 23rd the USSR warned Poland that it would denounce the Soviet-Polish Pact of Non-Aggression if the Polish government persisted in sending troops to the Czechoslovakia-Polish frontier. A partial mobilization in France was ordered on 24 September. On the 25th the British fleet and its auxiliary air force units were mobilized. Hitler spoke at the *Sportspalast* on the 26th, stating that the Czechoslovaks would have to come to terms peaceably with their non-German minorities. Chamberlain sent a message to Hitler that Britain would support France if it were drawn into war over Czechoslovakia. A final appeal to Britain to avoid war was sent by Hitler on the 27th. A conference among Italy, France, Germany, and Britain was called.

The signing of the Four-Power Agreement at Munich on 30 September 1938 terminated the crisis for France and the U.K. Czechoslovakia was forced to accept the terms. War with Germany had been temporarily avoided. The Soviet termination date was sometime early in October, once German troops were in occupation of all the German-claimed territories and war had been averted.

Other involved actors were Italy and the U.S. Mussolini formally proposed the terms—secretly drawn up by the German foreign office—that were incorporated in the Agreement. President Roosevelt sent personal appeals to all actors on 26 and 27 September to refrain from the use of force. There was no League of Nations involvement in this crisis.

(See *Master Table*, pp. 676–77.)

Sources
Documents on British Foreign Policy (DBFP) 1949–52; *Documents Diplomatiques Français (DDF)* 1964; *Documents on German Foreign Policy (DGFP)* 1948; Baynes 1942; Beloff 1947–49; Bonnefous 1965, 1967; Braddick 1968–69; Bruegel 1973; Bullock 1962; Butler and Sloman 1975; Carr 1945; Cowling 1975; Dilks 1971; Eden 1962; Eubank 1965; Feiling 1946; Fuchser 1982; Henderson 1940; Lacaze 1995; Laffan 1951; Middlemas 1972; Perman 1962; Robbins 1968; Schuman 1939; Shirer 1964, 1985; Smelser 1975; Smith 1982; Taylor 1979; Thorne 1967; Weinberg 1980, 1988; Wheeler-Bennett 1948.

(68) Czechoslovakia's Annexation

Germany's overt threat of annexation precipitated a crisis for Czechoslovakia on 14–15 March 1939.

Background and Pre-crisis
The period between **Munich** and the annexation, October 1938 to March 1939, witnessed national and societal unrest in Czechoslovakia. Slovak and Ruthenian nationalities, supported by Germany and Hungary, were making increasing demands for independence. There was a rapid deterioration in Czechoslovakia's economic situation, apparently generated by the secession of important industrial areas of the Sudetenland and Teschen after September, as a result of the Munich Agreement. This economic and societal disruption formed the basis of Hitler's claim that, as Czechoslovakia was composed of dissatisfied nationalities precipitating social unrest that culminated in economic deterioration, it was in fact no longer a viable state.

On 17 December 1938 Hitler, assuming no resistance, directed his armed forces to make preparations to occupy the rest of Czechoslovakia. This directive was followed by a final order on 12 March, at the height of the Slovak tension, for the invasion of Czechoslovakia and its incorporation into the Reich. The following day the Czechoslovak President, Emil Hacha, requested an interview with Hitler. On 14 March both Ruthenia and Slovakia proclaimed their independence from Czechoslovakia.

Crisis
On the morning of 14 March Hitler informed Hacha that German troops had already occupied the important industrial town of Moravska Ostrava and that they were now poised all along the perimeter of Bohemia and Moravia. The crisis for Czechoslovakia had been triggered. Hitler, while ignoring the issue of Slovak independence, stated that, if the Czechoslovak president invited the entry of German troops, Czechoslovakia would be allowed to remain autonomous after incorporation into the Reich. If the Czechoslovak army resisted, Czechoslovakia would be annihilated.

Faced with this ultimatum, Hacha phoned his government in Prague early in the morning of the 15th and advised capitulation. After receiving their consent, he signed the note of surrender that had been drawn up earlier by the German foreign office. The crisis ended at 6 A.M. on 15 March, when German troops poured into Bohemia and Moravia. There was no resistance. The same day they entered Prague. A proclamation of Bohemia-Moravia and Slovakia as German protectorates followed.

The USSR took no action during the critical days of the crisis. The U.K. declared that its post-Munich guarantee of Czechoslovakia's territorial integrity and independence against unprovoked aggression was no longer applicable because the declaration of Slovak independence had put an end to the state whose frontiers London had promised to guarantee. An official protest from France was its only activity in the crisis. There was no League of Nations involvement.

(More than half a century elapsed before the beginning of a formal state-to-state reconciliation. On 21 January 1997, Chancellor Kohl of Germany and Czech Prime Minister Klaus signed a declaration expressing mutual regrets: the former, for the occupation and annexation of Bohemia and Moravia in March 1939 and for Nazi "policies of violence"; the latter, for the expulsion of 2.5 million Sudeten Germans from the restored Czechoslovakia in the aftermath of World War II. As expected, both the Sudeten Germans, concentrated in Bavaria since the mid-1940s, and right-wing Czechs objected strenuously to the concessions made by their respective governments.)

(See *Master Table*, pp. 676–77.)

Sources
Bullock 1962; Deutscher 1949; Kennan 1967; Laffan and Toynbee 1953; Mamatey 1973; *New York Times* December 1996, January 1997; Schuman 1939; Shirer 1964; Thorne 1967; Vital 1967; Watt 1989; Weinberg 1980.

Finland/Russia

There were four crises in the protracted conflict between Finland and Russia (USSR) from 1919 to 1961, as follows.

Case #9   **Finnish/Russian Border: Karelia,** in 1919–20;
  #76   **Finnish War,** in 1939–40;
  #122   **Soviet Note to Finland I,** in 1948;
  #189   **Soviet Note to Finland II,** in 1961.

Case #76—**Finnish War**—was related to early crises in the **World War II** PC, notably #75—**Soviet Occupation of the Baltic;** and #77—**Invasion of Scandinavia.** Cases #122 and 189—**Soviet Note to Finland I, II**—were influenced by the Cold War (see *Master Table*).

General Background

Finland's association with Russia dates to 1809 when it was ceded by Sweden to the czarist empire after defeat in war. It was organized as an autonomous grand duchy, with the czar serving as grand duke. So it remained until the last year of World War I.

Finland proclaimed its independence on 6 December 1917. Early in January it was recognized by the new Bolshevik regime in Russia, as well as by Sweden, France, and Germany. And in March 1918, under the terms of the Treaty of Brest-Litovsk, Russia was compelled, formally, to give up Finland, along with Poland, the Baltic states, Ukraine, and Transcaucasia.

During its early days Finland experienced a struggle between communist and anti-communist forces. Sporadic clashes erupted into civil war by late January 1918. During the next few months "White" Russian forces pushed Finnish and Soviet Russian units deep into East Karelia. The civil war ended in May 1918.

(9) Finnish/Russian Border: Karelia

The first of several international crises between Russia and Finland since the end of World War I lasted from 20 April 1919 to 14 October 1920.

Crisis
On 20 April 1919 a "volunteer" force of Finnish soldiers, backed by the Finnish government, crossed into East Karelia and seized Olonets, triggering a crisis for Russia. Foreign Affairs Commissar Chicherin demanded an explanation. And several members of the Finnish Economic Commission in Petrograd (St. Petersburg) were arrested. Both Prime Minister Castren and Foreign Minister Enrooth denied any Finnish territorial designs on Olonets but reaffirmed Finland's military support for the "volunteers."

On 6 May Finland's independence was recognized by the U.K. and the U.S. Finnish and Russian batteries exchanged fire on 17 and 18 May. (It is unclear who fired the first shot.) This triggered a crisis for Finland and escalated Russia's crisis. Sporadic fighting continued through May. Chicherin sent several protest notes to Helsinki, notably a letter to his Finnish counterpart on 6 June declaring that Russia considered itself free to take "all necessary steps" to eliminate "Finnish aggression," further escalating Finland's crisis. In the fighting that followed, Finnish forces experienced several setbacks.

Peace talks began in September 1919; but Finland renewed its offensive into East Karelia in October. After months of hostilities, negotiations resumed in June 1920. And a peace agreement, the Treaty of Tartu (Dorpat), was signed on 14 October 1920 marking an end to this crisis over territory.

Four major powers were involved in this crisis. Germany tried to mediate the conflict. Activity by France and the U.S. was confined to statements in support of Finland. And the U.K., in addition to supportive statements, dispatched naval vessels to the Baltic at Finland's request in order to enhance its bargaining position in the negotiations.

Although the League of Nations Council first met nine months before the end of this crisis, the global organization was not involved.

(See *Master Table,* pp. 666–67.)

Sources
Documents on British Foreign Policy (DBFP) 1949a (Woodward and Butler); Boulter 1928; Butler 1961; Degras 1953; Hovi 1980; Kirby 1975; Smith 1958.

(76) Finnish War

A crisis for Finland, Sweden, France, and the U.K., centering on the Finnish/Russian War, began on 6 October 1939 and ended on 13 March 1940.

Background
The city of St. Petersburg is 32 kilometers from the Finnish border, south of the Karelian Peninsula. Treaties signed by the Soviet Union with Estonia, Latvia, and Lithuania in September and October 1939 granted Moscow the right to build bases in the three Baltic states (see Case #75—**Soviet Occupation—Baltic,** in **Europe: Non-PCs**). In addition to a base in Estonia at the southwestern edge of the Gulf of Finland, the Soviets wanted a base at the northern end, along with territorial changes that would protect it from future attack, either by the U.K. or Germany. From early 1938 until mid-1939 requests for such border changes had been discussed by Soviet diplomats in Helsinki with the Finnish foreign minister. Pressure on Finland began once the treaties with the Baltic states had been signed. On 5 October Molotov requested the Finnish ambassador to the Soviet Union to inform his government that the USSR wished the Finnish foreign minister or some high-ranking delegate to come to Moscow to discuss concrete political questions in view of the altered international situation—the outbreak of World War II and the German-Soviet partition of Poland.

Crisis
In the absence of a reply by 6 October strong pressure was applied to the ambassador of Finland. A crisis was triggered for Finland when its ambassador in Moscow related the Soviet demands the same day. A negotiator was selected by Finland with clear instructions to convey its determination to stand firm. And Moscow was so informed on the 10th. The same day Finland called for partial mobilization and evacuation of some cities, along with a practice air raid and blackout in Helsinki.

Negotiations took place between 12 and 14 October. The Soviets presented their "minimum demands," which included the transfer of islands close to the USSR shore and the port of Itanko, moving the border 35 kilometers farther away from St. Petersburg; and concessions in the northern peninsula of Rybachi, including the port of Petsamo. The Finnish mission returned to Helsinki for further instructions. On 27 October Finland appealed to Sweden for military aid in case of war. The following day the appeal was rejected by the prime minister of Sweden. The last round of negotiations produced lesser Soviet demands, but Helsinki refused to consider them. The negotiators returned to Finland on 14 November.

An incident involving the firing of seven shots occurred in a town on the Soviet side of the Karelian border on 26 November. Moscow accused Finland of violating their Non-Aggression Pact; and a vehement press campaign was launched against Finland. The Soviets refused Finland's request to investigate the incident and withdrew its diplomats on 29 November, denouncing the Pact. On the 30th the USSR attacked Finland. The Finnish cabinet declared a state of war that day and appointed Marshal Mannerheim Commander in Chief of the Armed Forces. The government resigned on 1 December and was reorganized under a new Prime Minister, Ryti. On the 2nd the Soviet Union set up and recognized a Finnish Democratic Government in captured territory. The same day Finland appealed to the League of Nations, which invited the Soviet Union to attend an Assembly session. Moscow refused on 4 December; and on the 14th the League Assembly condemned the Soviet Union as an aggressor and requested that members give Finland material and humanitarian aid. The Soviet Union was expelled from the League, by then an empty shell.

During December France and the U.K. began to consider sending forces to aid Finland, with a view to stopping the flow of Swedish iron shipments through Narvik to Germany. In order to do this troops had to cross neutral Norway and Sweden. Sweden, physically closer to Finland and politically friendly, saw the situation as dangerous and feared being drawn into the conflict, particularly with Germany. When the first official offer by Britain and France to send troops to Finland via Sweden was made on 27 December 1939, a crisis was triggered for Sweden which, together with Norway, insisted that no troops pass through its territories. On 4 January the German ambassador to Finland made it clear that Germany would view Allied troops in northern Sweden and Norway as a casus belli. The Soviets, who had been surprised at Finnish perseverance and success, finally broke Finland's line on 14 January 1940, triggering a crisis for France and the U.K.: they were suddenly faced with the real prospect of a Soviet victory in a strategic area and a need to send aid to Finland before the spring thaw shifted the military conditions once more. They responded on 5 February with a finalized plan for action in Finland which was accepted by the Joint Allied Supreme War Council.

Sweden, which had been brokering negotiations between the Finnish foreign minister and the Soviet ambassador to Sweden, became more alarmed over the Allied plans. A press-leaked story about the negotiations and appeals from Finland for aid determined the Swedish major response to the crisis: on 19

February the king of Sweden officially refused to aid Finland. Throughout February and March, Britain and France continued to ignore Sweden's and Norway's refusals to grant passage for their troops and pressed Finland to accept Allied armies on its soil. Finland preferred to continue negotiations for an armistice with the Soviet Union via Sweden.

Moscow, which had originally expected little resistance and popular support for a communist government in Finland, finally agreed to an armistice while demanding stiffer conditions. The armistice was signed on 13 March 1940, terminating the crisis for all four actors.

Offers to mediate were made by the United States, Italy, and Germany.

(See *Master Table,* pp. 680–81.)

Sources

DGFP 1940 (1949); Beloff 1949; Bullock 1962; Calvocoressi and Wint 1972; Carlgren 1977; Churchill 1948; Dallin 1942; Degras 1953; *Finnish Blue Book* 1940; Jakobson 1961; Maude 1976; Nevakivi 1976; *RIIA* 1947; Schuman 1941; Snell 1963; Tanner 1957; Ulam 1974; Upton 1964; Walters 1952; Weinberg 1954, 1994.

(122) Soviet Note to Finland I

Finland was in a state of crisis with the USSR from 22 February until 6 April 1948.

Pre-crisis

On 9 February 1948 there was a meeting of representatives of the Nordic states. The Soviet Union felt that Nordic cooperation, backed by the West and, specifically, by the United States, posed a threat to Soviet hegemony in northern Europe.

Crisis

On 22 February the Soviet Union sent a Note to the Finnish government requesting a meeting of high-level officials for the purpose of concluding a Treaty of Mutual Friendship, Cooperation, and Non-Aggression. Such a treaty would effectively prevent Finland from adopting a pro-Western stance. Finland responded on 8 March 1948 by sending a delegation to Moscow.

The crisis ended on 6 April 1948 with the signing of a treaty. There was no violence and no overt threats by the Soviet Union. The negotiations seemed to proceed smoothly, and all parties appeared satisfied with the outcome. However, a message from Stalin was construed as containing an implied threat of Soviet military action if Finland did not comply with Moscow's proposal. The crisis was a turning point in Finnish/Soviet relations: it led to a basic change in Finland's foreign policy orientation and created the phenomenon of "Finlandization," namely, curtailing the freedom of action in international relations of a formally sovereign state in the emerging global cold war. The U.S. and the UN were not involved.

(See *Master Table*, pp. 688–89.)

Sources
Finnish Political Science Association 1969; Jakobson 1968; Maude 1976; Vloyantes 1975.

(189) Soviet Note to Finland II

Another crisis for Finland vis-à-vis the USSR occurred between 30 October and 24 November 1961.

Pre-crisis
Cold war tensions resulting from the erection of the **Berlin Wall** in August 1961 (see Case #185, in **Multiregional PCs: East/West**) and the breakdown of disarmament talks in September contributed to Soviet concern about the January 1962 presidential and parliamentary elections in Finland. Five coalition parties had united to back the candidacy of Olair Honka for president and presented a serious challenge to incumbent President Kekkonen. The Soviets perceived the possibility of Kekkonen's defeat as a political threat that would affect Finland's neutrality and its general pro-Soviet foreign policy. Finland, always sensitive to the wishes of its giant neighbor, perceived a military threat from the Soviet Union if it deviated too much from previous policy.

Crisis
On 30 October 1961 a Note was sent by the Soviet Union to Finland calling for consultations between the two governments "to ensure the defense of both countries from the threat of a military attack by Western Germany and allied states." The Finnish response, on 7 November, was a decision to send Foreign Minister Karzalaimen for talks with Soviet Foreign Minister Gromyko. Further negotiations between Kekkonen and Khrushchev resulted in the termination of the crisis on 24 November 1961, postponing military consultations between the two countries.

There was no UN involvement in this crisis.

(In 1962 Kekkonen was re-elected to the presidency.)

(See *Master Table*, pp. 700–701.)

Sources
Jakobson 1968; Vloyantes 1975.

France/Germany

There were five international crises in the **France/Germany** protracted conflict from 1920 to 1936, as follows.

Case #12   **Rhenish Rebellions,** in 1920;
     #20   **German Reparations,** in 1921;
     #27   **Ruhr I,** in 1923;
     #30   **Ruhr II,** in 1924;
     #51   **Remilitarization of the Rhineland,** in 1936.

Many other crises during the inter–world war period had a Franco/German PC dimension, such as the four **Spanish Civil War** cases—#52, 54, 65, 67; Cases #60—**Anschluss;** #62—**Czechoslovakia's May Crisis;** #64—**Munich;** #70—**Danzig;** and several crises in the **World War II PC,** notably Cases #74—**Entry into World War II;** #77—**Invasion of Scandinavia;** culminating in #78—**Fall of Western Europe;** and, finally, #94—**D-Day** (see *Master Table*).

General Background

The protracted conflict between France and Germany is among the longest and most intense in the history of international relations. It extends back in time at least three centuries, much longer in the judgment of some scholars. Notable eras of conflict are as follows: the Napoleonic Wars, 1799–1815; the Franco/Prussian War, 1870–71, with France's humiliation and defeat; and the two world wars of the twentieth century, with Germany suffering the ignominy of defeat and occupation, and France the defeat of 1940 and four years of occupation, as well as an enormous cost in human and material losses. It was the outcome of World War I that created the setting for a cluster of Franco/German international crises in the 1920s and 1930s.

(12) Rhenish Rebellions

France and Germany experienced a crisis over the Rhineland and the Ruhr from 3 April to 17 May 1920.

Pre-crisis
In the aftermath of Germany's defeat in World War I the stability of the newly proclaimed Weimar Republic (November 1918) was undermined by several internal uprisings. The most serious was a promonarchist putsch in Berlin by Wilhelm Kapp in mid-March 1920. Although he held power for only four days, 13–17 March, this incident triggered widespread rebellion, especially a Sparta-

cist (Communist) revolt in the Ruhr mining districts. Coping with these challenges was made more difficult by the Versailles Treaty requirement (Article 160) of a reduction of German armed forces to 100,000 by 31 March 1920, as well as by Article 43, which forbade German occupation of the Ruhr Neutral Zone.

In an attempt to suppress these rebellions the German government made two requests on 15 and 17 March for authority to send troops into the Ruhr. France refused. The U.K., backed by the other members of the Supreme Council at the Paris Peace Conference, Italy, Japan, and the U.S., took the position that it would be preferable to allow the Germans to crush the rebellions rather than to involve the Allies in German internal disputes. On the 20th, amplified on the 28th, France offered to accept the entry of German troops into the restricted zone if, as a quid pro quo, Allied troops occupied parts of Germany, to last as long as the German presence in the Ruhr. The U.K., perceiving this as a cover for long-term French occupation, disapproved, as did the Supreme Council. On 30 March Chancellor Müller informed the Reichstag that French consent to Germany's request had been granted and that 2 April had been set for the initial dispatch of troops to the Ruhr. On 31 March France withdrew its offer by making it conditional on approval by the Rhineland Commission.

Crisis

Despite British advice to Germany to delay implementation of its plan, forces of the Reichswehr entered the Ruhr Neutral Zone on 3 April and suppressed the Spartacist revolt with great severity. That act triggered a crisis for France, which perceived a threat to its influence in Western Europe generally and, in particular, the Franco/German border area. France responded on the 4th by placing its armed forces on alert and, more important, by occupying Frankfurt and Darmstadt on the 6th. That in turn triggered a crisis for Germany, which viewed France's unilateral act as a threat to its political regime.

Germany strongly opposed the French occupation of its territory, warning of "the gravest political and economic results." On the 8th the U.K. sent a sharp note to Paris condemning France's action, as well as boycotting the Conference of Ambassadors. This blunt criticism was elaborated two days later by a carrot-stick *démarche* from one ally to another: British Foreign Secretary Curzon told French Ambassador Cambon that, if France admitted it had erred in acting unilaterally and if it promised to refrain from such actions in the future, the U.K. would consider the matter "cleared up." Premier Millerand, who considered Anglo-French solidarity more important than the temporary presence of German troops in the Ruhr, gave the necessary assurances on 11 April, with a reciprocal German announcement the same day that all German forces in the Ruhr not required to put down the rebellion would be withdrawn immediately. Then on 24 April Germany informed France that its troops in the Ruhr were being withdrawn thereby terminating France's crisis. On the 26th, at the San Remo Conference, Millerand agreed to withdraw French forces as soon as German troops were evacuated. French (and supporting Belgian) troops began their withdrawal from

Germany on 17 May ending Germany's crisis and the international crisis as a whole. In an infrequent crisis outcome both France and Germany perceived the outcome as a victory.

Belgium, as noted, was a highly involved actor. Italy, the U.S., and Japan were less involved, supporting the high-profile and active British posture on the optimal path to effective crisis management. The League of Nations declined a German request that it attempt to resolve the dispute. The League Council held its first meeting less than three months before the outbreak of this crisis and was not involved.

(See *Master Table*, pp. 668–69.)

Sources
Documents on British Foreign Policy (DBFP) 1958, 1960 (Butler et al.); Boulter 1928; Carsten 1984; McDougall 1978; Toynbee 1927c.

(20) German Reparations

Germany, Belgium, and the Netherlands experienced a crisis over reparations payments from 3 March to 11 May 1921.

Pre-crisis
The Treaty of Versailles, signed on 28 June 1919, incorporated the principle of reparations by Germany following World War I. A schedule of reparations payments was formulated at a conference of victorious European powers in Paris in January 1921 and was reaffirmed at a conference in London in February–March. France was insistent on their enforcement. German counterproposals on 1 March were rejected.

Crisis
An ultimatum by the Allies led by France and the U.K. on 3 March 1921 triggered a crisis for Germany. This was followed by a threat of sanctions on the 7th. The next day Duisburg, Ruhrort, and Dusseldorf were occupied by French forces. President Ebert decried the occupation of German territory as a breach of the Versailles Treaty but acknowledged that Germany was "not in a position to oppose force with force." German ambassadors to London, Paris, and Brussels were recalled. On 10 March Germany appealed to the League of Nations, but Secretary-General Drummond ignored the petition. The League remained aloof throughout this crisis.

Both the Belgians and the Dutch were quietly opposed to the French occupation of the Ruhr: the former viewed it as a danger to Belgium's security; and the latter feared being drawn into a Franco/German conflict. For Belgium, a crisis was triggered by Prime Minister Briand's speech to the French Senate on 5 April indicating that France would act unilaterally and occupy the entire Left Bank of the Rhine if Germany did not meet its financial obligations by 1 May.

Belgium was concerned about both the consequences of not joining France against Germany—"a violent storm would burst against them"—and of participating in a French-led occupation, not knowing how far France would go in its punitive action. It also feared that French control of the Ruhr would make the Belgian economy more dependent on France. Reluctantly Belgium agreed to join France in its declared intention to occupy the Ruhr on 2 May, if necessary. The Netherlands, too, was concerned about the likely negative spillover effects of French occupation of the Ruhr, specifically the possibility of Franco/German military hostilities at Duisburg, which lay close to the Dutch frontier.

The trigger to Holland's crisis was partial mobilization of France's armed forces on 2 May in preparation for occupation of the Ruhr. The same day the Dutch foreign minister sought U.S. diplomatic intervention to dissuade France from proceeding with the occupation; and Belgium's premier informed the U.S. ambassador in Brussels that the occupation "was to be avoided if at all possible."

The U.K. was loyal to France throughout this crisis. A joint Anglo-French ultimatum on 5 May set in motion the de-escalation of the crisis by renewing the threat of occupation of the Ruhr if Germany did not accept the schedule of payments by the 12th. The German government resigned in protest. Its successor under Wirth accepted the conditions on the 11th terminating the crisis for all three actors and the German Reparations crisis as a whole.

(The issue of reparations generated other crises in 1923 and 1924—see Cases #27 and 30 below.)

(See *Master Table*, pp. 668–69.)

Sources
Documents on British Foreign Policy (DBFP) (Butler et al., Medlicott et al.) 1967, 1968; *Foreign Relations of the United States (FRUS) 1921*, vol. 2; Baudhuin 1946; Boulter 1928; Helmreich 1976; Mahaim 1926; McDougall 1978; Toynbee 1927c.

(27) Ruhr I

Poland, Germany, and the Netherlands experienced a crisis arising from the reparations issue from 22 January to 27 September 1923.

Pre-crisis
The conflict over German reparations continued to create tension after the crisis of 1921. By December 1922 Germany was declared to be in default regarding deliveries of lumber. And in early January 1923 it was declared in default of coal deliveries. On 10 January France and Belgium informed Germany that a commission of engineers, including Italians, would enter the Ruhr escorted by French and Belgian troops to facilitate the delivery of coal. The next day the Ruhr was occupied, an act that brought a strong protest from the German government. It also prompted Bolshevik Russia to make Poland aware that any Polish designs on

German territory, notably Upper Silesia, would not be tolerated. The Soviets were trying to neutralize Poland and to improve Russo-German relations, in the hope that this would pave the way for the spread of communism in Germany.

Crisis
Threats from Moscow generated a Polish perception of threat, time pressure, and higher probability of hostilities with Russia, on 22 January 1923. This concern was evident in the remark by a Polish minister to the German foreign office the same day, that Russian military moves made his government "very nervous." There was no clear termination date for Poland; rather, it faded in late July 1923.

Germany, the principal actor in this international crisis, did not perceive a crisis until 28 February, when its government expressed concern about civilian disturbances precipitated by the occupation of the Ruhr. The major German response was to approve a series of economic ordinances beginning on 16 March in support of passive opposition to the occupation; but Germany also negotiated with its adversaries.

The Netherlands entered the crisis on 9 March as a result of fear of the prospects for a new European war generated by information communicated to one of its ministers by French officials. It responded four days later by seeking— and getting—British assurances about the occupation of the Ruhr.

The German government fell in August. And its successor began to reassess the tactic of passive resistance. On 27 September Germany capitulated by calling off passive resistance, terminating the crisis for Germany and the Netherlands and the larger international crisis over the Ruhr.

There were many involved actors in Ruhr I: the three crisis actors; Belgium and France, Italy, Japan, the U.K., the U.S., and the USSR, along with the Vatican. Belgium expressed concern over the occupation; while the U.K. reassured Belgium by terming the occupation illegal. The League of Nations was not involved.

(See *Master Table,* pp. 670–71.)

Sources
See sources for Case #30; and Korbel 1963; Kossmann 1978; Polonsky 1972; von Riekhoff 1971.

(30) Ruhr II

Germany and France were the adversaries in another crisis over reparations from 29 April to 30 August 1924.

Pre-crisis
Despite Germany's abandonment of passive resistance to demands for reparations payments, tensions between the West European victor and vanquished in World War I became more acute. The Dawes Plan of 9 April 1924, which

specified a schedule of German payments for five years, was accepted by Germany a week later; but it insisted on immediate evacuation of the Ruhr. However, France (and Belgium) refused to withdraw from the Ruhr until 12 months of reparations payments were made. A standoff ensued, and tensions escalated.

Crisis

France's demand precipitated a crisis for Germany on 29 April: it feared that French Premier Poincaré's behavior was designed to foment a crisis thereby permitting France to use more coercive measures to achieve its aims—humiliation of Germany and weakening its economy. France's pressure on Germany to comply, and Germany's reluctance to pay further reparations without a guarantee of French withdrawal from the Ruhr and its demilitarization, maintained a high level of stress.

France perceived a crisis on 8 July, as evident in newly elected Premier Herriot's expression of concern for the military security of France: when Germany was "strong enough to refuse" to pay reparations, it would instigate a "new war." On 9 August the German delegation to a conference in London agreed to implement the Dawes Plan provisions on reparations. And on the 16th Germany signed a protocol with France and Belgium ending Germany's second Ruhr crisis: it was agreed that the occupation of the Ruhr would end by August 1925. For France, the second Ruhr crisis ended on 30 August, when the London Conference agreements were formally adopted, one day after the Reichstag ratified the protocol.

The U.K., the U.S., Japan, and Italy were highly involved in the negotiations that led to crisis resolution. Yugoslavia and to a lesser extent Greece, Romania, and Portugal were also involved in the negotiations. The League of Nations was not involved.

(See *Master Table,* pp. 670–71.)

Sources

DBFP (Medlicott et al.) 1976, 1978, 1985; Boulter 1928; Dexter 1967; Helmreich 1976; Rogers 1934; Sauvy 1972; Toynbee 1926.

(51) Remilitarizatlon of Rhineland

The international crisis over Germany's remilitarization of the Rhineland took place between 7 March and 16 April 1936. The actors were Belgium, Czechoslovakia, France, Poland, Romania, the U.K., and Yugoslavia.

Background

The international status of the Rhineland, an area separating Germany from France and Belgium, had been determined at Versailles at the end of World War I, and in the Locarno Pact of 1 December 1925. Germany was forbidden to maintain or construct any fortifications either on the left bank of the Rhine or on the right bank to a line drawn 50 kilometers to the east of the river. The Locarno Pact pledged Germany, France, and Belgium to nonaggression and pacific settlement. It guaranteed established frontiers and the demilitarization of the Rhineland. If the Reich armed this demilitarized zone, France was legally authorized to declare it an unprovoked act of aggression, and Britain, Italy, and Belgium would all be bound to come at once to France's aid. France had secured itself by alliances with Poland and the Little Entente states (Czechoslovakia, Romania, and Yugoslavia) which had built their security against German aggressiveness upon these military alliances with France. The Germans claimed that France's 1935 military pact with the Soviet Union, exclusively directed against Germany, was a violation of the Locarno Pact. Hitler proceeded to fulfill his election promises when plans were laid for Germany's reoccupation of the Rhineland.

Crisis

On 7 March 1936 three German battalions entered and occupied the demilitarized zone of the Rhineland, triggering a crisis for Belgium, Czechoslovakia, France, Poland, Romania, the U.K., and Yugoslavia. The border countries, France and Belgium, had assumed since the end of World War I that the Rhineland would remain permanently demilitarized. Britain had formally obligated itself to protect them. Moreover, it had been a cornerstone of British foreign policy that a threat to France and Belgium was, by nature of their geographic proximity, also a threat to the U.K. The Little Entente states and Poland, which were now obliged to act in France's defense, perceived their own safety and security to be threatened in the event of France's collapse. Each actor in the Remilitarization of the Rhineland crisis sought a pacific solution that might condemn Germany overtly but at the same time allow for a negotiable settlement.

France responded immediately with a cabinet decision on 7 March to act through the League and consult the Locarno guarantors in order to achieve a German withdrawal; a military solution was rejected as too dangerous. Czechoslovakia also responded that day with a declaration to conform its attitude exactly to that of France in every contingency. The following day Romania and Yugoslavia responded more reticently: they suggested to France that a peaceful solution to the crisis be sought but refused to commit themselves in the event of a forceful confrontation with Germany or the imposition of economic sanctions. The British responded on 9 March with a cabinet decision to consult with Hitler, the Locarno powers, and the League Council in the hope of negotiating a coordinated compromise settlement. A military response and economic sanctions were rejected. On 10 March Belgium's response was contained in a statement by its prime minister that it would demand at least a partial restoration of the status quo. He intimated that economic sanctions should be used; but when it became clear that this was not viewed favorably by the other Locarno powers it was withdrawn. That day, too, Poland declared that the Franco-Polish treaty covered unprovoked aggression against France proper, and as the remilitarization of the Rhineland did not fall into that category it would not act forcefully in the present crisis or support economic sanctions against Germany.

Members of the League Council began meetings in London on 13 March. On the 19th all members of the Council except Germany endorsed a White Paper condemning German action in the Rhineland as a threat to European unity. The Council proposed the appointment of a committee to recommend measures to be adopted to safeguard peace. Tentative solutions were put forth concerning the partial withdrawal of German troops and the establishment of an international force in a new and narrow demilitarized zone of 20 kilometers between Germany, France, and Belgium. They were rejected outright by Hitler, who threatened that a punitive resolution by the League Council would be regarded by Germany as an unfriendly act. This specter of war, together with Italy's reluctance to cooperate and Germany's veto, finally paralyzed the League completely: the Council meeting dissolved on 23 March 1936, terminating the crisis for Belgium, Czechoslovakia, Poland, Romania, and Yugoslavia. The crisis for France and the U.K. lasted until 16 April as France continued to insist that Britain compensate it for the loss of security on its eastern border. On 2 April Britain agreed to hold staff talks with the French on 15 and 16 April. These talks concluded the punitive phase of the crisis; and from that point on no further demands were made directly to Berlin over the Rhineland issue.

Involved in the Remilitarization of the Rhineland crisis were the seven crisis actors, along with Germany, Italy, and the Soviet Union. Italy, although a guarantor of the Locarno Pact, had moved away from the Western powers in the ensuing decade and had developed closer ties with Germany. The Soviet Union did not depend upon France's military strength for its security. Indeed Soviet decision makers perceived that, should the crisis lead to armed conflict, it would be located in Western Europe and would not affect the USSR. As for the U.S., Secretary of State Hull made it plain that he considered the Rhineland remilitarization to be a European development in which the United States was not involved.

A far-reaching effect of the Remilitarization of the Rhineland crisis on Belgium was the termination of the Franco-Belgian treaty of 1920 and Belgium's formal declaration of neutrality in October 1936. More generally, Hitler's first major gamble in international politics succeeded: the Versailles powers acquiesced, paving the way for **Munich** in 1938 (see Case #64, in **Czechoslovakia/Germany PC**) and, the next year, the outbreak of World War II (see Case #74, in **Multiregional PCs: World War II**).

(See *Master Table,* pp. 674–75.)

Sources
Bullock 1962; Emmerson 1977; Schuman 1939; Shirer 1964; Taylor 1966; Walters 1952; Weinberg 1970.

Italy / Albania / Yugoslavia

The protracted conflict among **Albania, Italy, and Yugoslavia** generated five international crises from 1921 to 1953, as follows.

Case #23   **Albanian Frontier,** in 1921;
#34   **Hegemony over Albania,** in 1926–27;
#71   **Invasion of Albania,** in 1939;
#104   **Trieste I,** in 1945;
#142   **Trieste II,** in 1953.

The **Trieste I** crisis occurred in the closing days of World War II and was influenced by the **World War II PC,** notably Cases #94—**D-Day,** in 1944–45; and #100—**Final Soviet Offensive,** in 1945 (see *Master Table*).

This conflict was quiescent during most of the Cold War; but the Albania/Yugoslavia dimension reemerged during the lengthy civil war in Yugoslavia since 1991 (see Cases #397—**Yugoslavia I,** in 1991–92; and #403—**Yugoslavia II,** in 1992–95, in **Europe: Non-PCs**).

General Background

After more than four centuries of Ottoman rule, Albania proclaimed its independence and formed a provisional government on 28 November 1912. Albania's independence was acknowledged by the European powers after the Balkan Wars of 1912–13; but the task of delimiting both its northern and southern borders remained incomplete when World War I erupted in August 1914. Under the provisions of the (secret) Treaty of London (26 April 1915), which enticed Italy into World War I on the side of the Triple Entente, Albania's independence was recognized and a commission was set up to determine its boundaries. However, during World War I Italy occupied most of southern Albania, while the Serbs and Montenegrins occupied the northern part.

Albania's appeal to the major powers at the Versailles Peace Conference to fix its boundaries went unheeded even though the Albanian and Greek governments pledged in May 1920 to accept a decision by the conference. Albania experienced de facto independence following an agreement with Italy on 2 August 1920, which led to the withdrawal of Italian forces from Albanian territory except for the island of Saseno. This short-lived independence was reinforced by Albania's admission to the League of Nations as a full member in December 1920; but its borders were still not demarcated.

(23) Albanian Frontier

Albania and Yugoslavia were enmeshed in a crisis over territory from 7 July to 18 November 1921.

Pre-crisis
In April and June 1921 Albania appealed to the League of Nations to delimit its frontiers. Greece and Yugoslavia sought to forestall this process because of their own territorial ambitions vis-à-vis Albania. Minor skirmishes occurred between Albanian and Yugoslav forces.

Crisis
In the first week of July 1921, around the 7th, Yugoslav troops occupied previously demilitarized territory triggering a crisis for Albania. As early as 13 July Yugoslav officials expressed their anticipation of an Albanian attack, triggering a crisis for Belgrade. It came on 9 August, when Albanian forces occupied Yugoslav territory. Full-scale war ensued and continued until November.

Under the authority of the League of Nations, the Conference of Ambassadors, then comprising Belgium, France, Italy, Japan, and the U.K., defined the Albania/Yugoslavia border in mid-November 1921. Moreover, the U.K. attempted, unsuccessfully, to invoke Article XVI of the League Covenant with a call for military action against Yugoslavia. The latter development accentuated Yugoslavia's perception of a potential grave military threat by the major powers. Together these two events had a positive impact: on 18 November 1921 the Albanian and Yugoslav representatives to the League accepted the border delimitation and pledged friendly relations. Albania was formally recognized. Their crisis was resolved.

Yugoslavia, which still controlled the northern part of Albania, withdrew its forces in 1921 under pressure from the League.

The most highly involved actors were the League of Nations Council and the U.K. Greece and Romania issued statements during the crisis. Albania misperceived Russian military involvement in support of Yugoslavia.

(See *Master Table*, pp. 670–71.)

Sources
Baerlein 1922; Boulter 1928; Dedijer 1974; Dexter 1967; Stickney 1926; Swire [1929] 1971; Toynbee 1927c; Walters 1952.

(34) Hegemony over Albania
Yugoslavia, Albania, and Italy were enmeshed in a crisis from 28 November 1926 until 22 November 1927.

Pre-crisis
From the outset Italy and Yugoslavia had competed for influence over Albania, both regarding it as vital to their national security. Tension eased in 1924 with a Treaty of Friendship between them, the Pact of Rome. Albania was proclaimed a republic in January 1925. Its frontiers were fixed by a formal agreement among the most interested major and regional powers—France, Greece, Italy, the U.K., and Yugoslavia—on 30 July 1926.

Crisis

Tension rose dramatically on 27 November 1926 with the signing of the Treaty of Tirana by Italy and its Albanian protégé, Ahmed Bey Zog (who became King of Albania in 1928). Italy was granted the right to dispatch troops to Albania if the latter was invaded, thereby making Albania a de facto Italian protectorate.

The Treaty of Tirana triggered a crisis for Yugoslavia the following day. Belgrade was slow to respond: in February 1927 it ordered a general reorganization of the army and tested its mobilization capability. In mid-March Albania became a crisis actor perceiving Komitadji rebels massing on its frontier as under the control of Yugoslavia. Albania responded by sending troops to the border. And Yugoslavia's testing of its mobilization system created a crisis for Italy on 17 March.

Italy's pledge of support if Albania was invaded, supplemented by minor troop movements to the island of Saseno, neutralized the perceived threat from Yugoslavia to Albania and terminated the latter's foreign policy crisis on 23 March. For Yugoslavia the crisis ended with the enhancement of its security through a Treaty of Friendship with France on 11 November designed to counter Italy's aggrandizement in southeast Europe. And Italy's crisis, along with the international crisis over Albania, ended with the second Treaty of Tirana on 22 November 1927 that created a defensive alliance between Italy and Albania. Yugoslavia (and France) acquiesced in this reassertion of Italian primacy.

The U.K., Germany, Czechoslovakia, and, later, Japan were involved politically through efforts to ease tensions between Italy and Yugoslavia. The League of Nations Council offered to mediate the conflict, but Italy declined.

(The "special relationship" between Albania and Italy forged by the two treaties of Tirana [1926, 1927] and their 20-year defensive military alliance [1927] marked the beginning of an Italian protectorate over Albania lasting until World War II.)

(See *Master Table*, pp. 670–71.)

Sources
DBFP (Medlicott et al. 1970, 1971); Cassels 1970; Currey 1932; Macartney and Cremona 1938; Marmullaku 1975; Swire [1929] 1971; Toynbee 1929b.

(71) Invasion of Albania

A crisis for Albania, France, Greece, and the U.K. occurred between 25 March and 13 April 1939.

Background
In 1928 a new constitution transformed Albania into a hereditary constitutional monarchy with Ahmed Zog crowned as King. Zog was given broad authority and ruled as a dictator until 1939. During the 1930s, on several occasions, King Zog attempted to break away from Italy but was forced to back down when Italian

diplomatic, economic, and military pressure was applied. By 1938 the Italians had become impatient with Zog and looked for a way to assume direct control over Albania.

Crisis

A crisis for Albania was triggered on 25 March 1939 when Italy presented a treaty draft, in the form of an ultimatum: it proposed the stationing of Italian troops in the main centers and on the frontiers of Albania, along with the full participation of the Italian minister in Tirana in the Albanian Council of Ministers. The pact was rejected by King Zog and, at the beginning of April, he presented counterproposals with new concessions. Mussolini was not placated. As Italian/Albanian negotiations were taking place, rumors spread about the completion of Italian military preparations for invasion, with a concentration of army and naval forces in southern Italy. Despite violent anti-Italian demonstrations throughout Albania, Zog issued a public declaration on 3 April denying the worsening of relations with Italy. Following a cabinet meeting the next day the king indicated to the Greek minister, then doyen of the diplomatic corps, that Italian demands would mean control over all the essentials of Albanian life and the establishment of an Italian protectorate on Greece's borders. Representatives of France, the U.K., and the Balkan Entente were informed that Italian demands would be rejected by force. Also on the 4th Mussolini set a deadline of 6 April for the acceptance of Italy's demands. Albania's major response was a decision by the council of ministers, on the 6th, to reject the Italian ultimatum; a negative reply was sent the same day. Preparations for resistance were made, including the distribution of arms.

Italian forces invaded Albania on 7 April, triggering a crisis for France, Greece, and the U.K. France perceived the fall of Albania as a prelude to an Italian-German offensive from the North Sea to Egypt. The Greek government was convinced that, once Albania had been annexed, the Italians would invade Corfu. And the U.K., fearing that the situation might undermine its influence and the status quo in the Mediterranean, became concerned about a possible Italian invasion of Greece.

The crisis for Albania ended on 8 April when the king and other Albanian officials fled to Greece. The Italians entered the capital that day. On the 9th Greek Prime Minister Metaxas informed the British minister that the Italians intended to attack Corfu between 10 and 12 April. On the same day two Greek destroyers were manned and made ready for action.

At an urgent meeting on 9 April the French National Defense Committee decided to move the French Atlantic fleet to the Mediterranean, to send reinforcements to Tunis and French Somaliland, and to call up reservists. The British major response occurred on 11 April, after precautions had been taken in Malta, air services to Italy had been suspended, and military leaves canceled. That day, at a meeting of the cabinet's foreign policy committee, a statement was approved warning Italy that any aggression against Greek territory would be regarded as a threat to the vital interests of Great Britain.

The crisis for France, Greece, and the U.K. ended on 13 April 1939. The British prime minister declared a guarantee of the independence of Greece and Romania. A similar guarantee was made by France's Premier Daladier the same day. These assurances terminated the crisis for Greece as well. There was no League of Nations activity, despite Albania's protest on 8 April. On 13 April the new Albanian puppet regime followed Italy's lead and withdrew from the League.

(See *Master Table,* pp. 678–79.)

Sources
Carr 1945; Ciano 1947; Clogg 1980; Knox 1982; Koliopoulos 1977; Pano 1968; Polo and Pato 1981; Schuman 1941; Shirer 1964; Smith 1982; Taylor 1968; Woodhouse 1968.

(104) Trieste I

The first international crisis over Trieste took place from 1 May to 11 June 1945. The U.K., the U.S., and Yugoslavia were the crisis actors.

Background
The city of Trieste (and the "Julian region" of which it was the centerpiece) was contested by rival powers throughout history because of its commercial and geopolitical importance: it was the principal outlet to the Adriatic for central Europe. Trieste had long performed this valuable function for the Hapsburg empire, until its demise in 1918.

In the prevalent mood of intense nationalism accompanying its unification, Italy claimed Trieste as *terra irredenta* (unredeemed land) as soon as Venice and Rome had been incorporated into the Italian state in 1866 and 1870. It has been unremitting in this claim ever since. So too was the new Yugoslavia from the time it was formed in 1918.

Italy's claim was at the heart of the issue of its participation in World War I. Thus in the (secret) Treaty of London (26 April 1915) France, the U.K., and Russia agreed to give Italy the Julian region, including Trieste, along with Trentino (South Tyrol to Austria) and the Dalmatian coast as territorial compensation for its entry into the war on the side of the Triple Entente. Italian forces occupied Trieste on 3 November 1918 amid the collapse of the Austro-Hungarian empire.

Dissatisfied by President Wilson's attempt at compromise at the Versailles Conference, Italy achieved its goal in November 1920: the Treaty of Rapallo gave Italy the Julian region. The cost, in terms of relations with the new Yugoslavia, which claimed Trieste with the same tenacity, was high—permanent tension and periodic crises during the inter–world war period. Then, in 1941, the U.K.'s Foreign Minister, Anthony Eden, promised Yugoslavia "favorable consideration" of its claim for territorial revision regarding the Julian region after the war—in return for Yugoslavia's support during the war: it was perceived in Belgrade—and Rome—as an implied reversal of the 1915 Treaty of London concession to Italy's territorial claim. And it sowed the seeds of subsequent conflict. That conflict emerged in the closing weeks of World War II.

With the crumbling of German resistance in 1945 military cooperation between the Soviet Union and the Western allies began to be eroded by political and ideological disputes related to the postwar settlement: the fundamental differences in their economic systems, political regimes, and ideological beliefs and their historically competing interests led to cracks in the Grand Alliance. It gave way to intense competition and potential conflict over spheres of influence in war-ravaged Europe.

Prime Minister Churchill urged the U.S. to seize as much territory in Europe as possible. Trieste was the first to reflect the emerging clash of interests between East and West. As German troops retreated from Italy, Anglo-American forces reached the northeast—to find that Tito had preceded them with his Yugoslav Partisans.

Crisis

On 1 May 1945 a crisis was perceived by the U.K. when Churchill received a cable from the Supreme Allied Commander in the Mediterranean reporting the presence of Tito's forces in Trieste. The following day the news reached the U.S. and triggered a crisis. That day, too, the Anglo-Americans occupied Trieste triggering a crisis for Yugoslavia.

Tension in the Trieste area mounted during the next week as the Yugoslavs began setting up a local administration and carrying out political purges while restricting the movements of Anglo-American forces. On 11 May President Truman cabled Churchill suggesting that Tito be informed, through their respective ambassadors in Belgrade, that the Yugoslav Government must immediately agree to the control of its forces by the Supreme Allied Commander in the Mediterranean. Churchill agreed, and a directive was issued to the Joint Chiefs of Staff. Yugoslavia rejected the Allied demands on 17 May. The U.S. and U.K. response, on 21 May, was taken in conjunction with earlier inquiries by Truman to the Joint Chiefs of Staff regarding possible military measures should Tito refuse to yield. Field Marshal Alexander's troops, reinforced by American units, crossed into the Yugoslav-occupied zone of Trieste. Later that day Yugoslavia announced its willingness to negotiate: the Anglo-American forces were far too strong for Yugoslavia to consider military resistance, especially as the USSR remained aloof from the crisis.

Talks were held at Devon at the end of May between General Morgan of the Allies and Yugoslav army representatives, and later in Belgrade among representatives of the three governments. The crisis ended without violence, when

Yugoslavia withdrew its troops on 11 June 1945, two days after it yielded to U.K.-U.S. demands.

The city was demilitarized and divided into two zones, one controlled by an Allied (U.K.-U.S.) military government, the other by Yugoslavia. In a Memorandum of Understanding among Italy, the U.K., and the U.S., Rome was given a larger share in the administration of the Allied-controlled zone.

Italy was an involved actor, with basic interests in the outcome. The crisis served to intensify the conflict over Trieste, for Yugoslavia was an aggrieved party and later became involved in a series of tense situations that eventually escalated to a renewed crisis in 1953 (see Case #142 below).

The League of Nations had virtually ceased to exist since the beginning of World War II.

(See *Master Table,* pp. 684–85.)

Sources
Auty 1970; Byrnes 1947; Churchill 1953; Duroselle 1966; Grew 1953; Novak 1970; Truman 1955.

(142) Trieste II

There were two crisis actors in the second international crisis over Trieste— Yugoslavia and Italy. It began on 8 October and ended on 5 December 1953.

Crisis
On 8 October 1953 Britain and the United States announced their intention to terminate the Allied Military Government in Trieste, to withdraw their troops, and to relinquish the administration to the Italian government. This triggered a crisis for Yugoslavia, which responded two days later by lodging a formal protest with London and Washington and informing the UN. The frontier was closed, Yugoslav military reserves were called up, and warships were moved into the area. Those acts on the 10th triggered Italy's crisis. Italy's major response, on 17 October, was to place three divisions at the Yugoslav frontier on emergency posting.

The decision by the U.K. and U.S. to evacuate Trieste was postponed while diplomatic efforts continued to convene a conference. On 5 December 1953 an agreement was announced in Rome and Belgrade for the simultaneous withdrawal of Italian and Yugoslav forces from the border. This ended the crisis for both actors.

(The political outcome of the dispute took the form of a Memorandum of Understanding, signed on 5 October 1954 by the U.S., the U.K., Italy, and Yugoslavia, which granted the northern zone to Italy and the southern zone to Yugoslavia.)

(See *Master Table,* pp. 692–93.)

Sources
See sources for Case #104; and Clissold 1975; Croci 1991; Donelan and Grieve 1973; Eden 1960; Eisenhower 1963.

Lithuania/Poland

The protracted conflict between **Lithuania** and **Poland** over the city of Vilna (Vilnius) generated three international crises from 1920 to 1938, as follows.

> Case #17 **Vilna I,** in 1920;
> #36 **Vilna II,** in 1927;
> #61 **Polish Ultimatum,** in 1938.

There were also three closely related crises: Cases #4—**Baltic Independence,** in 1918–20; #13—**Polish/Russian War,** in 1920; and #75—**Soviet Occupation—Baltic,** in 1939 (see *Master Table*).

General Background

Vilna first appears in world history as the capital of the newly founded state of Lithuania under the leadership of Gedymin (1316–41). During succeeding centuries the city was frequently contested by two expansionist powers in eastern Europe, Lithuania and Poland. And for lengthy periods Vilna was part of a Polish-Lithuanian kingdom. From the second partition of Poland (1793) until 1918 Lithuania, including Vilna, was part of the czarist Russian empire.

Lithuania's independence was proclaimed on 11 December 1917. Russia was compelled to recognize its independence under the terms of the Treaty of Brest-Litovsk on 3 March 1918 (see Case #4—**Baltic Independence,** in **Europe: Non-PCs**). Germany recognized the new state on 23 March and forged an alliance with Lithuania on 14 May.

(17) Vilna I

A crisis between Poland and Lithuania over the long-disputed city of Vilna lasted from 12 July until 29 November 1920.

Pre-crisis
Bolshevik forces captured Vilna on 5 January 1919 but lost it to the Poles on 4 April. On 8 December 1919 the Allied powers fixed the Polish/Lithuanian boundary (the "Curzon Line") leaving Vilna in Lithuania. A closely related crisis between Poland and Russia had begun in April 1920 (see Case #13—**Polish/Russian War,** in **Poland/Russia PC**).

Crisis

Russo/Lithuanian hostilities (1919–20) ended with the Treaty of Moscow on 12 July 1920. The Bolshevik regime, then at war with Poland, recognized Lithuania including Vilna. In return, the Russians were allowed to cross Lithuanian territory to engage the Poles. That provision triggered a crisis for Poland. It responded two days later with an attack on Lithuanian forces near Vilna triggering a crisis for Lithuania. Full-scale war continued through the summer.

Poland appealed to the League of Nations on 5 September. Mediation by the League Council led to an agreement on the 20th providing for a cease-fire and for Lithuania's neutrality in the Polish/Russian War; Vilna remained part of Lithuania. The (abortive) Treaty of Suwalki, incorporating these terms, was signed on 7 October.

Hours later Polish General Zeligowski crossed the frontier and occupied Vilna on the 9th. However, his attempts at further expansion into the Lithuanian heartland failed. Further mediation by the League of Nations led indirectly to a mutually accepted Protocol on 29 November 1920 calling for a plebiscite to decide the fate of Vilna. This agreement brought hostilities—and the Vilna I crisis—to an end.

Russia was highly involved in this crisis, providing direct military aid to Lithuania; and it was ultimately responsible for Poland's military failure in this international crisis.

(The Vilna plebiscite, held on 8 January 1922 under Zeligowski's supervision, showed, not surprisingly, a majority in favor of union with Poland. That status was formalized on 18 April. Lithuania rejected the outcome and severed relations with Poland. So it remained until 1927, following the **Vilna II** crisis [see Case #36 below].)

(See *Master Table,* pp. 668–69.)

Sources
de Chambon 1933; Dexter 1967; Dziewanowski 1969; Kaslas 1976; Natkevicius 1930; Toynbee 1927c; Walters 1952.

(36) Vilna II

Lithuania and Poland experienced another crisis over the long-disputed city of Vilna from mid-October to 10 December 1927.

Background
Poland's annexation of Vilna in 1922, following its self-supervised plebiscite, was rejected by Lithuania, which viewed itself in a state of war with Poland until 1927. Marshal Pilsudski returned to power in May 1926, first as Poland's Premier and Minister of War, later as President. He was a vocal advocate of a strong nationalist policy toward Vilna.

Crisis

A crisis for Lithuania was triggered in mid-October 1927 by the closure of Lithuanian schools and the arrest of Lithuanian teachers and priests in Poland, allegedly in retaliation for the persecution of Polish teachers in Lithuania. The renewed tension was accentuated by Poland's high-profile celebration in Vilna of the seventh anniversary of its occupation of the city, in the presence of General Zeligowski, who led the 1920 occupying army, and President Pilsudski.

Lithuania's response took the form of a Note to the League of Nations and a personal appearance by Premier Voldemaras before the League Council on 15 October, warning of the danger of war and the threat to Lithuania's independent existence. That dramatic act, in turn, created a crisis for Poland.

The great powers and the League Council did not take the threat to peace seriously: Lithuania's complaint was merely added to the agenda for the next regular Council session. France and the U.K. tried in vain to persuade Lithuania to withdraw its Note and to accept an offer of good offices. Poland declared that it would not use force to resolve the dispute over Vilna. The Soviet Union criticized Poland—and France—for seeking the former's annexation of Lithuania.

Pilsudski raised the tension level significantly just before the Council meeting in December by publicly criticizing Voldemaras and acknowledging that he had contemplated mobilizing Poland's armed forces with a view to invading Lithuania.

The crisis ended on 10 December, when the League Council, backed by the major powers, passed an omnibus resolution. Both parties were urged to declare an end to the state of war between them. The Council called on Poland to recognize Lithuania's independence and territorial integrity. It established a committee to report on alleged mistreatment of Lithuanian nationals in Poland. And the two parties were requested to restore normal relations. The Soviet delegate, Litvinov, helped to persuade Lithuania's president to accept the package. And the leaders of Poland and Lithuania sealed the change in relations with a public handshake.

(Negotiations to resume normal relations began at the end of March 1928. Poland's continued occupation of Vilna remained a stumbling block. In March 1938 another crisis [see Case #61] led to Lithuania's acceptance of a Polish ultimatum to restore diplomatic relations or face an invasion.)

(See *Master Table,* pp. 672–73.)

Sources
Dziewanowski 1977; Roos 1966; Walters 1952.

(61) Polish Ultimatum

A Polish ultimatum created a crisis for Lithuania from 13 to 19 March 1938.

Background and Pre-crisis
After Vilna was annexed to Poland in 1922, an intense campaign was carried out by Lithuania to retrieve its capital in medieval times, including a refusal to

conduct diplomatic or commercial relations with Poland. In 1936 the Polish foreign minister failed in his attempt to restore relations with Lithuania through the League of Nations. Lithuania refused to have its Vilna claim set aside and was willing to open only river traffic and communications, as well as consular facilities. Minority and frontier incidents contributed to the animosity between the two states. In February 1937 the visit of the Soviet chief of staff to Lithuania was followed by rumors of Soviet support for Lithuania's position, but these were denied. The incidents on the border were dealt with by local authorities within the framework of the 1928 Lithuanian-Polish agreement on frontier traffic. On the night of 10–11 March 1938 a Polish soldier was killed by Lithuanian frontier guards. Lithuania proposed solving the incident by a mixed commission of local authorities.

Crisis

A crisis for Lithuania was triggered on 13 March when the Polish government rejected its proposal and issued an official communiqué referring to a pending decision on steps for dealing with the situation existing between Poland and Lithuania. Rumors of Polish military action began to spread through Europe, which indeed had been Poland's initial intention. When Polish Foreign Minister Beck returned to the cabinet the following day, the military option was postponed. On 17 March Poland handed an ultimatum to the Lithuanian minister to Estonia. It demanded the restoration of normal relations by 31 March and gave the Lithuanian government 48 hours to reply. Vilna was not mentioned. The Lithuanian cabinet met all night, and parliament was summoned. German advice was sought. Having an interest in Memel, Germany counseled Lithuania to accept the Polish demands. German forces moved to the border. The U.K. and France also advocated Lithuanian compliance. The Lithuanian response on 19 March, to accept the ultimatum, also marked the termination of its crisis.

The League of Nations was minimally involved in this crisis, advising Poland to be reasonable and Lithuania to accept Polish terms. The Soviet Union, while refusing to supply military aid, supported Lithuania by informing Poland that Moscow reserved the right to take action in the event of a Polish attack on Lithuania.

(In subsequent months diplomatic relations and road and rail communications were reestablished. This was followed by a period of relative harmony between the two states. Vilna remained under Polish control until early in World War II. In September 1939 the city was occupied by Soviet troops, as part of the USSR's share in the fourth [German-Soviet] partition of Poland. Then, on 10 October, under the terms of a mutual assistance pact, the USSR ceded Vilna and its hinterland to Lithuania in return for military bases. [See Case #75—**Soviet Occupation—Baltic,** in **Europe: Non-PCs.**]

On 21 July 1940 Lithuania, including Vilna, along with Latvia and Estonia, was formally incorporated into the USSR. The Baltic states regained their independence in 1991.)

(See *Master Table*, pp. 676–77.)

Sources
Cienciala 1968; Gerutis 1969; Toynbee 1953b; Walters 1952.

Poland/Russia

There were four international crises in the protracted conflict between Poland and
Russia from 1920 to 1981, as follows.

Case #13   **Polish/Russian War,** in 1920;
#110   **Communism in Poland,** in 1946–47;
#154   **Poland Liberalization,** in 1956;
#315   **Solidarity,** in 1980–81.

Other crises impinged upon the **Poland/Russia** conflict, notably the following:
Cases #17—**Vilna I,** in 1920; #36—**Vilna II,** in 1927; #61—**Polish Ulti-
matum** in 1938; #74—**Entry into World War II,** in 1939; and #75—**Soviet
Occupation of Baltic States,** in 1939 (see *Master Table*).

General Background

As World War I drew to a close the Polish Republic was proclaimed on 3
November 1918. The Treaty of Versailles (June 1919) authorized the rebirth of
Poland as an independent state after more than a century of occupation by Russia,
Prussia, and Austria, the result of the partitions of Poland in 1772, 1793, and
1795. From the outset the preeminent Polish leader, General Pilsudski, embarked
on an expansionist foreign policy, west, east, north, and south, in an effort to
recreate Poland's eighteenth-century boundaries.

(13) Polish/Russian War

A crisis-war between Russia and Poland erupted on 25 April 1920 and lasted
until 12 October.

Pre-crisis
On 27 March 1920 the Poles demanded Russian acquiescence in the restoration
of their border of 1772, with a plebiscite to be held in the region west of that
boundary. Russia rejected the demand but made several attempts to find a compromise. The Poles were adamant. The result was full-scale war.

Crisis
On 25 April 1920, three days after securing a green light from "White" Russian
commanders, Poland launched a major offensive toward the Ukraine triggering a
crisis for Soviet Russia. Kiev was captured on 7 May. Russian forces regrouped
and launched a counterattack in mid-May triggering a crisis for Poland. The latter

was compelled to evacuate its Ukrainian-occupied territories, including Kiev, on 11 June. A major Russian offensive began in mid-July, assisted by a Russo-Lithuanian agreement on 12 July that allowed Russian troops to use Lithuanian territory to prosecute the war. (This was to trigger a separate crisis—see Case #17—**Vilna I**, in **Lithuania/Poland PC.**) The Poles were defeated near Vilna (Vilnius) on 15 July. The Russian advance penetrated deep into Polish territory, barely 20 miles from Warsaw on 14 August. Poland had appealed to the Allies earlier (7 July) for help and had obtained military aid from France including military advisers. By late August Polish forces turned the tide and expelled the Russians from ethnically Polish territory.

The two adversaries, exhausted by the war, agreed to an armistice on 18 September 1920. Peace talks began in Latvia's capital on 23 September and led to a preliminary agreement on 12 October ending the crises for Poland and Russia and the international crisis as a whole.

As noted, France and Lithuania were involved actors, the first actively supporting Poland, the second passively assisting Russia. British offers of mediation were rejected by Russia.

The League of Nations was not involved in this crisis. Poland did not seek its assistance. And Russia, not a member at the time, declared that it would reject any attempt at League intervention.

(The Treaty of Riga, signed on 18 March 1921, defined the frontier between the two adversaries. Poland was the clear victor, for it was awarded a border 200 kilometers east of the old Curzon Line. Russia's partial compensation was an end to the war, a high-priority goal because of the multiple dangers to the survival of the Bolshevik regime arising from civil wars against several autonomous White Russian armies and military intervention by major powers in the Far East and North Russia. [See Cases #1—**Russian Civil War I—Siberia;** and #3—**Russian Civil War II—North Russia, in Multiregional PCs: East/West.**])

(See *Master Table,* pp. 668–69.)

Sources
Kennan 1960; Langer 1972; Ullman 1972.

(110) Communism in Poland

The USSR experienced a crisis with Poland, from 30 June 1946 to 19 January 1947.

Pre-crisis
The post–World War II situation in Poland was extremely tense as thousands of armed persons, belonging to various underground movements, aimed at sabotaging the Communist-controlled Lublin coalition government established in 1944. The presence of Soviet troops added to the complex environment.

Crisis

On 30 June 1946 the Provisional Government of Poland held a preelection referendum that pointed to the fact that the strongest political force in the country was Mikolajczyk's Peasant Party. This triggered a crisis for the USSR, which feared Poland's withdrawal from the Soviet bloc. The Polish Communist leaders were summoned immediately to Moscow for consultations. The major Soviet response came on 28 August when, at a meeting in Moscow with leaders of both the Polish United Workers Party *(PUWP)* and the Peasant Party, Stalin dictated the results of the forthcoming elections in Poland, demanding that Mikolajczyk ally his party with the Polish Communists.

On 19 January 1947 elections were held and were predictably won by the alliance of the *PUWP* and Peasant Party, despite charges of gross irregularities. As Poland's potential defection from the Soviet bloc had been prevented, the Soviet crisis was over.

The U.K. and the U.S. were involved politically with notes and statements vis-à-vis the elections and border issues. The UN was not involved. There was no violence.

(See *Master Table,* pp. 686–87.)

Sources

Brzezinski 1967; Campbell and Herring 1975; Dziewanowski 1959; Korbonski 1965; Leslie 1980; Mikolajczyk 1948.

(154) Poland Liberalization

The USSR and Poland were enmeshed in a crisis from 15 to 22 October 1956.

Pre-crisis

During the summer and autumn of 1956 the Soviet Union faced threats to its hegemonial position in Eastern Europe, particularly in Hungary and Poland: economic stagnation was accompanied by increasing demands for greater political freedom internally, as well as more independence from Soviet dictation in foreign policy. On 28 June a demonstration of Polish workers in Poznan turned into a riot that was brutally suppressed by the Polish government, with hundreds killed or wounded. The Polish leadership eventually took decisions that gradually led to the rehabilitation of Wladsylaw Gomulka, a member of the Politburo purged in 1948 for Titoism. Politically, he was one of the few Communist leaders acceptable to the Polish masses.

Crisis

The trigger to the Soviet Union's crisis was Gomulka's return to power on 15 October 1956: he and three allies were invited to rejoin the Politburo of the Polish United Workers Party. The Soviets perceived this dramatic internal shift in power in Poland as a threat to their hegemony. Moscow's response, after the

Polish Communist leadership rejected a Khrushchev "invitation" to go to Moscow for a discussion, was a decision on 17 October to send a delegation of Soviet leaders, Khrushchev, Molotov, etc., to attend the *PUWP* Plenum. When this decision became known in Poland on the 18th, a reciprocal crisis was triggered. Poland's response, the next day, took the form of a threat by Gomulka to broadcast the news that Soviet troops were marching on Warsaw, a fact confirmed by Khrushchev. Such a broadcast could have led to widespread demonstrations. Seven Soviet divisions were put on alert; and patrols along the East German border with Poland were increased. Khrushchev finally relented and ordered a halt to Soviet troop movements when he perceived that the *PUWP* was in control of the situation and would not allow anti-Soviet demonstrations. Moreover, the veiled threat of the USSR was determined sufficient to keep the Polish leadership within acceptable boundaries.

The crisis over Poland's liberalization ended on 22 October 1956 with the close of the meetings of the Polish Plenum. Khrushchev, now back in Moscow, telephoned his best wishes to Gomulka. The crisis outcome was a compromise. While Gomulka remained in power, the Soviets retained effective control over Poland.

The U.S. was marginally involved in this crisis. The UN was not involved. (See *Master Table*, pp. 694–95.)

Sources
Bethell 1969; Crankshaw 1966; Gibney 1959; Gluchowski 1995; Lewis 1959; Tatu 1981; Ulam 1971, 1974.

(315) Solidarity

Poland, the USSR, Czechoslovakia, and East Germany were enmeshed in another major intra–Soviet-bloc upheaval from 14 August 1980 to 13 December 1981 (see Cases #141—**East German Uprising,** in 1953; #155—**Hungarian Uprising,** in 1956; and #227—**Prague Spring,** in 1968, in **Europe: Non-PCs**).

Background
Since the formation of Poland's Communist regime in 1944 there had been several violent outbursts of internal discontent, notably in 1970 and 1976, which led to major changes in both the party and state leadership. In the summer of 1980, too, a wave of industrial unrest gripped Poland in response to marked increases in food prices. However, violence was conspicuously absent from strikes and demonstrations led by Solidarity, an independent trade union headed by Lech Walesa, later the first President of Poland in the post-communist era. Yet for the Soviet Union, as for the U.S. in the Americas, unrest anywhere in Eastern Europe was perceived as a risk to Moscow's hegemony. This concern had already given rise to the Brezhnev Doctrine, during the **Prague Spring** crisis in 1968 (see Case #227, in **Europe: Non-PCs**): this asserted the concept of limited

sovereignty among members of the bloc and the Soviet Union's right to intervene in the domestic affairs of any member when bloc interests—as defined by Moscow—were threatened by internal events.

Crisis

On 14 August 1980, 17,000 Polish workers at the Lenin shipyard in Gdansk went on strike and occupied the huge industrial complex. They also presented a series of demands, some of which were perceived as political in nature by the Communist leaders of Poland. These events triggered a crisis for Poland and the USSR.

Warsaw's initial reaction was a government statement the next day criticizing the strikers' demands and noting the expectation of bloc allies that Poland's Communist regime would resolve its problems. Moscow's response was slow in coming—and indirect. The defense ministers and, separately, the foreign ministers of the Warsaw Treaty Organization (*WTO* or Warsaw Pact) met on 15–17 and 19–20 October to consider the challenge, more than two months after the initial strike by Solidarity. Prime Minister Pinkowski and the First Secretary of the Polish United Workers Party *(PUWP),)* Kania, were frequently summoned to Moscow for talks with Brezhnev.

A crisis for two other bloc members, East Germany (the DDR) and Czechoslovakia, was triggered on 30 August by a 21-point agreement between a Polish government commission and a delegation from the "Inter-Factory Strike Committee": the Gdansk Accords seemed to include political concessions to the strikers. East Germany responded on 28 October by promulgating "temporary" measures restricting visits by Polish citizens to the DDR. And Czechoslovakia reacted on 11 November with a set of rules restricting the purchase of Czechoslovak currency by Polish citizens.

Contingency plans for a large-scale *WTO* military intervention envisaged 15 Soviet tank and motorized divisions, drawn from the DDR, Czechoslovakia, and several military districts of the USSR, reinforced by three Czechoslovak and East German divisions and another dozen Soviet divisions—a formidable force. In mid-November 1980 the *WTO* concentrated troops on the Polish border, the major response of the three bloc members. And the USSR's defense ministry postponed the regular half-yearly rotation of one quarter of all Soviet conscripts.

Pressure from the USSR, East Germany, and Czechoslovakia for greater resolve by Poland's Communist rulers continued. The buildup of *WTO* forces near the Polish border led to a report by the Intelligence Oversight Committee of the U.S. House of Representatives in January 1981 asserting that the prospect of a Soviet invasion remained "very high." On 4 March Moscow demanded from the *PUWP* leaders that the course of events in Poland be reversed. On 18 March *WTO* forces held maneuvers. Tension increased at the end of March and persisted through the spring.

On 5 June the Central Committee of the Communist Party of the Soviet Union *(CPSU)* sent a strongly worded letter to its Polish counterpart, expressing disappointment at the lack of leadership under Kania. On 10 September Moscow demanded "radical measures" from the Polish Communist leadership. These were taken on the night of 12–13 December 1981. Almost the entire leadership of Solidarity, including Walesa, was arrested. Martial law was declared. And a "Military Council for National Salvation," led by General Jaruzelski, was created. These acts ended the crisis for all four actors.

Western reaction was muted. U.S. Secretary of State Haig declared on 13 December that the U.S. was "seriously concerned" by Poland's declaration of martial law and by the arrests. Several members of *NATO* adopted symbolic diplomatic and economic steps to indicate their displeasure. The UN was not involved in this crisis.

(See *Master Table,* pp. 722–23.)

Sources
Keesing's 1980, 1981; Kramer 1995a, 1995b; *New York Times* 1980, 1981.

Spain

The protracted conflict within—and for the control of—**Spain** was characterized by full-scale war throughout. Four of its battles or military campaigns generated international crises, as follows.

Case **#52 Spanish Civil War I—Onset,** in 1936–37;
 #54 Spanish Civil War II—Almería, in 1937;
 #65 Spanish Civil War III—Ebro, in 1938;
 #67 Spanish Civil War IV—Last Phase, in 1938–39.

General Background

The ideological and clerical conflict in the 1920s and 1930s concerning democracy, communism, fascism, and the role of the Catholic Church provided the background for the civil war in Spain. That war was strongly linked to emerging conflicts and coalitions among the major European powers: from its outset until its conclusion, Italy and Germany were the patrons of the Nationalist cause, while the Soviet Union played that role for the Republic (Loyalists). France and the U.K. were not directly involved.

(52) Spanish Civil War I—Onset

Spain experienced the first of four international crises during the long civil war, from 17 July 1936 to 18 March 1937.

Pre-crisis
On 16 January 1936 a Popular Front was forged by the small Communist Party, the Socialists, the Left Republicans, the Republican Union, the Catalán Left, and

the marxist *POUM* parties of Spain. The Anarcho-Syndicalists of Catalonia and Madrid did not join the Front, which was viewed by all conservatives and the church with alarm. The Popular Front was dominated by middle-class liberals, the communist elements adhering to a nonrevolutionary line. In the general elections a month later the Popular Front won 265 seats of a total of 473. President Alcalá Zamora was replaced by Manuel Azaña on 10 May 1936, but reform made slow progress. Strikes and anticlerical demonstrations prevailed. The Communists opposed immediate socialization of land and nationalization of industry in favor of a more disciplined evolution. The Socialists promoted a form of proletarian rule. The wealthy and the aristocracy saw symptoms of incipient social revolution and secretly mobilized to overthrow the Popular Front. In April 1936 Hans Hellermann became the leader of Spain's Nazi Party, which consisted largely of German nationals. By July moral and material help from Italy, Germany, and Portugal was received regularly by fascist conspirators. The revolt was to begin in Spanish Morocco and move on the capital, Madrid. It began on 17 July.

Crisis
The uprising on the Spanish mainland began on 18 July 1936 and triggered a crisis for Republican Spain. The following day inquiries were made as to the scope of the rebellion; and orders were given to the remaining loyal troops in Spanish Morocco to resist. The Soviet Union was concerned that a fascist regime in Spain would change the European power balance to the USSR's detriment and Germany's and Italy's favor. Spain's major response to the internal military challenge was an order from newly appointed Prime Minister Giral y Pereira, on 19 July, to arm the *CNT* (trade union of the Anarchist Party) and the *UGT* (General Union of Workers, led by the Spanish Socialist Party, later under Communist control). Giral perceived that these unions formed the only possible effective resistance to the fascist (Falange) rebellion, which spread rapidly to one-third of the garrisons in north and northwest Spain but failed to gain support in the key cities—Madrid, Barcelona, Valencia, and Bilbao. He ordered the trade unions to enter into active combat against the rebels, while appealing to Premier León Blum of France on 20 July to send arms and planes. That day General Franco took command of the Moors and Spain's Foreign Legion.

The death of General José Sanjurjo in a plane crash on the 20th left Generals Francisco Franco and Emilio Mola the two figures in command of the rebellion, Franco in the south and in Spanish Morocco, Mola in the north. Three days later "La Junta de la Defensa Nacional" was formed in Burgos as the executive body of the rebel movement. And on 29 September, two days after the rebel victory at Toledo—the Battle of Alcazar—the junta named Franco Head of Government and Generalíssimo of the Nationalists' land, sea, and air forces. (Mola was to die in a plane crash in June 1937.)

The initial rebel siege of Madrid from 7 November 1936 to 9 January 1937 and again in February failed. Málaga in the deep south fell to the rebels on 8 February. Most important was the Republican (Loyalist) victory at the Battle of Guadalajara on 18 March 1937, eliminating the pressure on Madrid and terminating Spain's first crisis of the civil war.

During the onset phase of that war three major powers and one small power were actively involved—Italy, Germany, and Portugal on the side of the rebels, the USSR supporting the Republican government. However, none perceived the conditions—threat, time pressure, higher likelihood of war—that would have qualified them as crisis actors. France and the U.K. took the lead in forming the Non-Intervention Committee, comprising most European states; and the U.S. remained aloof. (Spain's principal adversary throughout was a nonstate actor, namely, that segment of the Spanish army that rose in revolt against the Republic in July 1936.)

Initial contact by the rebels with Italy and Germany began in the first week of the uprising. Both pledged assistance within days, as did Portugal. Italy dispatched transport, aircraft, and military equipment in late July; and Germany sent the Condor Legion, with 100 planes, in November. And on the 28th Italy signed a secret treaty of friendship and assistance with the rebel leader.

The Soviets sent arms and equipment to the Republican government early in the war. It also played a key role in organizing the dispatch of International Brigades of volunteers to fight alongside the Loyalist forces, starting in October 1936.

France promised aid to the Republican government on 20 July but reneged five days later. And early in August it initiated a nonintervention plan, along with the U.K. It also suspended the export of all war materiel to Spain. The Non-Intervention Committee began regular meetings in London in September 1936, formally supported by all European states. However, it was undermined by Italy's and Germany's recognition of the Franco-led Burgos regime on 18 November 1936.

Spain protested to the League of Nations against foreign intervention and requested a meeting of the Council. It convened on 12 December but took no action—except to attempt to strengthen the U.K.–France–dominated nonintervention regime.

(Foreign intervention was a prominent feature throughout the civil war. After the flurry of prorebel activity in the early months, Germany and Italy provided large-scale additional military assistance in early 1937. On the Loyalist side, about 40,000 volunteers from more than a dozen countries in Europe, along with the United States and Canada, fought in the International Brigades, though no more than 18,000 at any one time; and another 20,000 foreigners served in medical and auxiliary units. France gave passive aid to the Republic by opening its frontier in the spring of 1938. And massive German military aid to the rebels in the autumn of 1938 was crucial for their final triumph [see Case #67— **Spanish Civil War IV—Last Phase** below].)

(See *Master Table,* pp. 674–75.)

Sources
Cameron and Stevens 1973; Carr 1945; Churchill 1948; Ciano 1947; Delzell 1970; Deutscher 1949; van der Esch 1951; Payne 1963; Preston 1986, 1994; Schuman 1939; Smith 1982; Thomas 1961; Walters 1952; Weinberg 1970; Wiskemann 1966.

(54) Spanish Civil War II—Almería

Italy, Germany, and Spain were engaged in an acute intra-war crisis from 24 to 31 May 1937.

Pre-crisis
Barely a month after the Republican victory in the Battle of Guadalajara (8–18 March 1937), Europe's great powers signed an agreement (20 April), designed to curtail the dispatch of arms to the protagonists in the Spanish civil war. However, it was ignored by the three most highly involved powers, Italy and Germany supporting the rebels, the USSR aiding the Republic.

On 26 April the city of Guernica in the Basque region of northern Spain was bombed into near oblivion by German planes, a precedent for the mass bombing of Coventry, Rotterdam, Dresden, and other cities during World War II.

Within the Republican-controlled part of Spain, civil strife among the myriad of leftist factions reached a peak: pro-Moscow Communist forces crushed a rebellion by anarchists and Trotskyites in Barcelona. Their pressure, too, led to the ouster of Socialist leader Largo Caballero from the premiership, a post he had held, with Communist backing, since early September 1936. He was replaced on 16 May by Juan Negrín, a physiology professor at the University of Madrid.

Crisis
On 24 May a crisis for Italy was triggered by a Republican air attack on the island of Palma de Mallorca which, inter alia, hit the Italian cruiser, *Barletta,* killing six Italian seamen. The *Barletta* was part of the Non-Intervention Committee's Naval Control, designed to monitor the dispatch of weapons to both sides in the civil war. But the port of Palma de Mallorca was a known center for arms shipments to the nationalist rebels—and had been assigned to France for this regulatory task, suggesting that the Italian ship's presence in Palma could not have been by chance.

The Non-Intervention Committee condemned the attack on the 25th. So too did the League Council the next day. However, Italy did not respond to a perceived threat to its self-image as a major power and, therefore, to its influence. That task was undertaken by its ally in the Spanish civil war, Germany, in a similar incident soon after.

On 26 May the battleship, *Deutschland,* then lying in port at Ibiza, was hit by two Republican planes, killing 31 German seamen and wounding 83. An enraged Hitler responded by ordering a retaliation raid. This was carried out on the 31st, when a German cruiser and four destroyers demolished 35 buildings and killed 19 persons by indiscriminate shelling of the Republican-controlled port of Almería. Germany and Italy also withdrew, temporarily, from the Non-Intervention Committee's naval patrol, returning to the fold on 16 July.

The naval bombing of Almería triggered a brief, but acute, crisis for Spain. At a meeting of the Republican cabinet in Valencia one of the most influential figures in the Negrín government, the Basque leader, Prieto, seriously proposed bombing the German fleet in the Mediterranean, fully aware of the possible escalation to major power war. After an intense discussion, President Azaña and most of the cabinet—and Moscow—opposed the idea; and the Almería "incident" was ignored. Spain's decision not to respond to the German attack thus ended the crisis for all three actors. The Almería crisis sheds much light on foreign intervention in the Spanish civil war.

(See *Master Table*, pp. 674–75.)

Sources
See sources for Case #52; and Weinberg 1980.

(65) Spanish Civil War III—Ebro

Republican Spain experienced another intra-war crisis in its prolonged civil war, from 30 October to 18 November 1938.

Pre-crisis
The war raged on, the Loyalists actively supported by the USSR and the International Brigades, the Nationalists by Italy and Germany. Moreover, many ships, notably those of interested European major powers, were attacked by "unknown" submarines, especially in the summer of 1937. An agreement reached on 14 September, with Germany and Italy absent, authorized ships of the Non-Intervention naval patrol to respond in kind if attacked. The indiscriminate raids continued, however. And the patrols failed to prevent massive foreign intervention throughout the Spanish civil war, mainly because the primary motive of the U.K. and France, the prime movers of "Non-Intervention," was to avoid hostilities with Germany and Italy. The latter was given a zone off the Mediterranean to patrol, which enabled it to continue sending military equipment to the rebels via Majorca.

There were many important military campaigns. The Battle of Brunette took place in July 1937, with a reverse outcome to that at Guadalajara, that is, a Nationalist victory, and very high Loyalist casualties (25,000 killed). The Republic's moderately successful Aragón offensive took place in August. And the rebels ultimately triumphed in the bitter, costly, three-month Battle of Teruel in February 1938. Barcelona was bombed by the rebels in mid-March. By mid-April 1938 rebel forces had reached the sea at Vinaroz, cutting off Catalonia from the rest of Republican Spain.

These were important developments, militarily; but none was—or catalyzed—an international crisis.

The Battle of the Ebro was to become a decisive engagement of the Spanish civil war. It began with a surprise attack by Republican forces on 24 July, designed to reduce the pressure on Valencia. Its initial success generated a sense of defeatism among the rebels in Burgos, Franco's capital. The Loyalist advance was stopped on 2 August. Nevertheless, Republican optimism about the war's outcome increased in August–September, kindled by a hope that preoccupation with the Czechoslovak crisis would lead to Germany's withdrawal from the Spanish civil war. That hope was shattered on 19 September when Germany, in the midst of the **Munich** crisis (see Case #64, in **Czechoslovakia/Germany PC**), reaffirmed its support for the Nationalists. A Republican attempt on 2 October to set in motion a negotiated solution was rebuffed by the rebels. And Soviet support for the Republic now declined sharply, largely because, having failed to forge an alliance with France and the U.K. against Nazism, Moscow began a basic shift in policy that was to culminate in the Molotov-Ribbentrop pact of August 1939.

Crisis
The Battle of the Ebro was transformed into an international crisis for Republican Spain on 30 October 1938 when the rebels launched a major counteroffensive at Sierra de Caballs. By that time the International Brigades, then with about 13,000 volunteers, had disbanded. These included 7,000 who were at the front in the Battle of the Ebro. By contrast, Italian involvement in the war was at its peak, with 48,000 troops actively engaged and 10,000 more offered by Mussolini.

Nationalist forces reached the Ebro River on 3 November, a turning point in the war. By the 10th there were only six artillery batteries west of the river. The Battle of the Ebro ended on 18 November in total defeat for the Republic, with an estimated 30,000 killed, among 70,000 casualties, compared to 33,000 on the Nationalist side. This crisis for Republican Spain had ended, a prelude to the last phase—and crisis—of the civil war.

(See *Master Table*, pp. 676–77.)

Sources
See sources for Cases #52 and 54.

(67) Spanish Civil War IV: Last Phase

Republican Spain's last intrawar crisis during the Spanish civil war lasted from 23 December 1938 to 31 March 1939.

Pre-crisis
As a result of their triumph in the Battle of the Ebro (see Case #65 above), General Franco's rebels were confident that they could now win the war. They

planned their Catalonia campaign for 10 December 1938. It was postponed until the 15th and then to the 23rd. A decisive input was a massive flow of arms from Germany in November.

Crisis

The Nationalists' "Christmas Offensive," with the Italian forces in Spain playing a central role in their campaign, began on 23 December with a crossing of the Segre River. This triggered an intra-war crisis for Republican Spain. By 3 January 1939 the Loyalists' defense line was pierced. Italian Foreign Minister Ciano warned of direct intervention by "regular" Italian divisions if France intervened on behalf of the Republic. But, as always during the Spanish civil war, this was unlikely. Tarragona fell to the rebels on 17 January. And the great prize of Barcelona, symbol of the Republic, fell on the 26th.

Panic led to a mass migration of Catalans toward the French border: between 27 January and 10 February half a million Spaniards, including 250,000 members of the Republican army, crossed into France. The Nationalists' Catalan campaign ended on 9 February in total triumph.

By then the remnants of the Loyalists' regime had crumbled. On 1 February Premier Negrín had offered three conditions of surrender—a guarantee of Spain's independence, a guarantee of the right of Spain's people to choose their own government, and freedom from persecution. These were rejected by Franco. Most of the Republic's leaders fled to France.

France and the U.K. recognized the Nationalist regime in Burgos on 27 February, despite vocal opposition from the moderate Left in both parliaments. The next day President Azaña resigned from the Republican presidency. Negrín left for France on 6 March. Finally, on 31 March 1939, the Nationalist forces occupied Madrid, ending Republican Spain's last intra-war crisis and the Spanish civil war. On 1 April the United States recognized the Franco regime, leaving the USSR as the only major European power that refused to recognize the outcome of the war.

The League of Nations was embroiled in the Spanish civil war from the outset, but never decisively. It began a series of discussions on Spain in 1936. The attempt by the League Council to pass a resolution in 1938 failed to achieve unanimity. Its only role was to supervise the withdrawal of volunteers enrolled in the International Brigades. It did not contribute to crisis abatement or, more generally, to conflict resolution.

(See *Master Table,* pp. 676–77.)

Sources

See sources for Cases #52 and 54.

Middle East: Protracted Conflicts

Arab/Israel

The **Arab/Israel** protracted conflict generated 25 international crises from 1947 to 1993, as follows.

Case #120 **Palestine Partition/Israel Independence,** in 1947–49;
#128 **Sinai Incursion,** in 1948–49;
#134 **Hula Drainage,** in 1951;
#143 **Qibya,** in 1953;
#149 **Gaza Raid–Czech. Arms,** in 1955–56;
#152 **Suez Nationalization-War,** in 1956–57;
#153 **Qalqilya,** in 1956;
#173 **Rottem,** in 1960;
#203 **Jordan Waters,** in 1963–64;
#220 **El Samu,** in 1966;
#222 **Six Day War,** in 1967;
#226 **Karameh,** in 1968;
#229 **Beirut Airport,** in 1968–69;
#232 **War of Attrition,** in 1969–70;
#251 **Libyan Plane,** in 1973;
#253 **Israel Mobilization,** in 1973;
#255 **October–Yom Kippur War,** in 1973–74;
#270 **Entebbe Raid,** in 1976;
#275 **Syria Mobilization,** in 1976;
#289 **Litani Operation,** in 1978;
#324 **Iraq Nuclear Reactor,** in 1981;
#327 **Al-Biqa Missiles I,** in 1981;
#337 **War in Lebanon,** in 1982–83;
#357 **Al-Biqa Missiles II,** in 1985–86;
#409 **Operation Accountability,** in 1993.

Several recurrent themes appear in the Arab/Israel PC cases. They involve **existence** (see Cases #120, 222, 324); **power politics and territorial claims** (see Cases #232, 253, 255, 275); **influence** (see Cases #327, 337, 357); **terror and reprisals** (see Cases #143, 149, 152, 153, 173, 220, 226, 229, 251, 270, 289, 409); and **resources** (see Cases #134, 203).

Along with the **World War II** and **East-West PCs,** the Arab/Israel protracted conflict has the largest number of international crises. The conflict remains unresolved.

General Background

The Arab/Israel interstate conflict began half a century ago (1947–48). As an intercommunal conflict it dates back more than a century, from the beginning of the "Return" of Jews to the Land of Israel in 1881. And as a civilizational conflict the hostility between Islam and Judaism can be traced to the founding of Islam in the seventh century B.C.E.

There had been serious outbreaks of violence between Jews and Arabs in Palestine over many years following the Balfour Declaration (1917) and the establishment of a British Mandate over Palestine (1922), notably the riots in 1921 and 1929 and the Arab Revolt from 1936 to 1938. The situation in Palestine in 1945–47 reflected the intensified struggle of the Jews for national independence after the European Holocaust during World War II and the Arab rejection of a Jewish state in what Jews regarded as their historic homeland. The Jewish demand for statehood became increasingly vocal. The Arab governments declared their determination to object by force to any plan that would authorize the creation of a Jewish state.

(120) Palestine Partition/Israel Independence

The first of many international crises in the protracted Arab/Israel conflict had six direct participants: Iraq, Egypt, Lebanon, Jordan, Syria, and Israel. It lasted from 29 November 1947 until 20 July 1949.

Pre-crisis
Viewed in interstate terms the conflict generated a crisis only with the birth pangs of the Jewish state in 1947–48. The situation in Palestine deteriorated rapidly as it became clear to all parties that the U.K., the Mandatory Power, was planning to relinquish its control over the area. As riots and instability increased, the decision regarding the future political solution for Palestine was placed on the UN agenda.

Crisis
The UN General Assembly Resolution of 29 November 1947, calling for the partition of Palestine into two independent states, one Arab, the other predominantly Jewish, triggered a crisis for Egypt, Iraq, Jordan, Lebanon, and Syria. Their initial response was a four-day summit meeting of Arab states on 8 December. On the 17th the Arab League reaffirmed its determination to maintain Palestine as an Arab state and announced plans to recruit an army of volunteers from League members.

The other Arab states objected to Jordan's plan to annex all of Palestine when the British Mandate ended. No further action was taken until May 1948.

Arab attacks on Jewish settlements in Palestine preceded the British evacuation; but regular Arab armies did not enter the area until the end of the Mandate on 14 May 1948.

The proclamation of the State of Israel on 14–15 May 1948, though anticipated, sharply escalated the crisis for the five Arab states. Plans for a combined army of Arab League forces, to be organized under an Iraqi commander, fell through; and directives were sent to each country to dispatch regular forces to Palestine. All the Arab states perceived a serious threat—the loss of territory that for centuries had been an integral part of the "Arab world." They responded by invading Israel on 15 May—Syria and Lebanon in the north, Jordan and Iraq in the east, and Egypt in the south. The Arab invasion triggered an existence crisis for the new state. Israel responded the same day by dispatching its newly formed regular army to fight on all fronts. A struggle for influence among Arab states and their fear that Jordan's King Abdullah would enlarge his domain by annexing all of Palestine and part of Syria accentuated the Arab decision to fight but created the seeds of disunity and disharmony in the first Arab/Israel war.

The crisis ended at different times for different participants. Fighting in the north ended on 30 October 1948 for Lebanon and Syria in defeat; but it was their armistice agreements with Israel on 23 March and 20 July 1949, respectively, that marked the termination of their crisis. With Iraq, unlike the four other Arab states, there was no formal agreement to end the war; but fighting effectively ceased after 18 July 1948. Fighting ended for Egypt with its defeat in Sinai in early January 1949 (see Case #128 below); and an armistice agreement was signed on 24 February 1949. The war ended for Israel after it captured Eilat on the Red Sea, and the Israeli government ratified the armistice agreement with Egypt on 10 March 1949. Israel and Jordan signed their armistice agreement on 3 April 1949. The last of the four armistice agreements was signed with Syria on 20 July 1949.

The UN was intensely involved in this crisis, arranging four truce agreements and brokering all the armistice agreements through the mediation of Count Folke Bernadotte and, after his assassination, Under-Secretary-General Ralph Bunche. The two superpowers and the former Mandatory Power were actively involved: the USSR as the primary source of weapons for the State of Israel acting indirectly through Czechoslovakia; the U.S. and the U.K. playing an important political role within and outside the UN.

(See *Master Table*, pp. 688–89.)

Sources

Foreign Relations of the United States (FRUS) 1947, vol. 5, 1948, vol. 5, 1949, vol. 5; Abdullah 1978; Abidi 1965; Baaklini 1976; Ben Gurion 1969, 1971; Bethell 1979; Black and Morris 1991; Bowyer-Bell 1969; Bullock 1983; Cattan 1969; Clifford 1991; Donovan 1977a; Dupuy 1978; Eagleton 1957; Flapan 1987; Glubb 1957; Goitein 1965; Hadawi 1964; Herzog 1982; Howley 1950;

Hurewitz 1950; Lenczowski 1962; Lie 1954; Longrigg 1953; Lorch 1966; Louis and Stookey 1986; al-Marayati 1961; McCullough 1992; Millis 1951; Morris 1987; O'Ballance 1957; Pogue 1987; Pollak and Sinai 1976; Rusk 1990; Safran 1969; Schoenbaum 1988; Shimoni 1987; Shlaim 1988; Spiegel 1985; Sykes 1973; Tessler 1994; Torrey 1964; Truman 1956; Weizmann 1949; Zayid 1965.

(128) Sinai Incursion

An intra-war crisis for Egypt, the U.K., and Israel occurred during the first Arab/Israel War and lasted from 25 December 1948 to 10 January 1949.

Background
The first of many Arab/Israel wars had begun on 15 May 1948 (see Case #120 above), with the end of the British Mandate, Israel's proclamation of independence, and the invasion by five Arab states. Egypt's refusal to negotiate an armistice agreement led Israel to increase its efforts to conquer southern territory.

Crisis
On 25 December 1948 Israeli forces launched an attack on the Egyptian army in the south, crossing into the Egyptian-held Sinai peninsula and triggering crises for Egypt and Britain. After an unsuccessful attempt to rally Arab League states to its aid, Egypt responded to this territorial threat on 31 December by appealing to the U.K. to press for a Security Council resolution demanding Israeli withdrawal. Britain, relying on its unrenewed 1936 treaty with Egypt, triggered a crisis for Israel by sending an ultimatum, via the U.S. embassy, on the 31st, demanding the evacuation of Egyptian territory no later than 8 January 1949. Israel responded to this threat of military intervention by changing the direction of its forces while still remaining in Sinai. The crisis was escalated further when Israel shot down five British planes over Israeli territory that had been sent to observe the Israeli withdrawal from Sinai. Britain reacted strongly by sending military reinforcements to its base in Aqaba, Jordan, on 7 January. That day Israel ordered its troops out of the area, in response to a Security Council call for a cease-fire. This withdrawal was completed by 10 January 1949, the termination date for all three crisis actors.

The U.S. was highly involved politically: it pressed Israel to comply with the U.K. demand. The USSR was aloof from this crisis.

(See *Master Table*, pp. 688–89.)

Sources
See sources for Case #120.

(134) Hula Drainage

Syria and Israel were enmeshed in a crisis over the Hula Valley in the Demilitarized Zone *(DMZ)* between them from 12 February to 15 May 1951.

Background
This was the first Arab/Israel interstate crisis since the end of the 1948–49 war. Its origins lay in a continuing dispute over control of the sources of the Jordan River and rights in the "No-Man's Land" on the Israel/Syrian border.

Crisis
A crisis for Syria was triggered on 12 February 1951, the day Israel's Palestine Land Development Company *(PLDC)* began work on the Hula drainage project in the *DMZ* north of Lake Tiberias (the *Kinneret,* Sea of Galilee). Its goals were to drain the lake and surrounding marshes, eliminate malaria in the area, reclaim 6,250 hectares (about 15,000 acres) of land for agriculture, and use the accumulated water to irrigate other parts of Israel.

Syria contended that Israel's project violated their 1949 Armistice Agreement, under which the *DMZ* was a no-man's land. It also perceived a threat from an adverse change in the balance of power with its enemy if the Hula Valley became an economically productive area under de facto Israeli control. On the 14th Damascus appealed to the UN Security Council to compel Israel to halt the project. Israel refused to do so, citing the concession granted to the *PLDC* by the British Mandatory Power in 1934 and claiming that the land fell under its jurisdiction according to Mandate maps. Syria countered with a claim to the town of al-Hamma and all territory in the *DMZ* east of the southern part of Lake Tiberias. On 15 March Arabs in civilian dress opened fire on a bulldozer of the Israeli company working in the Hula area. This triggered a crisis for Israel, which charged that they were Syrian soldiers, while Syria disclaimed responsibility for the acts of "Arab landowners." The next day Israel informed the UN Mixed Armistice Commission *(MAC)* that it would suspend operations in the Hula Valley for a week. Discussions in the *MAC* were deadlocked, with intermittent firing incidents.

Tension escalated dramatically on 4 April, when Syrian soldiers killed seven Israeli policemen near al-Hamma, in the southern part of the *DMZ.* Israel retaliated the next day with an air attack on the Syrian outpost and the police station of al-Hamma. Both sides appealed to the Security Council, blaming each other for a violation of their Armistice Agreement. Two Syrian planes were shot down on the 11th.

While Security Council deliberations were taking place, a further sharp escalation occurred early in May. On the 2nd Syrian forces overran the Israeli post at Tel al-Mutillah, just beyond the *DMZ.* After several counterattacks from 3 to 6 May and heavy casualties—40 Israelis and more Syrians—Israeli troops regained control of Tel al-Mutillah.

The Security Council passed a resolution on 8 May calling for a cease-fire and the withdrawal of military forces from the *DMZ*. Hostilities ended on the 11th, following an agreement mediated by the *MAC* that day. It was formalized on the 15th, terminating the Hula Drainage crisis.

The UN and its *MAC* played a crucial role in abating the crisis, as noted, through mediation and the Security Council resolution. The Council did not assign responsibility for the incidents on the ground, including the killing of the Israeli policemen, but criticized Israel's use of air power in the *DMZ*. Both the U.S. and the USSR were politically involved but had only a marginal effect on crisis abatement.

(On the larger issue of the Hula Drainage dispute, another Security Council resolution, on 18 May, adopted a pro-Syria stance: it ordered the *PLDC* to cease operations in the *DMZ* until the chairman of the Israel/Syria *MAC* arranged an agreement to resume the project. Israel agreed on 30 May to stop work, except on Jewish-owned land in the area, a compromise approved by the *MAC* chairman, but not by Syria.)

(See *Master Table*, pp. 690–91.)

Sources
Bar-Yaacov 1967; Ben Gurion 1969; Goichon 1964; Rabinovich 1991; Seale 1965.

(143) Qibya

There was one crisis actor—Jordan. The crisis was triggered on 14 October 1953. It had no exact termination date.

Background and Pre-crisis
After the Arab/Israel War of 1948–49 (see Case #120 above), Arab refugees who had fled Palestine were placed in camps in Jordan where anti-Israel sentiments flourished. Infiltrations from Jordan into Israel began in 1951. In October 1953 the situation was exacerbated when Jordanian infiltrators murdered an Israeli woman and her two children.

Crisis
On 14 October 1953 a Jordan crisis was triggered when the Israel Defense Forces retaliated against the village of Qibya in Jordan, killing 69 civilians and destroying 45 houses. Jordan responded on the 16th by conferring with the U.S. and Britain, lodging a complaint with the Security Council, and calling for a meeting of the Arab League. This resulted in condemnation of Israel by both forums. Israel public opinion prompted its leaders to decide to refrain from attacks on civilian targets in the future. Infiltrations stopped for a while but were resumed after a few months.

The U.S. was involved politically, with little effect on the substance or timing of the outcome. The USSR remained aloof from this crisis.

(See *Master Table*, pp. 692–93.)

Sources
Blechman 1972; Shwadran 1959.

(149) Gaza Raid–Czech. Arms

The crisis between Egypt and Israel began on 28 February 1955 and ended on 23 June 1956.

Background
During the early 1950s Israel suffered from repeated terrorist attacks by infiltration into Israeli territory, particularly from Gaza, which was then controlled by Egypt. Five reprisal raids into Egyptian territory were carried out by Israel from 1950 to 1955.

Crisis
Israel's retaliatory raid into Gaza on 28 February 1955, in which 39 Arabs were killed and 32 injured, triggered a crisis for Egypt. On 20 March Egypt appealed to the UN Security Council and the Arab League. Its major response, on 20 April, was a request by Nasir to Zhou Enlai to contact Moscow about supplying arms to Egypt. The crisis ended for Egypt on 28 September 1955 when, with Soviet approval, an arms agreement was signed with Czechoslovakia.

This marked the trigger for Israel's crisis. By 11 December 1955, when an agreement between France and Israel for the purchase of French Mystères was signed, Israel had answered cumulative terrorist attacks by four more raids into Egyptian territory. On 5 April 1956 a large raid into Gaza resulted in 59 deaths and 93 wounded. However, Israel's major response was a letter to the prime minister of France on 12 April 1956 requesting massive amounts of arms. Another agreement was signed for six more French Mystères on 23 April. The termination date for Israel's crisis was 23 June 1956 when a third arms deal was signed with France that would provide substantial French arms to Israel, and enable Israeli decision makers to correct the imbalance in military capability that had occurred as a result of the Czech. arms agreement with Egypt and Syria.

The Security Council passed a resolution condemning Israel for the Gaza Raid. The Secretary-General visited the area in the hope of mediating between the two parties, but the UN did not contribute to crisis abatement. The Arab League held discussions but did not pass any resolution.

The U.S. was politically involved in this crisis. The Soviet Union provided military aid to Egypt.

(See *Master Table,* pp. 692–93.)

Sources
Bar-Zohar 1967; Brecher 1974; Dayan 1966; Lacouture 1973; Love 1969.

(152) Suez Nationalization-War

There were six crisis actors in this two-stage Middle East crisis: France, the U.K., Egypt, the USSR, the U.S., and Israel. The crisis lasted from 26 July 1956 until 12 March 1957.

Background
The end of empire with respect to Egypt extended over more than three decades, with three notable events: termination of Britain's protectorate and the formal proclamation of Egypt's independence in February 1922; the Anglo-Egyptian treaty of August 1936, calling for the withdrawal of British forces from Egypt except for 10,000 troops in the Suez Canal Zone—in time of war the number might be increased—and a 20-year alliance; and as a final act the Anglo-Egyptian Agreement of October 1954, which provided for the evacuation of all 70,000 British troops from their Suez base within 20 months, that is, by June 1956.

Pre-crisis
On several occasions during the early part of 1956 Egypt had voiced its concern about the continued presence of British forces in the Canal Zone. Cairo had also declared its support for the Algerian *Front Liberation National (FLN)* in its struggle for independence from France. In the meantime the Egyptian monarchy had been overthrown by the Free Officers in 1952; and Colonel Jamal Abd-ul Nasir had emerged as the dominant political figure in Egypt in 1953. Among his ambitious reform goals was the construction of a massive dam at Aswan to harness the waters of the Upper Nile for irrigation and hydroelectric purposes. The U.S. and the U.K. initially pledged financial support for the Aswan Dam project but withdrew their offer in the spring of 1956 because of Nasir's increasing alignment with the USSR, as evident in the Czech.-Egyptian arms deal of September 1955 (see Case #149 above), which transformed the arms balance in the Arab/Israel domain.

Israel had been subjected to a steady increase of cross-border infiltrations from Egypt-controlled Gaza and the Sinai Peninsula since 1953. It was even more acutely concerned about the flow of arms to Egypt from Czechoslovakia in 1955–56.

Crisis
On 26 July 1956, "Liberation Day," the fourth anniversary of the military regime, Nasir responded to the Anglo-American volte-face on the Aswan Dam by proclaiming the nationalization of the Suez Canal. A 99-year lease to the Anglo-French Suez Canal Corporation was due to expire in 1968. This dramatic act, perceived in London and Paris as portending grave economic and military consequences, triggered a crisis for the two Western powers. On the 30th multilateral talks were initiated—by the U.K., the U.S., France, and Australia—in order to

find a peaceful solution. When these talks, as well as an appeal by Britain and France to the United Nations and three international conferences in the summer of 1956, did not result in satisfaction for the aggrieved parties, France initiated bilateral talks with Israel in August aimed at a military riposte. Britain joined its two allies at a conference at Sèvres held between 22–25 October, where they decided to launch a joint military attack on Egypt's Sinai Peninsula.

Crises for Egypt and the USSR were triggered by an Israeli invasion of Sinai, Israel's Sinai Campaign, on 29 October 1956. Two days later British and French forces landed in the Canal Zone. Egypt responded on 30 October with military resistance, a call for general mobilization, and an appeal to the Soviet Union for military and diplomatic assistance. On 5 November Moscow dispatched a harsh Note to the three invading powers and the United States, referring to the "dangerous consequences" of the aggressive war in Egypt, warning that London, Paris, and Tel Aviv lay under the threat of Soviet missiles and indicating the USSR's intention to use force if the situation were not rectified immediately. This escalated the crisis for Britain and France and triggered a crisis for Israel: all three states perceived a threat of grave damage to their urban centers and population at large. The Soviet Note also triggered a crisis for the United States, threatening its allies, its deterrent credibility, and its international influence.

Britain and France complied at once and agreed to a cease-fire, which came into effect the following day, 6 November. They also stated their intention to withdraw all their forces from the Canal Zone. This marked the termination of the Suez crisis for these two states.

The Soviet Note was received in Israel just after its prime minister had broadcast a "victory" speech to parliament, declaring the 1949 armistice lines "null and void." Israel conferred with France, but in the absence of a credible French military commitment against the Soviet threat, it acquiesced. This took the form of a declaration on 8 November that Israel would evacuate Sinai once arrangements for an emergency international peacekeeping force in Sinai had been concluded. This terminated the crisis for the two superpowers.

The process of Israel's withdrawal, with periodic eruptions of high tension, lasted four months. Its crisis—and with it Egypt's crisis and the Suez Nationalization-War crisis as a whole—ended on 12 March 1957 when Israel's withdrawal from Sinai was completed.

The U.S. responded on 6 November by declaring a semialert and indicated that it would not stand by idly if London and Paris were bombed. Tel Aviv was conspicuously omitted from this warning to Moscow. Although countering the Soviet threat, Washington also pressed its allies to withdraw their forces.

The UN, too, was intensely active, culminating in a decision by the General Assembly to send an Emergency Force to police Sinai and Gaza from which all foreign forces were to be withdrawn. *NATO*, as the regional security organization of the West, was also involved through a strong counterthreat by the *NATO* Supreme Commander on 13 November 1956.

(See *Master Table*, pp. 694–95.)

Sources
Documents Diplomatiques Français (DDF) 1956 (1988); *FRUS 1955–57,* vol. V (1987); Adams 1958; Bar-On 1994; Bar-Zohar 1964; Barker 1964; Beaufre 1969; Ben Gurion 1963, 1964, 1969; Black and Morris 1991; Blake 1975; Bowie 1974; Brecher 1974; Bromberger 1957; Campbell 1989; Childers 1962; Dayan 1966, 1976; Duff 1969; Eayrs 1964; Eban 1972, 1992; Eden 1960; Eisenhower 1965; Epstein 1964; Farnie 1969; Feske 1994; Finer 1964; Golan 1958; Goodspeed 1967; Horne 1989; Johnson 1957; Kyle 1991; Lloyd 1978; Louis and Owen 1989; Love 1969; Mackintosh 1962; Macmillan 1971; Middle East Research Center, Cairo 1956; Murphy 1964; Neustadt 1970; Nutting 1958, 1967; Peres 1970; Pineau 1976; Robertson 1964; Rosner 1963; Safran 1969; Shuckburgh 1986; Smolansky 1974; Spiegel 1985; Stephens 1971; Thomas 1970; Troen and Shemesh 1990.

(153) Qalqilya

A crisis for Jordan and Israel took place from 13 September until late October 1956.

Background and Pre-crisis
Infiltration into Israeli territory from neighboring Arab states occurred with increasing frequency during the six years prior to the Sinai Campaign. Acts of reprisal against the Arab state from whose territory infiltrators crossed into Israel were numerous and swift (see Cases #134, 143, and 149 above). Most recently, during July and August 1956, dozens of Israelis were killed or wounded as a result of several infiltrations of *feda'iyyun* (guerrilla) groups from Jordan.

Crisis
On 13 September 1956 Israeli forces blew up a police station in the Jordanian village of Garandal. King Hussein's response, the following day, was a decision to visit Iraq to consult Prime Minister Nuri al-Sa'id about the possible stationing of Iraqi troops in Jordan. After several other incidents from Jordan, including the firing on Israeli archaeologists meeting at a border settlement, Israel carried out another reprisal on the Jordanian village of Husan. A third reprisal raid took place on 10 October at Qalqilya in response to a Jordanian ambush of an Israeli bus.

On the 12th Iraq issued a statement that it was ready to send troops to Jordan immediately, if requested to do so. This triggered a crisis for Israel. Foreign Minister Golda Meir responded the next day by declaring that the stationing of Iraqi troops in Jordan would be a threat to Israel's integrity and that in such an event Israel would retaliate. In addition, Israel's ambassadors to the major powers were called home for consultation, and a request was made to convene the UN Security Council.

Israel's crisis ended on 15 October with a Jordanian declaration that Iraqi forces would not enter Jordan at that time but would do so if Israel attacked. The crisis for Jordan faded at the end of October. At that time British planes from Cyprus flew over Jordan in a symbolic gesture to reinforce the Jordan regime which had been undermined by the Qalqilya raid.

The UN Secretary-General met with the representatives of the powers and the two crisis actors and warned of Security Council intervention if peace did not prevail in the area. After the raid on Qalqilya, General Burns, the head of the UN Observer Forces, attempted to stop the fighting but was not successful. The U.S. was involved politically; the USSR was not active.

(See *Master Table*, pp. 694–95.)

Sources
See sources for Case #107.

(173) Rottem

A crisis for Egypt and Israel occurred between 15 February and 8 March 1960.

Background
Acts of terror in Israel by infiltrators crossing the border from Syria, and a subsequent Israeli retaliation raid in early February 1960, preceded this crisis. At that time Egypt and Syria constituted a single political entity, the United Arab Republic (UAR) (see Case #162—**Formation of UAR,** in 1958, in **Middle East: Non-PCs**).

Crisis
On 15 February 1960 President Nasir received a message from the Soviet embassy in Cairo claiming that Israel's troops were massing on its northern border, with an intention to attack Syria. In order to offset this danger, Egypt began secret troop maneuvers across the Suez Canal in Sinai toward the Israeli border, on the 19th. On 23 February Israeli intelligence notified Prime Minister (and Minister of Defense) Ben Gurion that the major part of the Egyptian army had crossed the Canal and was situated near Israel's southern border. This triggered a crisis for Israel. The following day Israel responded by moving its forces southward in army maneuvers, termed *Rottem* by the Israel Defense Forces. Egypt's crisis ended on 1 March 1960 when its forces began to return to their bases west of the Canal. Israel reciprocated soon after. And, one week later, on 8 March, Israel's prime minister departed for an official visit to the United States. This act indicated a reduction of tension and the end of Israel's crisis.

The Soviet Union was politically involved in support of Egypt (the UAR). The U.S. and the UN were not involved in this crisis.

(See *Master Table*, pp. 698–99.)

Sources
MER 1960; Rabin 1979; Schiff and Haber 1976.

(203) Jordan Waters

The crisis for the five actors, Jordan, Lebanon, Syria, Egypt, and Israel, started on 11 December 1963 and ended on 5 May 1964.

Background and Pre-crisis
The dispute between Israel and the neighboring Arab states concerning the utilization of the Jordan waters was long-standing (see Case #134—**Hula Drainage,** in 1951, above). Since the mid-1940s several plans had been drawn up for its resolution, but only one, the "Revised" Unified Johnston Plan of 1955, was approved and agreed upon at the technical level by both Israel and the Arab states. However, at a meeting of the Arab League Political Committee, it was rejected in principle because of its supposed bias toward Israel. After Israel's Sinai Campaign in 1956 (see Case #152 above) all further hopes of Arab/Israeli acceptance of any regional water proposal were destroyed, and both sides felt free to proceed in developing their own unilateral water projects.

In 1958 Jordan started working on a water scheme, and in 1959 Israel began the National Water Carrier plan for carrying water to the Negev by pumping it from Lake Tiberias. During the early months of 1960 concern by the Arab states, particularly Syria, deepened, with the Arabs claiming that Israel's water scheme would endanger Arab security because Israel could now settle larger numbers of immigrants, thereby increasing its potential military power.

Under Syrian pressure a conference of Arab military chiefs of staff was held in Cairo from 7 to 10 December 1963 in order to draw up a common Arab strategy against the Israeli diversion plan, due to be completed at the end of 1963. The conference also agreed to prepare an agenda for the forthcoming December meeting of the Supreme Arab Defense Council.

Crisis
A crisis for all four Arab states (Jordan, Lebanon, Syria, and Egypt) was triggered on 11 December, the day after the Arab chiefs of staff conference, when Israel's minister of labor stated that the National Water Carrier would be operated despite pressure from the Arab states or any other country. Nasir responded on 23 December 1963 by proposing a meeting of all Arab heads of state to consider Israel's plan to divert the Jordan waters. Realizing the Arab armies were not capable of defeating Israel, Nasir hoped to check the trend toward war that was being proposed by Syria. A Summit Conference was held on 13–16 January 1964 in Cairo under the auspices of the Arab League and attended by all 13 members of the League. At the conference it was decided unanimously not to go to war with Israel but to divert the three tributaries of the Jordan River and to set

up a joint (unified) military command to protect the Arab states. An official communiqué at the end of the conference, on 16 January, represented the response to the crisis by Egypt, Jordan, Syria, and Lebanon.

The announcement of the Arab Summit Conference decisions on 16 January triggered a crisis for Israel, which perceived a grave threat to its vital water supplies. On 19 January Israel responded by an official cabinet statement repeating its determination to carry out the plans for using the waters of the Jordan River.

Both superpowers, as well as the United Nations, issued strong warnings to Israel and the Arabs against using armed force.

The crisis ended on 5 May 1964 when it was officially announced by Israel that the project was completed and that it would go into operation in the summer of 1964. The announcement set off an outburst of indignation in the Arab press at the failure of the Arab governments to stop the project, but no further action was taken by them.

(See *Master Table,* pp. 702–3.)

Sources
Alexander and Kitrie 1973; Brecher 1974; Jansen 1964; Kadi 1966; Kerr 1970; Khouri 1985; Lowi 1993; Mehdi 1964; *MEJ* Chronology 1963, 1964; Nimrod 1965a, 1965b, 1965c; Saliba 1968; Stevens 1965.

(220) El Samu

The two actors in this crisis, a prelude to the Six Day War (see Case #222 below), were Israel and Jordan. It began on 12 November 1966 and ended on the 15th of that month.

Pre-crisis
A series of border infiltrations and terrorist attacks on Israel emanating from Jordan took place from the summer of 1966 onward.

Crisis
On 12 November an Israel crisis was triggered when an army command car was blown up by a mine near the Jordanian border. Three soldiers were killed and six wounded. In an effort to deter Jordan from further aid to the Palestinian infiltrators, Israel responded the following day with a commando raid on the village of El Samu, in Jordan, where Palestinian supporters were concentrated. Jordan's response to the raid was mobilization of its army. Heavy fighting took place, and Israel withdrew a few hours later. Jordan appealed to the Security Council and issued an internal state of alert, especially against possible riots on the West Bank. Jordan ended the state of alert on the 15th, terminating the crisis for both countries.

The Secretary-General of the UN met with the ambassadors of both actors,

but the UN did not resolve the crisis. The U.S. was politically involved in this crisis; the USSR was not.
(See *Master Table,* pp. 706–7.)

Sources
See the sources for Case #222.

(222) Six Day War

The six actors in this Middle East crisis were Israel, Jordan, Egypt, the United States, Syria, and the Soviet Union. It began on 17 May and ended on 11 June 1967.

Background and Pre-crisis
Tension along the Israel/Syria border had been increasing since the autumn of 1966 due to the stepping up of attacks by Palestinian guerrillas based in Syria. On 7 April 1967 six Syrian MIG fighter planes were downed in an air battle over the Israel/Syria border. Israel repeatedly warned Syria that a massive reprisal would be inevitable if Damascus did not stop active support of Palestinian raids into Israel. On 14 May both Syria and Egypt announced a state of emergency based upon Soviet-inspired reports that Israel was concentrating troops on its northern border.

Crisis
Two hostile acts by Egypt on 17 May 1967 triggered a crisis for Israel: an overflight of Israel's nuclear research center at Dimona and the dispatch of two additional Egyptian divisions into Sinai (others had crossed the Canal in the preceding two days). On the 18th UN Secretary-General U Thant acceded to President Nasir's demand, two days earlier, to withdraw the United Nations Emergency Force *(UNEF)* from Sinai. (It had functioned since the 1956 Suez War [see Case #152 above].) Army reserves were mobilized in Israel and Egypt on the 19th and 21st. And on 23 May Egypt announced the closure of the Strait of Tiran, thus blockading the Israeli port of Eilat. The British and U.S. governments termed this act a violation of international law, while the Soviet Union blamed Israel for the dangerous situation in the Middle East. Efforts by the U.S. and the U.K. to form a naval flotilla failed. The U.S. Sixth Fleet moved toward the eastern Mediterranean. The Security Council met at the request of Canada and Denmark. On 30 May a Defense Pact was signed between Jordan and Egypt.

Israel's major response to its crisis was a decision on 4 June to launch a preemptive strike. This was implemented by an air attack on Egypt's air force bases on 5 June, destroying Egyptian air power and triggering a crisis for Jordan and Egypt. Despite an Israeli assurance to Jordan via the United Nations that, if Jordan kept out of the war, Israel would not initiate any military action against its eastern neighbor, Jordan responded the same day by opening fire on Jerusalem and bombing Netanya. Israel destroyed the small Jordanian air force and, by noon of 7 June, captured the Jordan-controlled Old City of Jerusalem. Egypt's response, on 5 June, was to launch a counterattack against Israel.

The crisis trigger for the United States was a message from Premier Kosygin on 6 June threatening Soviet intervention. The crises for Syria and the Soviet Union were triggered on the 9th by Israeli advances on the Golan Heights. Syria responded immediately by bombarding Israeli border settlements. The next day the Soviets responded with a "hot line" telephone call from Kosygin to Johnson threatening Soviet action unless Israel halted operations at once. The major U.S. response was an immediate order by President Johnson to change the course of the Sixth Fleet and to cut the 100-mile restriction from the Syrian coast to 50 miles, signaling that the U.S. was prepared to resist Soviet intervention in the Arab/Israel war. Syria accepted a cease-fire on 10 June. The following day the cease-fire came into effect for all the other actors, terminating the 1967 Middle East Crisis.

Five East European states, together with the Soviet Union, severed diplomatic relations with Israel, namely, Bulgaria, Czechoslovakia, Hungary, Poland, and Yugoslavia. The UN helped to escalate the crisis, by the removal of *UNEF,* but it also contributed to the more rapid termination of the crisis through the efforts of the Security Council and cease-fire resolutions. The political activity of the two superpowers, especially that of the U.S., had an important impact on the course of the crisis and its outcome.

(See *Master Table,* pp. 706–7.)

Sources
Bar-Siman-Tov 1987; Bar-Zohar 1970; Black and Morris 1991; Brecher 1974; Brecher with Geist 1980; Bull 1976; Burdett 1970; Churchill and Churchill 1967; Dayan 1976; Dobrynin 1995; Draper 1968; Eban 1977; Glassman 1975; Heikal 1973, 1978; Higgins 1969; Hussein 1969; Johnson 1971; Khalidi 1975; Kimche and Bawly 1968; Lacouture 1992; Lall 1970; Laqueur 1968; *MER* 1971; Neff 1984; O'Ballance 1972; Quandt 1977, 1993; Rafael 1972; Riad 1981; Rusk 1990; Safran 1969; Schoenbaum 1988; Schueftan 1977; Spiegel 1985; Stein 1991; Stein and Tanter 1980; Stephens 1971.

(226) Karameh

This crisis between Israel and Jordan lasted from 18 to 22 March 1968.

Pre-crisis
From 15 February to mid-March 1968 Israel reported 37 sabotage raids from Jordan causing death and injuries among Israeli soldiers and civilians.

Crisis
A crisis for Israel was triggered on 18 March when an Israeli school bus went over a mine near the Jordan border; two children were killed and 28 wounded.

Defense Minister Dayan issued a warning to Jordan to prevent further border crossings by Palestinian *feda'iyyun*. The bus incident and Dayan's warning also triggered a crisis for Jordan: King Hussein stated that on that day he perceived a threat of full-scale invasion from Israel. Israel's response was a raid on the village of Karameh, a *feda'iyyun* base in Jordan, on 21 March. There was also an appeal to the United Nations. The Jordanian response was to dispatch armed forces to the site. Heavy fighting followed, with severe losses on both sides. Israel's crisis ended when its forces withdrew on 21 March. Jordan's crisis ended the following day, when it reopened the Allenby bridge linking the Israel-occupied West Bank and Jordan.

UN activity took the form of a discussion in the Security Council; no resolution was passed. Both the U.S. and the USSR were politically active in this crisis, with little effect.

(See *Master Table,* pp. 706–7.)

Sources
MEJ Chronology 1968; *MER* 1968.

(229) Beirut Airport

A crisis for Lebanon began on 28 December 1968. The crisis ended sometime in January 1969.

Pre-crisis
On 26 December 1968 the Lebanon-based *PFLP* (Popular Front for the Liberation of Palestine) attacked an Israeli civilian plane at Athens International Airport. One passenger was killed. Israel's policy had long been to retaliate against the host country in the hope of compelling the Arab states to restrain Palestinian attacks on Israeli citizens and property.

Crisis
The crisis trigger for Lebanon was Israel's retaliation raid on Beirut International Airport on 28 December 1968, destroying 13 jetliners belonging to the Middle East Airlines and other Lebanese-owned planes. There was no loss of life. The Lebanese security forces did not intervene. Lebanon's major response, the following day, was a complaint against Israel to the Security Council. Two days later Lebanon declared a state of alert and mobilized reserve forces. The raid on Beirut accentuated Lebanon's civil tensions and triggered an internal political crisis in that country. The international crisis ended some time in January 1969.

There was widespread condemnation of the Israeli raid, including a protest by the Vatican. On 7 January 1969 France reiterated its policy of a total embargo on all military supplies destined for Israel. The U.S. offered aid to Lebanon and put its Sixth Fleet on low-level alert. The Soviet Union confined its political activity to statements at the United Nations. The Security Council passed a resolution condemning Israel.

(See *Master Table,* pp. 708–9.)

Sources
MER 1968.

(232) War of Attrition

Israel, Egypt, and the USSR were the actors in this two-stage crisis-war from 8 March 1969 until 7 August 1970.

Background and Pre-crisis
During the June Six Day War of 1967 (see Case #222 above) Israel occupied the Sinai Peninsula, along with the Golan Heights, the West Bank and Gaza Strip, and East Jerusalem. In the autumn of 1968 Egypt's leaders perceived that the strategic balance had turned in its favor permitting a limited military initiative against Israel along the Canal. Accordingly Egyptian artillery bombarded Israeli positions on the east bank of the Canal in September and October. Israel responded with a display of force—the destruction of Egypt's power station at Naj Hamadi on 31 October. Egypt desisted from further military activity; and several months of tranquility followed on the Sinai front.

Crisis
On 8 March 1969 Egypt launched the War of Attrition with intense artillery fire against Israel's "Bar Lev Line" on the east side of the Canal. This triggered a crisis for Israel. After heightened losses in May, June, and July, Israel responded with air raids into Egypt on 20 July catalyzing a crisis for Egypt. As a result a planned Egyptian offensive to cross the Canal was set aside. Israeli threat perceptions declined. And when Israeli air raids were suspended on 28 July the first crisis for both actors, along with the first stage of the War of Attrition, came to an end.

The fighting escalated in October, when Israeli air raids destroyed SAM-2 batteries and Egyptian antiaircraft systems. But the catalyst to the second stage of the crisis-war and an intra-war crisis for Egypt was Israeli deep-penetration raids into Egypt beginning on 7 January 1970. Nasir, concerned that the raids might generate domestic pressure that would endanger his regime, appealed to the Soviet Union for aid: during a visit to Moscow starting on 22 January he requested Soviet military advisors and the introduction of a sophisticated missile air defense system into Egypt. Nasir's threat to resign if his requests were not met triggered a crisis for the Soviet Union. It responded favorably: by 19 March Soviet missile batteries were installed in Egypt near the Canal triggering Israel's second—intrawar—crisis of the War of Attrition. Israel responded with intensive bombing of these antiaircraft sites on 24 March. And in a rare direct Israeli encounter with Soviet military personnel during the entire Arab/Israel conflict Israeli- and Soviet-piloted aircraft clashed on 18 April.

Intense U.S. pressure led to a cease-fire on 7 August based upon Secretary of State Rogers's Plan "B" (19 June 1970) terminating the War of Attrition. Rogers's Plan "A" (9 December 1969), designed to bring about a peaceful solution on the principle of land for peace, remained unfulfilled until the Egypt-Israel Peace Treaty of 1979.

Big Four talks—the U.S., the USSR, the U.K., and France—under the auspices of the UN contributed marginally to crisis abatement. The Soviet Union supplied arms and missiles to Egypt and influenced it to abandon plans for a cross-Canal military operation in 1969. In addition to mediation efforts the U.S. also employed delaying tactics in the delivery of Phantom jets to Israel as a form of pressure to accept a cease-fire. On the whole both superpowers played an important role in crisis management. The Arab League held a conference in December 1969 but had no impact on the crisis outcome.

(See *Master Table,* pp. 708–9.)

Sources
Bar-Siman-Tov 1980; Brecher 1974; Breslauer 1983; Dayan 1976; Eban 1977; George 1983; Glassman 1975; Heikal 1975; Kissinger 1979; *MEJ* Chronology 1969, 1970; *MER* 1969–70; Quandt 1977, 1993; Rabin 1979; Riad 1981; Rubinstein 1977; Stephens 1971; Whetten 1974.

(251) Libyan Plane

The appearance of a Libyan plane over Israeli-occupied territory created a 30-minute crisis for Israel on 21 February 1973.

Background
Several weeks prior to this event, Israel's cabinet had been alerted to a terrorist plot to hijack an airliner which would be packed with explosives and crashed into an Israeli population center.

Crisis
On 21 February 1973 a plane was spotted on Israeli radar heading in the direction of Israel's nuclear plant in Dimona. Apparently a Libyan Boeing-727 with 113 passengers on board had strayed over the eastern side of the Suez Canal, then occupied by Israel. Israeli fighter planes immediately intercepted the intruding aircraft, demanding identification. Twenty minutes of sustained warnings and signals to the pilot brought no results. Orders were requested from higher military officers. The Army Chief of Staff, Lieutenant-General David Elazar, ordered the air force to shoot down the plane. Israeli pilots responded by so doing. When

the plane crashed, 30 minutes after it had been spotted, the crisis for Israel was terminated.

Immediately thereafter the Israelis learned that the plane had been a civilian airliner from Libya and that it had not represented a security threat. There were very few survivors. Most of the passengers were Egyptian, some German. The pilot was French. Israel subsequently paid compensation to the families of the dead. Following the crisis Israel was condemned by most members of the international system. France conducted a separate investigation. There was no UN or superpower activity during the crisis because of its brevity.

(See *Master Table,* pp. 712–13.)

Sources
ACR 1973; *ARB* 1973; *Keesing's* 1973; *New York Times* 1973.

(253) Israel Mobilization

A crisis for Israel in its relations with Egypt began on 10 April 1973 and ended in late June of that year.

Background and Pre-crisis
After the Arab defeat in the 1967 War (see Case #222 above), the Egyptians began to rebuild their armed forces, in conjunction with efforts to find a diplomatic solution to Arab (mainly Egypt's and Syria's) dissatisfaction over Israeli control of the Sinai Desert, the Golan Heights, the West Bank, and East Jerusalem. Anwar al-Sadat succeeded Nasir as President of Egypt in 1970 and persuaded Moscow to resupply weapons on a large scale. In early 1973 newly appointed Egyptian Chief of Staff Ahmed Ismail visited Moscow and conducted negotiations for additional Soviet arms. His visit to Washington, however, was less successful. In February President Nixon emphasized that the United States had no intention of putting pressure on Israel to withdraw from the Sinai Peninsula and all other territories captured during the Six Day War. Shortly thereafter news of U.S. agreement to supply Israel with 48 Phantoms and 36 Skyhawks was leaked to the press. Egyptian coordination with the Syrians began in February 1973, and a joint attack was scheduled for May of that year. At the beginning of April Sadat stated publicly that Egypt was preparing for war with Israel. He also announced a large Egyptian army exercise.

Crisis
On 10 April 1973 Israel's Chief of Staff, Lieutenant-General David Elazar, received intelligence reports of an intended Egyptian attack slated for 15 May: further, that Iraq and Libya had each sent 16 fighter planes to Egypt. Israeli intelligence maintained, however, that Sadat would back down before the actual launching of the war. This estimate was not accepted by Elazar. Israel responded

by placing its army on alert on 13 April and by canceling all leaves. War preparations began, and reserve units were called into active service.

Toward the end of June, after the Nixon-Brezhnev talks on the 22nd, Israel became convinced that Egypt did not intend to go to war at that time, and the crisis came to an end. Sadat subsequently explained that the postponement of the war was due to a scheduling of a second summit conference in Washington for May. Elazar came under severe criticism by Israel's finance minister for the economic cost of the April mobilization, while the Israel intelligence estimates were vindicated. This proved to be a crucial factor in Elazar's reluctance to order general mobilization and misconceptions that characterized Israeli thinking just before the successful Egyptian attack on 6 October 1973 (see Case #255 below).

There was no superpower or UN involvement in this crisis.

(See *Master Table,* pp. 712–13.)

Sources
Bartov 1981; Black and Morris 1991; Herzog 1975; Insight Team of the *Sunday Times* 1974; Meir 1975; *MEJ* Chronology 1973.

(255) October–Yom Kippur War

The October–Yom Kippur crisis began on 5 October 1973 and ended on 31 May 1974. The crisis actors were Israel, Syria, the United States, Egypt, and the Soviet Union.

Background and Pre-crisis
The West Bank of the Jordan River, the Golan Heights, the Gaza Strip, and the entire Sinai Peninsula had been occupied by Israel since the Six Day War of June 1967 (see Case #222 above). In March 1969 Egypt launched a War of Attrition against Israeli forces in the Sinai. In August 1970 a cease-fire was accepted by both sides with plans to put into effect a U.S. plan for peace in the region (see Case #232 above). The plan was never implemented. In April 1973 Israeli forces were put on alert, including a large mobilization, when its leaders suspected Egyptian mobilization and war exercises to be a prelude to an invasion of Israel (see Case #253 above). The invasion never took place.

On 13 September 1973 Israel and Syria fought an air battle in which 13 Syrian MIGs and one Israeli Mirage were shot down. When Syria did not react immediately to this dramatic defeat, Israel became suspicious that Damascus was planning a more basic action. Israeli forces in the north were strengthened, and precautionary measures were also taken in the south. Syria's massing of three infantry divisions, tanks, and artillery, and a mobilization of Syrian reserves in the north, along with the evacuation of Soviet military advisors and their families from Damascus and Cairo, were all noted by Israeli intelligence. The Israel Defense Forces *(IDF)* was put on the highest state of alert. Nevertheless, Israeli intelligence, as late as 3 October 1973, perceived the outbreak of war to be very unlikely. This erroneous judgment was based upon two Israeli misperceptions: that Egypt's inferior air power would not permit it to launch a war against Israel, and that Syria would not "go it alone," without Egyptian active participation.

Crisis

On 5 October 1973 a movement of Egyptian forces toward the Suez Canal and a change from a defensive to an offensive posture triggered a crisis for Israel. At the same time, Israel's intelligence service belatedly reported an impending Egyptian attack across the Canal scheduled for the following day. Israel immediately raised the *IDF* alert level and strengthened its forces along the northern and southern borders. The war began on 6 October with a simultaneous attack by Egyptian and Syrian forces. Egypt's successful crossing of the Suez Canal on the 7th and Syria's advance on the Golan Heights catalyzed an Israeli intra-war crisis (IWC): perceiving a grave danger, it adopted the "Samson Option," the use of Israeli nuclear weapons to stem the Egyptian/Syrian resort to counterattacks on the coastal plain. A few days later, on 14 October 1973, Israel's nuclear weapons were returned to storage. By 10 October, after heavy losses, Israeli forces succeeded in reversing the tide of battle in the north, triggering a crisis for Syria. Syria's response was multiple: it stepped up resistance, called upon Egypt to increase military pressure on Israel in the south, and appealed to the Soviet Union for aid. During the next three days Israeli forces advanced 10 kilometers beyond the 1967 cease-fire lines into Syrian territory.

On 12 October Israeli Prime Minister Meir agreed to a cease-fire in place. Its rejection by Egypt and Syria triggered a crisis for the United States, which feared a possible confrontation with the USSR. All seven Soviet airborne divisions had been placed on an increased state of readiness. The heavy Soviet commitment to the Arabs, in the form of resupplying arms by air and sea, indicated to Washington that Moscow would not tolerate a humiliating Arab defeat comparable to that in 1967.

The successful Egyptian operation to cross the Suez Canal was followed on 14 October by a large-scale tank battle in which Egypt suffered a severe defeat. On the 16th the Israelis crossed the Canal, threatening to surround the Egyptian Third Army. A crisis for Egypt was triggered on the 18th when Sadat became aware of the worsening position. Egypt's response was to pressure the Soviet Union to obtain a cease-fire agreement, which was accepted by Israel and Egypt on 22 October. When the Egyptians continued their attempt to destroy Israeli tank concentrations in order to open up an escape route for the Third Army, fighting broke out once more, with Israel strengthening its positions on the Egyptian side of the Canal.

Israeli violations of the 22 October cease-fire agreement triggered a crisis for the Soviet Union. Moscow responded on the 24th with a movement of naval vessels and a Note from President Brezhnev to President Nixon containing a clear warning that, unless the Israeli onslaught on the west bank of the Suez Canal was stopped at once, the USSR might intervene unilaterally. The U.S.

responded with mounting pressure on Israel to stop fighting and to allow nonmilitary supplies to reach the Third Army. At the same time, Nixon issued a sharp reply to Moscow: most of the U.S. armed forces, including the Strategic Air Command with its nuclear capability, were put on a high state of alert, namely "Defensive Condition 3."

The crisis escalated further when, on 25 October, a Soviet freighter arrived in Alexandria reportedly carrying nuclear weapons. Finally, on 26 October 1973, a U.S.-Soviet–sponsored Security Council resolution calling for a cease-fire was accepted by all the parties.

Talks between Egypt and Israel, with the active participation of U.S. Secretary of State Kissinger, continued for two months and concentrated on withdrawal to the post–Six Day War lines, the problem of the encircled Third Army, and the exchange of prisoners. A one-day symbolic Geneva Conference was convened on 21 December. Israel agreed to withdraw to 20 kilometers from the Canal and the size of both forces was reduced. A Disengagement Agreement was signed on 18 January 1974, ending the crisis for Egypt.

The negotiations between Israel and Syria took much longer. Kissinger mediated once more. Israel's demand for a complete list of all Israeli prisoners of war was negotiated by Kissinger in February 1974. In March Syria announced that it had decided to resume the war immediately. Shelling of Israeli-held positions in the north and firing back and forth continued throughout the spring of 1974. On 2 May the U.S. secretary of state began a month of shuttle diplomacy, traveling between Damascus and Jerusalem, with side trips to Riyad, Amman, and Cairo.

In the final agreement Israel returned parts of the Syrian town of Quneitra but kept control over two of the three strategic hills in the area where heavy weapons were forbidden. A UN buffer zone was established. The Israeli demand that Syria commit itself to a cessation of all terrorist activities was refused. As in the case of the Israel-Egypt Agreement, a U.S. Memorandum of Understanding was given to Israel. The Agreement was announced on 29 May and was signed on 31 May 1974, terminating the crisis for Israel, Syria, the Soviet Union, and the United States.

The superpowers, as crisis actors, were involved at a high level. Each supplied massive arms and equipment, as well as political support, to its client state. The cease-fire agreements were worked out between their representatives. Premier Kosygin arrived in Cairo on 16 October to persuade Egypt to accept a cease-fire. Kissinger visited Moscow on 19–20 October and hammered out a draft resolution for the Security Council, calling for an immediate cease-fire. The Council adopted this resolution within hours and authorized the creation of a UN force to police the Golan Heights.

(See *Master Table,* pp. 712–13.)

Sources

Adan 1980; Aruri 1975; Bandmann and Cordova 1980; Bar-Siman-Tov 1987; Bartov 1981; Black and Morris 1991; Blechman and Hart 1982; Brecher 1974b;

Brecher with Geist 1980; Cordesman and Wagner 1990, vol. I; Dawisha 1980–81; Dayan 1976; Dobrynin 1995; Dowty 1984; Eban 1977, 1992; Freedman 1975; Garthoff 1985; Golan 1977, 1984; Golan 1976; Heikal 1975, 1978; Herzog 1975; Isaacson 1992; Kalb and Kalb 1974; Kissinger 1982; Lebow and Stein 1994; Insight Team of the *Sunday Times* 1974; Meir 1975; *MEJ* Chronology 1973, 1974; Monroe and Farrar-Hockley 1974–75; Nixon 1978; Porter 1984; Primakov 1973; Pry 1984; Quandt 1977, 1993; Rubinstein 1977; Sadat 1978; Sagan 1979; Schiff 1975; Shazli 1980; Shimoni 1987; Spiegel 1985.

(270) Entebbe Raid

Jewish hostages were held in Entebbe in a *PLO*-generated crisis for Israel and Uganda from 27 June to 4 July 1976.

Background

Guerrilla war against Israel by the Palestine Liberation Organization *(PLO)* took several forms, including the hijacking of planes from Israel's national carrier, El Al, or other airlines carrying Israeli passengers. After strict security controls were instituted, these acts diminished in number. However, the security conditions at some airports remained less stringent. One of these was Athens.

Crisis

On 27 June 1976 an Air France plane en route from Tel Aviv to Paris was hijacked shortly after a stopover in Athens by an armed group belonging to the Popular Front for the Liberation of Palestine *(PFLP)*, including persons from Germany's Bader-Meinhof terrorist organization. This triggered a crisis for Israel. The pilot was forced to fly to Libya where the plane spent nine hours. Later it reached Entebbe in Uganda. The passengers were taken to the airport's former terminal building and divided into two groups—Israelis and Jews, and members of other nationalities. The latter were released shortly thereafter. The French crew remained with the former.

When it became apparent that Uganda's President, Idi Amin, had no intention of pressing for the release of the Jewish and Israeli passengers, Israel began to consider a military operation for their rescue. A decision to that effect was made on 1 July. On the 3rd three Hercules transport planes carrying Israeli commando troops landed in Entebbe, fought Ugandan soldiers in a one-hour battle, and succeeded in rescuing the hostages still being held at the airport. The arrival of Israeli troops and the military hostilities triggered a very short crisis for Uganda. The crisis ended on the 4th when the rescue team, together with the hostages, landed safely in Israel after a stop for fuel at Nairobi Airport. After the rescue, Amin blamed Kenya for aiding Israel and instituted several economic measures against its neighbor. In Arab League discussions Israel was condemned for the raid on Uganda, but no resolution was passed.

The UN, the U.S., and the USSR were not involved in this crisis. (See *Master Table,* pp. 714–15.)

Sources
ACR 1976; *AR* 1976; *ARB* 1976; Ajomo 1977; Ben-Porat and Schiff 1977; Dan 1976; Grahame 1980; Green 1976; Maoz 1981; Ofer 1976; Rabin 1979; Stevenson 1976; Ya'akobi 1980.

(275) Syria Mobilization

A Syrian army advance toward southern Lebanon precipitated a crisis for Israel from 21 November to 13 December 1976.

Background and Pre-crisis
In an attempt to avoid the partition of Lebanon during the latter's civil war, Syrian troops entered Lebanon in January 1976 (see Case #265—**Lebanon Civil War I, in Middle East: Non-PCs**). By September Syria had defeated Palestinian and Lebanese Muslim leftists and remained in control of large areas of the country. In the middle of October a summit meeting of the heads of state of Arab countries took place in Riyadh, Saʿudi Arabia. On 18 October a comprehensive peace plan for Lebanon was signed, setting up an Arab Deterrent Force, consisting almost entirely of Syrian troops. By 20 November Syria controlled all the key points in Lebanon with the exception of the area south of the Litani River bordering Israel. A tacit agreement was reached with Israel marking the Litani as the "Red Line," whereby both countries avoided confrontation.

Crisis
On 21 November, as Syrian forces pushed toward south Lebanon, Israel perceived a crisis, recognizing that Syria might break the tacit Red Line agreement, thereby undermining Israel's influence in Lebanon. Israel responded the following day by concentrating infantry and tanks along its northern border with Lebanon. In Jerusalem Prime Minister Rabin met with U.S. Ambassador Lewis to discuss the situation on 23 November, while in Washington talks were held between Ambassador Dinitz and U.S. Secretary of State Kissinger. The Syrians halted at the Litani River. By 13 December the situation stabilized and the tacit agreement between the two countries was restored, a process to which the U.S. contributed greatly. The USSR and the UN were not involved in this crisis.

(See *Master Table,* pp. 716–17.)

Sources
MECS 1976–77; *MEJ* Chronology 1976.

(289) Litani Operation

An Israeli retaliatory invasion caused a crisis for Lebanon from 14 March to 13 June 1978.

Background and Pre-crisis

PLO bases in Lebanon, supplied with Soviet weapons, had long been in operation as training camps for Palestinian guerrillas making frequent, mostly unsuccessful, incursions into Israeli territory. On 11 March 1978 11 Palestinians entered Israel by sea and attacked vehicles on the main highway 11 kilometers north of Tel Aviv. Thirty-five Israelis were killed and another 70 wounded before Israeli police, in a fierce clash, killed or captured all of the terrorists.

Crisis

Israeli troops, supported by the air force, crossed into southern Lebanon in a major attack against *PLO* bases, triggering a crisis for Lebanon on 14 March 1978. On the 17th Lebanon requested the Security Council to discuss the Israeli invasion. The Council met on the 19th and called for Israel's immediate withdrawal, along with the placement of a UN peacekeeping force in the area occupied by Israel. Lebanon's foreign minister met with ambassadors in Beirut to explain Lebanon's position. The hostilities ended at the end of March, but Israeli forces remained in Lebanon until 13 June 1978 when the last stage of the withdrawal was carried out. This terminated the crisis for Lebanon.

The Soviet Union and the United States were involved politically. Vice President Mondale acknowledged Israel's right to defend its borders against terrorist incursions but called for an Israeli withdrawal. The United States supported the Security Council resolution. The Soviet Union condemned the Israeli invasion and abstained in the Council vote. The United Nations Interim Force in Lebanon *(UNIFIL)*, established in 1978, remained in southern Lebanon through the Lebanon War of 1982 and for years thereafter.

(See *Master Table,* pp. 718–19.)

Sources

MECS (1977–78); *MEJ* Chronology 1978.

(324) Iraq Nuclear Reactor

Israel and Iraq experienced a crisis from January until 19 June 1981 over the development and, later, the destruction of the Osirak nuclear reactor.

Background

Iraq had long been Israel's most implacable enemy. It was the only Arab participant in the 1948–49 war that did not sign an armistice agreement with Israel (see

Case #120 above). Moreover, for decades it was in the vanguard of the Arab coalition against Israel, in word and deed.

Since the overthrow of its Hashemite monarchy in 1958 (see Case #165— **Lebanon-Iraq Upheaval, in Middle East: Non-PCs**), and especially after the Ba'ath Party came to power in 1963, Iraq sought to forge a nuclear capability. A pro-Soviet policy led to the construction of a small nuclear research reactor in 1968. In 1975 President Saddam Hussein secured a French commitment to build a larger reactor for "research." Israel's diplomatic efforts from 1976 to 1979 to persuade France to desist from this commitment proved to be in vain. A bomb exploded at Marseilles's harbor on 6 April 1979, with serious damage to a reactor that France had built and that was being dispatched to Iraq.

Pre-crisis
On 28 October 1980 Israel's cabinet made a decision in principle to attack the Osirak nuclear reactor near Baghdad. No date was specified; but a tentative date was set—soon after Israel's anticipated elections in November 1981. The rationale was expressed on several occasions by Prime Minister Begin: a nuclear weapon in the hands of any Arab state posed a threat to Israel's existence. A nuclear Iraq under Saddam Hussein was perceived as especially dangerous.

Crisis
A crisis for Israel was triggered by a French announcement in January 1981 that the Osirak reactor would be fully operational by 14 July. Israel Air Force *(IAF)* plans for a preemptive strike were approved by the cabinet on 15 March, to be implemented before the November election lest Begin be replaced by a Shimon Peres-led Labor government which, it was assumed, would be unwilling to implement this decision. On 3 May the Begin cabinet decided to act by the 10th.

The *IAF* attack occurred on 7 June, destroying the Osirak nuclear reactor and, for some years, Iraq's embryonic nuclear capability. The *IAF* raid ended Israel's crisis. Simultaneously, it catalyzed a brief crisis for Iraq—until 19 June, laying bare its vulnerability to Israeli retaliation and Iraq's relative military weakness.

(The initial world reaction was widespread condemnation of Israel—by the U.S., the USSR, France, the UN, and others the next day. Several days later the U.S. expressed its displeasure by suspending the delivery of F-16 planes to Israel, while approving a large-scale arms transfer, including Advanced Warning Airborne Command System (AWACS) aircraft, to Sa'udi Arabia. On 17 July the U.S. suspension was lifted. However, it was only in the context of the Gulf crisis and war a decade later that the major Western powers changed their public stance on Israel's 1981 destruction of Iraq's nuclear reactor.).

(See *Master Table*, pp. 724–25.)

Sources
Bishara 1982; Dupuy and Martell 1985; Haig 1984; *Keesing's* 1981; *MECS* 1980–81; *MEJ* Chronology 1981; Nakdimon 1993; Perlmutter et al. 1982; Weissman and Krosney 1981.

(327) Al-Biqa Missiles I

Syria and Israel, inveterate foes for almost half a century, were enmeshed in one of two missile crises over Lebanon in the 1980s from 28 April to 24 July 1981 (see also Case #357 below).

Background
Lebanon was, formally, a member of the Arab coalition against Israel since the beginning of the Arab/Israel conflict in 1947–48. However, it participated only in the first war of the protracted conflict (see Case #120 above). During most of the next two decades the Israel/Lebanon border was quiet, apart from several *PLO* raids from southern Lebanon since the mid-1960s, which became more frequent after its expulsion from Jordan in 1970 (see Case #238—**Black September,** in **Middle East: Non-PCs**). One of Israel's most dramatic responses was the destruction of 13 planes at Beirut Airport in December 1968 (see Case #229 above). In May 1970 and February 1972, Israeli armor and planes attempted, with little success, to destroy *PLO* and, later, Hizbullah bases in southern Lebanon in retaliation for cross-border raids against Israeli settlements in northern Israel. It was a pattern that continued into the mid-1990s (see Case #409 below).

The outbreak of civil war in Lebanon in April 1975 made a complex situation more unstable. Syria, which had long assumed a hegemonial role in Lebanon, intervened, occupied the Biqa (Bekaa) Valley in eastern Lebanon, and established its primacy in the entire country in 1976 by skillful "divide and rule" tactics, shifting its alignment with the Christian and Muslim-Druze-*PLO* contending factions in what developed into a 16-year civil war (1975–91). A ceasefire in October 1976 led to the creation of a 30,000-man Arab Deterrent Force *(ADF)* by the Arab League: Syria was the preeminent contributor from the outset; and from 1979 the *ADF* was a purely Syrian force. At the same time the U.S. brokered a "Red Line" agreement between Israel and Syria in 1976 that specified legitimate acts and constraints on their behavior in Lebanon (see Case #275 above). The 1981 missile crisis centered on alleged violation of the Red Line agreement.

Pre-crisis
In the spring of 1981 the Lebanese Forces, the largest Christian militia, were ensconced in the strategic town of Zahle astride the Beirut-Damascus highway. Aware of impending general elections in Israel, which Begin's Likud-led coali-

tion seemed likely to lose, the Christian *Falange* leaders tried to draw Israel into Lebanon's civil war—and succeeded.

Crisis

On 28 April 1981 Israeli planes shot down two Syrian helicopters carrying supplies to Syrian troops on Mount Sanin overlooking Zahle. Syria responded the next day by deploying SAM-3 ground-to-air missiles in Lebanon and attacking the Christian militia in Zahle. As threatened by Israel's prime minister, Israeli planes destroyed the Syrian missile bases on 28 May.

Both Israel and Syria accused each other of violating the 1976 Red Line agreement: by the use of Syrian air power against any party to the civil war and the introduction of missiles into Lebanon; and by Israel's intervention in the civil war with air power far north of the Israel/Lebanon border.

On 5 May the U.S. dispatched Philip Habib as a special envoy to mediate between the parties and to end the crisis. Moreover, in response to continuing Israeli bombing raids against Syrian positions and the *PLO* headquarters in Beirut, on 10 and 17 July, the U.S. froze the delivery of F-16 planes to Israel on 18 July; they were released on 11 August, after the cease-fire.

Crisis abatement was the result of mediation and pressure on both sides— the U.S. vis-à-vis Israel, and Sa'udi Arabia vis-à-vis Syria and the *PLO*. A cease-fire was negotiated separately with the *PLO*—formally with the Lebanon government—and Israel. It took effect on 24 July, ending the crisis for both Syria and Israel, the two state crisis actors, and the Al-Biqa crisis as a whole.

The U.S., as noted, played the decisive role in crisis resolution. The USSR supported Syria verbally and politically; and it held joint landing maneuvers with Syrian forces as an indicator of its intent if the crisis threatened to overthrow the Syrian regime. The UN was not involved in this crisis.

(See *Master Table,* pp. 724–25.)

Sources

See sources for Case #337; and *Keesing's* 1981; *MECS* 1980–81, 1981–82; *MEJ* Chronology 1981.

(337) War in Lebanon

Lebanon, Syria, and Israel were the crisis actors in the Lebanon War from 5 June 1982 until 17 May 1983.

Background

From the beginning of the Arab/Israel protracted conflict in 1947–48 (see Case #120 above) until 1970, the border between Israel and Lebanon was relatively quiescent. However, as a result of the *PLO*'s severe defeat in a military confrontation with the regime of King Hussein in 1970 (see Case #238—**Black Sep-**

tember, in **Middle East: Non-PCs**), most of its forces were transferred from Jordan to bases in south Lebanon. From there they launched raids into northern Israel in a prolonged guerrilla campaign.

The *PLO* also became enmeshed in Lebanon's intercommunal strife, a near constant in the Christian-Muslim struggle for control of the government and army in Lebanon since 1943. Full-scale civil war erupted in April 1975.

On 14 March 1978, the Israel Defense Forces *(IDF)* invaded Lebanon in retaliation for a *PLO* raid in Israel's heartland, north of Tel Aviv, three days earlier, in which 35 Israelis were killed and 70 others wounded. Hostilities ended at the end of March, but *IDF* units did not withdraw until 13 June 1978 (see Case #289 above).

Pre-crisis

An Israeli decision in principle to attack *PLO* bases in Lebanon was made on 21 April 1982. On 9 May 100 Katyusha rockets were fired from south Lebanon into Israel's northern Galilee settlements. *IDF* troops were dispatched to the Lebanese border several days later. On 3 June Israel's Ambassador to the U.K., Shlomo Argov, was gravely wounded in a terrorist attack in London. Israeli planes bombed *PLO* sites in Beirut.

Crisis

At the instigation of Israel Defense Minister Sharon, *IDF* forces responded to the London incident by activating a long-standing "Peace for Galilee" operation: they invaded Lebanon on 5 June along three fronts, triggering a crisis for Lebanon. Jerusalem signaled Damascus via Washington that its forces would not cross into Syria unless Israel was attacked by Syrian forces. However, the rapid *IDF* advance in Lebanon brought Israeli forces into direct conflict with Syrian troops in the Biqa Valley of Lebanon on 7 June, catalyzing a crisis for Syria. This was accentuated on 8–9 June by an air battle that reportedly led to the shooting down of 60 Syrian planes. The direct confrontation with Syria led to a crisis for Israel.

Initial U.S. mediation, through special envoy Philip Habib, led to a cease-fire between Israel and Syria on 11 June. However, continued *IDF/PLO* clashes led to a renewal of Israel/Syria hostilities. By 24 June *IDF* forces succeeded in cutting the strategic Beirut-Damascus highway, the key to Syria's military control over Lebanon. And by early July *IDF* forces laid siege to Beirut.

Persistent mediation by U.S. Ambassador Habib led to a complex agreement that resolved the crisis for Israel and Syria—but not the Lebanon War—on 1 September 1982. By that date the withdrawal of Syrian forces from Beirut, which began on 21 August, was complete. *PLO* forces completed their withdrawal from Lebanon on 1 September to nine locations in the Arab world, temporarily ceasing to be a meaningful military force in the Arab/Israel conflict. And *IDF* forces pulled back from the outskirts of Lebanon's capital. The crisis for Lebanon ended with the (abortive) peace agreement with Israel on 17 May 1983.

The UN and the U.S. were very active in efforts to resolve the crisis and terminate the Lebanon War. As early as 6 June the Security Council adopted a resolution calling for an immediate cessation of hostilities and the withdrawal of Israeli forces to the recognized Israel-Lebanon border. A Security Council resolution on 20 June calling on both *PLO* and *IDF* forces to withdraw from the Beirut area was vetoed by the U.S. Altogether, nine UN resolutions were passed during the Lebanon War, including those on 1 and 12 August by the Security Council and 19 August by the General Assembly, most of them condemning Israel; but not one was heeded.

The U.S. role was far more consequential. On 8 July, along with France and Italy, it announced a willingness to send troops to Lebanon in order to reestablish stability. On 19 July Washington temporarily suspended military aid to Israel because of its invasion of Lebanon. On 5 August it called upon Israel to withdraw to the prewar cease-fire lines. As noted, the U.S. mediated an initial Israel/Syria cease-fire, and the agreement of 1 September 1982, which ended the Lebanon War, though not all hostilities. Washington, through Secretary of State Shultz, also brokered the abortive Israel/Lebanon agreement of 17 May 1983.

The USSR adopted a low profile vis-à-vis the Lebanon War, compared with its role in the 1956, 1967, and 1973 Arab/Israel wars (see Cases #152, 222, 255 above). It condemned Israel several times. Two messages were sent to *PLO* Chairman Arafat expressing verbal support for his cause. And, most substantively, it sent military aid to Syria to replace losses during the fighting. The Arab League did not meet until after the end of the Lebanon War. At a summit conference in Fez, Morocco, on 6–9 September, it proposed a peace plan for the Arab/Israel conflict, which was rejected by Israel.

(Direct talks between the governments of Israel and Lebanon under U.S. auspices, beginning in late December 1982, led to the initialing of a peace agreement on 17 May 1983. It included the creation of an Israeli "security zone" in south Lebanon designed to protect Israeli settlements in northern Galilee against *PLO* or other trans-border attacks. Syria, the most influential external power in the internal affairs of Lebanon, opposed the agreement as a grave danger to its security; and the Israel/Lebanon peace agreement was never ratified.)

(Low-intensity military hostilities in Lebanon and a massive *IDF* presence in Lebanon continued until 1985. *IDF* forces continued to control the "security zone" more than a decade later.)

(See *Master Table*, pp. 726–27.)

Sources

Black and Morris 1991; Cobban 1984; Cordesman and Wagner 1990, vol. I; Dupuy 1986; Dupuy and Martell 1985; Evron 1987; Feldman and Rechnitz-Kijner 1984; Haig 1984; Herzog 1982; Khalidi 1986; Khalidi 1979; Rabinovich 1985; Reagan 1990; Schiff 1983; Schiff and Yaari 1984; Shultz 1993; Sofer 1988; Tanter 1990; Vertzberger 1997; Yaniv 1987.

(357) Al-Biqa Missiles II

Syria and Israel were embroiled in the second crisis over the Biqa (see Case #327 above) from 19 November 1985 to 15 January 1986.

Background and Pre-crisis
The Israel Air Force *(IAF)* has been conducting regular reconnaissance flights over Lebanon since the mid-1970s. These were accepted by Syria, the dominant power in Lebanon, in the 1976 "Red Line" agreement, which governed Israeli/Syrian military relations vis-à-vis Lebanon until the outbreak of the Lebanon War in 1982 (see Case #337 above). Although incidents did occur— sometimes Israeli planes, at other times Syrian planes, withdrew to avoid a direct military confrontation—this U.S.-brokered agreement maintained relative stability in a volatile region. According to the commander of the *IAF* at the time, Syria attempted to interfere with Israel's reconnaissance flights over Lebanon on several occasions in November 1985.

Crisis
On 19 November 1985 two Syrian MIG aircraft were shot down by two Israeli planes over Lebanon; according to Israel, this occurred after Syrian fighters threatened Israeli planes on reconnaissance missions over Lebanon. This incident, very common in the Israeli/Syrian protracted conflict, triggered a crisis for Syria.

Tension rose on 24 November when Syria responded by deploying SAM-6 missiles in the Biqa (Bekaa) Valley and along the Beirut-Damascus road. However, those missiles were soon withdrawn following U.S. pressure.

Israel's crisis was triggered on 15 December, when Syria redeployed SAM-6 and SAM-8 missiles close to the Lebanon border. Israel reacted the same day by accusing Syria of also deploying long-range SAM-2 missiles in southwestern Syria, posing a threat to mutually agreed Israeli reconnaissance missions over Lebanon. The Syrian government claimed on 16 December that the redeployment was a defensive move. Israel, in turn, through Defense Minister Rabin, warned on 27 December that the *IDF* would respond to the threatening missiles "whatever the cost."

Tension between the two long-time adversaries declined in early January 1986 as a result of U.S. mediation: Syria agreed not to interfere with *IAF* reconnaissance missions; and Israel agreed not to attack Syrian missile sites as long as they did not threaten Israeli reconnaissance flights over Lebanon. On 15 January the *IAF* announced that Syria's long-range missiles had been withdrawn from Lebanon. That Syrian act ended the crisis for both states.

(See *Master Table,* pp. 728–29.)

Sources
Keesing's 1986; *MECS* 1985–86.

(409) Operation Accountability

Israel and Lebanon were embroiled in a crisis from 10 to 31 July 1993.

Background
Low-intensity violence has been the norm in Israel/Lebanon relations since the failed "Litani Operation" by the Israel Defense Forces *(IDF)* in March 1978. During its 1982 "Peace for Galilee" campaign, that is, the Lebanon War, Israel created a "security zone" in south Lebanon to protect its northern towns and settlements from frequent shelling by hostile forces, notably from several factions within the Palestine Liberation Organization *(PLO)* or the Iranian-backed *Hizbullah* ("Party of God"). These raids intensified during the *Intifada* (the Uprising) by Palestinians against Israel's continued occupation of the West Bank and Gaza Strip from December 1987 until the signing of the Israel/*PLO* Oslo Accord in August 1993. There were frequent raids and retaliations across the Israel/Lebanon border—by both sides. One of these escalated to a full-scale crisis in 1993.

Crisis
A crisis for Israel was triggered on 10 July by a Hizbullah attack in the security zone that killed five *IDF* soldiers and wounded many others. Israel's initial response was a public demand by Prime Minister Rabin the same day that Syria curb the activities of the Hizbullah, whose headquarters were located in the Biqa Valley of Lebanon, where Syria held sway. Simultaneously Israel deployed more troops and firepower to its border with Lebanon.

On 19 July, after another Hizbullah attack in which several Israeli soldiers were wounded, the *IDF* was authorized to take whatever steps were necessary to protect the northern border. Rabin, who also held the Defense portfolio, issued another warning to both Syria and the Hizbullah. Another Israeli soldier was killed on the 23rd. Two days later came Israel's major response, the launching of "Operation Accountability." Heavy air raids and intense artillery attacks on south Lebanon villages, as well as Hizbullah bases all over Lebanon, triggered a crisis for Lebanon.

The aim of Israel's massive retaliation was to catalyze a flight of large numbers of people in south Lebanon to Beirut in an attempt to compel the government of Lebanon to stop Hizbullah's attacks on Israeli soldiers in the security zone and Israeli civilians in towns and villages near the northern border. Operation Accountability was dramatically successful at one level—half a million Lebanese refugees fled north to the capital. But even this was at a high cost in terms of external images of Israel: their flight was vividly portrayed by TV cameras for tens of millions of viewers around the world. As for the aim of curbing the Hizbullah via pressure from Lebanon, this was politically unrealistic: since the beginning of its civil war in 1975, and even after that war ended in 1991, Lebanon was incapable of protecting its territory or people from any invader, Israel or Syria, *PLO* or Hizbullah; it had become a client state, totally dependent on Syria.

UN Secretary-General Boutros-Ghali publicly condemned Israel on 28 July for creating a massive refugee problem. The government of Lebanon complained to the UN Security Council on the 30th, its major response to the crisis. The Council passed a resolution critical of Israel and called for its withdrawal from all Lebanese territory. On the 31st a cease-fire between the *IDF* and Hizbullah was arranged through U.S. mediation: the *IDF* agreed to desist from military operations north of the security zone, that is, against villages in south Lebanon; and Hizbullah pledged to stop firing missiles into northern Israel. Thus ended the crisis over Operation Accountability. However, tension and low-intensity violence continued intermittently in the Israel/Lebanon border area.

The U.S. criticized the scope of Operation Accountability and its humanitarian costs; it also mediated a cease-fire. Russia remained aloof.

(There was an exact replay of Operation Accountability in April 1996. Hizbullah fired Katyusha rockets into towns and villages of northern Israel, triggering a crisis for Israel. The *IDF*'s massive response, "Operation Grapes of Wrath," catalyzed a large-scale migration from south to north Lebanon, triggering a crisis for Lebanon. Once more, the U.S. brokered an agreement, restoring the "rules of the game," namely, no military acts against civilians in the border area.)

(See *Master Table,* pp. 736–37.)

Sources
Jerusalem Post 1993, 1996; *Keesing's* 1993, 1996; *New York Times* 1993, 1996.

Iran/Iraq

There were seven international crises in the **Iran/Iraq** protracted conflict from 1959 to 1988, five of them during their "long war," 1980–88, as follows.

Case #172 **Shatt-al-Arab I,** in 1959–60;
      #234 **Shatt-al-Arab II,** in 1969;
      #317 **Onset of Iran/Iraq War,** in 1980;
      #335 **Khorramshahr,** in 1982;
      #348 **Basra-Kharg Island,** in 1984;
      #361 **Capture of al-Faw,** in 1986;
      #385 **Iraq Recapture of al-Faw,** in 1988.

Among related crises, the most notable were those between Iraq and Kuwait, including the **Gulf** crisis-war of 1990–91 and the **Iraq Troop Deployment—Kuwait** crisis in 1994, in **Iraq/Kuwait PC** (see Cases #393 and 412). (See *Master Table.*)

General Background

The long war between the two major regional powers in the Gulf can be traced to multiple sources of conflict. One was the rivalry between Mesopotamia and Persia in antiquity. This was accentuated by intrareligious tension since the seventh century between Shi'ite Islam in Persia (Iran) and the orthodox Sunni strand of Islam in Mesopotamia (Iraq). It was further exacerbated by oppression of the latter's large Shi'ite minority.

There were, too, tangible disputes, notably over control of the Shatt-al-Arab waterway in the Gulf and of key strategic points along their lengthy land border, as well as over their respective parts of Kurdistan. Their rivalry extended to a continuing struggle for regional influence in the oil-rich Gulf area.

The rise to power of Ayatullah Khomeini in Iran in 1979 was perceived as a long-term threat by the secular Ba'ath-dominated Iraqi regime because of its unconcealed messianic character. At the same time the internal disarray within Iran, accompanying the transition from Pahlavi authoritarianism to Shi'ite fundamentalism, seemed to provide a unique opportunity to achieve President Saddam Hussein's goal of Iraqi hegemony in the Gulf and primacy within the Arab world. What was unfolding for Khomeini, by contrast, was an ideological and religious struggle for domination of the Islamic world. In short, there were multiple and deep roots of conflict between Iran and Iraq.

As for the Shatt-al-Arab, an international agreement in 1937 determined, in accord with previous Ottoman Turkey/Iran agreements, that the Shatt was wholly Iraqi territory except for a length of three miles opposite Abadan, where the frontier was to run along the *thalweg* (the line of greatest depth) of the river. According to the treaty, Iraq would collect transit dues from passing ships and would be responsible for the upkeep of the waterway. After the overthrow of the Hashemite kingdom in Iraq, in July 1958, the shah of Iran began, once more, to express his dissatisfaction with the 1937 agreement.

(172) Shatt-al-Arab I

A crisis for Iraq and Iran over their joint waterway lasted from 28 November 1959 to 4 January 1960.

Crisis
The trigger for Iraq was a press conference on 28 November 1959 where the Shah described the status quo concerning the Shatt-al-Arab as "intolerable." Prime Minister Qassem's response, the trigger for Iran, was a reiteration of Iraq's claim to the waterway on 2 December. Border clashes were reported on 10 and 15 December. Iran's frontier guards were reinforced on the 15th. Iraq sent a protest two days later. On the 22nd Iraq claimed that numerous Iranian border violations had occurred, including an 11-kilometer penetration of its territory. On

23 December Iran placed its military forces on full alert; previously Iran had been moving troops to the Iraqi border. By the last week in December both actors had expressed a willingness to negotiate their differences. The termination date for both was 4 January 1960 when an Iranian ship was allowed to pass through the Shatt unmolested.

The U.S. and U.K. mediated by proposing talks between the adversaries; and the USSR broadcast propaganda against Iran. The UN was not involved in this crisis.

(See *Master Table*, pp. 696–97.)

Sources
Chubin and Zabih 1974; Dann 1969; *MEJ* Chronology 1960.

(234) Shatt-al-Arab II

The second crisis for Iran and Iraq over the Shatt-al-Arab lasted from 15 April to 30 October 1969.

Crisis
Iran's crisis was triggered on 15 April 1969 when its ambassador to Baghdad was informed by Iraq's deputy foreign minister that Iraq regarded the Shatt-al-Arab as part of its territory and requested ships flying Iran's flag to lower their flag when entering the estuary. Furthermore, no Iranian nationals were to be aboard. If the demands were not met, Iraq would use force and would not allow vessels destined for Iranian ports to use the river. Iran responded on 19 April by declaring the 1937 treaty null and void and demanded its renegotiation. Iran's deputy foreign minister warned that any violation of Iran's sovereign rights would be met with full retaliation. The nullification of the 1937 treaty was the crisis trigger for Iraq. On 20 April Iraq responded by reiterating the validity of the treaty and reserved the right to take legal and legitimate action. Iran then concentrated its forces around Khorramshahr and Abadan and put its navy on full alert, while Iraqi forces were placed on alert at the port of Basra.

On 22 April, as a show of force, Iran sent a freighter through the Shatt, escorted by naval craft and protected by an umbrella of jet fighters. It was the first Iranian vessel to pass through the Shatt flying Iran's flag since the outbreak of the crisis. An Iraqi naval launch allowed the vessel to go through. This act constituted the Iraqi response to the crisis. Another escorted Iranian vessel passed through the Shatt unmolested on the 25th.

On 28 April Iraq circulated a document to UN delegates complaining of Iran's actions in the Shatt-al-Arab. This charge was answered on 5 May by Iran, which appealed to the UN Secretary-General to send a representative to Iran in order to witness the influx of Iranians expelled from Iraq who had been subjected to inhumane treatment by Iraqi authorities. Notes were also sent to the Security Council. During October the addresses to the General Assembly by the foreign ministers of both states contained accusations against one another in the Shatt-al-Arab crisis. The *CENTO* Ministerial Council conferred in Teheran on 26 and 27 May and issued a signed communiqué by Iran, Pakistan, Turkey, the U.K., and the U.S., disclosing discussion of the dispute.

The crisis ended on 30 October 1969 when the information ministers of Iran and Iraq decided to terminate the propaganda campaign against each other, with the hope that this would prepare the atmosphere for a peaceful settlement between the two countries. Several Middle East states attempted to mediate: Jordan, Kuwait, Saʿudi Arabia, and Turkey. Whereas Iraq was ready to accept mediation, Iran was not. A full-scale war between Iran and Iraq, catalyzed by the Shatt-al-Arab dispute, was to break out in September 1980 (See Case #317 below).

Neither the U.S. nor the USSR was involved in this crisis.

(See *Master Table*, pp. 708–9.)

Sources
Chubin and Zabih 1974; *MEJ* Chronology 1969; *MER* 1969–70; Ramazani 1972; Shimoni 1987.

(317) Onset of Iran/Iraq War

Iran and Iraq experienced several crises during Gulf War I, 1980–88. The first lasted from 17 September until 30 November 1980.

Pre-crisis
The specific focus of conflict, which erupted into full-scale war in mid-September 1980, was the Shatt-al-Arab. Despite the 1937 agreement there were interstate crises between Iran and Iraq in 1959–60 and 1969 (see Cases #172, 234 above). Another agreement between them was reached in Algiers on 6 March 1975; and a more formal "reconciliation" treaty was signed in Baghdad on 13 June 1975 recognizing the Shatt-al-Arab as the common border between Iran and Iraq.

(Mis)calculating that the turmoil in Iran following the ouster of the shah offered a unique opportunity to assert Iraqi primacy over the Shatt-al-Arab, Saddam Hussein expressed dissatisfaction with the 1975 accord on several occasions in 1979. Relations between the two states became increasingly tense, exacerbated by growing unrest among the predominantly Arab population in Iran's southwestern province of Khuzestan. There were also increasingly shrill mutual accusations of hostility and responsibility for cross-border land and air clashes.

In March 1980 Iraq began to launch commando raids into Iranian territory. On 7 April Iran placed its armed forces on full alert and responded with an anti-Iraqi propaganda campaign. On the 16th Iran announced the formation of a "Revolutionary Islamic Army for the Liberation of Iraq" and called upon the people of Iraq to revolt against the Baʾath regime. The same day Saddam Hussein warned that war could not be excluded from the escalating conflict and demanded

Iran's recognition of the Arab character of Khuzestan. And on 10 September he linked the clashes to Iraq's territorial claims.

Crisis

On 17 September 1980 President Saddam Hussein announced in Iraq's National Assembly the formal abrogation of the 1975 treaty; and he proclaimed full Iraqi sovereignty over the Shatt-al-Arab waterway. This triggered Iran's first crisis of Gulf War I. Four days later Iraqi forces launched a major offensive, occupying much of the border area including parts of Khorramshahr. They also almost completely encircled Iran's principal oil refinery at Abadan. And on the 22nd Iraqi planes attacked six Iranian air bases and four army bases.

Iran responded on the 23rd with powerful counterattacks on air bases in the heart of Iraq, at Baghdad, Basra, Mosul, Habaniya, Kut, and Nasiriya, triggering a crisis for Iraq. The same day Iraq occupied about 120 square kilometers of Iranian territory, after encountering only minor resistance. Its main offensive was in the direction of Khuzestan and Iran's key oil facilities. By 28 September Iraq was poised to seize all of southwestern Iran. The battle raged on, with the adversaries striking oil and other economic targets, bombing towns, sinking naval vessels, etc. On 5 October both Abadan and Khorramshahr were reported to be ablaze, and the Iraqi city of al-Faw to be deserted. The same day Iraq's governing body, the Revolutionary Command Council *(RCC)*, withdrew a conditional cease-fire offer of 24 September and vowed to "continue the just and honorable battle whatever its duration and the sacrifices required."

On 17 November 1980 Teheran Radio claimed that Iranian troops had driven Iraqi forces from Susangerd. On the 19th, noting the absence of any further advances by Iraqi troops, Iran's President Bani-Sadr called for "total victory" over Iraq's Saddam Hussein: this marked the end of Iran's crisis. By 30 November, according to a consensus of foreign journalists reporting from the battlefront, Iraqi forces had dug in and a stalemate followed, terminating the onset crisis—and the first phase—of the Iran/Iraq War.

The U.S. posture, proclaimed by President Jimmy Carter on 22 September 1980, was "strict neutrality." However, because of the grave danger of curtailed oil supplies to U.S. allies in Europe and Japan, by mid-October some 60 warships of the U.S., the U.K., France, and Australia were patrolling the Strait of Hormuz, the vital passageway that links the Gulf and the Indian Ocean. The USSR, too, from the beginning, proclaimed a policy of strict noninterference, while accusing the U.S. of attempting to exploit the conflict for Cold War ends. In reality, the Soviet Union and its East European clients provided limited arms supplies to both Iran and Iraq. The former also received weapons from Syria, Libya, and Israel, while France and North Korea sent arms to Iraq.

There were several failed efforts to mediate the Iran/Iraq conflict in the onset phase as, in fact, throughout the eight-year war. The UN Security Council unanimously called for a cease-fire, to take effect on 25 September. On 5 Novem-

ber the UN Secretary-General was asked by the Security Council to send a special representative to the area of conflict. Similarly, the Islamic Conference Organization *(ICO)* sent a Good Offices mission headed by the president of Pakistan. And the Non-Aligned Movement sent a mediation committee on 21 October. All third party efforts at crisis management were to no avail.
(See *Master Table*, pp. 722–23.)

Sources
Abdulghani 1984; Chubin and Tripp 1988; Cordesman and Wagner 1990, vol. II; Day 1987; Gordon 1981; Grummon 1982; Ismael 1982; Joyner 1990; Karsh 1987, 1989; *Keesing's* 1980; Khadduri 1988; al-Khalil 1989; King 1987; *MECS* 1980–81; *MEJ* Chronology 1980; *New York Times* 1980; O'Ballance 1988; Pipes 1982; Ramazani 1986; Safran 1988; Segal 1988; Tahir-Kheli and Ayubi 1983.

(335) Khorramshahr

In the second phase of their long war (1980–88) Iraq experienced an intra-war crisis (IWC) with Iran from 22 March to 30 July 1982.

Pre-crisis
The front line created by Iraq's initial advance into Iranian territory in September 1980 (see Case #317 above) had been pushed back by Iran up to 25 miles by September 1981. That month Iran's forces lifted the siege of Abadan, site of its principal oil refinery, and launched a new offensive capturing the town of Busta-neh in November 1981. By early 1982, although the war seemed to have reached a stalemate, the military initiative had passed to Iran, which repulsed several Iraqi counterattacks in February.

Iran launched another major offensive against Iraq in mid-March. This succession of Iranian military successes led to an increase of tension among the Arab Gulf states, which had supported Iraq both verbally and financially, mainly because they feared that Iran, if victorious, would be in a position to "export" its revolution to nearby neighbors.

Early efforts by regional organizations and the UN to mediate an end to the conflict were unsuccessful. The war became a protracted armed conflict, with the primary objective of both parties changing from the capture of new territory to the overthrow of the enemy's political regime.

Crisis
Iraq's IWC began on 22 March 1982, when Iran launched an offensive against Iraqi forces in the border region west of Dezful. During the next six days Iran scored its greatest victory in the war so far: Iraq was forced to withdraw from 350 square kilometers of Iran's territory.

Iraq's major response was to fortify the Iranian city of Khorramshahr, occupied in the first phase of the war, to ensure that it would not be outflanked from the west: the city became a strategic objective with high political symbolic value.

On 30 April Iran launched "Operation Jerusalem" to expel Iraqi forces from their last major stronghold in Iran—areas of southern Khuzestan and Khorramshahr. The city was recaptured on 23–24 May 1982.

In the face of defeat, Iraq initiated a unilateral cease-fire on 9 June and a unilateral withdrawal from 5,500 square kilometers of Iranian-occupied territory the next day. However, the intra-war crisis had not yet run its course. Iran was adamant about its conditions for peace, notably the overthrow of Saddam Hussein and the Ba'ath regime in Iraq.

Iran's military advance once more generated fear in the Arab Gulf states and Sa'udi Arabia, along with concern in the U.S. and the U.K. about a possible Iranian invasion of Iraq. That concern materialized with Iran's "Operation Ramadan" on 13 July, designed to cut the main roads linking Basra to the north and thereby to isolate Iraq's major southern port. By the 30th, however, Iran's attempts to achieve a strategic breakthrough in southern Iraq lost momentum ending the IWC over Khorramshahr.

Many states and international organizations were involved actors in the second (Khorramshahr) phase of the Iran/Iraq War (Gulf War I). The USSR, for many years Iraq's patron and principal arms supplier, continued to deliver advanced weapons including aircraft—as much as Iraq could pay for in hard currency. So too did France. The U.S. sold Iraq a small number of civilian transport planes, easily converted into military aircraft. Sudan sent a small number of volunteers to fight alongside the Iraqis. Algeria tried to mediate the conflict.

On 28 May 1982 the UN Secretary-General renewed his call for an end to the war, along with an offer to mediate. The Security Council adopted another— of many—cease-fire resolutions. And the UN General Assembly adopted a resolution on 22 October calling for a cease-fire and a peaceful resolution of the conflict. So too did the Islamic Conference Organization *(ICO)*. In July 1982 the Arab League condemned Iran's invasion of Iraq.

The Swedish political leader, Olaf Palme, served as a UN envoy in March 1982. The Gulf Cooperation Council *(GCC)* attempted mediation in June but strongly favored Iraq with large-scale financial support. Quiet diplomacy was attempted by the Soviets and by Egypt. All efforts at third party intervention, in this phase as throughout the Iran/Iraq War, came to naught.

(The long war continued unabated. In late September 1982 Iranian forces attacked Iraqi positions near Abadan. And on 1 November Iran launched another attack on Basra, aimed once more at cutting the road to Baghdad between Kut and the area northeast of Al-Aamorah and at the recapture of territory still held by Iraqi forces on the southern front. An Iranian attack to the north near Mandali occurred on 7 November with limited gains. By late November a stalemate was evident, with the opposing armies dug in for the winter.

From mid-August 1982 to January 1983 Iraq launched frequent air strikes, mainly against economic targets—Kharg Island and shipping in Iranian waters; but it, too, failed to achieve a strategic breakthrough or to recapture Iraqi territory lost to Iran in 1982. The long war had become a stalemate.

(See *Master Table*, pp. 724–25.)

Sources
See sources for Case #317; and *Keesing's* 1982; *MECS* 1981–82; *New York Times* 1982.

(348) Basra–Kharg Island

During the third phase of the Iran/Iraq War (1980–88) Iraq and Iran, along with Kuwait and Saʿudi Arabia, experienced a fresh crisis from 21 February to 11 July 1984.

Pre-crisis
The year 1983 witnessed several inconclusive attacks and counterattacks by the two protagonists in the war. The first was a major Iranian offensive in the area of Misan west of Dezful on 7 February *(Wal Fajr I)* but the initiative quickly petered out. Iraq counterattacked in late March but made no progress. A fresh Iranian offensive from 10–17 April, aimed at capturing the heights along the front north of Fuka, was indecisive. Iraq responded with air strikes on Iranian civilian targets in May and sought a cease-fire, without success. On 23 July Iran launched another offensive and advanced 15 kilometers within Iraq.

Iran's strategy of attrition was designed to exert pressure on the weakening Iraqi economy with the aim of toppling the Saddam Hussein regime. *Wal Fajr IV*, from 30 July to 10 August 1983, aimed at clearing the heights above Mehran. Iraq responded with more intense missile and air raids on Iranian towns and oil installations—and the use of mustard gas against Iranian troops. A major target was Iran's oil export installations on Kharg Island. Iran countered with attacks on shipping in the Gulf. However, none of these attacks in 1983 achieved the goal of a decisive defeat of the enemy's forces.

Crisis
In February 1984 Iran launched four separate attacks on Iraqi forces, one in the north on the 12th near Nowdeshah, the other three in the south. It was *Wal Fajr VI*, launched on 21 February near Dehloran and aimed at cutting the vital Basra-Baghdad road, that triggered an intra-war crisis for Iraq. However, as was often the case in the Iran/Iraq War, it turned into a battle of attrition: Iran's sole victory was the conquest of the oil drilling complex on Majnoon Island, the site of rich oil fields in southern Iraq.

Iraq responded with a major attack on Iranian oil installations on Kharg Island on 1 March 1984 triggering an IWC for Iran. The latter's "Operation

Badr" from 11 to 23 March, designed to capture Basra or cut it off from the rest of Iraq, reached the Basra-Baghdad road. Perceiving a threat of grave damage if Iranian forces succeeded, Iraq committed an elite Republican Guard division and its air force to the defense of Basra. By the 18th they recaptured all of Iraq's lost positions.

Kuwait became a crisis actor on 13 May 1984 when one of its tankers, transporting oil to the U.K., was damaged near Bahrain. Another Kuwaiti tanker was hit the following day. Kuwait accused Iran of the hostile acts. Iran responded that, if the passage to and from Kharg Island was not safe, no other routes in the Gulf would be secure. Sa'udi Arabia became a direct participant in the Basra–Kharg Island crisis as a result of the "tanker war": one of its ships was set ablaze on 16 May by Iranian aircraft firing within Sa'udi territorial waters north of the port of al-Jubay.

Kuwait's response to Iran's attacks was a request on 30 May for U.S. Stinger antiaircraft missiles, along with a U.S. naval escort for its tankers. Sa'udi Arabia responded militarily on 5 June: Sa'udi F-15s, assisted by U.S. advanced early-warning (*AWACS*) reconnaissance planes, shot down an Iranian F-4 fighter.

Crisis termination occurred on different dates for the four actors. As noted, Iraq's intra-war crisis ended on 18 March when it succeeded in thwarting Iran's attempt to capture Basra or to isolate that city from the rest of the country. Iran's IWC ended on 10 June when it agreed with Iraq to a moratorium on the shelling of civilian areas, brokered by the UN Secretary-General. On 20 June Sa'udi Arabia created an air defense zone, blocking further Iranian incursions into its airspace and ending its crisis. And Kuwait's crisis ended on 11 July, when it signed an arms deal with the USSR. This marked the end of the Basra–Kharg Island crisis as a whole; but the war continued unabated for another four years.

As in earlier phases of the Iran/Iraq War, all attempts to end the war—by the UN, the Gulf states, the Non-Aligned Movement, and various Islamic organizations—failed, though, as noted, the UN Secretary-General arranged a brief moratorium on the bombing of civilian areas.

France continued to be a major arms supplier to Iraq, whose war effort was heavily financed by Kuwait and Sa'udi Arabia. The U.S. goal throughout Gulf War I was to keep the Strait of Hormuz open to the steady flow of oil to its allies in Europe and Japan. Secretly it provided Iraq with valuable technological assistance and intelligence information throughout the war, and antiaircraft missiles and a naval escort for Sa'udi ships. The USSR provided arms to Iraq, notably SS-12 ground-to-ground missiles. Other suppliers of military equipment to Iraq were Egypt, Brazil, China, and Chile.

Except for Syria, the Arab world supported Iraq: both the Gulf Cooperation Council and the Arab League condemned Iran. And the latter sought UN intervention. On 21 May 1984 the Security Council adopted a resolution calling on all parties to respect freedom of navigation in the Gulf. By late August both superpowers shifted their stance from apparent impartiality to open support for Iraq.

(See *Master Table,* pp. 728–29.)

Sources
See sources for Case #317 (Chubin and Tripp, Cordesman and Wagner, Karsh, O'Ballance); and Abdulghani 1984; *Keesing's* 1984; *MECS* 1984; *New York Times* 1984.

(361) Capture of al-Faw

Iraq, Iran, and, briefly, Kuwait and Saʿudi Arabia were the actors in this intra-war crisis from 9 February until early April 1986.

Background and Pre-crisis
The Iran/Iraq War, which erupted in mid-September 1980 (see Case #317 above), showed no signs of winding down after more than four years of costly campaigns—heavy casualties on both sides—and periods of stalemate (see Cases #335 and 348 above).

There were no less than nine land attacks by Iran and three Iraqi counter-attacks in 1985. Notable was an Iranian attack in March in the area of the *al-Huwayza* marshes of southern Iraq that, for a time, closed the main road between Basra and Baghdad. An Iraqi counteroffensive repelled the Iranian penetration, with heavy casualties on both sides. During March there was also an exchange of air and missile raids on Teheran and Baghdad and other major cities, the first in four years. A visit by the UN Secretary-General to both states in April, in quest of a basis for peace talks, came to naught. After a long lull in the war of attrition against each other's oil installations, Iraq launched a series of air attacks against Kharg Island in August and September 1985, which succeeded, temporarily, in disrupting Iranian oil exports. In an attempt to diversify its facilities, Iran developed a floating terminal at Sirri Island. Both parties also continued to attack merchant ships in the Gulf, the "tanker war": from March to September more than 130 ships had been hit. All this was a prelude to a fresh intra-war crisis.

Crisis
A crisis for Iraq was triggered on 9 February 1986, when Iranian forces began a series of offensives in the south. Those aimed at Qurna and Majnoon failed to achieve their objective. However, on 10–11 February Iranian troops took *Umm al-Rassas*, lost it the next day, but advanced on the al-Faw Peninsula near Siba, and very near to Kuwait's island of Bubiyan, which was long coveted by Iraq (see Case #252—**Iraq Invasion of Kuwait**, in 1973, in **Iraq/Kuwait PC**). Iranian forces also began operations along the al-Faw–Basra road in order to divert Iraqi forces. Iran now threatened Iraq's only access to the Gulf and, potentially, its Umm Qasr naval base.

It was Iran's dramatic advance, notably the capture of al-Faw, and the fear of Iraq's defeat that triggered a brief crisis (11–13 February) for Kuwait and Saʿudi Arabia, key financial backers for Iraq's enormously expensive war effort. Their response was to take the lead in an Arab *démarche* to the UN: on 13 February the foreign ministers of Iraq, Jordan, Kuwait, Morocco, North Yemen, Saʿudi Arabia, and Tunisia requested a meeting of the UN Security Council and a condemnation of Iran's "aggression."

The UN Secretary-General was also active at this time—a mini–shuttle diplomacy in the Gulf to try to avoid a spillover of the Iran/Iraq War to Kuwait. Iran was cooperative: on 13 February President Khamenei assured Kuwait that Iran would respect its neutrality, provided it did not allow Iraq to use its territory for military operations against Iran. This eased the tension and ended the crisis for Kuwait and Saʿudi Arabia. At the end of February the Security Council again called for a cease-fire, which was not heeded.

By mid-February Iran controlled the strategically and symbolically important port and town of al-Faw but at an estimated cost of 8,000–10,000 casualties in five days of intense fighting; Iraq's losses were 3,000–5,000. On 14 February 1986 Iraq launched a counteroffensive aimed at regaining control of al-Faw. This catalyzed an intra-war crisis for Iran. Iraq also announced the expansion of its naval exclusion zone to include the coast of Kuwait. By 20 March another stalemate set in, with Iran still in control of al-Faw. Iran's casualties for the entire campaign were 27,000–30,000, Iraq's losses, 5,000–8,000. Iran also created a second front in Iraqi Kurdistan: its *Wal Fajr IX* offensive drove Iraqis and Kurds from 40 villages near Suleimaniya.

The al-Faw crisis faded in early April. Iran retained control of the town of al-Faw, including 200 square kilometers of the Faw Peninsula. But Iraq was able to prevent further Iranian advances in the south. So the situation remained until the last major battle of the Iran/Iraq War in the spring of 1988 (see Case #385 below).

(See *Master Table*, pp. 730–31.)

Sources
See sources for Case #317 (Chubin and Tripp, Cordesman and Wagner, Karsh, O'Ballance); and *Keesing's* 1986; *MECS* 1986.

(385) Iraq Recapture of al-Faw

Iran experienced its last intra-war crisis (IWC) of the eight-year Iran/Iraq War from 18 April to 8 August 1988.

Background
The long war in the Gulf region began in September 1980 when Iraq invaded its neighbor (see Case #317 above). There were several IWCs in the following years (see Cases #335, 348, 361 in 1982, 1984, 1986, above). Both sides suffered heavy casualties. There was little change in the strategic balance. And for most of the time the protagonists were locked in a stalemate.

The key Iraqi port of al-Faw at the entrance to the long-disputed Shatt-al-Arab estuary (see Cases #172, 234 above), with a history of conflict over this waterway going back to the Ottoman period before World War I, had fallen to Iran on 9 February 1986. On 14 May 1986 Iraqi forces made their first land incursion into Iran since the battle for Khorramshahr in 1982.

Pre-crisis
For the last two years of the war there was a renewed stalemate. Iraq's primary goal in this phase was to damage the Iranian economy, notably its oil exports. Iran's objectives were to punish Iraq as the initiator of the costly war, to oust Saddam Hussein from power in Baghdad, and to receive massive war reparations from Iraq. In light of these goals Iran rejected several Iraqi offers of a cease-fire, including one by Saddam Hussein in January 1987: on 12 February Ayatullah Khomeini declared that the war against Iraq was a "Holy Crusade" that could end only in victory. On 20 March 1988 Khomeini reaffirmed his determination to persist until final victory.

Iran used its Kurdish allies in a war of attrition against Iraq in the mountainous north. Iraqi planes continued to attack tankers in the Gulf and the Strait of Hormuz, in an attempt to undermine Iran's capability to sustain the long war. The naval war in the Gulf was internationalized in the spring of 1987, including an Iraqi attack on a U.S. frigate in the Gulf on 17 May, changing U.S. attitudes toward Gulf War I, but not to the extent of making Washington a direct participant. Iran and Iraq exchanged air raids on civilian targets in many cities of the two warring states, including Baghdad and Teheran. Iran also renewed pressure on Kuwait to desist from further material aid to Iraq, by naval attacks on Bubiyan Island on 30 March and 20 April 1988.

Crisis
On 18 April 1988, after a fierce battle, Iraqi forces recaptured the port of al-Faw, the first of a series of victories that would lead to the end of the war. Iraq launched another successful offensive on 25 May on the town of Shalamchech, which Iran had occupied in January 1987. An Iranian counteroffensive was unsuccessful. Nonetheless Iran refused all UN entreaties to negotiate with Iraq, directly or even indirectly.

In late May the UN Secretary-General began a new cease-fire initiative, but neither of the protagonists was receptive. On 2 June Iran, through its new commander in chief of the armed forces (and later, president), Rafsanjani, declared that there would be no compromise. On 18 June Iraq began a new offensive, attacking Mehran. A week later it reconquered Majnoon Island and the northern outskirts of Basra.

By the summer of 1988 Iran had yielded all of its military gains of the preceding six years. It was a turning point in the war, indicating that defeat was possible, and for Iraq, a signal that victory was attainable. Saddam Hussein declared on 28 June that "final victory is very near"; and on 12 July Iraq began to advance into Iran. From a position of strength Iraq proposed peace talks on the 18th. The two superpowers and the UN also pressed for negotiations, through

Security Council Resolution 598. Iran, suffering from a shortage of arms and several defeats on the battlefield, and under growing external pressure from the major powers, agreed to negotiate: on 20 July Khomeini announced Iran's acceptance of a cease-fire, a decision he described as "more deadly than taking poison." Iraq, however, insisted on direct negotiations on all aspects of the conflict. The fighting, the last IWC, and the Iran/Iraq War ended on 8 August 1988.

(None of the basic issues in dispute, including borders, was resolved by the war. The two Gulf powers had suffered massive losses and were weakened, internally and externally.)

(See *Master Table*, pp. 732–33.)

Sources
See sources for Case #317; and Chubin 1989; *MECS* 1988; *MEJ* Chronology 1988.

Iraq/Kuwait

The protracted conflict between Iraq and Kuwait generated six crises from 1961 to 1994, as follows.

Case #183 **Kuwait Independence,** in 1961;
　　#252 **Iraq Invasion—Kuwait,** in 1973;
　　#393 **Gulf War,** in 1990–91;
　　#398 **Bubiyan,** in 1991;
　　#406 **Iraq No-Fly Zone,** in 1992;
　　#412 **Iraq Troop Deployment—Kuwait,** in 1994.

The five international crises in the Iran/Iraq War, from Case #317—**Onset of Iran/Iraq War,** in 1980, to Case #385, **Iraq Recapture of al-Faw,** in 1988, were related to the outbreak of the **Gulf War** in 1990 (see **Iran/Iraq PC**). (See *Master Table*.)

General Background

Kuwait was a marginal pearl-diving and trading settlement on the edge of the Arabian peninsula until World War II. The ruling family, the al-Sabahs, was chosen in 1756 by migrant Bedouin tribes from the Najd Desert to administer the realm. Kuwait became a British protectorate in 1899. And the British acquired what became an extraordinarily valuable oil concession in 1934. On the eve of its independence crisis Kuwait had a population of less than two million, of whom fewer than a third were Kuwaitis. Two-thirds were Sunni Muslims, one-third Shi'ite. An oil boom in the 1950s was to transform Kuwait into the wealthiest state in the world per capita.

The norm in Iraq/Kuwait relations was a persistent challenge to Kuwait's legitimacy as an independent state. Iraq's territorial claim to the emirate of Kuwait can be traced to the era of Ottoman rule over both of these entities. The basis of Iraq's contention was the fact that, from 1875 until the end of the Ottoman Empire, Kuwait had been part of the autonomous province *(vilayet)* of Basra, which was included in an independent Iraq in 1920. Iraq's claim was pressed by all Iraq's rulers after the end of the British Mandate in 1932: by Hashemite kings until the overthrow of the monarchy in 1958; by General Qassem in 1961; by Ba'ath leaders until August 1991 when, during the **Gulf War** (see Case #393 below), Kuwait was briefly (re)incorporated into Iraq as its nineteenth province; and until November 1994 (see Case #412 below).

(183) Kuwait Independence

Iraq, Kuwait, and the U.K. were the direct participants in a crisis over Kuwait's independence from 19 June until 13 July 1961.

Crisis

Kuwait was granted its independence by the U.K. on 19 June 1961, accompanied by a mutual defense treaty. This triggered a crisis for Iraq. On the 25th Prime Minister Qassem vigorously renewed the claim that Kuwait was an integral part of Iraq and threatened action, including violence, to nullify Kuwait's independence. This catalyzed a crisis for Kuwait. Perceiving a threat to its existence, Kuwait responded on the 30th with a formal request to Britain for assistance under the provisions of their defense agreement. This in turn generated a crisis for the U.K. On 1 July it began a rapid military buildup in Kuwait: within one week British forces numbered 6,000.

The same day Kuwait appealed to the UN Security Council. The Council discussed the matter; but a draft resolution critical of Iraq was vetoed by the USSR. Moreover, Egypt's proposal for the withdrawal of British troops did not secure a Security Council majority. In July 1961 the Arab League admitted Kuwait to membership in the face of Iraq's protests and established a Pan-Arab force of mostly Jordanians and Sa'udi Arabians to defend Kuwait.

The Kuwait Independence crisis ended on 13 July when Iraq's military attaché in the U.K. denied that Iraq intended to attack Kuwait or that it had concentrated troops on the border.

The U.S. was not involved in this crisis.

(With recognition by the Arab world the emir of Kuwait requested British troops to leave; the evacuation was completed by October 1961. After the downfall of General Qassem in February 1963 Iraq recognized Kuwait's independence—but not the finality of the Iraq/Kuwait border. [This was to remain a source of persistent tension and was a precipitating cause of the Gulf crisis-war in 1990–91—see Case #393 below.] Iraq, which had boycotted the Arab League after its admission of Kuwait, withdrew its claim to all of Kuwait in the autumn of 1963.

On 10 November 1994, for the first time, Iraq formally recognized Kuwait's sovereignty, independence, and territorial integrity within its borders as demarcated after the 1991 war. This was in accord with a UN Security Council resolution during the October 1994 **Iraq Troop Deployment—Kuwait** crisis [see Case #412 below].)

(See *Master Table,* pp. 698–99.)

Sources
Bartlet 1977; Bogdanor and Skidelsky 1970; Dann 1969; Fitzimmons 1964; Goodspeed 1967; Hassouna 1975; Horne 1989b; Kerr 1971; Khadduri 1969; Macmillan 1973; al-Marayati 1966; *MEJ* Chronology 1961; *MER* 1961; Northedge 1974; Shwadran 1962.

(252) Iraq Invasion—Kuwait

A crisis for Kuwait began on 20 March and ended on 8 June 1973.

Pre-crisis
By 1973 Iraq's pressure on Kuwait to make territorial concessions that would enable an Iraqi creation of a new base for petroleum and military operations in the Persian Gulf had increased. A year earlier Kuwait had refused a large loan to Iraq. The USSR supported Iraqi claims to two Kuwaiti islands, Bubiyan and Warba, as it was expected that Iraq would permit the USSR to establish a naval facility there. Soviet support of Iraq was perceived by Kuwait, Iran, and other Western-aligned states in the Middle East as threatening. And Kuwait's growing rapprochement with Iran and Saʿudi Arabia disturbed Iraqi decision makers.

Crisis
On 20 March 1973 Iraqi troops crossed the border into Kuwait, with a view to annexing part of the disputed territory along their 99-mile border. Kuwait immediately sent troops, but they were defeated by the superior Iraqi forces, who then occupied the Kuwaiti outpost of Sametah where a number of huts were established. When Kuwait surrounded these huts with mosques the Iraqi forces were contained. The next day, at an emergency session of the Kuwaiti cabinet and parliament, a decision was taken to negotiate rather than fight.

Kuwait's insistence on Iraq's withdrawal, and the latter's refusal to do so, brought mediation efforts by Arab League Secretary-General Riad to a standstill. On 6 April the two foreign ministers met, after which Iraqi forces were withdrawn and an announcement was made by both parties that they accepted the Palestine Liberation Organization *(PLO)* leader, Yasser Arafat, as mediator. The debate centered around Kuwait's refusal to concede or to lease the islands to Iraq. The following day Kuwait offered a substantial investment in Iraqi development projects and special treatment for Iraqis residing in Kuwait.

The crisis ended on 8 June 1973 when an agreement was reached between the two states that included an Iraqi increase of freshwater supplies to Kuwait from the Shatt-al-Arab, but there were no Kuwaiti concessions on the islands. Following the agreement both Kuwait and Sa'udi Arabia completed substantial arms deals with the U.S. and the U.K., respectively, while Iraq obtained increased arms supplies from the USSR.

Mediation attempts were made by Egypt, Lebanon, and Syria; and Iran and Sa'udi Arabia offered military support to Kuwait. There were reports of 15,000 Sa'udi troops in Kuwait shortly after the beginning of the crisis.

The U.S., the USSR, and the UN were not involved in this crisis.

(See *Master Table*, pp. 712–13.)

Sources
MEJ Chronology 1973; *Keesing's* 1973; *New York Times* 1973.

(393) Gulf War

Kuwait, the U.S., Iraq, and Sa'udi Arabia were the main participants in a crisis-war over the Gulf from 2 August 1990 to 12 April 1991. The other crisis actors were Bahrain, Egypt, France, Israel, Oman, Qatar, Syria, United Arab Emirates (UAE), the U.K., and the USSR.

Background
Iraq's oil production, which was vital to its economy, declined drastically during the Iran/Iraq War from 1980 to 1988 (see **Iran/Iraq PC**). As a result Iraq was experiencing great difficulty in repaying loans received during that war from Arab states, notably Kuwait and the UAE, amounting to billions of dollars. Iraq requested cancellation of the debts; they refused.

Iraq expounded two arguments. One was that, in carrying the full human and material burden of war against Iran, it was defending the vital interests of all Arab states in the Gulf region against a fundamentalist regime intent on establishing its hegemony and taking control of their vast oil resources. The second was that these loans derived mainly from the large increase in their oil revenues due to the sharp reduction in Iraq's oil exports during the war years. For both reasons, argued Iraq, these "loans" should be regarded as contributions to a common war effort and should be canceled.

Pre-crisis
President Saddam Hussein's verbal attacks on Kuwait and the UAE began at an Arab League meeting on 28 May 1990. He accused them of waging economic war against Iraq by overproducing oil and causing a collapse in world oil prices. On 17 July, a week after the Gulf states agreed to cut their oil production, Hussein threatened that "if words fail to protect Iraq's interests, something effective must be done." The next day Iraq's Foreign Minister, Tariq Aziz, accused Kuwait of stealing a vast amount of oil from the southern section of the disputed

Rumaila oil field since 1980, worth $2.4 billion. Kuwait responded by placing its army on alert and by rejecting Iraq's claims and charges. Iraq moved forces to the Saʿudi Arabian border on the 23rd.

Talks between Iraq and Kuwait began on 31 July amid rising tension, despite informal mediation efforts by some Arab leaders. That day, too, six Iraqi divisions were concentrated along the border with Kuwait. The talks were suspended after only one session, when Kuwait rejected Iraq's demand for the strategically valuable Bubiyan and Warba islands.

Crisis

On 2 August 1990 Iraqi forces invaded Kuwait and occupied the emirate within six hours. This triggered the gravest of all possible crises for Kuwait, a threat to its existence as a state. The occupation of Kuwait and its huge oil resources was also perceived by the United States as a basic value threat. A U.S. statement on the 2nd condemned Iraq's invasion and called for the immediate and unconditional withdrawal of all Iraqi forces from Kuwait and the restoration of its legitimate government. The same day the UN Security Council adopted Resolution 660, the first of 15 during the crisis, calling for Iraq's complete and immediate withdrawal from Kuwait. The Arab League also condemned the invasion and called for Iraq's immediate withdrawal.

On the 3rd Iraqi forces concentrated on the Saʿudi Arabian border. In an emergency meeting on the 4th the Council of Europe decided to impose sanctions against Iraq. The UN Security Council, too, imposed wide-ranging sanctions against Iraq on 6 August.

A U.S. announcement on 7 August of its intent to deploy troops to Saʿudi Arabia marks the beginning of a massive military buildup of U.S. forces in the Gulf region. On the 8th the U.S. announced that up to 50,000 troops might be dispatched to Saʿudi Arabia to press for Iraq's compliance with UN resolutions.

Iraq's Revolutionary Command Council *(RCC)* responded the same day by annexing Kuwait "in a comprehensive, eternal, and inseparable merger." On the 10th, 12 of the Arab League members supported a resolution to send a Pan-Arab force to Saʿudi Arabia: the decision obliged only the supporting states. *NATO* members decided at a special meeting in Brussels to respond individually to the crisis, not through collective action.

On 12 August Saddam Hussein initiated a "linkage" between the Gulf conflict and the Palestinian issue, a tactic he employed throughout the crisis to win support from the Arab and Muslim worlds. The U.S., the U.K., and Israel rejected the linkage. France and the European Community supported it.

In a further escalatory step on the 16th, Iraq took thousands of foreigners, mostly Westerners, as hostages. A UN resolution three days later demanded their release. On 21 September the *RCC* called on Iraq's citizens to prepare for the "mother of all battles." On the 23rd Saddam Hussein threatened to attack Saʿudi oil fields, unfriendly Arab states, and Israel if UN economic sanctions were to "strangle" Iraq.

On 30 October President Bush secretly approved a military plan to launch an air and naval strike against Iraq in mid-January 1991 and a ground campaign in February. This decision triggered a full-scale crisis for the U.S. because it generated the three defining conditions of a crisis—basic value threat, namely the human and material costs of war, finite time, and the higher likelihood of military hostilities. In a follow-up action, Bush announced on 8 November the deployment of 150,000 more troops to the Gulf region. Hussein responded by announcing on the 19th the deployment of 250,000 more troops to Kuwait and southern Iraq.

On 29 November, at U.S. urging, the Security Council adopted Resolution 678, authorizing the "use (of) all necessary means" by member-states to secure Iraq's compliance with all its earlier resolutions: it specified a deadline of 15 January 1991 for Iraq's withdrawal from Kuwait, triggering a crisis for Iraq and for the U.S.'s allies as well—all the other crisis actors noted previously. Saddam Hussein rejected the resolution the next day. In a conciliatory gesture on 30 November, Bush offered to invite Iraq's Foreign Minister, Tariq Aziz, to Washington and to send the U.S. Secretary of State, James Baker, to Baghdad soon after "to discuss all aspects of the Gulf Crisis." The *RCC* accepted the offer of high-level talks. And on 6 December Hussein announced the release of all foreign hostages.

The Gulf states met in Doha on the 22nd for a summit meeting of the Gulf Cooperation Council *(GCC)*. They noted that the multinational force was coming "at the request of the *GCC* and will leave the region when the *GCC* states request." They also called for Iraq's unconditional withdrawal from Kuwait and reparations payment for the damage done.

On 2 January 1991 *NATO* decided to dispatch aircraft to protect Turkey from a possible Iraqi attack. A coalition of 28 states was formed, led by the U.S.: its most visible members were the U.K., France, and three Arab states, Saʿudi Arabia, Egypt, and Syria. The USSR was not an active member of the coalition but supported all UN resolutions during the crisis, including authorization of military action against Iraq. At the same time, Moscow took some dramatic diplomatic initiatives to resolve the crisis and prevent military intervention against Iraq.

The Aziz-Baker meeting took place in Geneva on 9 January: it ended in total impasse. On the 11th Baker requested Saʿudi approval of U.S. plans to intervene; and on the 15th Bush made a formal commitment to war. The U.S. informed the Saʿudi and Israeli ambassadors and coalition leaders of the decision on the 16th. The Soviet foreign minister was informed early in the morning of 17 January that coalition forces would attack Iraq an hour later. The USSR asked for additional time to make a last attempt to influence Saddam Hussein; and almost immediately after the war began it urged Iraq's leader to announce the beginning of a withdrawal from Kuwait.

The war, named "Operation Desert Storm," began with a massive bombardment of Iraq. Iraq responded with antiaircraft fire; but the U.S.-led coalition force had enormous superiority in firepower. Iraq retaliated by launching Scud missiles against Sa'udi Arabia and Israel. Intensive U.S. pressure succeeded in preventing an Israeli military riposte. In the early days of the war many of Iraq's most advanced planes flew to Iran for sanctuary. During the 38-day air campaign Iraq experienced saturation bombing.

The USSR was quiet during the first three weeks of Operation Desert Storm. In February President Gorbachev launched a high-profile mediation campaign to end the war. On the 9th the Soviet leader publicly condemned Iraq's invasion of Kuwait, warned (the U.S.) against going beyond the mandate defined by the UN, and called upon Saddam Hussein to adopt "realism." A Soviet mission to Baghdad by an academic specialist on Asia, Primakov, led to Iraq's conditional offer on the 15th: withdrawal from Kuwait; a guarantee of all Iraq's "historical rights"; abdication by the ruling al-Sabah family of Kuwait; and Israel's complete withdrawal from all occupied Arab territories. The offer was categorically rejected. A Tariq Aziz visit to Moscow then generated a six-point plan on the 22nd. The U.S. rejected the plan and issued an ultimatum to Iraq the same day to begin large-scale withdrawal from Kuwait the next day. Saddam Hussein rejected the ultimatum.

The military intervention plan was set on 11 February. The combined land, air, and sea attack on Iraqi forces began early in the morning of 24 February. In four days the Iraqi forces were mauled—but not decimated—by the coalition's ground forces. On the 27th the U.S. declared a unilateral "suspension of offensive combat operations." Iraq accepted the informal cease-fire on the 28th. The terms for an interim cease-fire were codified and adopted by the UN Security Council on 2 March—Resolution 686. Iraq accepted on the 6th. The conditions for a long-term cease-fire were set down in Resolution 687, passed by the Council on 3 April. Iraq acquiesced on the 6th.

U.S. troops began to leave Iraq on 8 April. On the 9th the Security Council authorized the deployment of a peacekeeping force of 1,440 to patrol a demilitarized zone along the Iraq/Kuwait border. The beginning of the implementation of the formal cease-fire on 12 April 1991 marked the end of the Gulf War crisis.

(See *Master Table*, pp. 734–35.)

Sources
Foreign Broadcast Information Service—Daily Report/Near East/South Asia (FBIS—DR/NESA) May 1990–April 1991; Baker 1995; Brecher 1993; Cigar 1992; Freedman and Karsh 1993; *Keesing's* 1990, 1991; Miller and Mylroie 1990; *New York Times* 1990, 1991; Powell 1995; Schofield 1991; Schwarzkopf 1992; Sciolino 1991; Sifry and Cerf 1991; Stein 1992; Woodward 1991.

(398) Bubiyan

Kuwait experienced a brief (2–3 day) crisis with Iraq starting on 28 August 1991.

Pre-crisis
Following the Gulf crisis-war, there were several incidents between Kuwait and Iraq, notably on 15 August 1991 when Kuwait accused Iraq of violating the cease-fire in the Demilitarized Zone between the two states.

Crisis
On 28 August 1991 Kuwait accused Iraq of landing troops on the Kuwaiti island of Bubiyan in order to retrieve weapons and military equipment abandoned by Iraq there during the Gulf War. This generated a perception of higher-than-normal threat to its territorial integrity, triggering a crisis for Kuwait.

It responded by protesting to the UN Security Council against "a clear violation of the [Gulf War] cease-fire agreement." Members of the UN Iraq-Kuwait Observer Mission *(UNIKOM)* visited Bubiyan on the 29th to investigate the incident. The next day Kuwaiti planes and helicopters resumed their patrols over the island. The crisis, with very minor clashes, faded by the end of August.

The U.S. provided Kuwait with political support. The USSR remained aloof from this crisis, as did the Arab League and the Gulf Cooperation Council.

(See *Master Table*, pp. 736–37.)

Sources
FBIS—DR/NESA August–September 1991; *Keesing's* 1991; *New York Times* 1991.

(406) Iraq No-Fly Zone

Iraq experienced a post–Gulf War crisis from 18 August to 8 September 1992 over the "no-fly zone" imposed by the U.S., the U.K., and France.

Background and Pre-crisis
Notwithstanding its military defeat in January–February 1991 (see Case #393— **Gulf War**), Iraq's regime continued a long-standing policy of repression against its Kurdish minority in the north and the Shia in the south. The victors in the war, led by the U.S., created "safe havens" for the Kurds in April 1991, following their failed rebellion against Saddam Hussein's regime and the mass flight— estimated at almost two million refugees—into the mountains of Iraqi Kurdistan. That Western interventionist regime in northern Iraq was still in force, in a modified form, six years after the war.

The idea of a no-fly zone south of the 32nd Parallel emerged from reports in early August 1992 of increasing Iraqi military activity and violations of human rights among the Shia population in southern Iraq.

On 11 August, at a UN Security Council meeting convened at the request of France, the U.K., and the U.S., the UN rapporteur on human rights in Iraq reported that there was documentary evidence of a systematic policy by Iraq to destroy the Shia Arabs of the marshlands and their culture. The Council did not pass a resolution; but this meeting was perceived—by Iraq, the Western powers, and others—as a step toward enforcing Iraq's compliance with the provision of Security Council Resolution 688, passed at the end of the Gulf War, demanding that Iraq's regime cease suppressing its Kurdish and Shia minorities. On 12 August Iraq dismissed Mr. van der Stoel's report as "inaccurate."

Crisis

On 18 August 1992 senior officials from France, the U.K., and the U.S. announced that they had decided to impose an "air exclusion zone" over Iraq. This was followed by a U.K. announcement of the dispatch of six Tornado jets to take part in an allied operation to protect the population of southern Iraq. These two announcements triggered a crisis for Iraq, which perceived a threat to its sovereignty and territorial integrity. On 20 August France announced that it would send 10 Mirage-2000 jets to the region. The U.S. already had more than 200 planes in the area.

Iraq's initial response, on the 20th, was to denounce the Western plan for an exclusive zone—an "imperialist conspiracy" aimed at dismembering Iraq. The same day Egypt expressed concern for the sovereignty and integrity of Iraq's territory. Turkey, too, announced that it opposed any plan "directed against the integrity of Iraq." And on 23 August official statements from Algeria, Jordan, Libya, Sudan, Syria, Yemen, and the Arab League expressed concern about the integrity of Iraq, warning that the plan would increase tension in the region.

On 26 August U.S. President Bush officially announced the establishment of the exclusion zone by France, Russia, the U.K., and the U.S., in order to protect the Shia population of southern Iraq. The decision imposed an immediate ban on flights by Iraqi helicopters and aircraft south of the 32nd Parallel.

Iraq was officially notified about the decision through its Permanent Representative at the UN, Abdul Amir al-Anbari.

Al-Anbari responded by denouncing the decision as an "illegal act" that required "clear and firm" Arab opposition and warned that "Iraq will choose the proper way and the proper time to confront this outrageous aggression." Algeria, Jordan, Sudan, Syria, and Yemen condemned the decision as a dangerous precedent in the region and as an indicator of the West's intention of partitioning Iraq into three blocks—Kurdish in the north, Sunni in the center, and Shia in the south. Egypt and Sa'udi Arabia, the leading Arab allies in the U.S.-led, anti-Iraq coalition of 1990–91, expressed reservations. Only Kuwait publicly approved the plan.

In late August, with the no-fly zone in effect, Iraq increased its ground campaign against Shia rebels in the south. However, Baghdad showed tacit compliance with the decision: it ordered its air force to keep away from the exclusion zone and instructed its ground forces not to fire at Western aircraft.

The major powers who initiated the no-fly zone strengthened their military power in the area. France sent another four Mirage jets. And Russia, throughout the 1990 crisis and war the most empathetic toward Iraq, announced on 1 September that it would send two warships to the Gulf.

On 5 September King Hassan of Morocco issued a strong warning against the West's "dangerous policy" toward Iraq. Foreign ministers from the six-member Gulf Cooperation Council *(GCC)*, dominated by Sa'udia Arabia, met in Jiddah on 8–9 September and accepted the enforcement of the no-fly zone over southern Iraq.

On 8 September Iraq's government reassured U.S., British, and French pilots monitoring the 'air exclusion zone' that they had nothing to fear if forced to land on Iraqi territory because of mechanical problems.

The crisis for Iraq seemed to end on 8 September with Iraq's compliance and statements that reduced tension among the confronting parties.

(Four years later a fresh crisis—between Iraq and the United States—erupted over both no-fly zones. Iraqi troops and armor entered the Kurdish safe haven in September 1996, in support of one of the two factions vying for power in Iraqi Kurdistan for decades, the Kurdistan Democratic Party. The U.S., viewing this incursion as a violation of the safe haven—and a threat to its vital interests in the Gulf region, responded with two missile attacks against Iraqi air defenses in the southern no-fly zone; direct military intervention in the north was not politically feasible. After a symbolic Iraqi retaliation against a U.S. plane flying a reconnaissance mission in the south, both adversaries refrained from further escalation of the 1996 Iraq no-fly zone crisis.)

(See *Master Table,* pp. 736–37.)

Sources
Baker 1995; *Keesing's* 1992; *New York Times* 1992, 1996.

(412) Iraq Troop Deployment—Kuwait

Kuwait, Sa'udi Arabia, the United States, and Iraq were enmeshed in another Gulf crisis from 7 October to 10 November 1994.

Pre-crisis
During the years that followed the Gulf War the U.S., the U.K., Kuwait, and Sa'udi Arabia were steadfast in their determination to maintain the sanctions regime until Iraq had fully complied with all UN demands as set out in the 7 March 1991 resolution, including an explicit demand that Iraq recognize Kuwait's sovereignty and territorial integrity. Russia and France adopted a softer line, calling for the gradual lifting of sanctions, primarily because they perceived major economic benefits from Iraq's return to the international community.

In late September 1994 President Saddam Hussein had to stop subsidizing food prices. This caused a large price increase that led to internal unrest in Iraq. Baghdad renewed its demand that UN sanctions be lifted on humanitarian grounds—Iraqi children were suffering the ill effects of malnutrition, and the population at large was experiencing the adverse effects of a persistent shortage of medicines and general medical services. Hussein warned that Iraq would retaliate if the Security Council, at its next scheduled meeting on 10 October, decided to renew economic sanctions, especially the oil embargo. In this atmosphere of escalating tension, very similar to the prelude to the 1990–91 Gulf crisis-war, Iraqi forces began to move toward Kuwait on 2 October. On the 4th Saddam Hussein condemned the U.S. insistence on retaining the sanctions, which continued to cripple the Iraqi economy.

Crisis
Iraq's deployment of troops near its border with Kuwait on 7 October 1994, estimated at 40,000–50,000, triggered a crisis for Kuwait and Saʿudi Arabia: it threatened their territorial integrity and rekindled memories of Iraq's invasion of Kuwait in 1990. Iraq's massive military buildup in a few days also triggered a crisis for the U.S., a renewed threat to its influence and economic (oil) interests in the region. (Since the Gulf War the U.S. has been committed to protect the Gulf states from Iraqi attacks.)

The gravity of the threat perceived by the U.S. was evident in several statements and actions on the 7th: "the most threatening moves Iraq had taken since the Gulf War," according to unnamed U.S. officials; Iraq's moves "are not routine . . . and therefore cause us concern," said Defense Secretary Perry; and President Clinton expressed his resolve not to permit Baghdad to threaten the UN into lifting sanctions.

Among the "precautionary" steps, Clinton ordered the aircraft carrier *Eisenhower,* to the Red Sea, along with the *Aegis* cruiser equipped with Tomahawk missiles. The U.S. also sent 4,000 troops to Kuwait the same day. These military moves triggered a crisis for Iraq. There were other visible expressions of U.S. resolve. At a meeting with the Saʿudi Foreign Minister, Saʿud al-Faisal, on the 7th, Clinton reaffirmed the U.S. commitment to Saʿudi Arabia's security. In a telephone call Secretary of State Christopher reassured Kuwait's foreign minister of U.S. support and its readiness to respond firmly to Iraq's "aggression." On 8 October Clinton, wanting to avoid President Bush's mixed signals of U.S. intent in 1990, warned Saddam Hussein in unmistakable words: "It would be a grave error for Iraq to repeat the mistakes of the past or to misjudge either American will or American power." The next day Clinton announced the dispatch of 36,000 more troops and planes to the Persian Gulf. On the 10th Iraq announced that its forces would be withdrawn from the Kuwaiti border.

In telephone calls on the 10th Clinton spoke with the leaders of the U.K., France, Russia, Egypt, and Turkey, seeking support for military action against Iraq, if necessary. The six leaders reportedly expressed support for "quick and vigorous military measures to defend Kuwait" and agreed to oppose Iraq's attempt to press the UN to lift the economic sanctions.

On 11 October Iraq began to withdraw forces from the Kuwaiti border. Nevertheless, the U.S. announced the same day the deployment of more troops and planes to the region and placed 155,000 ground troops on alert. A major U.S. concern was the danger that Iraq would indulge in similar threats in the future and create further international crises. Defense Secretary Perry emphasized that the U.S. did not want to maintain substantial forces in Kuwait for a long time.

The display of rapid U.S. resolve elicited gratitude from the six members of the Gulf Cooperation Council (Saʿudi Arabia, Kuwait, Bahrain, Qatar, Oman, and the United Arab Emirates): at a meeting with Christopher on the 12th their foreign ministers affirmed a commitment to pay the cost of deploying U.S. forces to the Gulf to defend Kuwait. The Gulf states also undertook to send their "Peninsula Shield Force" to help defend Kuwait.

Kuwait sought international support for a buffer zone in southern Iraq and called on the UN to press Iraq for information on the 600+ Kuwaiti hostages taken to Iraq during the 1990 invasion. The U.K. and France sent modest, symbolic forces to the region: the former, 900 troops, ships, and warplanes, the latter, a warship. King Hussein of Jordan, in contrast to 1991, condemned Iraq's provocation on 11 October. He did not deploy troops; but he expressed support for the possible use of military force by the U.S. and its allies to punish Saddam Hussein.

Among the many involved actors Russia was the most active on the diplomatic front. During a visit of Foreign Minister Kozyrev to Baghdad, Iraq and Russia announced an agreement on 13 October: Iraq would recognize Kuwait's sovereignty and borders; and this act would be linked to the lifting of some of the international sanctions within six months. The U.S. and U.K. responded the same day that there would be no negotiations with Iraq on terms for lifting the sanctions. To the contrary: U.S. officials, viewing Iraq as a long-term threat, spoke of requesting the UN to create a demilitarized zone in southern Iraq, from which Iraqi forces would be excluded.

On 15 October President Yeltsin wrote to Clinton, conveying his support for the Kozyrev-initiated idea of Iraq's recognition of Kuwait in exchange for the lifting of sanctions. Clinton replied with an expression of concern, since this was a sharp shift in Russia's long-standing support of the U.S. position of no negotiations on sanctions until after Iraq demonstrated full compliance with all UN resolutions.

The Security Council unanimously approved a U.S.-U.K.–initiated resolution on 10 October condemning Iraq's new threat to the Gulf region. It also demanded that Iraq withdraw immediately all its forces deployed in southern Iraq and avoid using force and aggressive acts to threaten its neighbors in the future, or to disturb UN activity in Iraq. Russia voted for the resolution, despite differences about how to deal with the Iraqi threat.

On 17 October Iraq's Revolutionary Command Council informed its National Assembly of the intention to recognize Kuwait. The foreign ministers of the six Gulf states, along with Egypt and Syria, met on 19 October in Cairo to discuss the crisis. Kuwait's foreign minister reaffirmed that Kuwait would not accept any solution less than Iraq's complete compliance with UN resolutions.

The Arab League called on Iraq to show restraint. It was U.S.-led resolve that determined the crisis outcome.

On 10 November Iraq's National Assembly formally declared "Iraq's recognition of the sovereignty of the state of Kuwait, its territorial integrity and political independence." This statement, signed by President Saddam Hussein, terminated the crisis for all the actors. All except Iraq were satisfied with the outcome; Iraq suffered an unqualified defeat.

(See *Master Table*, pp. 736–37.)

Sources
New York Times 8 October–11 November 1994.

Yemen

There were six international crises during the protracted conflict over Yemen from 1962 to 1979, as follows.

Case #195 **Yemen War I,** in 1962–63;
#209 **Yemen War II,** in 1964;
#212 **Yemen War III,** in 1964–65;
#219 **Yemen War IV,** in 1966–67;
#248 **North/South Yemen I,** in 1972;
#301 **North/South Yemen II,** in 1979.

General Background

The Imam Ahmad, who had been the absolute ruler of Yemen since 1948, died on 19 September 1962 and was succeeded by his son the Imam Muhammad al-Badr. One week later his monarchy was toppled by a coup d'état carried out by a group of military officers headed by Colonel Abdullah al-Sallal and aided by exiled Yemenis in Egypt who, prior to the coup, sent men and materials to uphold the new regime. Abdul Rahman al-Beidani, an exiled Yemeni diplomat living in Cairo, was named first Prime Minister of the Yemen Arab Republic (hereafter, the YAR or Yemen).

(195) Yemen War I

The four actors in the first phase of the long Yemen War were Jordan, Saʿudi Arabia, Egypt, and Yemen. This crisis lasted from 26 September 1962 to 15 April 1963.

Crisis
The coup in Yemen on 26 September triggered a crisis for Jordan and Saʿudi Arabia. Both feared the possibility that the fall of the monarchy in Yemen would

spread to their own kingdoms. They responded on 1 October with a delivery of arms to the Royalists led by the former imam. This triggered a crisis for Egypt and the YAR. On 4 October the Republican regime ordered general mobilization. Egypt, after sending a team to observe the situation on 13 October, decided to dispatch several thousand troops to Yemen by mid-November.

Civil war broke out between the Republicans in the south (the YAR), aided by Egypt, and the Royalists in the north, aided by arms and men from Jordan and Saʿudi Arabia. On 4 November Mecca Radio announced that Egyptian aircraft had attacked five Saʿudi villages. That day, too, a military alliance between Jordan and Saʿudi Arabia was made known. On the 10th a Joint Defense Pact between Yemen and Egypt was signed. Following the Egyptian raids on Saʿudi Arabia, a Saʿudi decision was made to carry out reprisal raids against the YAR. When the Republican government got word of this (via Jordanian officers who fled to Egypt), they warned of air attacks on the two countries.

The U.S. reacted by sending a warship to Jiddah as a warning against further Yemeni or Egyptian attacks on Saʿudi Arabia. Word was also given to Yemen that, in the event of an attack by the two states, all U.S. military aircraft would be withdrawn and the United States would adopt a neutral attitude. President Kennedy offered his good offices to bring about a peaceful solution and announced U.S. recognition of the Republican government on 19 December. Further Egyptian bombing of Saʿudi Arabia resulted in a Saʿudi call for general mobilization. Ralph Bunche, UN Under-Secretary-General for Special Political Affairs, visited Yemen from 1 to 4 March on a fact-finding mission on behalf of Secretary-General U Thant.

On 15 April 1963 Jordan recognized the YAR and withdrew from the war. A cease-fire and disengagement agreement signed that day marked the end of this crisis and the first phase of the Yemen War.

The USSR provided economic assistance to the YAR and, indirectly, through Egypt, military aid.

(See *Master Table*, pp. 700–701.)

Sources
Dawisha 1975; Gause 1990; Hassouna 1975; Heikal 1975; von Horn 1966; Ismael 1970; Kerr 1970; Kimche 1966; Little 1968; Mahjub 1974; *MEJ* Chronology 1962, 1963; O'Ballance 1971; Porter 1984; Sadat 1978; Safran 1988; Schmidt 1968; Stookey 1982; Wenner 1967.

(209) Yemen War II

Yemen, Egypt, and Saʿudi Arabia experienced intra-war crises from mid-May until 8 November 1964.

Pre-crisis
Fighting among the adversaries broke out immediately after the cease-fire of

April 1963 and continued throughout the year. President Sallal visited the Soviet Union in March and the PRC in June 1964. President Nasir visited Yemen in April 1964. (Jordan, which had at first supported the Yemen Royalists, gradually withdrew as its ties with Egypt became closer. It was not a crisis actor in any of the ensuing crises pertaining to the war in Yemen.) Reports by UN Secretary-General U Thant indicated a reduction in Egyptian forces in the area and an increase in supplies to the Royalists for the period preceding this crisis. The military situation had been fairly quiet, and the report indicated a stalemate. Republican and Egyptian forces controlled the mountains, the coastal plain, and the south of Yemen, while Royalists carried on guerrilla warfare in the mountain and desert areas of the north and east.

Crisis

In mid-May 1964 a retaliation attack was launched by the Royalists, triggering a crisis for the YAR and Egypt. Their response, in August, was the successful Horadeh offensive to seal the border with Sa'udi Arabia and thus prevent supplies from reaching Yemen. This triggered a crisis for Sa'udi Arabia. By 11 September the UN Yemen Observer Mission *(UNYOM)* had terminated its activities and left Yemen. The Sa'udi Arabian response to the crisis was Prince Faisal's visit to Alexandria on 11 September 1964 for talks with Nasir. Presidents Ben Bella of Algeria and Aref of Iraq served as mediators. Peace talks were held in early November, and a cease-fire came into effect on 8 November 1964, the termination date for all three actor-cases.

Neither the U.S. nor the USSR was involved in this crisis.

(See *Master Table,* pp. 704–5.)

Sources

See sources for Case #195.

(212) Yemen War III

This phase of the long war in Yemen, considered as crises for Egypt, Yemen, and Sa'udi Arabia, lasted from 3 December 1964 to 25 August 1965.

Pre-crisis

The peace talks, which were held in Sudan, led to a cease-fire on 8 November 1964, as well as an agreement to set up a National Congress to deal with the fundamental differences between the Republicans and the Royalists. By 20 November an announcement was made postponing the Congress; and on 13 December it was postponed indefinitely. The Royalist Foreign Minister, Ahmed al-Shami, made it clear that, if Royalist demands were not accepted, they would renew the fighting. The political confusion in Yemen was further intensified in December by an open split among the Republicans.

Crisis

On 3 December 1964 a Royalist offensive, backed by Saʿudi Arabia, was launched. Eventually they occupied most of the territory captured by the Republicans. This triggered a crisis for Egypt and Yemen. Their major response, on 10 January 1965, was the resumption of fighting. There were heavy casualties on both sides. The information minister of the Royalist government alleged on 23 January that Egyptian aircraft had dropped gas bombs, the crisis trigger for Saʿudi Arabia.

A Royalist request to the International Red Cross to investigate the charges was refused on the grounds that the use of gas was not forbidden by any International Red Cross convention. Fighting continued in the southeastern region, as well as in northern Yemen. Egyptian attempts in March and May to cut the Royalists' supply routes from Saʿudi Arabia failed. A strong Royalist offensive near Haral (Saʿudi frontier) on 7 June was repulsed. Yemen's Republican government lodged a complaint with the UN on 26 July, accusing Saʿudi Arabia of aiding the Royalists and claiming that, without Saʿudi support, the Royalists would have been defeated long before. Reports of large-scale Saʿudi and Iranian support were frequent from February 1965 onward.

Negotiations for a peace settlement, with Jordanian, Kuwaiti, and Algerian mediation, began in May 1965. After prolonged consultation in Cairo among the YAR leaders, President Sallal announced on 18 July a compromise agreement between the dissident Republicans and reaffirmed the proposals of the Khamner Conference. On 22 July President Nasir said that Egypt had reopened negotiations with Saʿudi Arabia concerning Egyptian troop withdrawal.

An agreement signed by President Nasir and King Faisal in Jiddah on 24 August provided for the following: an immediate cease-fire; the ending of Saʿudi aid to the Royalists; the withdrawal of Egyptian forces; the establishment of a provisional Yemen government; and the holding of a plebiscite in November 1966. The next day the Royalists stopped fighting; and the Egyptian forces began to withdraw from Yemen. This marked the end of the crisis—but not yet of the war or the protracted conflict.

The USSR continued to provide military aid to Egypt and the YAR. The UN and the U.S. were marginally involved in this crisis.

(See *Master Table*, pp. 704–5.)

Sources

See sources for Case #195.

(219) Yemen War IV

The last phase of the long war in Yemen took place between 14 October 1966 and 26 September 1967. There were three crisis actors: Saʿudia Arabia, Egypt, and Yemen.

Pre-crisis

On 23 November 1965 Yemeni Republican and Royalist delegations, together with observers from Egypt and Saʿudi Arabia, met to discuss the nature of the plebiscite agreed upon at Jiddah. The parties failed to reach agreement on any of the items on the agenda. Intermittent fighting continued. A new agreement for a peace settlement in Yemen was reached in Kuwait on 19 August 1966 but was never put into effect. The long war was renewed.

Crisis

On 14 October 1966 air raids began on Royalist-controlled villages in the northern mountains, a main target being the headquarters of the Royalists. Two Saʿudi villages were also bombed, the crisis trigger for Saʿudi Arabia. On 24 October intelligence reports that a strong concentration of Royalist tribesmen was gathering for an attack on the town of Saʾdah triggered another intra-war crisis for Egypt and Yemen. The YAR response, on 30 October, was a combined attack on Saʿudi troops and the Royalist Homdon tribe. Egypt's response was the use of poison gas in bombings of Halhal, a Royalist-held town, on 27 December 1966. Other gas bombings by Egypt were reported in January. Egypt's expeditionary force had reached 50,000–60,000.

The Saʿudi response to the crisis occurred the next day—a combined Royalist-Saʿudi attack on Yemen President Sallal's residence and a military post in the YAR capital, San'ā'. The Saʿudi Arabian delegate to the UN complained to the Secretary-General and warned that Saʿudi patience was at an end. On 28 February 1967 U Thant, whose offer of good offices was the main UN involvement, stated that he was powerless to deal with the matter. Jordan and Tunisia withdrew their recognition of the YAR. A UN General Assembly resolution of 5 December 1966 condemned the use of poison gas as contrary to international law, as well as to the policies of governments throughout the world.

The Republicans remained seriously divided during the early months of 1967. Military action was confined to sporadic Egyptian air raids on Royalist villages, in which poison gas bombs were reported to have been dropped. In March there were reports of a serious split among the Royalists. A reconciliation was reached on 10 April when a Royalist government-in-exile was formed. The crisis in May and the outbreak of war between Israel and Egypt beginning 5 June (see Case #222—**Six Day War**, in **Arab/Israel PC**) produced a transformation of the situation in Yemen: Egypt began withdrawing large numbers of troops. Yet a counteroffensive by Egyptian and Republican forces was launched in July. A Republican delegation visited Moscow to discuss Soviet military and economic aid to the YAR.

Under an agreement concluded in Khartoum between President Nasir and King Faisal on 31 August 1967, all Egyptian forces were to be withdrawn. They began their final evacuation of Yemen on 26 September, marking the termination date of the crisis.

The U.S. was marginally involved in this crisis; and the USSR continued to provide military aid to Egypt and the YAR.

(Sa'udi Arabia subsequently withdrew as well; but the civil war between Royalist and Republican Yemen simmered for another two years. An unwritten agreement was finally concluded whereby a number of Royalist leaders would be appointed to the presidential council and the government of Yemen. The YAR was officially recognized by Sa'udi Arabia, the U.K., and France in July 1970.) (See *Master Table*, pp. 706–7.)

Sources
See sources for Case #195; and *MER* 1967.

(248) North/South Yemen I

A major battle between (North) Yemen and South Yemen triggered a crisis for the two states from 26 September to 28 November 1972.

Pre-crisis
The U.K.'s withdrawal from Aden (South Yemen) in August 1967 led to the creation of the People's Democratic Republic of Yemen (hereafter, the PDRY or South Yemen). Relations between the two Yemens deteriorated in 1971 as the PDRY adopted a more radical pro-Soviet policy while the YAR established increasingly friendly relations with Sa'udi Arabia. The situation in the YAR was further complicated by rivalry between the traditionalist Fadi tribes of the northern provinces and the more progressive people of the southern provinces who looked for support to South Yemen. Irregular forces operating from Sa'udi Arabia made a series of unsuccessful raids into South Yemen between October 1970 and June 1971. A series of clashes on the border of the two Yemeni states occurred between February and May 1972. The USSR provided military aid and advisors to both sides. Each country accused the other of troop buildups along the border. During the summer of 1972 the long-standing border dispute resulted in a series of armed clashes.

Crisis
A major battle on 26 September 1972 over the border town of Qa'taba spread over a 45–75 mile front and triggered a crisis for both North and South Yemen. Fighting continued until 13 October when a cease-fire was concluded by an Arab League mission that was to provide military observers to monitor the cessation of hostilities. Nevertheless, fighting continued until 19 October when a new cease-fire agreement was reached.

A peace agreement and an agreement on unification were initialed in Cairo on 28 October by representatives of the two Yemens. Their presidents signed an agreement on unification on 28 November 1972 in Tripoli, Libya, terminating the crisis for both Yemens. Air services were resumed between North and South Yemen two days later.

Colonel Qaddhafi was reported to have taken an active part in the discussions. During the crisis Kuwait, Algeria, and Libya attempted mediation.

The UN, the U.S., and the USSR were not involved in this crisis.

(See *Master Table,* pp. 712–13.)

Sources
Abir 1974; Hassouna 1975; *MEJ* Chronology 1972.

(301) North/South Yemen II

War between North and South Yemen triggered a crisis for both from 24 February to 30 March 1979.

Pre-crisis
In the years following their 1972 crisis, relations between the Yemen Arab Republic (YAR) in the north and the People's Democratic Republic of Yemen (PDRY) in the south oscillated between statements of friendship and calls for unity, and expressions of hostility and border clashes. After the assassination of the YAR's president in June 1978 there was a sharp rise in tension between the two states, and relations with the PDRY were severed. The following month both heads of state were killed within days of each other. Accusations and counter-accusations of murder and penetration across each other's border followed. Despite *PLO* leader Yasser Arafat's attempt at mediation in September, serious border incidents continued, with both sides massing troops along the frontier. In December the YAR sent troops to restore control over some villages on the border. Localized clashes escalated into open hostility as the YAR charged the PDRY with training saboteurs, harboring foreign troops from Cuba, Ethiopia, and the USSR, and having aggressive designs. The PDRY rejected these accusations, claiming the YAR had made open declarations of war. Renewed attempts by Iraq, Kuwait, Syria, and the *PLO* to ease the tension and stop border clashes were made during the first half of February 1979.

Crisis
On 24 February 1979 North Yemen (the YAR) informed the U.S. ambassador that South Yemen (the PDRY) had launched a three-pronged attack across the border, with Soviet assistance, while the latter maintained it was successfully repulsing an attack launched by North Yemeni forces and had penetrated into the YAR capturing border towns. North Yemen called for an emergency meeting of the League of Arab States *(LAS)* to discuss South Yemen's "aggression" and appealed to the United States for arms.

Sa'udi Arabia placed its armed forces on a state of alert on the 28th. The Sa'udis, while remaining a staunch ally and supporter of North Yemen, also wished to improve their relations with the PDRY and sought to preserve the military balance in the area.

That day, too, the U.S. announced a speedup of delivery of Saʿudi-financed U.S. arms to North Yemen. This move reflected, at least in part, the profound impact of the Iranian revolution and a fear that Yemen would be the next target in a Soviet plan to dominate the region. The USSR was the main supplier of arms and weapons, directly, or indirectly through Cuba, to South Yemen.

On 2 March mediation efforts by Iraq, Syria, and Jordan succeeded in bringing about an agreement on a cease-fire to begin the next day. Nevertheless, fighting continued for two weeks after the 3 March agreement. On the 5th the *LAS* adopted a resolution calling for a cease-fire and agreed to form a follow-up committee to supervise its implementation and work toward normalizing relations between the two adversaries. A meeting in San'ā' between the chiefs of staff of both Yemens on 16 March resulted in a second cease-fire agreement. The withdrawal of YAR and PDRY troops began on the 18th and was completed the next day. The presidents of both states arrived in Kuwait on the 28th. On the 30th they announced a provisional agreement to unite their countries, terminating the crisis. (With the beginning of the unity talks after the Kuwait summit, a new atmosphere prevailed—both Yemens abstained from public accusations, and propaganda ceased immediately.)

The UN remained aloof during this crisis.

(The two Yemens united in 1990. In 1994, a full-scale war erupted between the two former independent states of (North) Yemen and South Yemen: the latter tried to secede but was not successful. It was in substance, though not in form, an international crisis in the still unresolved conflict between long-standing Yemeni adversaries.)

(See *Master Table,* pp. 720–21.)

Sources

Bidwell 1983; Bissell 1978; Garthoff 1985; *MECS* 1978–79; *MEJ* Chronology 1979; Peterson 1981, 1982; Safran 1988; Stookey 1982.

Multiregional: Protracted Conflicts

East/West

The **East/West** protracted conflict generated 21 international crises from 1918 to 1989, two in the early interwar years, all the others during the Cold War—from the end of World War II until the collapse of the Soviet bloc in 1989. The cases are as follows:

Case #1	Russian Civil War I (Siberia),	in 1918–20;
#3	**Russian Civil War II (Northern Russia),**	in 1918–19;
#106	**Kars-Ardahan,**	in 1945–46;
#111	**Turkish Straits,**	in 1946;
#112	**Greek Civil War II,**	in 1946–47;
#113	**Communism in Hungary,**	in 1947;
#114	**Truman Doctrine,**	in 1947;
#115	**Marshall Plan,**	in 1947;
#121	**Communism in Czechoslovakia,**	in 1948;
#123	**Berlin Blockade,**	in 1948–49;
#144	**Guatemala,**	in 1953–54;
#159	**Syria/Turkey Confrontation,**	in 1957;
#168	**Berlin Deadline,**	in 1958–59;
#181	**Bay of Pigs,**	in 1961;
#185	**Berlin Wall,**	in 1961;
#196	**Cuban Missiles,**	in 1962;
#233	**EC-121 Spy Plane,**	in 1969;
#239	**Cienfuegos Submarine Base,**	in 1970;
#303	**Afghanistan Invasion,**	in 1979–80;
#344	**Able Archer 83,**	in 1983;
#354	**Nicaragua MIG-21s,**	in 1984.

In addition to these direct East/West crises, the U.S. and the USSR and often other members of the two blocs were highly involved, sometimes as crisis actors, in many other international crises since the end of World War II that are classified in other protracted conflicts; for example, Case #133—**Korean War II,** in the **Korea PC;** and in two of the most important crises in the **Arab/Israel PC,** Cases #222—**Six Day War** and #255—**October–Yom Kippur War** (see *Master Table*).

As the central PC of the post–World War II era, the East/West protracted conflict spilled over to other PCs and international crises in all regions of the global system.

(1) Russian Civil War I (Siberia)

Bolshevik Russia, precursor to the Soviet Union (USSR), experienced three international crises during its civil war (1918–20). One occurred in Transcaucasia before theend of World War I and is therefore excluded from the ICB data set. Another, from May 1918 to 1 April 1920, took place in Siberia (see also **Russian Civil War II**—Case #3 below).

Pre-crisis
The Communist regime, which had attained power in Russia on 7 November 1917, opted to withdraw from World War I through a separate peace with Germany—the Treaty of Brest-Litovsk on 3 March 1918. The Western Allies were anxious to maintain an eastern front against Germany and wished to prevent the Germans from seizing large stocks of arms in Vladivostok (the Far East) and Murmansk and Archangelsk (northern Russia). In pursuit of these goals the Allies attempted to use the 40,000 troops of the Czech. Legion then in Siberia.

Crisis
The Czech. Legion, an anomalous nonstate actor *(NSA)*, refused to be disarmed by Bolshevik forces. Serious clashes between them ensued triggering a crisis for Russia in May 1918. Intermittent fighting lasted for almost two years: the Czech. Legion, fighting alongside the "Whites," acquired control of large parts of western Siberia and the Urals. However, the lack of sustained military support from the Allies led to the Czech. Legion's decision to evacuate Siberia on 1 April 1920 and to return to the recently created independent Czechoslovakia, thus ending the crisis.

Five state actors were highly involved in this crisis—Canada, France, Japan, the U.K., and the U.S. All landed troops in Siberia. However, only the Czech. Legion fought against the Bolsheviks. As in **Russian Civil War II** (see Case #3 below), Russia was victorious by default because the Czech. Legion decided to disengage without achieving its—or the Allies'—principal objective.

The League of Nations, whose Council first met on 16 January 1920, was not involved in this crisis.

(See *Master Table,* pp. 666–67.)

Sources
Bradley 1975; Jackson 1972; Kennan 1960; Ullman 1968.

(3) Russian Civil War II (Northern Russia)

For much of the period of **Russian Civil War I** in Siberia, Bolshevik Russia experienced another crisis with the Western Allies, in the Arctic region from 23 June 1918 until 27 September 1919.

Crisis

Among the wartime Allies, Canada, France, and the U.K. reacted to revolution-
ary developments in the former czarist empire and in particular to the Brest-
Litovsk treaty by landing troops in the two northern Russian ports of Murmansk
and Archangelsk beginning on 23 June 1918; the U.S. provided political support.
This multistate intervention triggered a crisis for Communist Russia which, as in
Russian Civil War I, perceived a grave threat to its political system. Russia
responded almost at once, in serious clashes with British forces and the "Whites."
Fighting continued intermittently for 15 months. The Allies had secured control
over the regions around the two northern ports but did not attempt to march on St.
Petersburg; and the Red Army lacked the power to push them into the sea. The
military stalemate and the harsh Russian winter took their toll on the morale of
Allied troops. Their evacuation was scheduled for the spring of 1919; but fighting
continued through the summer. The withdrawal of Allied forces was completed
on 27 September 1919, with Russia the victor by default, as in **Russian Civil
War I**.

There was no global organization at the time of the termination of this crisis.
(See *Master Table,* pp. 666–67.)

Sources

See sources for Case #1.

(106) Kars-Ardahan

The Kars-Ardahan crisis, the first in the East/West Cold War, lasted from 7 June
1945 to 5 April 1946. Turkey alone was a crisis actor, while the U.S., the USSR,
and the U.K. were highly involved.

Background

The territories of Kars and Ardahan are located in northeast Turkey bordering
Armenia. Following its defeat in the Russo/Turkish War, the Ottoman Empire
transferred Kars and Ardahan to Russia in 1878. They reverted to Republican
Turkey in March 1921. At the end of World War II long-standing Soviet designs
on the Turkish Straits were revived when the USSR requested a revision of its
1925 alliance with Turkey—due to changed conditions. A Soviet press campaign
was launched against Turkey.

Crisis

On 7 June 1945, at a meeting in Moscow with the Turkish ambassador, Foreign
Minister Molotov submitted a set of Soviet proposals to revise the 1936 Montreux Convention on the Straits. The demands, including the return of the Kars
and Ardahan territories, triggered a crisis for Turkey. Its ambassador informed
the Turkish government, which apprised the U.K. on 12 June. In Washington the
U.K. ambassador proposed a joint U.S.-U.K. *démarche,* to be presented before

the scheduled July Potsdam Conference; this was rejected by the U.S. at that time. Later in June and in early July information about the massing of Soviet forces on the Turkish frontier was relayed to Washington. The USSR, in exchanges with the U.S., presented its territorial demands for parts of Turkish Armenia, emphasizing the need for adequate security on the Black Sea coast, with free passage for Soviet warships and the right to close the Straits to all ships should it so desire. On 2 July Turkey responded by requesting aid from the U.K. and the U.S., emphasizing the dangerous situation in which the U.S. was being placed. This succeeded in getting Washington's agreement to bring the matter before Stalin at Potsdam.

When Churchill refused to consider Stalin's demands for bases in Turkey, Truman proposed a revision of the Montreux Convention under a three-power guarantee, to ensure free passage through the Straits for the ships of all states in peace and war. Discussion was postponed. As U.S. concern about Soviet ambitions increased, Washington decided on an unusual show of force. On 5 April 1946 the U.S. navy announced that the body of the deceased Turkish ambassador to the U.S. would be returned to Istanbul via the battleship *Missouri,* with full escort. This move, pointing to assured U.S. support, terminated the crisis for Turkey.

The situation remained stable throughout the summer until a renewal of Soviet demands triggered another, closely related crisis for Turkey in August 1946 (see **Turkish Straits**—Case #111 below).

Although the League of Nations formally continued to exist until April 1946, it was not involved in this crisis. The disputants discussed the idea of submitting this issue to the UN; but in the end the new global organization was not approached.

(See *Master Table,* pp. 686–87.)

Sources
See sources for Case #114 below.

(111) Turkish Straits

A second post–World War II crisis over the Straits, arising from renewed Soviet demands for a revision of the Montreux Convention, occurred for Turkey and the United States between 7 August and 26 October 1946.

Crisis
The crisis trigger for Turkey and the United States was a Note from the USSR on 7 August 1946, requesting a revised international regime for the Straits. Simultaneously, the Soviets began naval maneuvers in the Black Sea and a concentration of forces in the Caucasus. Turkey viewed this as additional pressure from the Soviets for bases on its territory. On 11 August Moscow broadcast the content of a series of documents allegedly found in the archives of the German foreign

office that recorded violent anti-Soviet statements by Turkey's former Premier and President Inönü. Ankara denied the authenticity of these documents two days later. The U.S. major response occurred on 20 August 1946: after meetings between President Truman and his top advisors, Washington opted for a show of force by sending army and naval forces into the area. With U.S. backing, Turkey was able to give a firm response on 22 August resisting the Soviet demands, while expressing a willingness to participate with all the original signatories in a conference to revise the Montreux Convention. Another Soviet Note followed on 24 September, milder in tone. On 9 October the United States sent a Note to the Soviet Union reaffirming its support for Turkey. The U.K. did the same.

Increased U.S. and British naval activity in the region preceded Turkey's total rejection of Soviet demands, which was contained in a Note to Moscow on 18 October. On the 26th the USSR relented: word was passed to London that, in the Soviets' opinion, a conference on the Straits at that time was premature, thereby terminating the crisis for both Turkey and the U.S. Moreover, once Soviet troops had begun to withdraw from Iran (see Case #108—**Azerbaijan,** in **Multiregional PCs: Iran/USSR**), there was a growing feeling in Turkey that the USSR would not use force to achieve its goal relating to the Straits.

The UN played no role. And violence was not used by any crisis actor. (See *Master Table,* pp. 686–87.)

Sources
See sources for Case #114; and *Foreign Relations of the United States (FRUS) 1946;* de Luca 1977.

(112) Greek Civil War II

Greece experienced an international crisis during its lengthy civil war; the crisis began on 13 November 1946 and ended on 28 February 1947.

Background
A Communist attempt to seize power in Greece in December 1944 was crushed by British forces. Many of the guerrillas escaped to Yugoslavia, Albania, or Bulgaria, all of which provided sanctuary and military support (see Case #98— **Greek Civil War I,** in **Europe: Non-PCs**). The civil war continued in the north of Greece with few lulls in the fighting.

Crisis
On 13 November 1946 a major attack was launched by Greek guerrillas at Skra. The seriousness of the situation triggered a crisis for Greece, which feared the possible effect on its political system. Aid to the Greek Communist rebels by the Communist regime in Yugoslavia made that country Greece's principal adversary.

A full-scale military operation against the rebels was launched by the Greek army on 18 November. On 3 December Greece also responded with an appeal to the United Nations Security Council. UN activity took the form of a fact-finding mission in January 1947 authorized by the Security Council. (An earlier Security Council discussion [Jan. 1946] on British forces in Greece ended without any UN action.) The mission found that infiltration across Greece's frontiers was indeed taking place. The crisis may be said to have ended on 28 February 1947, the day the U.S. government invited Greek officials to draft a letter asking for aid. Two weeks later President Truman requested Congress to provide economic and military assistance to the Athens regime (see Case #114 below).

The outcome of this specific crisis was a compromise because the conflict continued for more than two years after the termination of Greece's crisis with neighboring states aiding Greek Communist guerrillas. The Greek civil war ended on 10 July 1949 when Tito announced the closing of Yugoslavia's border to Greek guerrillas. One month later the Greek army launched an offensive and, within two weeks, the guerrillas were crushed. Prior to Tito's action the army had been unable to suppress the Greek communists, despite its military superiority.

(See *Master Table*, pp. 686–87.)

Sources
Alexander 1982; Berle 1975; Bullock 1983; Campbell and Herring 1975; Chandler 1959; Eagleton 1957; Kousoulas 1953; Kuniholm 1980; McNeil 1957; Miller 1967; O'Ballance 1966; Stavrakis 1989; Wittner 1982; Woodhouse 1976; Xydis 1963.

(113) Communism in Hungary

A crisis between the Soviet Union and Hungary began on 10 February and terminated on 1 June 1947.

Background and Pre-crisis
The Soviet army liberated Hungary from German occupation at the end of World War II and was the dominant factor in the Allied Control Commission *(ACC)* which administered the country after 1945. With Soviet support, the Hungarian Communist Party began to organize itself as a political force. In 1947 the government of Hungary was a coalition of the Smallholder, Social-Democratic, National Peasant, and Communist parties. Although the Smallholders had obtained a majority, the party was obliged by the Soviet-led *ACC* to form a coalition and grant the Communists the key post of Ministry of the Interior, thus enabling them to control the police. In December 1946 a conspiracy to overthrow the regime was uncovered, with the Secretary-General of the Smallholders Party, Bela Kovács, being implicated. An investigation by Hungarian police began.

Crisis
The trigger to the Soviet crisis was the change created by the signing of the Peace Treaty on 10 February 1947: it called for the withdrawal of occupation forces

from Hungary within six months. The Soviets perceived this to be a threat to their control of Hungary and responded on 26 February with the arrest of Kovács on charges of undermining the security of the Soviet occupation forces. This act triggered a crisis for Hungary, which viewed Kovács's arrest as a challenge to the elite and the regime. In March there was another purge of the Smallholders Party extending to members of parliament and ministers in the government. When Prime Minister Nagy was away from Hungary, on vacation in Switzerland, the Soviet authorities presented the Hungarian government with a record of the Kovács interrogation wherein Nagy was named as a fellow conspirator. When Nagy refused to return to the country for fear of arrest, he was asked to resign. This was accompanied by threats to the safety of his son, still in Hungary. Nagy decided to do so on 30 May. The termination for both crisis actors was his formal resignation on 1 June 1947. Hungarian political resistance had been broken (see Case #155—**Hungarian Uprising**, in 1956, in **Europe: Non-PCs**).

The U.S. and the U.K. asked for a three-power inquiry into Kovács's arrest. Notes with the USSR were exchanged. There was no UN involvement.

(See *Master Table,* pp. 686–87.)

Sources
Kertesz 1950; Kovrig 1970; Lahav 1976; Nagy 1948; Schoenfeld 1948; Seton-Watson 1956; Vali 1961.

(114) Truman Doctrine

An international crisis culminating in the proclamation of the Truman Doctrine lasted from 21 February to 22 May 1947. There were three crisis actors: Greece, Turkey, and the United States.

Background
Soviet demands for the transfer of Turkish territories in 1945 and 1946 deepened U.S. suspicion about USSR intentions in the eastern Mediterranean (see Cases #106 and 111 above). In Greece, civil war was raging, with support and bases for Greek Communists being supplied by Yugoslavia, Albania, and Bulgaria (see Case #112 above). Thus societal unrest and mass violence were rampant in Greece. Labor strikes erupted in the cities. And on 30 January 1946 martial law was declared. The U.K., struggling to restore economic stability at home following the massive dislocations of World War II, decided it could no longer bear the burden of military and economic aid to Greece and economic assistance to Turkey.

Crisis
The U.K. announcement on 21 February 1947 of its intention to discontinue aid to Greece and Turkey by 31 March triggered a crisis for the U.S., Greece, and Turkey. For the U.S., the issue was fear of Soviet hegemony in the eastern

Mediterranean region, while Greece and Turkey perceived a threat to their respective political regimes. Turkey felt obliged to keep its army fully mobilized in order to discourage and forestall Soviet aggression. Its major response, on 21 February, was to request aid from the U.S. Similarly, upon the advice of President Truman, Greece responded to the U.K. announcement by sending a formal Note to Washington on 27 February requesting U.S. aid. Truman asked Congress on 12 March to grant military and economic assistance to Greece and Turkey in order to offset communist threats. The crisis for all three states ended when an aid bill was signed on 22 May 1947. This marked the proclamation of the Truman Doctrine, with a U.S. offer of aid to countries threatened by the Communist bloc during the first stage of the Cold War.

There was no discussion about Turkey in the United Nations; but the Security Council established a commission to investigate Greek border violations. The report, issued in May 1947, called for an end to external assistance to Greek Communist guerrillas. A resolution to that effect, and with it further UN activity, was vetoed by the USSR.

(See *Master Table*, pp. 686–87.)

Sources
FRUS 1947, vol. 5; Acheson 1969; Berle 1975; Bisbee 1951; Bullock 1983; Chandler 1959; Clifford 1991; Donovan 1977a; Harris 1972; Howard 1974; Kennan 1967; Kilic 1959; Kuniholm 1980; Larson 1985; Leffler 1985; McCullough 1992; Millis 1951; Pogue 1987; Robinson 1963; Rusk 1990; Schoenbaum 1988; Seton-Watson 1956; Shaw 1977; Truman 1956; Vere-Hodge 1950.

(115) Marshall Plan

A crisis for the Soviet Union and Czechoslovakia over the Marshall Plan occurred between 3 and 11 July 1947.

Background
Severe winters in 1945 and 1946 and a drought in 1947 had caused great economic hardship in Czechoslovakia. The food supply was severely reduced, and all goods originally destined for domestic consumption had to be exported. Both unemployment and citizen discontent were rising rapidly. Consequently, when an invitation was issued by France and Great Britain to Czechoslovakia to attend a conference in Paris dealing with the Marshall Plan and U.S. conditions for aid, it was readily accepted and a delegation was sent.

Pre-crisis
The proposal of large-scale economic aid to Europe, in an address by U.S. Secretary of State Marshall at Harvard University on 5 June 1947, elicited a favorable response from Central and Eastern European states, notably Czechoslovakia and Poland. Soviet leaders were uncertain about U.S. motives but,

initially, were not hostile to the "Marshall Plan." In fact, they participated actively in the first Paris meeting on the plan from 26 June to 3 July.

It was during that meeting that Soviet perceptions changed. One reason was concern that Marshall Plan aid to Germany would lead to an increase in German industrial capacity, evoking memories of the havoc wreaked by an economically powerful Germany during the war. Another was a dispute over the procedure for submitting aid requests to the U.S. and its implications: the U.K. and France preferred a coordinated list for all of Europe produced by a multinational committee; the Soviets wanted to aggregate all individual requests and to submit them to Washington. Important as these issues were, their primary impact was to rekindle Soviet fears that the U.S., along with the U.K. and France, intended to use economic aid as an instrument to undermine Soviet hegemony in Central and Eastern Europe, areas where its control was tenuous barely two years after the end of World War II.

Crisis

It was this perception that triggered the USSR's Marshall Plan crisis, as evident in Molotov's volte face. The Soviet foreign minister's opening statement at the conference on 26 June was moderate. His closing speech on 3 July before his dramatic exit from the conference articulated this dramatic change: he accused the Western powers of planning to divide Europe into hostile camps; and he declared that Moscow would no longer cooperate with the Marshall Plan.

For several days, however, the Soviet attitude remained ambivalent. Thus the Czechoslovak cabinet's decision on 4 July to accept the Anglo-French invitation to participate in the next Paris meeting, scheduled for the 12th, was approved by Molotov on the 5th in a back-channel message to Prague. Czechoslovakia formally announced its acceptance of the invitation on the 7th. The next day Molotov demanded that Prague retract its acceptance.

By then Soviet skepticism, reinforced by negative assessments of U.S. motives (from the USSR's Ambassador to the United States, Novikov) and of the economic consequences (from its most influential economic planner, Varga) had turned to outright hostility. This was expressed by Stalin to a Czechoslovak government delegation, headed by Communist Party leader and Prime Minister Gottwald, along with the non-communist Ministers of Foreign Affairs and Justice, Masaryk and Dritna. On 9 July Stalin delivered an ultimatum calling upon Prague to rescind its acceptance of the invitation to participate in the Marshall Plan talks in Paris: he told the delegation that Czech. participation would be "an unfriendly act." This triggered a crisis for Czechoslovakia, which was virtually surrounded by Soviet troops. It responded the following day by compliance to Soviet wishes. The Czech. ministers in Moscow telephoned their cabinet colleagues in Prague and requested them to rescind the earlier decision to participate in the Paris meetings. The Czech. cabinet met at 4:00 A.M. and did so. The 11th of July was the termination date for both actors in the 1947 Marshall Plan crisis. There was no violence.

The UN was not involved in this crisis.

(A more far-reaching Soviet response to the threat posed by the Marshall Plan occurred after the crisis ended: at a conference of nine communist parties in Poland on 22–27 September 1947 the Communist Information Bureau *(COMINFORM)* was founded—to propagate the Soviet line internationally, through European communist parties. It was regarded in the West as a successor to the Communist (or Third) International *(COMINTERN)*, founded by Lenin in 1919 and disbanded in 1943 by Stalin as a gesture to his Western allies. At that conference its founder, Stalin aide Andrei Zhdanov, in a speech on "the International Situation," first propounded the Soviet doctrine that became paramount throughout the Cold War, namely, the division of Europe by the West into "two camps," which he traced primarily to the Marshall Plan.)

(See *Master Table,* pp. 686–87.)

Sources
FRUS 1947, vol. 3; Acheson 1969; Bullock 1983; Donovan 1977a; Hogan 1987; Kennan 1967; Kolko 1972; Korbel 1959, 1977; Leffler 1992; McCullough 1992; Parrish and Narinsky 1994; Pelling 1988; Pogue 1987; Shulman 1963; Szulc 1971a; Taubman 1982; Ulam 1973.

(121) Communism in Czechoslovakia

The Czech. regime crisis for the USSR and Czechoslovakia occurred from 13 to 25 February 1948.

Background and Pre-crisis
The 1946 elections in Czechoslovakia resulted in a coalition government in which the Communists were the largest single party. Klement Gottwald, the Communist leader, became Prime Minister, and Jan Masaryk, son of the first President, Thomas Masaryk, and a liberal belonging to no party, was appointed Foreign Minister. A campaign of intimidation against non-Communist ministers of the Czechoslovak cabinet began in the autumn of 1947. Elections were scheduled for May 1948. A preelection poll commissioned by the Ministry of the Interior pointed to a Communist Party defeat, although there were indications of genuine Czech. sentiment toward the USSR as liberator and protector against Germany. There was, as well, some popular sympathy with Soviet economic goals.

The desperate state of the national economy, increasing police malpractice, threats from the trade unions, and other political disturbances were present in Czechoslovakia in January and February 1948. In January the Czech. coalition government accused the Czech. secret police of direct cooperation with the Soviet *NKVD.* On 13 February all non-communist regional commanders of the police in Prague were suddenly retired or transferred. The cabinet ordered the Communist minister of the interior to reinstate the non-communist police. As a result of the nonimplementation of this order, 12 members of the cabinet resigned in protest.

Crisis

The Czech. cabinet resignations triggered a crisis for the USSR on 13 February 1948. The Soviets, fearing that early elections would adversely affect communist supremacy in Czechoslovakia, responded on the 19th by dispatching Deputy Foreign Minister Zorin to Prague, ostensibly to supervise an incoming shipment of Soviet wheat. He immediately called upon Czech. President Beneš suggesting that the USSR was interested in seeing Prime Minister Gottwald succeed in solving the cabinet crisis. This constituted the trigger for the Czech. crisis. The Czech. response, and the termination of the crisis for both actors, occurred on 25 February when Beneš, fearing Soviet military intervention, yielded to Zorin's and Gottwald's pressure and accepted the resignations of non-communist cabinet ministers, despite his own reluctance and demonstrations outside the president's palace.

The UN was not involved in this crisis.

(The bloodless coup enabled the Communists to retain control of Czechoslovakia. It was alleged that Soviet troops participated in the coup, directly or indirectly. On 10 March 1948 Foreign Minister Jan Masaryk was found dead—a suicide or a victim of assassination—on the ground below his apartment in the foreign ministry. Czechoslovakia maintained that the coup was an internal matter and declined a Security Council invitation on 6 April to participate in UN deliberations. A draft resolution by Argentina and Chile on 29 April calling for an inquiry into the regime changes was vetoed by the Soviet Union in the Security Council. The U.S. criticized Soviet behavior.)

(See *Master Table*, pp. 688–89.)

Sources

See sources for Case #115.

(123) Berlin Blockade

The crisis actors in the first of three international crises over Berlin were the USSR, France, the U.K., and the U.S. It began on 7 June 1948 and ended on 12 May 1949.

Background and Pre-crisis

Escalation of tension between the Western powers and the Soviet Union centered around the issue of occupied Germany. The Potsdam Agreement of 1945 divided Germany into four zones but decreed that the country was to be treated as one economic unit under the Allied Control Council *(ACC)*. The final breakdown of this agreement occurred when the Soviet representative walked out of a meeting of the Council on 20 March 1948. On 1 April the Russians temporarily restricted Western access to Berlin by the imposition of a "baby blockade." The U.K., the U.S., and France met once more in June.

Crisis

On 7 June 1948 the Western powers published the recommendations of the March 1948 London Conference, to which the Soviet Union had not been invited, to integrate their zones in Germany. This triggered a crisis for Moscow, which perceived a basic threat to its influence in Europe. The USSR responded on 24 June by blockading all Western transportation into and out of Berlin. The Soviets also cut off all electric current, coal, food, and other supplies to West Berlin.

This triggered a crisis for the U.S., the U.K., and France; the future of Germany and, with it, their influence in Europe was at stake. The response by the Western powers, on 26 June 1948, was to step up the airlift to Berlin, which had begun two months earlier, and to continue with plans for the rehabilitation of Germany as part of Western Europe. Talks to break the diplomatic deadlock began in August. By 21 March 1949 the blockade had been almost completely lifted. A full agreement was reached on 12 May, the termination date for all four crisis actors; it left Germany split into two embryonic states—the Federal Republic of Germany (FRG) and the German Democratic Republic (DDR).

Following a complaint by France, the U.K., and the U.S. in September 1948, a UN Security Council draft resolution calling for the lifting of the blockade and the resumption of talks was vetoed by the Soviet Union. A neutral commission was set up to study the currency problem, but it failed to get agreement of the Four Powers. Appeals by the UN Secretary-General and the president of the General Assembly also had no effect. Talks were held in the winter of 1949 between the Soviet and U.S. representatives to the UN. The status of Berlin catalyzed a second crisis in November 1958 (see Case #168—**Berlin Deadline** below).

(See *Master Table,* pp. 688–89.)

Sources

FRUS 1948, vol. 2, *1949;* Acheson 1969; Adomeit 1982; Balfour 1968; Bohlen 1973; Bullock 1983; Clay 1950; Davison 1958; Donovan 1977a, 1977b; Fischer 1951; Fish 1991; George and Smoke 1974; Grosser 1964; Jessup 1971, 1972; Kennan 1967; La Feber 1976; Lie 1954; McCullough 1992; Murphy 1964; Paterson 1973; Pogue 1987; Richardson 1994; Rusk 1990; Schoenbaum 1988; Shlaim 1983; Smith 1963, 1974; Sowden 1975; Tanter 1974; Truman 1956; Ulam 1971, 1974; Windsor 1963; Young 1990; Young 1968.

(144) Guatemala

Guatemala, the United States, and Honduras were engaged in a crisis with a pronounced Cold War dimension from 12 December 1953 until 29 June 1954.

Background

Agrarian reform and foreign investment control were instituted in Guatemala in 1951, with growing influence of the Communist Party. The U.S. perceived this development as a threat to its influence in Latin America.

Crisis

The Guatemala crisis was triggered on 12 December 1953 when Guatemala's government received information concerning a U.S. decision to support an anti-government "liberation" movement. The following month Guatemala responded with a decision to obtain arms from the Soviet bloc in order to arm a workers' militia. This information, confirmed to the U.S. on 10 February 1954, triggered a crisis for the U.S. Soviet arms began reaching Guatemala on 15 May and were viewed by the U.S. as a grave development. On 18 May Honduras, in the midst of a general strike causing substantial damage to its economy, perceived Guatemalan infiltration, along with rumors about arms reaching Honduran strikers via Guatemala, as a threat. Honduras responded on 25 May by recalling its ambassador to Guatemala.

After unsuccessful efforts by the U.S. to resolve the situation through conferences, negotiations, and promises to review Latin American economic problems, its major response occurred on 18 June when the U.S. proclaimed a complete embargo on arms shipments to Guatemala and backed an invasion led by Castillo Armas against the Arbenz government, then in power in Guatemala. Guatemala appealed to the Security Council and the Inter-American Peace Committee the next day for assistance, accusing Honduras (and Nicaragua) of aggression. On the 20th, the Soviets vetoed a Security Council resolution calling for no UN intervention until an investigation had been completed by the Organization of American States *(OAS)*. When the Guatemalan army refused to engage the Armas forces, Arbenz resigned, on 27 June. After an interim Diaz-led military junta stayed in control for two days, a new junta, led by Colonel Morzón, was set up on 29 June 1954 and suppressed the "Arbencista" political elite. This marked the termination date for all three crisis actors.

(The U.S.'s CIA-initiated Guatemala crisis and the overthrow of the Arbenz regime led to the longest internal war in Latin America's history. It began in 1961 and led to the death of more than 100,000—some estimates are as high as 200,000. After 35 years of civil strife, the armed forces and left-wing guerrillas signed a peace accord on 19 September 1996. This was the fifth major pact brokered by the U.N. since January 1994: the others dealt with human rights, poverty, land tenure, and war crimes. The military accord provided for a substantial reduction in the size, budget, and power of the armed forces, including the creation of a new, civilian-directed police force to take over the army's long-standing control over internal security.)

(In December 1996 the Guatemalan Government and the left-wing guerrilla coalition terminated their struggle with three pacts: a "definitive cease-fire"; an agreement on constitutional reforms and electoral procedures; and the process for reintegrating the guerrillas into Guatemalan society. The overarching peace accord was signed in Guatemala City on 29 December 1996.)

(See *Master Table,* pp. 692–93.)

Sources
Alexander 1954a, 1954b, 1957; Ball 1969; Bissell 1996; Braden 1971; Cottam 1994; Eisenhower 1963; Galich 1968; Gillin and Silvert 1956; Grant 1955; Hammond and Farrell 1975; Mecham 1961; Pike 1955; Roberts 1972; Rosenthal 1962; Schneider 1959; Shapira 1978; Silbert 1954; Slater 1967; Szulc 1971b; Taylor 1956; Toriello 1955; Whitaker 1954; Wise and Ross 1964; Ydigoras 1963.

(159) Syria/Turkey Confrontation

The three actors in this Middle East Cold War crisis were Turkey, the United States, and Syria. It began on 18 August and ended on 29 October 1957.

Background and Pre-crisis
Syria and the USSR signed a trade agreement in November 1955 and a cultural agreement in August 1956. The Syrian defense minister visited Moscow in July–early August 1957 with an extensive military shopping list, which had been accepted by the Soviets. Some armed clashes and border incidents took place between Syria and Turkey in the summer of 1957.

Crisis
On 18 August 1957 a number of changes in high-ranking positions were formalized in Syria, among them the appointment of pro-Soviet Colonel 'Afif Bizri as Chief of Staff of Syria's armed forces. This triggered a crisis for Turkey and the U.S., which feared that Syria had now moved into the Soviet camp. Turkey responded on 21 August with a series of frantic meetings with its Arab neighbors—Iraq, Jordan, Lebanon, and Saʿudi Arabia—and the deployment of troops along its border with Syria. On 7 September Washington reaffirmed the Eisenhower Doctrine, whereby the U.S. would come to the assistance of any Middle East state threatened by "international communism."

   This U.S. declaration triggered a crisis for Syria. Damascus responded the next day by announcing that it did not intend to attack any Arab state. Following Khrushchev's severe warning to Turkey, Premier Menderes replied on 21 September that Turkey had no aggressive intentions against Syria.

   Two Soviet warships that had been visiting Latakia since 21 September left the Syrian port on 2 October. On the 7th Khrushchev once again accused Turkey of planning to attack Syria; 30,000 Turkish troops were taking part in *NATO* exercises. The USSR and Syria repeated their allegation at the UN General Assembly on 16 October, specifically, that Turkey, with the support of U.S. advisors, was planning to attack Syria after Turkey's general elections on 27 October. Turkey's UN representative denied the charge.

   On 29 October 1957 Khrushchev unexpectedly appeared at a reception held at the Turkish embassy in Moscow, thereby signaling the end of Turkey's crisis and, with it, crisis termination for the other two actors as well. (This surprise move was apparently due to domestic considerations: Marshal Zhukov had been dismissed as Defense Minister, ostensibly as a consequence of his blunder in Syria, but in reality as a result of his challenge to Khrushchev's power.)

The U.S. shipped arms to Jordan. And its Sixth Fleet held maneuvers off Syria. However, its activity in the crisis was mainly political-diplomatic messages and speeches reaffirming commitments to Turkey. *NATO*'s Supreme Commander warned the USSR not to attack Turkey.

(During the last ten days of October, at Syria's request, the crisis was debated by the UN General Assembly. Syria withdrew its complaint on 1 November, a few days after Khrushchev's appearance at the Turkish embassy. By mid-November Turkish forces withdrew from Syria's border.)

(See *Master Table,* pp. 694–95.)

Sources
Eisenhower 1965; Horne 1989b; Karpat 1975; Kerr 1971; Kushner 1986; Mackintosh 1962; Macmillan 1971; *MEJ* Chronology 1957; Seale 1965; Smolansky 1974; Torrey 1964.

(168) Berlin Deadline

The crisis over the Berlin Deadline began on 27 November 1958 and lasted until 15 September 1959. The crisis actors were France, the U.K., the U.S., West Germany, East Germany, and the USSR.

Background
Since the end of World War II Berlin—and Germany as a whole—had been administered as four zones by the victorious powers: France, the U.K., the United States, and the Soviet Union. The **Berlin Blockade** crisis occurred in 1948–49 (see Case #123 above). An abortive **East German Uprising** took place in 1953 (see Case #141, in **Europe: Non-PCs**). The crises of 1956 in Poland and Hungary (see Cases #154 and 155, in **Europe: Non-PCs**) caused further apprehension in the Kremlin about the appeal of West Berlin for East Berliners and East Germans generally, offering them a haven from the rigors of socialism as practiced in the DDR. West Germany's role within *NATO* and its extensive rearmament were of primary concern to the Soviet Union.

Pre-crisis
In the summer and autumn of 1957 the USSR demonstrated new missile and rocket capabilities. In response, the U.S. proposed sending tactical nuclear weapons and intermediate-range ballistic missiles to Europe, including Germany, but under U.S. control. This was transformed into formal Western policy on 15 December, in the form of a *NATO* foreign ministers resolution. This reinforced Moscow's deep mistrust of the intentions of the U.S., the Western bloc, and West

Germany vis-à-vis East Germany and the Communist bloc generally. But Moscow did not yet manifest crisis behavior.

Moscow first tried to prevent this ominous development by calling for a nuclear-free zone in Central Europe, along with conventional force reductions and measures to prevent surprise attacks in Europe. It also announced unilateral troop reductions. The Kremlin then proposed a summit conference and threatened to deploy ballistic missiles in East Germany, Czechoslovakia, and Poland if *NATO* would not agree to the Soviet proposals. When none of the above had any effect on Western determination to rearm Germany, Khrushchev decided upon harsher measures. In a speech on 10 November 1958 he announced that the Soviet Union intended to turn over control of East Berlin, including all access routes to West Berlin, to East Germany (the German Democratic Republic or DDR), thus forcing the West to recognize and to deal with East Germany. High tension, normal in the Cold War, was approaching crisis intensity.

Crisis
Khrushchev, increasingly concerned about publicly announced U.S.-*NATO* plans to nuclearize the East/West conflict in Europe, especially the West German army, and to undermine the DDR, and under mounting pressure from East Germany's Walter Ulbricht, initiated a crisis for France, the U.K., the U.S., and West Germany by an ultimatum on 27 November 1958. A Note to the four Western ambassadors in Moscow proposed that West Berlin be demilitarized and declared a "Free City," a status that would be guaranteed by the Western powers, the Soviet Union, and, perhaps, the United Nations. If no agreement could be reached on this proposal within six months, the Soviet government would turn over to the DDR full sovereignty over East Berlin, including access routes to West Berlin. At a press conference the same day the Soviet leader denied that the six months constituted an ultimatum but stated that Moscow did indeed intend to carry out its proposals; and should the West use force against the Ulbricht regime, the USSR was committed militarily to the defense of East Germany as a Warsaw Pact ally. On 11 December the Tass news agency warned that a Western attempt to force its way into West Berlin by land, an option considered in the 1948 **Berlin Blockade** crisis (see Case #123 above), would lead to war. Foreign Minister Gromyko repeated the warning two weeks later.

After several rounds of negotiations among the three Western powers, their joint response, on 14 December 1958, was a communiqué that rejected the Soviet Note and its repudiation of USSR obligations to the Western powers to maintain the status quo in Berlin and vis-à-vis the access routes. After approval by the *NATO* Council, the formal replies of France, the U.K., and the United States were presented to Moscow on 31 December. West Germany's reply was presented on 5 January 1959.

The firm Western response triggered a crisis for both East Germany and the Soviet Union: a higher value threat—the continued viability of the DDR; a (self-imposed) time pressure, the 27 May 1959 deadline; and the distinctly higher probability of military hostilities with the West over the future status of West Berlin.

On 7 January 1959 the East German government announced its support for the Soviet proposal. On 10 January the Soviet Union responded to the reply of the Western powers by presenting a draft of a peace treaty with Germany to all countries who fought against Germany between 1939 and 1945. And on 16 February the three Western powers and West Germany sent replies with *NATO* approval, counterproposing a Foreign Ministers' Conference to deal with the problem of Germany. Moscow agreed to a Foreign Ministers' Conference for 2 March, but the proposed agenda was unacceptable to the West. The Soviet Union also demanded a summit conference for the end of April.

Further negotiations for lower and higher level conferences took place among the crisis actors. The UN Secretary-General attempted conciliation. On 19 March Khrushchev revealed his willingness to accede to a Foreign Ministers' Conference on 11 May if the agenda were limited to Berlin and a German peace treaty, implying the need for a summit meeting to discuss the larger issues of disarmament and European defense. This was made formal in Notes dated 28 March 1959. On 30 March the Soviet Union formally agreed to a May conference, in return for U.S. agreement to a summit conference the following year.

Nonetheless, the crisis escalated. Still suspicious of Soviet intentions, the U.S. began to reinforce its combat and support units in Europe, and U.S. transport planes prepared for an airlift. In May, as the deadline of the six months from 27 November approached, U.S. aircraft carriers with nuclear weapons aboard were redeployed to the Mediterranean, and marines were alerted for rapid movement to West Berlin.

An interim agreement was signed on 3 August 1959, after 25 sessions of the Foreign Ministers Conference, when President Eisenhower visited Khrushchev in Moscow. The formal agreement was signed on a return visit to Washington on 15 September, the crisis termination date for all the participants. The agreement called for the banning of all nuclear weapons and missiles from Berlin and the limiting of Anglo-French-U.S. forces in the city. Negotiations on Germany would be resumed.

(See *Master Table,* pp. 696–97.)

Sources
See sources for Case #185; and Ambrose 1984; Barraclough 1962, 1964; Embrée 1963; Harrison 1993a, 1993b; Hoopes 1973; Macmillan 1971; Richter 1994; Slusser 1978; Trachtenberg 1991; Zubok 1993.

(181) Bay of Pigs

Cuba and the United States were the adversaries in a crisis from 15 to 24 April 1961.

Background and Pre-crisis

A series of incursions into Caribbean and Central American states, in which Cuba was perceived to be involved, took place in 1959–60 (see Cases #170 and 178—**Central America/Cuba I, II, in Americas: Non-PCs**). In addition, the U.S. had become increasingly concerned about the strong ties that had developed between Cuba and the USSR. Relations between the U.S. and Cuba were strained; and the latter appealed to the Security Council at the end of 1960 charging the U.S. with plans to mount an invasion of Cuba using Cuban exiles trained in Guatemala. Diplomatic relations between the two countries were broken on 3 January 1961. In early April 1961 President Kennedy authorized an invasion of Cuba by the exiles, reasoning that, in the event of a failure, the remaining force would be able to establish guerrilla bases in the Cuban mountains. Support, or nonobjection to the invasion plans, was given to Kennedy by the CIA, the Defense Department, and the Joint Chiefs of Staff of the United States.

Crisis

On 15 April 1961 Cuban military and civilian centers were bombed by exiles flying U.S.-provided B-26 aircraft, triggering a crisis for Cuba. The U.S. crisis was triggered the same day when Cuba, at a meeting of the UN General Assembly, charged it with complicity in planning and financing the air attack. On the 17th Cuba responded with a declaration of a state of "national alert," an order to Cubans to fight, and a second appeal to the General Assembly charging the U.S. with aggression. While the United States ambassador to the UN denied the charge, the U.S. proceeded with support for the invasion on 18 April by an anti-Castro force made up of Cuban exiles.

A Note from the USSR to the U.S. on 18 April warned of a possible chain reaction to all parts of the globe arising from the invasion and reasserted Soviet support to Cuba to repel the attack. The U.S. responded that day through President Kennedy's answer to the Soviets: Kennedy emphasized that the U.S. "intends no military intervention" in Cuba, but would act to protect the hemisphere in case of military intervention by an outside force. The crisis ended for Cuba on 19 April when it defeated the invading force whose remnants were unable to escape to the mountains. It ended for the U.S. on the 24th when, reversing earlier disclaimers of U.S. involvement, the White House issued a statement by Kennedy assuming direct responsibility for the events leading to the Bay of Pigs fiasco.

A weak resolution was passed by the General Assembly calling upon all members to take action to reduce tensions.

(U.S./Cuba relations continued to deteriorate, the latter being supplied with weapons by the Soviet Union. In 1962 the much graver crisis over missiles in Cuba occurred [see Case #196 below].)

(See *Master Table,* pp. 698–99.)

Sources
See sources for Case #196; and Cuba Government 1964; Bissell 1996; Bonsal 1971; Bowles 1971; Cottam 1994; Dominguez 1978; Fontaine 1975; Johnson et al. 1964; Meyer and Szulc 1962; Mezerik 1962; Wyden 1979.

(185) Berlin Wall

The last Cold War crisis over Berlin was of direct concern to six actors: the DDR (East Germany), the USSR, France, the U.K., the FRG (West Germany), and the U.S. It began early in August and ended on 28 October 1961.

352Background
Soon after the end of World War II in Europe the U.S., the U.K., and France became parties to an uneasy agreement with the Soviet Union regarding the administration of Germany and its capital, Berlin: the Potsdam Agreement of 2 August 1945 partitioned Berlin (and Germany) into four zones of occupation; an Allied Control Council, representing the Four Powers, was to serve as an overall supervisory body. Acute crises between the Western powers and the Soviet Union occurred in 1948–49 and 1958–59 (see Cases #123—**Berlin Blockade;** and #168—**Berlin Deadline** above). (The **East German Uprising** [see Case #141, in **Europe: Non-PCs**] was an intra–Soviet-bloc crisis.)

Pre-crisis
In October 1960 the Soviet leader, Khrushchev, after canceling the Paris summit meeting with President Eisenhower over the U-2 affair, set the end of 1961 as the deadline for the signing of a German peace treaty, in the absence of which the USSR would sign a separate peace treaty with East Germany. President Kennedy's meeting with Khrushchev in Vienna on 3–4 June 1961 made no progress on Berlin. On returning to Moscow, Khrushchev repeated his ultimatum, while Kennedy announced to the American people that the U.S. would fight to defend its rights in Berlin and the freedom of West Berliners. He also called up military reserve units.

Crisis
A crisis for the DDR and the USSR crystallized at the beginning of August 1961: by that time the flow of East German refugees to the West had reached alarming proportions—100,000 during the first half of the year, including 20,000 in June, which rose to 30,000 in July. Under growing pressure from the East German leader, Walter Ulbricht, and the specter of an impending collapse of communist power in the DDR, Khrushchev, just before a Communist-bloc summit meeting in Moscow on 3–5 August, authorized Ulbricht to erect a wall around West Berlin. The implementation of this decision on 13 August was the major response to the crisis by the USSR and the DDR. It, in turn, triggered a crisis for France,

the U.K., West Germany, and the U.S. And it terminated East Germany's crisis because the wall ended the flow of refugees to the West.

West Germany responded on 16 August with a call from West Berlin's Mayor Willy Brandt to the West for effective action. An emergency session of the FRG parliament was held the next day. On the 17th and 18th the U.S., the U.K., and France responded by strengthening the Berlin garrison—1,500 U.S. troops were rushed to the city. On 22 August DDR forces announced the establishment of a no-man's land of 100 meters on each side of the Wall. West Berliners were warned to keep clear of that zone. Western forces began to patrol the area to the west while East German forces kept watch over their side.

The crisis ended for France, the U.K., and West Germany on 17 October when Khrushchev, at the Soviet 22nd Party Congress, withdrew his year-end deadline for the signing of a German peace treaty.

For the two superpowers the crisis lingered on another 11 days. A brief but ominous confrontation between U.S. and Soviet tanks from 25 to 28 October at "Checkpoint Charlie," the crossing point between the U.S. and the USSR sectors of Berlin, re-escalated the interbloc crisis. United States leaders perceived this incident as a test of U.S. resolve that was met successfully. Soviet leaders perceived it as a Western threat to penetrate the Wall and East Berlin. It was resolved by a tacit agreement between Kennedy and Khrushchev on 28 October for a parallel withdrawal of U.S. and Soviet tanks from a potentially dangerous violent clash.

Both *NATO* and the Warsaw Treaty Organization *(WTO)* were active in the crisis, each backing its own protagonists in the dispute. The UN was not involved in this crisis.

(The Western Allies and West Germany failed to demolish the Wall—that occurred spontaneously within East Germany in 1989; but they remained steadfast in maintaining their presence in Berlin. This resolve was communicated dramatically to the people of West Berlin by President Kennedy in his memorable "Ich bin ein Berliner" speech during his August 1963 visit to the city. A Four-Power agreement in 1971 stabilized the Berlin status quo for almost two decades. The conflict over Berlin remained unsolved until the reunification of East and West Germany in 1990.

The Soviet [and, after 1991, Russian] military presence in East Germany and Berlin lasted 49 years. More than half a million Russian troops and dependents were evacuated from 1991 to 1994. And the final symbolic withdrawal of the Four Powers' military contingents from Berlin occurred in August–September 1994.)

(See *Master Table,* pp. 700–701.)

Sources

Adomeit 1982; Anderson 1962; Barker 1963; Beschloss 1991; Betts 1987; Brandt 1976; Brinkley 1992; Bundy 1988; Cate 1978; Catudal 1980; Crankshaw

1966; E. L. Dulles 1972; Eisenhower 1965; Filene 1968; Garthoff 1991; Gelb 1986; George and Smoke 1974; Hilsman 1967; Horelick and Rush 1965; Horne 1989b; Khrushchev 1970; Kulski 1966; La Feber 1976; Macmillan 1972; Mc-Clelland 1968; Merritt 1968; Rusk 1990; Schick 1971; Schlesinger 1965; Schoenbaum 1988; Shapley 1993; Slusser 1973; Smith 1963; Sorensen 1965; Tanter 1974; Thomas 1962; Ulam 1974; Watt 1965; Windsor 1963; Wolfe 1970; Wyden 1989; Young 1968.

(196) Cuban Missiles

There were three crisis actors in the most ominous of all East/West crises, the United States, Cuba, and the Soviet Union. The crisis lasted from 16 October to 20 November 1962.

Pre-crisis
After the 1961 **Bay of Pigs** abortive invasion (see Case #181 above), Cuba became one of the central issues of U.S. foreign policy: the U.S. viewed Cuba as a potential source of communist-oriented subversive activities in Latin America. When the U.S. discovered the presence of Soviet military personnel in Cuba on 7 September 1962 it called up 150,000 reservists. The Soviets mobilized on the 11th. Although persistent rumors circulated concerning the deployment of Soviet missiles in Cuba, Soviet Ambassador Anatoly Dobrynin denied the charges, and Premier Khrushchev gave his personal assurances that ground-to-ground missiles would never be shipped to Cuba. On the eve of the Missile crisis Washington did not openly challenge the Soviet statements concerning the defensive character of the weapons being sent to Cuba.

Crisis
The U.S. crisis was triggered on 16 October when the CIA presented to President Kennedy photographic evidence of the presence of Soviet missiles in Cuba. The U.S. responded with a decision on the 20th to blockade all offensive military equipment en route to Cuba. When this was announced on 22 October, a crisis was triggered for Cuba and the USSR.

An urgent meeting of the UN Security Council was requested by both the U.S. and Cuba on the 22nd, and by the USSR the next day. On the 23rd as well, the Soviets accused the United States of violating the UN Charter and announced an alert of its armed forces and those of the Warsaw Pact members. That day Cuba responded by condemning the U.S. blockade and declaring its willingness to fight.

A resolution was adopted on the 23rd by the *OAS* calling for the withdrawal of the missiles from Cuba and recommending that member-states take all measures, including the use of force, to ensure that the government of Cuba would not continue to receive military material. On 24 October the Security Council adopted a resolution requesting the Secretary-General to confer with the parties:

U Thant began mediation by proposing that the Soviet Union and the United States enter into negotiations, during which period both the shipment of arms and the quarantine would be suspended.

Moscow's major response to the crisis was a letter from Khrushchev to Kennedy on 26 October offering the removal of Soviet offensive weapons from Cuba and the cessation of further shipments in exchange for an end to the U.S. quarantine and a U.S. assurance that it would not invade Cuba. The situation was exacerbated on the 27th when a U.S. U-2 surveillance plane was shot down. That day another Khrushchev letter was received in Washington offering the removal of Soviet missiles from Cuba in exchange for the removal of U.S. missiles from Turkey. U.S. mobilization and aerial reconnaissance flights were stepped up. And on the 27th President Kennedy sent the Soviet premier an acceptance of the proposals contained in the letter of 26 October while making no reference to Khrushchev's second letter of the 27th. The following day Khrushchev notified the U.S. government that he had ordered work on the missile sites in Cuba stopped. He agreed to ship the missiles back to the USSR and promised that UN observers would be allowed to verify the dismantling of the sites. At the same time he warned Washington that U-2 reconnaissance flights over Cuba must be stopped as well.

The crisis continued at a lower level of intensity for several more weeks due to Cuban President Castro's demands concerning a U.S. pledge not to invade his country. On 30 October U Thant began talks in Havana, and Kennedy agreed to lift the quarantine for the duration of the talks. When Cuba rejected UN inspection, the U.S. resumed the quarantine and air surveillance.

The Kremlin sent Deputy Premier Anastas Mikoyan to Cuba on 2 November to try to persuade Castro to allow UN inspection. When this proved unsuccessful, a U.S.-USSR agreement was reached on 7 November allowing U.S. inspection and interception of Soviet ships leaving Cuba and the photographing of the missiles. The following day the superpowers negotiated the removal of the IL-28 bombers which Castro had claimed were Cuban property. Castro's agreement was conveyed to the U.S. on 20 November 1962, which terminated the Missile crisis for all three actors. The U.S. naval quarantine was lifted immediately, but aerial surveillance continued until the agreement was completely carried out.

Three regional/security organizations were involved in this crisis—the *OAS, NATO,* and the *WTO.* Kennedy sent Dean Acheson to Paris on 23 October to brief *NATO's* Permanent Council on U.S. measures against Cuba. Involved were members of the Warsaw Pact, whose forces were put on alert, and Latin American states which offered military assistance to the U.S.

(See *Master Table,* pp. 702–3.)

Sources
Abel 1966; Allison 1971; Allyn, Blight, and Welch 1989–90; Bender 1975; Beschloss 1991; Blight and Welch 1989; Brenner and Blight 1995; Brinkley

1992; Brzezinski and Huntington 1964; Bundy 1988; Chayes 1974; Crankshaw 1966; Daniel and Hubbel 1963; Dinerstein 1976; Divine 1971; Dobrynin 1995; Draper 1965; Garthoff 1989, 1995; George 1991; George and Smoke 1974; Goldenberg 1965; Gromyko 1989; Halper 1971; Hershberg 1995; Hilsman 1967; Horelick 1964; Kennedy 1962, 1964; Kennedy 1969; Khrushchev 1970; Langley 1970; Larson 1963; Lebow and Stein 1994; Pachter 1963; Plank 1967; Rush 1970; Rusk 1990; Sagan 1985; Schlesinger 1965, 1978; Schoenbaum 1988; Shapley 1993; Sorensen 1965; Wainhouse 1966; Wohlstetter and Wohlstetter 1965; Young 1968; Zubok 1995.

(233) EC-121 Spy Plane

The United States experienced a crisis with North Korea from 15 to 26 April 1969 over the shooting down of a U.S. reconnaissance plane.

Background
The U.S. and North Korea had fought a bitter and costly war from 1950 to 1953 (see Cases #132, 133, 140—**Korean War I, II, III**, in **Korea PC**). Fifteen years later, they experienced another crisis, arising from North Korea's seizure of the U.S.S *Pueblo* and the capture of its crew in what the U.S. claimed was international waters (see Case #224—**Pueblo**, in **Korea PC**): that crisis began on 22 January 1968 but dragged on until December, less than four months before the outbreak of a new crisis between the two long-time adversaries.

Crisis
On 15 April 1969 a U.S. navy EC-121 reconnaissance plane with 31 men aboard was shot down by a North Korean aircraft over the Sea of Japan. In a radio broadcast North Korea claimed that the plane was flying deep into its territorial airspace. The U.S. countered with a statement that the plane had never left international airspace and responded with the dispatch into the Sea of Japan of Task Force 7—29 ships, including four aircraft carriers. In Washington, an ad hoc group of the National Security Council was formed to recommend to the president alternative ways to deal with the crisis. (This group was the beginning of the Washington Special Action Group *[WSAG]*, organized by National Security Advisor Henry Kissinger to assist in crisis management.)

The options presented to President Nixon ranged from diplomatic protests to strong military retaliation, for U.S. credibility and its influence as a superpower were perceived to be at stake. President Nixon ordered the resumption of reconnaissance flights accompanied by armed escorts, and the redisposition of the strong U.S. naval force into the Sea of Japan. The Soviet Union became involved early in the crisis when the Nixon administration requested Moscow's assistance, along with that of Japan and South Korea, in the search for the plane and its missing crewmen. On 22 April the USSR issued a mild protest against U.S.

activity in the Sea of Japan. The crisis ended on 26 April when the U.S. naval task force was moved from the Sea of Japan into the Yellow Sea, after no further incidents occurred.

The UN remained aloof during this crisis.

(See *Master Table,* pp. 708–9.)

Sources
Dobrynin 1995; Hersh 1983; Isaacson 1992; Kalb and Kalb 1974; Kissinger 1979; Koh 1969a; Nixon 1978; Simmons 1976; Zagoria and Zagoria 1981.

(239) Cienfuegos Submarine Base

This Cold War crisis for the United States occurred from 16 September to 23 October 1970.

Background and Pre-crisis
U-2 intelligence flights over Cuba had been conducted by the U.S. since the Missile crisis of 1962 (see Case #196 above). In 1968 a Soviet naval squadron visited Cienfuegos in Cuba. On 2 and 9 September 1970 two more Soviet naval visits took place. The Soviet Ambassador in Washington, Dobrynin, met with National Security Advisor Kissinger in August to determine U.S. intentions in light of the 1962 agreement on Cuba. In September U-2 planes picked up the first information on Soviet construction of a nuclear submarine base at Cienfuegos.

Crisis
Kissinger informed President Nixon on 16 September 1970 that U.S. intelligence flights had substantiated reports about construction of the Soviet base, the trigger for a U.S. crisis. Nixon warned Foreign Minister Gromyko that the U.S. was monitoring events carefully. On 25 September the story broke in the U.S. press. The U.S. major response, that day, was a warning from Kissinger to Dobrynin and a demand for an explanation. Dobrynin's answer, on the 27th, was that there had not been a violation of the 1962 agreement since no offensive weapons had been installed at Cienfuegos. At another meeting with Kissinger on 5 October, Dobrynin reaffirmed the validity of the 1962 agreement. Kissinger asked for a definition of a "base." On 13 October a Tass news agency communiqué denied that the Soviet Union was building a base in Cuba. Reports in the U.S. confirmed that a submarine tender had left Cienfuegos. On 22 October Gromyko, at a meeting with Nixon, reaffirmed the 1962 agreement once again. U-2 photos revealed a slowdown, and later a halt, in construction. On 23 October the U.S. crisis ended when Washington received a Soviet assurance that construction had been halted and that the Soviet naval force had left Cienfuegos.

The UN remained aloof during this crisis.

(The dispute continued until the spring of 1971, but tension decreased substantially, and the docking of Soviet submarines at other Cuban harbors was not perceived as a military threat to the United States.)

(See *Master Table,* pp. 710–11.)

Sources
Dobrynin 1995; Garthoff 1983, 1985; Gonzalez 1972; Isaacson 1992; Kalb and Kalb 1974; Kissinger 1979; Nixon 1978; Quester 1971.

(303) Afghanistan Invasion

The Soviet Union, Afghanistan, Pakistan, and the United States were enmeshed in a lengthy international crisis marking the onset of the prolonged war over Afghanistan (1979–91). The crisis lasted from mid-March 1979 until 28 February 1980.

Background and Pre-crisis
Two crucial events preceded the Afghanistan Invasion crisis and war. The last King of Afghanistan, Mohammad Zahir, was overthrown in a coup on 17 July 1973; and a republic was proclaimed by his first cousin and brother-in-law, Mohammad Daoud Khan, who had served as Prime Minister from 1953 to 1963. Daoud, in turn, along with 30 family members, was killed in a left-wing coup on 27 April 1978. This marked the end of the Mohammadzai lineage of the Durrani Pushtun, which had ruled Afghanistan for 150 years.

A revolutionary council took power in the new Democratic Republic of Afghanistan (the DRA), with three leaders representing competing factions on the left of the Afghan political system: Mohammad Taraki, leader of the People's Democratic Party of Afghanistan *(PDPA),* as President; Babrak Karmal as Vice-President; and Hafizullah Amin as Deputy Prime Minister.

From the outset the new left-wing rulers of Afghanistan relied upon the Soviet Union for funds to cover the payroll of civil servants, and for a commitment to support the new regime during a critical period in the modern history of Afghanistan. Because its coup lacked legitimacy within Afghanistan, the new ruling party, the *PDPA,* faced open rebellion during the subsequent months from a welter of antigovernment forces dominated by Muslim fundamentalists, later known as the *Mujahuddin.* The most serious challenge was the Herat Uprising in mid-March 1979. It was so serious that the *PDPA* Politburo turned to Moscow for assistance to ensure its survival.

Crisis
A crisis for the USSR was triggered by the Herat Uprising and by the *PDPA* appeal for urgent aid in mid-March 1979. Moscow decided at once to take whatever steps were deemed necessary to keep the Communists in power in Kabul. Operationally, the Soviets began a large-scale airlift to the *PDPA* regime on 26–27 March: cargo planes, light tanks, armored personnel carriers, and

helicopter gun ships. General Yepishev was sent to Kabul on 5 April; and *Pravda* articles began to blame the U.S., Pakistan, China, and Egypt for provoking and backing the Afghan rebels.

Within the *PDPA,* Taraki was replaced by Amin as the dominant figure after the Herat Uprising. However, an article in *Pravda* in mid-July clearly indicated that the Soviets were seeking a replacement for Amin. This triggered a crisis for Afghanistan. Amin then embarked on a hundred bloody days of repression to save his own position. Moscow, increasingly concerned about the ability of its client regime to survive, made the critical decision to invade Afghanistan, on 27 November 1979. Implementation began on 24 December, when troops of the 105th airborne division began to land at Kabul airport.

By 27 December Amin was dead. He was succeeded by the most loyal pro-Soviet Afghan leader, Babrak Karmal, long-time head of one of the two domi-nant *PDPA* factions, the *Parcham* (Flag) Group, formed by him in 1967 against the then-dominant *Khalq* Group. The two groups had renewed their cooperation in July 1977 to oppose the Daoud regime. But factional rivalry broke out again soon after the overthrow of Daoud and remained a constant until the collapse of the *PDPA* regime amid the withdrawal of Soviet forces from Afghanistan in 1991. The installation of Karmal as leader of Afghanistan marked the end of the USSR's and Afghanistan's initial crisis—but not the international crisis as a whole or the Afghan War; from that time on, until 1991, Afghanistan under Babrak Karmal was an appendage of the USSR in the Afghan War.

For both Pakistan and the U.S. a crisis was triggered by the Soviet invasion of Afghanistan on 24 December. An emergency meeting of the U.S.'s National Security Council was convened to cope with what President Carter termed the most serious superpower crisis of his presidency. The U.S. response took the form of a series of measures announced on 2 January 1980. The U.S. blocked the export of 17 million tons of grain to the Soviet Union, then facing a severe food shortage; stopped the sale of computers and other high tech equipment to the USSR; reduced the permissible catch by the Soviet fishing fleet in U.S. waters from 350,000 tons to 75,000 tons; delayed the opening of a Soviet consulate in New York; postponed the renegotiation of a cultural agreement with the Soviet Union, then under consideration; boycotted the Moscow Olympics in 1980; reassured the Pakistanis of U.S. security support; and visibly increased U.S./ China cooperation, including the sale of military equipment to Beijing.

That U.S. response also marks the beginning of the winding down of its Afghanistan Invasion crisis. The main reason was that, at the end of 1979, the U.S. administration and public opinion became preoccupied with the hostage crisis in Iran (see Case #309—**U.S. Hostages in Iran**, in **Middle East: Non-PCs**). Termination of the U.S.'s Afghanistan crisis is identified with a decision on 28 February 1980 to pursue a two-track policy: return to normal relations with the USSR; and continue a steady flow of arms aid, via Pakistan, to the many groups of anti-Soviet Afghan guerrillas until the Soviets withdrew from Afghanistan.

Pakistan's generals perceived the Soviet invasion as a graver threat than did the U.S., namely, the distinct possibility that the Soviets would invade Pakistan as well. For that reason and because of its geographic proximity to the USSR they responded much more cautiously than the U.S.: on 29 December 1979 Pakistan delivered a strongly worded message to Moscow condemning the invasion and calling for the immediate withdrawal of Soviet forces. At that early stage, however, Pakistan took no concrete action, unlike its later crucial role as a conduit for sustained U.S. covert operations in support of the Mujahuddin.

Washington, aware of Pakistan's sense of insecurity, especially because of the long-standing (1971) Indo-Soviet military alliance, sought to provide reassurance to General Zia, Pakistan's leader: this took the form of an offer of limited military aid, at a high level meeting with Carter's National Security Advisor, Brzezinski, in Rawalpindi on 2 February 1980. This marked the end of Pakistan's crisis.

The Soviet invasion of Afghanistan also generated concern in many states, notably Iran and the PRC. The UN Security Council and General Assembly addressed this conflict frequently, in 1979–80 and throughout the long war, which dragged on for more than a decade. So too did many regional and interregional organizations, including *ASEAN,* the European Community, *NATO,* the Non-Aligned Group, and the Islamic Conference. Frequent resolutions were passed by these organizations calling for the withdrawal of Soviet forces—but to no avail until 1991 when the Soviet Union, less than a year before its own disintegration into 15 independent states, concluded that the costs of continued occupation of Afghanistan vastly outweighed the benefits.

(See *Master Table,* pp. 720–21.)

Sources
Amer 1992; Amstutz 1986; Arnold 1985; Bradsher 1983; Brzezinski 1983; Carter 1982; Collins 1986; Cordesman and Wagner 1990, vol. 3; Dobrynin 1995; Hammond 1984; Hosmer and Wolfe 1983; Newell 1981; Nyrop and Seekins 1986; Vance 1983; Vertzberger 1982.

(344) Able Archer 83

The Soviet Union experienced a mini–nuclear crisis with the United States from 2 to 11 November 1983.

Background
Throughout the East/West protracted conflict one of the most important tasks of the intelligence services of the two superpowers was to monitor military exercises and alert procedures of the adversary. The most crucial were war games involving the planned use of nuclear weapons in both "first-strike" and retaliation scenarios.

Like the Warsaw Pact, *NATO* had conducted war games before, but its 1983 nuclear exercise, **Able Archer,** was more extensive than ever before. The Soviet misperception of the U.S.'s and *NATO*'s intentions was influenced by its image of the Reagan administration as unpredictable, with a president who was willing to use force to protect and enhance U.S. "national interests." In the 18 months before Exercise Able Archer the U.S. had dispatched forces to Lebanon (see Case #337—**War in Lebanon,** in 1982–83, in the **Arab/Israel PC**) and to Honduras to weaken the Sandinista regime in Nicaragua. It also engaged in a show of force against Libya (see Case #330—**Gulf of Syrte I,** in 1981, in **Africa: Non-PCs**). And on 25 October 1983, a week before Able Archer began, the Reagan administration launched its **Invasion of Grenada** (see Case #343, in **Americas: Non-PCs**).

Soviet mistrust and concern were also reinforced by an incident on 1 September 1983, when a Soviet fighter plane shot down a Korean airliner, KAL-007, which penetrated deep into Soviet airspace while on a flight from Alaska to Seoul; all passengers and crew were killed, including 60 Americans. This incident caused deep concern in the U.S. Reagan later wrote in his memoirs: "If anything, the KAL incident demonstrated how close the world had come to the precipice and how much we needed nuclear arms control." Given this series of events, all of which were perceived in the Soviet prism as hostile and threatening, the sudden discovery of Exercise Able Archer was interpreted as ominous by Soviet decision makers.

Crisis
On 2 November 1983 *NATO* began a military exercise code-named Able Archer. The large-scale war game embraced all *NATO* territory from Norway to Turkey between 2 and 11 November and included large amounts of arms and combat equipment. Its aim was to test nuclear release mechanisms in case of a nuclear first strike against the Soviet bloc.

Able Archer was misperceived by the USSR as preparation for, not a simulation of, a nuclear attack by the West. It therefore triggered a grave crisis for the USSR—the closest the two superpowers came to a direct nuclear confrontation since the **Cuban Missile** crisis in 1962 (see Case #196 above). During the exercise, U.S. intelligence, monitoring Soviet communications, was alarmed to hear that the USSR was expecting—and preparing for—a nuclear war in a short time. The Soviet misperception was profoundly influenced by *NATO*'s use of new communications procedures in Able Archer, which went through all alert stages, from normal to general alert.

The USSR first responded on 5 November, sending messages to the *KGB* residencies in Europe to warn of a Western surprise attack and ordering them to increase their vigilance. The same day a Politburo member, Romanov, in a public speech, described the international situation as "thoroughly white hot," a rarely used expression that indicated acute stress.

KGB agents in Germany reported on the 5th that U.S. bases had been placed on alert and that there were irregular troop movements. Moscow then sent urgent telegrams on the 8th–9th to its agents across Western Europe, warning of the

U.S.'s nuclear alert. The Soviet major response came on the 9th, when it placed its nuclear fighters on higher alert.

The U.S. was astounded by the Soviet perception and by its profound concern about an imminent nuclear threat. Nonetheless, the very high tension generated by Exercise Able Archer, a mini–Cuban Missile crisis, ended without violence or incidents between the two superpowers: with the end of *NATO*'s nuclear exercise on 11 November, the USSR's crisis terminated abruptly.

Although the incident was concealed by both sides, and little has been published since then, Able Archer seems to have had a profound effect on the East/West conflict. The day the crisis ended Reagan publicly called for the elimination of nuclear armaments in the world. The crisis also seems to have transformed Reagan's image of the "evil empire."

There was no UN involvement in this crisis.

(See *Master Table,* pp. 726–27.)

Sources
Andrew and Gordievsky 1990; Brook-Shepherd 1988; Fischer 1995; Oberdorfer 1991.

(354) Nicaragua MIG-21s

The United States and Nicaragua were engaged in a brief crisis (6–12 November 1984) over the reported dispatch of advanced fighter planes by the USSR to the pro-Soviet regime in Managua.

Background
After years of struggle against the Somoza dictatorship the left-wing Sandinista movement achieved power in 1979. Tension and mistrust between the U.S. and the Sandinista government, evident in the last year of the Carter administration, became acute when Reagan entered the White House at the beginning of 1981. By then Nicaragua had become informally aligned with the Soviet Union. The Reagan administration made it clear that it regarded the marxist regime "in America's backyard" as a threat to U.S. national security; and that it perceived the bilateral conflict with Managua as part of the Cold War with the USSR. It was in this hostile global context and an intense U.S. domestic political setting—the presidential election was due on 6 November 1984—that the MIG-21 crisis erupted.

Crisis
Reports surfaced in Washington on election day that a Soviet cargo ship, the *Bakuriani,* was en route to Nicaragua carrying MIG-21s for the Sandinista regime. To some in the newly reelected Reagan administration with a disposition to historical analogies, this was perceived as a minireplay of another, grave, superpower crisis in the Americas 22 years earlier, when Soviet ships were reported

carrying offensive missiles to a nuclear weapons base in Castro's Cuba (see Case #196—**Cuban Missiles** above).

The U.S. response, on the 7th, was to increase the number and visibility of military exercises the Pentagon was conducting in Nicaragua's neighbor, Honduras, and in general to "flex its muscles" on land and at sea in and near Central America. This show of strength and the accompanying hard-line rhetoric in Washington were perceived in Managua as signals of an imminent U.S. invasion. The specific act that triggered a crisis for Nicaragua was the pursuit by two U.S. frigates of a merchant vessel flying the Soviet flag—when the ship was already in Nicaraguan territorial waters and was about to enter the port of Corinto. Reports of violations of Nicaragua's airspace reinforced this image of hostile U.S. intent.

Nicaragua responded on the 9th by requesting an emergency meeting of the UN Security Council. Its fears and complaints of an imminent U.S. invasion were discussed, but the Council did not pass a resolution.

The crisis began to wind down the same day. Moscow announced that the *Bukuriani* was not carrying MIG-21s. U.S. officials quickly confirmed the Soviet statement. On the 12th the U.S. State Department issued a categorical statement that no preparations were being made to invade Nicaragua. This terminated the crisis for Nicaragua and the U.S., even though the Sandinista government issued an emergency communiqué the same day putting its people on "maximum alert" for a possible invasion. There was no violence in this crisis.

As noted, both superpowers were involved, the U.S. as a direct participant, the USSR passively. The UN Security Council provided a forum for debate, but no more. And the *OAS,* the regional organization of the Americas, was aloof.

(It was later reported by *Jane's Defense Weekly* that the Soviet vessel en route to Nicaragua had been carrying MIG-21s but had unloaded them in Libya before crossing the Atlantic. Still later, the International Court of Justice ruled that it did have jurisdiction in this case, and it "slapped the United States on the wrist" for its hostile acts against Nicaragua.)

(See *Master Table,* pp. 728–29.)

Sources
Clement 1985; Dobrynin 1995; Guttman 1984; Hopkins 1984, 1985; *Keesing's* 1984; *New York Times* 1984.

Greece/Turkey

There have been nine international crises in the **Greece/Turkey** protracted conflict, from 1920 to 1987, as follows.

Case #16   **Greece/Turkey War I,** in 1920;
    #18   **Greece/Turkey War II,** in 1921;
    #25   **Greece/Turkey War III,** in 1922;
   #202   **Cyprus I,** in 1963–64;

#223   **Cyprus II,** in 1967;
#257   **Cyprus III,** in 1974–75;
#272   **Aegean Sea I,** in 1976;
#349   **Aegean Sea II,** in 1984;
#376   **Aegean Sea III,** in 1987.

The **Greece/Turkey PC,** the longest in the twentieth century, remains unresolved.

General Background

The roots of the Greece/Turkey protracted conflict are embedded in a lengthy relationship of Turkish-Muslim domination. Greece was conquered in 1453 by Sultan Mohammed II and remained a part of the Ottoman Empire until 1829. Its independence resulted from a lengthy war of independence (1821–29) and the political intervention of the European powers.

Among the tangible sources of conflict was the predominantly Greek island of Cyprus. For many centuries part of the Ottoman Empire, it was occupied by U.K. forces in accord with a secret Anglo-Turkish agreement in 1878. Cyprus remained under British control until 1960 (see Case #202—**Cyprus I** below). Turkey also aspired to resume control over the island. A large Greek community in the Anatolian city of Smyrna (Izmir) was an additional source of conflict. But all of these specific foci of friction derived from a deep-rooted national, cultural, religious conflict that generated mutual hostility and distrust during the near four centuries of Turkey's harsh rule over the Greeks. As the Ottoman Empire disintegrated at the close of World War I, this protracted conflict shifted to a struggle over territory in Anatolia between these historic enemies.

Over the next 70 years their PC focused on three issues—**Smyrna** and, more generally, territory in Anatolia (see Cases #16, 18, 25 below); **Cyprus** (see Cases #202, 223, 257 below); and the resources of the **Aegean Sea** (see Cases #272, 349, 376 below).

(16) Greece/Turkey War I

The first of three interrelated post–World War I crises between these historic enemies in the eastern Mediterranean lasted from 22 June until 9 July 1920. Turkey was the sole crisis actor, with Greece as the triggering entity.

Pre-crisis
British forces occupied Constantinople (Istanbul) in March 1920 symbolizing the demise of the Ottoman Empire. On 18 April the main provisions of a draconian peace treaty were agreed upon by Allied leaders at the San Remo Conference. The Treaty of Sèvres was presented to the *Sublime Porte* (the government of the Ottoman Empire in Constantinople) on 10 June. The sultan's government was to

renounce all claims to non-Turkish territory. Hijaz, which later became part of
Saʿudi Arabia, was to be recognized as an independent state (see Case #29—
Hijaz/Najd War, in 1924–25, in **Middle East: Non-PCs**). Syria and Lebanon
were to become French protectorates (formally mandates under the aegis of the
League of Nations in 1922), Palestine, including Trans-Jordan (and Iraq soon
after), British Mandates. Smyrna was allocated to Greece for an interim period of
five years prior to a plebiscite (see Case #7—**Smyrna,** in 1919, in **Middle East:
Non-PCs**). The Dodecanese islands and Rhodes were given to Italy. And Thrace
and the remaining Aegean islands were assigned to Greece. The Straits and
Constantinople were to be internationalized, with the adjacent territory demilitarized. It was a "Carthaginian" peace.

Crisis
Concerned about the growing influence of Turkey's nationalists under Mustafa
Kemal Atatürk, the U.K. provided Greece with a green light to launch an attack
in Anatolia. Thus on 22 June 1920 Greek troops in Smyrna began a move to the
east triggering a crisis for Turkey: it was a major operation, as the Greeks crossed
four points of the Milne Line, laid down in Paris as the demarcation between
Greece and Turkey. The Turks, with few and ill-equipped troops in western
Anatolia, offered little resistance and, on Kemal's orders, retreated to the city of
Eskisehir. The Greeks were thus able to capture Bursa. They also landed another
force, which pushed south along the Sea of Marmara and recaptured Izmit. At the
same time, another Greek force occupied the major center of Adrianople (Edirne)
in Eastern Thrace.

The first Anatolian campaign was halted by Greece on 9 July 1920 in order
to prevent a dangerous dispersal of troops in the newly acquired territory over
which Greek control had not yet been consolidated. That unilateral act ended
Turkey's first crisis in the Greece/Turkey War of 1920–22.

Kemal Atatürk's nationalist forces suffered a defeat; but they scored military successes elsewhere. They also enhanced their claim to the succession to the
defunct Ottoman Empire, now a hollow shell of authority. And soon after they
achieved an important rapprochement with the Soviet regime: in a treaty of 16
March 1921 Batum was returned to Russia, with Kars and Ardahan recognized
by Moscow as part of Turkey. The latter became the focus of a crisis between
them soon after World War II (see Case #106—**Kars-Ardahan,** in the **East/
West PC**).

The U.K., as noted, was the most highly involved major power providing
military aid to the Greek advance. France was initially reticent but eventually
provided political support to Greece as well.

There was no involvement in this crisis by the newly established League of
Nations.

(The Treaty of Sèvres was imposed on the feeble Ottoman government in
Constantinople on 10 August 1920. Turkish nationalists led by Kemal Atatürk
vehemently opposed the draft, formed an alternative government, and secured

mass support for their attempt to create a new, modern, Western-type political regime [see also Case #11—**Cilician War,** in 1919–21 in **Middle East: Non-PCs**]. They rejected the treaty. And after a marked change in the balance of forces in Anatolia in 1922 in favor of Turkey [see Case #25—**Greece/Turkey War III** below], it was replaced by the less draconian Treaty of Lausanne on 24 July 1923. Turkey was still obliged to renounce all claims to the non-Turkish territories of the Ottoman Empire; but it recovered Eastern Thrace to the Maritza River, as well as some of the Aegean islands. The capitulations were abolished. Turkey was freed from reparations payments. The Straits were demilitarized; but if Turkey was at war enemy ships might be excluded. And a separate Greek/Turkish agreement provided for compulsory exchange of populations.)

(See *Master Table,* pp. 668–69.)

Sources
See sources for Case #7; and Anderson 1966; Emin 1930; Kinross 1964; Langer 1972; Smith 1973; Sonvel 1975.

(18) Greece/Turkey War II

A second—multiphase—international crisis during the Greece/Turkey War in Anatolia lasted from 6 January until 12 September 1921. Once more, Turkey was the crisis actor, Greece the triggering entity.

Pre-crisis
Greek Prime Minister Venizelos's defeat in the autumn 1920 elections and the subsequent return of exiled King Constantine intensified the dream of many Greeks for an Anatolian empire. The restoration of the old regime, however, gave France and Italy a pretext to disassociate themselves from Athens's ambitions; and they came to terms with Kemal Atatürk, leading to a withdrawal of their forces from Anatolia. Only the U.K. remained loyal to Greece. In the meantime Turkish nationalists achieved control over the stillborn Armenian state. They also concluded a military agreement with Bolshevik Russia in late April 1920 thereby securing their eastern flank, with the added benefit of potential Soviet military aid.

Crisis
Perceiving an opportunity for territorial gain in the midst of Turkey's turmoil, Greece launched a second—multiphase—campaign of the ongoing war east of Bursa on 6 January 1921. This triggered another crisis for Turkey. However, Greek forces met fierce resistance in the valley of Inönü and hurriedly retreated to Bursa four days later.

After a pause Greece resumed its offensive on 23 March, to the north of Bursa and in central Anatolia from Usak: the key goal was the Turkish nationalist stronghold of Eskisehir. The Greeks captured Afyonkarahisar and penetrated Turkish defenses near Inönü. But Turkish resistance again drove the Greeks back ending this phase on 1 April. They attacked once more on 10 July, from the south, with Eskisehir still the main target, but this time more successfully. The Turks were taken by surprise and were compelled to evacuate that strategic city in central Anatolia in late July.

The last phase of the Greek campaign in 1921 began on 13 August, this time in the direction of Ankara, the nationalist capital. Full-scale war raged for a month, until 12 September, by which time all Greek forces had been expelled to the west of the Sakarya River, Ankara's last natural defense line. Negotiations between the adversaries took place in London but played no role in crisis abatement. Violence and the balance of military power determined the outcome, which was a victory for Turkey, even though Greek forces had captured and held Eskisehir. The end of the second crisis of the Greece/Turkey War was a watershed event stopping hostilities for almost a year.

Three major powers were involved in Greece/Turkey War II. The U.K. provided political support to Greece, though less vigorously than in the first military campaign when Venizelos, whom Prime Minister Lloyd George admired, was in power in Athens. Russia provided military assistance to Turkey during the August 1920 phase of the fighting. And Italy, resentful of Greece after the **Smyrna** crisis (see Case #7, in **Middle East: Non-PCs**), was supportive of Turkey as well.

As with the other two Greece/Turkey War cases, the League of Nations was not involved in this crisis.

(See *Master Table*, pp. 668–69.)

Sources
See sources for Cases #7 and 16.

(25) Greece/Turkey War III

Greece experienced a crisis with Turkey in the last phase of their spasmodic war from 26 August to 15 September 1922.

Background
After Greece's severe defeat in the last stage of its 1921 military campaign in Anatolia the major powers initiated an armistice proposal. It was rejected by Mustafa Kemal because it did not provide for total Greek evacuation of Anatolia. The Turkish nationalists had also strengthened their position politically through a tacit alliance with France—the Andara Accord of October 1921. And Greece, facing serious economic problems at home, could not resume the war. The result was a lull in hostilities for more than 11 months.

Crisis
Turkish nationalist forces launched a surprise multipronged attack on 26 August 1922 designed to expel all Greek forces from Anatolia. This triggered a crisis for

Greece. The Turks, facing little resistance, recaptured Eskisehir, Afyon, and Dumlupinar. The Greeks were soon in full retreat. On 9 September they were compelled to relinquish the supreme prize, Smyrna (Izmir). By 15 September all Greek forces had evacuated Anatolia, marking the end of this crisis and the Greece/Turkey War of 1920–22. Turkey had won an unqualified victory; and Greece had suffered a humiliating defeat.

No other state actor was involved. The League of Nations too was inactive in this crisis.

The outcome reinforced deep-rooted mutual resentment and hostility that were further strengthened by crises over Cyprus and the Aegean Sea in the 1970s and 1980s (see Cases #202, 223, 257, 272, 349, 376 below).

(See *Master Table*, pp. 670–71.)

Sources
See sources for Cases #16 and 18; and Andreades 1930.

(202) Cyprus I

From 30 November 1963 until 10 August 1964 the historic rivals, Turkey and Greece, along with Cyprus, were direct participants in the first of several international crises over the new Mediterranean island-state.

Background
The Zurich and London Conferences of 1959 worked out arrangements for Cypriot independence, subject to the terms of a series of interrelated agreements known as the Zurich-London Accords. According to these Accords, the interests of both the Greek and Turkish communities in Cyprus were recognized and safeguarded under a republican form of government, with several provisions insuring the fair participation of both autonomous communities in legislative functions. Once Cyprus became independent, however, each community became suspicious of the other's intentions. The Turkish minority, feeling that it did not receive all of the rights granted by the constitution, made frequent use of its legislative veto power. President Makarios, who felt that effective operation of his government was being hampered, acted often without legislative approval.

Crisis
Turkey's crisis and the international crisis as a whole were triggered by a memorandum from the President of the Cypriot Republic, Archbishop Makarios, to Vice-President Kutchuk on 30 November 1963 containing 13 proposals for the amendment of the 1960 constitution which would change Cyprus into a unitary state with guarantees for the Turkish minority. The trigger for Cyprus and Greece was an announcement on 6 December by Turkish Foreign Minister Erkin, rejecting the amendment proposals as totally unacceptable. The Turkish government

also threatened to intervene in Cyprus if the constitution was altered in any way, accentuating a perception of high threat for Cyprus and Greece. Within this tense atmosphere, an incident on 21 December, when a Greek police patrol insisted on searching a Turkish car, sparked the outbreak of fighting between the Greek and Turkish communities in Nicosia, which spread quickly to other areas in Cyprus. Three days later the Greek Cypriot forces were on the verge of completely overrunning the Turkish section of the capital. On 24 December the Turkish Cypriots appealed to Turkey for assistance. Turkey replied that, if the fighting continued, it would intervene under the terms of the Treaty of Guarantee.

Turkey's major response, on 25 December, took the form of a series of non-violent military acts. Orders were given to the Turkish army contingent in Cyprus to move out of its camps and take positions controlling the road to Kyrenia. The Turkish fleet left the Istanbul area for the eastern Mediterranean. Its armed forces were put on alert. More troops were moved into areas that were in easy striking distance of Cyprus. And Turkish aircraft flew over Nicosia.

The Greek response, the same day, was an announcement that, if Turkey intervened in Cyprus, Greece would do likewise. Makarios, hoping to gain Security Council condemnation of the Zurich-London Accords, accused Turkey of interference in the internal affairs of Cyprus, at a session of the Security Council on 27 December. No resolution was passed at that time.

On 28 December Britain's Commonwealth Secretary, Duncan Sandys, met with Greek and Turkish Cypriot leaders, as well as with the ambassadors of Greece and Turkey in Cyprus. A cease-fire and the setting up of neutral zones on 29 December reduced the stress level for Turkey. The United States participated in the cease-fire talks. *NATO,* which was repeatedly warned by the USSR to keep out of the internal affairs of Cyprus, met in emergency session in Paris.

A conference in London on the Cyprus issue began on 15 January 1964. A British proposal for an international peace force composed of units from *NATO* members was ultimately accepted by Makarios if the forces were formally dispatched by—and responsible to—the UN. Soviet Premier Khrushchev protested *NATO* involvement in a letter on 7 February to the U.K., the U.S., France, Greece, and Turkey. In the middle of February a Turkish threat of intervention posed the danger of renewed fighting.

The UN Security Council convened on 14 February and adopted a resolution on 4 March to establish a UN Peacekeeping Force in Cyprus. On 13 March Turkey threatened to intervene militarily unless attacks against the Turkish community ceased immediately. The Peacekeeping Force was formed on 27 March, easing but not ending the concerns of Turkey and Greece.

Turkey's crisis escalated on 27 May 1964 when conscription orders to the Cypriot National Guard were announced for all men between the ages of 18 and 59. Despite British, Greek, and Turkish protests that the conscription bill was in violation of Cyprus's constitution, it was passed on 1 June. Greece and Turkey intensified their supply of arms to their communities on the disputed island. It was also learned that the Cyprus government was purchasing heavy arms from abroad. On 4 June, in response to the conscription bill, Turkey reaffirmed its protector role for Turkish Cypriots. However, in the face of a blunt U.S. warning the same day not to invade Cyprus, along with a threat to suspend U.S. military aid and to remain neutral if the Soviets intervened, Turkey's President Inönü announced on 5 June that it had abandoned plans to land forces in Cyprus. (Ten years later it was to do so [see Case #257—**Cyprus III** below].)

During June tension rose again with the return of Greek General Grivas to Cyprus. The Greek and Turkish prime ministers were invited to Washington for talks in late June. Proposals by U.S. special mediator Dean Acheson were rejected by Greece. During July the UN mediator held talks in Geneva with the Greek and Turkish ambassadors.

On 4 August Greek Cypriot patrol boats fired on vessels in the Turkish Cypriot harbor of Kokkina further escalating Turkey's crisis. During the next two days several Turkish Cypriot villages fell to Greek Cypriot forces, largely because of the restrictions placed upon the UN forces by Makarios. Turkey appealed to the Security Council on the 7th and warned Makarios of possible retaliation. The following day Greek Cypriot troops attacking Kokkina were bombed by the Turkish air force. On the 9th Greece issued a threat to Ankara that, if attacks did not cease within 36 hours, Greek Cypriots would be assisted with all military means at Greece's disposal. Greek planes flew over Cyprus that day. On 9 August, too, the Security Council adopted a cease-fire resolution. The *NATO* Council met as well. Makarios appealed to the USSR and received a promise of Soviet support if the island were invaded. Turkey was warned to stop its military operations. President Johnson sent urgent appeals to Cyprus, Greece, and Turkey to settle the crisis peacefully. An unconditional cease-fire was accepted by Cyprus and Turkey on 10 August 1964, ending the crisis for them and for Greece. Continuing tension escalated into crises with the same actors in 1967 and 1974 (see Cases #223 and 257 below).

(See *Master Table*, pp. 702–3.)

Sources
Ball 1982; Bitsios 1975; Black 1977; Day 1987; Denktash 1982; Ehrlich 1974; Kosut 1970; *MEJ* Chronology 1963, 1964; Miller 1967; Papandreou 1970; Salih 1978; Wiener 1980.

(223) Cyprus II

Another crisis over the Mediterranean island-state, among Turkey, Greece, and Cyprus, broke out on 15 November and ended on 4 December 1967.

Pre-crisis
The cease-fire of August 1964 was breached in 1967 in a clash between Turkish-Cypriot and Greek-Cypriot forces.

Crisis

The crisis trigger for Turkey was an attack by the Greek-Cypriot National Guard against two Turkish-Cypriot villages on 15 November 1967. Turkey responded on the 17th with a resolution by its Grand National Assembly that authorized the government to decide upon the number and destination of armed forces to be dispatched to the area to deal with any new situation that might occur and to call for General Grivas, head of the Greek forces in Cyprus, to be sent home. This constituted the crisis trigger for Cyprus and Greece.

The Greek response was to recall Grivas for consultations on 19 November. Greece also indicated that it was ready to negotiate. On 22 November UN Secretary-General U Thant sent a message to the three states urging them to avoid war. Cyprus, on 24 November, called for an urgent meeting of the Security Council, which subsequently met and discussed the situation. Discussions between Greece and Turkey took place with Cyrus Vance, former U.S. Deputy Secretary of Defense, as mediator. An agreement was reached on 1 December 1967 between Turkey and Greece. Cyprus signed on 4 December, terminating the crisis as a whole. Greece agreed to withdraw all troops from Cyprus that exceeded the number specified in the London and Zurich agreements of 1959–60. Turkey canceled large-scale preparations for an invasion of Cyprus.

(See *Master Table*, pp. 706–7.)

Sources

See sources for Case #202; and Adams and Cottrell 1968; Camp 1980; Crawshaw 1978; Denktash 1982; Duncan-Jones 1972; Foley and Scobie 1975; Markides 1977; *MER* 1967; Patrick 1976; Vanezis 1977; Volkan 1979.

(257) Cyprus III

This crisis lasted from 15 July 1974 until 24 February 1975. As in earlier crises over Cyprus, there were three actors: Cyprus, Turkey, and Greece.

Pre-crisis

The 1960 agreement among Greece, Turkey, and the U.K. for the maintenance of the status quo in Cyprus was undermined once more when a terrorist group, *EOKA-B*, advocating *enosis* (union with Greece), planned a coup against President Makarios. On 2 July 1974 in a letter to the Greek government, the president accused Greek officers in the Cypriot National Guard of plotting his assassination and demanded their removal. New policies were introduced by Cyprus to reduce their influence.

Crisis

On 15 July 1974 a military coup was engineered in Nicosia by officers from Athens, and parliamentary rule was overthrown, triggering a crisis for Cyprus.

Makarios escaped to London, and Nikos Sampson was installed as President. Heavy fighting followed. The Cypriot response, on the 19th, was an appeal to the UN Security Council and to the U.K. for assistance. The 15 July coup also triggered a crisis for Turkey, which then proceeded to mount a counterpolice action, after the military junta in Greece rejected its demand to restore Makarios as President of Cyprus. On 20 July, after rejecting pleas from the U.S., the U.K., and the UN for restraint, Turkey invaded Cyprus. Soon 40,000 Turkish troops were in control of the territory stretching from Kyrenia on the north coast to Nicosia. Fighting was extensive, and there were thousands of casualties. A crisis was triggered for Greece with the invasion on 20 July.

The superiority of the Turkish forces and the distance between Greece and Cyprus prevented a Greek counterattack: and the disastrous failure of the Greek military junta's attempt to precipitate *enosis* toppled the regime in Greece. On 23 July a civilian government was restored in Athens. Sampson resigned as President of Cyprus, and Glafkos Clerides was installed as Acting President.

Peace negotiations opened on 25 July attended by representatives from the U.K., Greece, and Turkey and an observer from the USSR. An agreement was signed on 30 July confirming a cease-fire and establishing a security zone between the Greek and Turkish forces. Talks, however, broke down on 4 August, and Turkish forces advanced to occupy the entire northern part of Cyprus, over 40 percent of the island's territory. Human rights violations against the Greek population were reported. Once Turkey had achieved its military objectives, it called for a cease-fire on 16 August, which went into effect immediately. Following a series of talks between Archbishop Makarios and Clerides during November, Makarios returned to Cyprus on 7 December 1974. In February 1975 a Turkish-Cypriot Federated State was proclaimed and, on 24 February, a Constituent Assembly for Turkish Cyprus was convened, ending the crisis for Turkey. By their failure to challenge this act, the crisis ended for Cyprus and Greece as well.

The UN played an active role in the third international crisis over Cyprus. An emergency meeting of the Security Council was held immediately after the coup on 15 July. Several resolutions were passed, calling for a cease-fire, an end to foreign military intervention in Cyprus and respect for its sovereignty, and the resumption of negotiations, as well as cooperation of the parties with UN forces. The abortive cease-fire agreements of 22 and 30 July were to come into effect under UN auspices. The UN Force in Cyprus *(UNFICYP)* supervised the cease-fire of 16 August. Talks between Acting President Clerides and the Turkish Cypriot leader, Denktash, were also held under UN auspices. On 13 December the *UNFICYP* mandate was extended for another six-month period.

The U.S., beset by the Watergate political crisis at home, was nevertheless active in efforts to mediate among the parties. Cyprus and Greece maintained that the absence of U.S. pressure on Turkey to stop military action encouraged Ankara. And when U.S. military aid to Turkey was stopped in December, relations between those two countries deteriorated. *NATO* was not active in the crisis. Greece, protesting that security organization's inability to restrain Turkey, withdrew its forces from *NATO*.

The Soviet Union made several military moves during the crisis. A Soviet task force moving toward Cyprus was reinforced at sea; and seven airborne divisions were put on alert. More than two decades later, the partition of Cyprus remained intact.

(See *Master Table*, pp. 712–13.)

Sources
See sources for Cases #202 and 223; and Callaghan 1987; Campbell 1976; Coulombis 1983; Kaplan 1981; Kissinger 1982; *MEJ* Chronology 1974, 1975; Nixon 1978; Wilson 1979.

(272) Aegean Sea I

Greece and Turkey experienced a crisis over disputed rights to Aegean Sea resources from 6 August to 25 September 1976.

Background and Pre-crisis
Greece had long claimed an exclusive right to the continental shelf off each of its Aegean islands. Turkey disputed the claim. Their protracted conflict flared up again on 15 July 1976, when Turkey's prime minister announced that a Turkish "research vessel," the *Sizmik I,* would prospect for oil in the Aegean Sea before the end of the month. On the 19th Greece threatened military retaliation if Turkey violated its jurisdiction in the Aegean. And on the 29th Greece dispatched several warships to patrol the area.

Crisis
The *Sizmik I* sailed from Canakkale on 6 August, accompanied by a Turkish minesweeper and military aircraft. This triggered a crisis for Greece, which filed a complaint with Turkey immediately. On the 12th Athens declared a state of alert for all Greek troops along the border with Turkey. Almost all of the Greek air force was moved to advanced bases. And the Greek navy began patrolling the eastern Aegean, where the Turkish vessel continued to take seismic soundings. Greece also complained to the UN Security Council and appealed to the International Court of Justice.

The Greek military response of 12 August triggered a crisis for Turkey. Both parties entered into negotiations under U.S. auspices. The Security Council passed a resolution urging negotiations; so too did the U.S. and the Soviet Union. In September the Turkish navy announced that its "research ship" would cease operations in the Aegean. On 25 September it returned to Turkish waters, termi-

nating the first of three crises on this aspect of the Greece/Turkey conflict (see Cases #349 and 376 below).
(See *Master Table*, pp. 716–17.)

Sources
Gross 1977; Robol 1977; Wilson 1979–80.

(349) Aegean Sea II

Greece experienced a two-day crisis with Turkey in the Aegean Sea from 8 to 10 March 1984.

Background
Following the first **Aegean Sea** crisis in 1976, Greece and Turkey signed an agreement in Berne, Switzerland, undertaking not to search for oil outside their territorial waters. But the boundary dispute remained unresolved. In the context of their enduring rivalry both Greece and Turkey were predisposed to perceive any act by their long-time adversary as threatening.

Crisis
The catalyst to Greece's 1984 crisis was a report from Greek intelligence that one of its warships was fired on by five Turkish destroyers in the northeast Aegean Sea on 8 March 1984. Following an emergency meeting of the Greek cabinet, Prime Minister Papandreou declared that this was the worst Turkish provocation since the massive invasion of Cyprus in 1974 (see Case #257 above). Greece responded the following day by placing its armed forces on alert and by recalling its ambassador from Ankara.

In an attempt to reduce the tension Turkey's embassy in Washington asserted the same day that Turkish warships were engaged in artillery maneuvers when a Greek warship and civilian vessel entered the firing zone. Turkey's prime minister also reported that Greece had been informed 15 days earlier of Turkey's planned naval exercise. The next day, 10 March, the Turkish stand was endorsed by the *NATO* ambassadors meeting in emergency session.

The winding down of this crisis was swifter and much less painful than earlier eruptions in the Greece/Turkey protracted conflict. On 10 March Greece announced that it had concluded Turkish warships had not intentionally fired on the Greek destroyer in the Aegean. It canceled the recall of its ambassador to Turkey and its planned military alert, thereby terminating the crisis with Turkey.

There was no UN or USSR activity in this crisis. The U.S. was involved only indirectly, through *NATO*.
(See *Master Table*, pp. 728–29.)

Sources
Keesing's 1984; *New York Times* 1984.

(376) Aegean Sea III

Greece and Turkey were enmeshed in another Aegean Sea crisis from 1 to 28 March 1987.

Pre-crisis
In January 1987 Greek Prime Minister Papandreou reiterated that the dialogue with Turkey should be based upon the status quo and offered to accept a judgment by the International Court of Justice, based upon the principle that islands have their own continental shelf. Turkey rejected the principle. And Greece rejected binding arbitration of the dispute. The situation was ripe for another crisis.

Crisis
The catalyst to Greece's crisis was an announcement by an international consortium on 1 March that its North Aegean Petroleum Company *(NAPC)* would begin prospecting for oil at the end of the month, 16 kilometers east of the island of Thassos, outside Greek territorial waters: Greece perceived Turkey's support of the *NAPC*'s plan and, therefore, a high value threat, time pressure, and a heightened likelihood of military hostilities with its historic rival. Athens declared that oil prospecting in international waters was the responsibility—and right—of the geographically contiguous state and hinted that it might take over control of the *NAPC*. This triggered a crisis for Turkey. Its deputy prime minister replied on 2 March that Turkey would do "whatever is necessary" if the *NAPC* began to prospect for oil in international waters.

In early March, too, the Turkish ship, *Piri Reis,* was sailing in the vicinity of Greek islands. Greece protested that the ship's course was provocative, while Turkey claimed that Greece was challenging a legitimate voyage. On 6 March Greece hinted again that it might take control over the *NAPC,* which was mining the oil field, Prinos, off the island of Thassos.

The crisis escalated sharply on 25 March, when Ankara authorized the Turkish Petroleum Corporation to search for oil in the Aegean Sea outside Turkish territorial waters, off the Greek islands of Lesbos, Lemnos, and Samothrace. The next day Greece warned that, if the Turkish "research vessel," *Sizmik I,* probed for oil in areas that, under international law, belonged to Greece, it would "take the necessary measures to ensure its sovereign rights." Greece generated even more stress for Turkey on the 27th when its prime minister threatened that its armed forces would "teach the Turks a very hard lesson" if Turkey continued its "aggressive acts." In a further escalatory act the same day Premier Papandreou renewed his charge that the U.S. favored Turkey in their conflict and, more important, threatened to close U.S. bases in Greece if hostilities broke out between Greece and Turkey. The U.S. was asked to suspend operations at its telecommunications base at Nea Makri, northeast of Athens.

The armed forces of Greece and Turkey were put on alert. The Secretary-General of Turkey's General Staff, Brigadier-General Ergence, warned that any Greek act to disturb the *Sizmik I* would be countered by "unhesitating retaliation." *NATO* ambassadors called on the disputants, both *NATO* members, to do everything to prevent resort to violence. And *NATO* Secretary-General Lord Carrington offered to mediate.

The crisis de-escalated abruptly. Later that day, 27 March, Prime Minister Turgut Ozol declared that Turkey would not prospect for oil outside its territorial waters unless Greece did so first. The next day Greece announced that it, too, would not explore for oil in disputed waters. And the *NAPC* announced that it had frozen plans to operate outside Greek territorial waters. Thus ended the third Aegean Sea crisis.

Neither the UN nor the USSR was involved. The U.S. was drawn in by virtue of its leadership role in *NATO* and the Western political community; but its activity was confined to political acts to help wind down the crisis between two *NATO* allies.

(Although the Greece/Turkey protracted conflict was relatively quiescent for almost a decade, it was far from resolved. This was evident from another minicrisis at the end of January 1996. The issue was sovereignty over two tiny (10 acre), uninhabited rock formations in the eastern Aegean Sea, known as Imia by Greece, and Kardak by Turkey, located four miles from the Turkish coast and 12 miles from the undisputed Greek island of Kalimnos in the Dodecanese chain. Both parties made unqualified claims of sovereignty, lodged diplomatic protests, and sent troops and warships to the islets. It was only the personal intervention of U.S. President Clinton that persuaded Greece and Turkey, nominally two *NATO* allies, to de-escalate the crisis, a replica of their two-day crisis in March 1984 (see Case #349—**Aegean Sea II** above).

(See *Master Table*, pp. 732–33.)

Sources
Keesing's 1987.

Iran/USSR

There were four international crises during the **Iran/Russia** (USSR) protracted conflict from 1920 to 1946, as follows.

Case #14   **Persian Border**, in 1920–21;
    #87   **Occupation of Iran**, in 1941–42;
    #96   **Iran–Oil Concessions**, in 1944;
   #108   **Azerbaijan**, in 1945–46.

While their relations fluctuated thereafter, the protracted conflict had come to an end.

General Background

The British and czarist Russian empires had been rivals in Central Asia for more than a century. A fundamental change was heralded by the Anglo-Russian entente of 1907. In global terms it aligned Russia with France and the U.K. against the Central Powers presaging the coalition pattern in World War I (the Triple Entente versus the Triple Alliance). In Central Asia, too, the Convention of 1907 was a turning point. Persia, a basic source of the historic rivalry—the "great game"—was divided into Russian and British spheres of influence, in the north and south, respectively, with a Persian regime in control of the central part of Iran, autonomous in domestic affairs but dependent on the two protecting powers in foreign policy. So it remained until the end of World War II.

(In addition, Russia acknowledged Britain's primacy in Afghanistan; and both empires recognized China's suzerainty over Tibet. In separate notes the same year the U.K.'s primacy in the Persian Gulf was acknowledged, with Britain indicating support for a change in the regime governing the Straits [Bosporus and Dardanelles] favorable to Russia.)

(14) Persian Border

Russia and Persia (Iran) experienced a crisis—the "Enzeli Affair"—from early May 1920 until 26 February 1921.

Background
After the collapse of the czarist empire in November 1917 the Bolshevik regime repudiated the 1907 Convention and related notes. Several efforts by Moscow to encourage Persia to establish diplomatic relations in 1918–19 failed. Britain's policy too underwent review: the foreign office favored continued British occupation of southern Persia as a bulwark against communist expansion toward the Persian Gulf; the War Office and the India Office disagreed. Lloyd George's cabinet decided in favor of withdrawal from Persia. As a result the Persian government faced an insoluble dilemma: it wished to curtail foreign, mainly British, influence but recognized that it lacked the military power to protect itself from Russian-controlled communist forces operating in Transcaucasia.

Crisis
The Bolshevik regime perceived the "White" Russian-controlled fleet in the Caspian Sea as a persistent threat to its fragile control of Transcaucasia. When in May 1920 elements of the White Russian navy withdrew to, and anchored in, Persia's Caspian port of Enzeli, Moscow perceived a graver threat, namely, secure sanctuary for a powerful force under the control of its enemy in the pro-

longed Russian civil war, a threat accentuated by the presence of hostile British troops in Enzeli. Thus on 18 May 1920 Russian naval and land forces, intent on seizing the anchored White Russian fleet, attacked and captured the Caspian seaport triggering a crisis for Persia. The British garrison in Enzeli complied with the demands of the Bolshevik commander and immediately withdrew from the town.

Persia reacted on the 19th by sending a protest note to the Secretary-General of the League of Nations claiming violation of Article 11 of the Covenant. (In fact, the Enzeli Affair was the first case submitted to the League Council by a member, as was another [Persia] Iran/USSR dispute to the UN Security Council, over Azerbaijan in January 1946 [see Case #108—**Azerbaijan** below].) Persia also asked the British government to send its troops back to Enzeli. And it attempted to respond to feelers from Moscow about diplomatic relations with the new regime in Russia.

After months of low-level talks, formal negotiations to resolve the dispute opened on 25 October 1920. The League Council discussed the matter in June 1920 but did not intervene: it informed the Persian foreign minister that it would take no action until the results of Persian/Russian negotiations were known. London refused to commit more troops to Persia. And Foreign Affairs Commissar Chicherin informed his Persian counterpart, Prince Firuz, that Soviet forces had been ordered to withdraw from Persia and that Russia wanted friendly relations with the Teheran regime.

Persian mistrust of Soviet intentions was fueled by the continued control of the northern Persian provinces of Gilan and Mazaneran on the part of communist forces in collusion with Jangali rebels, despite assurances that they had been withdrawn. Nonetheless, after lengthy negotiations Persia and Russia signed a Treaty of Friendship on 26 February 1921 terminating the Persian Border crisis: the Soviets pledged not to intervene in Persia's affairs unless a third party did so.

The U.K., the other occupying power, was militarily involved in this international crisis but passively, as noted. So too was France, whose troops aided the British contingent in Persia in 1920. The German consul in Tabriz supported a plan to oust Persia's Prime Minister, Mushir al-Dawlah. And the U.S. Minister to Persia, Caldwell, issued statements praising the Anglo-French action in Persia.

(Soviet forces remained in control of northern Persia until late October 1921. Only after their withdrawal on 15 December did the Iranian *Majlis* [national assembly] ratify the treaty.)

(See *Master Table*, pp. 668–69.)

Sources

Boulter 1928; Dexter 1967; Eudin and North 1957; Lenczowski 1949; Ramazani 1975; Rezun 1981; Sykes 1922; Temperley 1969; Ullman 1972; Walters 1952.

(87) Occupation of Iran

Iran's crisis over the Anglo-Soviet invasion of its territory began on 25 August 1941 and ended on 29 January 1942.

Background
Iran's neutrality at the onset of World War II was opposed by the U.K. and the Soviet Union because of that country's rich oil reserves and their need for strategic bases and communication routes. They particularly objected to the large number of Germans in Iran and demanded their expulsion by August 1941. Iran refused to comply, maintaining its right to control its own internal affairs.

Crisis
The Anglo-Soviet invasion on 25 August 1941 triggered a crisis for Iran, which promptly ordered its army to resist the attack. When resistance collapsed within 48 hours, Reza Shah abdicated in favor of his son Muhammad Reza. A decision was reached on 28 August at an extraordinary session of Iran's cabinet to cease fire and to continue diplomatic negotiations already in progress. Soviet troops occupied the north of the country, while the British occupied the south, joined, in 1942, by U.S. troops. Negotiations with Britain and the Soviet Union continued throughout the year. While the British assumed a more flexible position, the Soviets proceeded to increase their demands upon Iran. During the course of the negotiations Iran sought direct U.S. intervention. While the U.S. refused to participate in the talks at that time, it did serve as a mediator and was instrumental in bringing about a tripartite Treaty of Alliance signed on 29 January 1942. Under its terms, the U.K., the U.S., and the USSR undertook to respect Iran's sovereignty and to withdraw from that country within six months after the cessation of hostilities with the Axis powers. This ended Iran's crisis.

The League of Nations had ceased to exist de facto at the time of this crisis. (See *Master Table*, pp. 682–83.)

Sources
See sources for Case #108.

(96) Iran–Oil Concessions

A crisis for Iran over Soviet demands for oil concessions took place from 26 September to 9 December 1944.

Background and Pre-crisis
Contrary to the tripartite treaty of 1942, the USSR showed signs of continuing its occupation in order to keep northern Iran and its oil resources within the sphere of Soviet influence. At that time there were only two authorized oil

concessionaires in Iran: the Anglo-Iranian Oil Company in the southwest; and the Kavir-i-Khurian Company near Seronan, owned jointly by the Soviet Union and an Iranian group. The publication in August 1944 of a general Anglo-American agreement for oil concessions in the southeast aroused criticism by the communist-dominated Tudeh Party in a Majlis debate and disturbed the Soviets to the extent that they decided to revive their claims to oil concessions in northern Iran.

Crisis

A crisis for Iran was triggered on 26 September 1944 when the Soviet Assistant People's Commissar for Foreign Affairs, Kavtaradre, during a visit to Teheran, demanded oil concessions in five northern Iranian provinces. The Soviet demand was viewed by nationalist elements in Iran's government as being detrimental to Iran's national interests, as well as an infringement upon Iran's sovereignty. Iran's response was a decision to reject all (British, U.S., and Soviet) demands for oil concessions. Whereas Britain and the United States accepted the Iranian decision, the USSR rejected it and questioned the integrity of Iran's Prime Minister Sa'id. This was followed by a violent press campaign by the Tudeh Party attacking Sa'id's policies and demanding his resignation. The campaign led to mass demonstrations in Teheran and other cities against Sa'id. In Teheran, Soviet army trucks carried considerable numbers of Tudeh Party members to a demonstration in front of the Majlis, while Soviet army detachments with tanks protected the demonstrators against any counteraction by Iranian troops. The presence of Soviet troops paralyzed any activity on the part of the Iranians. Sa'id resigned on 8 November and a new government was formed by Mortera Quli Bayat. This new government was also attacked by the Tudeh Party in demonstrations and through the press. On 2 December the Majlis passed a law forbidding any minister to grant or negotiate oil concessions with foreign governments without parliamentary approval. The crisis ended when Kavtaradre and his delegation left Iran for Moscow on 9 December 1944.

Iran, which had looked toward the U.S. as a friendly third power, was disappointed that Washington did not openly oppose Soviet claims.

The League of Nations did not function in 1944.

(See *Master Table*, pp. 684–85.)

Sources

See sources for Case #108.

(108) Azerbaijan

There were four direct participants in the first major post–World War II international crisis—Iran, the U.K., the U.S., and the USSR. The Azerbaijan crisis lasted from 23 August 1945 to 9 May 1946.

Crisis

Another crisis for Iran vis-à-vis the USSR erupted on 23 August 1945 when the Tudeh Party attempted to take over the city of Tabriz, the Azerbaijani capital and the headquarters of Soviet occupation forces. Supported and protected by Soviet troops, the Tudeh occupied several government buildings and issued a manifesto demanding administrative and cultural autonomy for Azerbaijan. The following day the Iranian government sent a gendarme force to reassert central authority over the insurgents. The gendarmes, however, were denied entry to the Soviet zone of occupation. Tension eased toward the end of September when the Tudeh Party withdrew from government buildings, the Iranian governor regained his authority, and communications with Tehran were restored.

Iran's crisis escalated on 16 November 1945 with a Soviet-supported rebellion by Iran's Democratic Party for the autonomy of Azerbaijan. The Iranian government responded by sending an armed force to Tabriz on the 17th; they were, however, stopped near Qasvin by a Soviet military force.

The 16 November rebellion also triggered a crisis for the U.K., which perceived a threat to its influence in the Middle East. Britain delivered a Note to the Soviet Union on the 26th asking it to withdraw its troops from Iran by 2 March 1946. A similar Note had been sent two days earlier by the U.S. setting 1 January 1946 as the date for Soviet withdrawal. During the Moscow Conference of Foreign Ministers, on 19 December 1945, Foreign Secretary Bevin and Secretary of State Byrnes tried to settle the Iranian problem with Stalin. Bevin proposed that a joint commission of the Big Three be sent to Iran to investigate the Azerbaijan problem, but the proposal was rejected by the USSR.

Disenchanted by the outcome of the Moscow Conference and unable to do anything within northern Iran because of Soviet interference, the Iranian government, on 19 January 1946, requested a meeting of the newly created UN Security Council, alleging that Soviet interference in Iran's internal affairs would likely cause international friction. The U.K.'s major response was to introduce a resolution in the Security Council on 25 January calling for bilateral negotiations between Iran and the USSR. On the 30th the Council passed a modified resolution to that effect, which also requested the parties to inform the Council of the results. Moscow declared that direct negotiations were the best path to a settlement and rejected the Council's jurisdiction in the dispute. On 19 February Iranian Premier Qavam left for Moscow in an attempt to negotiate a solution.

During Qavam's negotiations in Moscow the deadline arrived for the evacuation of foreign troops from Iran (as stipulated in the January 1942 tripartite treaty). All U.S. troops had withdrawn by 1 January 1946; and Britain had declared that its troops would be out by the stipulated date of 2 March. By contrast, Radio Moscow announced on 1 March that, except for the northern provinces, Soviet forces would remain in other parts of Iran pending clarification of the situation. In fact, the USSR began to pour new forces into Iran: on 4 and 5

March Soviet troops and armored columns moved outward from Tabriz in three directions—toward the Turkish and Iraqi frontiers and toward Teheran.

The movement of Soviet troops in Iran, combined with an intensive Soviet diplomatic and propaganda offensive against Turkey, the main bastion against the USSR's advance into the Middle East, triggered a crisis for the United States on 4 March 1946: its global and regional influence was threatened. The U.S. responded on the 7th with a decision by Byrnes to send a sharply worded protest to Moscow and to instruct the U.S. delegation to the Security Council to take a firm position on the Iranian case. The Note, which was far stronger than any previous U.S. communication to the Soviet Union, was delivered in Moscow on 9 March and catalyzed a crisis for the USSR. It called on Moscow to explain Soviet troop movements and the continued presence of Soviet troops in Iran. The Soviet government, in a Tass news agency broadcast on 14 March, stated that Washington's report of troop movements was incorrect.

The State Department followed up its Note by declaring the same day that the U.S. would bring the dispute to the Security Council if the differences between the Soviet Union and Iran were not settled before the forthcoming Council meeting on 25 March, and if Iran itself did not raise the issue at the UN forum. In fact, on 18 March Iran did request the Security Council to place the Azerbaijan issue on its agenda. When the Soviets failed to keep the Iranian case off the Council's agenda, they attempted to postpone debate until 1 April. When this too was defeated, the Soviet delegate, Gromyko, left the Council chamber.

The strong position adopted by the U.S., the resistance of Iran, world public opinion, and the publicity of the Security Council meetings led the Soviet leadership to decide on 24 March to announce to the Council, two days later, that an agreement between the USSR and Iran had been reached and that Soviet troops would be withdrawn from Iran within 5–6 weeks if no unforeseen circumstances occurred. After that announcement the Iranian case was temporarily removed from the Security Council agenda. On 4 April 1946 Prime Minister Qavam concluded an agreement with the Soviets that declared that Iranian territory would be evacuated within six weeks of 24 March, that a joint Soviet-Iranian oil company would be established (to be ratified by the Majlis within seven months after 24 March), and that Moscow recognized Azerbaijan as an internal problem of Iran. Finally, on 9 May 1946, Soviet troops left Iran, terminating the Azerbaijan crisis for Iran, the U.K., the U.S., and the USSR.

(See *Master Table*, pp. 686–87.)

Sources

Foreign Relations of the United States (FRUS) 1946; Acheson 1969; Bullock 1983; Byrnes 1947; Campbell and Herring 1975; Chubin and Zabih 1974; Cottam 1988; Donovan 1977a; Eagleton 1957; Goodspeed 1967; Hamilton 1962; Hess 1974; Kuniholm 1980; Lenczowski 1949, 1962, 1978; Lie 1954; Lytle

1987; Ramazani 1964, 1975; Rossow 1956; Shwadran 1973; Truman 1956; Werth 1964; Zabih 1966.

Taiwan Strait

There were four international crises in the protracted conflict over the **Taiwan Strait** from 1948 to 1962, as follows.

Case #125 **China Civil War,** in 1948–49;
#146 **Taiwan Strait I,** in 1954–55;
#166 **Taiwan Strait II,** in 1958;
#192 **Taiwan Strait III,** in 1962.

General Background

The island of Taiwan (Formosa), with an area of 36 thousand square kilometers and a population of 20+ million, is separated from mainland China by the Taiwan Strait. For much of Taiwan's modern history China was the dominant power: it wrested the island from Dutch control in 1662 and ruled Taiwan until 1895. Following its defeat in the Sino/Japanese war (1894–95), China, in the Treaty of Shimonoseki (1895), ceded to Japan the island of Formosa (along with the Pescadores, Hainan, and the Liaotung Peninsula, and recognized Korea's independence).

During World War II the Cairo Declaration of 1943 provided that Japan must vacate all territories that it occupied since 1894. The return of Taiwan to the Republic of China was specified in the Potsdam Agreement of July 1945. China regained sovereignty over Taiwan (along with Inner Mongolia, Manchuria, and Hainan) in September 1945, a week after Japan's surrender at the end of the war.

Chiang Kai-shek's Nationalist (*Kuomintang* or *KMT*) government emerged from World War II in disarray due to the resumption of the civil war with the Chinese Communists, combined with severe inflation and economic difficulties. President Roosevelt, and after him President Truman, advocated political unification of the Nationalist government and the Communists. Accordingly, Truman sent George Marshall to China to mediate between the two conflicting parties, while giving active U.S. assistance to the Nationalists. The mediation mission, which lasted for 13 months, ended in failure, despite a cease-fire in 1946, when fighting resumed in Manchuria. U.S. pressure on Kuomintang leaders to bring the Communists into the Chinese government took the form of an arms embargo on China. By January 1947 Marshall concluded that there was no hope of accomplishing Chinese unification. He left China to assume the post of Secretary of State. Partial withdrawal of U.S. soldiers began.

As the situation in China deteriorated during April and May 1947, the U.S. decided to lift the arms embargo on 26 May; and the process of partial withdrawal came to an end. In an attempt to reappraise the U.S.'s China policy, a fact-finding mission, headed by General Wedemeyer, was sent to China. The Wedemeyer Report recommended a five-year program of large-scale U.S. economic aid to be administered by the Nationalist government with U.S. guidance, along with a U.S. supervisory force of 10,000 soldiers. Secretary of State Marshall, determined not to adopt any measure of military aid that might lead to U.S. intervention in China, shelved the report. On 18 February 1948 Truman signed a Foreign Assistance Act granting economic aid to China.

The military campaigns in mainland China during 1948 were of decisive importance. The Communists attacked in Manchuria and in Shantung and occupied Supingchieh, the gateway to Changchun.

(125) China Civil War

The international crisis resulting from the civil war in China involved Nationalist China and the United States as crisis actors from 23 September 1948 to 8 December 1949.

Crisis

On 23 September 1948 the strongly fortified city of Tsinan, Shantung's capital, fell to the Chinese Communists, triggering a crisis for the United States: the city was lost after the defection of an entire division of Nationalist soldiers. For the United States the Nationalist setback posed in increasingly acute form the threat of loss of U.S. influence in China and the question of granting large-scale military aid, including the eventual use of U.S. armed forces, to a government that had lost the confidence of its own troops and its own people. By the autumn of 1948 the whole of northeast China had fallen into Communist hands.

U.S. decision makers undertook an extensive policy review in October, and on the 26th the U.S. responded to the crisis with a decision not to commit military aid to Nationalist China, despite the near-certain consequences of Communist victory in the civil war. This decision ended the crisis for the United States.

Early in January 1949 Nationalist military strength was broken. Throughout that year the Communists gradually achieved control over the mainland. In the spring Nationalist forces began retreating to Taiwan.

The proclamation of the People's Republic of China (PRC) on 1 October 1949 expanded Nationalist China's internal crisis to international proportions. The response and termination occurred on the same date, 8 December 1949, when the Nationalists formally established the Republic of China (ROC) on the island of Taiwan, thereby tacitly acknowledging the PRC as ruler of mainland China. The United States backed Nationalist claims to be the sole representative of the people of China at the United Nations until 1971.

On 8 December 1949 the United Nations General Assembly passed a resolution calling on all states "to refrain from (a) seeking to acquire spheres of influence or to create foreign controlled regimes within the territory of China; (b) seeking to obtain special rights or privileges within the territory of China." This ended the crisis for China.

The Soviet involvement was political; substantial Soviet forces had been withdrawn from China by October 1948.

Three subsequent crises erupted over the Taiwan Strait and the larger issue of the unresolved China civil war, in 1954, 1958, and 1962 (see Cases #146, 166, and 192 below).

(See *Master Table,* pp. 688–89.)

Sources
U.S. Department of State 1967; Bernstein and Matusow 1966; Bianco 1971; Borg and Heinrichs 1980; Chang 1990; Chiang Kai-shek 1957; Donovan 1977b; Fairbank 1972, 1976; Kalicki 1975; Latourette 1952; Pogue 1987; Schurmann and Schell 1967–74; Truman 1956; Tsou 1963.

(146) Taiwan Strait I

There were three crisis actors in the first international crisis over the Taiwan Strait: the People's Republic of China (PRC), Nationalist China (Republic of China [ROC] or Taiwan), and the United States. The crisis began in early August 1954 and ended on 23 April 1955.

Background
The conflict over the Taiwan Strait began in 1949 after the Communist victory in China's civil war and the split between the PRC and the Nationalists on Taiwan (see Case #125 above). Neither side was content with this arrangement: each aimed at reunification, with the PRC advocating a Communist regime while Chiang Kai-shek wished to see the Mao Tse-tung–led government removed from the mainland.

Crisis
A crisis for the PRC was triggered in early August 1954 by fear of the impending creation of the Southeast Asia Treaty Organization *(SEATO).* It was formally established on 8 September. Zhou Enlai denounced *SEATO* in a speech on 11 August in which he emphasized the justice of any Communist attempt to reunify China. On 3 September 1954 the PRC bombarded the Nationalist-held offshore islands of Quemoy and Matsu. This triggered a crisis for the United States and Taiwan. Nationalist China's response, on 7 September, took the form of air strikes against the Chinese mainland. On the 12th the U.S. responded by deciding to send the Seventh Fleet to the area and appealing to the UN. On 2 December 1954 a defense treaty was signed between the U.S. and Taiwan, by which time the PRC had ceased the bombardment, ending Taiwan's first crisis.

The signing of a U.S.-Taiwan Defense Pact on 2 December 1954 escalated the crisis for the PRC. Its response, on 10 January 1955, was heavy bombardment of the Tachen Islands. This, in turn, triggered a second crisis for Taiwan. The latter responded some time in January 1955 by returning fire and staging battles on the three islands of Tachen, Quemoy, and Matsu. Taiwan subsequently evacuated the Tachen Islands. The U.S. responded to the escalation of the crisis with a request by President Eisenhower to Congress on 24 January to grant him a free hand in controlling the situation in the Taiwan area. The termination of Taiwan's second crisis occurred on 25 March 1955, after completion of the fortification of Quemoy and Matsu, with U.S. help. The crisis for the U.S. and the PRC ended on 23 April 1955 when Zhou Enlai offered to negotiate in the face of an increasing U.S. commitment and the reduced prospects for a successful PRC invasion. Taiwan did not participate in the talks.

During the course of the first Taiwan Strait crisis there was a shift from the plane of Communist-Nationalist confrontation to primary interaction between the PRC and the U.S. United States strategy was directed at building an alliance network of anti-communist states. The Secretary-General of the UN conducted talks, as did the Security Council, but no resolution was passed; and the UN had no effect on the abatement of the crisis. Although the formation of *SEATO* was the trigger to the crisis, that regional organization was entirely inactive during the crisis. The USSR was marginally involved during this crisis.

In 1958 the same three states experienced another crisis over the issue of Quemoy and Matsu (see Case #166 below).

(See *Master Table*, pp. 692–93.)

Sources
Foreign Relations of the United States (FRUS) 1952–54, 1955; Brands 1988; Branyan and Larsen 1971; Bueler 1971; Chang 1988, 1990; Chiang 1957; Clubb 1960; Day 1987; F. R. Dulles 1972; Eisenhower 1963; George and Smoke 1974; Guang 1992; Gurtov and Hwang 1980; Halperin and Tsou 1966; Hsieh 1962; Huang et al. 1992; Kalicki 1975; MacFarquhar 1972; Rushkoff 1981; Stolper 1985; Tsou 1958.

(166) Taiwan Strait II

A second international crisis in the Taiwan Strait, from 17 July to 23 October 1958, comprised three actors: Taiwan, the United States, and the People's Republic of China.

Background
East Asia again became a theater of armed conflict between communist and anticommunist forces in 1958, breaking an informal truce that prevailed in the region since 1955 (see Case #146 above). The unresolved issue of "one China" erupted once more, at the same time as a new crisis in the Middle East, when U.S. forces landed in Lebanon, British forces entered Jordan, and the Iraq monarchy was overthrown (see Case #165—**Iraq-Lebanon Upheaval,** in **Middle East: Non-**

PCs). The PRC was critical of Soviet silence on Middle East and East Asian events and decided to test Soviet and U.S. resolve by building up its forces in the coastal areas opposite the offshore islands of Quemoy and Matsu.

Crisis

By 17 July 1958 the massing of mainland China's military forces near the offshore islands had triggered a crisis for Taiwan. Khrushchev arrived in Beijing for conversations with Mao from 31 July to 3 August. On the 23rd of August, when the PRC began bombarding Quemoy and Matsu, a crisis was triggered for the United States. Taiwan responded that day by returning fire. The U.S. responded two days later by threatening to move into the area with the reinforced Seventh Fleet, a decision implemented with some restriction on the 27th. This, in turn, triggered a crisis for the PRC.

Between 2 and 4 September the U.S. administration met to frame a detailed policy position. On the 4th the PRC responded to the crisis by announcing the extension of its territorial waters to 12 miles offshore, thereby blockading Quemoy and Matsu. This threat to U.S. ships supplying the islands was promptly rejected by the U.S. in a statement by Secretary of State Dulles, who strongly implied that the U.S. would intervene if Quemoy were invaded, and that such an intervention might involve the use of nuclear weapons. Zhou Enlai suggested that ambassadorial talks between the PRC and the U.S. be resumed.

On 7 September Khrushchev sent a letter to Eisenhower in which he warned that "an attack on the PRC is an attack on the Soviet Union." Nevertheless, one week later it was clear that the Soviets intended to remain aloof from the crisis. Talks between the PRC and the United States were resumed in Warsaw on 14 September, ending the crisis for the latter. On the 30th the crisis ended for the PRC when Secretary Dulles declared that the U.S. favored the evacuation of Nationalist Chinese forces from the offshore islands if the PRC would agree to a cease-fire. Taiwan's crisis termination date was 23 October, when Chiang and Dulles issued a joint communiqué: this constituted a tacit understanding between Taiwan and the PRC, for there was a clear indication that an invasion of the mainland would not be supported by the U.S. Washington recommended a redefinition of Nationalist China's objectives.

The Soviet position was clarified in a Tass news agency statement on 5 October that excluded military support for Beijing's efforts to "liberate" Taiwan. However, while publicly disavowing Soviet military intervention in the crisis, Moscow extended covert aid in support of the PRC.

The General Assembly held discussions, but no resolution was passed. (See *Master Table,* pp. 696–97.)

Sources

See sources for Case #146; and Bundy 1988; Eisenhower 1965; Halperin 1966; Segal 1985; Thomas 1962; Whiting 1975b; Xiaobing et al. 1995–96; Zubok 1995–96.

(192) Taiwan Strait III

The PRC was the sole crisis actor. This crisis lasted from 22 April to 27 June 1962.

Pre-crisis
During the three years before this crisis there had been agricultural disasters and a significant shortage in consumer goods on the Chinese mainland. There was a mass exodus of Chinese across the borders; from Sinkiang into Soviet Central Asia and from Kwangtung into Hong Kong. In addition, during the period preceding the crisis there was tension along China's border with India (see Case #194—**China/India Border II**, in 1962–63, in **Asia: Non-PCs**). Beginning in January 1962, a series of bellicose statements by senior Nationalist officials alerted decision makers in the PRC that Chiang Kai-shek might be preparing an invasion of the mainland.

Crisis
The trigger for the PRC's crisis was an Easter message by Chiang Kai-shek to his people on 22 April 1962, which contained threats to invade the mainland. This was followed by a conscription of additional manpower to Taiwan's army. On 1 May a special new tax was imposed in order to support the "return to the mainland." Further, from 22 May more Nationalist statements were issued indicating plans for an invasion. On 29 May the PRC's Foreign Minister, Ch'en Yi, divulged the existence of specially trained agents who, together with anti-communist elements on the mainland, would join forces if a decision were made by Chiang Kai-shek to drop paratroops into Communist China. Ch'en Yi intimated that there would be U.S. support for this venture.

Alarmed by the possibility of U.S. intervention, the response of the PRC was a considerable troop buildup in Fukien Province beginning on 10 June. On 23 June a meeting was held between U.S. and PRC ambassadors in Warsaw, where U.S. Ambassador John Cabot denied that the U.S. would actively support a Taiwan invasion. On 27 June President Kennedy, at a news conference, reiterated U.S. policy: the U.S. would defend Taiwan against a PRC threat, but its policy was peaceful and defensive only. This was an indirect assurance that the U.S. would not support a Taiwanese attempt to invade the mainland. That statement marked a unilateral conclusion to the third **Taiwan** crisis.

Neither the UN nor the USSR was involved in this crisis.

(There was no full-scale international crisis between the PRC and Taiwan for more than three decades. However, the protracted conflict between the two China regimes erupted periodically—usually in the form of a Beijing-perceived threat from Taipei, supported by the U.S., to thwart the PRC's persistent claim to sovereignty over Taiwan, by reactivating the "Two Chinas" policy, renounced by the U.S. in 1971. The most recent crisis [**Taiwan Strait IV** in this PC] was triggered by a U.S.-permitted private visit of Taiwan President Lee Teng-hui to the United States in May 1995. China responded to this hostile act by doing the following: withdrawing its ambassador from Washington for five months, suspending high-level official visits, and holding show-of-force naval maneuvers near Taiwan in the summer and autumn of 1995. The PRC renewed its military pressure on Taiwan in February–March 1996, more intensely, and with even higher visibility; but, as in the summer of 1995, there was no violence between the adversaries. All these acts signaled—to Taiwan and the U.S.—the PRC's determination to reintegrate Taiwan into China, preferably by negotiation, but by force if necessary.)

(See *Master Table*, pp. 700–701.)

Sources
Brugger 1977; Cheng 1972; Hilsman 1967; Hinton 1966; Howe 1971; Kennedy 1964; Leng and Chiu 1972; Mendel 1970; Segal 1985; Simmonds 1970; Yahuda 1978.

World War II

World War II, the most intense of the long-war protracted conflicts since 1918, generated 24 international crises, all but the first intrawar crises (IWCs), as follows.

Case	#74	**Entry into World War II,** in 1939;
	#77	**Invasion of Scandinavia,** in 1940;
	#78	**Fall of Western Europe,** in 1940;
	#79	**Closure of Burma Road,** in 1940;
	#81	**Battle of Britain,** in 1940;
	#82	**East Africa Campaign,** in 1940–41;
	#83	**Balkan Invasions,** in 1940–41;
	#84	**Mid-East Campaign,** in 1941;
	#85	**Barbarossa,** in 1941;
	#88	**Pearl Harbor,** in 1941–42;
	#89	**Stalingrad,** in 1942–43;
	#90	**El Alamein,** in 1942–43;
	#91	**Fall of Italy,** in 1943;
	#92	**German Occupation of Hungary,** in 1944;
	#93	**Soviet Occupation of East Europe,** in 1944–45;
	#94	**D-Day,** in 1944–45;
	#95	**Fall of Saipan,** in 1944;
	#97	**Leyte Campaign,** in 1944;
	#99	**Luzon,** in 1945;
	#100	**Final Soviet Offensive,** in 1945;
	#101	**Iwo Jima,** in 1945;
	#103	**Okinawa,** in 1945;

#105   **French Forces/Syria**, in 1945;
#107   **Hiroshima-Nagasaki**, in 1945.

General Background

World War II and its myriad of international crises can be traced to the outcome of World War I, in particular, Germany's defeat, the "Carthaginian peace" imposed by the Versailles Treaty in 1919, and Nazi Germany's policy of revanchism in the 1930s.

The reascent of Germany to great power status from 1933 to 1939 was the pivotal development of the interwar period. Nazi policy was the catalyst to the growth of alliances and counteralliances in Europe, as well as the remilitarization of the European powers. Its insatiable expansionism led, in a period of six years, to the outbreak of the second cataclysmic war in the twentieth century, global in scope, massive in casualties, and revolutionary in its consequences.

The path to World War II is strewn with international crises, as the powers and their clients, beset by uncertainty and instability, sought to protect and enhance their "national interests." For Germany under Hitler this was equated with hegemony in Europe, including territorial aggrandizement in Central and Eastern Europe, wherever and whenever opportunities for Germany's achievement of *lebensraum* (living space) emerged. This is evident in the notable international crises culminating in the outbreak of World War II: Cases #45—**Austria Putsch**, in 1934; #51—**Remilitarization of the Rhineland**, in 1936; #60—**Anschluss**, in 1938; #62—**Czech. May Crisis**, in 1938; #64—**Munich**, in 1938; #68—**Czech. Annexation**, in 1939; #70—**Danzig**, in 1939; culminating in #74—**Entry into World War II** (see *Master Table*).

(74) Entry into World War II

The crisis immediately preceding—and following the onset of—World War II began on 20 August 1939 and ended on 28 September of that year. The following 21 countries were crisis actors: Australia, Belgium, Canada, Denmark, Estonia, Finland, France, Japan, Latvia, Lithuania, Luxembourg, the Netherlands, New Zealand, Norway, Poland, Romania, South Africa, Sweden, Switzerland, the U.K., and the USSR.

Pre-crisis
The **Czech. Annexation** crisis of March 1939 (see Case #68, in **Czech./Germany PC**) confronted the small states of Europe, especially Poland and Romania, with forebodings of a similar fate. In an effort to build an effective European coalition of anti-German forces, negotiations were initiated between the Western powers and the Soviet Union. The failure of these negotiations, to a large extent, was due to Poland's and Romania's refusal to allow the entry of Russian troops into their

territories, even for the purpose of assisting resistance to a possible German attack.

German-Soviet negotiations had been taking place since June, and on 15 August German Ambassador Schulenberg delivered a message to Soviet Foreign Minister Molotov stating that Ribbentrop was prepared to visit Moscow in order to bring about a permanent change in German-Soviet relations. Hitler wished Ribbentrop to be received at once, for his plans to invade Poland on 26 August were contingent upon the Soviet response. On 19 August the Soviets indicated their agreement to a meeting on the 26th.

Crisis

Triggers and Responses
The first state to perceive a crisis was *Latvia*. On 20 August Latvian Foreign Minister Munters received reports of plans for the partition of Eastern Europe between Germany and the Soviet Union. Latvia's representative in Berlin was instructed to obtain a formal statement from the German government that the security, integrity, and independence of the Baltic states would be maintained. Its major response, on 30 August, was a decision at a special meeting of the Latvian cabinet to introduce a number of defense measures, including mobilization.

On 21 August a crisis was triggered for the *Soviet Union* when Stalin received a personal message from Hitler accepting the Soviet draft for a Non-Aggression Pact and urging an earlier date for the Ribbentrop visit. Stalin interpreted this message as an ultimatum. If the German plan to invade Poland on the 26th was not met by strong action on the part of France and the U.K., Germany would be free to impose its views on the USSR. After short deliberations, Stalin agreed to Ribbentrop's arrival on 23 August. The signing of a Non-Aggression Treaty with Germany on 23 August was the USSR's major response.

On the evening of 21 August word was received in the capitals of *Japan, Poland,* and the *U.K.* that negotiations between Germany and the USSR for a Non-Aggression Pact were about to be concluded. Japan's Ambassador to Berlin, Oshima, protested to Germany that it would be an act of bad faith and a contravention of the Anti-Comintern Pact. At that time, a full-scale war was raging between Japan and the Soviet Union at **Nomonhan** (see Case #72, in **Asia: Non-PCs**), and the Japanese feared that the USSR would take advantage of their strengthened international position to exert added pressure on Japan in Asia. The Hiranuma cabinet responded by instructing Oshima to make a formal protest to the German government, which was delivered on 26 August.

In the U.K., news of the Pact was accompanied by reports of German troop movements toward the Polish frontier. At a cabinet meeting the following day, members decided on partial mobilization and a call to convene parliament on the 24th. The British were faced with a fait accompli, their inability to reach an agreement with Moscow; and the existence of the Molotov-Ribbentrop Pact did not alter the U.K.'s obligations to Poland. On 22 and 23 August Notes were exchanged between Chamberlain and Hitler, and on 25 August Hitler demanded that a Polish emissary arrive in Berlin within 24 hours. The British cabinet considered this unreasonable and refused to recommend to Poland that it comply with this demand. Diplomatic efforts continued until 1 September when German forces crossed the Polish frontier and began their invasion. On the 2nd the U.K. sent an ultimatum to Hitler, after no reply had been received to its Note of the previous day, offering to negotiate if German forces were withdrawn from Poland. And on the 3rd the U.K. declared war on Germany.

The impending Ribbentrop journey to Moscow was broadcast by Moscow Radio on 22 August. This news triggered a crisis for Australia, Belgium, Canada, Denmark, Estonia, Finland, France, Lithuania, Luxembourg, the Netherlands, New Zealand, Norway, Poland, Romania, Sweden, and Switzerland.

In *Australia,* Prime Minister Menzies stated on the 23rd that, if Britain were forced to go to war, it would not be alone. The following day Menzies issued a declaration confirming the unity in the ranks of the British Empire. The Australian response was Menzies's declaration of war on 3 September.

Belgium's King Leopold, addressing the Oslo powers (Belgium, Denmark, Finland, Luxembourg, the Netherlands, Norway, Sweden) on 23 August, appealed to the major powers to maintain peace. On the 25th, at a meeting of Belgium's Council of Ministers, it was decided to place the Belgian forces at home on a war footing: active divisions and first reserves were mobilized, automobiles and horses were requisitioned, and frontier patrols were posted. That day the prime minister gave the German chargé d'affaires assurances that the actions of the Belgian government constituted an affirmation of its independence and its wish to stay out of any conflict.

On 23 August *Canada*'s Prime Minister, Mackenzie King, declared that parliament would be summoned the moment the situation required it, stating that the powers of the War Reserve Act would be utilized to place Canada on a war footing. On the 26th Canada's foreign minister sent identical appeals to Germany, Poland, and Italy urging the avoidance of war and the solving of issues through conference and negotiation. The Canadian major response to the crisis was at an emergency cabinet meeting on 1 September. Canada vowed to stand by Britain. The mobilization of army and navy forces was to be completed, and measures were taken for Canada's defense and the granting of aid to Britain. On the 10th Canada declared war on Germany.

Despite a Non-Aggression Pact signed with Germany in May 1939, the 22 August announcement triggered a crisis for *Denmark,* which sought assurances from both Germany and the U.K. that its neutrality would be respected. On the 28th these assurances were given by Germany, and on the 30th by the U.K. Denmark's major response came on 1 September when the Rigodag met to ensure that Danish forces were adequate to carry out the task of protecting the country's neutrality.

A large concentration of Soviet troops stationed along the Estonian/USSR border posed a serious threat to *Estonia.* In the hope of maintaining German guarantees, Foreign Minister Selter responded to the German-Soviet Non-Aggression Pact by offering congratulations to the German government and stating his conviction that Germany, according to its Non-Aggression Treaties with Estonia and the Soviet Union, had prepared the ground for ensuring Estonian security.

For *Finland,* the assumption that permanent hostility between Germany and the Soviet Union would maintain a balance of power in the Baltic region was shattered on 22 August. Foreign Minister Errko feared that the signatories of the Pact would turn against neighboring Baltic states at a later date. The German ambassador to Helsinki was called in on 1 September with a request for assurances that Germany would respect Finland's neutrality; these were given.

In *France,* word of the Pact on 22 August produced a response of partial mobilization. All frontier troops were put on alert on the 23rd, and full mobilization of reserves began on the 24th. Hitler and Prime Minister Daladier exchanged letters on 25 and 27 August. France agreed to come to Poland's aid if it were attacked by Germany. After the attack on 1 September, the French Council of Ministers ordered a general mobilization for the following day. France, like Britain, sent an ultimatum to Hitler on the 2nd, to expire the next day. And on the 3rd France, too, declared war on Germany.

Lithuania viewed the Pact as a threat to its existence, despite the Non-Aggression Pacts that Lithuania, together with Latvia and Estonia, had signed with Germany and with the Soviet Union. Lithuania's response was a declaration of neutrality on 2 September.

Luxembourg attended the Oslo Powers Conference on 23 August, which called for peace. Its major response was an appeal on 31 August for the observance of Luxembourg's neutrality.

The response of *the Netherlands* was a cabinet decision on 25 August to maintain neutrality. The following day the German minister met with Queen Wilhelmina and conveyed German expectations that the Netherlands would not swerve from the neutrality decision. On the 28th a mobilization order was proclaimed, along with other measures for Holland's security. On 30 August assurances were also received from the U.K.

New Zealand, like other members of the British Commonwealth, perceived a crisis on 22 August when the grave threat facing the U.K. as a result of the Pact became known. The following day, with cabinet approval, Acting Premier Frazer declared that New Zealand would remain solidly behind Britain should war come. A state of emergency was proclaimed on 1 September; and war declared on the 3rd.

Ribbentrop's proposed journey to Moscow also became known in *Norway* on the 22nd. Norway responded on the 30th with an order for partial mobilization. Assurances of Germany's respect for Norway's neutrality were sought and received on 1 September.

After reports of extensive German military preparations on the 23rd, *Poland* mobilized one-third of its army. On 24 August, Foreign Minister Beck told the British ambassador that he considered the situation most grave. The following day the Anglo-Polish Agreement was signed. As further German troop concentrations were reported on the border, and German troops in Slovakia called upon the population to collaborate against Poland, the Polish government decided upon general mobilization on 29 August. It was announced on the 30th, despite the advice of the French and British ambassadors, whose countries were still negotiating with Germany. When the invasion took place, Poland's major response, on 1 September, was to fight the invaders while appealing to Britain and France to implement their guarantees.

Romania, caught between the two strongest powers in Europe, viewed the Pact as a grave threat to its sovereignty. Romania particularly feared Russian designs on Bessarabia and the implications for Romania's freedom of movement on behalf of Poland in the event of war. On 27 August Foreign Minister Gafencu told the German ambassador that Romania was determined to remain neutral even if France and Britain became involved in a war with Germany. On the 28th Romania began to fortify its frontier with the USSR along the valley of the Dniester River.

On 27th August *Sweden* responded to the crisis with a decision to maintain strict neutrality. A partial mobilization had been called on the previous day. On 1 September the king declared that all defense positions would be strengthened.

Switzerland's geographic position, bordering Germany, France, Austria, and Italy, placed it in an especially vulnerable position on 22 August. On the 28th the Bundesrat ordered the mobilization of frontier forces and all defense troops. Parliament was summoned the following day for a special session. On 30 August the United Federal Assembly appointed General Henri Guisan as Commander in Chief of the Swiss army. And the following day Switzerland reaffirmed its neutrality.

The German invasion of Poland on 1 September triggered a crisis for *South Africa.* The Hertzog-Smuts coalition was split over the question of South Africa's response to the crisis. Hertzog advocated neutrality, maintaining that the dispute was among the European powers and did not affect South Africa. General Smuts believed that South Africa should enter the war on the side of the U.K. The issue was placed before the House of Assembly. When no solution was forthcoming Prime Minister Hertzog requested the governor-general to dissolve parliament and call an election. The request was refused, the prime minister resigned, and the governor-general asked Smuts to form a cabinet. South Africa's major response was to declare war against Germany on 6 September.

Terminations
Japan's crisis ended on 28 August with the resignation of the Hiranuma cabinet.

On 31 August the crisis for *Switzerland* terminated when the Federal Council issued a declaration of neutrality after assurances had been received from

Germany and Italy. On that day as well, *Luxembourg's* crisis ended when it, too, received assurances of German observance of its strict neutrality.

On 1 September there were official declarations of neutrality by the Scandinavian countries—*Denmark, Finland, Norway,* and *Sweden; Romania,* too, declared neutrality that day, as did *Estonia* and *Latvia.*

Lithuania proclaimed neutrality the next day. Neutrality was declared by *Belgium* and *the Netherlands* on 3 September.

Australia, Britain, France, and *New Zealand* declared war against Germany on 3 September.

South Africa joined the war on the 6th, and *Canada* on the 10th.

Germany fought in *Poland* for 17 days. The conquest was completed on 17 September. That day the Soviet Union invaded Poland from the east, meeting the advancing German troops near Brest-Litovsk two days later.

The last actor to perceive crisis termination was the *Soviet Union,* on 28 September 1939. Despite the signing of the Pact, bad faith continued to exist between Germany and the USSR until additional agreements were signed on the 28th when the German and Soviet governments divided Poland.

By the end of this crisis, Australia, Canada, France, New Zealand, South Africa, and the U.K. were at war with Germany. Poland had been conquered. The Scandinavian countries, the Baltic states, and Belgium, Luxembourg, Romania, Switzerland, and Holland had declared neutrality. Japan was at war in Asia with China. And Moscow was serene in the misconception that Germany would not attack the USSR.

The League of Nations, although formally still in existence until 1946, had become moribund by 1939 and was not involved in any crisis during the long-war **World War II PC.**

(See *Master Table,* pp. 678–79.)

Sources
See sources for Cases #64, 68, 69, 70, 75; and Baldwin 1966; Grattan 1963; Hull 1948, vol. I; von Rauch 1970; Snell 1963; Weinberg 1994.

(77) Invasion of Scandinavia

The German invasion of Scandinavia generated a crisis for Norway, Denmark, the Netherlands, France, and the U.K. from 8 April to 10 June 1940.

Pre-crisis
The **Finnish War** (see Case #76, in **Finland/Russia PC**), which had ended in March 1940, emphasized the strategic importance of Scandinavia's waterways for both the Allies and Germany. Winston Churchill, then First Lord of the Admiralty, pressed for the mining of Norwegian waters, which were the passageway for Swedish ore to Germany. Early in 1940 the German tanker *Altmark,* sailing in Norwegian waters and carrying British prisoners of war, was boarded

by the British while moored in Jossingfjord, and the prisoners were released. Both Norway and Germany issued strong protests to London. Norway, which feared German retaliation, emphasized that the British ships had violated its neutrality. The *Altmark* incident accelerated German plans for the invasion of Norway and spurred British cabinet approval of Churchill's naval plans. Due to Britain's superior naval strength, Germany decided upon a surprise attack against Norway.

Crisis

On 8 April 1940 a crisis was triggered for Norway when it received intelligence reports predicting a German invasion the next day. Several U.K. vessels did spot and engage the Germans that day, but the British viewed these as isolated clashes. On 9 April the Germans invaded Denmark and Norway, creating a crisis for Denmark, France, and the U.K. A crisis was also triggered for the Netherlands, which perceived the invasion as presaging an attack on Holland, for it was the first German offensive since the "phony war" of the preceding winter and spring and was accompanied by perceptions of German plans to attack Western Europe. While Denmark and Norway perceived no more than grave damage at the outset, for Germany demanded free passage only, as the crisis escalated they perceived a threat to their existence in the form of German occupation.

The Norwegian and Danish responses occurred on 9 April. Norway's King Haakon offered to abdicate rather than capitulate. Norway reorganized its defenses and began strong resistance under a new Commander in Chief, General Ruge. Denmark held cabinet meetings with King Christian and, under his leadership, decided not to resist, ending its crisis on the 9th.

The U.K. and France had been considering the dispatch of troops to aid Norway. The German attack hastened their decision, on 13 April, to do so. Haphazard and insufficient planning prevented the success of the operation. The target areas were too narrow for the ships carrying artillery to land, and the landing sites were changed, confusing the troops. Norwegian forces had tried to keep landing areas and key ports free for the Allies.

On 19 April the Netherlands responded to the crisis by mobilizing its troops and issuing a strong statement of its intention to defend itself against German attack. Holland's tension eased as the German invasion concentrated on Denmark and Norway and, on 27 April, its crisis ended, with military preparations returning to normal.

The Anglo-French forces, together with the Norwegians, resisted for another month. In the interim, on 10 May, Britain's Prime Minister, Neville Chamberlain, resigned and was replaced by Winston Churchill. By the end of May the Allies had been badly beaten, and a decision was made to withdraw. The last troops were evacuated on 8 June 1940, following the French defeat in northern France (see Case #78 below), terminating the intrawar crisis for France and Britain. The king of Norway and his government left the country with the British and French on the 8th, and, on 10 June, a member of General Ruge's staff signed

an armistice with Germany, ending the last fighting around Narvik and terminating the crisis for Norway.
(See *Master Table*, pp. 680–81.)

Sources
Bullock 1962; Calvocoressi and Wint 1972; Carlgren 1977; Churchill 1948; Derry 1952; Olsson 1975; Petrow 1974; Royal Institute of International Affairs (RIIA) 1947; Schuman 1941; Snell 1963; Weinberg 1994; Ziemke 1960.

(78) Fall of Western Europe

The crisis over Germany's occupation of Western Europe occurred from 10 May to 22 June 1940. Belgium, Luxembourg, the Netherlands, Britain, and France were the crisis actors.

Pre-crisis
On 9 April 1940 German armed forces occupied Denmark and invaded Norway (see Case #77 above).

Crisis
Early in the morning of 10 May 1940 German armies, without warning, invaded Belgium, Luxembourg, and the Netherlands, triggering a crisis for those three countries and for France and Britain. The latter were cobelligerent partners in the ongoing European war; the cornerstone of Britain's defense policy had always been that a threat to France was perceived in London as a threat to itself. Thus, on 10 May, they responded by dispatching expeditionary forces into Belgium to cooperate with the Belgian army in its resistance. Diplomatic negotiations were also carried on. Belgium and the Netherlands responded on the 10th as well with military resistance. In Luxembourg there was no fighting. The royal family retired to its castle, refusing to communicate with the German invaders, and its crisis ended on the day of the invasion. In Holland, Rotterdam surrendered to the Germans after a fierce air attack, and the government, headed by Queen Wilhelmina, escaped to London on 13 May. Holland signed an armistice agreement with the Germans on 15 May 1940.

Between 17 and 21 May German mechanized divisions drove deep into northern France and succeeded in separating British and Belgian forces in Flanders from the main French armies. The fall of Brussels forced the British and Belgian troops back to Ostend and Dunkirk. On 26 May Boulogne fell to the Germans, and King Leopold ordered his army to capitulate. This was done on 28 May, terminating the crisis for Belgium. Two hundred and fifty thousand British troops were evacuated from the beaches of Dunkirk.

A broad attack on France was launched on 5 June. On the 10th Italy declared war against France and Britain. Paris was evacuated on the 13th. And on 17 June the U.K. crisis ended when it formally withdrew its troops from France and agreed to the latter's making a separate peace with the Germans. On that day Marshal Petain asked the Germans for an armistice. This was signed on 22 June 1940 ending the crisis for France and leaving three-fifths of the country under German occupation.

An immediate legacy of this intrawar crisis was a near confrontation between Britain and Vichy France as a result of the former's fear that the French fleet concentrated in Toulon would be handed over to Germany. The British signaled their determination to prevent this by sinking the French naval flotilla in Oran, North Africa, on 3 July 1940. The U.K. remained suspicious of Petain's intentions throughout the tenure of the Vichy French regime, as evident in the **Mid-East Campaign** crisis of 1941 (see Case #84 below).

(See *Master Table,* pp. 680–81.)

Sources
Bryant 1957; Butler 1956; Churchill 1949; Dallek 1979; Nere 1975; Schuman 1941; Shirer 1969; Weinberg 1980, 1994.

(79) Closure of Burma Road

The closure of the Burma Road by the Japanese created a crisis for the U.K. from 24 June to 14 July 1940.

Background
Throughout the 1930s Britain's support for the Nationalist regime in China was viewed by Japan as hostile to its interests. Britain's involvement in the European war provided Japan with an opportunity to proceed without hindrance to establish its proclaimed "New Order"—the "Greater East Asia Co-Prosperity Sphere." As the tide of the war turned against Britain, Japan increased its pressure.

Crisis
On 24 June Japan demanded that the U.K. cease assistance to Chiang Kai-shek, withdraw its troops from Shanghai, and close the transit routes for supplies to China through Hong Kong and the Burma Road. A force of about 5,000 Japanese troops took up positions along the border of the leased Kowloon territory in Hong Kong. The British perceived that, if they yielded to the Japanese demands, the security of the British Commonwealth would be compromised. Yet Britain could not afford to risk war with Japan, being already involved in the European and Mediterranean theaters.

The U.K.'s major response, on 27 June, was to seek American assurances that the U.S. would stand by Britain in resisting Japanese demands, either through an embargo on all exports to Japan or by sending U.S. warships to Singapore. The U.K. also requested U.S. cooperation in mediating a peace settlement between China and Japan. The U.S., while urging the U.K. to stand firm, rejected any plan for joint action. On the 30th the Hong Kong military authorities ordered the destruction of the frontier rail and road bridges over the Shumchun River. An evacuation of British women and children from Hong Kong to Manila and Australia followed.

A Japanese foreign ministry communiqué, on 8 July, demanded British reconsideration. On the 12th the U.K. informed U.S. Secretary of State Cordell Hull that Japan would declare war at any time unless the British government closed the Burma Road.

The crisis ended on 14 July 1940 when an Anglo-Japanese agreement was reached in Tokyo whereby all transit of war materials was stopped for three months. Four days later the agreement was communicated to the British parliament by the prime minister and the foreign secretary. The U.K., perceiving a high probability that Japan would enter the war on the side of the Axis, and unable to meet the threat without U.S. support, yielded to the Japanese demands.

(The Burma Road was cleared of Japanese forces in the spring of 1945 following a two-pronged attack on Japanese positions in northern Burma by Chinese troops under the direction of U.S. General Stilwell.)

(See *Master Table*, pp. 680–81.)

Sources
Boyle 1972; Hull 1948, vol. I; Jones 1954; Lowe 1977; Morley 1974.

(81) Battle of Britain

The battle, an intrawar crisis for the U.K., took place from 10 July to 15 September 1940.

Background and Pre-crisis
A Naval Agreement between the U.K. and Germany in 1935 and British concessions at **Munich** in 1938 (see Case #64, in **Czech./Germany PC**) led Hitler to expect U.K. cooperation for a quiet Western flank which would enable him to carry out a massive attack on the USSR. After Britain's declaration of war and Churchill's announcement, following the fall of France (see Case #78 above), that Britain would continue to fight alone, Hitler began to formulate a plan to invade the U.K. He envisioned a long and costly campaign requiring at the outset the transport of around 30–40 divisions by sea across the Channel. Since Germany lacked sufficient naval power to compete with Britain, the prerequisite to a successful crossing was absolute air superiority. As German ships began to collect along the coast of France, the Luftwaffe initiated its efforts to gain control of the air. After the fall of France and the Dunkirk evacuation, the U.K. appealed to the U.S. for military supplies. By the end of June U.S. guns and ammunition had reached British shores. In early July the Germans occupied islands in the English Channel.

Crisis

On 10 July 1940 the Luftwaffe began "Operation Eagle" by attacking towns near the coast of Britain. The U.K.'s response to the crisis was immediate, through *RAF* counterattacks. The German assault continued during July and August with fierce *RAF* opposition. On 8 August German planes bombed airfields and vital industries. On the 15th 1,000 German planes ranged as far north as Scotland. The British retaliated with raids on Berlin, Dusseldorf, Essen, and other German cities. On 3 September a defense agreement was concluded between the U.K. and the U.S. The 7th marked the highest British casualty count. And on 11 September the U.K. began continuous bombing of continental ports to frustrate German invasion preparations, including the assembling of ships for the future crossing of the English Channel.

As time went on it became clear that the Luftwaffe would not be able to gain complete air superiority. And the original target date for the German invasion ("Operation Sea Lion") was postponed several times. The Luftwaffe's strategy had been to draw the U.K.'s Fighter Command into a major engagement, first over the English Channel and then, on 15 September 1940, in a mass raid on London in an effort to deliver a final assault. The British resisted, preserved the Fighter Command by meeting the German attacks with a minimum of force, and pushed the Luftwaffe back across the Channel. This victory of 15 September 1940, proving that the *RAF* was still master of the skies over Britain, marked the termination of Britain's crisis, though night bombing of London and other British cities continued far into the winter.

Once the conditions for a successful German landing had been denied, Germany canceled the invasion plans. Hitler decided to proceed with an attack in the east without the subjugation of Britain. Italy dispatched an air force division—after the crisis proper had ended.

(See *Master Table*, pp. 680–81.)

Sources

Baldwin 1966; Bryant 1957; Bullock 1962; Calvocoressi and Wint 1972; Churchill 1949; Schuman 1941; Shirer 1964; Weinberg 1994.

(82) East Africa Campaign

The U.K. and Italy were the crisis actors in an IWC from 19 August 1940 until 17 May 1941.

Pre-crisis

On 10 June 1940 Italy declared war on Britain in the belief that the impending collapse of the Allies in Europe would make any serious Italian participation unnecessary. With the expected downfall of the British, Egypt, British Somaliland, and British East Africa would be added to Italy's existing possessions covering an immense area in northeast Africa. When Italy entered the war, the reinforcement of British forces through the Mediterranean became extremely dangerous. This threat intensified in July when the collapse of opposition in French Somaliland led to a French-Italian armistice. Large Italian forces had now been released for use against British Somaliland. During July Italy occupied Sudanese and Kenyan frontier posts. On 3 August the Italians crossed the frontier into British Somaliland.

Crisis

On 19 August 1940 the British were forced to evacuate British Somaliland. This setback at the hands of the Italians came as a shock to British public opinion. Although Italian attacks on Aden were now more easily facilitated, the protectorate had no significant strategic value for the U.K. Nevertheless, the location of an Italian East Africa on the flank of Britain's vital sea route, the Red Sea, was a threat to Britain's influence among its client states, and the forced evacuation triggered a crisis for the U.K. The British responded, months later, on 2 December 1940, with a decision to expel Italy from East Africa. The campaign in North Africa began on 8 December. The East African offensive began in February 1941 when the British advanced from the Anglo-Egyptian Sudan and Kenya into Ethiopia and Eritrea.

On 13 February Kismayu fell, and Mogadiscio (Mogadishu) submitted on the 25th. And on 17 March the Italians abandoned Sigjiga. The British advances had revealed the weakness of the Italian colonial forces, and internal disorder increased greatly. On the 22nd Neghelli in southern Ethiopia was occupied by British and Ethiopian forces.

The crisis trigger for Italy was at the Battle of Keren on 27 March 1941. The loss of 3,000 men in that battle broke the back of Italian resistance, which now abandoned hope of retaining control over Eritrea. Italy responded on 30 March with a decision to concentrate resistance at Amba Alagi. Mussolini was so informed by the Duke of Aosta, Supreme Commander of all Italian armed forces in East Africa. On 3 April the duke united the remainder of his reserve force with the remnants of the Italian Eritrean army.

On 6 April Addis Ababa capitulated. Prior to the defeat, Mussolini had instructed the duke not to abandon the capital unless absolutely necessary because it would be politically equivalent to losing the empire.

On 11 April President Roosevelt announced that the Red Sea and the Gulf of Aden were no longer combat zones within the meaning of U.S. neutrality and U.S. vessels could now carry war supplies to the British Middle East forces by this route.

The termination of the crisis for both the U.K. and Italy came on 17 May 1941 when the Duke of Aosta surrendered and signed an armistice agreement. Italian resistance in Eritrea collapsed by June. And before the end of 1941 all of East Africa was under British control.

(See *Master Table,* pp. 680–81.)

Sources
Churchill 1949; Ciano 1947; Collins 1947; Playfair 1954.

(83) Balkan Invasions

The Italian and German invasions of the Balkans created a crisis for Greece, Yugoslavia, the U.K., Turkey, Italy, and Germany. The duration of the crisis was from 28 October 1940 until 1 June 1941.

Background and Pre-crisis
The high geostrategic importance of the Balkans for Germany, the USSR, and the West stems from the fact that they guarded one access to the Mediterranean close to vital areas of the British Empire, namely, the Suez Canal and the Middle East. Together with Turkey and Romania, the Balkans dominate the Dardanelles, the access to the USSR and the Black Sea, and the mouth of the Danube River. They are also rich in natural resources, especially oil. In the summer of 1940, when three countries claimed Romanian territories, Hitler imposed a solution on Romania and Hungary in order to avoid war (see Case #80, in **Europe: Non-PCs**). On 8 October German troops entered Romania to "protect" the oil fields. Italy had long been interested in Yugoslavia and Greece as guardians of the opposite shore of the Adriatic, and Hitler had cautiously granted Mussolini a free hand in the area. When Italy attacked and occupied Albania in early 1939 (see Case #71—**Invasion of Albania**, in **Italy/Albania/Yugoslavia PC**), the balance in the area was altered. Mussolini, after a poor showing on the French front and ignorant of Hitler's plan vis-à-vis Romania, wished to present Hitler with a fait accompli by occupying Greece.

Crisis
On 28 October 1940 Italy's ambassador to Greece presented Premier Metaxas with an ultimatum to relinquish Greek bases for use by the Italian government. One-half hour before the ultimatum expired, Italy attacked Greece from Albania. Greece responded that day by mobilizing its forces and appealing to the U.K. for help under its guarantee, triggering a crisis for the U.K. Britain perceived a threat to the strategic balance in the area and therefore to its entire Middle East empire. Crises were also triggered for Yugoslavia, which feared for its own security should the port of Thessaloniki, Greece be occupied by the Italians, and for Turkey, which viewed Bulgaria as capable of seizing the military opportunity to take control of Greek areas of strategic importance to Turkey, as well as fearing a spillover that would endanger Turkey's neutral status. Yugoslavia and Turkey both responded on 1 November. Yugoslavia held a meeting of its Crown Council and ordered partial mobilization. Turkey's President İnönü announced that his country would stand by its allies and not tolerate a threat to its security. To back this up some Turkish troops were moved to the Bulgarian border—which ulti-

mately freed Greek soldiers, fighting in the vicinity, for campaigns elsewhere in Greece. The U.K., which had sent reinforcements to Crete and other Greek islands on 30 October, decided at a cabinet meeting on 3 November to increase its military and economic aid to Greece so as to enable that country to resist the Italian offensive.

The attack itself did not go well for Italy. Severe winter conditions and the fierce determination of the Greek forces ground the Italian offensive to a standstill. By the middle of November the Greeks were able to reorganize for an offensive, which, by 21 November, had forced the Italians back. The first crisis for Greece and Yugoslavia ended that day. The U.K.'s first crisis ended the following day, with the news of Greek successes on the battlefield.

The Greek offensive, which resulted, inter alia, in the capture of the strategic town of Koritsa, triggered a crisis for Italy and Germany. Hitler viewed Italian losses as detrimental to his strategy in the area, for Western victories would allow the British access to the Balkans and the Romanian oil fields. Italy responded on 5 December by sending its ambassador in Berlin to Hitler to request aid in Greece. Although the request was later withdrawn, Hitler had been convinced of the need to salvage the situation there. Accordingly, on 13 December, Germany began to plan for an invasion of Greece in February. It was eventually delayed until April. Germany's Soviet campaign was thus also delayed.

By the beginning of 1941 the military situation had stabilized somewhat. Hitler spent the winter in political maneuvering, easing the tension between Bulgaria and Turkey and countering strong British pressure on Turkey to support Greece. Hitler was instrumental in bringing about the signing of a Bulgaria-Turkey Friendship Pact on 17 February 1941, which terminated Turkey's crisis vis-à-vis Bulgaria. On 29 February Bulgaria adhered to the Tripartite Pact (Germany, Italy, Japan) and therewith allowed German troops to assemble on its territory to await the invasion of Greece.

In Yugoslavia the same German pressure was being applied, and there also was popular unrest and some civil violence as rival groups maneuvered for dominance in that multinational state. The Regent, Prince Paul, though willing in principle to join the Axis powers, did not wish it to become public knowledge. Nevertheless, he obligated Yugoslavia to provide forces, if necessary, and allowed the passage of German troops. On 4 March 1941 Prince Paul visited Hitler where he experienced strong pressure to adhere to the Tripartite Pact. This triggered a second crisis for Yugoslavia, as Germany threatened to occupy Thessaloniki, Greece and hand it over to Bulgaria or Italy. On 24 March 1941 Yugoslavia responded by agreeing to join the Pact, which was done the following day. On the night of the 26th a coup d'état took place in Yugoslavia. The new rulers were quick to state that they would adhere to previous policy, but the signs were unclear. Hitler, in fury, decided to invade Yugoslavia as well as Greece and did so on 6 April 1941, triggering a second crisis for Greece and the U.K. Efforts to coordinate military plans between the U.K. and Greece had met with difficulties.

Greece feared that too much British aid would bring Germany into the battle. The U.K. felt that what was acceptable to Greece was insufficient. Poor coordination and misunderstanding led to poor performance.

On 7 April the British pledged military support to Yugoslavia, and on the 8th the U.S. cabled Belgrade that it would provide material aid. Two days later, with a preliminary U.K. withdrawal in Greece, Hungary invaded Yugoslavia. The Greek response to the second crisis was a major withdrawal on 12 April. On 17 April Yugoslavia signed an armistice with Germany, which terminated its second crisis. And on the 23rd Greece surrendered, ending its crisis and that of Italy as well. The next day the Greek government requested that the British withdraw, and Bulgaria invaded Greece. The major U.K. response was a decision on 27 April to withdraw its forces to Crete.

Fighting continued as German forces attacked Crete, which had never been properly fortified. Nonetheless, it took over a month to force a final U.K. withdrawal from Crete, on 1 June, terminating the crisis for the U.K. and for Germany—and this IWC as a whole. In the final analysis the Balkan campaign delayed "Operation **Barbarossa**" by at least four weeks, more likely several months (see Case #85 below).

The U.S. sent a mediator to the Balkans in the spring and invoked the Neutrality Act in the fall of 1940. Australian and New Zealand troops fought alongside the British.

(See *Master Table,* pp. 682–83.)

Sources
Barker 1976; Cervi 1971; Churchill 1949, 1950a; Ciano 1947; van Creveld 1973; Cruickshank 1976; Kirkpatrick 1964; Ristic 1961; Smith 1982; Weinberg 1994.

(84) Mid-East Campaign

Military campaigns in the Middle East triggered crises for Iraq, the U.K., Germany, and Vichy France from 29 April to 14 July 1941.

Pre-crisis
At the beginning of 1941 the Middle East comprised an area of great concern to both sides in the European war. With a German-Italian threat to the Suez Canal, the British began to consider the Basra-Baghdad-Palestine route. On 3 April 1941 pro-Axis Rashid Ali staged a coup and reassumed power in Iraq. U.K. losses in the Balkans and Libya had been reflected in the growth of anti-British sentiment in Iraq, heightened by the fact that Baghdad had become the center of pro-Axis intrigue, leading to British fears of German control over Iraq. The British decided that the situation could be restored only by force. Despite Rashid Ali's assurances that he would honor the 1930 Anglo-Iraqi

Treaty, Britain was determined to restore the legitimate government to power in order to safeguard the Allies against Axis intervention in Iraq. On 17 April 1941 a British-Indian military contingent landed in Basra, in accordance with treaty provisions.

Crisis

A second British contingent landed on 29 April 1941, triggering a crisis for Iraq. That day Iraq responded by ordering its forces to Habbaniya, the principal British air base there. With Iraqi artillery surrounding the air base and other forces encircling the compound of the British embassy in Baghdad, on 29 April, a crisis was triggered for the U.K. The following day the Iraqi commander demanded the closure of the base. The British replied that any interference with flights would be treated as an act of war. The ambassador was given full authority to take any steps necessary, including air attacks, to assure the withdrawal of the Iraqis. While Iraq endeavored to take Habbaniya, the British responded with an attack on 1 May. Rashid Ali's early attempts to secure Axis military assistance had been unsuccessful, as Germany was occupied in Greece and in preparing for its attack on the USSR (see Case #85—**Barbarossa** below). Despite German pressure, Turkey refused to allow a transit of arms and troops through its territory. The only open channel left was Vichy-controlled Syria.

On 6 May Iraqi forces retreated from the hills overlooking the Habbaniya base. Troops from Palestine relieved the hard-pressed British garrison. On 12 May Germany came to Iraq's assistance by sending its Syrian-based bombers to attack British airfields in the Mosul region of Iraq. By 30 May the British had succeeded in crushing the rebellion in Iraq. Rashid Ali and his associates fled to Iran, and Iraq sued for an armistice, terminating its crisis. The following day, Germany announced an agreement on military collaboration between the German and Vichy France governments—despite persistent French pressure for German withdrawal from Syrian territory. The crisis ended for Germany when the Luftwaffe detachment from Syria was recalled on 6 June 1941.

On the 8th the British government announced that it would not tolerate Vichy collaboration with the Germans. Free French troops, with support from Imperial forces, entered Syria and Lebanon that day from Palestine, Transjordan, and Iraq, and triggered a crisis for Vichy France. It responded on 17 June with an attack on Quneitra and Marjayun, in the Golan Heights and south Lebanon, respectively. As the Allies began closing in on Damascus on the 20th, Vichy France asked the U.S. to inquire on what terms an armistice might be arranged. On 8 July General Dentz, the Vichy High Commissioner in Syria, received authority to negotiate. An agreement was finally reached on 14 July 1941, terminating the crisis for the U.K. and Vichy France.

(The latter fell in November 1942, when Germany occupied the rest of France.)

(See *Master Table*, pp. 682–83.)

Sources
Churchill 1950b; Khadduri 1960; Lenczowski 1962; Nyrop 1971; Palmer 1973; Penrose 1978; Weinberg 1994.

(85) Barbarossa

The Soviet Union's existence crisis arising from the German invasion culminated in a massive attack on Moscow. It lasted from 22 June to 5 December 1941.

Pre-crisis
The Italo-German campaign in the Balkans ended at the end of May 1941 with a greatly strengthened Axis position. As a result of the conquest of Greece and Crete, the Aegean Sea became unsafe for British ships (see Case #83—**Balkan Invasions** above). On 13 April Soviet and Japanese diplomats signed a Non-Aggression Pact at Moscow. In late May representatives from Finland, Hungary, Romania, and Bulgaria met with the German high command to coordinate plans to invade Russia. Hitler floated a rumor of Soviet intentions to attack Germany as a pretext for his own premeditated designs against the USSR.

Crisis
On 22 June 1941 the Germans, in a surprise attack, invaded the Soviet Union along a front of 2,000 miles, triggering a crisis for the USSR. Romanian and Finnish troops participated actively with those of Nazi Germany, while Hungary and Bulgaria provided free passage for German troops on their way east. The Soviets responded the same day with fierce resistance but were soon forced into a slow retreat. Prime Minister Churchill promised that the U.K. would extend all possible aid to the Soviets. A Mutual Assistance Pact was concluded between them on 13 July. During the month of July Riga, Latvia's capital, and Smolensk were captured by the Germans. On 19 August the Germans claimed all Ukrainian territory west of the Dnieper River, except Odessa, and on 4 September the siege of Leningrad began. During September Axis forces continued their advance, and by the end of the month the Germans had entered the Crimea on the southern end of the front and had commenced the battle for Moscow. This triggered a short but intense IWC for the USSR, which ended on 29 October, when the Germans were hurled back at the gates of the Soviet capital. Before then, in mid-October, the Soviet government had transferred its headquarters further east, to Kuybyshev.

On 30 October the United States expedited Soviet purchases of promised U.S. supplies by extending the USSR a credit of one billion dollars. This was later supplemented by a Master Lend-Lease Agreement in 1942. In early December the Soviets began a major counterthrust before the gates of Moscow. On 5 December the German high command decided to halt operations on the eastern front for the winter because German troops were exhausted, short of ammunition, suffering from the cold, and beset by logistical problems. The German halt outside of Moscow on 5 December 1941 ended the first stage of Germany's

Russian campaign and, with it, the Soviet intrawar crisis over the fate of its capital, as well as the Barbarossa crisis as a whole. Hitler had not fulfilled his objective—defeat of the Soviet Union within three months. Japan adhered to its Pact with the USSR and remained strictly neutral, but two days later launched the Pacific war with an attack on Pearl Harbor (see Case #88 below).

(See *Master Table*, pp. 682–83.)

Sources
Bullock 1962; Calvocoressi and Wint 1972; Cecil 1975; Churchill 1950a; de Gaulle 1971; Glantz and House 1995; Palmer 1973; Weinberg 1954, 1994.

(88) Pearl Harbor

The Japanese attack on the U.S. Pacific Fleet at Pearl Harbor crystallized a crisis for Japan, the United Kingdom, the Netherlands, Australia, New Zealand, Canada, the United States, Thailand, Germany, and Italy. The duration of the crisis was from 26 November 1941 until 7 June 1942.

Background and Pre-crisis
Japan's quest for empire was symbolized by the proclamation of the "Greater East Asia Co-Prosperity Sphere." It began with the invasion of Manchuria in 1931 (see Case #39—**Mukden Incident,** in **China/Japan PC**). During the 1930s the Imperial Army spread southward into China (see Cases #40—**Shanghai,** in 1932; #43—**Jehol Campaign,** in 1933; #56—**Marco Polo Bridge,** in 1937–38; all in **China/Japan PC**). Later its attention shifted to the Western colonial empires in Southeast Asia (British Malaya, Dutch Indonesia, French Indochina). These countries could supply Japan's need for raw materials so as to reduce its dependence on other countries, notably the U.S., for such strategic commodities as petroleum, rubber, and iron.

In 1941 both the U.S. and the U.K. stood in the way of complete Japanese control of the Far East and Southeast Asia. The U.S. had vested interests in the region since the early part of the century, and its army and navy occupied important bases around Manila Bay in the Philippines. The U.S. considered the Philippines a vital link in the defense line for the protection of the west coast and continental United States. The British had long controlled Malaya and Borneo, with Singapore serving as one of the most important U.K. bases for imperial defense.

The fall of France in 1940 (see Case #78—**Fall of Western Europe** above) had removed one of Japan's obstacles; and by 1941 the Konoye government had worked out an arrangement with Vichy France for the use of French Indochina as a military corridor and base. The Dutch government and royal family fled to London with the fall of the Netherlands on 12 May 1940. However, its government-in-exile, together with the Dutch East Indies government (headed by the governor-general), continued to run the affairs of Indonesia, which was rich in oil and rubber.

During 1940 the United States exerted economic pressure on Japan. On 25 July the President prohibited the export of U.S. petroleum, petroleum products, and scrap metal without license. A few days later an embargo was imposed on the export of aviation fuel to all countries outside the Western Hemisphere except for use by U.S. planes. The embargo was expanded to scrap iron and steel after the signing of the Germany-Italy-Japan Tripartite Pact on 26 September 1940. After Japan landed troops in French Indochina on 24 July 1941, talks between Japan and the United States were broken off and all Japanese assets in the United States were frozen, effectively cutting Japan off from its most important markets and sources of raw materials.

In August Prime Minister Konoye sought a meeting with President Roosevelt but was rebuffed. Later that month, at a joint army-navy meeting, the heads of the Japanese armed forces agreed in principle that, if diplomacy did not bring results by mid-October 1941, the use of force against the U.S. would be unavoidable; and they subsequently stated that the decision for war or peace must be made by 15 October. Between 25 September and 15 October Konoye was unsuccessful in gaining political control over the supreme command of the armed forces. The cabinet resigned on 16 October, and Konoye was replaced, on the 18th, by General Tojo, who retained the position of War Minister.

To the United States' surprise, Tojo decided to continue the diplomatic path and sent a second envoy, Kurusu, to Washington to help the resident ambassador, Nomura, in his efforts to reach an agreement. Meanwhile, secret plans for the military campaign against the United States continued. During the first two weeks of November the Japanese embassy in Washington received a steady stream of messages that would eventually make up two Japanese proposals, A and B. These messages were deciphered by U.S. naval intelligence, thus informing the U.S. of a new Japanese deadline of 25 November for U.S. acceptance of its final proposal. (The deadline, the U.S. discovered, was postponed to 29 November.) Japan's proposals were rejected by Secretary of State Cordell Hull.

Crisis

On 26 November 1941 Hull presented the two Japanese envoys with a Ten Point Plan, viewed by Japan as an ultimatum and triggering a crisis for Tokyo. At the same time that Nomura and Kurusu were talking with Hull, Admiral Nagumo's task force had been at sea for 24 hours en route to Pearl Harbor. However, it was still in Tojo's power to stop them. On 1 December Japan's major response was a decision for war, but negotiations with the United States continued until 7 December.

The attack on Pearl Harbor, on 7 December 1941, triggered a crisis for the United States as well as Australia, Canada, the Netherlands, New Zealand, and the U.K. The Americans suffered 2,400 deaths and over 1,000 wounded. The U.S. responded on 8 December with a declaration of war. The British responded to the attack on a friendly state, as well as to the attack on Malaya the same day, by declaring war on Japan. Canada did likewise on the 8th. The Netherlands' response, on 8 December, was to mobilize the army in the Netherlands East Indies and to declare a state of emergency.

The trigger to Thailand's crisis was a Japanese attack on its territory on 8 December. After only five hours of fighting, the Thai government surrendered and announced that it would allow Japanese forces to pass through its territory. Japan, it was contended, would respect Thailand's territorial integrity. On 8 December, too, when the United States and its allies declared war on Japan, a crisis was triggered for Italy and Germany. The following day Australia and New Zealand responded to the crisis with similar declarations of war. On 10 December Thailand announced that it would not fight together with the Allied forces, thereby ending its crisis. And on 11 December Italy and Germany declared war on the United States. On the 21st a 10-year alliance was signed at Bangkok between Japan and Thailand: the Thai government agreed to aid Japan and declared war on the U.S. and the U.K. on 25 January 1942.

On 25 December 1941 British and Canadian forces in Hong Kong surrendered to the Japanese. From 27 January to 1 March the Battle of the Java Sea took place: Allied naval units were largely destroyed, and the way was opened for the Japanese conquest of the East Indies. The end of the crisis for the Netherlands was its formal surrender on 5 March 1942. Singapore fell on 15 February 1942 when the Japanese, having penetrated Malaya, landed from the north. Sixty thousand prisoners were taken. The fall of Singapore, signaling apparent victory for Japan, terminated its crisis and the crisis for its Axis allies, Germany and Italy. The British surrender terminated the U.K. crisis, in defeat.

In March the British evacuated Rangoon, allowing Japan to occupy Burma; the Burma Road was subsequently closed. The Battle of the Coral Sea began on 7 May. Allied naval and air power frustrated a possible Japanese invasion of Australia by destroying 100,000 tons of Japanese shipping between New Guinea and the Solomon Islands. On 8 May, with the reduction of danger, the crisis ended for Australia and New Zealand. And on 4 June a Japanese naval force attacked Midway Island and was dispersed, with heavy losses, by U.S. air and naval units. The crisis for Canada and the United States ended on 7 June 1942.

The United States approached the Pan American Union on 10 December 1941, but no activity followed.

(See *Master Table*, pp. 682–83.)

Sources

Foreign Relations of the United States (FRUS), Japan 1931–1941, vol. II; Baldwin 1966; Barnhart 1987; Ben-Zvi 1987; Borg and Okamoto 1973; Butow 1961; Churchill 1950a; Dallek 1979; Feis 1950; Heinrichs 1988; Hosoya 1968; Hull 1948, vol. II; Ike 1967; Jones 1954; Langer and Gleason 1953; Morton 1959; Prange 1981, 1986; Richardson 1994; Schroeder 1958; Snell 1963; Thorne 1978; Toland 1970; Vandenbosch 1959; Watt 1967; Weinberg 1994; Weintraub 1991; Wohlstetter 1962.

(89) Stalingrad

The USSR and Germany were enmeshed in a turning-point intrawar crisis (IWC) over Stalingrad from 28 June 1942 to 2 February 1943.

Background

The city of Stalingrad was one of the three strategic prizes of the German military campaign that began with "Operation **Barbarossa**" on 22 June 1941 (see Case #85 above), along with Moscow and Leningrad. The former Volgograd, renamed in honor of the ruler of the Soviet Union, was cut off from its hinterland, both in the north and the south, in July 1942.

Crisis

On 28 June 1942 German forces launched another major offensive in the east, triggering an IWC for the Soviet Union. At stake was the entire southern part of the eastern front, with the vast oil resources of the Caucasus at risk. On 28 July Stalin, by his Special Order 227, recognized that the city of Stalingrad, too, was a major objective of the German campaign. That military offensive appeared on the point of succeeding, but the Wehrmacht had overstretched its lines.

Seizing the opportunity created by the vulnerability of German forces, the Red Army launched a massive counteroffensive northwest and southeast of Stalingrad on 19 November, aimed at encircling the city and crushing the German Sixth Army. This triggered what was to become the gravest IWC for Germany during World War II—until the **D-Day** offensive in the West in 1944 (see Case #94 below).

The following day Hitler issued a personal order to the commander of the Sixth Army to stand fast no matter the cost. During the course of the Battle of Stalingrad this "no retreat" decision was repeated several times—after Field Marshal Manstein's request on 25 November to withdraw and General Zeitzler's similar appeal during December. The German operation to break out of its encirclement, "Winter Gale," began on 12 December but suffered defeat after defeat. Soviet forces recaptured Velikye-Luki on 1 January and entered Mozdok on the 3rd to relieve Leningrad from a 17-month siege. On 8 January 1943 the Soviets presented Hitler with an ultimatum to surrender at Stalingrad: it was refused.

On the 10th, the last phase of the Battle of Stalingrad began with an enormous Soviet artillery bombardment. Another Soviet demand for the surrender of German forces was made on the 24th, again refused by Hitler. On 31 January Soviet forces captured Field Marshal von Paulus, the commander of German forces at Stalingrad. Twenty-two German divisions were cut off and reduced to 80,000 men. They were forced to capitulate on 2 February 1943, ending Germany's Stalingrad crisis in disastrous defeat: the Germans and their Axis allies lost more than half a million soldiers, killed or captured. The Soviet IWC ended the same day in resounding triumph. The tide of battle in the "Great Patriotic

War" was changed irrevocably, as Soviet armies began the long march through German-occupied eastern Europe, culminating in the occupation of Berlin in May 1945.

(See *Master Table*, pp. 682–83.)

Sources
Baldwin 1966; Ciano 1947; Erickson 1975, 1983; Gilbert 1950; Jukes 1985; Schroter 1958; Seaton 1970; Shirer 1964; Weinberg 1994; Ziemke 1968, 1987.

(90) El Alamein

The North Africa campaign, beginning with the Battle of El Alamein, was an intrawar crisis for Germany and Italy from 23 October 1942 to 13 May 1943.

Pre-crisis
In the summer of 1942 a number of military victories were achieved by the Axis powers in North Africa. The British had been considerably weakened by their dispatch of 60,000 troops to Greece and had been forced to abandon recent conquests in Libya. On 21 June German General Rommel, commanding eight Italian divisions along with the Afrika Corps, captured Tobruk, the key to British defenses in North Africa. By the end of the month Rommel had moved toward the British-held stronghold at El Alamein in Egypt. When fuel shortages became extreme, the Italians were forced to halt their advance.

Crisis
On 23 October 1942 the British Eighth Army, commanded by General Montgomery, attacked from its position at El Alamein and broke through the Axis lines, triggering a crisis for Germany and Italy. The battle, which turned the tide of the war in North Africa, lasted 16 days.

A major British attack on 1–2 November succeeded in breaking through the southern sector of the front and overrunning the Italian divisions in the area. Rommel contacted Hitler's headquarters and informed him of his intention to withdraw while opportunity still prevailed. On 3 November Hitler ordered Rommel to stand fast and use all men and weapons available to defend the Axis position; the Italian response was similar. Rommel adhered reluctantly to the order. By the time permission for withdrawal was given the following day it was too late to save anything but the motorized divisions of the Panzer Army.

On 8 November, an Anglo-American force, commanded by General Eisenhower, disembarked in French Morocco and Algiers in an amphibious operation hitherto unequaled in history. Within three days Vichy French resistance had collapsed. The British headed toward Tunisia. Tobruk was reoccupied on 12 November and Benghazi on the 20th—by British forces advancing from Egypt into Libya.

From 17 to 27 January Churchill, de Gaulle, and Roosevelt met in Casablanca. Eisenhower took command of the unified Allied North African operations. The British Eighth Army broke through the Mareth Line into southern Tunisia and met the advancing U.S. Second Army Corps on 8 April. The termination of the crisis for Germany and Italy was 13 May 1943 when all German and Italian troops in North Africa surrendered.

(See *Master Table*, pp. 684–85.)

Sources
Churchill 1950b; Ciano 1947; Eisenhower 1948; Liddell-Hart 1953; Mussolini 1949; Shirer 1964; Weinberg 1994; Woodward 1962.

(91) Fall of Italy

The Allied invasion of Italy triggered an intrawar crisis for Italy and Germany from 9 July to 11 September 1943.

Pre-crisis
The Anglo-American campaign in North Africa resulted in a crushing defeat for Germany and Italy in May 1943 (see Case #90 above).

Crisis
United States, British, and Canadian forces launched an attack on Sicily on 9 July 1943, triggering a crisis for Italy: its mainland was threatened; and there was an imminent danger of the collapse of Mussolini's Fascist regime. Italy's leader perceived capitulation as a threat to Italy's role and status as a great power and felt that it would lead to prolonged occupation by the Allies. Mussolini met with Hitler on 19 July in the hope of obtaining Hitler's consent to Italy's early withdrawal from the war; no concessions were granted. The Italian response, on 24 July, was the dismissal of Mussolini by the king, at a meeting of the Fascist Grand Council, and the appointment of a new government under Marshal Pietro Badoglio. The council, which had not met since 12 September 1939, criticized Mussolini for leading the country into disaster. The majority of the party leaders were convinced of the advisability of a conclusion of a separate peace and a return to constitutional monarchy.

The news of Mussolini's dismissal, on 25 July, triggered a crisis for Germany. Armistice proposals by Italy, expected within a week to 10 days, would jeopardize German strategic control of northern Italy and expose the Reich's southern flank. The following day Hitler ordered German forces into northern Italy. On 18 August Italian resistance in Sicily collapsed following thousands of casualties on both sides. Allied troops landed on the boot of southern Italy on 2 September. The next day an armistice agreement was signed between Italy and the Western powers, ending hostilities between the Anglo-American forces and those of the Badoglio regime. German and Italian forces evacuated Sicily on 8

September, terminating Italy's crisis with the Allies. On the 10th Italian forces surrendered to the Germans after they were defeated in the battle around Rome. The crisis ended for Germany on 11 September when all Italian territory, including Rome, was declared by the German army to be a theater of war under German military control.

(Mussolini, who had been held prisoner near Rome, was rescued by German troops, and proclaimed the establishment of a Republican Fascist Party in northern Italy, in alliance with the German army of occupation.)

(See *Master Table*, pp. 684–85.)

Sources
Bryant 1959; Churchill 1951; Deakin 1962; Eisenhower 1948; Graham and Bidwell 1986; Liddell-Hart 1953; Murphy 1964; Mussolini 1949; Shirer 1964; Smith 1982; Snell 1963; Weinberg 1994.

(92) German Occupation of Hungary

Hungary's intrawar crisis with Germany lasted from 13 to 19 March 1944.

Pre-crisis
After Italy's capitulation to the Allies in September 1943 (see Case #91 above), Germany began to consider the possibility of a similar fate for Hungary and Romania, and plans were made for German occupation of both countries. While Romania was perceived to be a lesser problem, it was known that Hungary had begun to send out feelers for an armistice agreement with the Allies. German plans for the occupation of Hungary were operationalized on 12 March, as Soviet forces moved rapidly toward the Hungarian frontier.

Crisis
The concentration of German troops around Vienna and on the Hungarian frontier triggered a crisis for Hungary on 13 March 1944. Two days later, Hitler demanded that Hungary's Regent, Admiral Horthy, meet with him. While Horthy deliberated his decision, fearing his detention and arrest while Germany occupied Hungary, the Allies decided finally to seek an armistice with Hungary and therefore dropped a U.S. mission into that country on 17 March to discuss terms of surrender. By 18 March Horthy had decided that he was compelled to see Hitler at any cost, and set out to do so.

Horthy was detained for one day, under the pretext of an air raid, and allowed to reach the Hungarian frontier as German troops began their invasion. On 19 March Hungary was occupied by Germany with no real resistance. The U.S. mission was turned over to the German forces, and Hungary's capitulation ended its crisis.

(See *Master Table*, pp. 684–85.)

Sources
Fenyo 1972; Macartney 1956–57; Shirer 1964; Speer 1970; Weinberg 1994; Werth 1964.

(93) Soviet Occupation of East Europe

Soviet offensives into Eastern Europe in 1944–45 created an intrawar crisis for Romania, Germany, and Hungary from 26 March 1944 to 13 February 1945.

Background and Pre-crisis
Romanian oil fields had been protected by Germany since 1939. And on 23 September 1940 Romania became a member of the Tripartite Pact (Germany, Italy, Japan), fighting alongside Germany against the Soviet Union. As the tide turned at the Battle of Stalingrad (see Case #89 above), Soviet troops began major offensives into Eastern Europe. In December 1943 the U.S. and the USSR, followed by the U.K., warned Romania, Bulgaria, and Hungary that Germany's defeat would mean a defeat for those countries as well. Romania's King Michael began to try to find ways to arrange an agreement with the Allies. By the end of March Soviet troops were marching toward Romania's borders.

Hungarian peace feelers throughout 1943 provoked German suspicions, resulting in its occupation by Germany on 19 March 1944, at the time that Hungarian Regent Horthy was meeting with Hitler. The economic situation in Hungary was severe from 1943, along with increased repression, as a result of the German occupation.

Crisis
A crisis for Romania was triggered on 26 March with the arrival of Soviet forces at its border, threatening defeat and occupation. A USSR announcement on 2 April declared that the Soviet Union did not wish to take over Romanian territory; nor did it aspire to create a new social order there. Soviet troops would enter the country only as needed to continue the resistance to enemy forces. On the 4th the Allies began mass bombings of Romania, especially oil production installations. One week later Soviet armistice terms were rejected by Romania. By 5 May oil production was down to half of its previous level.

Romania's major response, on 23 August, was King Michael's acceptance of armistice terms preferred covertly by the Soviet Union. An amnesty was declared for political prisoners, and a Government of National Union was set up: Romania would henceforth fight alongside the Allies. The Romanian response triggered a crisis for Germany, with the loss of an ally, and the threat of the Soviet thrust extending to Germany itself. The German response, the same day, was an order to seize the Romanian oil fields and the nearby harbor of Constanta, and to set up a pro-German government in Romania. On the 25th Germany bombed Bucharest while negotiations between the Soviets and the Romanians continued. On 12 September an armistice was signed in Moscow, ending the crisis for Romania.

Within a week Soviet forces approached the borders of Bulgaria, Yugoslavia, and Hungary. And on 22 September they expelled the Germans from Romania, ending Germany's crisis over Romania in defeat.

A crisis for Hungary was triggered on 22 September with an invasion by Soviet and Romanian forces. Hungary attempted to contact the Allies that day, and again on 10 October, when a provisional armistice was arranged in Moscow conditional on Hungary's joining the war against Germany. Hungary responded on 15 October with Horthy's proclamation of an armistice. Some Hungarian troops, however, joined the German forces. Hungary's response triggered another crisis for Germany, which responded on the 16th by placing Horthy under protective custody; and, as the Hungarians surrendered, German forces took over Budapest. Horthy finally signed the appointment of Szalasi, head of the pro-Nazi Arrow Cross movement, as Prime Minister.

By December 1944 the Red Army had begun a siege of Budapest, completely encircling the city by the 26th. The battle lasted two more months, and on 13 February 1945 Budapest fell, terminating the crisis for both Germany and Hungary in defeat, with the latter effectively out of the war.

Bulgaria held a series of negotiations with the Soviet Union and eventually withdrew from the Axis and entered the war against Germany.

(See *Master Table*, pp. 684–85.)

Sources
Bullock 1962; Erickson 1983; Fenyo 1972; Ionescu 1964; Macartney 1956–57; Shirer 1964; Weinberg 1994; Ziemke 1968.

(94) D-Day

An intrawar crisis for Germany was triggered by the Allied landing in Western Europe on 6 June 1944. It lasted until Germany's surrender on 7 May 1945.

Pre-crisis
By 1944 the tide of war had definitely turned in the Allies' favor. The end of Axis resistance in North Africa had been achieved by 13 May 1943 (see Case #90—**El Alamein** above). The Soviets had defeated the Germans at Stalingrad and at Kursk-Orel and were advancing rapidly through Eastern Europe (see Cases #89 and 93 above). German divisions in southern Italy had been forced to retreat (see Case #91 above). And the war in the Pacific was proceeding successfully for the U.S. (see Case #95 below). For many months careful and elaborate plans for the invasion of France had been made by the Supreme Headquarters of the Allied Expeditionary Forces, commanded by General Eisenhower. The chief base for

the concentration of troops and war materials was the U.K.; and the plan of the campaign had been rehearsed and prepared to the finest detail.

Crisis
An IWC was triggered for Germany on 6 June 1944 when British, American and Canadian forces invaded Nazi-occupied Western Europe. The German response was immediate: wherever they encountered Allied troops they fought back, hoping to prevent a firm Allied foothold on the Normandy coast. Within one week, however, a strip of beach 60 miles long had been occupied and artificial harbors were constructed—to offset the lack of port facilities for disembarkation. With the capture of Cherbourg on 27 June the Allies gained a major port. Throughout the summer they advanced into France and Belgium, and, on 2 September 1944, the U.S. First Army crossed the German frontier. The advance was halted when an Allied attempt to outflank the West Wall through the flat Dutch territory in the north failed, and survivors of an Allied airborne division, which had been dropped in Holland at Arnhem, had to be withdrawn. On 16 December the Germans broke through U.S. defense lines in the Belgian and Luxembourg sector. The Battle of the Bulge inflicted heavy losses, and the Allied forces were driven back to the Meuse. The gap was closed by the end of December when the Allies rallied to attack on both sides of the "Bulge."

From the beginning of 1945 the Allied drive into Germany from the west coordinated with the rapid and powerful Soviet offensive from the east (see Case #100 below). President Roosevelt, Prime Minister Churchill, and Marshal Stalin met at Yalta in the Crimea on 7 February to plan the final defeat and occupation of Germany. The U.S. First and Third Armies crossed into Germany in February and March, and the British and Canadians opened an offensive southeast of Nijmegen, Holland. By 12 April the U.S. Ninth Army had reached the Elbe River. On that day President Roosevelt died. Soviet forces fought their way into Berlin on the 25th. And on the 26th the armies of the U.S. and USSR met on the Elbe at Torgau. On 29 April German resistance in northern Italy broke. And on 1 May the Battle of Berlin began. A German radio announcement from Hamburg declared that Hitler had died that day. On 7 May a group of German army leaders sent envoys to Reims where they signed terms of surrender, ending the crisis for Germany and the war in Europe.

(See *Master Table,* pp. 684–85.)

Sources
Baldwin 1966; Bryant 1959; Calvocoressi and Wint 1972; Churchill 1951, 1953; Eisenhower 1948; Liddell-Hart 1970; Palmer 1973; Weigley 1981; Weinberg 1994.

(95) Fall of Saipan

The defeat at Saipan precipitated an IWC for Japan between 9 and 18 July 1944.

Background and Pre-crisis

The war in the Pacific had been turning against Japan since the Battle of Midway in June 1942. Toward the end of 1943 and the beginning of 1944 Japanese sea lanes came under continuous attack from the American and British navies. Although the Japanese leadership understood the gravity of the situation, the Japanese press continued to inform the public of the war's progress—in Japan's favor. In February 1944 the largest carrier-launched air armada in history attacked Japan's strategic Caroline Islands base at Truk, sinking 19–26 ships and destroying about 200 planes. Prime Minister Tojo carried out a major reorganization and consolidation of his cabinet on 19 February. He assumed the post of Chief of the Army General Staff and appointed Navy Minister Shimada as Chief of the Navy General Staff. For the first time in Japanese history administrative and command posts were held by the same persons.

Severe restrictions were placed on Japanese society. There was mobilization and reorganization of labor and business. Air raid defense networks were built, and entertainment centers were closed. As the pressure of the Allied forces grew, so did the opposition to Tojo within the Japanese elite. In June American forces delivered a series of devastating attacks upon Saipan, Tinian, Guam, and Rota in the Marianas. The strategic cordon of defense that Japan had created around the home islands vanished rapidly. The American invasion of Saipan, "Operation Forager," began with a bombardment of Japanese positions on 13 June 1944. The island's strategic importance was due to the fact that long-range American bombers, if installed on airstrips there, could threaten the Japanese people in their cities and towns.

Crisis

The defeat at Saipan on 9 July 1944 triggered another intrawar crisis for Japan, which perceived a threat of grave damage to its population centers. On the 13th Prime Minister Tojo sought advice from the Lord Privy Seal, the Marquis Kido, who had been Tojo's supporter for the position of Prime Minister. Kido presented the prime minister with three conditions aimed at changing the nature and style of his government. He demanded the separation of the war minister and army chief of staff posts, the replacement of the navy minister, and the formation of a United Front cabinet which would include members of the senior statesmen-group (*Jushin*), consisting of former prime ministers.

During the next four days Tojo attempted to reorganize his cabinet. Most ex–prime ministers refused to join and demanded Tojo's resignation. On 18 July Tojo resigned terminating this crisis for Japan.

(See *Master Table*, pp. 684–85.)

Sources

See sources for Case #88.

(97) Leyte Campaign

The U.S. invasion of Leyte in the Philippines created another IWC for Japan from 20 October to 26 December 1944.

Pre-crisis
The Japanese anticipated an early U.S. attempt to retake the Philippines; and in the summer of 1944 they began developing defense plans that included air and navy support. By September 1944 Japan had suffered serious reverses on both military and diplomatic fronts.

Crisis
On 20 October 1944 the advance units of the largest amphibious operation of the Pacific war (four U.S. divisions, ultimately involving a quarter of a million troops) landed on the island of Leyte. This began the campaign for the reconquest of the Philippines, triggering a crisis for Japan: Tokyo perceived a strategic threat to the home islands if the Philippines fell to the Americans. In the last major naval battle of World War II, the Japanese navy suffered a loss of 40 ships sunk, 46 ships damaged, and 405 planes destroyed. On land the scope of the campaign is evident in the casualties on Leyte: more than 15,000 Americans and more than 50,000 Japanese. The Philippines had been earmarked by Japan as the first in a series of decisive battles that was slated to end in Japan's overwhelming triumph. When the army agreed to concentrate its forces in a bold effort to rout the Americans, Prime Minister Koiso and the Japanese people were led to believe that a Japanese victory in Leyte would turn the tide of the war. Japan's response, on 24 October, was to withdraw its fleet from Philippine waters once they had failed to halt the Leyte invasion.

After the defeat Japan no longer had a fleet or air force that could mount an offensive. Japan was losing planes and pilots faster than they could be replaced. On 24 November the first large-scale B-29 raid on Japan began. This destroyed major Japanese aircraft factories. On 26 December the U.S. announced the successful completion of the Leyte campaign, granting control of the Pacific to the Allies, and ending Japan's IWC in total defeat.

(See *Master Table*, pp. 684–85.)

Sources
See sources for Case #88.

(99) Luzon

Following the American victory at Leyte, the U.S. invasion of Luzon created another IWC for Japan from 9 January to 3 March 1945.

Pre-crisis
After the defeat at Leyte, Japan's political and military leaders concentrated their hopes for victory on Luzon. As the situation deteriorated in the Philippines, the emperor called a meeting of the *Jushin* (senior statesmen) on 6 January 1945 to seek their advice on the future course. While the Japanese military had already lost the war, some of the Jushin advised, Japan's spirit could not be destroyed. For want of a better solution, they now proposed a concentration of forces against the U.S. in the hope that a victorious battle would permit Japan to end the war on more favorable terms.

Crisis
On 9 January two corps of the U.S. Sixth Army invaded Luzon, triggering a new crisis for Japan. They had gained an element of surprise by selecting an undesirable part of the coastline for landing. A combination of artillery, air bombardment, and the dogged advance of the U.S. infantry gradually led to progress. Although the Japanese forces were cut off from retreat in Manila, they continued to refuse to surrender. Other U.S. forces sought to secure Manila Bay. Finally, on 3 March, the American occupation of Manila was completed, terminating this crisis for Japan.
(See *Master Table,* pp. 684–85.)

Sources
See sources for Case #88.

(100) Final Soviet Offensive

An intrawar crisis for Germany in the East lasted from the beginning of the final Soviet offensive on 11 January until Germany's surrender on 7 May 1945. This crisis overlapped with the German IWC over the continuing Allied advance in Western Europe in 1944–45 (see Case #94—**D-Day** above). Both ended with Germany's capitulation.

Pre-crisis
The campaign was planned by the Soviets as a separate and well-defined offensive. The aim was to strike at the heart of the Third Reich. The Russian homeland had been liberated from Nazi conquest by July 1944; and by 29 August Soviet forces had reached the border of East Prussia. At this point they halted and deliberately did not penetrate German territory. Instead, they concentrated on the Baltic Peninsula and the Balkans. These areas were liberated in October and December of 1944. In January 1945 the Soviets turned their full attention to the planning of a two-pronged attack, against East Prussia in the north and Silesia in the center.

Crisis

An intrawar crisis for Germany was triggered on 11 January 1945 when the first part of the Soviet offensive began with a thrust from Poland into Silesia. For the first time Germany proper was threatened. The German response was immediate: they used every means available in order to halt the Soviet advance. On 13 January the second Soviet thrust advanced from Lithuania into East Prussia. By 1 February East Prussia had been conquered, and the Soviets advanced into Silesia capturing a long and broad front inside the eastern border of Germany along the Oder River from Zehden in the north to Ratibor in the south. By the end of March they held the entire area of eastern Germany. On 25 April 1945 the Soviets entered Berlin.

Meanwhile the Allies were advancing in western Germany, and the two armies met on the 25th. Thereafter, both armies converged on those parts of Germany that had not yet been conquered until the Third Reich finally collapsed and surrendered on 7 May 1945 to the Allied and Soviet Commands.

(See *Master Table,* pp. 684–85.)

Sources

Calvocoressi and Wint 1972; Churchill 1953; Clark 1965; Erickson 1983; Glantz and House 1995; Weinberg 1994; Werth 1964; Ziemke 1968.

(101) Iwo Jima

The Battle of Iwo Jima generated an intrawar crisis for Japan from 19 February to 16 March 1945.

Background and Pre-crisis

Iwo Jima, located among a group of volcanic islands midway between the Marianas and Japan, was of high strategic salience to the armies of both adversaries. Japan used it as a staging base for damaging raids on U.S. B-29s in the Marianas; and the U.S. found it imperative to capture the island, destroy the air base, and establish a position 750 miles from Yokahama. Iwo Jima received the longest and most intensive U.S. preinvasion bombardment of any objective in the Pacific war. Regular air raids had begun in August 1944; and soon thereafter they were a daily occurrence. Nevertheless, Japanese defenses were not destroyed. After the **Fall of Saipan** (see Case #95 above), the Japanese resolved to convert Iwo Jima into an impregnable fortress. As the bombs fell, they dug deeper underground.

Crisis

An IWC for Japan was triggered on 19 February 1945 when the U.S. launched a massive invasion of Iwo Jima. Firing from concealed points, the Japanese resisted the U.S. advance yard by yard in a stubborn and protracted battle that cost the U.S. 19,938 casualties, including 4,198 dead. On 8 March the Japanese began one of their most concerted counterattacks. It caught the U.S. marines off guard.

They, in turn, rallied for a great flanking movement that pressed the Japanese back toward the sea. Japanese losses were very high. The last phase of the battle began on 11 March with a more rapid U.S. advance. On 16 March one of the last segments of opposition was pushed into a small region on the northern end of the island where the Japanese fought defiantly until the end. Other pockets were eliminated, with difficulty. The crisis for Japan ended in defeat on the 16th.

The following day the Americans raised the U.S. flag on the island of Iwo Jima.

(See *Master Table,* pp. 684–85.)

Sources
See sources for Case #88.

(103) Okinawa

Japan's IWC over the island of Okinawa took place from 1 April to 21 June 1945.

Pre-crisis
By the spring of 1945 both time and space for Japan had run out. U.S. victories in the Philippines and Iwo Jima had chiseled away the outer walls of Japan's outposts of defense; and the route to final victory was controlled by Allied air and naval power. On 21 March a U.S. aircraft carrier, penetrating Japanese inland waters, attacked principal units of the Japanese Home Fleet, damaging 15 warships and destroying 475 planes. Japanese suicide attacks had become a calculated tactic as the U.S. proceeded to plan for the occupation of Okinawa, 325 miles from Japanese cities.

Crisis
On 1 April 1945 U.S. marines and army troops invaded Okinawa and triggered another intrawar crisis for Japan. A Japanese attempt to check this amphibious operation resulted in the sinking by U.S. aircraft of the Japanese battleship *Yamato,* two cruisers, and three destroyers. On 5 April the Koiso cabinet collapsed in Tokyo. That day, as well, the Soviets announced that they would not renew their Neutrality Pact with Japan. One of the most extensive suicide assaults of modern warfare was launched by Japan on 6 April. A five-hour battle ensued in which 135 kamikaze pilots sank six vessels and damaged 18 others. Heavy fighting in April brought the adversaries to a stalemate. Toward the end of the month a Japanese counterattack was launched. The U.S. advances were slowed down both by strong resistance and heavy rains. On 9 June the new Prime Minister, Suzuki, announced that Japan would continue to defend itself to the end and that unconditional surrender was out of the question. Official resistance on Okinawa ended on 21 June 1945. The Okinawa campaign was the climax of Japan's final resistance; it left little room for doubt as to the outcome of the Pacific war.

(See *Master Table,* pp. 684–85.)

Sources
See sources for Case #88.

(105) French Forces/Syria

Syria and France were the actors in a crisis involving French control over Syria, from 17 May to 3 June 1945.

Background and Pre-crisis
Syria's independence was formally recognized by France and the U.K. in 1941. France, however, remained the Mandatory Power until the end of World War II and allowed Syria to maintain a militia, but not an army. The *Comité Français de Libération Nationale (CFLN)*, under the leadership of General Charles de Gaulle, had been recognized by the U.K. and the U.S. as the French government-in-exile. On 25 August 1944 de Gaulle entered Paris and the *CFLN* was then recognized as the Provisional Government of the French Republic, with Charles de Gaulle as President.

With the defeat of Nazi Germany in May 1945, the president and National Assembly of Syria appealed to France for a new treaty that would curtail French privileges in Syria and transfer control over security and foreign affairs from the French Mandatory Power to the government of Syria. France wished to delay this step until the formal establishment of the United Nations. Sporadic riots and strikes against the French in Syria began on 8 May. In order to retain control, and as a security measure, de Gaulle ordered French troops into Syria.

Crisis
A crisis for Syria was triggered on 17 May 1945 when three French battalions landed in Beirut and proceeded to Syria in order to secure positions in Damascus and other major cities. On 28 May the Syrian militia, accompanied by rioting citizens, attacked all French posts in the country. De Gaulle accused the British of supplying arms to the Syrians. The riots triggered a crisis for France, which responded the same day by firing on the militia and bombing major Syrian cities. In two days of fighting an estimated 400 soldiers and civilians lay dead in Damascus, along with countless injured.

After the outbreak of violence the U.K. intervened and demanded that France agree to a cease-fire, evacuate its positions in the Syrian cities, and return all French forces to their barracks. Churchill intimated to de Gaulle that, if the French did not comply, the consequences might be collisions between British and French forces. A disagreement between France and the U.K. over the authority of British General Paget, the Commander in Chief of all Allied forces in the Middle East, had precipitated the U.K. ultimatum. Churchill regarded the French forces as still officially under the supreme command of General Paget until the end of the Pacific war, while de Gaulle assumed that Paget had completed his function once the war in Europe was over.

De Gaulle considered rejecting the British ultimatum, even in light of the possibility of hostilities between French and British forces; but the French parliament and press vehemently opposed French resistance. On 3 June France complied with the ultimatum and evacuated its positions ending the crisis for both itself and Syria.

On 1 June the USSR sent a memorandum to de Gaulle expressing concern about developments in the Middle East. The U.S. was approached by de Gaulle on the 2nd to participate in a conference to settle the crisis in Syria, as well as all other Mandate questions in the Middle East, including Palestine and Iraq. Washington, however, refused to involve itself in an issue that it considered to be exclusively of British and French concern. Moreover, the idea of inviting the USSR to the conference prompted President Truman to reject the idea. British troops replaced the French until 1946 when the United Nations terminated the French Mandate and acknowledged the Syrian Republic's full sovereignty. (See *Master Table*, pp. 684–85.)

Sources
Churchill 1953; de Gaulle 1971; Longrigg 1958; Palmer 1973; Willis 1968.

(107) Hiroshima-Nagasaki

Japan's final intrawar crisis began with the dropping of the first U.S. atom bomb on 6 August 1945 and terminated with its formal surrender on 2 September 1945.

Pre-crisis
Prime Minister Koiso, who had succeeded Tojo in July 1944, resigned on 8 April 1945. He was replaced by Admiral Suzuki, whose mission was to bring the war to an end, though the Japanese government and people were still committed publicly to continued resistance.

After the collapse of Germany in May (see Cases #94—**D-Day** and # 100—**Final Soviet Offensive** above), the Japanese were left without allies, and British and U.S. efforts concentrated on the Pacific theater. U.S. aircraft destroyed or immobilized the remnants of the Japanese navy and shattered Japan's industry. United States battleships shelled densely populated cities, and the air force dropped 40,000 tons of bombs on Japanese industrial centers in one month. Japanese morale began to disintegrate. On 20 June the emperor summoned the Supreme War Council and indicated his wish to seek peace with the Allies and to approach the Soviet Union with a request for mediation.

The Potsdam Conference began on 17 July 1945 with Churchill, Stalin, and Truman participating. The final text of their communiqué, dated 26 July, called for Japan's "unconditional surrender," while avoiding all mention of the future of the emperor, implying that the Allies would determine whether he would remain after the surrender. Japanese military forces would be disarmed, and Japan would be deprived of its imperial conquests. The Potsdam Declaration specified that

Japan would be welcomed back into the international community and that the occupation would end after the Allies had accomplished their objectives and the Japanese had chosen a responsible government by democratic means. "The alternative for Japan is prompt and utter destruction." Japan's prime minister, foreign minister, and navy minister were in favor of accepting the terms, but the war minister and the chief of staff were opposed.

Crisis

A grave intrawar crisis for Japan was triggered on 6 August when an atomic bomb was dropped on Hiroshima. Three-fifths of the city was destroyed. Japan's crisis was compounded on the 8th when the Soviet Union declared war and launched a major invasion of Japanese-occupied Manchuria. A continuing threat to Japan's existence as a state was manifested on the 9th, with the dropping of another nuclear bomb on Nagasaki. The same day the inner cabinet in Tokyo appealed to the emperor for a final expression of his wish. The emperor opted for peace. On the 10th Japan made an offer of surrender on the basis of the Potsdam Declaration, but on condition that it did not comprise "any demand which prejudices the prerogatives of His Majesty as a Sovereign Ruler."

The U.S. government refused to accept any such condition and replied with the formula: "from the moment of surrender, the authority of the Emperor and the Japanese Government to rule the state shall be subject to the Supreme Commander of the Allied Powers . . . " After lengthy consideration Japan, once again following the lead of the emperor, decided to surrender despite the rejection of a condition that had been considered essential. On 15 August the emperor told the Japanese nation that the war was at an end. The Suzuki cabinet resigned, and the formal terms of surrender were signed on 2 September aboard the U.S.S *Missouri* in Tokyo Bay, ending the war and the final intrawar crisis for Japan.

The Japanese home islands were placed under the rule of a U.S. army of occupation. The emperor remained as head of state. And the Japanese political and police officials continued to function. The capitulation of Japanese forces in China took place on 9 September. And China regained sovereignty over Inner Mongolia and Manchuria, as well as the islands of Formosa and Hainan. Hong Kong was reoccupied by the British, who accepted the formal Japanese surrender at Singapore on 12 September 1945.

(A debate has raged for 50 years over the U.S. decision to employ atomic bombs in the closing days of World War II. Some, notably those who made the decision [President Truman and the U.S. defense establishment, and their defenders], argued that it was necessary in order to save half a million Americans or more who would have been killed in a frontal invasion of Japan's home islands. Others, led by revisionist historians of the origins of the Cold War, have argued that Japan would have surrendered before the end of 1945 even if atomic bombs had not been dropped on Hiroshima and Nagasaki—and that the most senior U.S. decision makers knew this at the time.)

(See *Master Table*, pp. 684–85.)

Sources

Alperovitz 1965, 1995a, 1995b; Bernstein 1995; Bernstein and Matusow 1966; Brooks 1968; Buchanan 1964; Butow 1954; Byrnes 1947; Feis 1966; Hane 1972; Hewlett and Anderson 1990; Holloway 1994; Iriye 1981; Kase 1969; Knapp 1967; Kolko and Kolko 1972; Newman 1995; Rhodes 1986; Rusk 1990; Sansom 1948; Sherwin 1975; Shigemitsu 1958; Thorne 1972; Truman 1955; Weinberg 1994.

Africa: Non-Protracted Conflict (PC) Crises

Among the five regions, Africa generated the largest number of international crises in the twentieth century, 108 cases or 26 percent of the total from the end of 1918 to the end of 1994. This is especially visible since Africa was the most recent entry into the mainstream of world politics: until 1955 there were only four independent states in Africa: Egypt, Ethiopia, Liberia, and South Africa; and Egypt was primarily a Middle East actor. The upsurge of independence in Africa began in 1960, with the transfer of power from France to its colonies in Saharan Africa.

There are few crises located in Africa—in whole or in part—with consequences beyond that region. And those that have more wide-ranging effects were on the periphery of Africa: Cases #152—**Suez Nationalization-War,** in 1956–57; #222—**Six Day War,** in 1967; #255—**October-Yom Kippur,** in 1973–74, all of which included the Sinai desert but are classified as Middle East cases. The only pure Africa exceptions were Cases #47—**Ethiopian War,** in the inter-world war period of multipolarity; #260—**War in Angola,** in 1975–76; and #292—**Shaba II,** in 1978, in the polycentrism system-period. Among the protracted conflicts in Africa, most have—or appear to have—ended, namely, Rhodesia in 1980, Angola in 1992, and Chad/Libya in 1994, or are in the process of winding down. The others—**Ethiopia/Somalia** and **Western Sahara**—are less active in terms of international crises in the post–Cold War era (see *Master Table*).

The following pages present summaries of all non-PC crises that occurred in Africa, organized chronologically. Moreover, the 46 PC cases are listed, along with a reference to where the relevant summary can be found.

(47) Ethiopian War

One of the celebrated international crises of the inter–world war period, **Ethiopian War,** began on 6 December 1934 and lasted until 5 May 1936. There were four crisis actors: Ethiopia, the U.K., France, and Italy.

Background
Italy's entry into East Africa as a colonial power in the late nineteenth century was made possible by a British objective of reducing French influence in the region. Italian expansion continued until their severe defeat by Abyssinian (Ethiopian) troops at the Battle of Adowa in 1896. Eritrea was transferred to Italy by British royal decree in 1899. Mussolini's efforts to achieve domination

424

over Ethiopia began as early as 1923. In 1928 a Treaty of Friendship was signed; but Ethiopia refused to live up to its conditions, which granted Italy special privileges. In 1932 Mussolini sent his minister of the colonies to Eritrea to prepare it as a springboard for an invasion of Ethiopia. Thereafter roads and military installations in Eritrea were built and strengthened. Incidents occurred on the border as the Ethiopians became more and more apprehensive of Italy's designs.

Pre-crisis

Wal-wal (Ual-ual), a watering site in a loosely designated border area between Italian and Ethiopian territory, had been used frequently by tribes from British and Italian Somaliland who wandered freely in the area. It became the site of an Italian garrison. In November 1934 a British mission surveying the border between British Somaliland and Ethiopia arrived at the wells of Wal-wal with an armed Ethiopian escort. The Italian garrison commander perceived an imminent attack from tribesmen nearby and requested reinforcements, while the British mission withdrew from the area.

Crisis

On 6 December 1934 Mussolini demanded an unconditional apology, a large indemnity, and punishment of those responsible for an attack by Ethiopian tribesmen against the Italians at Wal-wal the previous day. This triggered a crisis for Ethiopian Emperor Haile Selassie, who claimed that the dispute fell under the arbitration clause of the 1928 Treaty of Friendship. The U.K. proposed a conciliatory solution that Italy refused to consider.

Ethiopia appealed to the League of Nations on 9 December. When no progress was forthcoming it requested League intervention on 3 January 1935. The Council encouraged direct negotiations between the parties and, later, arbitration. The item was removed from the Council's agenda when Italy agreed to bilateral talks. However, negotiations began to break down in March in the face of new preconditions by Italy and the buildup of its forces in Eritrea. On 17 March and 3 April there were two more Ethiopian appeals to the League.

France and the U.K. supported Italy's view that the League should await the outcome of pending arbitration. (In an earlier Franco-Italian agreement, 7 January, Paris gave Rome a free hand vis-à-vis Ethiopia. France, Italy, and the U.K. met on 11–14 April to form the Stresa Front against Germany. Italy then conceded that it would consent to arbitration with Ethiopia under the 1928 treaty. Further negotiations between the two adversaries and France and Great Britain centered around the 20 May 1935 League Council meeting, which adopted two resolutions on the timing and form of arbitration: 25 August was designated as the final date for a ruling. A U.K. offer of economic concessions to Italy amounting to economic control over Ethiopia and a large part of Ogaden, with an Ethiopian access to the sea through British Somaliland, was refused by Italy in June. The situation was further aggravated by the signing of an Anglo-German naval agreement in June, which allowed German naval expansion to 35 percent of the size of the British navy.

A three-power meeting without Ethiopian participation began in August 1935. Italy, which by then had assembled 250,000 troops in East Africa, rejected Anglo-French proposals and refused to state its final demands. Sometime during that month a U.K. perception that Mussolini might attack Britain in retaliation for its support of Ethiopia triggered a crisis for the U.K. (As early as January 1935 London had informed the emperor that "no assurances of even the most general and personal nature" could be given.)

In response to a perceived threat of possible war the U.K. reinforced its Mediterranean fleet on 3 September 1935. It also began negotiations with other Mediterranean states, especially Yugoslavia and Turkey. At the same time, the "Hoare-Laval Plan" (see below) ruled out Anglo-French military action against Italy. And the British foreign secretary assured Mussolini that the U.K. would not close the Suez Canal to Italian ships or impose economic sanctions.

In early September Ethiopia appealed to the Council once more, under Article 15 of the Covenant. On 9 September a League Committee of Five was appointed to discuss the dispute, as well as Italian claims that Ethiopia was unfit for League membership. League observers were requested to witness Italian mobilization and the forward movement of its troops. And when Ethiopia perceived war as imminent it informed the League on 29 September of its intention to mobilize.

On 3 October 1935 Italy, the triggering entity for the international crisis as a whole, began a full-scale attack on Ethiopia transforming the incipient crisis over Wal-wal into the Ethiopian War. In addition to military resistance the victim appealed to the League the following day. Mussolini justified the war, alleging Ethiopian "aggression." The League Council condemned Italian aggression on the 7th. And on the 11th the League Assembly called on members to impose sanctions against Italy.

France feared that strong League action might provoke Italy to leave the recently formed anti-German Stresa Front and realign with Germany. Thus the Council's action triggered a crisis for France. Premier Pierre Laval, who as Foreign Minister had negotiated the January 1935 carte blanche deal with Italy, attempted to slow down the imposition of sanctions by a special League Committee of Thirteen, which had been set up on 9 October to draft specific measures. Its recommendations, issued on 6 November, triggered a crisis for Italy because they included sanctions on oil imports, as well as other vital raw materials. Italy responded in early December by informing France's premier that such League action would seriously affect Franco-Italian relations.

Laval took measures to stall the imposition of oil sanctions and succeeded in preventing their adoption, preferring a compromise agreement between the adversaries. U.K. Foreign Secretary Hoare and Laval began talks on 7 December. The result was the Hoare-Laval Plan announced on 9 December. The plan called for three areas of Ethiopia bordering Eritrea and Italian Somaliland to be ceded to

Italy, and a large section of southern Ethiopia to be set aside for exclusive Italian exploitation. Ethiopia was to receive a corridor to the sea and the port of Assab in Eritrea.

The plan was uncovered by the press in Britain and published even before it was proposed to the belligerents. The subsequent backlash resulted in Hoare's resignation on 18 December 1935 and the fall of the Laval government in France on 22 January 1936. On 3 March the new French premier was able to thwart the final attempt to impose oil sanctions against Italy in favor of an appeal to the belligerents for conciliation.

Once the threat of effective League action was over, the crises for Italy, France, and the U.K. ended. Hitler's reoccupation of the Rhineland on 7 March 1936 (see Case #51—**Remilitarization of the Rhineland,** in **France/Germany PC**) diverted League attention from Italy. Meanwhile war raged in Ethiopia and escalated with the Italian use of mustard gas, despite League disapproval. Ethiopia appealed to the League, to other states, and to the world at large throughout April 1936. On 2 May Haile Selassie fled into exile through French Somaliland. On 5 May the capital, Addis Ababa, fell to Italy's forces; and Mussolini announced the end of the war and Italy's annexation of Ethiopia.

(The League Assembly lifted the sanctions against Italy in July 1936 and refused to recognize its conquest of Ethiopia. The United States passed the Second Neutrality Act on 29 February 1936 in response to the recommendations for oil sanctions against Italy.)

(See *Master Table,* pp. 674–75.)

Sources
Baer 1967; Boca 1969; Carr 1945; Cassels 1968; Chabad 1963; Drysdale 1964; Eagleton 1957; Eden 1962; Feis 1947; Garratt 1938; Haile Selassie 1976; Hallett 1974; Hull 1948, vol. I; Kirkpatrick 1964; Laurens 1967; Laval 1948; Lowe and Marzari 1975; Robertson 1977; Schaefer 1961; Schuman 1939; Sik 1970; Smith 1976, 1982; Torres 1941; Villari 1956; Walters 1952; Warner 1969; Young 1976; Zimmern 1935, 1936.

(66) Italy Threat to France

A crisis for France over this issue began on 30 November 1938 and ended on 31 March 1939.

Background
Differences between France and Italy were of long standing. France possessed an important trade route in East Africa through the railroad from Djibouti in Somaliland, where Italy's colonies of Eritrea and Italian Somaliland were located. Corsica, though Italian speaking, was under French control. Rivalries existed as well over satellites in the post–Hapsburg Empire states of eastern Europe. Italy's use of the Suez Canal in order to maintain contact with its East African colonies

became a source of tension as its objections to the high French-imposed tolls increased. As for the balance of power in Europe, France looked to Italy as a potential ally against Hitler.

On 14 April 1935 representatives from France, Italy, and Great Britain met at Stresa and aligned themselves formally against Germany. Soon after the Wal-wal incident (see Case #47 above), France signed an agreement with Italy in which small areas were ceded and a settlement of the Italian minority problem in Tunisia was reached. During the Italian war with Ethiopia (see Case #47 above), France exerted considerable effort not to alienate Italy. When the League Council condemned Italy as the aggressor in Ethiopia in October 1935 French Prime Minister and Foreign Minister Laval was able to prevent the adoption of any substantive sanctions, specifically oil sanctions and the closure of the Suez Canal to Italian shipping. In the period after Italy's annexation of Ethiopia, France made further efforts to improve relations with Italy: it recognized the annexation, signed a commercial agreement on 7 November 1938 and accredited a new French ambassador to the king of Italy–emperor of Ethiopia.

Crisis
A parliamentary upheaval during Foreign Minister Ciano's speech in Rome on 30 November 1938, which called for retribution over French control of Tunisia, Corsica, Nice, Savoy, and Djibouti, turned into a street demonstration that Mussolini addressed from his balcony in the Palazzo Venezia, and triggered a crisis for France. To French protests in Paris and Rome, the reply was that the Italian government could not be responsible for spontaneous demonstrations that did not reflect its views. An anti-French campaign was begun by the Italian press and, by 5 December, demonstrations and telegrams of support for France had come from Corsica and Tunisia. On 17 December the Italian government informed France that their bilateral agreement of January 1935 was now void and that France was obliged to produce new proposals. This was not divulged in Paris until five days later. France sent copies of the Italian Note to Germany and Britain and replied on 26 December that, as far as it was concerned, the 1935 agreement was still intact but that there was a need for new proposals on French and Italian interests in Africa.

France's major response, on 2 January 1939, was Prime Minister Daladier's departure for a visit to Corsica, Algeria, and Tunisia, where he stated before cheering crowds that France would stand firm in all its territories in the face of any Italian demands or threats. France also reinforced its forces in Africa and in the Mediterranean. On 14 January Chamberlain and Halifax arrived in Rome for Anglo-Italian negotiations. Despite the request of the French government for no intercession on the Franco-Italian dispute, some British intervention was attempted, but without success—France and Italy continued to exchange demands and France repeated its intention to defend its territory. The crisis continued until 31 March, a week before Italy's **Invasion of Albania** (see Case #71, in

Italy/Albania/Yugoslavia PC), when Mussolini stated that he would not press demands on France.

The United States cabled its support to France, while Great Britain and Germany supported Italy. The League of Nations was not involved.

(The issue did not die down, and throughout the war against Albania the Italian demands remained a source of dispute.)

(See *Master Table*, pp. 676–77.)

Sources
Adamthwaite 1977; Bonnefous 1967; Carr 1945; Ciano 1947; Clough 1970; Ebenstein 1973; Nere 1975; Smith 1982; Werth 1966.

(82) East Africa Campaign, 1940–41 (see Multiregional PCs: World War II)

(90) El Alamein, 1942–43 (see Multiregional PCs: World War II)

(136) Suez Canal

This crisis lasted from 30 July 1951 to 30 January 1952 and involved two crisis actors, Egypt and the United Kingdom.

Background
At the end of World War II Egypt had demanded the abrogation of the 1936 Anglo-Egyptian treaty on the Suez Canal and its unification with Sudan. When Britain promised self-determination to Sudan, Egypt's relations with the U.K. worsened, and talks between the two countries to renew the treaty allowing a British presence in the Canal Zone ran into difficulties. A shift toward radicalization in Egypt's political life occurred.

Crisis
On 30 July 1951 a crisis was triggered for Egypt by the U.K.'s reaffirmation of its rights to the Canal under the 1936 treaty and a call for U.S. support. Cairo viewed this as an implied threat of force and an explicit threat to Egypt's sovereignty over the Canal Zone. Egypt's response, on 8 October 1951, which triggered a crisis for the U.K., was a draft proposal to the Egyptian parliament calling for the abrogation of the treaty and demanding British evacuation of the Suez Canal Zone. The U.K. responded on 16 October by declaring a state of emergency for its forces in Egypt and a decision to reinforce troops in the Canal Zone, as well as to prohibit the export of arms to Egypt. Attempts to force the evacuation of British troops by a popular resistance movement caused prolonged and serious clashes. Guerrilla warfare in Egypt against the British continued for some time

until the country was in near-total disorder. Egypt's crisis ended on 27 January 1952 when King Farouk appointed a new government. The crisis for the U.K. ended on 30 January when the Egyptian prime minister called upon the British ambassador and agreed to resume talks.

The United States strongly supported the British position. The USSR was not involved. Egypt appealed to the UN in November 1951, and an inquiry committee was set up. (On 18 February 1952, subsequent to the crisis, a report was published that denied Egyptian allegations of Britain's use of forced labor to build its bases in Egypt.) The Political Committee of the Arab League passed a resolution on 3 September 1951 expressing full support for Egypt.

(See *Master Table,* pp. 690–91.)

Sources
Acheson 1969; Blake 1975; Childers 1962; Duff 1969; Eden 1960; Egyptian Ministry of Foreign Affairs 1951; Farnie 1969; Great Britain foreign office 1951; Hoskins 1950; Marlowe 1954; Morrison 1960; Moussa 1955; Royal Institute of International Affairs 1952; Sadat 1957; Schonfield 1952, 1969; Vatikiotis 1979; Watt 1957.

(158) France/Tunisia

Tunisia's three-stage crisis started on 31 May 1957 and ended on 17 June 1958.

Background
France, reluctant to give up its position as a colonial power, attempted to retain control over its North African colonies, especially Algeria. Following Tunisia's independence in 1956, France was granted the right to maintain military bases on Tunisian soil. However, Tunisian sympathy for Algeria's struggle for independence created hostile feelings toward the French military presence. Moreover, President Bourguiba saw this as a threat to his regime. France, frustrated by its inability to crush the Algerian Front Liberation National *(FLN),* accused Tunisia of providing sanctuary for retreating Algerian guerrillas, thus creating further tension between France and Tunisia which erupted in sporadic clashes.

Crisis
The trigger to Tunisia's crisis was a clash on 31 May 1957 between French troops and Tunisian soldiers and National Guards, in which seven Tunisians were killed. This took place on the Algerian-Tunisian frontier where about 2,000 Algerian refugees had crossed into Tunisia. Tunisia responded the next day by issuing a strong protest to France, along with a call for negotiations concerning the evacuation of French forces from Tunisia and an order forbidding the movement of French troops without the Tunisian government's authority.

Negotiations between France and Tunisia led to an announcement on 27 June that approximately 10,000 of the 25,000 French troops stationed there would be transferred to Algeria during the following six months, with the remainder confined to military bases. This marked the end of the first stage of this crisis. The outcome was unsatisfactory to both sides, and the tension between them remained high.

The second stage began on 8 February 1958, when French medium-range bombers attacked the Tunisian town of Sakiet Sidi Youssef along the Tunisian-Algerian border, killing 69 Tunisians. Although this action was not authorized by Paris, the French government defended it as a legitimate retaliation for Tunisia's assistance to Algerian *FLN* rebels. Tunisia responded later that day, following an emergency cabinet meeting: its ambassador to France was recalled; all French troop movements in Tunisia were henceforth forbidden unless approved by Tunisian authorities; and the demand was renewed for the evacuation of all French forces from Tunisia, apart from the naval base at Bizerta. Tunisia also appealed to the UN Security Council. The United States, faced with the dilemma of choosing between supporting France as a *NATO* ally and promoting U.S. regional influence in North Africa by supporting Tunisia, discouraged Security Council discussions and resolutions, always subject to a Soviet veto.

The debate in the Security Council ended when the U.S. and Britain offered their good offices in an attempt to resolve the dispute. France and Tunisia accepted this offer on 17 February and agreed to begin negotiations. However, the French National Assembly refused to support the government's decision to resume direct talks with Tunisia, and in May, tension increased as clashes broke out once more.

The trigger to the third stage of Tunisia's crisis with France was a violent clash at Remada on 24 May. Once again it responded by complaining to the Security Council, on 29 May. The Security Council debate was suspended on 2 June following an appeal by President de Gaulle to President Bourguiba to settle the differences between the two countries. The crisis came to an end on 17 June following direct negotiations, when France agreed to withdraw all its forces from Tunisia except those at Bizerta.

The USSR was not involved in this crisis.

(See *Master Table,* pp. 694–95.)

Sources
AR 1957; Barraclough 1962; Ling 1967; *MEJ* Chronology 1957.

(160) Ifni

Spain's crisis in North Africa began on 23 November 1957 and ended in April 1958.

Background
Ifni, a small Spanish enclave in southern Morocco on the Atlantic coast, was ceded to Spain in 1869 and occupied in 1934. In 1956, when Morocco became

independent, Spain ceded to the new kingdom the part known as Spanish Morocco on the Mediterranean coast but retained Spanish West Africa and the tiny enclave of Ifni. For several months prior to this crisis, armed bands of the Army for the Liberation of Sahara *(AOL)* had crossed into Ifni to harass Spanish forces. The *AOL* was also active in aiding Algeria in its struggle for independence from France (1954–62). Spain requested Morocco to impose its authority on the armed bands and replace them with units of the regular Moroccan army. Since no response was received, Spain decided to reinforce its garrison in Ifni.

Crisis
On 23 November 1957 large-scale fighting broke out between Spanish troops stationed in Ifni and 1,200 Moroccan irregulars, following an attack by the *AOL*. Spain's major response to a threat to its territory occurred the next day—heavy bombing of the invading forces. Moroccan government troops were sent to take up positions around Ifni. Several of the *AOL* camps were dismantled. Spain then threatened to carry the fighting into Agadir, a Moroccan town north of Ifni. Negotiations among several militant Saharan groups and King Mohammed V of Morocco, in the spring of 1958, enabled the king to solidify his authority and permitted Morocco to exercise a restraining influence over guerrilla operations. U.S. mediation led Spain to cede the Tekna protectorate and Tarfaya to Morocco in April, terminating the Ifni crisis.

The UN and the USSR were not active in this crisis.

(In January 1969 Spain ceded Ifni to Morocco.)

(See *Master Table,* pp. 694–95.)

Sources
AR 1957, 1958; Ben Ami 1977; Payne 1967; Touval 1972; Welles 1965; *WA* 1957, 1958; Whitaker 1961; Zartman 1964.

(163) Egypt/Sudan Border I

There was one crisis actor, Sudan. The crisis occurred between 9 and 25 February 1958.

Background
Egypt claimed two areas lying north of the 22nd Parallel that had been administered by Sudan since 1902.

A plebiscite on the formation of the United Arab Republic (Egypt and Syria) was scheduled for 21 February. Forthcoming Sudanese elections were to be held six days later. On 1 February 1958 the Egyptian government sent a note to the Sudanese government charging Sudan with making arrangements for elections in areas north of the 1899 frontier.

Crisis

On 9 February 1958 a crisis was triggered for Sudan when it received reports that Egyptian army units were being sent to the disputed area. There were several strands to Sudan's response: a statement on 18 February in reply to an Egyptian Note received that day, declaring Sudan's determination to defend its sovereign territory; the dispatch of Sudanese troops to the area; and a complaint to the UN Secretary-General the next day.

The Security Council met on 21 February but did not pass a resolution. However, Egypt, realizing that its case did not carry much weight, moved to settle the dispute expeditiously. On 25 February the Sudan government announced that the Egyptian flag had been taken down at Abu Ramada and that Egyptian forces had been removed. The crisis ended on 25 February without violence.

Neither the U.S. nor the USSR was involved in this crisis.

(See *Master Table,* pp. 694–95.)

Sources

AR 1958; Hassouna 1975; *MEJ* Chronology 1958; Shimoni 1987; Touval 1972.

(174) Ghana/Togo Border I

A crisis for Ghana lasted from early March to 1 April 1960.

Background and Pre-crisis

In 1956 a majority of voters in a plebiscite held in the Trust Territory of British Togoland voted to accede to Ghana instead of to the adjoining area under French jurisdiction. Counterdemands were made for the reunification of the two Togos and the creation of a Togolese state within its pre-1914 German colonial frontiers. In October 1958 the announcement by France that Togo would receive its independence in April 1960 revived the dispute. In October 1959 and again in January 1960 Prime Minister Nkrumah of Ghana called for the integration of the two countries after Togo's independence. The future President of Togo, Sylvanus Olympio, rejected the idea of a merger with Ghana.

Crisis

A crisis for Ghana was triggered in early March 1960 when a draft constitution for the Republic of Togo was uncovered by Ghanaian government agents. It laid claim to the territory of the formerly British Togoland, which had been incorporated into Ghana as the Volta region. Furthermore, a plot by irregular forces, inhabitants of the Volta region trained in Togo, to infiltrate and attack Ghana in the last week of March was uncovered. After France ignored a formal Ghanaian protest requesting that it take immediate action to prevent the territory under its administration from serving as a base for an armed attack against Ghana,

Nkrumah convened an emergency meeting of his cabinet. Cabinet members were asked to approve the following decisions taken by an ad hoc committee on 14 March: to strengthen security forces in the Volta region; to arrest opposition leaders and those involved in the plot; and to issue a public statement. Annual army exercises were carried out in the Volta region between 22 and 28 March, and an additional army battalion was sent to the region in April.

After the date of the expected invasion passed without incident the tension began to subside. The termination date was 1 April when a decision was made to send top-level Ghanaian delegates to Togo's independence celebrations. (Subsequent to the crisis, a meeting between Nkrumah and Olympio was held on 12 June 1960 where agreement was reached on a union for economic and political cooperation.)

Neither the U.S. or the USSR, nor the UN, was involved in this crisis. (See *Master Table*, pp. 698–99.)

Sources
AR 1960; Austin 1963; Dei-Anang 1975; Oliver 1972; Thompson 1969; Touval 1972; *WA* 1960; Widstrand 1969.

(176) Congo I-Katanga

The two crisis actors were Belgium and Congo. The crisis lasted from 5 July 1960 to 15 February 1962.

Background
Belgian Congo was granted independence on 30 June 1960. Lumumba became the first Prime Minister and Defense Minister and Kasavubu the first President. The country had been plagued by tribal fighting and serious disorders. A Treaty of Friendship and Cooperation was signed in Leopoldville between Congo and Belgium.

Crisis
The trigger for Belgium, on 5 July 1960, was a mutiny among soldiers of the Congolese *Force Publique* which rapidly turned into a general assault against Belgian and other European residents. Belgium responded on the 8th by announcing its intention to send troop reinforcements to Congo. A crisis was triggered for Congo two days later when Belgian troops went into action. Lumumba decried Belgium's alleged violation of their friendship treaty. A request to President Eisenhower to restore order was denied. Tshombe, leader of mineral-rich Katanga, announced its independence on 11 July, triggering a second Congo crisis. That day, too, Lumumba responded by appealing to the UN. Belgium announced on the 13th that it would not withdraw its troops. The Soviet Union issued a statement condemning what it termed Western and *NATO* aggression against Congo. On 14 July the UN Security Council passed a resolution to

establish a UN military force in Congo and requested the withdrawal of Belgium's forces. Lumumba demanded the withdrawal of Belgian diplomats as well and declared a state of war between the two countries.

The resolution did not, however, accept Lumumba's demands to oust Tshombe and reintegrate Katanga by force. The two adversaries accepted the Security Council's resolution, though without enthusiasm, ending their dyadic crisis on the 15th.

Lumumba's forces began receiving aid from the USSR, and the split between him and Kasavubu increased. Internal developments in Congo prevented a quick solution. On 14 September 1960 Colonel Mobutu announced that the army was taking control. A new central government was finally formed on 9 February 1961. An announcement of Lumumba's death was made on 13 February. On 21 March the UN Secretary-General's Conciliation Committee on the Congo recommended a federal form of government to preserve the country's unity and integrity. On 1 August President Kasavubu invited Adoula, a moderate, to form a new government.

The UN Security Council passed a resolution calling upon the Secretary-General to organize and dispatch an emergency military force. Pressure was exerted by the U.S. to bring Tshombe and Adoula together. And on 18 December 1961 a provisional cease-fire was announced that led to the Kitona Agreement of 21 December, with a unilateral declaration by Tshombe that the Katanga secession was over and a pledge to recognize the indivisible unity of Congo Republic. The crisis ended for Congo on 15 February 1962 when the Katanga Assembly ratified Tshombe's declaration and agreed to end its secession.

(See *Master Table*, pp. 698–99.)

Sources
AR 1960, 1961, 1962; van Bilsen 1962; Dayal 1976; Gerard-Libois 1966; Goodspeed 1967; Hilsman 1967; Hoskyns 1965; Lefever 1965, 1967; Miller 1967; Okumu 1963; Tondel 1963; Wigny 1961.

(177) Mali Federation

A crisis for Mali and Senegal occurred from 20 August to 22 September 1960.

Background
The Mali Federation, consisting of Senegal, the Soudan (later, Mali), Upper Volta, and Dahomey, was created in June 1959 and became independent one year later. Upper Volta and Dahomey left the Federation immediately thereafter, and the two remaining countries decided to appoint a federal president with wide authority. This appointment was the cause of a bitter dispute between Senegal and the Soudan over control of the presidency. Elections never took place because the Federation ended one week before the scheduled elections. Senegal, whose political system tolerated open opposition, among them Soudan sup-

porters, perceived itself to be in danger of being placed in a permanent minority despite the constitutional balance built into the Federation. It warned the Soudan to stop intervention into Senegal's internal affairs.

Crisis
A crisis was triggered for Mali, then known as the Soudan, on 20 August 1960 when Senegal President Senghor declared its independence from the Federation. Mali's President, Modibo Keita, proclaimed a state of emergency and called upon France to intervene. The Mali response, the same day, triggered a crisis for Senegal, whose president, on 20 August, broadcast an impassioned speech accusing Mali of desiring the colonization and enslavement of the Senegalese people. A state of emergency was declared in Senegal; the army took control of the capital, Dakar, and all Mali ministers, as well as soldiers who had been stationed in Senegal, were returned to Bamako, the capital of Mali, the following day. France, which had ignored Keita's call for intervention, recognized Senegal's independence on 11 September 1960.

On 22 September the Soudan ended the Federation and proclaimed its independence, adopting the name of Mali. When the Federation ceased to exist, the crisis ended for both actors.

Discussions were held in the Security Council, but no resolution was passed. The USSR gave political support to Mali. The U.S. was not involved.

(See *Master Table*, pp. 698–99.)

Sources
AR 1960; Carter 1962; Crowder 1962; Foltz 1965; *Keesing's* 1972; Snyder 1965; *WA* 1960; Zartman 1966.

(179) Ethiopia/Somalia, 1960–61 (see Ethiopia/Somalia PC)

(184) Bizerta

There were two actors in this crisis, France and Tunisia. It began on 17 July and ended on 29 September 1961.

Background
France continued to maintain a number of military bases in its former colony of Tunisia after Tunisia's independence in 1956. This caused tense relations which reached crisis proportions in 1957–58 (see Case #158 above). As a result France reduced its military presence to one large base at Bizerta.

Crisis
In spite of a vague promise by President de Gaulle to President Bourguiba that France would evacuate the base, the French began construction in July 1961 of

an additional runway designed to increase its military capability. On 17 July Bourguiba triggered a crisis for France when he issued an ultimatum giving the French approximately 48 hours to open negotiations on a timetable for withdrawal from Bizerta, or face a Tunisian-imposed blockade. France's response was a decision on the 18th to take military action; and on the 19th, when the Tunisians tried to block a French attempt to resupply the base, French paratroops and other forces launched a military assault against Tunisian positions, triggering a crisis for Tunisia.

Tunisia's response was multiple: on 20 July it appealed to the UN Security Council and also attempted to meet French violence with violence of its own. France was condemned in resolutions by the Security Council and the General Assembly. An Arab League resolution was also passed authorizing action by member-states in the form of volunteer military forces for Tunisia. However, none of these contributed to the abatement of the Bizerta crisis. The crisis ended on 29 September with an agreement between France and Tunisia that restored the status quo prior to Bourguiba's ultimatum. (After lengthy negotiations, France evacuated its base at Bizerta on 15 October 1963.)

Neither the U.S. nor the USSR was involved in this crisis.

(See *Master Table*, pp. 698–99.)

Sources
See sources for Case #158; and Hassouna 1975; Ruf 1971.

(191) Mali/Mauritania

A crisis for Mauritania lasted from 29 March 1962 to 18 February 1963.

Background and Pre-crisis
The border between Mauritania and Mali had been the subject of dispute since 1944. Nomadic tribes from both states crossed back and forth over the border. Prior to the independence of both countries, in 1960, conferences on future boundaries were held, but immediately after independence relations between the two states deteriorated. Guerrillas, thought to be organized by Morocco and based in Mali, carried out actions in Mauritania: there were several attempted assassinations of Mauritanian officials as well. In early 1962 Mauritania changed its position on the border question, successfully overcoming internal Moroccan-supported opposition.

Crisis
On 29 March 1962 six people were accused of murdering French officers at Nama in eastern Mauritania, triggering a crisis for that state. Mali was accused of harboring a Moroccan terrorist group that aimed at ridding Mauritania of the French in order to facilitate Moroccan territorial claims in the area. The response, on 6 April, was a presidential declaration that Mauritania would not allow any

attempt against the integrity of the country. On 7 June 1962 the Mauritanian UN representative charged that Moroccan terrorists, trained in bases in Mali, had raided border outposts in his country.

A political settlement was reached by the presidents of the two countries at Kayes, Mali, on 18 February 1963 ending the crisis. The nationals of both states were guaranteed nomadic rights and the use of wells in disputed areas. Compromise agreements were reached, although Mali gained more territory than Mauritania.

Neither the U.S. nor the USSR, nor the UN, was involved in this crisis. (See *Master Table*, pp. 700–701.)

Sources
AR 1962, 1963; Gerteiny 1967; Moore 1965; Touval 1972; WA 1962, 1963; Widstrand 1969; Zartman 1963, 1966.

(199) Algeria/Morocco Border

A crisis over territory between Algeria and Morocco lasted from 1 October to 4 November 1963.

Background
The dispute centered around areas of the Sahara held by Algeria that Morocco claimed had been part of the Moroccan state in precolonial times. Algeria countered that the disputed territory had been administered by the French and was liberated by the *Front Liberation National (FLN)*, along with the rest of Algeria. A long-standing nationalist revolt against French rule in Algeria (1954–62) exacerbated the situation.

Crisis
On 1 October 1963 Algeria's President Ben Bella announced that Moroccan troops had taken up positions in the disputed territory, triggering a crisis for Algeria. Further, he charged that the Moroccans were supplying aid to rebel leader Ait-Ahmad, a former member of the Algerian National Assembly, then controlling the nearby region of Kabylia. Algeria responded on 8 October when its forces clashed with Moroccan troops. This constituted the crisis trigger for Morocco, which subsequently withdrew. On 14 October Morocco responded by reinforcing its troops and reoccupying the lost outposts.

Efforts at negotiation were initiated by Algeria. Morocco, too, called for a peaceful settlement. The Bamako Agreement, signed on 30 October by both parties, was worked out through the mediation of Ethiopian Emperor Haile Selassie and Mali President Modiba Keita. However, fighting continued for several more days until a Malian officer monitoring the truce succeeded in bringing the fighting to an end on 4 November 1963, terminating the crisis.

In the agreement, Morocco obtained Algeria's consent to an examination of the border problem and an undertaking to cease propaganda attacks. Algeria secured Morocco's withdrawal from the positions it occupied during the fighting and an agreement to settle the dispute within the framework of the *OAU*. (In February 1964, Morocco withdrew its forces.)

In addition to the *OAU*, the Arab League was active in the crisis; but neither regional organization contributed to its resolution. (The *OAU*'s role occurred in the later stages of negotiation and reconciliation after the crisis ended.) Cuba and the United Arab Republic (UAR, Egypt) were perceived by Morocco to be partial to Algeria in the dispute.

The UN, the U.S., and the USSR remained aloof from this crisis. (See *Master Table*, pp. 702–3.)

Sources
Annuaire de l'Afrique du Nord 1963; Hassouna 1975; *MEJ* Chronology 1963; Touval 1972; Widstrand 1969; Wild 1966; Zartman 1966.

(201) Kenya/Somalia

Kenya experienced a crisis with Somalia from 20 November 1963 until 4 March 1964.

Background and Pre-crisis
In March 1963 the U.K. announced that it would grant internal self-government to the British colony of Kenya after the local parliamentary elections of 18–26 May 1963. Despite a demand from the Somali population residing in the Northern Frontier District (NFD) to secede from Kenya and unite with Somalia, it was also announced that the NFD would become the seventh region of Kenya. On 18 March Somalia severed diplomatic relations with the U.K. On 1 June Jomo Kenyatta became Kenya's first Prime Minister. The elections were boycotted by the Somali tribespeople of the NFD. In addition, Somali secessionists carried out a series of protest raids on military and police posts in the territory—according to a statement by Kenyatta, 33 attacks until 13 November. The Kenya government banned nonessential travel to the area and issued a statement to the effect that Kenya would not give up an inch of the area.

Crisis
The Vice-President of Kenya's eastern region, Ahmed Farah, stated on 20 November that Somalia was preparing to attack Kenya and had already secretly distributed arms to Kenya's Somalis. Kenya, he warned, should be ready for war with Somalia after independence on 12 December 1963. This marked the crisis trigger for Kenya. Fearing a full-scale insurrection in the north, Kenyatta issued an order on 28 November that he wanted all Somali raiders captured, dead or alive.

Kenya's major response, on 25 December, was a proclamation of a state of emergency along the 440-mile NFD. A five-mile prohibitive zone was established along the entire frontier. The next day Kenyan troops were placed on full alert; and on the 29th the border with Somalia was completely sealed. British troops stationed in Kenya were also sent to back up Kenya's security forces. On 28 December a military delegation from Ethiopia arrived to confer with Kenyan officials on the Somali border crisis, and a mutual defense treaty was ratified.

In February 1964 Kenya requested that the dispute be placed on the agenda of the *OAU* Council of Ministers. On 12 February an *OAU* resolution was passed detailing steps to settle the dispute and requesting the sides to refrain from propaganda. On 25 February 1964 the Kenyan state of emergency in the NFD was extended for another two months; but by the time of the 4 March elections the crisis had ended. Secessionist Somalis in the NFD participated in the election for the regional assembly, thus indicating their—and Somalia's—willingness to drop their secessionist demands.

The superpowers maintained a neutral position, but Somalia was receiving military aid from the Soviet Union and therefore regarded it as an ally. The UN was not involved.

(By mid-1967 a Zambian initiative to mediate the continued low-level conflict succeeded when Kenyan and Somali leaders promised to cease provocative acts and restore normal relations.)

(See *Master Table,* pp. 702–3.)

Sources
ARB 1964; Castango 1964; Farer 1979; Gorman 1981; Hoskyns 1969b; Laitin and Samatar 1987; Legum and Lee 1979; Selassie 1984; Touval 1972.

(204) Dahomey/Niger

On 21 December 1963 a crisis began for Niger and Dahomey, lasting until 4 January 1964.

Background
Civil disorder preceded a military revolt in Dahomey that replaced President Hubert Maga with the Commander of the Army, Colonel Soglo. A provisional government was set up on 29 October 1963. There was also a sharp increase in labor strikes and regime repression prior to the onset of the crisis. Since 1960 the government of Niger was in the hands of the authoritarian President Hamani Diori, a friend and ally of Dahomey's former president. The conflict originated with a dispute over ownership of the tiny island of Lete on the Niger River, which forms the frontier between the two countries.

Crisis
On 21 December 1963 the National Assembly of Niger alleged that Dahomey was preparing to send troops to occupy Lete Island. Niger's response to this

perceived threat, and the trigger for Dahomey, was an announcement on 22 December of the imminent expulsion of 16,000 Dahomeyans residing and working in Niger. President Soglo, on 27 December, responded with an order to close Dahomey's rail and road links to Niger, thus cutting off the Dahomeyan port of Cotonou from landlocked Niger. Both sides sent forces to the border but were deterred from military hostilities by French warnings. On 4 January delegations from both countries met at the frontier and issued a joint communiqué reopening the road and withdrawing forces. This was the result of mediation efforts by several neighboring countries, Gabon, Togo, and Nigeria, and a proposal by the President of the Union Africaine et Malagache, President Yameogo of Upper Volta.

Neither the U.S. nor the USSR, nor the UN, was involved in this crisis. (See *Master Table*, pp. 702–3.)

Sources
AD 1963, 1964; *AR* 1963, 1964; *ARec* 1963, 1964; *ARB* 1963, 1964; Touval 1972.

(205) Burundi/Rwanda

A crisis between Rwanda and Burundi began on 21 December 1963 and ended sometime in April 1964.

Background and Pre-crisis
Relations between Rwanda and Burundi had been strained since precolonial times. Both were traditional sacred kingdoms ruled by a *Mwami* (king). Each kingdom was populated by three ethnic groups: the Tutsi, the Hutu, and the Twa. The Tutsi traditionally dominated politics, the military, and social life in both kingdoms.

The Belgian-administered UN Trust Territory of Ruanda-Urundi achieved independence as two separate states on 1 July 1962: the southern part became the Kingdom of Burundi, and the northern part became the Republic of Rwanda. Attempts by the UN to bring about the creation of a single independent state had failed.

Between 1960 and 1964 some 200,000 members of the Tutsi tribe left Rwanda and settled in the border regions of neighboring states, the Congo, Uganda, Burundi, and Tanganyika. Many of the Tutsi, however, had not given up the hope of returning to Rwanda to reestablish the monarchy (officially abolished on 2 October 1961) and thus reestablish their traditional position as political and military rulers over the majority Hutu.

Early in December 1963 the Burundi government dispersed a group of about 5,000 Tutsi refugees who had gathered on the border with Rwanda apparently intending to unleash an armed attack against their former homeland.

Crisis

On 21 December 1963 a crisis was triggered for Rwanda when a band of about 5,000 Tutsi exiles, armed with bows and arrows and a few rifles, invaded Rwanda from Burundi territory. The Rwanda government responded the same day by meeting the invasion with force, broadcasting a warning to the Hutu population to be "on the alert" for Tutsi invaders, and by dividing the country into nine emergency regions. By 27 December the attack had reportedly been repulsed, but the level of tension had not decreased. Bitter attacks were directed against the remaining Tutsi population in Rwanda, which appeared to have been condoned and even supported by the government. These massacres created an international problem that immediately involved the UN.

A crisis for Burundi was triggered on 22 January 1964 when it was reported that troops of the Rwanda army had violated Burundi territory and "massacred" a number of Burundi inhabitants in the border area. The Burundi response was an appeal, on 28 January 1964, to the UN and the *OAU* to intervene and "to put an end to provocations by Rwanda." King Mwambutsa of Burundi also wrote to UN Secretary-General U Thant to complain of the frontier violations by Rwanda. The crisis ended some time in April, without a formal agreement: by then the threat of military hostilities had been reduced sufficiently for President Kayibanda of Rwanda to allow some of the Tutsi émigrés back into the country.

UN activity was limited to dealing with the refugee problem: a Special Representative was appointed for this purpose by the Secretary-General. The *OAU* was minimally involved through its good offices. Neither the U.S. nor the USSR was involved.

(The overthrow of the king in Burundi in November 1966 facilitated a final agreement in March 1967 whereby all Tutsi refugees could return to their homes after giving up their arms.)

(See *Master Table,* pp. 702–3.)

Sources

AD 1963, 1964; *AR* 1963, 1964; *ARec* 1963, 1964; *ARB* 1963, 1964; Lemarchand 1970; Melady 1974.

(207) East Africa Rebellions

A crisis for the U.K. occurred in several East African states from 19 to 30 January 1964.

Background

On 12 January 1964 a coup d'état took place in Zanzibar, a former British colony. Western observers claimed that there had been communist involvement. At that time Tanganyika, at Zanzibar's request, sent a group of armed police. The U.K. sent naval reinforcements to the coast off Dar es Salaam.

Crisis
On 19 January 1964 a crisis was triggered for the U.K. when soldiers of the First Battalion Tanganyika Rifles mutinied against their British and Tanganyikan officers. The European officers were captured and replaced by Africans. The rebel troops demanded an interview with President Nyerere, better pay, and the removal of the European officers. The Tanganyikan minister of the interior appealed to the U.K. to intervene in order to help control the rioting and looting. In the meantime British troops were moved from Aden to Kenya to protect British nationals in Tanganyika in case of a threat. On 21 January, in a broadcast by President Nyerere, the nation was informed that Tanganyika's internal crisis was over.

On 23 January soldiers of the Uganda Rifles mutinied and held their British officers prisoner. The U.K. received a request for aid from Prime Minister Obote and responded the same day by landing troops in Entebbe. Another request for British troops came from Tanganyika on 24 January when fighting broke out again. Troops were also rushed from Kenya to Tanganyika. Also on the 24th a brief revolt broke out in Kenya, and British troops stationed there, along with those offshore, were rushed to the scene.

On 27 January Nyerere of Tanganyika called for an emergency *OAU* meeting, but it did not meet. The British troops stayed in the area until 30 January when calm once more prevailed in the three former British colonies, Kenya, Tanganyika, and Uganda.

Neither the U.S. or the USSR, nor the UN, was involved in this crisis. (See *Master Table*, pp. 704–5.)

Sources
AR 1964; *ARec* 1964; *ARB* 1964.

(208) Ogaden I, 1964 (see Ethiopia/Somalia PC)

(211) Congo II

The formation of a rebel regime and the taking of hostages in Stanleyville led to a crisis for Congo (later, Zaire), Belgium, the United States, and the USSR lasting from 4 August to 30 December 1964.

Background and Pre-crisis
On 29 September 1963 President Kasavubu disbanded Congo's parliament after a series of increasingly repressive measures was passed against the political opposition. The deterioration of economic and social conditions, along with repression, led to societal unrest that manifested itself in tribal fighting, raids, and other arbitrary acts of violence—mainly in East Katanga and Upper Congo. Large-scale uprisings, led by the National Liberation Committee *(NLC)*, occurred during January and April 1964. On 30 June the UN Emergency Force, which had

been set up in 1960, left Congo. In July of that year Kasavubu requested Moise Tshombe to form a new government. The governments of Congo-Brazzaville, Burundi, and Mali were accused of giving support to the *NLC,* as were the USSR and China, which were providing arms and military training. Rebel activities against the central government increased, and large areas in the eastern part of the country, including Stanleyville, were under control of the rebel forces.

Crisis

The trigger to Congo's crisis was the formation of a Revolutionary Council in Stanleyville on 4 August 1964, with the *NLC* leader Christophe Gbenye as President, after rebel forces had occupied the city. Congo's response, on the 6th, was an appeal by Premier Tshombe to the United States and Belgium for direct military aid. Tshombe also took his case to the *OAU,* which resolved to set up an ad hoc committee to examine the situation and to act as a mediator between the central Congo government and the rebels.

The trigger for the United States and Belgium occurred on 26 September when Gbenye, who was holding 1,500 white foreign civilians as hostages in Stanleyville, announced that they would not be allowed to leave the city. Their safety was made contingent upon a cease-fire, the eschewing of bombings by the central government, and the termination of Western support. This was accompanied by threats of physical harm against the hostages if those conditions were rejected. The U.S.'s, and Belgium's, major response, on 22 November, was to dispatch paratroops to a British base in Congo to prepare for a military rescue of the hostages. On the 24th an emergency *NATO* meeting, requested by Belgium, expressed sympathy and support for the Western countries.

The paratroops occupied Stanleyville on 24 November and rescued the hostages within a few hours. The Congo government coordinated an attack on the rebels for the same time as the rescue mission. Control was handed back to the central government on 29 November, marking the termination date for Belgium and the United States.

A crisis for the USSR was triggered by the Belgian/U.S. rescue mission on 24 November. The Soviets feared that Tshombe's pro-Western regime would crush the rebels and thus reduce Soviet influence in the area. The USSR's response, on the 26th, was to accuse the U.S., Belgium, and Britain of aggressive intervention. The Soviet crisis ended on 17 December when its embassy in Kinshasa was closed down.

Discussions were held at the Security Council between 9 and 30 December. It adopted a resolution on 30 December, calling for a cease-fire in the fighting between the rebels and the central government, the removal of mercenaries, and a stop to foreign intervention. This terminated Congo's crisis and the international crisis as a whole.

(In early 1965 President Kasavubu dismissed Premier Tshombe and was himself ousted in a coup d'état led by Colonel Joseph Mobutu on 25 November

1965. Relations between Congo-Brazzaville and Congo-Kinshasa remained poor until 1970, when diplomatic relations and river traffic were finally restored.) (See *Master Table,* pp. 704–5.)

Sources
United States Department of State 1965 ARB 1964; Clarke 1968; Epstein 1965; Gappert and Thomas 1965; Gerard-Libois 1966; Gerard-Libois and van Lierde 1966; Gibbs 1994; Hoare 1967; Hoskyns 1969a; Kitchen 1965; Miller 1967; Nkrumah 1967; Reed 1965; Schlesinger 1973; Spaak 1971; Talon 1976; Tshombe 1967.

(217) Guinea Regime

A crisis for Guinea began on 9 October 1965 and ended in mid-December that year.

Background and Pre-crisis
Guinea's independence from France in October 1958 was followed by a severe curtailment of French aid and expertise. In the year prior to this crisis the political climate in Guinea was constantly troubled, the standard of living had dropped, and consumer goods were expensive and irregularly supplied. Many Guineans fled the country in search of more favorable economic conditions.

In July 1965 a meeting was held in Paris among the Presidents of the Ivory Coast (Houphouet-Boigny), Niger (Diori), and Upper Volta (Yameogo), with Tshombe from the Congo and two French ministers. According to Guinea's President, Sekou Touré, this group decided to provide funds and other aid to Guineans who wished to remove him from the presidency. Three attempts to overthrow the Guinean government between February and October 1965 were uncovered and halted.

Crisis
The crisis trigger for Guinea was internal: on 9 October 1965 the statutes of a new opposition party to the only authorized party in Guinea were deposited with the Guinean minister of the interior. On 12 October Mamadou Touré, leader of the *Parti de l'Unité Nationale de Guinee,* was arrested, and disorders in Guinea's second town, Kankan, were suppressed. Guinea's formal complaint to the *OAU* on 17 November alleged that subversive acts were being financed by the Ivory Coast, with a view to a coup d'état in Guinea. Houphouet-Boigny publicly refuted Sekou Touré's charges. On 7 December Guinea allegations against France were reiterated in the Political Committee of the United Nations General Assembly, which offered its good offices.

By mid-December Sekou Touré had succeeded in overcoming the threat to his regime, and the crisis ended through a tacit understanding by the parties.

The U.S. and the USSR were not involved in this crisis.

(See *Master Table,* pp. 704–5.)

Sources
AR 1965; *ARB* 1965; *WA* 1965.

(218) Rhodesia's UDI, 1965–66 (see Rhodesia PC)

(240) Conakry Raid

A crisis for the Republic of Guinea took place from 22 November to 11 December 1970.

Background
Guinean President Sekou Touré alleged Portuguese assassination attempts on his life during January and July 1964 and October 1970. Portugal accused the Republic of Guinea of harboring guerrillas wishing to oust Lisbon from the neighboring colonial territory of Portuguese Guinea (later Guinea-Bissau).

Crisis
On 22 November 1970, the trigger date, Radio Conakry of the Republic of Guinea announced an invasion by mercenaries from several sanctuaries, especially from the colonial territory of Portuguese Guinea. The same day, President Sekou Touré responded with force and appealed, on 22 and 23 November, for an emergency meeting of the Security Council and for troops from the United Nations and the *OAU* for "covert support."

The Security Council met from 22 to 24 November and called for the cessation of the attack and the withdrawal of the invading forces. It was decided to send a fact-finding commission to Guinea. The mission visited Guinea from 25 to 29 November. Its report, confirming the invasion of 350–400 men on 22 November and alleging support from an outside power, which seemed to be Portugal, was published on 4 December. The report also stated that the invasion was aimed at the overthrow of Sekou Touré, the freeing of Portuguese prisoners in the Republic of Guinea, and the weakening of the guerrilla forces who were active in Portuguese Guinea. Portugal rejected the UN report and denied participation in the invasion.

On 25 November Sekou Touré appealed to all friendly countries for military support. Kenya, Mali, Nigeria, and Sierra Leone offered to send troops. There were further incursions into Guinea by land on 27 November. Tanzania, Zambia, and the U.S. sent economic aid. Egypt sent arms and ammunition. Algeria and Libya were also reported to have sent military supplies. Political support for Guinea came from China, India, Ivory Coast, Senegal, and the Soviet Union. The Security Council passed a resolution on 8 December, the Western powers abstaining, warning Portugal against further attacks on African states, and called for immediate self-determination and independence for Portuguese Guinea. The termination date of the crisis was 11 December 1970, the day the Organization of African Unity *(OAU)* passed a unanimous resolution, initiated by Ethiopia,

Egypt, Libya, and Sudan, condemning Portugal and demanding reparations to Guinea. There was a subsequent tacit agreement to end the invasion.

(Portuguese Guinea became Guinea Bissau after it achieved independence in 1974.)

(See *Master Table,* pp. 710–11.)

Sources
ACR 1970; *AR* 1970; *ARB* 1970; *ARec* 1970; Bruce 1973; Hall 1981; Nelson et al. 1975; Riviere 1977.

(243) Chad/Libya I, 1971–72 (see Chad/Libya PC)

(244) Caprivi Strip

Zambia's crisis over the Caprivi Strip occurred from 5 to 12 October 1971.

Background
South Africa and Zambia share a common border along the Caprivi Strip, a long narrow strip of land in the far northeast corner of South Africa–ruled South-West Africa (later, Namibia). Large operational bases in the area were maintained by South African Defence and Police *(SADP)* forces against guerrilla infiltration. Economic conditions in Zambia deteriorated toward the end of 1970 when world copper prices were forced down.

Crisis
A crisis was triggered for Zambia on 5 October 1971 when South African Prime Minister John Vorster announced that a Union police vehicle along the Zambian border had been blown up by a land mine. He placed responsibility on Zambia, charging that it had made Zambia's territory available for "this sort of aggression." Units of the South African security forces crossed into Zambia in order to pursue alleged perpetrators. On 8 October Zambia requested a special session of the UN Security Council to discuss the "numerous violations of South African forces against the sovereignty, airspace and territorial integrity of Zambia." Zambia's President Kaunda announced that compulsory national service and Home Guards would reinforce the regular army as part of the country's defense system.

A Security Council resolution on the 12th, condemning South Africa and calling on it to respect the sovereignty of Zambia, terminated the crisis, although Zambia viewed the resolution as "watered down" and insufficient. Neither the U.S. nor the USSR was involved in this crisis.

(See *Master Table,* pp. 710–11.)

Sources
ACR 1971; *AR* 1971; *ARB* 1971; *ARec* 1971; Pettman 1974.

(245) Tanzania/Uganda I

A crisis for Tanzania and Uganda began on 20 October and ended on 25 November 1971.

Background and Pre-crisis
On 25 January 1971, while Uganda President Milton Obote was out of the country, a coup took place and General Idi Amin assumed power. Obote took refuge in Tanzania where he was joined by about 1,000 loyal Ugandan soldiers. Other Ugandans fled to southern Sudan. Amin viewed Tanzania and Sudan as possible jump-off points for military operations against his regime. Sharp hostility existed between Tanzanian President Nyerere and Amin. On 7 July Amin closed the border with Tanzania, alleging that guerrillas had infiltrated from Tanzania into Uganda. Further allegations, in early August, pointed to Tanzanian violations of Ugandan airspace and tank and troop movements into Ugandan territory. On 24 August Amin announced that his troops had clashed with Chinese-led Tanzanian forces. More reports of troop movements and bombings followed, and by the end of September accusations were steadily exchanged between the two countries.

Crisis
A crisis for Tanzania began on 20 October 1971 when it was announced that Ugandan air force jet fighters had destroyed a Tanzanian military camp that was perceived by Amin as a base for ex-President Obote and his men. On 24 October Uganda claimed that Tanzania had mobilized its forces on the border between the two states, triggering a crisis for Uganda. The Tanzanian response was a statement by the minister of information and broadcasting the next day, objecting to the Ugandan threat to destroy Tanzanian bases established north of the Kagera River and declaring its intention to meet with resistance any troop movements in that area. Amin responded on 1 November with a declaration of his determination to defend "every inch of Ugandan territory." There is evidence that both Uganda and Tanzania had moved troops to the border.

On 21 November Amin reestablished air and telephone communications with Tanzania. The crisis ended for both actors on 25 November. Nyerere, though still refusing to recognize Amin, announced his intention to reduce the number of troops on the border. These unilateral acts terminated the crisis.

The U.S., the USSR, and the UN remained aloof from this crisis.
(See *Master Table,* pp. 710–11.)

Sources
ACR 1971; *AR* 1971; *ARB* 1971; *ARec* 1971; Gukiina 1972; Kyemba 1977; Low 1973; Martin 1974.

(247) Tanzania/Uganda II

A second crisis for Uganda and Tanzania began on 17 September 1972 and ended on 5 October of that year.

Background
Military clashes between Uganda and Tanzania were reported for much of 1971. The two countries verged on a wider confrontation when Ugandan air force planes attacked border placements in Tanzania, triggering a crisis from 20 October until its termination on 25 November 1971 (see Case #245 above).

Crisis
On 17 September 1972 1,000 supporters of ex-President Obote in Tanzania invaded Uganda from Tanzania; no Tanzanian soldiers were among them. Idi Amin responded the following day by moving forces to the border region to meet the invasion and by bombing the town of Bukoba in Tanzania, triggering a crisis for Tanzania. Tanzania responded the same day by moving its Fourth Battalion of over 1,000 men to the border. Its crisis management technique was mediation, both through the *OAU* and Somalia.

The termination date for both actors was 5 October 1972, when they signed an agreement wherein both announced their intention to remove forces from the border area and to cease all military hostilities. Moreover, the two sides agreed to stop all hostile propaganda against each other and "to refrain from harboring or allowing subversive forces to operate in the territory of one state against the other."

Neither the U.S. or the USSR, nor the UN, was involved in this crisis.
(See *Master Table*, pp. 710–11.)

Sources
See sources for Case #245.

(250) Zambia Raid, 1973 (see Rhodesia PC)

(260) War in Angola, 1975–76 (see Angola PC)

(261) Moroccan March, 1975–76 (see Western Sahara PC)

(266) Uganda Claims

Ugandan claims to Kenyan territory caused a crisis for Kenya from 15 to 24 February 1976.

Background

Disputes between Uganda and the two other members of the East African Community, Kenya and Tanzania, had occurred for five years prior to this crisis. In 1971 and 1972 confrontations took place between Uganda and Tanzania over Idi Amin's allegations of Tanzanian support for exiled Ugandans (see Cases #245 and 247 above). During the next several years Idi Amin's behavior became more aggressive. There was a gradual deterioration of relations between Uganda and Kenya since 1975.

Crisis

On 15 February 1976 a crisis was triggered for Kenya when Idi Amin announced that large parts of Kenya and the Sudan historically belonged to Uganda and that he was investigating the possibility of claiming these territories. The disputed area extended to within 20 miles of Nairobi, Kenya's capital. Amin stated further that, despite his preference for peace, he would consider engaging Kenya in war in order to recover the territory. Should Uganda's access to the sea be denied by any country (Kenya or Tanzania), war would be the result. The following day another Amin statement, while withdrawing an actual claim to the areas, guaranteed the security of any Ugandans within that territory who sought independence. He also intimated that he was connected with the Luos secession movement in western Kenya. Kenya responded on 17 February when President Kenyatta addressed a mass rally, stating Kenya's readiness to fight to protect its territorial integrity. Amin cabled the *OAU* Secretary-General setting forth Ugandan claims, along with vague threats accompanying a denial of any intention to go to war. The *OAU* never met to discuss the issue. Amin approached the UN as well, but there was no activity by the global organization either. In Kenya protests were held in the town of Kakamega. On 20 February Kenyatta canceled two ministerial meetings of the East African Community and refused to participate in any further Community work until the issue between Uganda and Kenya was settled. On 23 February dockworkers in Mombassa boycotted Ugandan cargo. The crisis ended on 24 February when Kenyatta received a message from Amin disavowing any intention to seize territory from Kenya or Sudan.

(A telephone conversation between the two presidents was reported the following day dealing with matters other than territorial claims.)

The U.S. and the USSR were not involved in this crisis.

(See *Master Table*, pp. 714–15.)

Sources

ACR 1976; *ARB* 1976; Brownlie 1979; *Keesing's* 1976.

(267) Operation Thrasher, 1976 (see Rhodesia PC)

(268) Nouakchott I, 1976 (see Western Sahara PC)

(270) Entebbe Raid, 1976 (see Arab/Israel PC)

(271) Sudan Coup Attempt

A Libyan-backed attempt to overthrow President Numeiri caused a crisis for Sudan from 2 to 15 July 1976.

Background
With Sudan's independence on 1 January 1956 the predominantly Muslim north was united with the Christian and animist south. Regional diversity persisted in the postindependence period, with the most acute domestic problem being the question of Sudan's southern provinces, where open rebellion to the regime began in 1963. Harsh military action caused a large number of southern Sudanese to take refuge in neighboring countries. A guerrilla war began in January 1964. The unrest in the south was one of the main reasons for the bloodless military coup staged by a group of army officers under Colonel Numeiri in May 1969, which invested absolute powers in a National Revolutionary Council. Numeiri formally recognized southern autonomy and attempted to include southern political leaders in the government.

Negotiations with the Anya-Nya guerrilla organization, based in Uganda, began in 1971. The following year the civil war ended in Sudan, but hostilities in the south persisted. Relations between Sudan and Libya were strained. The former, together with Egypt and Sa'udi Arabia, was in the Western camp; Libya was strongly supported by the USSR. Libyan forces in Chad were another bone of contention between Libya, which wished them to remain, and Sudan, which advocated their withdrawal (see Case #243—**Chad/Libya I**, in **Chad/Libya PC**). Libya's leader, Qaddhafi, took advantage of Sudan's north/south problem and Numeiri's absence from the country to encourage an attempt to overthrow Sudan's government.

Crisis
Minutes after President Numeiri arrived at Khartoum airport, on his return from a visit to the United States and France, on 2 July 1976, grenades exploded in many parts of the city, and armed civilians advanced on the airport. The coup was suppressed by loyal government troops after some loss of life and considerable damage to property. Sudan accused Libya of designing the coup attempt and of an act of armed aggression: Libya, Numeiri claimed, provided training, arms, ammunition, and transport to the rebels. A complaint was lodged by Sudan in the Security Council on 4 July, and on the 6th Sudan broke off diplomatic relations with Libya. The crisis ended for Sudan with the signing of a joint Defense Agreement between Egypt and Sudan on 15 July: Libya was defined as the common enemy in the agreement.

The *OAU* and the Arab League were both involved in this crisis, although neither regional organization had any effect on the outcome: the latter urged President Numeiri to withdraw his complaint to the Security Council with a promise that his accusations against Libya would be investigated. The UN was inactive, as were both superpowers.

(See *Master Table*, pp. 714–15.)

Sources
ACR 1976; *AR* 1976; *ARB* 1976; *ARec* 1976; Nelson 1979.

(273) Nagomia Raid, 1976 (see Rhodesia PC)

(276) Operation Tangent, 1976–77 (see Rhodesia PC)

(277) Shaba I, 1977 (see Angola PC)

(278) Mapai Seizure, 1977 (see Rhodesia PC)

(280) Nouakchott II, 1977 (see Western Sahara PC)

(281) Egypt/Libya Clashes

Border clashes between Libya and Egypt created a crisis for these two north African states from 14 July to 10 September 1977.

Background
The problem of undemarcated boundaries between Egypt and Libya was long-standing. The personal enmity between President Sadat and Colonel Qaddhafi increased after the conclusion of the October 1973 war between Egypt and Israel, when the Libyan leader accused Sadat of working toward a thaw in Egypt/Israel relations, as well as developing stronger ties with the United States. Egypt, on the other hand, resented the increasing Muslim fundamentalism in Libya and feared the spread of Soviet influence then prevalent in that country. For several years the two African neighbors had accused each other of acts of sabotage and had carried on an almost unbroken propaganda campaign (see Case #314—**Libya's Threat to Sadat,** in 1980, below).

Crisis
A crisis was triggered for Libya when Egyptian armed forces attacked a Libyan border police fort on 14 July 1977. The Libyan response, on 19 July, was artillery fire on a Egyptian border post killing nine soldiers and capturing 14. This triggered a crisis for Egypt. On the 21st Egyptian forces, supported by tanks and aircraft, crossed the border into Libya. During August intermittent clashes continued, with each side accusing the other of aggression. Yasser Arafat, leader of the Palestine Liberation Organization, along with the presidents of Algeria and

Togo, succeeded in mediating the crisis. On 10 September Egyptian and Libyan troops withdrew from the border, terminating the crisis for both actors.

The United States provided arms and weapons to Egypt, as did the Soviet Union to Libya. Libya brought the matter before the United Nations, the Arab League, and the *OAU,* but no discussion took place.

(See *Master Table,* pp. 716–17.)

Sources
ACR 1977; *ARec* 1977; *ARB* 1977; *Keesing's* 1977; *MECS* 1977–78; *MEJ* Chronology 1977; Oliver and Crowder 1981.

(282) Ogaden II, 1977–78 (see Ethiopia/Somalia PC)

(283) Rhodesia Raid, 1977–78 (see Rhodesia PC)

(285) French Hostages in Mauritania, 1977 (see Western Sahara PC)

(286) Chimoio-Tembue Raids, 1977–78 (see Rhodesia PC)

(288) Chad/Libya II, 1978 (see Chad/Libya PC)

(290) Chad/Libya III, 1978 (see Chad/Libya PC)

(291) Cassinga Incident, 1978 (see Angola PC)

(292) Shaba II, 1978 (see Angola PC)

(293) Air Rhodesia Incident, 1978 (see Rhodesia PC)

(296) Fall of Amin

Tanzania, Uganda, and Libya were the actors in a crisis from 30 October 1978 to 10 April 1979 leading to the fall of Uganda's President Idi Amin.

Background
In 1971 General Idi Amin seized power in Uganda in a coup that overthrew the regime of President Milton Obote, who then took refuge in Tanzania. From that time onward relations between the two countries were hostile as Amin perceived President Nyerere of Tanzania as supporting a military overthrow of his regime. Crises between the two countries occurred in 1971 and 1972 (see Cases #245, 247 above). During the years that followed no overt clashes occurred, but there were mutual accusations of troop movements. In October 1978 serious mutinies

erupted in various Ugandan army barracks near the Tanzanian border. The mutineers were reported to have fled into Tanzania.

Crisis

On 30 October Ugandan troops invaded Tanzania and occupied the Kagera Salient, triggering a crisis for Tanzania. Idi Amin announced that he had annexed the area north of the Kagera River. A large Ugandan force followed the invading troops. Tanzania's resistance in the Salient on 31 October triggered a crisis for Uganda, but the Tanzanian major response was a counteroffensive launched on 11 November. Uganda responded on the 13th by withdrawing its forces from the Kagera Salient. By late November President Nyerere made it known that Tanzania would not be satisfied until Amin was overthrown. Sporadic fighting continued until the end of January 1979 as Tanzanian forces pushed across the Ugandan border. As they began to advance northward into Uganda, the tense border situation exploded in a series of violent exchanges. By mid-February the Tanzanian advance had come within 150 kilometers of Kampala. At that stage, Libya, an ally of Amin's Uganda, renewed its mediatory efforts, with little success. As Amin's position became more vulnerable, the Ugandan leader appealed to "all friendly countries" to come to his rescue with troops and military equipment. On 25 February the government of Libya perceived the possible downfall of Amin as a threat to its influence in the region. It responded to this crisis on 4 March by sending troops to Kampala to join an earlier contingent that had arrived in Entebbe, together with supplies, in mid-February.

Despite the new equipment and foreign reinforcements, Uganda suffered defeat after defeat until, by 25 March, Tanzanian artillery was firing on Kampala and Entebbe. On 6 April Tanzanian and anti-Amin Ugandan forces moved to the outskirts of Kampala; and, on the following day, they captured Entebbe. On 9 April it was reported that Libya paid the Ugandan National Liberation Forces (*UNLF*, the combined exiled anti-Amin forces) the equivalent of $20 million to allow Libya's expeditionary force to pull out of Uganda without being attacked. The crisis ended for Libya in defeat. The following day Amin fled from the capital, and the crisis ended for Uganda and Tanzania.

Amin's appeals to the *OAU*, the Arab League, and the UN, on 4 November 1978, to force the Tanzanians to stop fighting had failed, as did the mediation attempts by Kenya, Nigeria, and Zambia. Discussions in the *OAU* ad hoc committee on interstate conflicts were also fruitless; and on 2 March 1979 the *OAU* admitted that its efforts to reach a cease-fire had failed. UN Secretary-General Waldheim appealed to Tanzania and Uganda to stop fighting and offered his good offices to seek a solution.

United States involvement was political: on 6 March 1979 the State Department accused Libya of direct military involvement; this followed a statement by Secretary of State Vance calling for the withdrawal of Ugandan troops from the Kagera Salient at the onset of the crisis. A *Pravda* statement on 12 November 1978 accused Tanzania of aggression: the USSR had been a supplier of weapons and advisors to Amin's Uganda prior to the crisis, but there was no increase in this activity during the crisis. In March 1979 the Soviet Union reportedly withdrew advisors and military supplies from Uganda.

(See *Master Table,* pp. 718–19.)

Sources
ACR 1978, 1979; Amer 1992; *AR* 1978–79; *ARec* 1978–79; Avirgan and Honey 1982; Brzoska and Pearson 1994; Omara-Otunnu 1987; Smith 1980; Twaddle 1979.

(297) Angola Invasion Scare, 1978 (see Angola PC)

(299) Tan Tan, 1979 (see Western Sahara PC)

(300) Raids on *ZIPRA,* 1979 (see Rhodesia PC)

(302) Raids on *SWAPO,* 1979 (see Angola PC)

(304) Chad/Libya IV, 1979 (see Chad/Libya PC)

(305) Goulimime-Tarfaya Road, 1979 (see Western Sahara PC)

(307) Rhodesia Settlement, 1979–80 (see Rhodesia PC)

(308) Raid on Angola, 1979 (see Angola PC)

(311) Raid on Gafsa

Tunisia and Libya were the protagonists in a crisis from 27 January to 30 April 1980.

Background
Several issues contributed to strained relations between these North African Arab neighbors. One was a long-standing dispute over the delimitation of the continental shelf in the Gulf of Syrte (Sidra): a ruling by the International Court of Justice had not yet been made. Another was a failed Libyan attempt at union in January 1974: the merger was formally proclaimed, but Tunisia withdrew within a few weeks. These and other bilateral matters were exacerbated by acute differences in character and leadership style between President Bourguiba of Tunisia and Libya's Colonel Qaddhafi.

Crisis
A crisis for Tunisia was triggered on the night of 26–27 January 1980 when a group of 50 Tunisian insurgents crossing the border from Algeria attacked and captured army and police installations in the oasis town of Gafsa, killing 40

persons. Tunisian security forces regained control of the town in the evening of the 27th. Interrogation of prisoners revealed that they had been trained in Libya, with the goal of forming a pro-Libyan "revolutionary" government that would seek and receive Libyan military aid.

Tunisia immediately sought diplomatic, economic, and military aid from Western and Arab states. France sent military transport planes and advisors to Tunisia on 28 January, triggering a crisis for Libya. This was followed by the dispatch of three French warships and five submarines on the 30th to patrol off the Tunisian/Libyan coast. The same day Tunisia expelled Libya's ambassador. On the 31st the U.S. defense secretary announced that the delivery of military equipment to Tunisia would be expedited.

Libya, too, responded to its perceived threat with several measures. On 4 February the French embassy in Tripoli was burned by a crowd of demonstrators. France's cultural center in Benghazi was ransacked the same day. On the 5th France recalled its ambassador to Libya. On the 7th Qaddafi accused Paris of a new imperialism in Africa. Three days later he threatened war against France. An emergency meeting of Libya's General People's Congress on 12 February demanded that France withdraw its "invasion force" from Tunisia. It also called for an alliance with the "oppressed people" of Tunisia in their armed struggle to overthrow the Bourguiba regime. That day French military aircraft were withdrawn from Tunisia.

Crisis tension declined on 27 February when Qaddafi declared the confrontation with Tunisia over, after the "fall" of Tunisia's Prime Minister Hedi Nouira, who was hospitalized in Paris. The next day Libya's leader said that the possibility of a serious confrontation with France, too, had ended following President Giscard d'Estaing's statement on the 26th that French forces had not actively intervened in the Gafsa fighting.

Relations between Tunisia and Libya remained severely strained during March and the first half of April 1980, particularly after the execution on 12 April of 15 Tunisians convicted of participating in the Gafsa raid. By the end of April a more conciliatory tone was evident in statements by the two adversaries, and the crisis ended.

The most involved actor, other than the adversaries themselves, was France. Both Tunisia and Libya appealed to the *OAU* in early February: the former called for condemnation of Libya's alleged involvement in the raid on Gafsa; and Libya sought a censure of France for its "invasion of Tunisia." First, Africa's regional organization on 15 February and then the Arab League on 28 February adopted resolutions reaffirming the principle of noninterference in internal affairs and respect for national sovereignty. The Arab League also established a four-member mediation mission and called upon the two protagonists to take steps to normalize their relations. U.S. activity in this crisis consisted of the dispatch on 7 February of two air force transport planes with armored vehicles for the Tunisian army. The USSR and the UN were not involved in this crisis.

(See *Master Table,* pp. 722–23.)

Sources
ACR 1980; *AR* 1980; *ARB* 1980; *ARec* 1980; *Facts on File* 1980; *Keesing's* 1980; *MECS* 1979–80.

(312) Operation Iman, 1980 (see Western Sahara PC)

(313) Operation Smokeshell, 1980 (see Angola PC)

(314) Libya Threat to Sadat

Egypt and Libya were embroiled in a personalized crisis from the 11th to the end of June 1980.

Background and Pre-crisis
Almost from the moment they came to power—Muammar Qaddhafi in Libya through a military coup in 1969, Anwar al-Sadat, who succeeded Nasir as President of Egypt in 1970—their relations were marked by acute hostility. There were several sources of this animus. One was personal rivalry for Nasir's mantle of leadership in the Arab world. Another was Sadat's marked shift to a pro-U.S. policy during and after the **October–Yom Kippur War** of 1973–74 (see Case #255, in the **Arab/Israel PC**). Hostility was accentuated by a violent border dispute in 1977 (see Case #281—**Egypt/Libya Clashes**). Another source was Egypt's peace agreement with Israel in 1979, which Qaddhafi attacked virulently; in fact, Libya took the lead in the group of "resistance" or "steadfastness" Arab states in pressing, successfully, for the expulsion of Egypt from the Arab League. And finally they disagreed over Chad, with Libya supporting Goukouni Oueddi, Egypt backing Hissene Habré (see Case #304—**Chad/Libya IV**, in 1979—in the **Chad/Libya PC**). During the late 1970s Qaddhafi and Sadat engaged in frequent verbal attacks and some attempts at sabotage and assassination.

Crisis
A crisis for Egypt was triggered by Qaddhafi's blunt and provocative speech on 11 June 1980, marking the tenth anniversary of the evacuation of U.S. bases in Tripoli. Not only did Libya's leader declare that the freedom of the Libyan people was threatened so long as U.S. forces remained on Egyptian territory, he also unequivocally proclaimed Libya's "alliance with the Egyptian people and army in order to topple treason in Egypt" and urged a *jihad* (holy war) by all Muslims against the Egyptian regime.

Egypt responded on the 16th by declaring a state of emergency in the western part of Egypt, deploying troops to the region bordering Libya, and reimposing martial law regulations in force for 70 years that Sadat had lifted a month earlier. These measures triggered a crisis for Libya: Libya's Foreign Secretariat termed them equivalent to "a declaration of a state of war"; and it affirmed Libya's "legitimate right to self-defense." Libya added insult to the threat by holding the U.S. responsible for Egypt's "aggression," because "al-Sadat is not the master of his decisions."

Libya followed this up with a vigorous diplomatic campaign on 18 June, conveying its view of the crisis—as an Egyptian "threat to the stability of the region"—to the UN Secretary-General, the President of the UN Security Council, the Secretary-General of the Arab League, the *OAU*, the Islamic Conference Organization *(ICO)*, and the Non-Aligned Conference. The same day the Arab League Secretary-General concurred, terming Egypt's state of emergency and its massing of troops on Libya's border "a threat to Arab security and general security in the region."

At an African ministerial council meeting on 21 June the Arab rejectionist states led by Libya failed to expel Egypt from meetings of the *OAU* and the Arab-African Cooperation Organization, despite support from the Arab League. The strongest condemnation of Egypt from within the Arab world came from the Political Committee of the "National Front for Steadfastness and Confrontation," comprising Algeria, Libya, Syria, and the *PLO*. Tension continued to increase, with Libya accusing Egypt of making war preparations along its border.

On 26 June the commander of Libya's forces on the front with Egypt said that Libya would not be the first to launch a war but warned that Libya had enough power to repel any Egyptian attack. The next day Libya's Foreign Secretariat repeated its call to overthrow the Egyptian regime. On the 27th, too, Egypt's defense minister de-escalated the tension by denying any intention to attack Libya and explaining the arrival of U.S. planes—for a 90-day joint U.S.-Egyptian training exercise. The crisis faded rapidly after that statement. In sum, it was intense in hostile rhetoric but without violence.

The U.S. and the USSR were not involved, though both Libya and Egypt expressed concern during the crisis about active support to their adversary. The UN was only marginally involved.

(See *Master Table*, pp. 722–23.)

Sources
Foreign Broadcast Information Service—Daily Report/Middle East and Africa (FBIS–DR/MEA) 1980; *ACR* 1980; *AR* 1980; *ARB* 1980; *MECS* 1980–81.

(318) Libya Intervention in The Gambia

The Gambia experienced a crisis from 27 October to 7 November 1980 as a result of alleged Libyan involvement in an attempted coup.

Background and Pre-crisis
The Gambia's relations with Libya deteriorated in 1979. Most visibly, its government nationalized a transport company jointly owned with Libya, following

Tripoli's apparent failure to honor promises of economic aid. Most important was alleged Libyan involvement in internal attempts to overthrow The Gambia's government. A formal protest was sent to Libya in March 1980.

In a related incident, Senegal, The Gambia's long-time protector—de facto since the latter's independence in 1965, formally since their mutual defense agreement in 1976—severed diplomatic relations with Libya on 14 July 1980: President Senghor accused Libya of training a mercenary army and attempting to destabilize the governments of Chad, Mali, Niger, and Senegal in order to assert Libya's dominance over equatorial Africa.

Apart from The Gambia and Senegal, several of Libya's neighbors saw its "long arm" in attempts to overthrow their regimes, as in Chad since 1978 (see Cases #288, 290, 304—**Chad/Libya II, III, IV,** in **Chad/Libya PC**), and in Tunisia (see Case #311—**Raid on Gafsa** above).

Crisis

A crisis for The Gambia was triggered on 27 October 1980 by the murder of the deputy commander of its paramilitary Field Force. While the government later attempted to dispel rumors that this had been part of an attempted coup, Libya's embassy was closed and its staff expelled on 29 October.

The Gambia accused Libya of attempting to use its money and power to destabilize Gambian society. Specifically, Libya's diplomatic mission in the Gambian capital, Banjul, was accused of providing financial aid and training to two opposition groups in The Gambia, the Movement for Justice in Africa (*MOJA*-Gambia) and the Gambia Socialist Revolutionary Party *(GSRP),* seeking to spread confusion and disorder in The Gambia. On 30 October these radical groups were banned. On the 31st 150 Senegalese troops flew into Banjul at the request of The Gambia's long-time leader, Sir Dawda Jawara—he held power from 1965 to 1994—to take part in a previously scheduled joint training exercise under the terms of their defense agreement. These troops took up positions around the State House, around The Gambia's Field Force barracks at Bakai, and at Yundum airport.

Stress among The Gambia's decision makers declined in the succeeding days. The Senegalese troops remained in The Gambia for a week. Their departure on 7 November marked the end of the crisis.

There was no UN or regional organization involvement or superpower activity in this crisis.

(Eight months later, Senegalese troops again successfully defended the Jawara regime against an internal revolt [see Case #329 below].)

(See *Master Table,* pp. 722–23.)

Sources

ACR 1980–81; *AR* 1980; *ARB* 1980; *ARec* 1980; *Keesing's* 1980; *WA* 1980.

(320) East Africa Confrontation, 1980–81 (see Ethiopia/Somalia PC)

(321) Chad/Libya V, 1981 (see Chad/Libya PC)

(323) Mozambique Raid

Mozambique experienced an inconclusive crisis with the Union of South Africa from 30 January to late March 1981.

Background and Pre-crisis

South Africa targeted most of its neighbors as part of a lengthy struggle against the African National Congress *(ANC)* in the 1970s and 1980s. These generally brief crises took the form of cross-border raids against alleged *ANC* bases—in Zambia (see Case #244 above), in Angola (see Cases #297, 302, 308, 313, 331, in **Angola PC**), and in Lesotho (see Case #339 below).

On 26 November 1980 Prime Minister P. W. Botha publicly warned South Africa's neighbors that continued support for *ANC* guerrillas would result in cross-border raids by the South Africa Defence Forces *(SADF)*. On 28 January 1981 he announced the arrest of a *KGB* officer, Major Alexei Mikhailovich Kozlov, who was accused of spying in South Africa on behalf of the *ANC* and *SWAPO*.

Crisis

The trigger to Mozambique's crisis was a *SADF* raid on 30 January 1981, which destroyed *ANC* headquarters in Matola, a suburb of the capital, Maputo. The *SADF* reported 30 *ANC* members and two of its soldiers killed.

On 8 February the *ANC* president, Oliver Tambo, denied that there were *ANC* bases or training camps in Mozambique. The presence of Soviet warships in Mozambique waters at the time—the USSR and Mozambique had signed a treaty of cooperation in 1977—raised the stakes by adding a Cold War dimension to the South Africa/*ANC* conflict. On 19 February Soviet Ambassador Vdovin was reported to have warned of an "appropriate response" if "anyone attacks us or our friends." No such attacks occurred. There was a further minor border incident on 17 March; and the crisis faded late in March 1981, without an agreement, formal, informal, or tacit.

While the Soviet Union was involved in this crisis through the presence of a naval flotilla, the U.S. remained aloof. And the UN did not play a role in abating the crisis.

(See *Master Table*, pp. 724–25.)

Sources

ACR 1981–82; *AR* 1981; *ARB* 1981; *ARec* 1981; *Keesing's* 1981.

(328) Cameroon/Nigeria I

A long-standing border dispute generated the first of several crises between Nigeria and Cameroon from 15 May to 24 July 1981.

Background
On 31 May 1975 General Yakubu Gowon, Nigeria's Head of State, and President Ahmadou Ahidjo of Cameroon signed an agreement in the Cameroonian town of Maroua: the access channel to the port of Calabar was to remain within Nigeria's territorial waters; and the rights of Nigerian fishers within a two-kilometer strip were not to affect the territorial waters between the two states. However, after the fall of Gowon in July 1975, the Maroua Agreement was not ratified or implemented by Nigeria. The territorial waters dispute remained unresolved.

Crisis
On 15 May 1981 a Cameroonian patrol boat fired on Nigerian soldiers on the Cameroon/Nigeria border, killing five and wounding three. This triggered a crisis for Nigeria. On the 18th Nigeria's foreign minister issued a formal protest condemning the attack as occurring within Nigeria's territory and warned that Nigeria would "fight back" if pushed further.

This verbal response triggered a crisis for Cameroon. On the 24th President Ahidjo delivered a message to Nigeria's President Shehu Shageri, expressing "regret" for the killing and calling for a joint commission of inquiry to resolve the crisis. Nigeria rejected the proposal and demanded an unqualified apology, full reparations, and the punishment of Cameroon's soldiers who opened fire. It also pressed for international arbitration of the dispute.

Pressure for a military response, including pressure from the speaker of the house of representatives, grew in Nigeria. On 27 May a group of Nigerians damaged Cameroon's embassy in Lagos. Nigeria's attempt to place the issue on the *OAU* agenda at the Nairobi summit in June failed; and it boycotted the meeting. Mediation efforts in July by Kenya's foreign minister and the *OAU* Secretary-General were more successful. On 20 July Cameroon's president reportedly offered to pay compensation to the families of the five Nigerian soldiers. On the 22nd Ahidjo accepted an invitation to visit Nigeria. And on the 24th a letter from Shageri accepted Cameroon's offer of compensation, along with its agreement to international arbitration to resolve the border dispute. This terminated the first of several full-scale crises between these West African neighbors (see Cases #377 and 410 below).

There was no UN, U.S. or USSR involvement in this crisis.

(See *Master Table,* pp. 724–25.)

Sources
ACR 1981; *AR* 1981; *ARB* 1981; *WA* 1981; *Keesing's* 1981.

(329) Coup Attempt in The Gambia

Senegal experienced a foreign policy crisis as a result of a coup attempt in its neighbor and client, The Gambia, from 30 July 1981 to 29 January 1982.

Background
Dawda Jawara had been in power since The Gambia attained independence in 1965, at first as Prime Minister and from 1970 as President. Opposition groups had attempted to overthrow his regime on several occasions, mainly because of discontent over the state of the economy, and its dependence on groundnuts for most of its export earnings: one of these attempts generated an international crisis (see Case #318 above).

Crisis
On 30 July 1981, while Jawara was in London, the leftist 12-member National Revolutionary Council *(NRC)* led a coup against his regime, accusing the president of "corruption, tribalism, social oppression, and creating a bourgeois class." Within hours the *NRC* took control of the airport, the radio station, and most of the capital. They announced the suspension of the constitution and proclaimed their intention to establish a "dictatorship of the proletariat."

The same day The Gambia's president requested Senegal's military intervention—as in 1980 (see Case #318 above) thereby triggering a crisis for Senegal. President Diouf of Senegal responded on the 31st by dispatching 400 soldiers to its neighbor. By the 6th about 2,700 Senegalese troops were deployed in The Gambia. In the meantime, Jawara proclaimed a state of emergency upon his return to Banjul on 2 August.

On 19 August, at Diouf's initiative, the two states announced their intention to create a confederation, Senegambia. A summit meeting in The Gambia's capital led to an initial agreement. The inauguration of the confederation, with the signing of a treaty on 29 January 1982, marked the end of the crisis. (Two days later Senegalese troops left The Gambia.)

Verbal support for Senegal's military intervention was conveyed to Diouf by the U.S. president, the chairman of the *OAU,* and several African leaders. The USSR's Tass news agency denied allegations of involvement in the coup. The UN was not involved in the crisis.

(See *Master Table,* pp. 724–25.)

Sources
ACR 1981–82; *AR* 1981, 1982; *ARB* 1981, 1982; *ARec* 1981; *Keesing's* 1981; *WA* 1981.

(330) Gulf of Syrte I

Libya experienced two crises with the United States over the Gulf of Syrte (Sidra) in the 1980s. The first lasted from 12 August to 1 September 1981.

Background and Pre-crisis
Relations between Libya and the U.S. were characterized by undisguised hostility since Colonel Muammar Qaddhafi overthrew the Libyan monarchy and seized power in 1969. His anti-U.S. policy and pronouncements, military alignment with the Soviet Union, and frequent interventions in the domestic affairs of neighbors and more distant African states generated a U.S. image of Libya as "public enemy no. 1" in Africa.

Libya had persistently claimed the Gulf of Syrte (Sidra) as an "internal sea"; and in 1973 it extended the 12-mile limit of its claimed territorial waters north of the Gulf into the contiguous Mediterranean Sea. The U.S., by contrast, adhered to international convention, which viewed the Gulf as part of international waters, that is, the global commons. Thus, when U.S. reconnaissance flights over the central Mediterranean–Gulf of Syrte area began in 1972, tension increased. Qaddhafi warned the U.S. of a possible military confrontation if it continued to intrude into Libya's maritime space and airspace. Libya's active intervention in Chad throughout 1981 (see Case #321—**Chad/Libya V,** in **Chad/Libya PC**) further exacerbated the difficulties in its relationship with the U.S. This deterioration was accentuated by the closure of Libya's embassy in Washington on 6 May 1981. The ongoing dispute over Libya's territorial waters erupted a few months later.

Crisis
A crisis for Libya was triggered by a U.S. announcement on 12 August 1981 that its Sixth Fleet would hold maneuvers in the Mediterranean. Libya responded with a full military alert the same day. And on the 18th it accused the U.S. of violating Libya's territorial waters by holding naval exercises within the Gulf of Syrte. The next day two U.S. F-14s shot down two Libyan SU-22 fighters 60 miles from Libya's coast, but within the Gulf of Syrte—the only act of violence in this crisis. The U.S. also warned Libya against retaliation, threatening to use military force if Libya attacked U.S. aircraft or ships involved in the Sixth Fleet exercise.

On the 20th Qaddhafi declared that Libya was ready to defend its territorial waters even if it led to war with the U.S. or a World War III. President Reagan responded the same day that he had deliberately ordered the maneuvers in order to challenge Libya's claim to the disputed waters.

The crisis ended abruptly on 1 September when Libya's ruler threatened to attack U.S. nuclear bases in the Mediterranean and cause "an international catastrophe" if the U.S. once more intruded into Libya's Gulf of Syrte.

The USSR offered only verbal support to its client: Tass accused the U.S. of "terrorism." Acting through the Arab League and the Gulf Cooperation Council, all Arab states except Egypt and the Sudan criticized U.S. behavior. Both protagonists informed the UN Security Council of this incident; but there was no UN—or *OAU*—involvement.

(In effect, the 1981 crisis was a prelude to a more severe confrontation between the U.S. and Libya over the Gulf of Syrte, including serious clashes, in 1986 [see Case #363 below].)

(See *Master Table*, pp. 724–25.)

Sources
ACR 1981–82; *AR* 1981; *ARB* 1981; *Keesing's* 1981; *MECS* 1981–82.

(331) Operation Protea, 1981 (see Angola PC)

(332) Galtat Zemmour I, 1981 (see Western Sahara PC)

(338) Ogaden III, 1982 (see Ethiopia/Somalia PC)

(339) Lesotho Raid

Lesotho experienced a crisis with the Union of South Africa from 9 to 15 December 1982.

Background and Pre-crisis
Lesotho, like Angola and Zambia, experienced violent crises with South Africa from the early 1970s, as part of Pretoria's continuing struggle against the African National Congress *(ANC)* (see **Background** to Case #323 above). In early 1982, economic and political sites in Lesotho were attacked. On 26 May the Prime Minister of Lesotho, Chief Jonathan, accused the Pretoria regime of supporting these raids, a charge that was emphatically denied.

On 7 August Lesotho's Minister of Works, Jobo K. Rampeta, was killed in an ambush. The next day Pretoria sent a message of sympathy. On the 11th Lesotho rejected this apology. A border incident was reported the same day; and, once more, Lesotho accused South Africa of responsibility.

Crisis
A crisis for Lesotho was triggered on 9 December 1982 when the South Africa Defence Forces launched a raid against the homes of *ANC* members in its capital, Maseru, killing 32. The next day Chief Jonathan condemned the raid. A complaint to the UN led to a Security Council resolution on 15 December, condemning South Africa's attack. This terminated Lesotho's crisis.

Neither the U.S. nor the USSR was involved.

(On 9 February 1983 South Africa's foreign minister, in a letter to the UN

Secretary-General, rejected the resolution, asserted Pretoria's wish to negotiate nonaggression pacts with its neighbors, and claimed the right to take measures to defend the life and property of its citizens.)
(See also Case #360 below.)
(See *Master Table*, pp. 726–27.)

Sources
ACR 1982–83; *AR* 1982; *ARB* 1982; *ARec* 1982; *Keesing's* 1982.

(340) Libya Threat to Sudan

Sudan, Egypt, and Libya were enmeshed in a crisis from 11 to 22 February 1983.

Background and Pre-crisis
Sudan and Libya experienced a basic change in political regime almost simultaneously: a seizure of power by Brigadier-General Numeiri in Khartoum in May 1969; and a coup d'état led by Colonel Qaddhafi in Tripoli in September 1969, overthrowing the monarchy. Both proved to be durable leaders—Numeiri, until his ouster in 1985; and Qaddhafi, who is still in power. However, the two regimes differed markedly: Numeiri was pro-West; and Qaddhafi projected a messianic role, designed to transform the Arab world. The result was increasing tension and hostility between the two leaders and their states during the 1970s and early 1980s.

Sudan perceived continuous attempts at subversion by Qaddhafi, aimed at expanding his influence in Africa and the Arab world through mergers, as with Chad, Egypt, and Tunisia. Diplomatic relations were severed in 1976–77 and from 1981 to 1985. There were many border incidents and alleged overflights of Sudan's territory. One of these generated an international crisis.

Tension escalated in the autumn of 1983 with a visible increase in Libya's military presence, notably air power, near Sudan's northern border: MIG-23s and TU-22 bombers supplied by the Soviet Union were concentrated near the border.

Crisis
Evidence of a Libya military buildup and the perception in Khartoum and Cairo, by 11 February, of a Libyan plan to overthrow the Numeiri regime triggered a crisis for Sudan and Egypt. The next day Sudan complained to the UN and placed its forces on alert. Egypt, too, perceived Libya's military buildup as a threat, especially because of its commitments to Sudan under the terms of their mutual defense agreement in 1976 and their Charter of Integration in October 1982. Cairo responded on the 12th by sending fighter planes close to its border with Sudan and transport planes to Aswan in southern Egypt, within easy distance for a rapid deployment of troops to Sudan. President Mubarak also warned the U.S. of an impending Libyan attack on Sudan.

On 17 February the U.S. became militarily involved, though not as a full-fledged crisis actor: it dispatched four multipurpose AWACS reconnaissance planes to Egypt and the aircraft carrier, *Nimitz*, to the Red Sea off the coast of Sudan and Egypt. These signals of U.S. resolve to support Arab allies triggered a crisis for Libya. It responded the next day by concentrating more air power near the Egyptian border. On the 21st Sudan renewed its charge of a growing Libyan military buildup close to its border, despite U.S. and Egyptian assurances that the Libyan threat had declined. The same day Egypt accused Libya of interfering in Sudan's internal affairs and affirmed that it would assist Sudan's defense against military intervention. Sudan renewed this charge the next day and accused Libya of violating its airspace. However, on the 22nd Numeiri and Mubarak met in Khartoum to consider the implementation of their 1982 integration agreement: this reduced Sudan's stress and ended the 11-day crisis for all three actors, along with the international crisis as a whole.

The UN Security Council, on 22 February, provided a forum for debate on the crisis between Sudan and Libya; but it did not play a role in crisis management. And the USSR was not involved directly: its supply of arms to Libya made possible—but did not shape—Qaddhafi's behavior toward his neighbors.

(A year later, the same three actors were embroiled in another crisis [see Case #350 below].)

(See *Master Table*, pp. 726–27.)

Sources
ACR 1983–84; *AR* 1983; *ARB* 1983; *ARec* 1983; *Keesing's* 1983; *MECS* 1982–83.

(341) Chad/Nigeria Clashes

Chad and Nigeria experienced a border crisis from 18 April until 11 July 1983.

Background and Pre-crisis
Both of these states were granted independence in 1960—Chad by France, Nigeria by the U.K. Relations were cooperative until the late 1970s, when oil exploration in the undemarcated Lake Chad region portended substantial wealth for the beneficiary of the discovery of oil.

The bilateral relationship was complicated by the role of Nigerian soldiers as peacekeepers in Chad, under *OAU* auspices in 1979 and again in 1981 at the invitation of the then-victorious Goukouni regime. They were compelled to leave Chad by Habré, who replaced Goukouni in 1982.

The problem was compounded by the emergence of new islands in the Lake Chad region as a result of falling water levels in the lake. Some of these were being used as sanctuaries by anti-Habré Chadian forces, who were harassing Nigerian fishers.

Crisis

Amid incidents along the border, Nigerian soldiers were sent to Kinsara Island in the disputed Lake Chad area on 18 April 1983 to protect Nigerian fishers. This was perceived as a threat to territory and triggered a crisis for Chad. Its violent response the same day catalyzed a crisis for Nigeria. Serious clashes ensued until 24 April. At the end of April Chadian troops attacked—and recaptured—Kinsara Island. Nigeria responded with retaliatory raids.

In late May the intensity of the border clashes seemed to subside. Nigeria's foreign minister spoke, prematurely, about a peaceful solution based upon revived joint patrols of the border area, along with demarcation, by a committee appointed by the Chad Basin Commission, of the borders of its four member-states, Nigeria, Chad, Niger, and Cameroon.

Intermittent clashes continued until 2 July when the presidents of Chad and Nigeria met. An agreement signed on 11 July formally ended the fighting and reopened the disputed border, terminating the crisis. There were few casualties in the fighting, an estimated 75 Chadian soldiers and nine Nigerians.

The two superpowers, the UN, and the *OAU* were not involved in this crisis. (See *Master Table*, pp. 726–27.)

Sources

ACR 1982–83; *AR* 1983; *ARB* 1983; *ARec* 1983; Decalo 1987; *Keesing's* 1983.

(342) Chad/Libya VI, 1983–84 (see Chad/Libya PC)

(345) Maitengwe Clashes

Botswana experienced a crisis with Zimbabwe (the successor to Rhodesia) from 8 November to 21 December 1983.

Background

Two Zimbabwean political forces competed for power in the struggle against the white colonial regime in Rhodesia: the Zimbabwe African National Union *(ZANU)*, under the leadership of Robert Mugabe; and the Zimbabwe African People's Union *(ZAPU)*, led by Joshua Nkomo. The former won a decisive majority in the February 1980 elections preparatory to independence.

Authority was transferred to *ZANU* on 18 April 1980, with Mugabe as Prime Minister, later as President of the new state (see Case #307—**Rhodesia Settlement, in Rhodesia PC**). However, rivalry, including frequent clashes, continued during the early years of independence, largely due to the *ZANU*-led government's attempt to extend central authority to the *ZAPU*'s territorial base, Metabeleland. Some of the latter's forces sought—and received—sanctuary in neighboring Botswana, notably at the Dukwe refugee camp.

Crisis

In a "hot pursuit" operation against the alleged dissident training camp, a small contingent of Zimbabwean forces penetrated four kilometers into Botswana near Maitengwe on 8 November 1983. Minor clashes with Botswana border guards triggered a foreign policy crisis for Zimbabwe's much weaker neighbor. Botswana responded by strengthening several border posts and by requesting an urgent meeting of their Joint Defense and Security Commission. The Zimbabwe minister of state tried to reassure Botswana of its peaceful intentions at the commission's meeting on 10 November.

A second incident occurred on 20 December, with Zimbabwe acknowledging for the first time that its forces had intruded into Botswana. The crisis was defused as a result of a meeting between senior officials of the two states on the 21st.

There was no involvement by the U.S., the USSR, the UN, or the *OAU*. Maitengwe was a low-intensity crisis, with minor violence, a spillover from the internal politics of Zimbabwe in the pre- and early postindependence years.

(See *Master Table,* pp. 726–27.)

Sources

ACR 1983–84; *AR* 1984; *ARec* 1983; *ARB* 1983; *Keesing's* 1984.

(346) Ethiopia/Sudan Tension

Sudan perceived a crisis with Ethiopia from 20 November 1983 to 20 February 1984.

Background and Pre-crisis

A protracted civil war between the Muslim-led government in the north and predominantly Christian forces in the south had created havoc and made Sudan vulnerable to external intervention. The internal situation deteriorated in May 1983 following Khartoum's attempts to weaken the south, through an imposed administrative division of the south into three zones and the rotation of southern army units to the north, along with the exploitation of newly discovered oil in the south for the benefit of the north. The result was mutiny in the army and mass desertions of southern soldiers, and a sharpening of civil strife.

In September 1983 President Numeiri accused Ethiopia, Iran, Libya, and the USSR of plotting against his regime. On 15 November 11 foreign workers and 18 Sudanese were kidnapped by rebel forces based in Ethiopia. Two days later Sudan claimed that these rebel forces had attacked southern Sudan.

Crisis

The crisis trigger for Sudan was an alleged massing of 1,000 Ethiopian troops on its border, supported by 150 Cuban and Soviet advisors, financed by Libya. This "foreign conspiracy" was denounced on 20 November by Sudan's First Vice-President, General Omar Mohamed Al-Taib. The same day Sudan proclaimed a state of emergency and placed its armed forces on a state of maximum alert. In a delayed reaction, President Mengistu of Ethiopia denied Sudan's allegations on 24 January 1984, as did Ethiopia's foreign minister in Paris, claiming that the situation on the border was "very calm."

Sudan claimed on 19 December that its forces had broken the siege of Nasir, about 30 kilometers from the border. Tension and low-intensity conflict persisted until 20 February when Sudan's foreign minister announced unilateral steps to end its hostile verbal campaign against Ethiopia as a goodwill gesture. This marked the termination of Sudan's crisis with its neighbor.

The U.S., the UN, and the *OAU* were not involved. The USSR, as noted, was accused by Sudan of a "Kremlin plan" to undermine Sudan's territorial integrity and political stability.

(See *Master Table*, pp. 726–27.)

Sources
ACR 1983–84; *AR* 1983, 1984; *ARB* 1983, 1984; *ARec* 1983, 1984; *Keesing's* 1983, 1984.

(347) Operation Askari, 1983–84 (see Angola PC)

(350) Omdurman Bombing

Sudan, Egypt, and Libya were the direct participants in a brief crisis, beginning on 16 March 1984; the crisis faded.

Background
Throughout its lengthy tenure (1969–85) the Numeiri military regime in Sudan viewed Libya and Ethiopia, aided by the USSR, as engaged in persistent subversion to undermine its hold on power in Khartoum. On two previous occasions Libya's acts and Sudan's perceptions led to international crises (see Cases #340 and 346 above).

Crisis
On 16 March 1984 a sole Tupolev (TU-22) bomber attacked the twin city of Sudan's capital, Omdurman. This triggered a crisis for Sudan—and Egypt, the latter because of its commitments under their 1976 mutual defense agreement. On the 17th Sudan's military regime immediately placed its armed forces on alert. The same day Egypt dispatched senior army officers to Khartoum as a signal of its concern and support. Both accused Libya of responsibility for the raid, a charge that it denied.

In response to a request by Sudan and Egypt the U.S. dispatched two AWACS surveillance aircraft on 18 March, triggering a crisis for Libya. Four days later Libya requested a meeting of the UN Security Council, which met on 27–28 March. As in February 1983 (see Case #340 above), Sudan accused

Libya of the raid and, more generally, of intervention in its affairs; and Libya charged the U.S. with acts of aggression. As in the earlier crisis, too, President Mubarak of Egypt went to Khartoum on 25 March in a gesture of solidarity with the Numeiri regime. Thousands of Egyptian soldiers were by then deployed in Sudan. No finite end to this crisis can be identified.

The U.S., as noted, actively supported Sudan and Egypt. The USSR provided passive backing to Libya. The UN did not play an active role in crisis management. And the two regional organizations, the *OAU* and the Arab League, remained aloof.

(See *Master Table,* pp. 728–29.)

Sources
ACR 1984–85; *AR* 1984; *ARB* 1984; *ARec* 1984; *Keesing's* 1984.

(355) Botswana Raid

Botswana experienced a crisis with the Union of South Africa from 14 to 21 June 1985.

Background and Pre-crisis
From 1978 until 1988 South Africa used its superior military power to launch frequent raids against neighboring states—some at the level of full-scale invasion—alleging that Angola, Botswana, Lesotho, Mozambique, Zambia, and Zimbabwe were providing sanctuaries for African National Congress *(ANC)* fighters. Most of these incursions were directed at Angola (see **Background** to Case #323 above; and Case #380 in **Angola PC**).

On 16 March 1984 the Nkomati Accord between Mozambique and South Africa neutralized the former as a sanctuary for the *ANC*. Pretoria, concerned that the *ANC* would move its bases from Mozambique to Botswana, pressed Botswana to sign a similar agreement; but it refused. Botswana accused South Africa of applying economic, as well as military and political, pressure. In September 1984 South Africa reiterated that it would take whatever action was necessary to ensure its security.

Crisis
On 14 June 1985 the *SADF* launched a raid on 10 alleged centers of *ANC* guerrillas in the capital of Botswana, Gaborne. Botswana denied the charge. In protest, the U.S. recalled its ambassador from Pretoria. The U.K. protested to South Africa's ambassador in London. India and other members of the Non-Aligned Movement denounced the raid. So too did the *OAU* and the UN Secretary-General.

Most visible in this chorus of criticism was the UN Security Council. In its Resolution 568 passed on 21 June, the Council unanimously condemned South Africa's act and demanded that it pay "full and adequate compensation." This ended the crisis for Botswana—but not South Africa's ubiquitous raids. The USSR was not involved.

(The next day, Pretoria threatened to invade Botswana if it did not change its policy toward the *ANC*. And on 19 May 1986 it launched another raid against Botswana, as well as Zambia and Zimbabwe [see Case #365 below].)

(See *Master Table*, pp. 728–29.)

Sources
ACR 1985–86; *AR* 1985; *ARB* 1985; *ARec* 1985; *Keesing's* 1985.

(356) Expulsion of Tunisians

Tunisia experienced a crisis with Libya from 21 August to 26 September 1985 over the mass expulsion of Tunisians.

Background and Pre-crisis
The relations between these two North African Arab neighbors were chronically unstable. Since the **Raid on Gafsa** (see Case #311 above), there was an improvement, especially between the summer of 1984 and the spring of 1985. As a result, a cooperation agreement was signed between them at the end of December 1984, covering trade, security, industry, employment, and culture. Nonetheless, because of declining oil revenues and a costly development program, Libya decided to expel 38,000 foreign workers in August 1985, of whom 30,000 were Tunisians. Tunisia protested this unilateral act. Qaddhafi tried to pressure Tunisia into a political union. On 18 August Tunisia accused Libya of violating its airspace: it closed the Libyan cultural center, news agency, and airline in Tunis, expelled 253 Libyans who were accused of threatening its internal and external security, and declared 30 Libyan diplomats persona non grata.

Crisis
On 21 August 1985 Libya accused Tunisia of participating in an "imperialist" anti-Libya plot, triggering a crisis for its neighbor. A buildup of Libyan troops near the border with Tunisia—and Egypt—was reported. The next day Tunisian forces were placed on alert, to prevent a possible attack by Libya. On the 23rd and again on 31 August and 23 September, Tunisia accused Libya of violating its airspace and of preparing for war. It also summoned home the remaining Tunisian migrant workers in Libya.

On 26 September Tunisia broke diplomatic relations with Libya and announced the suspension of air traffic between the two countries. This terminated Tunisia's crisis; but relations with Libya remained strained.

The Arab League and, independently, Morocco and Kuwait tried to mediate the crisis, without success. The U.S. on 26 August, and Algeria's president during a visit to Tunisia on 2 September, announced their support of Tunisia's territorial integrity. Neither the USSR nor the UN was involved in this crisis.

(Ten years later, in September 1995, another exodus from Libya occurred: Qaddhafi publicly acknowledged that he was expelling thousands of Palestinians from Libya—to punish *PLO* leaders for agreeing to limited self-rule, in negotiations with Israel. Attempted mediation by Egypt was not successful.)
(See *Master Table*, pp. 728–29.)

Sources
ACR 1985; *AR* 1985; *ARB* 1985; *ARec* 1985; *Keesing's* 1985; *MECS* 1985–86.

(358) Egypt Air Hijacking

Egypt and Libya were enmeshed in a crisis from 23 November to 3 December 1985.

Background
Tension between these North African neighbors had existed for more than a decade. Libya's Colonel Qaddhafi, who overthrew the Libyan monarchy in 1969, was an ardent Nasirite and considered himself the successor to Egypt's charismatic leader when he died in 1970. Relations between Qaddhafi and President Sadat of Egypt, during his tenure from 1970 to 1981, were, at best, distant: they differed on ideology, policies toward the U.S. and the USSR, attitudes toward the legitimacy of political terrorism, and peace with Israel. Relations with President Mubarak, who continued Sadat's policies in all these domains, were no better: the Libyan leader's mercurial behavior and his image as inspirer, protector, and supporter of militant antiestablishment groups within and outside the Arab world fostered mistrust and instability in the Egypt/Libya relationship.

Crisis
A crisis for Egypt was triggered on 23 November 1985 by an air piracy incident: five members of an anti-Mubarak group, "Egypt Revolution," took control of an Egypt Air flight from Athens to Cairo, with 92 passengers. One of the hijackers was killed and an Egyptian security guard was wounded in an exchange of fire during the flight. Egypt and several Western states condemned Libya for giving active support to the terrorists, who were thought to be members of the anti-Arafat "Al-Fatah Revolutionary Command," headed by Abu Nidal. Egypt put its armed forces on alert, along with a military buildup on its border with Libya, triggering its crisis.

The plane landed in Malta, despite the refusal of its civil aviation authorities to authorize a landing. The hijackers demanded that the plane be refueled; but Malta's Prime Minister, Dr. Carmelo Bonnici, insisted that all passengers first be released. The hijackers set the West European, North American, Australian, and Israeli passport holders apart from the rest and shot some of them, killing one person.

Egypt's major response to its crisis was an antiterrorist military operation.

On the 24th, 75 Egyptian commando troops were secretly dispatched to the airport in Malta; three U.S. officers joined the Egyptian force. That evening they stormed the plane. During the fighting and fire that ensued, about 60 people were killed.

The U.S., the U.K., and Israel supported the Egyptian rescue mission. Malta's prime minister declared that he supported the assault because the hijackers continued to shoot hostages and threatened to blow up the plane in midair. The Greek ambassador protested to Malta's foreign minister on the 26th for not consulting Athens before allowing the Egyptian rescue mission, since a large number of passengers were Greek nationals. The same day, President Mubarak claimed that the leader of the hijacking group was living in a Tripoli hotel. Egypt requested the extradition of the one surviving hijacker; but this was denied, in the absence of an extradition treaty between Egypt and Malta.

Despite rumors of an impending Egyptian attack on Libya, tension eased. And on 3 December Mubarak declared that it was impossible for Egypt to "fight an Arab or African brother." This terminated the crisis with Libya.

There was no UN, Arab League, or *OAU* involvement in this crisis. The U.S. was active on the periphery of the rescue mission. And the USSR confined its activity to verbal criticism of the charges of Libyan complicity in the hijacking.

(See *Master Table*, pp. 728–29.)

Sources
ACR 1985; *AR* 1985; *ARB* 1985; *ARec* 1985; *Keesing's* 1985; *MECS* 1985–86.

(359) Burkina Faso/Mali Border

Mali and Burkina Faso, formerly Upper Volta, experienced a second crisis over the Agacher Strip from 20 December 1985 to 18 January 1986.

Background and Pre-crisis
The Agacher area between these two West African states, reputedly rich in minerals, was in dispute since both were granted independence by France in 1960. In 1979 the parties agreed on procedures to resolve their dispute. By September 1985 a joint border commission had succeeded in demarcating 1,000 kilometers of their common border. However, relations became badly strained a month earlier when Burkina Faso expelled the Secretary-General of the Francophone West African Economic Community, a Malian, because he criticized the President of Burkina Faso. (Captain Thomas Sankara, who became President of Upper Volta in 1983, changed its name to Burkina Faso in 1984.)

Crisis
The crisis trigger was a non-violent act by Burkina Faso around 20 December 1985—an attempt to conduct a census in the Agacher region under police guard.

This led to violent incidents, which escalated on the 25th, when Mali troops attacked towns within the disputed area. Burkina Faso planes and soldiers penetrated deep into Mali territory on the 26th. Four days of serious clashes left an estimated 400 persons dead. A cease-fire was achieved on the 30th through Nigerian and Libyan mediation under *OAU* auspices and took effect the next day, monitored by a small (16-person) Observer Group from the states of the Non-Aggression and Defense Aid Agreement and Benin. Moreover, the parties, who had agreed in principle to submit the border dispute to the International Court of Justice in September 1983, did so in December 1985.

Crisis termination was achieved at a multistate conference in the Ivory Coast on 17–18 January: the two protagonists agreed to withdraw their forces from the disputed territory, thereby terminating the crisis.

Neither the U.S. nor the USSR was involved in this crisis. The *OAU*, as noted, played an indirect mediating role. The UN Secretary-General appealed to the two parties on 27 December 1985 to exercise maximum restraint; and he offered good offices to the *OAU*.

(See *Master Table*, pp. 728–29.)

Sources
ACR 1985–86; *AR* 1986; *ARB* 1985, 1986; *ARec* 1986; Day 1987; Johnson 1986; *Keesing's* 1986; *WA* 1986.

(360) South Africa Raid on Lesotho

Lesotho experienced another crisis with the Union of South Africa from 20 December 1985 to 25 January 1986.

Background and Pre-crisis
The Pretoria regime's regional goal during the 1980s was nonaggression pacts with its neighbors. The policy was successful with Swaziland (February 1982) and Mozambique (March 1984). However, it failed vis-à-vis Botswana (see Case #355 above).

Lesotho, too, resisted South Africa's pressure (see Case #339 above). In early 1985 relations improved when the totally encircled kingdom imposed stricter security controls along the border. However, in October 1985 Lesotho unexpectedly requested the UN to take "urgent, necessary and appropriate measures to deter and disarm the oppressive regime" in South Africa.

Crisis
Two raids on its capital, Maseru, on 20 December 1985, killing nine people, triggered a crisis for Lesotho. South Africa, the alleged culprit, denied its involvement but reaffirmed its concern over the continued presence of hostile, pro-*ANC* groups in its neighbor states.

On 30 December the UN Security Council unanimously adopted a resolution condemning South Africa's unprovoked violent acts against Lesotho and demanded compensation to the victim state. On 1 January 1986 Pretoria imposed a de facto blockade of Lesotho, justifying it as necessary to prevent "terrorist *[ANC]* infiltration" into South Africa. In fact, the blockade was designed to achieve several goals: to persuade Lesotho to sign a nonaggression agreement; to expel *ANC* activists; and to stop the activities of Soviet-bloc advisors in Lesotho.

Lesotho responded on 14 January with an appeal to the UN, the U.K., and the U.S. to mount an airlift of food and essential supplies to the besieged kingdom. If necessary, it warned, it would turn to the Soviet bloc for assistance. As a consequence of the blockade the Prime Minister, Chief Jonathan, was deposed on 20 January: the king was given power to rule by decree, advised by the military.

South Africa welcomed the internal change in Lesotho, as evident in the easing of the blockade on 20 January. The two states signed a mutual security agreement on the 21st. And border restrictions were completely lifted on the 25th, marking the end of Lesotho's—and the international—crisis.

The U.S. and the USSR were marginally involved.

(See *Master Table,* pp. 728–29.)

Sources
ACR 1985–86; *AR* 1986; *ARB* 1986; *ARec* 1986; *Keesing's* 1986.

(362) Chad/Libya VII, 1986 (see Chad/Libya PC)
(363) Gulf of Syrte II

Libya and the United States were embroiled in a second crisis over the Gulf of Syrte (Sidra) from 24 March until 21 April 1986.

Background and Pre-crisis
Like the Mediterranean Sea, into which it flowed, the Gulf of Syrte was traditionally viewed as international waters. Since October 1973, however, Qaddafi's Libya had claimed the entire Gulf as its territorial waters. This was first challenged in 1981 soon after Reagan entered the White House: U.S. naval exercises in the Gulf sparked a confrontation and crisis with Libya (see Case #330 above).

This process was replicated in the second crisis. In January 1986 Washington announced its intent to hold two naval exercises in the Gulf, on 23–30 January and 11–14 February. U.S. naval aircraft intercepted Libyan planes during those maneuvers; but there was no violence. On 20 March the Pentagon announced that several ships of the U.S.'s Sixth Fleet would cross into the Gulf south of latitude 32'30. On the 23rd U.S. naval aircraft flew south of that designated line; but that act was almost routine by then.

Crisis
A full-scale foreign policy crisis for Libya was triggered by the implementation of the 20 March announcement, that is, the entry into the Gulf of Syrte of three

U.S. naval vessels on 24 March. Libya, perceiving this act as a grave threat to its territorial integrity, fired two Soviet-made SAM-5 missiles on U.S. carrier-based planes, causing no damage. U.S. planes then attacked a Libyan missile ship and a corvette, as well as mounting raids on the radar installations of Libyan batteries at Syrte. Another clash occurred on the 25th, with conflicting and disputed claims of casualties from another U.S. air attack. President Qaddhafi's initial verbal reaction, the same day, took the form of tit-for-tat: "this is not a time for speaking . . . it is a time for war."

U.S. naval maneuvers ended on 27 March, four days ahead of schedule. On the 28th Secretary of State Shultz warned that U.S. forces would take further action against Libya if necessary. Tension increased on 2 April when a bomb exploded on a TWA plane flying from Rome to Athens: four passengers were killed. The U.S. accused Libya of being involved; Libya denied any responsibility; and Shultz later acknowledged this.

While the U.S. was deeply involved from the outset, triggering Libya's crisis, it experienced all three conditions of a foreign policy crisis only on 5 April, when a bomb exploded in a discotheque frequented by U.S. soldiers in West Berlin: one U.S. soldier and a Turkish woman were killed, with 155 persons injured. On the 7th the U.S. Ambassador to West Germany, Richard Burt, linked this terrorist act to Libya. On the 9th Libya denied any involvement. The same day, Reagan referred to Qaddhafi as a "mad dog" and warned of U.S. retaliation.

On the 9th, too, the U.S. president approved a proposal for air strikes against Libya; among his security advisors, only Defense Secretary Weinberger dissented. The major response to the crisis was implemented on 15 April, in the form of air raids on Tripoli and Benghazi: the attack was described by Reagan as "a single engagement in a long battle against terrorism." The U.S. neither affirmed nor denied that the primary goal of the raids was to kill Qaddhafi; but one of his children was among the reported 100 civilian casualties in Tripoli (and 30 in Benghazi).

The successful air strikes on Libya's two largest cities drastically reduced stress for the U.S., terminating its crisis. But it was not until a draft resolution sympathetic to Libya was debated in the UN Security Council on 21 April that Libya's crisis—and the second international crisis over the Gulf of Syrte—came to an end: although the resolution was vetoed by the U.S. and the U.K., its condemnation of U.S. actions ensured that another U.S. air raid on Libya would not occur, at least in the near future.

Many international organizations and states were involved in this interstate crisis. The UN Security Council debated the issue from 26 to 31 March and, as noted, voted overwhelmingly in favor of a resolution critical of U.S. air raids on Libya: despite the U.S.-U.K. veto, it effectively terminated the crisis. The USSR and several Arab states—Algeria, Morocco, and Sa'udi Arabia, along with the PLO and Iran—criticized the U.S. naval exercises and strongly condemned the U.S. air raids. So too did the Arab League; but it rejected Libya's demand that member-states sever diplomatic and economic relations with Washington. Europe, too, was involved. Foreign ministers of the European Community met on 14 April: they urged restraint by both adversaries, criticized Libya as the source of terrorism, but did not accede to the U.S. request to impose economic sanctions on Libya. Earlier, France and West Germany expelled some Libyan diplomats.

(During the next decade Libya was treated as a pariah state by the U.S.—and the UN—over its refusal to hand over two Libyans suspected of causing the bombing of a Pan American flight over Lockerbie in Scotland in 1988, with hundreds of casualties, mostly U.S. citizens. UN sanctions were imposed; but there was no further full-scale crisis between Libya and the U.S.)

(See *Master Table*, pp. 730–31.)

Sources
ACR 1986; *AR* 1986; *ARB* 1986; *Keesing's* 1986; *New York Times* 1986; Reagan 1990; Shultz 1993.

(365) South Africa Cross-Border Raid

Botswana, Zambia, and Zimbabwe experienced a crisis with the Union of South Africa in May 1986.

Background and Pre-Crisis
The African National Congress *(ANC)*, the largest organization of black South Africans opposed to the white regime in Pretoria, was founded in 1912. For almost half a century it pursued non-violence as the path to racial equality. In 1960 it adopted a strategy of military struggle against the apartheid system and was outlawed. Its campaign of guerrilla attacks from neighboring states, notably Botswana, Zambia, and Zimbabwe, reached a peak in 1985–86. On 15 May 1986 President Botha warned these three "front-line states," all of which were vulnerable to South Africa's military and economic power, of the risk of providing a sanctuary for *ANC* fighters.

Crisis
The crisis trigger for these three states was "punitive" air and commando raids by the South African Defence Forces on 19 May against selective *ANC* targets in Botswana, Zambia, and Zimbabwe. The U.S. condemned the attack the same day but persisted with its policy of "constructive engagement" and opposition to economic sanctions against South Africa.

On 20 May the six front-line states of southern Africa opposed to the apartheid regime—Angola, Mozambique, and Tanzania, along with the three targets of South Africa's cross-border raid—condemned the Pretoria regime and called upon the international community to impose mandatory, comprehensive, economic sanctions in order to bring about "peace and stability in the region." The *OAU* called for world pressure to prevent further Union of South Africa raids against its neighbors. The Secretary-General of the Arab League, too, urged sanctions. By contrast, South Africa's President Botha, clearly seeking U.S. understanding and support, compared the cross-border raid to the U.S. air raid on Libya two months earlier (see Case #363 above).

At the UN, the Secretary-General condemned the raids as violations of the territorial integrity and sovereignty of the three target states and of the UN Charter. A Security Council draft resolution calling for mandatory economic sanctions, sponsored by Senegal on behalf of the OAU and by Zambia speaking for the front-line states, received a large majority but was vetoed by the U.K. and the U.S. on 23 May. After the Security Council's vote the crisis faded in late May. The USSR was marginally involved in this crisis.

(See *Master Table,* pp. 730–31.)

Sources
ACR 1985–86; *AR* 1986; *ARB* 1986; *ARec* 1986; *Keesing's* 1986.

(366) Rebel Attack on Uganda

Uganda experienced a crisis with Sudan from 19 August 1986 to early June 1987.

Background and Pre-crisis
Sudan has been beset with internal turmoil since its independence in 1956. During the early years (September 1963–March 1972) civil strife took the form of the "Anya-Nya" war against non-Muslim rebels in the south, who relied upon bases in neighboring states, notably Uganda. There were frequent cross-border raids by Sudanese forces, meetings between leaders of Sudan and Uganda, some agreements to cooperate against the rebels, persistent high tension. The costly Anya-Nya war between Sudan and the Southern Sudanese Liberation Movement—there were several hundred thousand, mostly civilian, casualties—ended on 12 March 1972, with Ethiopian mediation. However, domestic strife and low-intensity conflict between Sudan and Uganda—and within both states—persisted through the 1970s and into the 1980s.

A brief respite in a parallel internal war in Uganda began on 17 December 1985, when Yoweri Museveni, leader of the National Resistance Army *(NRA),* and General Tito Okello, head of Uganda's Military Council, signed a "peace agreement" in Nairobi ending the former's attempts to overthrow Uganda's regime. Kenya and Tanzania, the mediators, undertook to create a peacekeeping force to monitor the cease-fire. It was short-lived. The *NRA* resumed its military campaign on 17 January 1986 and took control of Kampala on the 26th. Museveni became President three days later. However, civil strife between the *NRA,* now in power, and rebel troops of the former Military Council, led by General Okello, continued during the next six months.

Crisis

Uganda's internal conflict acquired an interstate dimension on 19 August, when some 400 rebel troops crossed the border from Sudan and attacked the strategically important town of Gulu in Uganda. Museveni accused Sudan of supporting the rebels. Khartoum denied any involvement but acknowledged that it was difficult to control the border with Uganda because of widespread instability in southern Sudan, alluding to the long-standing civil war against the renamed Sudan People's Liberation Army *(SPLA)*. Uganda, in turn, denied that it was supporting the *SPLA*. In September the Kampala regime unilaterally closed the border with Sudan temporarily.

Civil strife in Uganda continued until an amnesty for all rebel forces went into effect on 11 June 1987. Several days earlier, President Museveni and Sudan's Prime Minister, Sadiq el-Mahdi, met in Khartoum. They agreed on measures to enhance border security, trade relations, and extradition, thereby ending their crisis.

There was no involvement by either of the superpowers, the UN or the *OAU*. (See *Master Table,* pp. 730–31.)

Sources

ACR 1986, 1987; *AR* 1986, 1987; *ARB* 1986, 1987; *ARec* 1986, 1987; *Keesing's* 1986, 1987.

(367) Mozambique Ultimatum

Malawi experienced a crisis with Mozambique from 11 September to 18 December 1986.

Background and Pre-crisis

Mozambique's relations with its neighbors had deteriorated since the early 1980s. On the one hand, South Africa accused it of providing a sanctuary for the African National Congress and allowing *ANC* fighters to launch raids into South Africa from its territory (see Case #323 above). Moreover, Mozambique accused Malawi of supporting the *Resistencia Nacional Mocambicana,* the Mozambique National Resistance *(MNR):* this charge was publicly made by the Chief of Staff of Mozambique's armed forces, Colonel-General Sebastiao Mabote, in July 1986.

Crisis

On 11 September 1986, at a minisummit of black African leaders in the Malawi town of Blantyre, President Machel of Mozambique threatened to deploy missiles along the border with Malawi and to close the border. This triggered a crisis for Malawi. President Banda of Malawi denied any kind of involvement in *MNR* activities. President Kaunda of Zambia also threatened to close its borders with both Mozambique and Malawi unless the latter changed its policy.

Banda responded on the 17th by announcing that he would no longer permit the *MNR* to maintain bases in Malawi and by proposing a joint security commission with Mozambique. And in early October he issued an expulsion order against *MNR* fighters in Malawi. Bilateral relations improved thereafter, despite an accusation by Foreign Minister Botha of South Africa on 6 November that Zimbabwe and Mozambique were involved in a plot to overthrow the regime of President Banda. There were some minor clashes—but not as a technique of crisis management; rather, both parties relied on negotiation. The crisis ended amicably on 18 December with an accord on mutual cooperation and a protocol covering defense, state security, and public order.

There was no involvement in this crisis by the UN, the *OAU*, the U.S., or the USSR.

(See *Master Table*, pp. 730–31.)

Sources
ACR 1986; *AR* 1986; *ARB* 1986; *ARec* 1986; *Keesing's* 1986.

(368) Attempted Coup—Togo

Togo experienced a crisis with Ghana from 23 September 1986 to 5 February 1987.

Background
As part of the "scramble for Africa" among Europe's great powers, Togoland became a German protectorate in 1884. During World War I an Anglo-French agreement (1916) over the "spoils of war" divided Togoland, with the French part, Togo, attached to French West Africa. It became a UN Trust Territory in 1946, with France as the Trusteeship power. After a UN plebiscite it became an autonomous republic in 1956. Along with the rest of France's empire in Africa, Togo became independent, on 27 April 1960. Its first head of state, Sylvanus Olympio, was overthrown by an army coup in 1963. Nicholas Grunitzky, who succeeded him, was ousted in 1967 by another army coup led by the Chief of Staff, Lieutenant-Colonel Etienne Eyadema, who remained in power for more than two decades. Since 1963 French military intervention was permitted under the terms of a France-Togo defense agreement.

Crisis
A crisis for Togo was triggered by another attempted military coup, on 23 September 1986. The rebels' objective was to seize the radio station and the military barracks which also served as the president's residence and the headquarters of the governing party, the *RPT (Rassemblement du Peuple Togolais)*. Togo accused Ghana of supporting the coup. Fourteen persons were killed in clashes with security forces in the capital, Lomé. Many of the 60 rebels were captured during that sole outbreak of violence.

Togo managed its crisis with Ghana by non-violent means. On the 24th a curfew was imposed, the Lomé international airport was closed, and Togo's borders with Ghana and Benin were closed. The next day Eyadema requested French military assistance in accordance with the 1963 defense agreement. France responded on the 26th, dispatching 150 paratroops and jet aircraft. The same day Zaire, too, sent troops to support Eyadema. On the 28th President Mobutu of Zaire visited Togo, as did representatives from Ivory Coast, Benin, Niger, Morocco, and Liberia in a show of support. On the 29th Togo again accused Ghana—and Burkina Faso—of training the rebels; both denied any involvement. In October and November about 300 Ghanaians were charged with illegal entry into Togo and were deported.

The *OAU* sent a fact-finding mission, which reported on 26 November without supporting or rejecting Togo's charges. By then the crisis was winding down, though it lingered for another two months. Burkina Faso sent a delegation to Lomé on 13 January 1987 for the celebration of Eyadema's 20 years in power. Togo reopened its border with Ghana on 2 February. And on the 5th Togo, in an official announcement, absolved Ghana of any involvement in the attempted coup. This ended the crisis.

The UN, the U.S., and the USSR were not involved in this crisis.

(In March, Togo's foreign minister called for a restoration of normal relations.)

(See *Master Table,* pp. 730–31.)

Sources
ACR 1986–87; *AR* 1986, 1987; *ARB* 1986, 1987; *ARec* 1986, 1987; *Keesing's* 1986, 1987; *WA* 1986, 1987.

(370) Chad/Libya VIII, 1986–87 (see Chad/Libya PC)

(373) Todghere Incident, 1987 (see Ethiopia/Somalia PC)

(375) Sand Wall, 1987 (see Western Sahara PC)

(377) Cameroon/Nigeria II

Nigeria experienced a minor border crisis with Cameroon from 2 May to 26 September 1987.

Crisis
As with most African borders, that between Cameroon and Nigeria is porous and imprecise at several points. On 2 May 1987 a small number of Cameroonian troops intruded into Nigeria's Borno Province, triggering a crisis for Nigeria. However, on 1 July Nigeria's President Babangida described it as a minor incident.

On 24 September Nigeria's Chief of Army Staff, Major-General Abacha, visited Cameroon—to affirm the "commitment of Nigeria toward peace and progress and toward the stability and peaceful coexistence between Cameroon and Nigeria." Abacha said that his visit had given the two countries an opportunity to correct some wrong impressions. Two days later, on 26 September, a joint military border patrol was formed to monitor the border. That act terminated a low-intensity crisis in West Africa.

The UN, the U.S., the USSR, and the *OAU* were not involved in this crisis.

(On 29 September, Cameroon's Army Chief of Staff arrived in Nigeria: Brigadier-General James held talks at the airport with General Abacha on the incursions into Nigeria by Cameroonian soldiers. Relations between Nigeria and Cameroon entered a new positive phase following the visit of Babangida to Cameroon on 8–11 December. This did not, however, prevent other border incidents, including one full-scale crisis [see Case #410 below—**Cameroon/Nigeria III,** in 1993–94].)

(See *Master Table,* pp. 732–33.)

Sources
AR 1987; *ARB* 1987; *ARec* 1987; *Keesing's* 1987.

(380) South Africa Intervention in Angola, 1987–88 (see Angola PC)

(382) Kenya/Uganda Border

Kenya and Uganda experienced a brief border crisis from 14 to 28 December 1987.

Background
Tension between these East African neighbors increased as a result of Uganda's decision in May 1987 to transport its coffee crop and fuel by its own national railroad, which was less expensive than the Kenyan road system. Kenya retaliated by imposing strict border controls on traffic from Uganda, which caused heavy delays. Uganda blamed Kenya for closing the border unilaterally.

Crisis
Both states perceived a crisis the same day, 14 December 1987. Ugandan troops reportedly crossed the border first, near the town of Busia, triggering a crisis for Kenya. In the clashes that ensued, which triggered a crisis for Uganda, 15 Ugandans were reportedly killed. On the 18th Kenya ordered Uganda's high commissioner to leave the country.

President Daniel Arap Moi of Kenya and President Museveni of Uganda met at the border town of Malaba on the 28th and agreed on a series of steps to ease the tension. Security forces were to be pulled back from the frontier by both sides and replaced by regular police. Moreover, the border was to be reopened to regular traffic. These conciliatory acts terminated the crisis.

There was no involvement by the UN, the *OAU,* the U.S., or the USSR in this crisis.

(See *Master Table,* pp. 732–33.)

Sources
ACR 1987; *AR* 1987; *ARB* 1987; *ARec* 1987; *Facts on File* 1987; *Keesing's* 1987.

(386) Libyan Jets

The United States and Libya were engaged in a brief, dramatic crisis from 21 December 1988 to 12 January 1989.

Background
During the 1980s there were several violent incidents between Libya and the U.S., including two crises over the Gulf of Syrte (Sidra) (see Cases #330 and 363 above). Tension flared again at the end of 1988.

Crisis
A crisis for the U.S. was triggered by the crash of a Pan American plane over Lockerbie, Scotland, on 21 December 1988: Libya was the prime suspect in the explosion that caused the deaths of 257 passengers, most of them U.S. citizens. This dramatic catalyst was reinforced by U.S. intelligence reports that Libya had embarked on the production of chemical weapons at a plant near Rabta, 60 kilometers south of the capital, Tripoli. U.S. sanctions were imposed on Libya on 28 December.

At the beginning of 1989 a U.S. task force, headed by the aircraft carrier, *John F. Kennedy,* was holding maneuvers in the central Mediterranean, near Libya. On 4 January two Libyan MIG-23s were shot down by two U.S. fighters over international waters, 110 kilometers from the Libyan coast, triggering a crisis for Libya.

The reaction in the international community was widespread criticism of U.S. actions. On 5 January the USSR, Libya's patron and arms supplier for a decade, accused the U.S. of "state terrorism" and "political adventurism." That day, too, only a U.K. veto saved the U.S. from an embarrassing European Community statement that failed to support the U.S. version of events. On 11 January a draft UN Security Council resolution deplored U.S. acts and called on the U.S. to suspend its military maneuvers off Libya's coast: the resolution was vetoed by France, the U.K., and the U.S. And the next day an emergency meeting of the Arab League and the Islamic Conference condemned U.S. aggression. A visible decline in tension between Libya and the U.S. from that day marked the end of their third crisis in the 1980s.

(See *Master Table,* pp. 734–35.)

Sources

Foreign Broadcast Information Service—Daily Report/Near East/South Asia (FBIS—DR/NESA) 1988, 1989; *ACR* 1989; *AR* 1989; *ARB* 1989; *ARec* 1989; *Keesing's* 1989.

(387) Mauritania/Senegal

Senegal and Mauritania were enmeshed in a lengthy crisis from 21 August 1989 to 18 July 1991.

Background and Pre-crisis

Both were part of the French empire in West Africa. For many years they formed a single electoral unit and were represented by the same senator in France's legislature. Mauritania was separated from Senegal politically in 1946. The two states became independent in 1960, Senegal initially as part of the Mali Federation—along with Soudan (later, Mali), Upper Volta, and Dahomey—from which it seceded in August 1960 (see Case #177 above).

The population of Senegal is entirely black African, that of Mauritania mixed Arab in the north, black African in the south. The border region, the most arable part of Mauritania, was cultivated by black Africans, competing with Senegalese across the Senegal River for limited water resources. At the root of the interstate conflict was increasing desertification, which drove Arab nomadic herders south toward black African farmlands on both sides of the border. As the value of the arable land rose, Mauritania denied Senegalese access to its land.

A series of nonmilitary violent incidents occurred in April 1989, notably on "Black Tuesday," the 25th, when hundreds were killed and injured leading to a wave of refugees. By early June 75,000 Senegalese and 170,000 Mauritanians had been airlifted to their homelands. And in July Mauritanian officials were forcibly expelling thousands of Senegalese workers across the river boundary to Senegal.

Crisis

It was this economically driven tension and violence between the people of the two countries that led to the crisis trigger for both states: on 21 August Senegal's ambassador to Mauritania was declared persona non grata; and the same day Senegal severed diplomatic relations with Mauritania.

The first of several military clashes occurred in October 1989. The armed forces of both states were strengthened in November and later by a spillover from a long-standing hostility and rivalry between Syria and Iraq: the former supported Senegal, the latter, Mauritania. Heavy artillery was exchanged in January 1990 affecting villages on both sides of the border. And intermittent outbreaks of violence occurred during the next 18 months. This low-intensity African crisis ended on 18 July 1991 with an agreement in principle to restore diplomatic relations.

UN involvement was low-key—a fact-finding mission dispatched by the Secretary-General, which had no effect on crisis abatement. Neither did mediation efforts by the *OAU*. Both the U.S. and the USSR were aloof from this crisis. (See *Master Table,* pp. 734–35.)

Sources
ACR 1989, 1990, 1991; *AR* 1989, 1990, 1991; *ARB* 1989, 1990, 1991; *ARec* 1989, 1990, 1991; *Keesing's* 1989, 1990, 1991; *New York Times* 1989.

(390) Galtat Zemmour II, 1989 (see Western Sahara PC)

(394) Rwanda/Uganda Cross-Border Raids

Rwanda experienced an ethnic crisis with Uganda from 30 September 1990 to 29 March 1991.

Background
Ethnic conflict between the Hutu and Tutsi communities has been endemic in Rwanda (and neighboring Burundi) since long before independence in July 1962. Until a successful Hutu revolt in 1959 the Tutsi dominated politics and the military. Thousands of Rwanda Tutsi fled to nearby states, Burundi, the Congo (later, Zaire), Tanganyika (later, Tanzania), and, most important, Uganda. It was in Uganda that thousands of Tutsi refugees organized themselves into a disciplined armed force, the Rwanda Patriotic Front *(RPF),* with the goal of regaining power in Rwanda. (They ultimately did so, at the end of a lengthy civil war and in the aftermath of the 1994 Hutu-organized genocide against the members of the Tutsi community who had not fled Rwanda.)

Crisis
A crisis for Rwanda was triggered on 30 September 1990 by an *RPF* incursion from its bases in Uganda that threatened the Hutu-dominated regime of President Juvenal Habyarimana. Inconclusive clashes in the capital, Kigali, occurred on 4–5 October.

Rwanda's initial response was to arrest 3,000 members of the Tutsi community, eliciting expressions of concern from Belgium and the U.S. A cease-fire took effect on the 24th but collapsed quickly. Fighting resumed near the Rwanda/Uganda border in late October and, after a lull, again on 12 December and on 4 and 23 January 1991—there were further incursions by the *RPF* from across the Uganda border.

On several occasions Rwanda accused the Uganda army of assisting the *RPF,* a charge that was always denied.

During the episodic fighting between Rwanda's army and the *RPF* over a period of six months, many efforts were made to resolve the crisis by diplomacy. A Belgian diplomatic initiative began as early as 15 October 1990 (see below). On 26 October a regional summit conference in Zaire agreed on the creation of a joint monitoring group to supervise a cease-fire. Another regional meeting was held in Kenya in February. Talks between the presidents of Rwanda and Uganda in Tanzania on 17 February 1991 led to an agreement for an immediate cease-fire. A regional conference two days later in Tanzania called on the *OAU* and the UN to assist the return of refugees to Rwanda.

There was renewed fighting on 9 March and several days thereafter. Finally, at the initiative of Zaire, a cease-fire was signed by Uganda's government and the *RPF* on 18 March and was formalized on 29 March. This marked the end of the crisis—but not of the deep-rooted Hutu-Tutsi ethnic conflict in Rwanda, which was to generate one of the cataclysmic acts of genocide in the twentieth century, the slaughter of up to a million Tutsi by Hutu armed forces and police in 1994.

Among external powers, Belgium, the former colonial power in Rwanda as administrator of the UN Trust Territory, and Zaire were the most highly involved states in this crisis. As noted, Belgium sought an end to the fighting as early as 15 October 1991, through a diplomatic initiative in cooperation with the *OAU:* Rwanda's president refused to negotiate with the *RPF.* Belgium also sought the creation of an African peacekeeping force and offered logistical and financial support. And it sent an elite battalion of 600 soldiers, along with arms and ammunition, to assist the Rwanda army. Zaire dispatched 1,000 troops to assist the Rwanda army, in accordance with their mutual defense agreement; and it played the key role in arranging the March 1992 cease-fire. France sent 150 paratroopers to protect Europeans resident in Rwanda.

The UN, the U.S., and Russia were not involved.

(See *Master Table*, pp. 734–35.)

Sources
ACR 1990, 1991; *AR* 1990, 1991; *ARB* 1990, 1991; *Keesing's* 1990, 1991.

(395) Liberia/Sierra Leone

Sierra Leone experienced a foreign policy crisis from 23 March to 31 October 1991.

Background
Sierra Leone's crisis was a direct spillover from Liberia's lengthy, complex civil war, which began in 1989. Several groups vied for power in a conflict that wrecked havoc in Africa's oldest independent state: President Samuel Doe, backed by Liberia's army; the National Patriotic Front of Liberia *(NPFL),* led by Charles Taylor; and a small rebel armed group controlled by Prince Yormie Johnson. After Doe's murder on 11 September 1990, the remnants of his forces came under the command of Nimely David, head of the presidential guard. Moreover, there was an interim government of Liberia headed by Amos Sawyer, an academic and lawyer, based in Freetown, the capital of Sierra Leone; and there also was the United Liberation Movement of Liberia for Democracy *(UL-IMO),* also based in Freetown and supported by Libya.

Crisis

A crisis for Sierra Leone was triggered on 23 March 1991 when 25 people were killed on its territory in a cross-border raid by Taylor's troops. Burkina Faso, which provided the *NPFL* with military and logistical assistance, was perceived as the source of threat to its territory by Sierra Leone's President, Joseph Saidu Momoh.

Sierra Leone responded at once by dispatching 2,000 troops to the border area; and on 31 March they occupied part of Lofa County in Liberia. Heavy fighting in April and May led to the killing of an estimated 3,000–5,000 Sierra Leone civilians and Liberian refugees by the *NPFL*—which denied any involvement. By mid-May *NPFL* forces had penetrated 150 kilometers into Sierra Leone's territory.

Peace talks, intended to terminate Liberia's civil war, were held on 30 June at Yammoussoukro in the Ivory Coast, attended by the leaders of Burkina Faso, The Gambia, Ivory Coast, Nigeria, and Togo, but to no avail. By 7 September all Liberian rebel forces had been expelled from Sierra Leone's territory.

At the fourth in a series of summit meetings on Liberia's civil war, held on 29–31 October 1991 in the Ivory Coast, an agreement was reached. The *NPFL* agreed to surrender the territory it controlled within Liberia to *ECOMOG* (Economic Community of West African States Monitoring Group), a creation of *ECOWAS* (Economic Community of West African States), a regional organization that played a crucial role in abating the crisis (see below). All foreign forces in Sierra Leone were to withdraw immediately; and a buffer zone between Liberia and Sierra Leone was to be created. This (temporary) suspension of the civil war in Liberia marked the end of Sierra Leone's crisis. Thereafter, when civil strife resumed in Liberia, it did not spill over the Sierra Leone border. (Liberia's civil war began to wind down in November 1994.)

The most active and effective external actor was the regional international organization of West Africa, *ECOWAS*. It attempted, unsuccessfully, to mediate between Doe's government and Taylor's *NPFL* in mid-1990. In August 1990 it sent a multinational force *(ECOMOG)* to Liberia, 4,000–5,000 troops, mostly Nigerians and, secondarily, Ghanaians, to impose a cease-fire. In November 1991 *ECOMOG,* now about 8,000, separated the warring factions in Liberia, thereby facilitating the elusive quest for a political solution. In short, the regional organization attempted mediation, contributed peacekeepers, and served as an observer force. Some west African states were involved in Liberia's civil war outside of *ECOMOG:* Burkina Faso, as noted; and the Ivory Coast and Togo, which provided passive support to the *NPFL.*

Superpower involvement in this crisis was minimal to nil. On 12 April 1991 Sierra Leone sought—but did not receive—U.S. military assistance. Washington's role was confined to a diplomatic effort to end the civil war: its Assistant Secretary of State for Africa, Herman Cohen, brokered a truce on 22 September 1991. The USSR and the UN were completely uninvolved.

(The lengthy civil war in Liberia, with an estimated 150,000 killed since

December 1989, appeared to be winding down in August–September 1995; following an *ECOWAS*-brokered peace accord, signed on 19 August by all the militias, a temporary coalition government of the contending factions was formed in Monrovia on 1 September. However, renewed factional strife and the flight of thousands of refugees at the end of 1995 and in early January 1996, and still another major eruption of violence in April–May 1996, leading to a descent into anarchy in Monrovia, revealed the fragility of the Liberia peace accord.)

(Sierra Leone, too, experienced a civil war from 1991 to 1996. It ended with a peace agreement on 30 November 1996 between the Sierra Leone government and the Revolutionary United Front, brokered by the Ivory Coast.)

(See *Master Table*, pp. 734–35.)

Sources
ACR 1991; *AR* 1991; *ARB* 1991; *ARec* 1991; *Keesing's* 1990, 1991; *New York Times* 1990, 1991, 1995, 1996; *WA* 1991; Weller 1994.

(396) Ghana/Togo Border II

Ghana experienced a crisis with Togo from 11 April to 5 October 1991.

Background
The relations between these west African neighbors had been strained for more than 30 years. Opponents of various regimes in Togo had sought refuge in Ghana.

Crisis
A crisis for Ghana was triggered on 11 April 1991, when Togolese soldiers threatened to fire at demonstrators who had fled across the border to Ghana. Togo closed the border and increased its military presence there. Ghana's Foreign Minister, Obed Asamoah, criticized Togo's behavior as designed to create an international incident, to enable Togo to seek outside help to solve serious internal problems: Togo was then experiencing mounting street violence, strikes, and harsh repression of all dissent by its security forces.

To avert a serious spillover from Togo's domestic crisis, Ghana's defense forces were placed on alert, to intervene if the safety of Ghanaians in Lomé, Togo's nearby capital, came under threat. Several cross-border violent incidents occurred; but a major confrontation between the armed forces of the two states was avoided. The low-intensity crisis continued until 5 October, when Ghana and Togo agreed to reopen their frontier.

(See *Master Table*, pp. 736–37.)

Sources
ACR 1991; *AR* 1991; *ARB* 1991; *WA* 1991.

(399) Foreign Intervention in Zaire

Zaire, along with Belgium and France, was enmeshed in a crisis arising from internal turmoil from 23 September to 4 November 1991.

Background
The former Belgian Congo became independent on 30 June 1960 and was almost immediately confronted with an international crisis triggered by a mutiny among its soldiers (see Case #176 above). The occupation of Stanleyville by rebel forces and the formation of a Revolutionary Council on 4 August 1964 led to another Congo crisis with high-profile foreign military intervention (see Case #211 above). In November 1965 Colonel Mobutu seized power in a coup d'état—and remains Head of State in Zaire (formerly Congo) 32 years later.

Crisis
As in 1960 and 1964 a crisis for Zaire, Belgium, and France was triggered by an internal challenge on 23 September 1991: the catalyst was rioting by regular troops of Zaire's army and their occupation of Kinshasa Airport, in protest against low wages. The Mobutu regime correctly perceived this as a serious threat to Zaire's political system. For France and Belgium, as for Belgium and other states in the two earlier crises in the Congo, turmoil in Zaire's army posed a threat to influence in this raw material–rich state, the largest in central Africa.

Belgium and France responded on the 24th by announcing their intention to dispatch troops to Zaire to protect and evacuate foreign (Western) residents. The next day President Mobutu termed the riots in Kinshasa the worst since those that accompanied the coming of independence, in July 1960. Opposition parties, which protested against impending foreign intervention, proposed Etienne Tsisekedi as Premier of a "public salvation government" to cope with the riots. Mobutu acquiesced on 30 September, under pressure from the U.S., France, and Belgium. And on 3 October the newly appointed premier, in open opposition to the president's policy, asked France and Belgium not to withdraw their troops prematurely.

More clashes occurred in Kinshasa in mid-October. Tension between the president and premier escalated over the allocation of ministerial portfolios between Mobutu supporters and the opposition. Mobutu dismissed Tsisekedi on 20 October. The result of this act and the deteriorating economic situation was an eruption of violence in major cities of Zaire from 21 to 27 October.

The evacuation of European residents from Zaire by Belgium and France was nearly complete by 25 October. And Belgium and France announced that they would withdraw shortly. France also announced the suspension of economic aid to Zaire. On the 27th Mobutu announced that he would remain in office, despite growing domestic and international pressure to resign. Four days later a group of opposition parties, the "Sacred Coalition," intensified its struggle with the president by forming a parallel regime in Kinshasa.

French troops departed on the 31st. Belgian troops followed on 4 November. This marked the end of Belgium's and Zaire's foreign policy crises and the international crisis as a whole, even though internal turmoil, violence, and political opposition to Mobutu continued for years.

The U.S. provided transport planes for the Belgian-French evacuation project. The USSR and the UN were not involved in this crisis.

(See *Master Table*, pp. 736–37.)

Sources
ACR 1991; *AR* 1991; *ARB* 1991; *ARec* 1991; *Facts on File* 1991; *FBIS–DR/CA* 1991; *Keesing's* 1991; *New York Times* 1991.

(402) Egypt/Sudan Border II

Egypt and Sudan experienced another crisis over a long-standing border dispute from late January to late June 1992.

Background
The Hala'ib region of southeast Egypt along the Red Sea has long been a source of contention. The 1899 agreement between Egypt and the U.K., which established an Anglo-Egyptian condominium over Sudan, determined that the border between Egypt and Sudan was to run along a straight west-east line. However, for convenience, Sudan was given authority to administer the Hala'ib area, almost 20,000 square kilometers, north of the line, and Egypt, an area south of the line. Over time Sudan began to claim political and economic rights in the Hala'ib area, for example, the right of its residents to vote in Sudanese elections, and the right to exploit its economic resources. However, Sudan never openly challenged Egypt's sovereignty over this area. Until Sudan's independence in 1956 the issue never became a focus of conflict; and thereafter Egypt allowed Sudan to administer the area.

Overt conflict was rare. However, on one occasion, in February 1958, Egypt and Sudan were embroiled in a crisis over Cairo's attempt to take control of the area by force. Although it remained non-violent, troops were dispatched, and Sudan complained to the UN Secretary-General about Egypt's "aggression" (see Case #163—**Egypt/Sudan Border I** above).

Crisis
A crisis for Egypt was triggered toward the end of January 1992 when Sudan granted a Canadian oil company a concession to explore for oil in Hala'ib. Egypt contested this right early in February by advising oil companies around the world that Sudan did not have the authority to sign exploration agreements on any land north of their political boundary as laid down in the 1899 condominium agreement. However, it expressed the hope to settle the dispute quietly and did not

issue an official protest. Sudan, by contrast, argued that "administrative" rights included the right to utilize the area's potential economic resources.

This low-intensity crisis escalated on 4 April when armed clashes occurred between Egyptian and Sudanese forces in the disputed area. President Mubarak sent an apology to Sudan's ruler, General Hassan a-Bashir. Two joint commissions were created—to examine the clash and to seek a resolution of the dispute. They met from 22 April to 5 May, without result. Other attempts were made to settle the disagreement through quiet diplomacy; but they too were unsuccessful.

The crisis ended as a result of the external actor's behavior: the Canadian company stopped its exploration in the Hala'ib region at the end of June, thereby removing the object of contention.

There was no involvement by the U.S., Russia, the UN, the *OAU,* or the Arab League.

(Tension declined but did not entirely dissipate after the termination of oil exploration. In August 1992 Egypt placed all mosques in the Hala'ib region under its control. Roads were constructed to give Egypt readier access to the region. And in mid-December Egyptian troop reinforcements were reportedly dispatched to the area. In December, too, Sudan sent a memo to the UN Security Council explaining its position on the dispute; but it did not seek UN intervention. And in mid-December Egypt's foreign minister declared that any dispute with Sudan could be resolved peacefully.)

(In June 1995 the Hala'ib dispute was reactivated—in the aftermath of an attempted assassination of Mubarak upon his arrival in Addis Ababa for an *OAU* summit. Egypt's president explicitly charged Sudan with collusion in this act and called upon the Sudanese people to overthrow its fundamentalist Islamic government. Several soldiers on both sides were reportedly wounded and, according to Sudan, two policemen killed, in a border clash in the Hala'ib region on 27 June 1995. But this episode, too, faded without serious consequences. The dispute remains unresolved.)

(See *Master Table,* pp. 736–37.)

Sources
FBIS–DR/NESA 1992; *AR* 1992; *ARB* 1992; *ARec* 1992; *MECS* 1992–93; *New York Times* 1992, 1995.

(410) Cameroon/Nigeria III

Nigeria and Cameroon were embroiled in another crisis over territory from the end of December 1993 until late November 1994.

Background
The borderland area of Bakassi consists largely of Nigerian nationals, mostly fishers. However, Nigeria had no legal claim to the territory. An Anglo-German

treaty in 1913 had assigned the territory to the then-British colony of Southern Cameroon. And in the postindependence period Nigeria acknowledged Cameroon's sovereignty in the 1975 Maroua treaty.

Crisis

A crisis for Nigeria was triggered at the end of December 1993 when Cameroonian troops raided the fishing village of Abana, killing six persons. Nigeria responded on 3 January by occupying Diamond and Djsbana, Cameroonian islands in an oil-producing sector of the Gulf of Guinea. That act catalyzed a crisis for Cameroon, which, in turn, responded by dispatching troops in an attempt to reassert its claim to the islands.

From that initial tit-for-tat exchange the crisis oscillated between expressions of conciliation and minor clashes. Thus, on 6 January 1994, Cameroon's President, Paul Biya, and Nigeria's Foreign Minister, Baba Gana Kingibe, met in a friendly atmosphere and decided to establish joint patrols in the disputed area. On 17 February there were renewed clashes. Ten days later a French military mission arrived in Cameroon under the terms of their 1974 defense agreement. Nigeria reacted angrily, its foreign minister attacking France on 2 March for internationalizing the dispute.

Crisis diplomacy intensified in March. Cameroon submitted the dispute to the International Court of Justice and requested both the UN Security Council and the *OAU* to mediate. It also accepted a mediation offer by Togo. The foreign ministers of Nigeria and Cameroon met on 9–10 March. Peaceful crisis management suffered a setback when Cameroon's president made the withdrawal of Nigerian troops from the islands a condition for a summit meeting.

The *OAU* became active on 24 March when it passed a resolution calling on both parties to do the following: withdraw their troops from the disputed area; exercise restraint; take measures to restore confidence; and continue their negotiations. Neither party was pleased with this package. Again in mid-April the *OAU* tried to mediate by dispatching a delegation to the two capitals. Their task was aggravated by the apparent use of the Bakassi dispute by both heads of state to enhance domestic support for their authoritarian rule.

There was progress at a summit meeting between Biya and the head of Nigeria's military regime, General Abacha, in Tunis on 13 June: they agreed to set up a joint committee with a Togolese chairman to seek a peaceful solution. A commitment to finding a lasting solution to their territorial dispute was reaffirmed at a joint meeting on 4–6 July. However, a summit meeting scheduled for 18 July was postponed. And on 18 September 10 Cameroonian soldiers were killed in a surprise attack by Nigerian troops.

Thereafter the crisis de-escalated—and faded in late November. This is evident in expressions of "delight" at the maintenance of peace despite the continuing territorial dispute, at a meeting between Nigeria's president and foreign minister with Cameroon's ambassador on 6 December 1994. The dispute remains unresolved; but the 1993–94 crisis faded into a mutual acceptance of the status quo.

Neither the U.S. nor Russia was involved in the crisis. The UN did not respond to attempts by Cameroon to draw it into the dispute. Only the *OAU*, as noted, was active in crisis management.

(Despite the long-standing de facto cease-fire in the dispute over Bakassi, violence flared up again in late April 1996.)

(See *Master Table,* pp. 736–37.)

Sources
AR 1994; *ARB* 1994; *ARec* 1994; *Keesing's* 1994; *WA* 1994.

Americas: Non-Protracted Conflict (PC) Crises

There were 48 international crises in the Americas from 1918 until the end of 1994. Of these, 18 occurred in the context of a protracted conflict (PC), within this region (Costa Rica/Nicaragua, Honduras/Nicaragua, or Ecuador/Peru) or in a multiregional PC (East/West). The other 30 crises erupted within the Americas but were not part of a protracted conflict.

Only one international crisis that took place in the Americas was of global significance: Case #196—**Cuban Missiles,** in 1962; but this was a multiregional crisis, with direct participation by the two superpowers. Another, Case #336— **Falklands/Malvinas,** in 1982, achieved high visibility by virtue of its multiregional character. Several others attracted attention; but this, too, was due to their salience to the **East/West PC:** Cases #144—**Guatemala,** in 1953–54; #181—**Bay of Pigs,** in 1961; #239—**Cienfuegos Submarine Base,** in 1970; #294—**Nicaraguan Civil War,** in 1978–79; and #354—**Nicaragua MIG-21s,** in 1984. All the other crises in the Americas were of bilateral and, occasionally, of regional importance (see *Master Table*).

The following pages present summaries of all non-PC crises that occurred in the Americas, organized chronologically. Moreover, the 18 PC cases are listed along with a reference to where the relevant summary can be found.

(2) Costa Rican Coup, 1918–19 (see Costa Rica/Nicaragua PC)

(19) Costa Rica/Panama Border

A crisis between Panama and Costa Rica over disputed territory lasted from 21 February to 24 August 1921.

Background
Costa Rica and Panama (and earlier, Colombia, which held sovereignty over Panama until 1903) had long claimed title to the territory of Pueblo Nuevo de Coto along their common border. Numerous efforts to settle the boundary dispute, in 1825, 1856, 1865, 1876, 1880, and 1886, had failed. The most recent attempt, the White (arbitration) Award of 1914, ruled in favor of Costa Rica. Panama continued to occupy the territory claiming that U.S. Supreme Court Justice White had exceeded his authority. And for six years Costa Rica did not act to implement the White Award.

Crisis
The status quo changed drastically on 21 February 1921: Costa Rican forces unexpectedly occupied a village in the de Coto region triggering a crisis for Panama. On the 27th Panamanian police struck back creating a crisis for Costa Rica. Minor clashes ensued for several days. On the 28th U.S. Secretary of State Hughes warned both states not to use violence to solve the dispute. Secretary-General Drummond of the League of Nations initiated a fact-finding inquiry into the dispute on the 28th. On 2 March Panama appealed to the League to punish Costa Rica for sending troops into the disputed area. On the 4th the League Council called on the foreign ministers of the disputants to adhere to their obligations as League members. On the 7th–8th Costa Rica, then Panama, agreed to suspend hostilities. The U.S. offered to arbitrate on 16 March and warned Panama that the U.S. would enforce the White Award, if necessary. To indicate its resolve a battalion of U.S. marines was dispatched to the Canal Zone. Panama continued to reject the White Award—which Costa Rica had accepted from its inception—until 24 August 1921 when, under the threat of U.S. military intervention, it relented and set in motion withdrawal from the disputed territory thereby terminating the crisis.

The Pan American Union was not involved in this Central American crisis.

(Costa Rica regained formal possession of the de Coto region on 9 September. An international commission was later established to resolve residual land disputes but Panama refused to participate.)

(See *Master Table,* pp. 668–69.)

Sources
Foreign Relations of the United States (FRUS) 1921, vol. 2 [pub. 1936]; Dexter 1967; Howland 1929; Ireland [1938] 1971; McCain 1937; Munro 1974; Weil 1972.

(33) Nicaragua Civil War I

Nicaragua experienced a crisis with Mexico from 17 August 1926 until 15 May 1927.

Background
Several months after a (periodic) withdrawal of U.S. marines, in August 1925, Nicaragua was again embroiled in civil war: it erupted because opponents of President Emiliano Chamorro interpreted U.S. nonrecognition of his regime as carte blanche to overthrow him. Moreover, Mexico's President Plutarco Calles seized upon the opportunity of internal disarray to reassert Mexico's influence in Central America by aiding the Liberal opposition to Chamorro.

Crisis
The trigger to Nicaragua's foreign policy crisis was the Chamorro government's awareness on 17 August 1926 that a Mexican auxiliary warship had set sail with

men and arms to aid Nicaraguan rebels. Nicaragua responded on the 24th by notifying the Secretary-General of the League of Nations. Mexico denied the allegation on 30 August; but it refused to comply with the request of U.S. President Coolidge on 15 September to impose an embargo on arms and ammunition destined for Nicaragua.

Chamorro resigned on 30 October because of continued U.S. nonrecognition. His successor, Adolfo Diaz, elected by the Nicaragua Congress on 11 November as an interim leader pending a national election, was recognized by Washington on 17 November. However, Juan Sacasa, the Liberal Vice President under Chamorro who had fled Nicaragua, returned on 2 December, was proclaimed President by Liberal supporters, and was recognized by Mexico on 7 December.

U.S. marines returned to Nicaragua in December 1926, ostensibly to protect U.S. and other foreign citizens and property. They also assisted the Diaz regime in the civil war. Nonetheless, the Liberal forces behind Sacasa continued to advance, leading Washington on 5 January 1927 to lift the embargo on arms sales to Nicaragua. This was followed by an arms agreement with Diaz on 25 February 1927.

U.S. policy throughout Nicaragua's civil war was to undermine Mexico's competing influence in Central America. Its decisive intervention in the crisis was the dispatch of Henry L. Stimson to Nicaragua on 31 March with instructions to mediate and end the civil war. The presidential envoy was able to get both factions to agree on all points except the continuation of Diaz as President. On 4 May Stimson achieved an agreement: Diaz was to complete his term of office; the Liberal rebels, led by José Maria Moncada, were to disarm; and the U.S. would supervise the 1928 presidential election. The next day an amnesty was declared. And on 15 May Stimson wrote to Secretary of State Kellogg that the civil war was over. For Nicaragua the assurance of a continuing U.S. military presence eliminated fears of further Mexican exploitation of civil strife thereby ending its foreign policy crisis.

There were many involved actors in Nicaragua's civil war of 1926–27. Offers to mediate by Costa Rica, Guatemala, and El Salvador were declined. The U.S., as noted, was highly involved, militarily and politically, serving as the crucial agent of crisis management. The U.K. sent a warship in February 1927 to evacuate British citizens. And the League of Nations' Secretary-General dispatched a fact-finding mission in response to Nicaragua's Note of 24 August 1926 regarding Mexico's intervention; but there was no further League activity. The Pan American Union was not involved in this crisis.

(See *Master Table,* pp. 670–71.)

Sources
FRUS 1925, vol. 2 [pub. 1940], *1926,* vol. 2 [1941], *1927,* vol. 1 [1942]; Beals 1926; Cox 1927; Denny 1929; Howland 1929; Langer 1972; Munro 1974; Stimson 1927; Toynbee 1929b; Wood 1961.

(37) Chaco I

A crisis between Bolivia and Paraguay occurred between 5 December 1928 and 12 September 1929.

Background
The Chaco Boreal consists of 116,000 square miles of territory that had been claimed by Bolivia and Paraguay for 150 years. The area is mostly swamp, with very few inhabitants, and its agricultural or industrial value was as yet unexplored. It represented the only Bolivian access to the sea. Army patrols and forts were maintained by each state on its side of the Chaco. Notwithstanding agreements between Bolivia and Paraguay in 1913 and 1915, the dispute remained unresolved.

Crisis
A crisis for Bolivia was triggered on 5 December 1928 when Paraguayan troops captured and destroyed a Bolivian fort. The Bolivian government immediately severed diplomatic relations with Paraguay, mobilized its reserve forces, and, on 14 December, retaliated with a military attack to reoccupy the captured fort and occupy a second one. This triggered a crisis for Paraguay, which regarded Bolivia's military advance as a serious threat to its territory. On 17 December Paraguay proclaimed general mobilization and sent reinforcements north to halt what was believed to be an impending assault.

The adversaries seemed to be on the brink of a war that neither desired. Paraguay appealed to the League of Nations. But the prime mover in mediation was the Pan American Conference on Conciliation and Arbitration, a body that had been organized by the Pan American Union, a predecessor of the Organization of American States *(OAS)*. The conference was composed of representatives from the U.S., Colombia, Cuba, Mexico, and Uruguay, as well as the two crisis actors. The activities of the Conference led to a Conciliation Protocol signed in Washington on 3 January 1929. It called for a restoration of the status quo ante and the resumption of diplomatic relations between the two states, and set up a commission of inquiry. A proposed arbitration convention on 31 August 1929 was rejected by both parties. The crisis ended on 12 September 1929 when Bolivia and Paraguay ratified a resolution presented by the commission.

(The status quo as of December 1928 was restored on 4 April 1930, but no effort had been made to resolve the basic territorial dispute. The issue erupted again in 1932 [see Case #41—**Chaco II** below].)

The League of Nations Council warned the two parties against further military activity and urged them to resolve the dispute peacefully. However, its mediation effort yielded to the Pan American Conference when the Pan American Union took up the matter. The United States was the most important contributor to crisis abatement, along with other members of the Pan American Union.

(See *Master Table,* pp. 672–73.)

Sources
See sources for Case #41.

(41) Chaco II

A second crisis over Chaco between Paraguay and Bolivia began on 18 June 1932 and lasted until 12 June 1935.

Pre-crisis
The issue of ownership of the vast undeveloped Chaco region remained in dispute since the crisis of 1928–29 (see Case #37 above). During the intervening years there were some incidents, but no serious fighting took place. On 11 November 1931 negotiations between the adversaries began on the question of a settlement of their territorial differences. A draft nonaggression pact was under consideration when the second crisis broke out.

Crisis
A Bolivian attack and occupation of a fort were reported on 18 June 1932 to the headquarters of the chief of the Paraguayan General Staff. On 15 July Paraguay responded with an attack on a Bolivian fort built after the 18 June incident. Three days later the loss of the fort was reported, triggering a crisis for Bolivia, which perceived a threat to its political regime. Bolivia responded during the night of 18 July by holding a special emergency cabinet meeting where the president ordered a major reprisal and the immediate capture of the areas of Corralo and Toledo. This was done on 27 and 28 July, and Boqueron was occupied by Bolivian forces on 31 July 1932.

A Paraguayan counterattack during August 1932 succeeded in recapturing these forts and also pushed the Bolivian army back several miles from the positions held prior to the outbreak of the crisis. A Bolivian counterattack occurred during November and December 1932.

On 10 May 1933 Paraguay declared war. A truce was proposed in December 1933, but on 6 January 1934 fighting resumed. On 17 November 1934 the Paraguayans captured a principal Bolivian supply base.

Paraguay had appealed to the League of Nations Council in 1932, under Articles 10 and 11 of the Covenant. With U.S. approval, the Council sent a commission of inquiry. When a truce broke down, Bolivia appealed to the League under Article 15. The dispute was transferred to the 15th Session of the League Assembly in November 1934, and an inquiry committee was formed to prepare a report. Its recommendations were the cessation of hostilities, the withdrawal and demobilization of armies, temporary policing of the evacuated zone, and neutral arbitration. They were accepted by Bolivia and rejected by Paraguay.

On 16 January 1935 the advisory committee of the Assembly unanimously adopted a recommendation to League members to lift their arms embargo on Bolivia but to maintain it against Paraguay. Paraguay announced its intention to leave the League on 23 February, and the next day the recommendations went into effect.

Paraguay occupied most of the Chaco in a series of military campaigns. But military advantage began to swing in Bolivia's favor. The final phase of the negotiations for an armistice in the Chaco began on 27 May 1935 when Argentina, Brazil, Chile, Peru, Uruguay, and the United States began negotiations with the now exhausted states of Bolivia and Paraguay over a new protocol based upon the League of Nations' recommendations, with some modifications to pacify Paraguay. An agreement was reached on 9 June and signed on 12 June 1935, ending the crisis for both actors. The agreement provided for the cessation of hostilities and the holding of a peace conference. About 90,000 soldiers died in South America's deadliest war of the twentieth century.

President Roosevelt issued a proclamation on 28 May 1934 prohibiting the sale of arms to Bolivia and Paraguay. This was eventually agreed to by France, Germany, Italy, the Soviet Union, and the U.K.

Mediation was attempted by the neutral Commission of Washington (Colombia, Cuba, Mexico, Uruguay, and the U.S.); by the *ABCP* group (Argentina, Brazil, Chile, Peru); and by the united efforts of all the neutral American states of the Pan American Conference at Montevideo in December 1933.

(Peace was not formally restored until 10 July 1938 and was approved by a plebiscite on 10 August. The peace treaty provided for arbitration of the boundaries. An arbitral award, by six American presidents, on 10 October 1938, gave most of the Chaco territory to Paraguay, along with an outlet to the sea via the Paraguay River for Bolivia.)

(See *Master Table*, pp. 672–73.)

Sources
Eagleton 1957; Estigarribia 1969; Fagg 1967; Hull 1948, vol. I; Ireland [1938] 1971; Kain 1938; Klein 1969; Lindsay 1935; Osborne 1965; Schurz 1929; Thomas 1956; Walters 1952; Warren 1949; Wood 1966; Zimmern 1936; Zook 1960.

(42) Leticia
A crisis for Colombia and Peru over Leticia began on 8 September 1932 and terminated on 25 May 1933.

Background and Pre-crisis
The frontier between Colombia and Peru was in dispute until 1922 when the Salomon-Lozano Treaty was signed by the two states. The agreement provided that Peru recognize Colombian sovereignty over the Leticia Trapeze—a narrow strip of territory running from the Putumayo River to the Amazon.

During the night of 31 August–1 September 1932 a group of armed Peruvians attacked and occupied the river port of Leticia, the capital of the Colombian district of the Amazon. Colombian troops were dispatched to repel the "aggressors." Peru denied responsibility for the attack, citing communists and enemies of the Peruvian government as having carried out the incursion. However, rumors of Peruvian President Sanchez Cerro's support for the seizure, as well as for a revision of the Salomon-Lozano Treaty, began to spread.

Crisis

On 8 September 1932 the U.S. ambassador to Colombia reported to the State Department that Colombian President Olaya perceived the possibility of war with Peru over the latter's support for the occupiers of Leticia. With a view to restoring its control over Leticia, Colombia responded in early September 1932 by sending a small naval expedition to retake the territory. The expedition had to pass through the Panama Canal and then 2,000 miles up the Amazon River. On 22 September the government of Colombia issued a special loan for national defense. During November Ecuador sent a Note to the League of Nations about the conflict between Colombia and Peru.

On 27 December 1932 the Colombian expedition arrived at the mouth of the Amazon River, triggering a crisis for Peru. At that time Peruvian reinforcements were reported to be assembling near Leticia. Colombia formally asked for League of Nations intervention on 2 January 1933 and again requested a special session on the 21st.

On 6 February General Victor Ramos, commander of the Peruvian forces, cabled a warning to the Colombian consul in Lima stating that the entry of the Colombian flotilla into the Amazon was a hostile act and he had therefore ordered military measures to prevent its arrival at Leticia. Following a request by the commander of the Colombian expedition to allow him to occupy Tarpaca peacefully, Peru bombed the Colombian gunboats on 14 February 1933. Tarpaca was captured the following day by Colombian forces.

During March and April Colombian troops captured several Peruvian posts. The assassination of President Cerro in Peru on 30 April decreased the possibility of further military clashes. On 2 May direct negotiations began between the new Peruvian President, Benavides, and his close personal friend, Alfonso Lopez, a leader of the Liberal Party in Colombia, who was to become its President the following year. On the 10th the League Council's advisory committee submitted a new proposal, and on 25 May 1933 an agreement was signed by representatives of Colombia and Peru, transferring control of Leticia from the Peruvian forces to a League of Nations commission of three (Brazil, Spain, and the U.S.) for one year, terminating the crisis for both actors.

The League of Nations played a crucial role in crisis abatement. The Council discussed the Leticia issue on 24 and 26 January 1933 and sent Notes to both parties. On 13 March it unanimously adopted a report calling on Peru to withdraw all its forces from Leticia and all support from Peruvian occupiers of Colombia's territory—as a prelude to negotiations on Peru's grievances. (Both parties rejected arbitration.) The Council also appointed an advisory committee to monitor the crisis. Its new proposals, submitted on 10 May, proved to be the basis of negotiations between the adversaries, leading to the agreement of 25

May. (Moreover, the League Commission administered the disputed territory for a year. Leticia was transferred to Colombia in June 1934, following a treaty between the two parties on 24 May 1934.)

The U.S. responded to a Colombian appeal by sending a Note to Peru requesting that it allow the restoration of Colombian control over Leticia. Later, in March 1933, the U.S. participated in the deliberations of the League of Nations Advisory Committee. The U.K. also applied pressure, mostly on Peru, to cooperate with the League. Brazil tried to mediate, unsuccessfully.

(See *Master Table*, pp. 672–73.)

Sources
Eagleton 1957; Fluharty 1957; Hull 1948, vol. I; Walters 1952; Wood 1966.

(50) Ecuador/Peru Border I, 1935 (see Ecuador/Peru PC)

(57) Postage Stamp Crisis, 1937 (see Honduras/Nicaragua PC)

(58) Dominican Republic/Haiti I

A crisis for Haiti began on 5 October 1937 and terminated on 31 January 1938.

Background
The Haitian economy had been seriously affected by the Great Depression in the United States, and large numbers of Haitian cane cutters migrated to the neighboring Dominican Republic and to Cuba. During 1936 and 1937 a plot by Trujillo, the ruler of the Dominican Republic, to undermine the government of Haiti was uncovered. Both countries had signed the General Convention of Inter-American Conciliation in 1929. When most of the sugar mills in Trujillo's Dominican Republic and Batista's Cuba closed down, the Haitians sought work in other fields. On 2 October 1937 Trujillo declared that Haitian trespassers would no longer be tolerated, while indicating that the slaughter of Haitians that began the day before at Banica, with 300 victims, would continue. That evening Trujillo ordered a new massacre of Haitian nationals in the vicinity of the Dominican Republic/Haiti border, which continued until 4 October.

Crisis
Haiti's President Vincent received word of the massacres on 5 October 1937. On the 10th a Note was delivered to the Dominican Republic expressing his doubts that the government of the Dominican Republic could have associated itself with these events and requesting investigation and compensation. An official joint declaration by the two countries in Washington on 23 October stated that relations between them had not been impaired. Nevertheless, as domestic unrest

grew and both began concentrating troops at the border, Haitian decision makers perceived a threat of a Dominican Republic invasion. On 12 November Haiti's major response was to request U.S., Mexican, and Cuban mediation. The Dominican Republic at first refused to cooperate with the commission set up by the three mediating countries, claiming that the magnitude of the dispute did not warrant mediation. On 18 December, four days after Vincent invoked the 1928 Pact and the use of a mediating commission, Trujillo consented to mediation. Negotiations were carried on directly, as well as through meetings in Washington, diplomatic channels, and the good offices of the Pope. Trujillo agreed to the draft settlement with minor revisions; and it was accepted and signed by both countries on 31 January 1938, ending their crisis.

The Haiti government's request to invoke the Inter-American Convention for Conciliation was within the framework of the Pan American Union. The mediation undertaken by the regional organization's commission consisting of representatives from Argentina, Guatemala, and Peru was very effective in abating the crisis and contributed to more rapid termination. The League of Nations was not involved in this crisis.

(See *Master Table,* pp. 676–77.)

Sources
Crassweller 1966; Diedrich and Burt 1969; Hicks 1968; Mecham 1961.

(86) Ecuador/Peru Border II, 1941–42 (see Ecuador/Peru PC)

(117) Cuba/Dominican Republic

This Caribbean crisis had only one actor, the Dominican Republic, and lasted from 26 July until 28 September 1947.

Background
President Trujillo, the dictator of the Dominican Republic since 1930, had seized control of all the instruments of power (army, courts, press, economy) and had crushed all opposition. The result was a large number of political exiles from the Dominican Republic seeking shelter in neighboring states such as Cuba and Guatemala. They in turn were joined by exiles, mercenaries, adventurers, and criminals from other states in the region. This group was known as the "Caribbean League."

These states, with Cuba the most supportive, supplied weapons, training, bases, and money, as well as ideological support, to the League's activities. The crisis, therefore, was the result of a military threat to the Trujillo regime by the Caribbean League, with Cuba taking the lead. The exiles began gathering at Cayo Conlites (Cuba) as early as January 1946, with the Cuban government providing training and support.

Crisis

By 26 July 1947 the Trujillo regime perceived the exiles to be a serious military threat. Dominican precautions in the form of blackouts were instituted on that day. The Dominican Republic's major response occurred on 18 August when Trujillo voiced the possibility of war breaking out and suggested setting up an international commission to investigate the matter. The Dominican armed forces were put on alert. On 28 September the Cubans disbanded the revolutionary forces at the same time as the U.S. began to be negatively involved—prohibiting the purchase of U.S. weapons. The immediate threat subsided, but the conflict was to continue for several more years, with later involvement of the *OAS;* and a crisis erupted in 1949 (see Case #130—**Luperon** below).

The UN and the USSR were not involved in this crisis.

(See *Master Table,* pp. 686–87.)

Sources

Atkins and Wilson 1972; Crassweller 1966; Espaillat 1963; Furniss 1950; de Galindez 1973; Mecham 1961; Nanita 1951; Pattee 1967; Pochando 1974; Szulc 1971b; Wiarda 1969, 1970; Wilgus 1963.

(126) Costa Rica/Nicaragua I, 1948–49 (see Costa Rica/Nicaragua PC)

(130) Luperon

This minicrisis involved one actor only, the Dominican Republic. It started on 19 June 1949 and terminated two days later.

Background

Tension in the Caribbean region was high, and there had been several attempts by the Caribbean League to overthrow Trujillo, the Dominican Republic's authoritarian ruler (see Case #117—**Cuba/Dominican Republic** above).

Crisis

On 19 June 1949 a planeload of 15 mercenaries from Guatemala landed at Luperon in the Dominican Republic. The plane was destroyed by the Dominican navy, and the expedition was crushed immediately. Although this did not represent a large-scale military threat, Trujillo took the incident seriously and on 21 June sent a protest note to Cuba, along with threatening words to Guatemala— the Dominican Republic's major response to a perceived threat to its political regime. That day the Cuban government announced its determination to stop the enlistment of men to fight as mercenaries, and the crisis terminated, although tension in the area remained high until December 1951, the culmination of all *OAS* activity to settle the disputes in the region.

The U.S., the USSR, and the UN were not involved in this crisis. (See *Master Table*, pp. 690–91.)

Sources
See sources for Case #117.

(144) Guatemala, 1953–54 (see Multiregional PCs: East/West)

(147) Costa Rica/Nicaragua II, 1955 (see Costa Rica/Nicaragua PC)

(156) Mocorón Incident, 1957 (see Honduras/Nicaragua PC)

(169) Mexico/Guatemala Fishing Rights

A crisis between these two states lasted from 29 December 1958 to 1 February 1959.

Background
Mexico observed a nine-mile territorial water limit off its shores while Guatemala regarded its own territorial waters as extending to 12 miles. Mexican fishers had been fishing for shrimp in what Guatemala considered its territorial waters.

Crisis
On 29 December 1958 the president of Guatemala articulated his perception of a crisis stemming from an economic threat from Mexico and warned it of impending attack if its fishers did not leave Guatemalan waters. Guatemala's response, and the trigger for Mexico, occurred on 31 December when Guatemalan planes strafed three Mexican shrimp boats off the Pacific coast, killing three fishers and wounding 14 others. Mexico's response was a severe protest to Guatemala on 3 January 1959. The crisis ended for Mexico on 12 January 1959, the day 200 Mexican shrimp boats began fishing in the same general area of the incident, after receiving an official promise from the Guatemalan government that its planes would not attack them. The termination date for Guatemala was 1 February 1959, the day the president of Mexico proposed a peaceful settlement with Guatemala and requested information about its terms for a settlement. Guatemala responded favorably.

The UN, the U.S., and the USSR were not involved in this crisis. (See *Master Table*, pp. 696–97.)

Sources
See general list, especially *Keesing's* 1959 and *New York Times* 1959.

(170) Central America/Cuba I

This crisis involved four actors: Panama, Nicaragua, the Dominican Republic, and Haiti. It began on 25 April 1959 and ended toward the close of 1959.

Pre-crisis
The Batista dictatorship in Cuba collapsed on 1 January 1959 when Fidel Castro established control. The new Cuban government welcomed exiles from Latin American countries and aided them in organizing revolutionary activities. All four actor-cases derived from invasions in which exiles and the Cuban armed forces tried to establish a revolutionary government in each of the four states previously noted. In all, a grave economic situation existed, and domestic unrest was prevalent.

Crisis
The first to experience a crisis was Panama, where a boat carrying 80–90 foreign invaders landed on 25 April 1959. Panama responded the following day by requesting assistance from the *OAS,* which agreed to supply arms, as well as to send an inquiry committee. Castro, recognizing *OAS* disapproval, denounced the invaders on 28 April and sent two government officials to persuade the invaders to surrender. They did so on 1 May. The following day an *OAS* international naval patrol off the Panama coast was authorized. The crisis terminated for Panama on 4 May 1959 when the naval and aerial patrols were called off and the *OAS* investigating committee returned to Washington.

On 1 June a small force of Nicaraguan exiles from Costa Rica landed in two areas of Nicaragua. An emergency session of the *OAS* was held on 2 June, and a fact-finding mission was sent two days later to Costa Rica and Nicaragua. President Somoza accepted the Costa Rican expression of neutrality and did not view the latter as the source of threat to Nicaragua. On 11 June the rebellion was crushed as a result of a swift military response by Nicaragua. On 13 June Somoza accused Castro of personally preparing the master plan for the overthrow of the Nicaraguan government. The crisis ended on 14 June 1959 when a victory parade was held in Nicaragua.

The third in this series of low-intensity crises was an invasion of the Dominican Republic on 14 June 1959, which met with military resistance. The economic situation in the Dominican Republic was particularly grave, with mounting terror and government repression. On 24 June Trujillo declared that the invasion, assisted by the Cuban navy, had been repelled. A complaint was lodged against Cuba at the *OAS* on 2 July, but because of an unfavorable *OAS* attitude toward the Trujillo regime, the Dominican Republic did not request an emergency session. Tension remained high for several more months and dissolved slowly at the end of 1959.

Haiti was invaded on 13 August 1959, during a period of extreme instability and terror. The response occurred on the 16th with a Note to the *OAS* foreign ministers charging Cuba with responsibility. And on 5 September the Haiti government announced the surrender of the invaders.

The *OAS* was actively involved throughout this multiple crisis, assisting each state in its confrontation with the Cuban threat. Fact-finding missions were sent. Superpower involvement was relatively limited. The U.S. sought to maintain stability in the area by organizing a naval mission to patrol the Caribbean waters and authorizing it to shoot in order to bar any communist-led invasion attempt. The USSR was not involved in the crisis; but it made known its support of Castro's Cuban government.

(See *Master Table*, pp. 696–97.)

Sources
Atkins and Wilson 1972; Bayo 1967; Bonsal 1971; Castillero-Reyes 1962; Crassweller 1966; Diederich and Burt 1969; Dreier 1962; Duff and McGamant 1976; Galich 1968; Halperin 1972; Mecham 1961; Rosenthal 1962; Rotberg with Clage 1971; Szulc 1963; Veliz 1968; Ydigoras 1963.

(175) Failed Assassination—Venezuela

A crisis between Venezuela and the Dominican Republic occurred from 24 June to mid-September 1960.

Background
Diplomatic relations with the Dominican Republic were broken by Venezuela in June 1959. In February 1960 a charge of flagrant violations of human rights was made to the *OAS* against the Dominican Republic by the Venezuelan government.

Crisis
An assassination attempt on Venezuelan President Betancourt triggered the crisis on 24 June 1960. Dominican Republic complicity was suspected when it was learned that the plot was organized by Venezuelan exiles living there. In addition, the Dominican Republic radio reported the assassination attempt 15 minutes after it occurred. On the 25th Venezuela accused Trujillo of initiating it. This triggered a crisis for the Dominican Republic, which feared a Venezuelan attack on its territory. The Dominican Republic promptly denied all charges. Its major response, on 27 June, was to place the Dominican armed forces on alert and to call for general mobilization. The Congress met in emergency session the following day.

Venezuelan countermeasures consisted of placing its army on alert and issuing another formal accusation against the Dominican Republic. On 30 June a state of emergency was declared in Venezuela after Trujillo accused Venezuela of preparing for war in order to overthrow his regime. Venezuela's major response, on 1 July, was to call for an emergency session of the *OAS* and to press for a resolution of sanctions against the Dominican Republic. President Betancourt stated that, if no measures were taken against Trujillo by the *OAS,* Venezuela would act unilaterally. An investigation committee was appointed by the *OAS* on 8 July. On 20 August a resolution was passed condemning the Dominican Republic's "acts of aggression and intervention." It called upon the members of the *OAS* to break off diplomatic relations with the Dominican Republic and to impose an arms embargo, along with partial economic sanctions. This terminated the crisis for Venezuela.

During the *OAS* debate the United States attempted unsuccessfully to have a more conciliatory resolution passed, fearing a replacement of the Trujillo government by a communist regime. The U.S. then complied with the resolution by withholding the Dominican Republic's sugar quota and breaking off diplomatic relations.

On 5 September, at an urgent meeting of the Security Council, the USSR called for a resolution to act upon *OAS* sanctions, but it was not passed. The crisis for the Dominican Republic faded in mid-September.

(See *Master Table,* pp. 698–99.)

Sources
Atkins and Wilson 1972; Crassweller 1966; Wainhouse 1966.

(178) Central America/Cuba II

This crisis occurred from 9 November to 7 December 1960, with two actors, Nicaragua and Guatemala.

Background
In 1959 Panama, Nicaragua, the Dominican Republic, and Haiti were confronted with crises involving Cuban-supported rebels (see Case #170—**Central America/Cuba I** above). Each state succeeded, with *OAS* support, in repelling the invaders. In Guatemala, domestic political and economic instability was present, with high unemployment, demonstrations, strikes, and rapid inflation.

Crisis
Nicaragua was invaded once more on 9 November 1960 when exiles crossed into its territory from Costa Rica and captured two small towns. Martial law was imposed, and troops were rushed to the area. And on 13 November dissident units of the Guatemalan army seized a port 70 miles northeast of Guatemala City. President Ydigoras responded on 14 November by stating that the government had proof of Cuban involvement and appealed to the U.S. to dispatch naval and air patrols. The revolt in Guatemala collapsed on the 16th.

The Nicaraguan response was an appeal to the United States on 17 November. That day President Eisenhower announced that surface and air units of the United States navy would act to prevent invasions by communist-directed elements. The crisis for both Nicaragua and Guatemala ended when the U.S. president, having received assurances from both governments that coastal defense was no longer required, ordered the withdrawal of the Caribbean patrol on 7 December 1960.

During the crisis Guatemala and Nicaragua submitted a joint complaint about Cuban interference to the *OAS*. This was denied by Cuba, which protested the U.S. naval presence in the area, describing it as a violation of the principle of nonintervention and an act of aggression.

Soviet and Chinese newspapers and broadcasts took a similar stand. The UN was marginally involved.

(See *Master Table*, pp. 698–99.)

Sources
See sources for Case #170.

(181) Bay of Pigs, 1961 (see Multiregional PCs: East/West)

(196) Cuban Missiles, 1962 (see Multiregional PCs: East/West)

(198) Dominican Republic/Haiti II

The Dominican Republic and Haiti were the actors in a two-phase crisis from 26 April to 3 June 1963.

Background
The Dominican Republic's dictator, Trujillo, was assassinated in 1960; and members of his family fled to Haiti. Newly elected President Bosch feared that Trujillo's exiled relatives would try to regain power. An attempt on the lives of the children of Haiti's dictator Duvalier (Papa Doc) aroused suspicions of Dominican Republic complicity: the conspirators had sought refuge in the Dominican Republic embassy in the Haitian capital, Port-au-Prince.

Crisis
On 26 April 1963 Haitian policemen forcibly entered the Dominican Republic embassy and arrested opponents of Haiti's regime. This violation of diplomatic immunity triggered a crisis for the Dominican Republic. The next day President Bosch responded by issuing a 24-hour ultimatum to Haiti that triggered a reciprocal crisis. Bosch also appealed to the *OAS* and proposed a joint democratic Latin American force to oust Duvalier. On the 28th Haiti severed diplomatic relations with the Dominican Republic. The following day the Dominican Republic began stationing troops along its border with Haiti.

An *OAS* fact-finding mission arrived in Haiti on 30 April. On 5 and 6 May the crisis reached its peak. *OAS* officials shuttled between the two countries in an attempt at de-escalation. A new *OAS* five-nation mediation committee was created on the 8th. By 10 May the possibility of a Dominican Republic invasion of Haiti had lessened considerably. On the 14th Duvalier released the hostages, terminating the crisis for the Dominican Republic. This was followed by the demobilization of Dominican Republic forces. On 3 June Haiti's crisis ended with the publication of the final report by the *OAS* committee, which did not recommend further action against Haiti. The U.S., fearing for the lives of foreign citizens in Haiti, sent a naval task force. This was withdrawn after the final report of the *OAS,* and normal relations with Haiti were restored.

The UN Security Council met on 8–9 May at Haiti's request and discussed the issue but left action to the regional organization.

(See *Master Table,* pp. 702–3.)

Sources
MacDonald 1964; Martin 1966; Slater 1967; Tomasek 1968–69.

(200) Cuba/Venezuela

The duration of Venezuela's crisis with Cuba was one month, from 1 November to 1 December 1963.

Pre-crisis
During 1963 Venezuela's internal situation began to verge on civil war. There was a marked increase in communist guerrilla attacks on major targets within Caracas itself. President Betancourt had announced emergency legislation against Venezuela's left-wing parties and ordered the arrest of leading communists, following an assassination attempt. Betancourt's drive against the Left on the domestic scene was matched by attempts in his foreign policy to isolate Cuba and invoke *OAS* sanctions against the Castro regime. This policy was actively encouraged by the U.S. Presidential elections in Venezuela were scheduled for 1 December 1963.

Crisis
On 1 November 1963 the Venezuelan government discovered a significant arms cache on the Paraguana Peninsula, one of Venezuela's quiet, secluded beaches. A plan of operation to capture Caracas and prevent the elections of 1 December was also discovered. On 29 November the Cuban origin of the arms was confirmed. Venezuela took the matter to the *OAS* Council for action under Article 6 of the Rio Treaty. The crisis ended on 1 December with the successful conclusion of Venezuela's presidential election.

The UN and the USSR were not involved in this crisis.

(The *OAS* agreed to investigate Venezuela's charges on 3 December, after the termination of Venezuela's crisis: in February 1964 it supported Venezuela's charges against Cuba but did not call for sanctions against Cuba which, by that time, was no longer a member of the regional organization of the Americas.) (See *Master Table,* pp. 702–3.)

Sources
Ball 1969; Parkinson 1974; Slater 1967; Wainhouse 1966.

(206) Panama Flag

Panama and the U.S. experienced a brief crisis over the Panama Canal Zone from 9 to 12 January 1964.

Background and Pre-crisis
An "unequal" treaty, providing for U.S. control over the Panama Canal Zone and the Canal, was imposed on Panama in 1903. Persistent Panamanian opposition to the treaty for 60 years centered around the issues of full U.S. sovereignty over the Canal Zone, Panama's inability to fly its flag in the area, and inadequate payment, according to Panama, for unrestricted United States use of the Canal. As President Carter later acknowledged: "From the outset, Panamanians deeply resented this denial of their authority over part of their territory."

The flag issue was partly rectified in 1962 by an agreement that both flags would fly side by side at designated public sites. However, to reduce tension, the flying of both states' flags in front of Canal Zone schools was banned in December 1963.

Crisis
On 9 January 1964 a group of U.S. students in the Canal Zone raised the U.S. flag at Balboa High School. Massive rioting followed and was met by force: U.S. troops fired upon the Panamanian demonstrators, killing 26 and wounding 100, triggering a crisis for Panama.

The dramatic eruption of the crisis led Panama's President Chiari to break diplomatic relations with the United States the same day. He also filed a complaint with the *OAS* and the UN Security Council. Notification of these acts on 10 January triggered a U.S. crisis. The same day President Johnson responded by phoning Chiari to express his regret for the casualties and to call for joint efforts to restore calm. Chiari demanded a complete revision of all treaties affecting U.S./Panama relations. Johnson insisted that order must first be restored to the Canal Zone. He requested the *OAS* Peace Committee to investigate the matter. It took 48 hours to persuade the Panamanian president to agree to Johnson's proposal. When he did so, on 12 January, the crisis ended for both countries.

The UN was marginally involved in this crisis; the USSR was uninvolved. (Diplomatic relations were restored on 3 April 1964. And soon after, the

parties agreed to renegotiate the Panama Canal treaties, a process completed in 1979.)
(See *Master Table,* pp. 702–3.)

Sources
Bloomfield 1967; Carter 1982; Farnsworth and McKenney 1983; Geyelin 1966; Gurtov 1974; Johnson 1971; Jordan 1984; La Feber 1989; Liss 1967; Minor 1974; Stebbins 1966.

(215) Dominican Intervention

A crisis for the United States in Central America began on 24 April and ended on 31 August 1965.

Pre-crisis
In December 1962, more than a year after the assassination of its long-time dictator, Rafael L. Trujillo, the first free elections in 38 years were held in the Dominican Republic. Juan Bosch was inaugurated as President in February 1963. In September military officers, alleging communist control of the civilian regime, staged a coup. Donald Reid y Cabral acted as puppet President while real power lay in the hands of a three-man military junta.

Crisis
A crisis for the United States was triggered on 24 April 1965 when Bosch supporters overthrew the junta. Civil war broke out immediately. U.S. embassy personnel cabled President Johnson that American lives were in danger. The United States responded on 28 April with a decision to send 400 army paratroops and marines to the island. By 2 May the U.S. force was 14,000 and by 20 May 22,000. All foreign citizens were evacuated. The next day Johnson assigned U.S. military units the task of restoring order. On 30 April the U.S. called for an *OAS* meeting.

While fighting continued, intense diplomatic activity was taking place within the *OAS* and the UN, as well as bilateral U.S./Dominican negotiations. An *OAS* resolution called for a cease-fire, mediation, and the dispatch of an Inter-American Peace Force to the Dominican Republic. In the Security Council, Cuba and the USSR charged the United States with military intervention in the internal affairs of the Dominican Republic. A mild Security Council resolution on 14 May called for a cease-fire and authorized the Secretary-General to take appropriate action. U Thant appointed Dr. José Antonio Mayobri as his Personal Representative. Mayobri began mediation efforts with U.S. and Dominican delegates to the *OAS.*

An *OAS* committee of mediation secured an agreement in late June for a provisional government and, later, elections. "The Act of Dominican Reconciliation," signed on 31 August 1965, ended four months of civil war and, with it, the international crisis. All sides compromised by agreeing on Garcia-Godoy as Provisional President.

(Further military incidents occurred in late 1965 and 1966. Free elections were held once more, in June 1966, in which Joaquín Balaguer defeated Juan Bosch and was elected President of the Dominican Republic.)

(See *Master Table*, pp. 704–5.)

Sources
Barnet 1968; Baron 1968; Draper 1968b; Evans and Novak 1967; Fagen and Cornelius 1970; Ferguson 1973; Gleijeses 1978; Herring 1968; Johnson 1971; Lowenthal 1969, 1972; Mann 1965; Miller 1967; Moreno 1970; Parkinson 1974; Rusk 1990; Schoenbaum 1988; Slater 1969, 1970, 1978; Spiegel and Waltz 1971; Stuart 1975; Szulc 1965, 1971b, 1990; Wiarda 1969, 1970; Wilson 1966.

(221) Ché Guevara–Bolivia

Guerrilla activity, led by Cuban revolutionary Ché Guevara, caused a crisis for Bolivia from 23 March to 10 October 1967.

Pre-crisis
In October 1966 Ché Guevara left Cuba on a secret mission—to establish a guerrilla training camp in Bolivia to bring about the overthrow of the Bolivian government. La Paz newspapers began reporting the presence of guerrilla forces in the Santa Cruz region in early March 1967. There was no comment on these reports by Bolivian authorities.

Crisis
An ambush by guerrillas of a large Bolivian army patrol in the Santa Cruz region on 23 March 1967 triggered a crisis for Bolivia. The incident was reported by Bolivian President Barrientos in a broadcast to the nation on the 27th. Bolivia feared that the pro-Cuban guerrilla movement might serve as a catalyst to revolt and would spread antigovernment sentiment in the country. On 30 March Bolivian troops were moved to the southeast region, more forces were mobilized, and clashes with the guerrillas ensued. Bolivia's major response, the next day, was a request to the United States for arms and aid. A policy of containment was decided upon, and on 1 April Barrientos flew to the area in which 3,000 Bolivian soldiers had encircled the guerrillas until an effective fighting force could be trained. On 11 April the U.S. sent 40 advisors to train antiguerrilla forces, in addition to modern weapons, including helicopters.

Bolivia decreed a state of siege on 2 June, suspending constitutional guarantees, after Bolivian students and miners staged demonstrations in support of the guerrillas. Toward the end of June the Bolivian government confirmed officially that Ché Guevara was in command of a force of well-trained Cubans in southeast

Bolivia. Bolivia appealed to Argentina to send troops to assist in the counterinsurgency operation but received only supplies and arms.

The *OAS* Foreign Ministers Conference met in Washington on 21 September, at Venezuela's request. At the meeting Bolivian representatives made public captured guerrilla documents, diaries, and photographs. U.S. Secretary of State Dean Rusk urged the *OAS* to tighten the diplomatic, economic, and political isolation of Cuba. The *OAS* passed a resolution condemning Cuban subversive activities in the Western Hemisphere.

On 10 October Barrientos announced that Ché Guevara had been killed by government troops on the 8th and that his death had ended the guerrilla movement in Bolivia.

The UN and the USSR were not involved in this crisis.

(Twenty-eight years later, in October 1995, a retired Bolivian army general revealed that he had been an eyewitness to the hitherto-unconfirmed killing of the legendary revolutionary figure.)

(See *Master Table,* pp. 706–7.)

Sources
See general list.

(228) Essequibo I

A crisis for Guyana, in a long-standing territorial dispute with Venezuela, occurred from 9 July to sometime in August 1968.

Background
British Guiana (since 1966, Guyana) and Venezuela have long disputed a large tract of territory contiguous to the Essequibo River. In 1899 an arbitral tribunal awarded the bulk of the territory, 45,000 of 53,000 square miles, to British Guiana. Venezuela accepted the award in 1905—until 1962 when, at the UN General Assembly, it pressed for a revision of the boundary: it claimed the entire disputed territory, which comprised 62 percent of British Guiana's total land base. Venezuela recognized Guiana's independence in 1966 and participated with British Guiana and the U.K. in a tripartite commission to resolve the dispute within four years.

Crisis
On 9 July 1968 Dr. Raul Leoni, President of Venezuela, issued a decree that annexed to Venezuela the territorial waters lying from three to 12 miles along the coast of the Guyana Essequibo. Venezuelan naval craft were later reported patrolling outside the three-mile limit. Guyana's response was a protest note to Venezuela, a complaint to UN Secretary-General U Thant, protests to Latin American members of the United Nations, and a complaint by Guyana's foreign minister to President Johnson. It was reported that, although the U.S. wanted to

maintain a neutral position in the dispute, it did appeal to Venezuela to revoke the decree. Guyana declared Venezuela's decree to be null and void and announced that it would resist an invasion by Venezuela. The crisis faded in August 1968. The UN Secretary-General offered his good offices to settle the dispute. Barbados expressed concern about Venezuela's contemplated use of force in a Note from its prime minister to the foreign minister of Venezuela.

(There were minor military incidents in the disputed territory in 1969 and 1970—until Guyana, Venezuela, and the U.K. formally agreed in the Trinidad Protocol on 18 June 1970 to a 12-year "cooling-off period" on the border dispute [see Case #325—**Essequibo II** below].)

(See *Master Table,* pp. 708–9.)

Sources
Braveboy-Wagner 1984; Child 1985; Day 1987; Ince 1970.

(235) Football War

A crisis between El Salvador and Honduras began on 15 June and terminated on 30 July 1969.

Background and Pre-crisis
Honduras, a sparsely populated country, was the domicile of large numbers of Salvadorans who, since the 1920s, had left overcrowded El Salvador to farm, squat, or work on the banana plantations of Honduras. Reports of their ill-treatment were brought to the attention of El Salvador. In Honduras the economic situation at the end of the 1960s was bleak, with societal unrest increasing. The first football (soccer) game between teams of the two countries in the elimination rounds of the 1970 World Cup Championship was played in the Honduras capital, Tegucigalpa, on 8 June 1969. Following the opener, Salvadoran players complained of suffering at the hands of their hosts. Violence in the stadium followed. In the next game, on 15 June in San Salvador, Honduran players were subjected to reciprocal treatment by their hosts, and riots broke out once again.

Crisis
The aftermath of the second football game, combined with reports from large numbers of Salvadoran refugees fleeing from Honduras and alleging maltreatment and confiscation of property, triggered a crisis for El Salvador on 15 June 1969. El Salvador declared a state of alert and appealed to the *OAS*. On 26 and 27 June diplomatic relations between the two states were broken. Tension, accompanied by incidents along the border, continued until El Salvador's major response: troops crossed into Honduras on 14 July. Honduras responded the same day with air attacks on Salvadoran cities and ports. A cease-fire, due to effective *OAS* mediation, came about on 18 July. By this time casualties on both sides exceeded 2,000.

El Salvador's victories led to the conquest of sizable chunks of Honduran territory from which it refused to withdraw after the cease-fire. Subsequent threats of *OAS* sanctions against El Salvador convinced it to do so. A compromise agreement, brokered by the *OAS* secretary-general, came into effect on 30 July 1969, marking the termination of the crisis.

The U.S. embargo on arms to both countries was perceived by Honduras as favoring the better equipped Salvadoran army. At the same time, there was U.S. pressure on El Salvador to withdraw from the Honduran territory it had invaded. Costa Rica, Guatemala, and Nicaragua attempted to mediate at the beginning of the crisis, but without success.

The UN offered its good offices. The USSR was not involved.

(Thirteen years after the Football (Soccer) War the International Court of Justice ruled in favor of Honduras, awarding it two-thirds of the disputed territory. And another 13 years passed until, in the summer of 1995, El Salvador and Honduras agreed to begin demarcating their border.)

(See *Master Table,* pp. 708–9.)

Sources
Brzoska and Pearson 1994; Cable 1969; Day 1987; Holly 1979.

(239) Cienfuegos Submarine Base, 1970 (see Multiregional PCs: East/West)

(262) Belize I

The U.K. experienced a crisis from 1 to 30 November 1975 over Guatemala's threat to annex the British self-governing colony of Belize.

Background
Belize was proclaimed a U.K. colony (British Honduras), closely linked to Jamaica, in 1862. It became a separate administrative unit in 1884, with British troops stationed in the area since 1948. Guatemala formally claimed the territory after World War II. A brief incident, an attempted incursion by two dozen members of the Belize Liberation Army, occurred in 1962.

Guatemala's claim to Belize and threats to annex the disputed territory once it became independent were discussed at the UN General Assembly for about 10 years prior to this crisis. The U.K. retained responsibility for the defense of Belize, but, in all other aspects, the colony was self-governing. In 1972 Guatemala threatened to invade Belize but the incident faded without violence.

Crisis
On 1 November 1975 the U.K. perceived a likely invasion of Belize following increased Guatemalan military activity—a movement of troops and patrol boats near the Belize border. The U.K. responded on 5 November with the dispatch of

additional forces to strengthen the British garrison in Belize. A declaration by Guatemala that it intended to annex Belize was reported on the 7th. Talks were held during a visit by Edward Rowlands, U.K. Minister of State at the foreign office, to Guatemala and Belize. An agreement was reached on 30 November terminating the crisis: the two countries were to resume talks about the future of Belize in February 1976. Troops were subsequently withdrawn on both sides.

The UN Trusteeship Council contributed to crisis abatement by adopting a resolution on 20 November urging the resumption of negotiations between the U.K. and Guatemala. An earlier offer of UN arbitration had been rejected by Guatemala.

The U.S. and the USSR were not involved in this crisis.

(Two years later a second U.K. crisis occurred over Belize [see Case #279 below].)

(See *Master Table*, pp. 714–15.)

Sources
Calvert 1976; Day 1987; Dewar 1984; *Keesing's* 1975; Krohn 1987; Menon 1979; *New York Times* 1975; Thorndyke 1978; Zammit 1978.

(279) Belize II

Guatemalan claims to Belize caused a second crisis for the U.K. from 25 June to 28 July 1977.

Background and Pre-crisis
Belize's independence had been delayed for many years because of Guatemala's threats to invade the territory once it became independent, claiming historic rights to its annexation. In 1975 Britain perceived a threat that Guatemala would invade Belize (see Case #262—**Belize I** above). The issue had been discussed in the United Nations General Assembly year after year. In the early summer of 1977 the possibility of independence for Belize once more precipitated Guatemalan action. On 17 June Guatemala's defense minister stated that his country's forces were waiting for word from the president to begin the recovery of Belize.

Crisis
On 25 June 1977 Guatemalan troops were deployed to the Belize border area, and reservists were called up. This action triggered a crisis for the U.K., which was responsible for Belize's security. It was followed by a statement from President Garcia on 1 July affirming Guatemala's rights to the territory. The U.K. responded on 6 July by dispatching air, infantry, and naval forces to the area. HMS *Achilles* took up position in Belizean waters, and British troops were moved to within two miles of Guatemala's border. At the request of the United

States, British Minister of State Edward Rowlands visited Washington to hold talks with Secretary of State Cyrus Vance. Vance then held separate talks with Guatemala's Foreign Minister Adolfo Molina and a Belizean delegation led by Premier George Price. It was decided that Rowlands would visit Guatemala. He did so from 26 to 28 July. A communiqué was issued on the 28th in which both sides agreed to take steps to reduce the border tension adding that there would be no sudden move to independence for Belize, thus terminating the U.K. crisis over Belize.

The United States welcomed the outcome of the talks. The UN was not involved in this crisis.

(The independence of Belize was proclaimed in 1981.)

(See *Master Table*, pp. 716–17.)

Sources
See sources for Case #262.

(287) Beagle Channel I

The century-old dispute over the Beagle Channel erupted into a crisis for Chile and Argentina on 5 December 1977 and ended on 20 February 1978.

Background and Pre-crisis
Since the mid-nineteenth century Argentina and Chile contested the ownership of three tiny islands, Lennox, Nueva, and Picton, located at the eastern entrance to the Beagle Channel, a waterway 150 miles long and 3–8 miles wide in the southern tip of South America. The islands are inhabited by Chilean shepherds and patrolled by Argentinian torpedo boats. The two countries signed an agreement in 1972 referring the dispute to the International Court of Justice *(ICJ)*, which awarded the islands to Chile on 2 May 1977. Argentina's access to the Atlantic, to its Antarctic bases, and to the potential resources of oil, minerals, and fish in the South Atlantic and Antarctic regions was in jeopardy.

Crisis
On 5 December 1977 the Argentine government delivered a formal Note to Chile objecting to the terms of the court ruling. More important, it called up army reservists in the Mendoza border region the same day, triggering a crisis for Chile. Negotiations between Chile and Argentina ended on 28 December, and all further meetings were canceled. Chile's response, on 5 January, was a speech by President Pinochet stating that his government would henceforth pursue a more aggressive and pragmatic foreign policy. That day it was also reported that Chilean soldiers were being massed between Puerto Natales and Punta Arenas and that tank and infantry maneuvers were in progress with Chilean warships patrolling the Magellan Straits. This activity triggered a crisis for Argentina.

Argentinian vessels sailed for the Beagle Channel area and remained offshore on 8 January. Two days later Argentina's naval commander, while observing maneuvers, stated that the navy was ready for action; the air force commander inspected airfields on the Chilean border. The same day President Videla interrupted a vacation to return to Buenos Aires for consultations with the military junta.

Throughout January 1978 Argentina and Chile continued their preparations for a military confrontation. On 19 January Videla and Pinochet met in Mendoza to discuss matters of joint concern, especially the area in dispute. When Argentina once more rejected the ruling by the *ICJ,* a second meeting between the two presidents was postponed. However, on 20 February they did meet once more and signed the "Act of Puerto Montt" under which a joint negotiating committee was set up and given 180 days to resolve the dispute. The crisis ended for both actors that day with no change in the status quo.

The United States tried to persuade both parties to reduce tension and seek a solution through diplomatic means. The UN and the USSR were not involved.

(Almost two months after the 180-day negotiating period a second crisis over the Beagle Channel occurred [see Case #295 below].)

(See *Master Table,* pp. 718–19.)

Sources
Child 1985; Garrett 1985; Gwyne 1979; Kelley 1988; Princen 1987, 1992a, 1992b.

(294) Nicaragua Civil War II

An international crisis over the civil war in Nicaragua involved Costa Rica and Nicaragua from 10 September 1978 to 17 July 1979.

Pre-crisis
During 1978 there was severe unrest in Nicaragua, with widespread demonstrations and strikes in opposition to President Somoza's dictatorial regime. On 22 August the National Palace was temporarily seized by left-wing guerrillas of the Sandinista National Liberation Front *(SNLF),* who were supported by Costa Rica. The internal situation worsened in early September when regime repression increased, and the Sandinistas called for a national insurrection against Somoza. On the 9th heavy fighting broke out between the Nicaraguan National Guard and Sandinista supporters.

Crisis
A foreign policy crisis for Nicaragua was triggered on 10 September 1978 by a guerrilla attack from Costa Rica at the border town of Penas Blancas. According to Somoza, the 300-man invasion force was part of a plan to overthrow his regime, with the complicity of the Costa Rican government, President Cararo,

and other high officials. Nicaragua responded the same day with a counterattack and the reorganization of the National Guard to meet attacks throughout the country. The following day Somoza declared a partial state of siege.

A crisis for Costa Rica was triggered on 12 September by Nicaraguan bombing of its territory and "hot pursuit" by Nicaraguan forces across the border. The following day the state of siege was extended throughout Nicaragua. The Costa Rican response to the crisis was the signing of a mutual aid and cooperation agreement with Venezuela on 15 September, a day after the latter had sent four jet bombers to Costa Rica on a goodwill visit. Costa Rica had no official army; its defense was handled by a Civil Guard. Panama, too, sent arms to Costa Rica. On 16 September Nicaragua recalled its ambassadors from Costa Rica, Panama, and Venezuela, and, later, from Colombia.

On 18 September the Permanent Council of the *OAS* accepted a proposal to convene a meeting of foreign ministers to consider the situation in Nicaragua. At meetings that took place in Washington between 21 and 23 September, a resolution was passed affirming the principle of nonintervention and reaffirming Nicaraguan sovereignty over its internal affairs; and a decision was reached to send an investigation team to Nicaragua. A statement by the United States Department of State expressed concern at reported atrocities committed by the Nicaraguan National Guard. On 25 September the insurgents were defeated and factories and businesses reopened in Nicaragua, terminating its first crisis. On that day, too, Somoza announced that Nicaragua would accept U.S. mediation.

On 29 September Nicaragua's president agreed to a mediation team sponsored by the *OAS,* the mediating countries being the Dominican Republic, Guatemala, and the United States. Its first meeting was held on 16 October. However, by mid-January 1979 mediation efforts collapsed. And on 8 February the U.S. ended all military aid to Nicaragua.

Following clashes between Costa Rican Civil Guards and Nicaraguan National Guards on 21 November 1978, Costa Rica severed diplomatic relations with Nicaragua and began a call-up of 2,500 troops. A resolution was passed by the UN General Assembly on 15 December condemning Nicaragua for repressing its population and demanding that Nicaragua cease all acts endangering the security of its neighbors. UN activity made it difficult for Somoza to contend that his government was a victim of foreign communist aggression; and his regime became isolated. On the 27th Somoza threatened to invade Costa Rica if that country continued to assist the guerrillas. On 30 December Somoza met with the presidents of El Salvador, Guatemala, and Honduras, all of whom had been supporting him in the fight against the Sandinistas.

Sporadic fighting continued until 27 May 1979, when a second crisis was triggered for Nicaragua by an invasion of guerrillas from Costa Rica. Nicaragua responded the same day by repelling the invaders. The U.S. continued to refuse to sell arms to Nicaragua and, according to Somoza, convinced Israel to impose an arms embargo as well.

At the end of May Nicaragua called upon the Permanent Council of the *OAS* to invoke the Rio Treaty in response to the Costa Rican invasion. Costa Rica requested the same *OAS* action against Nicaragua on 3 June. The following day the *OAS* Council met and passed a resolution calling for the replacement of President Somoza's dictatorship by a democratic regime. A U.S. proposal to dispatch a peacekeeping force to Nicaragua was rejected by the *OAS*. Despite the embargo, U.S. military equipment found its way into the conflict zone. Heavy fighting continued throughout June. Toward mid-July the *OAS* agreed to a proposal whereby General Somoza would resign, a cease-fire would take place, and the left-wing revolutionary junta would assume power in Nicaragua. No agreement was reached between Somoza's government and the Sandinistas. The president fled Nicaragua on 17 July 1979, ending the crisis for Costa Rica and Nicaragua.

(The Sandinistas, in coalition with liberal democrats, assumed power in Nicaragua. During the Carter administration a $75 million loan was granted to Nicaragua, but the final payment was withheld by President Reagan in January 1981, when relations between the two countries deteriorated: the State Department charged that the Sandinista government was aiding guerrillas in El Salvador; Managua denied the charges.)

(See *Master Table,* pp. 718–19.)

Sources
Cottam 1994; Gordon and Munro 1982; Leogrande 1979.

(295) Beagle Channel II

A second crisis for Chile and Argentina over the Beagle Channel lasted from 16 October 1978 to 8 January 1979.

Pre-crisis
The first crisis over the Beagle Channel ended in February 1978 with a moratorium of 180 days in an attempt to settle the dispute (see Case #287 above). During that period six rounds of negotiations took place, with little progress. Soon after, Argentina began overt military preparations.

Crisis
On 16 October a crisis for Chile was triggered by Argentina's call-up of 50,000 reservists. Tank and troop movements, with minor clashes, were later reported near the Chilean border. Chile responded on the 24th by sending troops to the border and canceling naval maneuvers with the U.S. and Peru, due to take place 1,500 miles north of Chile, in the event that Argentina might try to occupy the disputed islands in the Beagle Channel.

On the day of the deadline, 2 November, the two states announced that they had reached an agreement on joint economic development of the Beagle region, but that the distribution of the maritime zones had still not been resolved. Chile's Foreign Minister, Herman Cubillos Sallato, proposed mediation by a friendly government. Argentina agreed on the 8th. On 11 December Sallato met with Argentina's Foreign Minister, Carlos Washington Paston, to designate a mediator. Pope John Paul II was chosen, but the talks collapsed after an Argentinian plan was rejected by Chile.

On 16 December a crisis for Argentina was triggered when Chile put 45,000 troops on full alert. It responded on the 21st with a complaint to the UN Security Council that Chile was creating a military imbalance in the disputed area by illegally deploying troops and artillery. The same day Chile asked for an urgent meeting of the *OAS* to prevent Argentina from attacking the islands; and the Pope announced that he would act as mediator. The offer was accepted by both states. On the 26th Cardinal Sumore arrived in Buenos Aires to start a mediation mission. The crisis ended for both actors with the signing of the Declaration of Montevideo on 8 January 1979, in which the two parties accepted the Pope's mediation and committed themselves not to use force in their relations with one another.

The Security Council discussed the problem but did not pass a resolution. On 10 November 1978 the United States called on the *OAS* to offer its services to the parties in order to avoid a violent conflict; but it did not become more deeply involved in the crisis despite U.S. and Chilean requests.

(The issue remained unresolved until 1984 when a Vatican-mediated treaty was signed by Argentina and Chile. The accord granted Chile sovereignty over the islands but limited its maritime rights to the Pacific waters, while Argentina won control of the waters on the Atlantic side of the Beagle Channel.)

There was no USSR involvement in this crisis.

(See *Master Table*, pp. 718–19.)

Sources
See sources for Case #287.

(310) Colombia/Nicaragua

Colombia and Nicaragua were the adversaries in a crisis over long-standing competing claims to the San Andrés Archipelago. It lasted from 12 December 1979 to 8 July 1981.

Background
The roots of this territorial conflict can be traced to the era of Spain's colonial rule. In 1803 a Spanish Royal Order allocated the islands of the San Andrés Archipelago, along with three uninhabited cays, Quita Sueño, Roncador, and Serrana, to the viceroyalty of Santa Fé de Bogotá, precursor to present-day Colombia and Panama, extending to the Mosquito Coast. In 1853 Nicaragua

claimed sovereignty over the Atlantic coast and its nearby islands. So too did independent Colombia.

The United States, which had controlled the economically valuable cays since 1869, took possession in 1919. On 24 March 1928 the Barcenas Meneses–Esguerra Treaty between Colombia and the U.S. recognized the former's sovereignty over the San Andrés Islands. A follow-up agreement between them on 10 April gave Colombia fishing rights around the cays but recognized that sovereignty over these reefs remained in dispute. Nicaragua, which was occupied by U.S. marines in 1928, accepted the Barcenas Meneses–Esguerra Treaty on 6 March 1930. A much later agreement between Washington and Bogotá, the Vasquez-Saccio Treaty of 8 September 1972, accorded sovereignty over the cays to Colombia and divided fishing rights equally between the two states. The treaty was ratified by Colombia—but not by the U.S. because of intense lobbying by the Somoza regime in Nicaragua. The ratification process was rescheduled for January 1980.

Crisis

On 12 December 1979 Nicaragua claimed jurisdiction over a 200-mile continental shelf, triggering a crisis for Colombia. Bogotá's initial response, on the 20th, was to repudiate the claim. On 26 January 1980 the United States urged a judicial solution to the territorial dispute.

Nicaragua escalated the crisis on 4 February by issuing a "white book" that claimed all of the San Andrés Archipelago; at the same time it indicated a willingness to negotiate. Two days later Colombia rejected negotiations with Nicaragua. Its major response to the crisis, on 7 February, was to reinforce bases in and around the San Andrés Islands and to deploy three surface warships and a submarine to the area. This high-visibility signal of Colombia's intent to use force, if necessary, triggered a crisis for Nicaragua. In the event, no violence occurred. Rather, Nicaragua responded with persistent pressure in an effort to block U.S. ratification of the 1972 treaty between Colombia and the United States. The ratification process took another 18 months, until 7 July 1981, when the U.S. Senate ratified the treaty, which formalized Colombia's sovereignty over the long-disputed islands and cays. This ended Colombia's crisis, in victory, and Nicaragua's crisis, in defeat.

The U.S., as noted, was very active throughout and played a crucial role in crisis resolution. Neither the USSR nor the OAS was involved. And the UN was involved only indirectly: Colombia referred its grievance to the UN Conference on the Law of the Sea, which was unable to settle the dispute.

(See *Master Table*, pp. 722–23.)

Sources

U.S. Congress (Senate) 1981; Day 1985; Drekonja-Kornat 1982; Hopkins 1983; Institute for the Study of Conflict 1981; *Keesing's* 1980, 1981; Kline 1983; Rudolph 1982.

(322) Ecuador/Peru Border III, 1981 (see Ecuador/Peru PC)

(325) Essequibo II

Guyana and Venezuela experienced another crisis over a large tract of disputed territory from 4 April 1981 to March 1983.

Background
Following the 1968 crisis (see Case #228, **Essequibo I** above), there were minor military incidents in 1969 and 1970, until Guyana, Venezuela, and the U.K. formally agreed to a 12-year "cooling-off" period, in the Port of Spain Protocol on 18 June 1970. Thereafter the boundary dispute was quiescent for a decade, until the approach of the expiry date.

Crisis
A crisis for Guyana was triggered by a Venezuelan government statement on 4 April 1981: it did not intend to renew the Port of Spain Protocol in 1982; and it opposed Guyana's Upper Mazaruni hydroelectric project in the disputed territory.

Whatever Venezuela's motives for this statement—to create an image of resoluteness for President Herrera before the 1983 presidential election, to exploit the economic and political vulnerability of Guyana, to strengthen its links with the U.S., since both Venezuela and the United States were concerned about Cuba's influence in the region, and/or pressure from Venezuelan nationalists to adopt a hard line—Guyana perceived a serious threat to its territorial integrity. It responded the same day by reaffirming its determination to carry on with the project, which was "crucial to the development of the nation." And on territory, Guyana President Burnham stated that his country would "not cede an inch."

In fact, during 1981 the crisis was characterized by a war of words and a diplomatic battle. Venezuela's ambassador to the *OAS* assured his colleagues in late May that there would be no armed conflict. More important, President Herrera declared on 2 June that Venezuela was committed to "keeping alive the historic claim to the Essequibo territory" and that his country would not renew the Port of Spain Protocol, which was due to expire on 18 June 1982. The U.K. was formally notified of Venezuela's position on the Protocol on 11 December 1981.

Apart from the war of words, there were other indicators of growing tension. In early June 1981, anticipating a possible internal or external attack, Guyana held a 10-day military exercise named "Operation Thunderflash."

Until the late summer of 1981 Venezuela remained the crisis initiator, putting growing pressure on a much weaker adversary. However, at the end of August a new catalyst emerged. Grave concern was expressed by Venezuela's foreign minister about the possible transfer of thousands of Cuban troops then in Angola to Guyana in the near future. That possibility triggered a crisis for

Venezuela, especially since Cuba, alone among Caribbean states, had given unqualified support to Guyana on this dispute: Venezuela perceived a threat to its territorial aspirations; finite time for response (the Port of Spain Protocol was due to expire on 18 June 1982); and heightened probability of involvement in military hostilities, due to Cuba's unconcealed and active support for Guyana and Guyana's public acknowledgment that, in the event of a Venezuelan attack, it would accept assistance "from any nation that wanted to give it."

In 1982 tension was sustained by the continued war of words. It escalated once again on 18 June 1982 with the expiration of the 12-year "cooling-off" period. On 8 July the Guyana Assembly insisted on Guyana's right to the territory. During the next three months President Burnham expressed his fear of an invasion and refused a Venezuelan proposal for bilateral negotiations. In addition, Guyana accused Venezuela of violating its airspace and producing border incidents, in a letter to the UN on 14 September 1982. The same month President Herrera reaffirmed that Venezuela "wants a peaceful solution."

During the first three months of 1983 Venezuela and Guyana disagreed on the modalities of peaceful crisis resolution. Venezuela proposed bilateral talks; Guyana wanted to submit the issue to the International Court of Justice or the UN Security Council.

The crisis ended in March 1983 when both adversaries formally referred the dispute to the UN Secretary-General. (During all of 1983 Javier Perez de Cuellar met with the leaders of the two states, but he did not succeed in finding a solution: the tangible dispute was accentuated by the personal antipathy between Herrera and Burnham.)

Neither the U.S. nor the USSR was involved in this crisis, though Venezuela tried to elicit U.S. support by playing the "Cuba card": the U.S. did not alter its stance of May 1981, namely, that it had "no position of substance on the issue."

(Other incidents occurred; for example, in December 1983 six Venezuelan fishing boats were seized by Guyana because they were allegedly fishing illegally in Guyana's territorial waters.)

(See *Master Table,* pp. 724–25.)

Sources
Braveboy-Wagner 1982–83; Day 1987; *ISLA* 1981, 1982, 1983; *Keesing's* 1981; *LACCR* 1981–82, 1982–83; *LAWR* 1981, 1982, 1983; Spinner 1984.

(326) Contras I, 1981 (see Honduras/Nicaragua PC)

(336) Falklands/Malvinas

The U.K. and Argentina were enmeshed in an increasingly violent interstate crisis over the Falklands/Malvinas Islands from 31 March until 14 June 1982.

Background

The thinly populated island archipelago south of Argentina (2,100 in 1995) was discovered in 1592 by John Davis, a British explorer, and came under British, French, and Spanish control. Spain, the hegemonial power in Latin America until the nineteenth century, bought out the French in 1770 and drove out the British in 1774. It held sway in the islands until 1811. Argentina asserted sovereignty over the islands soon after attaining its independence from Spain in 1816. However, the U.K. ousted Argentina in 1833 and has retained control over the Falklands, along with nearby South Georgia and the South Sandwich Islands, ever since.

Argentina never recognized U.K. sovereignty over the Malvinas and frequently challenged it: in 1927, 1946, 1948, and 1953, and in 1973, when it submitted a claim before the UN, all to no avail. Negotiations between Argentina and the U.K. since 1966, at UN initiative, led to stalemate.

Pre-crisis

On 1 March 1982 Argentina's foreign minister warned that, if an agreement on the islands were not reached shortly, Argentina would resort to "other means" to resolve the dispute. Two days later London expressed "deep anxiety" over this statement. On the 19th a group of 60 Argentine civilians raised the Argentine flag in South Georgia. Moreover, Buenos Aires rejected London's request to punish the transgressors and sent a ship with supplies to secure their well-being. On the 28th Argentina's foreign minister termed the situation "grave." And on the 30th British Foreign Secretary Lord Carrington responded that it was "potentially dangerous." The same day the president of the UN Security Council, which met at the U.K.'s request because it feared an imminent Argentine invasion of the islands, called on both parties to seek a diplomatic solution.

Crisis

The trigger to a crisis for the U.K. was a British intelligence report on 31 March that an Argentine invasion of the Falklands was imminent. Prime Minister Thatcher cabled President Reagan the same day seeking his personal intervention with President Galtieri, to no avail. The U.K. leaders decided on 1 April to send a task force to the South Atlantic, recognizing that it would take 26 days to reach the Falklands.

On 2 April Argentine troops took control of the islands after less than four hours of combat. UN Security Council Resolution 502, on 3 April, condemned the Argentine invasion and called for its immediate withdrawal. The same day Britain's prime minister announced the severance of diplomatic relations with Buenos Aires and pledged before parliament her determination to regain control of the islands.

The U.K.'s dispatch of a large naval task force to the South Atlantic on 5 April triggered a crisis for Argentina: its leaders did not expect a British military riposte to their invasion of the islands. The next day London imposed economic sanctions on Argentina—the U.K. was its major investor and trading partner. The European Community *(EC)* approved the sanctions on the 10th. Argentina responded three days later with economic sanctions on all *EC* products. The European parliament condemned the Argentine invasion on 22 April.

Argentina mobilized 100,000 reservists on 9 April. The *OAS,* meeting on 22 April at Argentina's request, did not condemn U.K. behavior. Three days later British forces regained control of South Georgia. Argentina proclaimed a technical state of war the same day and informed the Security Council.

On 26 April the U.S. imposed economic sanctions against Argentina. On the 28th, in a marked shift, the *OAS* adopted a resolution recognizing Argentina's sovereignty over the Malvinas and calling upon the U.K. to withdraw its forces. Full-scale war erupted from the moment the British naval task force reached the Falklands. Argentina's foreign minister accepted the idea of U.S. mediation on 6 May. On the 21st 5,000 British troops landed on East Falkland Island. On the 25th the UN Security Council adopted Resolution 505 requesting Secretary-General Perez de Cuellar to renew an offer of good offices in an attempt to resolve the conflict. The *OAS* adopted a resolution on 29 May condemning the U.K. On 3 June British marines began their attack on the main Argentine garrison at Port Stanley. Argentine troops surrendered on 14 June terminating the crisis for both Argentina and the U.K. The outcome was unqualified victory for the U.K. and humiliating defeat for Argentina. There were almost 1,000 casualties in the war over the Falklands/Malvinas, 250 British, 700 on the Argentine side.

As noted, the U.S. played a conspicuous role. It attempted to prevent the Argentine invasion. Then, through the efforts of Secretary of State Haig, Washington tried to mediate an accommodation between the parties. And when these efforts failed, the U.S. declared its support for U.K. rights in the Falklands. The USSR adopted a passive posture, though it supported Argentina's aspirations, verbally. As noted, too, the UN and the *OAS* passed resolutions condemning one or the other party and sought to resolve the crisis by mediation, without success.

(Diplomatic relations between Argentina and the U.K. were restored in 1992. And in mid-September 1995 they reached agreement over their disputed claims to large natural gas and oil resources in the vicinity of the islands, reportedly, two-thirds of the earnings to the U.K., one-third to Argentina. The dispute over territory remains unresolved.)

(See *Master Table,* pp. 726–27.)

Sources

Brzoska and Pearson 1994; Calvert 1982; Cordesman and Wagner 1990, vol. 3; Day 1987; Freedman 1982, 1988; Freedman and Gamba-Stonehouse 1990; Gamba 1987; Haig 1984; Hastings and Jenkins 1983; Lebow 1985; *Sunday Times* 1982; Thatcher 1993; Ullman 1985.

(343) Invasion of Grenada

The United States and Grenada were enmeshed in a brief military intervention crisis from 19 to 28 October 1983.

Background
Grenada, a long-time British colony in the Caribbean, became a self-governing state, with full internal autonomy, in March 1967. The first general election, that year, brought the Grenada United Labor Party *(GULP)* to power, with its leader, Eric M. Gairy, as Prime Minister. Gairy ruled the island with an iron hand until 1979, opposed by two groups of young professionals and intellectuals: the Joint Endeavor for Welfare, Education, and Liberation *(JEWEL);* and the Movement for Assemblies of the People *(MAP)*. These merged into the New Jewel Movement *(NJM)* in March 1973, the advocate of pragmatic nationalism and a radical populist alternative to Gairy and the *GULP.*

Grenada was granted independence on 7 February 1974. The widespread political unrest and civil disturbances of the preindependence period continued unabated. *GULP* won a bare majority in the 1976 general election; and Maurice Bishop, a founder of the *MAP,* became leader of the parliamentary opposition, now integrated into the United People's Party. A successful coup in March 1979 brought the marxist *NJM* to power, headed by Prime Minister Bishop and Deputy Prime Minister and Finance Minister Bernard Coard. The new People's Revolutionary Government created a one-party system, suspended the constitution, and banned the opposition. It also rapidly expanded Grenada's diplomatic network beyond the Caribbean and its mentor, Castro's Cuba, to the Soviet Union and many socialist Third World states.

Washington had long regarded the Caribbean as a region of vital importance and an area of U.S. hegemony, in accordance with the Monroe Doctrine (1823) dictum against any European intervention in the Western Hemisphere. Thus the USSR's perceived influence on the left-wing regime in Grenada, via Cuba, was a source of concern. This was accentuated by the construction of a large airport on the island, capable of handling large civilian and military planes.

Pre-crisis
U.S. perceptions of an increasingly hostile regime in the United States' "backyard" were further aggravated by a week-long tour of East European capitals by Prime Minister Bishop, followed by two days of talks in Havana in early October 1983. Soon after, factional disunity within the Grenada regime erupted. Prime Minister Bishop, a pragmatist, favored rapprochement with the U.S., while his hard-line deputy sought a close alignment with the Soviet bloc.

On 14 October Coard was forced to resign for an alleged plot to assassinate Bishop. However, three days later a coup in Grenada deposed the prime minister, and Coard took power. Bishop and five other ministers were placed under house arrest by General Hudson Austin, commander of the People's Revolutionary Army.

Long before the coup there had been speculation in Grenada that the U.S. was planning some form of military intervention, especially after President Reagan, on 23 March 1983, described the island's regime as a "threat to the security of the United States." Washington had expressed anxiety over Cuban participation in the construction of the Point Salinas international airport, viewing it as a potential military base for Soviet-bloc forces in the Americas. Relations between the U.S. and Grenada had been further strained by the growing tension between the Reagan administration and the Sandinista regime in Nicaragua, especially after joint U.S.-Honduras military maneuvers in August.

Crisis

On 19 October 1983 Bishop was freed by supporters but was quickly recaptured; in the firing that ensued, an estimated 200 persons were killed or wounded by Austin's troops. Soon after, Bishop and seven cabinet ministers and trade union leaders were executed. This act and a 96-hour curfew, imposed by Grenada's military authorities, triggered a crisis for the U.S.: Washington perceived a threat to its influence in the Caribbean and Central America, along with potential harm to U.S. citizens living in Grenada, about 1,000, mostly university students.

A Revolutionary Military Council *(RMC),* headed by General Austin, was formed on 20 October. The *RMC* gave repeated assurances for the safety of foreign nationals, opened the airport, and allowed them to leave. However, the dramatic and radical shift of power in Grenada triggered a sharp response. At an emergency session of the Organization of East Caribbean States *(OECS)* held on the 21st, a decision was made to impose immediate diplomatic and economic sanctions against Grenada's military regime and to "take appropriate action" to ensure the defense and security of the subregion. The *OECS* approached the U.S. for assistance. The same day a U.S. naval task force, including the assault ship *Guam* and led by the aircraft carrier *Independence,* was diverted to the Caribbean, ostensibly for the possible evacuation of U.S. citizens. This triggered a crisis for the new military regime in Grenada.

At an emergency meeting of the Caribbean Community and Common Market *(CARICOM)* heads of government on 22–23 October a decision was taken to impose economic and diplomatic sanctions against Grenada, similar to, but geographically more wide-ranging than, those agreed to at the subregional *(OECS)* level. On the 23rd, in another, distant, international crisis, the headquarters of U.S. marines in Lebanon was bombed, with more than 200 fatalities. That night, partly under the stress of the Lebanon crisis, Reagan decided to respond to the urgent request of the *OECS:* final military plans were made for an invasion. On the 24th the curfew imposed by Grenada's *RMC* was lifted, and the airport was opened for anyone who wanted to leave the island.

Early in the morning of 25 October 1,900 U.S. troops landed in Grenada, followed shortly after by a contingent of 300 soldiers from Jamaica, Barbados,

Dominica, Antigua, St. Lucia, and St. Vincent, to serve as a Caribbean Peacekeeping Force. Resistance by troops loyal to Grenada's *RMC,* supported by some Cuban construction workers on the island, was more intense than had been anticipated. By the 28th all the major military objectives of the U.S.-led multinational force had been secured. This ended the crisis for both the U.S. and Grenada.

Nicaragua asked the UN Security Council on 25 October for an urgent meeting to consider "the invasion of the Republic of Grenada by United States troops." A draft resolution was vetoed by the U.S. in the Security Council on the 27th. The USSR condemned U.S. intervention in Grenada.

(Coard and Austin were captured on the 31st. Final pockets of *RMC* resistance were quelled by 3 November. The governor-general formed an interim administration on the 15th to pave the way for a return to democracy. U.S. forces handed the task of maintaining internal security to the Caribbean Peacekeeping Force on 22 November. And by mid-December all U.S. combat troops had been withdrawn.)

(See *Master Table,* pp. 726–27.)

Sources
Adkin 1989; Amer 1992; Beck 1993; Burrowes 1988; Dunn and Watson 1985; Gilmore 1984; *Keesing's* 1984; Lewis 1987; Payne et al. 1984; Reagan 1990; Shultz 1993; Thorndike 1983, 1985; Valenta and Valenta 1986; Vertzberger 1997.

(354) Nicaragua MIG-21s, 1984 (see Multiregional PCs: East/West)

(369) Contras II, 1986 (see Honduras/Nicaragua PC)

(383) Contras III, 1988 (see Honduras/Nicaragua PC)

(389) Contras IV, 1989 (see Honduras/Nicaragua PC)

(391) Invasion of Panama

The United States and Panama were enmeshed in a military intervention crisis from 15 December 1989 to 3 January 1990.

Background
Washington played the decisive role in carving a sovereign state of Panama from Venezuela in 1903—in return for Panama's acceptance of U.S. construction and permanent control of the Panama Canal, linking the Atlantic and Pacific Oceans. This gave the U.S. an enduring strategic interest in the domestic and external affairs of a small state at the southern tip of Central America. U.S. ownership of the Panama Canal Zone "in perpetuity" attested to the U.S. perception of a vital interest.

The "loss" of the Canal Zone was deeply resented by Panama's political and military elites. That resentment was expressed during a brief January 1964 crisis triggered by the raising of the U.S. flag in the Canal Zone by U.S. students, in violation of a December 1963 banning of both states' flags at Canal Zone schools (see Case #206—**Panama Flag** crisis above).

The U.S. and Panama agreed to renegotiate the 1903 treaties, after diplomatic relations were restored in April 1964. In June 1967 Presidents Johnson and Robles reached agreement on three treaties, but strong opposition prevented their consideration in, let alone ratification by, the U.S. Congress. General Omar Torrijos, who seized power in Panama in 1968, renounced the agreements. President Nixon resumed the negotiations in 1970, and a set of principles was agreed upon in 1974. Once more, strong opposition by right-wing Republicans aborted ratification.

Finally, after prolonged and acrimonious negotiations, President Carter secured the ratification of two integrally related U.S.-Panama treaties, one in April 1978 providing for the transfer of the Canal Zone to Panamanian sovereignty in the year 2000, the second in September 1979, guaranteeing the Canal's permanent neutrality and the right of the U.S. to defend the Canal indefinitely into the future.

Viewed in larger regional and U.S. foreign policy perspectives, the 1989 invasion of Panama was a continuation of U.S. policy toward Central America and the Caribbean, and Mexico, throughout the twentieth century, another dramatic expression of the Monroe Doctrine of U.S. hegemony in the Western Hemisphere (1823). That long-standing policy was evident in the prolonged U.S. occupation of Haiti (1915–34) and inter alia in many international crises: among them, Cases #2—**Costa Rican Coup**, in 1918–19, in **Costa Rica/Nicaragua PC**; #19—**Costa Rica/Panama Border**, in 1921, in **Americas: Non-PCs**; #33—**Nicaragua Civil War I**, in 1926–27, in **Americas: Non-PCs**. Since the end of World War II, U.S. intervention occurred in Cases #144—**Guatemala**, in 1953–54, and #181—**Bay of Pigs**, in 1961, in **Multiregional PCs: East/West**; #215—**Dominican Intervention**, in 1965, and #343—**Invasion of Grenada**, in 1983, both in **Americas: Non-PCs**; #354—**Nicaragua MIG-21s**, in 1984, in **Multiregional PCs: East/West**; and #383—**Contras III**, in 1988, in **Honduras/Nicaragua PC**.

Pre-crisis

Both of Carter's Republican successors in the White House, Reagan (1981–89) and Bush (1989–93), perceived the revised Panama Canal treaties as an affront to U.S. primacy in the Western Hemisphere, an infringement of U.S. national security, and a threat to basic U.S. interests in the Caribbean. Moreover, during the last year of Reagan's presidency and the first two years of the Bush administration, Washington made persistent efforts to remove General Manuel Noriega, successor to Torrijos, from his dominant position in Panama's military and its political system.

The U.S. campaign to oust General Noriega began in February 1988 with the imposition of economic sanctions on Panama. In July Reagan considered covert military action against Noriega, but the U.S. Senate Intelligence Committee objected and aborted the plan. Bush continued Reagan's policy; and in April 1989 he called for free elections in Panama. These were held on 7 May; but the results were nullified on the 10th. The next day Bush announced further economic measures against Panama: sanctions had seriously undermined Panama's economy by then.

An attempted coup against Noriega on 3 October 1989 failed. Five days later Secretary of State Baker confirmed U.S. complicity in that covert act. In short, the U.S. invasion of Panama in December 1989 was the culmination of a prolonged U.S. covert campaign, which coincided with a two-and-a-half–year domestic political crisis within Panama.

Crisis
A crisis for the U.S. was triggered by an official statement in Panama City on 15 December proclaiming Noriega head of government. The next day a U.S. marine was killed by Panamanian soldiers. And Panamanian officials issued a declaration of a state of war with the United States. (Many critics, within the U.S. and abroad, regarded these events as a pretext for a long-planned invasion.)

Washington enunciated four reasons for the invasion: to safeguard the lives of U.S. citizens in Panama; to defend democracy in Panama; to apprehend Noriega and to bring him to trial on charges of direct involvement in drug trafficking from South America to the United States; and to ensure the integrity of the Panama Canal treaties.

The decision to intervene was made by President Bush on 17 December. Its implementation, through an invasion force of 26,000 troops on the 20th in "Operation Just Cause," triggered a crisis for Panama. On 21 December Panama's church leaders, guardians of the May 1989 election results, proposed that the winning candidate, Endara, be proclaimed President. This occurred after Noriega's surrender on 3 January, following an intense 12-day military campaign against him and his National Guard. This marked the end of the Invasion of Panama crisis.

Both the USSR and the *OAS* condemned U.S. military action. So too did the UN: on 29 December the General Assembly adopted a resolution deploring the U.S. intervention as a violation of international law.

(Noriega was flown to Florida for a lengthy detention and trial, leading to long-term imprisonment. U.S. economic sanctions against Panama were lifted; and in May 1990 the U.S. Congress approved a $420 million aid package to support the new Endara regime. However, during the next five years Panama's leaders frequently complained about the niggardly transfer of aid funds from the U.S.)

(See *Master Table,* pp. 734–35.)

Sources
Amer 1992; Baker 1995; Carter 1982; Dinges 1991; Donnelly et al. 1991;
Flanagan 1993; *Keesing's* 1989, 1990; *New York Times* 1989, 1990; Scranton
1991, 1992; Shultz 1993; Vertzberger 1997; Watson and Tsouras 1990; Weeks
and Zimbalist 1989.

(400) Ecuador/Peru Border IV, 1991 (see Ecuador/Peru PC)

(411) Haiti Military Regime

The United States and Haiti were embroiled in a crisis from mid-July to 15
October 1994.

Background and Pre-crisis
For most of its history Haiti was ruled by a foreign power. It was a colony of
Spain from the earliest days of European contact with the Americas at the end of
the fifteenth century. It was ceded to France in 1697 and remained a French
colony until a successful slave revolt and victory over a large French army sent
by Napoleon, leading to independence in 1804.

After a century of Haiti's isolation, the U.S. became the hegemonial power.
It began with the landing of marines in 1915 and an imposed treaty that made
Haiti a political and financial protectorate of the United States, initially for 10
years and then extended to 1936. Thereafter Haiti was ruled by despots, notably
the Duvaliers, father and son, from 1957 to 1990.

In the first democratic elections, held on 16 December 1990, Father Jean
Bertrand Aristide, a left-wing Roman Catholic priest, was elected President.
However, less than a year later (30 September 1991) he was ousted by a military
junta headed by Lieutenant-General Raoul Cedras. All attempts to restore Aristide to power failed, including an agreement to step down, brokered by the U.S.
and signed by the junta on 3 July 1993 (Governors Island Agreement).

From 1991 to 1994 Haiti was characterized by brutal repression and violation of human rights, including the killing of 3,000 civilians by paramilitary
"death squads." In desperation, Haitians sought refuge in the U.S.—on a massive
scale: in one eight-day period, 1–9 July 1994, an estimated 12,300 "boat people"
were rescued and sent to makeshift camps in Panama and then to the U.S. naval
base in Cuba, Guantanamo Bay.

Crisis
It was this dramatic upsurge of refugees that triggered a crisis for the U.S.: the
potential—and likely—flood of Haitian boat people was perceived by the Clinton administration as a threat to domestic stability at a time when the U.S. was
still in the grip of economic recession. This concern was accentuated by the

image of U.S. impotence in the face of a military junta in the poorest and weakest state in the Americas resisting all efforts by the hegemonial power to restore democracy to the island. These themes were central to Clinton's announcement on 15 September 1994 of impending U.S. intervention (see below).

A major escalation point in the crisis was UN Security Council Resolution 940, passed on 31 July 1994 by 12–0, with two abstentions (Brazil and China) and one member absent (Rwanda): it authorized member-states "to use all necessary means to facilitate the departure from Haiti of the military leadership." The phrase, "all necessary means," was identical to the wording of the Security Council's authorizing resolution in the Gulf crisis of 1990 (see Case #393— **Gulf War,** in **Middle East: Non-PCs**). As in 1990, too, it was designed to legitimize U.S. military intervention, in this case to oust the junta from power in Haiti. (In both crises it served that purpose.) Resolution 940 also reaffirmed all nine earlier Council resolutions on Haiti, six in 1993, three in 1994, again following the precedent of the Council's Resolution 678 on 29 November 1990 during the Gulf crisis.

During the next six weeks attention shifted to the U.S. Congress and to public opinion: both seemed hostile or indifferent to military intervention, especially in light of the emergent fiasco of the U.S.'s humanitarian intervention in Somalia. (Before the intervention only 31 percent of the public approved sending troops to Haiti; and even after its success only 41 percent approved.) Fearful of taking a grave political risk and hoping to forge a consensus, the Clinton administration attempted one more type of peaceful crisis management, namely, an "unofficial" mediation effort by three high-profile Americans, former President Carter, former Chairman of the Joint Chiefs of Staff, General Powell, and Senator Nunn, chairman of the Senate Armed Services Committee.

Their mission to Haiti on 16 September led to an agreement with the junta two days later, which provided the framework for non-violent crisis resolution. The three members of the junta, Cedras, his chief of staff, Brigadier-General Philippe Blamby, and Colonel Michel François, the chief of police, were to step down and leave Haiti. President Aristide was to be restored to power. And UN economic sanctions on Haiti, including a crippling trade embargo, were to be lifted.

What made the agreement possible was a strong public statement by Clinton on 15 September: in an address to the nation the president announced the decision to intervene militarily, linking it to the Monroe and Truman Doctrines. It was, he said, designed "to protect U.S. interests," which were specified as putting an end to the atrocities on the island, "to secure our borders and preserve stability in our hemisphere, and to promote democracy and uphold the reliability of our commitment around the world." He also announced the Carter mediation mission as a willingness "to go the final mile" in an effort to resolve the crisis without violence. He was unequivocal that the mission was not going to negotiate with the junta but merely to settle the modalities for their departure from power and from Haiti.

The Clinton announcement of an imminent invasion triggered a crisis for

Haiti, that is, the military junta. Only then did it perceive U.S. resolve to compel their abdication from power and their departure from Haiti. Their response was to accept these terms in the negotiations with the Carter mission from 16–18 September.

With the Carter-brokered agreement in hand, 20,000 U.S. troops landed in Haiti in the following week, with a mandate to remain up to six months, if necessary. They rapidly took control of the island, with virtually no opposition and minuscule violence. Cedras resigned as commander in chief of Haiti's armed forces on 10 October. Three days later he and Blamby left for Panama; François had already fled to the Dominican Republic. Finally, with much fanfare, Aristide returned to the island and the president's palace on 15 October, marking the end of the Haiti Military Regime crisis.

(See Master Table, pp. 736–37.)

Sources
Bemis 1943; *New York Times* July–November 1994.

Asia: Non-Protracted Conflict (PC) Crises

There were 90 international crises in Asia from the end of World War I to the end of 1994, almost 22 percent of the total number of cases, 412. Seventy-five percent of the crises in Asia occurred within the setting of a protracted conflict, 25 percent in a non-PC context.

There were several notable PCs in Asia: two long-war PCs, Indochina from 1946 to 1989 and the Sino/Japanese long-war PC from the onset of Japanese incursions into mainland China in 1927 until the end of World War II. The longest, still unresolved, protracted conflict is between India and Pakistan since both attained independence in 1947.

Among the best-known and/or most important crises in Asia are the following: **Marco Polo Bridge,** in 1937–38 (Case #56); **Pearl Harbor** and **Hiroshima-Nagasaki,** during World War II (Cases #88, 107); the **China Civil War,** in 1948–49 (Case #125); the **Korean War** crises, from 1950–53 (Cases #132, 133, 140); the first **Taiwan Strait** crisis, in 1954–55 (Case #146); the **China/India Border** crisis-war, in 1962–63 (Case #194); several Vietnam War cases, notably the **Gulf of Tonkin,** in 1964, and the **Tet Offensive,** in 1968 (Cases #210, 225); the India/Pakistan crisis over **Bangladesh,** in 1971 (Case #242); the Soviet **Afghanistan Invasion** crisis, in 1979–80 (Case #303); the **Kashmir III: India/Pakistan Nuclear** crisis in 1990 (Case #392); and the **North Korea Nuclear Crisis,** in 1993–94 (Case #408). (See *Master Table*). Overall, Asia resembles Europe much more than Africa or the Americas in the scope, variety, and intensity of its international crises in the twentieth century.

Of the 90 international crises in Asia, only the 22 non-PC cases are discussed in this section. The rest are examined within the context of the seven protracted conflicts in Asia, as noted in the introduction to Part III, "Cases." Among these, the long-war PC crises are concentrated in two clusters, the **Indochina** and **China/Japan PCs.** All the PC crises are noted in the following pages, with an indication of where, in Part III, they are presented in detail.

(1) Russian Civil War I: Siberia, 1918–20 (see Multiregional PCs: East/West)

(8) Third Afghan War

A crisis-war between Afghanistan and the U.K., acting through British India, lasted from 15 April until 8 August 1919.

Background

Modern Afghanistan emerged in 1747 as a loose union of previously autonomous tribes. From the outset its geography—a landlocked state in Central Asia between czarist Russia and British India—shaped its foreign policy. After a phase of expansion (1747–1800) and a period of foreign conflict, with Persia (Iran), the Sikh Empire in the Punjab, Russia, and India (1800–80), Afghanistan under Amir Abdur Rahman (1880–1901) accepted British tutelage in foreign affairs. This protectorate status continued under Amir Habibullah (1901–19), who tried, but failed, to secure London's acquiescence in full independence in return for Afghan neutrality during World War I.

Pre-crisis

On 2 February 1919 Habibullah wrote to the Viceroy of India, Lord Chelmsford, seeking Afghan representation at the Paris Peace Conference and recognition of Afghanistan's "absolute liberty, freedom of action and perpetual independence." The negative response from Delhi contributed to his growing unpopularity, which led to his assassination on 19 February. In the struggle for succession his son Amir Amanullah assumed the throne. On 3 March he reiterated the demand for recognition of "our independent and free Government of Afghanistan," in a letter to the viceroy of India. He repeated this in a public proclamation a few days later and again on 13 April at a public *darbar,* or court reception, attended by the British agent in Kabul.

Crisis

The viceroy's reply to Amanullah's letter of 3 March, sent on 15 April, reaffirmed the protectorate status quo: "the alliance between the two Governments . . . is based on the treaties and engagements" undertaken by his two predecessors. This rebuff initiated a crisis for Afghanistan. Amanullah responded at once by moving regular Afghan forces to the frontier with India: they arrived at the Khyber Pass on 2 May; and a skirmish with the Khyber Rifles occurred the next day. On the 4th Afghan troops cut the water supply to Landi Kotal, triggering a crisis for the U.K. Britain retaliated by closing the Khyber Pass. The viceroy wrote again on the 4th offering the amir an opportunity to disclaim responsibility for initiating hostilities, but it was too late. During 5–6 May Afghan forces occupied the towns of Kalat-I-Ghilzai and Khost. On the 9th British Indian forces counterattacked in the Khyber area.

Afghan forces suffered several setbacks during the next few weeks. As a result Amanullah sought negotiations for a cease-fire, which began in mid-June. Peace talks commenced in Rawalpindi, India, on 25 July. And a formal agreement was signed on 8 August 1919. Afghanistan's independence in foreign policy was acknowledged but the U.K.'s special status was reaffirmed. Thus ended the brief Third Afghan War and the international crisis for Afghanistan and the U.K.

(Formal recognition of complete Afghan independence from the British

Empire was accorded at the Kabul Conference, which ended on 8 December 1921.)
There was no global organization at the time of this crisis.
(See *Master Table*, pp. 666–67.)

Sources
Adamec 1967, 1974; Cmd. Paper 324 1919; Dupree 1980; Maprayil 1983; Molesworth 1962; Poullada 1973; Stewart 1973; Toynbee 1927a.

(35) Shantung, 1927–29 (see China/Japan PC)

(38) Chinese Eastern Railway

A crisis between the USSR and China over the Chinese Eastern Railway *(CER)* began on 10 July and ended on 22 December 1929.

Background and Pre-crisis
Under the terms of a Sino-Russian secret treaty in 1896, China consented to the construction and operation of the Chinese Eastern Railway across Manchuria by the Russian-controlled Russo-Chinese bank. In 1924 an agreement was signed between the USSR and China for the joint management of the *CER*. During the next three years the Soviets assumed near-total management of the vital railway, and proposals by the Chinese to alter the situation were rejected. Relations between the two states were strained, and an incident in 1927 in which the Soviet embassy in Peking (Beijing) was searched did not improve matters. In addition, Chinese Communist activities in the railway zone were facilitated by Soviet diplomatic channels.

On 27 May 1929 the Chinese raided the Soviet consulate in Harbin, arresting several of its officers and railway employees. Documents seized at the time were published in the Chinese press and pointed to Soviet interference in China. The provincial government, acting in the railway area on the authority of China's national government, ordered the takeover of the *CER* and assumed its management, occupied USSR institutions, and arrested Soviet railway officials and citizens. A formal protest by Moscow on 31 May included demands for the immediate release of prisoners and the return of documents and property that, if not met, would incur the withdrawal of diplomatic privileges to Chinese personnel in the Soviet Union.

Crisis
On 10 July 1929 a crisis was triggered for the USSR: Chinese Nationalists, in cooperation with Marshal Chang Hseuh-liang, the ruler of Manchuria, seized the Chinese Eastern Railway, arresting a number of Russian administrators of the railway and closing their offices. The Soviet ambassador responded with an ultimatum on the 13th demanding the full restoration of the status quo ante vis-

à-vis the *CER*. The Chinese were given three days to respond and to agree to a conference to settle problems involving the railway. Perceiving a threat to its political regime, China responded to the crisis with counterdemands on 16 July. Moscow broke off diplomatic relations on the 19th and sent troops to the border. Military preparations were also made by the Chinese, who published a manifesto alleging Soviet transgressions of the 1924 agreement. Meetings between the Soviet consul in Harbin and Chinese officials took place on 24 and 28 July and 2 August. Soviet raids into Chinese territory occurred throughout the discussions. When proposals advanced by each side were rejected by the other, the crisis escalated to violence.

On 12 August Soviet troops occupied three strategic towns in China near the border. Six thousand Chinese troops were mobilized on the 15th. Serious clashes occurred. By late December the Soviet advance threatened Harbin. Under duress, China signed a protocol on 22 December 1929 capitulating to Moscow's demands. This terminated both parties' foreign policy crises and the international crisis over the Chinese Eastern Railway.

Germany approached the Soviet Union on China's behalf in August and offered its good offices to settle the dispute. In October German attempts to conciliate were once more unsuccessful. During the crisis the United States, Britain, and France sent Notes to both belligerents requesting a halt to military activities. China responded favorably, but the USSR refused any third party mediation. A Japanese recommendation for talks at the local level, too, failed to produce any results.

The League of Nations was not involved in this crisis.
(See *Master Table*, pp. 672–73.)

Sources
Cameron et al. 1952; Clyde 1958; MacNair and Lach 1955; Thorne 1972; Vinacke 1959; Wu 1950.

(39) Mukden Incident, 1931–32 (see China/Japan PC)

(40) Shanghai, 1932 (see China/Japan PC)

(43) Jehol Campaign, 1933 (see China/Japan PC)

(55) Amur River Incident

A crisis between Japan and the USSR took place from 22 June to 4 July 1937.

Background and Pre-crisis
The issue of sovereignty over several small islands in the Amur River between the Soviet Union and Japanese-controlled Manchuria (Manchukuo) had long

been in dispute: the crisis in 1937 was the 185th incident of its kind along this border. Between August 1936 and June 1937 a series of political trials and severe purges took place in the Soviet Union. Some persons who stood trial were executed because of alleged espionage on behalf of the Japanese. Many of the top-ranking Soviet officers stationed in the Far Eastern territories were removed. Inter alia, the Japanese wished to test Soviet strength and determination, as well as its readiness for war. On 19 June 1937 a small number of Soviet troops entered the two islets of Sennufu and Bolshoi on the Amur and abducted some gold miners. The same day Soviet gunboats, which routinely patrolled the area, engaged Manchukuon forces.

Crisis
On 22 June Japan's General Staff received reports of Soviet military occupation of the disputed islands: these reports triggered a crisis for Japan. It responded on the 24th with an order to concentrate troops in the area and a protest to the Soviet consul-general at Harbin. The trigger to the crisis for the Soviet Union, on 28 June, was a demand, delivered by the Japanese ambassador in Moscow, that all Soviet forces be evacuated from the islands. On 29 June forces of Japan's Kwantung Army bombed and sank a Soviet gunboat, apparently at the initiative of the local field commander. That day Soviet negotiators indicated a willingness to remove their troops, and, on 2 July, the USSR announced that it would comply with Japanese demands. The crisis ended for both actors on 4 July, with the Soviet evacuation of the islands. Four days later the Sino/Japanese War broke out. This crisis was not brought before the League of Nations.
(See *Master Table*, pp. 674–75.)

Sources
See sources for Case #72; and Hane 1972; MacNair and Lach 1955; Vinacke 1959.

(56) Marco Polo Bridge, 1937–38 (see China/Japan PC)

(59) Panay Incident

The sinking of the USS *Panay* near Nanjing (Nanking) caused a crisis for the United States from 12 to 26 December 1937.

Pre-crisis
The Sino/Japanese conflict resulted in a mounting threat to the treaty rights and interests of Britain, France, and the United States in China. On 27 November 1937, as the fighting between the Chinese and Japanese armies drew close to the city of Nanking, U.S. Ambassador Johnson moved most of his staff to Hankow. The few U.S. officials remaining in the capital were to be evacuated by the U.S.

gunboat *Panay*, which had been ordered to stand by. On 9 December embassy personnel boarded the USS *Panay*, and, three days later, it docked about 28 miles above Nanking, along with three Standard Oil Company tankers.

Crisis

A crisis for the United States was triggered on 12 December 1937 when Japanese planes bombed and sank the *Panay*, along with the three Standard Oil Company ships. Japan's Foreign Minister, Hirota, expressed his apologies to the U.S. ambassador in Tokyo. In Washington, Japan's Ambassador, Saito, did likewise to Secretary of State Hull. President Roosevelt responded the following day with a message to Tokyo via Secretary Hull, expressing shock at the indiscriminate bombings and requesting that the emperor be informed of the president's response. Hull urged that Tokyo extend a full expression of regret and compensation. Further, the U.S. demanded guarantees from Japan that such incidents would not occur again.

As reports from China indicated that the Japanese attacks had been deliberate, indignation grew in Washington. On 17 December the U.S. cabinet met, and strong action was proposed by several members, especially Secretary of the Navy Claude Swanson. Roosevelt expressed concern at Chinese reaction if the assault went unrebuked, and asserted that a stronger response was necessary in order to foil a Japanese plan to force all Westerners out of Japan. An economic blockade was suggested, but no decision was made.

On 23 December a U.S. Board of Inquiry reported that the shelling of the *Panay* seemed to have been deliberate and premeditated. The following day, Hirota handed U.S. Ambassador Grew a Note admitting responsibility, offering amends, and giving assurances against reoccurrence of such an incident. The crisis ended for the United States with its formal acceptance of the Japanese Note on 26 December. The Roosevelt administration expressed satisfaction with Japan's apology and the latter's acceptance of all U.S. demands.

Toward the end of the crisis a U.S. naval officer was sent to London for technical discussions that would apply in the event that both countries declared war on Japan.

This crisis did not come before the League of Nations.

(See *Master Table*, pp. 676–77.)

Sources

Foreign Relations of the United States (FRUS), Japan 1931–1941, vol. I; Borg 1964; Craigie 1946; Grew 1953; Hull 1948, vol. I; Ickes 1974; Jones 1954; Lee 1973; MacNair and Lash 1955.

(63) Changkufeng

A crisis between Japan and the USSR over an incident at Lake Hasan occurred between 13 July and 11 August 1938.

Background and Pre-crisis
Both Soviet and Japanese border garrisons had been posted in the area of Lake Hasan (Changkufeng) on the Soviet-Manchukuo frontier since the initial Japanese occupation of Manchuria in 1931. Between 1935 and 1938 there were more than 50 border incidents among Soviet, Japanese, and Manchukuon forces, almost all minor skirmishes. Due to the complex terrain there were many areas where the frontier was not clear, including the Changkufeng hill area. In October 1937 there had been a minor clash in the vicinity, but Changkufeng itself was not involved. On 7 July 1938 local Japanese commanders received information of Soviet intentions to occupy the area, and on 11 July about 40 Soviet soldiers appeared atop Changkufeng and began construction of new fortified positions.

Crisis
On 13 July imperial headquarters in Tokyo perceived a crisis for Japan when they received information attesting to Soviet occupation of, and activity at, Changkufeng. The Korean army headquarters were also informed on that day. Both armies were preparing for a major campaign at Hangchow in the Sino/Japanese War, and their respective headquarters did not wish an escalation of the situation near Lake Hasan. The Japanese local commanders, seemingly acting independently, met the Soviet activity with military force. The major fighting began on 27 July, but there was no evidence to suggest official sanction by either a supreme military or civil decision-making body in Japan.

On 29 July the Soviets crossed the frontier at Shatsofeng, near Changkufeng, and began to construct positions there. On 31 July the Soviet Union perceived a crisis when its forces were involved in heavy fighting. The Soviets responded with a major counterattack on 2 August, the same day that Japan's major response occurred: the Japanese cabinet decided to settle the dispute through negotiation. Indeed, Japan's civilian authorities had been endeavoring to remove any possibility of further military clashes by ordering the withdrawal of Japanese troops from the area. Between 4 and 11 August Ambassador Shigemitsu and Foreign Affairs Commissar Litvinov met to discuss the possibilities of a peaceful settlement. By 7 August heavy artillery pieces were being employed by the Soviet forces as fighting continued. On 10 August Litvinov proposed a truce, which came into effect the following day, terminating the crisis for both actors.

This crisis was not submitted to the League of Nations.

(See *Master Table*, pp. 676–77.)

Sources
See sources for Case #72.

(72) Nomonhan

A crisis for the Soviet Union and Japan arising from an incident at Nomonhan occurred between 28 May and 15 September 1939.

Background
Nomonhan is an oasis in the Gobi Desert whose pastures have been used for centuries by Mongol nomads. The territory, partly under Japanese and partly under Soviet control in the 1930s, was inhabited by Mongols. Japanese troops were engaged as allies of Manchukuo, by virtue of the 1932 Japan-Manchukuo Treaty of Mutual Assistance; and Soviet forces were allies of Outer Mongolia under their 1936 Pact of Mutual Assistance. The Manchukuo government claimed that the Khalha River was the boundary between Manchukuo and Outer Mongolia, whereas the government of Outer Mongolia declared that the boundary lay a number of miles east of the river.

Crisis
On 28 May 1939 a clash took place on the Mongolia/Manchukuo border in which 39 Outer Mongolian planes were shot down and 150 Mongols killed by Japanese forces. This triggered a crisis for the Soviet Union, which perceived a territorial threat. Moscow warned Japan on the 31st that the Soviet Union would defend Outer Mongolia's borders as if they were its own. A counterattack by Soviet forces in the vicinity of Nomonhan on 18 June, accompanied by air attacks on key strategic points in the rear, triggered a crisis for Japan. The Japanese attacked again on 28 June. During July the Japanese military attaché in Moscow reported that the Soviets were sending reinforcements to the Far East and that a new offensive was expected around the middle of August. It was thought that Japanese strength in the area would be sufficient to halt an enemy offensive.

Fighting continued throughout July; the major Soviet response came on 20 August when Soviet-Mongolian troops inflicted a heavy defeat on the Japanese, including 17,000 casualties, a third of their forces in that battle. They were subsequently driven out of the disputed area. The major Japanese response, on 28 August, was a decision to commence discussions with the Soviets in Moscow without delay. All this occurred while Japan's Kwantung Army was planning a major counteroffensive with four fresh divisions. On the 30th an imperial order was sent to the Kwantung Army to desist from further operations in the Nomonhan area. After several days of negotiations, Foreign Ministers Togo and Molotov reached an agreement on 15 September 1939, providing for a cease-fire along the lines held that day and the setting up of a commission to settle the boundary problem.

This crisis did not come before the League of Nations.
(See *Master Table*, pp. 678–79.)

Sources
Coox 1977; Dallin 1948; Ikuhiko 1976; Jones 1954; Kutakov 1972; Maxon 1957; Wu 1950.

(73) Tientsin

An international crisis for the U.K. over Tientsin began on 14 June 1939 and terminated effectively on 29 August of that year.

Background and Pre-crisis
After Japan's proclamation of "The Greater East Asia Co-Prosperity Sphere," on 3 November 1938, Tokyo concentrated on tightening its hold over the occupied areas of China and on undermining China's currency. Japan put pressure on the International Settlements in Shanghai and Amoy, and the British Concession at Tientsin, maintaining that these foreign enclaves were blocking the absorption of occupied China into "A New Order of East Asia." The Japanese had four main grievances against Britain at Tientsin: the Chinese guerrillas allegedly used the British Concession as a base to launch anti-Japanese attacks and propaganda; circulation of the Chinese currency was allowed; the British banks refused to accept the Japanese-sponsored Peking (Beijing) regime's Federal Reserve Bank notes; and, finally, that silver reserves deposited by Chinese government banks in Tientsin were not reported to the Japanese authorities.

On 9 April 1939 an official of the Peking puppet regime was assassinated within the British Concession in Tientsin. Two of the arrested suspects confessed under Japanese interrogation but retracted when they were handed over to the British. When the British authorities in Tientsin refused to place the suspects under the jurisdiction of the pro-Japanese Peking regime for a trial, Japan sent the U.K. an ultimatum. Britain proposed an advisory committee to deal with the problem, but Japan refused.

Crisis
On 14 June 1939 a crisis was triggered for the U.K. when Japan imposed a blockade on the British and French Concessions in Tientsin, cutting off supplies and harassing persons entering and leaving the Concessions. Japan then demanded Britain's abandonment of the Chinese national government and its cooperation with the "New Order." London received information that the Japanese General Staff had plans for war with Britain that were supported by a faction of the Japanese army.

The Tientsin issue was discussed by the British cabinet on 14 June, when Foreign Secretary Halifax suggested serious consideration of economic sanctions, but this was postponed. While Halifax advocated retaliatory measures, a report from the Colonial Board of Trade and foreign office was issued advising against them. On the 18th a report from Britain's chief of staff concluded that it would not be justifiable to take any action that might lead to hostilities with Japan. On 19 June the foreign secretary authorized Ambassador Craigie to propose conducting negotiations over Tientsin in Tokyo. This was accepted by Japan on the 23rd. On 15 July Japan's prime minister proposed a formula in which British assistance to China would be withheld during the large-scale Japanese military operations. On the 24th the Craigie-Arita Agreement was reached between the two governments providing for British recognition of the "actual situation in China" and stating that British officials and subjects would be instructed to refrain from obstructing the Japanese army.

The Tokyo conference on the Tientsin issue opened on 27 July, with quick agreement on the proposals dealing with the restoration and maintenance of order in Tientsin. Negotiations reached an impasse on economic issues. The conference was adjourned on 20 August. The following day the British foreign office circulated a paper in which Britain declared that, in the event of hostilities with Japan, it would denounce the Anglo-Japanese Commercial Treaty, nationals would be evacuated from North China, and economic steps would be instituted against Japan. On that day, as well, Japan was stunned by the announcement of the German/Soviet Non-Aggression Pact (see Case #74—**Entry into World War II, in World War II PC**). Japan was at that time engaged in large-scale fighting against Soviet troops at **Nomonhan** (see Case #72 above). The Pact enabled the USSR to concentrate on the East Asian situation without fear for its European flank. After the fall of the Hiranuma government, the silver and currency questions lapsed and the danger of an Anglo/Japanese war became less probable. On 26 August a formula was suggested by the Japanese embassy in London, to which Halifax agreed on the 29th. The outbreak of war in Europe in September, however, prevented a formal agreement. A British attempt to get U.S. backing resulted in a Roosevelt statement on 26 July giving notice to Japan of the U.S.'s intention to terminate the U.S.-Japan Commercial Treaty of 1911.

The League of Nations was not involved in this crisis.

(See *Master Table*, pp. 678–79.)

Sources
See sources for Case #59.

(79) Closure—Burma Road, 1940 (see Multiregional PCs: World War II)

(88) Pearl Harbor, 1941–42 (see Multiregional PCs: World War II)

(95) Fall of Saipan, 1944 (see Multiregional PCs: World War II)

(97) Leyte Campaign, 1944 (see Multiregional PCs: World War II)

(99) Luzon, 1945 (see Multiregional PCs: World War II)

(101) Iwo Jima, 1945 (see Multiregional PCs: World War II)

(103) Okinawa, 1945 (see Multiregional PCs: World War II)

(107) Hiroshima-Nagasaki, 1945 (see Multiregional PCs: World War II)

(109) Indonesia Independence I, 1945–47 (see Indonesia PC)

(116) Indonesia Independence II, 1947–48 (see Indonesia PC)

(118) Junagadh, 1947–48 (see India/Pakistan PC)

(119) Kashmir I, 1947–49 (see India/Pakistan PC)

(124) Hyderabad, 1948 (see India/Pakistan PC)

(125) China Civil War, 1948–49 (see Taiwan Strait PC)

(127) Indonesia Independence III, 1948–49 (see Indonesia PC)

(129) Pushtunistan I, 1949–50 (see Afghanistan/Pakistan PC)

(132) Korean War I, 1950 (see Korea PC)

(133) Korean War II, 1950–51 (see Korea PC)

(135) Punjab War Scare I, 1951 (see India/Pakistan PC)

(138) Infiltration into Burma

A crisis for Burma over Chinese Nationalist troops on its territory occurred between 8 February 1953 and 15 October 1954.

Background

In 1949 *Kuomintang* (*KMT,* Chinese Nationalist) forces, who had retreated to southern China during the **China Civil War** (see Case #125, in **Taiwan Strait PC**), crossed into Burma as the Chinese Communists consolidated their position in the south. *KMT* forces, commanded by General Li Mi, occupied part of the Burmese state of Kengtung, which adjoined China and Thailand, and became an intolerable nuisance to Burma because of their alliance with, and supply of arms to, the local insurgents. They also served as a possible provocation for a Chinese Communist incursion into Burmese territory and drew 12,000 Chinese forces into an uncomfortable proximity to the border. By 1952 air drops and supplies from foreign air bases became frequent and blatant.

Crisis

On 8 February 1953 a crisis was triggered for Burma when local insurgents combined with 300 *KMT* troops to attack Loikaw, the capital of the state of Kayah. Additional attacks occurred on the 11th and 27th at other Burmese locations. Documents showed that the intention of the *KMT* was to overthrow the Union of Burma government. Burma contended that the *KMT* forces were being supplied by Nationalist-held Taiwan, with tacit U.S. agreement. Prime Minister U Nu responded to the threat to his regime with a statement on 2 March that his government intended to take the *KMT* question to the United Nations. On 17 March Burma notified the United States that their assistance agreements would be terminated by June. This step was taken so that the government would not be accused of complacency on the *KMT* issue due to its obligations to Washington.

Burma submitted a complaint to the Secretary-General of the UN on the 25th, and on the 31st requested that it be placed on the General Assembly agenda for debate. A resolution was introduced on 17 April condemning the Nationalist Chinese government and indicating necessary steps to disarm and withdraw the *KMT* troops from Burma. On the 21st the General Assembly adopted a resolution condemning the presence of foreign troops in Burma and insisting upon their withdrawal. The U.S. proposed a conference with Burma, Nationalist China, and Thailand to discuss the withdrawal of the *KMT* forces.

A four-nation Joint Military Commission under UN auspices was formed and met on 22 May 1953. Negotiations, as well as serious clashes between Burma and *KMT* troops, continued throughout the summer. Burma withdrew from the talks on 17 September. Eventually 7,000 *KMT* troops were airlifted to Nationalist China between November 1953 and May 1954. On 30 May General Li Mi announced the formal dissolution of his Yunnan anti-communist army and, on 30 July, the Joint Military Commission announced in Burma that its program had been completed. About 6,000 guerrillas remained in Burma.

Burma submitted a new request to the UN Secretary-General on 20 August, and on the 29th of September a report on the situation was submitted to the UN stating that Burma viewed the continued presence of Chinese Nationalist troops in its territory as a threat. On 15 October 1954 Burma's representative acknowledged that the partial removal of *KMT* troops "represented the limit of what could be accomplished by international action." The crisis terminated that day with a Burmese statement that the removal of foreign troops from its territory would be its responsibility alone.

The USSR was not involved.

(*KMT* troops, with U.S. and Taiwan aid, continued their operations in Burma until 1961 when they were finally driven into Thailand and Laos by the Burmese army.)

(See *Master Table*, pp. 690–91.)

Sources
Johnstone 1963; Maung 1969.

(139) Invasion of Laos I, 1953 (see Indochina PC)

(140) Korean War III, 1953 (see Korea PC)

(145) Dien Bien Phu, 1954 (see Indochina PC)

(146) Taiwan Strait I, 1954–55 (see Taiwan Strait PC)

(150) Pushtunistan II, 1955 (see Afghanistan/Pakistan PC)

(151) Goa I

The first Goa crisis for Portugal began on 10 August and lasted until 6 September 1955.

Background and Pre-crisis
After the British withdrawal from India in 1947 Portugal continued to reject all Indian requests for the reunification of its enclaves on the west coast of India into the Republic of India. This led to the closing of the Indian legation in Lisbon in June 1953.

Intensification of nationalist agitation within India, as well as within Portugal's enclaves, began in mid-1954 and resulted in mass arrests, curfews, and expulsions. In July of that year Dadra, Nagar Haveli, and Damao were seized by "Free Goan volunteers." The Indian government refused passage to Portuguese forces to reinstate control over these areas. The mass entry of "volunteers" into Goa in May and June became the symbol of a campaign for the peaceful liberation of Goa.

Crisis
On 10 August 1955 it was announced that, despite Nehru's disapproval, Indian "volunteers" would march into Goa in a peaceful mass invasion on 15 August,

India's Independence Day. This announcement triggered a crisis for Portugal, which responded by moving army units to the Indian/Goan border and sending its chief of staff to Goa. Prime Minister Cunha called upon the Indian government to ban the march.

On 15 August about 3,000 Indian demonstrators marched across the Goan border. Portuguese police and soldiers opened fire killing 20 and wounding many more. Lisbon protested to New Delhi on the 17th, accusing it of violating Portugal's sovereignty. India broke diplomatic relations with Portugal on the 19th.

On 4 September the All-India Congress Committee, the legislative body of India's governing Congress Party, declared that in the present situation it would be inappropriate for Indian nationals to enter Goa. This crisis ended on 6 September when Indian Prime Minister Nehru stated in parliament that India had no intention of taking any warlike measures over Goa. A second crisis over Goa erupted in 1961 (see Case #190 below).

The UN, the U.S., and the USSR were not involved in this crisis.

(See *Master Table*, pp. 692–93.)

Sources
See sources for Case #190.

(161) West Irian I, 1957 (see Indonesia PC)

(164) Abortive Coup Indonesia, 1958 (see Indonesia PC)

(166) Taiwan Strait II, 1958 (see Taiwan Strait PC)

(167) Cambodia/Thailand, 1958–59 (see Indochina PC)

(171) China/India Border I

A border crisis for the PRC and India began on 25 August 1959 and ended on 19 April 1960.

Background
The basis of India's claim to the North East Frontier Agency (NEFA) was the Simla Agreement of 1914 between British India and the semiautonomous Tibet government, and the accompanying McMahon Line. Although initialed by the representative of the central Chinese government, this agreement was not formally ratified by China then or later. The border issue was accentuated in 1958 when the Chinese Communist regime completed the construction of the Aksai Chin road in the state of Jammu and Kashmir in the west, linking Tibet to China's province of Sinkiang.

Crisis

On 25 August 1959 Indian patrols in the region of Longju, NEFA, were perceived by the PRC as challenging its version of where that border village lay— on the Indian or Chinese side. The PRC, perceiving a threat, responded that day by attacking Indian positions at Longju. This attack triggered a crisis for India. On the 28th Prime Minister Nehru informed the *Lok Sabha,* the lower house of India's parliament, that a Chinese detachment of 200–300 men had crossed into Indian territory at Longju three days earlier. At the same time he revealed correspondence between the two governments since 1954 on alleged Chinese border violations and other issues in Sino/Indian relations. On 20 October 1959 another incident occurred at the Kongka Pass in the Ladakh area of northeast Kashmir. In addition, China's Premier Zhou Enlai explicitly refused to recognize the existing McMahon Line and claimed large tracts of NEFA's territory.

India's response, on 1 November 1959, was an announcement by Nehru that the Indian army would assume control of the border posts in Ladakh, Kashmir, from police detachments. Nehru described those border incidents as challenges by China to India's territorial integrity. PRC suggestions for negotiations were followed by a series of letters between Nehru and Zhou Enlai. A meeting between the two leaders, convened on 19 April 1960, ended this initial crisis. The meetings led to the creation of a Joint Officials Committee to examine relevant documents and to report points of disagreement and agreement.

Superpower involvement was limited to diplomatic activity. The United States expressed strong sympathy for India's attempts to resolve the issue peacefully. The Soviets adopted a neutral position, which was viewed unfavorably by the PRC. (See Case #194—**China/India Border II** below.)

The UN was not involved in this crisis.

(See *Master Table,* pp. 696–97.)

Sources
See sources for Case #194; and Liu 1994.

(180) Pathet Lao Offensive, 1961 (see Indochina PC)

(182) Pushtunistan III, 1961–62 (see Afghanistan/Pakistan PC)

(186) Vietcong Attack, 1961 (see Indochina PC)

(187) West Irian II, 1961–62 (see Indonesia PC)

(190) Goa II

A second crisis for Portugal over Goa lasted from 11 to 19 December 1961.

Pre-crisis
There had been relative inactivity since Portugal's first crisis with India over **Goa** in 1955 (see Case #151 above). In April 1961 a bill was passed by the Indian Parliament enabling the merger of Dadra and Nagar Haveli with the Indian Union. During the debate Nehru stated that he did not rule out sending the Indian army into Goa. He repeated this warning in October. Meanwhile, Indian public opinion began demanding that more active steps be taken toward the integration of Goa. Tension between India and Portugal escalated with the reported buildup of Portuguese military strength in Goa, and, on 17 and 24 November, Indian ships were shot at from the Portuguese island of Anjadev. India announced, on 5 December, that precautionary troop movements were taking place. On 8 December Portugal charged that the Indian buildup threatened peace in the area and suggested that international observers be sent. Portugal appealed to the UN Security Council on 9 December.

Crisis
Portugal's crisis was triggered by a Nehru statement on 11 December that Indian patience was at an end and that he hoped the Portuguese would withdraw from Goa and the two smaller Portuguese enclaves, Damas and Diu. Portugal responded the same day by informing the UN Security Council that Indian forces were massing along the border and were ready to invade Goa. On 12 December Portugal announced that it had decided to evacuate European women and children from the disputed area in view of an imminent Indian attack: information received by Portugal anticipated an attack on 15 December. On that day UN Secretary-General U Thant sent a message to the prime ministers of India and Portugal requesting them not to allow the situation to deteriorate and proposing negotiations. Salazar acceded to the Secretary-General's request, but Nehru replied with a demand that Portugal leave Goa.

On 18 December 1961 Indian troops entered Goa. Portugal called for an urgent meeting of the Security Council. A resolution was introduced by Portugal's Western allies calling for a cease-fire, Indian withdrawal, and a peaceful settlement but it was defeated by a Soviet veto. The United States strongly criticized India's action. President Kennedy sent a message to Nehru urging that no force be used—U.S. ambassadors to Delhi and Lisbon had succeeded in postponing the invasion date a number of times.

The crisis for Portugal ended on 19 December 1961 with the entry of Indian troops and the signing of a surrender agreement ending four centuries of Portuguese rule over Goa.

(See *Master Table,* pp. 700–701.)

Sources
Brecher 1968; Dupree 1962; E. B. 1954; Galbraith 1969; Goodspeed 1967; Kaul 1967; Kay 1970; Marshall 1961; Maxwell 1970; Rao 1963; Rubinoff 1971; Salazar 1956; Wright 1962.

(192) Taiwan Strait III, 1962 (see Taiwan Strait PC)

(193) Nam Tha, 1962 (see Indochina PC)

(194) China/India Border II

A second border crisis between India and China, leading to full-scale war, began on 8 September 1962 and ended on 23 January 1963.

Background
Border clashes between India and China erupted into an international crisis in August 1959 (see Case #171—**China/India Border I** above). From 1960 to 1962 the dispute continued at a lower level of intensity until Chinese forces began to take control of more disputed territory in the Aksai Chin region, in the western sector. India demanded a return to the status quo ante as a condition for negotiations. The PRC refused and began to concentrate military forces on the northeast (NEFA) border. India continued with its "Forward Policy" in which military patrols attempted to establish posts in territories held or claimed by the Chinese.

Crisis
On 8 September 1962 Chinese forces crossed the Thag La Ridge on the McMahon Line, triggering India's perception of a threat to its territorial integrity, with a limited time to respond militarily due to the imminent approach of winter. The following day India began to plan "Operation Leghorn" to bring about the eviction of the Chinese. The beginning of its implementation on 4 October triggered a crisis for China, which perceived an imminent Indian military campaign beyond border incidents. On the same day China informed the Soviet chargé d'affaires in Beijing of India's plans. The PRC responded on 20 October with a massive simultaneous attack on the western and eastern sectors of the disputed frontier. That day Nehru received a letter from Khrushchev expressing concern at reports that India intended to settle the dispute militarily, warning of the inherent dangers and urging India to accept the Chinese proposals for talks. India's major response, on 24 October, was to take up the military option and to reject the PRC suggestion for mutual withdrawal to the 7 November 1959 "line of actual control," which would leave China in control of large tracts of disputed territory. On 29 October the U.S. ambassador in New Delhi offered U.S. military aid to India. So too did the U.K.

An intrawar crisis for India was triggered on 16 November with a second Chinese offensive. On the 19th Nehru appealed to President Kennedy to dispatch immediately 15 bomber and fighter squadrons to provide air cover for Indian cities against an anticipated Chinese attack. A U.S. aircraft carrier was ordered to leave its base in the Pacific and head toward the Bay of Bengal. Shortly thereafter the defeat of the Indian army was completed.

The crisis ended for China on 21 November when the PRC announced a unilateral cease-fire and, from 1 December, a withdrawal of Chinese forces 20 kilometers behind the actual control lines of 7 November 1959, in both the Aksai Chin (western sector) and the McMahon Line (eastern sector). That withdrawal date terminated India's IWC—but not yet its crisis as a whole.

Six Asian and African nonaligned states (Burma, Ceylon, Indonesia, Cambodia, Ghana, and the UAR [Egypt]) attempted mediation at the Colombo Conference in early January 1963. By the time India's *Lok Sabha* approved their proposals, on 23 January, the PRC had implemented its unilateral withdrawal, a de facto cease-fire was in place, and the crisis ended for India.

Australia, Canada, the U.K., and the U.S. sent aircraft and other military equipment to India. The USSR and Pakistan were peripherally involved.

(On 29 November 1996, 34 years after their border war, the presidents of India and China renounced the use of force to solve their territorial dispute, by pledging that "neither side shall use its military capability against the other." They also announced an agreement in principle on mutual withdrawal of forces from disputed areas along their 2,500 mile frontier, though details were deferred to further negotiations. It was a step toward resolution of the conflict between the world's two most populous states but less than final termination.)

The UN was not involved in this crisis.

(See *Master Table,* pp. 700–701.)

Sources
Barnds 1972; Bobrow et al. 1979; Brines 1968; Clubb 1972; Day 1987; Eekelen 1964; Fisher et al. 1963; Galbraith 1969; Gurtov and Hwang 1980; Hinton 1966; Hoffmann 1990; Kaul 1967; Kavic 1967; Lamb 1964; Maxwell 1970; Patterson 1964; Rowland 1967; Segal 1985; Thornton 1973; Vertzberger 1984; Whiting 1975a; Woodman 1969.

(197) Malaysia Federation

Malaysia (then Malaya) and Indonesia were crisis actors over the issue of the Malaysia Federation from 11 February 1963 until 9 August 1965.

Background
Malaya became an independent member of the (British) Commonwealth on 31 August 1957. Throughout the 1950s Great Britain attempted to create a viable political structure for its Southeast Asia colonies, to include Brunei, Malaya, Sabah (British Borneo), Sarawak, and Singapore. Plans for a Federation of Malaysia among these five political entities—an agreement was signed on 31 July 1962—conflicted with territorial claims of Indonesia and the Philippines. Hostility was first expressed in December 1962, when Indonesia covertly backed a revolt in Brunei for independence from the U.K. The rebellion was quelled within 10 days. Following this revolt, Indonesia's support became more open.

Crisis
The trigger to Malaya's crisis was President Sukarno's declaration on 11 February 1963 that Indonesia strongly opposed a Malaysia federation. Malaya responded two days later by announcing an immediate expansion of its armed forces. Talks between the U.K. and the five participating entities resulted in an agreement in London on 9 July 1963 for the formation of the Federation of Malaysia, which was signed by all except Brunei. This triggered a crisis for Indonesia. Its response, on 11 July, was a sharp statement of opposition claiming a violation of a 14 June 1963 agreement that a federation would be established only after the UN ascertained the wishes of the people involved. Tension declined on 5 August when a summit conference of Indonesian, Malayan, and Philippine heads of state agreed that the UN would ascertain the views of the people.

Tension was exacerbated on 14 September 1963 with the publication of the results indicating the people's preference for a Malaysia federation. The next day Indonesia declared that it would not recognize the Federation and recalled its ambassador to Kuala Lumpur. Malaya responded on 17 September by severing diplomatic ties with Indonesia and the Philippines. The U.S. suspended economic aid to Indonesia and sent Attorney-General Robert Kennedy to mediate, with no results. The International Monetary Fund then withdrew its offer of promised credit. The Soviet Union gave Indonesia only lukewarm political support. China supported Indonesia throughout the crisis.

As the confrontation faded, the crisis eased. Singapore seceded from Malaysia on 9 August 1965, an event that Indonesia viewed as the beginning of the breakup of the Federation, a "face-saver." Malaya, too, perceived a victory because Indonesia's confrontation policy ended without destroying the Federation.

UN involvement was limited to discussion.
(See *Master Table*, pp. 702–3.)

Sources
See sources for Case #187; and Allen 1968; Greene 1975; James and Small 1971; Mackie 1974.

(210) Gulf of Tonkin, 1964 (see Indochina PC)

(213) Pleiku, 1965 (see Indochina PC)

(214) Rann of Kutch, 1965 (see India/Pakistan PC)

(216) Kashmir II, 1965–66 (see India/Pakistan PC)

(224) Pueblo, 1968 (see Korea PC)

(225) Tet Offensive, 1968 (see Indochina PC)

(230) Vietnam Spring Offensive, 1969 (see Indochina PC)

(231) Ussuri River

There were many border incidents between the Soviet Union and China from the late 1950s onward. One reached crisis proportions, at the Ussuri River from 2 March to 20 October 1969.

Background and Pre-crisis
The ideological rivalry between the PRC and the USSR surfaced with Khrushchev's accession to power in the Soviet Union in 1955. His "de-Stalinization" speech at the 1956 Soviet Communist Party Congress exacerbated the rift. And an open split between Maoist China and post-Stalinist Russia crystallized at the conference of world Communist parties in 1960. Border talks in 1964 were unilaterally suspended by China. In 1965 the USSR initiated a military buildup along China's borders. The impact of China's traumatic Cultural Revolution in the late 1960s was still fresh. There had been large population transfers from urban to rural areas' in China. The **Prague Spring** crisis had terminated with a Soviet-bloc invasion of Czechoslovakia in August 1968 (see Case #227, in **Europe: Non-PCs**). And by 1969 Soviet preoccupation with Berlin had subsided, allowing Moscow to concentrate on China.

For several years before the 1969 crisis there had been clashes along the Sino/Soviet border, notably in January, on 7–9 and 23 December 1967, and in late January 1968. On 16 February 1969 the Chinese became aware that Soviet forces along the Ussuri River had been placed on the highest alert.

Crisis
A foreign policy crisis for the USSR, as distinct from an incident, was initiated by a Chinese ambush of Soviet troops on 2 March 1969. Moscow's response, which triggered a crisis for China, was a massive attack on 15 March against Chinese forces stationed along the Ussuri River. China responded militarily the day of the attack. There were considerable casualties on both sides. Tension continued along the border, but there were no further military hostilities.

Following the clashes there were mass demonstrations in Beijing and in Moscow. On 29 March the USSR issued the first of a series of moderate diplomatic notes urging China to negotiate. A joint Sino/Soviet Commission to regulate navigation on border rivers reconvened on 11 May and reached agreement on 8 August 1969. At the same time, clashes continued—on 16, 17, and 25 April, 2, 12–15, 20, 25, and 28 May, 10–11 June, 8 and 20 July, and 13 August. That day, too, the Soviets threatened to bomb China's nuclear facilities situated several thousand miles away in the remote province of Sinkiang. Beijing then agreed to negotiate on the larger border problems between the two countries.

After the Sinkiang threat, a brief meeting took place on 11 September between Premiers Kosygin and Zhou Enlai. Negotiations on Sino/Soviet border disputes began on 20 October, marking the termination date for both crisis actors. The talks proved to be inconclusive. But while the conflict continued, the polemics had been considerably toned down.

(There were several minor border incidents in subsequent years, notably in 1978.) U.S. activity was limited to political statements. The Warsaw Treaty Organization met, but it had no effect on abating the crisis. The UN remained aloof.

(See *Master Table*, pp. 708–9.)

Sources
An 1973; Berton 1969; Borisov and Koloskov 1975; Cohen 1991; Day 1987; Dmitriyev 1969; Gelber 1970; Gurtov and Hwang 1980; Hinton 1971, 1975, 1976; Horn 1973; Jacobsen 1974; Levine 1969; Lowenthal 1971; Maxwell 1973, 1978; Powell 1973; Rhee 1970; Robinson 1972, 1981; Shapiro 1969; Simon 1973; Sulzberger 1974.

(233) EC-121 Spy Plane, 1969 (see Multiregional PCs: East/West)

(237) Invasion of Cambodia, 1970 (see Indochina PC)

(241) Invasion of Laos II, 1971 (see Indochina PC)

(242) Bangladesh, 1971 (see India/Pakistan PC)

(246) Vietnam Ports Mining, 1972 (see Indochina PC)

(249) Christmas Bombing, 1972–73 (see Indochina PC)

(258) Final North Vietnam Offensive, 1974–75 (see Indochina PC)

(259) Mayaguez, 1975 (see Indochina PC)

(264) East Timor, 1975–76 (see Indonesia PC)

(274) Poplar Tree, 1976 (see Korea PC)

(284) Vietnam Invasion of Cambodia, 1977–79 (see Indochina PC)

(298) Sino/Vietnam War, 1978–79 (see China/Vietnam PC)

(303) Afghanistan Invasion, 1979–80 (see Multiregional PCs: East/West)

(306) Soviet Threat to Pakistan

Soviet statements implying USSR intervention in the event of war between Afghanistan and Pakistan created a low-threat crisis for Pakistan from 1 June to 3 July 1979.

Background
Hostile relations between Afghanistan and Pakistan date to Pakistani independence in 1947 when Afghanistan demanded the creation of a separate Pushtu-speaking Pathan state in part of Pakistan's North West Frontier Province. Several crises occurred over this issue, in 1949–50, 1955, and 1961–62 (see Cases #129, 150, 182—**Pushtunistan I, II, III,** in **Afghanistan/Pakistan PC**). Between 1976 and 1978 Kabul dropped its insistence on self-determination for the Pathans on the Pakistani side of the border, and an active search for a solution began. After the marxist coup in Afghanistan in April 1978 clashes between Afghan government forces and anti-communist rebels led to a large-scale influx of refugees into Pakistan. The nature and length of the border made it almost impossible for Pakistan to control the border crossings.

Crisis
A crisis was triggered for Pakistan by a statement in *Pravda* on 1 June 1979 accusing it of allowing Afghan rebel groups to attack Afghanistan from its territory, and indicating that the USSR would not remain indifferent. Pakistan, although perceiving its military strength as sufficient to cope with direct Afghan threats, viewed a Soviet-backed and Soviet-protected Afghanistan with alarm. The Soviet statement, which charged Pakistan with willingly providing border sanctuaries to the Afghan rebels, made it clear that Moscow would intervene in the event of war between Afghanistan and Pakistan. Pakistan responded the same day with a denial of Soviet allegations, adding that it adhered strictly to the five principles of peaceful coexistence and calling for a resumption of normal relations between Pakistan and Afghanistan.

On 11 June the Tass news agency charged that the U.S. was training Afghan rebel forces in Pakistan. This was denied by a spokesperson for the State Department: the U.S., as Pakistan's long-time patron, extended political support to its client.

The dialogue between Afghanistan and Pakistan was renewed on 1 July when Afghan Foreign Minister Shah Mohammad Dost arrived in Pakistan for talks with President Zia-ul-Haq. The crisis ended on 3 July with a joint decision to continue the talks: the two parties agreed to prepare the ground for a summit meeting. It was also agreed that the refugees in Pakistan would return to Afghanistan as soon as possible, on a voluntary basis.

(Agreement between the two parties did not alter the situation. The flow of Afghan refugees into Pakistan continued, as did attacks on Afghanistan by rebels operating from Pakistani sanctuaries. A summit meeting never took place. Six months later the USSR invaded Afghanistan and imposed a pro-Soviet regime (see Case #303—**Afghanistan Invasion, in Multiregional PCs: East/West**). Afghan anti-communist guerrillas engaged in warfare against Soviet forces lasting a decade.

The UN was not involved in this crisis.

(See *Master Table*, pp. 720–21.)

Sources
Cheema 1983; Ziring 1980.

(351) Vietnam Incursion into Thailand

Thailand alone experienced a crisis from 25 March to 17 April 1984 arising from a Vietnamese incursion into its territory.

Background
Relations between Vietnam and Cambodia (Kampuchea) have always been characterized by hostility and rivalry. Vietnam has long perceived itself as the rightful hegemonial power in Indochina and viewed its neighbors, Cambodia and Laos, as tributaries (or client states). During the era of French domination, through protectorates over Cambodia (1863), Vietnam (1874), and Laos (1893), overt conflict among the three colonial peoples was prevented by external domination. The members of France's Indochina Union became independent following its defeat in the first stage of the long Vietnam War (1946–1954)—Laos, Cambodia, and the two Vietnams, the communist North Vietnam, with its capital in Hanoi, and the anti-communist South, centered in Saigon. During the second stage of the Vietnam War (1964–75), Kampuchea was at times a junior ally of Hanoi, at other times a U.S. base for operations against Vietnam.

Their traditional conflict erupted into a lengthy crisis in September 1977, culminating in full-scale war from 15 December 1978 to 7 January 1979, when Vietnam installed a puppet regime in Kampuchea's capital, Phnom Penh (see Case #284—**Vietnam Invasion of Cambodia, in Indochina PC**). In that case Thailand was a secondary crisis actor. Thus the crisis generated by Vietnam's incursion into Thailand in March 1984 was an extension of the protracted conflict between Vietnam and Cambodia.

Crisis
A crisis was triggered for Thailand on 25 March 1984 by the intrusion of Vietnamese troops into its territory in pursuit of Khmer Rouge Cambodian rebels: Vietnam's cross-border raid, along with Thai military and civilian casualties, was perceived as seriously undermining Thailand's security.

Bangkok responded quickly along two paths: a military effort to force the Vietnamese back into Kampuchea; and a diplomatic offensive in both Washington and the UN. The first included minor clashes in the area of the Khmer Rouge camp, the Chong Phra Palai Pass linking Kampuchea and Thailand. The second led to tangible U.S. support.

Initially Washington announced an offer of military aid to Thailand on 15 April. Two days later, following a meeting with the Thai Premier, General Prem Tinsulanonda, President Reagan reaffirmed the sale of 40 M-48 tanks to "bolster the nation's defenses," along with an assurance of further military sales, as needed. That visible expression of support from a superpower terminated Thailand's crisis.

Unlike the U.S., which took an active role, the USSR, an ally of North Vietnam, remained aloof. The UN, though approached by Thailand and notwithstanding its earlier resolution calling for the withdrawal of Vietnam from Kampuchea, played a minor role in this crisis. One regional organization, the six-state Association of South East Asia Nations *(ASEAN),* supported Thailand, a member, by writing a letter to the UN condemning Vietnam's unprovoked violation of Thailand's border.

(See *Master Table,* pp. 728–29.)

Sources
Hinton 1987; *Keesing's* 1984; *New York Times* 1984; Vichit-Vadakan 1985.

(352) Sino/Vietnam Clashes, 1984 (see China/Vietnam PC)

(353) Three Village Border I

Thailand and Laos experienced the first of two crises over a disputed border from 5 June until mid-October 1984 (see Case #381 below).

Background
Laos, a landlocked state in Indochina, was traditionally dependent on Thailand for its imports of vital goods and for its foreign trade generally. During the final phase of the prolonged Vietnam War the geopolitics of Indochina were transformed: in 1975 Laos became a communist state, the Laos People's Democratic Republic (LPDR), and a client of the regional superpower, the triumphant, united Socialist Republic of Vietnam (SRV). The signing by Laos of a defense cooperation agreement with Vietnam in 1977 escalated the ever-present low-level tension between Laos and Thailand. There were, too, sporadic minor clashes between them over border delineations since 1975.

The dispute between Thailand and Laos that generated their 1984 and 1987–88 crises (see Case #381 below) centered on the location of three border villages— Ban Mai, Ban Kang, and Ban Savang, with an area of 19 square kilometers and a population of 1,000. Both states accepted the watershed principle of border demarcation but disagreed about where the watershed lay vis-à-vis the Mekong and Me Nam Chao Phraya Rivers.

The dispute derived from ambiguity in the Franco-Siam treaty of 1907, which defined the border in the disputed area as the Hoeng River. The ambiguity was due to the fact that the river had two tributaries: Laos took one as the demarcation, Thailand the other. The territorial dispute was accentuated by the settling of Thai communist guerrillas in two of these villages. Moreover, Thai construction teams began building a road through the disputed area, leading to clashes with Laotian militiamen.

Crisis
Until early June 1984 both parties seemed willing to allow local officials to settle their boundary dispute. However, on 5 June, according to the Thais, Laotians moved wooden border markers into the villages, asserting an explicit claim: this was perceived as a threat and triggered a crisis for Thailand. The next day Thai troops moved into the villages to expel the Laotians, triggering a crisis for the LPDR. Laotian troops responded in kind, and minor clashes ensued for several days.

By the 9th Laos decided in favor of crisis management via diplomacy and so informed the Thai ambassador in Vientiane. With the military situation stalemated, Thailand, on 15 July, proposed negotiations between the two interior ministers. The LPDR accepted on the 17th, thereby terminating Thailand's crisis: as the state in occupation of the disputed territory, it no longer perceived a threat or time pressure or the likelihood of military hostilities.

Two rounds of negotiations, on 21–23 July and 6–15 August, ended in deadlock. Thus Laos's crisis lingered until mid-October, when Thailand agreed to withdraw its troops from the three villages and to cease construction in the disputed area. The outcome was a compromise, for neither party achieved all of its goals. In terms of values, the crisis was asymmetrical: for Laos, it was perceived as a serious threat to territorial integrity; for Thailand, it was a low value threat.

Both superpowers remained aloof, as did the regional organizations, *SEATO* and *ASEAN*. Only the UN was involved. Laos submitted the dispute to the Security Council. However, the Council's debate on 22 October 1984 indicated sympathy for Thailand's contention that Laos had instigated the crisis to undermine its (successful) campaign for a seat in the Council.

(See *Master Table*, pp. 728–29.)

Sources
Chawla and Sardesai 1980; Dommen 1985; Hinton 1987; Vichit-Vadakan 1985.

(371) Sino/Vietnam Border, 1987 (see China/Vietnam PC)

(372) Punjab War Scare II, 1987 (see India/Pakistan PC)

(378) India Intervention in Sri Lanka

Prolonged ethnic strife in Sri Lanka generated a crisis with India from 3 June to 30 July 1987.

Background
The roots of this South Asian crisis lay in the one-way migration of Indian Tamils to Ceylon (later, Sri Lanka) during the extended period of British rule: from 1757 to 1947 in the Indo/Pakistani subcontinent, from 1796 to 1948 in Ceylon. During the nineteenth century Indian Tamils, pushed by the endemic poverty of their homeland, the South Indian province of Madras (later, Tamilnadu), and pulled by the opportunities for employment in the labor-intensive rubber plantations of Ceylon, migrated in large numbers. By the time of independence, the Hindu Tamils comprised approximately 20 percent of Ceylon's population, with a vast majority of Buddhist Sinhalese.

From the outset the Tamils, concentrated in the northern Jaffna Peninsula, perceived acute discrimination in all aspects of Sri Lanka's society, economy, and polity. Ethnic resentment erupted into open rebellion in 1983 under the leadership of the most militant and disciplined Tamil group, the Liberation Tigers of Tamil Eelam, the *LTTE,* best known as "the Tamil Tigers" or "the Tigers." Their goal for more than a decade has been an independent state for the Tamils of Sri Lanka, the vast majority of whom reside in the Northern and Eastern Provinces.

Pre-crisis
There have been several escalation points in an increasingly bitter ethnic conflict. One was a large-scale offensive launched by Sri Lanka's armed forces against the Tamil Tigers on 26 May 1987, "Operation Liberation." Not for the first time, the plight of their ethnic and religious kin generated a massive pressure group in Tamilnadu, a state in south India, which urged the government of India to intervene on behalf of Sri Lanka's Tamils. Prime Minister Rajiv Gandhi repeated earlier calls for restraint by Sri Lanka's government and urged a resolution of the conflict through negotiation. On 1 June India's high commissioner (ambassador) to Sri Lanka conveyed a proposal to send unarmed Indian ships, under Indian Red Cross auspices, to deliver relief supplies to the Tamils of Jaffna. Following an emergency cabinet meeting, Sri Lanka's government stated on the 2nd its willingness to consider the idea but vigorously opposed "unilateral action" by India which, it added, would be regarded as a violation of its "independence, sovereignty and territorial integrity."

Crisis
On 3 June a flotilla of 19 Indian fishing boats sailed from the Tamilnadu port of Rameswaram, carrying food, medicine, and kerosene. Officials from the Indian Red Cross and India's External Affairs Ministry and many journalists were aboard.

Three hours later, at 5:00 P.M., the Indian flotilla was stopped by Sri Lankan patrol boats off Kachchative Island and denied entry into Sri Lanka's territorial waters.

After four hours of futile talks, the Indian boats returned to Rameswaram. Sri Lanka's act triggered a crisis for India, posing a threat to its regional primacy. New Delhi's initial response, on 4 June, was a plan devised by the Indian cabinet's Political Affairs Committee, its standing crisis management body, to air-drop relief supplies to the Tamils in Jaffna. The plan was implemented the same day: five transport planes, escorted by four Mirage fighter aircraft, dropped 22 tons of supplies over the Jaffna Peninsula.

This unilateral Indian operation triggered a crisis for Sri Lanka, a direct challenge to its sovereignty over its northern province. Colombo, angered by the half-hour notice of the Indian operation—India claimed it had informed Sri Lanka three hours earlier—sent a formal complaint to New Delhi charging India with a clear violation of Sri Lanka's territorial integrity. Soon after, both parties followed the path of negotiation. The result was an interim agreement on 15 June, which permitted unarmed Indian vessels, without escort, to deliver relief supplies to Sri Lankan officials in Jaffna, for distribution to the Tamil residents. This agreement marked the end of the high stress crisis period but not yet of the crisis as a whole.

Food shipments began on 24 June and continued in July. Negotiations were held quietly at a high level. On 16 July President Jayawardene and members of the Sri Lanka cabinet met with India's high commissioner. A formal peace plan was submitted to Delhi on the 18th. Sri Lanka's parliament approved the plan on the 22nd. There was a setback on the 27th, when the Tiger leader, Prabhakaran, rejected the proposal. The next day, under pressure from India's prime minister, he softened his opposition. And four other militant Tamil groups indicated their support for the peace plan. Finally, during a festive visit to the island on 29–30 July by India's prime minister, an agreement was formally signed by all of the interested parties. Sri Lanka agreed to merge the Tamil-majority Northern and Eastern Provinces into one province. An island-wide cease-fire agreement went into effect. And India undertook to provide a peacekeeping force for the Tamil majority areas of Sri Lanka. To that end, 3,000 Indian soldiers arrived in Jaffna on 30 July to supervise the disarming of Tamil militants. Moreover, Indian planes transported 600 Sri Lankan troops to the capital, Colombo, to assist the police in asserting control over large numbers of Sinhalese demonstrating against the accord. With the agreement of 30 July, the India/Sri Lanka crisis over the Tamils of the island came to an end.

The UN, the U.S., and the USSR were not involved in this crisis.

The domestic ethnic conflict continues into the late 1990s.

(See *Master Table*, pp. 732–33.)

Sources

Hellmann-Rajanayagam 1994; *Keesing's* 1987; Kodikara 1989; Muni 1993; *New York Times* 1987; O'Ballance 1989; Rao 1988; de Silva 1982; de Silva 1995; Singer 1990, 1992; Vanniassingham 1988; Wilson 1988.

(381) Three Village Border II

Laos and Thailand were enmeshed in another crisis over disputed territory from 3 November 1987 to 17 February 1988.

Pre-crisis
In May 1987 Laos accused Thailand of massing troops close to the northern border, in order to protect illegal logging activities. Laos launched several attacks on Thai loggers, killing some of them.

Crisis
A crisis for Laos and Thailand was triggered simultaneously on 3 November 1987 when heavy fighting broke out in the disputed three village area (see Case #353—**Three Village Border I**, above). Laos claimed that the fighting began with Thai air and artillery attacks on Laotian soldiers in the Boten district of its Sayaboury Province. Thailand said it was attacking Laotian troops who had invaded the Chat Trakan district of its Phitsaulok Province.

Thailand's initial response was "Operation Soi Dao," designed to clear the disputed region of Laotian troops. Its major response occurred on 15 December when Thai F5 fighter planes bombed Laotian positions in the region. Laos appealed to the UN Secretary-General to intervene; Perez de Cuellar offered his good offices.

As heavy fighting continued, Laos agreed on 28 December to a third round of border talks with Thailand. However, by mid-January 1988 Thailand claimed that it had reasserted control over 70 percent of the area around Hill 1428. Fighting intensified on 1–2 February, as Thai planes launched heavy strikes against Laotian troop positions.

Talks between the two states, aimed at ending the armed border conflict, began on 16 February in Bangkok. Laos was represented by the Chief of the General Staff of the Laotian People's Army, General Sisavat Keobounphan. Thailand sent General Chaovalit Yongchaiyut, the commander of the Thai army.

The military leaders signed a cease-fire agreement on 17 February calling on their governments to begin negotiations to solve the dispute by the end of the month. That agreement terminated the crisis for both sides. (The cease-fire took effect two days later.)

(See *Master Table*, pp. 732–33.)

Sources
Asian Recorder 1988; *Facts on File* 1988; *Keesing's* 1988.

(384) Spratly Islands, 1988 (see China/Vietnam PC)

(388) Cambodia Peace Conference, 1989–90 (see Indochina PC)

(392) Kashmir III: India/Pakistan Nuclear, 1990 (see India/Pakistan PC)

(401) Nagornyy-Karabakh

An international crisis between Armenia and Azerbaijan, part of a lengthy, still-unresolved conflict over Nagornyy-Karabakh (N-K), erupted on 27 November 1991 and began to fade in mid-August 1992.

Background and Pre-crisis
In the turmoil that followed the Bolshevik Revolution of November 1917 (see Cases #1, 3—**Russian Civil War I, II,** in 1918–20, in **Multiregional PCs: East/West**), the southern regions of the czarist empire experienced a brief period of political independence: Georgia and Armenia declared their independence on 22 April 1918, Azerbaijan on 26 May 1918. By November 1920 the "Red" forces, freed by victory in the war against Poland (see Case #13—**Polish/Russian War,** in **Poland/Russia PC**), triumphed over the "Whites" in the south. Soviet-style governments were established in Georgia and Armenia, on 25 February and 2 April 1921. On 12 March 1922 the three regions were integrated into the Transcaucasian Soviet Socialist Republic, which became part of the newly created USSR on 30 December of that year. In December 1936, under the terms of the "Stalin Constitution," each became an "independent" republic in the 11-member USSR. So they remained until the dissolution of the USSR in December 1991.

Despite its overwhelming Armenian Christian population, Nagornyy-Karabakh, an enclave within Azerbaijan, was incorporated into the overwhelmingly Muslim republic of Azerbaijan in July 1921. Although it acquired the status of an Autonomous *Oblast* (District) in June 1923, this sowed the seeds of a bitter conflict between Armenia and Azerbaijan, which erupted in the late 1980s.

It began with street protests in N-K in October 1987. An attempt by an N-K delegation in Moscow between November 1987 and February 1988 to secure the transfer of the enclave to Armenia failed. There were mass demonstrations in N-K's capital, Stepanakert, on 11 February 1988. A week later Gorbachev, as Secretary-General of the Communist Party of the Soviet Union *(CPSU)*, termed the problem of nationalities "the most fundamental and most vital issue" for the USSR. On 20 February the N-K Soviet requested the transfer of the enclave to Armenia; this was rejected by the *CPSU* Central Committee two days later. And on 24 February Soviet troops were dispatched to the area of conflict.

Clashes, demonstrations, and pressure continued throughout 1988 and the first half of 1989. Among the most noteworthy occurrences in 1988 were the following: the Sumgait massacre on 29 February—32 killed and 197 injured in an anti-Armenian riot in a city near the Azeri capital, Baku; the reiterated demand of the N-K Regional Council (Soviet) on 12 March for a transfer of the disputed territory to Armenia; the replacement of the Communist Party leaders in Armenia and Azerbaijan on 21 May; Gorbachev's announcement on 28 June that the Soviet Union would not accept the Armenian demand; the first confrontation between troops and protesters in Armenia on 5 July, with one person killed, 36 injured; a unanimous vote of the N-K Regional Council on 12 July in favor of immediate secession from Azerbaijan; the proclamation of a state of emergency in N-K on 21 September; a mass demonstration and intervention by troops the next day; outbreaks of violence in Baku and two other cities in Azerbaijan on 22 November, causing the deaths of three soldiers and injuries to 126 civilians; a severe earthquake on 7 December that devastated northern Armenia; the arrest of most members of the pro-Armenian Karabakh committee on 10 December, leading to large-scale protests and clashes in Armenia's capital, Yerevan.

Direct rule over N-K was imposed by Moscow on 12 January 1989. And, as a measure of the cost of the escalating dispute, an official estimate of cumulative casualties on 7 February cited 87 civilians and four soldiers killed; more than 1,500 civilians, 115 soldiers, and 32 policemen injured. After a period of tranquility, Armenia proclaimed a union with N-K on 1 December 1989, an act against which Azerbaijan protested.

In the meantime the USSR was in the process of disintegration. Even before this was consummated, with the formation of the Commonwealth of Independent States (CIS) on 21 December 1991, Armenia and Azerbaijan attained their independence, on 23 and 30 August 1991, respectively. An agreement between them on 24 September to set their territorial dispute at rest proved to be stillborn.

Crisis

A crisis for Armenia was triggered on 27 November 1991 by Azerbaijan's abolition of the long-existing N-K Autonomous *Oblast*. When, in a referendum on 10 December, the population of N-K overwhelmingly voted for independence, a crisis was triggered for Azerbaijan. This choice was reaffirmed in elections in N-K on 28 December.

Rapid escalation of the crisis occurred: on 3 January 1992 Armenia's parliament supported the N-K demand for independence; Azerbaijan mobilized its armed forces; Armenia replied in kind; and military clashes occurred. Several attempts at mediation followed in January–April 1992: by the Conference on Security and Cooperation in Europe *(CSCE)*, which both Armenia and Azerbaijan had recently joined; by U.S. Secretary of State Baker, who visited both protagonists in February; by the UN Security Council, which passed two resolutions calling for a cease-fire by the conflicting parties; by Turkey, Iran, and Czechoslovakia—all for naught. And, although Armenia declared on 3 March that it had no territorial claims against Azerbaijan and that the dispute over N-K was Azerbaijan's "internal affair," confrontation and military hostilities continued.

A further escalation point was a massive, successful attack by Armenia against the important town of Shusha on 8 May. Turkey, a patron of Azerbaijan, threatened Armenia on the 13th that it would intervene militarily if Shusha and Lachin were not restored to Azerbaijan. Russia responded by signing an agreement with Armenia on 15 May pledging military aid if its security were threatened. On the 20th Turkey reassured Russia that it would not intervene with force.

Azerbaijan launched a counteroffensive on 12 June. Because of its military successes, Armenia suspended its participation in the *CSCE*-sponsored peace talks in Rome, with the involvement of Armenia, Azerbaijan, Belarus, Czechoslovakia, France, Germany, Italy, Sweden, Russia, Turkey, and the U.S. On 8 July Armenia rejected any formal link between N-K and Azerbaijan. On the 27th Azerbaijan accused Armenia of undermining its sovereignty. The N-K parliament accused Azerbaijan on 13 August of aggression, declared a six-month emergency, and ordered general mobilization. Although a finite end to the N-K crisis is not discernible, it can be viewed as fading from mid-August 1992 onward. The conflict over Nagornyy-Karabakh continues unresolved.

As noted, Russia was highly involved in this crisis, but only from May 1992. U.S. involvement was limited to its participation in the *CSCE*-sponsored Rome mediation effort. Many other states attempted to mediate the crisis and underlying conflict.

(See *Master Table,* pp. 736–37.)

Sources
Fraser et al. 1990; Hunter 1994; *Keesing's* 1988–93; Maggs 1993; Mouradian 1990; *New York Times* 1988–93; Rutland 1994; Suny 1993.

(404) Papua New Guinea/Solomon

These two island-states in the South Pacific experienced a crisis from 12 March until mid-September 1992.

Background
The root of this crisis was an ongoing secessionist conflict between Bougainville Island and Papua New Guinea (PNG) since the late 1980s. The rebel Bougainville Revolutionary Army *(BRA)* had compelled PNG forces to withdraw from their island in March 1990; but Bougainville's declaration of independence did not achieve international recognition. Negotiations between PNG and the *BRA* led to an accord in January 1991 to lift the crippling blockade of the island. In April 1991 PNG troops again landed on Bougainville leading to further clashes. Renewed fighting occurred in November 1991. A PNG offer of greater autonomy was rejected by the *BRA*, which relied on support from the Solomon Islands, an independent member of the Commonwealth since 1978.

Crisis
Internal strife in PNG acquired an interstate dimension with a PNG commando raid on the Solomon Islands on 12 March 1992, repeated on the 17th: it was

designed to destroy a fuel storage depot that PNG believed was used to supply the Bougainville Revolutionary Army's campaign for independence. (This PNG perception was based upon racial and cultural affinity of the people of Bougainville and the Solomons and the geographic proximity of the two islands.)

Prime Minister Solomon Mamaloni responded with a strong diplomatic protest. The PNG Prime Minister, Rabbie Namaliu, initially denied responsibility for the raid but later apologized for the "regrettable incident" to the Solomon Islands leader. At the same time, he renewed charges of military assistance to the *BRA* by the Solomons regime.

Another PNG commando raid on the Solomons occurred on 12 September. Once more the Solomons lodged a strong diplomatic protest and demanded an apology and compensation. They also deployed additional troops to the Shortland Islands. Several days later the PNG prime minister deplored the raid as "an atrocious act" and promised to punish those responsible, as well as to pay compensation to the Solomons. This terminated the crisis for both parties.

(There was a modest third-party intervention: Australia, Canada, and New Zealand, along with the Solomon Islands, formed a multinational supervisory team to interrupt the Papua New Guinea blockade of Bougainville.)

One consequence of the crisis was a report on 24 September that the Solomons had requested assistance from Japan and Taiwan to construct a military base in the area. Both remained aloof. So too did the UN, the U.S., and the USSR.

(See *Master Table*, pp. 736–37.)

Sources
Keesing's 1992.

(405) Sleeping Dog Hill

Thailand and Myanmar (formerly, Burma) experienced a crisis from 14 March to 25 December 1992 over the latter's cross-border "hot pursuit" raids.

Background
Since its attainment of independence from British rule on 4 January 1948, Burma's government and many minority communities (Karens, Kachins, etc.) were engaged in a prolonged military struggle for control of the borderlands of the new state. (That internal conflict remained unabated in 1995, though Burma's army imposed compliance on several minority groups in 1994 and 1995.)

Crisis
An international crisis for Thailand was triggered on 14 March 1992 when Myanmar forces, pursuing rebels near the border with Thailand, occupied the strategic Sleeping Dog Hill in Thai territory near Manerplaw. Thai forces were urged to withdraw from the area in order to avoid air and artillery attacks.

Thailand responded to a perceived threat to territory by placing its air force on alert and moving troops to the border. A fierce battle occurred on the 17th. The next day Thailand's interior minister warned Myanmar's military regime of the danger of continued occupation of Thai territory. And another inconclusive battle occurred the same day.

After an extended lull, a group of 10 Thai officials was arrested on 6 October while trying to reclaim Myanmar-occupied Thai villages. They were released on the 13th. In an extraordinary act on 4 December, Thai King Bhumibol called on both sides to settle the border dispute peacefully. The result was a meeting of military delegations from the two states a few days later. On 25 December Myanmar troops withdrew from Sleeping Dog Hill, terminating this crisis between two Southeast Asian neighbors.

The UN, the U.S., and Russia were not involved in this crisis.

(See *Master Table*, pp. 736–37.)

Sources
Keesing's 1991.

(407) Georgia/Abkhazia Civil War

The newly independent state of Georgia experienced a crisis with Russia from 25 September 1992 to 8 October 1993 during its prolonged civil war against a separatist movement in Abkhazia.

Background
The origins of Georgia can be traced to the first millennium B.C.E. However, its modern history began in 1800 when, in response to an appeal by the last king of Georgia for support against Persia, it was annexed by Russia. It was ruled until the end of World War I as an outlying province of the empire.

The collapse of czarist Russia and the turmoil accompanying the Bolshevik Revolution provided Georgia—and its Caucasian neighbors, Armenia and Azerbaijan—a "window of opportunity." The result was a short-lived independence, from April 1918 to February 1921, until the armies of the new Bolshevik regime established control over Transcaucasia. In March 1922 Georgia, Armenia, and Azerbaijan were merged into the Transcaucasian Soviet Socialist Republic (TSSR) and became a part of the USSR. In 1936, under the "Stalin Constitution," they became "independent" republics of the Soviet Union.

Pre-crisis
With the dissolution of the USSR at the end of 1991, Georgia, along with Armenia and Azerbaijan, became an independent state.

Abkhazia was an autonomous province in the northern part of Georgia near the border with the post-Soviet Russian Republic. The democratically elected first president of Georgia, Zviad Gamsakhurdia, a Georgian nationalist, was forced into exile in January 1992 by a rebellion led by former communists. Eduard Shevardnadze, the former Soviet Foreign Minister—and a former colonel in the KGB—became president.

Abkhazians, a distinctive ethnic group within Georgia, live mainly in the autonomous republics of Abkhazia and Adzarya, in which the port cities of Sukhumi and Batumi, Georgia's largest Black Sea harbors, are located. Abkhazian leaders demanded secession—the anti-Georgia movement in Abkhazia began its campaign against Georgia as early as 1977 but was suppressed by Soviet power. After the disintegration of the Soviet Union and the emergence of Georgia as a sovereign state, the long-standing low-intensity conflict within Georgia burst into a full-scale civil war, in which Russia supported the Abkhazians.

Fighting began in August 1992 between Georgian troops and Abkhaz separatists. Gamsakhurdia saw the eruption of war as an opportunity to return to power. The civil war threatened to draw Russia into conflict with Georgia, which accused Russia of actively supporting the rebels in order to protect its interests in the North Caucasus and the Black Sea region in general. Russia had a clear and stated goal of maintaining a strategic presence along Georgia's Black Sea coast, that is, a conception of Russia's "rights" in its neighboring "new states" as similar to those encompassed in the Brezhnev Doctrine (see Case #227—**Prague Spring**, in 1968, in **Europe: Non-PCs**). To Russia's nationalists and military, who were thought to be behind the Russian involvement in Georgia's civil strife, the secession of Abkhazia was viewed as both an opportunity to regain access to Black Sea resorts and "revenge" for Shevardnadze's role in the dissolution of the USSR.

Crisis

On 25 September 1992 Russia's Supreme Soviet (later, *Duma*) denounced Georgia's resort to violence in the interethnic conflict with the separatists of Abkhazia. It also passed a resolution suspending the delivery of Russian arms and equipment to Georgia. This triggered a crisis for Georgia, reinforcing its image of Russia as the patron of the Abkhaz separatists. Georgia accused Russia of interference in its domestic affairs.

After a lull in the fighting, serious clashes between Georgia's forces and the Abkhazian rebels resumed on 2 October. President Shevardnadze of Georgia blamed Russia for supplying arms to the separatists. Russia denied any involvement. But the next day President Boris Yeltsin warned that Russia would take "appropriate measures" if the lives of Russians in the conflict areas were threatened.

Relations with Russia worsened when the Georgian State Council announced that Georgia would take control of all Russian weapons and military equipment on its territory. The Russian Defense Minister, Marshal Pavel Grachev, warned that such an act would lead to "armed clashes." Georgia actually seized a Russian arms depot in southern Georgia on 2 November; and Marshal Grachev warned that Russia was prepared to use force in order to regain control of the depot.

Tension between Tbilisi and Moscow increased when, on 6 November, Georgia accused Russia of bombing Georgian positions in Sukhumi, the Abkhaz capital, and on the 8th, when Russia accused Georgia of involvement in the murder of three Russian soldiers in Abkhazia. In December 1992, after a Russian helicopter was shot down—it was delivering humanitarian aid to an Abkhazian town—Russia issued a protest and Defense Minister Grachev threatened again to take "measures of a military nature."

The Georgian Prime Minister, Tengiz Signa, said on 17 December that there was a crisis in relations between Georgia and Russia, but not a state of war. Georgia's parliament demanded the withdrawal of Russian troops from Abkhazia: despite the Russian denials of involvement in the civil war, 46 Russian servicemen had been killed in Georgia in 1992.

On 5 January 1993, Shevardnadze asked UN Secretary-General Boutros-Ghali to deploy a UN peacekeeping force to Abkhazia. Shevardnadze also urged the UN to call on Georgia's neighbors to remain neutral in the conflict. The next day a UN spokesperson said that time for UN intervention was not yet ripe. However, a UN mission arrived in Tbilisi on 20 January to ascertain the need for emergency aid for victims of ethnic conflict in the republic.

While fighting between Georgian forces and separatists continued, talks between Russia and Georgia were resumed in Tbilisi in January, with the goal of signing a friendship and cooperation accord between the two countries and to discuss the status of Russian troops in Georgia.

A major attack by separatists on Sukhumi, then held by Georgian forces, on 14–17 March, was materially aided by Russia. Georgia's parliament declared that the attack proved that Russia was escalating its undeclared war against Georgia. Russia again denied any involvement in the conflict. Yet, the bilateral talks continued, and a trade agreement was reached in March.

In April, Eduard Brunner was appointed by the UN Secretary-General as his Special Representative to assist in efforts to solve the Abkhazia conflict. Shevardnadze called for more active involvement by international organizations.

Violence continued in Georgia throughout June. On 16–22 June the Russian foreign minister held talks in Moscow with Georgian and Abkhaz delegations, in search of a cease-fire. As violence continued, Kozyrev threatened that "all necessary measures" would be taken against those responsible.

Georgian Prime Minister Tengiz Segna demanded on 7 July that Russia end its undeclared war against Georgia and called for the severance of diplomatic relations with Russia; the call was rejected by Shevardnadze.

Finally, on 27 July 1993 a peace agreement, mediated by Russia, was signed by Georgia and the Abkhaz separatists. Russia agreed to send troops as neutral peacekeepers, and the parties agreed on the need for UN observers to monitor the cease-fire. This agreement led to a sharp decline in tension between Georgia and Russia.

Shevardnadze and Yeltsin met in August and said that they were satisfied with the first steps toward a final settlement of the conflict over the future of Abkhazia.

On 25 August the UN Security Council approved the proposal to send 88 military observers to Georgia. The next day Georgia's army reported that all of its heavy military equipment and some troops had been withdrawn from the front line, as agreed in July. However, a surprise attack was launched on 16 September by Abkhaz separatists, and Sukhumi fell to the rebels after the major withdrawal of Georgian forces. On the 27th Shevardnadze accused Russia of "betrayal" and, specifically, of refusal to honor its obligations under the July cease-fire agreement, to enforce peace by military force if necessary.

In a letter to the UN Secretary-General, Shevardnadze wrote: "the world community should become aware that the evil empire is still thriving, still sowing seeds of death." Russia imposed sanctions on Abkhazia on 19–20 September but rejected Shevardnadze's call for the imposition of peace by the threat of force.

On 8 October, after a meeting with Yeltsin, Shevardnadze said that the Commonwealth of Independent States (CIS) was "the last chance to save the country" and agreed to join the loose successor to the USSR. (Georgia formally became a member of the CIS on 22 October.) Tension was defused, and the crisis ended.

(A peacekeeping force of 500 Russian marines arrived in Georgia on 4 November and was sent to western Georgia to protect main roads and railway lines. On 18 November the leader of Abkhazia's separatists, Vladislav Ardzinba, said that a referendum would be held to decide on unification with Russia.)

(The Georgia-Abkhaz agreement, mediated by the UN, was signed on 1 December in Geneva. The two sides agreed on a cease-fire and pledged to continue negotiations. They also agreed on the deployment of more international observers.)

(See *Master Table*, pp. 736–37.)

Sources
Keesing's 1992, 1993; *New York Times* 1992, 1993.

(408) North Korea Nuclear Crisis, 1993–94 (see Korea PC)

Europe: Non-Protracted Conflict (PC) Crises

From the end of 1918 until the end of 1994 there were 88 international crises in Europe, 21 percent of all crises. Almost two-thirds of Europe's crises (56) occurred before the end of World War II, and almost half of the 88 cases (39) took place in the inter–world war period of multipolarity, the zenith of Europe's centrality in global politics. As an indication of change in Europe's role and of relatively greater stability, only 14 of the 88 crises in Europe erupted after the close of World War II.

In terms of their *conflict setting,* 35 percent of Europe's international crises occurred outside a protracted conflict, 65 percent within a PC. Two protracted conflicts account for the vast majority of the PC crises in Europe—the **World War II** long-war PC and the **East/West** PC. If the former is excluded as a special case, with 16 crises, all but one of them IWCs, PC cases exceed those outside a PC setting, 39–33.

Many of the best-known and most carefully-researched crises were located in Europe: **Anschluss** and **Munich,** in 1938 (Cases #60, 64); **Entry into World War II,** in 1939 (Case #74); notable intrawar crises, **Fall of Western Europe** and **Battle of Britain,** in 1940 (Cases #78, 81); **Barbarossa,** in 1941 (Case #85); **Stalingrad,** in 1942–43 (Case #89); **D-Day,** in 1944–45 (Case #94); and after World War II, the **Berlin Blockade, Berlin Deadline,** and **Berlin Wall** crises, in 1948–49, 1958–59, and 1961 (Cases #123, 168, and 185); the **Hungarian Uprising,** in 1956–57 (Case #155); **Prague Spring,** in 1968 (Case #227); **Solidarity,** in 1980–81 (Case #315); and the two **Yugoslavia** crises that erupted in 1991 and 1992 (Cases #397, 403). (See *Master Table).*

Of the 88 international crises in Europe, only the 33 non-PC cases are discussed in the following pages. The 16 long-war PC crises are presented in the World War II cluster (see **Multiregional PCs: World War II**). The 39 other PC cases are summarized in the other six protracted conflicts in Europe, as noted in the introduction to Part III. All 55 PC cases are listed, along with a reference to where the relevant summary can be found.

(3) Russian Civil War II, 1918–19 (see Multiregional PCs: East/West)

(4) Baltic Independence

An international crisis between Russia and the Baltic states over the latter's assertion of independence occurred from 18 November 1918 to 11 August 1920.

Background
Of the three Baltic states Lithuania has a long history of independence and substantial power dating to its founding in 1316. At different times its territory included parts of Russia, Ukraine, and Poland, with suzerainty over Moldavia, Wallachia, and Bessarabia in southeastern Europe. Estonia, by contrast, was for most of its history under foreign control—by Denmark, the Teutonic Knights, and Sweden. Latvia, too, had never been independent before the twentieth century.

During World War I the Balts asserted their claim to independence on several occasions; but the tide of battle prevented its realization. From mid-July to mid-September 1915 the Central Powers stormed through Eastern Europe: czarist Russia suffered a series of severe military defeats leading to the loss of all of Lithuania (and Poland) and a million men.

Pre-crisis
On 28 November 1917, taking advantage of the turmoil accompanying the Bolshevik seizure of power in Russia three weeks earlier, the local *Diet* (legislature) in Tallinn proclaimed Estonia's independence. The new Soviet regime tried to reconquer a strategically important area but was blocked by the Germans. On 24 February 1918 Estonia again declared its independence—under German protection. Lithuania did the same on 16 February with the same outcome—an attempted Russian conquest and German occupation. Under the terms of the Treaty of Brest-Litovsk on 3 March 1918 Russia was compelled to recognize the independence of its three Baltic provinces, along with Finland, Poland, the Ukraine, and Transcaucasia. In reality, they were under German occupation until the end of World War I.

Crisis
With the defeat of Germany and rampant civil war in Russia, the Balts pressed their claim to independence: Latvia on 18 November 1918; and Estonia the next day by reaffirming the authority of the Provisional Government initially formed in February 1918 under German tutelage. Lithuania, too, challenged Soviet power by forming the first of many short-lived national governments on 11 November. Those challenges to Russia's territorial integrity created a crisis for the new Soviet regime. It responded almost at once, invading Estonia on 22 November, Lithuania and Latvia in December, creating an existence crisis for all three newly established Baltic states.

Russia's initial advances were impressive: its forces occupied three-fourths of Estonia; almost all of Latvia including the capital, Riga, on 4 January; and half of Lithuania including the capital, Vilna (Vilnius), on the 5th. But its success was short-lived. Estonian resistance, supported by British naval and air power, drove the Russians out by February 1919 leaving the Estonian government in effective control of most of its territory. The Russians were compelled to withdraw from Latvia by a German-Latvian force in March with the approval of the Allies. And in Lithuania Vilna was lost to Poland in April; it was restored to Lithuania by the Allies in December 1919. The severity of violence did not exceed serious clashes.

High tension persisted until December 1919, when bilateral peace talks began between the adversaries. Separate peace treaties were concluded incorporating formal Russian recognition of independence for each Baltic state: the Treaty of Tartu (Dorpat) with Estonia on 2 February 1920; the Treaty of Moscow with Lithuania on 12 July 1920; and the Treaty of Riga with Latvia on 11 August 1920. Each marked the end of the foreign policy crisis for the concerned Baltic state. The last agreement ended Russia's crisis and the international crisis over Baltic independence as a whole.

The League of Nations, which came into existence seven months before the end of this crisis, was not involved.

(The three Baltic states were occupied by Soviet forces in September–October 1939 [see Case #75—**Soviet Occupation: Baltic** below]. They were forcibly incorporated into the USSR on 21 July 1940. Soviet military bases were established in September and October 1940. Soviet control over the Baltic states was lost to Germany in 1941–42 and reacquired in September–October 1944. They reemerged as independent states with the disintegration of the Soviet Union in 1991.)

(See *Master Table,* pp. 666–67.)

Sources
Bradley 1975; Jackson 1972; Page 1970; Tarulis 1959; Ullman 1968.

(5) Teschen

Czechoslovakia and Poland were enmeshed in a crisis over Teschen, also known as Austrian Silesia, from 15 January 1919 to 28 July 1920.

Background
The duchy of Teschen is a small territorial enclave between Poland and Czechoslovakia. Both newly independent states laid claim to it after World War I. Rich in coal and heavy industry, Teschen also possessed a railroad leading to Slovakia. Inhabited by a mixture of Czechs, Poles, and Germans, the duchy offered an ethnic basis for both claims.

Pre-crisis
Polish and Czechoslovak national councils had been established in the disputed territory in October 1918. Warsaw had strengthened its influence by sending troops to the area. In November the two national councils agreed on their territorial jurisdiction, an agreement regarded as provisional by the Teschen Czechs. The Czechoslovak claim was supported by the U.K. and, especially, France. The U.S. and Italy backed Poland.

Crisis

In an attempt to present Prague with a fait accompli Warsaw announced on 15 January 1919 that elections would be held in Teschen later in the month for representatives to the Polish National Assembly. This triggered a crisis for Czechoslovakia, which feared that the election results would be interpreted by Warsaw as a popular wish to be part of Poland. Prague responded on 23 January, just three days before the elections, by dispatching troops to the district of Kewin, which was then administered by the Polish national council. That move triggered a crisis for Poland. A major battle was prevented only by the intervention of British and French officers.

Acting under the aegis of the victorious powers' Supreme Council (the Big Ten at the Paris Peace Conference), the Conference of Ambassadors produced a preliminary demarcation line in the duchy: Poland was to receive two-thirds of the territory including the principal town of Teschen, with the mining district, the railway station, and part of the railway allocated to Czechoslovakia. Warsaw accepted, but Prague refused. Serious clashes erupted in May 1919. The Supreme Council decided in favor of a plebiscite in September, but it was aborted. Clashes occurred again in March and May 1920. Finally, on 28 July, the Conference of Ambassadors secured the parties' agreement to a division of the disputed territory as set out above. This terminated the crisis over Teschen; but neither party was satisfied with the compromise then or later.

Although the League of Nations Council first met six months before the end of the Teschen crisis, the new global organization was not involved.

(See *Master Table*, pp. 666–67.)

Sources
Carr 1945; Perman 1962.

(6) Hungarian War

In one of several World War I "fall-out" crises Hungary experienced crisis and war with Czechoslovakia and Romania from 20 March to 3 August 1919.

Pre-crisis
The primary foreign policy objective of the Western powers in the aftermath of World War I was to reverse the revolutionary tide in Russia. At the same time small powers in Central–Eastern Europe aimed at expanding their territory at the expense of successors to the defeated Austro-Hungarian Empire. The new state of Hungary was at the crossroads of these two currents. Romania and Czechoslovakia were already violating the demarcation lines set by the 13 November 1918 Military Convention. France, concerned with strengthening Russia's western neighbors, tacitly encouraged the partition of Hungary. The Mihály Károlyi–led government in Budapest was not recognized by France, the U.K., or the U.S.

Crisis

International pressure on Hungary reached its peak on 20 March 1919 in the form of an ultimatum from the Supreme Council's delegate in Budapest, Lieutenant-Colonel Fernand Vix, to Károlyi: in accordance with a 26 February Paris Peace Conference decision the Hungarian government was instructed to accept the implementation of a neutral zone between Hungary and Romania. The ultimatum triggered a crisis for Hungary because of the following: it threatened the loss of extensive Hungarian territory, even more than indicated in the November 1918 Armistice; there was intense time pressure—30 hours—for acceptance; and because Vix, exceeding his orders, threatened military reprisals if the ultimatum were rejected. Károlyi responded to a perceived threat to Hungary's existence by rejecting the ultimatum and by resigning in favor of the pro-Soviet Socialist Béla Kun.

The ultimatum and the response increased the risk of war in Central Europe. There were, in fact, some clashes with the Czechoslovaks and the French, escalating to full-scale war on 16 April, when Romania invaded Hungary. Later that month Czechoslovakia attacked from the north. And the French were directly involved, occupying Hungarian towns in the south and, together with Italian military officers, advising the invading Czechoslovak troops. Hungary was able to resist and succeeded in launching a counteroffensive against the Czechoslovak forces on 11 May triggering a crisis for Prague. The Czechs were expelled from Hungarian territory; and Hungarian troops, with Polish military assistance, occupied part of Slovakia. At that point France intervened: on 8 and 15 June 1919 it sent two ultimatums to Budapest demanding its withdrawal from Slovakia. Hungary's government complied on the 16th thereby ending its brief intrawar crisis. Then on the 24th an armistice was signed between Hungary and Czechoslovakia ending the latter's crisis. Prague perceived the withdrawal of Hungarian troops as a victory.

War on Hungary's eastern front had receded, although the resumption of hostilities remained likely. And in fact Hungary launched an attack on 20 July triggering a crisis for Romania. Bucharest responded on the 24th with a counter-offensive, which quickly overcame Hungarian forces. And on 3 August Romanian troops occupied Budapest terminating this three-actor international crisis.

France, as noted, was very highly involved, the U.K. and the U.S. much less so. Russia provided statements of support to the communist regime in Hungary and relieved the pressure from Romania by diverting its attention to the northeast, sending an ultimatum on 1 May 1919, which triggered Romania's crisis over Bessarabia (see Case #10—**Bessarabia** below).

There was no global organization at the time of this crisis.

(See *Master Table,* pp. 666–67.)

Sources

Hadju 1979; Juhász 1979; Pastor 1976; Szilassy 1971; Volgyes 1971.

(9) Finnish/Russian Border, 1919–20 (see Finland/Russia PC)

(10) Bessarabia

The borderland of Bessarabia (Moldavia, later Moldova) was the focus of a crisis between Russia and Romania from 30 April 1919 to 2 March 1920.

Background

Bessarabia had a long history of foreign occupation, from the time the Bulgars, a Turkic people, settled there in 679 A.D.: the Mongols (1241); Lithuania (1396); Russia (1812); Turkey (1856); and Russia once more (1878).

The breakdown of law and order at the time of the Bolshevik Revolution led the provincial government in Bessarabia in late December 1917 to request both the Romanian government and the Russian army's *GHQ* to dispatch troops to the area. Romania did so; and its forces occupied Kishinev, capital of Bessarabia, on 13 January 1918. Bessarabia proclaimed its independence on 24 January, but it was not recognized by the powers.

Russia responded to Romania's military intervention by severing diplomatic relations with Bucharest on 13 January and insisting that Romanian troops be withdrawn from Bessarabia. Romania refused; and its military presence was backed by a Note in early February from the senior representatives of France, Greece, Italy, the U.K., and the U.S. to the *Rumtcerod,* or governing body in Odessa, as a measure designed to restore order; the question of sovereignty over Bessarabia was left open. Tension rose on 27 March and again on 9 April 1918, when the legislatures of Romania and Bessarabia passed an act of union. Chicherin, the Soviet Commissar for Foreign Affairs, protested to Bucharest on 27 March. (The events from 13 January to 27 March 1918 constitute a separate Russia/Romania crisis, but it is not treated as such here because it ended before November 1918, the onset of the ICB data set.)

Pre-crisis

Tension between Romania and Soviet Russia remained high during the next 12 months. This was exacerbated by two acts of formal recognition: of the Bessarabia-Romania union by the Central Powers in the Treaty of Bucharest on 7 May 1918; and of the Bessarabia-Romania "confederation" by the *Hetmanate,* or governing body, of independent Ukraine in June 1919 after initial opposition.

Crisis

Persistent tension escalated to international crisis when Romania formalized the union with Bessarabia on 30 April 1919. Russia perceived a serious threat to territory that had been internationally recognized as part of Russia in 1812 and again in 1878. It responded on 1 May with an ultimatum from Chicherin and Rakovsky, Chairman of the Council of Commissars for Soviet Ukraine, which triggered a crisis for Romania: Bucharest was given 48 hours to evacuate Bessarabia, or the Soviet regimes would act as they saw fit. Russia followed this with a declaration of war against Romania on 18 May. Serious clashes occurred but there was no decisive outcome, for the Red Army, faced with civil war against the "Whites," was unable to mount a concerted offensive against Romanian troops in Bessarabia. The military stalemate led to bilateral talks in early February 1920, though Romania refused to discuss the union with Bessarabia. An armistice was signed on 2 March ending the Bessarabia crisis, though not the long-standing conflict. The outcome was a victory for Romania, a defeat for Russia.

The League of Nations, whose Council first met less than two months before the end of this crisis, was not involved.

(Negotiations on a settlement of the basic dispute over territory broke down at the end of October 1920 following recognition of the Bessarabia-Romania union by France, Italy, Japan, and the U.K. on 28 October—though this treaty was not ratified until 1924 by Britain and France, and 1927 by Italy. The USSR formally recognized the loss of Bessarabia to Romania on 9 June 1934. However, it was occupied by Soviet troops on 28 June 1940 in accord with the Molotov-Ribbentrop Pact of August 1939 dividing eastern Europe into German and Soviet spheres of influence. After German occupation during World War II Bessarabia was reoccupied by Soviet forces in 1944 and was ceded by Romania in 1946. It remained part of the USSR until the collapse of the Soviet Union in 1991, when it emerged as the independent state of Moldova.)

(See *Master Table,* pp. 666–67.)

Sources
Boldur 1927; Boulter 1928; Clark 1927; Degras 1953; Langer 1972; Popovici 1931; Roucek 1971; Toynbee 1927c.

(12) Rhenish Rebellions, 1920 (see France/Germany PC)

(13) Polish/Russian War, 1920 (see Poland/Russia PC)

(15) Aaland Islands

Sweden and Finland experienced a crisis over the Aaland Islands from 5 June 1920 until 20 October 1921.

Background
For more than a century the grand duchy of Finland, including the Aaland Islands, had been an integral part of the czarist empire: it had been ceded to Russia by Sweden in 1809.

On 6 December 1917, a month after the Bolshevik revolution, Finland declared its independence, an act recognized by Russia, France, Germany, and Sweden in January 1918. However, on 29 December 1917 the residents of the Aaland Islands had asserted a right to self-determination and voted to join Sweden. On 2 March 1918, a day before the signing of the Treaty of Brest-Litovsk between Germany and Russia that recognized the independence of Finland, among many other czarist Russia possessions, Germany occupied the Aaland Islands at the request of Finland. German forces remained in Finland until late December 1918. On 1 June 1919 the islanders called for a plebiscite over the issue of joining Sweden. The issue remained dormant for almost a year.

Pre-crisis
On 7 May 1920 Finland's *Diet* (legislature) granted local autonomy to the Aaland Islands but ruled out secession. Tension rose at the beginning of June with the arrest of two islanders by Finland on a charge of treason.

Crisis
A formal Swedish protest was ignored. And Finland dispatched troops to the Aalands around 5 June. This precipitated a crisis for Sweden, which perceived that a direct military threat could be mounted from the islands. Some Swedes urged the use of force. Sweden responded on the 15th by recalling its minister to Helsinki and appealing to the League of Nations. This dual response, especially the latter act, catalyzed a crisis for Finland, which perceived a threat to territorial integrity and sovereignty over the Aalands.

On 11 July 1920 the U.K. brought the dispute between Sweden and Finland before the League Council under Article 11 of the Covenant. Finland, which was not then a League member, rejected the Council's competence. The next day the Council sought a decision by a committee of three jurists as to whether or not the League had the right to intervene in the dispute. On the basis of an affirmative ruling on 5 September the Council dispatched a neutral commission of inquiry to the Baltic, which deliberated from November 1920 to February 1921.

Acting on the findings of the commission the League Council, on 24 June 1921, confirmed Finland's sovereignty over the islands, with the requirement that they be demilitarized and given autonomy. Finland and Sweden accepted the recommendations on 27 June and agreed on guarantees for residents of the islands. The agreement, along with demilitarization and neutralization, was formalized on 20 October 1921 by a convention signed by many involved actors: Baltic states—Denmark, Estonia, Finland, Latvia, and Sweden; major powers—France, Germany, Italy, and the U.K.; and Poland. That formal act terminated the Aaland Islands crisis.

(In 1935 Finland, with the support of Sweden, both of which were concerned with growing insecurity in the Baltic, began to plan the refortification of the Aaland Islands. At the last session of the League of Nations Council in 1938–39 they sought Council approval. All the signatories to the 1921 convention had

approved the plan; but the USSR, a nonsignatory, balked and persuaded the Council not to pass a resolution on the matter.)
(See *Master Table*, pp. 668–69.)

Sources
Boulter 1928; *Current History* 1920, 1921; Dexter 1967; Eagleton 1957; Langer 1972; Oakley 1966; Scott 1977; Toynbee 1927c; Walters 1952.

(17) Vilna I, 1920 (see Lithuania/Poland PC)

(20) German Reparations, 1921 (see France/Germany PC)

(21) Karl's Return to Hungary

Three of the Austro-Hungarian Empire's successor states—Czechoslovakia, Yugoslavia, and Hungary—experienced a two-phase crisis from 27 March until 15 November 1921.

Background
Karl IV, the last Hapsburg Emperor of Austria-Hungary, abdicated in November 1918 and was exiled to Switzerland; but he did not abdicate his *right* to the throne.

Pre-crisis
Early in 1921 the Conference of Ambassadors, acting for the Supreme Council (Big Ten) at the Paris Peace Conference, issued a decree forbidding the restoration of the Hapsburg family to the vacant Hungarian throne. Moreover, several European governments issued statements indicating what recourse they might have if a Hapsburg reascended the throne in Budapest.

Crisis
On 27 March 1921 Karl unexpectedly returned to his homeland and called upon the Regent of Hungary, Admiral Horthy, to transfer his powers to the rightful ruler. This act triggered a crisis for Czechoslovakia and Yugoslavia. The latter responded two days later by declaring that it would regard any attempt to restore Karl as a casus belli. And Prague responded on the 30th with a Note to Hungary threatening diplomatic, economic, and military measures if Karl was not deported promptly. These warnings triggered a crisis for Hungary: they were perceived as threats of invasion and occupation, as well as a challenge to its political regime, by two neighbors then bound by a military alliance. Budapest responded on 1 April by adopting measures to deport Karl.

More pressure was imposed by the Conference of Ambassadors: it sent a

Note to Hungary warning of "disastrous consequences" if Karl was not removed. And on the 4th Czechoslovakia issued an ultimatum demanding Karl's deportation by the 7th. Yugoslavia supported the Czechoslovak action. So too did Romania. The first stage of this crisis—but not the international crisis as a whole—ended for all actors on 5 April when Karl was induced by Hungary, quietly, to return to Switzerland.

Hungary, Czechoslovakia, and Yugoslavia each perceived a second crisis over a renewed Hapsburg attempt to regain the Hungarian throne. In the months following Karl's resumed exile in Switzerland efforts were made to solve the "Hapsburg Question." While negotiations were in motion Karl suddenly returned to Hungary once more, on 20 October 1921, triggering a fresh foreign policy crisis for the same three states. The situation was aggravated by his arrival in German-speaking Burgenland, then a contentious issue for Hungary and Austria (see Case #24—**Burgenland Dispute** below)—and by the fact that royalist forces there rallied to Karl. In fact, he marched on Budapest with an improvised force.

On 22 October Hungary's government acknowledged a fear of invasion by its neighbors, with good reason. Czechoslovakia mobilized its army that day. And Yugoslavia did so the next day. The Conference of Ambassadors accentuated Hungary's concern by threatening to allow the Little Entente (Czechoslovakia, Yugoslavia, Romania) to act as it saw fit in the crisis. On 29 October the first two Little Entente allies issued an ultimatum threatening to invade Hungary unless the Hapsburg Question was resolved. Karl was arrested, handed over to the Allies, and exiled on 1 November to Portugal's island of Madeira (where he died in 1922).

Under pressure from the victorious Allies, Hungary's National Assembly passed a law on 10 November 1921 excluding a Hapsburg restoration to the throne forever. As a result Yugoslavia demobilized its forces on the 12th and Czechoslovakia on the 15th indicating the end of the international crisis as a whole arising from Karl's attempt to regain the throne of Hungary.

(The former imperial family was also barred from neighboring Austria. When the Hapsburg heir defied this law 75 years later, in March 1996, President Klestil urged the repeal of an "anachronistic" law, noting that Karl's aged sons did not pose a threat to Austria.)

There were many involved actors. France, Italy, Japan, and the U.K., acting through the Conference of Ambassadors, as noted, adopted a tough stand against a Hapsburg restoration. Romania, even as a passive member of the Little Entente, was perceived by Hungary as another potential invader. Austria was perceived by Hungary as actively supporting the royalist forces backing Karl. Spain and Switzerland, along with Austria, were involved in the negotiations to find a suitable exile for Karl. Poland sent a protest note to Hungary. And Portugal provided a place of exile for Karl. This case also revealed the power and solidarity of the Little Entente in the early 1920s.

The League of Nations was not involved in this crisis.

(See *Master Table,* pp. 668–69.)

Sources
DBFP (Medlicott et al.) 1980; Boulter 1928; Dedijer 1974; Horthy 1957; Kertesz 1953; Toynbee 1927c; Vondracek 1937.

(22) Austrian Separatists

Yugoslavia and Austria experienced a crisis from 11 May to 21 June 1921 over the threat of secession by several Austrian provinces and their merger with Germany.

Background
The Republic of Austria was proclaimed on 13 November 1918, the day after the abdication of Karl IV, the last emperor of Austria-Hungary. Under the terms of the Treaty of Saint-Germain, signed by Austria on 10 September 1919, the union of Austria with Germany *(anschluss)* was forbidden except with the League of Nations's consent. Almost at once and continuing through 1920 and 1921 some Austrian provinces attempted to secede and to join the new German Republic, despite statements by the Allied Powers from as early as December 1919 that they would use all means available to prevent the *anschluss* of Austria or any Austrian province with Germany.

Pre-crisis
Despite France's warning that it would withhold aid to Austria if a plebiscite in Tyrol called for 24 April 1921 was held, the people of Tyrol voted in favor of union with Germany. The Tyrol precedent led Salzburg to announce its own plebiscite on 29 May. This generated anxiety among Austria's neighbors and the major powers.

Crisis
Salzburg's announcement, especially the possibility of its merger with Germany, triggered a crisis for Yugoslavia on 11 May 1921. It responded with an implied threat to occupy the Austrian province of Carinthia if the Salzburg plebiscite were held. The rumor reached Vienna on 12 May, triggering a crisis for Austria. The Mayr government could not prevent the plebiscite on 29 May which, like Tyrol, also strongly supported union with Germany. France and Italy intimated to Austria's ministers in Paris and Rome that they might occupy Austria to prevent an *anschluss*.

Czechoslovakia, Poland, and Romania protested against the plebiscites. The attitude of Germany and the U.K. was more muted, the former favoring, the latter opposing, the Austrian separatists. Tension rose when the province of Styria called its own plebiscite for 3 June.

The Mayr cabinet resigned on 1 June. A new Austrian cabinet was formed on 21 June under Schöber. The crisis was resolved by assurances from the other Austrian provinces that plebiscites would not be held for at least six months and by the suspension of the Tyrol and Salzburg thrust to separation and union with Germany.

Many states, as noted, exhibited varying degrees of involvement: Yugoslavia and Austria as the crisis actors; France and Italy, with a threat to occupy Austria; and a lower political profile by Germany, Poland, Romania, and the U.K.

The League of Nations was not involved.

(The crisis over Austrian separatists was gestating at the same time as the first stage of the crisis arising from the deposed Emperor Karl's attempts to regain the Hungarian throne [see Case #21—**Karl's Return to Hungary** above]. Integration into Germany was to occur in March 1938 under the threat of imminent invasion by Nazi Germany [see Case #60—**Anschluss** below].)

(See *Master Table,* pp. 668–69.)

Sources
Ball 1937; Bauer [1925] 1970; Langer 1972; Taylor 1963.

(23) Albanian Frontier, 1921 (see Italy/Albania/Yugoslavia PC)

(24) Burgenland Dispute

Hungary and Austria experienced a crisis over the disputed territory of Burgenland (German West Hungary) from 28 August until 28 December 1921.

Pre-crisis
The treaties of St. Germain (10 September 1919) and Trianon (4 June 1920) had assigned the predominantly German-speaking area of Burgenland, only 15 miles from Vienna, to Austria. The date of the transfer from Hungary was fixed for 28 August 1921.

Crisis
Austrian police entered Burgenland that day, triggering a crisis for Hungary. In minor clashes they were rebuffed by regular and irregular Hungarian forces, triggering a crisis for Austria the same day. The next day its chancellor acknowledged the likelihood of more serious developments in Burgenland. Several days later Austria's government asserted that the peace of the republic was threatened.

Through the mediation of Italy's foreign minister a plebiscite was incorporated in the Venice Protocol, 13 October. Austria, however, was dissatisfied with some of the provisions and ratified the Protocol only under pressure from the great powers. The plebiscite, held in December 1921, gave most of Burgenland—except Odenburg—to Austria and ended the crisis for both on 28 December.

Among the involved actors were three major powers, as noted: Italy mediated the Venice Protocol, which France and the U.K. pressed Austria to accept. Czechoslovakia's offer of mediation was declined by Austria.

The League of Nations, to which Austria appealed, was nonresponsive. (See *Master Table,* pp. 670–71.)

Sources
DBFP (Medlicott et al.) 1980; Bauer [1925] 1970; Burghardt 1962; Horthy 1957; Kertesz 1953; Mitrany 1933.

(27) Ruhr I, 1923 (see France/Germany PC)

(28) Corfu Incident

Greece was confronted with a foreign policy crisis over the island of Corfu from 31 August to 29 September 1923.

Pre-crisis
The commission appointed by the Conference of Ambassadors to delimit the Albania/Greece border (see Case #23—**Albanian Frontier,** in 1921, in **Italy/Albania/Yugoslavia PC**) resumed its work in May 1923. From the outset the relations between the commission, especially its Italian Chairman, General Enrico Tellini, and Greece were strained: the Greek delegate openly claimed that he was partial to Albania's claims.

On 27 August Tellini and three assistants were murdered by unknown assailants at Kakavia near the Greek/Albanian frontier within Greek territory. Two days later Italy delivered a seven-point ultimatum to Athens demanding compliance within 24 hours. The Greek prime minister made counterproposals on the 30th, to no avail. The next day a protest note from the Conference of Ambassadors, with Italy's concurrence, was presented to Greece.

(It was learned later that, in July–August 1923, a secret decision was taken at the highest level, by Mussolini himself, to occupy Corfu in case Greece reacted adversely to Italy's proclamation of sovereignty over the Dodecanese Islands, long part of Greek territory. Military preparations to that end were taken in August.)

Italy's behavior was a classic example of a "pure opportunity" crisis actor. According to a definitive biography of Mussolini, "[H]e was casting about for some striking act of international brigandage that would eclipse memories of D'Annunzio's invasion of Fiume. . . . [I]n July 1923, . . . he ordered plans to be prepared for a landing on the Greek island of Corfu . . . in reply to the Greek 'provocations' that he intended to organize" [Smith 1982, 72].

Crisis
On 31 August, the same day as the protest note from the Conference of Ambassadors, Italian naval forces shelled and occupied the unfortified Greek island of

Corfu, triggering a crisis for Greece. Denouncing the seizure of Corfu as a "warlike" act, Greece appealed to the League of Nations on 1 September under Articles 12 and 15 of the Covenant. On the 2nd it pledged cooperation to the Conference of Ambassadors and proposed an international inquiry.

The League Council debated the issue on the 4th despite Italy's contention that it lacked competence in the matter; but the Council virtually withdrew from the task of crisis management by transferring the dispute to the Conference of Ambassadors. The Conference ruled in favor of Italy on the 5th: Greece was ordered to pay an indemnity of 50 million lira to Italy, clearly implying Greece's guilt for the Tellini murders. Four days later Greece accepted the demands of the Conference and Italy regarding reparations, in principle. Italy was to evacuate Corfu, which it did on 27 September; but it escaped censure for its self-declared "temporary occupation" of the island. The crisis ended on the 29th, when Greece agreed to pay the indemnity under protest.

There were many involved actors in the Corfu Incident of 1923: the members of the Conference of Ambassadors—Belgium, France, Japan, and the U.K., apart from Italy; Albania and Yugoslavia; and the League of Nations Council.

(A related dispute between the U.K. and Albania over mine-laying operations in the Corfu Channel during World War II, which caused damage and casualties to ships of the Royal Navy in 1946, was resolved by an even-handed ruling of the International Court of Justice in April 1949 without becoming a full-blown international crisis: the *IJC* awarded damages to the U.K., but British mine-sweeping operations in 1946 were termed a violation of Albanian sovereignty [see also Case #71—**Invasion of Albania,** in 1939, in **Italy/Albania/Yugoslavia PC**].)

(See *Master Table,* pp. 670–71.)

Sources
Documents on British Foreign Policy (DBFP) (Medlicott et al.) 1983; Barros 1965; Carr 1945; Cassels 1970; Dexter 1967; Eagleton 1957; Smith 1982; Toynbee 1927c; Walters 1952.

(30) Ruhr II, 1924 (see France/Germay PC)

(32) Bulgaria/Greece Frontier

An armed confrontation between Greece and Bulgaria occurred from 19 October to 15 December 1925.

Background
Like most Balkan frontiers during the inter–world war era the border between Greece and Bulgaria in 1925 was tense and prone to military incidents.

Crisis

A minor incident between Greek and Bulgarian border guards on 19 October 1925—one Greek soldier was killed—triggered a crisis for Greece: due to distorted intelligence and faulty communications it was misreported to Athens as a large-scale premeditated Bulgarian attack and was perceived as threatening Greece's security. The Greek response was swift: on 20 October an army corps was ordered to the frontier; and on the 22nd Greek troops, reportedly supported by artillery and air power, crossed the border, triggering a crisis for Bulgaria.

Sofia massed troops in the area; but in order to secure great power support it responded to the crisis primarily by diplomatic means. During the first few days Bulgaria requested a cease-fire. On the 22nd it appealed to the League of Nations requesting an immediate meeting of the League Council to resolve the crisis.

Within an hour of his receipt of the Bulgarian telegram early in the morning of 23 October the League's Secretary-General called an emergency meeting of the Council for the 26th, the earliest possible date. He also informed the (French) President of the Council, Briand, who immediately exhorted both parties to cease all military movements at once and withdraw their troops behind their own frontiers.

The extraordinary meeting of the League Council on 26 October demanded confirmation within 24 hours that orders for the withdrawal of (Greek) troops had been issued, to be completed within 60 hours. The U.K., France, and Italy were "requested" to send their military attachés to monitor the withdrawal. Under League and great power pressure, Greece complied, ordering the suspension of hostilities two and a half hours before a scheduled launching of an offensive on Petric, a center of activity of the anti-Greek, Macedonian revolutionary organization, the *Komitadji*. Its forces were withdrawn by 29 October.

The League Council then dispatched a commission of inquiry, after securing from both parties a commitment to accept and implement its decision, that is, compulsory arbitration. Responsibility for the incident was divided: Bulgaria, for the killing of a Greek soldier; Greece, for the breach of the peace causing heavy casualties and material damage in Bulgarian border villages. Greece was ordered to pay a nominal indemnity (45,000 pounds sterling) to Bulgaria. The crisis ended on 15 December, when both parties accepted the Council's ruling. However, conflict over the frontier persisted.

There were many involved actors, both major and minor powers. The U.K., France, and Italy strongly supported the League's pressure on Greece to terminate the hostilities. Romania, Yugoslavia, Germany, and Turkey were less involved. The League of Nations played the pivotal role in crisis management: "The Graeco-Bulgarian dispute was the culminating moment of this [first] phase of the history of the League" (Zimmern 1936, 372).

(See *Master Table,* pp. 670–71.)

Sources
Barros 1970; Boulter 1928; Dexter 1967; Eagleton 1957; Logio 1936; Macartney
1928; Walters 1952; Zimmern 1936.

(34) Hegemony over Albania, 1926–27 (see Italy/Albania/Yugoslavia PC)

(36) Vilna II, 1927 (see Lithuania/Poland PC)

(45) Austria Putsch

The crisis over the attempted *putsch* (plot to overthrow the government) in
Austria occurred between 25 and 31 July 1934. Austria, Czechoslovakia, Italy,
and Yugoslavia were crisis actors.

Background and Pre-crisis
Chancellor Dollfuss began ruling Austria by emergency decrees in March 1932
and built his dictatorship on the anti-Nazi and anti-marxist principles of the
Heimwehr (Home Guard) militia. All elections were prohibited after the Nazis
won nine of the 20 seats in the Innsbruck municipality. In May 1933 about 100
Austrian Nazis were arrested at a political demonstration. A Nazi campaign of
terror led to the formal suppression of the Austrian Nazi Party, the *NSDAP*. The
party went underground. Germany's aggressive policy toward Austria increased
in the summer of 1933. Dollfuss's efforts to secure support abroad succeeded in
acquiring moral and financial support for Vienna from France and the U.K. His
appeal to his patron, Mussolini, led to an Italian warning to Hitler on 5 August
and subsequent assurances of Italian support. A series of provocative German
broadcasts directed at Austria were initiated from the Bavarian capital. Italy,
France, and Britain sent representatives to Berlin to discuss the cessation of
German subversive activity in Austria, with partial success, although the broadcasts continued. On 11 August 1933 there was a shooting incident on the Austro-
German frontier. On the 14th alleged documents of the Austrian Nazi Party were
published, but their authenticity was denied by the Party. On 3 October there was
an unsuccessful assassination attempt on Dollfuss. Attempts at reconciliation
between Austria and Germany did not produce results.

On 12 February 1934 the headquarters of the Socialist Party in Linz was
stormed. A strike by the electrical workers paralyzed Austria. Arrests of most of
the Socialist leaders followed. Three days of heavy fighting between the Heimwehr and the Socialists followed. Martial law was proclaimed, together with the
dissolution of the Socialist Party, trade unions, and all affiliated organizations.
On 1 May the Austrian cabinet declared a new constitution: the country would
henceforth be ruled by the clerical fascists of the Heimwehr. Dollfuss assumed
the portfolios of public security, foreign affairs, and war, apart from the chancel-
lorship. Hitler and Mussolini met in Venice on 14 June to discuss the Austrian

question. On 12 July the Austrian cabinet decreed the death penalty for unauthorized possession of explosives following discovery that a new supply of arms was pouring across the German border. A Czechoslovakian worker was beaten and hung by the police in Vienna on the 24th. A cabinet meeting was rescheduled for the following day.

Crisis
On 25 July 1934 Austrian Nazis attacked the chancery and killed Dollfuss, triggering a crisis for Austria, Czechoslovakia, and Italy. Austria's response, the same day, was to repress the rebellion and arrest participating members of the SS unit. The vice-chancellor took charge of the government. Two days later Czechoslovakia, fearing that a German invasion of Austria would lead to an Italian invasion as well, threatened to move troops in the direction of Vienna to protect its own territory. Italy, determined to prevent an *anschluss* (union) of Austria with Germany, responded immediately by rushing troops to the border at the Brenner Pass on 25 July and by warning Hitler that, if the Germans invaded Austria, Italy would cross that border. At that time Dollfuss's family was in Italy, as Mussolini's guests, and were awaiting the chancellor's arrival on the 27th.

The Italian response of 25 July triggered a crisis for Yugoslavia, which had a long-standing dispute with Italy over Carinthia. Italian troops at the Brenner Pass constituted a serious security problem for Yugoslavia. Its response, that day, was a threat to move forces, mobilization, the strengthening of frontier guards, and the movement of some troops to the Moribor area on the Yugoslav/Austrian border.

The crisis ended for Austria, Czechoslovakia, and Italy on 31 July, by which time the Austrian militia had completed the suppression of Nazi uprisings that had belatedly broken out in the provinces. Yugoslavia's crisis ended that day as well, as a result of Italy's decision not to send troops into Austria. Germany's decision to pull back from an attempted anschluss constituted a tacit agreement with Italy not to take such action then or later without the latter's approval.

France, the U.K., and Germany were involved actors. The first two feared a war in Europe as a consequence of a successful putsch, while Hitler decried its failure, fearing Western blame for the attempt and not being militarily prepared as yet for a showdown with Britain and France.

There was no League of Nations activity in this crisis.
(See *Master Table*, pp. 672–73.)

Sources
See sources for Case #60; and Ball 1937; Weinberg 1970.

(46) Assassination of King Alexander

The international crisis that followed the assassination of Yugoslavia's King Alexander began on 8 October and ended on 10 December 1934. The crisis actors were Yugoslavia and Hungary.

Background
In 1921 King Alexander became the ruler of the Croatian, Serbian, and Slovene peoples. In 1929 he proclaimed a royal dictatorship and changed the name of the state to Yugoslavia. A new constitution was proclaimed in 1931, based on the will of the Serbs and the suppression of the minority Croats and Slovenes. Croatian refugees fled to Italy, Bulgaria, and especially Hungary where they organized terrorist acts against Alexander's tyranny. The attempt to halt the movement of terrorists led to shooting and border incidents between Yugoslavia and Hungary. Alexander accused Hungary of giving aid to Yugoslavia's enemies. Budapest denied the allegation and brought the Croatian claim before the League of Nations. French Foreign Minister Louis Barthou extended an invitation to King Alexander to visit Paris in October 1934. He wished to confer with the monarch on future policies toward Austria and Italy.

Crisis
On 8 October 1934, hours after King Alexander reached Marseilles, he and Louis Barthou were killed by a Macedonian assassin bearing a Hungarian passport. This triggered a crisis for Yugoslavia. Leaders of the Croatian terrorist organization were arrested in Italy at the French government's request, but Rome refused to extradite them to France or allow for their interrogation. Anti-Italian demonstrations broke out in Yugoslav towns. The Quai d'Orsay (a synonym for France's foreign ministry), on the eve of a Franco-Italian rapprochement, persuaded Yugoslavia to minimize the evidence of Italian complicity and to concentrate its anger on Hungary.

The delayed Yugoslav response, and the crisis trigger for Hungary, was a Yugoslav appeal to the League of Nations on 22 November, alleging that the assassins had been selected at Janka Puszta and had left Hungary freely with Hungarian passports. Budapest denied most of the charges in its response of 24 November. (Hungary had first approached the League Council, on 12 May, complaining of conditions on the frontiers of the two states.)

Threats of war passed, but feelings between the two countries were bitter and angry. A report was presented to the League affirming that certain Hungarian authorities had, at least by negligence, failed to prevent and repress political terrorism, with the result that the task of the assassins had been facilitated. Hungary was asked to make further investigations and report the result. The League discussions ended with a resolution requesting Hungary to "take at once appropriate punitive action in the case of any of its authorities whose culpability may have been established" and to report back to the Council. A commission of experts was set up to study the possibility of an international convention to discourage terrorism. The crisis terminated on 10 December 1934 when both states accepted the League resolution.

(In December, too, Belgrade initiated a brutal eviction of several thousand innocent Hungarian peasants from its territory but stopped when indignant protests were issued from abroad. In January 1935 Hungary informed the Council

that a detailed investigation had disclosed no official responsibility for the Marseilles crime.)
(See *Master Table*, pp. 672–73.)

Sources
Bullock 1962; Carr 1945; von Papen 1952; Schuman 1939; Shirer 1964; Walters 1952; Weinberg 1970.

(48) Bulgaria/Turkey

A two-stage non-violent crisis between Bulgaria and Turkey occurred between 6 March and 31 August 1935.

Background and Pre-crisis
On 8 February 1934 the Balkan Pact was signed by Greece, Romania, Turkey, and Yugoslavia: it provided mutual guarantees for the security of their borders; and each promised not to take action regarding any Balkan nonsignatory without previous discussions. Bulgaria had long refused to recognize the status quo established by the post–World War I peace treaties. On 1 March 1935 the followers of Venizelos in Greece staged an uprising in Athens, Macedonia, and Crete as a protest against royalism. Turkey began concentrating troops on its borders with Bulgaria and Greece.

Crisis
On 6 March Bulgaria's foreign minister expressed his country's alarm at the troop concentrations and complained of anti-Bulgarian propaganda in the Turkish press. Two days later Bulgaria responded with an aide-mémoire to the League of Nations charging Turkey with "aggression" and requesting League action, thereby triggering a crisis for Ankara. At a press conference Turkey denied unfriendly intentions, declared that its troop concentrations were directed at Greece, countercharged that there was a Bulgarian military buildup along the border, and affirmed its intent to maintain the status quo in the Balkans. This had the desired effect. On 10 March Bulgaria withdrew its memo from the League and asserted its peaceful intentions ending the first stage of this crisis for both actors.

Relations between Bulgaria and Turkey remained tense during the next five months. In March Kemal Atatürk was reelected President of Turkey for the next four years. Turkey continued its active policy of rearmament because of distrust of Italy's intentions in the eastern Mediterranean. In July the Turkish War Ministry ordered the fortification of Kirklareli near Bulgaria's southern border on the Black Sea. Bulgaria's nationalists desired an outlet to the Aegean Sea through the Turkish Gulf of Saros.

On 3 August 1935, as the Turkish fortifications at Kirklareli neared completion, Bulgaria's War Council met in emergency session and decided on immediate construction of strong permanent fortifications around the southern Bulgarian town of Haskovo. The Bulgarian perception of threat rose further when the Turkish army began carrying out maneuvers in Eastern Thrace near the border. On 23 August the Turkish minister to Bulgaria informed his government of the growing anxiety in Bulgaria regarding Turkish military maneuvers, especially in view of the fact that they were attended by all high-ranking Turkish officers. He also reported on the growing resentment at the anti-Bulgarian articles in the Turkish press. By 25 August the concentration of Turkish troops on the Bulgarian border was reported to have reached the strength of three army corps.

On 31 August, although half of the Turkish army was on maneuvers, the crisis ended with a visit to Sofia by Turkish Foreign Minister Aras resulting in a joint statement disapproving anti-Bulgarian attacks in the Turkish press.

The League of Nations was not involved in this crisis.

(See *Master Table*, pp. 674–75.)

Sources
Albrecht-Carrié 1965; Schuman 1939.

(49) Kaunas Trials

Lithuania's crisis with Germany over the Kaunas trials lasted from 28 March to 25 September 1935.

Background
The Versailles Treaty following World War I placed the city of Memel under Allied sovereignty. It was occupied by Lithuania in 1923, and the following year the League of Nations awarded Memel a special status under Lithuanian sovereignty. A dissatisfied Germany, which declared its intention to regain the city, was eagerly supported by Memel's German inhabitants. Parallel to the Nazi rise to power in Germany, Nazi and Nazi-front organizations became active in Lithuania. In 1934 an accusation of conspiracy against Lithuania was made against 122 Nazis who were tried in Kaunas. On 26 March 1935 they were found guilty.

Crisis
In response to the Kaunas trials Germany closed its border with Lithuania and imposed economic sanctions. This triggered a crisis for Lithuania on 28 March. Even before the trial had ended Memel police and border guards had been alerted to the possibility of an uprising or even an invasion. When Hitler urged the three guarantor powers (Britain, France, and Italy) to take action, they handed a protest note to Lithuania together with a threat to bring the issue to the League.

Tension reached its peak when, on 17 May, a Lithuanian appeals court upheld all the sentences except one. That day Germany moved its troops to the border, as did Lithuania while calling up reserve forces. During the period between May and September tension remained high, with Germany's repeated declarations of hostility. On 25 September elections were held in Memel, and their results led to a temporary reduction of tension. A détente between Germany and Lithuania was reached when the latter agreed to new amendments in its electoral laws.

The League of Nations played no role in this crisis.

(See *Master Table*, pp. 674–75.)

Sources
Gehase 1946; Gerutis 1969; Schuman 1939; Shirer 1964; Weinberg 1970.

(51) Remilitarization of the Rhineland, 1936 (see France/Germany PC)

(52) Spanish Civil War I, 1936–37 (see Spain PC)

(54) Spanish Civil War II, 1937 (see Spain PC)

(60) Anschluss

The **Anschluss** crisis between Austria and Germany took place between 12 February and 14 March 1938.

Background
Relations between Germany and Austria, after the 1934 **Putsch** attempt (see Case #45 above), had been governed by the Agreement of July 1936. The interpretation of that agreement, however, was marked by wide differences of opinion on the part of the two states. The government of Austria hoped to work these out in a meeting with Hitler. Accordingly, on the evening of 11 February 1938 Chancellor Schuschnigg left for Germany accompanied by his secretary of foreign affairs.

Crisis
A crisis for Austria began on 12 February 1938 when Hitler presented Schuschnigg with an ultimatum: the Austrian government was to recognize the Nazi Party and National Socialism as perfectly compatible with loyalty to Austria; the Minister of the Interior would be the Nazi Seyss-Inquart; an amnesty for all imprisoned Austrian Nazis was to be proclaimed within three days; and dismissed Nazi officials and officers would be reinstated. Finally, the Austrian economy was to be integrated with that of Germany, and Fischboek was to be appointed Minister of Finance. The Austrian chancellor signed the papers agreeing to Hitler's demands the same day.

By the end of the first week of the crisis Schuschnigg had decided upon some action to ensure the Austrian government's mastery of its own house. He called for a plebiscite on 13 March in which the Austrian people would be invited to declare whether or not they were in favor of an independent Austria.

The crisis trigger for Germany occurred on 9 March when Hitler was informed of Austria's plans to hold a plebiscite. A surprised Führer, furious at this obstruction of his plans, responded the next day with a decision to invade Austria. A special messenger was sent to Mussolini asking him not to interfere. By the 11th German army trucks and tanks were already on their way south. Schuschnigg offered to delay the plebiscite, but Göring demanded his resignation and the appointment of Seyss-Inquart as Chancellor. President Miklas at first refused to do so, but at midnight on 11 March he complied as preparations for a German invasion of Austria proceeded seriously. On 13 March Seyss-Inquart secured the passage of a law by the Austrian government annexing Austria to the Third Reich. On the 14th the crisis ended for both actors when Hitler made his triumphal visit to Vienna. This was accompanied by strong anti-Semitic demonstrations.

While Austria had no illusions about Britain's and France's willingness to act in its favor, it perceived that opposition by Italy might serve as a deterrent to Hitler. When Italy refused to take any action against Germany, Austrian decision makers concluded that they had no choice but to comply with Hitler's demands.

The League of Nations was not involved in this crisis.

(See *Master Table*, pp. 676–77.)

Sources
Ball 1937; Bullock 1962; Carr 1945; Edmondson 1978; Gedye 1939; Gehl 1963; von Papen 1952; Schuman 1939; Shirer 1964; Smith 1982; Thorne 1967; Villari 1956; Weinberg 1980.

(61) Polish Ultimatum, 1938 (see Lithuania/Poland PC)

(62) Czech. May Crisis, 1938 (see Czech./Germany PC)

(64) Munich, 1938 (see Czech./Germany PC)

(65) Spanish Civil War III, 1938 (see Spain PC)

(67) Spanish Civil War IV, 1938–39 (see Spain PC)

(68) Czech. Annexation, 1939 (see Czech./Germany PC)

(69) Memel

Germany's demand for the annexation of Memel created a crisis for Lithuania from 15 to 22 March 1939.

Background and Pre-crisis
Memel and its surrounding area, once part of East Prussia, were awarded to Lithuania by the Versailles Treaty, under the supervision of a League High Commissioner, and were formally incorporated in 1923. The city, German-speaking, was made semiautonomous on 7 May 1924 and was guaranteed by France, Britain, Italy, and Japan. The surrounding area, Lithuanian-speaking, was placed under Lithuania's sovereignty. Increasing tension between the area's populations followed, especially after the Nazi accession to power in Berlin in 1933.

In 1934 many prominent Germans were arrested in Memel and were accused of planning a Nazi putsch there (see Case #49—**Kaunas Trials** above). The Germans retaliated by boycotting Lithuanian agricultural produce. By 1936 the situation had normalized, and a trade treaty was signed between the two countries. The Nazi Party, though illegal, grew in Memel, and more arrests took place in the late spring of 1937. Elections were due to be held in late 1938; and despite Lithuanian electoral law concessions, Nazi strength grew in Memel during the campaign, with the anticipation of a reintegration into Germany after the Austrian **Anschluss** of March 1938 (see Case #60 above). After the elections German representation had improved to slightly over 80 percent of the Memel *Diet* (legislature). The new Lithuanian government, formed in December 1938, endeavored to be firm on the issue of Memel's autonomy, while Nazification and demands for incorporation into the Reich continued and German pressure increased. In early March 1939 the German press took up a renewed anti-Lithuanian campaign. On the 13th the Lithuanian prime minister perceived the danger of a German coup in Memel and related this to the British chargé d'affaires: he anticipated an announcement at the forthcoming meeting of the Memel Diet.

Crisis
On 15 March, when Germany took over Bohemia and Moravia, the remnant of Czechoslovakia (see Case #68—**Czech. Annexation**, in **Czech./Germany PC**), a crisis over Memel was triggered for Lithuania. Nazi party leader Neumann addressed a special meeting of the Memel Diet, pressing for a radical change in the relations between Memel and Lithuania. Rumors of immediate Nazi annexation followed rapidly. At a meeting between the local Lithuanian governor and German party leaders the governor refused to consider any concessions. The following day his attitude became more conciliatory, and a promise was made to convene the Diet on 25 March.

On 20 March Lithuanian Foreign Minister Urbsys was summoned to Berlin and was handed an ultimatum to return Memel to Germany. He was also warned not to consult any other power. Nonetheless, he spoke to the British, French, and Polish military attachés, indicating that Lithuania's decision would depend on their willingness to provide aid. Upon his return to Kaunas, German troops were reported moving toward the frontier with Lithuania. Shortly thereafter, Germany demanded an agreement. The Lithuanian cabinet met on 20 March and accepted the ultimatum. Two communiqués, issued by Lithuania, were withdrawn upon German disapproval.

The crisis ended on 22 March with the formal approval of an agreement signed in Berlin. Hitler arrived in Memel the following day to an enthusiastic welcome. The agreement safeguarded Lithuanian economic access and a free harbor zone and pledged nonaggression between the two countries. Britain, France, and Poland, the other involved actors, denied aid to Lithuania.

The League of Nations was not involved in this crisis.

(See *Master Table,* pp. 676–77.)

Sources
Cienciala 1968; Gerutis 1969; Sabaliunas 1972; Schuman 1941; Shirer 1964; Thorne 1967; Toynbee 1953a; Weinberg 1980.

(70) Danzig

A crisis for Poland over Danzig took place between 21 March and 6 April 1939.

Background
The Treaty of Versailles declared Danzig, predominantly German-speaking, a free city. Poland was allowed to use the port, its only access to the sea. A strip of land lying east of Danzig and the local Polish provinces linked Germany with East Prussia. In 1934 Poland signed a Non-Aggression Pact with Germany, and in November 1937 Hitler officially disavowed his aim of incorporating Danzig into Germany.

On 4 October 1938 the Polish ambassador in Berlin met with Foreign Minister Ribbentrop. The latter proposed incorporating Danzig into the Reich, granting an extraterritorial railroad and road into Germany, while leaving Poland to maintain a road, railway, and free port in Danzig, and guaranteed markets, a recognition of boundaries, and an extension of the Polish-German Pact. Poland would also join the Anti-Comintern Pact. Polish Foreign Minister Beck declined and insisted on retaining Polish rights to Danzig while proposing a joint Polish-German guarantee to replace League of Nations protection. On 21 October Hitler began to plan for military action over Danzig. Beck met with Hitler and Ribbentrop in Germany in early January 1939. After the final German takeover in Czechoslovakia (see Case #68—**Czech. Annexation,** in **Czech./Germany PC**) and Hitler's demand to Lithuania for Memel, both in mid-March 1939 (see Case #69 above), the issue of Danzig flared up once again.

Crisis
Poland's crisis was triggered on 21 March 1939 when Ribbentrop placed Germany's demand for Danzig before Polish Ambassador Lipski. The Polish foreign minister sought support against German aggression, especially from Britain, which was at that time trying to establish joint guarantees with France and the

Soviet Union. On 21–22 March Anglo-French conversations took place in London. The addition of an economic threat to Romania by Germany induced the U.K. to try to reach an agreement with France for the support of the whole of Eastern Europe, including Polish aid to Romania, if necessary. On 26 March Poland responded to German demands by offering to consider simplifying road and rail communications to East Prussia and by rejecting any extraterritorial highway, as well as the annexation of Danzig to the Reich. Ribbentrop, mentioning Polish interests in the Ukraine and hinting that Hitler might conclude that there could be no understanding with Poland, asked for further Polish consideration, to which Lipski agreed. Meanwhile, the U.K. continued to maneuver for a Four-Power declaration, while dropping the Soviet Union from the list, at Poland's request. Britain finally agreed upon a declaration of support for Poland while, at the same time, soliciting Polish support for Romania and Yugoslavia. On 31 March Chamberlain announced in the House of Commons that the U.K. would offer support to Poland if there was any threat to its independence, and that France had agreed to do likewise. On 3 April Beck journeyed to London for further talks, receiving an official guarantee on 6 April that the U.K. "would feel themselves bound at once to lend the Polish Government all support in their power." This terminated the crisis for Poland in victory; but the ultimate outcome of the conflict over Danzig remained uncertain—until it was overrun by German forces five months later.

(The Danzig crisis of March–April 1939, like those over the German annexations of **Czechoslovakia** [Case #68] and **Memel** [Case #69 above] and the **Invasion of Albania** [Case #71, in **Italy/Albania/Yugoslovia PC**], was an integral part of the intense conflict throughout 1939 that was to culminate in the outbreak of World War II [Case #74, in **World War II PC**]. Danzig remained an important issue throughout the summer of 1939 as the city became semisecretly militarized and war approached. On 1 September Germany invaded Poland.)

The Soviet Union negotiated with Britain and France on forging a bloc against Germany but backed away when other demands were not met by the Western powers. This encouraged Polish suspicions of Moscow's motives and potential actions in support of Germany. The League of Nations was not active in this crisis.

(See *Master Table*, pp. 676–77.)

Sources
Bullock 1962; Carr 1945; Cienciala 1968; Debicki 1962; Polonsky 1972; Pounds 1964; Schuman 1941; Shirer 1964; Thorne 1967; Toynbee 1953a; Walters 1952; Weinberg 1980.

(71) Invasion of Albania, 1939 (see Italy/Albania/ Yugoslavia PC)

(74) Entry into World War II, 1939 (see Multiregional PCs: World War II)

(75) Soviet Occupation of the Baltic

A crisis for Estonia, Latvia, and Lithuania occurred between 26 September and 10 October 1939.

Background and Pre-crisis
The three Baltic states had asserted their independence from Russia in November 1918 (see Case #4, **Baltic Independence** above), and maintained their independence during the inter–world war period.

The German invasion of Poland on 1 September 1939 was followed by a Soviet invasion of that country on 17 September. By the end of that month Poland had been divided between Germany and the Soviet Union. The Soviets occupied 77,620 square miles of eastern Poland. Lithuania and Slovakia received small parts of Polish territory. On 22 September the Estonian Foreign Minister, Karl Selter, went to Moscow for negotiations on economic issues. While there, a demand was made that Estonia sign a mutual assistance pact that would grant the USSR a naval base and airfields in the then-independent state. Foreign Minister Molotov threatened Selter that, if the Estonian government refused to comply, Soviet demands would be obtained through other methods.

Crisis
On 26 September 1939 Selter informed his government of the Soviet demands, triggering a crisis for Estonia. This was accompanied by extensive flights of Soviet aircraft over Estonian territory and rumors of large Russian troop concentrations along the border. Estonia responded on the 28th by complying with the demands thereby ending its crisis.

On 1 October the Latvian Foreign Minister, Wilhelm Munters, was summoned to Moscow for discussions. He arrived on the 2nd and held conversations with Stalin and Molotov. A crisis was triggered the next day when the Soviets made a series of demands under the threat of war. Lithuania's Foreign Minister, Joseph Urbsys, arrived in Moscow on the 3rd as well, to receive similar demands, triggering a crisis for Lithuania. Latvia, realizing that British or French assistance was out of the question at that time, and aware of the fact that 16 Soviet divisions were concentrated on the Latvian border, responded by signing a mutual assistance pact on 5 October. This marked the end of Latvia's crisis. The pact allowed the USSR to gain control over the Gulf of Riga and several air and naval bases. Thirty thousand Soviet troops were to be garrisoned in Latvia.

Negotiations between the USSR and Lithuania were conducted for a week after the trigger date, with Moscow applying severe pressure. The Soviet-Lithuanian Pact, ending the crisis, was signed on 10 October. It provided for the restoration of the city of Vilna to Lithuania and allowed the USSR to establish air and land bases and to maintain 20,000 troops in Lithuania. Lithuania, while viewing the return of Vilna with much satisfaction, had become a Soviet satellite.

By that time the League of Nations had become an empty shell.

(The Soviet [and, after 1991, Russian] occupation of the Baltic states lasted 54 years, with as many as 200,000 troops. Lithuania, Latvia, and Estonia became independent in 1992. The withdrawal of Russian troops from Lithuania was completed in 1993, and from Latvia and Estonia on 31 August 1994.)

(See *Master Table,* pp. 678–79.)

Sources
Dallin 1960; Farr 1944; Gehase 1946; Roi 1948; Sabaliunas 1972; Schuman 1941; Spekke 1951; Svabe 1947; Tarulis 1959.

(76) Finnish War, 1939–40 (see Finland/Russia PC)

(77) Invasion of Scandinavia, 1940 (see Multiregional PCs: World War II)

(78) Fall of Western Europe, 1940 (see Multiregional PCs: World War II)

(80) Romanian Territory

Romania's crises over Bulgarian, Hungarian, and Soviet claims on its territories occurred between 26 June and 7 September 1940.

Background and Pre-crisis
After World War I Romania received disputed territories claimed by several of its neighbors, including the USSR, Hungary, and Bulgaria. In July 1935 Romania signed a Pact of Non-Aggression with the Soviet Union that involved tacit recognition of Romania's possession of Bessarabia and was the direct result of Hitler's election victory in Germany and Moscow's preoccupation with the situation in the Far East. The fall of France and the desperate position of Britain in the summer of 1940 (see Cases #78—**Fall of Western Europe;** and #81—**Battle of Britain,** in **Multiregional PCs: World War II**) caused shifts in the European balance that emphasized Romania's vulnerability. The USSR, in talks with Germany, indicated that it could no longer wait to solve the problem of Bessarabia, which had been Russian from 1812 to 1918. It became clear that, if one power pressed claims on Romania, others would seize the opportunity to follow suit. Both Hungary and Romania viewed Transylvania as an integral part of their history and territory. And Bulgaria had long been voicing its claims to southern Dobruja.

Crisis

On 26 June 1940 Soviet Foreign Minister Molotov handed the Romanian ambassador in Moscow a 24-hour ultimatum to evacuate Bessarabia. Further, as compensation for the years of loss, the USSR demanded northern Bukovina as well. Romania turned for aid to the Balkan Entente, without success, and to Germany, which advised acceptance of Soviet demands as the territories fell under the Soviet sphere according to the August 1939 Ribbentrop-Molotov agreement. Romania's major response, on 28 June 1940, was to yield. Nevertheless, military preparations and mobilization were also carried out. Advancing Soviet troops went beyond the areas designated in the agreement, and some minor clashes with Romanian forces occurred. Ultimately, the Soviets withdrew to the agreed boundaries and, on 2 July, the operation was completed, terminating Romania's crisis with the Soviet Union.

Encouraged by the Soviet victory, the Hungarian Nazi Party accused Romania, on 1 July 1940, of evicting Hungarians to make room for Bessarabian refugees, triggering Romania's crisis with Hungary over Transylvania. Hungarian leaders conferred with Hitler and Italy's Foreign Minister Ciano, where they were advised to attack only if there appeared to be no other way to achieve their aims. Romania compromised with a plan for a population exchange and some territorial concessions, but these were rejected. Its major response, on 13 July 1940, was an offer by King Carol to Hitler for an offensive-defensive alliance, clearly aimed at the possibility of receiving German support against Hungary, and a movement of troops. Hitler replied, on the 15th, that Romania must come to terms with Hungary. On 26–27 July Romania, upon the advice of Hitler and Mussolini, agreed to negotiate.

Meanwhile, in July, minor clashes occurred on the Bulgarian-Romanian border in connection with the Bessarabian refugees, and another crisis was triggered for Romania, this time with Bulgaria. While Romanian representatives met with Mussolini on 27 July, Hitler proposed negotiations to the Bulgarians. On 4 August 1940 Romania's major response to the Bulgarian crisis was to send a delegate to Germany empowered to open talks with the Bulgarians. A meeting was held on the 19th. As Bulgaria's claim was less drastic and generally justified, agreement was reached quickly. On 21 August, southern Dobruja was transferred. The formal agreement was signed on 7 September 1940 terminating Romania's crisis with Bulgaria.

The Hungarian claims were far more complex. After meetings on 16 and 24 August, negotiations broke off and both sides mobilized. Hungary's decision to invade followed air skirmishes. On 26 August German intervention was suggested by Ribbentrop. The following day, Hitler himself worked out the boundaries, and, on the 29th, he called upon Hungary and Romania to send envoys to Vienna. At the meeting Hungarian protests of inadequacies were shouted down while Romania's shock was simply ignored. Neither side had any real choice. After consulting the Crown Council, the Romanian minister accepted the terms of Hitler's imposed solution on 30 August 1940, terminating the crisis with

Hungary. In return, Hungary was obliged to grant its German minority a privileged status, amounting to pro-Reich autonomy. The borders remained stable for several years as the war progressed.

Although the League of Nations existed, formally, it was not involved. (See *Master Table,* pp. 680–81.)

Sources
Bantea 1970; Fischer-Galati 1969; Gafencu 1945; Macartney 1956–57; Pavel 1944; Waldeck 1943.

(81) Battle of Britain, 1940 (see Multiregional PCs: World War II)

(83) Balkan Invasions, 1940–41 (see Multiregional PCs: World War II)

(85) Barbarossa, 1941 (see Multiregional PCs: World War II)

(89) Stalingrad, 1942–43 (see Multiregional PCs: World War II)

(91) Fall of Italy, 1943 (see Multiregional PCs: World War II)

(92) German Occupation of Hungary, 1944 (see Multiregional PCs: World War II)

(93) Soviet Occupation of East Europe, 1944–45 (see Multiregional PCs: World War II)

(94) D-Day, 1944–45 (see Multiregional PCs: World War II)

(98) Greek Civil War I

A crisis for the U.K. over Greece lasted from 3 December 1944 to 15 January 1945.

Background
After the withdrawal of the German occupation forces from Greece in October 1944, there was an intense struggle for power among Greece's political factions. The British, who were determined to impose a settlement that would ensure stability and their strong presence in the country, were in direct opposition to

Greece's Communists. The Caserta Agreement, signed on 20 September 1944, called for all guerrilla forces in the country to be placed under Greek government command, headed by British General Scobie.

Crisis

The crisis trigger for the U.K. was an exchange of fire between Greek Communist demonstrators and the police on 3 December 1944. This touched off a violent civil war that was perceived by Britain as a threat to its influence in the international system. More specifically, a communist takeover in Greece would virtually end all British influence in the region. Prime Minister Churchill responded the next day by ordering General Scobie to intervene with his forces and to open fire if necessary. Churchill flew to Athens on 24 December in an effort to bring the various factions together and settle the crisis. In the course of serious clashes, British and Greek troops succeeded in driving the Greek Communists out of Athens.

The U.K.'s crisis ended on 15 January 1945 with the implementation of a truce agreement. The United States was not active in this crisis, though Churchill and Roosevelt corresponded regularly. State Department criticism of British intervention was viewed unfavorably by Churchill. On the other hand, USSR inactivity was viewed favorably because it meant that Stalin was living up to the terms of the "spheres of influence" agreement struck at an earlier meeting in Moscow. The civil war in Greece erupted into another crisis for Britain in 1946 (see Case #112—**Greek Civil War II,** in 1946–47, in **Multiregional PCs: East/West**).

The League of Nations was moribund by 1944–45.

(See *Master Table*, pp. 684–85.)

Sources

See sources for Case #112.

(100) Final Soviet Offensive, 1945 (see Multiregional PCs: World War II)

(102) Communism in Romania

A crisis between the Soviet Union and Romania lasted from 24 February to 6 March 1945.

Background

The Soviet August 1944 offensive against Germany prompted a palace revolt in Bucharest on 23 August 1944, and Romania became part of the Allied war effort against Germany (see Case #93—**Soviet Occupation of East Europe,** in **Multiregional PCs: World War II**). Predominant Soviet influence in Romania was recognized by the Allies in September 1944. Following the palace coup there was a succession of governments. Radescu was appointed Prime Minister in December 1944. The domestic political situation during his tenure was very fluid, and the country became increasingly paralyzed between Right and Left. Disturbances occurred in factories, with communist attempts to take over workshop committees. In February 1945 unrest steadily mounted, with violent criticisms in the Soviet media. The Romanian press was suppressed.

Crisis
A Soviet crisis was triggered on 24 February 1945 when rioting erupted in Bucharest. That evening Premier Radescu broadcast a call to resist all foreign attempts at intervention in Romania's affairs. The USSR response was the dispatch of Deputy Foreign Minister Vyshinsky to Bucharest on 27 February. Moscow demanded that Radescu be replaced immediately on the grounds that he was incapable of maintaining order. When King Michael refused to consider this, Vyshinsky issued an ultimatum to appoint the "democratic choice" as Premier, Petru Groza, the Soviet candidate for the position. He also informed the king that his refusal would be interpreted as a hostile act against the Soviet Union. Simultaneous with Vyshinsky's ultimatum, the Soviet Command in Bucharest moved Romanian troops from the capital to the front, eliminating the king's chances of resistance while one million Soviet troops remained within striking distance of the capital. This ultimatum, on 28 February, triggered a crisis for Romania. Soviet demands were complied with on 1 March. The termination date for both crisis actors was 6 March 1945, when Groza was installed as Prime Minister after the king had overcome domestic opposition.

The League of Nations was not functioning in 1945.

(See *Master Table*, pp. 684–85.)

Sources
Bishop and Crayfield 1948; Byrnes 1947; Fischer-Galati 1969, 1970; Ionescu 1964.

(104) Trieste I, 1945 (see Italy/Albania/Yugoslavia PC)

(110) Communism in Poland, 1946–47 (see Poland/Russia PC)

(112) Greek Civil War II, 1946–47 (see Multiregional PCs: East/West)

(113) Communism in Hungary, 1947 (see Multiregional PCs: East/West)

(114) Truman Doctrine, 1947 (see Multiregional PCs: East/West)

(115) Marshall Plan, 1947 (see Multiregional PCs: East/West)

(121) Communism in Czech., 1948 (see Multiregional PCs: East/West)

(122) Soviet Note to Finland I, 1948 (see Finland/Russia PC)

(123) Berlin Blockade, 1948–49 (see Multiregional PCs: East/West)

(131) Soviet Bloc/Yugoslavia

A prolonged crisis for Yugoslavia began on 19 August 1949 and faded in November 1951.

Background
Relations between the Soviet Union and Yugoslavia began deteriorating soon after World War II. In January 1948 the Soviet Union communicated its displeasure with what it perceived as Yugoslavia's increasingly independent domestic and foreign policy. In the next few months there were further Russian charges and Yugoslav denials of disloyalty to international communism. In the summer of 1948 Yugoslavia was expelled from the Soviet-dominated Communist Information Bureau *(COMINFORM)*.

Crisis
On 19 August 1949 the Yugoslav government received an ultimatum from Soviet Foreign Minister Molotov that was perceived as a possible prelude to a military invasion; there was, in fact, a show of force by the Soviet division in Yugoslavia, but Moscow acted so as to avoid involvement in military hostilities against Tito's regime. Yugoslavia responded the same day by placing its forces on alert and conducting military maneuvers along the border. The crisis gradually faded.

In November 1951 Yugoslavia lodged a formal complaint with the UN against the "hostile actions" by the Soviet Union and its Eastern European allies. The General Assembly passed a resolution noting Yugoslavia's readiness to seek a peaceful solution. U.S. involvement consisted of economic aid to Yugoslavia. Sanctions by the *COMINFORM* were imposed on Yugoslavia and, later, by the Soviet bloc's economic organization, *COMECON*. This crisis led to a basic shift in Yugoslavia's foreign policy orientation and marked a precedent for a Soviet doctrine of the right of intervention, what became known as the "Brezhnev Doctrine" almost two decades later (see Case #227—**Prague Spring** below).
(See *Master Table*, pp. 690–91.)

Sources
Calvocoressi 1954; Clissold 1975; Ulam 1952; Windsor 1978.

(137) Catalina Affair

The crisis for Sweden began on 16 June 1952. The exact termination date is unknown but was probably sometime in July 1952.

Background
Sweden, separated from the USSR by Finland and the Baltic Sea, maintained its neutrality during the Soviet invasion of Finland in 1939 (see Case #76—**Finnish War**, in **Finland/Russia PC**) and during World War II. Swedish-Soviet relations after 1945 were cautious, but correct. In February 1952 a spy ring working in the service of the USSR was uncovered in Sweden.

Crisis
On 16 June 1952 two Soviet fighters shot down a Swedish Catalina flying boat that was taking part in a search for a Swedish training plane that had disappeared with its crew of eight men three days earlier. In response, Sweden placed its army on alert on the 18th. An exchange of Notes between the two countries followed. On 19 June several members of the Soviet embassy in Stockholm left Sweden to return to Moscow. The following day the Swedish foreign minister interrupted a visit to Italy to return home. There was no precise termination date: it was determined as sometime in July after the fourth and last Note relating directly to the crisis was sent by Sweden. There was no reply from the USSR, implying a tacit understanding to let the matter drop.

The incident was condemned by the United States in a statement by Secretary of State Dean Acheson.

There was no UN involvement.

(See *Master Table*, pp. 690–91.)

Sources
A. H. H. 1952; Swedish Royal Ministry for Foreign Affairs 1957.

(141) East German Uprising

A crisis for the Soviet Union over East German riots began on 17 June and terminated on 11 July 1953.

Background
The East German uprising in 1953 can be traced to a hard-line decision of the ruling Socialist Unity Party *(SED)* on 12 July 1952, calling for "the Construction of Socialism" in East Germany (the DDR): higher taxes; priority to heavy indus-

try; collectivization of agriculture; hostility to the churches; and remilitarization. Dissent grew steadily.

Following Stalin's death in March 1953, greater attention was devoted to consumer goods by the USSR, and the DDR's Walter Ulbricht was advised to follow suit. Nevertheless, on 28 May 1953 an increased production quota system was introduced in East Germany. This prompted a strike by construction workers on 16 June, a spontaneous demonstration directed against the ruling party on strictly economic grounds. Toward the end of the day, although the government had agreed to roll back the new quotas, a general strike was called for the following day.

Crisis

On 17 June 1953 workers went on strike and marched in East Berlin and 400 other towns in the DDR. Economic grievances took on political overtones, while throngs of people rioted. This triggered an external crisis for the USSR (as well as a major domestic crisis for East Germany). A state of emergency was declared in the DDR, and martial law was introduced. Moscow's response, the same day, was to send tanks and Soviet troops stationed in bases inside the DDR to East Berlin where they were supported by East German paramilitary police. These forces succeeded in quelling the rebellion, after 125 died and thousands were arrested.

The Soviets perceived these riots as a dangerous precedent—as it was to be for the **Hungarian Uprising** in 1956–57 (see Case #155 below) and a threat to their East European bloc. On 11 July martial law was lifted in the DDR, ending Moscow's crisis. It also put the official seal on a gradual process that led to the reduction of the Soviet presence. The Western powers limited themselves to psychological warfare, especially via the Radio in the American Sector *(RIFS)*, and diplomatic notes on the need to cease hostilities, as well as urging German reunification.

The UN was not involved in this crisis.

(See *Master Table*, pp. 692–93.)

Sources
Baring 1972; Harrison 1993a, 1993b; Ostermann 1994, 1995.

(142) Trieste II, 1953 (see Italy/Albania/Yugoslavia PC)

(154) Poland Liberalization, 1956 (see Poland/Russia PC)

(155) Hungarian Uprising

Hungary and the USSR were enmeshed in a crisis that began on 23 October 1956 and faded in January 1957.

Background
Threats to USSR hegemony in Eastern Europe began to appear in the summer and fall of 1956. A crisis over Poland occurred in October (see Case #154— **Poland Liberalization, in Poland/Russia PC**). At that time Hungary was ruled by a Soviet-backed government headed by Communist leader Matyas Rakosi. There was growing unrest due to a severe economic situation, lack of democracy, and the aggravating presence of Soviet troops.

Crisis
On 23 October 1956 an estimated 200,000 Hungarian demonstrators, including workers, students, and soldiers, massed in Budapest and other major cities. They called for the withdrawal of Soviet troops, the return of Imre Nagy to power, progress toward democratization, and the development of Soviet-Hungarian relations on the basis of absolute equality. This was the trigger to the Soviet crisis, a perceived threat to unity in the Soviet bloc. Moscow responded on 1 November with a decision to remove the new government by military action.

A crisis was triggered for Hungary the same day: the Nagy government received reports of massive Soviet armor and tank formations crossing the Hungarian frontier. Hungary responded immediately by announcing its withdrawal from the Warsaw Pact. A message was also sent to the UN Secretary-General requesting that the issue of Hungarian neutrality be placed before the General Assembly. On 4 November the General Assembly passed a resolution calling for Soviet withdrawal from Hungary; but this had no effect on the Soviet Union's actions or the termination of the crisis.

On 4 November the Soviets removed the Nagy government by force and installed in power a more compliant puppet regime. Nagy was later shot. The Soviet crisis ended on 14 November with the end of Hungarian armed resistance. For Hungary, crisis termination occurred in January 1957, when organized resistance by Hungarian workers was crushed.

The U.S. issued a protest against Soviet interference in Hungary, but acquiesced in the reassertion of Moscow's hegemony in Budapest.

(See *Master Table*, pp. 694–95.)

Sources
Soviet Documents on the Hungarian Revolution 1995; *UN Special Committee on the Problem of Hungary* 1957; Campbell 1989; Fejpoe 1957; Geist 1995; Goodspeed 1967; Granville 1995; Khrushchev 1970; Kiraly 1984; Lasky 1957; Lomax 1976; Meray 1959; Molnar 1968; Rainer 1995; Vali 1961.

(168) Berlin Deadline, 1958–59 (see Multiregional PCs: East/West)

(185) Berlin Wall, 1961 (see Multiregional PCs: East/West)

(189) Soviet Note to Finland II, 1961 (see Finland/Russia PC)

(202) Cyprus I, 1963–64 (see Multiregional PCs: Greece/Turkey)

(223) Cyprus II, 1967 (see Multiregional PCs: Greece/Turkey)

(227) Prague Spring

There were six actors in the Prague Spring crisis: East Germany, Poland, Bulgaria, Hungary, the Soviet Union, and Czechoslovakia. It lasted from 9 April to 18 October 1968.

Background and Pre-crisis
During late 1967 domestic unrest and political conflict within the Czechoslovak Communist Party led to the overthrow of Antonin Novotný as First Secretary of the Communist Party on 5 January 1968 and as the State President on 23 March 1968. Alexander Dubček, his successor as party leader, proposed an "Action Program" that was accepted by the Czechoslovak Party Central Committee. The program proposed solutions to the Czech. economic crisis, the Slovak question, the rehabilitation of party leaders sentenced during the purges of the 1950s, and a way to deal with the dissent of students and intellectuals. Censorship was abolished, economic controls and central planning by the government were reduced and restructured, and new members were appointed to political posts. A more independent foreign policy was pledged, but it would conform to the interests of the Warsaw Treaty Organization *(WTO)* in general and the USSR in particular.

Polish leader Wladyslaw Gomulka and East German leader Walter Ulbricht feared that the infection of liberalism, already in its early stages in their countries, would spread and undermine their respective positions. In the Soviet Union apprehension increased that the "Prague Spring" would encourage Ukrainian nationalist sentiment; and the possibility emerged that liberalization would spill over into neighboring states. Furthermore, the unity and strength of the Warsaw Pact as a whole were seen to be in jeopardy with Czechoslovakia's decreased reliability as an ally. The possibility of military intervention in Czechoslovakia alarmed Hungary and Bulgaria, which perceived a threat to their own political regimes.

Warsaw Pact delegates met in Dresden in March 1968 to discuss the situation. Military exercises of the *WTO* were decided upon, to be held in June 1968.

Crisis
The publication of Czechoslovakia's Action Program on 9 April 1968 triggered a crisis for East Germany and Poland. A crisis was triggered for Bulgaria and

Hungary on 8 May after they had participated in a meeting with delegates from the Soviet Union, Poland, and East Germany: it was at that time that Bulgaria and Hungary became seriously alarmed over the situation in Czechoslovakia, since military intervention now appeared as a very real possibility. The stability of East Europe, including Bulgaria's own regime, seemed at stake. Hungary was concerned over the possibility of having to participate in a military attack initiated by the Soviet Union and East Germany.

An open letter in Prague on 27 June, "Two Thousand Words," which called for the speeding up of Czechoslovak democratization and criticizing the conditions inside the Czechoslovak Communist Party prior to the January reforms, triggered a crisis for the Soviet Union: Moscow interpreted this letter as proof that the political situation in Czechoslovakia was out of control. Due to increasing tension, the Warsaw Pact Command delayed removing its troops from Czechoslovakia upon completion of the military exercises held there.

The responses of Hungary, Bulgaria, Poland, and East Germany were contained in an ultimatum to Czechoslovakia on 15 July. A letter, signed by the USSR and these four East European states, singled out the Two Thousand Words manifesto as a threat to the vital interests of the whole communist community. When the Czechoslovak head of defense and security criticized the Warsaw Pact structure, the USSR demanded his dismissal. Dubček acceded, signaling that military resistance was no longer a realistic option for Czechoslovakia. Intense diplomatic negotiations followed at a meeting held between Czechoslovak leaders and nine of the 11 members of the Soviet Politburo. The result was verbal promises to resolve the crisis, confirmed on 3 August by the Bratislava Declaration. *WTO* troops were withdrawn from Czechoslovakia but remained concentrated along its borders.

Ulbricht met with Dubček on 12 August and reported to the Soviet Politburo that the Czechoslovak leaders were unwilling to live up to the terms of the Bratislava agreement. Reports about the enthusiastic reception in Prague of Yugoslav President Tito and Romanian party leader Ceaucescu irritated the Soviets, who feared Czechoslovak influence on other Pact members that might undermine their loyalty to the Soviet Union. The major response of the Soviet Union, East Germany, and Poland to the crisis, the invasion of Czechoslovakia, was decided on 17 August after three days of talks among their military leaders.

Dubček, who continued to disregard unmistakable signs of a new Soviet debate on Czechoslovakia and who did not wish to create anti-Soviet feelings, did not inform the Czechoslovak President, Svoboda, about warnings received from Hungarian leader Kádár or those contained in a letter from the Soviet Politburo on 19 August. The invasion of Czechoslovakia began on 20 August. It was the crisis trigger for Czechoslovakia and the termination date for Bulgaria, Hungary, East Germany, and Poland. The Warsaw Pact armies acquired total control of Czechoslovak territory within 36 hours. The Czechoslovak response, on the 21st, was compliance. Svoboda flew to Moscow for talks with the Soviet leadership and pressed for the release of Czechoslovak leaders Dubček, Černík, and Smrkovský, who had been taken prisoner during the invasion. With Czechoslovak promises to control and arrest "counterrevolutionary" elements, the Moscow Protocol was signed on 18 October 1968 legalizing the presence of Soviet troops in Czechoslovakia and terminating the crisis for the USSR and Czechoslovakia.

The destruction of the Czechoslovak reform movement was viewed as a victory by Bulgaria, East Germany, Poland, and the USSR. However, Hungary was not pleased by the triumph of the hard-liners within the Soviet bloc, since it might threaten Hungary's own modest reform movement.

A UN Security Council draft resolution censuring the invasion as a violation of the UN Charter was vetoed by the Soviet Union on 21 August.

U.S. President Johnson condemned the Soviet actions and canceled all diplomatic activities scheduled with the USSR regarding future *SALT I* (Strategic Arms Limitation Treaty) talks. *NATO* foreign ministers discussed the situation on 8 October, but no meaningful decisions were taken.

(See *Master Table,* pp. 708–9.)

Sources
Bethell 1969; Bohlen 1973; Brandt 1976; K. Dawisha 1978, 1980, 1984; Golan 1971, 1973; Grey 1967; Johnson 1971; Jones 1975; Kramer 1992, 1993; Mlynar 1980; Paul 1971; Shawcross 1970; Skilling 1976; Szulc 1971a; Tatu 1981; Valenta 1979a, 1979b; Vertzberger 1997; Westwood 1973; Windsor and Roberts 1969; Wolfe 1970.

(254) Cod War I

The first crisis between the U.K. and Iceland over cod fishing rights began on 14 May and ended on 13 November 1973.

Background and Pre-crisis
In 1972 a dispute between Iceland, on the one hand, and Britain and West Germany, on the other, centered around Iceland's unilateral extension of its territorial waters from a 12-mile limit to 50 miles. This severely curtailed the fish catch available to other countries. Several incidents occurred as a result of the harassment of British and West German trawlers by Icelandic gunboats. Further incidents of ramming and exchanges of fire were reported in March and April 1973.

Crisis
On the night of 14 May 1973 Icelandic gunboats fired on British trawlers, triggering a crisis for the U.K. On the 16th British fishers threatened to leave the disputed waters if protection were not assured. London responded on 19 May by dispatching Royal Navy ships to Icelandic waters, triggering a crisis for Iceland. The following day, Iceland banned *RAF* aircraft from landing at the Keflavik *NATO* base, while protesting to the U.K. Talks between the two prime ministers

began on 2 October. On 13 November 1973 the parliament of Iceland approved an agreement whereby Iceland set aside certain areas within the newly accepted 50-mile limit for British fishers, terminating the crisis for both actors.

Two regional/security organizations, *NATO* and the Council of Europe, were involved, but neither was effective in abating the crisis. The U.S. limited its involvement to a statement about the dispute. A proposal for mediation came from Norway. USSR involvement was more substantial, however. Continued *NATO* use of the Keflavik air base, which was necessary for the implementation of important *NATO* antisubmarine warfare operations, was already an issue in Icelandic politics. Iceland's request to the USSR for a show of force during the crisis was answered by a special Soviet naval exercise: 10 Russian ships and 10 submarines were dispatched as a signal to the U.K. There was also a reported request from Iceland to the Soviet Union for a gunboat to strengthen Iceland's coast guard.

A second **Cod War** crisis occurred between Iceland and the U.K. in 1975–76 (see Case #263 below).

The UN was not involved in this case.

(See *Master Table,* pp. 712–13.)

Sources
Barston and Hannesson 1974; Day 1985; Hart 1976; Kaplan 1981; Katz 1973; Mitchell 1976; Vayrynen 1973.

(257) Cyprus III, 1974–75 (see Multiregional PCs: Greece/Turkey)

(263) Cod War II

Disputes over fishing rights in waters contiguous to Iceland precipitated another crisis for the U.K. and Iceland from 23 November 1975 to 1 June 1976.

Pre-crisis
In November 1973 an agreement was reached between Iceland and the U.K. that set the former's territorial waters as 50 miles offshore, within which certain areas were set aside for British fishers (see Case #254 above). On 15 July 1975 the government of Iceland announced its intention to extend its territorial waters to 200 miles off the Icelandic coast, as of 15 October; further, all foreign vessels would be forbidden to fish inside the new limit. During November Icelandic gunboats harassed British trawlers fishing for cod within the 200-mile limit.

Crisis
On 23 November 1975 British trawler skippers warned the U.K. that they would withdraw from Iceland's 200-mile zone unless they were assured of Royal Navy protection. On the 25th the British government, convinced of the danger to the welfare and safety of the fishers, decided to dispatch frigates to Icelandic waters,

triggering a crisis for Iceland. Iceland's foreign minister termed this U.K. move as "unmasked armed violence" and initiated talks between the two governments. The foreign ministers met in December 1975 and the prime ministers in January 1976. When these talks did not achieve progress, Iceland broke diplomatic relations with the U.K. on 18 February. Britain maintained the presence of the Royal Navy in Icelandic waters throughout the crisis, in order to protect the trawlers engaged in uninterrupted fishing. There were minor clashes. On 1 June 1976 an interim agreement between the two countries was signed in Oslo, allowing British trawlers fishing rights within the 200-mile zone, while limiting their number to an average of 24 trawlers a day.

Discussions were held in the UN Security Council from 2 to 11 December 1975; and talks between the two disputants were held under UN auspices. *NATO* and the Nordic Council discussed the military and economic issues of the crisis and met with the Icelandic and British leaders.

(A similar, though non-violent, crisis over fishing rights between Canada and Spain, backed by the European Union, erupted in March 1995, with Canada's seizure of a Spanish trawler in the North Atlantic for alleged "illegal fishing.")

(See *Master Table*, pp. 714–15.)

Sources
See sources for Case #254; and Jonsson 1982.

(272) Aegean Sea I, 1976 (see Multiregional PCs: Greece/Turkey)

(315) Solidarity, 1980–81 (see Poland/Russia PC)

(316) Libya/Malta Oil Dispute

Malta experienced a crisis with Libya over disputed offshore oil deposits from 20 August to 15 September 1980.

Background and Pre-crisis
Malta's political leaders hoped that the island-state could emulate the former colonial ruler, the U.K., and become self-sufficient in oil by exploiting offshore deposits. The most promising of these was the large Medina Bank 68 miles southeast of Malta's main island. Malta claimed jurisdiction over Mediterranean waters to a distance of 98 miles south of its southern coast, which was halfway between Malta and Libya. President Qaddhafi, however, as part of Libya's maritime claims that included the entire Gulf of Syrte (see Cases #330 and 363— **Gulf of Syrte I and II, in Africa: Non-PCs**), claimed two-thirds of the offshore waters, to a point 65 miles from the southern coast of Malta.

Libya and Malta had agreed in 1976 to submit their dispute to the International Court of Justice. Although Malta refrained during this period from prospecting in the disputed area, Libya proceeded with geological soundings. In July 1980 Malta's Prime Minister Mintoff responded belatedly by requesting the Texaco Oil Company to resume earlier prospecting in the Medina Bank on behalf of the government of Malta. In August Texaco chartered an oil rig from the Italian state oil company, which set out for the disputed area.

Crisis

On 20 August 1980 one of Libya's submarines and, soon after, a Libyan frigate began to harass the oil rig, triggering a crisis for Malta. Upon the advice of Italy's Foreign Ministry the Italian chartered vessel ceased operations at the Medina Bank. Malta responded to the threat by placing its minuscule air force on alert on 26 August. The next day 42 Libyan military personnel were expelled from the island-state. And on 30 August a Malta government statement accused Libya of endangering peace in the Mediterranean.

The UN became involved on 4 September, when the Security Council, at Malta's request, considered Libya's alleged "illegal act." However, the Council adjourned without taking any action.

Italy's intervention proved to be decisive for crisis management. On 15 September Italy and Malta exchanged notes formalizing an agreement on Malta's neutrality, announced a week earlier. Italy, an erstwhile protector of Malta, with historic interests in the central Mediterranean, recognized Malta's self-declared nonalignment and offered military aid and diplomatic support, in return for Malta's pledge not to join any alliance, not to permit foreign troops to be based on the island, and not to grant U.S. or USSR warships docking facilities. Italy also promised substantial economic assistance. That Italian initiative terminated Malta's foreign policy crisis and the international crisis as a whole.

(In the post-crisis phase UN Secretary-General Waldheim expressed his intention on 17 October to send a special envoy to Malta and Libya to mediate their dispute. On 13 November he submitted a report to the Security Council, indicating that Libya had undertaken unconditionally to seek ratification by Libya's People's Congress of a new agreement to seek adjudication by the International Court of Justice in December. Moreover, Libya reaffirmed its willingness to strengthen ties of friendship and cooperation with Malta.)

The U.S. and the USSR were not active in this crisis.

(See *Master Table*, pp. 722–23.)

Sources
ACR 1980; *AR* 1980; *ARB* 1980; *Keesing's* 1980.

(333) U-137 Incident

Sweden and the USSR were enmeshed in a crisis from 28 October to 6 November 1981 over the unauthorized entry of a Soviet submarine into a restricted Swedish military zone.

Background

The Soviet Union was heavily engaged in international crises elsewhere when the U-137 crisis occurred: in Afghanistan (see Case #303—**Afghanistan Invasion,** in 1979–80, in **Asia: Non-PCs**); and in Poland (see Case #315—**Solidarity,** in 1980–81, in **Europe: Non-PCs**). Nor was this the first—or the last—Soviet penetration of Sweden's territorial waters: on 18 September 1980 an unidentified (probably Soviet) submarine infiltrated and withdrew by 6 October.

Crisis

On 28 October 1981 a Swedish fisherman discovered a submarine near the naval base of Karlskrona in southern Sweden, a restricted military zone. The "whiskey-class" submarine had become wedged on the rocks; hence the alternative name of this crisis—"Whiskey on the Rocks." Sweden responded the same day with a protest note to Moscow by its foreign minister. The Soviet ambassador in Sweden explained that the submarine was unable to leave because of "technical problems" and sought permission for a Soviet rescue operation.

A Swedish ad hoc crisis decision-making group, comprising the prime minister, foreign minister, supreme commander of the armed forces, permanent under-secretary of foreign affairs, and others, also decided the following on the 28th: to turn down a request for the entry of Soviet rescue ships; to prevent any contact between Soviet embassy personnel in Stockholm and the crew of the submarine; and to have the national research defense agency inspect the submarine, for nuclear material was suspected. That cluster of decisions triggered a crisis for the USSR. Moscow perceived a multifaceted threat: to its superpower image; to its influence among nonaligned states; to its relations with Sweden; and to its image for probity regarding nuclear material.

At a meeting of Sweden's crisis group on the 29th preparations were made for possible violence in the Karlskrona area. However, it ruled out the use of force against the submarine for the time being. Foreign Minister Ola Ullsten told the Soviet ambassador the same day that Sweden had the right to question the submarine commander, to investigate the incident, and to conduct rescue operations. He also demanded an apology for the violation of Sweden's territorial waters. And he rejected a request to permit Soviet representatives to visit the submarine.

Swedish leaders left Stockholm for a quiet weekend in order to convey the impression that the situation was under control. On 1 November, the Prime Minister, Thorbjorn Falldin, briefed the Opposition leader, Olof Palme. An alert was announced on the 2nd because of a reported approach of Soviet vessels. And top-level consultations were held on the nuclear issue: Swedish experts believed that the crippled submarine contained nuclear weapons. The submarine commander was interrogated the same day. And the next day Swedish experts inspected the submarine.

On 2 and 3 November the Soviet ambassador conveyed Moscow's irritation at Sweden's behavior and the prolonged interrogation of the submarine commander, as well as its "aggressive tone." On the 4th the Soviet ambassador neither confirmed nor denied the presence of nuclear weapons in the submarine. This aspect of the crisis remained ambiguous throughout, with Sweden avoiding a direct accusation to that effect.

The Soviet Tass news agency reported the incident for the first time on 4 November, describing it as an "accidental violation of Sweden's sovereignty." More Soviet ships were detected approaching the crisis area; and a second Swedish protest note was dispatched. Sweden's decision to release the submarine was made on 5 November. Due to weather conditions, it departed on the 6th, terminating the crisis for both states. On the 11th Moscow apologized to Sweden. It was viewed by Sweden at the time as its most serious foreign policy crisis of the postwar era.

The UN and the U.S. were not involved in this crisis.

(In February 1995, Sweden's premier confirmed that most intrusions into its territorial waters during the preceding 20 years were minks—which generated sound patterns similar to those of submarines—not Soviet subs!)

(See *Master Table*, pp. 724–25.)

Sources
Agrell 1983, 1986; Leitenberg 1982; Lofgren 1984; O'Ballance 1984; Stern 1992; Stern and Sundelius 1992, 1994.

(344) Able Archer 83, 1983 (see Multiregional PCs: East/West)

(349) Aegean Sea II, 1984 (see Multiregional PCs: Greece/Turkey)

(376) Aegean Sea III, 1987 (see Multiregional PCs: Greece/Turkey)

(397) Yugoslavia I: Croatia, Slovenia

Yugoslavia (Serbia), Slovenia, and Croatia were embroiled in a grave crisis during the first phase of Yugoslavia's disintegration as a federal state, from 25 June 1991 to 3 January 1992.

Background
The three main ethnic constituents of twentieth-century Yugoslavia were the products of varied historical experience. For Serbia, it was Greek Orthodox Christianity and five centuries of Turkish (Muslim) rule: the Serbs suffered a decisive defeat at the Battle of Kossovo in 1389, when Serbia became a vassal state of the Turks; and it was incorporated into the Ottoman Empire in 1459. Serbia reemerged as an independent state in 1878 as part of the peace settlement

at the Congress of Berlin. Both the Slovenes and the Croats were predominantly Roman Catholic and fell within the cultural and political orbit of Central Europe, most recently as parts of the polyglot Austro-Hungarian empire from 1867 until its dissolution in 1918.

In the political vacuum created by World War I and the demise of the Dual Monarchy, the "South Slavs" united: on 4 December 1918 they proclaimed the Kingdom of the Serbs, Croats, and Slovenes, with young King Peter of Serbia as its monarch and Prince Alexander as Regent. Alexander succeeded to the throne upon Peter's death in 1921 and ruled until he was assassinated in 1934 (see Case #46—**Assassination of King Alexander** above). In 1929 he had proclaimed a dictatorship over the kingdom and renamed it Yugoslavia in a symbolic effort to eradicate the historic and ethnic divisions. Peter II served as king from 1934 to 1945, with power in the hands of Prince Paul as regent.

During World War II the Communist-led Yugoslav Partisans successfully resisted all German attempts to overrun Yugoslavia from 1941 to 1944. Belgrade, the Serbian capital, was liberated by Soviet and Yugoslav forces in October 1944.

In November 1945 the Constituent Assembly, with a majority held by the Communist-dominated National Front, proclaimed the Federal People's Republic of Yugoslavia. Josip Broz Tito was the dominant figure in Yugoslavia until his death in 1980. Thereafter the state was ruled by a collective presidency, with its chairperson rotating among the six republics of the federation—Serbia, Croatia, Slovenia, Bosnia-Hercegovina, Montenegro, and Macedonia. By 1990 communism as an ideology and political system was in disrepute throughout Eastern Europe. Economic deterioration during the preceding decade accentuated the always latent ethnic conflicts, which exploded in 1991 into crisis and war.

Pre-crisis
A wave of political and ethnic unrest erupted in the spring of 1991, with Croatia and Slovenia pressing to transform Yugoslavia into a confederation of independent states. These two republics organized their own armed forces and, during May and June, proceeded rapidly along the path to independence. Both held a referendum, which resulted in strong support for independence. And Slovenia began constructing border-crossing stations along the Croatian border.

The European Community *(EC)* and the U.S. announced that they would not recognize Croatia's and Slovenia's independence if this included secession from Yugoslavia. On 1 June the Yugoslav Prime Minister, Ante Markovic, condemned Croatia's and Slovenia's moves to secede and claimed they were illegal. On the 24th he asked Slovenia and Croatia not to declare their independence, warning that such a step could create economic and social catastrophe.

Crisis
Declarations of independence by Croatia and Slovenia on 25 June 1991 triggered a crisis for Yugoslavia (Serbia), for they threatened the continued existence of Yugoslavia as a federal state and Serbia's dominance. The federal government

responded the same day by condemning the declarations as illegal; and the federal Prime Minister, Markovic, called on the Yugoslav National Army *(JNA)* to take control of Yugoslavia's international borders. *JNA* tanks began to move toward Ljubljana, the Slovenian capital. These acts by Serbia-dominated Yugoslavia triggered a crisis for Slovenia and Croatia.

Minor clashes began in Slovenia, becoming more intense on 26 and 27 June, as *JNA* troops used force to take control of several border posts from Slovenian authorities and deployed tanks and troops around Slovenia's airport. In Croatia, Serbs stormed a police station, killing three persons. While the President of the newly proclaimed Croatia, Franjo Tudjman, made efforts to restrain violence, Slovenia's Defense Minister, Jansa, announced on the 27th that "Slovenia is at war"; and the Slovenian President, Milan Kucan, called on Slovenians to defend their sovereignty against Serb "aggression."

An *EC* mission, comprising the foreign ministers of Luxembourg, Italy, and the Netherlands, initiated the first cease-fire agreement in the Yugoslavia I crisis on 28 June; but the agreement broke down the next day, and minor clashes were renewed. The fighting escalated in Croatia during July; but it ended in Slovenia by 3 July and did not spread to the other republics. On the 2nd the Slovenian capital was heavily bombed by Yugoslavia's air force. After talks between Stjephan Mesic, the (Croat) President of the Federal Presidency of Yugoslavia, and Slovenian leaders that day, Slovenia agreed to release prisoners, and a cease-fire agreement was reached. On 3 July some *JNA* units began to withdraw from Slovenia. And on the 5th Slovenia announced that it had demobilized 10,000 soldiers in its defense force and began to lift blockades. Thus tension declined in Slovenia at the beginning of July.

A formal agreement, which was reached in talks between the *EC* mission and officials from Slovenia, Croatia, and the Federal Presidency on 7 July on the island of Brioni, marks the termination of Slovenia's crisis. Slovenia (and Croatia) agreed to suspend implementation of their independence, but not the declarations themselves. It was also agreed that, during a three-month cessation period, negotiations would begin on the future of all republics and provinces in the Yugoslav federation, and that hostilities would cease immediately. Further, the *JNA* would soon withdraw to its bases, and the Slovenian militia would be demobilized.

At an emergency meeting of the Conference on Security and Cooperation in Europe *(CSCE)* on 3–4 July in Prague a decision was made to dispatch an *EC*-based mission to Yugoslavia to supervise the cease-fire and to send a *CSCE* good offices mission to mediate among the parties. The *EC* foreign ministers decided on 5 July to impose an arms embargo and to freeze financial aid to Yugoslavia. A meeting of central European states on 26–27 July, including Yugoslavia and its neighbors (Italy, Austria, Hungary, and Czechoslovakia), issued a statement supporting the *EC* proposals to end the violence in Yugoslavia.

A hint of things to come—enlargement of the Yugoslavia crisis—became evident in August: discussions by Serb and Croat officials, with a view to partitioning Bosnia-Hercegovina, threatened the republic; and Sarajevo approached the *EC* and Turkey for support. (The Bosnia crisis was to erupt in March 1992 [see Case #403—**Yugoslavia II: Bosnia** below].)

In the meantime, Croatia's crisis intensified. On 22 August Croatia's President Tudjman warned that, unless Serbian "aggression" against Croatia ceased and the *JNA* withdrew from Croatia by the end of the month, "all necessary steps" would be taken to protect the new state. On 27 August a new cease-fire between Croatia's militia and the *JNA* was signed; but it was broken within hours. *EC* foreign ministers, meeting in Brussels, held Serbia responsible for the conflict, as did U.S. officials on the 29th. The *EC* proposed an international peace conference to resolve the crisis.

An international peace conference on Yugoslavia opened in London on 7 September. An arbitration commission of lawyers from France, Italy, and Germany was appointed. The meeting was brief and did not mark a major change in the crisis.

During September the war in Yugoslavia escalated, and Croatia lost about one-third of its territory (Krajina) to Serb forces in Croatia. (Croatian forces recaptured Krajina in a two-day campaign in August 1995.) All six Yugoslav republics and the President of the collective State Presidency, Mesic, and the (Croat) Federal Prime Minister, Markovic, signed another cease-fire agreement in Belgrade on 2 September. The agreement was reached through mediation by Dutch Foreign Minister Hans van den Broek. However, as often in the past and the future, the cease-fire broke down quickly, and heavy fighting in Croatia resumed. On 25 September, at France's initiative, the UN Security Council adopted Resolution 713, calling for a complete arms embargo on Yugoslavia and requesting the UN Secretary-General to assist with mediation.

Fighting spread for the first time to Serbian territory in early November 1991 as Croatian forces attacked Serbian villages. The most serious clashes between Serbs and Croats began on 18 November in Vukovar, Croatia: 900 people were killed; and the Croats were forced to surrender to the Serb-dominated *JNA*. This battle weakened the Croats and led to the end of the crisis within six weeks.

On 8 November the *EC* Council of Ministers imposed trade sanctions on Yugoslavia; and on the 25th it suspended Yugoslavia's special status in the European Parliament. President Bush said in December that the U.S. would also impose trade sanctions against Yugoslavia.

The first cease-fire mediated by the UN was signed on 23 November. *JNA* forces began to withdraw from Zagreb, the Croatian capital, on the 28th. However, fighting resumed in December.

With Germany taking the lead, the *EC* agreed in principle to recognize the independence of the seceding Yugoslav republics; and on 9 December an *EC* peace conference stated that Yugoslavia was "legally in process of dissolution." On the 10th the *EC* lifted its sanctions on four of the Yugoslav republics, but not Serbia and Montenegro, which were accused of aggression.

On 19 December two Serb enclaves in Croatia—the Serbian Autonomous Region of Krajina, and the Serb Autonomous Region of Slavonia, Baranja, and Western Srem—declared themselves the Serbian Republic of Krajina. The two regions did not have a common border; but together they encompassed a third of Croatia's territory. Serbia recognized the republic the next day.

On 20 December the parties signed another cease-fire agreement, the 15th brokered by UN special envoy (and former U.S. Secretary of State) Cyrus Vance. Politically, it was a compromise for both parties: Croatia retained its demand for independence but lost about one-third of its territory to Serbia. The cease-fire took effect on 3 January 1992. It was the first to last and create some stability. As such, the implementation of this agreement terminated the crisis for both Croatia and Yugoslavia (Serbia).

The UN was highly involved in this crisis, as noted: the Security Council's Resolution 713; successful mediation by the Secretary-General and his Special Representative, notably the cease-fire agreement that brought the crisis to an end. U.S. activity was limited to several political statements. The USSR was not visibly involved. The *EC* and the *CSCE,* by contrast, were highly involved and *NATO* modestly so.

(See *Master Table,* pp. 736–37.)

Sources
Baker 1995; Forbes et al. 1915; Glenny 1992; Kaplan 1993; *Keesing's* 1991, 1992; Magas 1993; *New York Times* 1991, 1992; Owen 1995; Silber and Little 1995; West 1941; Woodward 1995.

(403) Yugoslavia II: Bosnia

Yugoslavia (Serbia), Bosnia, and Croatia (and powerful minorities, notably the Bosnian Serbs) were entangled in a lengthy crisis over the fate of Bosnia-Hercegovina as a political entity. It began on 3 March 1992 and ended on 21 November 1995.

Background and Pre-crisis
The people of Bosnia-Hercegovina are, ethnically, part of the community of "South Slavs," including Serbs, Croats, Slovenes, and Montenegrins. By the end of the tenth century the people of eastern Bosnia, like those of modern Serbia, had accepted eastern Orthodox Christianity, while those of western Bosnia, like the Croats and Slovenes, had embraced Roman Catholicism.

The historical background, too, is complex. Bosnians and Serbs fought side by side in the decisive Battle of Kossovo in 1389; and like Serbia, Bosnia became part of the Ottoman Empire. There was one notable difference, with consequences for the crises of the 1990s. During the five centuries of Turkish rule the religious composition of Bosnia changed drastically, partly because of the immigration of Turks, partly because of the conversion of many Bosnians to Islam.

The result was that, at the time of Yugoslavia's dissolution, Muslims formed the largest religious-ethnic community in Bosnia, slightly more than half, compared to 31 percent for the Orthodox Serbs and 17 percent for the Catholic Croats.

Austria was given the right to occupy—but not to annex—Bosnia and Hercegovina in 1878, at the same time the major powers granted Serbia independence: Serbia's long-standing aspiration to control these two areas was rebuffed. More significantly, Bosnia and Hercegovina were annexed by the Austro-Hungarian Empire in October 1908, generating undisguised anger in Russia, Serbia, Montenegro, and Greece. That association lasted only a decade: with the dissolution of the Dual Empire at the end of World War I, Bosnia and Hercegovina became part of the Kingdom of Serbs, Croats, and Slovenes, created in 1918. And after World War II they became, together, one of the six constituent republics of the Federal People's Republic of Yugoslavia *(FPRY)*. In the post-Tito era, from 1980 to 1991, Bosnia-Hercegovina shared in the governance of Yugoslavia as a member of the collective and rotating Federal Presidency.

Bosnia-Hercegovina (hereafter, Bosnia) was not involved in the first stage of Yugoslavia's prolonged crisis-war from June 1991 to early January 1992 (see Case #397—**Yugoslavia I: Croatia, Slovenia** above); it remained a constituent republic of the Yugoslav federation. However, the reality of dissolution and the assertion of independence by two of Yugoslavia's republics penetrated Bosnia's political culture: a favorable attitude toward an independent Bosnia was already evident, especially among the Muslims, in 1991–92.

Crisis

Bosnia's Muslims and Croats voted strongly in favor of independence on 2 March 1992 and requested recognition by the European Union *(EU)* and its members (the European Community *[EC]* was renamed the European Union *[EU]* in February 1992, when the Maastricht Treaty came into effect). The Bosnian Serbs boycotted the referendum and warned of grave consequences. The next day Bosnia declared its independence. That act triggered a crisis for Yugoslavia, dominated more than ever by Serbia, and enraged the Bosnian Serbs. Fighting broke out at once between Bosnian Muslims and Croats on one side, the Yugoslav National Army (the *JNA*) and Bosnian Serbs on the other.

On 18 March, Bosnian Serb, Croat, and Muslim leaders signed an agreement in Lisbon to transform Bosnia-Hercegovina into three ethnic regions or cantons within a formally united independent state. However, on his return to Sarajevo, the (Muslim) President of Bosnia, Alija Izetbegovic, called on Bosnians to reject the division. He accused the governments of Serbia and Croatia of encouraging extreme Serb and Croat forces in Bosnia with the aim of partitioning Bosnia between them.

Largely at the urging of Germany, *EU* members recognized Bosnia's independence on 6 April. The U.S. did so on the 7th, recognizing Croatia and Slovenia as well. Other states recognized Bosnia's independence soon after, including Croatia, Czechoslovakia, Finland, Hungary, Poland, and Slovenia. In response to the *EU*'s recognition, ethnic Serbs declared a Serbian Republic of Bosnia the same day; and Yugoslav planes attacked Croatian towns in western Bosnia, triggering a crisis for Croatia. Fighting worsened on 14 April, as Serbian forces tried to create a corridor from Krajina, a Serb enclave in western Croatia, to Serbia itself. Sarajevo, the Bosnian capital, was subjected to an artillery barrage on 21 April, the first of hundreds of such attacks during the next three years. In fact, the pattern of behavior by all the crisis actors and the key involved actors—the major powers, the *EU,* the UN, Bosnian Serbs, and Bosnian Croats—during the prolonged second Yugoslavia crisis was established in the early days, as follows.

Bosnia—the use of force and diplomacy, and appeals to world public opinion, to maintain its existence as an independent state

Yugoslavia (Serbia)—support to the Bosnian Serbs, both military equipment and economic aid, to assist them in achieving their shared goal of "Greater Serbia" by any means, including "ethnic cleansing," that is, incorporating as much of Bosnia's territory as possible into Serbia, with as few non-Serb inhabitants as necessary; this behavior was moderated occasionally in order to satisfy pressure from the West, including the *EU* and *NATO,* and the UN, and to ease the burden of economic sanctions on Serbia proper

Croatia—the least consistent of all the actors, shifting alignments with different goals, sometimes with Serbia, with the aim of eliminating Bosnia and partitioning its territory between them, at other times with Bosnia, designed to weaken the Bosnian Serbs and to compel them to disgorge a substantial part of the 70 percent of the territory of Bosnia acquired by force of arms and "ethnic cleansing"

Bosnian Serbs—primary reliance on force and the policy of "ethnic cleansing" to take irrevocable control of most of Bosnia's territory for the Serb Republic of Bosnia, to realize the ultimate goal of Greater Serbia, supplemented by diplomacy, including political concessions to the UN or the *EU* when necessary, in order to prevent military intervention by the major powers or the lifting of the arms embargo, which adversely affected the Bosnian army much more than the Bosnian Serbs' military capability

Bosnian Croats—the use of force and "nuisance" tactics, to assert control over territory with a large Croat population, to be integrated into Croatia, and to undermine efforts at military and political cooperation between Bosnia and Croatia

The UN—moderating the fighting in Bosnia through its United Nations Protection Force *(UNPROFOR)* peacekeepers; reducing the suffering of civilians by designating exposed cities like Sarajevo, Bosnia's capital, "safe areas," and by as large and steady a supply of food and medicine to Bosnia's civilians as the Bosnian Serbs permitted; and seeking a peaceful solution of the conflict through economic sanctions—against the rump of

Yugoslavia—and diplomacy, notably comprehensive peace plans by special representatives of the Secretary-General

NATO—providing limited military support for *UNPROFOR* peacekeepers when necessary, through symbolic air strikes against the Bosnian Serbs, and verbal threats of retaliation

The *EU*—reliance on diplomacy, complementing that of the UN, to bring the parties to the bargaining table, exercised through an *EU* mediator, endless visits by foreign ministers of major European powers and others to all the actors, and cooperation with the U.S. and Russia through the "Contact Group," comprising the five major powers

(Since this pattern of behavior is evident throughout the Yugoslavia II crisis, the rest of this case summary will concentrate on escalation points and crucial developments.)

On 28 April 1992 the UN decided to extend its peacekeeping operation in Yugoslavia *(UNPROFOR)* to Bosnia-Hercegovina.

On 22 May Bosnia, Croatia, and Slovenia were admitted to the UN. On the 30th the Security Council adopted Resolution 757, imposing comprehensive sanctions on the Federal Republic of Yugoslavia *(FRY),* comprising Serbia and Montenegro. These included the severance of sports, cultural, and air links with the rest of the world; freezing government assets abroad, and an oil embargo. On 20 June Bosnia declared a state of war and general mobilization—five days after Bosnian President Izetbegovic and Croatian President Tudjman signed an agreement of friendship and cooperation, including military cooperation, "against the common enemy." As the war continued Bosnia's government repeatedly requested foreign military aid—but the embargo on arms remains in force. The U.S. Congress favored lifting the embargo; the *EU,* notably the U.K. and France, was steadfastly opposed.

As violence continued, amid horrific reports in the summer of 1992 of grave human rights violations, the UN Security Council and the UN Human Rights Commission strongly condemned the policy of forced deportation. Under the impact of intense media coverage of Bosnian Serb "ethnic cleansing," France, the U.K., Italy, Spain, and Belgium committed troops to a UN peacekeeping force.

Representatives of 20 states, including the six former republics of Yugoslavia, *EU* members, the five permanent members of the UN Security Council, and members of the *CSCE* met in London on 26–27 August 1992. The first of several futile efforts at "public crisis management," the conference condemned the expulsion of civilians. It also agreed on terms for a political settlement, including recognition of Bosnia by the other five Yugoslav republics, acceptance of present frontiers, guarantees for national minorities, and the right of return for those who were expelled from their homes. And it supported the idea of a UN peacekeeping force.

A follow-up "permanent" conference on Yugoslavia in Geneva began on 3 September. Following the Iraq precedent (see Case #406—**Iraq No-Fly Zone,** in **Iraq/Kuwait PC**), a UN Security Council resolution on 9 October 1992 banned military flights over Bosnia, to be enforced by *UNPROFOR*. Notwithstanding Croatia's military cooperation agreement with Bosnia, Croat forces in Bosnia took control of Mostar on 25 October and declared it the capital of the Croatian Community of Herceg-Bosnia.

In a seemingly endless quest for a viable diplomatic formula, the Geneva Conference, on 20 October, formally rejected the division of Bosnia into three ethnic republics. Instead it presented a plan for a decentralized republic, based on several regional governments and a central government in Sarajevo, responsible for foreign policy, defense, and trade.

Early in January 1993 the two principal mediators, Lord Owen (for the *EU*) and Cyrus Vance (for the UN), presented a comprehensive and complex three-part peace plan to the Geneva Conference on Yugoslavia: **territorial** provisions, calling for the reorganization of Bosnia into 10 provinces, with an attached map; **constitutional** principles, providing much autonomy to the provinces; and a **military** section, including a cease-fire and demilitarization. The Bosnian Serb leader, Radovan Karadzic, rejected the proposals, demanding the right of the Serbs to self-determination in a separate "state within a state." Bosnia's President Izetbegovic rejected the territorial section of the plan. And the Bosnian Croat leader, Boban, accepted the plan in full. Under strong pressure from Serbia's President Slobodan Milosevic, the Bosnian Serb Assembly voted in favor of the principles of the plan on 19–20 January. All three parties tried to increase their control over territory before a peace agreement was signed. Thus fighting escalated in the second half of January.

President Izetbegovic of Bosnia formally approved the military provisions of the Vance-Owen plan on 2 February and the all-important territorial section on the 25th. Only the Bosnian Serbs were adamant: on 25–26 April the Bosnian Serb Assembly rejected the proposed map. The *FRY* Foreign Minister, Vladislav Jovanovic, was sent to persuade the Serbs to accept the plan, in vain. The Bosnian Serbs were universally condemned. However, a cease-fire was accepted by all sides on 27 March 1993, allowing a relief convoy to enter Srebrenica.

On 27 April President Yeltsin warned the Bosnian Serbs that Russia would not protect them as long as they rejected the Vance-Owen plan. Croatia was warned by Western states in May that sanctions against Serbia would be lifted if it continued to support the Bosnian Croat forces. Meanwhile, Serb attacks continued against Bosnian Muslim areas.

The UN Security Council adopted Resolution 824 on 6 May 1993, declaring Sarajevo and five other towns "safe-areas," banning any armed attacks on them: Gorazde, Srebrenica, Tuzla, Zepa in the east, Bihac in the north. On 4 June the Security Council adopted Resolution 836, authorizing *UNPROFOR* to use force in cases of attacks against the six "safe areas" in Bosnia.

Typical of Croat maneuvering between the other two warring parties was an agreement by Presidents Milosevic (Serbia) and Tudjman (Croatia), announced to the Geneva Conference on 26 June 1993, to divide Bosnia into three ethnic states within a loose confederal Union of Republics of Bosnia-Hercegovina. Izetbegovic rejected the plan; but on 30 July he indicated acceptance, with reservations. Bosnian Muslims renewed their rejection of the Vance-Owen map at the end of August. And in September and October 1993 the Bosnian Assembly, the Bosnian Croat Assembly, and the Bosnian Serb Parliament all rejected the plan to partition Bosnia into three republics.

The impasse on the Vance-Owen peace plan continued. So too did the fighting, including the Bosnian Serb siege of Sarajevo and frequent attacks on "safe areas"; the impotence of *UNPROFOR,* based upon the extreme caution of all the major powers; their consensus against military intervention to end the fighting in Bosnia; U.S. verbal support of Bosnia; Russian attempts to shield Serbia and the Bosnian Serbs from more extreme UN-*EU-NATO* measures; the U.S.-*EU* disagreement on the arms embargo; UN resolutions, usually ignored; and cease-fire agreements, another in August 1993, violated sooner rather than later by one side or another. The plan for a "Union of Three Republics" was discussed at another international conference on Bosnia in Geneva at the end of November–early December 1993. Efforts were made to persuade the Bosnian Serbs to give up part of the land they controlled (approximately 70 percent of Bosnia's territory), in order to increase the size of the Muslim republic to about one-third of Bosnia's territory, mostly in central Bosnia, with several enclaves in the east. In return, the *EC* offered to lift the sanctions against Serbia gradually. Karadzic offered some territory—in exchange for the partition of Sarajevo into two cities, to be incorporated into the planned Muslim and Serb republics. Izetbegovic had two major concerns: the security of the new borders, for which he demanded a five-year *NATO* guarantee; and an outlet to the Adriatic Sea, at the port of Neum. In the absence of assurances on both points, he rejected the plan on 21 December.

One of the most shocking assaults on civilians occurred on 5 February 1994: a mortar bomb hit the main market of Sarajevo and killed dozens of civilians. Outraged Western leaders called for "the immediate lifting of the siege of Sarajevo by all means necessary, including air power." The response was swift. On the 9th *NATO* declared that it would execute immediately any future UN request for air strikes in Bosnia. Moreover, *NATO* ambassadors gave the Bosnian Serbs an ultimatum: withdraw or hand over to UN control all heavy weapons in the "safe areas" by midnight, 20–21 February, or face air strikes. The large-scale withdrawal of Serb heavy weapons began on 17 February, following an unexpected Russian intervention—an offer to replace the withdrawing Serb soldiers with 800 Russian troops; the first 400 Russians reached Sarajevo on the 20th. And on 28 February *NATO* aircraft first enforced the "no-fly zone" over Bosnia, shooting down four Soko G-4 aircraft.

Another shift in Croatia's zigzag policy and the convoluted diplomacy of the Bosnia crisis occurred on 8 March: agreements were signed in Washington to create a federation of Muslim- and Croat-controlled territory in Bosnia, to be divided into cantons on the Swiss model, and to form in the near future a Bosnia-

Croatia confederation. A constitution for the Bosnia federation and plans for a unified Croat-Muslim army in Bosnia were approved at simultaneous conferences in Vienna and Split from 4–8 March. While the federation and confederation formally came into existence, none of these agreements altered the course of the crisis. The Bosnian Serb Assembly, invited to join the Bosnia federation, declined on 24 March. A cease-fire agreement in June 1994 between the new Bosnian Federation of Muslims and Croats, and the Bosnian Serbs, lasted a month.

Among the major powers there were profound disagreements on policy toward Bosnia. Both the U.S. and Russia steadfastly refused to contribute any ground forces to *UNPROFOR;* but they differed substantially on many issues. The U.S. favored lifting the arms embargo, in order to "level the fighting field" between Bosnia and the Bosnian Serbs. It urged the adoption of a policy of "preventive bombardment" of Serb positions (which the U.K. and France, as well as Russia, opposed). The U.S. argued that sanctions against Serbia should be tightened and that the no-fly zone should be enforced by a Security Council resolution. Russia, traditionally pro-Serb, supported the Vance-Owen peace plan and the international peacekeeping force. However, it opposed the imposition of more sanctions against Serbia.

The West, too, was split over policy toward the Bosnia crisis. The U.S. was the most militant—verbally; the Europeans were cautious in word and deed. The U.S. Congress persistently urged the lifting of the UN arms embargo (and voted in favor of a unilateral U.S. termination of the embargo in July 1995). However, both presidents—Bush and Clinton—while favoring the policy, refused to act in direct conflict with the U.K. and France, *NATO* and the *EU,* especially since they bore the brunt of the peacekeeping operation on the ground, with thousands of troops, while the U.S. refused to participate in *UNPROFOR.* The Europeans, except for Germany, claimed that lifting the arms embargo would enlarge the scope and intensity of the war, with unpredictable and, almost certainly, dire consequences.

The U.S. was also much more activist on the issue of *NATO* air strikes against the Bosnian Serbs, designed to increase pressure on them to desist from more "ethnic cleansing," blocking food shipments to UN "safe areas," and attacks on UN peacekeepers. The air strikes almost always had momentary—or negative—results. (On one occasion, in June 1995, the Bosnian Serbs retaliated by taking several hundred *UNPROFOR* hostages in response to a U.S.-initiated *NATO* air strike.)

(In August 1995, the **Yugoslavia II** crisis escalated dramatically when the Croatian army, in a lightning three-day campaign, regained control of Krajina, the Serb majority area of Croatia, bordering on Serbia and Bosnia. Yugoslavia [Serbia] did not intervene, despite the forced exodus ["ethnic cleansing"] by Croatia of 150,000 Serb refugees to Serbia proper.)

(Another major escalation of the crisis-war over Bosnia was the Bosnian Serb capture of two UN "safe areas," Srebrenica and Zepa, on 11 and 25 July, followed by the massing of Bosnian Serb forces near Gorazde; the tightening of the Bosnian Serb siege of Sarajevo; and on 28 August, a shelling of a crowded market in the capital with 37 killed and 80 wounded, recalling a similar incident in February 1994, when 68 people were killed and more than 200 wounded. The effect of these escalation points was the first direct *NATO* military intervention, in the form of massive air attacks against Bosnian Serb positions at the beginning of September. That, in turn, was the catalyst to a renewed, intense, diplomatic process, leading to an agreed "Statement of Basic Principles" by the three warring parties on 8 September and a 21-day conference (1–21 November) at Dayton, Ohio, among the presidents of Bosnia, Croatia, and Serbia under U.S. auspices.)

The Dayton Accord, signed by all the parties including the now fully involved United States, on 21 November 1995, was a complex agreement with the following main provisions: (1) a division of **territory** between the Bosnian-Croat Federation (51 percent) and the autonomous Serb entity, the republic of Srpska (49 percent); (2) a **constitution** comprising a central government for Bosnia as a whole with a three-person group presidency, a two-house legislature, a court, and a central bank; and separate presidencies, legislatures, and armies for each of the two entities within Bosnia; (3) the mutual **withdrawal** of forces by both entities behind agreed cease-fire lines; and (4) the dispatch of a **peacekeeping** *NATO* force of 60,000 under U.S. command to monitor the cease-fire and control the airspace over Bosnia. Despite strong Bosnian Serb opposition "on the ground"— President Milosevic of Serbia negotiated on their behalf—the Dayton Accord marked the end of Bosnia's crisis—on 21 November 1995.

(The formal peace agreement was signed in Paris on 14 December by the presidents of Bosnia-Hercegovina, Croatia, and Serbia, in the symbolically important presence of the leaders of the Contact Group—France, Germany, Russia, the U.K., the U.S.—and Spain's Premier, then head of the European Union. Almost immediately after, the UN Security Council terminated the peacekeeping role of its *UNPROFOR* and authorized the dispatch of a *NATO* force of 60,000 troops to implement the withdrawal provisions of the Dayton Accord and to maintain peace in Bosnia.

All of the military provisions, including withdrawal of troops, were implemented in 1996, meeting the stipulated deadlines. The record on the civilian aspects of the Dayton Accord was mixed; but the elections for the central government of Bosnia-Hercegovina and its two constituent autonomous units were held, as planned, on 14 September 1996.)

(See *Master Table*, pp. 736–37.)

Sources
See sources for Case #397; and: *Keesing's* 1992, 1993, 1994, 1995; Kelly 1995; *New York Times* 1992, 1993, 1994, 1995, 1996; Riga 1992.

Middle East: Non-Protracted Conflict (PC) Crises

There were 78 international crises in the Middle East from the end of 1918 to the end of 1994. Its high proneness to international crises is evident in the fact that most states in this region attained their independence after World War II. Thus, only 11 of the 78 crises occurred before that watershed in world politics, which hastened the coming of independence to many states in the Middle East.

The Middle East generated some important and intense international crises. One contributed to the incipient Cold War—Case #108—**Azerbaijan**, in 1945–46. Several erupted within the **Arab/Israel PC**: Cases #120, 152, 222, 255—**Palestine Partition/Israel Independence**, in 1947–49; **Suez Nationalization-War**, in 1956–57; **Six Day War**, in 1967; **October–Yom Kippur War**, in 1973–74. And in the Gulf subregion of the Middle East, the **Onset of Iran/Iraq War** in 1980 (Case #317, in **Iran/Iraq PC**) and the **Gulf War** of 1990–91 (Case #393, in **Middle East: Non-PCs**) are notable (see *Master Table*). In sum, the Middle East was a high-profile crisis-war region since 1947.

The following pages present summaries of all non-PC crises that occurred in the Middle East, organized chronologically. Moreover, the 54 PC cases are listed along with a reference to where the relevant summary can be found.

(7) Smyrna

Greece and Italy were directly engaged in a crisis over Anatolia from early March to 29 July 1919.

Background and Pre-crisis
Turkey's defeat in World War I accelerated the dismemberment of the Ottoman Empire. France and the U.K. had already laid claim to its non-Turkish territories (see below). Constantinople was controlled, de facto, by the British; the Ottoman government had lost all autonomy in foreign policy. The Greeks had invaded Eastern Thrace and had made no secret of their claims to western Anatolia, especially to Smyrna (Izmir) with its large Greek population. However, spheres of influence had already been drawn by the Allies in Anatolia and the Middle East in secret agreements during the war.

The Treaty of St. Jean de Maurienne (21 April 1917) had awarded Italy primacy in the Adalia Province of southern Anatolia and in western Anatolia including Smyrna—in return for Italy's recognition of the Sykes-Picot Agreement of 9 May 1916. That agreement had divided the Arab Near East lands of the Ottoman Empire into British and French spheres of influence—Palestine and

Mesopotamia (Iraq) to the former, the coastal strip of Lebanon, Syria, Cilicia, and southern Kurdistan to the latter. Behind the scenes Britain's Prime Minister Lloyd George, a strong Hellenophile, was adamant about curtailing Italy's influence in the Near East.

Crisis

Acting under the terms of the Treaty of St. Jean de Maurienne, Italy began to occupy southern Anatolia in early March 1919. This triggered a crisis for Greece which, with the backing of the U.K. and France and, more quietly, the U.S., responded on 15 May 1919: 20,000 Greek troops landed in Smyrna. This triggered a crisis for Italy, which perceived a threat to its influence in the Near East. Minor clashes occurred in Smyrna between Greek and Turkish civilians and between Greek and Italian forces in the region.

Bilateral negotiations culminated in the Venizelos-Tittoni Agreement on 29 July 1919. Italy undertook to support Greece's claims in Thrace, northern Epirus, the Aegean Islands, and Smyrna. Greece, in turn, recognized Italian primacy in southwest Anatolia and pledged support for Italy's demands for a League of Nations Mandate over Albania. Moreover, Italy would retain Rhodes, and Greece received the Dodecanese Islands. This agreement ended the international crisis over Smyrna.

Although Greece achieved most of its territorial objectives, Greek/Turkish hostility, a constant in the eastern Mediterranean, was sharply intensified. (See Cases #16, 18, 25—**Greece/Turkey War I, II, III**, in 1920, 1921, 1922, in **Multiregional PCs: Greece/Turkey**.) Ottoman Turkey made the most concessions but did not experience a higher probability of war—with Greece or Italy— or time pressure. Thus Greece and Italy were the only crisis actors, with Turkey, the U.K., and France heavily involved in the Smyrna crisis.

There was no global organization at the time of this crisis.

(The terms of the Venizelos-Tittoni Agreement, along with those of Sykes-Picot, were later incorporated into the Treaty of Sèvres, 10 August 1920, between the Allies and the Ottoman Empire with some changes: a plebiscite was to be held in Smyrna and its hinterland after five years of Greek administration; and the Dodecanese Islands were given to Italy, the rest of the Aegean Islands to Greece. The Turks under Kemal Atatürk captured and largely destroyed Smyrna in September 1921 during the prolonged Greece/Turkey War [see Case #18— **Greece/Turkey War II**]. As a result Turkey regained control over all of Anatolia and recovered Eastern Thrace from Greece, in the Treaty of Lausanne, 24 July 1923, which replaced the Treaty of Sèvres.)

(See *Master Table*, pp. 666–67.)

Sources

Evans 1982; Graves 1941; Hale and Bagiz 1984; Kent 1984; Kinross 1964; Lewis 1961; Psomiades 1968.

(11) Cilician War

Turkey and France experienced a crisis-war in Anatolia from November 1919 to 20 October 1921.

Background
Secret agreements among the Great Powers during World War I had awarded France a sphere of influence in Cilicia, that is, southeastern Anatolia bordering on Syria (see **Background and Pre-crisis,** Case #7 above).

Crisis
As with Italy in the **Smyrna** crisis, France began to occupy its assigned area in November 1919, taking control of the three main cities—Maras, Aintab, and Urfa. This triggered a crisis for the new nationalist regime in Turkey under the leadership of Mustafa Kemal (Atatürk).

(Atatürk had succeeded in forging a National Pact through the summer and autumn of 1919, notably at the Erzurum and Sivas congresses in July–August and September. By December 1919 nationalist forces controlled Ankara, the agreed-upon capital of a renascent Turkey, and had liberated large parts of Anatolia. The *Sublime Porte,* the government of the Ottoman Empire in Constantinople, was reduced to an empty shell.)

Turkey responded to the French occupation in late January 1920, around the 20th, with an attack on French forces and their Armenian supporters in Maras, triggering a crisis for France. Hostilities escalated to full-scale war, and the French were evicted from Maras within three weeks. The parties agreed to a 20-day armistice on 23 May 1920; but the French broke the agreement on 10 June and opened another front in northern Anatolia.

British forces attempted to divert the Turkish nationalists by landing troops on the Anatolian coast off the Sea of Marmara. And Greece repeatedly attacked the Turks in 1920 and 1921 (see Cases #16 and 18, in **Multiregional PCs: Greece/Turkey**). Kemal Atatürk successfully resisted the Greek invasion and secured an agreement with Soviet Russia in December 1920 to relieve his eastern front.

As their military stalemate persisted, France and Turkey began secret negotiations in the summer of 1921. A formal agreement, the Ankara Accord, was voluntarily signed on 20 October 1921 ending the Cilician crisis-war: it had lasted almost two years and had been a considerable drain on French resources, in a region where French interests were secondary. France evacuated Cilicia and agreed to a special regime in Alexandretta, Syria, to safeguard the interests of the city's substantial Turkish population, in return for economic concessions, notably rights to sections of the Baghdad Railway.

The League of Nations was not involved in this crisis.

(Following the end of the Cilician War, France and Turkey entered upon an era of cooperation, though they were later enmeshed in a prolonged crisis over **Alexandretta,** from 1936 to 1939 [see Case #53 below].)

(See *Master Table,* pp. 666–67.)

Sources
See sources for Case #7.

(14) Persian Border, 1920–21 (see Multiregional PCs: Iran/USSR)

(16) Greece/Turkey War I, 1920 (see Multiregional PCs: Greece/Turkey)

(18) Greece/Turkey War II, 1921 (see Multiregional PCs: Greece/Turkey)

(25) Greece/Turkey War III, 1922 (see Multiregional PCs: Greece/Turkey)

(26) Chanak

Turkey and the U.K. experienced a crisis over the Neutral Zone of Chanak (Canakkale) from 23 September to 11 October 1922.

Pre-crisis
The ignominious Greek withdrawal from Anatolia on 15 September 1922 marked the end of the Greece/Turkey War (see Case #25—**Greece/Turkey War III**). An important spillover effect was the removal of the buffer between Turkish and British troops stationed on both sides of the Dardanelles. Public opinion in the U.K. and the West generally seemed strongly opposed to the resumption of hostilities in Anatolia. Moreover, the British media were adamant about the need to withdraw from Asia Minor. And Prime Minister Lloyd George's urgent request for military support from the British Dominions, on 18 September, met with an unmistakably negative response.

Crisis
The continuing risk of war prompted London to offer an armistice to Kemal Atatürk on 23 September triggering a crisis for the nationalist regime: an armistice was perceived as a cover for continued British occupation of Turkish territory. Kemal Atatürk responded the same day by dispatching troops into the Neutral Zone drawn around the city of Chanak on the Anatolian bank of the Dardanelles. This catalyzed a crisis for the U.K. There was no violence; in fact, Turkish forces halted their advance before reaching U.K. military installations.

British troops were put on a state of alert but were ordered not to fire first.

Three days later the U.K. sent an ultimatum to Kemal Atatürk via its ambassador to Turkey demanding evacuation of the Neutral Zone by Turkish forces. However, Lord Harrington believed that the Turks did not want war and did not deliver the ultimatum! He so informed London on 1 October. The same day, following French pressure and a meeting between the British Foreign Secretary, Lord Curzon, and Turkey's deputy foreign minister, Mustafa Kemal accepted the earlier offer of an armistice thus removing the need for a renewed British ultimatum. With war still lurking in the background, a conference began on the 3rd at Mudanya on the Anatolian side of the Sea of Marmara. After an initial deadlock on the 5th an armistice was signed on 11 October ending the Chanak crisis.

The agreement was a compromise for the U.K., a notable victory for Turkey. The former averted an undesirable war and succeeded in persuading Kemal Atatürk to remove his forces from the Neutral Zone around Chanak. Turkey obtained British recognition of its sovereignty over Istanbul, the Straits, and Eastern Thrace, the last at the expense of the Greeks. Moreover, the Mudanya armistice created the basis for a peace conference, which produced the much less punitive Treaty of Lausanne on 24 July 1923, replacing what for Turkey was the odious Treaty of Sèvres on 10 August 1920, a triumph for Kemal Atatürk.

The League of Nations was not involved in this case.

(See *Master Table,* pp. 670–71.)

Sources
See sources for Case #25.

(29) Hijaz/Najd War

Najd and Hijaz, two desert kingdoms in the Arabian Peninsula, precursors to Saʿudi Arabia, experienced a crisis-war from 7 March 1924 until 19 December 1925.

Background and Pre-crisis
Najd is the vast, sparsely populated, northern region of the Arabian Peninsula. Although formally a province of the Ottoman Empire from 1517 until the end of World War I, it was largely ignored by the *Sublime Porte* in Constantinople. It was unified by the orthodox Wahabi Muslims in the eighteenth century and was ruled continuously by the al-Saʿud dynasty except for a decade beginning in the early 1890s. Its capital, Riyadh, was reconquered in 1902 by Saʿud Ibn ʿAbd-ul-ʿAziz, who then steadily extended the Saʿudi domain to the entire Arabian Peninsula except the south—Yemen, Hadhramaut, and Oman.

Hijaz comprised the western region of Arabia. It extends from the Gulf of Aqaba and the border of the Kingdom of Jordan to ʿAsir with an area of 120,000–150,000 square miles. The home of Islam's two holiest cities, Mecca and Medina, Hijaz was the heartland of the Muslim faith. It also possessed political and economic importance, the latter due to substantial revenue deriving from the continuous flow of Muslim pilgrims and from Jidda, the main port of Arabia on the Red Sea.

Like Najd, Hijaz was an autonomous part of the Ottoman Empire for four centuries. A rebellion in 1916, part of the "Arab Revolt" against Turkish rule, led to a short-lived Kingdom of Hijaz (1916–25) under Hussein Ibn ʿAli, the Sharif of Mecca, a Hashemite and traditional rival of the Saʿudis, the great-grandfather of King Hussein of Jordan.

Tension between the two rivals for primacy in Arabia and Islam, the Saʿudis and the Hashemites, became acute in 1923 with clashes between Najd and Hijaz pilgrims; but the conflict was controlled by their common patron, the U.K., which had played that role since the Arab Revolt during World War I.

Crisis

Although ʿAbd-ul-ʿAziz sought and exploited any opportunity to extend the Saʿudi kingdom to all of Arabia, his decision to attack Hijaz was triggered by King Hussein's assumption on 7 March 1924 of the title of Caliph, which had been vacant since the end of the Ottoman Empire and had been abolished by the new secular Republic of Turkey. Hussein's move, although not recognized by the Muslim world, offended the orthodox Wahabis and especially their military core, the *Ikhwan*. It was perceived as a visible threat to the Saʿudi aspiration for hegemony in Arabia and primacy in Islam. The delayed Wahabi response was a military campaign against Hijaz beginning on 29 August 1924.

By 1 September Wahabi forces were at the gates of Taʾif, a summer resort for Hijaz and, later, Saʿudi Arabian notables, barely 40 kilometers from Mecca. This triggered a grave crisis for the king of Hijaz. Military resistance was in vain; and Taʾif fell on 5 September. The Wahabis advanced toward Mecca. Hussein abdicated on 3 October in favor of his son, ʿAli, and fled to Aqaba. Mecca was overrun on the 13th.

The Wahabis laid siege to the three remaining cities in Hijaz—Medina, Yanbu, and Jidda. The port city held out until 19 December 1925 marking the end of the crisis and the collapse of Hijaz as a state.

No great power, nor the League of Nations, was involved in this crisis.

(The Saʿudi ruler, ʿAbd-ul-ʿAziz, better known as Ibn Saʿud, assumed the title, King of Hijaz and Sultan of Najd, in 1926, changing it the following year to King of Hijaz and Najd, and held the title until 1932, when the united state was renamed "The Saʿudi Arabian Kingdom.")

(A geographically related crisis focusing on ʿAsir occurred a decade later [see Case #44—**Saʿudi/Yemen War**, in 1933–1934 below].)

(See *Master Table*, pp. 670–71.)

Sources

Benoist-Mechin 1955; Holden and Johns 1981; Iqbal 1977; Lacey 1981; Shimoni 1987; Toynbee 1927.

(31) Mosul Land Dispute

Turkey and the U.K. were enmeshed in a crisis over the Iraqi/Turkish borderland from 29 September to 15 November 1924.

Background
Mosul is an oil-rich area straddling the borders of northwestern Iraq, eastern Turkey, and northern Syria. Like the rest of the Arab Near East, Mosul was a province *(vilayet)* of the Ottoman Empire for four centuries, from 1517 until World War I.

Under the terms of the (secret) Sykes-Picot Agreement of 1916 Mosul was assigned to a postwar French zone of influence in the Middle East including Syria and Lebanon. However, in December 1918 French Premier Clemenceau agreed to British Prime Minister Lloyd George's request to transfer Mosul to what was anticipated to be the British zone of influence including Mesopotamia (Iraq), in exchange for British concessions on the Rhine. Nationalist Turkey, however, persisted in its claim to Mosul on ethnic and realpolitik grounds: its population was Kurdish—non-Arab, though Muslim; and the vilayet was not under British control at the time of the Mudrost Armistice in October 1918.

The Treaty of Sèvres in 1920, the initial, abortive peace agreement between the victorious Allies and Turkey, awarded Mosul to Iraq. The 1923 Treaty of Lausanne, the counterpart of the Versailles Treaty vis-à-vis Turkey, provided a procedure for resolving the territorial dispute but not its content: the U.K., by then the Mandatory Power in Iraq, and the Republic of Turkey, the successor to the Ottoman Empire, were to attempt to reach agreement by direct negotiations; if that failed the dispute was to be referred to the League of Nations Council. The U.K. did so in August 1924.

Pre-crisis
The Council requested—and received—from the disputants a commitment to accept its decision as binding. It then decided to dispatch a commission of inquiry to the contested area. In the meantime both claimants were taking measures to consolidate what each perceived to be its part of Mosul. This led to minor frontier skirmishes. The U.K. accused Turkey of crossing into Iraqi territory under British Mandate. Turkey responded with the charge that Royal Air Force sorties over Turkish territory violated the Treaty of Lausanne.

Crisis
A serious clash occurred in mid-September 1924. On the 29th the British chargé d'affaires in Constantinople called for the withdrawal of Turkish forces from the disputed zone within 48 hours, triggering a crisis for Turkey. Turkey replied in kind on 3 October catalyzing a crisis for the U.K.. The League Council called on the two parties to respect the status quo.

On 9 October the U.K. escalated the crisis by issuing an ultimatum to

Turkey to evacuate its forces by the 11th, with a threat to take "all necessary military measures" to restore the status quo ante if necessary. Turkey responded the next day with a Note to the Secretary-General of the League acknowledging the high probability of a violent confrontation and requesting the League to fix the boundary. The U.K. accepted the proposal on the 14th, in effect withdrawing its ultimatum of the 9th.

At Turkey's insistence—it challenged the Council's competence to set the boundary since the dispute concerned provisions of the Treaty of Lausanne—the League Council sought an advisory opinion from the World Court. The Court ruled that the Council had jurisdiction under Article 15 of the Covenant but that its decision required unanimity excluding the votes of the disputants; and its decision had to be accepted as binding.

A League-appointed commission investigated the competing claims. It reported that the majority population of Mosul, the Kurds, preferred independence to Turkish or Iraqi rule; if the options excluded independence they preferred being part of Iraq—on condition that Iraq remained a British Mandate for another 25 years. The commission recommended in favor of Iraq, contingent upon that condition or the return of most of Mosul to Turkey. Iraq—and the U.K.— accepted the condition. On that basis the Council defined an interim boundary, the "Brussels Line," and requested both parties to withdraw from the disputed zone by 15 November. The U.K. and Turkey accepted the ruling and the boundary, ending the crisis that day.

(The Mosul Land Dispute was formally resolved on 5 June 1926 with the signing of a tripartite agreement—the U.K., Turkey, Iraq—incorporating an agreed boundary between Turkey and Iraq.)

(In the context of this dispute the U.K. attempted to secure for Iraq control over a small piece of Turkish territory inhabited by the Christian Assyrian community—but failed.)

(See *Master Table*, pp. 670–71.)

Sources
Documents on British Foreign Policy (DBFP) (Medlicott et al. 1966); Boulter 1928; Dexter 1967; Edmunds 1957; Kinross 1965; Shimoni 1987; Toynbee 1926, 1927b; Walters 1952.

(44) Sa'udi/Yemen War

A crisis between Sa'udi Arabia and Yemen over territory began on 18 December 1933 and ended on 20 May 1934.

Background
In 1930 the former protectorate of 'Asir was incorporated into the Kingdom of Hijaz and Najd (later, Sa'udi Arabia), thus extending its territory to the Yemen border. The imam of Yemen then claimed a number of frontier districts between

the two states. Tribes residing in ʿAsir, aided by Yemen, staged a revolt against King Ibn Saʿud. Treaties of friendship had been signed between Saʿudi Arabia and Great Britain, and between Yemen and Italy.

Crisis

On 18 December 1933 the Saʿudis received information that Yemeni troops had entered ʿAsir. That day Saʿudi Arabia decided to initiate talks with Yemen. A conference was convened on 16 March 1934, but Yemen refused to withdraw from the disputed area. The Saʿudis opted for military action and, on 22 March 1934, ordered troops into ʿAsir. This triggered a crisis for Yemen. Saʿudi troops advanced into the disputed highland and along Yemen's coastal plain, to the port of Hudeida. British, French, and Italian warships were sent to the area, and their combined political and military pressure succeeded in halting the first Saʿudi advance.

Yemen resisted the Saʿudi assault at first, but, on 12 April, the imam cabled Ibn Saʿud requesting peace and announcing that his troops had been ordered to evacuate ʿAsir. Fighting continued during the talks on the terms of the armistice, held under a conciliation commission of Egyptians and Syrians. On 13 May 1934 Saʿudi Arabia officially announced an armistice: the imam had agreed to carry out the Saʿudi conditions. A peace conference began on 18 May, and on 20 May the crisis ended with the signing of the Treaty of Taʾif, which recognized Saʿudi Arabia's sovereignty over all of ʿAsir, including the oasis of Najran, the initial source of the dispute, and called for financial reparations from Yemen, in return for the withdrawal of Saʿudi forces from Yemeni territory.

The League of Nations was not involved in this crisis.

(This long-standing border dispute over the districts of ʿAsir, Jizan, and Najran generated another crisis between Saʿudi Arabia and Yemen in January–February 1995: Yemen reopened a claim to these territories which it acknowledged in a border agreement in 1973 had rightly been annexed by Saʿudi Arabia. However, unlike in 1933–34 the clashes occurred at many points along the Saʿudi Arabia/Yemen border. On 26 February 1995 they announced that a joint committee would demarcate the largely undefined 2,000-kilometer boundary.)

(See *Master Table*, pp. 672–73.)

Sources

Carr 1945; Ingrams 1963; Kohn 1934; *New York Times* 1995; Safran 1988; Shimoni 1987; Wenner 1967.

(53) Alexandretta

A lengthy five-stage international crisis over Alexandretta began on 9 September 1936 and lasted until 23 June 1939, with Turkey and France as crisis actors.

Background

The *Sanjak* of Alexandretta (Hatay) is a district in northwestern Syria that became a part of France's Syria Mandate in 1921, with strong opposition from

Turkey. The territory, which included a valuable harbor, has a large Turkish population and had been the subject of negotiation in 1926. Turkey considered the Sanjak and port of Alexandretta important to its security and objected to Arab (Syrian) rule over Turks. France maintained that separating Hatay from Syria would mean the latter's dismemberment. In addition, as guardian of the area, France could not risk the loss of reputation and prestige among other states. On the other hand, events in Europe preoccupied France, and it later looked to Turkey as a potential ally against Germany and Italy or, at least, as a neutral state.

Crisis

On 9 September 1936 a crisis for Turkey was triggered by the publication of the contents of a Treaty of Alliance between France and Syria, which identified the Sanjak of Alexandretta as part of Syrian territory. President Kemal Atatürk responded by promising his people on 2 November that Hatay would be returned to Turkey. The dispute was brought before the League of Nations by Turkey's foreign minister, who also expressed a willingness to enter into direct negotiations with France. On 7 January 1937 the Turks moved troops to the border, triggering a crisis for France. France responded on the 22nd by entering into talks with Turkey and welcoming League intervention. On the 27th both agreed to an autonomous government for the region, which remained nominally part of Syria. This ended the first stage of the crisis over Alexandretta. The French Mandate was to end in three years, with Syria and Lebanon becoming independent states, and safeguards were planned for the minorities.

The manner in which the agreement was reached encouraged Turkey to reopen the issue. On 3 June 1937 Turkish troops were again sent to the border when the French imposed a curfew in Alexandretta because of local disturbances. France responded on the 7th with an offer to hold direct negotiations in Paris. The matter was brought to the League of Nations by France and Turkey, and two core documents were envisaged. The League was to draw up a Statute providing for protection of minorities and Turkey's economic rights. A Fundamental Law was to define for the Sanjak autonomous governing institutions. They were both ratified in May 1937. A Treaty of Amity was signed by the adversaries on 4 July 1937, ending the second stage of the crisis.

Turkey, still dissatisfied, threatened France with war on 29 October 1937 if new demands for changes in the electoral regulations for the Sanjak were not met. On 16 December France once more opened negotiations with Turkey and agreed to the demands on 29 January 1938, ending the third stage of the crisis over Alexandretta.

On 4 June 1938 Turkey raised its demands to include Turkish participation in the military control of the Sanjak and moved its 7th Division from its base at Adana toward the frontier. That day France responded by holding talks with the Turkish ambassador in Paris. Further negotiations were carried out on 13 June, and the French cabinet instructed General Huntziger to yield. On 4 July 1938 another treaty of friendship was signed between France and Turkey.

On 5 April 1939 a rumor of Turkish annexation was strengthened by Turkish military maneuvers in the Sanjak and a further concentration of troops near the border. France reacted the same day by dispatching a warship to the area and strengthening its troop positions. Turkey demanded the cession of Hatay. Finally, on 23 June 1939 the crisis as a whole ended with a Declaration of Mutual Assistance and France's acquiescence in the transfer of Hatay to Turkey.

The League of Nations, as noted, played a key role in the early stages of this lengthy crisis. It drafted the Statute of the Sanjak, governing its relations with a future government of Syria, and the Fundamental Law of the Sanjak. It sent a commission and observers but withdrew them on 26 June 1938. The League commission also drafted the Electoral Law and fixed a date for elections. Elections were not held under League supervision but under Turkish and French military control. The U.K. pressured France to end the conflict and to yield to Turkey. Protests were made about French concessions to Turkey by Italy, Yugoslavia, and Iraq.

(See *Master Table*, pp. 674–75.)

Sources
Clough 1970; Hourani 1946; Kayali 1976; Kilic 1959; Longrigg 1958; Shaw and Shaw 1977; Tamkov 1976; Tibawi 1969; Vere-Hodge 1950; Walters 1952; Ziadeh 1957.

(84) Mid-East Campaign, 1941 (see Multiregional PCs: World War II)

(87) Occupation of Iran, 1941–42 (see Multiregional PCs: Iran/USSR)

(96) Iran–Oil Concessions, 1944 (see Multiregional PCs: Iran/USSR)

(105) French Forces/Syria, 1945 (see Multiregional PCs: World War II)

(106) Kars-Ardahan, 1945–46 (see Multiregional PCs: East/West)

(108) Azerbaijan, 1945–46 (see Multiregional PCs: Iran/USSR)

(111) Turkish Straits, 1946 (see Multiregional PCs: East/West)

(120) Palestine Partition/Israel Independence, 1947–49 (see Arab/Israel PC)

(128) Sinai Incursion, 1948–49 (see Arab/Israel PC)

(134) Hula Drainage, 1951 (see Arab/Israel PC)

(143) Qibya, 1953 (see Arab/Israel PC)

(148) Baghdad Pact

Egypt's crisis over the Baghdad Pact began on 24 February and ended in mid-October 1955.

Background and Pre-crisis
In February 1954 a Syrian army coup, with Iraqi involvement, ousted a pro-Egyptian regime in Damascus headed by Adib Shishakli. However, Iraqi hopes for a pro-Western Syria were not realized. An agreement between Turkey and Pakistan and bilateral military aid agreements between the U.S., Turkey, and Iraq were signed in April 1954. The United States and Pakistan signed a similar agreement the following month. Iraq announced its intention to join a pro-Western alliance and endeavored to prevent possible isolation in the Arab world by attempting to persuade other Arab states to join as well. On 16 January 1955 Egypt called for an emergency meeting of the Arab League, claiming that no member should become party to an agreement with the Western powers and that such a pact would likely undermine Arab sovereignty and independence. Cairo was unsuccessful in its efforts to have Iraq expelled from the Arab League.

Crisis
On 24 February 1955 Iran, Iraq, Pakistan, Turkey, and the U.K. created a regional anti-Soviet defense arrangement known as the Baghdad Pact, triggering a crisis for Egypt: Nasir viewed the Pact as a challenge to his leadership in the Arab world and a direct threat from the U.S. and the U.K. to overthrow his regime. At the end of February Egypt and Syria announced their intention to exclude Iraq from a new Arab alliance with Saʿudi Arabia and Yemen. Egypt's response, on 15 March, was a denunciation of the Pact and an accusation that the West was introducing great power rivalry and the Cold War into the Middle East, thus dividing the Arab world and threatening Egypt with encirclement. Egypt began to forge counteralliances with Jordan, Lebanon, and Syria; and the division of the Arab states into rival camps hardened.

The crisis ended in mid-October 1955 when Egypt and Syria concluded a Mutual Defense Pact. The United States participated in the negotiations and provided economic assistance but never formally joined the Pact. The Soviet Union provided arms and weapons to Egypt and Syria.

The UN was not involved in this crisis.

(In July 1958 a coup in Iraq overthrew the monarchy and established a

military dictatorship [see Case #165—**Iraq-Lebanon Upheaval** below]. Iraq subsequently left the Baghdad Pact.)
(See *Master Table,* pp. 692–93.)

Sources
Bowie 1974; Dekmejian 1971; Finer 1964; Hofstadter 1973; Lacouture 1973; Love 1969; Nutting 1967; Robertson 1964; Thomas 1970.

(149) Gaza Raid/Czech. Arms, 1955–56 (see Arab/Israel PC)

(152) Suez Nationalization-War, 1956–57 (see Arab/Israel PC)

(153) Qalqilya, 1956 (see Arab/Israel PC)

(157) Jordan Regime

A crisis over a threat to the regime of King Hussein occurred from 4 April to 3 May 1957.

Background and Pre-crisis
In October 1956 leftist nationalist parties won the parliamentary elections in Jordan, making Suleiman al-Nabulsi Prime Minister. Jordan joined a military alliance with Egypt, Syria, and Saʿudi Arabia. The treaty between the U.K. and Jordan was annulled in March 1957, and diplomatic relations were established with the USSR, which included the acceptance of an offer of Soviet aid. The British commander of Jordan's Arab Legion, Glubb Pasha, was dismissed and was replaced by General Ali Abu Nuwar, who favored closer ties with Nasirist Egypt. His country's increasingly rapid movements toward the Left alarmed King Hussein. The United States became concerned about a possible threat to the independence of Jordan and to the pro-Western regional alliance system established by the Baghdad Pact (see Case #148 above).

Crisis
The trigger to Jordan's crisis was an attempt on 4 April to overthrow the king. Hussein, perceiving a threat to his regime, accused Egypt and Syria of aiding anti-Hussein elements within Jordan. On 10 April King Hussein responded by dismissing the entire leftist cabinet. Riots and demonstrations followed but were controlled by suppressing all the political parties. Ali Abu Nuwar, the Chief of Staff, was dismissed, and the king succeeded in persuading army officers to support him. The United States, as well as Saʿudi Arabia, came to the king's assistance with military and economic aid. Units of the U.S.'s Sixth Fleet were

sent to the eastern Mediterranean, and their departure, on 3 May 1957, indicated that the crisis for the Hashemite Kingdom seemed to have ended.

The Soviet Union covertly supported the anti-Hussein plot. The UN was not involved in this crisis.

(See *Master Table*, pp. 694–95.)

Sources
Eisenhower 1965; *MEJ* Chronology 1957; Shimoni 1987.

(159) Syria/Turkey Confrontation, 1957 (see Multiregional PCs: East/West)

(162) Formation of UAR

The two crisis actors were Iraq and Jordan. The crisis began on 1 February and ended on 14 February 1958.

Background
An announcement by King Hussein of Jordan in April 1957 of the discovery of a Syrian-Egyptian plot against him led to the dismissal of the entire Jordanian cabinet and a political swing to the Right (see Case #157—**Jordan Regime** above). As a result Jordan's relations with Syria and Egypt worsened, and a violent anti-Jordan campaign of defamation ensued in those countries.

In Iraq, since Nuri Al-Saʿid's return to power in 1954, close collaboration with the West existed simultaneously with a repressive domestic regime. Discontent among the politically articulate elements of the population grew—Arab nationalists, liberals, communists, traditionalists, and army officers. And as the popularity of Egypt's Nasir increased, the Iraqi regime looked for ways to counter Egyptian influence on its citizens.

Crisis
A crisis was triggered for Iraq and Jordan when the merger of Egypt and Syria into the United Arab Republic (UAR) was proclaimed on 1 February 1958. This was perceived by the Hashemite rulers, King Hussein of Jordan and King Feisal of Iraq, as an act to incite the revolutionary pan-Arab movement and the Arab peoples to rise against existing Arab governments in order to join the UAR. The merger changed the Middle East subsystem: the Syrian Republic ceased to exist, and the new UAR was controlled by Nasir, giving it a population larger than all other Arab states combined. Hussein suggested a meeting with Feisal, which would include King Ibn Saʿud of Saʿudi Arabia, to discuss the possibility of a similar union. On 11 February an Iraqi delegation arrived in Amman. Their response was a joint Proclamation on 14 February 1958 establishing the Arab Federation. This marked the end of the crisis for both Iraq and Jordan. Saʿudi Arabia sent a representative to the talks but did not sign the Proclamation. At first

Nasir accepted the formation of the Federation, but two weeks later he attacked it as an arrangement between reactionaries who lacked the support of their subjects. There was no violence during this Middle East crisis. Neither the U.S. or the USSR, nor the UN, was involved in this crisis. (See *Master Table,* pp. 694–95.)

Sources
Cremeans 1963; Hussein 1962; Kerr 1970; Lenczowski 1962; *MEJ* Chronology 1958; St. John 1960; Shimoni 1987.

(165) Iraq-Lebanon Upheaval

Riots in Lebanon and a coup in Iraq precipitated an international crisis for four states, Lebanon, Jordan, the U.S., and the U.K., lasting from 8 May to the end of October 1958.

Background and Pre-crisis
A crisis in Lebanon occurred during a period of continuing unrest in the Middle East. The United States, in an effort to counter a Soviet threat to U.S. interests, tried to unify the pro-Western Arab states through the "Eisenhower Doctrine" in January 1957, pledging U.S. aid to any Middle East state attacked by "international communism." It was publicly supported by Lebanon alone. President Nasir's strong anti-Western policy was strengthened by the union of Syria and Egypt in February 1958, which weakened Sa'udi Arabia and Lebanon while bringing Iraq and Jordan closer together in an Arab Federation set up at the same time (see Case #162—**Formation of UAR** above).

In Iraq discontent focused on the Baghdad Pact of 1955 *(CENTO [Central Treaty Organization])* (see Case #148 above). A conspiratorial group of "Free Officers" hostile to the monarchy laid plans for a coup and elected Brigadier 'Abd-ul-Karim Qassem as Chairman of the Executive Committee.

Crisis
A crisis for Lebanon was triggered on 8 May 1958 by the murder of a reformist editor of a pro-communist Beirut newspaper, a vocal critic of President Camille Chamoun's Western orientation, including his attempt to amend Lebanon's constitution in order to run for a second term. Opposition elements believed the government was responsible for the assassination. Full-scale rioting ensued. On the 12th the Lebanese army took over security in Beirut, Tripoli, and other cities.

Lebanon responded to the crisis with several acts. Foreign Minister Malik accused the UAR of massive interference in Lebanon's internal affairs. Chamoun sent a message to Eisenhower inquiring about American action if he were to request U.S. assistance. On 21 May Lebanon lodged a formal complaint with the League of Arab States: its attempt to settle the dispute took the form of a neutral resolution without any call for action. And on 22 May Chamoun brought the matter to the UN Security Council.

The Council's discussions on 6 and 11 June resulted in a Swedish-sponsored resolution to dispatch an Observer Group to Lebanon to determine if there was infiltration from Egypt or Syria across the Lebanon border. The group's first report, submitted on 3 July, indicated no border infiltration. Lebanon criticized the report as being inconclusive and misleading. It also contended that the number of observers was insufficient to cover the entire border area and that their activity was ineffective.

On 14 July, a successful coup in Baghdad against the Hashemite monarch triggered a crisis for the United States. The same day U.S. marines were ordered to Lebanon in an attempt to end the violence and stabilize the area. The coup in Baghdad, followed by the dispatch of U.S. troops to Lebanon, triggered a crisis for Jordan and Britain. King Hussein appealed to the U.K. for help on the 16th; and the following day British paratroops landed in Jordan. By 31 July the situation in Lebanon was sufficiently calm to allow a special presidential election: Fu'ad Shihab was elected President.

When Security Council action was effectively blocked by a Soviet veto, an Emergency Session of the General Assembly was called for 8 August. After 15 meetings a mild resolution was adopted, calling on all parties to abide by the Arab League's principle of nonintervention.

A Five-Power Summit Conference called for by Khrushchev did not take place: on 5 August the Soviet leader withdrew his support for a conference. Events in Lebanon remained unstable; and it was not until 14 October that tension dissipated with the acceptance of the new government in Lebanon by all political factions, marking the end of the crisis for Lebanon and the U.S.

The crisis faded for the U.K. and Jordan toward the end of October 1958. At that time King Hussein voiced his perception that the crisis had terminated. The crisis ended with no agreement among the adversaries.

The USSR's involvement was mainly political, but Soviet warships moved westward through the Baltic during the crisis, an act interpreted as an attempt to prevent the victory of pro-U.S. Lebanese forces.

(See *Master Table*, pp. 696–97.)

Sources
Agwani 1965; Curtis 1964; Dowty 1984; Eisenhower 1965; Goodspeed 1967; Hassouna 1975; Heikal 1973; Hoopes 1973; Horne 1989; Hussein 1962; Kerr 1972; Macmillan 1971; *MEJ* Chronology 1958; Miller 1967; Murphy 1964; Penrose 1978; Quandt 1978; Qubain 1961; Shwadran 1959.

(172) Shatt-al-Arab I, 1959–60 (see Iran/Iraq PC)

(173) Rottem, 1960 (see Arab/Israel PC)

(183) Kuwait Independence, 1961 (see Iraq/Kuwait PC)

(188) Breakup of UAR

The duration of Egypt's crisis was from 28 September to 5 October 1961.

Background

A number of high-ranking right-wing Syrian officers in the army of the United Arab Republic formed an alliance with civilian politicians connected with the Syrian business class. Secret talks were held between these Syrians and Nasir's representative, Vice President Field Marshal ʿAmer, where strong dissatisfaction with the UAR was expressed.

Crisis

A coup in Syria on the night of 27–28 September 1961 triggered a crisis for Egypt on the 28th. The restoration of Syria's independence was demanded, and this was viewed by Nasir as a threat directed at Egypt's influence in the Middle East subsystem. Nasir immediately ordered the UAR armed forces to suppress the rebellion. Two thousand paratroops supported the First Army, followed by the entire UAR navy and more troop reinforcements in ships. The following day, the ports of Aleppo and Latakia were taken by the rebels. When Nasir learned this, he ordered the ships to turn back arguing that the reconquest of Syria was almost impossible unless a substantial part of the Syrian army remained loyal to the UAR. Egypt's primary crisis management technique was negotiations with Syrian leaders, but Cairo was unable to persuade them to continue Syria's merger with Egypt. The crisis terminated on 5 October when the end of the Union was admitted to have taken place. Nasir announced that he would not oppose the application of the new Syrian regime for readmission into the United Nations and the Arab League.

The UN, the U.S., and the USSR were not involved in this crisis.

(After the termination of the crisis, on 9 and 10 October, respectively, the USSR and the U.S. recognized the new regime in Syria.)

(See *Master Table*, pp. 700–701.)

Sources

See sources for Case #162; and *MEJ* Chronology 1961; *MER* 1961.

(195) Yemen War I, 1962–63 (see Yemen PC)

(203) Jordan Waters, 1963–64 (see Arab/Israel PC)

(209) Yemen War II, 1964 (see Yemen PC)

(212) Yemen War III, 1964–65 (see Yemen PC)

(219) Yemen War IV, 1966–67 (see Yemen PC)

(220) El-Samu, 1966 (see Arab/Israel PC)

(222) Six Day War, 1967 (see Arab/Israel PC)

(226) Karameh, 1968 (see Arab/Israel PC)

(229) Beirut Airport, 1968–69 (see Arab/Israel PC)

(232) War of Attrition, 1969–70 (see Arab/Israel PC)

(234) Shatt-al-Arab II, 1969 (see Iran/Iraq PC)

(236) Cairo Agreement—PLO

Syria's acquiescence in Palestinian Arab guerrilla activity caused a crisis for Lebanon from 22 October to 3 November 1969.

Pre-crisis
The political equilibrium within Lebanon was endangered when Palestinian Liberation Organization *(PLO)* guerrilla groups, based in Lebanon or infiltrating from across the Syrian border, stepped up their sabotage operations against Israel, bringing about retaliations in 1968. For some time clashes between forces of the Lebanon government and Palestinian guerrillas had been taking place. The clashes always centered around the issues that occupied Lebanon in the late 1960s and throughout the 1970s, namely, the *PLO*'s right to maintain bases in Lebanon and its demands to be allowed to operate from Lebanese soil against targets in Israel. Following an Israeli raid on Beirut's International Airport (see Case #229, in **Arab/Israel PC**) political upheavals in April 1969 left Lebanon with a caretaker government for seven months. Syrian intervention posed an ever-present threat to its political regime.

Crisis
On 22 October 1969 the *PLO* announced that serious clashes had occurred with Lebanese government forces after an attack on its bases in the south along the Israel border. This triggered a crisis for Lebanon. While continuing its military response against the guerrillas, Beirut began meetings with representatives of Egypt and Jordan on the 24th. Syria, which closed its border with Lebanon on 22 October and concentrated military units there, was also approached by Lebanon for negotiation, in a telephone conversation between the two presidents a day earlier. The crisis ended on 3 November when an agreement was reached be-

tween the Lebanese army and government and the *PLO* in Cairo, with the mediation of President Nasir. The Cairo Agreement granted the *PLO* wide-ranging rights to operate as a "state within a state" in Lebanon. Formally, it contained a modus operandi for the guerrilla groups, limiting their bases to the southeastern corner of Lebanon, as well as their sabotage operations against Israel. However, the overall effect was to curtail the sovereignty of Lebanon and its government's control over its own territory.

The United States and the Soviet Union gave political support to Lebanon and Syria, respectively. The UN was not involved in this crisis.

(Syria's border with Lebanon was reopened 11 days after the Cairo Agreement.)

(See *Master Table*, pp. 708–9.)

Sources
MEJ Chronology 1969; *MER* 1969–70.

(238) Black September

This Middle East crisis took place from 15 to 29 September 1970. There were four crisis actors: Syria, the United States, Israel, and Jordan.

Background and Pre-crisis
Palestinian guerrilla forces, encamped in Jordan, were creating serious internal problems for King Hussein throughout 1970. In June major fighting occurred in Amman between the *PLO* and the Jordan Legion. The king was forced to agree to full freedom of movement for the guerrillas. During the summer of 1970 there were more sporadic clashes. On 1 September Palestinian guerrillas sought to assassinate King Hussein for a second time in a period of three months. Fighting broke out immediately between Palestinians and King Hussein's forces in Jordan. After an unsuccessful attempt to hijack an Israeli plane on 4 September, the Popular Front for the Liberation of Palestine *(PFLP)* hijacked two civilian aircraft on the 6th, belonging to Switzerland and the U.S., and forced them to land on a desert strip outside Amman. Three days later a British *(BOAC)* plane was rerouted to join the other two. The *PFLP* hijackings were attempts to force the release of Palestinian prisoners held in Switzerland and the U.K.

Crisis
A crisis for Syria and the U.S. was triggered on 15 September 1970 by King Hussein's announcement of a drastic change in his cabinet, which would now include military personnel. His intention to confront the *PLO* challenge seemed clear. The U.S. feared the loss of an ally if Hussein were overthrown, and Syria perceived a decline in its influence in the region if the Palestinians were defeated. Syria responded on 19 September by invading Jordan, triggering a crisis for Jordan and Israel. Jordan's response was immediate; it engaged in battle with the

Syrian forces the same day and appealed to the U.S. for aid. Israel, at a cabinet meeting on 20 September, decided upon military action, if necessary, in order to prevent a Palestinian victory in Jordan, which was perceived as a grave threat to Israel's influence and security. The United States response was a decision on 21 September to provide umbrella support to Israel if the USSR and Egypt became involved; and National Security Advisor Kissinger, together with Israel's Ambassador to the U.S. (and former Chief of Staff), Rabin, worked out a possible joint plan of military action. This plan was approved by President Nixon. For Syria and the U.S., the crisis escalated with the entry of the Jordanian air force against the Palestinians on the 22nd. All Syrian tanks were withdrawn from Jordanian territory that day. As a result the Palestinian guerrillas were forced to leave Jordan; and they subsequently built strongholds in southern Lebanon.

The League of Arab States met in Cairo at Nasir's initiative, and a Jordan/Syria cease-fire agreement was signed on 27 September. While Hussein's victory was acknowledged, the agreement was a face-saving gesture for Syria because its forces had already been withdrawn, following a U.S.-backed Israeli threat to intervene militarily in support of Jordan. A declaration was issued supporting the rights of the Palestinians. The cease-fire was implemented on the 29th, which marked the termination date for all the crisis actors.

During the course of the crisis the U.S. placed airborne divisions in Germany and the U.S. on semialert. Ships of the Sixth Fleet were reported to be heading toward Lebanese shores. And the aircraft carrier *Saratoga* was ordered to the eastern Mediterranean. USSR involvement in the crisis consisted of political statements calling for a cease-fire and warning against outside intervention while pressuring Syria to pull out of Jordan. The Soviets also monitored U.S. naval operations off the Syrian coast.

The UN was not involved in this crisis.

(See *Master Table*, pp. 710–11.)

Sources
Bar-Siman-Tov 1983; Brandon 1972; Cooley 1973; Dowty 1984; Garfinkle 1985; Isaacson 1992; Kalb and Kalb 1974; Kerr 1970; Kissinger 1979; *MEJ* Chronology 1970; *MER* 1969–70; Nixon 1978; O'Neill 1978; Quandt et al. 1973; Quandt 1977, 1978, 1993; Rabin 1979; Stein 1987.

(248) North/South Yemen I, 1972 (see Yemen PC)

(251) Libyan Plane, 1973 (see Arab/Israel PC)

(252) Iraq Invasion of Kuwait, 1973 (see Iraq/Kuwait PC)

(253) Israel Mobilization, 1973 (see Arab/Israel PC)

(255) October–Yom Kippur War, 1973–74 (see Arab/Israel PC)

(256) Oman/South Yemen

South Yemen's active military assistance to Omani rebels created a crisis for Oman from 18 November 1973 to 11 March 1976.

Background
Fighting in Oman's eastern province of Dhofar between rebels and the sultan's army began in 1963. After independence in 1967 South Yemen increased support to the rebels. By 1970 the insurgents' control extended to all of Dhofar. The traditional sultan was deposed by his son in July 1970. This was followed by a lull in the fighting, and the more liberal sultan was able to gain some tribal support. After the British withdrawal from the Persian Gulf in 1971, the area was characterized by a power vacuum. Oman's independence was proclaimed at the end of 1971. In 1972 the Omani forces, strengthened by British, Iranian, and Jordanian troops, along with financial aid and arms from Sa'udi Arabia and the United Arab Emirates, succeeded in turning the campaign in their favor.

The focal point of tension between Oman and South Yemen had been the latter's support to the insurgents, along with Iraq, both in training (with arms supplied by the People's Republic of China) and in active participation in fighting. Rights over the Kuria Muria Islands, located off the Dhofar coast, were also in dispute. Clashes occurred on the Oman/South Yemen border in 1972, mainly as a result of an incursion into Dhofar by left-wing guerrillas operating from South Yemen. On 15 April 1973 Iran sent additional forces to Oman.

Crisis
On 18 November 1973 the Oman government announced that a military post had been attacked by South Yemen aircraft and that South Yemen forces were actively engaged in the fighting in Dhofar. Oman's response, on 22 December, was a successful military campaign to free the Muscat-Salala road held by the rebels. Oman's growing economic strength had enabled it to purchase large quantities of military equipment and to expand the army. On 28 January 1975 it was reported that guerrilla supply lines from South Yemen had been blocked. The rebels were completely cut off from supplies by October. And by the end of 1975 the insurgents had been driven out of their last strongholds in Dhofar and had crossed into South Yemen. A cease-fire, with Sa'udi mediation, was signed by South Yemen and Oman on 11 March 1976.

In May 1974 the League of Arab States *(LAS)* had created a conciliation commission that attempted to mediate, but without success. An *LAS* proposal for an international force to replace the non-Arab troops was refused by the sultan, who was willing to welcome it only if the Arab force consented to fight alongside the existing forces.

Oman received military assistance from the U.S. As South Yemen's relations with the Soviet bloc improved, the USSR increased arms supplies to the rebels.

The UN was not involved in this crisis.

(See *Master Table*, pp. 712–13.)

Sources
Lapidoth 1982; Litwak 1981; *MEJ* Chronology 1973–76; Owen 1973; Peterson 1981; Stookey 1982.

(265) Lebanon Civil War I

The civil war in Lebanon created a crisis for Syria from 18 January to 15 November 1976.

Background and Pre-crisis
The civil war in Lebanon began in April 1975: it was the culmination of years of gradual dislocation of Lebanese society, which developed into a polarization of the Christian and Muslim communities and signaled the possibility of the disintegration of Lebanon. Syria has always maintained that Lebanon and Syria are integral parts of Greater Syria and that the division of the two countries was artificially created by France to serve its colonial interests. Thus a possible partition of Lebanon was perceived by Syria as a threat to its vital security interests: first, as undermining Syria's image as the guardian of Arab nationalism and unity; and second, as giving Israel a pretext to move into southern Lebanon and occupy the area up to the Litani River. Syria's primary interest in 1975 was to mediate among the conflicting parties in Lebanon. Toward the end of that year victories by the Christian militias seemed to heighten the possibility of a partition of Lebanon. On 7 January 1976 Syria threatened to intervene militarily after the Christian Maronite militia, on 4 January, besieged the Palestinian camps, Tel al-Za'atar and Jisr al-Basha, in a concerted drive to clear the region of "alien" elements.

Crisis
On 18 January 1976 Lebanese Christian forces triggered a crisis for Syria when they overran Karantina, al-Maslakh, and al-Naba's, predominantly Muslim towns in the self-declared "Christian Heartland," north of Beirut, and proceeded to expel their residents. The following day Syria responded by dispatching to Lebanon the Yarmouk Brigade of the Syrian controlled Palestine Liberation Army, in response to appeals by Lebanese leftist Muslim leaders. On the 19th as well, Syria sent a delegation to Lebanon to try to impose an effective cease-fire. Shortly after Syria came to the rescue of the Muslim Lebanese and Palestinians, Syrian threat perceptions began to change.

President Asad had made a proposal to resolve the internal Lebanon conflict: retain the confessional system but replace the numerical proportionate basis of allocating political power with equality between the Christian and Muslim communities. This would entail a 50-50 representation in the legislature and a reduction of the Maronite president's authority in favor of the Sunni Muslim prime minister. The plan was accepted by the Christians but was rejected by the Muslims and the Palestinians. Thus Syria no longer saw the Christians as the catalyst to a Lebanese partition; rather, it was now the Muslim leftists and their *PLO* allies who, on the momentum of successive victories, threatened the fragile Lebanese equilibrium.

On 28 March Syria decided to place an embargo on all arms supplies to the leftist-*PLO* coalition. By 9 April Syria was sending clear signals to the leftists that Syrian troops concentrating on the Lebanese border would be brought into use if their intransigence persisted. On 1 June Syrian troops poured into Lebanon in order to force a resolution of the conflict. The immediate—and successful—goal was the relief of some Christian villages under siege. The Syrian advance against the Muslim leftist-*PLO* forces continued throughout the summer. On 28 September Syria decided to inflict a military defeat on them to be followed immediately by peace talks in which the Syrian point of view would be imposed. A concerted offensive, in alliance with Christian forces but restrained so as not to destroy the Muslim-*PLO* camp entirely, smashed all Palestinian forces in the Lebanese mountains. By 30 September all opposition in Lebanon to Syria's hegemony had been overcome and partition had been averted. However, the crisis lingered until an Arab Deterrent Force was authorized by the Arab League in October, composed of 20,000 to 30,000 Syrian troops, which occupied the center of Beirut on 15 November. Shortly thereafter, Syria reverted to its traditional pro-Palestinian stance after tension and clashes between Syrian and Christian forces, supporting the *PLO* against the Israeli-backed Christian militias.

Secretary-General Waldheim offered his good offices for UN mediation, but it was refused. U.S. activity consisted of verbal approbation of Syrian actions and serving as a conduit between Syria and Israel, relaying intentions and information. The USSR supported Syria until the 1 June invasion—to which it was strongly opposed. Arms deliveries to Damascus were halted. Syria's careful efforts not to provoke Israel by crossing the "Red Line" of the Litani River kept the latter out of the Lebanon fighting. During the crisis an Iraqi troop movement to the Syrian border precipitated another crisis for Syria from 9 to 17 June (see Case #269—**Iraqi Threat** below).

(See *Master Table,* pp. 714–15.)

Sources
A. I. Dawisha 1978, 1980; Heller 1980; *MECS* 1975–76, 1976–77; *MEJ* Chronology 1976; Meo 1977; Rabin 1979; Vocke 1978.

(269) Iraqi Threat

An Iraqi troop concentration on its border with Syria caused a crisis for Syria from 9 to 17 June 1976.

Background and Pre-crisis
Events in the Middle East in 1976 were complex. A civil war was raging in Lebanon, with Syrian military participation in an attempt to avert a partition of Lebanon (see Case #265—**Lebanon Civil War I** above). Syria's 1974 Disengagement Agreement with Israel (see Case #255—**October–Yom Kippur War,** in 1973, in **Arab/Israel PC**) had facilitated an uneasy truce between the two enemies, with Syria maintaining a division on its border in the Golan Heights. Iraq's relations with the rival Ba'ath regime in Syria were visibly tense. In addition, disputes between Iraq and Syria's ally, Iran, over the Shatt-al-Arab had never been solved (see Cases #172, 234, in 1959–60, 1969, in **Iran/Iraq PC**). In June 1976 Syria's preoccupation with events in Lebanon afforded Iraq an opportunity to attempt to weaken President Asad's regime.

Crisis
On 9 June 1976, in a sudden and surprise act, Iraq moved troops to its border with Syria, triggering a crisis for the latter. Part of Syria's army was engaged in the civil war in Lebanon, with much of its forces protecting Syria's border with Israel. A tacit agreement with Israel was sought to allow Syria to transfer troops from the Golan Heights. When this was achieved Syria responded on 13 June by removing its division from the Golan Heights and placing it on the Iraqi border. On 17 June the crisis ended when President Asad signaled the decline of threat perception by leaving the country for a three-day visit to France. Soon after the forces of both Iraq and Syria withdrew from the border to their original positions.

Neither the U.S. or the USSR, nor the UN or the Arab League, was involved in this crisis.

(See *Master Table*, pp. 714–15.)

Sources
MECS 1975–76; *MEJ* Chronology 1976.

(275) Syria Mobilization, 1976 (see Arab/Israel PC)

(289) Litani Operation, 1978 (see Arab/Israel PC)

(301) North/South Yemen II, 1979 (see Yemen PC)

(309) U.S. Hostages in Iran

A crisis for the U.S. and Iran over American hostages held in Iran lasted from 4 November 1979 to 20 January 1981.

Background and Pre-crisis

On 11 February 1979 an Islamic fundamentalist movement led by Ayatullah Khomeini established a new regime in Iran to replace the exiled Muhammad Riza Shah. During the course of government efforts to crush the power of the clergy— 90 percent of Iran's population belonged to Shiite Islam—Ayatullah Khomeini had been exiled from Iran in 1963, after leading students in a protest march against the shah. The shah's regime was protected by the *Savak*—a secret police force known for its harsh methods—and was bitterly opposed by many Iranians. The U.S. was viewed by anti-shah Iranians as propping up the shah, exploiting Iran's oil, profiting from the enormous sale of arms, and helping the Savak.

Two factions joined forces to overthrow the shah: a coalition of the clergy, masses of the Muslim faithful, and the traditional merchants of the bazaar; and the emerging class of Westernized nationalist students and intellectuals. On 26 October 1979, four days after the shah had been admitted to a New York hospital, young Iranian revolutionaries met and planned a sit-in at the U.S. embassy in Teheran. The previous week the provisional government of Prime Minister Mehdi Bazargan had turned marching demonstrators away from the U.S. embassy.

Crisis

On 4 November a crisis was triggered for the U.S. when some 400 Iranian students, acting under the inspiration of the new revolutionary regime in Teheran, broke away from one of Teheran's frequent demonstrations and stormed the U.S. embassy. U.S. marines held them back for a time with tear gas while diplomats within tried to shred secret documents. Minutes later the students occupied the embassy, indicating that this had been done in order to protest the admission of the shah to the U.S. for medical care. As support for the students grew, a decision was made to put the U.S. hostages on trial if Washington did not return the shah to Iran. This demand was rejected by the U.S. two days later. On the 6th, as well, the provisional Bazargan government collapsed.

In the following days President Carter sent two representatives, Ramsey Clark and William Miller, to Iran to seek to secure the release of the hostages. Khomeini would brook no compromise on his demand that the shah be returned to Iran for trial. On 10 November all Iranian students in the U.S. without legal documents were ordered to leave. Two days later U.S. oil purchases from Iran were discontinued. The following day U.S. and British naval vessels began maneuvers in the Arabian Sea. Iran called for a meeting of the Security Council on 13 November. All Iranian assets in the United States were frozen the following day, and the U.S. initiated action against Iran in the International Court of Justice.

On 20 November Iran suddenly released all black and female U.S. hostages. An internal political struggle began between the students and the clergy, on the one hand, and the secular political leaders in Iran, on the other.

After receiving medical treatment in the U.S., the shah went to Panama on 15 December. On that day, too, the International Court ordered the return of the U.S. embassy in Teheran to U.S. control, while the Iranians declared that the trial of the hostages would certainly take place. The U.S. approached the Security Council for economic sanctions, but the Soviet Union (and East Germany) voted against the draft resolution, thus preventing its approval.

Major efforts at negotiation began in January 1980. The UN set up a five-member commission under Secretary-General Waldheim to inquire into Iran's grievances. The U.S., in an effort not to provoke Iran further, delayed imposing formal economic sanctions on 6 February. On the 18th Iran's President Bani-Sadr authorized a visit by the UN commission. However, when it arrived in Iran on the 23rd, Khomeini announced that the hostage issue would be decided by the new Iranian *Majlis* (Parliament), to be elected in March. The ayatullah also called upon the militant students not to allow members of the commission to see the hostages until the commission's report was published. On 10 March the UN commission met with the Revolutionary Council. When the commission members felt they had reached an impasse, they gave up. Parliamentary elections in Iran were postponed on 22 March. The same day, at a meeting of the U.S.'s National Security Council, President Carter authorized a plan to rescue the hostages. The U.S. broke diplomatic relations with Iran on 7 April. And on the 11th the fateful U.S. decision was taken to send an airborne rescue mission to Iran. U.S. helicopters landed in Iran on 24 April. However, a collision between two helicopters, causing the death of eight U.S. soldiers, led Carter to abort the mission.

The U.S. attempt to rescue the hostages by military means triggered a crisis for Iran on 24 April 1980. By the end of the month Iran had responded by dispersing the hostages among 16 locations. Secretary of State Vance resigned on the 27th and was replaced by Senator Edmund Muskie. The shah died on 27 July in Egypt.

In September a German diplomat in Washington informed Muskie that a close associate of Khomeini wanted to meet urgently in Bonn with senior representatives of the U.S. government to work out conditions for the release of the hostages. A week later Sadeq Tabatabai met with U.S. Deputy Secretary of State Warren Christopher. The former agreed, on 22 September, to inform Khomeini of U.S. proposals, but on that day war broke out between Iran and Iraq, and the hostage issue was set aside. In November, two days before the U.S. presidential elections, the Iranian Parliament adopted the conditions outlined by Khomeini for the release of the hostages. Algeria was asked to serve as the mediator.

In December Iran demanded $24 billion from the U.S. to cover its claims on frozen Iranian assets and property taken by the shah and his family. However, by

early January 1981 the claim had been reduced to $9.5 billion. Christopher flew
to Algiers to work out a complex international agreement with Algeria's Foreign
Minister, Muhammad Ben Yahya. The final documents were signed in Algiers on
20 January; and later that day word was received in Washington that the hostages
had been freed—35 minutes after Ronald Reagan was installed as President of
the United States.

Unsuccessful negotiation and mediation efforts were made throughout the
crisis by Swiss and West German diplomats, as well as by private citizens. The
Pope and Yasser Arafat of the *PLO* also tried to mediate between the two
adversaries.

(See *Master Table*, pp. 722–23.)

Sources
Brzezinski 1983; Carter 1982; Christopher 1985; *Keesing's* 1979, 1980; *MECS*
1979–80, 1980–81; *New York Times* 1979, 1980; Sick 1985, 1991; Vance 1983.

(317) Onset of Iran/Iraq War, 1980 (see Iran/Iraq PC)

(319) Jordan/Syria Confrontation

Jordan experienced a crisis with Syria from 25 November to 14 December 1980.

Background
Instability has been the norm in the relations between these two Middle East
Arab neighbors. They ranged from confrontation, as in 1970 over the *PLO*–
Hashemite regime civil war in Jordan (see Case #238—**Black September**
above), to reconciliation, extending to an (abortive) agreement to establish a
federation between them, as in 1975–76. Relations deteriorated once more in
1978–80.

Syria's minority Alawi-led regime, perceiving itself as increasingly isolated
within the community of Arab states, accused Jordan of several hostile plans and
actions: intention to make peace with Israel and to regain control over the West
Bank and Gaza, at the expense of the *PLO;* harassing Syrians trying to cross the
border into Jordan; and most important, supporting the Muslim Brotherhood
within Syria in its attempts to overthrow the Asad regime. However, none of
these catalyzed a military-security crisis. This was a product of a Syrian initiative.

Crisis
On 25 November 1980 Damascus began moving armored units forward to positions on the Jordanian border. By the first week of December the military confrontation became ominous, with 30,000 Syrians and 24,000 Jordanians, supported by 1,000 tanks, facing each other. The confrontation lasted two weeks but

without violence. De-escalation was facilitated by Sa'udi Arabia's mediation. Syrian forces began to pull back on 5 December, Jordan's on the 10th. By the 11th most had redeployed to their pre-crisis positions. The military confrontation and, with it, the crisis ended on 14 December. But the fundamental distrust between the two regimes remained.

Both sides could claim political gains from the 1980 crisis. Jordan had demonstrated resolve and capability in the face of dramatic pressure from its much stronger neighbor. Syria had indicated the likely cost to Jordan of breaking ranks with its Arab allies in the conflict with Israel, of abandoning the *PLO*, and of continuing to meddle in Syria's internal affairs.

The U.S., the USSR, and the UN were not involved in this crisis.

(See *Master Table*, pp. 722–23.)

Sources
MECS 1980–81; *MEJ* Chronology 1980.

(324) Iraq Nuclear Reactor, 1981 (see Arab/Israel PC)

(327) Al-Biqa Missiles I, 1981 (see Arab/Israel PC)

(334) Coup Attempt in Bahrain

Bahrain and Sa'udi Arabia experienced a crisis with Iran from 13 December 1981 to 8 January 1982.

Background
Bahrain is a tiny oil-rich Gulf sheikhdom, comprising 33 islands between the Qatar Peninsula and the Sa'udi Arabian coast. It has an area of 230 square miles and a population of less than half a million, half of whom are foreigners.

Bahrain was a U.K. protectorate from 1861, formally since 1880, to 1971. London's announcement in 1968 that it would end the protectorate and withdraw British forces from the Gulf in 1971 led Iran to revive its long-standing claim to sovereignty over Bahrain, as part of its goal of hegemony in the Gulf. Iran also had a territorial claim, having ruled the island from 1753 to 1783.

Like all the small Gulf sheikhdoms, which became independent following the U.K.'s further retreat from empire, Bahrain was vulnerable to encroachments from the three competing major powers in the region, Iran, Iraq, and Sa'udi Arabia. Two upheavals nearby heightened Bahrain's sense of insecurity from external and (foreign-supported or foreign-inspired) internal sources: the fall of the shah and the emergence of an Islamic revolutionary regime under the leadership of Ayatullah Khomeini in 1979; and the outbreak of a war between Iran and Iraq in September 1980. As that war dragged on, the increasingly audible messianic fervor of Iran's fundamentalist regime generated more intense fear among the Gulf sheikhdoms.

Crisis

On 13 December 1981 Bahrain's Interior Ministry announced the arrest of a group of Bahrainis and other Gulf nationals accused of trying to overthrow the regime: their attempted coup triggered a crisis for the island-state. Iran was accused of inspiring, directing, and financing the plot.

Prince Naʿif of Saʿudi Arabia, too, accused Iran and termed the coup attempt a threat to Saʿudi Arabia and all Gulf states: the course of the Iran/Iraq War and the danger of an Iranian victory raised serious Saʿudi concerns about Iraq's ability to withstand the onslaught and the consequences of an Iranian triumph for the Saʿudi regime. Although there was some confusion about the source of the coup—some of its participants blamed Saʿudi Arabia at their trial—the context, the revolutionary zeal of Iran under Khomeini, and Saʿudi Arabia's fear that Iran aimed at undermining its own regime strongly point to Iran as the prime external source.

Bahrain responded with an official protest to Iran and declared its chargé d'affaires persona non grata. Saʿudi Arabia signaled its concern and protector role by signing a mutual security pact with Bahrain on 19 December; this response also marked the end of the Saʿudi crisis. Two months later, Saʿudi Arabia strengthened its hegemony among the Gulf states by signing similar agreements with three other members of the Gulf Cooperation Council, which was established that year—Oman, Qatar, and the United Arab Emirates.

Crisis termination for Bahrain can be dated as 8 January 1982: that day, bolstered by the security agreement with Saʿudi Arabia and implied support from Iran's most powerful foe, the United States, to which Bahrain had granted a de facto naval base in the 1970s, Bahrain banned Iranians from the sheikhdom, suspended economic relations with Iran, and declared martial law. (In May 1982 Bahrain's prime minister tried to denigrate the coup attempt by terming it an affair that "did not represent anything dangerous to us"; but by then the crisis was over and the danger from Iran had receded.)

The USSR and the UN were not active in this crisis.

(See *Master Table*, pp. 724–25.)

Sources

MECS 1981–82; *MEJ* Chronology 1981, 1982.

(335) Khorramshahr, 1982 (see Iran/Iraq PC)

(337) War in Lebanon, 1982–83 (see Arab/Israel PC)

(348) Basra-Kharg Island, 1984 (see Iran/Iraq PC)

(357) Al-Biqa Missiles II, 1985–86 (see Arab/Israel PC)

(361) Capture of al-Faw, 1986 (see Iran/Iraq PC)

(364) Al-Dibal Incident

Bahrain experienced a crisis with Qatar over disputed territory from 26 April until 15 June 1986.

Background
These two Persian Gulf ministates had been protectorates of the U.K., Bahrain from 1861, Qatar from 1916. Both were granted independence in 1971 as part of the last phase of Britain's retreat from empire in the Middle East.

Bahrain and Qatar had a long-standing dispute over the Hawar Islands adjacent to the Qatar Peninsula. There were periodic outbreaks of tension since the 1930s, but not a full-scale interstate crisis. In 1985 Bahrain began to construct a coast guard station on al-Dibal Island, within the disputed area.

Crisis
A crisis for Bahrain was triggered on 26 April 1986, when Qatari soldiers landed on al-Dibal, declared the island a "restricted zone," and arrested Bahraini officials. The raising of Qatar's flag on the 28th accentuated the perception of a threat to Bahrain's territorial integrity. On the 30th Bahrain denounced the occupation as "a violation of good-neighborliness."

The Netherlands, too, protested to Qatar because Qatari soldiers had seized a group of foreign workers employed by a Dutch construction company, *Ballast Nedam Groep.* Mediation by Oman, Saʿudi Arabia, and the United Arab Emirates, members of the Gulf Cooperation Council, along with Bahrain and Qatar, and Kuwait, led to an agreement: Qatari troops would withdraw from al-Dibal; and the tiny island would be evacuated by the Dutch construction company. All foreign workers were released on 12 May. And Qatari troops withdrew on 15 June, terminating the crisis.

There was no violence. The UN, the U.S., the USSR, and the Arab League were not involved in this minicrisis between ministates.

(See *Master Table,* pp. 730–31.)

Sources
Day 1987; *Keesing's* 1986; *MECS* 1986.

(374) Syrian Intervention in Lebanon

Syria experienced a crisis from 15 February to 6 April 1987 as a result of a sharp escalation in fighting among the contending factions in Lebanon.

Background and Pre-crisis
After three decades of coexistence between Lebanese Christians and Muslims, framed by the "National Pact" of 1943, civil war erupted in April 1975. It was

compounded by the presence of a large visible Palestinian refugee community in southern Lebanon, under the leadership of the *PLO*.

There were several international crises in Lebanon during the next decade (see Cases #265—**Lebanon Civil War I,** in 1976 above; #289—**Litani Operation,** arising from Israel's first major incursion into Lebanon, in 1978, in **Arab/Israel PC;** #337—**War in Lebanon,** triggered by Israel's large-scale invasion, in 1982–83, in **Arab/Israel PC**). Earlier, the Arab League had legitimized Syria's primacy in Lebanon by creating an Arab Deterrent Force *(ADF),* composed almost entirely of Syrian troops. Internal strife—among the paramilitary forces of *Amal,* the largest Shia militia in Lebanon, *Hizbullah,* the "Party of God," a pro-Iranian, extremist Shia militia in south Lebanon, the Druze forces in the Shouf mountains near Beirut, and *PLO* forces, mostly in the south—was endemic: from mid-October 1986 to January 1987 it became more visible, including the kidnapping of Western journalists and clergymen.

Crisis

Fighting between *Amal* and other competing groups in Lebanon escalated sharply on 15 February 1987: *Amal* militiamen laid siege to Palestinian refugee camps, blocking convoys of food and medical supplies. The renewed instability triggered a crisis for Syria, threatening its self-asserted hegemony over its western neighbor.

On the 19th Shia leaders, fearing an *Amal* defeat, requested Syrian intervention to take control of security in west Beirut—east Beirut was controlled by Christian militias, notably the Lebanese Forces. Factional fighting intensified on the 20th, with 200 killed. Internal instability was compounded by Hizbullah's escalation of cross-border raids into, and shelling of, northern Israeli border settlements. In fact, Syria perceived Iran, Hizbullah's mentor and arms supplier, as the source of threat to its primacy in Lebanon.

On 22 February Syria responded to a perceived threat to its influence in Lebanon by dispatching *ADF* (really Syrian) forces to take control over west Beirut. Only the *PLO* denounced this intervention. Even Israel, through Defense Minister Rabin, declared that Israel would not oppose the *ADF* (Syrian) deployment provided it was limited to Beirut. Within a day Syrian forces controlled all of west Beirut. However, on the 24th, they killed 26 Lebanese in the Bourj Hammoud district of the capital, including 18 members of Hizbullah and 3 from *Amal.* This led to a demonstration of 10,000 supporters of Hizbullah: the incident occurred while Iran's Foreign Minister, Ali Akbar Velayati, and its Revolutionary Guards Minister, Muhsin Rafiqdost, were meeting with President Asad in Damascus. On the 25th the head of Syria's forces in Beirut, Brigadier-General Ghazi Kan'an, announced that they would not be deployed in the south Beirut Shia suburbs. And on 4 March *Amal,* under Syria's pressure, freed 600 *PLO* prisoners.

Syria and Iran shared a common interest—hostility to Iraq. However, the former's secularism clashed with the latter's Islamic fundamentalism: Iran objected to antifundamentalist measures adopted by Syria, whose troops pressed Lebanese men to shave their beards and women not to wear the *chador* (veil): President Khamenei indicated Iran's displeasure with these acts and criticized Syrian soldiers on 6 March. Iran's interior minister conveyed this message to Asad the same day.

Syria's behavior was motivated by the determination to brook no interference with its hegemony in Lebanon. This included the posting of a 500-strong force along the Beirut-Sidon coast road and the use of Special Forces whenever deemed necessary. Finally, on 6 April a Syrian-mediated cease-fire agreement came into effect and ended the *Amal* siege of the Palestinian refugee camps: trucks carrying food and medical supplies were allowed to enter the camps. Although clashes between *Amal* and *PLO* forces erupted again near Sidon on 19 July—and continued to erupt periodically over the years—this specific crisis, with Iran perceived as the source of threat, ended with the cease-fire agreement of 6 April.

There was no UN or Arab League involvement in this crisis. Both superpowers, too, remained aloof.

(See *Master Table*, pp. 732–33.)

Sources
Keesing's 1987; *MECS* 1987–88; *MEJ* Chronology 1987.

(379) Mecca Pilgrimage

Saʿudi Arabia and Iran were embroiled in a crisis over Iranian pilgrims from 31 July to October 1987.

Background and Pre-crisis
No pilgrimage by Iranians to Islam's Holy Places since 1981 had passed without incident. Their annual demonstrations in the streets of Mecca and Medina challenged the Saʿudi concept of pilgrimage, the Saʿudi interpretation of Islam, Saʿudi control of the Holy Places, and the legitimacy of Saʿudi rule.

The first catalyst to tension between Iran and Saʿudi Arabia in 1987 was a statement by Iran's former pilgrimage representative, Musavi Khoiniha, a powerful hard-line figure in Iran. In a speech early in July Khoiniha reportedly said that a mere march or demonstration by Iranians would not suffice. He demanded that the Saʿudi regime allow Iranian pilgrims to enter the Great Mosque in Mecca at the end of their demonstration, where their representative would explain Iran's case regarding the Iran/Iraq War. That demand put the Saʿudi security forces on a high state of alert.

After difficult negotiations Iranian and Saʿudi officials reached an agreement that the demonstration would end half a kilometer before the Great Mosque. But tension remained high, so Saʿudi Arabia tried to persuade the Iranian pilgrimage representative, Hojjatolislam Mehdi Karrubi, to cancel the demonstration lest violence break out. Karrubi refused and declared that the Sa'udi government would be responsible for any disorder.

On 28 July Ayatullah Khomeini called on all Iranian pilgrims to take part in a "disavowal march" to "echo the crushing slogan of the disavowal of pagans and apostates of world arrogance, headed by the criminal USA," adding that "it is most disgraceful for Islamic countries and for heads of states that foreigners should penetrate the secret military centers of the Moslems." At the same time Iran's ruler called on the pilgrims "to avoid clashes, insults and disputes" and warned against those "intent on disruption."

Crisis

On 31 July 1987, during the annual *Haj* (pilgrimage) to Mecca, several hundred people were killed and many wounded in violent clashes between Sa'udi security forces and Iranian pilgrims. The clashes began during the demonstration of Iran's pilgrims: toward its end the march approached Sa'udi security guards, who refused to allow the demonstrators to move closer to the Great Mosque.

The Iranian demonstrators were invoking death threats against the U.S., Israel, and the Soviet Union. A confrontation began between the pilgrims and the Sa'udi security forces: the Sa'udis opened fire on the demonstrators. This incident triggered a crisis for Sa'udi Arabia and Iran that day.

Sa'udi Arabia denied firing on the pilgrims, claiming that those who were killed were crushed in a trample. Iran gave another version of the events, claiming that "Sa'udi police, in a pre-arranged joint Sa'udi-U.S. conspiracy . . . opened fire on Iranian pilgrims who were peacefully marching."

Iran's initial response, on 1 August, was to call for the overthrow of the Sa'udi regime. And 2 August was declared an official "Day of Hate" in Iran. The Iranian parliamentary Speaker (later, President of Iran), Hashemi Ali Akbar Rafsanjani, called for revenge, by "freeing the holy shrines from the mischievous and wicked Wahabis" and stated that "the Imam (Khomeini) dictates, [Sa'udi King] Fahd will not remain alive." The Iranian media accused the U.S. of responsibility for the "massacre."

Sa'udi spokesmen responded by accusing the Iranians of deliberate provocation. The Sa'udis refused to allow an Iranian delegation to enter Sa'udi Arabia on 2 August to investigate the deaths and to interview security officials.

On 25 August, for the first time, a senior Sa'udi official, Prince Na'if, sharply attacked Iran and publicly called for the overthrow of the regime in Teheran. The two sides continued to exchange accusations and insults throughout September. Late that month, Sa'udi Arabia denied Iran's accusation that it was unwilling to return 54 corpses of Iranian pilgrims who died in the clashes in Mecca. And at a UN General Assembly meeting on 22 September Iran's President Khamenei uttered threats against Sa'udi Arabia, which the Sa'udi delegate described as "meaningless" and totally unjustified.

The crisis faded in October 1987, with a Sa'udi victory and Iranian defeat. The Arab states supported the Sa'udis, except for Libya, which advocated placing the Mecca and Medina mosques under international Islamic control.

The U.S., the USSR, the UN, and the Arab League were not involved in this crisis.

(See *Master Table*, pp. 732–33.)

Sources
Foreign Broadcast Information Service, Daily Report; Near East/South Asia (FBIS—DR/NESA), August, September 1987; *Keesing's* 1987; Kramer 1988; *New York Times* 1987.

(385) Iraq Recapture of al-Faw, 1988 (see Iran/Iraq PC)

(393) Gulf War, 1990–91 (see Iraq/Kuwait PC)

(398) Bubiyan, 1991 (see Iraq/Kuwait PC)

(406) Iraq No-Fly Zone, 1992 (see Iraq/Kuwait PC)

(409) Operation Accountability, 1993 (see Arab/Israel PC)

(412) Iraq Troop Deployment—Kuwait, 1994 (see Iraq/Kuwait PC)

Table III.1. Master Table of Crises, 1918–1994

Column Definitions and Notes

Definitions

Crisis Number

International crises are numbered sequentially from 1 to 412.

The Kars-Ardahan crisis (no. 106; trigger date: 6/7/45) is listed after the Hiroshima-Nagasaki crisis (no. 107; trigger date: 8/6/45) because it was part of the bipolar system-period, not World War II.

International Crisis and Actors

Name of international crisis and name(s) of crisis actor(s). A crisis actor must be a sovereign state whose decision maker(s) perceive(s) a high threat to one or more basic values, finite time for response to the value threat, and a heightened probability of involvement in military hostilities; all three perceptions derive from a change in the state's external or internal environment.

When the international crisis included two or more crisis actors, the following procedures determined the order in which they appear in the table.

1. The trigger dates determine the sequence in which the actors are listed.
2. Where two or more actors have the same trigger date but different termination dates, the sequence in which they are listed is determined by the termination date.
3. Where two or more states have identical trigger dates and termination dates, they are listed alphabetically, except where it is clear from the case summary that one of the state actors experienced the first crisis.

Summary Page

Page on which the brief history of this international crisis in Part III begins.

Protracted Conflict (PC) or Region

If the international crisis occurred within a protracted conflict, the number identifies the protracted conflict. If the international crisis or the actor case occurred outside of a protracted conflict, the region in which the crisis occurred is identified (see p. 660).

Number   Protracted Conflict
 1 Angola
 2 Chad/Libya
 3 Ethiopia/Somalia
 4 Rhodesia
 5 Western Sahara
 6 Costa Rica/Nicaragua
 7 Ecuador/Peru
 8 Honduras/Nicaragua
 9 Afghanistan/Pakistan
10 China/Japan
11 China/Vietnam
12 India/Pakistan
13 Indochina
14 Indonesia
15 Korea
16 Czechoslovakia/Germany
17 Finland/Russia
18 France/Germany
19 Italy/Albania/Yugoslavia
20 Lithuania/Poland
21 Poland/Russia
22 Spain
23 Arab/Israel
24 Iran/Iraq
25 Iraq/Kuwait
26 Yemen
27 East/West
28 Greece/Turkey
29 Iran/USSR
30 Taiwan Strait
31 World War II

Number   Non-Protracted Conflict Region
40 Africa
41 Americas
42 Asia
43 Europe
44 Middle East

Trigger Date
The date on which the earliest crisis actor perceived threat, time pressure, and war likelihood.

Table III.1. Master Table of Crises, 1918–1994   661

Dates are listed as month/day/year. When the month, day, or year of the crisis trigger or termination date was unknown, it was recorded as 99. If the month and year were known, and the day could be approximated, the following convention was followed.

day 1 to day 10 = 66
day 11 to day 20 = 77
day 21 to end of month = 88

Termination Date

For the international crisis, the date on which the last actor perceived crisis termination (i.e., return to pre-crisis levels of threat, time pressure, and war likelihood). For individual actors, the date on which its decision makers perceived these factors.

System Level and Power Status

For the international crisis, system level is identified as the dominant system or a regional subsystem. For the crisis actor, power status is identified as potential impact on the external environment: superpower, great power, middle power, and small power. A state may be a small power in the global power hierarchy, but a middle or even great power within its subsystem. Thus, power status is determined by a state's capability at the system level in which its crisis occurred.

Triggering Entity

The state or nonstate actor that triggered the international crisis or a foreign policy crisis for the individual crisis actor.

Crisis Trigger

The specific act, event, or situational change that catalyzed the perceptions of threat, time pressure, and war likelihood:

Political—protests, threats, accusations, demands, subversion, alliance of adversaries, diplomatic sanctions, severance of diplomatic relations, violation of treaties.

Economic—embargo, dumping, nationalization of property, withholding of economic aid

External Change—intelligence reports, change in specific weapons, weapon system, offensive capability, change in global system or regional subsystem, challenge to legitimacy by international organization

Other Non-Violent

Internal Verbal or Physical Challenge to Regime or Elite—incitement by media, proclamation of new regime, fall of government, coup d'état, sabotage act, terrorism, assassination, riot, demonstration, strike, arrest, martial law, execution, mutiny, revolt

Non-Violent Military—show of force, war games or maneuvers, mobilization, movement of forces, change of force posture to offensive

Indirect Violent Act—revolt in another country, violent act directed at ally, friendly state, or client state

Violent Act—border clash, border crossing by limited forces, invasion of airspace, sinking of ship, sea-air incident, bombing of large target, large-scale attack, war

Gravity of Threat

For the international crisis, the most salient threat perceived during the course of the crisis. For an individual crisis actor, the most salient threat perceived by its decision makers during the crisis, from trigger to termination.

Other—unclassifiable

Limited—threat to population and territory, threat to social system such as forced migration, change of ethnic equilibrium, challenge to legitimacy of belief system

Economic—threat to economic interests such as control by another actor's economy, requisition of resources, loss of markets, blocked access to resources or markets

Political—threat of overthrow of regime, change of institutions, replacement of elite, intervention in domestic politics, subversion

Territorial Integrity—threat of integration, annexation of part of a state's territory, separatism

Influence—threat to influence in the international system or regional subsystem, threat of declining power in the global system and/or regional subsystem, diplomatic isolation, cessation of patron aid

Grave Damage—threat of large casualties in war, mass bombing

Existence—threat to survival of population, genocide, threat to existence of entity, of total annexation, colonial rule, occupation

Crisis Management Technique

The principal technique of crisis management, as distinct from a specific act. For the international crisis, this is the highest technique employed by any actor in the crisis, scaled from techniques involving negotiation and mediation through those involving violence.

Negotiation—formal, informal, bilateral, multilateral, international, diplomatic exchange

Adjudication or Arbitration

Mediation—by global or regional organization, ally, alliance partner

Multiple Not Including Violence

Table III.1. Master Table of Crises, 1918–1994   663

Non-Military Pressure—withholding of promised aid
Non-Violent Military—physical or verbal acts
Multiple Including Violence
Violence

The variable "Crisis Management Technique" identifies the most salient CMT for the crisis. In the Persian Border crisis (#14), while violence occurred in the international crisis (see "Violence" column), the primary crisis management technique was negotiation.

Violence
The most intense form of violence employed during the crisis, regardless of whether it was employed as a crisis management technique—*no violence, minor clashes, serious clashes, full-scale war.*

Superpower Activity (from Case #106 on)
Any substantive verbal or physical activity during an international crisis by the U.S. or the USSR (later Russia) from 1945–94.

None
Non-Intervention or Neutrality
Political—statements of approval or disapproval by authorized government officials
Economic—financial aid, or the withholding of aid from an actor
Propaganda
Covert—support for anti-government forces
Semi-Military—military aid or advisors, without participation in actual fighting
Direct Military—dispatch of troops, aerial bombing of targets, or naval assistance to a party at war
U.S. or USSR Crisis Actor

Global Organization Involvement
The substance of activity by the League of Nations or the United Nations during the course of the international crisis, or during the period in which a particular state was a crisis actor.

None
Other
Discussion—without resolution
Fact-Finding
Good Offices—minimal involvement in both the content and the process of resolving the dispute

Condemnation—includes implied or explicit demand to desist, request for member aid to victim of hostile activity

Call for Action—includes call for cease-fire, withdrawal, negotiation, member action to facilitate termination

Mediation—includes proposing a solution, offering advice, and conciliation of differences

Arbitration—formal binding settlement by arbitral body

Sanctions

Observers

Emergency Military Force

Outcome: Substance

The content of a crisis outcome in terms of the achievement/nonachievement of crisis actor goals, in the context of a specific foreign policy crisis. For the international crisis, the mix of actor outcomes dictates whether the overall outcome is ambiguous (stalemate and/or compromise) or definitive (victory and/or defeat).

Victory—achievement of basic goal(s); the crisis actor defeated a threatening adversary by counterthreats

Compromise—partial achievement of goal(s)

Stalemate—no effect on basic goal(s); no clear outcome to a crisis; no change in the situation

Defeat—nonachievement of basic goal(s); the crisis actor yielded or surrendered when an adversary threatened basic values

Outcome: Form

For the international crisis, forms include *formal agreement, semi-formal agreements, tacit understanding, unilateral act, imposed agreement, faded,* and *other.* For individual crisis actors, forms include a more elaborate breakdown of these categories.

TABLE III.1. Master Table of Crises, 1918–1994

NUM.	INTERNATIONAL CRISIS ACTORS	SUM. PAGE	PC OR REG.	TRIG. DATE	TERM. DATE	SYSTEM LEVEL POWER STATUS	TRIGGERING ENTITY	CRISIS TRIGGER
1	RUSSIAN CIVIL WAR I	333	27	05/99/18	04/01/20	MAINLY DOMINANT	NON-STATE ACTOR	VIOLENT
	Russia			05/99/18	04/01/20	Great power	Non-state actor	Violent
2	COSTA RICAN COUP	132	6	05/25/18	09/03/19	SUBSYSTEM	COSTA RICA	NON-VIOL. MI▮
	Nicaragua			05/25/18	12/15/18	Small power	Costa Rica	Non-viol. mil.
	Costa Rica			01/25/19	09/03/19	Small power	Non-state actor	Ext. change
3	RUSSIAN CIVIL WAR II	333	27	06/23/18	09/27/19	DOMINANT SYSTEM	MULTI-STATE	NON-VIOL. MI▮
	Russia			06/23/18	09/27/19	Great power	Multi-state	Non-viol. mil.
4	BALTIC INDEPENDENCE	571	43	11/18/18	08/11/20	MAINLY SUBSYSTEM	ESTONIA	INTERNAL CH/
	Russia			11/18/18	08/11/20	Great power	Estonia	Internal chal.
	Estonia			11/22/18	02/02/20	Small power	Russia	Violent
	Lithuania			12/99/18	07/12/20	Small power	Russia	Violent
	Latvia			12/99/18	08/11/20	Small power	Russia	Violent
5	TESCHEN	573	43	01/15/19	07/28/20	SUBSYSTEM	POLAND	POLITICAL
	Czechoslovakia			01/15/19	07/28/20	Small power	Poland	Political
	Poland			01/23/19	07/28/20	Middle power	Czechoslovakia	Non-viol. mil.
6	HUNGARIAN WAR	574	43	03/20/19	08/03/19	MAINLY SUBSYSTEM	MULTI-STATE	POLITICAL
	Hungary			03/20/19	08/03/19	Small power	Multi-state	Political
	Czechoslovakia			05/11/19	06/24/19	Small power	Hungary	Violent
	Hungary			06/08/19	06/16/19	Small power	France	Political
	Romania			07/20/19	08/03/19	Small power	Hungary	Violent
7	SMYRNA	625	44	03/66/19	07/29/19	MAINLY SUBSYSTEM	ITALY	NON-VIOL. MI▮
	Greece			03/66/19	07/29/19	Middle power	Italy	Non-viol. mil.
	Italy			05/15/19	07/29/19	Great power	Greece	Non-viol. mil.
8	THIRD AFGHAN WAR	535	42	04/15/19	08/08/19	MAINLY SUBSYSTEM	UK	POLITICAL
	Afghanistan			04/15/19	08/08/19	Small power	UK	Political
	UK			05/04/19	08/08/19	Great power	Afghanistan	Non-viol. mil.
9	FINNISH/RUSSIAN BDR.	232	17	04/20/19	10/14/20	MAINLY SUBSYSTEM	FINLAND	VIOLENT
	Russia			04/20/19	10/14/20	Great power	Finland	Violent
	Finland			05/18/19	10/14/20	Small power	Russia	Violent
10	BESSARABIA	576	43	04/30/19	03/02/20	SUBSYSTEM	ROMANIA	POLITICAL
	Russia			04/30/19	03/02/20	Great power	Romania	Political
	Romania			05/01/19	03/02/20	Small power	Russia	Political
11	CILICIAN WAR	627	44	11/99/19	10/20/21	SUBSYSTEM	FRANCE	NON-VIOL. MI▮
	Turkey			11/99/19	10/20/21	Middle power	France	Non-viol. mil.
	France			01/20/20	10/20/21	Great power	Turkey	Violent

GRAVITY OF THREAT	CRISIS MGMT. TECHNIQUE	VIOLENCE	GLOBAL ORG. INVOLVEMENT	OUTCOME: SUBSTANCE	OUTCOME: FORM
POLITICAL REGIME	VIOLENCE	SERIOUS CLASHES	NONE	DEFINITIVE	UNILATERAL
Political regime	Violence	Serious clashes	None	Victory	Unilateral-adv.
POLITICAL REGIME	MULTIPLE, NO VIOL.	NO VIOLENCE	NO ORG.	DEFINITIVE	UNILATERAL
LMD	Multiple, no viol.	No violence	No org.	Victory	Unilateral-self
Political regime	Multiple, no viol.	Minor clashes	No org.	Defeat	Unilateral-self
POLITICAL REGIME	VIOLENCE	SERIOUS CLASHES	NO ORG.	DEFINITIVE	UNILATERAL
Political regime	Violence	Serious clashes	No org.	Victory	Unilateral-adv.
EXISTENCE	VIOLENCE	SERIOUS CLASHES	NONE	DEFINITIVE	IMPOSED AGMT.
Territory	Violence	Serious clashes	None	Defeat	Imposed-imposee
Existence	Violence	Serious clashes	None	Victory	Imposed-imposer
Existence	Violence	Serious clashes	None	Victory	Imposed-imposer
Existence	Violence	Serious clashes	None	Victory	Imposed-imposer
TERRITORY	VIOLENCE	SERIOUS CLASHES	NONE	AMBIGUOUS	IMPOSED AGMT.
Territory	Violence	Serious clashes	None	Compromise	Imposed-imposee
Territory	Violence	Serious clashes	None	Compromise	Imposed-imposee
EXISTENCE	VIOLENCE	WAR	NO ORG.	DEFINITIVE	UNILATERAL
Existence	Violence	War	No org.	Defeat	Unilateral-adv.
Territory	Violence	War	No org.	Victory	Formal agmt.
Grave damage	Negotiation	No violence	No org.	Defeat	Compliance
Territory	Violence	War	No org.	Victory	Unilateral-self
TERRITORY	MULT. W/VIOL.	MINOR CLASHES	NO ORG.	AMBIGUOUS	FORMAL AGMT.
Territory	Mult. w/viol.	Minor clashes	No org.	Compromise	Formal agmt.
Influence	Mult. w/viol.	Minor clashes	No org.	Compromise	Formal agmt.
INFLUENCE	MULT. W/VIOL.	WAR	NO ORG.	AMBIGUOUS	FORMAL AGMT.
Political regime	Mult. w/viol.	War	No org.	Compromise	Formal agmt.
Influence	Mult. w/viol.	War	No org.	Compromise	Formal agmt.
TERRITORY	MULT. W/VIOL.	SERIOUS CLASHES	NONE	AMBIGUOUS	FORMAL AGMT.
Territory	Mult. w/viol.	Serious clashes	None	Compromise	Formal agmt.
Territory	Mult. w/viol.	Serious clashes	None	Compromise	Formal agmt.
TERRITORY	MULT. W/VIOL.	SERIOUS CLASHES	NONE	DEFINITIVE	FORMAL AGMT.
Territory	Mult. w/viol.	Serious clashes	None	Defeat	Formal agmt.
Territory	Mult. w/viol.	Serious clashes	None	Victory	Formal agmt.
TERRITORY	MULT. W/VIOL.	WAR	NONE	DEFINITIVE	FORMAL AGMT.
Territory	Mult. w/viol.	War	None	Victory	Formal agmt.
Influence	Mult. w/viol.	War	None	Defeat	Formal agmt.

(continued)

TABLE III.1.—Continued

NUM.	INTERNATIONAL CRISIS ACTORS	SUM. PAGE	PC OR REG.	TRIG. DATE	TERM. DATE	SYSTEM LEVEL POWER STATUS	TRIGGERING ENTITY	CRISIS TRIGGE
12	RHENISH REBELLIONS	237	18	04/03/20	05/17/20	MAINLY SUBSYSTEM	GERMANY	INDIRECT VI
	France			04/03/20	04/24/20	Great power	Germany	Indirect viol.
	Germany			04/06/20	05/17/20	Middle power	France	Non-viol. mil.
13	POLISH/RUSSIAN WAR	256	21	04/25/20	10/12/20	MAINLY SUBSYSTEM	POLAND	VIOLENT
	Russia			04/25/20	10/12/20	Great power	Poland	Violent
	Poland			05/15/20	10/12/20	Middle power	Russia	Violent
14	PERSIAN BORDER	375	29	05/66/20	02/26/21	MAINLY SUBSYSTEM	NON-STATE ACTOR	NON-VIOL. N
	Russia			05/66/20	02/26/21	Great power	Non-state actor	Non-viol. mil.
	Iran			05/18/20	02/26/21	Middle power	Russia	Violent
15	AALAND ISLANDS	577	43	06/05/20	10/20/21	SUBSYSTEM	FINLAND	NON-VIOL. N
	Sweden			06/05/20	10/20/21	Middle power	Finland	Non-viol. mil.
	Finland			06/15/20	10/20/21	Small power	Sweden	Political
16	GREECE/TURKEY WAR I	362	28	06/22/20	07/09/20	SUBSYSTEM	GREECE	VIOLENT
	Turkey			06/22/20	07/09/20	Middle power	Greece	Violent
17	VILNA I	252	20	07/12/20	11/29/20	SUBSYSTEM	LITHUANIA	POLITICAL
	Poland			07/12/20	11/29/20	Middle power	Lithuania	Political
	Lithuania			07/14/20	11/29/20	Small power	Poland	Violent
18	GREECE/TURKEY WAR II	364	28	01/06/21	09/12/21	SUBSYSTEM	GREECE	VIOLENT
	Turkey			01/06/21	09/12/21	Middle power	Greece	Violent
19	COSTA RICA/PANAMA BDR	494	41	02/21/21	08/24/21	SUBSYSTEM	COSTA RICA	NON-VIOL. N
	Panama			02/21/21	08/24/21	Small power	Costa Rica	Non-viol. mil.
	Costa Rica			02/27/21	08/24/21	Small power	Panama	Violent
20	GERMAN REPARATIONS	239	18	03/03/21	05/11/21	MAINLY SUBSYSTEM	MULTI-STATE	POLITICAL
	Germany			03/03/21	05/11/21	Middle power	Multi-state	Political
	Belgium			04/05/21	05/11/21	Small power	France	Political
	Netherlands			05/02/21	05/11/21	Small power	France	Non-viol. mil.
21	KARL'S RETURN HUNGARY	579	43	03/27/21	11/15/21	SUBSYSTEM	NON-STATE ACTOR	OTHER NON-
	Czechoslovakia			03/27/21	04/05/21	Small power	Non-state actor	Other non-viol
	Yugoslavia			03/27/21	04/05/21	Middle power	Non-state actor	Other non-viol
	Hungary			03/30/21	04/05/21	Small power	Multi-state	Political
	Yugoslavia			10/20/21	11/12/21	Middle power	Non-state actor	Other non-viol
	Czechoslovakia			10/20/21	11/15/21	Small power	Non-state actor	Other non-viol
	Hungary			10/20/21	11/15/21	Small power	Non-state actor	Internal chal.
22	AUSTRIAN SEPARATISTS	581	43	05/11/21	06/21/21	DOMINANT SYSTEM	NON-STATE ACTOR	POLITICAL
	Yugoslavia			05/11/21	06/21/21	Middle power	Non-state actor	Political
	Austria			05/12/21	06/21/21	Small power	Yugoslavia	Other non-viol.

GRAVITY OF THREAT	CRISIS MGMT. TECHNIQUE	VIOLENCE	GLOBAL ORG. INVOLVEMENT	OUTCOME: SUBSTANCE	OUTCOME: FORM
POLITICAL REGIME	NON-VIOL. MIL.	MINOR CLASHES	NONE	DEFINITIVE	UNILATERAL
Influence	Non-viol. mil.	No violence	None	Victory	Unilateral-adv.
Political regime	Negotiation	Minor clashes	None	Victory	Unilateral-adv.
EXISTENCE	VIOLENCE	WAR	NONE	AMBIGUOUS	FORMAL AGMT.
Territory	Violence	War	None	Compromise	Formal agmt.
Existence	Violence	War	None	Victory	Formal agmt.
TERRITORY	NEGOTIATION	MINOR CLASHES	DISCUSSION	AMBIGUOUS	FORMAL AGMT.
Political regime	Mult. w/viol.	Minor clashes	Discussion	Compromise	Formal agmt.
Territory	Negotiation	Minor clashes	Discussion	Victory	Formal agmt.
LMD	MEDIATION	NO VIOLENCE	MEDIATION	DEFINITIVE	FORMAL AGMT.
LMD	Mediation	No violence	Mediation	Defeat	Formal agmt.
Territory	Mediation	No violence	Mediation	Victory	Formal agmt.
TERRITORY	VIOLENCE	MINOR CLASHES	NONE	DEFINITIVE	UNILATERAL
Territory	Violence	Minor clashes	None	Defeat	Unilateral-adv.
TERRITORY	MULT. W/VIOL.	WAR	MEDIATION	AMBIGUOUS	FORMAL AGMT.
Territory	Mult. w/viol.	War	Mediation	Compromise	Formal agmt.
Territory	Mult. w/viol.	War	Mediation	Compromise	Formal agmt.
EXISTENCE	VIOLENCE	WAR	NONE	DEFINITIVE	UNILATERAL
Existence	Violence	War	None	Victory	Unilateral-self
TERRITORY	MULT. W/VIOL.	MINOR CLASHES	CALL FOR ACTION	DEFINITIVE	UNILATERAL
Territory	Mult. w/viol.	Minor clashes	Call for action	Defeat	Compliance
Territory	Mult. w/viol.	Minor clashes	Call for action	Victory	Unilateral-adv.
POLITICAL REGIME	NEGOTIATION	NO VIOLENCE	NONE	AMBIGUOUS	UNILATERAL
Political regime	Multiple, no viol.	No violence	None	Defeat	Compliance
Economic	Negotiation	No violence	None	Compromise	Unilateral-self
Economic	Negotiation	No violence	None	Victory	Spillover
POLITICAL REGIME	NON-VIOL. MIL.	NO VIOLENCE	NONE	DEFINITIVE	UNILATERAL
Political regime	Non-viol. mil.	No violence	None	Victory	Unilateral-adv.
Political regime	Non-viol. mil.	No violence	None	Victory	Unilateral-adv.
Political regime	Non-viol. mil.	No violence	None	Victory	Compliance
Political regime	Non-viol. mil.	No violence	None	Victory	Unilateral-adv.
Political regime	Non-viol. mil.	No violence	None	Victory	Unilateral-adv.
Political regime	Non-viol. mil.	No violence	None	Victory	Compliance
TERRITORY	NON-VIOL. MIL.	NO VIOLENCE	NONE	DEFINITIVE	UNILATERAL
Territory	Non-viol. mil.	No violence	None	Victory	Unilateral-ally
Territory	Negotiation	No violence	None	Victory	Compliance

(continued)

TABLE III.1.—*Continued*

NUM.	INTERNATIONAL CRISIS ACTORS	SUM. PAGE	PC OR REG.	TRIG. DATE	TERM. DATE	SYSTEM LEVEL POWER STATUS	TRIGGERING ENTITY	CRISIS TRIGGER
23	ALBANIAN FRONTIER	245	19	07/07/21	11/18/21	SUBSYSTEM	YUGOSLAVIA	NON-VIOL. MIL.
	Albania			07/07/21	11/18/21	Small power	Yugoslavia	Non-viol. mil.
	Yugoslavia			07/13/21	11/18/21	Middle power	Albania	Ext. change
24	BURGENLAND DISPUTE	582	43	08/28/21	12/28/21	SUBSYSTEM	AUSTRIA	NON-VIOL. MIL.
	Hungary			08/28/21	12/28/21	Small power	Austria	Non-viol. mil.
	Austria			08/28/21	12/28/21	Small power	Hungary	Violent
25	GREECE/TURKEY WAR III	365	28	08/26/22	09/15/22	SUBSYSTEM	TURKEY	VIOLENT
	Greece			08/26/22	09/15/22	Middle power	Turkey	Violent
26	CHANAK	628	44	09/23/22	10/11/22	MAINLY SUBSYSTEM	UK	POLITICAL
	Turkey			09/23/22	10/11/22	Middle power	UK	Political
	UK			09/23/22	10/11/22	Great power	Turkey	Non-viol. mil.
27	RUHR I	240	18	01/22/23	09/27/23	MAINLY SUBSYSTEM	USSR	POLITICAL
	Poland			01/22/23	07/88/23	Middle power	USSR	Political
	Germany			02/28/23	09/27/23	Middle power	Multi-state	Internal chal.
	Netherlands			03/09/23	09/27/23	Small power	Multi-state	Indirect viol.
28	CORFU INCIDENT	583	43	08/31/23	09/29/23	MAINLY SUBSYSTEM	ITALY	VIOLENT
	Greece			08/31/23	09/29/23	Middle power	Italy	Violent
29	HIJAZ/NAJD WAR	629	44	03/07/24	12/19/25	SUBSYSTEM	HIJAZ	POLITICAL
	Najd			03/07/24	12/19/25	Middle power	Hijaz	Political
	Hijaz			09/01/24	12/19/25	Small power	Najd	Violent
30	RUHR II	241	18	04/29/24	08/30/24	MAINLY SUBSYSTEM	FRANCE	POLITICAL
	Germany			04/29/24	08/16/24	Middle power	France	Political
	France			07/08/24	08/30/24	Great power	Germany	Other non-viol.
31	MOSUL LAND DISPUTE	631	44	09/29/24	11/15/24	MAINLY SUBSYSTEM	UK	POLITICAL
	Turkey			09/29/24	11/15/24	Middle power	UK	Political
	UK			10/03/24	11/15/24	Great power	Turkey	Political
32	BULGARIA/GREEK FRONT.	584	43	10/19/25	12/15/25	MAINLY DOMINANT	BULGARIA	VIOLENT
	Greece			10/19/25	12/15/25	Middle power	Bulgaria	Violent
	Bulgaria			10/22/25	12/15/25	Small power	Greece	Violent
33	NICARAGUA CIVIL WAR I	495	41	08/17/26	05/15/27	SUBSYSTEM	MEXICO	NON-VIOL. MIL.
	Nicaragua			08/17/26	05/15/27	Small power	Mexico	Non-viol. mil.
34	HEGEMONY OVER ALBANIA	246	19	11/28/26	11/22/27	SUBSYSTEM	MULTI-STATE	POLITICAL
	Yugoslavia			11/28/26	11/11/27	Middle power	Multi-state	Political
	Albania			03/77/27	03/23/27	Small power	Yugoslavia	Other non-viol.
	Italy			03/17/27	11/22/27	Great power	Yugoslavia	Non-viol. mil.

GRAVITY OF THREAT	CRISIS MGMT. TECHNIQUE	VIOLENCE	GLOBAL ORG. INVOLVEMENT	OUTCOME: SUBSTANCE	OUTCOME: FORM
TERRITORY	VIOLENCE	WAR	DISCUSSION	AMBIGUOUS	IMPOSED AGMT.
Territory	Violence	War	Discussion	Compromise	Formal agmt.
Grave damage	Violence	War	Discussion	Compromise	Imposed-imposee
TERRITORY	MULT. W/VIOL.	MINOR CLASHES	NONE	AMBIGUOUS	IMPOSED AGMT.
Territory	Mult. w/viol.	Minor clashes	None	Defeat	Formal agmt.
Territory	Mult. w/viol.	Minor clashes	None	Compromise	Imposed-imposee
TERRITORY	VIOLENCE	WAR	NONE	DEFINITIVE	UNILATERAL
Territory	Violence	War	None	Defeat	Unilateral-self
TERRITORY	MULTIPLE, NO VIOL.	NO VIOLENCE	NONE	AMBIGUOUS	FORMAL AGMT.
Territory	Multiple, no viol.	No violence	None	Victory	Formal agmt.
Influence	Multiple, no viol.	No violence	None	Compromise	Formal agmt.
POLITICAL REGIME	NEGOTIATION	NO VIOLENCE	NONE	AMBIGUOUS	UNILATERAL
Grave damage	Negotiation	No violence	None	Victory	Faded
Political regime	Multiple, no viol.	No violence	None	Defeat	Compliance
Grave damage	Negotiation	No violence	None	Other	Spillover
TERRITORY	ADJUD./ARBIT.	MINOR CLASHES	OTHER	DEFINITIVE	UNILATERAL
Territory	Adjud./Arbit.	Minor clashes	Other	Defeat	Compliance
EXISTENCE	VIOLENCE	WAR	NONE	DEFINITIVE	IMPOSED AGMT.
Influence	Violence	War	None	Victory	Imposed-imposer
Existence	Violence	War	None	Defeat	Imposed-imposee
ECONOMIC	NEGOTIATION	NO VIOLENCE	NONE	AMBIGUOUS	FORMAL AGMT.
Economic	Negotiation	No violence	None	Compromise	Formal agmt.
Economic	Mult. w/viol.	No violence	None	Compromise	Formal agmt.
TERRITORY	MEDIATION	MINOR CLASHES	ARBITRATION	AMBIGUOUS	SEMI-FORMAL AGMT.
Territory	Mediation	Minor clashes	Arbitration	Compromise	Semi-formal agmt.
Economic	Mediation	Minor clashes	Arbitration	Compromise	Semi-formal agmt.
TERRITORY	MULT. W/VIOL.	MINOR CLASHES	ARBITRATION	DEFINITIVE	SEMI-FORMAL AGMT.
Territory	Mult. w/viol.	Minor clashes	Arbitration	Defeat	Semi-formal agmt.
Territory	Mediation	Minor clashes	Arbitration	Victory	Semi-formal agmt.
POLITICAL REGIME	MEDIATION	MINOR CLASHES	FACT-FINDING	DEFINITIVE	UNILATERAL
Political regime	Mediation	Minor clashes	Fact-finding	Victory	Unilateral-ally
INFLUENCE	MULTIPLE, NO VIOL.	NO VIOLENCE	OTHER	DEFINITIVE	IMPOSED AGMT.
Influence	Multiple, no viol.	No violence	Other	Victory	Spillover
Political regime	Non-viol. mil.	No violence	Other	Victory	Imposed-imposee
Influence	Negotiation	No violence	Other	Victory	Imposed-imposer

(continued)

671

TABLE III.1.—Continued

NUM.	INTERNATIONAL CRISIS ACTORS	SUM. PAGE	PC OR REG.	TRIG. DATE	TERM. DATE	SYSTEM LEVEL POWER STATUS	TRIGGERING ENTITY	CRISIS TRIGGER
35	SHANTUNG	151	10	05/28/27	03/28/29	SUBSYSTEM	JAPAN	NON-VIOL. MIL.
	China			05/28/27	03/28/29	Middle power	Japan	Non-viol. mil.
	Japan			05/29/27	03/28/29	Great power	China	Political
36	VILNA II	253	20	10/77/27	12/10/27	SUBSYSTEM	POLAND	OTHER NON-VI◀
	Lithuania			10/77/27	12/10/27	Small power	Poland	Other non-viol.
	Poland			10/15/27	12/10/27	Small power	Lithuania	Verbal
37	CHACO I	497	41	12/05/28	09/12/29	SUBSYSTEM	PARAGUAY	VIOLENT
	Bolivia			12/05/28	09/12/29	Small power	Paraguay	Violent
	Paraguay			12/14/28	09/12/29	Small power	Bolivia	Violent
38	CHINESE E. RAILWAY	537	42	07/10/29	12/22/29	MAINLY SUBSYSTEM	NON-STATE ACTOR	NON-VIOL. MIL.
	USSR			07/10/29	12/22/29	Great power	Non-state actor	Non-viol. mil.
	China			07/13/29	12/22/29		USSR	Political
39	MUKDEN INCIDENT	153	10	09/18/31	02/18/32	MAINLY SUBSYSTEM	JAPAN	VIOLENT
	China			09/18/31	02/18/32	Middle power	Japan	Violent
	Japan			09/18/31	02/18/32	Great power	China	Violent
40	SHANGHAI	154	10	01/24/32	05/05/32	SUBSYSTEM	JAPAN	POLITICAL
	China			01/24/32	05/05/32	Middle power	Japan	Political
	Japan			01/29/32	05/05/32	Great power	China	Violent
41	CHACO II	498	41	06/18/32	06/12/35	SUBSYSTEM	BOLIVIA	VIOLENT
	Paraguay			06/18/32	06/12/35	Small power	Bolivia	Violent
	Bolivia			07/18/32	06/12/35	Small power	Paraguay	Violent
42	LETICIA	499	41	09/08/32	05/25/33	SUBSYSTEM	PERU	VIOLENT
	Colombia			09/08/32	05/25/33	Small power	Peru	Violent
	Peru			12/27/32	05/25/33	Small power	Colombia	Non-viol. mil.
43	JEHOL CAMPAIGN	155	10	02/23/33	05/31/33	SUBSYSTEM	JAPAN	VIOLENT
	China			02/23/33	05/31/33	Middle power	Japan	Violent
44	SAUDI/YEMEN WAR	632	44	12/18/33	05/20/34	SUBSYSTEM	YEMEN	VIOLENT
	Saudi Arabia			12/18/33	05/20/34	Middle power	Yemen	Violent
	Yemen			03/22/34	05/20/34	Small power	Saudi Arabia	Violent
45	AUSTRIA PUTSCH	586	43	07/25/34	07/31/34	MAINLY DOMINANT	NON-STATE ACTOR	INTERNAL CHAI
	Austria			07/25/34	07/31/34	Small power	Non-state actor	Internal chal.
	Czechoslovakia			07/25/34	07/31/34	Small power	Non-state actor	Non-viol. mil.
	Italy			07/25/34	07/31/34	Great power	Non-state actor	Indirect viol.
	Yugoslavia			07/25/34	07/31/34	Small power	Italy	Non-viol. mil.
46	ASSN./KING ALEXANDER	587	43	10/08/34	12/10/34	SUBSYSTEM	NON-STATE ACTOR	INTERNAL CHAI
	Yugoslavia			10/08/34	12/10/34	Middle power	Non-state actor	Internal chal.
	Hungary			11/22/34	12/10/34	Small power	Non-state actor	Political

672

GRAVITY OF THREAT	CRISIS MGMT. TECHNIQUE	VIOLENCE	GLOBAL ORG. INVOLVEMENT	OUTCOME: SUBSTANCE	OUTCOME: FORM
INFLUENCE	MULT. W/VIOL.	MINOR CLASHES	OTHER	AMBIGUOUS	FORMAL AGMT.
Political regime	Multiple, no viol.	Minor clashes	None	Compromise	Formal agmt.
Influence	Mult. w/viol.	Minor clashes	Other	Compromise	Formal agmt.
EXISTENCE	MEDIATION	NO VIOLENCE	MEDIATION	AMBIGUOUS	UNILATERAL
Existence	Mediation	No violence	Mediation	Compromise	Unilateral-ally
LMD	Mediation	No violence	Mediation	Compromise	Unilateral-ally
TERRITORY	MULT. W/VIOL.	MINOR CLASHES	GOOD OFFICES	AMBIGUOUS	FORMAL AGMT.
Territory	Mult. w/viol.	Minor clashes	Good offices	Stalemate	Formal agmt.
Territory	Multiple, no viol.	Minor clashes	Good offices	Stalemate	Formal agmt.
POLITICAL REGIME	MULT. W/VIOL.	SERIOUS CLASHES	NONE	DEFINITIVE	IMPOSED AGMT.
Economic	Mult. w/viol.	Serious clashes	None	Victory	Imposed-imposer
Political regime	Mult. w/viol.	Serious clashes	None	Defeat	Imposed-imposee
TERRITORY	MULT. W/VIOL.	SERIOUS CLASHES	FACT-FINDING	DEFINITIVE	UNILATERAL
Territory	Negotiation	Serious clashes	Fact-finding	Defeat	Unilateral-adv.
LMD	Mult. w/viol.	Serious clashes	Fact-finding	Victory	Unilateral-self
TERRITORY	MULT. W/VIOL.	SERIOUS CLASHES	CALL FOR ACTION	AMBIGUOUS	FORMAL AGMT.
Territory	Mult. w/viol.	Serious clashes	Call for action	Stalemate	Formal agmt.
LMD	Mult. w/viol.	Serious clashes	Call for action	Stalemate	Formal agmt.
GRAVE DAMAGE	MULT. W/VIOL.	WAR	SANCTIONS	AMBIGUOUS	FORMAL AGMT.
Grave damage	Mult. w/viol.	War	Sanctions	Compromise	Formal agmt.
Political regime	Mult. w/viol.	War	Sanctions	Compromise	Formal agmt.
TERRITORY	MULT. W/VIOL.	SERIOUS CLASHES	MEDIATION	DEFINITIVE	FORMAL AGMT.
Territory	Mult. w/viol.	Serious clashes	Mediation	Victory	Formal agmt.
LMD	Mult. w/viol.	Serious clashes	Mediation	Defeat	Formal agmt.
TERRITORY	MULT. W/VIOL.	WAR	DISCUSSION	DEFINITIVE	IMPOSED AGMT.
Territory	Mult. w/viol.	War	Discussion	Defeat	Imposed-imposee
TERRITORY	MULT. W/VIOL.	WAR	NONE	DEFINITIVE	IMPOSED AGMT.
Territory	Mult. w/viol.	War	None	Victory	Imposed-imposer
Influence	Mult. w/viol.	War	None	Defeat	Imposed-imposee
POLITICAL REGIME	VIOLENCE	MINOR CLASHES	NONE	DEFINITIVE	UNILATERAL
Political regime	Violence	Minor clashes	None	Victory	Unilateral-self
Influence	Non-viol. mil.	No violence	None	Victory	Spillover
Influence	Non-viol. mil.	No violence	None	Victory	Spillover
Territory	Non-viol. mil.	No violence	None	Victory	Unilateral-adv.
POLITICAL REGIME	MEDIATION	NO VIOLENCE	CALL FOR ACTION	DEFINITIVE	FORMAL AGMT.
Political regime	Mediation	No violence	Other	Victory	Formal agmt.
Influence	Mediation	No violence	Call for action	Defeat	Formal agmt.

(continued)

TABLE III.1.—Continued

NUM.	INTERNATIONAL CRISIS ACTORS	SUM. PAGE	PC OR REG.	TRIG. DATE	TERM. DATE	SYSTEM LEVEL POWER STATUS	TRIGGERING ENTITY	CRISIS TRIGGER
47	ETHIOPIAN WAR	424	40	12/06/34	05/05/36	MAINLY DOMINANT	ITALY	POLITICAL
	Ethiopia			12/06/34	05/05/36	Small power	Italy	Political
	UK			08/99/35	03/03/36	Great power	Italy	Political
	France			10/07/35	03/03/36	Great power	Non-state actor	Political
	Italy			11/06/35	03/03/36	Great power	Non-state actor	Economic
48	BULGARIA/TURKEY	589	43	03/06/35	08/31/35	SUBSYSTEM	TURKEY	NON-VIOL. MIL
	Bulgaria			03/06/35	03/10/35	Small power	Turkey	Non-viol. mil.
	Turkey			03/08/35	03/10/35	Middle power	Bulgaria	Political
	Bulgaria			08/03/35	08/31/35	Small power	Turkey	Non-viol. mil.
49	KAUNAS TRIALS	590	43	03/28/35	09/25/35	SUBSYSTEM	GERMANY	ECONOMIC
	Lithuania			03/28/35	09/25/35	Small power	Germany	Economic
50	ECUADOR/PERU BDR. I	136	7	11/01/35	11/30/35	SUBSYSTEM	ECUADOR	VIOLENT
	Peru			11/01/35	11/30/35	Small power	Ecuador	Violent
	Ecuador			11/14/35	11/30/35	Small power	Peru	Non-viol. mil.
51	REMILIT. RHINELAND	242	18	03/07/36	04/16/36	DOMINANT SYSTEM	GERMANY	NON-VIOL. MIL
	Belgium			03/07/36	03/23/36	Small power	Germany	Non-viol. mil.
	Czechoslovakia			03/07/36	03/23/36	Small power	Germany	Non-viol. mil.
	Poland			03/07/36	03/23/36	Middle power	Germany	Non-viol. mil.
	Romania			03/07/36	03/23/36	Small power	Germany	Non-viol. mil.
	Yugoslavia			03/07/36	03/23/36	Small power	Germany	Non-viol. mil.
	France			03/07/36	04/16/36	Great power	Germany	Non-viol. mil.
	UK			03/07/36	04/16/36	Great power	Germany	Non-viol. mil.
52	SPANISH CIVIL WAR I	261	22	07/17/36	03/18/37	MAINLY SUBSYSTEM	NON-STATE ACTOR	INTERNAL CHA*
	Spain			07/17/36	03/18/37	Middle power	Non-state actor	Internal chal.
53	ALEXANDRETTA	633	44	09/09/36	06/23/39	SUBSYSTEM	FRANCE	POLITICAL
	Turkey			09/09/36	06/23/39	Middle power	France	Political
	France			01/07/37	06/23/39	Great power	Turkey	Non-viol. mil.
54	SPANISH CIVIL WAR II	264	22	05/24/37	05/31/37	MAINLY SUBSYSTEM	SPAIN	VIOLENT
	Italy			05/24/37	05/31/37	Great power	Spain	Violent
	Germany			05/26/37	05/31/37	Great power	Spain	Violent
	Spain			05/31/37	05/31/37	Middle power	Germany	Violent
55	AMUR RIVER INCIDENT	538	42	06/22/37	07/04/37	MAINLY SUBSYSTEM	USSR	EXT. CHANGE
	Japan			06/22/37	07/04/37	Great power	USSR	Ext. change
	USSR			06/28/37	07/04/37	Great power	Japan	Political
56	MARCO POLO BRIDGE	156	10	07/08/37	01/16/38	SUBSYSTEM	JAPAN	VIOLENT
	China			07/08/37	12/13/37	Middle power	Japan	Violent
	Japan			07/09/37	01/16/38	Great power	China	Ext. change

674

GRAVITY OF THREAT	CRISIS MGMT. TECHNIQUE	VIOLENCE	GLOBAL ORG. INVOLVEMENT	OUTCOME: SUBSTANCE	OUTCOME: FORM
EXISTENCE	VIOLENCE	WAR	SANCTIONS	DEFINITIVE	UNILATERAL
Existence	Mult. w/viol.	War	Sanctions	Defeat	Compliance
Influence	Non-viol. mil.	No violence	None	Victory	Spillover
Grave damage	Mediation	No violence	Sanctions	Victory	Spillover
Economic	Violence	War	Sanctions	Victory	Unilateral-self
TERRITORY	NON-VIOL. MIL.	NO VIOLENCE	NONE	AMBIGUOUS	SEMI-FORMAL AGMT.
Territory	Negotiation	No violence	None	Stalemate	Unilateral-self
Influence	Negotiation	No violence	None	Victory	Unilateral-adv.
Territory	Non-viol. mil.	No violence	None	Compromise	Semi-formal agmt.
TERRITORY	NON-VIOL. MIL.	NO VIOLENCE	NONE	AMBIGUOUS	UNILATERAL
Territory	Non-viol. mil.	No violence	None	Stalemate	Unilateral-self
TERRITORY	MULTIPLE, NO VIOL.	MINOR CLASHES	NONE	AMBIGUOUS	SEMI-FORMAL AGMT.
Territory	Multiple, no viol.	Minor clashes	None	Compromise	Semi-formal agmt.
Territory	Adjud./Arbit.	Minor clashes	None	Compromise	Semi-formal agmt.
GRAVE DAMAGE	NEGOTIATION	NO VIOLENCE	CALL FOR ACTION	AMBIGUOUS	OTHER
Grave damage	Negotiation	No violence	Call for action	Defeat	Other-GO intv.
Grave damage	Negotiation	No violence	Call for action	Compromise	Other-GO intv.
Grave damage	Negotiation	No violence	Call for action	Compromise	Other-GO intv.
Grave damage	Negotiation	No violence	Call for action	Compromise	Other-GO intv.
Grave damage	Negotiation	No violence	Call for action	Compromise	Other-GO intv.
Grave damage	Negotiation	No violence	Call for action	Defeat	Other-ally
Grave damage	Negotiation	No violence	Call for action	Compromise	Other-ally
POLITICAL REGIME	VIOLENCE	WAR	OTHER	DEFINITIVE	UNILATERAL
Political regime	Violence	War	Other	Victory	Unilateral-self
TERRITORY	MULTIPLE, NO VIOL.	MINOR CLASHES	ARBITRATION	DEFINITIVE	IMPOSED AGMT.
Territory	Multiple, no viol.	Minor clashes	Arbitration	Victory	Imposed-imposer
Influence	Multiple, no viol.	Minor clashes	Arbitration	Defeat	Imposed-imposee
LMD	MULT. W/VIOL.	MINOR CLASHES	CALL FOR ACTION	AMBIGUOUS	UNILATERAL
Influence	Negotiation	Minor clashes	Call for action	Stalemate	Unilateral-ally
LMD	Violence	Minor clashes	None	Victory	Unilateral-self
LMD	Mult. w/viol.	Minor clashes	Condemnation	Stalemate	Unilateral-adv.
TERRITORY	MULTIPLE, NO VIOL.	MINOR CLASHES	NONE	DEFINITIVE	UNILATERAL
Territory	Multiple, no viol.	Minor clashes	None	Victory	Unilateral-adv.
Territory	Negotiation	Minor clashes	None	Defeat	Compliance
POLITICAL REGIME	VIOLENCE	WAR	CONDEMNATION	AMBIGUOUS	UNILATERAL
Political regime	Violence	War	Call for action	Defeat	Compliance
Influence	Mult. w/viol.	War	Condemnation	Compromise	Unilateral-self

(continued)

TABLE III.1.—Continued

NUM.	INTERNATIONAL CRISIS ACTORS	SUM. PAGE	PC OR REG.	TRIG. DATE	TERM. DATE	SYSTEM LEVEL POWER STATUS	TRIGGERING ENTITY	CRISIS TRIGGER
57	POSTAGE STAMP CRISIS	140	8	08/77/37	12/10/37	SUBSYSTEM	NICARAGUA	POLITICAL
	Honduras			08/77/37	12/10/37	Small power	Nicaragua	Political
	Nicaragua			08/30/37	12/10/37	Small power	Honduras	Non-viol. mil.
58	DOM. REP./HAITI I	501	41	10/05/37	01/31/38	SUBSYSTEM	DOMINICAN REPUBLIC	VIOLENT
	Haiti			10/05/37	01/31/38	Small power	Dominican Republic	Violent
59	PANAY INCIDENT	539	42	12/12/37	12/26/37	MAINLY SUBSYSTEM	JAPAN	VIOLENT
	US			12/12/37	12/26/37	Great power	Japan	Violent
60	ANSCHLUSS	591	43	02/12/38	03/14/38	DOMINANT SYSTEM	GERMANY	POLITICAL
	Austria			02/12/38	03/14/38	Small power	Germany	Political
	Germany			03/09/38	03/14/38	Great power	Austria	Political
61	POLISH ULTIMATUM	254	20	03/13/38	03/19/38	SUBSYSTEM	POLAND	POLITICAL
	Lithuania			03/13/38	03/19/38	Small power	Poland	Political
62	CZECH. MAY CRISIS	227	16	05/19/38	05/23/38	DOMINANT SYSTEM	GERMANY	NON-VIOL. MI
	Czechoslovakia			05/19/38	05/23/38	Small power	Germany	Non-viol. mil.
	France			05/19/38	05/23/38	Great power	Germany	Non-viol. mil.
	UK			05/19/38	05/23/38	Great power	Germany	Non-viol. mil.
	Germany			05/20/38	05/23/38	Great power	Czechoslovakia	Non-viol. mil.
63	CHANGKUFENG	540	42	07/13/38	08/11/38	MAINLY SUBSYSTEM	USSR	EXT. CHANGE
	Japan			07/13/38	08/11/38	Great power	USSR	Ext. change
	USSR			07/31/38	08/11/38	Great power	Japan	Violent
64	MUNICH	228	16	09/07/38	10/66/38	DOMINANT SYSTEM	NON-STATE ACTOR	INTERNAL CH
	Czechoslovakia			09/07/38	09/30/38	Small power	Non-state actor	Internal chal.
	France			09/12/38	09/30/38	Great power	Germany	Political
	UK			09/12/38	09/30/38	Great power	Germany	Political
	USSR			09/19/38	10/66/38	Great power	Czechoslovakia	Political
65	SPANISH CIVIL WAR III	265	22	10/30/38	11/18/38	MAINLY SUBSYSTEM	NON-STATE ACTOR	VIOLENT
	Spain			10/30/38	11/18/38	Middle power	Non-state actor	Violent
66	ITALY THREAT/FRANCE	427	40	11/30/38	03/31/39	MAINLY SUBSYSTEM	ITALY	POLITICAL
	France			11/30/38	03/31/39	Great power	Italy	Political
67	SPANISH CIVIL WAR IV	266	22	12/23/38	03/31/39	MAINLY SUBSYSTEM	NON-STATE ACTOR	VIOLENT
	Spain			12/23/38	03/31/39	Middle power	Non-state actor	Violent
68	CZECH. ANNEXATION	230	16	03/14/39	03/15/39	DOMINANT SYSTEM	GERMANY	POLITICAL
	Czechoslovakia			03/14/39	03/15/39	Small power	Germany	Political
69	MEMEL	592	43	03/15/39	03/22/39	MAINLY SUBSYSTEM	GERMANY	EXT. CHANGE
	Lithuania			03/15/39	03/22/39	Small power	Germany	Ext. change
70	DANZIG	594	43	03/21/39	04/06/39	DOMINANT SYSTEM	GERMANY	POLITICAL
	Poland			03/21/39	04/06/39	Middle power	Germany	Political

GRAVITY OF THREAT	CRISIS MGMT. TECHNIQUE	VIOLENCE	GLOBAL ORG. INVOLVEMENT	OUTCOME: SUBSTANCE	OUTCOME: FORM
TERRITORY	MEDIATION	NO VIOLENCE	NONE	AMBIGUOUS	FORMAL AGMT.
Territory	Mediation	No violence	None	Stalemate	Formal agmt.
Territory	Mediation	No violence	None	Stalemate	Formal agmt.
POLITICAL REGIME	MULTIPLE, NO VIOL.	MINOR CLASHES	NONE	DEFINITIVE	FORMAL AGMT.
Political regime	Multiple, no viol.	Minor clashes	None	Victory	Formal agmt.
LMD	NEGOTIATION	MINOR CLASHES	NONE	DEFINITIVE	SEMI-FORMAL AGMT.
LMD	Negotiation	Minor clashes	None	Victory	Semi-formal agmt.
EXISTENCE	NON-VIOL. MIL.	NO VIOLENCE	NONE	DEFINITIVE	UNILATERAL
Existence	Multiple, no viol.	No violence	None	Defeat	Compliance
Territory	Non-viol. mil.	No violence	None	Victory	Unilateral-self
TERRITORY	NEGOTIATION	NO VIOLENCE	GOOD OFFICES	DEFINITIVE	UNILATERAL
Territory	Negotiation	No violence	Good offices	Defeat	Compliance
GRAVE DAMAGE	NON-VIOL. MIL.	NO VIOLENCE	NONE	DEFINITIVE	UNILATERAL
Grave damage	Non-viol. mil.	No violence	None	Victory	Unilateral-adv.
Grave damage	Non-viol. mil.	No violence	None	Victory	Unilateral-adv.
Grave damage	Non-viol. mil.	No violence	None	Victory	Unilateral-adv.
Grave damage	Negotiation	No violence	None	Defeat	Unilateral-self
TERRITORY	MULT. W/VIOL.	SERIOUS CLASHES	NONE	AMBIGUOUS	FORMAL AGMT.
Territory	Mult. w/viol.	Serious clashes	None	Compromise	Formal agmt.
Territory	Mult. w/viol.	Serious clashes	None	Victory	Formal agmt.
GRAVE DAMAGE	NON-VIOL. MIL.	NO VIOLENCE	NONE	DEFINITIVE	IMPOSED AGMT.
Grave damage	Non-viol. mil.	No violence	None	Defeat	Compliance
Grave damage	Negotiation	No violence	None	Victory	Imposed-imposee
Grave damage	Negotiation	No violence	None	Victory	Imposed-imposee
Grave damage	Non-viol. mil.	No violence	None	Defeat	Spillover
GRAVE DAMAGE	VIOLENCE	WAR	NONE	DEFINITIVE	UNILATERAL
Grave damage	Violence	War	None	Defeat	Unilateral-adv.
TERRITORY	MULTIPLE, NO VIOL.	NO VIOLENCE	NONE	AMBIGUOUS	UNILATERAL
Territory	Multiple, no viol.	No violence	None	Stalemate	Unilateral-adv.
POLITICAL REGIME	MULT. W/VIOL.	WAR	NONE	DEFINITIVE	UNILATERAL
Political regime	Mult. w/viol.	War	None	Defeat	Unilateral-adv.
EXISTENCE	NEGOTIATION	NO VIOLENCE	NONE	DEFINITIVE	UNILATERAL
Existence	Negotiation	No violence	None	Defeat	Compliance
TERRITORY	NEGOTIATION	NO VIOLENCE	NONE	DEFINITIVE	IMPOSED AGMT.
Territory	Negotiation	No violence	None	Defeat	Imposed-imposee
TERRITORY	NEGOTIATION	NO VIOLENCE	NONE	DEFINITIVE	UNILATERAL
Territory	Negotiation	No violence	None	Victory	Unilateral-ally

(continued)

677

TABLE III.1.—Continued

NUM.	INTERNATIONAL CRISIS ACTORS	SUM. PAGE	PC OR REG.	TRIG. DATE	TERM. DATE	SYSTEM LEVEL POWER STATUS	TRIGGERING ENTITY	CRISIS TRIGGEI
71	INVASION OF ALBANIA	247	19	03/25/39	04/13/39	MAINLY SUBSYSTEM	ITALY	POLITICAL
	Albania			03/25/39	04/08/39	Small power	Italy	Political
	France			04/07/39	04/13/39	Great power	Italy	Indirect viol.
	Greece			04/07/39	04/13/39	Middle power	Italy	Indirect viol.
	UK			04/07/39	04/13/39	Great power	Italy	Indirect viol.
72	NOMONHAN	542	42	05/28/39	09/15/39	MAINLY SUBSYSTEM	JAPAN	INDIRECT VIC
	USSR			05/28/39	09/15/39	Great power	Japan	Indirect viol.
	Japan			06/18/39	09/15/39	Great power	USSR	Violent
73	TIENTSIN	543	42	06/14/39	08/29/39	MAINLY SUBSYSTEM	JAPAN	ECONOMIC
	UK			06/14/39	08/29/39	Great power	Japan	Economic
74	ENTRY WWII	388	31	08/20/39	09/28/39	DOMINANT SYSTEM	MULTI-STATE	POLITICAL
	Latvia			08/20/39	09/01/39	Small power	Multi-state	Political
	Japan			08/21/39	08/28/39	Great power	Multi-state	Political
	UK			08/21/39	09/03/39	Great power	Multi-state	Political
	USSR			08/21/39	09/28/39	Great power	Germany	Political
	Luxembourg			08/22/39	08/31/39	Small power	Multi-state	Political
	Switzerland			08/22/39	08/31/39	Small power	Multi-state	Political
	Denmark			08/22/39	09/01/39	Small power	Multi-state	Political
	Estonia			08/22/39	09/01/39	Small power	Multi-state	Political
	Finland			08/22/39	09/01/39	Small power	Multi-state	Political
	Norway			08/22/39	09/01/39	Small power	Multi-state	Political
	Romania			08/22/39	09/01/39	Small power	Multi-state	Political
	Sweden			08/22/39	09/01/39	Middle power	Multi-state	Political
	Lithuania			08/22/39	09/02/39	Small power	Multi-state	Political
	Australia			08/22/39	09/03/39	Small power	Multi-state	Political
	Belgium			08/22/39	09/03/39	Small power	Multi-state	Political
	France			08/22/39	09/03/39	Great power	Multi-state	Political
	Netherlands			08/22/39	09/03/39	Small power	Multi-state	Political
	New Zealand			08/22/39	09/03/39	Small power	Germany	Political
	Canada			08/22/39	09/10/39	Small power	Multi-state	Political
	Poland			08/22/39	09/17/39	Middle power	Multi-state	Political
	South Africa			09/01/39	09/06/39	Small power	Germany	Indirect viol.
75	SOVIET OCCUP.-BALTIC	596	43	09/26/39	10/10/39	MAINLY DOMINANT	USSR	POLITICAL
	Estonia			09/26/39	09/28/39	Small power	USSR	Political
	Latvia			10/03/39	10/05/39	Small power	USSR	Political
	Lithuania			10/03/39	10/10/39	Small power	USSR	Political

678

GRAVITY OF THREAT	CRISIS MGMT. TECHNIQUE	VIOLENCE	GLOBAL ORG. INVOLVEMENT	OUTCOME: SUBSTANCE	OUTCOME: FORM
EXISTENCE	MULT. W/VIOL.	WAR	NONE	AMBIGUOUS	UNILATERAL
Existence	Mult. w/viol.	War	None	Defeat	Unilateral-self
Influence	Negotiation	No violence	None	Stalemate	Unilateral-self
Territory	Negotiation	No violence	None	Stalemate	Unilateral-ally
Influence	Negotiation	No violence	None	Stalemate	Unilateral-self
TERRITORY	MULT. W/VIOL.	WAR	NONE	DEFINITIVE	FORMAL AGMT.
Territory	Mult. w/viol.	War	None	Victory	Formal agmt.
Territory	Mult. w/viol.	War	None	Defeat	Formal agmt.
INFLUENCE	NEGOTIATION	NO VIOLENCE	NONE	AMBIGUOUS	SEMI-FORMAL AGMT.
Influence	Negotiation	No violence	None	Compromise	Semi-formal agmt.
EXISTENCE	MULT. W/VIOL.	WAR	NONE	AMBIGUOUS	UNILATERAL
Existence	Negotiation	No violence	None	Stalemate	Unilateral-self
Influence	Negotiation	No violence	None	Defeat	Unilateral-self
Grave damage	Multiple, no viol.	No violence	None	Other	Unilateral-self
Grave damage	Negotiation	War	None	Compromise	Unilateral-ally
Grave damage	Negotiation	No violence	None	Other	Semi-formal agmt.
Grave damage	Multiple, no viol.	No violence	None	Victory	Semi-formal agmt.
Grave damage	Negotiation	No violence	None	Stalemate	Unilateral-self
Existence	Negotiation	No violence	None	Stalemate	Unilateral-self
Grave damage	Negotiation	No violence	None	Stalemate	Unilateral-self
Territory	Non-viol. mil.	No violence	None	Stalemate	Unilateral-self
Grave damage	Negotiation	No violence	None	Stalemate	Unilateral-self
Existence	Negotiation	No violence	None	Stalemate	Unilateral-self
Grave damage	Non-viol. mil.	No violence	None	Other	Unilateral-self
Grave damage	Multiple, no viol.	No violence	None	Other	Unilateral-self
Grave damage	Non-viol. mil.	No violence	None	Other	Unilateral-self
Grave damage	Multiple, no viol.	No violence	None	Victory	Unilateral-self
Grave damage	Non-viol. mil.	No violence	None	Other	Unilateral-self
Grave damage	Multiple, no viol.	No violence	None	Other	Unilateral-self
Existence	Mult. w/viol.	War	None	Defeat	Compliance
Other	Non-viol. mil.	No violence	None	Other	Unilateral-self
EXISTENCE	NEGOTIATION	NO VIOLENCE	NONE	AMBIGUOUS	IMPOSED AGMT.
Existence	Negotiation	No violence	None	Defeat	Imposed-imposee
Existence	Negotiation	No violence	None	Defeat	Imposed-imposee
Existence	Negotiation	No violence	None	Compromise	Imposed-imposee

(continued)

TABLE III.1.—Continued

NUM.	INTERNATIONAL CRISIS ACTORS	SUM. PAGE	PC OR REG.	TRIG. DATE	TERM. DATE	SYSTEM LEVEL POWER STATUS	TRIGGERING ENTITY	CRISIS TRIGGER
76	FINNISH WAR	233	17	10/06/39	03/13/40	MAINLY DOMINANT	USSR	POLITICAL
	Finland			10/06/39	03/13/40	Small power	USSR	Political
	Sweden			12/27/39	03/13/40	Middle power	Multi-state	Non-viol. mil.
	France			01/14/40	03/13/40	Great power	USSR	Indirect viol.
	UK			01/14/40	03/13/40	Great power	USSR	Indirect viol.
77	INVAS.-SCANDINAVIA	393	31	04/08/40	06/10/40	MAINLY DOMINANT	GERMANY	NON-VIOL. MI
	Norway			04/08/40	06/10/40	Small power	Germany	Non-viol. mil.
	Denmark			04/09/40	04/09/40	Small power	Germany	Violent
	Netherlands			04/09/40	04/27/40	Small power	Germany	Indirect viol.
	France			04/09/40	06/08/40	Great power	Germany	Indirect viol.
	UK			04/09/40	06/08/40	Great power	Germany	Indirect viol.
78	FALL OF WEST EUROPE	395	31	05/10/40	06/22/40	DOMINANT SYSTEM	GERMANY	VIOLENT
	Luxemburg			05/10/40	05/10/40	Small power	Germany	Violent
	Netherlands			05/10/40	05/15/40	Small power	Germany	Violent
	Belgium			05/10/40	05/28/40	Small power	Germany	Violent
	UK			05/10/40	06/17/40	Great power	Germany	Indirect viol.
	France			05/10/40	06/22/40	Great power	Germany	Indirect viol.
79	CLOSURE-BURMA ROAD	396	31	06/24/40	07/14/40	MAINLY SUBSYSTEM	JAPAN	POLITICAL
	UK			06/24/40	07/14/40	Great power	Japan	Political
80	ROMANIAN TERRITORY	597	43	06/26/40	09/07/40	MAINLY SUBSYSTEM	USSR	POLITICAL
	Romania			06/26/40	07/02/40	Small power	USSR	Political
	Romania			07/01/40	08/30/40	Small power	Hungary	Ext. change
	Romania			07/99/40	09/07/40	Small power	Bulgaria	Political
81	BATTLE OF BRITAIN	397	31	07/10/40	09/15/40	DOMINANT SYSTEM	GERMANY	VIOLENT
	UK			07/10/40	09/15/40	Great power	Germany	Violent
82	E. AFRICA CAMPAIGN	398	31	08/19/40	05/17/41	MAINLY SUBSYSTEM	ITALY	VIOLENT
	UK			08/19/40	05/17/41	Great power	Italy	Violent
	Italy			03/27/41	05/17/41	Great power	UK	Violent

GRAVITY OF THREAT	CRISIS MGMT. TECHNIQUE	VIOLENCE	GLOBAL ORG. INVOLVEMENT	OUTCOME: SUBSTANCE	OUTCOME: FORM
TERRITORY	**MULT. W/VIOL.**	**WAR**	**CALL FOR ACTION**	**DEFINITIVE**	**FORMAL AGMT.**
Territory	Mult. w/viol.	War	Call for action	Defeat	Formal agmt.
Grave damage	Negotiation	No violence	None	Victory	Spillover
Grave damage	Negotiation	No violence	None	Defeat	Spillover
Grave damage	Negotiation	No violence	None	Defeat	Spillover
EXISTENCE	**VIOLENCE**	**WAR**	**NONE**	**AMBIGUOUS**	**IMPOSED AGMT.**
Existence	Violence	War	None	Defeat	Imposed-imposee
Existence	Negotiation	Minor clashes	None	Defeat	Compliance
Grave damage	Non-viol. mil.	No violence	None	Stalemate	Spillover
Grave damage	Violence	War	None	Defeat	Unilateral-self
Grave damage	Violence	War	None	Defeat	Unilateral-self
EXISTENCE	**MULT. W/VIOL.**	**WAR**	**NONE**	**AMBIGUOUS**	**IMPOSED AGMT.**
Existence	Negotiation	Minor clashes	None	Defeat	Unilateral-self
Existence	Mult. w/viol.	War	None	Defeat	Imposed-imposee
Existence	Mult. w/viol.	War	None	Defeat	Compliance
Grave damage	Mult. w/viol.	War	None	Stalemate	Unilateral-self
Existence	Mult. w/viol.	War	None	Defeat	Imposed-imposee
GRAVE DAMAGE	**NEGOTIATION**	**NO VIOLENCE**	**NONE**	**DEFINITIVE**	**FORMAL AGMT.**
Grave damage	Negotiation	No violence	None	Defeat	Formal agmt.
TERRITORY	**MULTIPLE, NO VIOL.**	**MINOR CLASHES**	**NONE**	**DEFINITIVE**	**IMPOSED AGMT.**
Territory	Multiple, no viol.	Minor clashes	None	Defeat	Compliance
Territory	Multiple, no viol.	Minor clashes	None	Defeat	Imposed-imposee
Territory	Negotiation	Minor clashes	None	Defeat	Formal agmt.
EXISTENCE	**VIOLENCE**	**WAR**	**NONE**	**DEFINITIVE**	**UNILATERAL**
Existence	Violence	War	None	Victory	Unilateral-self
INFLUENCE	**VIOLENCE**	**WAR**	**NONE**	**DEFINITIVE**	**UNILATERAL**
Influence	Violence	War	None	Victory	Unilateral-self
Influence	Violence	War	None	Defeat	Compliance

(continued)

TABLE III.1.—Continued

NUM.	INTERNATIONAL CRISIS ACTORS	SUM. PAGE	PC OR REG.	TRIG. DATE	TERM. DATE	SYSTEM LEVEL POWER STATUS	TRIGGERING ENTITY	CRISIS TRIGGER
83	BALKAN INVASIONS	400	31	10/28/40	06/01/41	MAINLY DOMINANT	ITALY	VIOLENT
	Greece			10/28/40	11/21/40	Small power	Italy	Violent
	Yugoslavia			10/28/40	11/21/40	Small power	Italy	Indirect viol.
	UK			10/28/40	11/22/40	Great power	Italy	Indirect viol.
	Turkey			10/28/40	02/17/41	Middle power	Italy	Indirect viol.
	Italy			11/21/40	04/23/41	Great power	Greece	Violent
	Germany			11/21/40	06/01/41	Great power	Greece	Ext. change
	Yugoslavia			03/04/41	04/17/41	Small power	Germany	Political
	Greece			04/06/41	04/23/41	Small power	Germany	Violent
	UK			04/06/41	06/01/41	Great power	Germany	Indirect viol.
84	MID-EAST CAMPAIGN	402	31	04/29/41	07/14/41	MAINLY DOMINANT	UK	NON-VIOL.
	Iraq			04/29/41	05/30/41	Small power	UK	Non-viol. mil.
	UK			04/29/41	07/14/41	Great power	Iraq	Non-viol. mil.
	Germany			05/14/41	06/06/41	Great power	UK	Violent
	Vichy France			06/08/41	07/14/41	Small power	UK	Violent
85	BARBAROSSA	404	31	06/22/41	12/05/41	DOMINANT SYSTEM	GERMANY	VIOLENT
	USSR			06/22/41	12/05/41	Great power	Germany	Violent
	USSR			09/30/41	12/05/41	Great power	Germany	Violent
86	ECUADOR/PERU BDR II	136	7	07/05/41	01/29/42	SUBSYSTEM	PERU	VIOLENT
	Ecuador			07/05/41	01/29/42	Small power	Peru	Violent
	Peru			07/23/41	01/29/42	Small power	Ecuador	Violent
87	OCCUPATION OF IRAN	377	29	08/25/41	01/29/42	MAINLY DOMINANT	MULTI-STATE	VIOLENT
	Iran			08/25/41	01/29/42	Small power	Multi-state	Violent
88	PEARL HARBOR	405	31	11/26/41	06/07/42	DOMINANT SYSTEM	US	POLITICAL
	Japan			11/26/41	02/15/42	Great power	US	Political
	UK			12/07/41	02/15/42	Great power	Japan	Indirect viol.
	Netherlands			12/07/41	03/05/42	Small power	Japan	Indirect viol.
	Australia			12/07/41	05/08/42	Small power	Japan	Indirect viol.
	New Zealand			12/07/41	05/08/42	Small power	Japan	Indirect viol.
	Canada			12/07/41	06/07/42	Small power	Japan	Indirect viol.
	US			12/07/41	06/07/42	Great power	Japan	Violent
	Thailand			12/08/41	12/10/41	Small power	Japan	Violent
	Germany			12/08/41	02/15/42	Great power	US	Indirect viol.
	Italy			12/08/41	02/15/42	Great power	US	Indirect viol.
89	STALINGRAD	408	31	06/28/42	02/02/43	DOMINANT SYSTEM	GERMANY	VIOLENT
	USSR			06/28/42	02/02/43	Great power	Germany	Violent
	Germany			11/19/42	02/02/43	Great power	USSR	Violent

GRAVITY OF THREAT	CRISIS MGMT. TECHNIQUE	VIOLENCE	GLOBAL ORG. INVOLVEMENT	OUTCOME: SUBSTANCE	OUTCOME: FORM
EXISTENCE	VIOLENCE	WAR	NONE	AMBIGUOUS	UNILATERAL
Existence	Violence	War	None	Victory	Unilateral-self
Territory	Non-viol. mil.	No violence	None	Victory	Spillover
Influence	Violence	War	None	Victory	Spillover
Grave damage	Negotiation	No violence	None	Compromise	Formal agmt.
Influence	Violence	War	None	Compromise	Spillover
Influence	Violence	War	None	Victory	Unilateral-self
Existence	Mult. w/viol.	War	None	Defeat	Imposed-imposee
Grave damage	Violence	War	None	Defeat	Compliance
Influence	Violence	War	None	Defeat	Compliance
INFLUENCE	VIOLENCE	SERIOUS CLASHES	NONE	DEFINITIVE	IMPOSED AGMT.
Political regime	Mult. w/viol.	Serious clashes	None	Defeat	Compliance
Influence	Violence	Serious clashes	None	Victory	Imposed-imposer
Influence	Violence	Serious clashes	None	Defeat	Unilateral-self
Influence	Mult. w/viol.	Serious clashes	None	Defeat	Imposed-imposee
EXISTENCE	VIOLENCE	WAR	NONE	AMBIGUOUS	UNILATERAL
Existence	Violence	War	None	Stalemate	Unilateral-adv.
Existence	Mult. w/viol.	War	None	Defeat	Unilateral-adv.
TERRITORY	MULT. W/VIOL.	SERIOUS CLASHES	NONE	DEFINITIVE	FORMAL AGMT.
Territory	Mult. w/viol.	Serious clashes	None	Defeat	Formal agmt.
Territory	Mult. w/viol.	Serious clashes	None	Victory	Formal agmt.
EXISTENCE	NEGOTIATION	SERIOUS CLASHES	NONE	AMBIGUOUS	IMPOSED AGMT.
Existence	Negotiation	Serious clashes	None	Compromise	Imposed-imposee
EXISTENCE	VIOLENCE	WAR	NONE	AMBIGUOUS	UNILATERAL
Grave damage	Violence	War	None	Victory	Unilateral-self
Grave damage	Violence	War	None	Defeat	Compliance
Grave damage	Violence	War	None	Defeat	Compliance
Existence	Violence	War	None	Victory	Spillover
Existence	Multiple, no viol.	Minor clashes	None	Victory	Spillover
Grave damage	Violence	Serious clashes	None	Compromise	Spillover
Grave damage	Violence	War	None	Compromise	Unilateral-self
Existence	Negotiation	Minor clashes	None	Defeat	Compliance
Other	Non-viol. mil.	No violence	None	Victory	Spillover
Other	Non-viol. mil.	No violence	None	Victory	Spillover
GRAVE DAMAGE	VIOLENCE	WAR	NONE	DEFINITIVE	UNILATERAL
Grave damage	Violence	War	None	Victory	Unilateral-self
Grave damage	Violence	War	None	Defeat	Compliance

(continued)

TABLE III.1.—Continued

NUM.	INTERNATIONAL CRISIS ACTORS	SUM. PAGE	PC OR REG.	TRIG. DATE	TERM. DATE	SYSTEM LEVEL POWER STATUS	TRIGGERING ENTITY	CRISIS TRIGGE
90	EL ALAMEIN	409	31	10/23/42	05/13/43	DOMINANT SYSTEM	UK	VIOLENT
	Germany			10/23/42	05/13/43	Great power	UK	Violent
	Italy			10/23/42	05/13/43	Great power	UK	Violent
91	FALL OF ITALY	410	31	07/09/43	09/11/43	DOMINANT SYSTEM	MULTI-STATE	VIOLENT
	Italy			07/09/43	09/08/43	Great power	Multi-state	Violent
	Germany			07/25/43	09/11/43	Great power	Italy	Political
92	GERMAN OCCUP.-HUNGARY	411	31	03/13/44	03/19/44	DOMINANT SYSTEM	GERMANY	NON-VIOL. M
	Hungary			03/13/44	03/19/44	Small power	Germany	Non-viol. mil.
93	SOVIET OCCUP.-E. EUR	412	31	03/26/44	02/13/45	DOMINANT SYSTEM	USSR	NON-VIOL. M
	Romania			03/26/44	09/12/44	Small power	USSR	Non-viol. mil.
	Germany			08/23/44	09/22/44	Great power	Romania	Political
	Hungary			09/22/44	02/13/45	Small power	USSR	Violent
	Germany			10/15/44	02/13/45	Great power	USSR	Political
94	D-DAY	413	31	06/06/44	05/07/45	DOMINANT SYSTEM	MULTI-STATE	VIOLENT
	Germany			06/06/44	05/07/45	Great power	Multi-state	Violent
95	FALL OF SAIPAN	414	31	07/09/44	07/18/44	DOMINANT SYSTEM	US	EXT. CHANGE
	Japan			07/09/44	07/18/44	Great power	US	Ext. change
96	IRAN-OIL CONCESSIONS	377	29	09/26/44	12/09/44	MAINLY SUBSYSTEM	USSR	ECONOMIC
	Iran			09/26/44	12/09/44	Middle power	USSR	Economic
97	LEYTE CAMPAIGN	416	31	10/20/44	12/26/44	MAINLY DOMINANT	US	VIOLENT
	Japan			10/20/44	12/26/44	Great power	US	Violent
98	GREEK CIVIL WAR I	599	43	12/03/44	01/15/45	MAINLY DOMINANT	NON-STATE ACTOR	INDIRECT VI
	UK			12/03/44	01/15/45	Great power	Non-state actor	Indirect viol.
99	LUZON	416	31	01/09/45	03/03/45	MAINLY DOMINANT	US	VIOLENT
	Japan			01/09/45	03/03/45	Great power	US	Violent
100	FINAL SOVIET OFFENS.	417	31	01/11/45	05/07/45	DOMINANT SYSTEM	USSR	VIOLENT
	Germany			01/11/45	05/07/45	Great power	USSR	Violent
101	IWO JIMA	418	31	02/19/45	03/16/45	DOMINANT SYSTEM	US	VIOLENT
	Japan			02/19/45	03/16/45	Great power	US	Violent
102	COMMUNISM IN ROMANIA	600	43	02/24/45	03/06/45	MAINLY SUBSYSTEM	ROMANIA	INDIRECT VI
	USSR			02/24/45	03/06/45	Great power	Romania	Indirect viol.
	Romania			02/28/45	03/06/45	Small power	USSR	Political
103	OKINAWA	419	31	04/01/45	06/21/45	DOMINANT SYSTEM	US	VIOLENT
	Japan			04/01/45	06/21/45	Great power	US	Violent

NUM.	INTERNATIONAL CRISIS ACTORS	SUM. PAGE	PC OR REG.	TRIG. DATE	TERM. DATE	SYSTEM LEVEL POWER STATUS	TRIGGERING ENTITY	CRISIS TRIGGE
104	TRIESTE I	249	19	05/01/45	06/11/45	MAINLY DOMINANT	YUGOSLAVIA	NON-VIOL. M
	UK			05/01/45	06/09/45	Great power	Yugoslavia	Non-viol. mil.
	US			05/02/45	06/09/45	Great power	Yugoslavia	Non-viol. mil.
	Yugoslavia			05/02/45	06/11/45	Middle power	Multi-state	Non-viol. mil.
105	FRENCH FORCES/SYRIA	420	31	05/17/45	06/03/45	SUBSYSTEM	FRANCE	NON-VIOL. M
	Syria			05/17/45	06/03/45	Small power	France	Non-viol. mil.
	France			05/28/45	06/03/45	Small power	Syria	Violent
107	HIROSHIMA-NAGASAKI	421	31	08/06/45	09/02/45	DOMINANT SYSTEM	US	VIOLENT
	Japan			08/06/45	09/02/45	Great power	US	Violent

GRAVITY OF THREAT	CRISIS MGMT. TECHNIQUE	VIOLENCE	GLOBAL ORG. INVOLVEMENT	OUTCOME: SUBSTANCE	OUTCOME: FORM
GRAVE DAMAGE	VIOLENCE	WAR	NONE	DEFINITIVE	UNILATERAL
Grave damage	Violence	War	None	Defeat	Compliance
Influence	Violence	War	None	Defeat	Compliance
EXISTENCE	MULT. W/VIOL.	WAR	NONE	AMBIGUOUS	UNILATERAL
Existence	Mult. w/viol.	War	None	Defeat	Compliance
Grave damage	Violence	War	None	Compromise	Unilateral-self
EXISTENCE	NON-VIOL. MIL.	NO VIOLENCE	NONE	DEFINITIVE	UNILATERAL
Existence	Non-viol. mil.	No violence	None	Defeat	Compliance
GRAVE DAMAGE	VIOLENCE	WAR	NONE	AMBIGUOUS	UNILATERAL
Grave damage	Mult. w/viol.	War	None	Compromise	Imposed-imposee
Grave damage	Violence	War	None	Defeat	Compliance
Grave damage	Mult. w/viol.	War	None	Defeat	Compliance
Grave damage	Mult. w/viol.	War	None	Defeat	Compliance
EXISTENCE	VIOLENCE	WAR	NONE	DEFINITIVE	UNILATERAL
Existence	Violence	War	None	Defeat	Compliance
GRAVE DAMAGE	NEGOTIATION	NO VIOLENCE	NONE	DEFINITIVE	UNILATERAL
Grave damage	Negotiation	No violence	None	Defeat	Unilateral-self
ECONOMIC	NON-MIL. PRES.	NO VIOLENCE	NONE	DEFINITIVE	UNILATERAL
Economic	Non-mil. pres.	No violence	None	Victory	Unilateral-adv.
GRAVE DAMAGE	VIOLENCE	WAR	NONE	DEFINITIVE	UNILATERAL
Grave damage	Violence	War	None	Defeat	Compliance
INFLUENCE	MULT. W/VIOL.	SERIOUS CLASHES	NONE	DEFINITIVE	OTHER
Influence	Mult. w/viol.	Serious clashes	None	Victory	Other-misc.
GRAVE DAMAGE	VIOLENCE	WAR	NONE	DEFINITIVE	UNILATERAL
Grave damage	Violence	War	None	Defeat	Compliance
EXISTENCE	VIOLENCE	WAR	NONE	DEFINITIVE	UNILATERAL
Existence	Violence	War	None	Defeat	Compliance
GRAVE DAMAGE	VIOLENCE	WAR	NONE	DEFINITIVE	UNILATERAL
Grave damage	Violence	War	None	Defeat	Compliance
POLITICAL REGIME	NON-VIOL. MIL.	MINOR CLASHES	NONE	DEFINITIVE	UNILATERAL
Influence	Non-viol. mil.	No violence	None	Victory	Unilateral-adv.
Political regime	Negotiation	Minor clashes	None	Defeat	Compliance
GRAVE DAMAGE	VIOLENCE	WAR	NONE	DEFINITIVE	UNILATERAL
Grave damage	Violence	War	None	Defeat	Compliance

GRAVITY OF THREAT	CRISIS MGMT. TECHNIQUE	VIOLENCE	GLOBAL ORG. INVOLVEMENT	OUTCOME: SUBSTANCE	OUTCOME: FORM
TERRITORY	MULTIPLE, NO VIOL.	NO VIOLENCE	NONE	DEFINITIVE	UNILATERAL
Influence	Multiple, no viol.	No violence	None	Victory	Unilateral-adv.
Influence	Multiple, no viol.	No violence	None	Victory	Unilateral-adv.
Territory	Negotiation	No violence	None	Defeat	Compliance
GRAVE DAMAGE	VIOLENCE	SERIOUS CLASHES	NONE	DEFINITIVE	UNILATERAL
Grave damage	Violence	Serious clashes	None	Victory	Unilateral-adv.
Grave damage	Violence	Serious clashes	None	Defeat	Compliance
EXISTENCE	NEGOTIATION	WAR	NONE	DEFINITIVE	UNILATERAL
Existence	Negotiation	War	None	Defeat	Compliance

(continued)

685

TABLE III.1.—Continued

NUM.	INTERNATIONAL CRISIS ACTORS	SUM. PAGE	PC OR REG.	TRIG. DATE	TERM. DATE	SYSTEM LEVEL POWER STATUS	TRIGGERING ENTITY	CRISIS TRIGGER
106	KARS-ARDAHAN	334	27	06/07/45	04/05/46	MAINLY DOMINANT	USSR	POLITICAL
	Turkey			06/07/45	04/05/46	Middle power	USSR	Political
108	AZERBAIJAN	378	29	08/23/45	05/09/46	DOMINANT SYSTEM	NON-STATE ACTOR	INTERNAL CHAL.
	Iran			08/23/45	05/09/46	Small power	Non-state actor	Internal chal.
	UK			11/16/45	05/09/46	Great power	Non-state actor	Non-viol. mil.
	US			03/04/46	05/09/46	Superpower	USSR	Non-viol. mil.
	USSR			03/09/46	05/09/46	Superpower	US	Political
109	INDONESIA INDEP. I	204	14	09/29/45	03/25/47	SUBSYSTEM	MULTI-STATE	POLITICAL
	Netherlands			09/29/45	03/25/47	Middle power	Multi-state	Political
	Indonesia			10/02/45	03/25/47	Small power	Netherlands	Non-viol. mil.
110	COMMUNISM IN POLAND	257	21	06/30/46	01/19/47	MAINLY DOMINANT	POLAND	EXT. CHANGE
	USSR			06/30/46	01/19/47	Superpower	Poland	Ext. change
111	TURKISH STRAITS	335	27	08/07/46	10/26/46	MAINLY DOMINANT	USSR	POLITICAL
	Turkey			08/07/46	10/26/46	Middle power	USSR	Political
	US			08/07/46	10/26/46	Superpower	USSR	Political
112	GREEK CIVIL WAR II	336	27	11/13/46	02/28/47	MAINLY DOMINANT	NON-STATE ACTOR	INTERNAL CHAL.
	Greece			11/13/46	02/28/47	Small power	Non-state actor	Internal chal.
113	COMMUNISM IN HUNGARY	337	27	02/10/47	06/01/47	MAINLY DOMINANT	HUNGARY	EXT. CHANGE
	USSR			02/10/47	06/01/47	Superpower	Hungary	Ext. change
	Hungary			02/26/47	06/01/47	Small power	USSR	Internal chal.
114	TRUMAN DOCTRINE	338	27	02/21/47	05/22/47	DOMINANT SYSTEM	UK	ECONOMIC
	Greece			02/21/47	05/22/47	Small power	UK	Economic
	Turkey			02/21/47	05/22/47	Middle power	UK	Economic
	US			02/21/47	05/22/47	Superpower	UK	Political
115	MARSHALL PLAN	339	27	07/03/47	07/11/47	DOMINANT SYSTEM	US	POLITICAL
	USSR			07/03/47	07/11/47	Superpower	US	Political
	Czechoslovakia			07/09/47	07/11/47	Small power	USSR	Political
116	INDONESIA INDEP. II	205	14	07/21/47	01/17/48	SUBSYSTEM	NETHERLANDS	VIOLENT
	Indonesia			07/21/47	01/17/48	Small power	Netherlands	Violent
	Netherlands			07/31/47	01/17/48	Middle power	Non-state actor	Political
117	CUBA/DOMINICAN REP.	502	41	07/26/47	09/28/47	SUBSYSTEM	NON-STATE ACTOR	NON-VIOL. MIL.
	Dominican Republic			07/26/47	09/28/47	Small power	Non-state actor	Non-viol. mil.
118	JUNAGADH	165	12	08/17/47	02/24/48	SUBSYSTEM	NON-STATE ACTOR	POLITICAL
	India			08/17/47	11/09/47	Middle power	Non-state actor	Political
	Pakistan			11/01/47	02/24/48	Middle power	India	Non-viol. mil.

686

RAVITY OF THREAT	CRISIS MGMT. TECHNIQUE	VIOLENCE	US ACTIV.	USSR ACTIV.	GLOBAL ORG. INVOLVEMENT	OUTCOME: SUBSTANCE	OUTCOME: FORM
TORY	NEGOTIATION	NO VIOLENCE			NONE	AMBIGUOUS	UNILATERAL
ry	Negotiation	No violence	Semi-mil.	Semi-mil.	None	Stalemate	Unilateral-ally
TORY	NON-VIOL. MIL.	NO VIOLENCE			CALL FOR ACTION	DEFINITIVE	FORMAL AGMT.
ry	Non-viol. mil.	No violence	Political	Direct mil.	Call for action	Victory	Formal agmt.
nce	Negotiation	No violence	Political	Direct mil.	Call for action	Victory	Spillover
nce	Negotiation	No violence	US actor	Direct mil.	Call for action	Victory	Spillover
nce	Non-viol. mil.	No violence	Political	SU actor	Condemnation	Defeat	Formal agmt.
ENCE	MULT. W/VIOL.	WAR			DISCUSSION	AMBIGUOUS	FORMAL AGMT.
nce	Mult. w/viol.	War	None	Political	Discussion	Compromise	Formal agmt.
nce	Mult. w/viol.	War	None	Political	Discussion	Compromise	Formal agmt.
ENCE	NON-MIL. PRES.	NO VIOLENCE			NONE	DEFINITIVE	OTHER
nce	Non-mil. pres.	No violence	Political	SU actor	None	Victory	Other-misc.
TORY	MULTIPLE, NO VIOL.	NO VIOLENCE			NONE	DEFINITIVE	UNILATERAL
ory	Negotiation	No violence	Semi-mil.	Political	None	Victory	Unilateral-adv.
nce	Multiple, no viol.	No violence	US actor	Political	None	Victory	Unilateral-adv.
TICAL REGIME	MULT. W/VIOL.	WAR			FACT-FINDING	AMBIGUOUS	FADED
al regime	Mult. w/viol.	War	Political	Semi-mil.	Fact-finding	Compromise	Faded
TICAL REGIME	NON-VIOL. MIL.	NO VIOLENCE			NONE	DEFINITIVE	UNILATERAL
nce	Non-viol. mil.	No violence	Political	SU actor	None	Victory	Unilateral-adv.
al regime	Negotiation	No violence	Political	Direct mil.	None	Defeat	Compliance
TICAL REGIME	MULTIPLE, NO VIOL.	NO VIOLENCE			FACT-FINDING	DEFINITIVE	UNILATERAL
al regime	Negotiation	No violence	Economic	Political	Fact-finding	Victory	Unilateral-ally
al regime	Negotiation	No violence	Economic	Political	Fact-finding	Victory	Unilateral-ally
nce	Multiple, no viol.	No violence	US actor	Political	Call for action	Victory	Unilateral-self
TICAL REGIME	NON-VIOL. MIL.	NO VIOLENCE			NONE	DEFINITIVE	UNILATERAL
nce	Non-viol. mil.	No violence	Political	SU actor	None	Victory	Unilateral-adv.
al regime	Negotiation	No violence	Political	Political	None	Defeat	Compliance
ENCE	MULT. W/VIOL.	WAR			GOOD OFFICES	AMBIGUOUS	FORMAL AGMT.
nce	Mult. w/viol.	War	Political	Political	Good offices	Compromise	Formal agmt.
nce	Mult. w/viol.	War	Political	Political	Good offices	Compromise	Formal agmt.
TICAL REGIME	MULTIPLE, NO VIOL.	NO VIOLENCE			NONE	AMBIGUOUS	UNILATERAL
al regime	Multiple, no viol.	No violence	None	None	None	Stalemate	Unilateral-adv.
ITORY	MULTIPLE, NO VIOL.	MINOR CLASHES			NONE	DEFINITIVE	UNILATERAL
ory	Multiple, no viol.	Minor clashes	None	None	None	Victory	Unilateral-self
ory	Multiple, no viol.	No violence	None	None	None	Defeat	Other-misc.

(continued)

687

TABLE III.1.—Continued

NUM.	INTERNATIONAL CRISIS ACTORS	SUM. PAGE	PC OR REG.	TRIG. DATE	TERM. DATE	SYSTEM LEVEL POWER STATUS	TRIGGERING ENTITY	CRISIS TRIGGER
119	KASHMIR I	166	12	10/24/47	01/01/49	SUBSYSTEM	PAKISTAN	INDIRECT VIOL.
	India			10/24/47	01/01/49	Middle power	Pakistan	Indirect viol.
	Pakistan			10/27/47	01/01/49	Middle power	India	Non-viol. mil.
120	PAL. PRT./ISRAEL IND.	269	23	11/29/47	07/20/49	SUBSYSTEM	NON-STATE ACTOR	EXT. CHANGE
	Iraq			11/29/47	07/18/48	Middle power	Non-state actor	Ext. change
	Egypt			11/29/47	02/24/49	Middle power	Non-state actor	Ext. change
	Lebanon			11/29/47	03/23/49	Small power	Non-state actor	Ext. change
	Jordan			11/29/47	04/03/49	Small power	Non-state actor	Ext. change
	Syria			11/29/47	07/20/49	Small power	Non-state actor	Ext. change
	Israel			05/15/48	07/20/49	Small power	Multi-state	Violent
121	COMMUNISM IN CZECH.	341	27	02/13/48	02/25/48	DOMINANT SYSTEM	CZECHOSLOVAKIA	POLITICAL
	USSR			02/13/48	02/25/48	Superpower	Czechoslovakia	Political
	Czechoslovakia			02/19/48	02/25/48	Small power	USSR	Political
122	SOV. NOTE/FINLAND I	235	17	02/22/48	04/06/48	MAINLY SUBSYSTEM	USSR	POLITICAL
	Finland			02/22/48	04/06/48	Small power	USSR	Political
123	BERLIN BLOCKADE	342	27	06/07/48	05/12/49	DOMINANT SYSTEM	MULTI-STATE	POLITICAL
	USSR			06/07/48	05/12/49	Superpower	Multi-state	Political
	France			06/24/48	05/12/49	Great power	USSR	Non-viol. mil.
	UK			06/24/48	05/12/49	Great power	USSR	Non-viol. mil.
	US			06/24/48	05/12/49	Superpower	USSR	Non-viol. mil.
124	HYDERABAD	168	12	08/21/48	09/18/48	SUBSYSTEM	NON-STATE ACTOR	POLITICAL
	India			08/21/48	09/18/48	Middle power	Non-state actor	Political
125	CHINA CIVIL WAR	382	30	09/23/48	12/08/49	MAINLY DOMINANT	NON-STATE ACTOR	INDIRECT VIOL.
	US			09/23/48	10/26/48	Superpower	Non-state actor	Indirect viol.
	China			10/01/49	12/08/49	Middle power	Non-state actor	Internal chal.
126	COSTA RICA/NIC. I	133	6	12/11/48	02/21/49	SUBSYSTEM	NICARAGUA	VIOLENT
	Costa Rica			12/11/48	02/21/49	Small power	Nicaragua	Violent
127	INDONESIA INDEP. III	206	14	12/19/48	12/27/49	SUBSYSTEM	NETHERLANDS	VIOLENT
	Indonesia			12/19/48	12/27/49	Small power	Netherlands	Violent
	Netherlands			12/23/48	12/27/49	Middle power	Non-state actor	Political
128	SINAI INCURSION	271	23	12/25/48	01/10/49	SUBSYSTEM	ISRAEL	VIOLENT
	Egypt			12/25/48	01/10/49	Middle power	Israel	Violent
	UK			12/25/48	01/10/49	Great power	Israel	Indirect viol.
	Israel			12/31/48	01/10/49	Small power	UK	Non-viol. mil.
129	PUSHTUNISTAN I	148	9	03/77/49	10/05/50	SUBSYSTEM	PAKISTAN	NON-VIOL. MIL.
	Afghanistan			03/77/49	07/31/49	Small power	Pakistan	Non-viol. mil.
	Pakistan			09/30/50	10/05/50	Middle power	Afghanistan	Violent

GRAVITY OF THREAT	CRISIS MGMT. TECHNIQUE	VIOLENCE	US ACTIV.	USSR ACTIV.	GLOBAL ORG. INVOLVEMENT	OUTCOME: SUBSTANCE	OUTCOME: FORM
RITORY	VIOLENCE	WAR			FACT-FINDING	AMBIGUOUS	FORMAL AGMT.
itory	Violence	War	None	None	Fact-finding	Compromise	Formal agmt.
itory	Violence	War	None	None	Fact-finding	Compromise	Formal agmt.
STENCE	VIOLENCE	WAR			MEDIATION	DEFINITIVE	FORMAL AGMT.
ience	Violence	War	Political	Political	Mediation	Defeat	Other-misc.
itory	Violence	War	Political	Political	Mediation	Defeat	Formal agmt.
itory	Violence	War	Political	Political	Mediation	Defeat	Formal agmt.
itory	Violence	War	Political	Political	Mediation	Defeat	Formal agmt.
itory	Violence	War	Political	Political	Mediation	Defeat	Formal agmt.
tence	Violence	War	Political	Political	Mediation	Victory	Formal agmt.
ITICAL REGIME	NON-VIOL. MIL.	NO VIOLENCE			NONE	DEFINITIVE	UNILATERAL
ience	Non-viol. mil.	No violence	Economic	SU actor	None	Victory	Unilateral-adv.
tical regime	Negotiation	No violence	Economic	Political	None	Defeat	Compliance
ITICAL REGIME	NEGOTIATION	NO VIOLENCE			NONE	AMBIGUOUS	IMPOSED AGMT.
tical regime	Negotiation	No violence	None	Political	None	Compromise	Imposed-imposee
LUENCE	MULTIPLE, NO VIOL.	NO VIOLENCE			MEDIATION	DEFINITIVE	FORMAL AGMT.
ience	Multiple, no viol.	No violence	Direct mil.	SU actor	Mediation	Defeat	Formal agmt.
ience	Multiple, no viol.	No violence	Direct mil.	Direct mil.	Mediation	Victory	Formal agmt.
ience	Multiple, no viol.	No violence	Direct mil.	Direct mil.	Mediation	Victory	Formal agmt.
ience	Multiple, no viol.	No violence	US actor	Direct mil.	Mediation	Victory	Formal agmt.
RRITORY	VIOLENCE	MINOR CLASHES			DISCUSSION	DEFINITIVE	UNILATERAL
itory	Violence	Minor clashes	None	None	Discussion	Victory	Unilateral-self
ITICAL REGIME	VIOLENCE	WAR			CALL FOR ACTION	DEFINITIVE	UNILATERAL
ience	Negotiation	No violence	US actor	None	None	Defeat	Unilateral-self
tical regime	Violence	War	Political	Political	Call for action	Defeat	Other-GO intv.
ITICAL REGIME	MULTIPLE, NO VIOL.	MINOR CLASHES			DISCUSSION	DEFINITIVE	FORMAL AGMT.
tical regime	Multiple, no viol.	Minor clashes	Political	None	Discussion	Victory	Formal agmt.
STENCE	MULT. W/VIOL.	WAR			CALL FOR ACTION	DEFINITIVE	UNILATERAL
stence	Mult. w/viol.	War	Economic	Political	Call for action	Victory	Unilateral-adv.
ience	Mult. w/viol.	War	Economic	Political	Condemnation	Defeat	Compliance
RRITORY	MULT. W/VIOL.	SERIOUS CLASHES			CALL FOR ACTION	AMBIGUOUS	UNILATERAL
ritory	Mult. w/viol.	Serious clashes	Political	None	Call for action	Compromise	Unilateral-adv.
ience	Non-viol. mil.	No violence	Political	None	Call for action	Victory	Unilateral-adv.
D	Non-viol. mil.	Serious clashes	Political	None	Condemnation	Compromise	Compliance
RRITORY	VIOLENCE	SERIOUS CLASHES			NONE	DEFINITIVE	UNILATERAL
uence	Multiple, no viol.	Serious clashes	None	None	None	Defeat	Unilateral-adv.
ritory	Violence	Serious clashes	None	None	None	Victory	Unilateral-self

(continued)

689

TABLE III.1.—Continued

NUM.	INTERNATIONAL CRISIS ACTORS	SUM. PAGE	PC OR REG.	TRIG. DATE	TERM. DATE	SYSTEM LEVEL POWER STATUS	TRIGGERING ENTITY	CRISIS TRIGGER
130	LUPERON	503	41	06/19/49	06/21/49	SUBSYSTEM	NON-STATE ACTOR	VIOLENT
	Dominican Republic			06/19/49	06/21/49	Small power	Non-state actor	Violent
131	SOV. BLOC-YUGOSLAVIA	602	43	08/19/49	11/99/51	MAINLY DOMINANT	USSR	POLITICAL
	Yugoslavia			08/19/49	11/99/51	Middle power	USSR	Political
132	KOREAN WAR I	213	15	06/25/50	09/30/50	MAINLY DOMINANT	NORTH KOREA	VIOLENT
	South Korea			06/25/50	09/29/50	Small power	North Korea	Violent
	US			06/25/50	09/29/50	Superpower	North Korea	Indirect viol.
	China (PRC)			06/27/50	07/99/50	Great power	US	Non-viol. mil.
	Taiwan			06/28/50	09/30/50	Small power	China (PRC)	Non-viol. mil.
133	KOREAN WAR II	215	15	09/30/50	07/10/51	MAINLY DOMINANT	SOUTH KOREA	VIOLENT
	North Korea			09/30/50	07/10/51	Small power	South Korea	Violent
	China (PRC)			10/01/50	07/10/51	Great power	Non-state actor	Political
	USSR			10/07/50	12/26/50	Superpower	US	Indirect viol.
	US			10/31/50	07/10/51	Superpower	China (PRC)	Violent
	South Korea			12/26/50	07/10/51	Small power	Multi-state	Violent
134	HULA DRAINAGE	272	23	02/12/51	05/15/51	SUBSYSTEM	ISRAEL	OTHER NON-VIOL.
	Syria			02/12/51	05/15/51	Small power	Israel	Other non-viol.
	Israel			03/15/51	05/15/51	Small power	Syria	Violent
135	PUNJAB WAR SCARE I	169	12	07/07/51	08/99/51	SUBSYSTEM	PAKISTAN	NON-VIOL. MIL.
	India			07/07/51	08/99/51	Middle power	Pakistan	Non-viol. mil.
	Pakistan			07/10/51	08/99/51	Middle power	India	Non-viol. mil.
136	SUEZ CANAL	429	40	07/30/51	01/30/52	SUBSYSTEM	UK	POLITICAL
	Egypt			07/30/51	01/27/52	Middle power	UK	Political
	UK			10/08/51	01/30/52	Great power	Egypt	Political
137	CATALINA AFFAIR	603	43	06/16/52	07/99/52	MAINLY SUBSYSTEM	USSR	VIOLENT
	Sweden			06/16/52	07/99/52	Middle power	USSR	Violent
138	BURMA INFILTRATION	545	42	02/08/53	10/15/54	SUBSYSTEM	TAIWAN	NON-VIOL. MIL.
	Burma			02/08/53	10/15/54	Small power	Taiwan	Non-viol. mil.
139	INVASION OF LAOS I	180	13	03/24/53	99/99/53	SUBSYSTEM	NON-STATE ACTOR	NON-VIOL. MIL.
	France			03/24/53	99/99/53	Great power	Non-state actor	Non-viol. mil.
	Laos			04/05/53	99/99/53	Small power	Non-state actor	Violent
140	KOREAN WAR III	216	15	04/16/53	07/27/53	MAINLY DOMINANT	MULTI-STATE	VIOLENT
	US			04/16/53	07/27/53	Superpower	Multi-state	Violent
	China (PRC)			05/22/53	07/27/53	Great power	US	Other non-viol.
	North Korea			05/22/53	07/27/53	Small power	US	Ext. change
	South Korea			06/08/53	07/27/53	Small power	Multi-state	Political

GRAVITY OF THREAT	CRISIS MGMT. TECHNIQUE	VIOLENCE	US ACTIV.	USSR ACTIV.	GLOBAL ORG. INVOLVEMENT	OUTCOME: SUBSTANCE	OUTCOME: FORM
TICAL REGIME	VIOLENCE	MINOR CLASHES			NONE	AMBIGUOUS	UNILATERAL
cal regime	Violence	Minor clashes	None	None	None	Stalemate	Unilateral-adv.
TICAL REGIME	NON-VIOL. MIL.	NO VIOLENCE			OTHER	DEFINITIVE	FADED
cal regime	Non-viol. mil.	No violence	Economic	Semi-mil.	Other	Victory	Faded
TENCE	VIOLENCE	WAR			EMER. MIL. FORCE	AMBIGUOUS	UNILATERAL
ence	Violence	War	Direct mil.	Semi-mil.	Emer. mil. force	Victory	Unilateral-ally
ence	Violence	War	US actor	Semi-mil.	Emer. mil. force	Victory	Unilateral-self
tory	Non-viol. mil.	No violence	Direct mil.	Semi-mil.	Discussion	Stalemate	Other-misc.
ence	Non-viol. mil.	No violence	Direct mil.	Semi-mil.	Discussion	Stalemate	Spillover
TENCE	VIOLENCE	WAR			OTHER	AMBIGUOUS	SEMI-FORMAL AGMT.
e damage	Violence	War	Direct mil.	Direct mil.	Other	Compromise	Semi-formal agmt.
e damage	Violence	War	Direct mil.	Direct mil.	Other	Compromise	Semi-formal agmt.
tory	Non-viol. mil.	No violence	Direct mil.	SU actor	Other	Victory	Spillover
ence	Violence	War	US actor	Direct mil.	Other	Compromise	Semi-formal agmt.
ence	Violence	War	Direct mil.	Direct mil.	Other	Compromise	Semi-formal agmt.
RITORY	MULT. W/VIOL.	SERIOUS CLASHES			OBSERVERS	AMBIGUOUS	FORMAL AGMT.
tory	Mult. w/viol.	Serious clashes	Political	Political	Observers	Compromise	Formal agmt.
tory	Mult. w/viol.	Serious clashes	Political	Political	Observers	Compromise	Formal agmt.
RITORY	NON-VIOL. MIL.	NO VIOLENCE			GOOD OFFICES	AMBIGUOUS	TACIT UNDERSTANDING
tory	Non-viol. mil.	No violence	Political	None	Good offices	Stalemate	Tacit understanding
tory	Negotiation	No violence	Political	None	Good offices	Stalemate	Tacit understanding
RITORY	MULT. W/VIOL.	SERIOUS CLASHES			FACT-FINDING	AMBIGUOUS	SEMI-FORMAL AGMT.
tory	Mult. w/viol.	Serious clashes	Political	None	Fact-finding	Stalemate	Unilateral-self
ence	Non-viol. mil.	Serious clashes	Political	None	Fact-finding	Stalemate	Semi-formal agmt.
ER	MULTIPLE, NO VIOL.	MINOR CLASHES			NONE	AMBIGUOUS	TACIT UNDERSTANDING
r	Multiple, no viol.	Minor clashes	Political	Direct mil.	None	Stalemate	Tacit understanding
TICAL REGIME	NEGOTIATION	SERIOUS CLASHES			CALL FOR ACTION	DEFINITIVE	UNILATERAL
ical regime	Negotiation	Serious clashes	Political	None	Call for action	Victory	Unilateral-self
TICAL REGIME	VIOLENCE	SERIOUS CLASHES			NONE	AMBIGUOUS	FADED
ence	Violence	Serious clashes	Economic	None	None	Defeat	Faded
ical regime	Mult. w/viol.	Serious clashes	Semi-mil.	None	None	Stalemate	Faded
VE DAMAGE	MULT. W/VIOL.	SERIOUS CLASHES			DISCUSSION	AMBIGUOUS	FORMAL AGMT.
ence	Mult. w/viol.	Serious clashes	US actor	Political	Discussion	Victory	Formal agmt.
e damage	Mult. w/viol.	Serious clashes	Direct mil.	Political	Discussion	Compromise	Formal agmt.
e damage	Mult. w/viol.	Serious clashes	Direct mil.	Political	Discussion	Compromise	Formal agmt.
e damage	Mult. w/viol.	Serious clashes	Direct mil.	Political	Discussion	Compromise	Formal agmt.

(continued)

691

TABLE III.1.—Continued

NUM.	INTERNATIONAL CRISIS ACTORS	SUM. PAGE	PC OR REG.	TRIG. DATE	TERM. DATE	SYSTEM LEVEL POWER STATUS	TRIGGERING ENTITY	CRISIS TRIGGER
141	E. GERMAN UPRISING	603	43	06/17/53	07/11/53	MAINLY DOMINANT	NON-STATE ACTOR	INDIRECT VIOL.
	USSR			06/17/53	07/11/53	Superpower	Non-state actor	Indirect viol.
142	TRIESTE II	251	19	10/08/53	12/05/53	MAINLY SUBSYSTEM	MULTI-STATE	POLITICAL
	Yugoslavia			10/08/53	12/05/53	Middle power	Multi-state	Political
	Italy			10/10/53	12/05/53	Middle power	Yugoslavia	Non-viol. mil.
143	QIBYA	273	23	10/14/53	10/88/53	SUBSYSTEM	ISRAEL	VIOLENT
	Jordan			10/14/53	10/88/53	Small power	Israel	Violent
144	GUATEMALA	343	27	12/12/53	06/29/54	MAINLY DOMINANT	US	POLITICAL
	Guatemala			12/12/53	06/29/54	Small power	US	Political
	US			02/10/54	06/29/54	Superpower	Guatemala	Non-viol. mil.
	Honduras			05/18/54	06/29/54	Small power	Guatemala	Political
145	DIEN BIEN PHU	180	13	03/13/54	07/21/54	MAINLY DOMINANT	NON-STATE ACTOR	VIOLENT
	France			03/13/54	07/21/54	Great power	Non-state actor	Violent
	US			03/20/54	05/08/54	Superpower	France	Political
	UK			04/11/54	04/27/54	Great power	US	Political
146	TAIWAN STRAIT I	383	30	08/66/54	04/23/55	MAINLY DOMINANT	MULTI-STATE	POLITICAL
	China (PRC)			08/66/54	04/23/55	Great power	Multi-state	Political
	Taiwan			09/03/54	12/02/54	Small power	China (PRC)	Violent
	US			09/03/54	04/23/55	Superpower	China (PRC)	Indirect viol.
	Taiwan			01/10/55	03/25/55	Small power	China (PRC)	Violent
147	COSTA RICA/NIC. II	134	6	01/08/55	01/20/55	SUBSYSTEM	VENEZUELA	NON-VIOL. MIL.
	Costa Rica			01/08/55	01/20/55	Small power	Venezuela	Non-viol. mil.
	Nicaragua			01/16/55	01/20/55	Small power	Non-state actor	Ext. change
148	BAGHDAD PACT	636	44	02/24/55	10/77/55	MAINLY SUBSYSTEM	MULTI-STATE	POLITICAL
	Egypt			02/24/55	10/77/55	Middle power	Multi-state	Political
149	GAZA RAID-CZECH. ARMS	274	23	02/28/55	06/23/56	SUBSYSTEM	ISRAEL	VIOLENT
	Egypt			02/28/55	09/28/55	Middle power	Israel	Violent
	Israel			09/28/55	06/23/56	Small power	Multi-state	Non-viol. mil.
150	PUSHTUNISTAN II	148	9	03/27/55	11/99/55	SUBSYSTEM	PAKISTAN	POLITICAL
	Afghanistan			03/27/55	11/99/55	Small power	Pakistan	Political
	Pakistan			03/29/55	10/14/55	Middle power	Afghanistan	Political
151	GOA I	547	42	08/10/55	09/06/55	SUBSYSTEM	INDIA	POLITICAL
	Portugal			08/10/55	09/06/55	Small power	India	Political

GRAVITY OF THREAT	CRISIS MGMT. TECHNIQUE	VIOLENCE	US ACTIV.	USSR ACTIV.	GLOBAL ORG. INVOLVEMENT	OUTCOME: SUBSTANCE	OUTCOME: FORM
UENCE	VIOLENCE	SERIOUS CLASHES	•		NONE	DEFINITIVE	UNILATERAL
nce	Violence	Serious clashes	Political	SU actor	None	Victory	Unilateral-ally
ITORY	MULTIPLE, NO VIOL.	NO VIOLENCE			DISCUSSION	AMBIGUOUS	FORMAL AGMT.
ory	Multiple, no viol.	No violence	Political	None	Discussion	Compromise	Formal agmt.
ory	Multiple, no viol.	No violence	Political	None	Discussion	Compromise	Formal agmt.
TICAL REGIME	NEGOTIATION	SERIOUS CLASHES			CONDEMNATION	AMBIGUOUS	UNILATERAL
cal regime	Negotiation	Serious clashes	Political	None	Condemnation	Stalemate	Unilateral-adv.
TICAL REGIME	NON-VIOL. MIL.	MINOR CLASHES			OTHER	DEFINITIVE	UNILATERAL
cal regime	Non-viol. mil.	Minor clashes	Semi-mil.	Semi-mil.	Other	Defeat	Unilateral-self
nce	Multiple, no viol.	No violence	US actor	Semi-mil.	Other	Victory	Spillover
cal regime	Non-viol. mil.	No violence	Semi-mil.	Semi-mil.	Other	Victory	Unilateral-adv.
UENCE	MULT. W/VIOL.	WAR			NONE	AMBIGUOUS	IMPOSED AGMT.
ence	Mult. w/viol.	War	Political	Political	None	Defeat	Imposed-imposee
ence	Negotiation	No violence	US actor	Political	None	Defeat	Spillover
o	Negotiation	No violence	Political	None	None	Other	Unilateral-self
TENCE	VIOLENCE	SERIOUS CLASHES			DISCUSSION	AMBIGUOUS	SEMI-FORMAL AGMT.
tory	Mult. w/viol.	Serious clashes	Semi-mil.	Political	Discussion	Compromise	Semi-formal agmt.
ence	Violence	Serious clashes	Semi-mil.	Political	Discussion	Stalemate	Other-ally
ence	Multiple, no viol.	No violence	US actor	Political	Discussion	Stalemate	Semi-formal agmt.
tory	Violence	Serious clashes	Semi-mil.	Political	Discussion	Other	Unilateral-self
TICAL REGIME	MULT. W/VIOL.	MINOR CLASHES			NONE	DEFINITIVE	SEMI-FORMAL AGMT.
cal regime	Multiple, no viol.	Minor clashes	Semi-mil.	None	None	Victory	Semi-formal agmt.
cal regime	Mult. w/viol.	Minor clashes	Semi-mil.	None	None	Defeat	Semi-formal agmt.
UENCE	NON-VIOL. MIL.	NO VIOLENCE			NONE	AMBIGUOUS	OTHER
ence	Non-viol. mil.	No violence	Political	Semi-mil.	None	Compromise	Other-ally
TICAL REGIME	NON-VIOL. MIL.	SERIOUS CLASHES			MEDIATION	DEFINITIVE	OTHER
cal regime	Non-viol. mil.	Serious clashes	Political	Semi-mil.	Discussion	Victory	Other-ally
e damage	Non-viol. mil.	Serious clashes	Political	Semi-mil.	Mediation	Victory	Other-ally
RITORY	MULTIPLE, NO VIOL.	MINOR CLASHES			NONE	DEFINITIVE	SEMI-FORMAL AGMT.
tory	Multiple, no viol.	Minor clashes	None	Economic	None	Defeat	Semi-formal agmt.
tory	Multiple, no viol.	No violence	None	Economic	None	Victory	Unilateral-self
RITORY	VIOLENCE	MINOR CLASHES			NONE	AMBIGUOUS	UNILATERAL
tory	Violence	Minor clashes	None	None	None	Stalemate	Unilateral-adv.

(continued)

693

TABLE III.1.—Continued

NUM.	INTERNATIONAL CRISIS ACTORS	SUM. PAGE	PC OR REG.	TRIG. DATE	TERM. DATE	SYSTEM LEVEL POWER STATUS	TRIGGERING ENTITY	CRISIS TRIGGER
152	SUEZ NATN.-WAR	275	23	07/26/56	03/12/57	MAINLY DOMINANT	EGYPT	ECONOMIC
	France			07/26/56	11/06/56	Great power	Egypt	Economic
	UK			07/26/56	11/06/56	Great power	Egypt	Economic
	Egypt			10/29/56	03/12/57	Middle power	Israel	Violent
	USSR			10/29/56	11/08/56	Superpower	Israel	Indirect viol.
	US			11/05/56	11/08/56	Superpower	USSR	Other non-viol.
	Israel			11/05/56	03/12/57	Small power	USSR	Other non-viol.
153	QALQILYA	277	23	09/13/56	10/88/56	SUBSYSTEM	ISRAEL	VIOLENT
	Jordan			09/13/56	10/88/56	Small power	Israel	Violent
	Israel			10/12/56	10/15/56	Small power	Iraq	Political
154	POLAND LIBERALIZATION	258	21	10/15/56	10/22/56	MAINLY SUBSYSTEM	POLAND	EXT. CHANGE
	USSR			10/15/56	10/22/56	Superpower	Poland	Ext. change
	Poland			10/18/56	10/22/56	Middle power	USSR	Political
155	HUNGARIAN UPRISING	604	43	10/23/56	01/99/57	MAINLY SUBSYSTEM	NON-STATE ACTOR	EXT. CHANGE
	USSR			10/23/56	11/14/56	Superpower	Non-state actor	Ext. change
	Hungary			10/23/56	01/99/57	Small power	USSR	Ext. change
156	MOCORON INCIDENT	140	8	02/26/57	05/09/57	SUBSYSTEM	HONDURAS	POLITICAL
	Nicaragua			02/26/57	05/05/57	Small power	Honduras	Political
	Honduras			04/18/57	05/09/57	Small power	Nicaragua	Violent
157	JORDAN REGIME	637	44	04/04/57	05/03/57	SUBSYSTEM	NON-STATE ACTOR	INTERNAL CHAL.
	Jordan			04/04/57	05/03/57	Small power	Non-state actor	Internal chal.
158	FRANCE/TUNISIA	430	40	05/31/57	06/17/58	SUBSYSTEM	FRANCE	VIOLENT
	Tunisia			05/31/57	06/17/58	Small power	France	Violent
159	SYRIA/TURKEY CONFRNT.	345	27	08/18/57	10/29/57	MAINLY SUBSYSTEM	SYRIA	POLITICAL
	Turkey			08/18/57	10/29/57	Middle power	Syria	Political
	US			08/18/57	10/29/57	Superpower	Syria	Political
	Syria			09/07/57	10/29/57	Small power	US	Political
160	IFNI	431	40	11/23/57	04/99/58	SUBSYSTEM	NON-STATE ACTOR	VIOLENT
	Spain			11/23/57	04/99/58	Middle power	Non-state actor	Violent
161	WEST IRIAN I	207	14	12/01/57	99/99/99	SUBSYSTEM	INDONESIA	ECONOMIC
	Netherlands			12/01/57	99/99/99	Small power	Indonesia	Economic
162	FORMATION OF UAR	638	44	02/01/58	02/14/58	SUBSYSTEM	MULTI-STATE	POLITICAL
	Iraq			02/01/58	02/14/58	Middle power	Multi-state	Political
	Jordan			02/01/58	02/14/58	Small power	Multi-state	Political
163	EGYPT/SUDAN BORDER I	432	40	02/09/58	02/25/58	SUBSYSTEM	EGYPT	NON-VIOL. MIL.
	Sudan			02/09/58	02/25/58	Small power	Egypt	Non-viol. mil.

RAVITY OF THREAT	CRISIS MGMT. TECHNIQUE	VIOLENCE	US ACTIV.	USSR ACTIV.	GLOBAL ORG. INVOLVEMENT	OUTCOME: SUBSTANCE	OUTCOME: FORM
E DAMAGE	MULT. W/VIOL.	WAR			EMER. MIL. FORCE	AMBIGUOUS	UNILATERAL
damage	Mult. w/viol.	War	Political	Semi-mil.	Emer. mil. force	Defeat	Compliance
damage	Mult. w/viol.	War	Political	Semi-mil.	Emer. mil. force	Defeat	Compliance
damage	Mult. w/viol.	War	Political	Semi-mil.	Emer. mil. force	Victory	Unilateral-adv.
nce	Non-viol. mil.	No violence	Political	SU actor	Emer. mil. force	Victory	Spillover
nce	Non-viol. mil.	No violence	US actor	Semi-mil.	Emer. mil. force	Victory	Spillover
damage	Mult. w/viol.	War	Political	Semi-mil.	Emer. mil. force	Compromise	Compliance
TORY	MULT. W/VIOL.	SERIOUS CLASHES			DISCUSSION	AMBIGUOUS	UNILATERAL
	Mult. w/viol.	Serious clashes	Political	None	Discussion	Stalemate	Unilateral-ally
ory	Non-viol. mil.	Serious clashes	Political	None	None	Victory	Unilateral-adv.
ICAL REGIME	NEGOTIATION	NO VIOLENCE			NONE	AMBIGUOUS	TACIT UNDERSTANDING
nce	Multiple, no viol.	No violence	Propaganda	SU actor	None	Compromise	Tacit understanding
al regime	Negotiation	No violence	Propaganda	Political	None	Compromise	Tacit understanding
ICAL REGIME	VIOLENCE	SERIOUS CLASHES			CALL FOR ACTION	DEFINITIVE	UNILATERAL
nce	Violence	Serious clashes	Propaganda	SU actor	Condemnation	Victory	Unilateral-self
al regime	Violence	Serious clashes	Propaganda	Direct mil.	Call for action	Defeat	Other-misc.
TORY	MULT. W/VIOL.	MINOR CLASHES			NONE	AMBIGUOUS	FORMAL AGMT.
ory	Mult. w/viol.	Minor clashes	Political	None	None	Stalemate	Formal agmt.
ory	Mult. w/viol.	Minor clashes	Political	None	None	Stalemate	Formal agmt.
ICAL REGIME	NEGOTIATION	MINOR CLASHES			NONE	DEFINITIVE	UNILATERAL
al regime	Negotiation	Minor clashes	Semi-mil.	Covert	None	Victory	Unilateral-ally
ICAL REGIME	NEGOTIATION	MINOR CLASHES			DISCUSSION	AMBIGUOUS	SEMI-FORMAL AGMT.
al regime	Negotiation	Minor clashes	Political	None	Discussion	Compromise	Semi-formal agmt.
ICAL REGIME	MULTIPLE, NO VIOL.	NO VIOLENCE			DISCUSSION	DEFINITIVE	UNILATERAL
al regime	Multiple, no viol.	No violence	Semi-mil.	Semi-mil.	Discussion	Victory	Unilateral-adv.
nce	Multiple, no viol.	No violence	US actor	Political	Discussion	Victory	Unilateral-adv.
al regime	Multiple, no viol.	No violence	Political	Semi-mil.	Discussion	Victory	Unilateral-ally
ITORY	VIOLENCE	SERIOUS CLASHES			NONE	DEFINITIVE	FADED
ory	Violence	Serious clashes	Political	None	None	Victory	Faded
OMIC	NEGOTIATION	NO VIOLENCE			DISCUSSION	AMBIGUOUS	FADED
mic	Negotiation	No violence	Political	None	Discussion	Stalemate	Faded
ENCE	NEGOTIATION	NO VIOLENCE			NONE	AMBIGUOUS	OTHER
al regime	Negotiation	No violence	None	None	None	Stalemate	Other-ally
nce	Negotiation	No violence	None	None	None	Stalemate	Other-ally
ITORY	MULTIPLE, NO VIOL.	NO VIOLENCE			DISCUSSION	DEFINITIVE	UNILATERAL
ory	Multiple, no viol.	No violence	None	None	Discussion	Victory	Unilateral-adv.

(continued)

TABLE III.1.—*Continued*

NUM.	INTERNATIONAL CRISIS ACTORS	SUM. PAGE	PC OR REG.	TRIG. DATE	TERM. DATE	SYSTEM LEVEL POWER STATUS	TRIGGERING ENTITY	CRISIS TRIGGER
164	ABORT. COUP INDONESIA	208	14	02/21/58	05/20/58	SUBSYSTEM	NON-STATE ACTOR	NON-VIOL. MIL.
	Indonesia			02/21/58	05/20/58	Middle power	Non-state actor	Non-viol. mil.
165	IRAQ-LEB. UPHEAVAL	639	44	05/08/58	10/88/58	MAINLY SUBSYSTEM	NON-STATE ACTOR	INTERNAL CHAL.
	Lebanon			05/08/58	10/14/58	Small power	Non-state actor	Internal chal.
	Jordan			07/14/58	10/88/58	Small power	Iraq	Ext. change
	UK			07/14/58	10/88/58	Great power	Iraq	Ext. change
	US			07/14/58	10/14/58	Superpower	Iraq	Political
166	TAIWAN STRAIT II	384	30	07/17/58	10/23/58	MAINLY DOMINANT	CHINA (PRC)	NON-VIOL. MIL.
	Taiwan			07/17/58	10/23/58	Small power	China (PRC)	Non-viol. mil.
	US			08/23/58	09/14/58	Superpower	China (PRC)	Indirect viol.
	China (PRC)			08/27/58	09/30/58	Great power	US	Non-viol. mil.
167	CAMBODIA/THAILAND	182	13	07/24/58	02/06/59	SUBSYSTEM	CAMBODIA	POLITICAL
	Thailand			07/24/58	02/06/59	Small power	Cambodia	Political
	Cambodia			09/01/58	02/06/59	Small power	Thailand	Violent
168	BERLIN DEADLINE	346	27	11/27/58	09/15/59	DOMINANT SYSTEM	USSR	POLITICAL
	France			11/27/58	09/15/59	Great power	USSR	Political
	UK			11/27/58	09/15/59	Great power	USSR	Political
	US			11/27/58	09/15/59	Superpower	USSR	Political
	West Germany			11/27/58	09/15/59	Middle power	USSR	Political
	East Germany			12/31/58	09/15/59	Middle power	Multi-state	Political
	USSR			12/31/58	09/15/59	Superpower	Multi-state	Political
169	MEX./GUAT. FISHING	504	41	12/29/58	02/01/59	SUBSYSTEM	MEXICO	ECONOMIC
	Guatemala			12/29/58	02/01/59	Small power	Mexico	Economic
	Mexico			12/31/58	01/12/59	Middle power	Guatemala	Violent
170	CEN. AMERICA/CUBA I	505	41	04/25/59	12/88/59	SUBSYSTEM	NON-STATE ACTOR	VIOLENT
	Panama			04/25/59	05/04/59	Small power	Non-state actor	Violent
	Nicaragua			06/01/59	06/14/59	Small power	Non-state actor	Violent
	Dominican Republic			06/14/59	12/88/59	Small power	Non-state actor	Violent
	Haiti			08/13/59	09/05/59	Small power	Non-state actor	Violent
171	CHINA/INDIA BRD. I	548	42	08/25/59	04/19/60	MAINLY SUBSYSTEM	INDIA	NON-VIOL. MIL.
	China (PRC)			08/25/59	04/19/60	Great power	India	Non-viol. mil.
	India			08/28/59	04/19/60	Great power	China (PRC)	Violent
172	SHATT-AL-ARAB I	301	24	11/28/59	01/04/60	SUBSYSTEM	IRAN	POLITICAL
	Iraq			11/28/59	01/04/60	Middle power	Iran	Political
	Iran			12/02/59	01/04/60	Middle power	Iraq	Political

696

GRAVITY OF THREAT	CRISIS MGMT. TECHNIQUE	VIOLENCE	US ACTIV.	USSR ACTIV.	GLOBAL ORG. INVOLVEMENT	OUTCOME: SUBSTANCE	OUTCOME: FORM
TICAL REGIME	VIOLENCE	SERIOUS CLASHES			NONE	DEFINITIVE	UNILATERAL
ical regime	Violence	Serious clashes	Covert	Political	None	Victory	Unilateral-adv.
TICAL REGIME	MULT. W/VIOL.	MINOR CLASHES			OBSERVERS	AMBIGUOUS	UNILATERAL
ical regime	Mult. w/viol.	Minor clashes	Direct mil.	Semi-mil.	Observers	Compromise	Unilateral-self
ical regime	Non-viol. mil.	No violence	Semi-mil.	Political	Condemnation	Victory	Unilateral-self
ence	Non-viol. mil.	No violence	Semi-mil.	Political	Condemnation	Victory	Unilateral-ally
ence	Non-viol. mil.	Minor clashes	US actor	Semi-mil.	Observers	Victory	Unilateral-ally
VE DAMAGE	VIOLENCE	SERIOUS CLASHES			DISCUSSION	DEFINITIVE	TACIT UNDERSTANDING
e damage	Violence	Serious clashes	Semi-mil.	Political	Discussion	Victory	Tacit understanding
ence	Negotiation	No violence	US actor	Political	Discussion	Victory	Semi-formal agmt.
e damage	Mult. w/viol.	Serious clashes	Semi-mil.	Covert	Discussion	Victory	Tacit understanding
ITICAL REGIME	MULT. W/VIOL.	MINOR CLASHES			MEDIATION	AMBIGUOUS	SEMI-FORMAL AGMT.
ical regime	Mult. w/viol.	Minor clashes	None	Political	Mediation	Stalemate	Semi-formal agmt.
)	Mediation	Minor clashes	None	Political	Mediation	Stalemate	Semi-formal agmt.
LUENCE	NEGOTIATION	NO VIOLENCE			GOOD OFFICES	AMBIGUOUS	FORMAL AGMT.
ence	Negotiation	No violence	Political	Political	Good offices	Stalemate	Formal agmt.
ence	Negotiation	No violence	Political	Political	Good offices	Stalemate	Formal agmt.
ence	Negotiation	No violence	US actor	Political	Good offices	Stalemate	Formal agmt.
tory	Negotiation	No violence	Political	Political	Good offices	Stalemate	Formal agmt.
ical regime	Negotiation	No violence	Political	Political	Good offices	Stalemate	Formal agmt.
e damage	Negotiation	No violence	Political	SU actor	Good offices	Stalemate	Formal agmt.
NOMIC	MULT. W/VIOL.	MINOR CLASHES			NONE	AMBIGUOUS	SEMI-FORMAL AGMT.
omic	Mult. w/viol.	Minor clashes	None	None	None	Compromise	Semi-formal agmt.
omic	Negotiation	Minor clashes	None	None	None	Compromise	Semi-formal agmt.
ITICAL REGIME	MULT. W/VIOL.	MINOR CLASHES			OTHER	DEFINITIVE	UNILATERAL
ical regime	Negotiation	No violence	Semi-mil.	None	None	Victory	Other-GO intv.
ical regime	Mult. w/viol.	Minor clashes	Political	None	None	Victory	Unilateral-self
ical regime	Mult. w/viol.	Minor clashes	Political	None	Other	Victory	Other-misc.
ical regime	Negotiation	Minor clashes	Semi-mil.	None	None	Victory	Unilateral-adv.
RITORY	MULT. W/VIOL.	MINOR CLASHES			NONE	AMBIGUOUS	SEMI-FORMAL AGMT.
itory	Mult. w/viol.	Minor clashes	Political	Political	None	Stalemate	Semi-formal agmt.
tory	Negotiation	Minor clashes	Political	Political	None	Stalemate	Semi-formal agmt.
RITORY	MULTIPLE, NO VIOL.	MINOR CLASHES			NONE	AMBIGUOUS	TACIT UNDERSTANDING
itory	Multiple, no viol.	Minor clashes	Political	Propaganda	None	Stalemate	Tacit understanding
itory	Multiple, no viol.	Minor clashes	Political	Propaganda	None	Stalemate	Tacit understanding

(continued)

697

TABLE III.1.—*Continued*

NUM.	INTERNATIONAL CRISIS ACTORS	SUM. PAGE	PC OR REG.	TRIG. DATE	TERM. DATE	SYSTEM LEVEL POWER STATUS	TRIGGERING ENTITY	CRISIS TRIGGER
173	ROTTEM	278	23	02/15/60	03/08/60	SUBSYSTEM	ISRAEL	NON-VIOL. MIL.
	Egypt			02/15/60	03/01/60	Great power	Israel	Non-viol. mil.
	Israel			02/23/60	03/08/60	Middle power	Egypt	Non-viol. mil.
174	GHANA/TOGO BORDER I	433	40	03/66/60	04/01/60	SUBSYSTEM	TOGO	POLITICAL
	Ghana			03/66/60	04/01/60	Middle power	Togo	Political
175	FAILED ASS. VENEZUELA	506	41	06/24/60	09/77/60	SUBSYSTEM	NON-STATE ACTOR	INTERNAL CHAL.
	Venezuela			06/24/60	08/20/60	Middle power	Non-state actor	Internal chal.
	Dominican Republic			06/25/60	09/77/60	Small power	Venezuela	Political
176	CONGO I-KATANGA	434	40	07/05/60	02/15/62	MAINLY SUBSYSTEM	NON-STATE ACTOR	VIOLENT
	Belgium			07/05/60	07/15/60	Great power	Non-state actor	Violent
	Congo			07/10/60	07/15/60	Small power	Belgium	Violent
	Congo			07/11/60	02/15/62	Small power	Non-state actor	Internal chal.
177	MALI FEDERATION	435	40	08/20/60	09/22/60	SUBSYSTEM	NON-STATE ACTOR	INTERNAL CHAL.
	Mali			08/20/60	09/22/60	Small power	Non-state actor	Internal chal.
	Senegal			08/20/60	09/22/60	Small power	Mali	Political
178	CEN. AMERICA/CUBA II	507	41	11/09/60	12/07/60	SUBSYSTEM	NON-STATE ACTOR	VIOLENT
	Nicaragua			11/09/60	12/07/60	Small power	Non-state actor	Violent
	Guatemala			11/13/60	12/07/60	Small power	Non-state actor	Internal chal.
179	ETHIOPIA/SOMALIA	97	3	12/26/60	99/99/61	SUBSYSTEM	SOMALIA	VIOLENT
	Ethiopia			12/26/60	99/99/61	Middle power	Somalia	Violent
180	PATHET LAO OFFENSIVE	183	13	03/09/61	05/16/61	MAINLY DOMINANT	NON-STATE ACTOR	INDIRECT VIOL.
	US			03/09/61	05/16/61	Superpower	Non-state actor	Indirect viol.
	Thailand			04/10/61	05/16/61	Small power	Non-state actor	Indirect viol.
181	BAY OF PIGS	348	27	04/15/61	04/24/61	MAINLY SUBSYSTEM	NON-STATE ACTOR	VIOLENT
	Cuba			04/15/61	04/19/61	Small power	Non-state actor	Violent
	US			04/15/61	04/24/61	Superpower	Cuba	Political
182	PUSHTUNISTAN III	149	9	05/19/61	01/29/62	SUBSYSTEM	AFGHANISTAN	VIOLENT
	Pakistan			05/19/61	01/29/62	Middle power	Afghanistan	Violent
	Afghanistan			08/23/61	01/29/62	Small power	Pakistan	Political
183	KUWAIT INDEPENDENCE	313	25	06/19/61	07/13/61	SUBSYSTEM	UK	POLITICAL
	Iraq			06/19/61	07/13/61	Middle power	UK	Political
	Kuwait			06/25/61	07/13/61	Small power	Iraq	Political
	UK			06/30/61	07/13/61	Great power	Kuwait	Other non-viol.
184	BIZERTA	436	40	07/17/61	09/29/61	SUBSYSTEM	TUNISIA	POLITICAL
	France			07/17/61	09/29/61	Great power	Tunisia	Political
	Tunisia			07/19/61	09/29/61	Small power	France	Violent

GRAVITY OF THREAT	CRISIS MGMT. TECHNIQUE	VIOLENCE	US ACTIV.	USSR ACTIV.	GLOBAL ORG. INVOLVEMENT	OUTCOME: SUBSTANCE	OUTCOME: FORM
_UENCE	NON-VIOL. MIL.	NO VIOLENCE			NONE	AMBIGUOUS	TACIT UNDERSTANDING
ence	Non-viol. mil.	No violence	None	Political	None	Victory	Tacit understanding
ence	Non-viol. mil.	No violence	None	Political	None	Stalemate	Tacit understanding
RITORY	NON-VIOL. MIL.	NO VIOLENCE			NONE	DEFINITIVE	TACIT UNDERSTANDING
itory	Non-viol. mil.	No violence	None	None	None	Victory	Tacit understanding
ITICAL REGIME	NON-VIOL. MIL.	NO VIOLENCE			DISCUSSION	DEFINITIVE	OTHER
ical regime	Non-mil. pres.	No violence	Political	Political	Discussion	Victory	Other-GO intv.
ical regime	Non-viol. mil.	No violence	Political	Political	Discussion	Defeat	Other-misc.
ITICAL REGIME	MULT. W/VIOL.	SERIOUS CLASHES			EMER. MIL. FORCE	DEFINITIVE	OTHER
er	Mult. w/viol.	Serious clashes	Political	Political	Emer. mil. force	Defeat	Semi-formal agmt.
ical regime	Negotiation	Minor clashes	Political	None	Emer. mil. force	Victory	Semi-formal agmt.
e damage	Mult. w/viol.	Serious clashes	Political	Semi-mil.	Emer. mil. force	Victory	Other-non.-st.
RITORY	NON-VIOL. MIL.	NO VIOLENCE			DISCUSSION	DEFINITIVE	UNILATERAL
itory	Multiple, no viol.	No violence	None	Political	Discussion	Defeat	Unilateral-self
itory	Non-viol. mil.	No violence	None	Political	Discussion	Victory	Unilateral-adv.
ITICAL REGIME	NEGOTIATION	MINOR CLASHES			OTHER	DEFINITIVE	TACIT UNDERSTANDING
ical regime	Negotiation	Minor clashes	Semi-mil.	Propaganda	Other	Victory	Tacit understanding
ical regime	Negotiation	Minor clashes	Semi-mil.	Propaganda	Other	Victory	Tacit understanding
VE DAMAGE	VIOLENCE	SERIOUS CLASHES			NONE	AMBIGUOUS	FADED
e damage	Violence	Serious clashes	None	None	None	Stalemate	Faded
ITICAL REGIME	NON-VIOL. MIL.	NO VIOLENCE			NONE	DEFINITIVE	OTHER
ence	Negotiation	No violence	US actor	Political	None	Victory	Other-GO intv.
ical regime	Non-viol. mil.	No violence	Semi-mil.	Political	None	Victory	Other-GO intv.
ITICAL REGIME	VIOLENCE	MINOR CLASHES			CALL FOR ACTION	DEFINITIVE	UNILATERAL
ical regime	Violence	Minor clashes	Semi-mil.	Political	Call for action	Victory	Unilateral-self
ence	Non-mil. pres.	No violence	US actor	Political	Call for action	Defeat	Unilateral-self
RRITORY	VIOLENCE	MINOR CLASHES			NONE	AMBIGUOUS	SEMI-FORMAL AGMT.
itory	Violence	Minor clashes	Political	Semi-mil.	None	Compromise	Semi-formal agmt.
er	Mediation	Minor clashes	Political	Economic	None	Compromise	Semi-formal agmt.
STENCE	NON-VIOL. MIL.	NO VIOLENCE			DISCUSSION	DEFINITIVE	UNILATERAL
itory	Non-viol. mil.	No violence	None	Political	Discussion	Defeat	Unilateral-self
tence	Non-viol. mil.	No violence	None	Political	Discussion	Victory	Unilateral-adv.
nomic	Non-viol. mil.	No violence	None	Political	Discussion	Victory	Unilateral-adv.
VE DAMAGE	VIOLENCE	SERIOUS CLASHES			CONDEMNATION	AMBIGUOUS	FORMAL AGMT.
ence	Violence	Serious clashes	None	Economic	Condemnation	Compromise	Formal agmt.
e damage	Mult. w/viol.	Serious clashes	None	Economic	Call for action	Compromise	Formal agmt.

(continued)

TABLE III.1.—*Continued*

NUM.	INTERNATIONAL CRISIS ACTORS	SUM. PAGE	PC OR REG.	TRIG. DATE	TERM. DATE	SYSTEM LEVEL POWER STATUS	TRIGGERING ENTITY	CRISIS TRIGGER
185	BERLIN WALL	350	27	08/66/61	10/28/61	DOMINANT SYSTEM	NON-STATE ACTOR	INTERNAL CHAL.
	East Germany			08/66/61	08/13/61	Middle power	Non-state actor	Internal chal.
	USSR			08/66/61	10/28/61	Superpower	Non-state actor	Ext. change
	France			08/13/61	10/17/61	Great power	East Germany	Political
	UK			08/13/61	10/17/61	Great power	East Germany	Political
	West Germany			08/13/61	10/17/61	Middle power	East Germany	Political
	US			08/13/61	10/28/61	Superpower	USSR	Political
186	VIETCONG ATTACK	185	13	09/18/61	11/15/61	SUBSYSTEM	NON-STATE ACTOR	INTERNAL CHAL.
	South Vietnam			09/18/61	11/15/61	Small power	Non-state actor	Internal chal.
	US			09/18/61	11/15/61	Superpower	Non-state actor	Indirect viol.
187	WEST IRIAN II	209	14	09/26/61	08/15/62	SUBSYSTEM	NETHERLANDS	POLITICAL
	Indonesia			09/26/61	08/15/62	Great power	Netherlands	Political
	Netherlands			12/19/61	08/15/62	Middle power	Indonesia	Non-viol. mil.
188	BREAKUP OF UAR	641	44	09/28/61	10/05/61	SUBSYSTEM	NON-STATE ACTOR	INTERNAL CHAL.
	Egypt			09/28/61	10/05/61	Great power	Non-state actor	Internal chal.
189	SOV. NOTE/FINLAND II	236	17	10/30/61	11/24/61	SUBSYSTEM	USSR	POLITICAL
	Finland			10/30/61	11/24/61	Small power	USSR	Political
190	GOA II	549	42	12/11/61	12/19/61	SUBSYSTEM	INDIA	POLITICAL
	Portugal			12/11/61	12/19/61	Small power	India	Political
191	MALI/MAURITANIA	437	40	03/29/62	02/18/63	SUBSYSTEM	NON-STATE ACTOR	INTERNAL CHAL.
	Mauritania			03/29/62	02/18/63	Small power	Non-state actor	Internal chal.
192	TAIWAN STRAIT III	386	30	04/22/62	06/27/62	MAINLY DOMINANT	TAIWAN	POLITICAL
	China (PRC)			04/22/62	06/27/62	Great power	Taiwan	Political
193	NAM THA	186	13	05/06/62	06/12/62	MAINLY SUBSYSTEM	NON-STATE ACTOR	INDIRECT VIOL.
	Thailand			05/06/62	06/12/62	Small power	Non-state actor	Indirect viol.
	US			05/06/62	06/12/62	Superpower	Non-state actor	Indirect viol.
194	CHINA/INDIA BDR. II	551	42	09/08/62	01/23/63	MAINLY SUBSYSTEM	CHINA (PRC)	VIOLENT
	India			09/08/62	01/23/63	Great power	China (PRC)	Violent
	China (PRC)			10/04/62	11/21/62	Great power	India	Non-viol. mil.
	India			11/16/62	12/01/62	Great power	China (PRC)	Violent
195	YEMEN WAR I	324	26	09/26/62	04/15/63	SUBSYSTEM	NON-STATE ACTOR	INDIRECT VIOL.
	Jordan			09/26/62	04/15/63	Small power	Non-state actor	Indirect viol.
	Saudi Arabia			09/26/62	04/15/63	Middle power	Non-state actor	Indirect viol.
	Egypt			10/01/62	04/15/63	Great power	Saudi Arabia	Non-viol. mil.
	Yemen			10/01/62	04/15/63	Small power	Saudi Arabia	Non-viol. mil.

GRAVITY OF THREAT	CRISIS MGMT. TECHNIQUE	VIOLENCE	US ACTIV.	USSR ACTIV.	GLOBAL ORG. INVOLVEMENT	OUTCOME: SUBSTANCE	OUTCOME: FORM
TICAL REGIME	NON-VIOL. MIL.	NO VIOLENCE			NONE	AMBIGUOUS	TACIT UNDERSTANDING
cal regime	Negotiation	No violence	Direct mil.	Direct mil.	None	Victory	Unilateral-self
ence	Non-viol. mil.	No violence	Direct mil.	SU actor	None	Victory	Tacit understanding
ence	Negotiation	No violence	Direct mil.	Direct mil.	None	Defeat	Unilateral-adv.
ence	Negotiation	No violence	Direct mil.	Direct mil.	None	Defeat	Unilateral-adv.
omic	Negotiation	No violence	Direct mil.	Direct mil.	None	Defeat	Unilateral-adv.
ence	Negotiation	No violence	US actor	Direct mil.	None	Compromise	Tacit understanding
TICAL REGIME	MULT. W/VIOL.	MINOR CLASHES			NONE	DEFINITIVE	UNILATERAL
ical regime	Mult. w/viol.	Minor clashes	Semi-mil.	Covert	None	Victory	Unilateral-ally
ence	Non-viol. mil.	No violence	US actor	Covert	None	Victory	Unilateral-self
RITORY	MULTIPLE, NO VIOL.	MINOR CLASHES			GOOD OFFICES	DEFINITIVE	FORMAL AGMT.
tory	Multiple, no viol.	Minor clashes	Political	Semi-mil.	Good offices	Victory	Formal agmt.
ence	Negotiation	Minor clashes	Political	Semi-mil.	Good offices	Defeat	Formal agmt.
UENCE	NEGOTIATION	MINOR CLASHES			NONE	DEFINITIVE	UNILATERAL
ence	Negotiation	Minor clashes	None	None	None	Defeat	Unilateral-adv.
ITICAL REGIME	NEGOTIATION	NO VIOLENCE			NONE	AMBIGUOUS	SEMI-FORMAL AGMT.
ical regime	Negotiation	No violence	None	Political	None	Stalemate	Semi-formal agmt.
RITORY	MEDIATION	MINOR CLASHES			DISCUSSION	DEFINITIVE	IMPOSED AGMT.
itory	Mediation	Minor clashes	Political	Political	Discussion	Defeat	Imposed-imposee
RITORY	NEGOTIATION	MINOR CLASHES			NONE	AMBIGUOUS	FORMAL AGMT.
itory	Negotiation	Minor clashes	None	None	None	Compromise	Formal agmt.
ITICAL REGIME	MULTIPLE, NO VIOL.	MINOR CLASHES			NONE	AMBIGUOUS	UNILATERAL
ical regime	Multiple, no viol.	Minor clashes	Political	None	None	Stalemate	Unilateral-adv.
ITICAL REGIME	NON-VIOL. MIL.	NO VIOLENCE			NONE	DEFINITIVE	TACIT UNDERSTANDING
ical regime	Non-viol. mil.	No violence	Semi-mil.	Political	None	Victory	Tacit understanding
ence	Non-viol. mil.	No violence	US actor	Political	None	Victory	Tacit understanding
RITORY	VIOLENCE	WAR			NONE	DEFINITIVE	UNILATERAL
itory	Violence	War	Semi-mil.	Political	None	Defeat	Tacit understanding
itory	Violence	War	Semi-mil.	Political	None	Victory	Unilateral-self
ve damage	Mult. w/viol.	War	Semi-mil.	Political	None	Defeat	Unilateral-adv.
ITICAL REGIME	MULT. W/VIOL.	WAR			FACT-FINDING	AMBIGUOUS	FORMAL AGMT.
tical regime	Mult. w/viol.	War	Semi-mil.	Economic	Fact-finding	Stalemate	Unilateral-self
tical regime	Mult. w/viol.	War	Semi-mil.	Economic	Fact-finding	Stalemate	Formal agmt.
ence	Mult. w/viol.	War	Semi-mil.	Economic	Fact-finding	Stalemate	Formal agmt.
tical regime	Mult. w/viol.	War	Semi-mil.	Economic	Fact-finding	Stalemate	Formal agmt.

(continued)

TABLE III.1.—Continued

NUM.	INTERNATIONAL CRISIS ACTORS	SUM. PAGE	PC OR REG.	TRIG. DATE	TERM. DATE	SYSTEM LEVEL POWER STATUS	TRIGGERING ENTITY	CRISIS TRIGGER
196	CUBAN MISSILES	352	27	10/16/62	11/20/62	DOMINANT SYSTEM	USSR	EXT. CHANGE
	US			10/16/62	11/20/62	Superpower	USSR	Ext. change
	Cuba			10/22/62	11/20/62	Small power	US	Non-viol. mil.
	USSR			10/22/62	11/20/62	Superpower	US	Non-viol. mil.
197	MALAYSIA FEDERATION	552	42	02/11/63	08/09/65	SUBSYSTEM	INDONESIA	POLITICAL
	Malaysia			02/11/63	08/09/65	Small power	Indonesia	Political
	Indonesia			07/09/63	08/09/65	Great power	Multi-state	Political
198	DOM. REP./HAITI II	508	41	04/26/63	06/03/63	SUBSYSTEM	HAITI	OTHER NON-VIOL.
	Dominican Republic			04/26/63	05/14/63	Small power	Haiti	Other non-viol.
	Haiti			04/27/63	06/03/63	Small power	Dominican Republic	Political
199	ALGERIA/MOROCCO BDR.	438	40	10/01/63	11/04/63	SUBSYSTEM	MOROCCO	NON-VIOL. MIL.
	Algeria			10/01/63	11/04/63	Middle power	Morocco	Non-viol. mil.
	Morocco			10/08/63	11/04/63	Middle power	Algeria	Violent
200	CUBA/VENEZUELA	509	41	11/01/63	12/01/63	SUBSYSTEM	NON-STATE ACTOR	INTERNAL CHAL.
	Venezuela			11/01/63	12/01/63	Middle power	Non-state actor	Internal chal.
201	KENYA/SOMALIA	439	40	11/20/63	03/04/64	SUBSYSTEM	SOMALIA	NON-VIOL. MIL.
	Kenya			11/20/63	03/04/64	Small power	Somalia	Non-viol. mil.
202	CYPRUS I	366	28	11/30/63	08/10/64	SUBSYSTEM	CYPRUS	POLITICAL
	Turkey			11/30/63	08/10/64	Middle power	Cyprus	Political
	Cyprus			12/06/63	08/10/64	Small power	Turkey	Political
	Greece			12/06/63	08/10/64	Middle power	Turkey	Political
203	JORDAN WATERS	279	23	12/11/63	05/05/64	SUBSYSTEM	ISRAEL	ECONOMIC
	Jordan			12/11/63	05/05/64	Small power	Israel	Economic
	Lebanon			12/11/63	05/05/64	Small power	Israel	Economic
	Syria			12/11/63	05/05/64	Small power	Israel	Economic
	Egypt			12/11/63	05/05/64	Great power	Israel	Economic
	Israel			01/16/64	05/05/64	Middle power	Multi-state	Economic
204	DAHOMEY/NIGER	440	40	12/21/63	01/04/64	SUBSYSTEM	DAHOMEY	NON-VIOL. MIL.
	Niger			12/21/63	01/04/64	Small power	Dahomey	Non-viol. mil.
	Dahomey			12/22/63	01/04/64	Small power	Niger	Political
205	BURUNDI/RWANDA	441	40	12/21/63	04/99/64	SUBSYSTEM	NON-STATE ACTOR	VIOLENT
	Rwanda			12/21/63	04/99/64	Small power	Non-state actor	Violent
	Burundi			01/22/64	04/99/64	Small power	Rwanda	Violent
206	PANAMA FLAG	510	41	01/09/64	01/12/64	MAINLY SUBSYSTEM	US	INTERNAL CHAL.
	Panama			01/09/64	01/12/64	Small power	US	Internal chal.
	US			01/10/64	01/12/64	Superpower	Panama	Political

GRAVITY OF THREAT	CRISIS MGMT. TECHNIQUE	VIOLENCE	US ACTIV.	USSR ACTIV.	GLOBAL ORG. INVOLVEMENT	OUTCOME: SUBSTANCE	OUTCOME: FORM
AVE DAMAGE	NON-VIOL. MIL.	MINOR CLASHES			MEDIATION	DEFINITIVE	SEMI-FORMAL AGMT.
ave damage	Non-viol. mil.	Minor clashes	US actor	Semi-mil.	Mediation	Victory	Semi-formal agmt.
ave damage	Negotiation	Minor clashes	Direct mil.	Semi-mil.	Mediation	Defeat	Semi-formal agmt.
ave damage	Non-viol. mil.	No violence	Direct mil.	SU actor	Mediation	Defeat	Semi-formal agmt.
ISTENCE	NEGOTIATION	NO VIOLENCE			DISCUSSION	DEFINITIVE	OTHER
stence	Negotiation	No violence	Economic	Political	Discussion	Victory	Other-misc.
uence	Negotiation	No violence	Economic	Political	Discussion	Victory	Other-misc.
LITICAL REGIME	MULTIPLE, NO VIOL.	NO VIOLENCE			DISCUSSION	AMBIGUOUS	UNILATERAL
itical regime	Multiple, no viol.	No violence	Semi-mil.	Political	Discussion	Compromise	Unilateral-adv.
itical regime	Negotiation	No violence	Semi-mil.	Political	Discussion	Compromise	Other-GO intv.
RRITORY	MULT. W/VIOL.	SERIOUS CLASHES			NONE	AMBIGUOUS	FORMAL AGMT.
rritory	Mult. w/viol.	Serious clashes	None	None	None	Compromise	Formal agmt.
rritory	Mult. w/viol.	Serious clashes	None	None	None	Compromise	Formal agmt.
LITICAL REGIME	NEGOTIATION	NO VIOLENCE			NONE	DEFINITIVE	OTHER
itical regime	Negotiation	No violence	Political	None	None	Victory	Other-misc.
RRITORY	NON-VIOL. MIL.	MINOR CLASHES			NONE	DEFINITIVE	TACIT UNDERSTANDING
rritory	Non-viol. mil.	Minor clashes	None	None	None	Victory	Tacit understanding
AVE DAMAGE	MULT. W/VIOL.	SERIOUS CLASHES			EMER. MIL. FORCE	AMBIGUOUS	FORMAL AGMT.
itical regime	Mult. w/viol.	Serious clashes	Political	Political	Emer. mil. force	Stalemate	Formal agmt.
ave damage	Mult. w/viol.	Serious clashes	Political	Political	Emer. mil. force	Stalemate	Formal agmt.
itical regime	Non-viol. mil.	No violence	Political	Political	Emer. mil. force	Stalemate	Spillover
ONOMIC	NON-VIOL. MIL.	NO VIOLENCE			OTHER	DEFINITIVE	UNILATERAL
onomic	Non-viol. mil.	No violence	Political	Political	Other	Defeat	Unilateral-adv.
onomic	Non-viol. mil.	No violence	Political	Political	Other	Defeat	Unilateral-adv.
onomic	Non-viol. mil.	No violence	Political	Political	Other	Defeat	Unilateral-adv.
ave damage	Non-viol. mil.	No violence	Political	Political	Other	Defeat	Unilateral-adv.
onomic	Non-mil. pres.	No violence	Political	Political	Other	Victory	Unilateral-self
RRITORY	MULTIPLE, NO VIOL.	NO VIOLENCE			NONE	DEFINITIVE	SEMI-FORMAL AGMT.
ritory	Multiple, no viol.	No violence	None	None	None	Victory	Semi-formal agmt.
onomic	Multiple, no viol.	No violence	None	None	None	Victory	Semi-formal agmt.
LITICAL REGIME	MULT. W/VIOL.	SERIOUS CLASHES			FACT-FINDING	DEFINITIVE	OTHER
itical regime	Mult. w/viol.	Serious clashes	None	None	Fact-finding	Victory	Other-misc.
ritory	Negotiation	Serious clashes	None	None	Fact-finding	Victory	Other-misc.
FLUENCE	MULT. W/VIOL.	MINOR CLASHES			OTHER	AMBIGUOUS	IMPOSED AGMT.
1D	Negotiation	Minor clashes	Political	None	Other	Compromise	Imposed-imposee
uence	Mult. w/viol.	Minor clashes	US actor	None	Other	Compromise	Imposed-imposer

(continued)

703

TABLE III.1.—Continued

NUM.	INTERNATIONAL CRISIS ACTORS	SUM. PAGE	PC OR REG.	TRIG. DATE	TERM. DATE	SYSTEM LEVEL POWER STATUS	TRIGGERING ENTITY	CRISIS TRIGGER
207	E. AFRICA REBELLIONS	442	40	01/19/64	01/30/64	SUBSYSTEM	NON-STATE ACTOR	INDIRECT VIOL.
	UK			01/19/64	01/30/64	Great power	Non-state actor	Indirect viol.
208	OGADEN I	97	3	02/07/64	03/30/64	SUBSYSTEM	SOMALIA	VIOLENT
	Ethiopia			02/07/64	03/30/64	Middle power	Somalia	Violent
	Somalia			02/08/64	03/30/64	Small power	Ethiopia	Violent
209	YEMEN WAR II	325	26	05/77/64	11/08/64	SUBSYSTEM	NON-STATE ACTOR	VIOLENT
	Yemen			05/77/64	11/08/64	Small power	Non-state actor	Violent
	Egypt			05/77/64	11/08/64	Great power	Non-state actor	Violent
	Saudi Arabia			08/99/64	11/08/64	Middle power	Egypt	Violent
210	GULF OF TONKIN	187	13	07/30/64	08/77/64	MAINLY SUBSYSTEM	SOUTH VIETNAM	VIOLENT
	North Vietnam			07/30/64	08/77/64	Middle power	South Vietnam	Violent
	US			08/02/64	08/07/64	Superpower	North Vietnam	Violent
211	CONGO II	443	40	08/04/64	12/30/64	MAINLY SUBSYSTEM	NON-STATE ACTOR	INTERNAL CHAL.
	Congo			08/04/64	12/30/64	Middle power	Non-state actor	Internal chal.
	Belgium			09/26/64	11/29/64	Middle power	Non-state actor	Political
	US			09/26/64	11/29/64	Superpower	Non-state actor	Political
	USSR			11/24/64	12/17/64	Superpower	Multi-state	Indirect viol.
212	YEMEN WAR III	326	26	12/03/64	08/25/65	SUBSYSTEM	NON-STATE ACTOR	VIOLENT
	Egypt			12/03/64	08/25/65	Great power	Non-state actor	Violent
	Yemen			12/03/64	08/25/65	Small power	Non-state actor	Violent
	Saudi Arabia			01/23/65	08/25/65	Middle power	Yemen	Violent
213	PLEIKU	189	13	02/07/65	03/88/65	SUBSYSTEM	NON-STATE ACTOR	VIOLENT
	South Vietnam			02/07/65	03/02/65	Small power	Non-state actor	Violent
	US			02/07/65	03/02/65	Superpower	Non-state actor	Violent
	North Vietnam			02/19/65	03/88/65	Middle power	US	Violent
214	RANN OF KUTCH	170	12	04/08/65	06/30/65	SUBSYSTEM	PAKISTAN	VIOLENT
	India			04/08/65	06/30/65	Middle power	Pakistan	Violent
	Pakistan			04/08/65	06/30/65	Middle power	India	Violent
215	DOMINICAN INTERVENTN.	511	41	04/24/65	08/31/65	SUBSYSTEM	NON-STATE ACTOR	INDIRECT VIOL.
	US			04/24/65	08/31/65	Superpower	Non-state actor	Indirect viol.
216	KASHMIR II	171	12	08/05/65	01/10/66	SUBSYSTEM	PAKISTAN	VIOLENT
	India			08/05/65	01/10/66	Middle power	Pakistan	Violent
	Pakistan			08/25/65	01/10/66	Middle power	India	Violent
	India			09/16/65	09/21/65	Middle power	China (PRC)	Political
217	GUINEA REGIME	445	40	10/09/65	12/77/65	SUBSYSTEM	NON-STATE ACTOR	INTERNAL CHAL.
	Guinea			10/09/65	12/77/65	Small power	Non-state actor	Internal chal.

704

GRAVITY OF THREAT	CRISIS MGMT. TECHNIQUE	VIOLENCE	US ACTIV.	USSR ACTIV.	GLOBAL ORG. INVOLVEMENT	OUTCOME: SUBSTANCE	OUTCOME: FORM
LUENCE	VIOLENCE	MINOR CLASHES			NONE	DEFINITIVE	UNILATERAL
ıence	Violence	Minor clashes	None	None	None	Victory	Unilateral-self
RITORY	MULT. W/VIOL.	SERIOUS CLASHES			GOOD OFFICES	DEFINITIVE	FORMAL AGMT.
itory	Mult. w/viol.	Serious clashes	Semi-mil.	Semi-mil.	Good offices	Victory	Formal agmt.
itory	Mult. w/viol.	Serious clashes	Semi-mil.	Semi-mil.	Good offices	Defeat	Formal agmt.
ITICAL REGIME	MULT. W/VIOL.	WAR			OBSERVERS	AMBIGUOUS	FORMAL AGMT.
tical regime	Mult. w/viol.	War	None	None	Observers	Stalemate	Formal agmt.
ıence	Mult. w/viol.	War	None	None	Observers	Stalemate	Formal agmt.
ıence	Mult. w/viol.	War	None	None	Observers	Stalemate	Formal agmt.
)	VIOLENCE	MINOR CLASHES			DISCUSSION	AMBIGUOUS	UNILATERAL
)	Non-viol. mil.	Minor clashes	Direct mil.	Political	Discussion	Stalemate	Unilateral-adv.
ıence	Violence	Minor clashes	US actor	Political	Discussion	Stalemate	Unilateral-self
RITORY	VIOLENCE	SERIOUS CLASHES			CALL FOR ACTION	DEFINITIVE	UNILATERAL
itory	Mult. w/viol.	Serious clashes	Direct mil.	Semi-mil.	Call for action	Victory	Other-GO intv.
ıence	Violence	Minor clashes	Direct mil.	Semi-mil.	Condemnation	Victory	Unilateral-self
ıence	Violence	Minor clashes	US actor	Semi-mil.	Condemnation	Victory	Unilateral-self
ıence	Multiple, no viol.	No violence	Direct mil.	SU actor	Discussion	Defeat	Unilateral-adv.
ITICAL REGIME	MULT. W/VIOL.	WAR			OTHER	AMBIGUOUS	FORMAL AGMT.
ıence	Mult. w/viol.	War	Political	Semi-mil.	Other	Stalemate	Formal agmt.
tical regime	Mult. w/viol.	War	Political	Semi-mil.	Other	Stalemate	Formal agmt.
ıence	Mult. w/viol.	War	Political	Semi-mil.	Other	Stalemate	Formal agmt.
AVE DAMAGE	VIOLENCE	SERIOUS CLASHES			OTHER	AMBIGUOUS	UNILATERAL
)	Violence	Serious clashes	Direct mil.	Semi-mil.	Other	Stalemate	Unilateral-ally
ıence	Violence	Serious clashes	US actor	Semi-mil.	Other	Stalemate	Unilateral-self
ve damage	Violence	Serious clashes	Direct mil.	Semi-mil.	Other	Stalemate	Unilateral-adv.
RITORY	MEDIATION	SERIOUS CLASHES			OTHER	AMBIGUOUS	FORMAL AGMT.
itory	Mediation	Serious clashes	Political	Political	Other	Compromise	Formal agmt.
itory	Mediation	Serious clashes	Political	Political	Other	Compromise	Formal agmt.
LUENCE	MULT. W/VIOL.	MINOR CLASHES			CALL FOR ACTION	DEFINITIVE	FORMAL AGMT.
ıence	Mult. w/viol.	Minor clashes	US actor	Political	Call for action	Victory	Formal agmt.
RITORY	MULT. W/VIOL.	WAR			OBSERVERS	AMBIGUOUS	SEMI-FORMAL AGMT.
itory	Mult. w/viol.	War	Political	Political	Condemnation	Compromise	Semi-formal agmt.
itory	Mult. w/viol.	War	Political	Political	Observers	Compromise	Semi-formal agmt.
itory	Negotiation	No violence	Political	Political	None	Victory	Unilateral-adv.
ITICAL REGIME	MULTIPLE, NO VIOL.	NO VIOLENCE			GOOD OFFICES	DEFINITIVE	TACIT UNDERSTANDING
tical regime	Multiple, no viol.	No violence	None	None	Good offices	Victory	Tacit understanding

(continued)

705

TABLE III.1.—*Continued*

NUM.	INTERNATIONAL CRISIS ACTORS	SUM. PAGE	PC OR REG.	TRIG. DATE	TERM. DATE	SYSTEM LEVEL POWER STATUS	TRIGGERING ENTITY	CRISIS TRIGGER
218	RHODESIA'S UDI	104	4	11/05/65	04/27/66	SUBSYSTEM	RHODESIA	POLITICAL
	Zambia			11/05/65	04/27/66	Small power	Rhodesia	Political
219	YEMEN WAR IV	327	26	10/14/66	09/26/67	SUBSYSTEM	NON-STATE ACTOR	VIOLENT
	Saudi Arabia			10/14/66	09/26/67	Middle power	Non-state actor	Violent
	Egypt			10/24/66	09/26/67	Great power	Non-state actor	Non-viol. mil.
	Yemen			10/24/66	09/26/67	Small power	Non-state actor	Non-viol. mil.
220	EL SAMU	280	23	11/12/66	11/15/66	SUBSYSTEM	NON-STATE ACTOR	VIOLENT
	Israel			11/12/66	11/15/66	Middle power	Non-state actor	Violent
	Jordan			11/13/66	11/15/66	Small power	Israel	Violent
221	CHE GUEVARA/BOLIVIA	512	41	03/23/67	10/10/67	SUBSYSTEM	NON-STATE ACTOR	INTERNAL CHAL.
	Bolivia			03/23/67	10/10/67	Small power	Non-state actor	Internal chal.
222	SIX DAY WAR	281	23	05/17/67	06/11/67	MAINLY SUBSYSTEM	EGYPT	NON-VIOL. MIL.
	Israel			05/17/67	06/11/67	Middle power	Egypt	Non-viol. mil.
	Jordan			06/05/67	06/11/67	Small power	Israel	Violent
	Egypt			06/05/67	06/11/67	Great power	Israel	Violent
	US			06/06/67	06/11/67	Superpower	USSR	Political
	Syria			06/09/67	06/10/67	Small power	Israel	Violent
	USSR			06/09/67	06/11/67	Superpower	Israel	Indirect viol.
223	CYPRUS II	368	28	11/15/67	12/04/67	SUBSYSTEM	CYPRUS	INDIRECT VIOL.
	Turkey			11/15/67	12/01/67	Middle power	Cyprus	Indirect viol.
	Greece			11/17/67	12/01/67	Middle power	Turkey	Non-viol. mil.
	Cyprus			11/17/67	12/04/67	Small power	Turkey	Non-viol. mil.
224	PUEBLO	218	15	01/21/68	12/23/68	DOMINANT SYSTEM	NORTH KOREA	VIOLENT
	South Korea			01/21/68	04/17/68	Small power	North Korea	Violent
	US			01/22/68	12/23/68	Superpower	North Korea	Violent
	North Korea			01/25/68	12/23/68	Small power	US	Non-viol. mil.
225	TET OFFENSIVE	189	13	01/30/68	03/31/68	MAINLY SUBSYSTEM	NON-STATE ACTOR	VIOLENT
	South Vietnam			01/30/68	02/24/68	Small power	Non-state actor	Violent
	US			02/27/68	03/31/68	Superpower	Non-state actor	Political
226	KARAMEH	282	23	03/18/68	03/22/68	SUBSYSTEM	NON-STATE ACTOR	VIOLENT
	Israel			03/18/68	03/21/68	Great power	Non-state actor	Violent
	Jordan			03/18/68	03/22/68	Small power	Israel	Indirect viol.

GRAVITY OF THREAT	CRISIS MGMT. TECHNIQUE	VIOLENCE	US ACTIV.	USSR ACTIV.	GLOBAL ORG. INVOLVEMENT	OUTCOME: SUBSTANCE	OUTCOME: FORM
TENCE	MULTIPLE, NO VIOL.	NO VIOLENCE			SANCTIONS	AMBIGUOUS	UNILATERAL
ence	Multiple, no viol.	No violence	Economic	Political	Sanctions	Compromise	Unilateral-ally
TICAL REGIME	MULT. W/VIOL.	WAR			GOOD OFFICES	AMBIGUOUS	FORMAL AGMT.
ence	Mult. w/viol.	War	Political	Semi-mil.	Good offices	Compromise	Formal agmt.
ence	Mult. w/viol.	War	Political	Semi-mil.	Good offices	Defeat	Formal agmt.
ical regime	Mult. w/viol.	War	Political	Semi-mil.	Good offices	Compromise	Formal agmt.
VE DAMAGE	VIOLENCE	SERIOUS CLASHES			GOOD OFFICES	AMBIGUOUS	UNILATERAL
)	Violence	Serious clashes	Political	None	Good offices	Stalemate	Unilateral-adv.
e damage	Mult. w/viol.	Serious clashes	Political	None	Good offices	Victory	Unilateral-self
TICAL REGIME	MULT. W/VIOL.	SERIOUS CLASHES			NONE	DEFINITIVE	UNILATERAL
ical regime	Mult. w/viol.	Serious clashes	Semi-mil.	None	None	Victory	Unilateral-self
TENCE	VIOLENCE	WAR			CALL FOR ACTION	DEFINITIVE	IMPOSED AGMT.
ence	Mult. w/viol.	War	Political	Political	Condemnation	Victory	Imposed-imposer
tory	Violence	War	Political	Political	Call for action	Defeat	Imposed-imposee
tory	Violence	War	Political	Political	Call for action	Defeat	Imposed-imposee
ence	Multiple, no viol.	No violence	US actor	Political	Call for action	Victory	Spillover
e damage	Violence	War	Political	Political	Call for action	Defeat	Imposed-imposee
ence	Multiple, no viol.	No violence	Political	SU actor	Call for action	Defeat	Spillover
RITORY	NON-VIOL. MIL.	MINOR CLASHES			DISCUSSION	DEFINITIVE	FORMAL AGMT.
ence	Non-viol. mil.	No violence	Political	None	Discussion	Victory	Formal agmt.
ence	Mediation	No violence	Political	None	Discussion	Defeat	Formal agmt.
tory	Mediation	Minor clashes	Political	None	Discussion	Defeat	Formal agmt.
LUENCE	MULTIPLE, NO VIOL.	MINOR CLASHES			DISCUSSION	DEFINITIVE	IMPOSED AGMT.
ical regime	Negotiation	Minor clashes	Political	None	None	Victory	Semi-formal agmt.
ence	Multiple, no viol.	Minor clashes	US actor	Semi-mil.	Discussion	Defeat	Imposed-imposee
e damage	Multiple, no viol.	Minor clashes	Semi-mil.	Semi-mil.	Discussion	Victory	Imposed-imposer
VE DAMAGE	VIOLENCE	WAR			MEDIATION	DEFINITIVE	UNILATERAL
e damage	Violence	War	Direct mil.	Semi-mil.	Mediation	Defeat	Unilateral-ally
ence	Mult. w/viol.	War	US actor	Semi-mil.	Mediation	Defeat	Unilateral-self
VE DAMAGE	VIOLENCE	SERIOUS CLASHES			DISCUSSION	AMBIGUOUS	UNILATERAL
)	Violence	Serious clashes	Political	Political	Discussion	Stalemate	Unilateral-self
e damage	Violence	Serious clashes	Political	Political	Discussion	Victory	Unilateral-self

(continued)

707

TABLE III.1.—Continued

NUM.	INTERNATIONAL CRISIS ACTORS	SUM. PAGE	PC OR REG.	TRIG. DATE	TERM. DATE	SYSTEM LEVEL POWER STATUS	TRIGGERING ENTITY	CRISIS TRIGGER
227	PRAGUE SPRING	606	43	04/09/68	10/18/68	MAINLY SUBSYSTEM	CZECHOSLOVAKIA	POLITICAL
	East Germany			04/09/68	08/20/68	Middle power	Czechoslovakia	Political
	Poland			04/09/68	08/20/68	Middle power	Czechoslovakia	Political
	Bulgaria			05/08/68	08/20/68	Small power	Czechoslovakia	Political
	Hungary			05/08/68	08/20/68	Small power	Czechoslovakia	Political
	USSR			06/27/68	10/18/68	Superpower	Czechoslovakia	Political
	Czechoslovakia			08/20/68	10/18/68	Small power	USSR	Violent
228	ESSEQUIBO I	513	41	07/09/68	08/99/68	SUBSYSTEM	VENEZUELA	POLITICAL
	Guyana			07/09/68	08/99/68	Small power	Venezuela	Political
229	BEIRUT AIRPORT	283	23	12/28/68	01/99/69	SUBSYSTEM	ISRAEL	VIOLENT
	Lebanon			12/28/68	01/99/69	Small power	Israel	Violent
230	VIETNAM SPRING OFF.	191	13	02/22/69	06/08/69	MAINLY SUBSYSTEM	NORTH VIETNAM	VIOLENT
	US			02/22/69	03/18/69	Superpower	North Vietnam	Violent
	South Vietnam			05/12/69	06/08/69	Small power	North Vietnam	Violent
231	USSURI RIVER	554	42	03/02/69	10/20/69	MAINLY DOMINANT	CHINA (PRC)	VIOLENT
	USSR			03/02/69	10/20/69	Superpower	China (PRC)	Violent
	China (PRC)			03/15/69	10/20/69	Great power	USSR	Violent
232	WAR OF ATTRITION	284	23	03/08/69	08/07/70	MAINLY SUBSYSTEM	EGYPT	VIOLENT
	Israel			03/08/69	07/28/69	Great power	Egypt	Violent
	Egypt			07/20/69	07/28/69	Great power	Israel	Violent
	Egypt			01/07/70	08/07/70	Great power	Israel	Violent
	USSR			01/22/70	08/07/70	Superpower	Israel	Political
	Israel			04/19/70	08/07/70	Great power	USSR	Ext. change
233	EC-121 SPY PLANE	354	27	04/15/69	04/26/69	DOMINANT SYSTEM	NORTH KOREA	VIOLENT
	US			04/15/69	04/26/69	Superpower	North Korea	Violent
234	SHATT-AL-ARAB II	302	24	04/15/69	10/30/69	SUBSYSTEM	IRAQ	POLITICAL
	Iran			04/15/69	10/30/69	Great power	Iraq	Political
	Iraq			04/19/69	10/30/69	Great power	Iran	Political
235	FOOTBALL WAR	514	41	06/15/69	07/30/69	SUBSYSTEM	HONDURAS	VIOLENT
	El Salvador			06/15/69	07/30/69	Small power	Honduras	Violent
	Honduras			07/14/69	07/30/69	Small power	El Salvador	Violent
236	CAIRO AGREEMENT-PLO	642	44	10/22/69	11/03/69	SUBSYSTEM	NON-STATE ACTOR	VIOLENT
	Lebanon			10/22/69	11/03/69	Small power	Non-state actor	Violent

GRAVITY OF THREAT	CRISIS MGMT. TECHNIQUE	VIOLENCE	US ACTIV.	USSR ACTIV.	GLOBAL ORG. INVOLVEMENT	OUTCOME: SUBSTANCE	OUTCOME: FORM
TICAL REGIME	MULT. W/VIOL.	MINOR CLASHES			DISCUSSION	AMBIGUOUS	IMPOSED AGMT.
ical regime	Mult. w/viol.	Minor clashes	None	Direct mil.	None	Victory	Unilateral-ally
ical regime	Mult. w/viol.	Minor clashes	None	Direct mil.	None	Victory	Unilateral-ally
ical regime	Negotiation	Minor clashes	None	Direct mil.	None	Victory	Unilateral-ally
)	Mult. w/viol.	Minor clashes	None	Direct mil.	None	Compromise	Unilateral-ally
ence	Mult. w/viol.	Minor clashes	Political	SU actor	Discussion	Victory	Imposed-imposer
ical regime	Negotiation	Minor clashes	Political	Direct mil.	Discussion	Defeat	Imposed-imposee
RITORY	NEGOTIATION	NO VIOLENCE			GOOD OFFICES	AMBIGUOUS	UNILATERAL
tory	Negotiation	No violence	Political	None	Good offices	Stalemate	Unilateral-self
ITICAL REGIME	MEDIATION	MINOR CLASHES			CONDEMNATION	AMBIGUOUS	OTHER
ical regime	Mediation	Minor clashes	Political	Political	Condemnation	Stalemate	Other-misc.
STENCE	VIOLENCE	SERIOUS CLASHES			NONE	AMBIGUOUS	UNILATERAL
e damage	Violence	Serious clashes	US actor	None	None	Victory	Unilateral-self
ence	Mult. w/viol.	Serious clashes	Direct mil.	None	None	Compromise	Unilateral-ally
RITORY	MULT. W/VIOL.	SERIOUS CLASHES			NONE	AMBIGUOUS	SEMI-FORMAL AGMT.
itory	Mult. w/viol.	Serious clashes	Political	SU actor	None	Stalemate	Semi-formal agmt.
itory	Mult. w/viol.	Serious clashes	Political	Direct mil.	None	Stalemate	Semi-formal agmt.
VE DAMAGE	MULT. W/VIOL.	WAR			CONDEMNATION	AMBIGUOUS	FORMAL AGMT.
e damage	Mult. w/viol.	War	Political	Semi-mil.	Observers	Victory	Unilateral-self
e damage	Non-viol. mil.	Serious clashes	Political	Semi-mil.	Observers	Defeat	Unilateral-adv.
e damage	Mult. w/viol.	War	Political	Direct mil.	Condemnation	Compromise	Formal agmt.
ence	Mult. w/viol.	Minor clashes	Political	SU actor	Condemnation	Compromise	Spillover
e damage	Mult. w/viol.	War	Political	Direct mil.	Condemnation	Compromise	Formal agmt.
LUENCE	NON-VIOL. MIL.	MINOR CLASHES			NONE	AMBIGUOUS	UNILATERAL
ence	Non-viol. mil.	Minor clashes	US actor	Political	None	Stalemate	Unilateral-self
RITORY	NON-VIOL. MIL.	NO VIOLENCE			DISCUSSION	DEFINITIVE	SEMI-FORMAL AGMT.
itory	Non-viol. mil.	No violence	None	None	Discussion	Victory	Semi-formal agmt.
itory	Non-viol. mil.	No violence	None	None	Discussion	Defeat	Semi-formal agmt.
RITORY	MULT. W/VIOL.	WAR			GOOD OFFICES	AMBIGUOUS	FORMAL AGMT.
nomic	Mult. w/viol.	War	Political	None	Good offices	Stalemate	Formal agmt.
itory	Mult. w/viol.	War	Political	None	Good offices	Stalemate	Formal agmt.
ITICAL REGIME	MULT. W/VIOL.	SERIOUS CLASHES			NONE	AMBIGUOUS	IMPOSED AGMT.
ical regime	Mult. w/viol.	Serious clashes	Political	Political	None	Compromise	Imposed-imposee

(continued)

TABLE III.1.—Continued

NUM.	INTERNATIONAL CRISIS ACTORS	SUM. PAGE	PC OR REG.	TRIG. DATE	TERM. DATE	SYSTEM LEVEL POWER STATUS	TRIGGERING ENTITY	CRISIS TRIGGER
237	INVASION OF CAMBODIA	192	13	03/13/70	07/22/70	MAINLY SUBSYSTEM	CAMBODIA	POLITICAL
	North Vietnam			03/13/70	06/30/70	Middle power	Cambodia	Political
	Cambodia			03/23/70	07/22/70	Small power	Non-state actor	Political
	South Vietnam			04/10/70	07/22/70	Small power	North Vietnam	Indirect viol.
	US			04/21/70	06/30/70	Superpower	North Vietnam	Indirect viol.
238	BLACK SEPTEMBER	643	44	09/15/70	09/29/70	SUBSYSTEM	JORDAN	POLITICAL
	Syria			09/15/70	09/29/70	Middle power	Jordan	Political
	US			09/15/70	09/29/70	Superpower	Jordan	Political
	Israel			09/19/70	09/29/70	Great power	Syria	Indirect viol.
	Jordan			09/19/70	09/29/70	Small power	Syria	Violent
239	CIENFUEGOS SUB. BASE	355	27	09/16/70	10/23/70	DOMINANT SYSTEM	USSR	EXT. CHANGE
	US			09/16/70	10/23/70	Superpower	USSR	Ext. change
240	CONAKRY RAID	446	40	11/22/70	12/11/70	SUBSYSTEM	NON-STATE ACTOR	VIOLENT
	Guinea			11/22/70	12/11/70	Small power	Non-state actor	Violent
241	INVASION OF LAOS II	194	13	02/08/71	03/25/71	SUBSYSTEM	MULTI-STATE	VIOLENT
	Laos			02/08/71	03/25/71	Small power	Multi-state	Violent
	North Vietnam			02/08/71	03/25/71	Great power	Multi-state	Violent
242	BANGLADESH	172	12	03/25/71	12/17/71	SUBSYSTEM	PAKISTAN	VIOLENT
	Bangladesh			03/25/71	12/17/71	Small power	Pakistan	Violent
	Pakistan			03/26/71	12/17/71	Middle power	Non-state actor	Internal chal.
	India			10/12/71	12/17/71	Middle power	Pakistan	Non-viol. mil.
	Pakistan			11/21/71	12/17/71	Middle power	India	Violent
243	CHAD/LIBYA I	85	2	05/24/71	04/17/72	SUBSYSTEM	CHAD	EXT. CHANGE
	Libya			05/24/71	04/17/72	Middle power	Chad	Ext. change
	Chad			08/27/71	08/28/71	Small power	Non-state actor	Internal chal.
244	CAPRIVI STRIP	447	40	10/05/71	10/12/71	SUBSYSTEM	SOUTH AFRICA	VIOLENT
	Zambia			10/05/71	10/12/71	Small power	South Africa	Violent
245	TANZANIA/UGANDA I	448	40	10/20/71	11/25/71	SUBSYSTEM	UGANDA	VIOLENT
	Tanzania			10/20/71	11/25/71	Middle power	Uganda	Violent
	Uganda			10/24/71	11/25/71	Small power	Tanzania	Non-viol. mil.
246	VIETNAM PORTS MINING	195	13	03/30/72	07/19/72	MAINLY SUBSYSTEM	NORTH VIETNAM	VIOLENT
	South Vietnam			03/30/72	07/19/72	Small power	North Vietnam	Violent
	US			03/30/72	07/19/72	Superpower	North Vietnam	Violent
	North Vietnam			05/08/72	07/19/72	Middle power	US	Violent
247	TANZANIA/UGANDA II	449	40	09/17/72	10/05/72	SUBSYSTEM	NON-STATE ACTOR	VIOLENT
	Uganda			09/17/72	10/05/72	Small power	Non-state actor	Violent
	Tanzania			09/18/72	10/05/72	Middle power	Uganda	Violent

GRAVITY OF THREAT	CRISIS MGMT. TECHNIQUE	VIOLENCE	US ACTIV.	USSR ACTIV.	GLOBAL ORG. INVOLVEMENT	OUTCOME: SUBSTANCE	OUTCOME: FORM
TICAL REGIME	VIOLENCE	WAR			MEDIATION	AMBIGUOUS	UNILATERAL
ence	Violence	War	Direct mil.	Political	Mediation	Victory	Unilateral-adv.
cal regime	Violence	War	Direct mil.	Political	Mediation	Stalemate	Unilateral-adv.
ence	Violence	War	Direct mil.	Political	Mediation	Stalemate	Unilateral-self
ence	Violence	War	US actor	Political	Mediation	Stalemate	Unilateral-self
TICAL REGIME	MULT. W/VIOL.	WAR			NONE	DEFINITIVE	IMPOSED AGMT.
ence	Mult. w/viol.	War	Semi-mil.	Political	None	Defeat	Imposed-imposee
ence	Multiple, no viol.	No violence	US actor	Political	None	Victory	Imposed-imposer
nce	Multiple, no viol.	No violence	Semi-mil.	Political	None	Victory	Imposed-imposer
cal regime	Mult. w/viol.	War	Semi-mil.	Political	None	Victory	Formal agmt.
VE DAMAGE	NEGOTIATION	NO VIOLENCE			NONE	DEFINITIVE	UNILATERAL
damage	Negotiation	No violence	US actor	Semi-mil.	None	Victory	Unilateral-adv.
TICAL REGIME	MULT. W/VIOL.	SERIOUS CLASHES			CALL FOR ACTION	DEFINITIVE	OTHER
cal regime	Mult. w/viol.	Serious clashes	Economic	Political	Call for action	Victory	Other-GO intv.
VE DAMAGE	VIOLENCE	WAR			OTHER	AMBIGUOUS	UNILATERAL
damage	Non-mil. pres.	War	Direct mil.	Political	Other	Other	Unilateral-adv.
damage	Violence	War	Direct mil.	Political	Other	Victory	Unilateral-adv.
TENCE	VIOLENCE	WAR			CALL FOR ACTION	DEFINITIVE	IMPOSED AGMT.
ence	Violence	War	Semi-mil.	Political	Call for action	Victory	Spillover
damage	Violence	War	Semi-mil.	Political	Call for action	Defeat	Imposed-impose
damage	Violence	War	Semi-mil.	Political	Call for action	Victory	Imposed-imposer
ence	Violence	War	Semi-mil.	Political	Call for action	Defeat	Imposed-impose
TICAL REGIME	MULTIPLE, NO VIOL.	NO VIOLENCE			NONE	DEFINITIVE	UNILATERAL
ence	Multiple, no viol.	No violence	None	None	None	Defeat	Compliance
cal regime	Multiple, no viol.	No violence	None	None	None	Victory	Unilateral-adv.
RITORY	NEGOTIATION	MINOR CLASHES			CALL FOR ACTION	AMBIGUOUS	OTHER
ory	Negotiation	Minor clashes	None	None	Call for action	Stalemate	Other-GO intv.
RITORY	MULTIPLE, NO VIOL.	MINOR CLASHES			NONE	AMBIGUOUS	UNILATERAL
	Multiple, no viol.	Minor clashes	None	None	None	Stalemate	Unilateral-adv.
ory	Multiple, no viol.	Minor clashes	None	None	None	Stalemate	Unilateral-self
VE DAMAGE	MULT. W/VIOL.	WAR			DISCUSSION	AMBIGUOUS	SEMI-FORMAL AGMT.
ory	Mult. w/viol.	War	Direct mil.	Political	Discussion	Compromise	Semi-formal agmt.
nce	Mult. w/viol.	War	US actor	Political	Discussion	Compromise	Semi-formal agmt.
damage	Mult. w/viol.	War	Direct mil.	Political	Discussion	Compromise	Semi-formal agmt.
TICAL REGIME	MULT. W/VIOL.	MINOR CLASHES			NONE	AMBIGUOUS	FORMAL AGMT.
cal regime	Mult. w/viol.	Minor clashes	None	None	None	Victory	Formal agmt.
	Multiple, no viol.	Minor clashes	None	None	None	Compromise	Formal agmt.

(continued)

TABLE III.1.—Continued

NUM.	INTERNATIONAL CRISIS ACTORS	SUM. PAGE	PC OR REG.	TRIG. DATE	TERM. DATE	SYSTEM LEVEL POWER STATUS	TRIGGERING ENTITY	CRISIS TRIGGER
248	NORTH/SOUTH YEMEN I	329	26	09/26/72	11/28/72	SUBSYSTEM	SOUTH YEMEN	VIOLENT
	North Yemen			09/26/72	11/28/72	Small power	South Yemen	Violent
	South Yemen			09/26/72	11/28/72	Small power	North Yemen	Violent
249	CHRISTMAS BOMBING	196	13	10/23/72	01/27/73	MAINLY SUBSYSTEM	US	EXT. CHANGE
	South Vietnam			10/23/72	01/27/73	Small power	US	Ext. change
	US			12/04/72	01/27/73	Superpower	North Vietnam	Political
	North Vietnam			12/17/72	01/27/73	Middle power	US	Violent
250	ZAMBIA RAID	106	4	01/19/73	02/03/73	SUBSYSTEM	SOUTH AFRICA	NON-VIOL. MIL.
	Zambia			01/19/73	02/03/73	Small power	South Africa	Non-viol. mil.
251	LIBYAN PLANE	285	23	02/21/73	02/21/73	SUBSYSTEM	LIBYA	EXT. CHANGE
	Israel			02/21/73	02/21/73	Great power	Libya	Ext. change
252	IRAQ INVASION/KUWAIT	314	25	03/20/73	06/08/73	SUBSYSTEM	IRAQ	VIOLENT
	Kuwait			03/20/73	06/08/73	Small power	Iraq	Violent
253	ISRAEL MOBILIZATION	286	23	04/10/73	06/88/73	SUBSYSTEM	EGYPT	NON-VIOL. MIL.
	Israel			04/10/73	06/88/73	Great power	Egypt	Non-viol. mil.
254	COD WAR I	608	43	05/14/73	11/13/73	SUBSYSTEM	ICELAND	VIOLENT
	UK			05/14/73	11/13/73	Great power	Iceland	Violent
	Iceland			05/19/73	11/13/73	Small power	UK	Non-viol. mil.
255	OCT.-YOM KIPPUR WAR	287	23	10/05/73	05/31/74	MAINLY SUBSYSTEM	MULTI-STATE	NON-VIOL. MIL.
	Israel			10/05/73	05/31/74	Great power	Multi-state	Non-viol. mil.
	Israel			10/07/73	10/14/73	Great power	Multi-state	Violent
	Syria			10/10/73	05/31/74	Middle power	Israel	Violent
	US			10/12/73	05/31/74	Superpower	Multi-state	Political
	Egypt			10/18/73	01/18/74	Great power	Israel	Violent
	USSR			10/22/73	05/31/74	Superpower	Israel	Indirect viol.
256	OMAN/SOUTH YEMEN	645	44	11/18/73	03/11/76	SUBSYSTEM	SOUTH YEMEN	VIOLENT
	Oman			11/18/73	03/11/76	Small power	South Yemen	Violent
257	CYPRUS III	369	28	07/15/74	02/24/75	SUBSYSTEM	NON-STATE ACTOR	INTERNAL CHAL.
	Cyprus			07/15/74	02/24/75	Small power	Non-state actor	Internal chal.
	Turkey			07/15/74	02/24/75	Middle power	Non-state actor	Political
	Greece			07/20/74	02/24/75	Middle power	Turkey	Indirect viol.
258	FINAL N. VIETNAM OFF.	197	13	12/14/74	04/30/75	SUBSYSTEM	NORTH VIETNAM	VIOLENT
	South Vietnam			12/14/74	04/30/75	Small power	North Vietnam	Violent
	Cambodia			01/01/75	04/17/75	Small power	Non-state actor	Internal chal.
259	MAYAGUEZ	198	13	05/12/75	05/15/75	MAINLY SUBSYSTEM	CAMBODIA	VIOLENT
	US			05/12/75	05/14/75	Superpower	Cambodia	Violent
	Cambodia			05/13/75	05/15/75	Small power	US	Political

GRAVITY OF THREAT	CRISIS MGMT. TECHNIQUE	VIOLENCE	US ACTIV.	USSR ACTIV.	GLOBAL ORG. INVOLVEMENT	OUTCOME: SUBSTANCE	OUTCOME: FORM
RITORY	MULT. W/VIOL.	WAR			NONE	AMBIGUOUS	FORMAL AGMT.
tory	Mult. w/viol.	War	None	None	None	Stalemate	Formal agmt.
tory	Mult. w/viol.	War	None	None	None	Stalemate	Formal agmt.
STENCE	MULT. W/VIOL.	WAR			NONE	AMBIGUOUS	FORMAL AGMT.
ence	Mult. w/viol.	War	Political	Political	None	Compromise	Formal agmt.
ence	Mult. w/viol.	War	US actor	Political	None	Compromise	Formal agmt.
e damage	Negotiation	War	Direct mil.	Political	None	Compromise	Formal agmt.
RITORY	MULT. W/VIOL.	MINOR CLASHES			DISCUSSION	AMBIGUOUS	UNILATERAL
tory	Mult. w/viol.	Minor clashes	None	None	Discussion	Stalemate	Unilateral-adv.
VE DAMAGE	VIOLENCE	SERIOUS CLASHES			NONE	DEFINITIVE	UNILATERAL
e damage	Violence	Serious clashes	None	None	None	Victory	Unilateral-self
RITORY	NEGOTIATION	MINOR CLASHES			NONE	DEFINITIVE	FORMAL AGMT.
tory	Negotiation	Minor clashes	None	None	None	Victory	Formal agmt.
VE DAMAGE	NON-VIOL. MIL.	NO VIOLENCE			NONE	AMBIGUOUS	UNILATERAL
e damage	Non-viol. mil.	No violence	None	None	None	Stalemate	Unilateral-self
NOMIC	MULTIPLE, NO VIOL.	MINOR CLASHES			NONE	AMBIGUOUS	FORMAL AGMT.
omic	Multiple, no viol.	Minor clashes	Political	Semi-mil.	None	Compromise	Formal agmt.
omic	Multiple, no viol.	Minor clashes	Political	Semi-mil.	None	Victory	Formal agmt.
VE DAMAGE	MULT. W/VIOL.	WAR			CALL FOR ACTION	AMBIGUOUS	FORMAL AGMT.
e damage	Mult. w/viol.	War	Semi-mil.	Semi-mil.	Call for action	Compromise	Formal agmt.
e damage	Non-viol. mil.	War	Political	Political	None	Victory	Unilateral-ally
tory	Mult. w/viol.	War	Semi-mil.	Semi-mil.	Call for action	Compromise	Formal agmt.
ence	Multiple, no viol.	No violence	US actor	Semi-mil.	Call for action	Victory	Spillover
e damage	Mult. w/viol.	War	Semi-mil.	Semi-mil.	Call for action	Victory	Formal agmt.
ence	Multiple, no viol.	No violence	Semi-mil.	SU actor	Call for action	Compromise	Spillover
RITORY	MULT. W/VIOL.	SERIOUS CLASHES			NONE	DEFINITIVE	FORMAL AGMT.
tory	Mult. w/viol.	Serious clashes	Semi-mil.	Semi-mil.	None	Victory	Formal agmt.
VE DAMAGE	MULT. W/VIOL.	WAR			OBSERVERS	DEFINITIVE	UNILATERAL
e damage	Mult. w/viol.	War	Political	Semi-mil.	Observers	Defeat	Unilateral-adv.
ence	Mult. w/viol.	War	Semi-mil.	Semi-mil.	Call for action	Victory	Unilateral-self
ence	Negotiation	No violence	Political	Semi-mil.	Call for action	Defeat	Unilateral-adv.
ITICAL REGIME	VIOLENCE	WAR			GOOD OFFICES	DEFINITIVE	UNILATERAL
ical regime	Violence	War	Economic	Semi-mil.	Fact-finding	Defeat	Compliance
ical regime	Violence	War	Economic	None	Good offices	Defeat	Compliance
VE DAMAGE	VIOLENCE	SERIOUS CLASHES			GOOD OFFICES	DEFINITIVE	UNILATERAL
ence	Violence	Serious clashes	US actor	None	Good offices	Victory	Unilateral-adv.
e damage	Mult. w/viol.	Serious clashes	Direct mil.	None	Good offices	Defeat	Compliance

(continued)

TABLE III.1.—Continued

NUM.	INTERNATIONAL CRISIS ACTORS	SUM. PAGE	PC OR REG.	TRIG. DATE	TERM. DATE	SYSTEM LEVEL POWER STATUS	TRIGGERING ENTITY	CRISIS TRIGGER
260	WAR IN ANGOLA	69	1	07/12/75	03/27/76	MAINLY SUBSYSTEM	NON-STATE ACTOR	INDIRECT VIOL.
	Zambia			07/12/75	02/18/76	Small power	Non-state actor	Indirect viol.
	Zaire			07/12/75	02/28/76	Middle power	Non-state actor	Indirect viol.
	South Africa			08/08/75	03/27/76	Great power	Non-state actor	Indirect viol.
	Angola			08/15/75	02/24/76	Middle power	Non-state actor	Internal chal.
	Cuba			08/15/75	02/24/76	Middle power	Non-state actor	Ext. change
	USSR			08/15/75	02/24/76	Superpower	Non-state actor	Ext. change
	US			09/01/75	12/19/75	Superpower	Non-state actor	Indirect viol.
261	MOROCCAN MARCH	118	5	10/16/75	04/14/76	SUBSYSTEM	MOROCCO	POLITICAL
	Spain			10/16/75	11/14/75	Middle power	Morocco	Political
	Morocco			11/02/75	04/14/76	Middle power	Algeria	Political
	Algeria			11/14/75	03/06/76	Middle power	Morocco	Political
	Mauritania			12/10/75	04/14/76	Small power	Non-state actor	Violent
262	BELIZE I	515	41	11/01/75	11/30/75	SUBSYSTEM	GUATEMALA	NON-VIOL. MIL.
	UK			11/01/75	11/30/75	Great power	Guatemala	Non-viol. mil.
263	COD WAR II	609	43	11/23/75	06/01/76	SUBSYSTEM	ICELAND	INTERNAL CHAL.
	UK			11/23/75	06/01/76	Great power	Iceland	Internal chal.
	Iceland			11/25/75	06/01/76	Small power	UK	Non-viol. mil.
264	EAST TIMOR	210	14	11/28/75	07/17/76	SUBSYSTEM	NON-STATE ACTOR	POLITICAL
	Indonesia			11/28/75	07/17/76	Great power	Non-state actor	Political
265	LEB. CIVIL WAR I	646	44	01/18/76	11/15/76	SUBSYSTEM	NON-STATE ACTOR	INDIRECT VIOL.
	Syria			01/18/76	11/15/76	Great power	Non-state actor	Indirect viol.
266	UGANDA CLAIMS	449	40	02/15/76	02/24/76	SUBSYSTEM	UGANDA	POLITICAL
	Kenya			02/15/76	02/24/76	Middle power	Uganda	Political
267	OPERATION THRASHER	107	4	02/22/76	04/99/76	SUBSYSTEM	NON-STATE ACTOR	VIOLENT
	Rhodesia			02/22/76	03/99/76	Middle power	Non-state actor	Violent
	Mozambique			02/24/76	04/99/76	Small power	Rhodesia	Violent
268	NOUAKCHOTT I	121	5	06/08/76	06/08/76	SUBSYSTEM	NON-STATE ACTOR	VIOLENT
	Mauritania			06/08/76	06/08/76	Small power	Non-state actor	Violent
269	IRAQI THREAT	648	44	06/09/76	06/17/76	SUBSYSTEM	IRAQ	NON-VIOL. MIL.
	Syria			06/09/76	06/17/76	Middle power	Iraq	Non-viol. mil.
270	ENTEBBE RAID	290	23	06/27/76	07/04/76	SUBSYSTEM	NON-STATE ACTOR	OTHER NON-VIOL.
	Israel			06/27/76	07/04/76	Middle power	Non-state actor	Other non-viol.
	Uganda			07/03/76	07/04/76	Small power	Israel	Other non-viol.
271	SUDAN COUP ATTEMPT	451	40	07/02/76	07/15/76	SUBSYSTEM	NON-STATE ACTOR	INTERNAL CHAL.
	Sudan			07/02/76	07/15/76	Small power	Non-state actor	Internal chal.

GRAVITY OF THREAT	CRISIS MGMT. TECHNIQUE	VIOLENCE	US ACTIV.	USSR ACTIV.	GLOBAL ORG. INVOLVEMENT	OUTCOME: SUBSTANCE	OUTCOME: FORM
TICAL REGIME	VIOLENCE	WAR			CALL FOR ACTION	AMBIGUOUS	UNILATERAL
cal regime	Multiple, no viol.	No violence	Semi-mil.	Semi-mil.	Fact-finding	Compromise	Other-non.-st.
cal regime	Mult. w/viol.	Serious clashes	Semi-mil.	Semi-mil.	Fact-finding	Compromise	Unilateral-self
nce	Violence	War	Semi-mil.	Semi-mil.	Condemnation	Defeat	Unilateral-self
cal regime	Violence	War	Semi-mil.	Semi-mil.	Fact-finding	Victory	Other-non.-st.
nce	Violence	War	Semi-mil.	Semi-mil.	Call for action	Victory	Spillover
nce	Non-viol. mil.	No violence	Semi-mil.	SU actor	None	Victory	Spillover
nce	Multiple, no viol.	No violence	US actor	Semi-mil.	None	Defeat	Unilateral-self
RITORY	VIOLENCE	SERIOUS CLASHES			MEDIATION	AMBIGUOUS	OTHER
y	Negotiation	No violence	Political	None	Mediation	Compromise	Formal agmt.
ory	Violence	Serious clashes	Semi-mil.	Covert	Mediation	Victory	Other-ally
nce	Violence	Serious clashes	Semi-mil.	Covert	Mediation	Stalemate	Unilateral-self
ory	Violence	Serious clashes	Semi-mil.	Covert	Mediation	Compromise	Other-ally
UENCE	NON-VIOL. MIL.	NO VIOLENCE			CALL FOR ACTION	DEFINITIVE	SEMI-FORMAL AGMT.
nce	Non-viol. mil.	No violence	None	None	Call for action	Victory	Semi-formal agmt.
NOMIC	NEGOTIATION	MINOR CLASHES			DISCUSSION	AMBIGUOUS	FORMAL AGMT.
omic	Non-viol. mil.	Minor clashes	Political	None	Discussion	Compromise	Formal agmt.
omic	Negotiation	Minor clashes	Political	None	Discussion	Compromise	Formal agmt.
RITORY	VIOLENCE	SERIOUS CLASHES			CALL FOR ACTION	DEFINITIVE	UNILATERAL
ory	Violence	Serious clashes	None	None	Call for action	Victory	Unilateral-self
UENCE	VIOLENCE	SERIOUS CLASHES			GOOD OFFICES	DEFINITIVE	UNILATERAL
nce	Violence	Serious clashes	Political	Political	Good offices	Victory	Unilateral-self
RITORY	NEGOTIATION	NO VIOLENCE			OTHER	DEFINITIVE	SEMI-FORMAL AGMT.
ory	Negotiation	No violence	None	None	Other	Victory	Semi-formal agmt.
TICAL REGIME	VIOLENCE	SERIOUS CLASHES			CONDEMNATION	DEFINITIVE	OTHER
cal regime	Violence	Serious clashes	Political	Semi-mil.	Condemnation	Defeat	Other-ally
	Multiple, no viol.	Serious clashes	Political	Semi-mil.	Sanctions	Victory	Other-ally
TICAL REGIME	VIOLENCE	SERIOUS CLASHES			NONE	DEFINITIVE	UNILATERAL
cal regime	Violence	Serious clashes	None	None	None	Victory	Unilateral-self
TICAL REGIME	NON-VIOL. MIL.	NO VIOLENCE			NONE	AMBIGUOUS	UNILATERAL
cal regime	Non-viol. mil.	No violence	None	None	None	Stalemate	Unilateral-self
VE DAMAGE	VIOLENCE	MINOR CLASHES			NONE	DEFINITIVE	UNILATERAL
damage	Violence	Minor clashes	None	None	None	Victory	Unilateral-self
	Mult. w/viol.	Minor clashes	None	None	None	Defeat	Unilateral-adv.
TICAL REGIME	MULT. W/VIOL.	MINOR CLASHES			OTHER	DEFINITIVE	OTHER
cal regime	Mult. w/viol.	Minor clashes	None	None	Other	Victory	Other-ally

(continued)

TABLE III.1.—Continued

NUM.	INTERNATIONAL CRISIS ACTORS	SUM. PAGE	PC OR REG.	TRIG. DATE	TERM. DATE	SYSTEM LEVEL POWER STATUS	TRIGGERING ENTITY	CRISIS TRIGGER
272	AEGEAN SEA I	371	28	08/06/76	09/25/76	SUBSYSTEM	TURKEY	NON-VIOL. MIL.
	Greece			08/06/76	09/25/76	Middle power	Turkey	Non-viol. mil.
	Turkey			08/12/76	09/25/76	Great power	Greece	Non-viol. mil.
273	NAGOMIA RAID	108	4	08/09/76	11/99/76	SUBSYSTEM	RHODESIA	VIOLENT
	Mozambique			08/09/76	11/99/76	Small power	Rhodesia	Violent
274	POPLAR TREE	219	15	08/17/76	09/16/76	SUBSYSTEM	NORTH KOREA	VIOLENT
	US			08/17/76	09/16/76	Superpower	North Korea	Violent
	North Korea			08/19/76	09/16/76	Middle power	US	Non-viol. mil.
275	SYRIA MOBILIZATION	291	23	11/21/76	12/13/76	SUBSYSTEM	SYRIA	NON-VIOL. MIL.
	Israel			11/21/76	12/13/76	Great power	Syria	Non-viol. mil.
276	OPERATION TANGENT	109	4	12/20/76	03/31/77	SUBSYSTEM	RHODESIA	NON-VIOL. MIL.
	Botswana			12/20/76	03/31/77	Small power	Rhodesia	Non-viol. mil.
277	SHABA I	72	1	03/08/77	05/26/77	SUBSYSTEM	NON-STATE ACTOR	VIOLENT
	Zaire			03/08/77	05/26/77	Middle power	Non-state actor	Violent
	Angola			03/08/77	05/25/77	Middle power	Zaire	Political
278	MAPAI SEIZURE	110	4	05/29/77	06/30/77	SUBSYSTEM	RHODESIA	VIOLENT
	Mozambique			05/29/77	06/30/77	Small power	Rhodesia	Violent
279	BELIZE II	516	41	06/25/77	07/28/77	SUBSYSTEM	GUATEMALA	NON-VIOL. MIL.
	UK			06/25/77	07/28/77	Great power	Guatemala	Non-viol. mil.
280	NOUAKCHOTT II	121	5	07/03/77	07/88/77	SUBSYSTEM	NON-STATE ACTOR	VIOLENT
	Mauritania			07/03/77	07/88/77	Small power	Non-state actor	Violent
281	EGYPT/LIBYA CLASHES	452	40	07/14/77	09/10/77	SUBSYSTEM	EGYPT	VIOLENT
	Libya			07/14/77	09/10/77	Middle power	Egypt	Violent
	Egypt			07/19/77	09/10/77	Great power	Libya	Violent
282	OGADEN II	99	3	07/22/77	03/14/78	MAINLY SUBSYSTEM	NON-STATE ACTOR	VIOLENT
	Ethiopia			07/22/77	03/14/78	Middle power	Non-state actor	Violent
	Somalia			01/21/78	03/14/78	Small power	Ethiopia	Violent
283	RHODESIA RAID	111	4	08/31/77	08/14/78	SUBSYSTEM	RHODESIA	VIOLENT
	Zambia			08/31/77	08/14/78	Small power	Rhodesia	Violent
284	VIETNAM INV./CAMBODIA	199	13	09/24/77	01/07/79	SUBSYSTEM	VIETNAM	VIOLENT
	Cambodia			09/24/77	01/07/79	Small power	Vietnam	Violent
	Vietnam			09/24/77	01/07/79	Great power	Cambodia	Violent
	Thailand			02/09/78	12/15/78	Middle power	Cambodia	Violent
285	FRENCH HOSTAGES MAUR.	122	5	10/25/77	12/23/77	SUBSYSTEM	NON-STATE ACTOR	INDIRECT VIOL.
	France			10/25/77	12/23/77	Great power	Non-state actor	Indirect viol.
	Algeria			10/29/77	12/23/77	Middle power	France	Ext. change

GRAVITY OF THREAT	CRISIS MGMT. TECHNIQUE	VIOLENCE	US ACTIV.	USSR ACTIV.	GLOBAL ORG. INVOLVEMENT	OUTCOME: SUBSTANCE	OUTCOME: FORM
RITORY	MULTIPLE, NO VIOL.	NO VIOLENCE			CALL FOR ACTION	DEFINITIVE	UNILATERAL
itory	Multiple, no viol.	No violence	Political	Political	Call for action	Victory	Unilateral-adv.
nomic	Negotiation	No violence	Political	Political	Condemnation	Defeat	Unilateral-self
D	MULT. W/VIOL.	SERIOUS CLASHES			FACT-FINDING	AMBIGUOUS	OTHER
D	Mult. w/viol.	Serious clashes	Economic	Political	Fact-finding	Stalemate	Other-GO intv.
LUENCE	NON-VIOL. MIL.	MINOR CLASHES			OBSERVERS	AMBIGUOUS	FORMAL AGMT.
ience	Non-viol. mil.	Minor clashes	US actor	Political	Observers	Compromise	Formal agmt.
ience	Multiple, no viol.	Minor clashes	Semi-mil.	Political	Observers	Compromise	Formal agmt.
LUENCE	NON-VIOL. MIL.	NO VIOLENCE			NONE	AMBIGUOUS	TACIT UNDERSTANDING
ience	Non-viol. mil.	No violence	Political	None	None	Stalemate	Tacit understanding
D	MULTIPLE, NO VIOL.	MINOR CLASHES			CONDEMNATION	DEFINITIVE	UNILATERAL
D	Multiple, no viol.	Minor clashes	None	Political	Condemnation	Victory	Unilateral-self
LITICAL REGIME	MULT. W/VIOL.	SERIOUS CLASHES			NONE	DEFINITIVE	UNILATERAL
tical regime	Mult. w/viol.	Serious clashes	Semi-mil.	Semi-mil.	None	Victory	Unilateral-self
itory	Non-mil. pres.	No violence	Semi-mil.	Semi-mil.	None	Defeat	Unilateral-adv.
D	NEGOTIATION	SERIOUS CLASHES			CALL FOR ACTION	DEFINITIVE	OTHER
D	Negotiation	Serious clashes	Political	None	Call for action	Victory	Other-GO intv.
LUENCE	MULTIPLE, NO VIOL.	NO VIOLENCE			NONE	DEFINITIVE	SEMI-FORMAL AGMT.
ience	Multiple, no viol.	No violence	Political	None	None	Victory	Semi-formal agmt.
LITICAL REGIME	MULT. W/VIOL.	SERIOUS CLASHES			NONE	DEFINITIVE	UNILATERAL
tical regime	Mult. w/viol.	Serious clashes	None	None	None	Victory	Unilateral-self
D	MULT. W/VIOL.	SERIOUS CLASHES			OTHER	AMBIGUOUS	SEMI-FORMAL AGMT.
D	Mult. w/viol.	Serious clashes	Semi-mil.	Semi-mil.	Other	Stalemate	Semi-formal agmt.
D	Mult. w/viol.	Serious clashes	Semi-mil.	Semi-mil.	None	Stalemate	Semi-formal agmt.
RRITORY	MULT. W/VIOL.	WAR			NONE	DEFINITIVE	UNILATERAL
itory	Mult. w/viol.	War	Semi-mil.	Direct mil.	None	Victory	Unilateral-self
itory	Mult. w/viol.	War	Semi-mil.	Direct mil.	None	Defeat	Compliance
D	MULT. W/VIOL.	SERIOUS CLASHES			CALL FOR ACTION	DEFINITIVE	OTHER
D	Mult. w/viol.	Serious clashes	Political	None	Call for action	Victory	Other-non.-st.
STENCE	VIOLENCE	WAR			DISCUSSION	DEFINITIVE	UNILATERAL
stence	Mult. w/viol.	War	None	Semi-mil.	Discussion	Defeat	Unilateral-adv.
ve damage	Violence	War	None	Semi-mil.	None	Victory	Unilateral-self
itory	Negotiation	Minor clashes	None	None	None	Victory	Spillover
D	MULT. W/VIOL.	NO VIOLENCE			GOOD OFFICES	DEFINITIVE	OTHER
her	Mult. w/viol.	No violence	None	Political	Good offices	Victory	Other-non.-st.
D	Negotiation	No violence	None	Political	Good offices	Victory	Other-non.-st.

(continued)

717

TABLE III.1.—Continued

NUM.	INTERNATIONAL CRISIS ACTORS	SUM. PAGE	PC OR REG.	TRIG. DATE	TERM. DATE	SYSTEM LEVEL POWER STATUS	TRIGGERING ENTITY	CRISIS TRIGGER
286	CHIMOIO-TEMBUE RAIDS	112	4	11/23/77	03/22/78	SUBSYSTEM	RHODESIA	VIOLENT
	Mozambique			11/23/77	03/22/78	Small power	Rhodesia	Violent
287	BEAGLE CHANNEL I	517	41	12/05/77	02/20/78	SUBSYSTEM	ARGENTINA	NON-VIOL. MIL.
	Chile			12/05/77	02/20/78	Middle power	Argentina	Non-viol. mil.
	Argentina			01/05/78	02/20/78	Great power	Chile	Non-viol. mil.
288	CHAD/LIBYA II	85	2	01/22/78	03/27/78	SUBSYSTEM	CHAD	EXT. CHANGE
	Libya			01/22/78	02/24/78	Great power	Chad	Ext. change
	Chad			01/29/78	03/27/78	Small power	Non-state actor	Violent
289	LITANI OPERATION	292	23	03/14/78	06/13/78	SUBSYSTEM	ISRAEL	VIOLENT
	Lebanon			03/14/78	06/13/78	Small power	Israel	Violent
290	CHAD/LIBYA III	87	2	04/15/78	08/29/78	SUBSYSTEM	LIBYA	INDIRECT VIOL.
	France			04/15/78	07/88/78	Great power	Libya	Indirect viol.
	Libya			05/77/78	07/88/78	Great power	France	Indirect viol.
	Chad			06/22/78	08/29/78	Small power	Libya	Violent
291	CASSINGA INCIDENT	74	1	05/03/78	05/17/78	SUBSYSTEM	NON-STATE ACTOR	VIOLENT
	South Africa			05/03/78	05/17/78	Great power	Non-state actor	Violent
	Angola			05/04/78	05/06/78	Middle power	South Africa	Violent
292	SHABA II	75	1	05/11/78	07/30/78	SUBSYSTEM	NON-STATE ACTOR	VIOLENT
	Zaire			05/11/78	07/30/78	Middle power	Non-state actor	Violent
	Angola			05/11/78	07/30/78	Middle power	Zaire	Political
	Belgium			05/14/78	05/22/78	Middle power	Non-state actor	Indirect viol.
	US			05/14/78	05/22/78	Superpower	Non-state actor	Indirect viol.
	France			05/14/78	05/25/78	Great power	Non-state actor	Indirect viol.
293	AIR RHODESIA INCDNT.	113	4	09/03/78	10/31/78	SUBSYSTEM	NON-STATE ACTOR	VIOLENT
	Rhodesia			09/03/78	10/31/78	Middle power	Non-state actor	Violent
	Zambia			10/19/78	10/23/78	Small power	Rhodesia	Violent
294	NICARAGUA CIVIL WAR II	518	41	09/10/78	07/17/79	SUBSYSTEM	NON-STATE ACTOR	VIOLENT
	Nicaragua			09/10/78	09/25/78	Small power	Non-state actor	Violent
	Costa Rica			09/12/78	07/17/79	Small power	Nicaragua	Violent
	Nicaragua			05/27/79	07/17/79	Small power	Non-state actor	Violent
295	BEAGLE CHANNEL II	520	41	10/16/78	01/08/79	SUBSYSTEM	ARGENTINA	NON-VIOL. MIL.
	Chile			10/16/78	01/08/79	Middle power	Argentina	Non-viol. mil.
	Argentina			12/16/78	01/08/79	Great power	Chile	Non-viol. mil.
296	FALL OF AMIN	453	40	10/30/78	04/10/79	SUBSYSTEM	UGANDA	VIOLENT
	Tanzania			10/30/78	04/10/79	Middle power	Uganda	Violent
	Uganda			10/31/78	04/10/79	Small power	Tanzania	Violent
	Libya			02/25/79	04/09/79	Middle power	Tanzania	Indirect viol.

RAVITY OF THREAT	CRISIS MGMT. TECHNIQUE	VIOLENCE	US ACTIV.	USSR ACTIV.	GLOBAL ORG. INVOLVEMENT	OUTCOME: SUBSTANCE	OUTCOME: FORM
	NON-VIOL. MIL.	SERIOUS CLASHES			CALL FOR ACTION	AMBIGUOUS	UNILATERAL
	Non-viol. mil.	Serious clashes	Political	None	Call for action	Stalemate	Unilateral-self
TORY	MULTIPLE, NO VIOL.	NO VIOLENCE			NONE	AMBIGUOUS	FORMAL AGMT.
ory	Multiple, no viol.	No violence	Political	None	None	Stalemate	Formal agmt.
ory	Multiple, no viol.	No violence	Political	None	None	Stalemate	Formal agmt.
ICAL REGIME	MULT. W/VIOL.	WAR			NONE	AMBIGUOUS	FORMAL AGMT.
ce	Mult. w/viol.	War	None	None	None	Compromise	Semi-formal agmt.
al regime	Mult. w/viol.	War	None	None	None	Compromise	Formal agmt.
TORY	NEGOTIATION	SERIOUS CLASHES			CALL FOR ACTION	DEFINITIVE	UNILATERAL
ory	Negotiation	Serious clashes	Political	Political	Call for action	Victory	Unilateral-adv.
JENCE	VIOLENCE	WAR			NONE	AMBIGUOUS	SEMI-FORMAL AGMT.
ce	Violence	War	None	None	None	Victory	Semi-formal agmt.
ce	Mult. w/viol.	War	None	None	None	Compromise	Semi-formal agmt.
ory	Mult. w/viol.	War	None	None	None	Compromise	Other-non.-st.
JENCE	VIOLENCE	SERIOUS CLASHES			CONDEMNATION	AMBIGUOUS	SEMI-FORMAL AGMT.
ce	Violence	Serious clashes	Political	Semi-mil.	Condemnation	Stalemate	Semi-formal agmt.
	Negotiation	Serious clashes	Political	Semi-mil.	Call for action	Stalemate	Other-GO intv.
ICAL REGIME	VIOLENCE	SERIOUS CLASHES			NONE	AMBIGUOUS	FORMAL AGMT.
al regime	Mult. w/viol.	Serious clashes	Semi-mil.	Semi-mil.	None	Victory	Formal agmt.
	Negotiation	No violence	Semi-mil.	Semi-mil.	None	Compromise	Formal agmt.
ce	Violence	Serious clashes	Semi-mil.	Semi-mil.	None	Victory	Unilateral-self
ce	Non-viol. mil.	No violence	US actor	Semi-mil.	None	Victory	Unilateral-ally
ce	Violence	Serious clashes	Semi-mil.	Semi-mil.	None	Victory	Unilateral-self
E DAMAGE	MULT. W/VIOL.	SERIOUS CLASHES			CONDEMNATION	AMBIGUOUS	UNILATERAL
	Mult. w/viol.	Serious clashes	Political	None	Condemnation	Stalemate	Unilateral-self
damage	Mult. w/viol.	Minor clashes	Political	None	Other	Stalemate	Compliance
ICAL REGIME	VIOLENCE	WAR			CALL FOR ACTION	DEFINITIVE	UNILATERAL
al regime	Violence	War	Political	None	Call for action	Victory	Unilateral-self
	Mult. w/viol.	Minor clashes	Semi-mil.	None	Call for action	Victory	Unilateral-adv.
al regime	Mult. w/viol.	War	Political	None	None	Defeat	Unilateral-self
TORY	MULTIPLE, NO VIOL.	MINOR CLASHES			DISCUSSION	AMBIGUOUS	FORMAL AGMT.
ory	Multiple, no viol.	Minor clashes	Political	None	Discussion	Stalemate	Formal agmt.
ory	Multiple, no viol.	Minor clashes	Political	None	Discussion	Stalemate	Formal agmt.
ICAL REGIME	VIOLENCE	WAR			GOOD OFFICES	DEFINITIVE	UNILATERAL
ory	Violence	War	Political	Political	Good offices	Victory	Unilateral-adv.
al regime	Mult. w/viol.	War	Political	Political	Good offices	Defeat	Unilateral-self
ce	Violence	Serious clashes	Political	Political	None	Defeat	Unilateral-self

(continued)

TABLE III.1.—Continued

NUM.	INTERNATIONAL CRISIS ACTORS	SUM. PAGE	PC OR REG.	TRIG. DATE	TERM. DATE	SYSTEM LEVEL POWER STATUS	TRIGGERING ENTITY	CRISIS TRIGGER
297	ANGOLA INVASION SCARE	76	1	11/07/78	11/14/78	SUBSYSTEM	SOUTH AFRICA	EXT. CHANGE
	Angola			11/07/78	11/14/78	Middle power	South Africa	Ext. change
298	SINO/VIETNAM WAR	158	11	12/25/78	03/15/79	SUBSYSTEM	VIETNAM	INDIRECT VIOL.
	China (PRC)			12/25/78	03/15/79	Great power	Vietnam	Indirect viol.
	Vietnam			02/17/79	03/15/79	Great power	China (PRC)	Violent
299	TAN TAN	123	5	01/28/79	03/99/79	SUBSYSTEM	NON-STATE ACTOR	VIOLENT
	Morocco			01/28/79	03/99/79	Great power	Non-state actor	Violent
300	RAIDS ON ZIPRA	114	4	02/12/79	05/31/79	SUBSYSTEM	ZAMBIA	VIOLENT
	Rhodesia			02/12/79	05/31/79	Middle power	Zambia	Violent
	Angola			02/26/79	05/10/79	Middle power	Rhodesia	Violent
	Zambia			04/13/79	05/12/79	Small power	Rhodesia	Violent
301	NORTH/SOUTH YEMEN II	330	26	02/24/79	03/30/79	SUBSYSTEM	SOUTH YEMEN	VIOLENT
	North Yemen			02/24/79	03/30/79	Small power	South Yemen	Violent
	South Yemen			02/24/79	03/30/79	Small power	North Yemen	Violent
302	RAIDS ON SWAPO	77	1	03/06/79	03/28/79	SUBSYSTEM	SOUTH AFRICA	VIOLENT
	Angola			03/06/79	03/28/79	Middle power	South Africa	Violent
303	AFGHANISTAN INVASION	356	27	03/77/79	02/28/80	DOMINANT SYSTEM	NON-STATE ACTOR	INDIRECT VIOL.
	USSR			03/77/79	12/27/79	Superpower	Non-state actor	Indirect viol.
	Afghanistan			07/77/79	12/27/79	Small power	USSR	Political
	Pakistan			12/24/79	02/02/80	Middle power	USSR	Indirect viol.
	US			12/24/79	02/28/80	Superpower	USSR	Indirect viol.
304	CHAD/LIBYA IV	88	2	04/12/79	11/10/79	SUBSYSTEM	CHAD	POLITICAL
	Libya			04/12/79	11/10/79	Great power	Chad	Political
	Chad			06/25/79	11/10/79	Small power	Libya	Violent
	France			06/25/79	11/10/79	Great power	Libya	Indirect viol.
305	GOULIMIME-TARFAYA RD	125	5	06/01/79	06/25/79	SUBSYSTEM	NON-STATE ACTOR	VIOLENT
	Morocco			06/01/79	06/25/79	Middle power	Non-state actor	Violent
	Algeria			06/06/79	06/25/79	Middle power	Morocco	Political
306	SOVIET THREAT/PAK.	556	42	06/01/79	07/03/79	SUBSYSTEM	USSR	POLITICAL
	Pakistan			06/01/79	07/03/79	Middle power	USSR	Political
307	RHODESIA SETTLEMENT	115	4	07/15/79	03/04/80	SUBSYSTEM	NON-STATE ACTOR	INTERNAL CHAL.
	Rhodesia			07/15/79	03/04/80	Middle power	Non-state actor	Internal chal.
	Botswana			08/08/79	12/21/79	Small power	Rhodesia	Violent
	Mozambique			09/05/79	12/21/79	Small power	Rhodesia	Violent
	Zambia			11/17/79	01/31/80	Small power	Rhodesia	Violent
308	RAID ON ANGOLA	77	1	10/28/79	11/02/79	SUBSYSTEM	SOUTH AFRICA	VIOLENT
	Angola			10/28/79	11/02/79	Middle power	South Africa	Violent

720

RAVITY OF THREAT	CRISIS MGMT. TECHNIQUE	VIOLENCE	US ACTIV.	USSR ACTIV.	GLOBAL ORG. INVOLVEMENT	OUTCOME: SUBSTANCE	OUTCOME: FORM
/E DAMAGE	NON-VIOL. MIL.	NO VIOLENCE			OTHER	DEFINITIVE	UNILATERAL
damage	Non-viol. mil.	No violence	None	None	Other	Victory	Unilateral-adv.
/E DAMAGE	VIOLENCE	WAR			OTHER	AMBIGUOUS	UNILATERAL
nce	Violence	War	Political	Semi-mil.	Other	Stalemate	Unilateral-self
damage	Violence	War	Political	Semi-mil.	Other	Victory	Unilateral-adv.
ITORY	MULT. W/VIOL.	SERIOUS CLASHES			NONE	DEFINITIVE	OTHER
ory	Mult. w/viol.	Serious clashes	None	None	None	Victory	Other-non.-st.
	VIOLENCE	SERIOUS CLASHES			CONDEMNATION	AMBIGUOUS	UNILATERAL
	Violence	Serious clashes	None	None	Condemnation	Stalemate	Unilateral-self
	Non-viol. mil.	Minor clashes	None	None	None	Stalemate	Other-ally
	Non-viol. mil.	Serious clashes	None	None	None	Stalemate	Unilateral-self
ITORY	MULT. W/VIOL.	WAR			NONE	AMBIGUOUS	FORMAL AGMT.
ory	Mult. w/viol.	War	Semi-mil.	Semi-mil.	None	Compromise	Formal agmt.
ory	Mult. w/viol.	War	Semi-mil.	Semi-mil.	None	Compromise	Formal agmt.
	NEGOTIATION	MINOR CLASHES			CALL FOR ACTION	AMBIGUOUS	OTHER
	Negotiation	Minor clashes	None	None	Call for action	Stalemate	Other-GO intv.
TICAL REGIME	VIOLENCE	SERIOUS CLASHES			CALL FOR ACTION	AMBIGUOUS	UNILATERAL
nce	Violence	Serious clashes	Covert	SU actor	Condemnation	Victory	Unilateral-self
cal regime	Violence	Serious clashes	Covert	Direct mil.	None	Defeat	Unilateral-ally
cal regime	Negotiation	No violence	Semi-mil.	Direct mil.	Call for action	Stalemate	Other-ally
nce	Multiple, no viol.	No violence	US actor	Direct mil.	Call for action	Stalemate	Unilateral-self
TICAL REGIME	VIOLENCE	WAR			OTHER	AMBIGUOUS	UNILATERAL
nce	Mult. w/viol.	War	None	None	Other	Victory	Unilateral-adv.
cal regime	Mult. w/viol.	War	None	None	Other	Compromise	Unilateral-self
nce	Violence	War	None	None	Other	Compromise	Unilateral-ally
ITORY	MULT. W/VIOL.	MINOR CLASHES			DISCUSSION	DEFINITIVE	UNILATERAL
ory	Mult. w/viol.	Minor clashes	None	None	Discussion	Victory	Unilateral-self
ory	Non-viol. mil.	No violence	None	None	Discussion	Victory	Unilateral-adv.
ER	NEGOTIATION	NO VIOLENCE			NONE	AMBIGUOUS	SEMI-FORMAL AGMT.
	Negotiation	No violence	Political	Political	None	Stalemate	Semi-formal agmt.
TICAL REGIME	VIOLENCE	SERIOUS CLASHES			CALL FOR ACTION	DEFINITIVE	FORMAL AGMT.
cal regime	Mult. w/viol.	Serious clashes	Political	Semi-mil.	Call for action	Defeat	Unilateral-self
.	Violence	Minor clashes	None	None	Call for action	Victory	Formal agmt.
.	Violence	Serious clashes	None	Semi-mil.	Call for action	Victory	Formal agmt.
.	Non-viol. mil.	Serious clashes	None	None	Call for action	Victory	Semi-formal agmt.
)	NEGOTIATION	MINOR CLASHES			CALL FOR ACTION	AMBIGUOUS	OTHER
.	Negotiation	Minor clashes	None	None	Call for action	Stalemate	Other-GO intv.

(continued)

TABLE III.1.—*Continued*

NUM.	INTERNATIONAL CRISIS ACTORS	SUM. PAGE	PC OR REG.	TRIG. DATE	TERM. DATE	SYSTEM LEVEL POWER STATUS	TRIGGERING ENTITY	CRISIS TRIGGER
309	US HOSTAGES IN IRAN	649	44	11/04/79	01/20/81	MAINLY SUBSYSTEM	IRAN	POLITICAL
	US			11/04/79	01/20/81	Superpower	Iran	Political
	Iran			04/24/80	01/20/81	Middle power	US	Non-viol. mil.
310	COLOMBIA/NICARAGUA	521	41	12/12/79	07/08/81	SUBSYSTEM	NICARAGUA	POLITICAL
	Colombia			12/12/79	07/08/81	Small power	Nicaragua	Political
	Nicaragua			02/07/80	07/08/81	Small power	Colombia	Political
311	RAID ON GAFSA	455	40	01/27/80	04/30/80	NON-STATE ACTOR	NON-STATE ACTOR	INTERNAL CHAL.
	Tunisia			01/27/80	04/30/80	Small power	Non-state actor	Internal chal.
	Libya			01/28/80	04/30/80	Middle power	France	Non-viol. mil.
312	OPERATION IMAN	126	5	03/01/80	05/77/80	SUBSYSTEM	NON-STATE ACTOR	VIOLENT
	Morocco			03/01/80	05/77/80	Great power	Non-state actor	Violent
313	OPERATION SMOKESHELL	78	1	06/07/80	07/02/80	SUBSYSTEM	SOUTH AFRICA	VIOLENT
	Angola			06/07/80	07/02/80	Middle power	South Africa	Violent
314	LIBYA THREAT-SADAT	457	40	06/11/80	06/88/80	SUBSYSTEM	LIBYA	POLITICAL
	Egypt			06/11/80	06/88/80	Great power	Libya	Political
	Libya			06/16/80	06/88/80	Middle power	Egypt	Non-viol. mil.
315	SOLIDARITY	259	21	08/14/80	12/13/81	SUBSYSTEM	NON-STATE ACTOR	INTERNAL CHAL.
	Poland			08/14/80	12/13/81	Middle power	Non-state actor	Internal chal.
	USSR			08/14/80	12/13/81	Superpower	Non-state actor	Political
	Czechoslovakia			08/30/80	12/13/81	Small power	Non-state actor	Political
	East Germany			08/30/80	12/13/81	Middle power	Non-state actor	Political
316	LIBYA/MALTA OIL DISP.	610	43	08/20/80	09/15/80	SUBSYSTEM	LIBYA	NON-VIOL. MIL.
	Malta			08/20/80	09/15/80	Small power	Libya	Non-viol. mil.
317	ONSET IRAN/IRAQ WAR	303	24	09/17/80	11/30/80	SUBSYSTEM	IRAQ	POLITICAL
	Iran			09/17/80	11/19/80	Great power	Iraq	Political
	Iraq			09/23/80	11/30/80	Great power	Iran	Violent
318	LIBYA INTERV./GAMBIA	458	40	10/27/80	11/07/80	NON-STATE ACTOR	NON-STATE ACTOR	INTERNAL CHAL.
	Gambia			10/27/80	11/07/80	Small power	Non-state actor	Internal chal.
319	JORDAN/SYRIA CONFRNT.	651	44	11/25/80	12/14/80	SUBSYSTEM	SYRIA	NON-VIOL. MIL.
	Jordan			11/25/80	12/14/80	Small power	Syria	Non-viol. mil.
320	E. AFRICA CONFRONT.	100	3	12/05/80	06/29/81	SUBSYSTEM	MULTI-STATE	POLITICAL
	Somalia			12/05/80	06/29/81	Small power	Multi-state	Political
	Ethiopia			12/07/80	06/29/81	Middle power	Somalia	Political
	Kenya			12/07/80	06/29/81	Small power	Somalia	Political
321	CHAD/LIBYA V	89	2	01/06/81	11/16/81	SUBSYSTEM	LIBYA	POLITICAL
	France			01/06/81	11/16/81	Great power	Libya	Political
	Libya			01/11/81	11/16/81	Great power	France	Non-viol. mil.

RAVITY OF THREAT	CRISIS MGMT. TECHNIQUE	VIOLENCE	US ACTIV.	USSR ACTIV.	GLOBAL ORG. INVOLVEMENT	OUTCOME: SUBSTANCE	OUTCOME: FORM
UENCE	MULTIPLE, NO VIOL.	MINOR CLASHES			MEDIATION	AMBIGUOUS	FORMAL AGMT.
nce	Multiple, no viol.	Minor clashes	US actor	Political	Mediation	Compromise	Formal agmt.
cal regime	Multiple, no viol.	Minor clashes	Direct mil.	Political	Mediation	Compromise	Formal agmt.
ITORY	MULTIPLE, NO VIOL.	NO VIOLENCE			GOOD OFFICES	DEFINITIVE	UNILATERAL
ory	Multiple, no viol.	No violence	Political	None	Good offices	Victory	Unilateral-ally
ory	Multiple, no viol.	No violence	Political	None	Good offices	Defeat	Other-misc.
UENCE	MULT. W/VIOL.	SERIOUS CLASHES			NONE	DEFINITIVE	SEMI-FORMAL AGMT.
cal regime	Mult. w/viol.	Serious clashes	Semi-mil.	None	None	Victory	Semi-formal agmt.
nce	Non-viol. mil.	Serious clashes	Semi-mil.	None	None	Defeat	Semi-formal agmt.
ITORY	VIOLENCE	SERIOUS CLASHES			NONE	DEFINITIVE	FADED
ory	Violence	Serious clashes	None	None	None	Victory	Faded
VE DAMAGE	MULT. W/VIOL.	SERIOUS CLASHES			CONDEMNATION	AMBIGUOUS	UNILATERAL
damage	Mult. w/viol.	Serious clashes	None	None	Condemnation	Stalemate	Unilateral-adv.
TICAL REGIME	NON-VIOL. MIL.	NO VIOLENCE			OTHER	AMBIGUOUS	FADED
cal regime	Non-viol. mil.	No violence	None	None	Other	Victory	Faded
	Multiple, no viol.	No violence	None	None	Other	Stalemate	Faded
UENCE	MULTIPLE, NO VIOL.	NO VIOLENCE			NONE	DEFINITIVE	UNILATERAL
cal regime	Multiple, no viol.	No violence	Political	Semi-mil.	None	Victory	Unilateral-self
nce	Multiple, no viol.	No violence	Political	SU actor	None	Victory	Unilateral-ally
cal regime	Multiple, no viol.	No violence	Political	Semi-mil.	None	Victory	Unilateral-ally
cal regime	Multiple, no viol.	No violence	Political	Semi-mil.	None	Victory	Unilateral-ally
NOMIC	NEGOTIATION	NO VIOLENCE			DISCUSSION	AMBIGUOUS	UNILATERAL
omic	Negotiation	No violence	None	None	Discussion	Compromise	Unilateral-ally
ITORY	VIOLENCE	WAR			MEDIATION	AMBIGUOUS	UNILATERAL
ory	Violence	War	Semi-mil.	Semi-mil.	Mediation	Stalemate	Unilateral-self
ory	Violence	War	Semi-mil.	Semi-mil.	Mediation	Stalemate	Unilateral-self
TICAL REGIME	MULTIPLE, NO VIOL.	NO VIOLENCE			NONE	DEFINITIVE	UNILATERAL
cal regime	Multiple, no viol.	No violence	None	None	None	Victory	Unilateral-ally
TICAL REGIME	NON-VIOL. MIL.	NO VIOLENCE			NONE	DEFINITIVE	TACIT UNDERSTANDING
cal regime	Non-viol. mil.	No violence	Semi-mil.	Political	None	Victory	Tacit understanding
ITORY	NON-VIOL. MIL.	NO VIOLENCE			NONE	AMBIGUOUS	FORMAL AGMT.
ory	Non-viol. mil.	No violence	None	None	None	Victory	Formal agmt.
ory	Negotiation	No violence	None	None	None	Compromise	Formal agmt.
ory	Negotiation	No violence	None	None	None	Compromise	Formal agmt.
UENCE	NEGOTIATION	MINOR CLASHES			OTHER	DEFINITIVE	UNILATERAL
nce	Negotiation	No violence	Political	None	Other	Victory	Unilateral-adv.
nce	Negotiation	Minor clashes	Political	None	Other	Defeat	Unilateral-self

(continued)

723

TABLE III.1.—Continued

NUM.	INTERNATIONAL CRISIS ACTORS	SUM. PAGE	PC OR REG.	TRIG. DATE	TERM. DATE	SYSTEM LEVEL POWER STATUS	TRIGGERING ENTITY	CRISIS TRIGGER
322	ECUADOR/PERU BDR. III	137	7	01/22/81	04/02/81	SUBSYSTEM	PERU	VIOLENT
	Ecuador			01/22/81	04/02/81	Small power	Peru	Violent
	Peru			01/22/81	04/02/81	Middle power	Ecuador	Violent
323	MOZAMBIQUE RAID	460	40	01/30/81	03/88/81	SUBSYSTEM	SOUTH AFRICA	VIOLENT
	Mozambique			01/30/81	03/88/81	Small power	South Africa	Violent
324	IRAQ NUCLEAR REACTOR	292	23	01/99/81	06/19/81	SUBSYSTEM	IRAQ	EXT. CHANGE
	Israel			01/99/81	06/07/81	Great power	Iraq	Ext. change
	Iraq			06/07/81	06/19/81	Great power	Israel	Violent
325	ESSEQUIBO II	523	41	04/04/81	03/99/83	SUBSYSTEM	VENEZUELA	POLITICAL
	Guyana			04/04/81	03/99/83	Small power	Venezuela	Political
	Venezuela			08/88/81	03/99/83	Middle power	Guyana	Political
326	CONTRAS I	142	8	04/28/81	05/13/81	SUBSYSTEM	NICARAGUA	VIOLENT
	Honduras			04/28/81	05/13/81	Small power	Nicaragua	Violent
	Nicaragua			04/28/81	05/13/81	Small power	Honduras	Non-viol. mil.
327	AL-BIQA MISSILES I	294	23	04/28/81	07/24/81	SUBSYSTEM	ISRAEL	VIOLENT
	Syria			04/28/81	07/24/81	Great power	Israel	Violent
	Israel			04/29/81	07/24/81	Great power	Syria	Non-viol. mil.
328	CAMEROON/NIGERIA I	461	40	05/15/81	07/24/81	SUBSYSTEM	CAMEROON	VIOLENT
	Nigeria			05/15/81	07/24/81	Great power	Cameroon	Violent
	Cameroon			05/18/81	07/24/81	Small power	Nigeria	Political
329	COUP ATTEMPT-GAMBIA	462	40	07/30/81	01/29/82	SUBSYSTEM	GAMBIA	INDIRECT VIOL.
	Senegal			07/30/81	01/29/82	Middle power	Gambia	Indirect viol.
330	GULF OF SYRTE I	463	40	08/12/81	09/01/81	SUBSYSTEM	US	OTHER NON-VIOL
	Libya			08/12/81	09/01/81	Middle power	US	Other non-viol.
331	OPERATION PROTEA	79	1	08/23/81	09/30/81	SUBSYSTEM	SOUTH AFRICA	VIOLENT
	Angola			08/23/81	09/30/81	Middle power	South Africa	Violent
332	GALTAT ZEMMOUR I	127	5	10/13/81	11/09/81	SUBSYSTEM	NON-STATE ACTOR	VIOLENT
	Morocco			10/13/81	11/09/81	Great power	Non-state actor	Violent
333	U-137 INCIDENT	611	43	10/28/81	11/06/81	SUBSYSTEM	USSR	POLITICAL
	Sweden			10/28/81	11/06/81	Middle power	USSR	Political
	USSR			10/28/81	11/06/81	Superpower	Sweden	Political
334	COUP ATTEMPT-BAHRAIN	652	44	12/13/81	01/08/82	SUBSYSTEM	NON-STATE ACTOR	INTERNAL CHAL.
	Bahrain			12/13/81	01/08/82	Small power	Non-state actor	Internal chal.
	Saudi Arabia			12/13/81	12/19/81	Middle power	Iran	Other non-viol.
335	KHORRAMSHAHR	305	24	03/22/82	07/30/82	SUBSYSTEM	IRAN	VIOLENT
	Iraq			03/22/82	07/30/82	Great power	Iran	Violent

GRAVITY OF THREAT	CRISIS MGMT. TECHNIQUE	VIOLENCE	US ACTIV.	USSR ACTIV.	GLOBAL ORG. INVOLVEMENT	OUTCOME: SUBSTANCE	OUTCOME: FORM
RITORY	MULT. W/VIOL.	MINOR CLASHES			NONE	AMBIGUOUS	FORMAL AGMT.
ory	Mult. w/viol.	Minor clashes	Political	None	None	Stalemate	Formal agmt.
ory	Mult. w/viol.	Minor clashes	Political	None	None	Defeat	Formal agmt.
RITORY	NEGOTIATION	MINOR CLASHES			OTHER	AMBIGUOUS	FADED
ory	Negotiation	Minor clashes	None	Semi-mil.	Other	Stalemate	Faded
TENCE	MULT. W/VIOL.	MINOR CLASHES			CONDEMNATION	DEFINITIVE	UNILATERAL
ence	Mult. w/viol.	Minor clashes	Political	None	Condemnation	Victory	Unilateral-self
e damage	Negotiation	Minor clashes	None	Political	Call for action	Defeat	Unilateral-self
RITORY	MULTIPLE, NO VIOL.	NO VIOLENCE			MEDIATION	AMBIGUOUS	SEMI-FORMAL AGMT.
tory	Multiple, no viol.	No violence	None	None	Mediation	Stalemate	Semi-formal agmt.
tory	Negotiation	No violence	None	None	Mediation	Stalemate	Semi-formal agmt.
RITORY	NEGOTIATION	MINOR CLASHES			NONE	DEFINITIVE	SEMI-FORMAL AGMT.
tory	Negotiation	Minor clashes	None	None	None	Compromise	Semi-formal agmt.
tory	Negotiation	Minor clashes	None	None	None	Compromise	Semi-formal agmt.
UENCE	NON-VIOL. MIL.	MINOR CLASHES			NONE	AMBIGUOUS	FORMAL AGMT.
ence	Non-viol. mil.	Minor clashes	Political	Political	None	Victory	Formal agmt.
ence	Negotiation	Minor clashes	Political	Political	None	Stalemate	Formal agmt.
RITORY	NEGOTIATION	MINOR CLASHES			NONE	DEFINITIVE	SEMI-FORMAL AGMT.
tory	Negotiation	Minor clashes	None	None	None	Victory	Semi-formal agmt.
)	Negotiation	Minor clashes	None	None	None	Defeat	Semi-formal agmt.
UENCE	VIOLENCE	SERIOUS CLASHES			NONE	DEFINITIVE	FORMAL AGMT.
ence	Violence	Serious clashes	Political	None	None	Victory	Formal agmt.
RITORY	NON-VIOL. MIL.	MINOR CLASHES			NONE	DEFINITIVE	UNILATERAL
tory	Non-viol. mil.	Minor clashes	Direct mil.	None	None	Defeat	Unilateral-self
VE DAMAGE	MULT. W/VIOL.	SERIOUS CLASHES			DISCUSSION	AMBIGUOUS	UNILATERAL
e damage	Mult. w/viol.	Serious clashes	Political	Political	Discussion	Stalemate	Unilateral-self
RITORY	MULT. W/VIOL.	SERIOUS CLASHES			NONE	DEFINITIVE	UNILATERAL
tory	Mult. w/viol.	Serious clashes	Political	Political	None	Defeat	Unilateral-self
VE DAMAGE	NEGOTIATION	NO VIOLENCE			NONE	DEFINITIVE	UNILATERAL
e damage	Negotiation	No violence	None	SU actor	None	Victory	Unilateral-self
e damage	Negotiation	No violence	None	SU actor	None	Defeat	Unilateral-adv.
ITICAL REGIME	NEGOTIATION	NO VIOLENCE			NONE	DEFINITIVE	UNILATERAL
ical regime	Negotiation	No violence	None	None	None	Victory	Unilateral-self
ence	Negotiation	No violence	None	None	None	Victory	Other-ally
VE DAMAGE	MULT. W/VIOL.	WAR			CALL FOR ACTION	DEFINITIVE	UNILATERAL
e damage	Mult. w/viol.	War	Economic	Semi-mil.	Call for action	Defeat	Unilateral-adv.

(continued)

TABLE III.1.—Continued

NUM.	INTERNATIONAL CRISIS ACTORS	SUM. PAGE	PC OR REG.	TRIG. DATE	TERM. DATE	SYSTEM LEVEL POWER STATUS	TRIGGERING ENTITY	CRISIS TRIGGER
336	FALKLANDS/MALVINAS	524	41	03/31/82	06/14/82	SUBSYSTEM	ARGENTINA	EXT. CHANGE
	UK			03/31/82	06/14/82	Great power	Argentina	Ext. change
	Argentina			04/05/82	06/14/82	Great power	UK	Non-viol. mil.
337	WAR IN LEBANON	295	23	06/05/82	05/17/83	SUBSYSTEM	ISRAEL	VIOLENT
	Lebanon			06/05/82	05/17/83	Small power	Israel	Violent
	Syria			06/07/82	09/01/82	Great power	Israel	Violent
	Israel			06/09/82	09/01/82	Great power	Syria	Violent
338	OGADEN III	101	3	06/30/82	08/99/82	SUBSYSTEM	ETHIOPIA	VIOLENT
	Somalia			06/30/82	08/99/82	Small power	Ethiopia	Violent
	Ethiopia			07/26/82	08/99/82	Middle power	US	Non-viol. mil.
339	LESOTHO RAID	464	40	12/09/82	12/15/82	SUBSYSTEM	SOUTH AFRICA	VIOLENT
	Lesotho			12/09/82	12/15/82	Small power	South Africa	Violent
340	LIBYA THREAT/SUDAN	465	40	02/11/83	02/22/83	SUBSYSTEM	LIBYA	NON-VIOL. MIL.
	Sudan			02/11/83	02/22/83	Small power	Libya	Non-viol. mil.
	Egypt			02/11/83	02/22/83	Great power	Libya	Non-viol. mil.
	Libya			02/17/83	02/22/83	Middle power	US	Non-viol. mil.
341	CHAD/NIGERIA CLASHES	466	40	04/18/83	07/11/83	SUBSYSTEM	NIGERIA	VIOLENT
	Chad			04/18/83	07/11/83	Small power	Nigeria	Violent
	Nigeria			04/18/83	07/11/83	Great power	Chad	Violent
342	CHAD/LIBYA VI	91	2	06/24/83	12/11/84	SUBSYSTEM	LIBYA	VIOLENT
	Chad			06/24/83	10/10/84	Small power	Libya	Violent
	France			07/31/83	12/11/84	Great power	Libya	Indirect viol.
	Libya			08/09/83	11/10/84	Great power	France	Non-viol. mil.
343	INVASION OF GRENADA	527	41	10/19/83	10/28/83	SUBSYSTEM	GRENADA	INDIRECT VIOL.
	US			10/19/83	10/28/83	Superpower	Grenada	Indirect viol.
	Grenada			10/21/83	10/28/83	Small power	US	Non-viol. mil.
344	ABLE ARCHER 83	358	27	11/02/83	11/11/83	DOMINANT SYSTEM	US	NON-VIOL. MIL.
	USSR			11/02/83	11/11/83	Superpower	US	Non-viol. mil.
345	MAITENGWE CLASHES	467	40	11/08/83	12/21/83	SUBSYSTEM	ZIMBABWE	VIOLENT
	Botswana			11/08/83	12/21/83	Small power	Zimbabwe	Violent
346	ETHIOP./SUDAN TENSION	468	40	11/20/83	02/20/84	SUBSYSTEM	ETHIOPIA	NON-VIOL. MIL.
	Sudan			11/20/83	02/20/84	Small power	Ethiopia	Non-viol. mil.
347	OPERATION ASKARI	80	1	12/06/83	02/16/84	SUBSYSTEM	SOUTH AFRICA	VIOLENT
	Angola			12/06/83	02/16/84	Middle power	South Africa	Violent

GRAVITY OF THREAT	CRISIS MGMT. TECHNIQUE	VIOLENCE	US ACTIV.	USSR ACTIV.	GLOBAL ORG. INVOLVEMENT	OUTCOME: SUBSTANCE	OUTCOME: FORM
RITORY	MULT. W/VIOL.	WAR			CONDEMNATION	DEFINITIVE	IMPOSED AGMT.
itory	Mult. w/viol.	War	Political	Political	Other	Victory	Imposed-imposer
itory	Mult. w/viol.	War	Political	Political	Condemnation	Defeat	Imposed-imposee
LUENCE	MULT. W/VIOL.	WAR			CALL FOR ACTION	AMBIGUOUS	SEMI-FORMAL AGMT.
itory	Negotiation	War	Political	Political	Call for action	Stalemate	Other-ally
ence	Mult. w/viol.	War	Political	Semi-mil.	Call for action	Compromise	Semi-formal agmt.
ence	Mult. w/viol.	War	Political	Political	Condemnation	Compromise	Semi-formal agmt.
RRITORY	MULT. W/VIOL.	SERIOUS CLASHES			NONE	AMBIGUOUS	OTHER
itory	Mult. w/viol.	Serious clashes	Semi-mil.	None	None	Stalemate	Other-misc.
itory	Violence	Serious clashes	Semi-mil.	None	None	Stalemate	Other-misc.
RITORY	NEGOTIATION	MINOR CLASHES			CONDEMNATION	AMBIGUOUS	OTHER
itory	Negotiation	Minor clashes	Political	None	Condemnation	Stalemate	Other-GO intv.
ITICAL REGIME	NON-VIOL. MIL.	NO VIOLENCE			DISCUSSION	AMBIGUOUS	UNILATERAL
tical regime	Multiple, no viol.	No violence	Semi-mil.	None	Discussion	Victory	Unilateral-self
ence	Non-viol. mil.	No violence	Semi-mil.	None	Discussion	Victory	Unilateral-self
ence	Non-viol. mil.	No violence	Semi-mil.	None	Discussion	Compromise	Unilateral-adv.
RITORY	MULT. W/VIOL.	SERIOUS CLASHES			NONE	DEFINITIVE	FORMAL AGMT.
itory	Mult. w/viol.	Serious clashes	None	None	None	Victory	Formal agmt.
itory	Mult. w/viol.	Serious clashes	None	None	None	Victory	Formal agmt.
ITICAL REGIME	MULT. W/VIOL.	MINOR CLASHES			DISCUSSION	AMBIGUOUS	SEMI-FORMAL AGMT.
tical regime	Multiple, no viol.	Minor clashes	Semi-mil.	Political	Discussion	Defeat	Semi-formal agmt.
ence	Mult. w/viol.	Minor clashes	Semi-mil.	Political	Discussion	Compromise	Semi-formal agmt.
ence	Negotiation	Minor clashes	Semi-mil.	Political	Discussion	Victory	Semi-formal agmt.
LUENCE	VIOLENCE	SERIOUS CLASHES			DISCUSSION	DEFINITIVE	UNILATERAL
ence	Violence	Serious clashes	US actor	Political	Discussion	Victory	Unilateral-self
tical regime	Mult. w/viol.	Serious clashes	Direct mil.	Political	Discussion	Defeat	Unilateral-adv.
STENCE	NON-VIOL. MIL.	NO VIOLENCE			NONE	AMBIGUOUS	FADED
tence	Non-viol. mil.	No violence	Direct mil.	SU actor	None	Stalemate	Faded
O	NEGOTIATION	MINOR CLASHES			NONE	DEFINITIVE	OTHER
O	Negotiation	Minor clashes	None	None	None	Victory	Other-misc.
ITICAL REGIME	NON-VIOL. MIL.	NO VIOLENCE			NONE	DEFINITIVE	UNILATERAL
tical regime	Non-viol. mil.	No violence	None	Semi-mil.	None	Victory	Unilateral-self
AVE DAMAGE	MULT. W/VIOL.	SERIOUS CLASHES			CALL FOR ACTION	AMBIGUOUS	FORMAL AGMT.
ve damage	Mult. w/viol.	Serious clashes	Political	Political	Call for action	Compromise	Formal agmt.

(continued)

TABLE III.1.—*Continued*

NUM.	INTERNATIONAL CRISIS ACTORS	SUM. PAGE	PC OR REG.	TRIG. DATE	TERM. DATE	SYSTEM LEVEL POWER STATUS	TRIGGERING ENTITY	CRISIS TRIGGER
348	BASRA-KHARG ISLAND	307	24	02/21/84	07/11/84	SUBSYSTEM	IRAN	VIOLENT
	Iraq			02/21/84	03/18/84	Great power	Iran	Violent
	Iran			03/01/84	06/10/84	Great power	Iraq	Violent
	Kuwait			05/13/84	07/11/84	Small power	Iran	Violent
	Saudi Arabia			05/16/84	06/20/84	Middle power	Iran	Violent
349	AEGEAN SEA II	372	28	03/08/84	03/10/84	SUBSYSTEM	TURKEY	VIOLENT
	Greece			03/08/84	03/10/84	Middle power	Turkey	Violent
350	OMDURMAN BOMBING	469	40	03/16/84	99/99/84	SUBSYSTEM	LIBYA	VIOLENT
	Sudan			03/16/84	99/99/84	Small power	Libya	Violent
	Egypt			03/16/84	99/99/84	Great power	Libya	Indirect viol.
	Libya			03/18/84	99/99/84	Middle power	US	Ext. change
351	VIET./INCURS.	557	42	03/25/84	04/17/84	SUBSYSTEM	VIETNAM	VIOLENT
	Thailand			03/25/84	04/17/84	Middle power	Vietnam	Violent
352	SINO/VIETNAM CLASHES	160	11	04/02/84	06/88/84	SUBSYSTEM	CHINA (PRC)	VIOLENT
	Vietnam			04/02/84	06/88/84	Great power	China (PRC)	Violent
	China (PRC)			04/28/84	06/88/84	Great power	Vietnam	Indirect viol.
353	THREE VILLAGE BDR. I	558	42	06/05/84	10/77/84	SUBSYSTEM	LAOS	NON-VIOL. MIL.
	Thailand			06/05/84	07/17/84	Middle power	Laos	Non-viol. mil.
	Laos			06/06/84	10/77/84	Small power	Thailand	Violent
354	NICARAGUA MIG-21S	360	27	11/06/84	11/12/84	DOMINANT SYSTEM	USSR	EXT. CHANGE
	US			11/06/84	11/12/84	Superpower	USSR	Ext. change
	Nicaragua			11/07/84	11/12/84	Small power	US	Non-viol. mil.
355	BOTSWANA RAID	470	40	06/14/85	06/21/85	SUBSYSTEM	SOUTH AFRICA	VIOLENT
	Botswana			06/14/85	06/21/85	Small power	South Africa	Violent
356	EXPULSION-TUNISIANS	471	40	08/21/85	09/26/85	SUBSYSTEM	LIBYA	NON-VIOL. MIL.
	Tunisia			08/21/85	09/26/85	Small power	Libya	Non-viol. mil.
357	AL-BIQA MISSILES II	298	23	11/19/85	01/05/86	SUBSYSTEM	ISRAEL	VIOLENT
	Syria			11/19/85	01/05/86	Great power	Israel	Violent
	Israel			12/15/85	01/05/86	Great power	Syria	Non-viol. mil.
358	EGYPT AIR HIJACKING	472	40	11/23/85	12/03/85	SUBSYSTEM	NON-STATE ACTOR	VIOLENT
	Egypt			11/23/85	12/03/85	Great power	Non-state actor	Violent
	Libya			11/24/85	12/03/85	Middle power	Egypt	Non-viol. mil.
359	BURKINA FASO/MALI BDR	473	40	12/20/85	01/18/86	SUBSYSTEM	BURKINA FASO	NON-VIOL. MIL.
	Mali			12/20/85	01/18/86	Small power	Burkina Faso	Non-viol. mil.
	Burkina Faso			12/25/85	01/18/86	Small power	Mali	Violent
360	S.A. RAID ON LESOTHO	474	40	12/20/85	01/25/86	SUBSYSTEM	SOUTH AFRICA	VIOLENT
	Lesotho			12/20/85	01/25/86	Small power	South Africa	Violent

RAVITY OF THREAT	CRISIS MGMT. TECHNIQUE	VIOLENCE	US ACTIV.	USSR ACTIV.	GLOBAL ORG. INVOLVEMENT	OUTCOME: SUBSTANCE	OUTCOME: FORM
E DAMAGE	VIOLENCE	WAR			MEDIATION	AMBIGUOUS	SEMI-FORMAL AGMT.
damage	Violence	War	Semi-mil.	Semi-mil.	Mediation	Stalemate	Unilateral-self
ice	Violence	War	Semi-mil.	Semi-mil.	Mediation	Stalemate	Semi-formal agmt.
nic	Negotiation	Minor clashes	Semi-mil.	Semi-mil.	Call for action	Defeat	Other-ally
nic	Mult. w/viol.	Minor clashes	Semi-mil.	Semi-mil.	Call for action	Victory	Unilateral-self
	NEGOTIATION	MINOR CLASHES			NONE	AMBIGUOUS	SEMI-FORMAL AGMT.
	Negotiation	Minor clashes	None	None	None	Compromise	Semi-formal agmt.
ICAL REGIME	NON-VIOL. MIL.	MINOR CLASHES			DISCUSSION	AMBIGUOUS	FADED
al regime	Non-viol. mil.	Minor clashes	Semi-mil.	None	Discussion	Victory	Faded
ice	Non-viol. mil.	No violence	Semi-mil.	None	Discussion	Victory	Faded
ice	Negotiation	No violence	Semi-mil.	Political	Discussion	Compromise	Faded
	NEGOTIATION	MINOR CLASHES			OTHER	AMBIGUOUS	UNILATERAL
	Negotiation	Minor clashes	Semi-mil.	None	Other	Stalemate	Unilateral-ally
JENCE	VIOLENCE	SERIOUS CLASHES			OTHER	AMBIGUOUS	FADED
nce	Violence	Serious clashes	Political	Semi-mil.	Other	Stalemate	Faded
ory	Violence	Serious clashes	Political	Semi-mil.	Other	Stalemate	Faded
ITORY	MULT. W/VIOL.	MINOR CLASHES			DISCUSSION	AMBIGUOUS	UNILATERAL
	Mult. w/viol.	Minor clashes	None	None	Discussion	Compromise	Semi-formal agmt.
ory	Mult. w/viol.	Minor clashes	None	None	Discussion	Compromise	Unilateral-adv.
TICAL REGIME	NON-VIOL. MIL.	NO VIOLENCE			DISCUSSION	AMBIGUOUS	UNILATERAL
nce	Non-viol. mil.	No violence	US actor	Semi-mil.	Discussion	Stalemate	Unilateral-adv.
cal regime	Negotiation	No violence	Semi-mil.	Semi-mil.	Discussion	Stalemate	Unilateral-self
ITORY	NEGOTIATION	MINOR CLASHES			CALL FOR ACTION	AMBIGUOUS	OTHER
ory	Negotiation	Minor clashes	Political	None	Call for action	Stalemate	Other-GO intv.
TICAL REGIME	MULTIPLE, NO VIOL.	NO VIOLENCE			NONE	DEFINITIVE	UNILATERAL
cal regime	Multiple, no viol.	No violence	Political	None	None	Victory	Unilateral-self
UENCE	NON-VIOL. MIL.	MINOR CLASHES			NONE	AMBIGUOUS	TACIT UNDERSTANDING
nce	Non-viol. mil.	Minor clashes	Political	Political	None	Stalemate	Tacit understanding
nce	Negotiation	Minor clashes	Political	Political	None	Victory	Tacit understanding
TICAL REGIME	MULT. W/VIOL.	MINOR CLASHES			NONE	DEFINITIVE	UNILATERAL
r	Mult. w/viol.	Minor clashes	Semi-mil.	Political	None	Victory	Unilateral-self
cal regime	Negotiation	No violence	Semi-mil.	Political	None	Victory	Unilateral-adv.
RITORY	VIOLENCE	SERIOUS CLASHES			GOOD OFFICES	AMBIGUOUS	FORMAL AGMT.
ory	Violence	Serious clashes	None	None	Good offices	Stalemate	Formal agmt.
cal regime	Violence	Serious clashes	None	None	Good offices	Stalemate	Formal agmt.
TICAL REGIME	NEGOTIATION	MINOR CLASHES			CALL FOR ACTION	DEFINITIVE	FORMAL AGMT.
cal regime	Negotiation	Minor clashes	Political	Political	Call for action	Defeat	Formal agmt.

(continued)

729

TABLE III.1.—Continued

NUM.	INTERNATIONAL CRISIS ACTORS	SUM. PAGE	PC OR REG.	TRIG. DATE	TERM. DATE	SYSTEM LEVEL POWER STATUS	TRIGGERING ENTITY	CRISIS TRIGGER
361	CAPTURE OF AL-FAW	309	24	02/09/86	04/66/86	SUBSYSTEM	IRAN	VIOLENT
	Iraq			02/09/86	04/66/86	Great power	Iran	Violent
	Kuwait			02/11/86	02/13/86	Small power	Iran	Indirect viol.
	Saudi Arabia			02/11/86	02/13/86	Middle power	Iran	Indirect viol.
	Iran			02/14/86	04/66/86	Great power	Iraq	Violent
362	CHAD/LIBYA VII	92	2	02/10/86	03/88/86	SUBSYSTEM	LIBYA	VIOLENT
	Chad			02/10/86	03/88/86	Small power	Libya	Violent
	France			02/10/86	03/88/86	Great power	Libya	Indirect viol.
	Libya			02/16/86	03/88/86	Great power	France	Violent
363	GULF OF SYRTE II	475	40	03/24/86	04/21/86	SUBSYSTEM	US	NON-VIOL. MIL.
	Libya			03/24/86	04/21/86	Middle power	US	Non-viol. mil.
	US			04/05/86	04/15/86	Superpower	Non-state actor	Violent
364	AL-DIBAL INCIDENT	654	44	04/26/86	06/15/86	SUBSYSTEM	QATAR	VIOLENT
	Bahrain			04/26/86	06/15/86	Small power	Qatar	Violent
365	S.A. CROSS BORDER RAID	477	40	05/19/86	05/88/86	SUBSYSTEM	SOUTH AFRICA	VIOLENT
	Botswana			05/19/86	05/88/86	Small power	South Africa	Violent
	Zambia			05/19/86	05/88/86	Small power	South Africa	Violent
	Zimbabwe			05/19/86	05/88/86	Middle power	South Africa	Violent
366	REBEL ATTACK-UGANDA	478	40	08/19/86	09/20/86	SUBSYSTEM	NON-STATE ACTOR	VIOLENT
	Uganda			08/19/86	09/20/86	Small power	Non-state actor	Violent
367	MOZAMBIQUE ULTIMATUM	479	40	09/11/86	12/18/86	SUBSYSTEM	MOZAMBIQUE	POLITICAL
	Malawi			09/11/86	12/18/86	Small power	Mozambique	Political
368	ATTEMPTED COUP-TOGO	480	40	09/23/86	02/05/87	SUBSYSTEM	NON-STATE ACTOR	INTERNAL CHAL.
	Togo			09/23/86	02/05/87	Small power	Non-state actor	Internal chal.
369	CONTRAS II	143	8	12/04/86	12/12/86	SUBSYSTEM	NICARAGUA	VIOLENT
	Honduras			12/04/86	12/12/86	Small power	Nicaragua	Violent
	Nicaragua			12/06/86	12/12/86	Small power	Honduras	Violent
370	CHAD/LIBYA VIII	93	2	12/12/86	09/11/87	SUBSYSTEM	LIBYA	VIOLENT
	Chad			12/12/86	09/11/87	Small power	Libya	Violent
	Libya			01/02/87	09/11/87	Great power	Chad	Violent
371	SINO/VIETNAM BORDER	161	11	01/05/87	01/10/87	SUBSYSTEM	CHINA (PRC)	VIOLENT
	Vietnam			01/05/87	01/08/87	Great power	China (PRC)	Violent
	China (PRC)			01/05/87	01/10/87	Great power	Vietnam	Violent
372	PUNJAB WAR SCARE II	174	12	01/77/87	02/19/87	SUBSYSTEM	PAKISTAN	NON-VIOL. MIL.
	India			01/77/87	02/19/87	Great power	Pakistan	Non-viol. mil.
	Pakistan			01/23/87	02/19/87	Middle power	India	Non-viol. mil.

GRAVITY OF THREAT	CRISIS MGMT. TECHNIQUE	VIOLENCE	US ACTIV.	USSR ACTIV.	GLOBAL ORG. INVOLVEMENT	OUTCOME: SUBSTANCE	OUTCOME: FORM
RITORY	VIOLENCE	WAR			CONDEMNATION	AMBIGUOUS	UNILATERAL
tory	Violence	War	Semi-mil.	None	Condemnation	Defeat	Unilateral-self
omic	Negotiation	No violence	Semi-mil.	None	Condemnation	Stalemate	Unilateral-adv.
omic	Negotiation	No violence	Semi-mil.	None	Condemnation	Stalemate	Unilateral-adv.
tory	Violence	War	Semi-mil.	None	Condemnation	Victory	Unilateral-self
RITORY	VIOLENCE	SERIOUS CLASHES			OTHER	AMBIGUOUS	FADED
tory	Mult. w/viol.	Serious clashes	Semi-mil.	Political	Other	Stalemate	Faded
ence	Violence	Serious clashes	Semi-mil.	Political	Other	Stalemate	Faded
tory	Violence	Serious clashes	Semi-mil.	Political	Other	Stalemate	Faded
RITORY	VIOLENCE	MINOR CLASHES			DISCUSSION	DEFINITIVE	OTHER
tory	Violence	Minor clashes	Direct mil.	Political	Discussion	Defeat	Other-GO intv.
ence	Violence	Minor clashes	US actor	Political	Discussion	Victory	Unilateral-self
RITORY	NEGOTIATION	MINOR CLASHES			NONE	AMBIGUOUS	FORMAL AGMT.
tory	Negotiation	Minor clashes	None	None	None	Compromise	Formal agmt.
)	NEGOTIATION	MINOR CLASHES			DISCUSSION	AMBIGUOUS	OTHER
)	Negotiation	Minor clashes	Political	Political	Discussion	Stalemate	Other-GO intv.
)	Negotiation	Minor clashes	Political	Political	Discussion	Stalemate	Other-GO intv.
)	Negotiation	Minor clashes	Political	Political	Discussion	Stalemate	Other-GO intv.
TICAL REGIME	MULT. W/VIOL.	MINOR CLASHES			NONE	DEFINITIVE	UNILATERAL
ical regime	Mult. w/viol.	Minor clashes	None	None	None	Victory	Unilateral-self
)	NEGOTIATION	MINOR CLASHES			NONE	DEFINITIVE	FORMAL AGMT.
)	Negotiation	Minor clashes	None	None	None	Defeat	Formal agmt.
TICAL REGIME	NON-VIOL. MIL.	MINOR CLASHES			NONE	DEFINITIVE	SEMI-FORMAL AGMT.
ical regime	Non-viol. mil.	Minor clashes	None	None	None	Victory	Semi-formal agmt.
TICAL REGIME	VIOLENCE	MINOR CLASHES			DISCUSSION	AMBIGUOUS	UNILATERAL
tory	Violence	Minor clashes	Semi-mil.	None	Discussion	Stalemate	Unilateral-self
ical regime	Negotiation	Minor clashes	Semi-mil.	None	Discussion	Stalemate	Unilateral-adv.
RITORY	VIOLENCE	WAR			OTHER	AMBIGUOUS	SEMI-FORMAL AGMT.
tory	Violence	War	Semi-mil.	Political	Other	Compromise	Semi-formal agmt.
tory	Violence	War	Semi-mil.	Political	Other	Compromise	Semi-formal agmt.
RITORY	VIOLENCE	SERIOUS CLASHES			NONE	AMBIGUOUS	UNILATERAL
tory	Violence	Serious clashes	None	None	None	Stalemate	Unilateral-self
tory	Violence	Serious clashes	None	None	None	Stalemate	Unilateral-self
RITORY	MULTIPLE, NO VIOL.	NO VIOLENCE			NONE	AMBIGUOUS	FORMAL AGMT.
tory	Multiple, no viol.	No violence	None	None	None	Stalemate	Formal agmt.
tory	Multiple, no viol.	No violence	None	None	None	Stalemate	Formal agmt.

(continued)

TABLE III.1.—Continued

NUM.	INTERNATIONAL CRISIS ACTORS	SUM. PAGE	PC OR REG.	TRIG. DATE	TERM. DATE	SYSTEM LEVEL POWER STATUS	TRIGGERING ENTITY	CRISIS TRIGGER
373	TODGHERE INCIDENT	102	3	02/12/87	04/66/87	SUBSYSTEM	ETHIOPIA	VIOLENT
	Somalia			02/12/87	04/66/87	Small power	Ethiopia	Violent
374	SYRIAN INT./LEBANON	654	44	02/15/87	04/06/87	SUBSYSTEM	NON-STATE ACTOR	INDIRECT VIOL.
	Syria			02/15/87	04/06/87	Great power	Non-state actor	Indirect viol.
375	SAND WALL	128	5	02/25/87	05/04/87	SUBSYSTEM	NON-STATE ACTOR	VIOLENT
	Morocco			02/25/87	05/04/87	Great power	Non-state actor	Violent
	Mauritania			04/77/87	05/04/87	Small power	Morocco	Non-viol. mil.
	Algeria			04/77/87	05/04/87	Middle power	Morocco	Non-viol. mil.
376	AEGEAN SEA III	373	28	03/01/87	03/28/87	MAINLY SUBSYSTEM	TURKEY	POLITICAL
	Greece			03/01/87	03/28/87	Middle power	Turkey	Political
	Turkey			03/01/87	03/28/87	Middle power	Greece	Political
377	CAMEROON/NIGERIA II	481	40	05/02/87	09/26/87	SUBSYSTEM	CAMEROON	NON-VIOL. MIL.
	Nigeria			05/02/87	09/26/87	Great power	Cameroon	Non-viol. mil.
378	INDIA INT./SRI LANKA	560	42	06/03/87	07/30/87	SUBSYSTEM	SRI LANKA	NON-VIOL. MIL.
	India			06/03/87	07/30/87	Great power	Sri Lanka	Non-viol. mil.
	Sri Lanka			06/04/87	07/30/87	Small power	India	Non-viol. mil.
379	MECCA PILGRIMAGE	656	44	07/31/87	10/99/87	SUBSYSTEM	NON-STATE ACTOR	INTERNAL CHAL.
	Saudi Arabia			07/31/87	10/99/87	Middle power	Non-state actor	Internal chal.
	Iran			07/31/87	10/99/87	Great power	Saudi Arabia	Violent
380	S. AFRICA INT./ANGOLA	81	1	10/03/87	08/22/88	SUBSYSTEM	SOUTH AFRICA	VIOLENT
	Angola			10/03/87	08/22/88	Middle power	South Africa	Violent
	South Africa			12/10/87	08/22/88	Great power	Angola	Violent
381	THREE VILLAGE BDR. II	562	42	11/03/87	02/17/88	SUBSYSTEM	LAOS	VIOLENT
	Laos			11/03/87	02/17/88	Small power	Thailand	Violent
	Thailand			11/03/87	02/17/88	Middle power	Laos	Violent
382	KENYA/UGANDA BORDER	482	40	12/14/87	12/28/87	SUBSYSTEM	UGANDA	VIOLENT
	Kenya			12/14/87	12/28/87	Middle power	Uganda	Violent
	Uganda			12/14/87	12/28/87	Small power	Kenya	Violent
383	CONTRAS III	144	8	03/06/88	03/28/88	SUBSYSTEM	NICARAGUA	VIOLENT
	Honduras			03/06/88	03/28/88	Small power	Nicaragua	Violent
	Nicaragua			03/16/88	03/28/88	Small power	US	Non-viol. mil.
384	SPRATLY ISLANDS	162	11	03/14/88	04/88/88	SUBSYSTEM	CHINA (PRC)	VIOLENT
	Vietnam			03/14/88	04/88/88	Great power	China (PRC)	Violent
	China (PRC)			03/14/88	04/88/88	Great power	Vietnam	Violent
385	IRAQ RECAPTURE-FAW	310	24	04/18/88	08/08/88	SUBSYSTEM	IRAQ	VIOLENT
	Iran			04/18/88	08/08/88	Great power	Iraq	Violent

732

GRAVITY OF THREAT	CRISIS MGMT. TECHNIQUE	VIOLENCE	US ACTIV.	USSR ACTIV.	GLOBAL ORG. INVOLVEMENT	OUTCOME: SUBSTANCE	OUTCOME: FORM
RITORY	VIOLENCE	SERIOUS CLASHES			NONE	AMBIGUOUS	FORMAL AGMT.
tory	Violence	Serious clashes	Political	None	None	Stalemate	Formal agmt.
UENCE	VIOLENCE	SERIOUS CLASHES			NONE	DEFINITIVE	IMPOSED AGMT.
ence	Violence	Serious clashes	None	None	None	Victory	Imposed-imposer
RITORY	VIOLENCE	SERIOUS CLASHES			NONE	AMBIGUOUS	SEMI-FORMAL AGMT.
itory	Violence	Serious clashes	None	None	None	Victory	Semi-formal agmt.
itory	Multiple, no viol.	Serious clashes	None	None	None	Stalemate	Semi-formal agmt.
ence	Negotiation	Serious clashes	None	None	None	Stalemate	Semi-formal agmt.
NOMIC	MULTIPLE, NO VIOL.	NO VIOLENCE			NONE	AMBIGUOUS	SEMI-FORMAL AGMT.
nomic	Negotiation	No violence	Political	None	None	Stalemate	Semi-formal agmt.
nomic	Multiple, no viol.	No violence	Political	None	None	Stalemate	Semi-formal agmt.
RITORY	MULTIPLE, NO VIOL.	NO VIOLENCE			NONE	DEFINITIVE	FORMAL AGMT.
itory	Multiple, no viol.	No violence	None	None	None	Victory	Formal agmt.
ITICAL REGIME	NEGOTIATION	NO VIOLENCE			NONE	AMBIGUOUS	FORMAL AGMT.
ence	Negotiation	No violence	None	None	None	Victory	Formal agmt.
tical regime	Negotiation	No violence	None	None	None	Compromise	Formal agmt.
ITICAL REGIME	MULT. W/VIOL.	MINOR CLASHES			NONE	DEFINITIVE	FADED
tical regime	Non-viol. mil.	Minor clashes	Semi-mil.	None	None	Victory	Faded
ence	Mult. w/viol.	Minor clashes	Semi-mil.	None	None	Defeat	Faded
VE DAMAGE	MULT. W/VIOL.	SERIOUS CLASHES			CONDEMNATION	AMBIGUOUS	FORMAL AGMT.
ve damage	Mult. w/viol.	Serious clashes	Semi-mil.	Semi-mil.	Call for action	Compromise	Formal agmt.
ve damage	Mult. w/viol.	Serious clashes	Semi-mil.	Semi-mil.	Condemnation	Compromise	Formal agmt.
RRITORY	MULT. W/VIOL.	SERIOUS CLASHES			GOOD OFFICES	AMBIGUOUS	FORMAL AGMT.
itory	Mult. w/viol.	Serious clashes	None	None	Good offices	Compromise	Formal agmt.
itory	Mult. w/viol.	Serious clashes	None	None	Good offices	Compromise	Formal agmt.
NOMIC	NEGOTIATION	MINOR CLASHES			NONE	AMBIGUOUS	SEMI-FORMAL AGMT.
nomic	Negotiation	Minor clashes	None	None	None	Compromise	Semi-formal agmt.
nomic	Negotiation	Minor clashes	None	None	None	Compromise	Semi-formal agmt.
ITICAL REGIME	MULT. W/VIOL.	MINOR CLASHES			NONE	DEFINITIVE	UNILATERAL
itory	Mult. w/viol.	Minor clashes	Semi-mil.	None	None	Victory	Unilateral-ally
tical regime	Adjud./Arbit.	Minor clashes	Semi-mil.	None	None	Defeat	Unilateral-adv.
RRITORY	VIOLENCE	SERIOUS CLASHES			NONE	AMBIGUOUS	FADED
itory	Violence	Serious clashes	None	None	None	Stalemate	Faded
itory	Violence	Serious clashes	None	None	None	Stalemate	Faded
RRITORY	VIOLENCE	WAR			CALL FOR ACTION	DEFINITIVE	SEMI-FORMAL AGMT.
itory	Violence	War	Semi-mil.	Semi-mil.	Call for action	Defeat	Semi-formal agmt.

(continued)

733

TABLE III.1.—Continued

NUM.	INTERNATIONAL CRISIS ACTORS	SUM. PAGE	PC OR REG.	TRIG. DATE	TERM. DATE	SYSTEM LEVEL POWER STATUS	TRIGGERING ENTITY	CRISIS TRIGGER
386	LIBYAN JETS	483	40	12/21/88	01/12/89	SUBSYSTEM	LIBYA	VIOLENT
	US			12/21/88	01/12/89	Superpower	Libya	Violent
	Libya			01/04/89	01/12/89	Middle power	US	Violent
387	MAURITANIA/SENEGAL	484	40	08/21/89	07/18/91	SUBSYSTEM	MAURITANIA	POLITICAL
	Senegal			08/21/89	07/18/91	Middle power	Mauritania	Political
	Mauritania			08/21/89	07/18/91	Small power	Senegal	Political
388	CAMBODIA PEACE CONF.	202	13	08/30/89	01/27/90	MAINLY SUBSYSTEM	NON-STATE ACTOR	POLITICAL
	Cambodia			08/30/89	01/27/90	Small power	Non-state actor	Political
	Vietnam			08/30/89	01/27/90	Great power	Non-state actor	Political
389	CONTRAS IV	145	8	09/09/89	11/07/89	SUBSYSTEM	NICARAGUA	VIOLENT
	Honduras			09/09/89	11/07/89	Small power	Nicaragua	Violent
390	GALTAT ZEMMOUR II	130	5	10/07/89	11/88/89	SUBSYSTEM	NON-STATE ACTOR	VIOLENT
	Morocco			10/07/89	11/88/89	Middle power	Non-state actor	Violent
391	INVASION OF PANAMA	529	41	12/15/89	01/03/90	SUBSYSTEM	PANAMA	POLITICAL
	US			12/15/89	01/03/90	Superpower	Panama	Political
	Panama			12/20/89	01/03/90	Small power	US	Violent
392	KASHMIR III-NUCLEAR	176	12	01/14/90	06/88/90	SUBSYSTEM	PAKISTAN	POLITICAL
	India			01/14/90	06/88/90	Great power	Pakistan	Political
	Pakistan			01/15/90	06/88/90	Middle power	India	Political
393	GULF WAR	315	25	08/02/90	04/12/91	MAINLY DOMINANT	IRAQ	VIOLENT
	Kuwait			08/02/90	04/12/91	Small power	Iraq	Violent
	US			10/30/90	04/12/91	Superpower	Multi-state	Political
	Bahrain			11/29/90	04/12/91	Small power	Multi-state	Political
	Egypt			11/29/90	04/12/91	Middle power	Multi-state	Political
	France			11/29/90	04/12/91	Great power	Multi-state	Political
	Iraq			11/29/90	04/12/91	Middle power	Multi-state	Political
	Israel			11/29/90	04/12/91	Middle power	Multi-state	Political
	Oman			11/29/90	04/12/91	Small power	Multi-state	Political
	Qatar			11/29/90	04/12/91	Small power	Multi-state	Political
	Saudi Arabia			11/29/90	04/12/91	Middle power	Multi-state	Political
	Syria			11/29/90	04/12/91	Middle power	Multi-state	Political
	United Arab Emirates			11/29/90	04/12/91	Small power	Multi-state	Political
	UK			11/29/90	04/12/91	Great power	Multi-state	Political
394	RWANDA/UGANDA	485	40	10/01/90	02/17/91	SUBSYSTEM	NON-STATE ACTOR	VIOLENT
	Rwanda			10/01/90	02/17/91	Small power	Non-state actor	Violent
395	LIBERIA/SIERRA LEONE	486	40	03/23/91	10/31/91	SUBSYSTEM	NON-STATE ACTOR	VIOLENT
	Sierra Leone			03/23/91	10/31/91	Small power	Non-state actor	Violent

GRAVITY OF THREAT	CRISIS MGMT. TECHNIQUE	VIOLENCE	US ACTIV.	USSR ACTIV.	GLOBAL ORG. INVOLVEMENT	OUTCOME: SUBSTANCE	OUTCOME: FORM
FLUENCE	MULT. W/VIOL.	MINOR CLASHES			DISCUSSION	AMBIGUOUS	TACIT UNDERSTANDING
fluence	Mult. w/viol.	Minor clashes	US actor	Political	Discussion	Victory	Tacit understanding
fluence	Negotiation	Minor clashes	Direct mil.	Political	Discussion	Stalemate	Tacit understanding
CONOMIC	MULT. W/VIOL.	MINOR CLASHES			DISCUSSION	AMBIGUOUS	SEMI-FORMAL AGMT.
onomic	Mult. w/viol.	Minor clashes	None	None	Discussion	Compromise	Semi-formal agmt.
onomic	Mult. w/viol.	Minor clashes	None	None	Discussion	Compromise	Semi-formal agmt.
OLITICAL REGIME	MULT. W/VIOL.	MINOR CLASHES			DISCUSSION	DEFINITIVE	SEMI-FORMAL AGMT.
litical regime	Mult. w/viol.	Minor clashes	Political	Semi-mil.	Discussion	Victory	Semi-formal agmt.
fluence	Negotiation	Minor clashes	Political	Semi-mil.	Discussion	Victory	Spillover
MD	NEGOTIATION	MINOR CLASHES			OBSERVERS	DEFINITIVE	SEMI-FORMAL AGMT.
MD	Negotiation	Minor clashes	None	None	Observers	Victory	Semi-formal agmt.
RRITORY	MULT. W/VIOL.	SERIOUS CLASHES			CALL FOR ACTION	AMBIGUOUS	FADED
rritory	Mult. w/viol.	Serious clashes	None	None	Call for action	Stalemate	Faded
FLUENCE	MULT. W/VIOL.	SERIOUS CLASHES			CONDEMNATION	DEFINITIVE	UNILATERAL
fluence	Violence	Serious clashes	US actor	Political	Condemnation	Victory	Unilateral-self
litical regime	Mult. w/viol.	Serious clashes	Direct mil.	Political	Call for action	Defeat	Unilateral-adv.
XISTENCE	MULT. W/VIOL.	SERIOUS CLASHES			NONE	AMBIGUOUS	UNILATERAL
rave damage	Mult. w/viol.	Serious clashes	Political	Political	None	Stalemate	Unilateral-adv.
sistence	Mult. w/viol.	No violence	Political	Political	None	Stalemate	Unilateral-adv.
XISTENCE	MULT. W/VIOL.	WAR			CALL FOR ACTION	DEFINITIVE	IMPOSED AGMT.
sistence	Mult. w/viol.	War	Direct mil.	Political	Call for action	Victory	Other-ally
fluence	Mult. w/viol.	War	US actor	Political	Call for action	Victory	Imposed-imposer
rave damage	Multiple, no viol.	No violence	Semi-mil.	None	Call for action	Victory	Other-ally
fluence	Mult. w/viol.	War	Semi-mil.	Political	Call for action	Victory	Imposed-imposer
fluence	Mult. w/viol.	War	Semi-mil.	Political	Call for action	Victory	Imposed-imposer
rave damage	Mult. w/viol.	War	Direct mil.	Political	Call for action	Defeat	Imposed-imposee
rave damage	Non-viol. mil.	Minor clashes	Semi-mil.	None	Call for action	Victory	Other-ally
rave damage	Multiple, no viol.	No violence	Semi-mil.	None	Call for action	Victory	Other-ally
rave damage	Multiple, no viol.	No violence	Semi-mil.	None	Call for action	Victory	Other-ally
rave damage	Mult. w/viol.	War	Semi-mil.	None	Call for action	Victory	Imposed-imposer
fluence	Mult. w/viol.	War	Semi-mil.	Political	Call for action	Victory	Imposed-imposer
rave damage	Multiple, no viol.	No violence	Semi-mil.	None	Call for action	Victory	Other-ally
fluence	Mult. w/viol.	War	Semi-mil.	Political	Call for action	Victory	Imposed-imposer
MD	MULT. W/VIOL.	SERIOUS CLASHES			NONE	AMBIGUOUS	TACIT UNDERSTANDING
MD	Mult. w/viol.	Serious clashes	Political	Neutral	None	Compromise	Tacit understanding
RRITORY	VIOLENCE	SERIOUS CLASHES			NONE	DEFINITIVE	FORMAL AGMT.
rritory	Violence	Serious clashes	Political	None	None	Victory	Formal agmt.

(continued)

TABLE III.1.—*Continued*

NUM.	INTERNATIONAL CRISIS ACTORS	SUM. PAGE	PC OR REG.	TRIG. DATE	TERM. DATE	SYSTEM LEVEL POWER STATUS	TRIGGERING ENTITY	CRISIS TRIGGER
396	GHANA/TOGO BORDER II	488	40	04/11/91	10/05/91	SUBSYSTEM	TOGO	NON-VIOL. MIL.
	Ghana			04/11/91	10/05/91	Small power	Togo	Non-viol. mil.
397	YUG. I-CROAT./SLOVEN.	613	43	06/25/91	01/03/92	SUBSYSTEM	MULTI-STATE	INTERNAL CHAL.
	Yugoslavia			06/25/91	01/03/92	Middle power	Multi-state	Internal chal.
	Slovenia			06/25/91	07/07/91	Small power	Yugoslavia	Non-viol. mil.
	Croatia			06/25/91	01/03/92	Small power	Yugoslavia	Non-viol. mil.
398	BUBIYAN	318	25	08/28/91	08/88/91	SUBSYSTEM	IRAQ	VIOLENT
	Kuwait			08/28/91	08/88/91	Small power	Iraq	Violent
399	FOREIGN INTERV.-ZAIRE	489	40	09/23/91	11/04/91	SUBSYSTEM	NON-STATE ACTOR	INDIRECT VIOL.
	Belgium			09/23/91	11/04/91	Middle power	Non-state actor	Indirect viol.
	France			09/23/91	10/31/91	Great power	Non-state actor	Indirect viol.
	Zaire			10/25/91	11/04/91	Middle power	Multi-state	Political
400	ECUADOR/PERU BDR. IV	138	7	10/06/91	10/15/91	SUBSYSTEM	PERU	NON-VIOL. MIL.
	Ecuador			10/06/91	10/15/91	Small power	Peru	Non-viol. mil.
	Peru			10/06/91	10/15/91	Middle power	Ecuador	Political
401	NAGORNYY-KARABAKH	563	42	11/27/91	08/77/92	SUBSYSTEM	NON-STATE ACTOR	INTERNAL CHAL.
	Armenia			11/27/91	08/77/92	Small power	Non-state actor	Internal chal.
	Azerbaijan			12/10/91	08/77/92	Small power	Armenia	Internal chal.
402	EGYPT/SUDAN BDR. II	490	40	01/88/92	06/88/92	SUBSYSTEM	SUDAN	POLITICAL
	Egypt			01/88/92	06/88/92	Great power	Sudan	Political
	Sudan			04/04/92	06/88/92	Small power	Egypt	Violent
403	YUG. II-BOSNIA	617	43	03/03/92	99/99/99	SUBSYSTEM	BOSNIA	POLITICAL
	Serbia			03/03/92	99/99/99	Middle power	Bosnia	Political
	Bosnia			03/02/92	99/99/99	Small power	Serbia	Violent
	Croatia			04/06/92	99/99/99	Middle power	Serbia	Violent
404	PAPUA/SOLOMON	565	42	03/12/92	09/77/92	SUBSYSTEM	PAPUA/NEW GUINEA	VIOLENT
	Solomon Islands			03/12/92	09/77/92	Small power	Papua/New Guinea	Violent
	Papua/New Guinea			09/77/92	09/77/92	Small power	Solomon Islands	Non-viol. mil.
405	SLEEPING DOG HILL	566	42	03/14/92	12/25/92	SUBSYSTEM	BURMA	VIOLENT
	Thailand			03/14/92	12/25/92	Middle power	Burma	Violent
	Burma			03/18/92	12/25/92	Small power	Thailand	Violent
406	IRAQ NO-FLY ZONE	319	25	08/18/92	09/08/92	DOMINANT SYSTEM	MULTI-STATE	POLITICAL
	Iraq			08/18/92	09/08/92	Middle power	Multi-state	Political
407	GEORGIA/ABKHAZIA	567	42	09/25/92	10/08/93	SUBSYSTEM	USSR	POLITICAL
	Georgia			09/25/92	10/08/93	Middle power	USSR	Political

NUM.	INTERNATIONAL CRISIS ACTORS	SUM. PAGE	PC OR REG.	TRIG. DATE	TERM. DATE	SYSTEM LEVEL POWER STATUS	TRIGGERING ENTITY	CRISIS TRIGGER
408	N. KOREA NUCLEAR CR.	221	15	03/66/93	10/21/94	SUBSYSTEM	NON-STATE ACTOR	OTHER NON-VIOL.
	North Korea			03/66/93	10/21/94	Middle power	Non-state actor	Other non-viol.
	South Korea			03/12/93	10/21/94	Small power	North Korea	Political
	US			03/12/93	10/21/94	Superpower	North Korea	Political
409	OPTN. ACCOUNTABILITY	299	23	07/10/93	07/31/93	SUBSYSTEM	NON-STATE ACTOR	VIOLENT
	Israel			07/10/93	07/31/93	Great power	Non-state actor	Violent
	Lebanon			07/25/93	07/31/93	Small power	Israel	Violent
410	CAMEROON/NIGERIA III	491	40	12/88/93	11/88/94	SUBSYSTEM	CAMEROON	VIOLENT
	Nigeria			12/88/93	11/88/94	Great power	Cameroon	Violent
	Cameroon			01/03/94	11/88/94	Small power	Nigeria	Non-viol. mil.
411	HAITI MIL. REGIME	532	41	07/77/94	10/15/94	SUBSYSTEM	NON-STATE ACTOR	POLITICAL
	US			07/77/94	10/15/94	Superpower	Non-state actor	Political
	Haiti			09/15/94	10/15/94	Small power	US	Other non-viol.
412	IRAQ DEPLOY./KUWAIT	321	25	10/07/94	11/10/94	MAINLY DOMINANT	IRAQ	NON-VIOL. MIL.
	Kuwait			10/07/94	11/10/94	Small power	Iraq	Non-viol. mil.
	Saudi Arabia			10/07/94	11/10/94	Middle power	Iraq	Non-viol. mil.
	US			10/07/94	11/10/94	Superpower	Iraq	Non-viol. mil.
	Iraq			10/07/94	11/10/94	Middle power	US	Non-viol. mil.

736

GRAVITY OF THREAT	CRISIS MGMT. TECHNIQUE	VIOLENCE	US ACTIV.	USSR ACTIV.	GLOBAL ORG. INVOLVEMENT	OUTCOME: SUBSTANCE	OUTCOME: FORM
D	NEGOTIATION	MINOR CLASHES			NONE	AMBIGUOUS	TACIT UNDERSTANDING
D	Negotiation	Minor clashes	Neutral	Neutral	None	Stalemate	Tacit understanding
STENCE	MULT. W/VIOL.	WAR			SANCTIONS	AMBIGUOUS	FORMAL AGMT.
tence	Mult. w/viol.	War	Political	Political	Sanctions	Compromise	Formal agmt.
tence	Mult. w/viol.	War	Political	Political	Mediation	Compromise	Formal agmt.
e damage	Mult. w/viol.	War	Political	Political	Mediation	Compromise	Formal agmt.
RITORY	MULT. W/VIOL.	MINOR CLASHES			OBSERVERS	DEFINITIVE	FADED
itory	Mult. w/viol.	Minor clashes	Political	None	Observers	Victory	Faded
ITICAL REGIME	MULT. W/VIOL.	SERIOUS CLASHES			NONE	DEFINITIVE	UNILATERAL
ence	Mult. w/viol.	Serious clashes	Semi-mil.	None	None	Victory	Unilateral-self
ence	Mult. w/viol.	Serious clashes	Semi-mil.	None	None	Victory	Unilateral-self
ical regime	Mult. w/viol.	Serious clashes	Political	None	None	Victory	Unilateral-adv.
RITORY	NEGOTIATION	NO VIOLENCE			NONE	AMBIGUOUS	SEMI-FORMAL AGMT.
itory	Negotiation	No violence	Political	None	None	Compromise	Semi-formal agmt.
D	Negotiation	No violence	Political	None	None	Compromise	Semi-formal agmt.
RITORY	MULT. W/VIOL.	SERIOUS CLASHES			CALL FOR ACTION	AMBIGUOUS	FADED
D	Mult. w/viol.	Serious clashes	Political	Semi-mil.	Call for action	Stalemate	Faded
itory	Mult. w/viol.	Serious clashes	Political	Semi-mil.	Call for action	Stalemate	Faded
RITORY	NEGOTIATION	MINOR CLASHES			NONE	AMBIGUOUS	UNILATERAL
itory	Negotiation	Minor clashes	Neutral	Neutral	None	Stalemate	Unilateral-adv.
nomic	Negotiation	Minor clashes	Neutral	Neutral	None	Stalemate	Unilateral-self
STENCE	MULT. W/VIOL.	WAR			EMER. MIL. FORCE	MD	MD
e damage	Mult. w/viol.	War	Direct mil.	Political	Sanctions	MD	MD
tence	Mult. w/viol.	War	Direct mil.	Political	Emer. mil. force	MD	MD
e damage	Mult. w/viol.	War	Direct mil.	Political	Mediation	MD	MD
D	MULT. W/VIOL.	MINOR CLASHES			NONE	AMBIGUOUS	SEMI-FORMAL AGMT.
D	Mult. w/viol.	Minor clashes	None	None	None	Compromise	Semi-formal agmt.
D	Mult. w/viol.	Minor clashes	None	None	None	Compromise	Semi-formal agmt.
RITORY	MULT. W/VIOL.	SERIOUS CLASHES			NONE	AMBIGUOUS	UNILATERAL
itory	Mult. w/viol.	Serious clashes	None	None	None	Victory	Unilateral-adv.
ical regime	Mult. w/viol.	Serious clashes	None	None	None	Compromise	Unilateral-self
ITICAL REGIME	NEGOTIATION	NO VIOLENCE			DISCUSSION	DEFINITIVE	UNILATERAL
ical regime	Negotiation	No violence	Direct mil.	Direct mil.	Discussion	Defeat	Compliance
RITORY	MULT. W/VIOL.	SERIOUS CLASHES			OBSERVERS	AMBIGUOUS	FORMAL AGMT.
itory	Mult. w/viol.	Serious clashes	None	Covert	Observers	Compromise	Formal agmt.

GRAVITY OF THREAT	CRISIS MGMT. TECHNIQUE	VIOLENCE	US ACTIV.	USSR ACTIV.	GLOBAL ORG. INVOLVEMENT	OUTCOME: SUBSTANCE	OUTCOME: FORM
UENCE	NEGOTIATION	NO VIOLENCE			SANCTIONS	AMBIGUOUS	FORMAL AGMT.
ence	Negotiation	No violence	Political	None	Sanctions	Compromise	Formal agmt.
e damage	Negotiation	No violence	Political	None	Sanctions	Compromise	Other-ally
ence	Negotiation	No violence	US actor	None	Sanctions	Compromise	Formal agmt.
D	MULT. W/VIOL.	MINOR CLASHES			CONDEMNATION	AMBIGUOUS	TACIT UNDERSTANDING
D	Mult. w/viol.	Minor clashes	Political	None	Condemnation	Compromise	Tacit understanding
itory	Mediation	Minor clashes	Political	None	Call for action	Victory	Spillover
RITORY	MULT. W/VIOL.	SERIOUS CLASHES			NONE	AMBIGUOUS	FADED
tory	Mult. w/viol.	Serious clashes	Neutral	Neutral	None	Stalemate	Faded
tory	Mult. w/viol.	Serious clashes	Neutral	Neutral	None	Stalemate	Faded
UENCE	NEGOTIATION	MINOR CLASHES			SANCTIONS	AMBIGUOUS	IMPOSED AGMT.
ence	Negotiation	Minor clashes	Direct mil.	None	Call for action	Victory	Imposed-imposer
ical regime	Negotiation	Minor clashes	US actor	None	Sanctions	Compromise	Imposed-imposee
STENCE	NON-VIOL. MIL.	NO VIOLENCE			CONDEMNATION	DEFINITIVE	UNILATERAL
ence	Non-viol. mil.	No violence	Semi-mil.	Political	Condemnation	Victory	Unilateral-adv.
ical regime	Non-viol. mil.	No violence	Semi-mil.	Political	Condemnation	Victory	Unilateral-adv.
ence	Non-viol. mil.	No violence	US actor	Political	Condemnation	Victory	Unilateral-adv.
ence	Non-viol. mil.	No violence	Semi-mil.	Political	Condemnation	Defeat	Compliance

PART IV. ANALYSIS

Introduction

The international system has undergone dramatic changes since the end of World War I. The number of independent states has grown from approximately 60 in 1918 to almost 190 today. The system itself has evolved from multipolarity in the interwar years, through bipolarity in the 1945–62 period, polycentrism from 1963 through the end of the Cold War in 1989, and finally to the still largely uncharted waters of the post–Cold War era. The role of international and regional organizations has changed, as has the impact of major powers on crises in this century. Perhaps the only constant in this 76-year span of history has been the steady increase in the use of force as a means for settling communal, regional, and international disputes.

In this part of the book, we present a detailed analysis of the international system in the twentieth century from the vantage point of international crisis. Data from the International Crisis Behavior Project, spanning the years from the end of 1918 to the end of 1994, are examined in an effort to uncover patterns in crises during this century. The framework for analysis is provided by seven key attributes of the international system and its member-states. **Polarity** and **geography** are fundamental systemic characteristics within which interstate crisis behavior unfolds. **Ethnicity** and **regime type** provide important contexts for decision making in crises. The extent to which events occur within a **protracted conflict setting** and the choice of crisis management techniques—particularly **violence**—provide a context for the international community to judge the danger that a crisis poses for the system as a whole or to one of its subsystems. And all contribute to the extent to which **third parties**—international or regional organizations, and major powers—will attempt intervention and whether such intervention will prove successful in crisis abatement.

Our analyses will examine the phenomenon of crisis in terms of the following broad dimensions.

What has been the impact of changes in the **polarity** of the international system on the characteristics of crises and the behavior of states experiencing them?

Does **geography** play a role in the frequency of crisis, the presence of violence, and susceptibility to resolution of crises?

Do crises that originate in **ethnicity** differ in fundamental ways from non-ethnic crises?

Are crises involving actors with **democratic regimes** substantially different from those that do not?

Do crises that occur within ongoing **protracted conflicts** differ in fundamental ways from those that occur outside of this setting?

Under what conditions is **violence** likely to be the primary crisis management technique utilized by adversarial actors in a crisis?

Under what circumstances can **third parties,** either international organizations or major powers, be effective in abating international crises?

In the sections that follow, we will address these and related questions by drawing on the vast body of information contained in the ICB data sets. While the preceding questions do not by any means exhaust the range of issues relating to the phenomenon of crisis, they comprise some of the central questions with which researchers have grappled as they have tried to understand the dynamics of the crisis process, from onset, through escalation, to de-escalation and termination. Each of the seven sections concludes with a summary of major findings.

Two procedural issues must be addressed before we move to the analysis. First, crises that occurred during World War II were excluded from several portions of the analyses on the grounds that the war years constituted a disruption to the patterns of polarity that have characterized the international system in this century. Since polarity is both a major analytic variable and a contextual variable in many of the analyses in Part IV, it was felt that excluding those cases (32 international crises and 80 foreign policy cases) would help sharpen our findings on crisis in general.

The second issue concerns intra-war crises (IWCs) more generally. An additional 44 international crises and 157 actor-cases are excluded from most analyses to follow, on the grounds that their occurrence within an ongoing war renders them noncomparable to the main body of crises in the twentieth century. The only exception is the inclusion of IWCs when we examine the roles of global organizations and major powers as third-party intermediaries, and when we focus explicitly on protracted conflicts. To assist the reader, each of the seven sections that follow will indicate what portions of the data set are included in the analysis.

One methodological issue must also be addressed. Very early in this enterprise we decided that our ability to communicate clearly to a wide audience of scholars and practitioners interested in crisis phenomena would be severely constrained were we to utilize elaborate multivariate statistical procedures. We have introduced control variables in several sections of Part IV, and the section on democracy in fact uses logit analysis to probe multivariate relationships. But in general, we have tried to stay with contingency tables to present our data and findings, in keeping with the nominal nature of most of our measurements. Thus, while subsequent, more detailed analyses may well benefit from the use of multivariate statistics, they are not widely employed in this volume.

As described in Part II, the International Crisis Behavior data sets are comprised of 67 variables at the international system level of analysis and 85 variables at the foreign policy (actor) level of analysis. Many of these variables are used in the following analyses, and each will be defined when it is introduced for the first time. For a complete list of ICB variables, see Part II. Readers interested in the complete set of definitions and the data sets themselves may acquire them as Study #9286 from the Interuniversity Consortium for Political and Social Research at the University of Michigan.

Polarity

Introduction

One of the enduring questions in international politics concerns the link between systemic structure and international conflict. Historians have speculated about polarity and stability across the centuries. Empirical social scientists have collected and analyzed data about polarity and the frequency and intensity of warfare. Theorists have engaged in rigorous, deductive assessments of the logic underlying the presumed linkage. Yet, despite the abundance of scholarly effort, the issue remains unresolved.

The debate first crystallized in the aftermath of the Cuban Missile crisis, when Waltz (1964) made a cogent case for **bipolarity** as an inherently more stable system. He argued that two preeminent major power adversaries or integrated blocs with acknowledged patron-leaders would have a shared interest in maintaining the global balance and the power to do so. This arrangement would produce more predictable behavior by all actors, including the bloc leaders; a lower likelihood of miscalculation—of capability, coalitions, and intent—so often the generator of war; the "recurrence of crises" but their more effective control in the mutual interest of preserving the status quo; and the lesser danger of destabilization by weak third states.[1]

Deutsch and Singer (1964), supporting Kaplan's (1957:34–36) view that **multipolarity** is more stable, emphasized the greater uncertainty about likely outcomes of conflict in a multipolar system and, therefore, the greater caution in initiating potentially disruptive behavior. They also looked favorably on the following: the wider range of options, leading to crosscutting cleavages, which could reduce the rigidity of alignments and conflicts among states; the dispersion of attention among members of a multipolar system; and slower-to-mature arms races in an environment of changing alliances.[2]

Rosecrance (1966) criticized the two competing hypotheses and advocated an intermediate international system, **bimultipolarity,** as likely to be the most stable. His reasoning, too, was plausible. Each bipolar bloc leader would engage in both cooperative and competitive relations, restraining conflict but preventing hegemony by its adversary. So too would the lesser states. Zero-sum games would be avoided; conflicts would be limited in stakes; the possibility of war would be less; and the consequences of war would be more tolerable.[3]

Disagreement persists over the relative contribution to international stability of various types of systems. Would a structure with two dominant powers (bipolarity) or a structure characterized by a dispersion of power among several great powers (multipolarity) be more stable? What is the likely impact of a system that is bipolar along some dimensions and multipolar on others (polycentrism)? And how will the still-evolving dimensions of the post–Cold War international system after 1989 affect global stability? These and other questions will serve as the backdrop for the analyses that follow.

Having briefly related the positions taken by the major theorists in the formative stage of the "great debate" over polarity and stability,[4] we now turn to an empirical examination of this question. While much of the prior research has relied on data on conflict in general and war in particular as indicators of the relative stability of different systems (see, for example, Sabrosky 1985), our approach focuses on international crisis as the central unit of analysis (Brecher and Wilkenfeld 1989, 1991; Brecher, James, and Wilkenfeld 1990). Crisis, in a sense, is the initial indicator of a fundamental conflict of interests among two or more states. As described in more detail in the definition of international crisis in Part I, crisis is marked by a distortion in the type and/or an increase in the intensity of disruptive interactions among adversaries that poses a challenge to the existing structure of the global system, dominant system, or subsystem. Whether or not a crisis escalates to armed conflict and even full-scale war, and thus to more severe international instability, depends upon a number of factors.

Definitional Issues: Polarity and Stability

The first task is to define polarity and to delineate the various types of system structures. Our treatment of polarity refers to the number of power and decision centers in an international system. The concept of power center is similar to the more traditional notion of major powers, which in turn comprises both "great powers" and "superpowers." Major powers command human and material resources such that their foreign policy decisions shape the dominant or central subsystem of world politics. Superpowers, a term generally reserved for the U.S. and the USSR (later, Russia) in the post–World War II era, can determine the fate of the planet through their control of weapons of mass destruction. A cluster of great powers designates power multipolarity, and the presence of two superpowers indicates power bipolarity. Yet the exclusive focus on power, or military capability, does not facilitate the discussion of polarity in broader conceptual terms.

The concept of decisional center, as distinct from power center, lies at the heart of our revised definition of polarity. While a power center refers to a state that possesses sufficient military capability to sustain its territorial viability in peace and war and significantly influence the behavior of allies, clients, and neighbors, a decision center is characterized by autonomy of choice over a wide range of external issues, political, economic, and cultural. However, such a state may lack the military capability to defend its territorial integrity unilaterally or to serve as the pivot of an alliance providing security against external threats to its members' political independence.

Polarity, conceived as a two-dimensional concept, moves beyond the single, *military capability* criterion of autonomy and also beyond the *military-security issue-area* to the growing recognition that decisional autonomy by members of the international system may exist on some issues but not on others. Elsewhere we provide a detailed discussion of a variety of international systems that are theoretically possible (Brecher, James, and Wilkenfeld 1990; see also Keohane and Nye 1977, 1987). The discussion that follows will focus exclusively on systems with particular relevance to that portion of the twentieth century under examination in this volume. A more detailed discussion of these international systems can be found in Part I.

Bipolarity indicates a concentration of military power and political decision in two relatively equal actors, whether individual units or tight coalitions: the two polar centers are preeminent in determining the conditions of stability, the limits of independent behavior by bloc members or unaffiliated actors, and the outcomes of major wars in the system. Bipolarity, in the wider meaning of hostile centers of power and decision, applies to the global system from mid-1945 to late 1962.

Multipolarity signifies diffusion of military power and political decision among three or more relatively equal units. The entire period between World Wars I and II was a multipolar system par excellence, with seven relatively equal great powers recognized by each other and by all other members of the system as sharing the apex of the power pyramid: France, Germany, Great Britain, Italy, Japan, the Soviet Union, and the United States.[5]

Polycentrism identifies a hybrid structure, with two preeminent centers of military power and multiple centers of political decision. As such, it resembles both bipolarity and multipolarity. The current empirical referent for polycentrism at the global level is from 1963 to 1989. Power bipolarity and decision bipolarity in world politics are not synonymous in that other state centers of decision could no longer be controlled by the U.S. and the USSR.

Some scholars have begun to argue that, with the collapse of the Soviet Union and the establishment of republics among the Russian-led Commonwealth of Independent States (CIS), the international system has evolved from "pure" polycentrism to something more akin to **unipolarity**, with the United States as the dominant power.

Figure IV.1 presents the distribution of international crises across the four system-periods and World War II.

We turn next to the concept of system **stability** and the twofold rationale for the choice of **crisis** (rather than **war**) as the dependent variable in all of the analyses to follow. Elsewhere (Brecher and Wilkenfeld 1991) we discussed at great length our dissatisfaction with the literature that identifies stability with a simple indicator measuring the presence or absence of *war*.[6] We argue that crisis is a much more comprehensive indicator of conflict and disruption than war, for war is a subset of crisis. Some crises are accompanied by violence, whether minor or serious clashes or full-scale wars, while others are not. Yet all crises, like war, cause disruption in an international system; that is, they are sources of

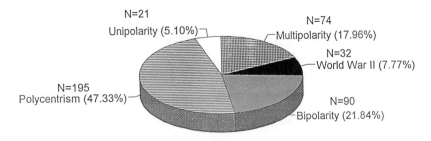

N=21
Unipolarity (5.10%)

N=74
Multipolarity (17.96%)

N=32
World War II (7.77%)

N=195
Polycentrism (47.33%)

N=90
Bipolarity (21.84%)

Figure IV.1. Twentieth-Century International Crises

instability. Stated conceptually, crisis occupies a much larger part of conflict space than does war (see Figure I.1). Empirically too, crisis has been a much more pervasive phenomenon: all but one of the interstate wars identified by the Correlates of War project for the period in which the COW and ICB data sets overlap (Small and Singer 1982:303–7) are included in the ICB data set. Thus, by focusing on crisis, rather than war, we tap a much larger segment of the conflict domain of world politics. And these analyses include war or, more broadly, the violence dimension of interstate conflict (see the "Protracted Conflict" section later in Part IV).

Another major difference between the bulk of the polarity literature previously cited and our inquiry is its scope; they focus on **great power** conflict only. This restrictive view excludes an array of hostile disruptive interactions in the international system, namely, crises—with or without violence—among middle and small powers. While the impact of conflict among the giants is unquestionably more significant for the stability of the international system as a whole, the lesser political earthquakes do destabilize parts of the system, often with spillover effects on relations among the great powers. In short, our scope is truly global, encompassing interstate crises everywhere, embracing all political regimes, economic and social systems, and all cultures. We can—and do—explore and compare parts of the whole, such as great power crises, or crises in Asia, or multipolarity crises. Our much broader database permits these partial "cuts," as well as an analysis of the crisis phenomenon as a whole.

The key to the crisis-based conception of stability and instability is the concept of change, but not necessarily drastic change, whether or not brought on by full-scale war. These drastic changes lie at the extreme of the stability/ instability continuum, while change refers to any shift from an existing pattern of interaction between two or more actors in the direction of greater conflict or cooperation. The former type of change frequently escalates to crisis and, less often, to war. Crisis, like war, whether or not accompanied by violence, represents change and causes disruption, leading to instability. Stability is redefined as change within explicit bounds or normal fluctuations (Azar et al. 1978).

Polarity-Stability Model

Our central thesis regarding polarity is that international systems vary in terms of the stability that they exhibit. The general proposition is that stability is greatest in a system of two preeminent powers (bipolarity), somewhat weaker in a system with greater dispersion of power (multipolarity), and lowest in a system of two major powers and multiple decisional centers (polycentrism).[7] In this sense, we take a position closer to that of Waltz (1964), although our formulation extends the argument into the realm of international crises. System stability will be measured in terms of the attributes of crises that characterize each system.

The rationale for this ranking can be stated in terms of the costs of security regimes. Each type of international structure—bipolarity, multipolarity, poly-centrism—entails different security-related costs to its members: costs of decision making and costs of implementation. The former refer to time spent on bargaining in order to reach agreement on the components of a security regime for the international system. Clearly, such costs increase with the number of decision centers. Thus, for this dimension, polycentrism and multipolarity would be more costly than bipolarity. Implementation encompasses fixed and variable costs. Problems arising from collective action suggest that two power centers would experience lower fixed costs—pertaining to the creation of the working components of a security regime—than three or more power centers, hence favoring bipolarity and polycentrism. Variable costs, referring to ongoing system management, are expected to be greater when a system has an unequal number of power and decisional centers. This would argue in favor of greater instability of polycentrism. Combining the two sets of costs, bipolarity clearly ranks first with regard to stability. As for the other two structures, fixed costs of implementation are higher for multipolarity, while polycentrism has higher variable costs. In this tradeoff, multipolarity is deemed better off, hence polycentrism is hypothesized to be the most unstable structure.

The expectation that polycentrism will be the most unstable type of international system is reinforced by several interrelated processes and a structural trait that, together, produce exceptionally high variable costs. First, the larger number of autonomous decision centers in polycentrism increases the theoretically possible number of adversarial pairs and coalitions that tend, per se, to generate more disruption. This tendency is accentuated by the status/capability gap—legal sovereignty with little military power—that affects most of these entities.

Four specific sources of instability can be discerned in this structure: uncertainty about likely behavior in future interstate relations; likely miscalculation about probable alignment and coalitions, especially on the periphery of the global system; attempts at manipulation of the weak by the strong, notably the bloc leaders; and continuous striving by weak actors for alliance or protector relationships with more powerful states. All this compounds the tendency to frequent disruptive interaction that is inherent in a system with many politically autonomous members—polycentrism.

Finally, the concentration of military power in two states or blocs (power bipolarity) induces a stable equilibrium in their direct relationship. However, this does not extend to the weaker autonomous decision centers on the periphery of the system, which are frequently engaged in disruptive conflicts, crises, and wars, leading to (often intense) destabilization. Furthermore, the bloc leaders tend to a policy of permissiveness about disruptive interactions among less powerful members of the system, including war, as long as destabilization on the periphery does not spill back to the central core of the international system. (This is especially evident in most of Africa's interstate crises since 1960.) For all of these reasons, polycentrism is hypothesized as the least stable international system (Brecher, James, and Wilkenfeld 1990).

A series of hypotheses spells out the postulated rank ordering from most unstable system (polycentrism) to most stable (bipolarity), with multipolarity occupying a middle ground. These hypotheses explore aspects of the links between types of international systems and indicators of system stability/instability: crisis characteristics (frequency of crisis, trigger, stress, crisis management); major power activity (involvement and effectiveness); and crisis outcomes (termination and legacy). Taken together, these constitute the elements of an index of stability for the international system.

Hypothesis 1: The frequency of crises will be highest in polycentrism, followed by multipolarity and bipolarity.

Hypothesis 2: The rate of violence in crisis triggers will be highest in polycentrism, followed by multipolarity and bipolarity.

Hypothesis 3: Decisional stress will be highest in polycentrism, followed by multipolarity and bipolarity.

Hypothesis 4: Violence in crisis management will be most severe in polycentrism, followed by multipolarity and bipolarity.

Hypothesis 5: Major power activity will be lowest in polycentrism, followed by multipolarity and bipolarity.

Hypothesis 6: Major power effectiveness as third parties will be lowest in polycentrism, followed by multipolarity and bipolarity.

Hypothesis 7: Crises in polycentrism will be least likely to terminate in agreement, followed by multipolarity and bipolarity.

Hypothesis 8: Crises in polycentrism will be least likely to terminate in tension reduction, followed by multipolarity and bipolarity.

Hypothesis 1 argues that the structural characteristics of international systems affect the **frequency** of crises; that is, we expect the decentralization in a polycentric system will result in a proliferation of crises, while a bipolar system, in which the two superpowers maintain reasonably tight control over their allies and clients, will be characterized by the fewest crises.

Violence in both crisis triggers (Hypothesis 2) and crisis management (Hypothesis 4) is expected to be most pronounced in polycentrism and lowest in bipolarity, because the decentralized nature of the power configuration in a poly-centric system will mean loss of control; and the result will be greater use of violence in both the initiation of crisis and in the way nations cope with crises. In bipolarity, where the use of violence is fraught with considerable danger not only for the actors involved but also for the international system as a whole, violence levels in both triggers and crisis management are expected to be lower.

The **trigger** to an international crisis, as noted, is the specific act, event, or situational change that catalyzes a crisis for the earliest crisis actor, that is, perception of value threat, time pressure, and likely military hostilities. For purposes of this analysis, triggers are grouped into four categories: **non-violent,** including political acts (e.g., severance of diplomatic relations), economic acts (e.g., nationalization of foreign property), and external change (e.g., change in weapon system); **internal,** including verbal or physical challenge to a regime or elite (e.g., coup d'état); **non-violent military,** that is, mobilization of forces; and **violent,** including indirect (attack on an ally) and direct violent acts (invasion of territory).

Severity of violence identifies the most severe form of behavior adopted in coping with the crisis by any of the actors involved. These range from **no violence, minor clashes, serious clashes,** to **war.**

Hypothesis 3 proposes that decision makers in polycentrism will experience higher stress than those in bipolarity or multipolarity. As noted in Part II, the indicator of **stress** is composed of a measure of the type of threat perceived by the decision makers and the power status of the adversary. Grave threat (threat to existence or threat to influence of a major power) and large negative discrepancy between the power of an actor and its adversary combine to produce the highest values on this indicator. Medium stress can result from the threat to such values as political regime, territory, and grave damage, combined with a moderate discrepancy in power status. Low levels on the stress indicator can result from a threat to relatively minor values and near parity among the adversaries. Stress is calculated first for each of the actors in an international crisis. The highest value for any actor in the crisis is then taken as the stress level for the international crisis as a whole.

Hypotheses 5 and 6 address the issues of **activity** and **effectiveness of major powers** in international crises of the twentieth century. Once again, the complex decentralized nature of polycentrism dictates both a limited role and limited effectiveness for the powers in international crises. Such involvement is any substantive verbal or physical activity in an international crisis by the seven great powers of the 1918–39 period, and by the superpowers since 1945.

Activity is grouped into three categories: **No/low activity,** including political and economic activity; **covert/semi-military,** including military advisors, without participation in combat; and **military,** for example, dispatch of troops in support of an ally during a war. The effectiveness of such activity in crisis abatement refers to the powers' role in preventing the outbreak of hostilities or in contributing to the termination of an international crisis. The categories for effec-

SYSTEM STRUCTURE   STABILITY / INSTABILITY

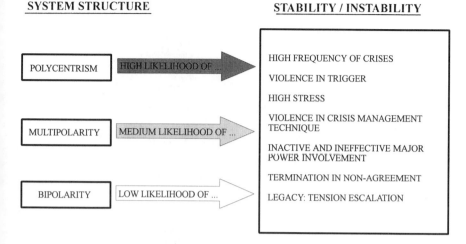

Figure IV.2. Polarity-Stability Model

tiveness are **no activity, ineffective, marginal, important,** and **single most important** factor in crisis abatement.

Hypotheses 7 and 8 address the outcome characteristics of crises, as they are affected by the type of international system in which they occur. Our argument is that the complexity of the polycentric system will detract from the ability of crisis adversaries to reach some form of agreement in their disputes. Similarly, we posit that polycentrism is likely to lead to a larger number of conflicts that persist, resulting in repeated outbreaks of crises among the main protagonists.

Form of outcome is classified as **formal agreement, semi-formal agreement, tacit agreement, unilateral act, imposed agreement,** and **faded or other. Crisis legacy** refers to whether or not the same principal adversaries were involved as actors in another crisis within a five year period following termination.[8] If yes, then the outcome is classified as one of **escalation of tension,** and if not, then it is classified as **de-escalation of tension.**

Figure IV.2 is a schematic representation of the polarity-stability model.

Crisis Characteristics and the International System

We turn first to the findings on a group of hypotheses that focuses on the link between type of international system and crisis characteristics.

Hypothesis 1 deals with the frequency of crises in the four international systems. Data on the distribution of crisis initiations over time are presented in Figure IV.3 and Table IV.1.[9] In Figure IV.3,[10] a general tendency toward a larger number of crises per year as we progress from 1918 to 1987 is visually apparent, with a significant decline thereafter. This recent sharp reduction in the number of

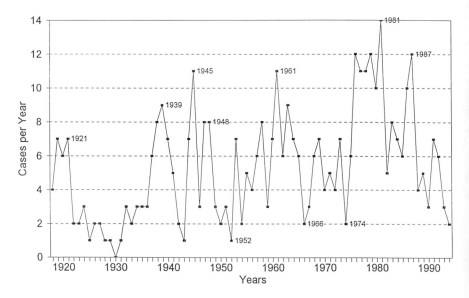

Figure IV.3.   International Crises, 1918–94 (N = 412)

international crises per year has both a substantive and statistical explanation. The decline in the power of the Soviet Union in the late 1980s, culminating in its disintegration into 15 independent states, coupled with the emergence of the United States as the dominant military power in the system, profoundly affected the nature and frequency of international conflict and crisis. While the global system remains dangerous, the defining characteristics of international crisis—increased disruptive interactions between two or more adversaries, high probability of military hostilities, and a challenge to the structure of the international system, either global, dominant, or subsystem—are no longer met by many of the types of conflict situations that typify the post–Cold War unipolar era. One need only think of the proliferation of conflicts based on ethnicity, nationality, and religion to detect this problem.

A secondary reason for the sharp decline in international crises may be rooted in the paucity of reliable source material from which to identify and code crises in the most recent period. In this sense, the ICB data set is an evolving data bank, which not only seeks to incorporate the most recent crises but also consciously attempts to add crises that were missed because of the lack of source material at the time of the initial coding of the most recent period.[11]

The upward trend in crisis frequency through 1987 noted above is highlighted in Table IV.1, which shows that the average number of crises per year increased 54% from multipolarity to bipolarity and an additional 20% from bipolarity to polycentrism. In 1981, for example, a year of very high crisis activity (see also 1976–1980—all during polycentrism), there were 14 international crises with a total of 21 states as crisis actors (two of these states, Libya and

TABLE IV.1. Patterns of Crises in the Twentieth Century[a]

System (a)	Years (b)	Number of years (c)	Number of crises (d)	Average: crisis/ year (e) e=d/c	Percent increase (f)
Multipolar	1918-39[b]	20.75	64	3.08	
Bipolar	1945-62[c]	17.30	82	4.74	+ 54%
Polycentric	1963-89	27.00	161	5.96	+ 20%
Unipolar	1990-94	5.00	21	4.20	- 42%

[a] All World War II cases and 52 intrawar crises from the other four system-periods are excluded from this and subsequent tables in the analysis of polarity.
[b] November 1918 to end August 1939.
[c] September 1945 to end December 1962.

Israel, were each involved in two crises that year): **Chad/Libya V, Ecuador/Peru Border III, Mozambique Raid, Iraq Nuclear Reactor, Essequibo II, Contras I, Al-Biqa Missiles I, Cameroon/Nigeria I, Coup Attempt-Gambia, Gulf of Syrte I, Operation Protea, Galtat Zemmour I, U-137 Incident, Coup Attempt—Bahrain** (see *Master Table,* pp. 722–25). Thus, using the criteria of the sheer volume of crisis activity in the global system, polycentrism exhibits the most acute signs of instability.[12]

We continue by examining the distribution of **triggers** to crises across polarity configurations (Hypothesis 2). This refers to the specific act, event, or situational change that catalyzes a crisis for the earliest actor in an international crisis, that is, its perception of value threat, time pressure, and likely military hostilities. We employ four categories of trigger in this analysis: *non-violent,* including political and economic acts; *internal,* for example, a verbal or physical challenge to a regime; *non-violent military,* for example, mobilization of reserves; and *violence,* direct violent acts (that is, attack on the actor itself) and indirect violence (that is, attack on an alliance partner).

Table IV.2 presents the ICB data on the relative frequency of the four types of triggers for each of the three system-periods. (At the bottom of this table and all others in this section, we also present chi-square and significance levels for paired comparisons between the distributions for each system.)

On the assumption that a violent trigger is the most destabilizing condition under which a crisis can erupt, polycentrism exhibits the greatest degree of system instability: 54% of the crises in that system were triggered by some form of violence, compared to 25% for multipolarity and 27% for bipolarity.

How is this marked difference to be explained? Among the distinguishing characteristics of the polycentric system is the emergence of a large number of new states (in Africa and Asia), many of which achieved independence through violence. It is notable that this pattern of violence carried over into the international crises of this system-period. In contrast, nearly half of all bipolarity crises (1945–62), occurring as they did in a period of structural rigidity, both in terms

TABLE IV.2. Polarity and Crisis Trigger

	Non-violent	Internal challenge	Non-violent military	Violent	TOTAL
Multipolarity	28 44%	5 8%	15 23%	16 25%	64 21%
Bipolarity	40 49%	10 12%	10 12%	22 27%	82 27%
Polycentrism	34 21%	14 9%	26 16%	87 54%	161 52%
TOTAL	102 33%	29 9%	51 17%	125 41%	307 100%

X^2 = 33.70, p = .00

Multipolarity-Bipolarity: X^2 = 3.57, p = .31
Multipolarity-Polycentrism: X^2 = 18.32, p = .00
Bipolarity-Polycentrism: X^2 = 23.86, p = .00

of the number of states in the system and the tightness of its alliance configuration, were triggered by non-violent events such as political and economic acts, more than double the proportion for crises in polycentrism.

The chi square and significance tests for the paired comparisons of systems (see bottom of Table IV.2) reveal that trigger uniquely distinguishes polycentrism from both multipolarity and bipolarity. Of particular interest is the sharp distinction between bipolarity and polycentrism, systems that, although sequential chronologically, are in fact quite different in terms of the degree of control and the suppression of conflict that the superpowers were able to impose over the other actors in the systems. Typical of the 40 bipolarity crises triggered by non-violence (49% of the total) were the following: the U.K. announcement on 21 February 1947 of its intention to discontinue aid to Greece and Turkey, triggering a crisis for the U.S., Greece, and Turkey—the **Truman Doctrine** crisis (economic act); the 24 February 1955 creation of the Baghdad Pact by the U.K., Iraq, Iran, Turkey, and Pakistan, triggering a crisis for Egypt—the **Baghdad Pact** crisis (political act); Guatemala's perception of an economic threat from Mexico on 29 December 1958, resulting from a dispute over fishing rights—**Mexico/ Guatemala Fishing Rights** crisis (economic act); and Gomulka's return to power in Poland on 15 October 1956, which was perceived by the USSR as a threat to its hegemony—**Poland Liberalization** crisis (external change). Conversely, typical of the violent acts that triggered 54% of the polycentrism crises were the following: the 8 April 1965 Indian and Pakistani attacks on each others' police posts in the disputed part of Kutch, triggering crises for India and Pakistan simultaneously—the **Rann of Kutch** crisis; the Chinese ambush of Soviet troops on 2 March 1969—the **Ussuri River** crisis; and the crossing by Iraqi troops into Kuwait on 20 March 1973, triggering a crisis for Kuwait—the **Iraq Invasion of Kuwait** crisis.

Decisional stress is the third crisis dimension we employ to examine the instability of a system (Hypothesis 3). In this context, we classify international crises according to the highest level of stress experienced by any of the actors in a

TABLE IV.3. Polarity and Level of Stress

	Low stress		Medium stress		High stress		TOTAL	
Multipolarity	13	20%	33	52%	18	28%	64	21%
Bipolarity	30	37%	16	19%	36	44%	82	27%
Polycentrism	56	35%	64	40%	41	25%	161	52%
TOTAL	99	32%	113	37%	95	31%	307	100%

$X^2 = 20.63$, p = .00

Multipolarity-Bipolarity: $X^2 = 16.65$, p = .00
Multipolarity-Polycentrism: $X^2 = 4.73$, p = .09
Bipolarity-Polycentrism: $X^2 = 12.64$, p = .00

crisis. Our expectation is that the complex nature of decentralization of power in polycentrism will result in the highest levels of decisional stress.

Table IV.3 presents the ICB findings on stress and instability. The paired comparisons among the three systems reveal that the distribution of stress levels in bipolarity is significantly different from both multipolarity and polycentrism. Bipolarity exhibits the largest proportions of crises with high stress values—44% of all bipolarity crises were characterized by high stress. The 36 bipolarity crises exhibiting high stress consist of two types. Some are cases in which superpowers are crisis actors, and in which one or the other perceives very high stress deriving from a credible threat to a basic national interest. Examples include the U.S. and the USSR in **Azerbaijan** 1945–46 and **Berlin Blockade** 1948–49, the U.S. in the **Truman Doctrine** crisis of 1947 and **Berlin Deadline** crisis 1958–59, and the USSR in the **Marshall Plan** crisis 1947. The second type involved crisis actors that, by virtue of a threat to their very existence, and/or a direct confrontation with a superpower, experienced extreme stress: Finland in the **Soviet Note** crises of 1948 and 1961, Israel in the **Palestine Partition/Israel Independence** crisis of 1947–49, Poland and Hungary in their respective 1956 crises with the USSR, Cuba in the **Bay of Pigs** 1961, Tunisia in its struggle with France in the **Bizerta** crisis of 1961.

Thus, on the stress indicator, contrary to Hypothesis 3, bipolarity is the most unstable international system. This suggests that a system with highly centralized power distribution among its members is a fertile ground for high stakes crises. Thus, whatever tendency there was for the centralization of the power structure to limit instability in bipolarity was overwhelmed by the impact of the East-West rivalry and its attending high levels of stress, often resulting from a threat to existence.[13] But this is not to say that because the overall level of stress in crisis has decreased in polycentrism crises, we are living in a more conflict-free international environment. Rather, we have found that even conflict situations involving relatively low levels of stress escalate to full-blown international crises at higher rates under polycentrism than was the case in other international systems (see Table IV.1).

TABLE IV.4. Polarity and Severity of Violence in Crisis Management

	No violence as CMT		Minor clashes		Serious clashes		War		TOTAL	
Multipolarity	29	45%	10	16%	11	17%	14	22%	64	21%
Bipolarity	36	44%	20	24%	18	22%	8	10%	82	27%
Polycentrism	63	39%	32	20%	48	30%	18	11%	161	52%
TOTAL	128	42%	62	20%	77	25%	40	13%	307	100%

X^2 = 10.78, p = .10

Multipolarity-Bipolarity: X^2 = 5.27, p = .15
Multipolarity-Polycentrism: X^2 = 7.34, p = .06
Bipolarity-Polycentrism: X^2 = 2.16, p = .54

A fourth indicator of system stability/instability is the severity of violence employed in crisis management, ranging from *no violence, minor clashes, serious clashes,* to *full-scale war* (Hypothesis 4). The pattern observed earlier with respect to violence in crisis triggers is apparent in Table IV.4 as well: not only are polycentrism crises far more likely than those of the other two systems to be triggered by violence, crisis actors in polycentrism are also more likely to use more severe forms of violence—particularly serious clashes—in crisis management, a difference that was most pronounced between polycentrism and multipolarity. Serious clashes were a particularly frequent crisis management technique (CMT) for actors in polycentrism crises (30%), including such cases as **Algeria/Morocco Border** 1963, **Ogaden I** 1964, **Ussuri River** 1969, **Mayaguez** 1975, **Invasion of Grenada** 1983, **Syrian Intervention in Lebanon** 1987. Interestingly, multipolarity includes both the highest rate of nonuse of violence in crisis management (45%) and the highest rate of resort to full-scale war (22%). From an overall violence perspective—combining serious clashes and full-scale war—the crises that occurred during polycentrism and multipolarity were more destabilizing than those of bipolarity.

In sum, three key indicators of crisis characteristics reveal polycentrism to be the most unstable system: frequency of crisis and violence (the latter both as a trigger to crises and, together with multipolarity, in severity of violence in crisis management). And although bipolarity exhibited the highest level of stress for decision makers among the systems, overall bipolarity crises exhibit the least destabilizing characteristics.

Major Power Activity in Crises

The second set of hypotheses examines system instability from the perspective of major power activity in crises, both the degree of activity and the extent of effectiveness as third-party intermediaries.

In essence, Hypotheses 5 and 6 attempt to differentiate between major

TABLE IV.5.   Polarity and Major Power Activity

	No/low	Covert/ semi-military	Military	TOTAL
Multipolarity	18 28%	21 33%	25 39%	64 21%
Bipolarity	49 60%	23 28%	10 12%	82 27%
Polycentrism	101 63%	44 27%	16 10%	161 52%
TOTAL	168 55%	88 29%	51 16%	307 100%

$X^2 = 35.73$, p = .00

Multipolarity-Bipolarity:	$X^2 = 18.93$, p = .00
Multipolarity-Polycentrism:	$X^2 = 32.16$, p = .00
Bipolarity-Polycentrism:	$X^2 = .35$, p = .84

power roles as crisis actors and as crisis managers. In the first, the argument is that the more directly involved the powers are as actors in the crises of their era, the greater the instability of the system. Thus, the focus is on extent of activity as an indicator of instability. The second of these hypotheses examines the effectiveness of the powers' intervention in crises: it argues that the more effective such activity is in crisis abatement, the more stable the international system.[14]

Major power activity is any substantive verbal or physical involvement in an international crisis by the seven great powers (from 1918–39) or the two superpowers (from 1945 onward). Such activity is grouped into three categories: *no/low,* including political and economic activity; *semi-military,* including the dispatch of military advisors or military aid, or covert activity; and *direct military,* for example, the dispatch of troops. For purposes of this analysis, the highest level of activity by any one of the seven great powers in multipolarity (France, Germany, Italy, Japan, the U.K., the U.S., the USSR), or any one of the two superpowers in bipolarity and polycentrism (the U.S., the USSR), served as the basis for coding major power activity in an international crisis. This coding scheme was applied both to cases in which the major power was a crisis actor and to those in which it was an involved actor.

Table IV.5 reports the findings on major power activity in crises across the three international systems (Hypothesis 5). Two important findings emerge. First, there is a remarkable similarity in the patterns exhibited by the two post–World War II international systems, with approximately 62% of their crises showing no or very low superpower activity. Second, multipolarity crises had a .72 probability of exhibiting either covert/semi-military or direct military activity on the part of one or more of the seven great powers, almost twice the rate for the superpowers in bipolarity and polycentrism.

Even if one notes the smaller number of states and the larger number of great powers during multipolarity, these findings on major power behavior in crisis situations point to a fundamental difference in the way the powers conceived of their roles in international politics before and after World War II. The

756   Analysis

TABLE IV.6. Polarity and Major Power Effectiveness

	No activity		Ineffective		Marginal		Important or most important		TOTAL	
Multipolarity	10	16%	24	37%	6	10%	24	37%	64	22%
Bipolarity	13	17%	36	48%	7	9%	20	26%	76	26%
Polycentrism	59	38%	52	34%	14	9%	30	19%	155	52%
TOTAL	82	28%	112	38%	27	9%	74	25%	295[a]	100%

$X^2 = 21.00$, p = .00

Multipolarity-Bipolarity: $X^2 = $ 2.22, p = .53
Multipolarity-Polycentrism: $X^2 = 13.50$, p = .00
Bipolarity-Polycentrism: $X^2 = 10.89$, p = .01

[a] This table excludes cases in which all seven great powers were actors (during multipolarity) and cases in which the two superpowers were actors (during the post-World War II system).

great powers of the multipolar (inter–world war) system-period exhibited a behavior pattern more characteristic of the flexible alliance structure of the balance of power system of nineteenth-century Europe. The findings also highlight the fact that multipolarity crises were geographically concentrated in the core of the international system (Europe), where most of the great powers were located, while many bipolarity and polycentrism crises were located on the periphery of the dominant (major power) system. Multipolarity is clearly the most unstable of the three systems from the perspective of this indicator. Since both post-1945 systems were dominated by two superpowers, the evidence supports the contention that power bipolarity is inherently more stable than a system with multiple centers of power.

The effectiveness of major power activity refers to their role in crisis management, that is, in preventing the outbreak of military hostilities or in contributing to the abatement of an international crisis. The findings on Hypothesis 6 are reported in Table IV.6. The ICB data clearly show that the proportion of crises in which there was no activity by the powers increased from multipolarity and bipolarity to polycentrism (16%, 17%, 38%), while the number of crises with effective power involvement decreased substantially (from 37% for multipolarity, to 26% for bipolarity, to only 19% for polycentrism). The bivariate statistical analyses clearly show polycentrism as significantly distinct from the other two systems. From the point of view of effective major power activity in crisis abatement, polycentrism is the least stable of the three systems under consideration—the superpowers were either inactive or ineffective in 72% of the crises. Stated differently, as the primary locus of international crises shifted from the center (dominant system) to the periphery (subsystems), the interests of the superpowers decreased concomitantly, and both the level of activity of the superpowers and their effectiveness have revealed a parallel decrease.

In sum, the role of major powers in international crises is complex. In multipolarity, great powers participated as actors in a large proportion of crises, thus contributing to the instability of that system. However, when the focus changes to the effectiveness of major powers as third parties in crisis abatement, it is polycentrism that exhibits the most abysmal record insofar as the superpowers were concerned—they were conspicuously aloof and ineffective. Thus, when assessing the roles of the powers in crises, we must clearly differentiate between the powers as crisis actors and as crisis managers, as well as among system structures.

Crisis Outcomes and International Systems

The final perspective on the interrelationship of system instability and crisis focuses on outcomes, that is, the form and legacy of crisis termination.

We turn first to the different forms that crisis termination can take (Hypothesis 7). One can differentiate between crises that terminate in **agreement**—a formal agreement such as a cease-fire or a **semi-formal agreement** such as an oral declaration or exchange of letters; those that terminate through a **tacit understanding**—a mutual understanding by adversaries, unstated and unwritten; a **unilateral act,** an **imposed agreement;** and **faded,** whereby the crisis simply fades with no known termination date.

The distribution of ICB cases from the end of 1918 to the end of 1989, in terms of polarity and the form of crisis outcome, does not exhibit any major differences among the systems (and hence no table is presented). Roughly 35% of all international crises terminate in formal and semi-formal agreements, a pattern that holds for all three polar systems.

A final indicator of system instability is crisis legacy, measured as the effect of crisis outcome on the tension level between the principal adversaries after the termination of a crisis (Hypothesis 8). **Tension escalation** is indicated by one or more crises between the adversaries during the subsequent five-year period, while **tension reduction** means that crises did not recur in that time frame.

As evident in Table IV.7, multipolarity and polycentrism exhibited high rates of tension escalation, 45% and 42%, respectively. This contrasts with a 30% propensity for escalation among bipolarity crises. The low 35% rate for termination in agreement, exhibited by all three systems and alluded to previously, appears to have spilled over into a relatively low rate of tension reduction for multipolarity and polycentrism, less so for bipolarity. Closer examination of the bipolarity cases reveals that crises in that system-period that terminated either in tacit agreements or unilateral acts had much higher rates of tension reduction than was the case for either multipolarity or polycentrism. Bipolarity tacit understanding cases resulting in conflict reduction included **Punjab War Scare I** 1951, **Poland Liberalization** 1956, **Taiwan Strait II** 1958, **Central America/ Cuba II** 1960, **Berlin Wall** 1961. Bipolarity unilateral acts resulting in conflict

TABLE IV.7. Polarity and Crisis Legacy

	Escalation of tensions		Reduction of tensions		TOTAL	
Multipolarity	29	45%	35	55%	64	21%
Bipolarity	25	30%	57	70%	82	28%
Polycentrism	63	42%	88	58%	151	51%
TOTAL	117	39%	180	61%	297[a]	100%

$X^2 = 4.00$, p = .13

Multipolarity-Bipolarity:	$X^2 = 3.39$, p = .06
Multipolarity-Polycentrism:	$X^2 = .24$, p = .63
Bipolarity-Polycentrism:	$X^2 = 2.85$, p = .09

[a] There were 10 cases with missing data on crisis legacy.

reduction included **Truman Doctrine** 1947, **East German Uprising** 1953, **Hungarian Uprising** 1956, **Iraq/Lebanon Upheaval** 1958, **China/India Border II** 1962.

Summary

Table IV.8 presents a summary of the bivariate findings on the relationship between polarity and stability, with the latter measured on a number of characteristics of crisis, from behavior to outcome. The bivariate findings reported in this section strongly point to polycentrism as the most unstable system from the point of view of the characteristics of international crises. Of the eight indicators, polycentrism had the highest instability scores (designated by X) on four (aver-

TABLE IV.8. Ranking of International Systems on Indicators of Instability

Indicators of instability	Multipolarity	Bipolarity	Polycentrism
Frequency of crises			X
Violence in trigger			X
Stress		X	
Severity of violence			X
Low major power activity	X		
Low major power effectiveness			X
Form of outcome (rate of agreement)	Inconclusive	Inconclusive	Inconclusive
Crisis legacy		T	T

age frequency of crises per year, violence in crisis trigger, severity of violence employed in crisis management, and ineffectiveness of major power intervention) and was tied as the most unstable (designated by T) on another indicator (outcome leading to escalation of tension or crisis legacy—tied with bipolarity). Multipolarity evidenced instability on one indicator (extent of activity by the great powers), while bipolarity showed instability on the indicator of stress and tied with polycentrism on crisis legacy. Thus, the ICB data on crises in the twentieth century point to polycentrism as the most unstable international system. The evidence is less conclusive in terms of its ability to differentiate between bipolarity and multipolarity in terms of which evidences greater stability. While these findings provide partial reinforcement for the polarity/stability arguments originally propounded by Waltz (1964), more work is needed in developing a theoretical statement that takes account of the unique features of crises and their impact on the international system, as well as the unique features of the still-emerging post–Cold War unipolar system.

Geography

Geographic factors have long been a central concern in research on international conflict. From the time that humans first formed as collectivities, the border where two groups meet has been a potential source of conflictual interactions. Empirically, geography and territory are a strong presence in conflict situations: most interstate wars identified by the Correlates of War Project occurred between neighboring states or involved a major state in a colonial expansion (Small and Singer 1982; see also Holsti 1991). In addition, neighbors are responsible for two-thirds of all Militarized International Disputes (MIDs), and this frequency increases with the intensity of threat (Gochman 1990).

Recent theoretical frameworks utilized in empirical studies of geography and conflict adopt one of three major approaches: geography as a facilitating cause, as an underlying cause, or as a direct cause of conflict (Diehl 1991; Vasquez 1993). This research began with the work of Sprout and Sprout (1965), who abandoned environmental determinism for "environmental possibilism." State action is seen as a result of the interplay in the "ecological triad," an entity, its environment, and the entity-environment relationship. While states respond to their geographic environment, they are not determined; the environment enables and also constrains leaders' processes of decision (Starr 1991). Geography is one of several environmental factors that increase or inhibit the likelihood of war between two states. These include the effects of location, size, climate, distribution of population, and natural resources.

The large empirical literature on diffusion and interaction develops out of the Sprouts' environmental possibilism, as applied by Starr (Starr 1978; Siverson and Starr 1991). In Starr's framework, opportunity and willingness are necessary conditions for war, conditions partially determined by geography. Opportunity, or "the possibility of interaction between entities or behavioral units of some kind" (Starr 1978:364), related to the Sprouts' possibilism, and willingness, "the process by which (leaders) *recognize opportunities* and then, given these opportunities, become willing to choose war as a behavioral alternative" (Starr 1978:370), pick up on the Sprouts' probabilism and cognitive behaviorism. In other words, Starr views geopolitical factors in the environment as providing a structure of opportunities and constraints (Starr 1991:4). Geographical concerns, such as the presence of shared borders, thus become a facilitating condition for military conflict.

The interaction argument inherent in this framework argues that wars arise out of contiguity, as contiguity causes interaction, which causes uncertainty and conflicts of interest, which can lead to violence (Bremer 1982). Frequency of war therefore is a function of geographic opportunity. Empirical evidence is provided from studies of borders and diffusion. Richardson (1960) was the first to show that the more borders a state has, the more likely it is to be involved in conflict. States close to each other interact more often (Cobb and Elder 1970). Midlarsky (1975) shows that the greater the number of borders, the more uncertainty is created, which he links to war. Starr and Most (1976, 1978) argue, however, that borders per se do not cause conflict, but structure risks and opportunities. Gleditsch and Singer (1975) discovered that the average distance between warring states is significantly less than the average distance between all states. Diehl's (1985) study of major powers confirms that it is not shared borders alone, but geographic proximity that is the facilitating condition; besides increased opportunity, he argues that proximity increases the willingness to fight.

The literature on diffusion provides a related argument to that of geographic proximity. The crucial difference between the research on borders and that of diffusion is that in diffusion "geographic proximity allows the spread of existing war or conflict in some cases (although not in all), and the border effect does not rely on concurrent or previous conflict for war to occur" (Diehl 1991:18). Salience and ease of interaction are at the core of Starr's "interaction model" (1991), which posits interaction opportunities as necessary for diffusion of war; they also indicate the direction of diffusion.

Significant empirical findings on diffusion include the fact that a state with a warring neighbor is three to five times more likely to experience war than is a state without a neighbor at war (Most and Starr 1980, 1983). Starr and Most (1985) also find that diffusion occurs where there is a large number of interactions between states; number of interactions is increased by shared borders, indicating a relation between the two bodies of work. Noncolonial borders are also stronger agents of diffusion than colonial borders, and land borders are stronger than sea borders.

Unlike the diffusion literature, which sees geography as a facilitating condition for conflict, Vasquez (1993, 1995) argues that the operating factor is not contiguity and interaction but **territoriality,** the natural tendency for humans to occupy and defend territory. Territoriality is thus an underlying cause; it is seen as underlying in that territorial disputes usually produce a sequence of results leading to war, giving rise to the practice of "power politics"; it is a cause in that when territorial disagreements are settled peacefully, it is unlikely that there will be such disputes in the future between the two adversaries. Building on the previous evidence showing that contiguous states fight, Vasquez highlights Wallensteen's (1981) finding that contiguous major state dyads have higher than average military confrontations and wars. Diehl (1985) also notes that in enduring rivalries, contiguous disputes are much more likely to escalate, while Bremer (1982) finds that the probability of war between contiguous states is 35 times higher than for noncontiguous states.

The third strand of the current literature takes Vasquez's argument a step further and points to certain geographical characteristics as the source, or major cause, of certain forms of conflict. Territory can take on important characteristics in and of itself and lead to future conflict. Diehl and Goertz (1988) identify and elaborate two aspects of territorial importance: intrinsic and relative. Intrinsic importance is the value that the territory has for any given state and is measured in reference to the size of the area in the exchange and the number of people living in the area. Relative importance is the varying value that territory may have for different states and is measured by geographic location and by whether it is colonial or noncolonial. A modest relationship was found between territorial importance and propensity for violence in territorial changes (Goertz and Diehl 1992b).

This discussion has shown that a wide and diverse body of theory on geography and conflict points to geography as a facilitating condition, an underlying cause, and a source of conflict. In the study of crisis, the centrality of geography has been manifest in at least three different factors: (1) the distribution of international crises across geographic regions, and regional distributions on such dimensions as the frequency and severity of violence, and the involvement of third parties in international crisis management; (2) the effect of geographic proximity/distance of crisis adversaries on the types of triggers, crisis management techniques, and outcomes of crises; and (3) the impact of the location of the crisis to the crisis actor on threat perception, major power activity, and outcomes. Factors (1) and (2) focus on characteristics of the international crisis as a whole, while (3) adopts the perspective of individual states as crisis actors.

Geographic location, adversarial proximity, and **proximity of crisis to the actor** will serve as the foci for an examination of the interplay of geography and crisis.[15] For **geographic location,** we pose a set of general questions to guide the presentation of ICB data. For **adversarial proximity** and **proximity of the crisis to the actor,** models and sets of hypotheses will be proposed for subsequent analysis. As is the case throughout most of Part IV, we exclude intra-war crises from the present analysis (see introduction to Part IV for a discussion of this exclusion). Thus, we deal with 336[16] international crises and 658 foreign policy crises for the 1918–94 period. We turn first to a broad examination of the regional location of crises.

Geographic Location of Crises

The following questions guide our initial examination of the geography-crisis nexus.

1. How are international crises distributed across the major regions of the globe?
2. Is the distribution of international crises by region related to the polarity of the system?
3. Does the severity of crisis-related violence vary across regions?
4. Does geographic location affect the likelihood and extent of major power or international organization involvement in crises?

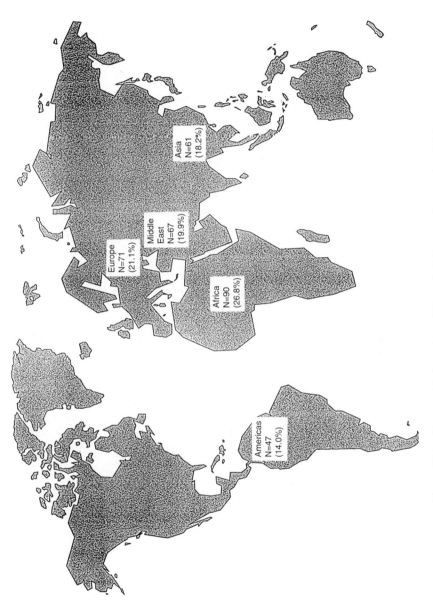

Figure IV.4.   Geographic Location of Twentieth-Century International Crises

TABLE IV.9.   Distribution of International Crises by Region

	Multipolarity 1918-39		Bipolarity 1945-62		Polycentrism 1963-89		Unipolarity 1990-94		TOTAL	
Africa	2	2%	10	11%	72	80%	6	7%	90	27%
Americas	9	20%	12	26%	23	50%	2	4%	46	14%
Asia	9	15%	24	39%	22	36%	6	10%	61	19%
Europe	34	51%	17	26%	13	20%	2	3%	66	20%
Middle East	10	15%	19	29%	31	48%	5	8%	65	20%
TOTAL	64	20%	82	25%	161	49%	21	6%	328[a]	100%

X^2 = 96.23, p = .00

[a] Eight non-intrawar crises that occurred during the period 1939-45 are excluded from this table.

The most general question pertaining to the geography-crisis nexus deals with the distribution of crises across the five major regions of the globe. Figure IV.4 provides a regional breakdown across the entire 76-year span of the twentieth century under examination. While no region has been immune to international crises, Africa is at one end of the frequency spectrum with 27%, while the Americas are at the other with 14%. This very high figure for Africa relates to states that achieved independence for the most part only at the beginning of polycentrism. The vast majority of the 90 African crises are clustered during a relatively short span of time, 30 of the 76 years. We address these issues as we turn to polarity.

These aggregate figures conceal important differences among the regions that are highlighted by the incorporation of system polarity into the analysis (see Table IV.9). Three regions exhibit a preponderance of crises in polycentrism— Africa (80%), the Americas (50%), the Middle East (48%). Europe exhibits the reverse, with 51% of its crises occurring in multipolarity[17] and much smaller proportions for the other system-periods. In fact, Europe was the site of over half the international crises in the multipolar system (34 of 64 cases), dropping to only 8% of all international crises during polycentrism (13 of 161) and 10% (2 of 21) of the cases during unipolarity. Africa, on the other hand, went from the region with the lowest proportion of crises in both multipolarity and bipolarity to the region with the highest proportion—almost half—of international crises in polycentrism, more than double the proportion for any other region.

A second perspective on the distribution of crises by region on polarity takes yearly crisis rates into account. While the Americas and the Middle East maintained relatively stable rates of crises per year—the Americas with .69 crises per year for bipolarity and .85 for polycentrism, the Middle East with 1.15 crises per year for bipolarity, 1.10 for polycentrism—Africa showed both the highest yearly rate of 2.67 for polycentrism and also the most marked increase—up from a .59 rate in bipolarity. These patterns, and Africa's in particular, contrast sharply

TABLE IV.10.   System-Level Crises: Comparison of Europe (Multipolarity) and Africa (Polycentrism)

	Subsystem		Mainly subsystem		Mainly dominant		Dominant		TOTAL	
Europe: multipolarity	13	38%	10	29%	2	6%	9	27%	34	100%
Africa: polycentrism	69	96%	3	4%	0	0%	0	0%	72	100%

with Europe, which had rates of 1.64 for multipolarity, .98 for bipolarity, and .44 for polycentrism.[18]

Part of the explanation for the stark disparity between patterns for Europe and Africa in particular derives from the fact that the African continent was dominated by colonial powers until the end of the bipolar system in the early 1960s. However, a shift in conflict patterns across the international systems is also evident. That is, while Europe was the locus of 53% of all crises during multipolarity (and Africa only 3%), Africa was the locus of 45% of all polycentrism crises (and Europe only 8%). There was, of course, a qualitative difference between the types of crises in the two regions. Table IV.10 shows that, for Europe during multipolarity, 33% of its crises occurred at the mainly dominant or dominant system level, including **Remilitarization of the Rhineland** 1936, **Anschluss** 1938, **Munich** 1938, **Czech. Annexation** 1939, and **Entry into World War II** 1939. In Africa during polycentrism, on the other hand, 96% of its 72 crises occurred at the subsystem level, with only three—**Congo II** 1964, **War in Angola** 1975–76, and **Ogaden II** 1977–78—spilling over into the dominant system because of superpower participation. Thus a shift in the balance of crises over time from Europe to Africa has accompanied a shift from the center or dominant system to the periphery or the subsystem level of world politics. This is a trend that we will return to as we delve more deeply into regional patterns of crisis.

A third factor that will help fine-tune the aggregate analysis of the geography-crisis nexus concerns the extent of violence associated with international crises (see Table IV.11).[19] For this analysis, we introduce the variable VIOL, which identifies the extent of violence in an international crisis as a whole, regardless of whether or not it was employed in crisis management. Particularly striking is the finding that 56% of all European crises exhibited no violence. Closer examination of the data on European crises sheds additional light on the dramatic changes in crisis patterns for Europe that we noted previously. Europe accounted for 40% of all international crises in which no violence occurred (almost double the proportion for any other region), while at the same time it accounted for 21% of all international crises involving war (10 of 47 cases), virtually all of the latter occurring during multipolarity.

Two significant integrative processes, with origins in the bipolar system, help explain this dramatic downturn in violence in Europe's crises: the establish-

TABLE IV.11.   Geography and Violence in International Crises

	No violence		Minor clashes		Serious clashes		War		TOTAL	
Africa	18	20%	33	37%	34	38%	5	5%	90	27%
Americas	14	30%	24	51%	5	11%	4	8%	47	14%
Asia	9	15%	18	29%	22	36%	12	20%	61	18%
Europe	40	56%	12	17%	9	13%	10	14%	71	21%
Middle East	19	28%	19	28%	13	20%	16	24%	67	20%
TOTAL	100	30%	106	31%	83	25%	47	14%	336	100%

$X^2 = 65.72$, p = .00

ment of *NATO* in 1949, leading to the elimination of interstate war in Western Europe, and the establishment of the Warsaw Pact in 1955, leading to the virtual elimination of war in Eastern Europe. In addition, superpower bloc rivalry, along with qualitative changes in military technology (the nuclear dimension) led each bloc to eschew direct intervention in the other bloc, for example, the U.S. re the **Hungarian Uprising** 1956 and **Prague Spring** 1968, the USSR re **Guatemala** 1953 and the **Dominican Republic** 1965. Finally, the preeminence of the superpowers reduced the frequency of resort to violence by their client-allies.

Two additional regions—Asia and the Middle East—accounted for a large proportion of wars. Examination of the cases reveals that the bulk occurred in the post–World War II era. For Asia, these crisis-wars included **Kashmir I** 1947, **Korean War I** 1950, **China/India Border II** 1962, **Kashmir II** 1965, **Bangladesh** 1971, **Vietnam Invasion of Cambodia** 1977, **Sino/Vietnam War** 1978.[20] For the Middle East, the list of crisis-wars included **Palestine Partition/Israel Independence** 1947, **Suez Nationalization-War** 1956, **Six Day War** 1967, **North/South Yemen I** 1972, **October–Yom Kippur War** 1973, **Iran/Iraq War** 1980, **War in Lebanon** 1982, **Gulf War** 1990. Africa, despite the fact that it accounted for almost half of the crises in the polycentric system, shows the lowest proportion of cases with full-scale war (5%). Two-thirds of the African crises involved minor or serious clashes. In sum, while the African region was the site of the largest proportion of crises in the period under study, these crises were, for the most part, peripheral to the central concerns of the major actors in the international system and were least likely to exhibit violence escalating to full-scale war.

A fourth question growing out of a system perspective on international crises asks whether geographic location affects the extent of major power activity, either when they themselves are actors, or when they are third parties. That is, do the major powers respond differently to crises that occur in the core of a system than to those that occur in the periphery? The ICB data reported in Figure IV.5 reflect the dramatic transition from a Eurocentric multipower international system before World War II to a more diffuse superpower-dominated global

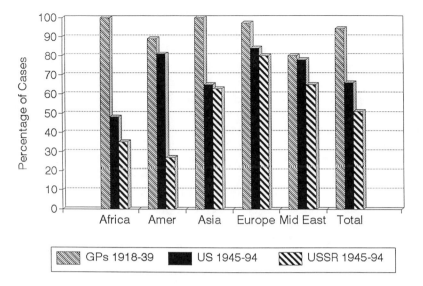

Figure IV.5. Percent Involvement by Major Powers

system from 1945 onward. While there is a good deal of regional variation, we note that the great powers—France, Germany, Great Britain, Italy, Japan, the U.S., and the USSR—were involved to some degree in over 90% (see Total bars) of all crises for the interwar period. A large proportion of these multipolarity crises with great power activity were in Europe (33 of the 64). A separate analysis reveals that among the 64 multipolarity crises in which one or more of the great powers was active, 26 (41%) showed direct military involvement.

Post–World War II patterns offer a sharp contrast. The U.S. was active in 66% of all international crises, while the Soviet Union was active in 51%. Furthermore, additional analysis reveals that direct military activity was reflected in only 20 of the 174 crises in which the U.S. was active (11%), and in only 13 of the 133 crises with Soviet activity (10%)—contrasting with the 43% rate of direct military activity for the great powers in multipolarity. Although the United States was active in a larger proportion of crises than was the USSR in all five regions, this discrepancy was most pronounced in Latin America (81% involvement for U.S. versus 27% for USSR), where the U.S. continued to exhibit hegemonic behavior, and the Middle East (78% versus 65%), where the superpowers actively competed for influence in a "gray zone." The rates of activity in Africa (48% versus 35%, respectively) are considerably lower, reflecting that region's secondary status in the struggle for power and influence between the two superpowers (see Blechman and Kaplan 1978; Kaplan 1981).

Finally, we consider global organization (GO) involvement and geography: (a) Are there regional differences in global organization involvement? and (b) when global organizations became involved, in which regions was their involvement effective in crisis abatement?[21] **Global organization involvement** is dichotomized into cases of no League of Nations or United Nations involvement, and cases in which involvement at some level occurred—general, Secretary-General, (General) Assembly, and (Security) Council. **Global organization effectiveness** was classified as follows: no GO involvement; GO involvement did not contribute to crisis abatement or escalated the crisis; GO involvement contributed marginally to crisis abatement; and GO involvement was an important or the most important factor in crisis abatement.

International crises were virtually evenly divided between those showing no GO involvement and those in which some involvement occurred.[22] And the regions themselves showed an almost identical 50/50 split for involvement, with the exception of the Americas, which exhibited 62% global organization involvement, and Europe with only a 40% level. Among the 161 crises in which the League or the UN became involved, only 40 or 25% showed such involvement to have been effective in terms of crisis abatement, (for effective, we include cases in which the global organization was effective or the most effective element in crisis abatement). Regional effectiveness-to-involvement ratios ranged from Europe at 40%, the Middle East at 31%, the Americas at 21%, Asia at 19%, to Africa at 18%.

It is worth taking a closer look at Africa and the Americas, since both had relatively active regional organizations during the post–World War II era. The two regions exhibit quite different patterns. For the Americas, while the UN was effective in only six of the 45 post–World War II crises, the Organization of American States was effective in 12 of the 45. The UN and the *OAS* were jointly effective in crisis abatement in only two crises in which they were both involved—**Cuban Missiles** in 1962 and **Nicaraguan Civil War** in 1978–79. In Africa, by contrast, the UN was effective in only eight of the 90 post–World War II crises, and the Organization for African Unity was effective in only four. There were no crises in which both the *OAU* and the UN were effective. So whereas in the case of the Americas, the *OAS* picked up slack left by the ineffectiveness of the UN in the region, Africa did not have the same safety valve available.

In sum, across the 1918 to 1994 time span, the data show Africa to be the most crisis-prone region, with the vast majority of its crises occurring during polycentrism, and virtually all at the subsystem level. Europe, on the other hand, experienced half of its crises during multipolarity, most at the dominant system level, with a steady decline since. Asia and the Middle East accounted for large proportions of crises associated with war, with the bulk occurring in the post–World War II era. Africa, while accounting for the largest proportion of post–World War II crises, had the smallest proportion of crises escalating to full-scale war. Great powers were involved in 90% of all crises in the interwar period, while the U.S. was involved in only two-thirds of post–World War II crises, and the USSR in only one-half. Finally, while involvement rates for global organizations by region showed little variation, effectiveness in terms of crisis abatement was greatest in Europe, lowest in Africa.

Adversarial Proximity

We now turn to the first of two models that employ the concept of geographic proximity in explaining crisis phenomena. We propose first an **Adversarial Proximity–Crisis Model,** which grows out of a series of questions pertaining to the circumstances under which the geographic proximity/distance of the principal crisis adversaries will affect crisis characteristics. Does geographic proximity between crisis adversaries affect the likelihood that crisis eruption will be violent? In the event of violence in a crisis, is it likely to be more severe when the crisis adversaries are geographically contiguous? Do crisis outcomes—substance and form—differ in cases where the adversaries share a common border from those where they are geographically apart? Are crises between immediate neighbors more likely to be part of a protracted conflict (enduring rivalry) than are those between adversaries that are geographically distant from each other?

Specifically, the model presented in Figure IV.6 generates the following hypotheses for testing.

Hypothesis 9: The greater the proximity of the crisis adversaries, the more likely it is that the crisis will be triggered by violence.

Hypothesis 10: The greater the proximity of the crisis adversaries, the more likely it is that violence will be employed in crisis management.

Hypothesis 11: The greater the proximity of the crisis adversaries, the more likely it is that the crisis will terminate in agreement.

Hypothesis 12: The greater the proximity of the crisis adversaries, the more likely it is that the crisis will be part of a protracted conflict.

Regarding the proximity-violence link (Hypotheses 9 and 10): contiguity allows adversaries to undertake military action by moving troops and equipment to a common border; that is, violence is made easier and, therefore, more likely. Distant adversaries can be expected to display a wider range of crisis behavior, since launching military action under such circumstances is a considerably more serious undertaking.

Proximity also plays a role in the manner in which crises can be expected to terminate. Contiguous or nearby adversaries may need to achieve agreements (Hypothesis 11), such as a cease-fire or separation of forces, in order to bring closure to a situation that is more likely to generate immediate and acute concern for the populations involved. More distant adversaries may be able to sustain a greater degree of ambiguity in crisis termination, since the lack of closure through agreement is less likely to be a constant source of irritation to their populations.

Finally, Hypothesis 12 postulates that proximate adversaries are more likely than their distant counterparts to be part of protracted conflicts. The reason is that the conditions that give rise to conflict and crisis among proximate adversaries are likely to linger, since they often involve issues such as population, territory,

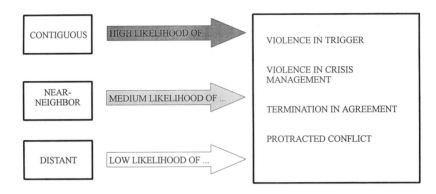

Figure IV.6.   Adversarial Proximity–Crisis Model

and language/culture. They are provoked by more frequent contacts between adversaries, thereby increasing the likelihood that such conflicts will become protracted.

Twentieth-century crises were classified according to the geographic proximity of the principal adversaries. As with the coding of power discrepancy and other ICB relational variables, the adversary need not have been a crisis actor in the case at hand. Figure IV.7 presents the distribution of the 336 international crises (excluding IWCs) according to whether the adversaries were contiguous (shared a border), near neighbors (same geographic region), or distant. Clearly, the vast majority of crises—73%—involved adversaries that were contiguous, with an additional 12% involving near neighbors. As hypothesized, there is an expectation that this geographic factor will have an important role in differentiating crises across a broad range of characteristics.

Only 52 crises (15%) in this 76-year span of the twentieth century involved geographically distant adversaries. As expected, these distant crises had some unique features. Forty percent of the distant crises (21) occurred during bipolarity, the system with the tightest alliance structure of the entire century. In

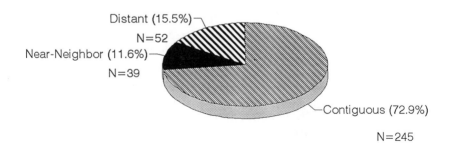

Figure IV.7.   Adversarial Proximity (*N* = 336)

TABLE IV.12. **Adversarial Proximity and Trigger**

	Non-violent		Internal challenge		Non-violent military		External violence		TOTAL	
Contiguous	81	33%	16	7%	40	16%	108	44%	245	73%
Near neighbors	11	28%	9	23%	6	16%	13	33%	39	12%
Distant	21	40%	6	12%	10	19%	15	29%	52	15%
TOTAL	113	34%	31	9%	56	17%	136	40%	336	100%

$X^2 = 14.69$, p = .02

addition, 21 distant crises (40%) were played out at the mainly dominant or dominant system level, four times the rate for contiguous or near-neighbor crises. Among the dominant system crises with distant principal adversaries were **Truman Doctrine** 1947, **Berlin Blockade** 1948–49, **Berlin Deadline** 1958–59, **Berlin Wall** 1961, and **Cuban Missiles** 1962, all part of the East/West protracted conflict. We will return to these characteristics in the context of patterns of violence and outcomes relating to geographic proximity/distance of adversaries.

Table IV.12 reports on the relationship between adversarial proximity/distance and crisis trigger (Hypothesis 9). Crises among contiguous adversaries were more frequently triggered by external violence than were more distant crises—44% contiguous, 33% near neighbor, 29% distant. Table IV.13 reveals a considerably different pattern for crisis management technique. While the level of violence in crisis management is highest among contiguous adversaries as expected (Hypothesis 10), the extent of violence employed in crisis management increased for all three categories of adversarial proximity, with the greatest increase apparent among distant crisis adversaries—29% violence in crisis triggers (Table IV.12), 44% violence in crisis management technique (Table IV.13). Later in Part IV we will examine data that point to low decision maker stress as one of several factors contributing to the possibility of violent responses to non-violent triggers, along with such other factors as deteriorating internal conditions and power parity among crisis actors.[23] Among the distant international crises in which non-violent triggers were followed by violence in crisis management were **Suez Canal** 1951–52, **Taiwan Strait I** 1954–55, **Suez Nationalization-War**

TABLE IV.13. **Adversarial Proximity and Crisis Management Technique**

	Negotiation		Pacific		Non-violent military		Violence		TOTAL	
Contiguous	38	15%	42	17%	34	14%	131	54%	245	73%
Near neighbors	14	36%	6	15%	3	8%	16	41%	39	12%
Distant	6	12%	12	23%	11	21%	23	44%	52	16%
TOTAL	58	17%	60	18%	48	14%	170	51%	336	100%

$X^2 = 14.72$, p = .02

TABLE IV.14. Adversarial Proximity and Form of Outcome

	Agreement		Tacit		Unilateral		Other		TOTAL	
Contiguous	97	40%	13	5%	81	33%	53	22%	244	73%
Near neighbors	9	23%	2	5%	19	49%	9	23%	39	12%
Distant	13	25%	5	10%	26	50%	8	15%	52	15%
TOTAL	119	35%	20	6%	126	38%	70	21%	335	100%

X^2 = 11.51, p = .07

1956–57, **Congo II** 1964, **Iraq Nuclear Reactor** 1981, **Falklands/Malvinas** 1982, **Kashmir III–Nuclear** 1990.

The relationship between adversarial proximity and form of outcome is explored in Table IV.14. Two findings are prominently displayed. Crises involving contiguous actors have a 40% rate of termination in agreement, compared to considerably lower rates for crises involving more distant adversaries (Hypothesis 11). In addition, contiguous crisis adversaries are considerably less likely to experience termination through unilateral acts than is the case for more distant adversarial protagonists. Both findings support the notion that for crisis adversaries that share a common border, there is a greater felt need for formal termination of a crisis through agreement, lest they continue to experience stress and threat. With greater distance, the adversaries can tolerate a less formal outcome, since the distance between them serves as a buffer preventing all but the most extreme provocations from escalating to crisis.

Before reading too much into these findings, we need to be aware that further analysis reveals that contiguous crises also have the highest rate for termination in ambiguity, which we define as either stalemate or compromise for some or all of the actors involved. So although a comparatively large number of agreements ensue, they are unlikely to lead to permanent resolution of crises among proximate adversaries.

These latter findings are reinforced by the data on adversarial proximity and protracted conflict (Hypothesis 12).[24] In Table IV.15, we note that contiguous and distant crises are considerably more likely than crises among near neighbors to

TABLE IV.15. Adversarial Proximity
and Protracted Conflict

	Non-protracted conflict		Protracted conflict		TOTAL	
Contiguous	114	46%	131	54%	245	73%
Near neighbors	29	74%	10	26%	39	12%
Distant	21	40%	31	60%	52	15%
TOTAL	164	49%	172	51%	336	100%

X^2 = 12.18, p = .00

have occurred in the context of protracted conflicts. Crises involving contiguous actors tend for the most part to be over local issues such as territory, resources, and population and are not easily permanently resolved, even if agreement is achieved—see, for example, India/Pakistan (1947–present), Arab/Israel (1947–present). At the opposite extreme, those crises involving the most distant adversaries have tended to be dominant system crises, many as part of the East/West protracted conflict, which were also difficult to resolve. It is the crises involving near neighbors that have the greatest possibility of more permanent resolution, involving as they often do small powers with less vital interests.

To summarize, three of the four hypotheses derived from the Adversarial Proximity–Crisis Model (Figure IV.6) have been supported: the more proximate the adversarial actors, the more likely it was that the crisis was triggered by violence, that violence was employed in crisis management, and that termination involved the reaching of agreement among the parties. We have also seen that both contiguous and distant sets of crisis actors were more likely than near neighbors to be locked in protracted conflict, although the nature of these protracted conflicts was likely to be different for the two types of crises.

Proximity of Crisis to the Actor

Having examined crisis characteristics and outcomes from the perspective of the international crisis as a whole, we now shift our attention to the foreign policy actors and focus on the impact of the proximity of the actor to the geographic location of the crisis. Specifically, the **Proximity of Crisis to Actor Model** builds upon the following questions. Do international crises occurring on the actor's home territory differ from more distant crises in terms of the types of events or acts that trigger them? Are "home territory" crises likely to generate the use of more severe forms of violence in crisis management than is the case for actors in more remote crises? Do the outcomes of crises, in terms of form and substance, differ for actors involved in crises on their home territory from outcomes for more remote crises? Are actors in home territory crises more likely than others to be part of a protracted conflict?

The **Proximity of Crisis to Actor Model** (see Figure IV.8) generates the following hypotheses.

Hypothesis 13: States involved in crises on their home territory are more likely than others to experience violent triggers.

Hypothesis 14: States involved in crises on their home territory are more likely than others to employ severe violence in crisis management.

Hypothesis 15: States involved in crises on their home territory are more likely than others to terminate their crises in agreement.

Hypothesis 16: States involved in crises on their home territory are more likely than others to be part of a protracted conflict.

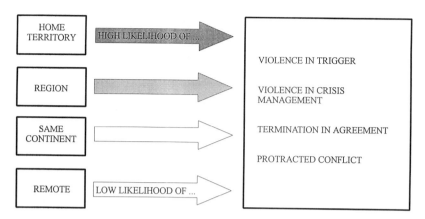

Figure IV.8.   Proximity of Crisis to Actor Model

The reader will note that these hypotheses parallel Hypotheses 9–12—where the focus was on the international crisis as a whole—and is referred to the discussion of those hypotheses for their rationale.

For purposes of this analysis, crises are classified into those that occur on the actor's home territory, within its subregion, on the same continent, and in a more remote location. Figure IV.9 shows that 59% of all foreign policy crises occur on the home territory of a crisis actor, and an additional 21% occur in its region. Eleven percent of all actor-level crises occur in a geographically remote location for the crisis actor. A closer examination of these latter cases indicates that 47 of these 72 crisis actors were either great powers in the multipolar system or superpowers in bipolarity and polycentrism, attesting to the fact that it is primarily states with significant global agendas and the capability to project power far beyond their territories that tend to become involved in crises beyond their immediate subregions. Most of the exceptions involved the U.K. (10 cases) and France (nine cases) after World War II, where at least for a certain period of

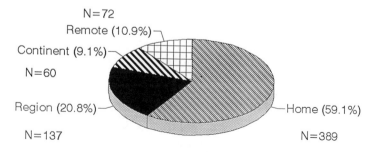

Figure IV.9.   Geographic Proximity of Crises to Actors, Foreign Policy Crises (N = 658)

TABLE IV.16. Geographic Proximity and Crisis Trigger

	Non-violent		Internal challenge		Non-violent military		Violence		TOTAL	
Home territory	127	33%	36	9%	80	21%	146	37%	389	59%
Subregion	59	43%	0	0%	33	24%	45	33%	137	21%
Same continent	37	62%	1	2%	12	20%	10	16%	60	9%
Remote	33	46%	0	0%	9	12%	30	42%	72	11%
TOTAL	256	39%	37	6%	134	20%	231	35%	658	100%

$X^2 = 46.62$, $p = .00$

time and in certain regions they continued to exercise the type of global reach that had typified their international behavior during multipolarity. Others for the most part involved former colonial powers: the Netherlands in **West Irian I** 1957, Belgium in **Congo II** 1964, **Shaba II** 1978, and **Foreign Intervention in Zaire** 1991. One notable exception to this pattern was the classification in this group of Israel in the **Entebbe Raid** of 1976.

We turn first to those events that trigger crises for individual states and ask whether they tend to differ, depending upon how close the crisis is to the territory of the crisis actor. The data presented in Table IV.16 clearly show that violent triggers are preeminent in proximate (i.e., home territory and subregion) crises, whereas those crises that are more distant (i.e., same continent) are predominantly triggered by non-violent events (Hypothesis 13). The exception to this pattern is the group of crisis actors involved in geographically remote crises, for which violent triggers are again prominent. As would be expected, a large proportion of these latter cases—more than three times the rate for the entire population—involved crises that were triggered by indirect violent acts (i.e., violence directed at an ally, friend, or client state). Further analysis reveals that in terms of threat perception, the dominant threat for states experiencing crises in their home territory or subregion are threats to territory and political system, while threats to influence in the international system were dominant among actors involved in remote crises.

Clearly, then, from a geographic perspective, the global system is characterized by at least two types of crisis actors. The first group comprises those actors for which a crisis is both proximate geographically and threatening to basic values. The more proximate such crises, the more likely it is that they will be triggered by violence. The second group is composed primarily of great powers and superpowers, which exercise considerable global reach, and for which many crises in which they become involved are remote from their home territory. For this group, the threat is more often than not to their influence in the international system, rather than an immediate territorial or political concern. Many of the most serious international crises typically involve some mix of both types of crisis actors at some or all stages of the crisis. Among these crises were

TABLE IV.17.   Geographic Proximity and Crisis Management
a.   Crisis Management Technique

	Negotiation		Other pacific		Non-violent military		Violence		TOTAL	
Home territory	105	27%	86	22%	40	10%	157	41%	388	59%
Subregion	38	28%	20	15%	29	21%	50	36%	137	21%
Same continent	20	33.3%	14	33.3%	17	28.3%	9	15%	60	9%
Remote	15	21%	18	25%	14	19%	25	35%	72	11%
TOTAL	178	27%	138	21%	100	15%	241	37%	657	100%

X^2 = 31.78, p = .00

b.   Severity of Violence in Crisis Management

	No violence in CM		Minor clashes		Serious clashes		War		TOTAL	
Home territory	178	46%	85	22%	101	26%	25	6%	389	59%
Subregion	83	61%	16	12%	21	15%	17	12%	137	21%
Same continent	49	82%	8	13%	2	3%	1	2%	60	9%
Remote	46	64%	9	12.5%	9	12.5%	8	11%	72	11%
TOTAL	356	54%	118	18%	133	20%	51	8%	658	100%

X^2 = 51.17, p = .00

some of the most dangerous of the last half century: **Azerbaijan** 1945–46, **Korean War I** 1950, the **Berlin** crises of 1948–49, 1958–59, and 1961, **Suez Nationalization-War** 1956–57, **Taiwan Strait II** 1958, **Cuban Missiles** 1962, **Congo II** 1964, **Six Day War** 1967, **Prague Spring** 1968, **October–Yom Kippur War** 1973–74, **War in Angola** 1975, **Shaba II** 1978, **Afghanistan Invasion** 1979–80, **Gulf War** 1990–91, **Iraq Deployment/Kuwait** 1994.

Once a crisis has been triggered (either violently or otherwise), the interaction of geography and violence becomes rather complex. When violence (compared to other techniques) is viewed from the perspective of **crisis management** (Hypothesis 14 and Table IV.17a), there is a moderate tendency for it to be more prominent among more proximate crises (41% for crises on home territory, 36% for same region, 15% for same continent, but back up to 35% for remote crises). Virtually no difference is found among the four categories of proximity insofar as the tendency to use negotiation as a crisis management technique is concerned— 27%. However, when we consider the **severity of violence in crisis management** (see Table IV.17b), clear differences emerge among the four categories of proximity. Whereas 54% of crisis actors employ some violence when a crisis is on their home territory, this drops to 39% for the subregion and only 18% for crises on the same continent (Hypothesis 14). Once again, the major powers that were involved in remote crises saw more violence than would have been expected, 36%.

TABLE IV.18.   Geographic Proximity and Termination
in Agreement

	Agreement (formal, semi-formal, tacit)		No agreement		TOTAL	
Home territory	158	41%	230	59%	388	59%
Subregion	46	34%	88	66%	134	21%
Same continent	13	22%	47	78%	60	9%
Remote	20	28%	52	72%	72	11%
TOTAL	237	36%	417	64%	654	100%

$X^2 = 11.33$, p = .01

Hypothesis 15 postulates that actors in home territory crises are more likely than others to terminate their crises in agreement. The data in Table IV.18 provide modest support for this hypothesis. Additional analyses found that, despite this tendency to terminate in agreement, proximity and perception of victory (in terms of achievement of foreign policy goals) are inversely related; that is, while proximity may induce agreement, such agreement may be limited in its ability to deliver on major goals of the crisis actors.

Finally, the data provide no support for Hypothesis 16; that is, crises on the home territory of the actor are no more likely than others to be part of a protracted conflict.

In conclusion, the analyses focusing on foreign policy crises show that the closer the crisis is geographically to the crisis actor, the more likely it is that the crisis will be triggered by violence. When threat perception is introduced into the mix, we find that many of the most serious crises in the international system are composed of a mix of smaller states for which the crisis is proximate and gravely threatening, and major powers for which the crisis is often remote and a threat to their influence in the international system. We have found that the more proximate the crisis to the actor, the more likely it is that intense violence will be used in crisis management. Finally, we have observed that crises in the actor's home territory and subregion are more likely than others to terminate in agreement, although such agreements are least likely in such proximate crises to result in the achievement of the foreign policy goals of the crisis actor.

Summary

Our examination of the geography-crisis nexus focused on geographic location, adversarial proximity, and proximity of the crisis to the actor.

Regarding geographic location, we have found that over time and across international systems, there has been a shift from Europe, the most frequent locus of crisis during multipolarity, to the Third World in general, and to Africa in particular, during polycentrism. We have also noted the corresponding finding that European crises during multipolarity exhibited a high proportion that were part of the dominant or mainly dominant system. The overwhelming proportion of crises in Africa during polycentrism occurred at the subsystem level. Europe accounted for an unusually large proportion of violent crises during multipolarity, a mantle passed to Asia and the Middle East in the post–World War II era. Finally, the data reveal a dramatic change in major power activity by region: great power activity in multipolarity crises across all regions was uniformly higher than corresponding rates for either the U.S. or the USSR in the post–World War II years.

Our examination of data relative to the adversarial proximity model revealed three strong relationships: crises between contiguous states were more likely than others to be triggered by violent acts and to exhibit violence in crisis management, while contiguous crises were more likely than others to end through agreements.

Finally, we explored the impact of the proximity of the crisis to the actors on their behavior and outcomes. Not surprisingly, those actors that were involved in the most remote crises tended overwhelmingly to be the great powers in multipolarity and the superpowers in bipolarity and polycentrism, attesting to their global reach. High threat produced violent triggers in crises on home territory and in the same region, while threat to influence produced violence in more distant crises. The more proximate the crisis, the more likely it was that the actor used severe violence in crisis management. Finally, while actors involved in crises on their home territory were most likely to terminate these crises through agreements, such agreements were unlikely to lead to the achievement of the state's foreign policy objectives.

Ethnicity

A casual observer of the international system in the late 1990s might conclude, with some justification, that the defining characteristic of the current decade is the prominence of conflicts with ethnic overtones, be they in southern and central Africa, the former Yugoslavia, the former Soviet republics, or elsewhere. Yet ethnicity was, until recently, a neglected factor in world politics, linked to the struggle for self-determination in Africa, Asia, and the Middle East against the imperial powers of the West. It has acquired high visibility only since the end of the Cold War.

The catalyst for much of the ethnic conflict in the spotlight today was the disintegration of the USSR and the withdrawal of Soviet power from Eastern Europe in 1989–91: this unleashed new forces that cast a fresh light on the role of ethnicity in interstate, as well as intrastate, politics. Minorities, long suppressed or dormant under communist rule, emerged as sources of discontent, for example, ethnic Hungarians in Romania, ethnic Turks in Bulgaria, ethnic Germans in Poland. A second dramatic expression of this new phenomenon was the minority status accorded to 25 million ethnic Russians in peripheries of the former USSR —in the Baltic states, Ukraine, Moldova, Tadjikistan, and other former (Muslim) Central Asian Republics of the Soviet Union. The unthinkable, during most of the 70 years of Soviet power, now became a reality.

In the post-Tito federation of Yugoslavia, too, ethnopolitics emerged, at first in Slovenia and Slovakia in 1991 and, later, in Bosnia-Hercegovina. The avalanche of ethnic identity and the demand for ethnic sovereignty shaped the debate and the violent conflict that ensued.

One indicator of ethnicity's newly recognized salience is the intense, dramatic attention given to several conflicts by the media: between Armenia and Azerbaijan over the disputed enclave of Nagornyy-Karabakh; the Yugoslav inferno; civil wars between Georgia and its Abkhazian minority; Sri Lanka and the secessionist wing of its Tamil minority; the struggle for power between the Tutsi and the Hutu in Rwanda; and the ongoing conflict among tribal clans in Somalia, among many others.

Another indicator of ethnicity's salience is the emergence of a critical mass of literature on ethnicity and politics during the past few years, notably systematic work attempting to place this phenomenon in a broader analytic context— see, for example, the work of Gurr (1992, 1993a, 1993b), Heisler (1990), and Horowitz (1985). Even more relevant to the present study are an increasing number of studies dealing with ethnic conflict and international politics in general, notably work by Rosenau (1964), Said and Simmons (1977), Suhrke and Noble

(1977), and more recently by Carment (1993), Carment and James (1995), Chazan (1991), de Silva and May (1991), Heraclides (1991), Midlarsky (1992), Ryan (1988), and Schechterman and Slann (1993).

Are the ethnic conflicts that are highly visible in the international system today uniquely associated with the conditions of the contemporary post–Cold War unipolar system, or are they a variant of a phenomenon that has long characterized international politics? If it is the latter, what have we learned from the historical record that will better equip us to anticipate and manage such occurrences in the future?

The relationship between ethnic or communal conflict and international system factors has been explored in a number of ways. Gurr (1992:4–5), for example, proposes four general international dimensions to communal conflicts within states.

1. International conditions that facilitate the mobilization of communal groups by contributing to their sense of common identity, cohesion, organization, and capacity for political action.
2. International conditions that prompt regimes into policies that exacerbate relations with communal minorities.
3. Logistic assistance and sanctuary for contenders.
4. International facilitation of mediation, negotiation, and accommodation.

Zartman (1992) also discusses the conditions under which internationalization of communal strife may occur. In his treatment, communities may overflow boundaries to encompass fellow members in neighboring states, in an effort to seek support or sanctuary. The neighbor may see the conflict as a security threat and join the home state in suppressing the communal group. Or it may see the conflict as an opportunity to pursue its own interests against the home state. Finally, in some cases, the neighbor may find it in its interests to serve as a mediator in the dispute.[25]

One aspect of ethnopolitics that has not yet been explored to any meaningful extent is the relationship between ethnicity and international crisis, one element of the oft-postulated linkage between domestic conditions and international behavior. Clearly, the most dangerous ethnic conflicts from the point of view of system stability are those that spill over into the international system as crises and become part of the existing rivalries among international actors. Given the relatively low level of attention accorded ethnicity until recently, it is all the more surprising to discover that 35% of all international crises from the end of World War I through 1994 had an ethnopolitical dimension.[26]

In this section we focus on the relationship between ethnicity and crisis, or, more precisely, the effects of *interstate* ethnic conflict on the configuration of crises in the international system. To that end, a model of ethnicity and crisis will be specified, a general proposition on the link framed, and a set of hypotheses deduced. These will be tested against the International Crisis Behavior (ICB) **system level** data set covering most of the twentieth century.

Definitions

The concept of **interstate ethnic conflict** comprises disputes deriving from both secessionist and irredentist pressures. According to Carment (1993a:22–23) "An **interstate secessionist conflict** [emphasis added] . . . in which one or more ethnic groups seek a reduction of control or autonomy from a central authority through political means . . . leads to an interstate crisis in four non-mutually exclusive instances: (1) when ethnic groups refuse to recognize the political authorities that can trigger a foreign policy crisis for the state in question (internal challenge . . .); (2) trigger foreign policy crises for the state's allies . . . ; (3) invite external involvement based on . . . one or more state interlocutors supporting the secessionist group . . . ; and (4) invite external involvement of one or more states based on ethnic affinities supporting the state-centre triggering an international crisis." "[A]n **irredentist conflict** [emphasis added] is the claim to the territory of an entity—usually an independent state—wherein an ethnic in-group is in a numerical minority. . . . The redeeming state can be an ethnic nation-state or a multi-ethnic plural state. The territory to be redeemed is sometimes regarded as part of a cultural homeland, as part of a historic state, or as an integral part of one state. The claim to territory . . . [and] an irredentist conflict leads to interstate ethnic crisis in three non-mutually exclusive ways: (1) by triggering a foreign policy crisis for one or more states . . . ; (2) external threats made by one or both states; [and] (1) and (2) can trigger (3) foreign policy crises for allies of the two states."

The analyses reported in this section are based on the combining of the secessionist and irredentist cases into a single measure of interstate ethnic conflict; that is, our analyses differentiate simply between interstate crises that are characterized by ethnopolitical conflict and those that are not.

Ethnicity-Crisis Model

Some international crises are driven by ethnic conflict. Others erupt outside that setting, that is, without the condition of intergroup conflict based upon separate identity. This distinction between ethnic and non-ethnic conflict is central to the present analysis. The guiding research questions are as follows: are there differences between international crises that are ethnicity driven, ethnicity related, or non-ethnic and, if so, what are they?[27] Specifically, does the attribute of ethnicity affect any or all of the crucial dimensions of crisis, from onset to termination? And, further, are the effects of ethnicity upon crisis accentuated or moderated by, or are they impervious to, a setting of protracted conflict?[28]

Underlying these questions is a general proposition about ethnicity and crisis, and a set of hypotheses derived therefrom.

PROPOSITION: *International ethnicity crises differ from non-ethnicity crises along a number of dimensions, from type of trigger and values at stake, through the role of violence in crisis management, and the extent of involvement by the major powers and the global organization, to the type of crisis outcome, both content and form. A setting of protracted conflict will sharpen the differences between ethnicity and non-ethnicity crises.*

The presence or absence of ethnicity generates a set of expectations about the process and management of crises. Specifically, it is postulated that international crises with a pronounced ethnic element will be characterized by a greater likelihood of the following.

Hypothesis 17: violence in crisis triggers;

Hypothesis 18: higher stakes, that is, a perceived threat to more basic values;

Hypothesis 19: more severe violence in crisis management;

Hypothesis 20: political rather than military activity on the part of the major powers;

Hypothesis 21: more involvement and greater effectiveness of the global organization;

Hypothesis 22: more ambiguous crisis outcomes, that is, stalemate or compromise; and

Hypothesis 23: nonformal agreements in the termination of crises.

It is also postulated (**Hypothesis 24**) that a setting of protracted conflict between the crisis adversaries will accentuate each of these traits, resulting in three crisis configurations: ethnicity crises within a protracted conflict; ethnicity crises outside a protracted conflict; and non-ethnic crises. In other words, protracted conflict becomes an intervening variable in the ensuing analyses. The concept of protracted conflict refers to an environment of ongoing disputes among adversaries, with fluctuating interaction ranging from violence to near tranquility, multiple issues, spillover effects on all aspects of their relations, and the absence of mutually recognized or anticipated termination.[29]

We now turn to a discussion of the individual elements of the Ethnicity-Crisis Model. The first attribute to be explained is crisis **onset** or trigger. This refers to the act, event, or situational change that catalyzes the crisis. Values range from political (protest, accusation, demand, severance of relations, alliance formation), economic (embargo, dumping, etc.), non-violent military (mobilization of reserves, change of force posture to the offense, etc.), indirect violent (directed at an ally or client state, etc.), to direct violent (military attack).

The postulate that ethnicity crises are more likely than others to be **triggered** by violence (Hypothesis 17) derives from the effects of ethnic conflict. One is mutual mistrust. Another is the expectation of violence from an adversarial ethnic group. Ethnicity also generates several layers of disharmony and issues in dispute. Moreover, the values at stake are likely to be basic in an ethnic conflict, creating a predisposition to initiate a crisis by violence, lest the adversary do so first—preemption, the first law of state behavior in an international system of anarchy.

In non-ethnicity crises, by contrast, there is no logical reason to anticipate a violent rather than a non-violent trigger. The type of trigger will depend upon the specific configuration of a crisis—the attributes of the adversaries, the centrality of the issue(s) in dispute, the power balance, etc. However, the long-term effects of ethnicity, especially intense mistrust, which spill over to perceptions and behavior, are absent from these crises. Thus, while violence *may* be present in triggers to non-ethnicity crises, it is no more likely than non-violence; and it is less probable than violence in ethnicity crises.

The likelihood of a violent trigger to ethnicity crises will also be influenced by the conflict setting in which an interstate crisis erupts (Hypothesis 24). A protracted conflict (PC) between the same adversaries creates cumulative hostility, which accentuates the anticipated effects of ethnic conflict. Moreover, the periodic resort to violence in a protracted conflict—one of its defining characteristics—reinforces the belief by all adversaries that violence will reoccur; and this creates a further inducement to preemptive violence at the onset of an interstate crisis. This additional stimulus to violence is not present in ethnicity— or non-ethnicity—crises outside of a protracted conflict. In short, all other things being equal, a hierarchy of likelihood of violence in crisis onset is postulated: ethnic crises within a PC; ethnic crises outside a PC; and non-ethnic crises.

The second crisis attribute to be explained is **value threat,** that is, the most salient threat during an international crisis perceived by the crisis actors. This ranges from threats to economic interests (trade restrictions, termination of aid, etc.), threat of limited military damage, threat to the political system (overthrow of a regime, intervention in domestic politics), influence in the international system, territorial integrity (annexation of territory, partition, etc.), and a threat of grave damage (large casualties in war), to the most basic value, existence (politicide).

The reason for anticipating a more basic value threat in ethnicity crises (Hypothesis 18) is the clash between ethnic adversaries over core values—group identity, language, culture; often this clash extends over a lengthy period, as part of a protracted conflict. By contrast, threatened values in non-ethnicity crises are specific to the issues in immediate dispute, without the hostile state of mind engendered by ethnic conflict. The setting of protracted conflict accentuates the value component too: ethnicity—and non-ethnicity—crises within a PC are shaped by the psychological legacy of ongoing and pervasive conflict. Basic values are more likely to be threatened in an environment of deep, abiding mistrust of, and hostility toward, the adversary as a consequence of earlier clashes or crises. As with triggers, value threats are less likely to take the most extreme form in crises outside of a PC setting.

Hypothesis 19 focuses on the severity of violence in **crisis management:** the primary technique used by states to protect threatened values in a crisis, ranging from no violence, minor clashes, serious clashes, to full-scale war. The model postulates that ethnicity crises, and even more so ethnicity crises within a protracted conflict, are more likely than other crises to be characterized by violence in the response of crisis actors. Why should this be so?

Violence is prevalent, perhaps inherent, in ethnic disputes. It is, too, a central and endemic attribute of a protracted conflict. As long as ethnic adversaries see no end to their glaring differences and disputes, and view their conflict in zero-sum terms, the dynamics of their hostile relationship create a disposition to violence in crisis management, as in crisis onset. The persistence of competition over values and the deep-rooted expectation of violence generate a reliance on violent behavior in crises. This is especially so when an ethnicity crisis erupts within a protracted conflict. In non-ethnicity and non-PC crises, by contrast, adversaries function in an environment of less frequent and less severe violence. Crisis actors are as likely to rely on negotiation, mediation, or some other peaceful technique of crisis management as on violence in coping with a crisis. In short, an environment of ethnic conflict is more conducive to violence in crisis management. The "lessons of history" strengthen that tendency. A non-ethnic and, even more so, a non-PC setting does not.

Hypothesis 20 focuses on **major power activity** in crises. This ranges from no activity, through low-level activity (political, economic, and propaganda), to semi-military (covert support, military aid or advisors) and direct military activity (dispatch of armed forces). This hypothesis postulates more political than military activity by major powers in ethnicity crises.

The rationale is that, despite their greater disposition to violence, ethnicity crises are less likely to spill over beyond the territory of the adversarial actors and will therefore be less destabilizing for the dominant system in world politics. Major powers in the dominant system have a vested interest in system stability, in order to ensure their continued status at the top of the system hierarchy. Since ethnicity crises are less dangerous to that system's stability, major powers are more inclined to confine their activity in such crises to political intervention—if any activity at all.

A protracted conflict setting for an ethnicity crisis has a dual effect. It reinforces the preference of major powers for political activity; but it increases the likelihood of some kind of intervention by the powers. The reason is that such crises pose a greater challenge to dominant system stability than non-PC crises. Thus major powers, playing the role of system managers, are more inclined to attempt to reduce the severity, scope, and duration of violence in such crises, to prevent destabilizing escalation. Non-ethnicity crises, especially those outside a PC setting, are more likely to be managed by the adversarial actors through nonviolent techniques, thus reducing the pressure on major powers to become involved at all. In short, major powers are expected to be most active in ethnicity crises within a protracted conflict and least active in non-ethnicity crises; and their activity is likely to be political rather than military.

Global organization involvement in crises ranges from low (fact-finding, good offices, etc.), through medium (mediation, call for action by adversaries, etc.), to high involvement (observers, sanctions, emergency military force). Hypothesis 21 postulates that ethnicity crises, especially those within a PC setting, will be characterized by more active and effective involvement on the part of the world body than non-ethnicity cases.

The rationale is similar to that cited for expected major power activity. Ethnic conflict accentuates mistrust and hostility between crisis adversaries. As such, it is an additional—and serious—obstacle to successful direct negotiation between the parties, often even to setting these in motion. Mediation facilitates communication and concessions, with minimal "loss of face." And the global organization engenders less mistrust by ethnic groups than major powers or even the relevant regional organization, which aids in bringing about mutually acceptable crisis termination. Thus, when victory is unattainable or the costs are perceived as excessive, an ethnicity-crisis actor is likely to turn to the world body to play a mediating role. Non-ethnicity-crisis actors will tend to do the same in this situation, but the tendency will be less pronounced than in ethnicity related interstate crises.

As with major power activity, too, a protracted conflict setting will accentuate reliance on the global organization. For one thing, crises within a PC generally, ethnicity crises even more so, leave the parties dissatisfied and their tendency to violence undiminished. For another, the world body is perceived to have less self-interest in the outcome than other third parties. For this reason, it is likely to be effective in crisis management. And since, like the major powers, it attempts to manage the global system to maximize stability and non-violent change, it has a vested interest in mediation. In short, it is more highly disposed to intervene in ethnicity crises in order to achieve accommodation, if not resolution, of the underlying conflict.

The last dimension of the Ethnicity-Crisis Model relates to **outcome,** both **content** and **form.** It is postulated that ethnicity crises will terminate with more ambiguous outcomes (Hypothesis 22) and less agreement (Hypothesis 23) than non-ethnicity crises. Once more, the context of protracted conflict will accentuate these tendencies.

Ethnicity crises tend to be eruptions in a continuing conflict over core values. Whatever value is at stake in a particular crisis, ethnic adversaries do not identify its outcome in decisive terms: regardless of the outcome, the underlying conflict remains. Indecisive results, like compromise or stalemate, symbolize an unresolved conflict. Subsequent crises are anticipated by both—or all—the adversaries. In this respect, as in many others, the impact of ethnicity is similar to that of protracted conflict.

When the latter is the setting for an interstate crisis—and ethnicity and protractedness are often associated—this tendency to ambiguous outcomes is even more pronounced, for crises within a PC are akin to phases in a multiissue continuing dispute. The parties anticipate more crises—and violence—in the future. An end to their conflict is nowhere in sight or too distant and uncertain of attainment to serve as a reliable basis for choice and behavior in any crisis situation. They are prisoners of expectations rooted in the dynamics of a protracted conflict. Such conflicts are extremely difficult to resolve, even without the ethnic dimension. The ethnicity dimension only exacerbates the conflict and its periodic crisis eruptions between the same adversaries. By contrast, non-ethnicity crises—and non-PC crises—have more autonomous starting and termination points. They are usually less threatening than ethnicity—and PC—crises. They are not affected by the legacy of an ongoing conflict sharpened by identity, a we-they syndrome. Actors can address the specific crisis. Outcomes will therefore be clearer and unlinked to other crises and outcomes. Victory and defeat can be more readily identified and accepted as such.

As for the form of outcome: because ethnicity crises are viewed by the protagonists as interim stages, termination represents a decline in the intensity of threat perception and hostility, a pause between two phases of acute, ongoing, conflictual interaction. An agreement to end a crisis is an acknowledgment by the parties that the specific source of the crisis has been overcome, but the ethnic conflict remains. Thus termination is more likely to take the form of an imposed agreement, tacit understanding, or a faded crisis, until the next outbreak of ethnic strife. A voluntary agreement is least likely in an ethnicity crisis. Once more, a PC environment increases the likelihood of nonagreement in an ethnicity crisis. By contrast, a non-ethnicity crisis lends itself to a more formal agreement. It can be treated by the parties as an aberration from a normal relationship of cooperative interaction. In short, ethnicity—and protractedness—spills over to the mode of crisis termination, as with other crisis attributes.[30]

As can be seen from the preceding discussion, we began this inquiry with a set of expectations about the effects of ethnicity on the configuration of interstate crises. These are specified in the preceding Ethnicity-Crisis Model, along with the logical underpinnings of these expectations. Hypotheses were derived from the model and then tested with data from the ICB data set for international crises from the end of 1918 to the end of 1994. Figure IV.10 presents a schematic representation of the Ethnicity-Crisis Model.

What does the evidence from twentieth-century interstate crises indicate about these hypotheses and the Ethnicity-Crisis Model? To this task we now turn, using the abundant data on crisis, protracted conflict, and ethnicity accumulated by the ICB project.

Findings

The hypotheses discussed previously will be tested with two data sets on ethnicity and crisis. The essential difference between them lies in the necessary condition for designating a case an ethnicity crisis. The first is more inclusive, identifying as an ethnicity crisis any case in which ethnicity was a factor in the behavior of one or more adversaries and in the unfolding of the crisis: "the central question is: was ethnicity a salient aspect of any component or phase of the conflict?" (Carment 1993a). The data on this variable are designated *ethnicity*

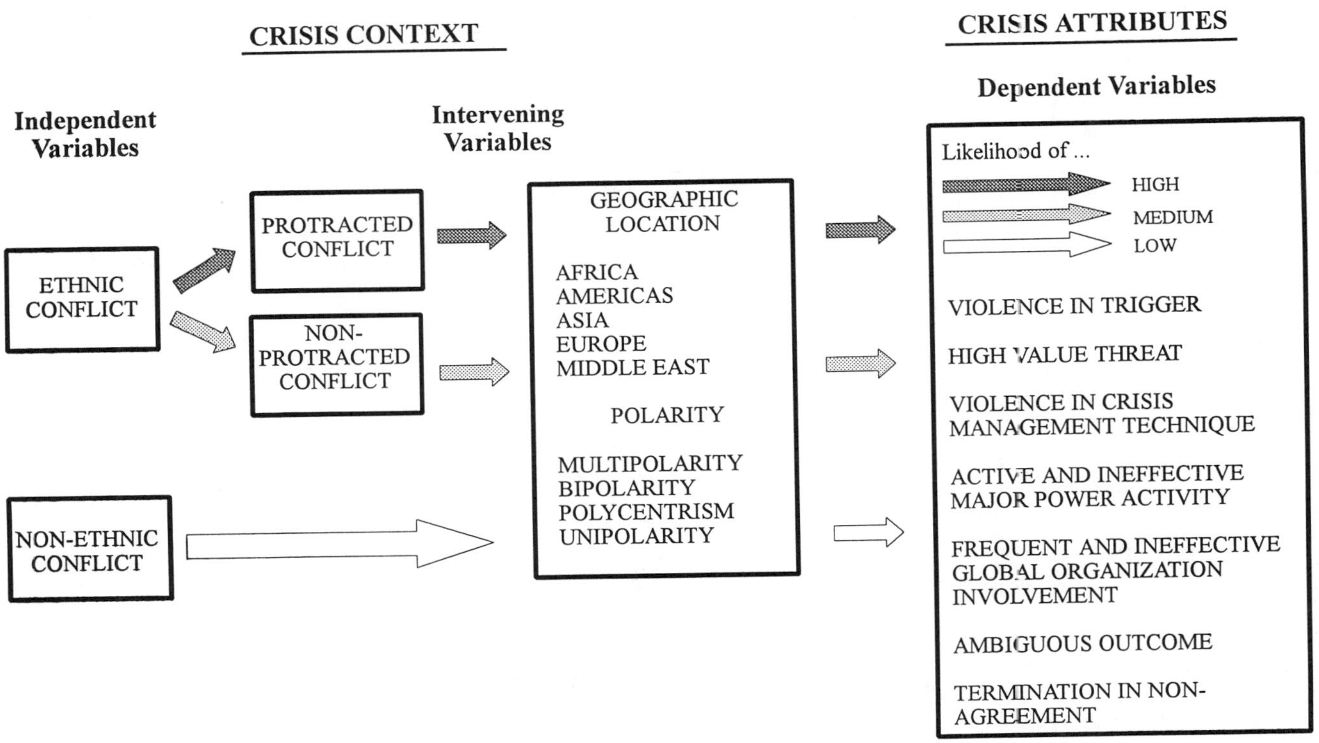

CRISIS CONTEXT

CRISIS ATTRIBUTES

Independent Variables	Intervening Variables	Dependent Variables

Independent Variables

ETHNIC CONFLICT

NON-ETHNIC CONFLICT

Intervening Variables

PROTRACTED CONFLICT

NON-PROTRACTED CONFLICT

GEOGRAPHIC LOCATION

AFRICA
AMERICAS
ASIA
EUROPE
MIDDLE EAST

POLARITY

MULTIPOLARITY
BIPOLARITY
POLYCENTRISM
UNIPOLARITY

Dependent Variables

Likelihood of ...

HIGH
MEDIUM
LOW

VIOLENCE IN TRIGGER

HIGH VALUE THREAT

VIOLENCE IN CRISIS MANAGEMENT TECHNIQUE

ACTIVE AND INEFFECTIVE MAJOR POWER ACTIVITY

FREQUENT AND INEFFECTIVE GLOBAL ORGANIZATION INVOLVEMENT

AMBIGUOUS OUTCOME

TERMINATION IN NON-AGREEMENT

Figure IV.10. Ethnicity-Crisis Model

related. This variable has merit. However, given the ubiquity of ethnic diversity in most states, it seems to us far too broad a criterion, leading to the inclusion of cases in which ethnicity is a marginal attribute of the crisis. The second—ICB— variable is more focused: ethnicity must be the preeminent causal factor in the behavior of a crisis actor and in the configuration of the crisis. This variable is designated *ethnicity driven.* This dual testing will shed maximal light on the core question: does the presence or absence of ethnicity, whether related or central, affect the character of a crisis; or are ethnicity and non-ethnicity crises essentially the same—in origin, evolution, value threat, the reliance on violence, the substance and form of outcome?

We consider intra-war crises to be special cases of international crises in general and exclude them from the present analysis of ethnicity. Furthermore, since many of the analyses reported subsequently examine the impact of polarity, we also exclude the 1939–45 period, on the grounds that this world war international system does not conform to the general characteristics of polarity. Therefore, the following analysis examines 328 international crises, of which 118 or 36%[31] were *ethnicity related* and 78 or 24% were *ethnicity driven.*[32]

Before turning to testing of the hypotheses specified earlier, it will be useful to examine ethnicity and crisis from the vantage point of **polarity** and **geography.** Indeed, we will have occasion to return to these two perspectives throughout our discussion as a way of sharpening the focus on ethnicity and crisis. Tables IV.19 and IV.20 present relevant data.

With regard to polarity, we focus on four systems. **Multipolarity** refers to a structure of diffuse military power and multiple centers of autonomous political decisions—among three or more units (e.g., 1918–39). **Bipolarity** indicates a concentration of power and decision in two relatively equal actors that limit the independent behavior of bloc members or unaffiliated actors (e.g., 1945–62). **Polycentrism** identifies a hybrid structure, with two preeminent centers of military power and multiple centers of political decision (e.g., 1963–89). Finally, **Post–Cold War Unipolarity** (1990–) is used to designate the still emerging international system that has evolved from the end of the Cold War and the disintegration of the Soviet Union.[33]

TABLE IV.19.   Polarity and Ethnic Crises

	Ethnic protracted conflict		Ethnic non-protracted conflict		Non-ethnic conflict		TOTAL	
Multipolarity	13	20%	19	30%	32	50%	64	20%
Bipolarity	14	17%	9	11%	59	72%	82	25%
Polycentrism	33	20%	22	14%	106	66%	161	49%
Unipolarity	1	5%	7	33%	13	62%	21	6%
TOTAL	61	19%	57	17%	210	64%	328	100%

$X^2 = 17.41$, p = .01

TABLE IV.20.   Geography and Ethnic Crises

	Ethnic protracted conflict		Ethnic non-protracted conflict		Non-ethnic conflict		TOTAL	
Africa	17	19%	25	28%	48	53%	90	27%
Americas	3	6.5%	3	6.5%	40	87%	46	14%
Asia	16	26%	8	13%	37	61%	61	19%
Europe	13	20%	13	20%	40	60%	66	20%
Middle East	12	19%	8	12%	45	69%	65	20%
TOTAL	61	19%	57	17%	210	64%	328	100%

$X^2 = 21.98$, p = .00

Ethnicity related crises were proportionately more prominent under multi-polarity than in either of the three later systems (Table IV.19), 50% compared to 28% of bipolarity crises, 34% of polycentrism crises, and 38% of post–Cold War unipolarity crises. It seems that the dynamics present in the three post–World War II international systems were somewhat more conducive to the management of interstate ethnic conflicts, at least in terms of minimizing the extent to which they spilled over into the international system as full-blown international crises. This latter finding, of course, must be tempered with our knowledge that the post–Cold War unipolar era, when fully analyzed (beyond the five years under examination here), may yield results more closely resembling multipolarity; that is, once again, the system's institutions will exhibit difficulty in coping with eth-nic conflict.[34] It should be noted that, in the following discussion of the ethnicity driven variable, ethnicity was equally prominent in the multipolar and post–Cold War unipolar systems.

Turning to geographic location (Table IV.20), we note important distinctions among the five regions. Ethnicity related crises in protracted and non-protracted conflict settings are most frequent in Africa, accounting for 47% of its interna-tional crises. Since this is the region with the largest number of crises overall (90, virtually all since the end of World War II, especially since 1960), this finding has important implications for crisis trends in the contemporary global system, par-ticularly since it can be anticipated that tribal (ethnic) identity and conflict will continue to be an important factor in most regions of Africa indefinitely. The Americas, with only 14% ethnicity related crises, are notable at the other extreme of the ethnicity spectrum. The findings for Asia reveal that the large majority of ethnicity related crises occurred within protracted conflicts (16 of 24), whereas the opposite is true for Africa (17 of 42).

The analytic portion of this inquiry focuses on a number of crisis attributes that are presumed to be affected by the combined impact of ethnicity and pro-tracted conflict. Specifically, we propose that certain tendencies, such as extent of violence, degree of threat, activity by third parties, definitiveness of outcome, etc., will be accentuated under the combined influence of ethnicity and protrac-

TABLE IV.21. Ethnicity, Protracted Conflict, and Crisis Trigger

	Non-violent		Internal challenge		Non-violent military		Violence		TOTAL	
Ethnic PC	23	38%	2	3%	9	15%	27	44%	61	19%
Ethnic non-PC	16	28%	7	12%	13	23%	21	37%	57	17%
Non-ethnic	70	33%	22	11%	32	15%	86	41%	210	64%
TOTAL	109	33%	31	10%	54	16%	134	41%	328	100%

$X^2 = 6.09$, p = .41

tedness, somewhat less strongly observed in non-protracted ethnic conflicts, and least in evidence among non-ethnic conflicts. It is to these themes that we now turn.

Table IV.21 addresses the relationship between **ethnicity** and **crisis trigger** (Hypothesis 17). Overall, the data do not reveal a statistically significant pattern. Ethnicity related crises within protracted conflicts are no more likely than ethnicity related crises in non-PCs or non-ethnic conflicts to be triggered by violence.

Tables IV.21a and IV.21b isolate the 61 international crises that were ethnicity related and occurred within a protracted conflict setting. Earlier we hypothesized that this group of crises would be most likely to exhibit violence in their

TABLE IV.21a. Violent Triggers and Ethnic PC Crises: Geography

	No violence		Violence		TOTAL	
Africa	3	18%	14	82%	17	28%
Americas	1	33%	2	67%	3	5%
Asia	10	62%	6	38%	16	26%
Europe	12	92%	1	8%	13	21%
Middle East	8	67%	4	33%	12	20%
TOTAL	34	56%	27	44%	61	100%

$X^2 = 18.53$, p = .00

TABLE IV.21b. Violent Triggers and Ethnic PC Crises: Polarity

	No violence		Violence		TOTAL	
Multipolarity	10	77%	3	23%	13	21%
Bipolarity	11	79%	3	21%	14	23%
Polycentrism	12	36%	21	64%	33	54%
Unipolarity	1	100%	0	0%	1	2%
TOTAL	34	56%	27	44%	61	100%

$X^2 = 11.14$, p = .01

TABLE IV.22. Ethnicity, Protracted Conflict, and Threat to Values

	Low threat		Political		Territory		Influence		Grave damage		Existence		TOTAL	
Ethnic PC	3	5%	4	7%	36	59%	2	3%	8	13%	8	13%	61	19%
Ethnic non-PC	4	7%	9	16%	35	61%	3	5%	1	2%	5	9%	57	17%
Non-ethnic	19	9%	78	37%	51	24%	31	15%	18	9%	13	6%	210	64%
TOTAL	26	8%	91	28%	122	37%	36	11%	27	8%	26	8%	328	100%

$X^2 = 62.13$, $p = .00$

triggers. A regional breakdown (Table IV.21a) exhibits considerable diversity. African ethnicity related crises are much more likely to exhibit violent triggers in ethnic PCs than are other regions—the contrast with Europe is particularly striking.[35] With regard to polarity, Table IV.21b reveals that violent triggers are considerably more likely to characterize ethnicity related crises in PCs during polycentrism than for either bipolarity or multipolarity.[36]

Combining these two findings, we note that 16 of the 17 African ethnicity related PC crises with violent triggers occurred during polycentrism, while 13 of the 21 polycentric crises with violent triggers were African. These 13 African polycentric cases with violent triggers include **Ogaden I, II, III** 1964, 1977–78, 1982; **Shaba I** and **II** 1977, 1978; **French Hostages Mauritania** 1977; **Raids on SWAPO** 1979; **Chad/Libya VI, VII, VIII** 1983–84, 1986, 1986–87; **Todghere Incident** 1987; **Sand Wall** 1987; **Galtat Zemmour II** 1989. The close association of African crises with violence conforms to the preeminence of ethnic differentiation and ethnic conflict among the multitribal states of Africa, compared with other regions.

Table IV.22 reports on the relationship between **ethnicity** and **threat to values** (Hypothesis 18). We note that ethnicity related crises differ from non-ethnicity crises with respect to the most serious of all threats perceived by crisis actors, in that two types of threats stand out. Ethnicity related PC crises show a 26% rate for threats to existence and threat of grave damage, compared to 11% for non-PC ethnicity related crises and 15% for non-ethnic conflict cases. In addition, territorial threats account for 60% of all ethnicity related crises, regardless of whether or not the crisis occurred within a protracted conflict, more than twice the proportion among non-ethnicity crises (24%). Thus, as hypothesized, the findings generally point to higher threat among ethnic protracted conflicts, and to a preponderance of threats to the territory of the state.[37]

Table IV.23 examines the relationship between **ethnicity** and **severity of violence in crisis management** (Hypothesis 19). We observe modest support for the hypothesis, in that the tendency to employ violence in crisis management increases as we move from non-ethnicity crises to ethnicity related crises in protracted conflicts, coupled with a tendency for actors in the latter to use more severe violence.

TABLE IV.23.   Ethnicity, Protracted Conflict, and Severity of Violence in CMT

	No violence		Minor clashes		Serious clashes		War		TOTAL	
Ethnic PC	19	31%	11	18%	17	28%	14	23%	61	19%
Ethnic non-PC	19	33%	12	21%	21	37%	5	9%	57	17%
Non-ethnic	94	45%	47	22%	46	22%	24	11%	210	64%
TOTAL	132	40%	70	21%	83	25%	43	14%	328	100%

$X^2 = 13.60$, p = .03

TABLE IV.23a.   Severity of Violence and Ethnic PC Crises: Geography

	No violence or minor		Serious clashes/war		TOTAL	
Africa	5	29%	12	71%	17	28%
Americas	3	100%	0	0%	3	5%
Asia	7	44%	9	56%	16	26%
Europe	9	69%	4	31%	13	21%
Middle East	6	50%	6	50%	12	20%
TOTAL	30	49%	31	51%	61	100%

$X^2 = 8.04$, p = .09

TABLE IV.23b.   Severity of Violence and Ethnic PC Crises: Polarity

	No violence or minor		Serious clashes/war		TOTAL	
Multipolarity	10	77%	3	23%	13	21%
Bipolarity	8	57%	6	43%	14	23%
Polycentrism	12	36%	21	64%	33	54%
Unipolarity	0	0%	1	100%	1	2%
TOTAL	30	49%	31	51%	61	100%

$X^2 = 7.50$, p = .06

In Tables IV.23a and IV.23b we focus on the 61 ethnicity related PC crises and their tendency to exhibit severe violence. From the standpoint of regions, the findings again show that African ethnicity related PC crises not only have a greater tendency to be triggered by violence, but actors in these crises have the greatest tendency to employ severe violence in crisis management (71% severe violence in Africa, compared to an overall average of 51%). This conspicuous tendency toward violence in African crises explains the strong propensity to violence in polycentrism PC crises, since the largest proportion of polycentrism cases are located in Africa. But polycentrism is not totally dominated by African protracted conflict cases. Asia, too, provides several examples of ethnicity related PC crises with both violent triggers and severe violence in crisis management during polycentrism: **Rann of Kutch** 1965, **Kashmir II** 1965–66, **Bangladesh** 1971, all part of the India/Pakistan PC.

But it is bipolarity that shows the greatest mismatch between violence in crisis triggers (21%—see Table IV.21b) and severe violence in crisis management (43%) among ethnicity related crises in protracted conflicts. That is, ethnicity related crises within protracted conflicts, in the immediate aftermath of World War II, were particularly vulnerable to the use of force in crisis management when the crisis was triggered by a non-violent act, perhaps a legacy of the war. Three bipolarity cases fit this mold: **Indonesia Independence I** 1945–47, **Palestine Partition/Israel Independence** 1947–49, **Pushtunistan I** 1949–50.

Tables IV.24 and IV.25 deal with **major power activity** in ethnicity related international crises, and the effectiveness of such activity in crisis abatement. With regard to major power activity (Table IV.24), we had hypothesized that political would be more prevalent than military activity in ethnicity crises, and a protracted conflict setting would accentuate that trend (Hypothesis 20). The results in Table IV.24 show that, as hypothesized, political activity was more frequent, proportionately, in ethnicity related PC crises than in ethnic non-PCs, although ethnicity related PCs and non-ethnicity PCs are indistinguishable. It is interesting to note that major powers remained inactive in 40% of ethnicity related non-PC cases, more than twice the inactivity rate for the other two types of crises.

Table IV.24a indicates that political activity by major powers in ethnicity related protracted conflict cases is most frequent in Asia and the Middle East, accounting for 50% and 33% of the crises in those regions, respectively. Table IV.24b reveals that political activity by major powers was most pronounced during bipolarity—more than twice the rate for the other system-periods. Seven international crises satisfied all of these criteria: ethnicity related protracted conflict, Asia or the Middle East, bipolar international system, and political activity by major powers. They were as follows: for Asia, **Indonesia Independence I** 1945–47, **Pushtunistan II** 1955, **West Irian I** 1957–, **Cambodia/Thailand** 1958–59, and **Pushtunistan III** 1961–62; and for the Middle East, **Palestine Partition/Israel Independence** 1947–49, and **Shatt-al-Arab I** 1959–60.

In Table IV.25, we find no evidence to support the notion that the likelihood of effective major power activity is affected by an ethnic or protracted conflict setting. Once again, ethnicity related non-PC cases are least likely to exhibit any sort of major power activity, regardless of its effectiveness. In Table IV.25a, we note that ethnicity related PC crises often exhibited effective major power activity when they occurred in Europe (85%), not surprising since most European crises occurred during multipolarity, and most great powers of that era were European powers. Table IV.25b indicates that only in multipolarity did great power activity have a high likelihood (77%) of being effective. European crises

TABLE IV.24. Ethnicity, Protracted Conflict, and Major Power Activity

	No MP activity		Low level or political		Covert or semi-military		Military		TOTAL	
Ethnic PC	13	21%	20	33%	20	33%	8	13%	61	19%
Ethnic non-PC	23	40%	10	18%	17	30%	7	12%	57	17%
Non-ethnic	47	22%	69	33%	54	26%	40	19%	210	64%
TOTAL	83	25%	99	30%	91	28%	55	17%	328	100%

$X^2 = 12.62$, p = .05

TABLE IV.24a. MP Political Activity and Ethnic PC Crises: Geography

	No activity or other		Political activity		TOTAL	
Africa	14	82%	3	18%	17	28%
Americas	1	33%	2	67%	3	5%
Asia	8	50%	8	50%	16	26%
Europe	10	77%	3	23%	13	21%
Middle East	8	67%	4	33%	12	20%
TOTAL	41	67%	20	33%	61	100%

$X^2 = 6.04$, p = .20

TABLE IV.24b. MP Political Activity and Ethnic PC Conflict: Polarity

	No activity or other		Political activity		TOTAL	
Multipolarity	11	85%	2	15%	13	21%
Bipolarity	6	43%	8	57%	14	23%
Polycentrism	24	73%	9	27%	33	54%
Unipolarity	0	0%	1	100%	1	2%
TOTAL	41	67%	20	33%	61	100%

$X^2 = 8.06$, p = .04

during multipolarity showing effective great power activity include **Vilna I** and **II** 1920, 1927, **Albanian Frontier** 1921, **Hegemony over Albania** 1926–27, **Remilitarization of the Rhineland** 1936, **Polish Ultimatum** 1938, **Czech. May Crisis** 1938, **Munich** 1938.

Tables IV.26 and IV.27 provide comparable analyses for **global organization involvement** and **effectiveness** (Hypothesis 21). As Table IV.26 clearly shows, GOs (the League of Nations in the interwar period, the United Nations since 1945) were considerably more likely to become involved through medium- or high-level activity in ethnicity related crises within PCs than in either ethnicity related non-

TABLE IV.25.   Ethnicity, Protracted Conflict, and Major Power Effectiveness

	No MP activity		Ineffective		Marginal		Important or most important		TOTAL	
Ethnic PC	15	25%	18	29%	4	7%	24	39%	61	19%
Ethnic non-PC	21	38%	13	24%	4	7%	17	31%	55	17%
Non-ethnic	44	21%	58	28%	19	9%	88	42%	209	64%
TOTAL	80	25%	89	27%	27	8%	129	40%	325	100%

$X^2 = 7.41$, p = .28

TABLE IV.25a.   MP Effectiveness and Ethnic PC Crises: Geography

	No activity or not effective		Important or most important		TOTAL	
Africa	15	88%	2	12%	17	28%
Americas	1	33%	2	67%	3	5%
Asia	12	75%	4	25%	16	26%
Europe	2	15%	11	85%	13	21%
Middle East	7	58%	5	42%	12	20%
TOTAL	37	61%	24	39%	61	100%

$X^2 = 18.93$, p = .00

TABLE IV.25b.   MP Effectiveness and Ethnic PC Crises: Polarity

	No activity or not effective		Important or most important		TOTAL	
Multipolarity	3	23%	10	77%	13	21%
Bipolarity	12	86%	2	14%	14	23%
Polycentrism	21	64%	12	36%	33	54%
Unipolarity	1	100%	0	0%	1	2%
TOTAL	37	61%	24	39%	61	100%

$X^2 = 12.15$. p = .01

PC or non-ethnic crises. It is at what we term the "medium" level of activity—condemnation, call for action by adversaries, mediation—that GOs are most likely to undertake intervention—25% for ethnicity related PC cases, compared with 9% for ethnicity related non-PCs and 18% for non-ethnic crises. We note from Table IV.26a that the Middle East and Europe were the regions with the highest probability by far of involvement by global organizations (42% and 46%, respectively). Table IV.26b indicates that the polycentric international system exhibited the highest rate of global organization involvement (42%). Combining these two findings produces the following list of international crises: for the Middle East— **Six Day War** 1967, **War of Attrition** 1969–70; **October–Yom Kippur War**

TABLE IV.26.   Ethnicity, Protracted Conflict, and Global Organization Involvement

	No GO involvement		Low		Medium		High		TOTAL	
Ethnic PC	23	38%	19	31%	15	25%	4	6%	61	19%
Ethnic non-PC	33	58%	11	19%	5	9%	8	14%	57	17%
Non-ethnic	103	49%	58	28%	39	18%	10	5%	210	64%
TOTAL	159	48%	88	27%	59	18%	22	7%	328	100%

$X^2 = 14.15$, p = .03

TABLE IV.26a.   GO Involvement and Ethnic PC Crises: Geography

	No or low GO involvement		Medium or high GO involvement		TOTAL	
Africa	13	76%	4	24%	17	28%
Americas	3	100%	0	0%	3	5%
Asia	12	75%	4	25%	16	26%
Europe	7	54%	6	46%	13	21%
Middle East	7	58%	5	42%	12	20%
TOTAL	42	69%	19	31%	61	100%

$X^2 = 4.08$, p = .39

TABLE IV.26b.   GO Involvement and Ethnic PC Crises: Polarity

	No or low GO involvement		Medium or high GO involvement		TOTAL	
Multipolarity	10	77%	3	23%	13	21%
Bipolarity	12	86%	2	14%	14	23%
Polycentrism	19	58%	14	42%	33	54%
Unipolarity	1	100%	0	0%	1	2%
TOTAL	42	69%	19	31%	61	100%

$X^2 = 4.66$, p = .20

1973–74, **Onset Iraq/Iran War** 1980; for Europe—**Cyprus I, II, III** 1963–64, 1967, 1974–75, **Aegean Sea I** 1976—all on the European "periphery."

In Table IV.27, we note that global organizations are more likely to be **effective** in ethnicity related crises within protracted conflicts than in other cases: 20% effectiveness for ethnicity related PC cases, 13% for non-ethnic PC cases, and 10% for non-ethnic crises. Tables IV.27a and IV.27b fill out this picture by showing that GO effectiveness was most frequent in ethnicity related PC crises in Europe (the system-periods are indistinguishable on this dimension [Table IV.27b]). The GO was highly effective in the three **Cyprus** crises, 1963, 1967, and 1974, **Kashmir II**

TABLE IV.27.   Ethnicity, Protracted Conflict, and Global Organization Effectiveness

	No GO involvement		Ineffective		Marginal		Important or most important		TOTAL	
Ethnic PC	23	38%	18	29%	8	13%	12	20%	61	19%
Ethnic non-PC	34	62%	8	14%	6	11%	7	13%	55	17%
Non-ethnic	108	51%	71	34%	10	5%	21	10%	210	64%
TOTAL	165	51%	97	30%	24	7%	40	12%	326	100%

$X^2 = 18.06$, p = .01

TABLE IV.27a.   GO Effectiveness and Ethnic PC Crises: Geography

	GO not involved or ineffective		GO effective		TOTAL	
Africa	13	76%	4	24%	17	28%
Americas	3	100%	0	0%	3	5%
Asia	11	69%	5	31%	16	26%
Europe	6	46%	7	54%	13	21%
Middle East	8	67%	4	33%	12	20%
TOTAL	41	67%	20	33%	61	100%

$X^2 = 4.76$, p = .31

TABLE IV.27b.   GO Effectiveness and Ethnic PC Crises: Polarity

	GO not involved or ineffective		GO effective		TOTAL	
Multipolarity	9	69%	4	31%	13	21%
Bipolarity	10	71%	4	29%	14	23%
Polycentrism	21	64%	12	36%	33	54%
Unipolarity	1	100%	0	0%	1	2%
TOTAL	41	67%	20	33%	61	100%

$X^2 = .82$, p = .84

1965, and **Aegean Sea I** 1976. In combination, these findings support the hypothesis that global organizations are both more active and more effective in crises within protracted conflicts. This is significant since, as observed previously, the record of major power activity and effectiveness in crisis abatement is at best mixed.

We conclude with two assessments of the **outcome** of international crises from the perspective of ethnicity, **substance** and **form** (Hypotheses 22 and 23). In Table IV.28, we note a very sharp distinction between crises within ethnicity related protracted conflicts on the one hand, 57% ambiguous outcomes, and 34% for ethnicity related non-PC cases. The high rate of ambiguous outcomes for ethnicity related PC crises, that is, termination in stalemate or compromise, at-

TABLE IV.28.   Ethnicity, Protracted Conflict, and
Substance of Crisis Outcome

	Ambiguous outcome		Definitive outcome		TOTAL	
Ethnic PC	35	57%	26	43%	61	19%
Ethnic non-PC	19	34%	37	66%	56	17%
Non-ethnic	108	51%	102	49%	210	64%
TOTAL	162	50%	165	50%	327	100%

$X^2 = 7.86$, p = .02

TABLE IV.28a.   Substance of Outcome and Ethnic PC
Crisis: Geography

	Ambiguous outcome		Definitive outcome		TOTAL	
Africa	13	76%	4	24%	17	28%
Americas	3	100%	0	0%	3	5%
Asia	9	56%	7	44%	16	26%
Europe	5	38%	8	62%	13	21%
Middle East	5	42%	7	58%	12	20%
TOTAL	35	57%	26	43%	61	100%

$X^2 = 7.88$, p = .10

TABLE IV.28b.   Substance of Outcome and Ethnic PC
Crises: Polarity

	Ambiguous outcome		Definitive outcome		TOTAL	
Multipolarity	6	46%	7	54%	13	21%
Bipolarity	8	57%	6	43%	14	23%
Polycentrism	20	61%	13	39%	33	54%
Unipolarity	1	100%	0	0%	1	2%
TOTAL	35	57%	26	43%	61	100%

$X^2 = 1.55$, p = .67

tests to inconclusive terminations, due presumably to the intractable nature of the underlying conflicts involved. As evident in Table IV.28a, ambiguous outcomes in ethnic PC crises were frequent in Africa (76%) and Asia (56%), while the Middle East and Europe showed reasonably strong tendencies toward definitive outcomes. Table IV.28b indicates that, while definitiveness was more visible in multipolarity crises, ambiguity typified the post–World War II bipolar and poly-centric cases.

Finally, Table IV.29 deals with the relationship between ethnicity and form of outcome in different conflict settings. Contrary to what was hypothesized previously, ethnicity related PC crises terminated in agreement more frequently

TABLE IV.29.   Ethnicity, Protracted Conflict, and Form of Crisis Outcome

	Agreement		Tacit		Unilateral		Imposed		Faded/other		TOTAL	
Ethnic PC	30	49%	1	2%	15	24%	6	10%	9	15%	60	19%
Ethnic non-PC	24	43%	3	5%	15	27%	8	14%	6	11%	56	17%
Non-ethnic	63	30%	16	8%	93	44%	9	4%	29	14%	210	64%
TOTAL	117	36%	20	6%	123	38%	23	7%	44	13%	327	100%

$X^2 = 23.15$, p = .00

TABLE IV.29a.   Agreement and Ethnic PC Crises: Geography

	Other termination		Agreement		TOTAL	
Africa	10	59%	7	41%	17	28%
Americas	0	0%	3	100%	3	5%
Asia	7	44%	9	56%	16	26%
Europe	8	62%	5	38%	13	21%
Middle East	6	50%	6	50%	12	20%
TOTAL	31	49%	30	51%	61	100%

$X^2 = 4.23$, p = .38

TABLE IV.29b.   Agreement and Ethnic PC Crisis: Polarity

	Other termination		Agreement		TOTAL	
Multipolarity	8	62%	5	38%	13	21%
Bipolarity	6	43%	8	57%	14	23%
Polycentrism	16	48%	17	52%	33	54%
Unipolarity	1	100%	0	0%	1	2%
TOTAL	31	51%	30	49%	61	100%

$X^2 = 1.99$, p = .57

(49%) than did ethnicity related non-PC (43%) or non-ethnicity crises (30%). As Table IV.29a indicates, the tendency among ethnicity related PC cases to terminate in agreement was more evident in Asia and the Middle East, while Table IV.29b indicates that bipolarity was the international system most conducive to agreement.

How can we explain the seemingly contradictory tendency for ethnicity related PC crises to end with ambiguous outcomes, while at the same time exhibiting a high rate of termination in agreement? Twelve ethnicity related PC cases exhibited these contradictory tendencies, but eight of them fit our definition of negative crisis legacy—that is, a further crisis involving the same adversaries within five years. In other words, while agreement was achieved, perhaps made necessary by the intensity of the conflict involved and, probably, geographic proximity, these agreements were often the result of stalemate or compromise and did not stand the test of time. The eight crises that exhibited this pattern were as follows: **Indonesia Independence I** 1945–47, **Cyprus I** 1963–64, **Rann of Kutch** 1965, **War of Attrition** 1969–70, **East Africa Confrontation** 1980–81, **Chad/Libya VI** 1983–84, **Chad/Libya VIII** 1986–87, **Punjab War Scare II** 1987.[38]

Centrality of Ethnicity in International Crisis

Thus far, we have examined the impact of ethnicity in terms of the presence or absence of an ethnic component in a crisis: that is, the analysis did not differentiate between crises that were ethnically related and crises in which ethnicity was the dominant factor in causing or exacerbating a crisis. The more rigorous notion—an ethnicity driven crisis—will now be examined to see whether it sheds additional light on the relationship between ethnicity and various dimensions of international crises.[39]

It is important to note that whereas 36% of all international crises (excluding intra-war crises and World War II cases) were ethnicity related, only 24% were driven by ethnicity. While one-third of (pre–World War II) multipolarity and (post–Cold War) unipolarity crises were ethnicity driven, this was true of only one-fifth of the bipolarity and polycentrism crises. This provides some preliminary evidence that the current unipolar international system, freed of some of the constraints imposed by Cold War bipolarity along the power dimension, is once again falling victim to the spread of international conflict fueled by ethnic cleavages both within and between states.

Data on the variable ethnicity driven also allow us to differentiate more sharply among geographic regions in terms of frequency of crises. Two regions exhibit particularly high levels of ethnicity driven crises—Europe with 39% and Asia with 34%, compared to 16% for the other three regions. Interestingly, while Africa exhibited the highest rate among all regions for the ethnic dimension in general—47%—this rate drops to only 21% for ethnicity driven cases. That is, while ethnicity played a role in almost half of Africa's crises, it was central, or causally linked to crisis origin, in only a fifth of those crises—for example, in four of the six cases in the Ethiopia/Somalia protracted conflict, and in five of the ten cases in the Western Sahara protracted conflict.

We turn now to an examination of the combined impact of ethnicity driven and protracted conflict on four key attributes of crisis: violence, threat, third-party activity, and outcome. Regarding violence, one critical finding stands out: among ethnicity related PCs, roughly the same proportion of crises were triggered by violence and exhibited severe crisis management techniques—44% to 51%, respectively. However, among ethnicity driven PCs, the comparable numbers were 49% and 66%. In other words, the combined impact of ethnicity driven for the crisis actors and the fact that the crisis was embedded in a protracted conflict made for a volatile confrontation in which violence was likely to escalate.

It is noteworthy that in all other respects, there is little difference among ethnicity driven, ethnicity related, and non-ethnic international crises. Threat to territory was preeminent for both types of ethnicity crises. Major power activity was neither more prominent nor more effective among ethnicity driven PCs than it was among non-PCs and non-ethnic crises. Similarly, ethnicity driven did not make it more likely that global organizations would become involved, nor was their involvement more effective. And whereas ethnicity related PCs were more likely than others to terminate in agreement, this was not the case for ethnicity driven PCs.

In sum, the more focused perspective on ethnicity afforded by the ethnicity driven variable has allowed us to refine further our assessment of the role of ethnicity in international conflict. The end of the Cold War has been accompanied by a significant although less than dramatic increase in the proportion of ethnicity driven crises in the international system. Africa, the region that has seen the most dramatic increase in crises in general and ethnicity related crises, is nonetheless unexceptional in terms of its proportion of ethnicity driven crises. Finally, ethnicity driven protracted conflicts stand out from all the rest in terms of the level of violence employed in crisis management, and in the tendency of violence to escalate from the level present in the crisis trigger. In all other respects, the greater frequency and higher visibility of ethnicity in the international arena has not impacted on the manner in which these crises play out, or in the reaction of the international community to their management. Thus, from the more focused perspective that the *ethnicity driven* variable affords, the evidence on twentieth-century crises indicates clearly, contrary to conventional wisdom, that the presence or absence of ethnicity has, at most, a marginal effect on the unfolding of an interstate crisis.

Summary

We began this analysis by postulating that ethnicity related international crises differ from non-ethnic crises along a number of key dimensions of crisis behavior, intervention, and outcome. We further postulated that a protracted conflict environment accentuates these differences. Finally, we proposed that two contextual variables, geography and polarity, help to sharpen the analysis of crises with ethnic conflict dimensions. These relationships were summarized in the Model of Ethnicity and Crisis.

While the extensive findings have been summarized in the analysis reported on earlier, several key relationships arc worth highlighting here, because they have important implications for the international system as it charts its course in the uncertain waters of the post–Cold War era. In particular, we would emphasize the following.

(1) Ethnicity related crises occurring within protracted conflicts are especially susceptible to escalating violence. In particular, these crises are likely to exhibit severe violence in crisis management (serious clashes and full-scale war), even if the initial trigger was non-violent. Thus, the level of existing hostility among the actors in protracted conflicts has a tendency to cause escalation from non-violence to violence, or from low to severe violence.

(2) Ethnicity related crises occurring within protracted conflicts are characterized by a higher level of threat perception on the part of the principal adversaries. In particular, their decision makers perceive threats to existence, grave damage, and territorial loss, whereas crises occurring outside this context are more likely to be characterized by political threat or threat to influence.

(3) While global organizations are both more involved and more effective as third parties in ethnicity related crises within protracted conflicts, the involvement of major powers displays only a marginal effect on crisis management. In fact, the activity of major powers often has the tendency to exacerbate a crisis.

(4) While ethnicity related crises occurring within protracted conflicts show a high rate of termination in agreement, the agreements tend to be of short duration and unstable. These agreements tend to be achieved through stalemate and compromise and often do not address the key issues of the conflict. Hence, it is not surprising that these agreements contain the seeds of subsequent conflict and crisis, as evidenced by the high rate of recurrence of crisis between the same adversaries within a relatively short time frame.

(5) Ethnicity driven crises within protracted conflicts stand out from other crises in the prevalence of violence in crisis management, and in the tendency for that violence to escalate. We have also noted an increase in ethnicity driven crises in the post–Cold War unipolar system, a return to the high rates that typified the multipolarity of the interwar years.

These are clearly warning signals as we move into an international system that appears to be characterized by an increasingly high rate of ethnicity in international crises, while many of the protracted conflicts of the previous system remain unresolved. Such crises are more likely to escalate to violence, while existing systemic crisis management techniques are often ineffective. There are important consequences for the international system of crises that exhibit an ethnic dimension, and it is this concern that should guide future work on ethnicity, crises, and world politics.

Democracy

Introduction

One of the most widely researched topics in international politics in recent years has been the *theory of democratic peace.* Wars between democracies are extremely rare. This well-articulated theory, coupled with an enormously robust empirical result, has led Levy (1988, see also Levy 1994) to refer to the peace between democracies as "the closest thing we have to a law in international politics."

Building upon early theoretical work by Kant ([1795] 1969) and recent expositions by Doyle (1986) and Rummel (1979, 1983), many studies have provided strong empirical support for the theory, along with explanations of factors that contribute to the democratic peace. These include Bremer (1992, 1993), Bueno de Mesquita and Lalman (1992), Chan (1993), Dixon (1993, 1994), Ember et al. (1992), Gleditsch (1992, 1995), Maoz and Abdolali (1989), Maoz and Russett (1992, 1993), Mintz and Geva (1993), Morgan (1993), Morgan and Campbell (1991), Morgan and Schwebach (1992), Raymond (1994), Rousseau et al. (1996), Rummel (1995), Russett (1993, 1995), Small and Singer (1976), Starr (1992). Several case studies have explored the democratic peace in order to shed light on this phenomenon—Owen (1994), Ray (1993, 1995). Gowa (1995) and James and Mitchell (1995) have proposed serious changes to the theory. Several recent studies have attempted to debunk the theory or have challenged its empirical support—Cohen (1994), Layne (1994), Russett et al. (1994), Spiro (1994), Weede (1984, 1992). For comprehensive reviews of this burgeoning literature, see Hagan (1994) and Hermann and Kegley (1995).

The basic outline of the theory posits that, although democracies are no less prone than nondemocracies to engage in violence in pursuit of their interests, democracies rarely employ war as a means for resolving conflicts with other democracies. Several of the recent studies have explicitly attempted to identify the characteristics of democracies that serve as brakes on the escalation of disputes to military violence. As Russett (1993; see also Maoz and Russett 1993) points out, the contending explanations fit into two categories—a *normative* model and a *structural* model. While the normative model (to be elaborated subsequently) contends that democracies do not fight each other because norms of compromise and cooperation prevent their conflicts from escalating to violence, the structural model posits that political mobilization processes impose institutional constraints on the leaders of two democracies in conflict, rendering violent conflict infeasible.

In this section, we propose a set of hypotheses derived from the normative explanatory model, while expanding the reach of the democratic peace theory to encompass international crisis behavior. We will argue that, for nations locked in crisis, the presence or absence of democratic norms of conflict resolution will dictate whether or not such crises are likely to escalate to violence. Therefore, our first task is to explore in greater detail the logic of the normative explanation for the democratic peace.

The normative model is based on the assumption that nation-states externalize the norms of domestic political processes in interstate interactions. The character of interstate behavior is indicative of the norms that guide and shape domestic political institutions. Political behavior in democracies is distinguished by an emphasis on peaceful political competition. Political disputes are resolved through negotiations and compromise. The victors in democracies cannot permanently dissolve the defeated. Rather, the defeated are permitted to survive and continue in their attempts to achieve their interests.

These so-called democratic norms contrast sharply with "nondemocratic norms." In nondemocratic states, political competition is not necessarily guided by peaceful norms. The role of violence and coercion is more pronounced. As a result, the losers in political competition are often denied opportunities to continue political competition. It may be that the lack of rules to protect losers in political competition contributes to an unwillingness to compromise in disputes and leads to incentives for pursuing more extreme political outcomes.

Maoz and Russett explain that the anarchic nature of the international system implies that conflict interactions between democracies and nondemocracies will be dominated by the norms of the nondemocracy. Confronted with nondemocratic norms in an international dispute, democracies must protect themselves from being exploited and pattern their behavior on the basis of nondemocratic norms to ensure survival. Only when both disputants are democracies can democratic norms take over and guide interstate behavior. In this case, the externalization of domestic political norms will lead to heightened expectations that the dispute can be resolved peacefully through negotiation and compromise. The willingness to resort to force will be dampened. Thus, it follows that conflicts between democracies should result more frequently in peaceful outcomes than in violence.

Implications of the Normative Model for International Crises

The unit of analysis for this section is an international crisis. Our focus is on the following question: how does the presence of democratic states in an international crisis affect crisis behavior? To answer that question, we extend the argument set forth under the normative model and apply it to international crises.

According to the normative model, nations externalize norms from domestic politics into international disputes. When two democratic nations confront each other, the injection of these norms into their conflict interactions signals a willingness by each to make compromises rather than escalate the conflict to the point of military hostilities. With heightened mutual expectations for compromise, the prospect for peacefully negotiated settlement is greater. The logic for this argument leads to implications that enable us to make distinctions among various types of international crises depending upon the number and types of crisis actors involved.

Since international crises often involve more than two actors, it is possible for democratic nations to be aligned with nondemocratic nations in a coalition against an opposing coalition. For example, consider a three-actor crisis involving nations **a, b,** and **d.**

Nation **d** is democratic and nations **a** and **b** are not.
Nation **a** is aligned with **d** against **b.**

By the logic of the normative model, this crisis is quite different from one involving two democracies (a D-D crisis, for short) or one involving a democracy and a nondemocracy (a D-ND crisis).

The three-actor crisis is different from a D-D crisis because nation **d**'s ability to inject democratic norms into conflict interactions is tempered by its primary motivation to protect itself from possible exploitation by **b.** Moreover, within the coalition, **d**'s ability to signal willingness to compromise is hindered by its alliance with nondemocratic **a.** In effect, if **d** aligns with **a**, **d**'s ability to send a clear signal about its willingness to compromise is diminished. As **d** aligns itself with more and more nondemocracies, that signal becomes increasingly diluted. By the logic of the normative model, the likelihood of military hostilities is higher in this three-actor crisis than in the D-D crisis.

There is also a theoretical difference between the three-actor crisis and the D-ND crisis. Again, assume a democracy's ability to inject crisis interactions with democratic norms is diminished to an increasing degree by increases in the number of nondemocratic alliance partners. In that case, the D-ND crisis is different in terms of the likelihood for escalation because the sole democracy is not aligned with another nondemocratic actor. Although it still must contend with a nondemocratic opponent, the democratic nation's ability to externalize domestic political norms is not dampened by a nondemocratic coalition partner. Ceteris paribus, the three-actor crisis is expected to have a higher likelihood of escalation than the D-ND crisis.

The argument we put forward here focuses both on the proportion of democracies within each of the opposing coalitions and on the overall proportion of democracies in the crisis. The coalition proportion is important because a democracy's ability to project its norms into crisis interactions will be limited to the extent that it shares coalition decision making with nondemocracies.

The overall proportion of democracies in a crisis is also important. According to the normative model, the mutual expectation that norms favoring compromise will be reciprocated plays an important role in defusing dyadic disputes

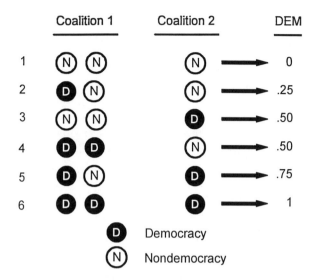

Figure IV.11.   DEM and Variations of a Three-Actor Crisis

involving two democracies. Thus, a high proportion of democracies in one coalition is not sufficient to assure that norms favoring compromise will prevail in the dispute. Rather, a preponderance in both coalitions is critical.

We propose a simple measure that is sensitive to both the coalitional proportion and overall proportion of democracies in crisis. The measure, DEM, is

$$\text{DEM} = \frac{(p_1 + p_2)}{2}$$

where p_1 is the proportion of democracies in one coalition and p_2 is the proportion in the other. Simply put, DEM is the average proportion of democracies in each of the opposing coalitions in the crisis.[40]

Figure IV.11 illustrates how DEM works in the case of a three-actor crisis. The figure shows all of the theoretically possible combinations of crisis actors in terms of their regime type. Looking at the figure, one can see how DEM is sensitive to different configurations of democracies in crisis. The measure makes theoretical distinctions among the various types of crises depending on the overall proportion of democracies in the crisis and the proportion in each coalition.

For example, consider the difference between variations 4 and 5. Two democracies are involved in each crisis. However, variation 4 is different from 5 in that both democracies are aligned together in 4 but are unaligned in 5. The measure for variation 4 is .50 and .75 for variation 5. Although the overall proportion of democracy is the same in each version, the average coalitional proportion in variation 5 is higher. With a democracy in each of the opposing coalitions, the projection of democratic norms into the crisis can be reciprocated. Consequently, the mutual expectations for negotiated settlement are higher in variation

5 than in 4. The DEM measure reflects this characteristic of the crisis by giving a higher score to variation 5. For the same reason, no theoretical distinction is made between variations 3 and 4. The crises are similar in that one of the coalitions is purely nondemocratic. Although the overall proportion of democracies is higher in 4, there are no democracies in the opposing coalition to reciprocate the projection of democratic norms into crisis interactions. For that reason, DEM treats both crises equivalently by giving each a score of .50.[41]

Propositions about Democracies and International Crisis

Using the DEM indicator discussed above as a measure of the prevalence and coalitional distribution of democratic nations in a crisis, we present a set of propositions consistent with the normative model of democratic peace. The propositions address the interaction between the prevalence of democracy and crisis characteristics in two key domains: (1) the extent of violence; and (2) the likelihood and effectiveness of third-party intervention. Our empirical investigation is rooted in the following two general propositions about the relationship between the prevalence of democracies in crisis and crisis behavior.

PROPOSITION 1: *Democracies and Crisis Violence—As the prevalence of democracies in a crisis increases (as measured by DEM), the likelihood of escalation of military hostilities decreases.*

PROPOSITION 2: *Democracies and the Involvement and Effectiveness of International Organizations as Crisis Intermediaries—As the prevalence of democracies in a crisis increases (as measured by DEM), the involvement of international organizations in a crisis will be greater, and effectiveness in crisis abatement will be enhanced.*

Democracies and Crisis Violence

Since the dependent variables in this study are dichotomous, logit analysis is an appropriate method for estimating the impact of DEM on the likelihood of military violence occurring in crises. We begin with a preliminary examination of the relationship between the prevalence of democracies in a crisis and the propensity for the crisis to involve violence. We start with bivariate analysis to determine first whether DEM is a good predictor of violence on its own. The following hypotheses pertaining to the extent of violence in crisis are derived from Proposition 1.

Hypothesis 25: As the prevalence of democracy among the crisis actors increases, the likelihood of violence during any stage of the crisis decreases.

Hypothesis 26: As the prevalence of democracy among the crisis actors

increases, the likelihood that violence will be the primary crisis management technique for crisis actors decreases.

Hypothesis 27: As the prevalence of democracy among the crisis actors
increases, the likelihood of severe violence as the primary crisis management technique decreases.

Hypothesis 28: As the prevalence of democracy among the crisis actors
increases, the likelihood that violence will be important in obtaining
foreign policy goals decreases.

A range of indicators of violence is employed in order to gain a broad
picture of the extent to which violence occurred in crisis settings. The aim is to
assess not only the extent to which a crisis ultimately escalated to the point where
violence was employed as the most prominent crisis management technique, but
also whether it occurred at any point during the evolution of the crisis as a whole.
That is to say, this set of indicators allows us to examine the relationship between
the prevalence of democracy in crisis and characteristics of violence beyond the
basic question of whether or not it occurred. We use four different measures of
violence included in the ICB data set. We briefly describe each variable in order
to point out the differences in the precise characteristics of crisis violence each is
designed to measure.

The primary measure of **violence** is the ICB variable VIOL. This variable
indicates an overall characterization of the nature of violence, if any, that occurred over the entire duration of the crisis. The variable is coded with four
different values: (1) no violence, (2) minor clashes, (3) serious clashes, and (4)
full-scale war. We dichotomize VIOL such that cases with values (1) and (2) will
be coded as having no or low violence, and cases with values (3) and (4) are
considered high violence.

The variable **crisis management technique** (CRISMG) is a measure of the
primary technique employed by the crisis actors to resolve a crisis. Its values
range from negotiation and other non-violent techniques such as mediation and
arbitration, through non-military pressure, non-violent military, and violence. A
dichotomous variable for CRISMG is coded as non-violent when CRISMG is
coded as negotiation, mediation, non-military pressure, non-violent uses of the
military (i.e., military maneuvers), or combinations of any of the preceding, and
as violent when crisis management techniques involve actual military operations,
combat, and casualties. Note that it is possible for violence to occur in crisis, but
for it not to be considered the primary crisis management technique.[42] Hence,
there is an important distinction between VIOL and CRISMG.

When the primary crisis management technique is violence, SEVVIOSY
measures the **severity** of that violence. Its coded values are identical to VIOL.
We dichotomize SEVVIOSY in the same way as VIOL. The difference between
VIOL and SEVVIOSY is that the latter measures the extent of violence in those
cases where violence was considered the primary crisis management technique.
If violence was not the primary crisis management technique, then SEVVIOSY

is coded as "no violence." Although VIOL is somewhat more general than SEVVIOSY, it is not surprising that the two variables correlate strongly (Pearson correlation $= .91$, $p < .01$, two-tailed).

Finally, the fourth measure of violence is CENVIOSY, which measures the **centrality** of violence in a crisis. That is to say, if violence was used in the crisis as the primary crisis management technique, this variable denotes how important that violence was in obtaining foreign policy goals for the crisis decision makers. CENVIOSY is coded on a four-point scale for the role of violence in the crisis. The scale is as follows: (1) no violence, (2) violence minor, (3) violence important, and (4) violence preeminent. We dichotomize CENVIOSY such that crises coded with values 3 or 4 are cases where violence was central.

The **democracy** variable DEM as discussed earlier is based on the ICB variable REGIME. That variable distinguishes between democratic and various types of authoritarian regimes, including civil authoritarian, direct military rule, indirect military rule, and military dual authority. Criteria for identifying democratic regimes are the following: competitive elections; pluralist representation in the legislature; several autonomous centers of authority in the political system; competitive parties; and a free press. Coding decisions were made in terms of actual practices at the time of a crisis, rather than constitutional or other formal legal provisions.

The analysis of hypotheses relating democracy to violence will be based on ICB data from 1918 to 1994. However, a number of cases will be excluded. First, as with earlier sections, intra-war crises are excluded, since they have already escalated to violence and war and hence their inclusion would confound the results. In addition, cases were excluded either because coalition relationships could not be accurately determined or because, in certain single-actor cases, the precise adversarial arrangements could not be ascertained. Ultimately, 257 cases were included in the present analysis. Figure IV.12 illustrates how these crises are distributed across the four quartiles of DEM.

Analysis of Democracy and Crisis Violence

Table IV.30 presents the results of logit regression involving DEM on the four different measures of crisis violence. For all four measures of the dependent variable, the parameter estimates for DEM are in the hypothesized direction and all are significant, at least at the .10 level. Of the four dependent variables, DEM predicts SEVVIOSY best. The coefficient estimate in that case is significant at the .01 level. Recall that SEVVIOSY measures the severity of violence in a crisis *when violence was considered the primary crisis management technique.* VIOL is the more general variable because it measures the extent of violence regardless of whether or not it was considered the primary crisis management technique. The coefficient estimate in that model is significant at the .05 level.

The estimated coefficients can be used to find estimates for the relationship between DEM and the probability of violence in crisis. According to the esti-

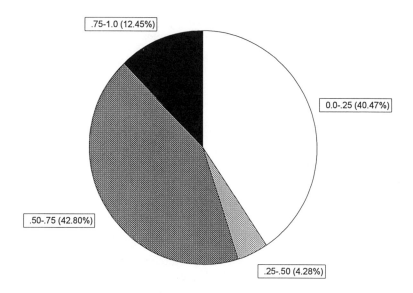

.75-1.0 (12.45%)

0.0-.25 (40.47%)

.50-.75 (42.80%)

.25-.50 (4.28%)

Figure IV.12.   Distribution of Crises on DEM by Quartile

mated model for the VIOL variable, the probability of violence in a crisis with DEM = 0.0 is .52. With DEM = 0.50, the probability of violence is .39. When all the nations in a crisis are democracies (DEM = 1.00), the probability of violence is estimated at .27. Incidentally, there were 33 crises where all the crisis actors were democracies; only seven of these resulted in violence during the course of the crisis. The seven crises involving democracies with a DEM score of 1.00 and with VIOL showing either serious clashes or full-scale war are as follows: the three crises over **Indonesia Independence** 1945–49 (Indonesia and the Netherlands); **Kashmir I** 1947–49 (India and Pakistan); **Guatemala** 1953–54 (Guatemala, Honduras, the U.S.); **Aborted Coup in Indonesia** 1958 (Indonesia and the U.S.); and **Cyprus** 1963–64 (Cyprus, Greece, Turkey). It could be

TABLE IV.30.   Logit Analysis of Democracy
and Crisis Violence

Dependent variables	Coefficient	Standard error	t-ratio
VIOL	-1.07	.40	-2.70[b]
SEVVIOSY	-1.21	.40	-3.00[a]
CRISMG	-0.59	.38	-1.55[c]
CENVIOSY	-0.60	.38	-1.57[c]

[a] p < .01 (one-tail)
[b] p < .05 (one-tail)
[c] p < .10 (one-tail)

argued that the three early Indonesia crises involved only a democracy in the making, and not a full-scale democracy. And by 1958, Indonesian democracy was under some stress.

Overall, the results of the bivariate analysis suggest strong support for Hypotheses 25 and 27. Although DEM is a good predictor of whether violence occurs at all in crisis (VIOL), it is not as good a predictor of whether violence is the primary crisis management technique (CRISMG). Further, although increases in the proportion of democracies in crisis are associated with decreases in the severity of violence as the primary crisis management technique (SEVVIOSY), it is not as good a predictor of the centrality of violence in achieving foreign policy goals (CENVIOSY).

Before drawing any further conclusions from this analysis, we must introduce controls for some other important factors that are often used to explain the likelihood of violence in crisis. If the explanatory power of DEM is weak, the inclusion of control variables will confound the effects of DEM in the logit model. Only after accounting for other important control variables will it be possible to make an assessment as to the explanatory power of DEM.

Multivariate Analysis: Controlling for Potentially Confounding Effects

Before presenting the multivariate analysis, we first comment on the choice of variables to include as controls. As noted earlier, the purpose of this multivariate analysis is to assess the explanatory power of the prevalence of democracies in crisis independent of the effects of other powerful predictors. Tapping the literature on international crisis, we have selected control variables that have been shown to be strong predictors of crisis violence in order to provide the most stringent test of the hypotheses. Inclusion of these variables will potentially confound the explanatory power of DEM in multivariate analysis. Stronger versions of the hypotheses will posit that DEM will diminish the likelihood of crisis violence *independently of other important predictors of crisis violence.* Empirical support for these stronger versions of the hypotheses requires that DEM remain a significant explanatory variable in models that include these other control variables.

The three variables to be included as controls are crisis trigger (TRIG), gravity of threatened values (GRAV), and protracted conflict (PC).[43] These variables have all been introduced in earlier sections of Part IV. In general, we expect that crises triggered by violent acts will be more likely than others to exhibit violent behavior, that crises exhibiting grave threat to values will also produce more violence, and that crises within protracted conflicts are more likely than others to exhibit violence.

In introducing these important control variables, we propose variants on Hypotheses 25–28. We hypothesize that the prevalence of democratic nations in crisis will have a significant impact on crisis violence *independent of the explan-*

atory effects of other important control variables. Thus, we test variants of
Hypotheses 25–28 to assess the impact of DEM after controlling for violence in
crisis trigger (TRIG), gravity of threatened values (GRAV), and whether or not
the crisis was part of a protracted conflict (PC). The variant for Hypothesis 25
follows (where VIOL is the dependent variable).

> Hypothesis 25a: As the prevalence of democracy among crisis actors
> increases, the likelihood of violence in crisis decreases, independent
> of the extent of violence in crisis trigger, extent of value threat, and
> protracted conflict.
> Hypotheses 26a–28a follow analogously for dependent variables
> CRISMG, SEVVIOSY, and CENVIOSY.

Table IV.31 presents the results of logit analysis for the four models corresponding to each of the four different measures for crisis violence. The dependent
variable corresponding to each model is indicated at the top of the table. The
model with VIOL as the dependent variable performs best. Recall that VIOL
measures the overall use of violence in the crisis regardless of whether it is used
as the primary crisis management technique. The model predicts 71.6% of the
cases correctly, and the McKelvey-Zavoina R^2 is 30.7%.[44] With the exception of
PC (protracted conflict), each of the coefficient estimates for the independent
variables is significant and in the predicted direction. We should note that the
coefficient estimate for PC is nearly significant in the VIOL model with $p = 0.06$.
The model using SEVVIOSY as the dependent variable also performed well,
although the number of correctly predicted cases as well as the McKelvey-
Zavoina R^2 is not as high as in the VIOL model.

TABLE IV.31. **Logit Analysis of Democracy and Potentially Confounding
Control Variables**

Independent variables	VIOL	SEVVIOSY	CRISMG	CENVIOSY
Democracy	-1.13[b] (0.45)	-1.21[b] (0.44)	-0.41 (0.41)	-0.41 (0.41)
Trigger	1.49[a] (0.29)	1.37[a] (0.28)	1.29[a] (0.28)	1.30[a] (0.28)
Gravity of threat	0.64[b] (0.23)	0.69[b] (0.23)	0.50[c] (0.22)	0.61[b] (0.22)
Protracted conflict	0.48 (0.30)	0.16 (0.30)	-0.16 (0.29)	-0.23 (0.29)
% Predicted correctly	71.6%	66.9%	63.0%	63.8%
McKelvey-Zavoina R^2	30.7%	27.2%	17.4%	18.6%

The number to the left is a coefficient estimate from logit regression. The
number in parentheses is the standard error.

[a] $p < .001$
[b] $p < .010$
[c] $p < .025$

For each of these two models (i.e., VIOL and SEVVIOSY) it is important to note that the impact of DEM remains statistically significant despite the inclusion of powerful control variables. In explaining overall crisis violence and the severity of violence when employed as a crisis management technique, the prevalence of democratic actors in a crisis appears to be a very important variable. The results indicate strong support for the hypothesis that the prevalence of democracies in international crisis is an important predictor of crisis violence independent of other variables that have traditionally been identified as important in explaining crisis escalation.

As in the bivariate analysis, the models including CRISMG and CENVIOSY did distinctly worse than VIOL and SEVVIOSY. For both the CRISMG and CENVIOSY models, the coefficient estimate is not significant.

Several crises comprised entirely of democracies were characterized by violent crisis management techniques having central importance. Among these are the first **Chaco** crisis 1928–29 (Bolivia and Paraguay); the **Mexican-Guatemala Fisheries** crisis 1958–59 (Mexico and Guatemala); and the **Panama Flag** crisis 1964 (Panama and U.S.). For each of these crises, despite the centrality of violent crisis management techniques, the severity of violence was limited to minor clashes. Recall that footnote 42 lists all the crises where VIOL is coded for violence and DEM = 1.0. The reader may wonder why these are not included in that list. For these three crises, VIOL was coded as "non-violent" because the level of violence did not exceed minor clashes. But, although the overall level of violence was slight, it was still considered the primary crisis management technique.

These crises illustrate a refinement in our understanding of how democracies utilize armed force against each other. While the theory of democratic peace posits that full-scale war is unlikely to erupt between democracies, we find that smaller outbreaks of violence are possible between democracies in the context of crisis. Moreover, although minor in scale, such crisis violence may play an important role for actors in reaching crisis objectives. However, when crisis actors adopt violent crisis management techniques, the *severity* of crisis violence is dampened as the prevalence of democracies increases. It is in that respect that the theory of democratic peace makes its connection to international crisis.

In summary, using a measure that accounts for the overall proportion and coalition proportion of democracies in crisis, we have found that the prevalence of democracies in crisis is an important explanatory variable for overall crisis violence. As DEM increases, the likelihood that crisis violence will result in any form decreases. When crisis actors choose to use violence as their crisis management technique, the severity of violence lessens as the prevalence of democracies in the crisis increases. These results are robust against the inclusion of control variables that are known to be very strong predictors of crisis violence themselves. However, the prevalence of democracies in crisis does not seem to be related to whether the primary crisis management technique is violent or not. Finally, when crisis actors choose to use violence as their crisis management technique, the prevalence of democracies in crisis is not significantly related to the importance of that violence in reaching crisis goals. We will comment further on the relationship between the proportion of democracies in crisis and the likelihood of escalation at the end of the section on democracy.

A further comment is warranted before proceeding. In an interesting investigation of how dyadic characteristics affect the likelihood of war, Bremer (1992) found that the involvement of a democracy in the dyad, whether reciprocated or not, led to a significant decrease in the probability of war. This led him to conclude

> Because war onset in undemocratic dyads is about 4 times as likely as between mixed (i.e., one democratic, one undemocratic) pairs of states, it appears that the contention of some that both states must be democratic before the war-inhibiting effect of democracy is felt is unsupported. (Bremer 1992:329)

Put differently, Bremer's results suggest that, by itself, the presence of a democracy in a conflict changes the complexion of that dispute in terms of the odds of escalation. The results reported here support Bremer's conclusion. As noted in footnote 41, the DEM measure makes theoretical distinctions between crises even when all the democratic crisis actors are on one side. While a balance of democracies across opposing coalitions will increase DEM, it remains the case that DEM increases (with a limit of .5) when democracies are added to only one side.

We did consider an alternative measure to DEM (described in footnote 40) that was less sensitive to the balance of democracy across opposing coalitions. This was simply the overall proportion of democracies involved in the crisis. Although we do not report the results of those analyses here, the alternative measure performed similarly to DEM. Thus, as Bremer explains, there may be reason to doubt whether reciprocity is a necessary condition for the effects of democracy to work on limiting the likelihood of escalation. Until a more complete control is made for the effects of reciprocity, however, no concrete conclusions can be drawn.

Let us turn now to an examination of the relationship between DEM and the likelihood and effectiveness of third-party intervention.

Democracy and Global Organization Involvement and Effectiveness

The logic behind the normative model of democratic peace leads to a set of intuitively appealing propositions regarding the likelihood of third-party involvement in international crisis (see Proposition 2). Third parties interested in facilitating peaceful settlements to disputes are more likely to become involved in crises composed largely of democratic nations where norms favoring compromise are presumed to prevail. Dixon (1993) examines this relationship between democracy and the involvement of third parties and finds support for this proposition in a set of post–World War II political and security disputes. We test a similar hypothesis. Specifically,

Hypothesis 29: As the prevalence of democracies in crisis (measured by DEM) increases, the likelihood of involvement by an international organization increases.

The approach adopted here differs in several important respects from Dixon (1993). First, the sets of cases are different. The focus here is on international crises; and the temporal domain (1918–94) is longer. Second, the measure of democracy utilized here is significantly different from Dixon's. His "weak link" measure gives a democracy score for a dispute equal to the lower of the democracy scores of the two opposing coalitions.[45] These differences are important to keep in mind for interpreting the results reported below.

Tables IV.32 and IV.33 show the results for the test of Hypothesis 29 for global and regional organizations, respectively. DEM has been collapsed into three categories. The involvement of a global or regional organization can take the form of discussion with or without resolution, fact-finding, provision of good offices, mediation, arbitration, observer groups, sanctions, or use of peacekeeping forces. Seven cases are missing from Table IV.32 because no global organization was in existence for those crises. For Table IV.33, 51 cases are missing because no regional organization was in existence.

The tables indicate little support for Hypothesis 29 in the data. Looking at Table IV.32, we note that the relationship between global organization involvement and DEM is in the hypothesized direction. The frequency with which global organizations become involved in crises increases gradually as DEM increases, but the overall cell distribution is not significant. For regional organizations (Table IV.33), the frequency distribution across the cells is significant, but not in the hypothesized direction. Regional organizations are nearly as likely to become involved in cases with a low DEM score as in cases with high DEM.

TABLE IV.32.   Democracy and Global Organization
Involvement in International Crises

	GO not involved		GO involved		TOTAL	
DEM <.5	61	54%	52	46%	113	45%
DEM =.5	50	48%	54	52%	104	42%
DEM >.5	13	39%	20	61%	33	13%
TOTAL	124	50%	126	50%	250	100%

X^2 = 2.34, p = .31

TABLE IV.33.   Democracy and Regional Organization Involvement in International Crises

	RO not involved		RO involved		TOTAL	
DEM <.5	40	46%	47	54%	87	42%
DEM =.5	56	62%	34	38%	90	44%
DEM >.5	12	41%	17	59%	29	14%
TOTAL	108	52%	98	48%	206	100%

$X^2 = 6.33$, $p = .04$

These results are especially puzzling in light of the strong support Dixon (1993) found for the relationship between democracy and third-party involvement. However, as we pointed out earlier, there are important differences in the way Dixon measured the extent of democracy from the method employed here. Since Dixon found support for hypotheses similar to Hypothesis 29 for only the post–World War II period, we checked only crises occurring over this period, too. The results for the post-World War II crises, however, were the same as those for the overall period. In addition, as Dixon points out, his results differ in this respect from earlier studies by Holsti (1966), Nye (1971), Haas et al. (1972), and Butterworth (1976) in that these studies focused on management procedures and their effectiveness rather than merely on the presence of a managing agent (Dixon 1993:52). That is precisely the direction in which our next hypothesis leads.

Although the evidence from twentieth-century crises does not seem to support Hypothesis 29, it remains plausible to presume that international organizations will be most effective in abating crisis tensions when the crisis is composed primarily of democratic nations. Whatever factors contribute to getting international organizations involved in crises (and the preceding results suggest that the prevalence of democratic nations is not one of them), one can still make a theoretically compelling argument that international organizations will be most effective in settings where most of the crisis actors are democratic. Hypothesis 30 follows.

Hypothesis 30: As the prevalence of democracies in crisis (measured by DEM) increases, the likelihood that international organization involvement will be effective in abating the crisis increases.

We measure the effectiveness of global and regional organization with ICB variables GLOBEFCT and ROEFCT. These variables identify the extent to which the organization's involvement contributed to the abatement of the crisis in terms of preventing hostilities. Tables IV.34 and IV.35 show the results of the test

TABLE IV.34. Democracy and Global Organization Effectiveness in International Crises

	GO not effective		GO effective		TOTAL	
DEM <.5	92	81%	21	19%	113	45%
DEM =.5	77	74%	27	26%	104	42%
DEM >.5	26	79%	7	21%	33	13%
TOTAL	195	78%	55	22%	250	100%

$X^2 = 1.73$, $p = .42$

of Hypothesis 30. For global organizations (Table IV.34), DEM does not appear to have any impact on effectiveness. There is little difference in the frequency of effective involvements across the three groupings of DEM. Interestingly, however, there is a strong relationship between DEM and the effectiveness of regional organizations (see Table IV.35). For those crises where DEM is greater than .50, regional organizations were effective in approximately 38% of their involvement. This "success rate" is more than 20% higher than for the other two groupings of DEM. In summary, we find partial support for Hypothesis 30. Although the prevalence of democracy is not associated with the effectiveness of global organizations in crisis abatement, the relationship between democracy and the effectiveness of regional organizations is statistically significant.

Summary

This section has drawn upon extended arguments from the normative model of democratic peace and applied them to international crisis. Its focus was on the mix of regime types for states involved in crisis, and it proposed a measure for the prevalence of democracies in crisis. Based on the logic of the normative model, several hypotheses pertaining to the relationship between this measure and crisis behavior were proposed and tested.

TABLE IV.35. Democracy and Regional Organization Effectiveness in International Crises

	RO not effective		RO effective		TOTAL	
DEM <.5	74	85%	13	15%	87	42%
DEM =.5	76	84%	14	16%	90	44%
DEM >.5	18	62%	11	38%	29	14%
TOTAL	168	82%	38	18%	206	100%

$X^2 = 8.53$, $p = .01$

It was found that the prevalence of democracy in crisis is a significant predictor of overall crisis violence and the severity of violence when used as the primary crisis management technique. This result remained robust even when controls were introduced for a number of other important predictors of violence in crisis—violence in crisis trigger, gravity of threat to values, and protracted conflict. However, the prevalence of democracies in crisis did not explain whether crisis actors would adopt violence as the primary crisis management technique or the importance of violence as a crisis management technique in reaching foreign policy goals.

Stated differently, it was found that a preponderance of democracies in an international crisis diminished the likelihood of overall violence and the severity of violent crisis management techniques. However, the proportion of democracies in crisis is not a good predictor for whether crisis actors will choose violence as the primary crisis management technique in the first place. In crises with high democratic proportions, violence as the crisis management technique is less likely to be severe but may remain an important factor in achieving foreign policy goals. In crises with low democratic proportions, violence as the primary crisis management technique is more likely to be severe, and violence is also likely to play an important role in achieving crisis goals.

Additionally, the investigation suggests the possibility that democracies need not be involved equally on either side of a crisis in order for the democratic effect to work. As discussed in the preceding, typical articulations of the normative model of democratic peace posit that a balance of democracies is a necessary feature of the overall dynamic. In this analysis, increases in DEM are possible even when the involvement of a democracy on one side of a crisis is not reciprocated by the involvement of another on the other side. Seen in that manner, the findings presented here are consistent with those put forth by Bremer (1992). This analysis also provides evidence that should caution researchers when extrapolating beyond the propositions of the normative model for democratic peace and the impact of democracies on violent escalation. No evidence was found to link democracy in crisis to a higher likelihood of international organization involvement. Looking at the effectiveness of international organizations also produced mixed results. While regional organizations were more effective in crises with a high DEM, global organizations were not.

In the end, the theory of democratic peace speaks mostly to the relationship between the prevalence of democracies in a dispute and the characteristics of violence. However, this analysis has shown that the theory is not necessarily limited only to an explanation of the likelihood of violent escalation. This analysis suggests insights into *how* violence is used as a crisis management technique in conflicts between democracies. *For international crises involving a high proportion of democracies, violence may be used with central importance for achieving crisis objectives, but it will rarely be severe.* The fact that DEM was not a good predictor for the choice of crisis management technique means that actors in crises with a high DEM do resort to violent crisis management techniques from time to time. Moreover, the results show that there are some instances when DEM was high when violence was often considered an important means toward achieving crisis objectives. However, when violent crisis management techniques are adopted, the severity of violence is generally limited when the prevalence of democracies is high.

Protracted Conflict

International crises in the twentieth century can be classified according to those that unfold in the context of a protracted conflict, versus those that occur as more isolated eruptions. Virtually every key dimension of crisis is affected by its conflict setting: from the types of events likely to trigger a crisis, the timing and extent of violence utilized by the actors, the extent and effectiveness of crisis management by crisis actors and third parties, and the substance and form of crisis outcomes. In previous sections of Part IV, we have employed protracted conflict as a key explanatory variable. Here we propose a **Protracted Conflict– Crisis Model** and derive a series of hypotheses to be tested with the ICB data set covering the years 1918–94.

What distinguishes protracted conflict (PC) from other forms of conflictual relations among states? Protracted conflicts have been defined by Azar et al. (1978:50) as

> hostile interactions which extend over long periods of time with sporadic outbreaks of open warfare fluctuating in frequency and intensity. They are conflict situations in which the stakes are very high—the conflicts involve whole societies and act as agents for defining the scope of national identity and social solidarity. While they may exhibit some breakpoints during which there is a cessation of overt violence, they linger on in time and have no distinguishable point of termination. . . . Protracted conflicts, that is to say, are not specific events or even clusters of events at a point in time; they are processes.[46]

Table IV.36 presents a list of protracted conflicts in the twentieth century, classified by region. There have been 31 protracted conflicts since the end of World War I, some lasting several decades or more. These 31 PCs account for 245 international crises or 60% of all crises for the period in question. Some protracted conflicts are composed of recurrent crises over virtually the same issue, for example, the Chad/Libya crises from 1971 to 1994 over control of the mineral-rich territory along their border, or the Western Sahara crises since 1975 over control of the territory known by that name. Other protracted conflicts exhibit crises over diverse issues, as in the India/Pakistan conflict—Kashmir, the Indus River system, evacuee property, Bengali refugees, East Pakistan/Bangladesh, etc., or the Arab/Israel conflict, encompassing such issues as territory, refugees, settlements, access to holy sites, water resources, and terrorism.

No region has been immune to this type of conflict, although only in Europe

TABLE IV.36. Protracted Conflicts in the Twentieth Century

	Duration of protracted conflict[a]	Number of international crises	Number of foreign policy crises
Africa			
1. Angola	1975-88	11	18
2. Chad/Libya	1971-94	8	20
3. Ethiopia/Somalia	1960-	6	11
4. Rhodesia	1965-80	11	18
5. Western Sahara	1975-	10	15
Americas			
6. Costa Rica/Nicaragua	1918-55	3	5
7. Ecuador/Peru	1935-	4	8
8. Honduras/Nicaragua	1937-	6	10
Asia			
9. Afghanistan/Pakistan	1949-	3	6
10. China/Japan	1927-45	5	8
11. China/Vietnam	1978-	4	8
12. India/Pakistan	1947-	9	19
13. Indochina	1946-90	18	41
14. Indonesia	1945-76	7	11
15. Korea	1950-	6	12
Europe			
16. Czech./Germany	1938-45	3	3
17. Finland/Russia	1919-61	4	5
18. France/Germany	1920-45	5	10
19. Italy/Albania/Yugo.	1921-53	5	9
20. Lithuania/Poland	1920-38	3	5
21. Poland/Russia	1920-81	4	9
22. Spain	1936-39	4	6
Middle East			
23. Arab/Israel	1947-	25	58
24. Iran/Iraq	1959-	7	14
25. Iraq/Kuwait	1961-	6	12
26. Yemen	1962-79	6	16
Multi-regional			
27. East/West	1918-89	21	60
28. Greece/Turkey	1920-	9	16
29. Iran/USSR	1920-46	4	4
30. Taiwan Strait	1948-	4	10
31. World War II	1939-45	24	62
TOTAL		245	509

[a] A protracted conflict is deemed to have terminated when the nation-state adversaries in that PC are no longer engaged in overt hostile behavior. For example, although the civil war in Angola continues into the late 1990s, South Africa and Angola, the principal adversaries in the Angola protracted conflict, ceased overt hostilities after their 1987-88 crisis (Case #380).

have all interstate protracted conflicts ended, the last the Poland/Russia PC from 1920 to 1981.[47] At the other end of the spectrum, three of the four protracted conflicts in the Middle East remain unresolved—Arab/Israel (1947–), Iran/Iraq (1959–), and Iraq/Kuwait (1961–). Some protracted conflicts erupt with great frequency, for example, the Arab/Israeli PC with 25 international crises and 58 crisis actors to date, the East/West PC with 21 international crises and 60 crisis actors until its termination in 1989, and the Indochina PC with 18 crises and 41 crisis actors between 1946 and 1990. Others have involved few flare-ups, such as Costa Rica/Nicaragua, Czechoslovakia/Germany, and Afghanistan/Pakistan, each with three international crises. There was great variety, too, in the duration of protracted conflicts: while some lasted less than a decade, others spanned more than four decades, such as Ecuador/Peru and Honduras/Nicaragua in the Americas, India/Pakistan and Korea in Asia, Arab/Israel in the Middle East, and Greece/Turkey in Multiregional; all of these lengthy protracted international conflicts remain unresolved.

Part III presented summaries of each of the 412 international crises that constitute the ICB data set. The 245 international crises that occurred within protracted conflicts are presented there as integral parts of these conflicts. The interested reader should consult Part III while reading the material presented in the following.

Given this wide variation in terms of duration, geographic location, number of eruptions, variety of issues, etc., is it folly to postulate any meaningful patterns for crises with respect to their conflict setting? Our argument is precisely that, despite their diversity, crises occurring within protracted conflicts exhibit characteristics that clearly differentiate them from crises occurring outside such a context. Our analyses will be guided by a Protracted Conflict–Crisis Model composed of a general proposition and a set of hypotheses derived from the model.

Protracted Conflict–Crisis Model

PROPOSITION: *International crises within a PC differ from those outside a PC along a number of dimensions, from type of trigger and values at stake, through the role of violence in crisis management, the extent of involvement by the major powers and global organizations, and their effectiveness in crisis abatement, to the substance and form of outcome.*

More specifically, it is postulated that international crises within PCs are characterized by the following.

Hypothesis 31: the more visible presence of violence in crisis triggers;

Hypothesis 32: higher stakes, that is, a perceived threat to more basic values;

Hypothesis 33: greater reliance on violence in crisis management;

Hypothesis 34: a resort to more severe types and levels of violence in crisis management;

Hypothesis 35: a primary role for violence in crisis management;

Hypothesis 36: more political and less military activity by the major powers;

Hypothesis 37: greater effectiveness of major power activity in crisis abatement;

Hypothesis 38: more involvement by global organizations;

Hypothesis 39: more effectiveness of global organization involvement in crisis abatement;

Hypothesis 40: more ambiguous crisis outcomes, that is, stalemate or compromise; and

Hypothesis 41: fewer agreements in the termination of crises.

Figure IV.13 is a schematic representation of the Protracted Conflict–Crisis Model to be explored in this section.

The notion that international crises within protracted conflicts are more likely than others to be triggered by violence (Hypothesis 31) derives from a PC's distinctive characteristics. First, prolonged hostility between the same adversaries creates mutual mistrust and expectation of violent behavior. The likely presence of multiple issues within an ongoing conflict (a characteristic of many, but not all, protracted conflicts) strengthens this anticipation. Also, the periodic resort to violence in the past reinforces the belief that violence will indeed recur. And finally, the importance of the values at stake creates a disposition to initiate a

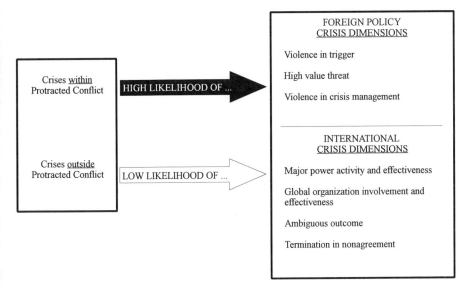

Figure IV.13.   Protracted Conflict–Crisis Model

crisis by violent acts, as well as a disposition to expect violence from one's adversary. By contrast, in crises outside of protracted conflict, there is no reason to expect a preponderance of violent triggers. Rather, the use or nonuse of violence in crisis triggers will be tied more closely to the individual characteristics of the crisis itself—the nature of the issues involved, the power balance among the adversaries, etc.

Hypothesis 32 postulates that crises within PCs are more likely than others to be characterized by a perceived threat to more basic values. The reason lies in a central feature of a protracted conflict, namely, a deep, abiding clash over multiple values, whether between ideologies, civilizations, or belief systems. While each specific crisis within an ongoing protracted conflict may focus on a limited goal or issue, it is linked to the enduring values in conflict over a prolonged period. By contrast, threatened values in other crises are specific to the issues in immediate dispute, without the psychological baggage of ongoing conflict. Thus, crises within a protracted conflict tend to involve more basic values.

Hypotheses 33, 34, and 35 pertain to aspects of violence in crisis: crisis management technique, severity of violence, and centrality of violence. It is more likely for crises in PCs to exhibit violence in crisis management, for this violence to be more central to the achievement of foreign policy goals, and for the violence to be more severe. The dynamics of interactions among adversaries locked in protracted conflict create a predisposition to violence. By contrast, in non-protracted conflict situations, adversaries operate in an atmosphere largely free from a history of violence, thus opening the door for the use of non-violent crisis management techniques. And even in situations where violence is considered necessary, there is no a priori disposition to intense violence.

Hypothesis 36 postulates that major power activity in other states' protracted conflicts will be more political in nature and less military. Given their greater disposition to violence, crises occurring in PCs are likely to be more destabilizing. Since such destabilization is likely to threaten the dominant status of the powers in the international system, it is likely that major powers will focus most of their intervention in the political realm, where the risk of escalating to violence is minimized.

Closely related is Hypothesis 37, which argues that major power activity is likely to be more effective in crises within protracted conflicts. These powers fear being drawn into PCs by client states, and an increase in the inherent danger of confrontation with another power, both providing considerable motivation for a commitment to expedite crisis resolution. This greater commitment is likely to enhance the probability of such intervention being effective. Conversely, the major powers are more likely to allow non-PC crises to run their course without risking influence, status, and resources. In short, the risks for them are not as great.

Hypotheses 38 and 39 postulate that crises within protracted conflicts will be characterized by more active global organization involvement, and that such involvement will be effective in crisis abatement. Since protracted conflict poses a continuing challenge to the global community and its representative institutions, and since the periodic crises arising from these conflicts are likely to leave the parties dissatisfied and their tendency toward violence undiminished, GOs are strongly disposed to intervene in such crises in order to seek accommodation and resolution. While more involvement need not necessarily lead to greater effectiveness in crisis abatement, the increased attention and greater expertise in the issues of the conflict are likely to lead to such an outcome.

With regard to crisis outcome, Hypothesis 40 proposes that crises within protracted conflicts are more likely to lead to ambiguous outcomes (stalemate or compromise rather than defeat or victory), and Hypothesis 41 posits a lesser propensity to termination in agreement. Since crises within PCs are phases in continuing disputes, their outcomes are not necessarily identified in decisive terms. That is, regardless of the outcome, the conflict is likely to continue—indecisive results symbolize an unresolved conflict. Crises outside of a protracted conflict pose a lesser threat and are not affected by an ongoing conflict. Similarly, because crises in PCs are viewed by the protagonists as interim stages of an ongoing hostile interaction, termination is viewed as a decline in threat perception between this and the next phase of an acute conflict. Thus, formal agreements are less likely than are tacit or imposed outcomes. By contrast, crises outside PCs lend themselves to agreements, with less reference to residual disputes between the actors.

Operationalization

As noted earlier, 60% of all international crises between 1918 and 1994 cluster into 31 protracted conflicts. The 245 international crises that form these clusters constitute the international system-level data set for the analyses that follow. Similarly, the 509 states that were actors in these crises constitute the foreign policy actor-level data set for the analyses to be reported.

Several international crises were "mixed," in the sense that actors within them were members of different protracted conflicts, and these actors were assigned to PCs accordingly. So, for example, the **Six Day War** of 1967 and the **October–Yom Kippur War** of 1973 were assigned to the Arab/Israel protracted conflict. However, while Egypt, Israel, Jordan, and Syria were assigned as actors to the Arab/Israel PC, the U.S. and the USSR, also actors in these crises, were assigned to the East/West PC, since these two Middle East wars were also important escalation points in the ongoing East/West protracted conflict.

These details are important, because the following analysis will utilize both actor- and international-level data sets. Trigger, value threat, and behavior are crisis dimensions that are most appropriately assessed at the actor level of analysis, because they originate with state decisions. Major power and global organization activity and effectiveness, as well as the form and substance of crisis outcome, apply to the international crisis as a whole. For both actor- and international-level analyses, unlike in other sections of Part IV, intra-war crises (IWCs) are included. This decision is motivated by the assessment that crises occurring within wars are prime examples of protracted conflict. World War II cases are excluded only when the impact of major powers and global organizations is examined.[48] Finally, although the ICB data at both levels provide a breakdown of cases according to whether they were non-protracted conflicts, protracted conflicts, or long-war protracted conflicts, we will collapse the latter two categories into one single protracted conflict category.

Findings

The first element in the analysis of protracted conflict setting relates to crisis trigger (Hypothesis 31). We expect that crises occurring within PCs are more likely than others to be triggered by violence, largely due to the deep-rooted mistrust and hostility resulting from the long-standing conflict among the actors.

The findings on crisis trigger are reported in Table IV.37, with trigger dichotomized into non-violent and violent. The data clearly show a stronger propensity for crises within PCs to be triggered by violence (51%) than in a non-PC setting (36%). We are not arguing that crises occurring outside of protracted conflicts are unlikely to be triggered by violent acts—clearly a large number of such crises are. Rather, the contention is that, in the special circumstance of protracted conflict, such a tendency toward violent triggers should be more pronounced than usual. And that is what the findings show.

The second component of the crisis profile for actors in protracted conflicts is threatened values, specifically, the tangible or intangible interest perceived by the principal decision maker(s) of a crisis actor to be the object of gravest threat at any time during its foreign policy crisis (Hypothesis 32). While the values for this variable range from limited threat to a threat to existence, we grouped the values as follows: *low threat* = economic, limited military damage, threat to influence of nonmajor power; *medium threat* = political regime, territory, threat of grave damage; *high threat* = threat to influence of major power, threat to existence.

Table IV.38 exhibits only a modest tendency in the hypothesized direction: while crises in a non-PC setting exhibited high threat in 15% of the cases, this tendency increased to 21% among actors in PC crises. Although the results are in the predicted direction and are approaching statistical significance, they basically

TABLE IV.37.   Crisis Triggers and Conflict Setting

	Non-violent trigger		Violent trigger		TOTAL	
Non-protracted conflict	247	64%	140	36%	387	43%
Protracted conflict	249	49%	256	51%	505	57%
TOTAL	496	56%	396	44%	892	100%

$X^2 = 18.70$, p = .00

TABLE IV.38.   Threatened Values and Conflict Setting

	Low gravity of threat		Medium gravity of threat		High gravity of threat		TOTAL	
Non-protracted conflict	92	24%	238	61%	57	15%	387	43%
Protracted conflict	116	23%	284	56%	105	21%	505	57%
TOTAL	208	23%	522	59%	162	18%	892	100%

$X^2 = 5.53$, p = .06

show that actors within and outside of protracted conflicts exhibit a wide range of threat perception.[49]

We have postulated a particularly important role for violence in crisis management when crises occur within protracted conflicts (Hypotheses 33, 34, 35). To assess this impact, three indicators are employed: crisis management technique (non-violent or violent), severity of violence (low or no violence versus severe violence—serious clashes and full-scale war), and centrality of violence in crisis management (low or no violence versus violence playing an important or preeminent role).

Tables IV.39, IV.40, and IV.41 reveal that the postulated relationships hold for all three indicators: crises in protracted conflicts are more likely than their non-PC counterparts to exhibit the following: violence in crisis management (55%–41%); severe violence (51%–30%); and violence as central to the achievement of foreign policy goals (54%–37%). The evidence pertaining to all three violence-related hypotheses is unmistakable: crises that occurred within protracted conflicts contained much more—and more severe—violence, with a more central role for violence as the primary crisis management technique than did crises outside a PC setting.

To this point, the analyses of the hypotheses have required that we focus on the actor level of analysis. We now shift focus to characteristics of the international crisis as a whole, and our empirical setting will be the international crisis level of analysis. We begin this stage of the analysis with an examination of the

TABLE IV.39.   Crisis Management Technique (CMT) and Conflict Setting

	Non-violent CMT		Violent CMT		TOTAL	
Non-protracted conflict	228	59%	159	41%	387	43%
Protracted conflict	228	45%	276	55%	504	57%
TOTAL	456	51%	435	49%	891	100%

$X^2 = 16.39$, p = .00

TABLE IV.40.   Severity of Violence and Conflict Setting

	Low or no violence		Severe violence		TOTAL	
Non-protracted conflict	271	70%	116	30%	387	43%
Protracted conflict	248	49%	257	51%	505	57%
TOTAL	519	58%	373	42%	892	100%

$X^2 = 39.40$, p = .00

role of third parties in international crises. Although they are quite different in their objectives and impact, we examine the roles of both the great powers (GPs) (1918–45) and superpowers (SPs) (1945–94), as well as the role of global organizations (GOs) (the League of Nations from 1919 to 1939 and the United Nations from 1945 to the end of 1994).

Turning first to the great powers–superpowers (hereafter referred to as major powers), it should be noted that we excluded from this analysis the actions of powers when they were themselves crisis actors (as opposed to third parties) in a crisis. That is, when any of the seven great powers of the 1918–39 period— France, Germany, Italy, Japan, the U.K., U.S., or USSR—were actors (direct participants) in a crisis, their actions were excluded from the analysis. Examples of excluded cases are as follows: Russia in **Baltic Independence** 1918–19, Italy in **Smyrna** 1919, France in **Cilician War** 1919–21, and Italy, France, and the U.K. in the **Ethiopian War** 1934–36. For the 1945–94 period, we excluded entire international crises where both superpowers were crisis actors, for example, **Berlin Wall** 1961, **Cuban Missiles** 1962, **October–Yom Kippur War** 1973–74. In addition, when a single superpower was a crisis actor, its actions were also excluded, for example, the U.S. in **Truman Doctrine** 1947 and in **Taiwan Strait I** 1954–55, and the USSR in **Hungarian Uprising** 1956–57 and **Prague Spring** 1968.

Overall, as evident in Table IV.42, the major powers were considerably less likely to remain aloof from crises in PCs (20%) than they were from non-PC cases (34%). We postulated that, when major powers become involved as third

TABLE IV.41.   Centrality of Violence and Conflict Setting

	Violence not central		Violence central		TOTAL	
Non-protracted conflict	243	63%	144	37%	387	43%
Protracted conflict	234	46%	270	54%	504	57%
TOTAL	477	54%	414	46%	891	100%

$X^2 = 23.56$, p = .00

TABLE IV.42. Major Power Activity and Conflict Setting

	No major power activity		Low-level activity		Semi-military activity		Military activity		TOTAL	
Non-protracted conflict	52	34%	66	42%	30	19%	8	5%	156	44%
Protracted conflict	41	20%	85	43%	62	31%	12	6%	200	56%
TOTAL	93	26%	151	42%	92	26%	20	6%	356[a]	100%

$X^2 = 10.34$, p = .02

[a]Fifty-Six cases in which either the U.S. or the USSR was a crisis actor were excluded from this analysis.

parties in crises within PCs, such involvement was more likely to take a political than a military form (Hypothesis 36). The data presented in Table IV.42 do not fully support this proposition. However, if semi-military and military activity are combined, PC crises are considerably more likely than non-PC cases to exhibit this type of major power intervention (37% for PCs, 24% for non-PCs). Low-level, including political, activity is equally prevalent for PC and non-PC crises.

Table IV.43 presents findings on the effectiveness of major power activity as third parties in terms of crisis abatement (Hypothesis 37). Here we find results that run counter to our expectations. That is, when major powers become involved as third parties in PC crises, they are not likely to be more effective, even marginally so, than in non-PC cases. In fact, they are considerably more likely to be ineffective in PC crises (46%–34%). The intractable nature of protracted conflicts would appear to make these less amenable to successful intervention by the major powers.

Since these findings were disappointing, we decided to disaggregate the data by examining the great powers in the 1918–39 period separately from the super-powers in the post–World War II period. In addition, we looked separately at the

TABLE IV.43. Major Power Effectiveness and Conflict Setting

	No major power activity		Ineffective		Marginal		Important or most important		TOTAL	
Non-protracted conflict	52	34%	53	34%	16	10%	34	22%	155	44%
Protracted conflict	41	20%	91	46%	15	8%	53	26%	200	56%
TOTAL	93	26%	144	41%	31	9%	87	24%	355[a]	100%

$X^2 = 9.97$, p = .02

[a]Fifty-six cases in which either the U.S. or the USSR was a crisis actor were excluded from this analysis. There was one case with missing data.

U.S. and the USSR as third parties in this latter period. In this discussion, we will focus exclusively on effectiveness in crisis abatement.[50]

Disaggregation highlights sharp differences in the rates of activity for the great powers in the 1918–39 period, compared to the two superpowers in the post–World War II years. One or more of the great powers was active as a third party in 86% of all international crises from 1918 to 1939, compared to a 61% rate for the U.S. and a 47% rate for the USSR (Russia after 1989) from 1945 to 1994.[51] When we single out crises within protracted conflicts, activity was only marginally higher for the great powers and the U.S. but considerably higher for the USSR (57% for PC crises compared to 33% for non-PC cases).

Effectiveness, too, differed sharply: great powers were effective in 37% of the PC crises in which they were active as third parties, compared to 22% for the U.S. and only 9% for the USSR. For example, great powers were considered to have been the most important factors in crisis abatement in the following PC crises, among others: the U.S. in the **Costa Rican Coup** 1918–19 (Costa Rica/Nicaragua PC); the U.K. and France in **German Reparations** 1921 (France/Germany PC); the U.K., the U.S., Japan, Italy in **Ruhr II** 1924 (France/Germany PC); and the U.K. in **Shanghai** 1932 (China/Japan PC). In the post–World War II era, the U.S. was the most important factor in crisis abatement in the following: the **Mocorón Incident** 1957 (Honduras/Nicaragua PC); **Abortive Coup in Indonesia** 1958 (Indonesia PC); **Pushtunistan III** 1961 (Afghanistan/Pakistan PC); **Taiwan Strait III** 1962 (Taiwan Strait PC); **Cyprus II** 1967 (Greece/Turkey PC); **War of Attrition** 1969–70 (Arab/Israel PC); **Al-Biqa Missiles I** 1981 and **Al-Biqa Missiles II** 1985–86 (Arab/Israel PC). The USSR was the most important factor in crisis abatement in only two cases: **Gaza Raid–Czech. Arms** 1955–56 (Arab/Israel PC); and **Syria/Turkey Confrontation** 1957 (East/West PC).

We turn now to an examination of global organization involvement and effectiveness in protracted conflicts (Hypotheses 38 and 39). We have hypothesized that crises within PCs will reflect a higher frequency of GO involvement and greater effectiveness. As we proposed previously regarding great power and superpower activity, this expectation is based on the serious nature of protracted conflicts and the danger to the international system that they pose.

Table IV.44 exhibits modest support for Hypothesis 38, in that global organizations were involved in 60% of PC crises, compared to 47% for non-PC cases. Virtually all of this difference is evident for medium-level global organization involvement—mediation, resolutions calling for action, and condemnation.

Overall, as Table IV.45 shows, global organizations were no more effective in PC than in non-PC crises. This finding led us to further disaggregate the data in order to examine GO involvement and effectiveness by region. Here we find considerable diversity: GO involvement ranged from a low of 27% for the 11 PC crises in the Americas to a high of 63% for the 44 PC crises in the Middle East. But involvement does not translate into effectiveness; in fact, the regions showed reasonable uniformity in the effectiveness of GOs (both marginal and decisive)

TABLE IV.44.   Global Organization Involvement and Conflict Setting

	No GO involvement		Low level GO involvement		Medium level GO involvement		High level GO involvement		TOTAL	
Non-protracted conflict	85	53%	43	26%	22	14%	11	7%	161	43%
Protracted conflict	86	40%	62	29%	54	26%	11	5%	213	57%
TOTAL	171	46%	105	28%	76	20%	22	6%	374[a]	100%

$X^2 = 9.88$, p = .02

[a] World War II cases are excluded because of the ambiguous status of the global organization from 1939-45.

as a proportion of the total number of protracted conflicts in which they became involved. Effectiveness varied from a low of 29% for Asia, 34% for the Middle East, to 50% for Africa. While Africa showed relatively high effectiveness, much of this GO involvement was marginal at best, with only minor impact on crisis abatement.

Several examples will help sharpen this picture. The three regions with the largest number of PC crises were Asia with 52, Africa with 46, and the Middle East with 44. In Africa, the GO was more than marginally effective in only four PC crises: **Operation Thrasher** 1976 and **Mapai Seizure** 1977 (Rhodesia PC), and **Operation Smokeshell** 1980 and **Operation Askari** 1983–84 (Angola PC). For Asia, the seven effective global organization cases were **Indonesia Independence II** 1947–48, **III** 1948–49, and **West Irian II** 1961–62 (Indonesia PC), **Kashmir I** 1947–49 and **II** 1965–66 (India/Pakistan PC), **Cambodia/Thailand** 1958–59 (Indochina PC), and **North Korea Nuclear** 1993–94 (Korea PC). Finally, for the Middle East, the eight cases of effective GO involvement were **Palestine Partition/Israel Independence** 1947–49, **Hula Drainage** 1951, **Suez Nationalization-War** 1956–57, **Litani Operation** 1978 (Arab/Israel PC), **Basra–Kharg Island** 1984 and **Iraq Recapture al-Faw** 1988 (Iran/Iraq PC), and **Iraq Deployment/Kuwait** 1994 (Iraq/Kuwait PC).

TABLE IV.45.   Global Organization Effectiveness and Conflict Setting

	No GO involvement		GO ineffective		GO marginal		GO effective		TOTAL	
Non-protracted conflict	88	55%	45	28%	10	6%	17	11%	160	43%
Protracted conflict	89	42%	77	36%	19	9%	28	13%	213	42%
TOTAL	177	47%	122	33%	29	8%	45	12%	373[a]	100%

$X^2 = 6.48$, p = .09

[a] World War II cases are excluded because of the ambiguous status of the global organization from 1939-45.

TABLE IV.46.   Substance of Outcome and Conflict Setting

	Ambiguous outcome		Definitive outcome		TOTAL	
Non-protracted conflict	72	43%	96	57%	168	41%
Protracted conflict	130	54%	113	46%	243	59%
TOTAL	202	49%	209	51%	411	100%

$X^2 = 4.50$, p = .03

Finally, two hypotheses (40 and 41) deal with crisis outcome and the effect of conflict setting. The substance of crisis outcome variable, which was dichotomized into ambiguous—compromise or stalemate—and definitive—victory or defeat—assesses the mix of outcomes for individual crisis actors and assigns an overall value for the international crisis as a whole. Table IV.46 reports the findings for the substance of outcome. As hypothesized, PC crises were somewhat more likely to terminate in ambiguous outcomes. This supports the notion that it is precisely these ambiguous outcomes that perpetuate the protracted conflict, with more eruptions to be expected.

The final hypothesis deals with form of outcome, that is, whether or not a crisis ends in some form of voluntary agreement. As evident in Table IV.47, there was virtually no difference between PC and non-PC crises in terms of their relative propensity to end in agreement.

Summary and Profiles

The concept of protracted conflict has been analyzed from the perspectives of the crisis actor (Hypotheses 31–35) and the international crisis as a whole (Hypotheses 36–41). All five of the actor-level hypotheses were supported: crisis actors within protracted conflicts are more likely to experience violent triggers, to perceive more basic threat, and to employ violence with high severity and prominence in crisis management. Only three findings of note emerged from the system-level hypotheses for protracted conflict: PC crises are more likely than

TABLE IV.47.   Form of Agreement and Conflict Setting

	Formal agreement		Semi-formal agreement		Tacit agreement		Non-agreement		TOTAL	
Non-protracted conflict	38	23%	22	13%	10	6%	98	58%	168	41%
Protracted conflict	51	21%	26	11%	10	4%	156	64%	243	59%
TOTAL	89	21%	48	12%	20	5%	254	62%	411	100%

$X^2 = 1.85$, p = .60

others to exhibit semi-military activity by the major powers, global organization involvement is most likely to be at the medium level of activity, and the outcomes of these crises are more likely to be ambiguous—stalemate or compromise. The data did not support hypotheses relating to the greater effectiveness of major powers and global organizations in protracted conflicts, nor did they support the expectation that such crises are less likely to terminate in formal agreement among the parties.

Given the strong results when PC crises were examined at the actor level, our summary will focus exclusively on that level of analysis. Table IV.48 presents information on the 37 foreign policy crises (see column 4) that exhibit all five of the dimensions found to be closely associated with protracted conflict: direct or indirect violence in the crisis trigger; high value threat (i.e., threat to influence when a major power is the actor and threat to existence for all actors); violence or multiple acts including violence in crisis management; severe violence as the main crisis management technique; and violence used as a central means for achieving foreign policy objectives.

The majority of actor-cases in this table—20 of the 37—are drawn from what we have classified as "long-war protracted conflicts"—World War II, Korea, Indochina. Others come from among the most serious and destabilizing protracted conflicts in the twentieth century: India/Pakistan, Arab/Israel, East/West, and Taiwan Strait. Many other severe crises exhibit some but not all of the traits identified in this study. The severity of these 20 crises makes all the more disturbing the lack of strong major power and global organization activity and effectiveness. Thus, while a number of cases listed in Table IV.47 exhibit involvement by these third parties, their effectiveness was negligible. Table IV.48 lists 18 protracted conflict international crises that occurred after the end of World War II.[52] The UN was involved in all but one of these crises, that is, a 93% involvement rate compared to an overall post–World War II involvement rate of only 56%. Nevertheless, it played an important role (never *the* most important role) in crisis abatement in only three of these 18 cases—**Indonesia Independence II** and **III** 1947–48, 1948–49, and **Palestine Partition/Israel Independence** 1947–49. The U.S. had a somewhat different experience, since it was itself an actor in all but five of the 18 post–World War II international crises that fit the PC profile. Among these five, it was an important factor in crisis abatement in two: **Indonesia Independence II** and **III**. The USSR was an actor in only two post–World War II PC crises and was an effective third party in only one of the remaining 14—**Vietnam Ports Mining** 1972.

What, then, can we say in conclusion about the distinctive character of crises occurring within protracted conflicts? At the actor level, we found considerable evidence to support the contention that these actors find themselves in quite different situations from the corresponding non-protracted conflict actors, and that these differences are reflected in the manner in which their crises are triggered, the gravity of the perceived threat, and the types of crisis management techniques that are employed. And while it is clear from an international system

TABLE IV.48. Actors Conforming to Profile of Crises in Protracted Conflicts

Protracted conflict[a]	International crisis[b]	Year	Actor(s) fitting profile[c]
Poland/Russia (21)	Polish/Russian War (13)	1920	Poland
Greece/Turkey (28)	Greece/Turkey War II (18)	1921	Turkey
World War II (31)	Fall of West Europe (78)	1940	Netherlands, Belgium, Fra
World War II (31)	Battle of Britain (81)	1940	U.K.
World War II (31)	East Africa Campaign (82)	1940	U.K., Italy
World War II (31)	Balkan Invasions (83)	1940	Greece, U.K. (2),Italy
World War II (31)	Barbarossa (85)	1941	USSR (2)
World War II (31)	Pearl Harbor (88)	1941	Australia
World War II (31)	El Alamein (90)	1942	Italy
World War II (31)	Fall of Italy (91)	1943	Italy
World War II (31)	D-Day (94)	1944	Germany
World War II (31)	Final Soviet Offensive (100)	1945	Germany
Indonesia (14)	Indonesia Independence II (116)	1947	Indonesia
Arab/Israel (23)	Palestine Part./Israel Ind. (120)	1947	Israel
Indonesia (14)	Indonesia Independence III(127)	1948	Indonesia
Korea (15)	Korean War I (132)	1950	South Korea, U.S.[d]
Korea (15)	Korean War II (133)	1950	South Korea, U.S.[d]
Korea (15)	Korean War III (140)	1953	U.S.[d]
Taiwan Strait (30)	Taiwan Strait I (146)	1954	Taiwan
Indochina (13)	Gulf of Tonkin (210)	1964	U.S.
Indochina (13)	Pleiku (213)	1965	U.S.
Indochina (13)	Vietnam Spring Offensive (230)	1969	South Vietnam
Indochina (13)	Invasion of Cambodia (237)	1970	U.S.
India/Pakistan (12)	Bangladesh (242)	1971	Pakistan
Indochina (13)	Vietnam Ports Mining (246)	1972	U.S.
Indochina (13)	Mayaguez (259)	1975	U.S.
Indochina (13)	Vietnam Invasion of Cambodia (284)	1978	Cambodia
East/West (27)	Afghanistan Invasion (303)	1979	USSR

[a] Number in parentheses refers to PC number.
[b] Number in parentheses refers to crisis number.
[c] The 37 foreign policy crises actors listed in column 4 exhibit all of the following characteristics.
   Protracted conflict setting
   Indirect or direct violence in trigger
   Threat to influence of major power or threat to existence
   Violence in crisis management
   Severe violence as crisis management technique
   Violence central in achieving foreign policy objectives.
[d] In Korean War I and Korean War II, South Korea was classified as part of the Korean protracted
   conflict; the U.S. was classified as part of the East/West PC. In Korean War III, with a more limited
   scope, the U.S. was classified as part of the Korean PC.

perspective that PC crises are taken seriously, that is, both the global organizations and the major powers become involved as third parties at a higher rate than
in non-PC cases, their effectiveness in crisis abatement shows no appreciable
difference from the overall record for international crises.

Violence

While it is commonplace to assume that international crises and violence go hand in hand, the International Crisis Behavior Project has demonstrated that the two need not be linked. Readers will have already noted from the ICB definition of crisis that, while a perceived heightened probability of violence is assumed to exist in crisis situations for individual states, violence frequently does not occur during the course of a crisis. Before we examine the role of violence in crisis, it will be useful to view from a number of perspectives the degree to which violence is present in international crises in general, and in the behavior exhibited by crisis actors.

For the international system as a whole, four ICB indicators give us a very rich picture of the pattern of violence in twentieth-century crises. The most general indicator, VIOL, assesses the extent to which violence was present at any point in a crisis, from onset through termination. Significantly, 29% of all international crises in this century involved no violence at all, among them some of the most serious and threatening of our age: **Remilitarization of the Rhineland** 1936, **Munich** 1938, **Azerbaijan** 1945–46, **Berlin Blockade** 1948–49, **Berlin Deadline** 1958–59, **Berlin Wall** 1961, **Cuban Missiles** 1962, **Iraq Deployment/Kuwait** 1994.[53]

A second variable, CRISMG, identifies the primary crisis management technique (CMT) employed by the actors in an international crisis. These are arrayed along a scale from the most pacific—negotiation, adjudication, mediation—through non-violent military, to violence. Here, we find that only 168 or 51% of international crises exhibited some form of violence as the primary crisis management technique. A third variable, SEVVIOSY or severity of violence, indicates that among these 168 violent crises, 27% exhibited only minor clashes as the primary CMT, with an additional 48% exhibiting serious clashes and 25% showing full-scale war. Finally, from CENVIOSY or centrality of violence—the relative importance that decision makers attached to violence in pursuing their goals in a crisis—we learn that, among the 168 crises in which some form of violence was employed in crisis management, violence was viewed as the preeminent CMT in only 70 or 42% of the cases.

The aggregate figures on the limited resort to violence in twentieth-century crises adds an important dimension to our perception of conflict in the international system. All too often, the student of international politics is confronted with findings based on Correlates of War (Small and Singer 1982) or Militarized International Disputes (Gochman and Maoz 1984), where conflict and violence appear to be inseparable. An orientation that does not presuppose that all crises among nations must always lead to violence allows us to expand our concept of conflict resolution to incorporate a whole range of effective non-violent strategies. Throughout our discussions of the various dimensions of violence in crises, we have offered a variety of explanations as to why certain crises were more likely than others to have been triggered by violence, to have escalated to violence, or to have employed violence in crisis management. It is noteworthy that, while much of the attention of both the scholarly and policy communities has focused on those crisis situations in which violence or even war is preeminent, a very large proportion of crises never reach this point. Whether these latter cases can be explained by factors such as power discrepancy, alliance configuration, or regional differences, they remain an important group to contend with as we seek explanations for crisis phenomena.

All this notwithstanding, we do not want to minimize the important role that violence plays in twentieth-century crises. This role has been carefully examined in the preceding sections on polarity, geography, ethnicity, democracy, and protracted conflict, and will be discussed in the final section on third parties. It is useful to survey here the most salient of our findings on violence.

Polarity

Crises during polycentrism (1963–89) were by far the most likely to be triggered by violence (53%), followed by multipolarity (1918–39) (33%) and bipolarity (1945–62) (24%). We have noted that polycentrism was characterized by a rapid expansion in the number of states in the system (particularly in Africa and Asia), many of which achieved independence through violence. We emphasized that this pattern of violence carried over into their behavior in the international system. By contrast, bipolarity exhibited relative stability in terms of the number of states in the system and the tightness of its alliance configuration. Multipolarity occupies a middle ground between the extremes of polycentrism and bipolarity.

Actors in polycentrism crises were more likely to employ severe violence in conflict management—particularly serious clashes—than in bipolarity and multipolarity. Once again, the legacy of violence among newly independent states helps explain this propensity to use violence in crisis management.

Geography

Patterns of violence in crisis management vary across regions and, within regions, across systems. Europe accounted for 39% of all international crises with no violence—largely the product of bipolarity and polycentrism—but was also the locus of 22% of all crises involving war in the international system—largely the by-product of multipolarity and World War II. Two regions—Asia and the Middle East—accounted for an unusually large proportion of wars in the post–World War II era, while Africa accounted for a very high proportion of crises in which violence short of war was employed, virtually all in the polycentric system.

Crises between contiguous or near-neighbor adversaries were more likely to be triggered by violence than were crises between more distant adversaries. However, among major powers, even more distant crises were often triggered by violent acts—attesting to the global reach of their alliance commitments.

The more proximate a crisis was to an actor—home territory or subregion—the more likely it was to have been triggered by a violent act. Here again, major powers were often the exception, almost always indicating violence involving a client state.

The more proximate a crisis, the more likely it was that violence occurred at some point in its evolution. Once again, the exception to this finding involved major powers.

Ethnicity

Ethnicity and protracted conflict setting combined to make violence considerably more likely in African crises than for any other region.

Ethnicity and protracted conflict setting combined to make crises in polycentrism more prone to violent triggers than crises in either bipolarity or multipolarity. For both of these findings, it appears to be the combination of extreme ethnic conflict, particularly in Africa during polycentrism, and the protracted nature of African conflicts, which stands out.

Ethnicity in bipolar protracted conflicts had the effect of increasing the likelihood of violence in crisis management. This occurred even when the crisis was initially triggered by a non-violent act.

Democracy

As the proportion of democracies among the actors in an international crisis increases, the likelihood of violence decreases. Furthermore, when crisis actors choose violence as their primary crisis management technique, the severity of violence lessens as the prevalence of democracies in the crisis increases. These findings remain strong even after the introduction of such well-accepted explanatory factors as violence in the crisis trigger, gravity of threat, and protracted conflict setting. These crisis-related findings add a significant new dimension to the theory of democratic peace.

Protracted Conflict

Actors in protracted conflict crises were more likely to experience violent triggers and to employ more severe violence in crisis management. Coupled with the finding that value threat was likely to be greater in PC cases, these findings point to the more extreme danger that such crises pose to the international system, by virtue of their propensity to escalate to violence.

Third-Party Intervention

Bipolarity and polycentrism exhibited a positive relationship between violent triggers and the propensity for the UN to become involved. As a corollary, these post–World War II crises triggered by violence were more likely than others to have entailed the involvement of high-level UN organs—the General Assembly and Security Council.

For bipolarity and polycentrism, the more severe the violence in a crisis, the more likely it was that the UN would become involved. In addition, for bipolarity, the more intense the violence, the more likely it was that high-level organs would attempt to manage a crisis.

Virtually all of these findings on violence have been drawn from the perspective of the international crisis as a whole. Yet the ultimate choice of whether or not to employ violence in interstate behavior in general and in crisis management in particular is, by definition, a state-level decision. Why certain actors choose violence in the first place or engage in behavior that escalates to violence during the course of a crisis are central concerns for students of foreign policy behavior.

As we shift our focus to the state level of analysis, one of the most significant aspects of crisis behavior has to do with the circumstances in which action-reaction or tit-for-tat patterns of response are chosen, as well as the circumstances in which such patterns break down. The remainder of this section will focus on the conditions under which states in crises engage in, or deviate significantly from, matching behavior.

Trigger-Response Mechanism

We begin this analysis by introducing the concept of "matching." In conflict and crisis situations, matching behavior is defined as a reciprocal relationship between incoming behavior (crisis trigger) and outgoing behavior (crisis response). In particular, we are interested in the degree to which the crisis management technique, both in type and severity, matches the event that triggered the crisis for the state in question.

Our basic premise is that exclusive of other factors, there is no intrinsic reason to expect a state to overreact or underreact to incoming stimuli. Thus, in the case of an incoming non-violent act, such as a protest, threat, demand, or accusation, the expectation is that a state will respond with a similar type of act. Similarly, violent acts are expected to engender violent responses. The fundamental research question is this: for crisis situations, what factors contribute to disruptions that may occur in the matching process?

There has been considerable empirical work on the behavior-begets-behavior phenomenon in conflict and non-conflict interactions. In a study of conflict interactions among Middle East states, Wilkenfeld (1975) found that the level of conflict received was the crucial predictor of conflict sent. In a more elaborate study of 56 nations between 1966 and 1970, Wilkenfeld et al. (1980) found that action-reaction matching behavior was the overwhelming factor in explaining the use of military force. Other studies have also examined the behavior-begets-behavior linkage at the international level (see, for example, Zinnes and Wilkenfeld 1971; Wilkenfeld 1975; Most and Starr 1980; Hoole and Huang 1989; Hensel and Diehl 1994; Sayrs 1992). And, of course, the important work of Axelrod (1984) typifies the game-theoretic approach to this phenomenon. The action-reaction process is somewhat less imposing as an explanatory factor for non-military conflict and drops out of the picture altogether when non-violent, predominantly diplomatic behavior is the focus (Wilkenfeld et al. 1980).[54]

In this section we will focus on the manner in which the behavior-begets-behavior dynamic plays out in the context of an international crisis. Specifically, we will explore the disruptive impact on the trigger-response dynamic of key factors drawn from three different levels of analysis: the individual, the state, and the system (Waltz 1959). The specific factors posited as potentially disruptive are as follows: (a) degree of stress experienced by crisis decision makers; (b) socio-political conditions internal to a state at the time that its major response to a crisis must be formulated; and (c) the power relationship between a state and its principal adversary in a crisis (i.e., the triggering entity). It is expected that these factors will help explain deviations in state behavior in crisis from the matching behavior that would normally be expected under conditions of stimulus-response theory.

Stress

At the individual level of analysis, we focus on the impact of stress on decision makers. According to Holsti and George (1975:257),

> it is customary to regard stress as the anxiety or fear an individual experiences in a situation which he perceives as posing a severe threat to one or more values. . . . Psychological stress occurs either when the subject experiences damage to his values or anticipates that the stimulus situation may lead to it.

In the study of foreign policy behavior, stress refers to a state of mind among decision makers brought on by an environmental challenge requiring a response within a limited time; that is, stress is a psychological condition usually associated with anxiety and/or frustration produced by crisis and threat.

It is assumed that the lower the level of stress being experienced by crisis decision makers, the greater the likelihood that behavior will deviate from a strictly linear matching pattern.[55] Underlying this view is the premise that high stress, as evidenced by the combination of threat to basic values and a power differential in favor of one's principal adversary, evokes greater attentiveness on the part of decision makers to both the content and intensity of incoming actions as the proper responses are formulated. That is, decision latitude is circumscribed by the greater need to respond meaningfully and accurately in highly threatening situations. Conversely, under conditions of low stress, such matching is not as critical, since the threat is lower and the dangers inherent in the situation are not viewed by the decision makers as grave. As a consequence, greater decision latitude exists, and we can expect to find some breakdown in the behavior-begets-behavior linkage.[56]

Sociopolitical Conditions

There is extensive literature in the social sciences in general (Simmel 1955; Coser 1956), and in international politics in particular, on the relationship between societal factors and the occurrence of violence, either within or between nations (for reviews of this literature, see Wilkenfeld 1973; Gurr 1980; Stohl 1980; Ward and Widmaier 1982; Levy 1989). While such relationships are extraordinarily complex, the cumulative body of empirical evidence points generally to a linkage between deteriorating sociopolitical conditions and a propensity by some political leaders to employ diversion mechanisms such as external aggression.

The condition of international crisis differs substantially from the setting in which the internal-external conflict hypotheses have been examined previously. In a non-crisis situation, our expectation is that the decision maker, bent on employing a diversion mechanism such as external violence, has some decision latitude in terms of the timing, the target, and the intensity of such behavior. For decision makers whose states are locked in a crisis situation, the range of choices has essentially been eliminated: there are a specific source of threat (usually, although not always, another state), a specific triggering act that must be urgently addressed (i.e., finite time for response), and an intensity associated with the triggering act. Under these circumstances, the employment of a diversion mechanism is undertaken at the risk of sending the wrong signal in a situation that is already fraught with the danger of undesired escalation.

In crisis situations, therefore, we would expect that, when internal sociopolitical conditions have been deteriorating prior to a crisis, matching behavior will break down. Non-violent triggers will exhibit a greater-than-expected tendency to produce violent responses (as decision makers attempt to engage in diversion mechanisms). On the other hand, non-violent responses to violent crisis triggers will be exceedingly rare.

Power Relations among Adversaries

A third theoretical perspective deals with the question of power relations among adversaries and how this impacts on state behavior. One branch of this literature focuses on power transition and argues that war is most likely when power is approximately equally distributed among nations or, more precisely, when the power of the challenger approaches—or begins to exceed—that of its more powerful opponent (Organski 1968; Organski and Kugler 1980; Kugler and Organski 1989). Balance of power theorists (Claude 1962; Wright 1965) argued that equality of power among nations diminishes the chance of war, based primarily on the argument that uncertainty over outcomes caused by approximate power parity leads actors to make more careful calculations. Steinberg (1981) argued that, during the confrontation stages of a dispute, a challenger state with equal or less military capability than its opponent will pattern its behavior closely to that of its opponent, and a more powerful challenger will act primarily according to its own objectives. Leng (1980) also found that states frequently reciprocate conflict behavior by an opponent, particularly under conditions of power parity.[57]

We propose that the choice of a response to a triggering event in a crisis situation will depend in part on the power relations between the adversaries. Specifically, following the power transition direction of the theoretical argument, we propose that power parity is the situation most likely to lead to a breakdown of matching behavior, since it is in this context that the adversaries may risk an overreaction (i.e., a violent response to a non-violent trigger). Situations typified by power discrepancy among adversaries are quite different from those where there is power parity. In the case of positive power discrepancy (a target state more powerful than a triggering entity), the target state need not necessarily employ violence in order to achieve its crisis objectives. In the case of negative power discrepancy (a target state weaker than a triggering entity), the target state would be ill-advised to employ violence in the face of a non-violent trigger emanating from a more powerful adversary.

In general, then, we argue that the type of matching behavior that has been identified empirically in conflict studies in general is expected to persist under conditions of crisis. The present study attempts to shed light on those particular and unusual circumstances under which significant deviations from matching occur during crises. In this regard, we propose three factors for consideration: the level of stress experienced by the decision makers, sociopolitical conditions in the state experiencing the crisis, and power relations among the adversaries.

To this point we have not differentiated between two types of matching behavior: non-violent to non-violent, and violent to violent. While deviations from both patterns occur, we do not expect the same explanatory factors to account for these two types of deviations. Although the subsequent analysis presents findings for both types of matching, the hypotheses to be developed

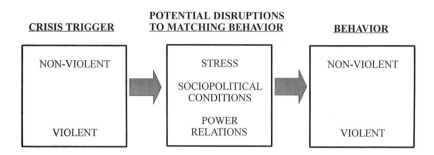

POTENTIAL DISRUPTIONS
CRISIS TRIGGER   TO MATCHING BEHAVIOR   BEHAVIOR

NON-VIOLENT	STRESS	NON-VIOLENT
	SOCIOPOLITICAL CONDITIONS	
VIOLENT	POWER RELATIONS	VIOLENT

Figure IV.14. Trigger-Behavior Transition Model

have been formulated with the non-violent to non-violent match in mind. It is useful to point out that in an important recent study, Hensel and Diehl (1994) examined the circumstances under which states that are challenged militarily choose responses that do not involve military force. Among the factors they posit as explaining non-military responses to military challenges in militarized international disputes are issue salience, the initiator's level of hostility, relative capabilities, preoccupation with domestic conditions, and learning (see Hensel and Diehl 1994:485–89).

Three hypotheses will guide the analysis that follows.

Hypothesis 42: The higher the level of stress being experienced by crisis decision makers, the less the likelihood of deviation from matching behavior (individual level).

Hypothesis 43: The greater the deterioration in sociopolitical conditions within the state experiencing crisis, the greater the likelihood of deviation from matching behavior (societal level).

Hypothesis 44: The closer the crisis actor is to power parity with its adversary, the greater the likelihood of deviation from matching behavior (interstate level).

Figure IV.14 presents the **Trigger-Behavior Transition Model.**

Specification of Variables

As noted, the primary focus in this section is on the identification of factors that help explain deviations from pure matching behavior. In particular, we are interested in explaining those cases in which the level of violence as a crisis management technique deviated significantly from the level of violence in the crisis trigger. Therefore, the independent variable will be crisis trigger, the dependent variables will be measures of violence in crisis behavior, and the intervening variables will consist of measures of stress, sociopolitical conditions, and power relations among adversaries.

The level of analysis is state behavior in crisis, rather than the international crisis as a whole. The ICB data set contains data on 895 crisis actors for the period 1918–94. All 80 World War II actor-cases were excluded from the analysis, on the grounds that the high level of stress that typified these cases meant that there was virtually no variance to be explained. However, all other intra-war crises were retained in the data set. Thus, we will be working with a set of 815 cases in the following analysis.

Crisis Trigger

Trigger, as noted, refers to the act, event, or change that generates a perception of threat to basic values among the decision makers of a state. **Non-violent triggers** include the following types: political (protests, alliance of adversaries), economic (embargo), external change (weapon system), non-violent internal change (proclamation of new regime), and non-violent military (mobilization). **Violent triggers** include direct (border clashes), indirect (violence against a client state), and violent internal change.

Crisis Behavior

Three indicators are used to assess the type of crisis management behavior engaged in by a state. This act need not be the first response of a state to the crisis trigger, but rather that act which was so clear in its intent that it came to characterize the crisis as a whole for that actor. For example, in the crisis for Great Britain and France triggered by Egypt's nationalization of the Suez Canal (**Suez Nationalization-War** 1956), while bilateral and multilateral attempts to resolve the crisis were undertaken, ultimately violence was employed in late October 1956 as their primary crisis management technique.

Crisis management technique has been dichotomized into **non-violent,** including negotiation and other pacific and non-violent military acts (threat to use violence), and **violent,** including all forms of violence.

Centrality of violence refers to the relative importance that decision makers attached to the use of violence in crisis management. It has been dichotomized into **non-violent,** if violence played no role or only a minor role, and **violent,** if violence was preeminent or important.

Severity of violence is dichotomized into **non-violent,** referring to no violence or minor violence, and **violent,** in cases where serious clashes or full-scale war occurred.

Table IV.49 presents the various forms that matching behavior can take and the percentages of crises associated with each form. That is, matching can take two distinct forms: non-violent trigger and non-violent response, and violent trigger and violent response. The table shows that both forms of matching are

TABLE IV.49. Matching Behavior in International Crises

Trigger	Behavior	Classification	Frequency	Percentage	Total
Crisis management technique					
Non-violent	Non-violent	Matching	309	69	
Non-violent	Violent	Non-matching	137	31	
			446		
Violent	Violent	Matching	245	68	
Violent	Non-violent	Non-matching	118	32	
			363		80
Centrality of violence					
Non-violent	Non-violent	Matching	321	72	
Non-violent	Violent	Non-matching	125	28	
			446		
Violent	Violent	Matching	235	65	
Violent	Non-violent	Non-matching	128	35	
			363		80
Severity of violence					
Non-violent	Non-violent	Matching	340	76	
Non-violent	Violent	Non-matching	107	24	
			447		
Violent	Violent	Matching	212	58	
Violent	Non-violent	Non-matching	151	42	
			363		81

more prevalent than non-matching, confirming that behavior in crisis conforms to patterns observed in conflict behavior in general. We are particularly interested in the approximately 28% of cases with non-violent triggers in which violent responses were observed, and in the 37% of cases with violent triggers in which non-violent responses were observed. We turn now to the intervening variables that have been posited as possible explanations for these deviations.

Intervening Variables

An indicator of **stress** was developed that takes account of both the threat to basic values that the crisis poses and the power status of one's adversary in a crisis.[58] Threat to basic values ranges from limited threat and threat to influence of a minor power at the low end of the scale, through economic, political, territorial, threat to major power influence, threat of grave damage, and, at the highest level, threat to existence. Power relations among adversaries is a relational variable based on a four-point scale: small power, middle power, great power, and super-power. Level of stress is then trichotomized into low, medium, and high.

A second indicator measures **sociopolitical conditions.** Its first component measures societal unrest, or the level of internal disruption as evidenced by assassinations, terrorism, general strikes, demonstrations, and riots. The second component measures mass violence, assessing the extent of such phenomena as insurrection, civil war, and revolutionary behavior. The indicator has three categories: no change in either societal unrest or mass violence from levels existing prior to a crisis; moderate deterioration in either societal unrest or mass violence; and serious deterioration in both societal unrest and mass violence.

The final indicator assesses the **power discrepancy** between the crisis actor and its principal adversary in a crisis (this latter need not be, but most often is, the actor that triggered the crisis). A power score was determined for each crisis actor and its principal adversary on the basis of data on size of population, GNP, territorial size, alliance capability, military expenditure, and nuclear capability. The final measure used here distinguishes between power discrepancy (either positive or negative) and power parity.

Findings

It will be recalled that matching behavior can take on two forms: non-violent triggers with non-violent responses, and violent triggers with violent responses. Table IV.50 presents a summary of findings for matching behavior when the crisis is triggered by a non-violent act. The findings are organized by the three types of intervening factors: stress, sociopolitical conditions, and power relations. The percentages of matching behavior are all in the predicted directions, and six of the nine sets were derived from contingency tables for which significant chi-squares were found.

For example, the results for Hypothesis 42 show that the lower the level of stress experienced by a crisis decision maker, the less likely it is that non-violent triggers will result in non-violent responses as a means for achieving foreign policy goals (Centrality of Violence—CEN)—65% matching for low stress, 68% matching for medium stress, and 78% matching for high stress. Similarly, the more serious the deterioration in sociopolitical conditions within the crisis actor at the time of a crisis, the less likely it is that non-violent triggers will be matched by non-violent crisis management techniques (CMT)—78% match for no change/improvement in sociopolitical conditions, 66% matching for moderate deterioration, and 53% matching for actors for which serious deterioration in sociopolitical conditions has occurred. Finally, crises in which power parity among adversaries exists are less likely than cases of power discrepancy to exhibit matching behavior between non-violent triggers and less severe forms of responses (SEV)—80% matching for power discrepancy and 69% matching for power parity.

TABLE IV.50.   Matching Behavior for Non-violent Crisis Triggers

Stress: Hypothesis 42	Non-violent trigger non-violent CMT[a]	Non-violent trigger non-violent CEN[b]	Non-violent trigger non-violent SEV[c]
Low stress	63%	65%	72%
Medium stress	65%	68%	74%
High stress	75%[d]	78%[e]	79%
Sociopolitical conditions: Hypothesis 43			
No change or improvement	78%	80%	82%
Moderate deterioration	66%	68%	75%
Serious deterioration	53%[f]	55%[f]	59%[f]
Power relations: Hypothesis 44			
Power discrepancy	74%	76%	80%
Power parity	66%	66%	69%[d]

[a] Crisis management technique.
[b] Centrality of violence.
[c] Severity of violence.
[d] Based on contingency table for which X^2 p<.10
[e] Based on contingency table for which X^2 p<.05
[f] Based on contingency table for which X^2 p<.01

Table IV.51 focuses on attempts to explain deviations from violent trigger–violent crisis management matching behavior. Two important findings stand out. First, only two of the nine relationships examined show a statistically significant impact for the intervening variables in explaining these deviations. Second, to the extent that any direction at all can be established, the data point in the opposite direction to what had been hypothesized. Clearly, then, while the three factors of stress, sociopolitical conditions, and power relations help substantially in explaining deviations from the non-violent trigger to non-violent response dynamic, we will need to identify other factors to explain deviations from violence to violence matching.

While a detailed analysis of the interaction effects among the three intervening variables would be potentially valuable, the dichotomous and trichotomous nature of all the key variables precludes all but extremely rudimentary multivariate analysis.

Table IV.52 presents a summary of cases that fall into various categories of disruption of the trigger-behavior matching dynamic. The focus here is exclusively on disruptions that take the form of violent responses to non-violent triggers. The three control variables have all been set at the values found to be

TABLE IV.51.   Matching Behavior for Violent Crisis Triggers

Stress: Hypothesis 42	Violent trigger violent CMT[a]	Violent trigger violent CEN[b]	Violent trigger violent SEV[c]
Low stress	65%	58%	47%
Medium stress	68%	65%	57%
High stress	68%	67%	66%[e]
Sociopolitical conditions: Hypothesis 43			
No change or improvement	64%	62%	55%
Moderate deterioration	70%	68%	61%
Serious deterioration	76%	73%	73%[d]
Power relations: Hypothesis 44			
Power discrepancy	65%	64%	57%
Power parity	71%	71%	62%

[a] Crisis management technique.
[b] Centrality of violence.
[c] Severity of violence.
[d] Based on contingency table for which X^2 p<.10
[e] Based on contingency table for which X^2 p<.05

associated with the highest levels of disruption (see Table IV.50): serious deterioration in sociopolitical conditions, power parity among adversaries, and low level of stress.

Each of the three conditions is associated with a relatively large number of cases of deviations from matching: 27 for sociopolitical conditions, 21 for power parity, and 21 for low stress. These numbers drop dramatically when we begin to

TABLE IV.52.   Disruptions in Trigger-Behavior Matching: Non-violent Triggers and Violent Crisis Management Techniques

Serious deterioration in sociopolitical conditions	Power parity among adversaries	Low decision maker stress	Number of crises
X	X	X	1
X	X		4
X		X	2
X			27
	X	X	7
	X		21
		X	21

combine disruptive factors. Four crisis actors chose violent responses to non-violent triggers when sociopolitical conditions were deteriorating and power parity existed: China in **Shanghai** 1932, Peru in **Leticia** 1932–33, Algeria in **Algeria/Morocco Border** 1963, and Yemen in **Yemen War IV** 1966–67. Two crisis actors exhibited violent responses to non-violent triggers when sociopolitical conditions were deteriorating and the level of decision maker stress was low: Peru in **Leticia** 1932–33, and France in **Bizerta** 1961. And seven crisis actors chose violent responses to non-violent triggers when power parity existed and decision maker stress was low: USSR in **Chinese Eastern Railway** 1929, Peru in **Leticia** 1932–33, Indonesia in its three **Independence** crises of 1945–47, 1947–48, and 1948–49, and Egypt in the **Yemen War** crises of 1962–63 and 1966–67. Finally, only Peru in the **Leticia** crisis of 1932–33 exhibited a violent response to a non-violent crisis trigger when all three disruptive conditions were present. Clearly, then, there is virtually no interaction among the three disrupting factors.

Summary

A key aspect of the research reported here is that crises, like conflict situations in general, exhibit a very high degree of matching behavior across all three types of behavioral linkages examined—trigger–crisis management technique, trigger–centrality of violence, and trigger–severity of violence. We have also found support for the postulated disruptive nature of the three factors examined, with the primary disruption observable in the non-violent trigger to non-violent response pattern. Thus, for stress, it was found that disruption occurred primarily under conditions of relatively low threat to values. For sociopolitical factors—societal unrest and mass violence—disruption occurred when there was serious deterioration in these conditions. Finally, the results show that disruption in matching behavior was most likely when the power relations among the adversaries were at approximate parity.

Third-Party Intervention

This final analytic section examines the roles of third parties in international crises. The involvement of third parties in the search for pacific settlement of disputes has been an enduring part of world politics in the twentieth century, enshrined in the Covenant of the League of Nations and, after World War II, in the United Nations Charter. Regional organizations such as the Organization of American States and the Organization of African Unity, together with security organizations such as *NATO* and the Warsaw Pact, have also played significant roles as third parties in regional conflicts. Finally, individual states, notably (but not exclusively) the great powers of the interwar period and the superpowers since 1945, have also been deeply involved in attempts to resolve conflicts, crises, and disputes among other states.

A widely employed definition of third-party intervention was proposed by Young (1967:34): "Any action taken by an actor that is not a direct party to the crisis, that is designed to reduce or remove one or more of the problems of the bargaining relationship and, therefore, to facilitate the termination of the crisis itself." The rationale for such intervention derives from the essentially anarchic character of the international system. Parties to a dispute can often achieve accommodation only through the intervention of a disinterested party, for example, Egypt and Israel, with U.S. mediation, 1977–79.

Research on third-party involvement in interstate disputes has generated a large body of literature, mostly from the perspective of traditional international law and organization.[59] Social science contributions have also been substantial.[60] Bobrow (1981) has provided a useful summary of the functions that third parties can perform, based on prior work by Young (1967) and Touval (1975).

In principle, third parties can contribute to crisis regulation and settlement in two ways. First, they can make a direct positive contribution. Familiar examples include focusing the parties on a particular termination agreement, devising a formula to avoid hard issues, providing an agenda, and manipulating timing. Second, third parties can work to weaken constraints on the primary parties; that is, they can make it easier for the primary parties to do what they in some sense like to do anyway. Third parties do this by lowering the net costs associated with a more flexible bargaining position, including the internal political penalties. In effect, third parties provide face-saving assistance for the primary conflict participants. They may do so by providing rationalizations for the disavowal of previous stands, by certifying the benefits of an agreement, and by providing insurance against the risks should an agreement fail.

Our examination of third-party intervention in international crises will focus on the circumstances in which such intervention is likely to occur, what form it takes, and the conditions under which it is most likely to be effective in crisis management and resolution. In the first part of this section, we will focus on international organizations, specifically the League of Nations from 1920 to 1939, and the United Nations from 1945 onward. In the second part, we will turn to an examination of the great powers of the interwar period, and the super-powers after World War II, in their roles as international crisis managers.[61]

Global Organizations in International Crises

The analysis to follow will focus on three aspects of global organization (GO) intervention in crisis. First, we will be concerned with the **forum** of such involvement in terms of specific organs that play an active role in crisis management, that is, the Council, Assembly, and Secretary-General for the League of Nations, and the Security Council, General Assembly, and Secretary-General for the United Nations. Second, we will examine the **level** of such involvement, that is, low level (fact-finding, discussion without resolution, good offices, general), medium level (mediation, condemnation, call for action), and high level (arbitration, sanctions, observers, emergency military forces). Third, we will assess the **effectiveness** of GO involvement in abating a crisis, that is, in preventing hostilities or contributing to crisis termination. League or UN involvement was considered to have been effective when it was the single most important contributor to crisis abatement, when it had an important impact along with action by other international actors, and when it had a marginal but positive effect.[62]

To set the stage for the empirical analysis sketched out above, we begin with an examination of the record of global organizations in terms of crisis intervention. Throughout this section, since the focus is primarily on third-party intervention, intra-war crises will remain in the data set. Only the crises between the outbreak and end of World War II (a period in which the global organizations were inactive), and five 1918–19 crises that began before the League of Nations came into existence, are excluded from the present analyses.

Table IV.53 presents the record of global organization involvement in summary form. It is immediately obvious that the two organizations displayed quite different patterns. The League became involved in only 36% of crises during its years of existence; however, it was effective in 14 of those 25 interventions, or 56%. The UN, on the other hand, while becoming involved in 56% of all crises in the post–World War II period, was effective in only 60 of these 173 interventions, or 35%. Notable among the 14 effective League interventions were four cases in which it was the most important contributor to crisis abatement: **Aaland Islands** 1920–21, **Mosul Land Dispute** 1924, **Bulgaria/Greek Frontier** 1925,

TABLE IV.53. Crisis Intervention by Global Organizations

	Number of crises	Number of crises with GO intervention	Intervention rate	Number of effective interventions	Effectiveness rate
League of Nations	69	25	36%	14	56%
United Nations	306	173	56%	60	35%

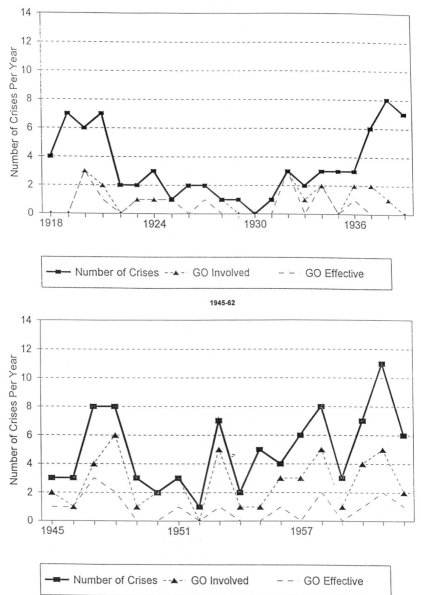

Figure IV.15. International Crises and GO Involvement: *a,* 1918–39; *b,* 1945–62; *c,* 1963–94

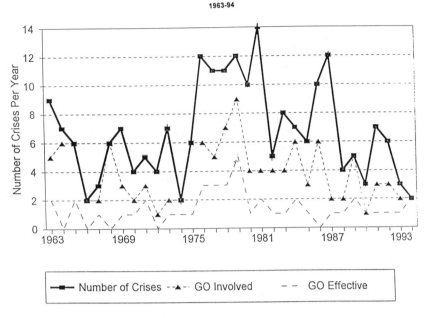

1963-94

Figure IV.15. Continued

and **Vilna II** 1927. The United Nations record of interventions in which it was the most important contributor to crisis abatement includes only five cases: **Caprivi Strip** 1971, **Operation Thrasher** 1976, **Mapai Seizure** 1977, **Essequibo II** 1981–83, and **Lesotho Raid** 1982. It is interesting to note that four of these five cases are Africa crises.

A second perspective on the record of global organizations across the entire period under examination is provided by Figures IV.15a, IV.15b, and IV.15c. Three variables are plotted on a yearly basis: number of international crises (C); number of crises in which the global organization became involved (I); and number of crises in which the global organization was effective (E). A visual examination of these plots shows reasonably strong relationships among these variables, and that is confirmed by a correlation analysis:[63] $r_{C,I} = .71$, $r_{C,E} = .53$, $r_{I,E} = .65$ (all significant at $p < .01$); that is, changes in the number of crises per year are correlated with changes in both involvement and effectiveness of global organizations. However, a careful examination of the data points to two disquieting trends. First, despite these correlations, for most years, there is a rather large discrepancy between the number of international crises and both involvement and effectiveness rates. Second, there is also a considerable gap between involvement and effectiveness rates themselves.

In order to gain more insight into the trends identified in the preceding, an examination of residuals was undertaken. The residuals pertain to the number of effective interventions, as predicted by the number of crises per year. Visual examination of Figure IV.15 reveals six peak periods of crisis activity: 1920–21, 1937–39, 1947–48, 1960–63, 1976–81, and 1986–87. It is interesting to note that several of these peak crisis periods correspond to major transition points in the international system: the late 1930s and the transition from multipolarity to a world war system; the late 1940s and the transition from embryonic bipolarity with the U.S., the USSR, and the U.K.-Commonwealth as power centers, to tight bipolarity; the early 1960s, characterized by the transition to polycentrism, with the two superpowers maintaining their dominance in military capability but with a diffusion of influence among other decision-making centers; and the late 1980s and transition to the post–Cold War era.

Three of those six peak periods contain years in which the residuals reveal far greater than expected effective involvement on the part of the relevant global organization: 1920, 1948, and 1979; that is, these were periods in which the League or the UN did better than expected in terms of effectiveness in crisis abatement. Crises in those years in which the global organization played an effective role in crisis abatement were **Aaland Islands** 1920–21 (League of Nations Most Important), **Persian Border** 1920–21 (League Marginal), **Vilna I** 1920 (League Important), **Palestine Partition/Israel Independence** 1947–49 (UN Important), **China Civil War** 1948–49 (UN Marginal), **Indonesia Independence III** 1948–49 (UN Important), **Raids on Zipra** 1979 (UN Marginal), **Raids on SWAPO** 1979 (UN Marginal), **Goulimime-Tarfaya Road** 1979 (UN Marginal), **Raid on Angola** 1979 (UN Marginal), and **U.S. Hostages in Iran** 1979–81 (UN Important). For two periods of high crisis activity, examination of the residuals attested to particularly low effectiveness levels for the global organization: 1937–39 and 1986–87. The former, a period of high crisis frequency and low global organization involvement presaged the outbreak of this century's largest international conflict—World War II. It would appear that the international system managed to weather the 1986–87 period of high crisis frequency and low global organization involvement and effectiveness, despite the Gulf War of 1990–91—the ICB data reveal a decided downturn in the frequency of international crises in the post–Cold War era (see Figure IV.15).

While we have touched on polarity in our discussion of the distribution of global organization involvement and effectiveness over time, we turn now to address this factor explicitly. GO involvement in international crises increased from 36% for the League in the pre–World War II multipolarity system, to 54% for the UN in bipolarity, 58% for polycentrism, and 50% in the post–Cold War unipolar system. It is interesting to note that the combined percentage of UN involvement in post–World War II crises of 56% is considerably higher than that found by E. Haas (1986), where the focus was on a set of 319 disputes between July 1945 and September 1984, of which 137 or 43% were referred to the UN. This discrepancy may point to an important distinction between international organization intervention in these two types of conflict—crisis and dispute.

TABLE IV.54. Global Organization Organs Involved in Crisis Management

	General		Secretary-General		(General) Assembly		(Security) Council		TOTAL	
Multipolarity	2	8%	1	4%	3	12%	19	76%	25	12%
Bipolarity	6	12%	5	10%	9	19%	29	59%	49	25%
Polycentrism	12	11%	24	21%	6	5%	71	63%	113	57%
Unipolarity	0	0%	1	9%	1	9%	9	82%	11	6%
TOTAL	20	10%	31	16%	19	10%	128	64%	198	100%

$X^2 = 14.66$, p = .10

Table IV.54 provides a more detailed breakdown on GO involvement in crises for the four system-periods. The patterns are quite different and point to an evolution in GO involvement that mirrors important structural changes in the international system. Relatively constant across all systems is the role of the Security Council (Council, for the League), handling between 59% and 82% of all crises in which the global organization became involved. The relative prominence of the Secretary-General and the General Assembly (Assembly, for the League) changed markedly across the system-periods. Crisis management for the League during multipolarity and for the UN during bipolarity relied considerably on the Assembly (12% and 19%, respectively), but the role of the UN General Assembly diminished to only 5% of crises in the polycentric system. Polycentrism, on the other hand, showed a prominent role for the Secretary-General in crisis management—21%—compared to only 4% for multipolarity and 10% for bipolarity. This latter finding is a reflection of the large increase in UN membership (from 50 in 1945 to 159 in 1985 and 185 in 1994), making centralized organizational activity more unwieldy. Polycentrism crises in which the Secretary-General was both active and at least marginally effective in crisis management were **Burundi/Rwanda** 1963–64, **Cyprus II** 1967, and **Three Village Border II** (Thailand/Laos) 1987–88. Interestingly, the post–Cold War unipolar crises show a dramatic move away from the Secretary-General and back to the Security Council as the primary locus of GO involvement.

With these general trends in mind, let us turn to the three-pronged analysis of the role of the global organization in international crises: **forum, level,** and **effectiveness.** Two general research questions will guide the design and analysis to follow.

1. What is the relationship between the attributes of international crises and the extent of global organization involvement?
2. Under what conditions and at what level is global organization intervention in international crises likely to lead to favorable outcomes?

Crisis Attributes and Global Organization Involvement

The data presented thus far reveal that global organizations became involved in barely half of the 375 international crises between 1918 and 1994 (the World War II period was excluded since neither global organization was functioning at that time). Given their mandate in the area of international conflict and crisis, what explains this relatively low involvement? On the surface, it could be plausibly argued that the League and later the UN, with primary interest in the maintenance of international peace and security, become involved in those situations that posed the most serious threat to peace and security. Traditionally, this threat has been judged in terms of such indicators as extent of violence, number of participants, and involvement by major powers. The following hypotheses are proposed for this portion of the analysis.

> Hypothesis 45: The more serious an international crisis, the more likely it is that the global organization will intervene.[64]
>> Hypothesis 45a: The more violent a crisis trigger, the more likely it is that the global organization will become involved.
>> Hypothesis 45b: The higher the level of stress among crisis decision makers, the more likely it is that the global organization will become involved.
>> Hypothesis 45c: The more intense the violence employed as a crisis management technique, the more likely it is that the global organization will become involved.
>> Hypothesis 45d: The larger the number of crisis actors, the more likely it is that the global organization will become involved.
>> Hypothesis 45e: The higher the level of major power activity in a crisis, the more likely it is that the global organization will become involved.

Figure IV.16 is a schematic representation of Hypothesis 45 and its five subhypotheses.

Findings

For purposes of the following analyses, crisis triggers are grouped as follows: non-violence (political, economic, external change, internal challenge), non-violent military, and external violence. We have hypothesized that the more serious the crisis—in this case, the more violent the trigger—the more likely was global organization involvement to occur.

Table IV.55 presents the findings on the relationship between type of **trigger** and extent of global organization involvement (Hypothesis 45a). The data reveal only a weak trend in the direction of greater GO involvement when crises were triggered by violent acts. Furthermore, there were no important distinctions

SERIOUSNESS
OF CRISIS

GLOBAL
ORGANIZATION
INVOLVEMENT

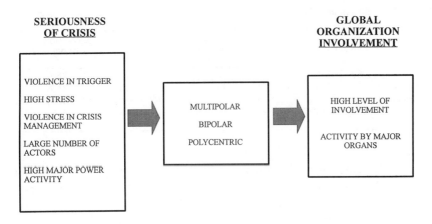

Figure IV.16.   Global Organization Involvement Model

among the various global organization forums in terms of the types of crises—
violent or non-violent—most likely to fall in their domain, with all three types of
triggers indicating that the Security Council was the most likely organ to be
invoked. It is worth noting again that a very high proportion of crises in which
the General Assembly became involved occurred during bipolarity (9 of 19
General Assembly cases, or 47% of the total), compared to only six General
Assembly cases during the entire polycentric era. The nine bipolarity crises with
General Assembly involvement included **China Civil War** 1948–49, **Soviet
Bloc–Yugoslavia** 1949–51, **Korean War II** (October) 1950–51, **Burma Infil-
tration** 1953–54, **Korean War III** 1953, **Suez Nationalization-War** 1956–57,
Hungarian Uprising 1956–57, **Syria/Turkey Confrontation** 1957, and **Bay of
Pigs** 1961. We will return to the question of effectiveness later in the discussion.

Table IV.56 deals with the level of decision maker **stress** and GO involvement. We have hypothesized that the more serious (higher) the level of stress, the
more likely there is to be GO involvement (Hypothesis 45b).

TABLE IV.55.   Trigger and Global Organization Involvement in International Crises

	No GO involvement		General		Secretary-General		(General) Assembly		(Security) Council		TOTAL	
on-violence	75	51%	9	6%	9	6%	8	5%	47	32%	148	40%
on-violent military	29	55%	4	7%	2	4%	1	2%	17	32%	53	14%
iolence	73	42%	7	4%	20	11%	10	6%	64	37%	174	46%
OTAL	177	47%	20	6%	31	8%	19	5%	128	34%	375	100%

^{2} = 9.49, p = .30

TABLE IV.56.   Stress and Global Organization Involvement in International Crises

	No GO involvement		General		Secretary-General		(General) Assembly		(Security) Council		TOTAL	
Low stress	65	53%	13	11%	5	4%	5	4%	34	28%	122	33%
Medium stress	63	46%	4	3%	19	14%	4	3%	47	34%	137	36%
High stress	49	42%	3	3%	7	6%	10	9%	47	40%	116	31%
TOTAL	177	47%	20	6%	31	8%	19	5%	128	34%	375	100%

$X^2 = 26.84$, $p = .00$

As hypothesized, as the level of stress rises, so does the probability of global organization involvement—from 47% for low stress, 54% for medium stress, to 58% for high stress. Also interesting is the finding that stress levels are positively related to Security Council involvement—28%, 34%, and 40%, respectively. Further analysis of the data reveals that the relationship between stress and level of Security Council involvement is particularly strong for polycentrism and post–Cold War unipolarity, where the Security Council dealt with 24 of 30, and 6 of 7 high stress cases, respectively. For example, the post–Cold War high stress cases handled by the Security Council were **Gulf War** 1990–91, **Yugoslavia II—Bosnia** 1992–95, **Iraq No-Fly Zone** 1992, **Operation Accountability** 1993, **Haiti Military Regime** 1994, **Iraq Deployment/Kuwait** 1994. And three of these cases included threats to existence—Kuwait in 1990–91 and 1994, and Bosnia in 1992–95.

Turning to Table IV.57, we focus on the question of whether seriousness of crisis, as measured by the **severity of violence** employed by the crisis actors, predicts the extent of global organization involvement. The data provide strong support for Hypothesis 45c. The two GOs became involved in 70% of all full-scale wars, compared to an involvement rate of only 51% for all other crises. Further analysis reveals that 12 of the 20 full-scale war cases occurred during the interwar years, where a weak League of Nations was stymied in its peacekeeping attempts almost from the outset. The eight crisis-wars from which the UN remained aloof were as follows: **China/India Border II** 1962–63, **Black September** 1970, **North/South Yemen I** and **II** (1972, 1979), **Christmas Bombing** 1972–73, **Ogaden II** 1977–78, and **Chad/Libya II** and **III** 1978.

Table IV.58 explores the relationship between the **number of actors** in a crisis and the extent of global organization involvement. We have proposed that the larger the number of crisis actors, the more likely it is that GOs will become involved (Hypothesis 45d). Crises have been classified as single-actor cases, those involving two to three actors, and those involving four or more actors. The relationship is strongly supported: while only 39% of single-actor crises and 57% of midsized crises showed global organization involvement, the figure rose to 71% GO involvement for crises with large numbers of actors. Furthermore, the larger the number of actors in the crisis, the more likely it was that the Security Council (Council, for the League) was the organ most involved.

TABLE IV.57. Severity of Violence and Global Organization Involvement in International Crises

	No GO involvement		General		Secretary-General		(General) Assembly		(Security) Council		TOTAL	
No violence	72	53%	11	8%	7	5%	3	2%	43	32%	136	36%
Minor clashes	39	53%	5	7%	3	4%	3	4%	23	32%	73	20%
Serious clashes	46	47%	4	4%	10	10%	6	6%	33	33%	99	26%
Full-scale war	20	30%	0	0%	11	17%	7	10%	29	43%	67	18%
TOTAL	177	47%	20	6%	31	8%	19	5%	128	34%	375	100%

$X^2 = 29.29$, p = .00

TABLE IV.58. Number of Actors and Global Organization Involvement in International Crises

	No GO involvement	General	Secretary-General	(General) Assembly	(Security) Council	TOTAL
Single-actor crisis	74 61%	8 7%	4 3%	5 4%	31 25%	122 33%
2-3 actor crisis	92 43%	10 5%	23 11%	11 5%	79 36%	215 57%
4+ actor crisis	11 29%	2 5%	4 11%	3 8%	18 47%	38 10%
TOTAL	177 47%	20 6%	31 8%	19 5%	128 34%	375 100%

$X^2 = 20.15$, $p = .01$

**.BLE IV.59. Major Power or Superpower Activity and Global Organization Involvement
International Crises**

1918-39

	No GO involvement		General		Secretary-General		Assembly		Council		TOTAL	
» MP activity	4	100%	0	0%	0	0%	0	0%	0	0%	4	6%
w MP activity	9	45%	1	5%	0	0%	0	0%	10	50%	20	29%
gh MP activity	31	69%	1	2%	1	2%	3	7%	9	20%	45	65%
)TAL	44	64%	2	3%	1	1%	3	4%	19	28%	69	100%

= 10.43, p = .24

1945-94

	No GO involvement		General		Secretary-General		General Assembly		Security Council		TOTAL	
» SP activity	57	66%	5	6%	6	7%	1	1%	17	20%	86	28%
w SP activity	35	36%	7	7%	9	9%	5	5%	42	43%	98	32%
gh SP activity	41	34%	6	5%	15	12%	10	8%	49	41%	121	40%
)TAL	133	44%	18	6%	30	10%	16	5%	108	35%	305	100%

= 29.36, p = .00

The final portion of this analysis deals with the relationship between the extent of **major power activity** in crisis and the likelihood of global organization involvement (Hypothesis 45e). Major power activity has been trichotomized into cases of no activity, those in which one or more major powers was engaged in political, economic, or propaganda activity (low), and cases in which the powers' activity reflected covert, semi-military, or direct military activity (high).

Table IV.59 reports the findings for the seven great powers in the 1918–39 period, and the two superpowers for the post-1945 era.[65] As noted previously, the interwar period reveals a much higher rate of great power activity in crises than was the case for the superpowers—94% versus 72%. Despite this disparity, we find that only 36% of multipolarity crises showed League involvement, compared to a rate of 56% for the combined post–World War II systems. Furthermore, these latter cases showed a constant rate of Security Council activity (42%) when the superpowers were active in an international crisis, whereas for multipolarity, when great power activity was high, Council activity dropped dramatically. In the case of the post–World War II systems, the duopoly of power facilitated collective action through the Security Council in cases where the superpowers had some degree of mutual interest in limiting escalation.

By way of summary, there were three international crises between 1918 and 1994 that perfectly fit the profile of a serious crisis as it has been operationalized here: violent trigger, high decision maker stress, severe violence (full-scale war), large number of crisis actors, and major powers as crisis actors. These were as follows: **Korean War I**—25 June 1950, when North Korean forces crossed the 38th Parallel and triggered a crisis for South Korea and the United States; **Korean War II**—1 October 1950, when South Korean forces crossed the 38th Parallel and advanced rapidly, triggering a crisis for North Korea; and the **Gulf War** of 1990–91, in which the Iraqi invasion and occupation of Kuwait precipitated crises for 14 states, the most serious crisis of the post–Cold War international system. Security Council action was critical in all three crises, although in **Korean War II** the action shifted to the General Assembly under the umbrella of its Uniting for Peace Resolution.

Global Organization Involvement and Crisis Outcome

The second general question posed earlier in this section focuses on the conditions under which global organization intervention affects crisis outcomes. In particular, we are concerned with identifying the conditions under which GO involvement in a crisis is likely to lead to favorable outcomes, both from the point of view of the individual actors (satisfaction of goals) and of the peace and security of the international system (defusing of tensions). In this regard, we are guided by the following general hypothesis and subhypotheses.

> Hypothesis 46: The more involved the GO is in an international crisis, the more likely it is that outcomes will be favorable to the participants and the international system in general.
> > Hypothesis 46a: The more involved the GO, the more likely it is that a definitive outcome will be achieved.
> > Hypothesis 46b: The more involved the GO, the more likely is the achievement of agreement among the crisis actors.
> > Hypothesis 46c: The more involved the GO, the more likely it is that parties will be satisfied with the outcome.
> > Hypothesis 46d: The more involved the GO, the more likely it is that long-term tensions among the parties will be reduced.

Findings

Our discussion of the impact of global organization involvement in crises will focus on the three central organs that played the dominant roles in crises in the twentieth century: the UN Security Council (Council, for the League), the Secretary-General, and the UN General Assembly (Assembly, for the League). For each organ, we will examine both the patterns exhibited by the different system-periods and the impact of GO involvement on four outcome variables: substance, form, satisfaction with outcome, and escalation/reduction of tensions. The results of these analyses are summarized in the following.[66]

Security Council

The overwhelming majority of crises in which global organizations became involved (64%) were taken up by the Security Council, and there was little variation in this rate across the four polarity systems. There was, however, considerable variation in terms of crisis outcomes, particularly between bipolarity and polycentrism: for bipolarity as compared with polycentrism, Security Council activity was associated with relatively high levels of definitive outcomes (52% versus 37%) and reduction in tensions (72% versus 49%). It is interesting to note that while post–Cold War unipolarity crises showed a high rate of Security Council involvement, similar in that respect to bipolarity, it had a very low rate for tension reduction. As noted previously, a definitive outcome involves a combination of perceived victory and/or defeat in terms of actors' foreign policy objectives, as opposed to stalemate or compromise. Tension reduction is defined as termination such that the same principal adversaries do not again become involved in an international crisis with each other during the subsequent five-year period.

Among the 29 bipolarity cases of Security Council intervention in crises, 12 or 41% fit the definitive/tension reduction pattern, and four of these showed Security Council activity to have been effective: **Azerbaijan** 1945–46, **Indonesian Independence III** 1948–49, **Egypt/Sudan Border I** 1958, and **Goa II** 1961. By contrast, only 16 of 71 polycentrism cases (22%) of Security Council intervention had definitive outcomes and reduction of tensions, and in only six of these was the Security Council effective: **Conakry Raid** 1970, **Bangladesh** 1971, **Cyprus III** 1974–75, **Aegean Sea I** 1976, **Cambodia Peace Conference** 1989–90, and **Contras IV** 1989. No cases fit this pattern for the post–Cold War unipolar system.

Secretary-General

As noted earlier, 16% of all crises in which global organizations were involved had the Secretary-General as the most active organ. An examination of these cases by polarity reveals that the large majority of these cases—24 of 31—are found in the polycentric system. Thus we will focus primarily on that system.

The enhancement of the role of the Secretary-General in polycentrism represents a movement away from collective crisis management attempts by both the Security Council and the General Assembly. But enhanced activity did not necessarily mean success for the Secretary-General. Indeed, these 24 crises were characterized by higher than average ambiguous terminations (compromise or stalemate), termination through unilateral acts (rather than agreement), and a high rate of tension escalation. Six polycentric crises fit this rather pessimistic mold, and all showed the Secretary-General to have been ineffective in crisis management: **Pleiku** 1965, **El Samu** 1966, **Invasion of Cambodia** 1970, **Invasion of Laos II** 1971, **Chad-Libya IV** 1979, **Capture of al-Faw** 1986. During the entire 27-year span of polycentrism, the Secretary-General, despite that office's enhanced role, was effective in crisis management in only three cases:

Burundi/Rwanda 1963–64, **Cyprus II** 1967, and **Three Village Border II** 1987–88.[67]

General Assembly

The (General) Assembly was the most active organ in 12% of multipolarity crises and 19% of bipolarity crises, but in only 5% of crises during polycentrism. Despite the wide disparity between bipolarity and polycentrism, the outcomes were similar: a 67% rate of definitive outcomes, a 54% rate of satisfaction with outcome, but a 53% rate of tension escalation. Multipolarity patterns contrasted sharply, with high rates of ambiguous outcomes (67%) and a 100% rate of escalation of tensions. During the entire 76-year period under examination, seven cases showed effective (General) Assembly activity: **Shanghai** 1932, **China Civil War** 1948–49, **Burma Infiltration** 1953–54, **Suez Nationalization-War** 1956–57, **French Hostages in Mauritania** 1977, **Nicaraguan Civil War** 1978–79, and **Georgia/Abkhazia** 1992–93.

Summary: Global Organizations and International Crises

In this section, we examined the record of the League of Nations and the United Nations in terms of involvement and effectiveness as third-party intermediaries in crises. We observed that, despite a higher effectiveness rate for the League than for the UN, this did not prevent the international system from hurtling toward world war in the late 1930s. We noted that, for some years of particularly frequent crisis activity—1920, 1948, 1979—global organization involvement was highly effective, while for other frequent crisis periods—1937–39, 1986–87—global organization involvement was ineffective. And we observed an evolution in global organization involvement mirroring important structural changes in the international system: while the (Security) Council accounted for almost two-thirds of GO involvement throughout the 76-year period under study, the role of the (General) Assembly declined precipitously during polycentrism, while the role of the Secretary-General was enhanced. Preliminary indications from the post–Cold War unipolarity system indicate a reinvigoration of the role of the Security Council.

We also observed that the more serious crises, defined by such measures as violence in triggers and crisis management, high stress levels, large number of actors, and high activity by major powers as actors, produced global organization involvement at the highest levels during bipolarity. This trend was somewhat less pronounced for polycentrism but not in evidence at all during multipolarity. Finally, in terms of crisis outcomes, we found that the three primary conflict management organs of the global organizations—(Security) Council, Secretary-General, (General) Assembly—had sharply different records as crisis managers. The Security Council was particularly effective during bipolarity, often producing definitive outcomes and a reduction in tension. As noted, the Secretary-

General was very active in polycentrism, although the outcomes were largely ambiguous and unilateral and produced higher tension. General Assembly involvement was most notable in bipolarity and polycentrism, where it tended to produce definitive outcomes and satisfaction with those outcomes, although its occurrence was a rarity in polycentrism. To this point, the General Assembly has been identified with only one post–Cold War international crisis—**Georgia/Abkhazia** 1992–93—where its impact was marginal.

Major Powers as Intermediaries in International Crises

The analysis of major powers as crisis intermediaries is made more complex by the necessity to differentiate those crises in which the powers were themselves crisis actors from those in which they played legitimate intermediary roles. Any comparison between the crisis roles of global organizations and major powers must bear in mind that, whereas GOs are by definition always third parties, there is often a thin line between major powers functioning as crisis actors and major powers in their roles as third parties.

We turn our attention first to an overview of the activity of great powers in international crises before disaggregating the data in terms of third parties and crisis actors. As we have done in other sections, we will employ a control for polarity. Thus, for the multipolar system, we focus on the activities of the seven great powers: France, Germany, Great Britain, Italy, Japan, the United States, and the Soviet Union. For the bipolarity, polycentrism, and post–Cold War unipolar systems, we will focus exclusively on the two superpowers: the U.S. and the USSR (later, Russia). Our initial scan of these systems explores the different types of activities exhibited by these actors.

The degree of involvement of great powers in the international crises of the multipolar system (1918–39) was considerably higher than the comparable rate for superpowers during bipolarity, polycentrism, and post–Cold War unipolarity (1945–94). Great powers were at least minimally involved in fully 86% of all international crises for multipolarity, compared to only 67% for the U.S. and 52% for the USSR during the post–World War II systems.

Two explanations for this sharp difference come to mind. First, the fact that there were seven great powers during multipolarity and only two superpowers thereafter, coupled with the fact that there were far fewer states in the multipolar system, produces an a priori higher probability of great power activity in crises during multipolarity. Second, the core of the international system during multipolarity was Europe, the geographic locus of five of the seven great powers, and hence, it would be expected that a large proportion of multipolarity crises would involve the great powers of the period. We have already seen that in the post–World War II systems, and particularly during polycentrism, the locus of the vast majority of international crises shifts to the periphery of the international system, with most attracting little attention or interest on the part of the U.S. and the USSR. While the former explanation may be based in part on a statistical artifact,

TABLE IV.60. Superpower Activity in International Crises, 1945–94[a]

	No USSR activity			Low level USSR activity			Semi-military/covert USSR activity			USSR military activity			TOTAL	
No U.S. activity	84	85%	58%	10	10%	11%	5	5%	9%	0	0%	0%	99	33%
Low level U.S. activity	43	37%	29%	45	38%	51%	21	18%	39%	8	7%	57%	117	39%
Semi-military/covert U.S. activity	15	26%	10%	19	33%	22%	21	37%	39%	2	4%	14%	57	19%
U.S. military activity	4	14%	3%	14	48%	16%	7	24%	13%	4	14%	29%	29	9%
TOTAL	146	48%		88	29%		54	18%		14	5%		302[b]	100%

$X^2 = 95.64$, $p = .00$

[a] Percentage figures on left refer to U.S. activity and are summed across rows; percentage figures on right refer to USSR activity and are summed down columns.

[b] There were four cases with missing data on one of the superpower activity variables.

the latter provides evidence of a significant change in the way the major powers of the international community perform the function of crisis management.

The crisis data for bipolarity, polycentrism, and unipolarity lend themselves to a particularly interesting comparative analysis of U.S. and USSR activity. We note from Table IV.60 that of the 302[68] post–World War II international crises until the end of 1994, the U.S. was involved at some level in 67% (see total column) and the USSR in 52% (see total row), indicating frequent involvement in international crises by both states. Nevertheless, the higher overall level of U.S. involvement might be explained by a number of factors.

First, the U.S. was more globally oriented than the USSR during the immediate post–World War II period, when the latter was preoccupied with managing and consolidating communist regimes (Ulam 1974:408), particularly in Eastern Europe, but also at other points around its periphery as in North Korea and (unsuccessfully) in Iran. Moreover, not until Khrushchev's rhetoric for wars of "national liberation" in the Third World in the mid- to late 1950s did the USSR develop a more globalist foreign policy (Nacht 1985:11). Paralleling the USSR's rise to globalism was a military buildup that provided it with a global naval capability and nuclear parity with the U.S. The U.S., on the other hand, was at the center of the international system from the end of World War II. International efforts to stabilize and institutionalize the postwar international system demanded an active and global U.S. presence. U.S. efforts to fill the vacuum left by the retreat of Great Britain around the world caused the U.S. to become active internationally at an unprecedented level. U.S. willingness and capability to rebuild the international economy through the Bretton Woods monetary system (1944) and the Marshall Plan (1947) are indicators of U.S. globalism at that time.

A second factor that may have contributed to less USSR activity in other states' crises was caution in Soviet foreign policy generally; this tended to inhibit the use of military force in situations where the U.S. was integrally involved and in situations where long-term commitments were seen by the USSR as likely (Adomeit 1982:322).[69] Studies of political uses of military force in the postwar era by the U.S. (Blechman and Kaplan 1978) and the Soviet Union (Kaplan 1981) also indicated greater Soviet caution and lower activity: there were more incidents cited for the U.S. (215 from January 1946 to May 1975) than for the USSR (190 from June 1944 to February 1979). Particularly in crises, which often require quick action and also present riskier foreign policy situations, Soviet caution tended to preclude participation, especially if the USSR was inclined to be risk averse, as Triska and Finley (1968:347) concluded. In this regard, Soviet intervention in Afghanistan, from 1979 to 1989, can be viewed as an unusual case for the USSR.

Table IV.60 presents a cross-tabulation of the 302 post–World War II crises for types of activity by the U.S. and the USSR. There were 84 international crises (28% of the total) in which neither superpower was involved. All but one of these crises—**Aegean Sea II** 1984—were located in the Third World. This should not be surprising, given the peripheral nature of the Third World in the larger competition between the superpowers. Furthermore, of these 84 cases, 61% occurred in Africa. This finding confirms many of the ideas in the international relations literature about regional aspects of superpower competition. Africa has been peripheral to U.S. and Soviet foreign policy efforts. For the U.S., many of the conflicts in Africa were residual problems of colonialism and decolonization. Hence, because of extensive commitments elsewhere, U.S. decision makers seem to have decided to remain aloof from Africa or to leave its postcolonial crises to the former European rulers. Until the mid-1970s U.S. foreign policy toward Africa was "low profile and cautious" (Oye et al. 1983:337). The only major exceptions were **Congo II** 1964, **War in Angola** 1975–76, **Gulf of Syrte I** and **II** 1981 and 1986, and **Libyan Jets** 1988–89.

For the USSR, too, Africa was an area of secondary concern. The first real venture into African politics did not occur until 1959, after Guinea declared its independence from France. And, while the Soviets did become involved in Africa thereafter, for example, in **Congo II** (1964) and **Ogaden II** 1977–78, Africa remained outside its sphere of high interest until recently. The Angolan and *SWAPO* (Namibia) commitments tended to raise superpower competition in southern Africa to a higher level.

More striking than the data on noninvolvement cases is the fact that 47% of the total (141 cases—the addition of the southeast nine cells in Table IV.60) saw some activity by both superpowers in the same crisis. Further, in those crises in which one superpower was highly involved (direct military, semi-military, or covert activity), the level of involvement for the other superpower tended to be lower. Of the crises with direct military activity—29 for the U.S. and 14 for the USSR—there were only four crises in which both were active militarily: **Berlin Blockade** 1948–49, **Korean War II** 1950–51, **Berlin Wall** 1961, **Iraq No-Fly Zone** 1992. Yet the events in all four crises basically support the overall findings in relation to U.S./USSR confrontation: caution on the part of the superpowers with little likelihood of high risk direct military confrontation.

During the Berlin Blockade, the USSR had ample opportunity to escalate the crisis, due to the continued U.S. airlift, but it refrained from doing so. Instead, Soviet forces were used for the ground blockade, while U.S. forces were engaged in the airlift. In the Korean War II crisis, Soviet forces in the Far East were merely put on alert due to the potential of U.S. troops advancing to the Korea-Soviet border; the crisis ended for the USSR when the tide of battle shifted in favor of the PRC and North Korea. The Berlin Wall crisis also showed super-power caution and restraint: although various instances of "saber rattling" did occur, neither superpower did more than reinforce its troops in Berlin, possibly to signal commitment rather than intent to fight. Ultimately, although the possibility of direct military conflict was slightly higher in the Berlin Wall crisis, both superpowers were able to avoid a direct confrontation, just as in the previous two instances of minimal military activity. This suggests that the behavior of both the U.S. and the USSR was constrained by their roles in the global system. In 1992, France, Russia, the U.K., and the U.S. established a "no-fly zone" over southern

Iraq in order to protect the Shia population from attacks by the Iraqi government. In this post–Cold War international crisis, the U.S. and Russia were operating on the same side.

Overall, although U.S. activity is somewhat higher than that for the USSR, the basic patterns of involvement showed only marginal difference in the distribution of cases across the three types of activity. Subsequent analyses will attempt to pinpoint some of the circumstances under which such differences are likely to occur.

We turn next to a more detailed examination of the effectiveness of major powers as third-party intermediaries in international crises of the twentieth century. Since our focus is now explicitly on major powers as third parties rather than as crisis actors, we exclude from the following analyses any instances in which the powers themselves were actors in the crisis. For multipolarity, we exclude from our assessment of great power activity and effectiveness any activity on the part of a great power crisis actor. For bipolarity and polycentrism, since the ICB data set contains separate U.S. and USSR activity and effectiveness variables, this means excluding from the U.S. analysis those crises in which the U.S. was a crisis actor, and similarly for the USSR.

The initial set of analyses focuses on the relationship between level of activity and extent of effectiveness in crisis abatement. We hypothesize that as the level of activity increases, effectiveness will also increase. Level of activity ranges from low level (including political, economic, and propaganda involvement), covert or semi-military (covert activity or military aid or advisors), to direct military activity (including dispatch of troops, air and naval assistance).[70] Activity was considered to have been effective when it contributed marginally to crisis abatement, when it had an important impact, and when it was deemed to be the single most important contributor to crisis abatement.

Table IV.61 presents the findings on activity and effectiveness, examined across the three system-periods: multipolarity, bipolarity, and polycentrism.[71] The data for multipolarity (Table IV.61a) run exactly counter to our expectations. As the level of activity increased from low to semi-military and covert, to direct military, the effectiveness of the great powers declined—from 74% to 37% and 21%. Only three crises coupled high activity (military) with the highest level of effectiveness—**Baltic Independence** 1918–20 with the USSR and Germany active militarily; **Remilitarization of the Rhineland** 1936 with German military activity; and **Spanish Civil War II** 1937, with German and Italian military activity. Notable failures in crisis abatement, where high-level great power third-party activity actually exacerbated the crisis, included the following: the U.K. and France in **Greece/Turkey War I** 1920; U.K., Russia, Italy in **Greece/Turkey II** 1921; France, Italy, Japan, U.K. in **Corfu Incident** 1923; Italy, Germany, USSR in **Spanish Civil War I** 1936–37. This combination of either failure of intervention, or exacerbation of an existing crisis, is uniquely identified with the multipolar system and is directly related to the intense involvement of the powers in the central conflict arena of the era, most of which played out in

TABLE IV.61a. Great Powers as Third-Party Intermediaries, 1918–39

	Great powers not effective		Great powers effective		TOTAL	
Low level GP activity	8	26%	23	74%	31	48%
Covert or semi-military	12	63%	7	37%	19	30%
Military activity	11	79%	3	21%	14	22%
TOTAL	31	48%	33	52%	64	100%

X^2 = 13.10, p = .00

TABLE IV.61b. U.S. as Third-Party Intermediary

(1) Bipolarity	U.S. not effective		U.S. effective		TOTAL	
Low level U.S. activity	21	56%	16	44%	37	80%
U.S. covert/semi-military	1	11%	8	89%	9	20%
TOTAL	22	48%	24	52%	46	100%

(2) Polycentrism						
Low level U.S. activity	38	60%	25	40%	63	66%
U.S. covert/semi-military	17	52%	16	48%	33	34%
TOTAL	55	57%	41	43%	96	100%

Part (1) X^2 = 6.04, p = .01; part (2) X^2 = .68, p = .41

TABLE IV.61c. USSR as Third-Party Intermediary

(1) Bipolarity	USSR not effective		USSR effective		TOTAL	
Low level USSR activity	22	71%	9	29%	31	70%
USSR covert/semi-military	11	79%	2	21%	13	30%
TOTAL	33	75%	11	25%	44	100%

(2) Polycentrism						
Low level USSR activity	39	82%	8	18%	47	58%
USSR covert/semi-military	25	78%	9	22%	34	42%
TOTAL	64	79%	17	21%	81	100%

Part (1) X^2 = .91, p = .34; part (2) X^2 = 1.06, p = .30

Europe. By contrast, low-level great power activity was deemed to have been effective at a 74% rate, including seven crises in which such activity was the most important contributor to crisis abatement: **Teschen** 1919–20, **Burgenland Dispute** 1921, **Ruhr II** 1924, **Vilna II** 1927, **Shanghai** 1932, **Italian Threat to France** 1938–39, **Danzig** 1939.

The data for the United States and the Soviet Union (Tables IV.61b and IV.61c) in the post–World War II era present quite a different picture. The transition from the multipolar system with seven great powers to bipolarity involved a considerable shift in patterns of activity. For the U.S. during bipolarity, there is a strong positive relationship between level of activity and effectiveness—just the opposite of the finding for the great powers during multipolarity. In bipolarity, although the U.S. engaged in what we have classified as high-level third-party activity in only 20% of the cases in which it became involved, that activity was effective in crisis abatement eight out of nine times, including **Kars Ardahan** 1945–46, **Costa Rica/Nicaragua II** 1955, **Jordan Regime** 1957, **Abortive Coup—Indonesia** 1958, **Central America/Cuba I** 1959, **Central America/Cuba II** 1960, **China/India Border II** 1962–63, **Yemen War I** 1962–63. The single failed case of U.S. high-level involvement was **Invasion of Laos I** 1953.

In polycentrism, while the rate of U.S. high-level activity in crises increased to 34%, the proportion of cases in which such high-level activity was effective dropped from 89% for bipolarity to 48% for polycentrism. In fact, low-level and high-level U.S. activity were almost indistinguishable in terms of their effectiveness.

For the USSR in the postwar era, the data revealed virtually no relationship between level of activity and effectiveness. Effectiveness rates were far below those of the U.S., averaging about 22% of crises in which the USSR became involved.[72]

Our final cut on third-party effectiveness in crises will focus on regional differences. As Table IV.62a shows, 56% of all international crises in which great powers became involved as third parties in the interwar period were located in Europe, with the great powers exhibiting effectiveness in roughly half of those cases (19 of 36).

The international system underwent dramatic change in the post–World War II era (see Tables IV.62b and IV.62c), with European crises constituting only 24% of all cases in which the U.S. became active in bipolarity and only 10% in polycentrism. Comparable figures for the USSR are 14% for bipolarity and 5% for polycentrism. The new realities of polycentrism, including the sharp rise in

TABLE IV.62a.   Great Power Effectiveness as Intermediary, by Region

	Great powers not effective		Great powers effective		TOTAL	
Africa	1	50%	1	50%	2	3%
Americas	1	12%	7	88%	8	12.5%
Asia	7	70%	3	30%	10	16%
Europe	17	47%	19	53%	36	56%
Middle East	5	62%	3	38%	8	12.5%
TOTAL	31	48%	33	52%	64	100%

$X^2 = 6.66, p = .16$

TABLE IV.62b.   U.S. Effectiveness as Intermediary, by Region

(1) Bipolarity	U.S. not effective		U.S. effective		TOTAL	
Africa	2	50%	2	50%	4	9%
Americas	0	0%	6	100%	6	13%
Asia	4	31%	9	69%	13	28%
Europe	10	91%	1	9%	11	24%
Middle East	6	50%	6	50%	12	26%
TOTAL	22	48%	24	52%	46	100%

(2) Polycentrism						
Africa	26	70%	11	30%	37	38.5%
Americas	3	21%	11	79%	14	15%
Asia	9	75%	3	25%	12	12.5%
Europe	5	50%	5	50%	10	10%
Middle East	12	58%	11	42%	23	24%
TOTAL	55	57%	41	43%	96	100%

Part (1) X^2 = 15.23, p = .00; part (2) X^2 = 11.91, p = .02

TABLE IV.62c.   USSR Effectiveness as Intermediary, by Region

(1) Bipolarity	USSR not effective		USSR effective		TOTAL	
Africa	3	100%	0	0%	3	7%
Americas	2	67%	1	33%	3	7%
Asia	12	60%	8	40%	20	45%
Europe	6	100%	0	0%	6	14%
Middle East	10	83%	2	17%	12	27%
TOTAL	33	75%	11	25%	44	100%

(2) Polycentrism						
Africa	27	90%	3	10%	30	37%
Americas	4	67%	2	33%	6	7%
Asia	15	75%	5	25%	20	25%
Europe	3	75%	1	25%	4	5%
Middle East	15	71%	6	29%	21	26%
TOTAL	64	79%	17	21%	81	100%

Part (1) X^2 = 5.96, p = .20; part (2) X^2 = 3.70, p = .45

the number of African crises, are reflected in heightened activity rates for both superpowers (almost all of this activity was low-level), but low effectiveness rates (30% for the U.S., 10% for the USSR). While activity levels for the superpowers in Africa were on the rise, the data show a decline in activity rates for Asia, accompanied by a sharp decline in effectiveness as well. Finally, it is worth noting that the Americas remain a region in which U.S. activity has been consistently effective in crisis abatement (100% for bipolarity, 79% for polycentrism).

Summary: Major Powers as Third Parties in International Crises

International crisis data for the twentieth century show that the great powers of the multipolar system were considerably more likely than their superpower counterparts in the post–World War II era to have been involved as both actors and intermediaries in international crises. This finding reflects the larger number of great power actors in multipolarity, the smaller number of states in that system-period, and the European locus of most of the crises of that era.

A close examination of the superpowers as actors and intermediaries reveals the great care with which the U.S. and the USSR interacted on the global stage. While half of all international crises exhibited both U.S. and USSR activity, they were almost never active at a high level simultaneously. In fact, there were only four crises—**Berlin Blockade** 1948–49, **Korean War II** 1950–51, **Berlin Wall** 1961, and **Iraq No-Fly Zone** 1992—in which both superpowers were involved militarily, and in the last case the U.S. and Russia entered on the same side.

Level of activity by great powers as intermediaries was inversely related to effectiveness during multipolarity, positively related during bipolarity for the U.S., and unrelated to effectiveness for the USSR.

Finally, the data on geographic region and crisis activity and effectiveness reflect the decline in the centrality of Europe in terms of both activity and effectiveness, and the rise of Africa in the polycentric system, although effectiveness in Africa remained at a low point for both superpowers.

Conclusions

Part IV presents an analysis of international crises from the perspective of seven key contextual attributes of the international system and its member-states: **polarity** and **geography** as fundamental structural characteristics in which international crises unfold; **ethnicity** and **regime type (democracy/nondemocracy)** as constraints and influences on decision making in crisis; the **conflict setting** and **extent of violence** as criteria by which the international community judges the potential danger a crisis poses for the system as a whole; and **third-party intervention** as a potential response by the system and its actors. Each of these contextual attributes was examined with data on international crises spanning almost the entire twentieth century. Each of the seven sections concludes with a summary of key findings pertaining to the more than 50 hypotheses examined in this study. Our final task is to explore the significance of these empirical findings for the international system as it approaches the beginning of the twenty-first century.

The turn of the century coincides with the emergence of a new international system, the outlines of which are just beginning to crystallize. With the end of the Cold War and the demise of the Soviet Union, the United States has emerged (perhaps somewhat reluctantly) as the dominant—some would argue hegemonic—power in the international system. The record of crises in the twentieth century attests to the destabilizing characteristics of polycentrism and the relatively stabilizing influences of bipolarity. If the international system is indeed headed toward a period of unipolarity, is it likely to be less crisis prone than earlier systems? Does the fact that the system managed the transition from polycentrism to unipolarity without an international catastrophe similar to the one that accompanied the end of multipolarity in 1939 signal a maturing of the international system and its actors and institutions? It could be argued that, if the U.S. accepts the mantle of hegemony, with the interventions and international peacekeeping involvements which this entails, we might expect the current unipolar system to resemble bipolarity in terms of the relative control that the major powers managed to maintain, despite the periodic eruptions of the system and its subsystems.

ICB research has revealed a basic change over time in the locus of crises in the twentieth century. We have carefully documented a shift from Europe, the center of crises during multipolarity (1918–39), to the Third World in general, and to Africa in particular, since the end of World War II. Structurally, this change has been accompanied by a decline in crises at the dominant system level and an increase within subsystems. Moreover, contiguous crisis actors were more

874

likely to experience and employ violence in their crises. Not surprisingly, great powers and superpowers, with the widest global reach, were most likely to be involved in crises far from their borders. Global reach will continue to be an important factor in the twenty-first century, with the U.S. clearly the only power at present capable of effective intervention in crises far from its borders. And while polycentrism was characterized by the predominance of crises on the geopolitical periphery, the disquieting signals from the republics of the former Yugoslavia and the former Soviet Union point to the outbreak of many critical crises in the geopolitical near-core.

Is ethnicity the emerging international social force of the twenty-first century, as suggested by its close association with some high visibility crises of the post–Cold War era; or is its current high profile likely to pass once the international system and its member-states make the accommodations necessary to recognize its roots and cope with its demands? ICB data point to a relatively steady rate of crises with ethnic dimensions throughout the twentieth century, but some of their unique characteristics bear watching: crises with ethnic dimensions, particularly if they occur within protracted conflicts, are particularly susceptible to escalating violence, undoubtedly attributable to the high level of perpetual hostility existing among the adversaries. These crises are also characterized by very high levels of threat perception, particularly when territorial issues are involved. And crises with ethnic dimensions are characterized by a high rate of dissatisfaction with the terms of the agreements that are often associated with their termination, that is, they are poised for subsequent and serious eruptions. International organizations have generally been more involved and more effective as intermediaries in ethnic crises than have been the major powers.

Just as the international relations literature has found a strong general link between democracy and peace, so too, ICB research has confirmed this link among states involved in international crises: the higher the proportion of democracies among the adversarial actors in a crisis, the less likely it is that violence will be employed in crisis management; and, when employed, the less likely it is that such violence will escalate to a high level. If, as some would argue, the end of the Cold War and the breakup of the Soviet Union are evidence of the victory of democracy over totalitarianism, then the findings reported here should foreshadow an era of less frequent and less serious crises.

Left unanswered in the euphoria over the emergence of new democracies in virtually every corner of the globe is the question of whether a system dominated by a plurality of democracies will exhibit the same "peaceful" tendencies that were associated with democracies when they were relatively few in number. At issue, too, is the question of exactly what democracy is; that is, are free elections a sufficient indicator, or do we still need the tradition of democratic norms, to go along with the trappings of democratic structure, to reap the stabilizing benefits seemingly associated with democracy?

The majority of twentieth-century international crises occurred in the context of an ongoing protracted conflict. These crises were more likely than others to have been triggered by violence, to involve the perception of grave threat, and to entail the use of violence in crisis management. Despite these indicators of seriousness, the international community has been unable to deal with these crises effectively, either through its international organizations or through the actions of its major powers. The end of the twentieth century is exhibiting a flurry of third-party activity around some high-profile protracted conflicts—most notably the Arab/Israel conflict—but others go on either unattended or in spite of international and regional efforts. Protracted conflicts and the crises that they spawn are likely to be with us into the next century, with lessons concerning effective coping mechanisms insufficiently learned.

A great deal has been learned about the role of violence in international crises. Polycentrism was particularly susceptible to violence in both triggers and crisis management. Regions differed in terms of the extent and severity of violence. At the same time, regardless of region, contiguity was a strong predictor of violence among crisis adversaries. As noted, ethnicity, too, was a strong predictor of violence in crisis. Democracy among crisis adversaries dampened the tendency toward the use of violence in crisis management. And the more protracted the conflict in which a crisis was embedded, the more likely it was for the trigger to be violent and for actors to have employed violence in crisis management. Finally, decision maker stress, societal unrest, and power discrepancy among adversaries all contribute to the likelihood that violence in crises will escalate. How the international system of the twenty-first century goes about handling some of these key contributing factors to violence will be crucial in determining whether its crises will differ significantly from those of earlier systems.

Finally, what is the prognosis for crisis management by international organizations and major powers? We have observed an evolution in global organization involvement in international crises accompanying important structural changes in the system: while the Security Council has consistently accounted for roughly two-thirds of international organization activity, the role of the General Assembly declined during polycentrism, while that of the Secretary-General was enhanced. The post–Cold War unipolar system provides some preliminary evidence of a reinvigorated role for the Security Council, but time will tell whether this increased activity will be accompanied by greater effectiveness. Great powers during multipolarity were far more likely to become involved in international crises than the two superpowers during bipolarity and polycentrism. Indeed, a close examination of the superpowers as actors and intermediaries reveals the great care with which they interacted in the global arena—the U.S. and the USSR were almost never involved in the same crisis at a high level simultaneously. How the U.S. chooses to adapt its foreign policy to the new realities of the unipolar international system will have enormous import for the stability of that system. As that government picks and chooses its interventions strategically— Haiti and Bosnia but not Rwanda or Liberia—the system will experience either enhanced or diminished crisis activity.

Overall, we have endeavored to provide a framework within which crises and protracted conflicts can be examined from a comparative perspective. Although we have provided a panorama of crises in the twentieth century, we have not provided answers to all questions about crises. Hopefully, foreign policy decision makers will learn from this multidimensional research as they endeavor to avoid repeating the mistakes of the past. For the scholarly community, we have tried to strengthen the tradition of cumulation of knowledge in the crucial domain of crisis and conflict, and particularly with regard to the seven key themes that have guided this analysis.

Notes to Part IV

1. The greater stability of a bipolar structure was also argued by Riker (1962:182–87) and Zoppo (1966:601).

2. Prior to the explicit phase of the debate on polarity and stability, Morgenthau (1948:271–72) had noted that the possibility of more—and changing—coalitions contributed to stability through uncertainty, just as a balancer in a multipolar system could maintain or restore a viable balance of power by appropriate behavior, in its own interests, as well as those of adversarial states or coalitions. Wright (1942:755) and Gulick (1955:94–95), arguing in a similar vein, and Masters (1961:789) also supported multipolarity.

3. Other mixed models include Hanrieder's (1965) **heterosymmetrical bipolarity,** Hoffmann's (1968:21–46; 356–64) **multihierarchical system,** Young's (1968) **discontinuities** model, and Spiegel's (1972:127–28) **bimodal** structure.

4. The various types of polarity and contributions to the literature after the initial debate were discussed in Part I.

5. The period 1939–45 was essentially a self-contained transition from the multipolar system of the 1920s and 1930s to the bipolar system after 1945; that is, it exhibited many centers of decision, resembling the former, along with intense intercoalitional conflict and intracoalitional cohesion, like the latter.

6. Others who have tackled this issue with wider definitions of system stability include Gochman and Maoz (1984), Midlarsky (1988, 1991), and Pearson and Baumann (1988).

7. Twenty-one international crises occurred during the unipolar international system—1990–94. Due to their small number, and the lack of well-developed theory relating the attributes of late twentieth-century unipolarity to stability, we do not include these cases in our general empirical examination of polarity and stability.

8. A half decade seemed to the ICB researchers to be a reasonable span of time to assume that a crisis eruption is a direct outgrowth of a previous crisis between the same parties.

9. The findings on the average number of crises per year are not weighted by the number of states in the global system at any point in time. The rationale derives from competing hypotheses in the bipolarity/multipolarity literature; that is, that the larger number of states in the system is likely to induce more/less conflict.

10. In order to provide as complete a picture as possible on crises in the twentieth century, Figure IV.3 includes all 412 international crises: intra-war crises, World War II cases, and the 21 unipolarity crises.

11. For a discussion of the ICB procedures for updating previously coded cases, see Part II.

12. Table IV.1 shows that as the number of states in the system grew, so too did the number of states involved in crises and the number of crises. In fact, with an average of 76 states in multipolarity, 84 in bipolarity, and 150 in polycentrism, the actual probability of a state being involved in a crisis in any given year varied only slightly from one system to

the next. This, in turn, prevents us from drawing any conclusions about the relative crisis proneness of systems, other than to point out that regardless of other factors, polycentrism shows the largest number of crises per year.

While size of system—number of states in a system—clearly has a bearing on the number of states potentially involved in crisis and the number of potential crises, there is no a priori reason to expect these factors to influence the nature of the crises themselves. That is, such characteristics of crises as triggers, threat to values, extent of violence, and crisis outcomes should not be affected by the relative frequency of crises in the four system-periods. The number of actors in the system should not affect the distribution of cases across categories of variables. Therefore, a control for system size in subsequent analyses is not deemed necessary.

13. It could be argued that instability for a system results both from the level of stress *and* the ability of states to act on that stress. The lack of autonomy to act on stress during bipolarity explains its accumulation within that system. The authors are grateful to Patrick James for this insight.

14. The "Third-Party Intervention" section that follows deals explicitly with the major powers as third-party intermediaries in crises. The reader is referred to that section for a more complete discussion of this aspect of the analysis.

15. Issues surrounding the concept of territoriality and its impact on conflict and crisis are beyond the scope of the present analysis. Nevertheless, the territorial factor is addressed in the ICB variable TERRDISP, available with the rest of the ICB data sets.

16. In the previous section on polarity, the number of international crises was 307. That set excluded all crises that occurred between the outbreak and the termination of World War II, as well as all 21 unipolarity crises. In the present section, we include both the set of 21 unipolarity crises and also eight crises between 1939 and 1945 that were not intra-war crises. These eight crises were **Soviet Occupation—Baltic** 1939, **Finnish War** 1939–40, **Romanian Territory** 1940, **Ecuador/Peru Border II** 1941–42, **Iran–Oil Concessions** 1944, **Greek Civil War I** 1944–45, **Trieste I** 1945, and **French Forces/Syria** 1945.

17. Recall that intra-war crises, and hence virtually all of the crises in World War II, are excluded from these analyses.

18. The relatively small number of cases in the five-year span of the post–Cold War unipolar system under examination here precludes useful comparison.

19. It should be borne in mind that this analysis excludes intra-war crises; that is, the analysis assesses the extent to which violence occurred in crises that did not occur in the midst of an ongoing war.

20. Again, the reader is cautioned that intra-war crises are excluded from this analysis. Thus, all Vietnam War crises, with the exception of **Gulf of Tonkin** 1964, which initiated the war, were excluded.

21. A more complete discussion of global organization involvement can be found in the "Third-Party Intervention" section that follows.

22. Tables are not presented because of the lack of variation across the regions on these indicators.

23. For recent analyses of the circumstances under which states may react with violence to non-violent crisis triggers, see Wilkenfeld (1991), Hensel and Diehl (1994), James and Harvey (1992), Harvey (1995), Harvey and James (1996).

24. For an extended discussion of the concept of protracted conflict, see the "Protracted Conflict" section that follows.

25. See also Heraclides (1991) for an interesting treatment of external involvement in ethnic conflict.

26. The original Carment (1993) data set on ethnicity and crisis covered the period 1918–88; it was updated by the ICB Project through 1994.

27. Corollary questions, which are outside the scope of the present volume, include the following: (1) Has the impact of these crises on the international system been different from that of nonethnopolitical crises? (2) Have international systemic characteristics and dynamics impacted on the nature of ethnopolitical crises?

28. The concept of protracted conflict utilized in these analyses (see Part I) is different from Gurr's use of the term "protracted communal conflict," which refers obviously to the extent to which communal group members took part in antistate terrorism or rebellion over a sustained (at least 15-year) period (Gurr 1992).

29. Recently, the concept of "enduring rivalries" has received considerable attention in the international conflict literature (Goertz and Diehl 1992; Huth and Russett 1993). The concept of protracted conflict employed in the present study is closer in origin to that developed by Azar in his work on protracted social conflict (see Azar 1972; Azar et al. 1978). For a fuller discussion of the concept of protracted conflict, see Part I.

30. Hypothesis 24, on the effects of protracted conflict, has been alluded to frequently in the presentation of the Ethnicity-Crisis Model. It does not require separate attention here.

31. The figure of 35% cited earlier was based on the entire set of 412 international crises.

32. The data set that is being used to evaluate the model contains fewer ethnicity crises than that originally generated by Carment (1993a, 1993b). Furthermore, the original Carment coding has been updated by the ICB Project through 1994.

33. For a more comprehensive discussion of the concept of polarity as employed by the ICB Project, see Part I.

34. For the five years of unipolarity, the eight nonintra-war crises with ethnic dimensions were **Kashmir III–Nuclear** 1990, **Rwanda/Uganda** 1990–91, **Yugoslavia I— Croatia/Slovenia** 1991–92, **Nagorny-Karabakh** 1991–92, **Yugoslavia II—Bosnia** 1992–95, **Papua/Solomon** 1992, **Georgia/Abkhazia** 1992–93, **Cameroon/Nigeria III** 1993–94.

35. Since only three cases in the Americas were ethnicity related crises in the context of a protracted conflict, they will not be included in this and subsequent discussions of regional patterns.

36. Since there was only one post–Cold War ethnicity related crisis within a protracted conflict (**Kashmir III–Nuclear** 1990—**India/Pakistan PC**), that category will not be discussed here and in subsequent analyses in this section.

37. Since the analyses of geography and polarity did not produce any meaningful findings, these tables are not reproduced here.

38. A crucial, related question on outcome—when, that is, under what conditions, is an **international conflict,** as distinct from a crisis, most likely to end—remains unresolved. A recently developed concept, which has attracted much attention, is the notion of "ripe for resolution"; a conflict winds down and terminates only when the conditions are "ripe," notably intolerable fatigue by the conflicting parties (Zartman 1989; Haas 1990; Stedman 1991).

39. Rather than presenting another set of tables based on this revised formulation of ethnicity, we will present the results in summary form only.

40. We considered an alternative measure for DEM for this study. This measure was simply the overall proportion of democracies in the crisis with no regard to coalitional proportions. However, this measure had an important flaw. Without accounting for the coalitional proportion of democracies in the crisis, this measure was not tied explicitly to the theoretical dictates of the normative model. It is interesting to note, however, that this alternative measure correlates very highly with DEM (Pearson corr. = .986, p, .01; two-tailed test).

For yet another alternative index of democracy, see Dixon (1993:51).

41. Notice that there need not be democracies on each side of the crisis for DEM to increase. Although the normative model of democratic peace typically posits reciprocation as a necessary condition, our measure treats reciprocity as an important part of the puzzle but not a necessary condition. We comment again on this issue later in this section.

42. Crises of this nature include **Burma Infiltration** 1953–54 (between Burma and Taiwan); the crisis over **Qibya** in Jordan 1953 (between Israel and Jordan); **Guatemala** 1953–54 (among the U.S., Honduras, and Guatemala); and the **Chimoio-Tembue Raids** 1977–78 (between Mozambique and Rhodesia). Although violence occurred in these crises, non-violent crisis management techniques were the dominant means used by crisis actors.

43. An additional control for contiguity will be explored in future studies.

44. The McKelvey-Zavoina R^2 is a goodness-of-fit measure for logit and probit models. Like the R^2 statistic in OLS regression, the McKelvey-Zavoina R^2 statistic serves as a measure of the proportion of variance explained by the independent variables in the model. It should not be surprising to note that the McKelvey-Zavoina R^2 is relatively low for all of the models reported in Table IV.31. After all, we are not suggesting that these are complete models for explaining the occurrence of crisis violence. Rather, we use the models to focus only on the explanatory impact DEM has on the propensity for crises to result in violence.

45. See Dixon (1993) for the full description of this measure.

46. For additional discussion of the definitional issues relating to protracted conflict, see Azar (1979, 1985), Azar and Farah (1981), Brecher (1984), Brecher and Wilkenfeld (1989:chaps. 9–11), and Hewitt et al. (1991). It should be noted that the ICB definition of protracted conflict has dropped the condition of "sporadic outbreaks of open warfare." The concept of protracted conflict is related to, but not totally analogous to, the concept of "enduring rivalry," which has been dealt with extensively in the IR literature during the past several years—see, for example, Goertz and Diehl (1992a, 1992b), Huth and Russett (1993), Maoz and Russett (1993). For additional discussion of the ICB concept of protracted conflict, see Part I.

47. It could be argued that the crises involving the former republics of Yugoslavia since 1991 constitute protracted conflicts (many going back hundreds of years). However, we view the present phase of this important historical protracted conflict as beginning with the breakup of Yugoslavia a decade after the death of Tito in 1980.

48. In the tables that follow, the actor-level analyses are based on 895 cases, while the international-level analyses are based on 412 cases. In fact, due to sporadic missing data, the actual N's are somewhat lower.

49. A related variable used elsewhere in this volume to assess decision maker stress during a crisis also failed to differentiate between PC and non-PC crisis actors.

50. For the sake of brevity, we will verbally summarize the voluminous tabular material upon which these findings are based.

51. Of course, there were seven great powers in the interwar period, operating in a much smaller international system, so their higher rate of involvement is not unexpected.

52. The remaining 12 international crises in Table IV.48 occurred before the League of Nations came into existence or during World War II, when the League was moribund; the UN did not yet exist.

53. For the analyses of VIOL, CRISMG, SEVVIOSY, and CENVIOSY, where the focus is on violence in the crisis as a characteristic of the crisis as a whole, intra-war crises are excluded.

54. A number of additional studies have focused on other aspects of the action-reaction dynamic in conflict behavior in general, and crisis situations in particular: Bobrow (1982), Howell (1983), Hybel and Robertson (1978), Leng (1984, 1993a, 1993b), Leng and Walker (1982), Levy (1989) and Phillips (1973).

55. While all foreign policy crises are presumed to exhibit some degree of threat to decision makers' basic values and hence stress, crises vary according to the level of such threat.

56. For a more extended discussion of stress and crisis behavior, see Wilkenfeld, Brecher, and Hill (1989); for a discussion of the general impact of stress on foreign policy behavior, see Brecher (1993), Holsti (1965).

57. The literature on crisis bargaining also focuses on the notion of matching or reciprocity. Thus, Gochman and Leng (1983:101) proposed the following hypothesis: "The relative military-industrial capabilities of disputants are associated with the degree of reciprocity that characterizes interstate bargaining in militarized disputes. Bargaining among adversaries of relatively equal capabilities is more likely to be reciprocal in nature than is bargaining among unevenly matched adversaries." See also Leng (1983, 1993a, 1993b).

58. For a full discussion of the indicators of stress, sociopolitical conditions, and power relations, see Part II.

59. Claude (1964), David Davies Institute (1972), Eagleton (original 1932, revised 1957), Falk and Mendlovitz (1966), Goodspeed (1967), Henkin (1968), James (1969), Nicholas (1971), Stone (original 1954, revised 1973).

60. Bercovitch (1992), Bercovitch and Rubin (1992), Bercovitch and Rubin (1993), Butterworth (1976), Finlayson and Zacher (1980), E. Haas (1983, 1986), Haas et al. (1972), Hewitt (1996), Mitchell and Webb (1988), Pelcovits and Kramer (1976), Pricen (1992), Touval (1992), Touval and Zartman (1985), Young (1967), Zacher (1979), Zartman (1989), Zartman and Touval (1985).

61. We do not consider the role of regional and security organizations in the present volume, due to the generally small number of cases in which such intervention took place. However, the ICB data sets do contain information on these cases (see list of variables in Part II), which can be particularly helpful in the analysis of certain regional conflicts and crises.

62. In earlier treatments of global organization effectiveness, cases where the global organization was deemed to have been only marginally effective were not included in the overall effectiveness score (see Wilkenfeld and Brecher 1984; Brecher and Wilkenfeld 1989).

63. While a correlation coefficient is not necessarily the most efficient measure of association for time series data, it is employed here largely to supplement what is visually obvious.

64. Finlayson and Zacher (1980) suggest that alignment configuration is an important factor in determining whether or not the UN will become involved in a particular crisis. In essence, they suggest that the one type of conflict that is most likely to evoke UN attention is that involving threats or acts of force by aligned against nonaligned states. While we find this notion intriguing, its implications are beyond the scope of the present analysis.

65. Both measures utilized here provide data on the highest level of activity by any of the great powers or superpowers in an international crisis.

66. In the interests of saving space, a decision was made to exclude the voluminous tabular material upon which the following discussion is based.

67. Overall, only four additional international crises during the entire 76-year period showed the Secretary-General to have been effective in crisis management: **Cambodia/Thailand** 1958–59, **West Irian II** 1961–62, and **Cuban Missiles** 1962 during bipolarity; and **North Korea Nuclear Crisis** 1993–94, in the post–Cold War unipolar system.

68. There were four crises for which there were missing data on one or more of the variables examined here.

69. Dawisha (1984) also supports at least some of these assertions in her study of Soviet intervention in Czechoslovakia in 1968. She states that Romania and Yugoslavia both felt that one of the main reasons the USSR intervened during the **Prague Spring** crisis was because it perceived the risk of Western military counteraction to be negligible.

70. Due to a paucity of crises in which either superpower engaged in direct military activity when it was not itself a crisis actor (one crisis in bipolarity and two during polycentrism), direct military activity was merged with semi-military and covert activity for the analyses of superpower activity and effectiveness.

71. In the post–Cold War unipolar system, there were only nine crises with U.S. third-party activity and only three with Russian third-party activity. These small numbers precluded meaningful statistical analysis, and they are excluded in the subsequent analysis.

72. In fact, further analysis reveals that USSR activity actually exacerbated crises in 13% of the cases, compared to an exacerbation rate of 6% for the U.S.. Among these USSR cases were **Kars-Ardahan** 1945–46, **Turkish Straits** 1946, **Greek Civil War II** 1946–47, **Guatemala** 1953–54, **Congo I–Katanga** 1960–62, **Shaba I, II** 1977, 1978.

BIBLIOGRAPHY

References for Preface and Parts I, II, and IV

Adomeit, Hannes. *Soviet Risk-Taking and Crisis Behavior: A Theoretical and Empirical Analysis.* London: Allen & Unwin, 1982.

Allan, Pierre. *Crisis Bargaining and the Arms Race: A Theoretical Model.* Cambridge, MA: Ballinger, 1983.

Allison, Graham T. *The Essence of Decision: Explaining the Cuban Missile Crisis.* Boston, MA: Little, Brown, 1971.

———. "Conceptual Models and the Cuban Missile Crisis." *American Political Science Review* 63 (September 1969): 689–718.

Andriole, Stephen J. "The Levels of Analysis Problems and the Study of Foreign, International and Global Affairs: A Review Critique and Another Final Solution." *International Interactions* 5, nos. 2–3 (1978): 113–33.

Andriole, Stephen J., Jonathan Wilkenfeld, and Gerald W. Hopple. "A Framework for the Comparative Analysis of Foreign Policy Behavior." *International Studies Quarterly* 19, no. 2 (1975): 160–98.

Anglin, Douglas G. *Zambian Crisis Behaviour: Confronting Rhodesia's Unilateral Declaration of Independence, 1965–66.* Montreal and Kingston: McGill-Queen's University Press, 1994.

Axell, Karin. "States in Armed Conflict 1992." Uppsala, Sweden: Report No. 36, Department of Peace and Conflict Research, Uppsala University, 1993.

Axelrod, Robert. *The Evolution of Cooperation.* New York: Basic Books, 1984.

Azar, Edward E. "Protracted International Conflicts: Ten Propositions." *International Interactions* 12, no. 1 (1985): 59–70.

———. "Peace amidst Development: A Conceptual Agenda for Conflict and Peace Research." *International Interactions* 6, no. 2 (1979): 123–43.

———. "Conflict Escalation and Conflict Reduction in an International Crisis: Suez, 1956." *Journal of Conflict Resolution* 16, no. 2 (1972): 183–201.

Azar, Edward E., and N. Farah. "The Structure of Inequalities in Protracted Social Conflicts: A Theoretical Framework." *International Interactions* 7, no. 4 (1981): 317–35.

Azar, Edward E., Paul Jureidini, and Ronald McLaurin. "Protracted Social Conflict: Theory and Practice in the Middle East." *Journal of Palestine Studies* 8, no. 1 (1978): 41–60.

Bercovitch, Jacob. "The Structure and Diversity of Mediation in International Relations." In *Mediation in International Relations: Multiple Approaches to Conflict Management,* edited by Jacob Bercovitch and Jeffrey Z. Rubin, 1–29. New York: St. Martin's Press, 1992.

Bercovitch, Jacob, and Jeffrey Langley. "The Nature of the Dispute and the Effectiveness of International Mediation." *Journal of Conflict Resolution* 37, no. 4 (1993): 670–91.

Bercovitch, Jacob, and Jeffrey Z. Rubin, eds. *Mediation in International Relations: Multiple Approaches to Conflict Management.* New York: St. Martin's Press, 1992.

Blechman, Barry M. "The Impact of Israel's Reprisals on Behavior of the Bordering Arab Nations Directed at Israel." *Journal of Conflict Resolution* 16, no. 2 (1972): 155–81.

Blechman, Barry M., and Stephen S. Kaplan, *Force without War: U.S. Armed Forces as a Political Instrument*. Washington, DC: Brookings Institution, 1978.

Bobrow, Davis B. "Uncoordinated Giants." In *Sage International Yearbook of Foreign Policy Studies*, vol. 7, edited by Charles W. Kegley, Jr. and Pat McGowan, 23–49. Beverly Hills, CA: Sage, 1982.

———. "The Perspective of Great Power Foreign Policy." In *Dynamics of Third Party Intervention: Kissinger and the Middle East*, edited by J. Rubin. New York: Praeger, 1981.

Boulding, Kenneth E. "General Systems Theory—The Skeleton of Science." *Management Science* 2 (1956): 197–208.

Bouthoul, Gaston, and René Carrère. *Le Défi de la Guerre, 1749–1974*. Paris: Presses Universitaires de France, 1976.

Brady, Linda P. "Threat, Decision Time and Awareness: The Impact of Situational Variables on Foreign Policy Behavior." Ph.D. diss., Ohio State University, 1974.

Brams, Steven J. *Theory of Moves*. New York: Cambridge University Press, 1994.

Brams, Steven J., and E. Marc Kilgour. *Game Theory and National Security*. New York: Basil Blackwell, 1988.

Brecher, Michael. *Crises in World Politics: Theory and Reality*. Oxford: Pergamon Press, 1993.

———. "International Crises and Protracted Conflicts." *International Interactions* 11, no. 3 (1984): 237–97.

———. "State Behavior in International Crisis: A Model." *Journal of Conflict Resolution* 23, no. 3 (1979a): 446–80.

———, ed. *Studies in Crisis Behavior*. New Brunswick, NJ: Transaction Books, 1979b.

———. "International Relations and Asian Studies: The Subordinate State System of Southern Asia." *World Politics* 15 (January 1963): 213–35.

Brecher, Michael, and Hemda Ben Yehuda. "System and Crisis in International Politics." *Review of International Studies* 11, no. 1 (1985): 17–36.

Brecher, Michael, with Benjamin Geist. *Decisions in Crisis: Israel, 1967 and 1973*. Berkeley, CA: University of California Press, 1980.

Brecher, Michael, and Patrick James. *Crisis and Change in World Politics*. Boulder, CO: Westview Press, 1986.

Brecher, Michael, Patrick James, and Jonathan Wilkenfeld. "Polarity and Stability: New Concepts, Indicators and Evidence." *International Interactions*. 16, no. 1 (1990): 49–80.

Brecher, Michael, Blema Steinberg, and Janice Stein. "A Framework for Research on Foreign Policy Behavior." *Journal of Conflict Resolution* 13, no. 1 (1969): 75–101.

Brecher, Michael, and Jonathan Wilkenfeld. "International Crises and Global Instability: the Myth of the 'Long Peace.'" In *The Long Postwar Peace*, edited by Charles W. Kegley, Jr., 85–104. New York: HarperCollins, 1991.

———. *Crisis, Conflict and Instability*. Oxford: Pergamon Press, 1989.

———. *Crises in the Twentieth Century*. Vol. 1, Handbook of International Crises. Oxford: Pergamon Press, 1988.

Bremer, Stuart A. "Democracy and Militarized Interstate Conflict, 1816–1965." *International Interactions* 18, no. 3 (1993): 231–49.

————. "Dangerous Dyads: Conditions Affecting the Likelihood of Interstate War, 1816–1965." *Journal of Conflict Resolution* 36, 2 (1992): 309–41.

————. "The Contagiousness of Coercion: The Spread of Serious International Disputes, 1900–1976." *International Interactions* 9, 1 (1982): 29–55.

Bueno de Mesquita, Bruce. "The War Trap Revisited: A Revised Expected Utility Model." *American Political Science Review* 79, no. 1 (1985): 156–77.

————. *The War Trap.* New Haven, CT: Yale University Press, 1981.

————. "Systemic Polarization and the Occurrence and Duration of War." *Journal of Conflict Resolution* 22, no. 2 (1978): 241–67.

————. "Measuring Systemic Polarity." *Journal of Conflict Resolution* 19, no. 2 (1975): 187–216.

Bueno de Mesquita, Bruce, and David Lalman. *War and Reason: Domestic and International Imperatives.* New Haven, CT: Yale University Press, 1992.

Butterworth, Robert L. *Managing Interstate Conflict, 1945–74: Data with Synopses.* Pittsburgh, PA: University of Pittsburgh, 1976.

C.A.C.I. "Analysis of the Soviet Crisis Management Experience: Technical Report." Arlington, VA: Defense Advanced Research Projects Agency, C.A.C.I. No. N00014-77-C-0135, 1978.

Cannizzo, Cynthia. "Capability Distribution and Major-Power War Experience, 1816–1965." *Orbis* 21, no. 4 (1978): 947–57.

Carment, David. "The International Politics of Ethnic Conflict: The Interstate Dimensions of Secession and Irredenta in the Twentieth Century, A Crisis-Based Approach." Ph.D. Diss. McGill University, Montreal, 1993a.

————. "The International Dimensions of Ethnic Conflict: Concepts, Indicators, and Theory." *Journal of Peace Research* 30, no. 2 (1993b): 137–50.

Carment, David, and Patrick James. "Internal Constraints and Interstate Ethnic Conflict." *Journal of Conflict Resolution* 39, no. 1 (1995): 82–109.

Carr, Edward H. *The Twenty Years' Crisis, 1919–1939.* London and New York: Macmillan, 1939.

Carroll, Berenice A. "How Wars End: An Analysis of Some Current Hypotheses." *Journal of Peace Research* 4 (1969): 295–321.

Chan, Steve. "Democracy and War: Some Thoughts on a Future Research Agenda." *International Interactions* 18, no. 3 (1993): 205–13.

————. "Mirror, Mirror, on the Wall . . . Are the Freer Countries More Pacific?" *Journal of Conflict Resolution* 28, no. 4 (1984): 345–369.

Chazan, Naomi, ed. *Irredentism and International Politics.* Boulder, CO: Lynne Reinner, 1991.

Claude, Inis L. Jr. *Swords into Plowshares: The Problems and Progress of International Organization.* 3rd ed. New York: Random House, 1964.

————. *Power and International Relations.* New York: Random House, 1962.

Cobb, Roger W., and Charles Elder. *International Community: A Regional and Global Study.* New York: Holt, Rinehart, & Winston, 1970.

Cohen, Raymond. "Pacific Unions. A Reappraisal of the Theory that 'Democracies Do Not Go to War with Each Other'." *Review of International Studies* 20 (July 1994): 207–23.

Coser, Lewis. *The Functions of Social Conflict.* New York: Free Press, 1956.

Cusack, Thomas R., and Wolf-Dieter Eberwein. "Prelude to War: Incidence, Escalation and Intervention in International Disputes, 1900–1976." *International Interactions* 5, no. 1 (1982): 9–28.

David Davies Memorial Institute of International Studies. *International Disputes: The Legal Aspects.* London: Europa Publications, 1972.

Dawisha, Adeed I. *Syria and the Lebanese Crisis.* London: Macmillan, 1980.

Dawisha, Karen. *The Kremlin and the Prague Spring.* Berkeley, CA: University of California Press, 1984.

Deitchman, Seymour J. *Limited War and American Defense Policy.* Washington, DC: Institute of Defense Analysis, 1964.

Deutsch, Karl W. *Politics and Government.* 2d ed. Boston, MA: Houghton Mifflin, 1974.

Deutsch, Karl W., and J. David Singer. "Multipolar Power Systems and International Stability." *World Politics* 16, no. 3 (1964): 390–406.

Diehl, Paul. "Geography and War: A Review and Assessment of the Empirical Literature." *International Interactions* 17 (1991): 11–27.

———. "Contingency and Military Escalation in Major Power Rivalries, 1816–1980." *Journal of Politics* 47 (1985): 1203–11.

Diehl, Paul, and Gary Goertz. "Territorial Changes and Militarized Conflict." *Journal of Conflict Resolution* 32, 1 (1988): 103–22.

Dixon, William J. "Democracy and the Peaceful Settlement of International Conflict." *American Political Science Review* 88, no. 1 (1994): 14–32.

———. "Democracy and the Management of International Conflict." *Journal of Conflict Resolution,* 37, no. 1 (1993): 42–68.

Domke, William K. *War and the Changing Global System.* New Haven, CT: Yale University Press, 1988.

Donelan, Michael D., and M. J. Grieve. *International Disputes: Case Histories, 1945–1970.* London: Europa Publications, 1973.

Dowty, Alan. *Middle East Crisis: U.S. Decision Making in 1958, 1970, and 1973.* Berkeley, CA: University of California Press, 1984.

Doyle, Michael W. "Liberalism and World Politics." *American Political Science Review* 80, no. 4 (1986): 1151–69.

Eagleton, Clyde. *International Government.* New York: Ronald Press, 1932, 3d ed. 1957.

East, Maurice A. "Size and Foreign Policy Behavior: A Test of Two Models." *World Politics* 25 (July 1973): 556–76.

East, Maurice A., and Charles F. Hermann. "Do Nation-Types Account for Foreign Policy Behavior?" In *Comparing Foreign Policies: Theories, Findings and Methods,* edited by James N. Rosenau, 269–303. New York: John Wiley, 1974.

Eckhardt, William, and Edward E. Azar. "Major World Conflicts and Interventions, 1945 to 1975." *International Interactions* 5, no. 1 (1978): 75–110.

Ember, Carol, Melvin Ember, and Bruce Russett. "Peace between Participatory Polities: A Cross-Cultural Test of the 'Democracies Rarely Fight Each Other' Hypothesis." *World Politics* 44, no. 4 (1992): 573–99.

Falk, Richard A., and Saul H. Mendlovitz, eds. *The Strategy of World Order.* Vol. 3, *The United Nations.* New York: World Law Fund, 1966.

Finlayson, J. A., and Mark W. Zacher. *The United Nations and Collective Security: Retrospect and Prospect.* United Nations Association of America, 1980.

Frei, Daniel, ed. *Managing International Crises.* Beverly Hills, CA: Sage, 1982.

Gaddis, John L. "Great Illusions, the Long Peace, and the Future of the International

System." Chap. 2 in *The Long Post War Peace,* edited by Charles W. Kegley Jr. New York: HarperCollins, 1991.

———. *The Long Peace.* New York: Oxford University Press, 1987.

———. "The Long Peace: Elements of Stability in the Post War International System." *International Security* 10, no. 4 (1986): 99–142.

Garnham, David. "The Causes of War: Systemic Findings." Chap. 2 in *Polarity and War,* edited by A. Ned Sabrosky. Boulder, CO: Westview Press, 1985.

Geller, Daniel, and Daniel M. Jones. "The Effect of Dynamic and Static Balances on Conflict Escalation in Rival Dyads." Paper presented at the annual meeting, American Political Science Association, 1991.

George, Alexander L., ed. *Avoiding War: Problems of Crisis Management.* Boulder, CO: Westview Press, 1991.

———. *Managing U.S.-Soviet Rivalry.* Boulder, CO: Westview Press, 1983.

———. *Presidential Decisionmaking in Foreign Policy: The Effective Use of Information and Advice.* Boulder, CO: Westview Press, 1980.

George, Alexander L., and Richard Smoke. *Deterrence in American Foreign Policy: Theory and Practice.* New York: Columbia University Press, 1974.

Ghoshal, U. N. "The System of Inter-State Relations and Foreign Policy in the Early Arthasastra State." *India Antiqua.* Leiden: E. J. Brill, 1947.

Gilpin, Robert. *War and Change in World Politics.* New York: Cambridge University Press, 1981.

Gleditsch, Nils P. "Geography, Democracy, and Peace." *International Interactions.* 20, no. 4 (1995): 297–323.

———. "Democracy and Peace." *Journal of Peace Research* 29, no. 4 (1992): 369–76.

Gleditsch, Nils P. and J. David Singer. "Distance and International War, 1816–1965." In *Proceedings of the International Peace Research Association Fifth General Conference.* Oslo: International Peace Research Association, 1975.

Gochman, Charles S. "The Geography of Conflict: Militarized Interstate Disputes since 1918." Paper presented at the annual meeting, International Studies Association, Washington, DC, 1990.

Gochman, Charles S., and Russell J. Leng. "Realpolitik and the Road to War." *International Studies Quarterly* 27, no. 1 (1983): 97–120.

Gochman, Charles S., and Zeev Maoz. "Militarized Interstate Disputes, 1816–1976: Procedures, Patterns, and Insights." *Journal of Conflict Resolution* 28, no. 4 (1984): 585–615.

Goertz, Gary, and Paul F. Diehl. "Enduring Rivalries: Theoretical Constructs and Empirical Patterns." *International Studies Quarterly* 37, no. 2 (1993): 147–71.

———. "The Empirical Importance of Enduring Rivalries." *International Interactions* 18, no. 2 (1992a): 151–63.

———. *Territorial Change and International Conflict.* London: Routledge, 1992b.

Goldmann, Kjell. "Detente and Crisis." *Cooperation and Conflict* 18 (1983): 215–32.

Goodspeed, Stephen S. *The Nature and Function of International Organization.* New York: Oxford University Press, 1967.

Gowa, Joanne. "Democratic States and International Disputes." *International Organization* 49, no. 3 (1995): 511–22.

Greaves, Colonel Fielding V. "Peace in Our Time—Fact or Fable?" *Military Review* (December 1962): 55–58.

Gulick, Edward V. *Europe's Classical Balance of Power.* Ithaca, NY: Cornell University Press, 1955.

Gurr, Ted R. *Minorities at Risk: Origins and Outcomes of Ethnopolitical Conflicts.* Washington, DC: US Institute of Peace, 1993a.

———. "Why Minorities Rebel: A Global Analysis of Communal Mobilization and Conflict since 1945." *International Political Science Review* 14, no. 2 (1993b): 161–201.

———. "The Internationalization of Protracted Communal Conflicts since 1945." In *The Internationalization of Communal Strife,* edited by Manus I. Midlarsky. London and New York: Routledge, 1992.

———. "On the Outcomes of Violent Conflict." In *Handbook of Political Conflict,* edited by Ted R. Gurr, 238–94. New York: Free Press, 1980.

Haas, Ernst B. "Why We Still Need the United Nations." University of California Policy Papers in International Affairs, No. 26. Berkeley, CA: Institute of International Studies, 1986.

———. "Regime Decay: Conflict Management and International Organizations, 1945–1981." *International Organization* 37, no. 2 (1983): 189–256.

Haas, Ernst B., Robert L. Butterworth, and Joseph S. Nye. *Conflict Management by International Organizations.* Morristown, NJ: General Learning Press, 1972.

Haas, Michael. "Research on International Crisis: Obsolescence of an Approach?" *International Interactions* 13, no. 1 (1986): 23–58.

———. "International Subsystems: Stability and Polarity." *American Political Science Review* 64, no. 2 (1970): 98–123.

Haass, Richard N. *Conflicts Unending.* New Haven, CT: Yale University Press, 1990.

Hagan, Joe D. "Domestic Political Systems and War Proneness." *Mershon International Studies Review* 38, supp. 2 (1994): 183–207.

Hanrieder, Wolfram F. "The International System: Bipolar or Multibloc?" *Journal of Conflict Resolution,* 9 (1965): 299–307.

Hart, Jeffrey A. "Power and Polarity in the International System." In *Polarity and War.* edited by A. Ned Sabrosky, 25–40. Boulder, CO: Westview Press, 1985.

Harvey, Frank P. "Rational Deterrence Theory Revisited: A Progress Report." *Canadian Journal of Political Science* 28, no. 3 (1995): 403–36.

Harvey, Frank P., and Patrick James. "Nuclear Crisis as a Multistage Threat Game: Toward an Agenda for Comparative Research." *International Political Science Review* 17, no. 2 (1996): 197–214.

Heisler, Martin. "Ethnicity and Ethnic Relations in the Modern West." In *Conflict and Peacemaking in Multiethnic Societies,* edited by Joseph V. Montville. Lexington, MA: Lexington Books, 1990.

Heldt, Birger, ed., with contributions by Birger Heldt and Peter Wallensteen. "States in Armed Conflict 1990–91." 2d ed. Uppsala, Sweden: Report No. 35, Department of Peace and Conflict Research, Uppsala University, 1993.

Henkin, Louis. *How Nations Behave: Law and Foreign Policy.* New York: Praeger, 1968.

Hensel, Paul R., and Paul F. Diehl. "It Takes Two to Tango: Nonmilitarized Response in Interstate Disputes." *Journal of Conflict Resolution* 38, no. 3 (1994): 479–506.

Heraclides, Alexis. *The Self-Determination of Minorities in International Politics.* Portland, OR: Frank Cass, 1991.

Hermann, Charles F., ed. *International Crises: Insights from Behavioral Research.* New York: Free Press, 1972.

————. *Crisis in Foreign Policy: A Simulation Analysis.* Indianapolis, IN: Bobbs-Merrill, 1969a.

————. "International Crisis as a Situational Variable." In *International Politics and Foreign Policy: A Reader,* rev. ed., edited by James N. Rosenau, 409–21. New York: Free Press, 1969b.

————. "Some Consequences of Crisis Which Limit the Viability of Organizations." *Administrative Science Quarterly* 8 (1963): 61–82.

Hermann, Charles F., and Robert E. Mason. "Identifying Behavioral Attributes of Events that Trigger International Crises." In *Change in the International System,* edited by Ole R. Holsti, Randolph M. Siverson, and Alexander L. George, 189–210. Boulder, CO: Westview Press, 1980.

Hermann, Margaret G., and Charles W. Kegley Jr. "Rethinking Democracy and International Peace: Perspectives from Political Psychology." *International Studies Quarterly* 39, no. 4 (1995): 511–33.

Herz, John H. "Idealist Internationalism and the Security Dilemma." *World Politics* 2, no. 2 (1950): 157–80.

Hewitt, J. Joseph. "The Strategic Prospects of Mediating International Disputes." Ph.D. diss., University of Maryland, 1996.

Hewitt, J. Joseph, Mark A. Boyer, and Jonathan Wilkenfeld. "Familiarity and Contempt: Protracted Conflicts and Crises." Paper presented at the annual meeting, International Studies Association, 1991.

Hewitt, J. Joseph, and Jonathan Wilkenfeld. "Democracy and International Crisis." *International Interactions* 22, no. 2 (1996): 123–42.

Hoffmann, Stanley A. *Gulliver's Troubles; or, the Setting of American Foreign Policy.* New York: Council on Foreign Relations, 1968.

Hoffmann, Steven A. *India and the China Crisis.* Berkeley, CA: University of California Press, 1990.

Holsti, Kalevi J. *Peace and War: Armed Conflicts and International Order 1648–1989.* Cambridge: Cambridge University Press, 1991.

————. "Resolving International Conflicts: A Taxonomy of Behavior and Some Figures on Procedures." *Journal of Conflict Resolution* 10, no. 3 (1966): 272–96.

Holsti, Ole R. "Crisis Decision Making." In *Behavior, Society, and Nuclear War,* vol. 1, edited by Philip E. Tetlock, Jo L. Husbands, Robert Jervis, Paul C. Stern, and Charles Tilly, 8–84. New York: Oxford University Press, 1989.

————. *Crisis, Escalation, War.* Montreal and Kingston: McGill-Queen's University Press, 1972.

————. "The 1914 Case." *American Political Science Review* 59, 2 (1965): 365–78.

Holsti, Ole R., and Alexander L. George. "The Effects of Stress on the Performance of Foreign Policy Makers." *Political Science Annual* 6 (1975): 255–319.

Hoole, Francis W., and Chi Huang. "The Global Conflict Process." *Journal of Conflict Resolution* 33, no. 1 (1989): 142–63.

Hopf, Ted. "Polarity, the Offense-Defense Balance, and War." *American Political Science Review* 85, no. 2 (1991): 475–93.

Hopple, Gerald W., and Paul J. Rossa. "International Crisis Analysis: Recent Developments and Future Directions." In *Cumulation in International Relations Research,* edited by P. Terrence Hopmann, Dina A. Zinnes, and J. David Singer, 65–97. Denver, CO: Monograph Series in World Affairs, vol. 18, book 3, University of Denver, 1981.

Hopple, Gerald W., Jonathan Wilkenfeld, Paul J. Rossa, and Robert N. McCauley. "Societal and Interstate Determinants of Foreign Conflict." *Jerusalem Journal of International Relations* 2 (summer 1977): 30–66.

Horelick, Arnold L. "The Cuban Missile Crisis: An Analysis of Soviet Calculations and Behavior." *World Politics* 16, no. 3 (1964): 363–89.

Horowitz, David L. *Ethnic Groups in Conflict.* Berkeley, CA: University of California Press, 1985.

Howell, Llewellyn D. "A Comparative Study of the WEIS and COPDAB Data Sets." *International Studies Quarterly* 27, no. 2 (1983): 149–59.

Huth, Paul, and Bruce Russett. "General Deterrence between Enduring Rivals: Testing Three Competing Models." *American Political Science Review* 87, no. 1 (1993): 61–73.

Huth, Paul, Daniel M. Jones, and Zeev Maoz. "Enduring International Rivalries: An Operational Definition and Case Identification Criteria." Mimeo, University of Michigan and Haifa University, 1991.

Hybel, Alex R., and Dale B. Robertson. "Assessing the Dynamic Reaction of the USSR to American and Chinese Actions and to its Nuclear Gap with the U.S." *International Interactions* 4, no. 2 (1978): 125–54.

Jackson, William D. "Polarity in International Systems: A Conceptual Note." *International Interactions* 4, no. 1 (1977): 87–96.

James, Alan. *The Politics of Peacekeeping.* New York: Praeger, 1969.

James, Patrick. "Structural Realism and the Causes of War." *Mershon International Studies Review* 39, Supp. no. 2 (1995): 181–208.

———. *Crisis and War.* Montreal and Kingston: McGill-Queen's University Press, 1988.

James, Patrick, and Frank P. Harvey. "The Most Dangerous Game: Superpower Rivalry in International Crises, 1948–1985." *Journal of Politics* 54, no. 1 (1992): 25–53.

James, Patrick, and Glenn E. Mitchell II. "Targets of Covert Pressure: The Hidden Victims of the Democratic Peace." *International Interactions* 21, no. 1 (1995): 85–107.

Jukes, Geoffrey. *Hitler's Stalingrad Decisions.* Berkeley, CA: University of California Press, 1985.

Kant, Immanuel. *Perpetual Peace.* New York: Columbia University Press, [1795] 1969.

Kaplan, Morton A. *System and Process in International Politics.* New York: John Wiley, 1957.

Kaplan, Stephen S. et al. *Diplomacy of Power: Soviet Armed Forces as a Political Instrument.* Washington, DC: Brookings Institution, 1981.

Kegley, Charles W. Jr., and Gregory A. Raymond. "Must We Fear a Post-Cold War Multipolar System?" *Journal of Conflict Resolution* 36, no. 3 (1992): 573–85.

Kellog, James C. "A Synopsis of Military Conflict 1945–1964." Unpublished paper, Bendix Systems Division, Arms Control Project Office, Ann Arbor, MI, n.d.

Kende, Istvan. "Wars of Ten Years (1967–1976)." *Journal of Peace Research* 15, no. 3 (1978): 227–41.

———. "Twenty-five Years of Local Wars." *Journal of Peace Reseaarch* 1 (1971): 5–22.

Keohane, Robert O. *After Hegemony: Cooperation and Discord in the World Political Economy.* Princeton, NJ: Princeton University Press, 1984.

Keohane, Robert O., and Joseph S. Nye Jr. "Power and Interdependence Revisited." *International Organization* 41, no. 4 (1987): 725–53.

———. *Power and Interdependence.* Boston, MA: Little, Brown, 1977.

Kugler, Jacek and A. F. K. Organski. "The Power Transition: A Retrospective and Prospective Evaluation." In *Handbook of War Studies,* edited by Manus I. Midlarsky, 171–94. Boston, MA: Unwin and Hyman 1989.

Lake, David A. "Powerful Pacifists: Democratic States and War." *American Political Science Review* 86, no. 1 (1992): 24–37.

Layne, Christopher. "Kant or Cant: The Myth of the Democratic Peace." *International Security* 19, no. 2 (1994): 5–49.

———. "The Unipolar Illusion: Why New Great Powers Will Rise." *International Security* 17, no. 4 (1993): 5–51.

Lebow, R. Ned. *Between Peace and War: The Nature of International Crisis.* Baltimore, MD: Johns Hopkins University Press, 1981.

Lebow, Richard N., and Janice G. Stein. *We All Lost the Cold War.* Princeton, NJ: Princeton University Press, 1994.

Leiss, Amelia C., and Lincoln P. Bloomfield et al. *The Control of Local Conflict: A Design for Arms Control and Limited War in the Developing Areas.* Cambridge, MA: Center for International Studies, MIT, 1967.

Leng, Russell J. *Interstate Crisis Behavior, 1816–1980: Realism versus Reciprocity.* Cambridge: Cambridge University Press, 1993a.

———. "Reciprocating Influence Strategies in Interstate Crisis Bargaining." *Journal of Conflict Resolution* 37, no. 1 (1993b): 3–41.

———. "Reagan and the Russians: Crisis Bargaining Beliefs and the Historical Record." *American Political Science Review* 78, no. 2 (1984): 338–55.

———. "When Will They Ever Learn? Coercive Bargaining in Recurrent Crises." *Journal of Conflict Resolution* 27, no. 3 (1983): 379–419.

———. "Influence Strategies and Interstate Conflict." In *The Correlates of War,* Vol. 2, *Testing Some Realpolitik Models,* edited by J. David Singer, 124–57. New York: Free Press, 1980.

Leng, Russell J., and J. David Singer. "Militarized Interstate Crisis: The BCOW Typology and Its Application." *International Studies Quarterly* 32, no. 1 (1988): 155–73.

Leng, Russell J., and Stephen G. Walker. "Comparing Two Studies of Crisis Bargaining: Confrontation, Coercion, and Reciprocity." *Journal of Conflict Resolution* 26, no. 4 (1982): 571–91.

Leng, Russell J., and H. G. Wheeler. "Influence Strategies, Success, and War." *Journal of Conflict Resolution* 23, no. 4 (1979): 655–84.

Levy, Jack S. "The Democratic Peace Hypothesis: From Description to Explanation." *Mershon International Studies Review* 38, Supp. 2 (1994): 352–54.

———. "The Diversion Theory of War." In *Handbook of War Studies,* edited by Manus I. Midlarsky, 259–88. Boston, MA: Unwin Hyman, 1989a.

———. Domestic Politics and War." *Journal of Interdisciplinary History,* 18, no. 4 (1988): 653–73.

———. "The Polarity of the System and International Stability: An Empirical Analysis." In *Polarity and War,* edited by A. Ned Sabrosky, 41–60. Boulder, CO: Westview Press, 1985.

Lindgren, Karin, ed., with contributions by Christer Ahlström, Ramses Amer, Björn Hagelin, Birger Heldt, Karin Lindgren, Kjell-Åke Nordquist, Peter Wallensteen, Håkan Wiberg. "States in Armed Conflict 1989." Uppsala, Sweden: Report No. 32, Department of Peace and Conflict Research, Uppsala University, 1991.

Luard, Evan. *War in International Society.* New Haven, CT: Yale University Press, 1987.

Mansfield, Edward D. "Concentration, Polarity, and the Distribution of Power." *International Studies Quarterly* 37 (March 1993): 105–28.

Maoz, Zeev. *National Choices and International Processes.* Cambridge: Cambridge University Press, 1990.

———. *Paths to Conflict: International Dispute Initiation 1816–1976.* Boulder, CO: Westview Press, 1982.

Maoz, Zeev, and Nasrin Abdolali. "Regime Types and International Conflict, 1816–1976." *Journal of Conflict Resolution* 33, no. 1 (1989): 3–35.

Maoz, Zeev, and Ben D. Mor. "Enduring Rivalries: The Early Years." *International Political Science Review* 17, no. 2 (1996): 141–60.

Maoz, Zeev, and Bruce Russett. "Normative and Structural Causes of Democratic Peace, 1946–1986." *American Political Science Review* 87, no. 3 (1993): 624–38.

———. "Alliances, Wealth, Contiguity, and Political Stability: Is the Lack of Conflict between Democracies a Statistical Artifact?" *International Interactions* 17, no. 3 (1992): 245–67.

Masters, Roger D. "A Multi-Bloc Model of the International System." *American Political Science Review* 55, no. 4 (1961): 780–98.

Mattingly, Garrett. *Renaissance Diplomacy.* London: Jonathan Cape, 1955.

McClelland, Charles A. "The Beginning, Duration, and Abatement of International Crises: Comparisons in Two Conflict Arenas." In *International Crises: Insights from Behavioral Research,* edited by Charles F. Hermann, 83–105. New York: Free Press, 1972.

———. "Access to Berlin: the Quantity and Variety of Events, 1948–1963." In *Quantitative International Politics: Insights and Evidence,* edited by J. David Singer, 159–86. New York: Free Press, 1968.

———. "Action Structures and Communication in Two International Crises: Quemoy and Berlin." *Background* 7 (1964): 201–15.

———. "Applications of General Systems Theory in International Relations." *Main Currents in Modern Thought* 12 (1955): 27–34.

McCormick, James M. "Evaluating Models of Crisis Behavior: Some Evidence from the Middle East." *International Studies Quarterly* 19, no. 1 (1975): 17–45.

Mearsheimer, John J. "Back to the Future: Instability in Europe after the Cold War." *International Security* 15, no. 1 (1990), 5–56.

Midlarsky, Manus I. "Polarity and International Stability." *American Political Science Review* 87, no. 1 (1993): 173–79.

———, ed. *The Internationalization of Communal Strife.* London: Routledge, 1992.

———. "International Structure and the Learning of Cooperation: The Postwar Experience." In *The Long Postwar Peace,* edited by Charles W. Kegley, Jr., 105–22. New York: HarperCollins, 1991.

———. "Hierarchical Equilibria and the Long-run Instability of Multipolar Systems." In *Handbook of War Studies,* edited by Manus I. Midlarsky, 55–81. Boston, MA: Unwin Hyman, 1989.

———. *The Onset of World War.* Boston, MA: Unwin Hyman, 1988.

———. *On War: Political Violence in the International System.* New York: Free Press, 1975.

Mintz, Alex, and Nehemia Geva. "Why Don't Democracies Fight Each Other? An Experimental Study." *Journal of Conflict Resolution* 37, no. 3 (1993): 484–503.

Mitchell, Christopher R., and K. Webb, eds. *New Approaches to International Mediation.* Westport, CT: Greenwood Press, 1988.

Modelski, George. "Kautilya: Foreign Policy and International System in the Ancient Hindu World." *American Political Science Review* 58, no. 3 (1964): 549–60.

Mor, Ben D. *Decision and Interaction in Crisis: A Model of International Crisis Behavior.* Westport, CT: Praeger, 1993.

Morgan, T. Clifton. *Untying the Knot of War.* Ann Arbor, MI: University of Michigan Press, 1994.

———. "Democracy and War: Reflections on the Literature." *International Interactions* 18, no. 3 (1993): 197–203.

Morgan, T. Clifton, and Sally H. Campbell. "Domestic Structure, Decisional Constraints, and War." *Journal of Conflict Resolution* 35, no. 2 (1991): 187–211.

Morgan, T. Clifton, and Valerie L. Schwebach. "Take Two Democracies and Call Me in the Morning: A Prescription for Peace?" *International Interactions* 17, no. 4 (1992): 305–20.

Morgenthau, Hans J. *Politics among Nations.* 5th ed. New York: Knopf, 1973. 1st ed. 1948.

Most, Benjamin A., and Harvey Starr. "Conceptualizing 'War': Consequences for Theory and Research." *Journal of Conflict Resolution* 27, no. 1 (1983): 137–59.

———. "Diffusion, Reinforcement, Geopolitics and the Spread of War." *American Political Science Review* 74, no. 4 (1980): 932–46.

Nacht, Michael. *The Age of Vulnerability: Threats to the Nuclear Stalemate.* Washington, DC: Brookings Institution, 1985.

Nicholas, Herbert G. *The United Nations.* New York: Oxford University Press, 1971.

Nomikos, Eugenia V., and Robert C. North. *International Crisis: The Outbreak of World War I.* Montreal and Kingston: McGill-Queen's University Press, 1976.

Nordlander, Ylva, ed., with contributions by Karin Axell, Birger Heldt, Erik Melander, Kjell-Åke Nordquist, Thomas Ohlson, Peter Wallensteen, and Carl Åsberg. "States in Armed Conflict 1993." Uppsala, Sweden: Report No. 38, Department of Peace and Conflict Research, Uppsala University, 1994.

North, Robert C. "Research Pluralism and the International Elephant." *International Studies Quarterly* 11, no. 4 (1967): 394–416.

Nye, Joseph S. *After the Cold War: International Institutions and State Strategies in Europe, 1989–1991.* Cambridge, MA: Harvard University Press, 1993.

———. *Bound to Lead: The Changing Nature of American Power.* New York: Basic Books, 1990.

———. *Peace in Parts.* Boston, MA: Little, Brown, 1971.

Organski, A. F. K. *World Politics.* 2d ed. New York: Knopf, 1968.

Organski, A. F. K., and Jacek Kugler. *The War Ledger.* Chicago, IL: University of Chicago Press, 1980.

Owen, John M. "How Liberalism Produces Democratic Peace." *International Security* 19, no. 2 (1994): 87–125.

Oye, Kenneth, Donald Rothchild, and Robert J. Lieber, eds. *Eagle Defiant: US Foreign Policy in the 1980s.* Boston, MA: Little, Brown, 1983.

Paige, Glenn D. *The Korean Decision.* New York: Free Press, 1968.

Paul, T. V. "Time Pressure and War Initiation: Some Linkages." *Canadian Journal of Political Science* 28, no. 2 (1995), 255–76.

———. *Asymmetric Conflicts: War Initiation by Weaker Powers.* Cambridge: Cambridge University Press, 1994.

Pearson, Frederic S., and Robert A. Baumann. "International Military Interventions: Iden-
tification and Classification." *International Interactions* 14, no. 2 (1988): 173–80.
Pelcovits, Nathan A., and Kevin L. Kramer. "Local Conflict and UN Peacekeeping: The
Uses of Computerized Data." *International Studies Quarterly* 20, no. 4 (1976): 533–
52.
Phillips, Warren R. "The Conflict Environment of Nations." In *Conflict Behavior and
Linkage Politics,* edited by Jonathan Wilkenfeld, 124–47. New York: David McKay,
1973.
Pricen, Thomas. *Intermediaries in International Conflict.* Princeton, NJ: Princeton Univer-
sity Press, 1992.
Rapkin, David P., and William R. Thompson, with Jon A. Christopherson. "Bipolarity and
Bipolarization in the Cold War Era." *Journal of Conflict Resolution* 23, no. 2 (1979):
261–95.
Ray, James Lee. *Democracy and International Conflict.* Columbia, SC: University of
South Carolina Press, 1995.
———. "Wars between Democracies: Rare, or Nonexistent?" *International Interactions*
18, no. 3 (1993): 251–76.
Raymond, Gregory A. "Democracies, Disputes, and Third-Party Intermediaries." *Journal
of Conflict Resolution,* 38, no. 1 (1994): 24–42.
Richardson, Lewis F. *Statistics of Deadly Quarrels.* Pittsburgh, PA: Boxwood Press, and
Chicago, IL: Quadrangle Books, 1960.
Riker, William H. *The Theory of Political Coalitions.* New Haven, CT: Yale University
Press, 1962.
Robinson, James A. "Crisis." In *International Encyclopedia of the Social Sciences,* vol. 3,
edited by David L. Sills, 510–14. London and New York: Collier-Macmillan, 1968.
———. *The Concept of Crisis in Decision-Making.* Washington, DC: National Institute of
Social and Behavioral Science. Symposia Studies Series No. 11, 1962.
Rosecrance, Richard N. "Bipolarity, Multipolarity, and the Future." *Journal of Conflict
Resolution* 10, no. 3 (1966): 314–27.
———. *Action and Reaction in World Politics.* Boston, MA: Little, Brown, 1963.
Rosenau, James N. *Turbulence in World Politics: A Theory of Change and Continuity.*
Princeton, NJ: Princeton University Press, 1990.
———. "Pre-Theories and Theories of Foreign Policy." In *Approaches to Comparative
and International Politics,* edited by R. Barry Farrell, 27–92. Evanston, IL: North-
western University Press, 1966.
———, ed. *International Aspects of Civil Strife.* Princeton, NJ: Princeton University
Press, 1964.
Rousseau, David L., Christopher Gelpis, Dan Reiter, and Paul K. Huth. "Assessing the
Dyadic Nature of the Democratic Peace." *American Political Science Review* 90, no.
3 (1996): 512–33.
Rummel, R. J. "Democracy, Power, Genocide, and Mass Murder." *Journal of Conflict
Resolution* 39, no. 1 (1995): 3–26.
———. "Libertarianism and International Violence." *Journal of Conflict Resolution* 27,
no. 1 (1983): 27–71.
———. *War, Power, Peace.* Beverly Hills, CA: Sage, 1979.
———. "Some Empirical Findings on Nations and Their Behavior." *World Politics* 16, no.
2 (1969): 226–41.
———. "The Relationship between National Attributes and Foreign Conflict Behavior."

In *Quantitative International Politics: Insights and Evidence,* edited by J. David Singer, 187–214. New York: Free Press, 1968.

Russett, Bruce M. "The Democratic Peace: 'And Yet it Moves'." *International Security* 19, no. 1 (1995): 164–75.

———. *Grasping the Democratic Peace: Principles for a Post-Cold War World.* Princeton, NJ: Princeton University Press, 1993.

———. "The Mysterious Case of Vanishing Hegemony; or, Is Mark Twain Really Dead?" *International Organization* 39, no. 2 (1985): 207–31.

Russett, Bruce M., Christopher Layne, David E. Spiro, and Michael W. Doyle. "Correspondence: The Democratic Peace." *International Security* 19, no. 4 (1995): 164–84.

Ryan, Stephen. "Explaining Ethnic Conflict: The Neglected International Dimension." *Review of International Studies* 14, no. 3 (1988): 161–77.

Sabrosky, A. Ned. "Alliance Aggregation, Capability Distribution, and the Expansion of Interstate War." In *Polarity and War,* edited by Ned Sabrosky, 145–89. Boulder, CO: Westview Press, 1985.

Said, Abdul, and Luiz R. Simmons, eds. *Ethnicity in an International Context.* New Brunswick, NJ: Transaction Books, 1977.

Saperstein, Alvin M. "The 'Long Peace'—Result of a Bipolar Competitive World?" *Journal of Conflict Resolution* 35, no. 1 (1991): 68–79.

Sayrs, Lois W. "The Effect of Provocation on Foreign Policy Response: A Test of the Matching Hypothesis." *International Interactions* 18, no. 2 (1992): 85–100.

Schechterman, Bernard, and Martin Slann, eds. *The Ethnic Dimension in International Relations.* Westport, CT: Praeger, 1993.

Schuman, Frederick L. *International Politics.* New York: McGraw-Hill, 1933.

Shlaim, Avi. *The United States and the Berlin Blockade, 1948–1949: A Study of Crisis Decision-Making.* Berkeley, CA: University of California Press, 1983.

de Silva, K. M., and Ronald J. May, eds. *Internationalization of Ethnic Conflict.* London: Pinter Publishers, 1991.

Simmel, George. *Conflict and the Web of Group-Affiliations.* Glencoe, IL.: Free Press [1908], 1955.

Singer, J. David. "The Level-of-Analysis Problem in International Relations." *World Politics* 14, no. 1 (1961): 77–92.

Singer, J. David, Stuart Bremer, and John Stuckey. "Capability Distribution, Uncertainty, and Major Power War, 1820–1965. In *Peace, War, and Numbers,* edited by Bruce M. Russett, 19–48. Beverly Hills, CA: Sage, 1972.

Singer, J. David, and Melvin Small. *The Wages of War 1816–1965: A Statistical Handbook.* New York: John Wiley, 1972.

———. "Alliance Aggregation and the Onset of War 1815–1945." In *Quantitative International Politics: Insights and Evidence,* edited by J. David Singer, 247–86. New York: Free Press, 1968.

Singer, Marshall R. *Weak States in a World of Powers.* New York: Free Press, 1972.

SIPRI. *Yearbook of World Armaments and Disarmament 1968–69.* Stockholm: Almquist and Wiksell; New York: Humanities Press, 1969.

Siverson, Randolph M., and Harvey Starr. *The Diffusion of War: A Study of Opportunity and Willingness.* Ann Arbor, MI: University of Michigan Press, 1991.

Siverson, Randolph M., and Michael R. Tennefoss. "Interstate Conflicts: 1815–1965." *International Interactions* 9, no. 2 (1982): 147–78.

Small, Melvin, and J. David Singer. *Resort to Arms: International and Civil Wars, 1816–1980.* Beverly Hills, CA: Sage, 1982.

———. "The War-Proneness of Democratic Regimes, 1816–1965." *Jerusalem Journal of International Relations* 1, no. 4 (1976): 50–69.

Snyder, Glenn H. "Crisis Bargaining." In *International Crises: Insights from Behavioral Research,* edited by Charles F. Hermann, 217–56. New York: Free Press, 1972.

Snyder, Glenn H., and Paul Diesing. *Conflict among Nations: Bargaining, Decision Making, and System Structure in International Crises.* Princeton, NJ: Princeton University Press, 1977.

Snyder, Richard C., H. W. Bruck, and Burton Sapin. *Foreign Policy Decision-Making.* New York: Free Press, 1962.

Sorokin, Pitirim A. *Social and Cultural Dynamics.* Vol. III, *Fluctuation of Social Relationships, War, and Revolution.* New York: American Book Co., 1937.

Spiegel, Steven L. *Dominance and Diversity.* Boston, MA: Little, Brown, 1972.

Spiro, David E. "The Insignificance of the Liberal Peace." *International Security* 19, no. 2 (1994): 50–86.

Sprout, Harold, and Margaret Sprout. *The Ecological Perspective on Human Affairs.* Princeton, NJ: Princeton University Press, 1965.

Starr, Harvey. "Democracy and War: Choice, Learning and Security Communities." *Journal of Peace Research* 29, no. 2 (1992): 207–13.

———. "Joining Political and Geographic Perspectives: Geopolitics and International Relations." *International Interactions* 17, no. 1 (1991): 1–9.

———. "'Opportunity' and 'Willingness' as Ordering Concepts in the Study of War." *International Interactions* 4, no. 4 (1978): 363–87.

Starr, Harvey, and Benjamin A. Most. "The Forms and Processes of War Diffusion." *Comparative Political Studies* 18, no. 2 (1985): 206–27.

———. "A Return Journey: Richardson, 'Frontiers,' and Wars in the 1946–1965 Era." *Journal of Conflict Resolution* 22, no. 3 (1978): 441–67.

———. "The Substance and Study of Borders in International Relations Research." *International Studies Quarterly* 20, no. 4 (1976): 581–620.

Stedman, Stephen J. *Peacemaking in Civil War: International Mediation in Zimbabwe, 1974–1980.* Boulder, CO: Lynne Rienner, 1991.

Stein, Janice G., and Raymond Tanter. *Rational Decision-Making: Israel's Security Choices, 1967.* Columbus, OH: Ohio State University Press, 1980.

Steinberg, Blema S. "Purpose and Behavior: The Cuban Missile Crisis Revisited." *International Interactions* 8, no. 3 (1981): 189–227.

Stohl, Michael. "The Nexus of Civil and International Conflict." In *Handbook of Political Conflict,* edited by Ted R. Gurr, 297–330. New York: Free Press, 1980.

Stoll, Richard J. "Bloc Concentration and the Balance of Power." *Journal of Conflict Resolution* 28, no. 1 (1984): 25–50.

Stone, Julius. *Legal Controls of International Conflict.* New York: Rinehart, 1954; rev. ed. 1973.

Strange, Susan. "The Persistent Myth of Lost Hegemony." *International Organization* 41, no. 4 (1987): 551–74.

Stremlau, John J. *The International Politics of the Nigerian Civil War, 1967–1970.* Princeton, NJ: Princeton University Press, 1977.

Suhrke, Astri, and Lela Garner Noble, eds. *Ethnic Conflict and International Relations.* New York: Praeger, 1977.

Tanter, Raymond. "International Crisis Behavior: An Appraisal of the Literature." In *Studies in Crisis Behavior,* edited by Michael Brecher, 340–74. New Brunswick, NJ: Transaction Books, 1979.

Thompson, William R. *On Global War: Historical-Structural Approaches to World Politics.* Columbia, SC: University of South Carolina Press, 1988.

———. "Polarity, the Long Cycle, and Global Power Warfare." *Journal of Conflict Resolution* 30, no. 4 (1986): 587–615.

———. "The Regional Subsystem: A Conceptual Explication and a Propositional Inventory." *International Studies Quarterly* 17, no. 1 (1973): 89–117.

Thucydides. *A History of the Peloponnesian War.* Translated by Benjamin Jowett. Oxford: Shendene Press, 1930.

Tillema, Herbert K. *International Armed Conflict since 1945: A Bibliographic Handbook of Wars and Military Interventions.* Boulder, CO: Westview Press, 1991.

Touval, Saadia. "The Superpowers as Mediators." In *Mediation in International Relations: Multiple Approaches to Conflict Management,* edited by Jacob Bercovitch and Jeffrey Z. Rubin, 232–48. New York: St. Martin's Press, 1992.

———. "Biased Intermediaries: Theoretical and Historical Considerations." *Jerusalem Journal of International Relations* 1, no. 1 (1975): 51–70.

Touval, Saadia, and I. William Zartman. *International Mediation in Theory and Practice.* Boulder, CO: Westview Press, 1985.

Triska, Jan F., and David D. Finley. *Soviet Foreign Policy.* New York: Macmillan, 1968.

Ulam, Adam. *Expansion and Coexistence.* New York: Praeger, 1974.

Valenta, Jiri. *Soviet Intervention in Czechoslovakia, 1968: Anatomy of a Decision.* Baltimore, MD: Johns Hopkins University Press, 1979a.

Vasquez, John A. "Why Do Neighbors Fight? Proximity, Interaction, or Territoriality." *Journal of Peace Research* 32, no. 3 (1995): 277–93.

———. *The War Puzzle.* Cambridge: Cambridge University Press, 1993.

Vertzberger, Yaacov Y. I. *Risk-Taking and Decisionmaking: Foreign Military Intervention Decisions.* Stanford, CA: Stanford University Press, 1997.

———. *The World in Their Minds: Information Processing, Cognition, and Perception in Foreign Policy Decisionmaking.* Stanford, CA: Stanford University Press, 1990.

———. *Misperceptions in Foreign Policymaking: The Sino-Indian Conflict, 1959–1962.* Boulder, CO: Westview Press, 1984.

Wagner, R. Harrison. "What Was Bipolarity?" *International Organization* 47, no. 1 (1993): 77–106.

Wainhouse, David W., in association with Bernard G. Bechhoefer. *International Peace Observation: A History and Forecast.* Baltimore, MD: Johns Hopkins University Press, 1966.

Walker, Richard L. *The Multi-State System of Ancient China.* Hamden, CT: Shoe String Press, 1953.

Wallace, Michael D. "Polarization: Towards a Scientific Conception." Chap. 6 in *Polarity and War,* edited by A. Ned Sabrosky. Boulder, CO: Westview Press, 1985.

———. "Alliance Polarization, Cross-Cutting, and International War, 1815–1964: A Measurement Procedure and Some Preliminary Evidence." *Journal of Conflict Resolution* 17, no. 4 (1973): 575–604.

Wallensteen, Peter. "Incompatibility, Confrontation, and War: Four Models and Three Historical Systems, 1816–1976." *Journal of Peace Research* 18, 1 (1981): 57–90.

Wallensteen, Peter, ed., with contributions by Hayward R. Alker, Karin Lindgren, Peter Wallensteen, and G. Kenneth Wilson. "States in Armed Conflict 1988." Uppsala, Sweden: Report No. 30, Department of Peace and Conflict Research, Uppsala University, 1989.

Wallensteen, Peter, and Karin Axell. "Conflict Resolution and the End of the Cold War, 1989–1993." *Journal of Peace Research* 31, no. 3 (1994): 333–49.

Waltz, Kenneth N. *Theory of International Politics.* Reading, MA: Addison-Wesley, 1979.

———. "International Structure, National Force, and the Balance of World Power." *Journal of International Affairs* 11, no. 2 (1967): 215–31.

———. "The Stability of a Bipolar World." *Daedalus* 93, no. 3 (1964): 881–909.

———. *Man, the State, and War.* New York: Columbia University Press, 1959.

Ward, Michael D., and Ulrich Widmaier. "The Domestic-International Conflict Nexus: New Evidence and Old Hypotheses." *International Interactions* 9, no. 1 (1982): 75–101.

Wayman, Frank W. "Bipolarity and War: The Role of Capability Concentration and Alliance Patterns among Major Powers, 1816–1965." *Journal of Peace Research* 21, no. 1 (1984): 61–78.

Wayman, Frank W., and T. Clifton Morgan. "Measuring Polarity in the International System." In *Measuring the Correlates of War,* edited by J. David Singer and Paul F. Diehl, 139–58. Ann Arbor, MI: University of Michigan Press, 1990.

Weede, Erich. "Some Simple Calculations on Democracy and War Involvement." *Journal of Peace Research* 29, no. 4 (1992): 377–83.

———. "Democracy and War Involvement." *Journal of Conflict Resolution,* 28, no. 4 (1984): 649–64.

Whiting, Allen S. *China Crosses the Yalu: The Decision to Enter the Korean War.* Stanford, CA: Stanford University Press, 1960.

Wiener, Anthony J., and Herman Kahn, eds. *Crisis and Arms Control.* New York: Hudson Institute, 1962.

Wilkenfeld, Jonathan. "Trigger-Response Transitions in Foreign Policy Crises." *Journal of Conflict Resolution* 35, no. 1 (1991): 143–69.

———. "A Time-Series Perspective on Conflict Behavior in the Middle East." In *Sage International Yearbook of Foreign Policy Studies,* vol. 3, edited by Patrick J. McGowan, 177–212. Beverly Hills, CA.: Sage, 1975.

———, ed. *Conflict Behavior and Linkage Politics.* New York: David McKay, 1973.

Wilkenfeld, Jonathan, and Michael Brecher. *Crises in the Twentieth Century.* Vol. 2, *Handbook of Foreign Policy Crises.* Oxford: Pergamon Press, 1988.

———. "International Crises, 1945–1975: The UN Dimension." *International Studies Quarterly* 28, no. 1 (1984): 37–59.

———. "Superpower Crisis Management Behavior." In *Foreign Policy: US/USSR, Sage International Yearbook of Foreign Policy Studies,* vol. 7, edited by Charles W. Kegley, Jr., and Pat McGowan, 185–212. Beverly Hills, CA: Sage, 1982.

Wilkenfeld, Jonathan, Michael Brecher, and Stephen R. Hill. "Threat and Violence in State Behavior." In Michael Brecher and John Wilkenfeld, *Crisis, Conflict and Instability,* 177–93. Oxford: Pergamon Press, 1989.

Wilkenfeld, Jonathan, Gerald W. Hopple, Paul J. Rossa, and Stephen J. Andriole. *Foreign Policy Behavior.* Beverly Hills, CA: Sage, 1980.

Wilson, G. Kenneth, and Peter Wallensteen. "Major Armed Conflicts in 1987." Uppsala, Sweden: Report No. 28, Department of Peace and Conflict Research, Uppsala University, 1988.

Wood, David. "Conflict in the Twentieth Century." London: International Institute for Strategic Studies (IISS). Adelphi Paper No. 48, May 1968.

Wright, Quincy. *A Study of War.* 2 vols. Chicago, IL: University of Chicago Press, 1942; rev. ed., 1965.

Young, Oran R. *The Politics of Force: Bargaining during International Crises.* Princeton, NJ: Princeton University Press, 1968.

———. *The Intermediaries: Third Parties in International Crises.* Princeton, NJ: Princeton University Press, 1967.

Zacher, Mark W. *International Conflicts and Collective Security, 1946–77.* New York: Praeger, 1979.

Zartman, I. William. "Internationalization of Communal Strife: Temptations and Opportunities of Triangulation." In *The Internationalization of Communal Strife,* edited by Manus I. Midlarsky. London and New York: Routledge, 1992.

———. *Ripe for Resolution: Conflict and Intervention in Africa.* New York: Oxford University Press, 1989.

Zartman, I. William, and Saadia Touval. "International Mediation: Conflict Resolution and Power Politics." *Journal of Social Issues* 41, no. 2 (1985): 27–45.

Zinnes, Dina A., and Jonathan Wilkenfeld. "An Analysis of Foreign Conflict Behavior of Nations." In *Comparative Foreign Policy,* edited by Wolfram F. Hanrieder, 167–213. New York: McKay, 1971.

Zoppo, Ciro E. "Nuclear Technology, Multipolarity and International Stability." *World Politics* 18, no. 4 (1966): 579–606.

Sources for Case Summaries (Part III)

General Sources

Africa
Africa Contemporary Record (London) *(ACR)*
Africa Diary (New Delhi) *(AD)*
Africa Report (Washington) *(AR)*
Africa Research Bulletin (ARB)
African Currents
African Recorder (ARec)
Annuaire de l'Afrique du Nord
Annual Register
Asian Affairs (New York)
Asian Recorder
Asian Survey (Berkeley, CA)
Axell, Karin, ed., with contributions by Birger Heldt, Erik Melander, Peter Wallensteen, and Karin Axell. "States in Armed Conflict 1992. Uppsala, Sweden: Report No. 36, Department of Peace and Conflict Research, Uppsala University, 1993.
Blechman, Barry M., and Stephen S. Kaplan. *Force Without War: U.S. Armed Forces as a Political Instrument.* Washington, DC: Brookings Institution, 1978.
Butler, David, and Anne Sloman. *British Political Facts.* London: Macmillan, 1975.
Butterworth, Robert L. *Managing Interstate Conflict, 1945–74: Data with Synopses.* Pittsburgh, PA: University of Pittsburgh, 1976.
C.A.C.I. "Analysis of the Soviet Crisis Management Experience: Technical Report." Arlington, VA: Defense Advanced Research Projects Agency, C.A.C.I. No. N00014-77-C-0135, 1978.
Data India (New Delhi)
Documents Diplomatiques Français (Paris) *(DDF)*
Documents on British Foreign Policy (London) *(DBFP)*
Documents on German Foreign Policy (Berlin) *(DGFP)*
Economist (London)
Events
Everyman's United Nations (New York: UN Department of Public Information)
Facts on File
Foreign Broadcast Information Service—Daily Report/Central Africa (FBIS-DR/CA) (U.S. Government, Washington, DC)
Foreign Broadcast Information Service—Daily Report/China (FBIS-DR/China) (U.S. Government, Washington, DC)
Foreign Broadcast Information Service—Daily Report/Latin America (FBIS-DR/LAT) (U.S. Government, Washington, DC)

Foreign Broadcast Information Service—Daily Report/Middle East and Africa (FBIS-DR/MEA) (U.S. Government, Washington, DC)

Foreign Broadcast Information Service—Daily Report/Near East and South Asia (FBIS-DR/NESA) (U.S. Government, Washington, DC)

Heldt, Birger, ed., with contributions by Birger Heldt and Peter Wallensteen. "States in Armed Conflict 1990–91." 2d ed. Uppsala, Sweden: Report No. 35, Department of Peace and Conflict Research, Uppsala University, 1993.

Information Services on Latin America (ISLA) (monthly) (Berkeley, CA)

International Financial Statistics

Jerusalem Post

Kaplan, Stephen S., et al. *Diplomacy of Power: Soviet Armed Forces as a Political Instrument.* Washington, DC: Brookings Institution, 1981.

Keesing's Contemporary Archives (Keesing's)

Langer, William L., ed. *Encyclopedia of World History.* 5th ed. 2 vols. Boston, MA: Houghton, Mifflin, 1972.

Latin America and Caribbean Contemporary Records (LACCR)

Latin America Weekly Report (London) *(LAWR)*

Lindgren, Karin, ed., with contributions by Christer Ahlström, Ramses Amer, Björn Hagelin, Birger Heldt, Karin Lindgren, Kjell-Åke Nordquist, Peter Wallensteen, Håkan Wiberg. "States in Armed Conflict 1989." Uppsala, Sweden: Report No. 32, Department of Peace and Conflict Research, Uppsala University, 1991.

The Middle East

Middle East Contemporary Survey (New York) *(MECS)*

Middle East Journal (Washington, DC) *(MEJ)*

Middle East Record (Tel Aviv, New York) *(MER)*

Mideast Mirror

New York Times and Index

New Yorker

Newsweek (New York)

Nordlander, Ylva, ed. with contributions by Karin Axell, Birger Heldt, Erik Melander, Kiell-Åke Nordquist, Thomas Ohlson, Peter Wallenstein, and Carl Åsberg. "States in Armed Conflict 1993." Uppsala, Sweden: Report No. 38, Department of Peace and Conflict Research, Uppsala University, 1994.

Pacific Community

Pan American Union Bulletin

Richardson, Lewis F. *Statistics of Deadly Quarrels.* Pittsburgh, PA: Boxwood Press and Chicago, IL: Quadrangle Books, 1960.

Shimoni, Yaacov. *Biographical Dictionary of the Middle East.* New York: Facts on File, 1991.

Singer, J. David, and Melvin Small. *The Wages of War 1816–1965: A Statistical Handbook.* New York: John Wiley, 1972.

Siverson, Randolph M., and Michael R. Tennefoss. "Interstate Conflicts: 1815–1965." *International Interactions* 9, no. 2 (1982): 147–78.

Small, Melvin, and J. David Singer. *Resort to Arms: International and Civil Wars, 1816–1980.* Beverly Hills, CA: Sage, 1982.

Snyder, Glenn H. and Paul Diesing. *Conflict among Nations: Bargaining, Decision Making, and System Structure in International Crises.* Princeton, NJ: Princeton University Press, 1977.

Statesman's Yearbook (London)

Strategic Survey

Studies in Comparative Communism

Survey of International Affairs (London)

Tillema, Herbert K. *International Armed Conflict since 1945: A Bibliographic Handbook of Wars and Military Interventions.* Boulder, CO: Westview Press, 1991.

Time (New York)

United Nations Security Council Official Records (New York) *(UNSCOR)*

Wallensteen, Peter, ed., with contributions by Hayward R. Alker, Karin Lindgren, Peter Wallensteen, and G. Kenneth Wilson. "States in Armed Conflict 1988." Uppsala, Sweden: Report No. 30, Department of Peace and Conflict Research, Uppsala University, 1989.

Wallensteen, Peter, and Karin Axell. "Conflict Resolution and the End of the Cold War, 1989–1993." *Journal of Peace Research* 31, no. 3 (1994): 333–49.

West Africa (WA)

Wilson, G. Kenneth, and Peter Wallensteen. "Major Armed Conflicts in 1987." Uppsala, Sweden: Report No. 28, Department of Peace and Conflict Research, Uppsala University, 1988.

World Today (London) *(WT)*

Wright, Quincy. *A Study of War.* 2 vols. Chicago, IL: University of Chicago Press, 1942; rev. ed., 1965.

Zacher, Mark W. *International Conflicts and Collective Security, 1946–77.* New York: Praeger, 1979.

Primary Sources

Academy of Sciences of Democratic People's Republic of Korea. *History of the Just Fatherland Liberation War of the Korean People.* Pyongyang, 1961,

Accounts and Papers: East India, Papers Regarding the Hostilities with Afghanistan, 1919. Vol. 37, no. 6, Cmd. 324. London: His Majesty's Stationery Office (HMSO). 1919.

Burma, Government of the Union of. *Kuomintang Aggression against Burma.* Rangoon: Ministry of Information, 1953.

Cold War International History Project. *Bulletin.* Washington, DC. Woodrow Wilson Center for Scholars (CWIHP).

Cuba, Government of. *History of an Aggression.* Havana: Ediciones Venceromos, 1964.

Documents Diplomatiques Français, 1956. Paris: Imprimerie Nationale, 1988. *(DDF)*

Documents Diplomatiques Français, 1932–1939. First series (1932–35). 6 vols. Second series (1936–39). 9 vols. Paris: Imprimerie Nationale, 1964–74. *(DDF)*

Documents on British Foreign Policy, 1919–1939. First Series. 26 vols. Edited by William N. Medlicott et al. London: Her Majesty's Stationery Office (HMSO), 1985. *(DBFP)*

———. 1st ser., vol. 24. Edited by W. Medlicott et al. London: HMSO, 1983. *(DBFP)*

———. 1st ser., vol. 22. Edited by W. Medlicott et al. London: HMSO, 1980. *(DBFP)*

———. 1st ser., vol. 21. Edited by W. Medlicott et al. London: HMSO, 1978. *(DBFP)*

———. 1st ser., vol. 20. Edited by W. Medlicott et al. London: HMSO, 1976. *(DBFP)*

———. 1st ser., vol. 16. Edited by W. Medlicott et al. London: HMSO, 1968. *(DBFP)*

————. 1st ser., vol. 15. Edited by Rohan H. Butler et al. London: HMSO, 1967. *(DBFP)*

————. 1st ser., vol. 11. Edited by Rohan H. Butler, J. Bury, and M. Lambert. London: HMSO, 1961. *(DBFP)*

————. 1st ser., vol. 9. Edited by Rohan H. Butler et al. London: HMSO, 1960. *(DBFP)*

————. 1st ser., vol. 8. Edited by Rohan H. Butler and J. Bury. London: HMSO, 1958. *(DBFP)*

————. Series 1A, vol. 4. Edited by W. Medlicott et al. London: HMSO, 1971, *(DBFP)*

————. Series 1A, vol. 3. Edited by W. Medlicott et al. London: HMSO, 1970, *(DBFP)*

————. Series 1A, vol. 1. Edited by W. Medlicott et al. London: HMSO, 1966. *(DBFP)*

Documents on British Foreign Policy, 1919–1939. Third Series (1938–39). 10 vols. London: HMSO, 1949–52. *(DBFP)*

————. 3rd ser., vol. 1. Edited by E. Llewellyn Woodward and Rohan H. Butler. London: HMSO, 1949a. *(DBFP)*

————. 3rd ser., vol. 2. Edited by E. Llewellyn Woodward and Rohan H. Butler. London: HMSO, 1949b. *(DBFP)*

Documents on German Foreign Policy, 1918–1945, ser. D, vol. 1. London: HMSO, 1949. *(DGFP)*

Egyptian Ministry of Foreign Affairs. *Records of Conversations, Notes and Papers Exchanged between the Royal Egyptian Government and the United Kingdom Government (March 1950–November 1951),* Cairo 1951.

Gay, George, and H. Fisher. *Public Relations of the Commission for Relief in Belgium: Documents.* Vols. 1 and 2. Stanford, CA: Stanford University Press, 1929.

Great Britain, Foreign Office. *Anglo-Egyptian Conversations on the Defence of the Suez Canal and on the Sudan (1950–51).* London: HMSO, 1951.

HEARINGS Before the Committee on International Relations and its Subcommittee on International Political and Military Affairs. "Seizure of the Mayaguez." Washington, DC: United States Government Printing Office (hereafter USGPO), 1975.

Historic Documents of 1979. "Soviet Invasion of Afghanistan, December 25–31, 1979." Washington, DC: *Congressional Quarterly,* 1980.

League of Nations Journal (Geneva)

Soviet Documents on the Hungarian Revolution, 24 October–4 November 1956. CWIHP. *Bulletin* 5 (spring 1995): 22–23, 29–34.

Statistical Yearbook of the League of Nations (Geneva)

Statistical Yearbook of the United Nations (New York)

Swedish Royal Ministry for Foreign Affairs. *Documents on Swedish Foreign Policy, 1952.* New Series, I:C:2. Stockholm: 1957.

United Nations. Statistical Abstracts of Latin America (New York)

United Nations. *Report of the Security Council Special Mission to the Republic of Guinea Established under Resolution 289 (1970).* United Nations Security Council Official Records (UNSCOR), Twenty-fifth Year, Special Supplement no. 2 (1971).

United Nations. *Report of the Special Committee on the Problem of Hungary.* General Assembly Official Records *(GAOR),* Eleventh Session, Supp. 18 (A/3592), 1957.

United States Congress. Senate. "Treaty with Colombia Concerning the Status of Quita Sueno, Roncador, and Serrana." *Senate Executive Report.* 97th Cong, 1st sess. Washington, DC: USGPO, 1981: 1–28.

United States Department of State Bulletin (Washington, DC).

United States Department of State. *The China White Paper, August 1949.* Stanford, CA: Stanford University Press, 1967.

————. *The Conflict in Korea.* Public Affairs, Publication 4266, October 1951.

————. "Congo, Realities and US Policy." Washington, DC: USGPO, 1965.

United States Department of State. *Foreign Relations of the United States (FRUS)* (Washington, DC).

————. *Foreign Relations of the United States 1955–57.* Vol. 2 *China,* vol. 5, *The Near East, South Asia, and Africa.* Washington, DC: USGPO, 1986, *(FRUS)*

————. *Foreign Relations of the United States 1952–54.* Vol. 12, bk. 1, *East Asia and the Pacific;* Vol. 14, *China and Japan.* Washington, DC: USGPO, 1984, 1985. *(FRUS)*

————. *Foreign Relations of the United States 1950.* Vol. 5, *The Near East, South Asia, and Africa;* vol. 6, *East Asia and the Pacific;* vol. 7, *Korea.* Washington, DC: USGPO, 1976, 1977, 1978. *(FRUS)*

————. *Foreign Relations of the United States 1949.* Vol. 5, *The Near East, South Asia, and Africa;* vol. 6, *East Asia and the Pacific.* Washington, DC: USGPO, 1976, 1977. *(FRUS)*

————. *Foreign Relations of the United States 1948.* Vol. 2, *Germany and Austria;* vol. 3, *Western Europe;* vol. 4, *Eastern Europe: the Soviet Union;* vol. 5, bk. 2, *The Near East, South Asia and Africa.* Washington, DC: USGPO, 1973, 1974, 1974, 1976. *(FRUS)*

————. *Foreign Relations of the United States 1947.* Vol. 3, *Western Europe;* vol. 5, *The Near East, South Asia, and Africa.* Washington, DC: USGPO, 1971 *(FRUS)*

————. *Foreign Relations of the United States 1946.* Vol. 7, *The Near East and Africa.* Washington, DC: USGPO, 1969. *(FRUS)*

————. *Documents on German Foreign Policy, 1918–1945.* From the Archives of the German Foreign Ministry. Washington, DC: USGPO, 1948. *(FRUS)*

————. *Foreign Relations of the United States 1928.* Vol. 2. Washington, DC: USGPO, 1943. *(FRUS)*

————. *Foreign Relations of the United States, Japan 1931–1941.* Vols. 1, 2. Washington, DC: USGPO, 1943. *(FRUS)*

————. *Foreign Relations of the United States 1927.* Vol. 1, bk. 3. Washington, DC: USGPO, 1942. *(FRUS)*

————. *Foreign Relations of the United States 1926.* Vol. 2. Washington, DC: USGPO, 1941. *(FRUS)*

————. *Foreign Relations of the United States 1925.* Vol. 2. Washington, DC: USGPO, 1940. *(FRUS)*

————. *Foreign Relations of the United States 1921.* Vol. 2. Washington, DC: USGPO, 1936. *(FRUS)*

————. *Foreign Relations of the United States 1920.* Vol. 1. Washington, DC: USGPO, 1935. *(FRUS)*

————. *Foreign Relations of the United States: The Lansing Papers 1914–1920.* Vol. 2. Washington, DC: USGPO, 1940. *(FRUS)*

————. *Foreign Relations of the United States 1919.* Vol. 1. Washington, DC: USGPO, 1934. *(FRUS)*

————. *Foreign Relations of the United States 1918.* Washington, DC: USGPO, 1930. *(FRUS)*

————. *Foreign Relations of the United States 1917.* Washington, DC: USGPO, 1926. *(FRUS)*

United States in World Affairs (New York: Harper & Row).

"The Question of the Aaland Islands." In *League of Nations—Official Journal* 5 (July–August 1920).
World Economic Survey of the League of Nations (General).

Secondary Sources

A. H. H. "A Note on the Swedish-Russian Dispute: Repercussions in Sweden." *World Today* (London) 8 (September 1952): 388–92.
Abdulghani, Jasim M. *Iraq and Iran: The Years of Crisis.* Baltimore, MD: Johns Hopkins University Press, 1984.
Abdullah King of Jordan. *My Memoirs Completed: Al-Takmilah.* New York: Longman, 1978.
Abel, Elie. *The Missiles of October: The Story of the Cuban Missile Crisis.* Philadelphia and New York: J. B. Lippincott, 1966.
Abidi, Aqil H. H. *Jordan: A Political Study, 1948–1957.* London: Asia Publishing House, 1965.
Abir, Mordechai. *Oil, Power and Politics.* London: Frank Cass, 1974.
Acheson, Dean. *The Korean War.* New York: Norton, 1971.
———. *Present at the Creation: My Years in the State Department.* New York: New American Library, 1969.
———. *Our Far Eastern Policy: Debate, Decisions and Action.* Washington, DC: Department of State, Division of Publications, Office of Public Affairs, 1951a.
———. "American Policy toward China: Statement before a Joint Senate Committee, June 4, 1951." Washington, DC: USGPO, 1951b.
Adamec, Ludwig. *Afghanistan's Foreign Affairs to the Mid-Twentieth Century: Relations with the USSR, Germany and Britain.* Tucson, AZ: University of Arizona Press, 1974.
———. *Afghanistan 1900–1923: A Diplomatic History.* Berkeley, CA: University of California Press, 1967.
Adams, Michael. *Suez and After—Year of Crisis.* Boston, MA: Beacon Press, 1958.
Adams, Nina S., and Alfred W. McCoy, eds. *Laos: War and Revolution.* New York: Harper & Row, 1970.
Adams, Thomas W., and Alvin J. Cottrell. *Cyprus, between East and West.* Baltimore, MD: Johns Hopkins University Press, 1968.
Adamthwaite, Anthony. *France and the Coming of the Second World War, 1936–1939.* London: Frank Cass, 1977.
Adan, Avraham. *On the Banks of the Suez.* San Francisco, CA: Presidio, 1980.
Adkin, Mark. *Urgent Fury: The Battle for Grenada.* Lexington, MA: DC Heath, 1989.
Adomeit, Hannes. *Soviet Risk-Taking and Crisis Behavior.* London: Allen & Unwin, 1982.
Agrell, Wilhelm. "Behind the Submarine Crisis: Evolution of the Swedish Defense Doctrine and Soviet War Planning." *Cooperation and Conflict* 21 (1986): 197–217.
———. "Soviet Baltic Strategy and the Swedish Submarine Crisis." *Cooperation and Conflict* 18 (1983): 269–81.
Agung, I. *Twenty Years of Indonesian Foreign Policy 1945–1965.* The Hague: Mouton, 1973.
Agwani, Mohammed S. *The Lebanese Crisis, 1958: A Documentary Study.* London: Asia Publishing House, 1965.

Ajomo, M. Ayo. "The Entebbe Affair: Intervention in International Law." Lagos: Nigerian Institute of International Affairs, Lecture Series, No. 13, 1977.

Albrecht-Carrié, René. *A Diplomatic History of Europe since the Congress of Vienna.* London: Methuen, 1965.

Alexander, George M. *The Prelude to the Truman Doctrine: British Policy in Greece, 1944–47.* London: Oxford University Press, 1982.

Alexander, Robert J. *Communism in Latin America.* New Brunswick, NJ: Rutgers University Press, 1957.

———. "The Guatemalan Communists." *Canadian Forum* 34 (July 1954a): 81–83.

———. "The Guatemalan Revolution and Communism." *Foreign Policy Bulletin* 3314 (April 1954b): 4–7.

Alexander, Yonah, and Nicholas N. Kittrie, eds. *Crescent and Star: Arab and Israeli Perspectives on the Middle East Conflict.* New York: AMS Press, 1973.

Allen, Richard H. S. *Malaysia; Prospect and Retrospect: The Impact and Aftermath of Colonial Rule.* New York: Oxford University Press, 1968.

Allison, Graham T. *The Essence of Decision: Explaining the Cuban Missile Crisis.* Boston, MA: Little, Brown, 1971.

Allyn, Bruce J., James G. Blight, and David A. Welch. "Essence of Revision." *International Security* 14, no. 3 (1989–90): 138–49.

Alperovitz, Gar. *The Decision to Drop the Atomic Bomb: and the Architecture of an American Myth.* New York: Knopf, 1995a.

———. "Hiroshima: Historians Reassess." *Foreign Policy* 99 (summer 1995b): 15–34.

———. *Atomic Diplomacy: Hiroshima and Potsdam: The Use of the Atomic Bomb and the American Confrontation with Soviet Power.* New York: Penguin Books, 1965.

Ambrose, Stephen E. *Eisenhower: The President 1952–1969.* Vol. 2. New York: Simon and Schuster, 1984.

Amer, Ramses. "The United Nations and Foreign Military Interventions: A Comparative Study of the Application of the Charter." Uppsala, Sweden: Report No. 33, Department of Peace and Conflict Research, Uppsala University, 1992.

Ameringer, Charles D. *Don Pepe: A Political Biography of José Figueres of Costa Rica.* Albuquerque, NM: University of New Mexico Press, 1978.

Amoo, Samuel G., and I. William Zartman. "Mediation by Regional Organizations: The Organization of African Unity (OAU) in Chad." In *Mediation in International Relations: Multiple Approaches to Conflict Management,* edited by Jacob Bercovitch and Jeffrey Z. Rubin, 131–48. New York: St. Martin's Press, 1992.

Amstutz, J. Bruce. *Afghanistan: the First Five Years of Soviet Occupation.* Washington, DC: National Defense University, 1986.

An, Tai-Sung. "Turmoil in Indochina: The Vietnam-Cambodian Conflict." *Asian Affairs* 5 (March–April 1978): 245–56.

———. *The Sino-Soviet Territorial Dispute.* Philadelphia, PA: Westminster, 1973.

Anderson, David L. *Trapped by Success: The Eisenhower Administration and Vietnam, 1953–1961.* New York: Columbia University Press, 1991.

Anderson, Evelyn. "East Germany." *Survey* 44–45 (October 1962): 54–65.

Anderson, Jack, with George Clifford. *The Anderson Papers.* New York: Random House, 1973.

Anderson, Matthew S. *The Eastern Question, 1774–1923.* New York: St. Martin's Press, 1966.

Andreades, Andreas M. *Les Effets Economiques et Sociaux de la Guerre en Grèce.* Edited by James Shotwell. New Haven, CT: Yale University Press, 1930.

Andrew, Christopher M., and Oleg Gordievsky. *KGB: The Inside Story of Its Foreign Operations from Lenin to Gorbachev.* New York: Harper Perennial, 1990.

Anglin, Douglas G. *Zambian Crisis Behaviour: Confronting Rhodesia's Unilateral Declaration of Independence, 1965–1966.* Montreal and Kingston: McGill-Queen's University Press, 1994.

———. "Zambian Crisis Behavior: Rhodesia's Unilateral Declaration of Independence." *International Studies Quarterly* 24, no. 4 (1980): 581–616.

Appleman, Roy E. *Disaster in Korea: The Chinese Confront MacArthur.* College Station, TX: Texas A&M University Press, 1989.

Armbrister, Trevor. *A Matter of Accountability: The True Story of the Pueblo Affair.* London: Barrie & Jenkins, 1970.

Armstrong, J. P. *Sihanouk Speaks.* New York: Walker, 1964.

Arnold, Anthony. *Afghanistan: The Soviet Invasion in Perspective.* Rev. ed. Stanford, CA: Hoover Institution Press, 1985.

Artaud, Denise. "Conclusion." In *Dien Bien Phu and the Crisis of Franco-American Relations, 1954–1955,* edited by Lawrence S. Kaplan, Denise Artaud, and Mark R. Rubin, 251–68. Wilmington, DE: SR Books, 1990.

Aruri, Naseer H., ed. *Middle East Crucible: Studies on the Arab-Israeli War of October 1973.* Wilmette, IL: Medina University Press International, 1975.

Atkins, G. Pope, and Larmen C. Wilson. *The US and the Trujillo Regime.* New Brunswick, NJ: Rutgers University Press, 1972.

Austin, Anthony. *The President's War: The Story of the Tonkin Gulf Resolution and How the Nation Was Trapped in Vietnam.* Philadelphia, PA: Lippincott, 1971.

Austin, Dennis. "The Uncertain Frontier: Ghana-Togo." *Journal of Modern African Studies* 1, no. 2 (1963): 139–45.

Auty, Phyllis. *Tito: A Biography.* Harlow: Longman, 1970.

Avery, William P. "Origins and Consequences of the Border Dispute between Educador and Peru." *Inter-American Economic Affairs* 38 (1984–85): 65–77.

Avirgan, Tony, and Martha Honey. *War in Uganda: The Legacy of Idi Amin.* Westport, CT: L. Bill, 1982.

Ayal, Eliezer B. "Some Crucial Issues in Thailand's Economic Development." *Pacific Affairs* 34 (summer 1961): 157–64.

Ayoob, Mohammed, and K. Subrahmanyam. *The Liberation War.* New Delhi: S. Chand, 1972.

Ayub Khan, Mohammad. *Friends, Not Masters: A Political Autobiography.* London: Oxford University Press, 1967.

Baaklini, Abdo I. *Legislative and Political Development, Lebanon, 1842–1972.* Durham, NC: Duke University Press, 1976.

Baer, George W. *The Coming of the Italian-Ethiopian War.* Cambridge, MA: Harvard University Press, 1967.

Baerlein, Henry. *A Difficult Frontier (Yugoslavs and Albanians).* London: Leonard Parsons, 1922.

Bajanov, Evgueni. "Assessing the Politics of the Korean War, 1949–51." *CWIHP. Bulletin.* 6–7 (winter 1995–96): 54, 87–91.

Bajpai, Kanti P. *Brass Tacks and Beyond: Perception and Management of Crisis in South Asia.* New Delhi: Manohar, 1995.

Baker, James A. III, with Thomas M. DeFrank. *The Politics of Diplomacy: Revolution, War and Peace, 1989–1992.* New York: G. P. Putnam's Sons, 1995.

Baldwin, Hanson W. *Battles Lost and Won: Great Campaigns of World War II.* New York: Konecky and Konecky, 1966.

Balfour, Michael L. G. *West Germany: A Contemporary History.* New York: Praeger, 1968.

Ball, George W. *The Past Has Another Pattern.* New York: Norton, 1982.

Ball, Margaret M. *The O.A.S. in Transition.* Durham, NC: Duke University Press, 1969.

———. *Post-War German-Austrian Relations: The Anschluss Movement, 1918–1936.* Stanford, CA: Stanford University Press, 1937.

Ball, Nicole. *Regional Conflicts and the International System: A Case Study of Bangladesh.* Brighton, U.K.: Institute for the Study of International Organizations, University of Sussex, 1974.

Ballard, Roger. "Kashmir Crisis: View from Mitpur." *Economic and Political Weekly* (Bombay) (2–9 March 1991): 513–17.

Bamba, Nobuya. *Japanese Diplomacy in a Dilemma: New Light on Japan's China Policy 1924–1929.* Vancouver, BC: University of British Columbia Press, 1972.

Bandmann, Yona, and Yishai Cordova. "The Soviet Nuclear Threat towards the Close of the Yom Kippur War." *Jerusalem Journal of International Relations* 5, no. 1 (1980): 94–110.

Bantea, Eugen, Nicholae Constanza, and Gheorghe Zaharia. *Romania in the War against Hitler's Germany, August 1944–May 1945.* Bucharest: Meridiane Publishing House, 1970.

Bar-On, Mordechai. *The Gates of Gaza: Israel's Road to Suez and Back, 1955–1957.* New York: St. Martin's Press, 1994.

Bar-Siman-Tov, Yaacov. *Israel, the Superpowers and the War in the Middle East.* New York: Praeger, 1987.

———. *Linkage Politics in the Middle East: Syria between Domestic and External Conflict, 1961–1970.* Boulder, CO: Westview Press, 1983.

———. *The Israeli-Egyptian War of Attrition, 1969–1970: A Case-Study of Limited Local War.* New York: Columbia University Press, 1980.

Bar-Yaacov, Nissim. *The Israel-Syrian Armistice: Problems of Implementation, 1949–1966.* Jerusalem: Magnes Press, 1967.

Bar-Zohar, Michael. *Embassies in Crisis: Diplomats and Demagogues behind the Six Day War.* Englewood Cliffs, NJ: Prentice-Hall, 1970.

———. *Ben-Gurion: The Armed Prophet.* Englewood Cliffs, NJ: Prentice-Hall, 1967.

———. *Suez: Ultra Secret.* Paris: Librairie Fayard, 1964.

Baring, Arnulf. *Uprising in East Germany: June 17, 1953.* Ithaca, NY: Cornell University Press, 1972.

Barker, Arthur J. *Suez: The Seven Day War.* London: Faber & Faber, 1964.

Barker, Elisabeth. *British Policy in Southeast Europe in the Second World War.* London: Macmillan, 1976.

———. "The Berlin Crisis, 1958–1962." *International Affairs* (London) 39 (January 1963): 59–73.

Barnds, William J. *India, Pakistan, and the Great Powers.* New York: Praeger, 1972.

Barnet, Richard J. *Intervention and Revolution: The United States in the Third World.* New York: World Publishing Co., 1968.

Barnhart, Michael A. *Japan Prepares for Total War: The Search for Economic Security, 1919–1941.* Ithaca, NY: Cornell University Press, 1987.

Baron, Dona. "The Dominican Republic Crisis of 1965: A Case-Study of the Regional vs.

the Global Approach to International Peace and Security." In *Columbia Essays in International Affairs (III): The Dean's Papers, 1967,* edited by Andrew W. Cordier, 1–37. New York: Columbia University Press, 1968.

Barraclough, Geoffrey. *Survey of International Affairs, 1959–1960.* Royal Institute of International Affairs (hereafter, RIIA). London: Oxford University Press, 1964.

———. *Survey of International Affairs, 1956–1958.* RIIA. London: Oxford University Press, 1962.

Barratt, John. "Southern Africa: A South African View." *Foreign Affairs* 55 (October 1976): 147–68.

Barros, James. *The League of Nations and the Great Powers: The Greek-Bulgarian Incident, 1925.* Oxford: Clarendon Press, 1970.

———. *The Corfu Incident of 1923: Mussolini and the League of Nations.* Princeton, NJ: Princeton University Press, 1965.

Barston, R. P., and Hjalmar W. Hannesson. "The Anglo-Icelandic Fisheries Dispute." *International Relations* (UK) 4 (November 1974): 559–84, 628.

Bartlet, Christopher J. *A History of Postwar Britain, 1945–1974.* London: Longman, 1977.

Bartov, Hanoch. *Dado: Forty-Eight Years and Another Twenty Days.* 2 vols. (in Hebrew). Tel Aviv: Ma'ariv Library, 1981.

Baudhuin, Fernand. *Historique Economique de la Belgique 1914–1939.* Vols. 1 and 2. Brussels: E. Bruylant, 1946.

Bauer, Otto. *The Austrian Revolution.* Translated by H. Stenning. 1925. Reprint, New York: Burt Franklin, 1970.

Baynes, Norman H., ed. *The Speeches of Adolph Hitler, April 1922–August 1939.* 2 vols. London: Oxford University Press, 1942.

Bayo, Armando. *Panamá.* La Habana: Instituto del Libro, 1967.

Beals, Carleton. "Mexico Seeking Central American Leadership." *Current History* 24, no. 6, (1926).

Beasley, William G. *The Modern History of Japan.* New York: Praeger, 1964.

Beaufre, André. *The Suez Expedition 1956.* London: Faber & Faber, 1969.

Beck, Robert J. *The Grenada Invasion: Politics, Law, and Foreign Policy Decisionmaking.* Boulder, CO: Westview Press, 1993.

Bellows, Thomas J. "Proxy War in Indochina." *Asian Affairs* 7 (September–October 1979): 13–30.

Beloff, Max. *The Foreign Policy of Soviet Russia, 1929–1941.* 2 vols. London: Oxford University Press, 1947–49.

Bemis, Samuel F. *The Latin American Policy of the United States: An Historical Interpretation.* New York: Harcourt, Brace & World, 1943.

Ben-Ami, S. *Spain between Dictatorship and Democracy, 1936–1977* (in Hebrew). Tel Aviv: Am Oved, 1977.

Ben-Gurion, David. *Israel: A Personal History.* Tel Aviv: Sabra, 1972.

———. *Recollections* (in Hebrew). Tel Aviv: Am Oved, 1971.

———. *The Restored State of Israel* (in Hebrew). Tel Aviv: Am Oved, 1969.

———. *The Sinai Campaign* (in Hebrew). Tel Aviv: Am Oved, 1964.

———. *Israel: Years of Challenge.* New York: Holt, Rinehart & Winston, 1963.

Ben-Porat, Yeshayahu, and Ze'ev Schiff. *Entebbe Rescue.* London: Delacorte Press, 1977.

Ben-Zvi, Abraham. *The Illusion of Deterrence: The Roosevelt Presidency and the Origins of the Pacific War.* Boulder, CO: Westview Press, 1987.

Bender, Gerald J. "Kissinger in Angola: Anatomy of Failure." In *American Policy in Southern Africa: The Stakes and the Stance,* 2d. ed., edited by René Lemarchand, 63–143. Washington, DC: University Press of America, 1981.

———. "Angola, the Cubans, and American Anxieties." *Foreign Policy* 31 (summer 1978): 3–30.

Bender, Lynn D. *The Politics of Hostility: Castro's Revolution and United States Policy.* Hato Rey, PR: Inter-American University Press, 1975.

Benoist-Mechin. *Ibn Seoud et la naissance d'un royaume.* Paris: Editions Albin Michel, 1955.

Berger, Carl. *The Korea Knot—A Military-Political History.* Philadelphia, PA: University of Pennsylvania Press, 1957.

Berle, Adolf A. *Tides of Crisis.* Westport, CT: Greenwood, 1975.

Berman, Larry. *Lyndon Johnson's War: The Road to Stalemate in Vietnam.* New York: Norton, 1989.

Bermann, Karl. *Under the Big Stick: Nicaragua and the United States since 1848.* Boston, MA: South End Press, 1986.

Bernstein, Barton J. "Hiroshima, Rewritten." *New York Times,* 31 January 1995, A21.

———. "The Policy of Risk: Crossing the 38th Parallel and Marching to the Yalu." *Foreign Service Journal* 54 (March 1977): 16–22, 29.

Bernstein, Barton J., and Allen J. Matusow, eds. *The Truman Administration: A Documentary History.* New York: Harper & Row, 1966.

Berton, Peter. "The Territorial Issue." *Studies in Comparative Communism* 2 (July–October 1969): 131–49.

Beschloss, Michael R. *The Crisis Years: Kennedy and Khrushchev, 1960–1963.* New York: HarperCollins, 1991.

Bethell, Nicholas. *The Palestine Triangle.* London: André Deutsch, 1979.

———. *Gomulka: His Poland and His Communism.* New York: Holt, Rinehart & Winston, 1969.

Betts, Richard K. *Nuclear Blackmail and Nuclear Balance.* Washington, DC: Brookings Institution, 1987.

Bianco, Lucien. *Origins of the Chinese Revolution, 1915–1949.* Stanford, CA: Stanford University Press, 1971.

Bidwell, Robin. *The Two Yemens.* Singapore: Longman/Westview Press, 1983.

Billings-Yun, Melanie. *Decision against War: Eisenhower and Dien Bien Phu, 1954.* New York: Columbia University Press, 1988.

van Bilsen, A. J. "Some Aspects of the Congo Problem." *International Affairs* (London) 38 (January 1962): 41–51.

Bird, Leonard A. *Costa Rica, the Unarmed Democracy.* London: Sheppard Press, 1984.

Birdwood, Christopher B. *Two Nations and Kashmir.* London: Robert Hale, 1956.

Bisbee, Eleanor. *The New Turks: Pioneers of the Republic, 1920–1950.* Philadelphia, PA: University of Pennsylvania Press, 1951.

Bishara, Ghassan. "The Political Repercussions of the Israeli Raid on the Iraqi Nuclear Reactor." *Journal of Palestine Studies* 11, (spring 1982): 58–76.

Bishop, Robert, and E. S. Crayfield. *Russia astride the Balkans.* London: Evans Brothers, 1948.

Bissell, Richard E. "Soviet Use of Proxies in the Third World: The Case of Yemen." *Soviet Studies* 30 (January 1978): 87–106.

Bissell, Richard M. Jr., with Jonathan E. Lewis and Frances T. Pudlo. *Reflections of a Cold Warrior: From Yalta to the Bay of Pigs.* New Haven, CT: Yale University Press, 1996.

Bitsios, Dmitri S. *Cyprus, the Vulnerable Republic.* Thessaloniki, Greece: Institute for Balkan Studies, 1975.

Black, Ian, and Benny Morris. *Israel's Secret Wars: A History of Israel's Intelligence Services.* New York: Grove Weidenfeld, 1991.

Black, Naomi. "The Cyprus Conflict." In *Ethnic Conflict in International Relations,* edited by A. Suhrke and L. Nobel, 43–92. New York: Praeger, 1977.

Blake, Gerald H. *The Suez Canal: A Commemorative Bibliography, 1975.* Durham, England: Centre for Middle Eastern and Islamic Studies, University of Durham, Occasional Papers, Series No. 4, 1975.

Blanchard, Wendell. *Thailand: Its People, Its Society, Its Culture.* New Haven, CT: Human Relations Area Files Press, 1958.

Blechman, Barry M. "The Impact of Israel's Reprisals on Behavior of the Bordering Arab Nations Directed at Israel." *Journal of Conflict Resolution* 16, (June 1972): 155–81.

Blechman, Barry M., and Douglas M. Hart. "The Political Utility of Nuclear Weapons: The 1973 Middle East Crisis." *International Security* 7 (summer 1982): 132–56.

Blight, James G., and David A. Welch. *On the Brink: Americans and Soviets Reexamine the Cuban Missile Crisis.* New York: Hill & Wang, 1989.

Blinkenberg, Lars. *India-Pakistan: The History of Unsolved Conflicts.* Copenhagen: Munksgaard, Dansk Udenrigspolitisk Instituts Skrifter, 4, 1972.

Bloomfield, Lincoln P. *The United Nations and U.S. Foreign Policy: A New Look at the National Interest.* Boston, MA: Little, Brown, 1967.

Bobrow, Davis B., Steve Chan, and John A. Kringen. *Understanding Foreign Policy Decisions: The Chinese Case.* New York: Free Press, 1979.

Boca, Angela D. *The Ethiopian War, 1935–1941.* Chicago, IL: University of Chicago Press, 1969.

Bogdanor, Vernon, and Robert Skidelsky, eds. *The Age of Affluence: 1951–1964.* London: Macmillan, 1970.

Bohlen, Charles E. *Witness to History, 1929–1969.* New York: Norton, 1973.

Boldur, Alexandre. *La Béssarabie et les Relations Russo-Roumaines.* Paris: J. Gamber, 1927.

Bone, Robert C. Jr. *The Dynamics of the Western New Guinea (Irian Barat) Problem.* Ithaca, NY: Cornell University Press, 1962.

Bonnefous, Edouard. *Histoire de la Troisième République.* Vol. 7, *La Course vers l'Abime: la fin de la IIIe République (1938–1940).* Paris: Presses Universitaires, 1967.

———. *Histoire de la Troisième République.* Vol. 6, *Vers la Guerre; du Front Populaire à la Conférénce de Munich (1936–1938).* Paris: Presses Universitaires, 1965.

Bonsal, Philip W. *Cuba, Castro and the United States.* Pittsburgh, PA: University of Pittsburgh Press, 1971.

Borg, Dorothy. *The United States and the Far Eastern Crisis of 1933–1938.* Cambridge, MA: Harvard University Press, 1964.

Borg, Dorothy, and Waldo Heinrichs, eds. *The Uncertain Years: Chinese-American Relations, 1947–1950.* New York: Columbia University Press, 1980.

Borg, Dorothy, and Shumpei Okamoto, eds. *Pearl Harbor as History: Japanese-American Relations 1931–1941.* New York: Columbia University Press, 1973.

Borisov, Oleg B., and B. T. Koloskov. *Soviet-Chinese Relations, 1945–1970.* Bloomington, IN: Indiana University Press, 1975.

Boulter, Veronica. *Survey of International Affairs 1925: Supplement.* RIIA. London: Oxford University Press, 1928.

Bowie, Robert R. *Suez 1956: International Crises and the Role of Law.* New York: Oxford University Press, 1974.

Bowles, Chester. *Promises to Keep: My Years in Public Life, 1941–1969.* New York: Harper, 1971.

Bowman, Isaiah. "The Ecuador-Peru Boundary Dispute." *Foreign Affairs* 20 (July 1942): 757–61.

Bowyer Bell, John. *The Long War: Israel and the Arabs since 1946.* Englewood Cliffs, NJ: Prentice-Hall, 1969.

Boyle, John H. *China and Japan at War 1937–1945: The Politics of Collaboration.* Stanford, CA: Stanford University Press, 1972.

Braddick, Henderson B. *Germany, Czechoslovakia and the "Great Alliance" in the May Crisis, 1938.* Denver, CO: University of Denver Monograph Series in World Affairs, no. 6, 1968–69.

Braden, Spruille. *Diplomats and Demagogues: The Memoirs of Spruille Braden.* N. Rochelle, NY: Arlington House, 1971.

Bradley, John F. N. *Civil War in Russia, 1917–1920.* London: B. T. Batsford, 1975.

Bradsher, Henry S. *Afghanistan and the Soviet Union.* Durham, NC: Duke University Press, 1983.

Brandon, Henry. *The Retreat of American Power.* Garden City, NY: Doubleday, 1972.

———. *Anatomy of Error: The Secret History of the Vietnam War.* London: André Deutsch, 1970.

Brands, H. W. Jr. "Testing Massive Retaliation: Credibility and Crisis Management in the Taiwan Straits." *International Security* 12 (spring 1988): 124–51.

Brandt, Ed. *The Last Voyage of USS Pueblo.* New York: Norton, 1969.

Brandt, Willy. *People and Politics: The Years 1960–1975.* Boston, MA: Little, Brown, 1976.

Branyan, Robert L., and Lawrence H. Larsen, eds. *The Eisenhower Administration 1953–1961: A Documentary History.* New York: Random House, 1971.

Braveboy-Wagner, Jacqueline A. *The Venezuela-Guyana Border Dispute: Britain's Colonial Legacy in Latin America.* Boulder, CO: Westview Press, 1984.

———. "The Venezuela-Guyana Border Dispute." *Latin America and Caribbean Contemporary Record* 2 (1982–83): 229–44.

Brecher, Michael. *Crises in World Politics: Theory and Reality.* Oxford: Pergamon Press, 1993.

———. *Decisions in Israel's Foreign Policy.* London: Oxford University Press, 1974a.

———. "Israel and the Rogers Peace Initiatives: Decisions and Consequences." *Orbis* 18 (summer 1974b): 402–26.

———. *India and World Politics: Krishna Menon's View of the World.* London: Oxford University Press, 1968.

———. *The Struggle for Kashmir.* New York: Oxford University Press, 1953.

Brecher, Michael, with Benjamin Geist. *Decisions in Crisis: Israel 1967 and 1973.* Berkeley, CA: University of California Press, 1980.

Brenner, Philip, and James G. Blight. "Cuba, 1962: The Crisis and Cuban-Soviet Relations: Fidel Castro's Secret 1968 Speech." *CWIHP. Bulletin* 5 (spring 1995): 1, 81–87.

Breslauer, George W. "Soviet Policy in the Middle East, 1967–1972: Unalterable Antagonism or Collaborative Competition?" Chap. 4. in *Managing U.S.-Soviet Rivalry: Problems of Crisis Prevention,* edited by Alexander L. George. Boulder, CO: Westview Press, 1983.

Brind, Harry. "Soviet Policy in the Horn of Africa." *International Affairs* 60 (winter 1983–84): 75–95.

Brines, Russell. *The Indo-Pakistani Conflict.* London: Pall Mall Press, 1968.

Brinkley, Douglas. *Dean Acheson: The Cold War Years 1953–1971.* New Haven, CT: Yale University Press, 1992.

Bromberger, Merry, and Serge Bromberger. *Secrets of Suez.* London: Pan Books, 1957.

Brook-Shepherd, Gordon. *The Storm Birds.* London: Weidenfeld and Nicolson, 1988.

Brooks, Lester. *Behind Japan's Surrender: The Secret Struggle That Ended an Empire.* New York: McGraw-Hill, 1968.

Brown, David J. Latham. "Recent Developments in the Ethiopia-Somaliland Frontier Dispute." *International and Comparative Law Quarterly* 10 (January 1961): 167–78.

Brownlie, Ian. *African Boundaries: A Legal and Diplomatic Encyclopedia.* Berkeley, CA: University of California Press, 1979.

Bruce, Neil. *Portugal's African Wars.* London: Institute for the Study of Conflict, 1973.

Bruegel, Johann W. *Czechoslovakia before Munich: The German Minority Problem and British Appeasement Policy.* Cambridge: Cambridge University Press, 1973.

Brugger, William. *Contemporary China.* London: Croom Helm, 1977.

Bryant, Arthur. *Triumph in the West, 1943–1946.* London: Collins, 1959.

———. *The Turn of the Tide.* Garden City, NY: Doubleday, 1957.

Brzezinski, Zbigniew. *Power and Principle: Memoirs of the National Security Adviser 1977–1981.* New York: Farrar, Straus, Giroux, 1983.

———. *The Soviet Bloc: Unity and Conflict.* Rev. and enl. ed. Cambridge, MA: Harvard University Press, 1967.

Brzezinski, Zbigniew, and Samuel P. Huntington. *Political Power: USA/USSR.* New York: Viking Press, 1964.

Brzoska, Michael, and Frederic S. Pearson. *Arms and Warfare: Escalation, De-escalation, and Negotiation.* Columbia, SC: University of South Carolina Press, 1994.

Buchanan, Albert R. *The United States and World War II.* New York: Harper & Row, 1964.

Bucher, Commander Lloyd M. *Bucher: My Story.* Garden City, NY: Doubleday, 1970.

Bueler, William M. *U.S.-China Policy and the Problem of Taiwan.* Boulder, CO: Colorado Associated University Press, 1971.

Bull, General Odd. *War and Peace in the Middle East.* London: Leo Cooper, 1976.

Bullock, Alan L. G. *Ernest Bevin: Foreign Secretary, 1945–1951.* London: Heinemann, 1983.

———. *Hitler: A Study in Tyranny.* New York: Harper & Row, 1962.

Bundy, McGeorge. *Danger and Survival: Choices about the Bomb in the First Fifty Years.* New York: Random House, 1988.

Burchett, Wilfred G. *The China-Cambodia-Vietnam Triangle.* Chicago, IL: Vanguard Books, 1981.

Burdett, Winston. *Encounter with the Middle East: An Intimate Report of What Lies behind the Arab-Israeli Conflict.* London: André Deutsch, 1970.

Burghardt, Andrew. *Borderland: A Historical and Geographical Study of Burgenland, Austria.* Madison, WI: University of Wisconsin Press, 1962.

Burke, John P., and Fred I. Greenstein, with the collaboration of Larry Berman and Richard Immerman. *How Presidents Test Reality: Decisions on Vietnam, 1954 and 1965.* New York: Russell Sage Foundation, 1989.

Burke, S. M. *Mainsprings of Indian and Pakistani Foreign Policies.* Minneapolis, MN: University of Minnesota Press, 1974.

———. *Pakistan's Foreign Policy: An Historical Analysis.* London: Oxford University Press, 1973.

Burrowes, Reynold A. *Revolution and Rescue in Grenada.* New York: Greenwood Press, 1988.

Buszynski, Les. "Vietnam Confronts China." *Asian Survey* 20 (August 1980): 829–43.

Butler, David, and Anne Sloman. *British Political Facts: 1900–1975.* 4th ed. London: Macmillan, 1975.

Butler, Rohan H. *Grand Strategy.* 7 vols. London: HMSO, 1956–76.

Butow, Robert J. C. *Tojo and the Coming of the War.* Princeton, NJ: Princeton University Press, 1961.

———. *Japan's Decision to Surrender.* Stanford, CA: Stanford University Press, 1954.

Buttinger, Joseph. *Vietnam: A Dragon Embattled.* Vol. 2, *Vietnam at War.* New York: Praeger, 1967.

Byrnes, James F. *Speaking Frankly.* New York: Harper, 1947.

Cable, Vincent. "The 'Football War' and the Central American Common Market." *International Affairs* 45 (October 1969): 658–71.

Callaghan, James. *Time and Chance.* London: Collins, 1987.

Calvert, Peter. *The Falklands Crisis: The Rights and the Wrongs.* New York: St. Martin's Press, 1982.

———. "The Belize Conundrum." *The Economist* 264 (16 July 1977): 15.

———. "Guatemala and Belize." *Contemporary Review* 228 (January 1976): 7–12.

Calvocoressi, Peter. *Survey of International Affairs 1951.* RIIA. London: Oxford University Press, 1954.

Calvocoressi, Peter, and Guy Wint. *Total War: Causes and Courses of the Second World War.* Harmondsworth: Penguin, 1972.

Cameron, Meribeth E., Thomas H. D. Mahoney, and George E. McReynolds. *China, Japan and the Powers.* New York: The Ronald Press, 1952.

Cameron, Norman, and R. H. Stevens, eds. and trans. *Hitler's Table Talk, 1941–44: His Private Conversations.* London: Weidenfeld & Nicolson, 1973.

Camp, Glen D. "Greek-Turkish Conflict over Cyprus." *Political Science Quarterly* 95 (spring 1980): 43–70.

Campbell, John C. "The Soviet Union, the United States, and the Twin Crises of Hungary and Suez." In *Suez 1956: The Crisis and Its Consequences,* edited by W. Roger Louis and Roger Owen. Oxford: Clarendon Press, 1989.

———. "The United States and the Cyprus Question." In *Essays on the Cyprus Conflict,* edited by Van Coufoudakis. New York: Pella, 1976.

Campbell, Thomas M., and George C. Herring, eds. *The Diaries of Edward R. Stettinius, Jr., 1943–1946.* New York: New Viewpoints, 1975.

Caridi, Ronald J. *The Korean War and American Politics.* Philadelphia, PA: University of Pennsylvania Press, 1968.

Carlgren, Wilhelm M. *Swedish Foreign Policy during the Second World War.* London: E. Benn, 1977.

Carr, Edward H. *International Relations since the Peace Treaties.* Rev. ed. London: Macmillan, 1945.

Carsten, Francis L. *Britain and the Weimar Republic: The British Documents.* London: Batsford Academic and Educational Ltd., 1984.

Carter, Gwendolyn M. *African One-Party States.* Ithaca, NY: Cornell University Press, 1962.

Carter, Gwendolyn M., and Patrick O'Meara, eds. *Southern Africa in Crisis.* Bloomington, IN: Indiana University Press, 1977.

Carter, Jimmy. *Keeping Faith: Memoirs of a President.* New York: Bantam Books, 1982.

Cassels, Alan. *Mussolini's Early Diplomacy.* Princeton, NJ: Princeton University Press, 1970.

———. *Fascist Italy.* London: Routledge & Kegan Paul, 1968.

Castango, A. A. "The Somali-Kenyan Controversy: Implications for the Future." *Journal of Modern African Studies* 3 (July 1964): 165–88.

———. "Conflicts in the Horn of Africa." *Orbis* 4 (summer 1960): 204–15.

Castillero-Reyes, Ernesto. *Historia de Panamá.* Panama City: Republic of Panama, 1962.

Cate, Curtis. *The Ides of August: The Berlin Crisis, 1961.* New York: M. Evans, 1978.

Cattan, Henry. *Palestine, the Arabs and Israel: The Search for Justice.* London: Longman, 1969.

Catudal, Honoré M. *Kennedy and the Berlin Wall Crisis: A Case Study in US Decision Making.* Berlin: Berlin Verlag, 1980.

Cecil, Robert. *Hitler's Decision to Invade Russia, 1941.* London: Davis-Poynter, 1975.

Cervi, Mario. *The Hollow Legions: Mussolini's Blunder in Greece, 1940–1941.* Garden City, NY: Doubleday, 1971.

Chabad, Federico. *A History of Italian Fascism.* London: Weidenfeld & Nicolson, 1963.

de Chambon, Henri. *La Lithuanie Moderne.* Paris: Editions de la Revue Parlementaire, 1933.

Chan, Steve. "Chinese Conflict Calculus and Behavior: Assessment from a Perspective of Conflict Management." *World Politics* 30 (April 1978): 391–410.

Chandler, Geoffrey. *The Divided Land: An Anglo-Greek Tragedy.* London: Macmillan, 1959.

Chang, Gordon H. *Friends and Enemies: The United States, China, and the Soviet Union, 1948–1972.* Stanford, CA: Stanford University Press, 1990.

———. "To the Nuclear Brink: Eisenhower, Dulles, and the Quemoy-Matsu Crisis." *International Security* 12 (spring 1988): 96–122.

Chang, Pao-min. "A New Scramble for the South China Sea Islands." *Contemporary Southeast Asia* 12, no. 1 (1990): 20–39.

———. *The Sino-Vietnamese Territorial Dispute.* New York: Praeger, 1986.

Chawla, Sudershan, and D. R. Sardesai. *Changing Patterns of Security and Stability in Asia.* New York: Praeger, 1980.

Chayes, Abram. *The Cuban Missile Crisis: International Crises and the Role of Law.* London: Oxford University Press, 1974.

Cheema, Pervaiz Iqbal. "The Afghanistan Crisis and Pakistan's Security Dilemma." *Asian Survey* 23 (March 1983): 227–43.

Chege, Michael. "The Revolution Betrayed: Ethiopia 1974–9." *Journal of Modern African Studies* 17 (September 1979): 359–80.

Chen, King C. *China's War with Vietnam, 1979: Issues, Decisions, and Implications.* Stanford, CA: Hoover Institution Press, 1987.

Cheng, Peter. *A Chronology of the People's Republic of China from October 1, 1949.* Ottawa: Rowman & Littlefield, 1972.

Chew, Allen F. *The White Death: The Epic of the Soviet-Finnish Winter War.* East Lansing, MI: Michigan State University Press, 1971.

Chiang Kai-shek. *Soviet Russia in China: A Summing-Up at 70.* London: Harrap, 1957.

Child, Jack. *Geopolitics and Conflict in South America: Quarrels among Neighbors.* New York: Praeger, 1985.

Childers, Erskine B. *The Road to Suez: A Study of Western-Arab Relations.* London: Macgibbon & Kee, 1962.

Chopra, Pran. *India's Second Liberation.* Boston: MIT Press, 1974.

Choudhury, Golam W. *The Last Days of United Pakistan.* Bloomington, IN: Indiana University Press, 1974.

———. *Pakistan's Relations with India, 1947–1966.* New York: Praeger, 1968.

Christensen, Thomas. "Threats, Assurances, and the Last Chance for Peace: The Lessons of Mao's Korean War Telegrams." *International Security* 17, no. 1 (1992): 122–54.

Christopher, Warren et al. *American Hostages in Iran: The Conduct of a Crisis.* New Haven, CT: Yale University Press, 1985.

Chubin, Shahram. "Iran and the War: From Stalemate to Ceasefire." In *The Gulf War: Regional and International Dimensions,* edited by H.W. Maull and O. Pick. London: Pinter, 1989.

Chubin, Shahram, and Charles Tripp. *Iran and Iraq at War.* Boulder, CO: Westview Press, 1988.

Chubin, Shahram, and Sepehr Zabih. *The Foreign Relations of Iran: A Developing State in a Zone of Great-Power Conflict.* Berkeley, CA: University of California Press, 1974.

Chung, Chin O. *Pyongyang between Peking and Moscow: North Korea's Involvement in the Sino-Soviet Dispute, 1958–1975.* Tuscaloosa, AL: University of Alabama Press, 1978.

Churchill, Randolph S., and Winston S. Churchill. *The Six Day War.* London: Heinemann, 1967.

Churchill, Winston. *The Second World War.* 6 vols. London: Cassell, 1948–53.

———. *The Gathering Storm.* Vol. 1. London: Cassell, 1948.

———. *Their Finest Hour.* Vol. 2. London: Cassell, 1949.

———. *The Grand Alliance.* Vol. 3. London: Cassell, 1950a.

———. *The Hinge of Fate.* Vol. 4. London: Cassell, 1950b.

———. *Closing the Ring.* Vol. 5. London: Cassell, 1951.

———. *Triumph and Tragedy.* Vol. 6. London: Cassell, 1953.

Ciano, Count Galeazzo. *Ciano's Diary 1939–1943.* London: Heinemann, 1947.

Cienciala, Anna Maria. *Poland and the Western Powers, 1938–1939: A Study in the Interdependence of Eastern and Western Europe.* London: Routledge & Kegan Paul, 1968.

Cigar, Norman. "Iraq's Strategic Mindset and the Gulf War: Blueprint for Defeat." *Journal of Strategic Studies* 15, no. 1 (1992): 1–29.

Clark, Alan. *Barbarossa: The Russian-German Conflict, 1941–1945.* London: Hutchinson, 1965.

Clark, Charles. *Bessarabia: Russia and Roumania on the Black Sea.* New York: Dodd, Mead & Company, 1927.

Clark, Mark W. *From the Danube to the Yalu.* New York: Harper Brothers, 1954.

Clarke, S. J. G. *The Congo Mercenary: History and Analysis.* Johannesburg: South African Institute of International Affairs, 1968.

Clay, Lucius D. *Decision in Germany.* Garden City, NY: Doubleday, 1950.

Clement, Peter. "Moscow and Nicaragua: Two Sides of Soviet Policy." *Comparative Strategy* 5, no. 1 (1985): 75–91.

Clifford, Clark. *Counsel to the President: A Memoir.* New York: Random House, 1991.
Clissold, Stephen. *Yugoslavia and the Soviet Union, 1939–1973: A Documentary Survey.* London: Oxford University Press, 1975.
Clogg, Richard. *A Short History of Modern Greece.* Cambridge: Cambridge University Press, 1980.
Clough, Shepard B. *France: A History of National Economics, 1789–1939.* New York: Octagon Books, 1970.
Clubb, Oliver E. *Twentieth Century China.* 2d ed. New York: Columbia University Press, 1972.
———. "Formosa and the Offshore Islands in American Policy." *Political Science Quarterly* 74 (winter 1960): 517–31.
Clyde, Paul Hibbert. *The Far East.* 3d ed. Englewood Cliffs, NJ: Prentice-Hall, 1958.
Cobban, Helena. *The Palestine Liberation Organization.* Cambridge: Cambridge University Press, 1984.
Cohen, Arthur A. "The Sino-Soviet Border Crisis of 1969." Chap. 12 in *Avoiding War: Problems of Crisis Management,* edited by Alexander L. George. Boulder, CO: Westview Press, 1991.
Collins, Joseph J. *The Soviet Invasion of Afghanistan: A Study in the Use of Force in Soviet Foreign Policy.* Lexington, MA: D. C. Heath, 1986.
———. *War in Peacetime—The History and Lessons of Korea.* Boston, MA: Houghton Mifflin, 1969.
Collins, Robert J. *Lord Wavell, 1883–1941: A Military Biography.* London: Hodder & Stoughton, 1947.
Connell-Smith, Gordon. *The Inter-American System.* London: Oxford University Press, 1966.
Cooley, John K. *Green March, Black September: The Story of the Palestinian Arabs.* London: Frank Cass, 1973.
Coox, Alvin D. *The Anatomy of a Small War: The Soviet-Japanese Struggle for Changkufeng-Khasan, 1938.* Westport, CT: Greenwood Press, 1977.
Cordesman, Anthony H., and Abraham R. Wagner. *The Lessons of Modern War.* Vol. I, *The Arab-Israeli Conflicts, 1973–1989;* Vol. II, *The Iran-Iraq War;* Vol. III, *The Afghan and Falklands Conflicts.* Boulder, CO.: Westview Press, 1990.
Cottam, Martha L. *Images and Intervention: U.S. Policies in Latin America.* Pittsburgh, PA: University of Pittsburgh Press, 1994.
Cottam, Richard W. *Iran and the United States: A Cold War Case Study.* Pittsburgh, PA: University of Pittsburgh Press, 1988.
Coulombis, Theodore A. *The United States, Greece, and Turkey: The Troubled Triangle.* New York: Praeger, 1983.
Cowling, Maurice. *The Impact of Hitler: British Politics and British Policy 1933–40.* Cambridge: Cambridge University Press, 1975.
Cox, Isaac. "Nicaragua and the United States 1909–1927." In *World Peace Foundation Pamphlets* 10, no. 7 (1927): 703–887.
Craigie, Robert L. *Behind the Japanese Mask.* London: Hutchinson, 1946.
Crankshaw, Edward. *Khrushchev: A Biography.* London: Collins, 1966.
Crassweller, Robert D. *Trujillo: The Life and Times of a Caribbean Dictator.* New York: Macmillan, 1966.
Crawshaw, Nancy. *The Cyprus Revolt: An Account of the Struggle for Union with Greece.* London: Allen & Unwin, 1978.

Cremeans, Charles D. *The Arabs and the World: Nasser's Arab Nationalist Policy.* New York: Praeger, 1963.

van Creveld, Martin L. *Hitler's Strategy 1940–1941: The Balkan Clue.* Cambridge: Cambridge University Press, 1973.

Croci, Osvaldo. "The Trieste Crisis, 1953." Ph.D. diss, McGill University, Montreal, 1991.

Crocker, Chester A. *High Noon in Southern Africa: Making Peace in a Rough Neighborhood.* New York: W. W. Norton, 1992.

Crouch, Harold A. *The Army and Politics in Indonesia.* Ithaca, NY: Cornell University Press, 1978.

Crowder, Michael. *Senegal: A Study in French Assimilation Policy.* London: Oxford University Press, 1962.

Cruickshank, Charles G. *Greece 1940–41.* London: Paris-Poynter 1976.

Cumings, Bruce. *The Origins of the Korean War.* Vol. 2, *The Roaring of the Cataract, 1947–1950.* Princeton, NJ: Princeton University Press, 1990.

———. *The Origins of the Korean War.* Vol. 1, *Liberation and the Emergence of Separate Regimes, 1945–1947.* Princeton, NJ: Princeton University Press, 1981.

Cumings, Bruce, and Kathryn Weathersby. "An Exchange on Korean War Origins." CWIHP. Bulletin 6–7 (winter 1995–96): 120–22.

Current History. "Sweden and the Aland Award." 5 (April–September 1921): 543–44.

———. "Conservative Trend in Scandinavia: Fall of Sweden's Socialist Ministry—Status of the Aland Situation." 5 (October 1920–March 1921): 425–27.

———. "Developments in Scandinavian Countries—Aland: A Fiume of the North." 4 (April–September 1920): 790–92.

Currey, Muriel. *Italian Foreign Policy, 1918–1932.* London: Ivor Nicholson and Watson, 1932.

Curtis, Gerald L. "The United Nations Observation Group in Lebanon." *International Organization* 18 (autumn 1964): 738–65.

Dahm, Bernhard. *History of Indonesia in the Twentieth Century.* London: Pall Mall Press, 1971.

Dallek, Robert. *Franklin Delano Roosevelt and American Foreign Policy, 1932–1945.* New York: Oxford University Press, 1979.

———. *Soviet Conduct in World Affairs.* New York: Columbia University Press, 1960.

Dallin, David J. *Soviet Russia and the Far East.* New Haven, CT: Yale University Press, 1948.

———. *Soviet Russia's Foreign Policy, 1939–1942.* New Haven, CT: Yale University Press, 1942.

Damis, John J. *Conflict in Northwest Africa: The Western Saharan Dispute.* Stanford, CA: Hoover Institution Press, 1983.

Dan, Uri. *Operation Uganda.* Jerusalem: Keter, 1976.

Daniel, James, and John G. Hubbell. *Strike in the West: The Complete Story of the Cuban Crisis.* New York: Holt, Rinehart & Winston, 1963.

Dann, Uriel. *Iraq under Qassem, a Political History 1958–1963.* New York: Praeger, 1969.

Darling, Frank C. "Marshal Sarit and Absolutist Rule in Thailand." *Pacific Affairs* 33 (December 1960): 347–60.

Das Gupta, Jyoti Bhusan. *Indo-Pakistan Relations 1947–1955.* Amsterdam: Djambatan, 1958.

Davidson, Phillip B. *Vietnam at War: The History, 1946–1975.* New York: Oxford University Press, 1991.

Davis, Harold E., John J. Finan, and F. Taylor Peck. *Latin American Diplomatic History: An Introduction.* Baton Rouge, LA: Louisiana State University Press, 1977.

Davis, Nathaniel. "The Angola Decision of 1975: A Personal Memoir." *Foreign Affairs* 57 (fall 1978): 109–24.

Davison, Walter P. *The Berlin Blockade: A Study in Cold War Politics.* Princeton, NJ: Princeton University Press, 1958.

Dawisha, Adeed I. *Syria and the Lebanese Crisis.* London: Macmillan, 1980.

———. "The Impact of External Actors on Syria's Intervention in Lebanon." *Journal of South Asian and Middle East Studies* 2 (fall 1978): 22–43.

———. "Intervention in Yemen: An Analysis of Egyptian Perceptions and Policies." *Middle East Journal* 29, no. 1 (1975): 47–64.

Dawisha, Karen. *The Kremlin and the Prague Spring.* Berkeley, CA: University of California Press, 1984.

———. "Soviet Decision-Making in the Middle East: The 1973 October War and the 1980 Gulf War." *International Affairs* (London) 57 (winter 1980–81): 43–59.

———. "Soviet Security and the Role of the Military: The 1968 Czechoslovakia Crisis." *British Journal of Political Science* 10 (July 1980): 341–63.

———. "The Soviet Union and Czechoslovakia, 1968." *Jerusalem Journal of International Relations* 3 (winter–spring 1978): 143–71.

Day, Alan J., ed. *Border and Territorial Disputes.* 2d ed. Burnt Mill, Harlow, Essex, U.K.: Longman, 1987.

———, ed. *Maritime Affairs—A World Handbook: A Reference Guide to Maritime Organizations, Conventions and Disputes to the International Politics of the Sea.* Burnt Mill, Harlow, Essex, U.K.: Longman, 1985.

Dayal, Rajeshwar. *Mission for Hammarskjöld: The Congo Crisis.* London: Oxford University Press, 1976.

Dayan, Moshe. *Story of My Life.* New York: Morrow, 1976.

———. *Diary of the Sinai Campaign.* New York: Harper & Row, 1966.

Deakin, F. W. *The Last Days of Mussolini.* Harmondsworth, U.K.: Penguin, 1962.

Dean, William F., with William L. Worden. *General Dean's Story.* London: Weidenfeld & Nicolson, 1954.

Debicki, Roman. *Foreign Policy of Poland 1919–1939: From the Rebirth of the Polish Republic to World War II.* New York: Praeger, 1962.

Decalo, Samuel. *Historical Dictionary of Chad.* 2d ed. Metuchen, NJ: Scarecrow Press, 1987.

———. "Regionalism, Political Decay, and Civil Strife in Chad." *Journal of Modern African Studies* 18 (March 1980a): 23–56.

———. "Chad: The Roots of Centre-Periphery Strife." *African Affairs* 79 (October 1980b): 491–509.

Dedijer, Vladimir, et al. *History of Yugoslavia.* Edited by Marie Longyear. Translated by Kordija Kveder. New York: McGraw-Hill, 1974.

Deeb, Mary Jane. *Libya's Foreign Policy in North Africa.* Boulder, CO: Westview Press, 1991.

Degras, Jane, ed. *Soviet Documents on Foreign Policy 1917–41.* RIIA, vol. 3. London: Oxford University Press, 1953.

Dei-Anang, Michael. *Administration of Ghana's Foreign Relations, 1957–1965: A Personal Memoir.* London: Institute of Commonwealth Studies, by Athlone Press, 1975.

Dekmejian, Richard H. *Egypt under Nasir: A Study in Political Dynamics.* Albany, NY: SUNY Press, 1971.

Delzell, Charles F. *Mediterranean Fascism 1919–1945.* New York: Macmillan, 1970.

Denktash, Rauf R. *The Cyprus Triangle.* Boston: Allen & Unwin, 1982.

Denny, Harold. *Dollars for Bullets: The Story of American Rule in Nicaragua.* New York: Dial Press, 1929.

Derry, Thomas. *The Campaign in Norway.* London: HMSO, 1952.

Deutscher, Isaac. *Stalin: A Political Biography.* London: Oxford University Press, 1949.

Dewar, Michael. *Brush Fire Wars: Minor Campaigns of the British Army since 1945.* New York: St. Martin's Press, 1984.

Dexter, Byron. *The Years of Opportunity: The League of Nations, 1920–1926.* New York: Viking Press, 1967.

Diederich, Bernard, and A. Burt. *Papa Doc—Haiti and Its Dictator.* London: Bodley Head, 1969.

Dien, Bui. "A New Kind of War in Southeast Asia." *Asian Affairs* 6 (May–June 1979): 273–81.

Dilks, David, ed. *The Diaries of Sir Alexander Cadogan, 1938–1945.* London: Cassell, 1971.

Dinerstein, Herbert S. *The Making of a Missile Crisis: October 1962.* Baltimore, MD: Johns Hopkins University Press, 1976.

Dinges, John. *Our Man in Panama.* New York: Random House, 1991.

Dingman, Roger. "Atomic Diplomacy during the Korean War." *International Security* 13 (winter 1988–89): 50–91.

Divine, Robert A. *The Cuban Missile Crisis.* Chicago, IL: Quadrangle Books, 1971.

Dmitriyev, Yuri. "Far Away on the Border." *Current Digest of the Soviet Press* 21 (2 April 1969): 4.

Dobrynin, Anatoly. *In Confidence.* New York: Times Books/Random House, 1995.

Dominguez, Jorge I. *Cuba: Order and Revolution.* Cambridge, MA: Belknap Press, 1978.

Dommen, Arthur J. "Laos in 1984: The Year of the Thai Border." *Asian Survey* 25 (January 1985): 114–21.

———. *Conflict in Laos: The Politics of Neutralization.* Rev. ed. New York: Praeger, 1971.

Donelan, Michael D., and M. J. Grieve. *International Disputes: Case Histories, 1945–1970.* London: Europa, 1973.

Donnelly, Thomas M., Margaret Roth, and Caleb Baker. *Operation JUST CAUSE: The Storming of Panama.* New York: Lexington Books, 1991.

Donovan, Robert J. *Conflict and Crisis: The Presidency of Harry S. Truman, 1945–1948.* New York: Norton, 1977a.

———. *Tumultuous Years: The Presidency of Harry S. Truman 1949–1953.* New York: Norton, 1977b.

Dowty, Alan. *Middle East Crisis: U.S. Decision-Making in 1958, 1970, and 1973.* Berkeley, CA: University of California Press, 1984.

Draper, Theodore. *Israel and World Politics: Roots of the Third Arab—Israeli War.* New York: Viking Press, 1968a.

———. *The Dominican Revolt: A Case Study in American Policy.* New York: *Commentary* Report, 1968b.

———. *Castroism: Theory and Practice.* London: Pall Mall Press, 1965.

Dreier, John C. *The Organization of American States and the Hemisphere Crisis.* New York: Harper & Row, 1962.

Drekonja-Kornat, Gerhard. "El Diferendo Entre Colombia Y Nicaragua." *Foro Internacional,* 27 (October–December 1982): 133–45.

Druks, Herbert. *From Truman through Johnson: A Documentary History.* New York: Robert Speller, 1971.

Drysdale, John. *The Somali Dispute.* New York: Praeger, 1964.

Duff, Ernest A., and John F. McGamant. *Violence and Repression in Latin America: A Quantitative and Historical Analysis.* New York: Free Press, 1976.

Duff, R. E. B. *100 Years of the Suez Canal.* Brighton, U.K.: Clifton, 1969.

Duiker, William J. *China and Vietnam: The Roots of Conflict.* Berkeley, CA: Institute of East Asian Studies, University of California, 1986.

Dulles, Eleanor L. *The Wall: A Tragedy in Three Acts.* Columbia, SC: University of South Carolina Press, 1972.

Dulles, Foster Rhea. *American Policy toward Communist China: The Historical Record, 1949–1969.* New York: Crowell, 1972.

Duncan-Jones, Anne. "The Civil War in Cyprus." In *The International Regulation of Civil Wars,* edited by Evan Luard, 148–68. London: Thames and Hudson, 1972.

Duncanson, Dennis. "China's Vietnam War: New and Old Strategic Imperatives." *World Today* 35 (June 1979): 241–49.

Dunn, Peter M., and Bruce W. Watson, eds. *American Intervention in Grenada: The Implications of Operation "Urgent Fury."* Boulder, CO: Westview Press, 1985.

Dupree, Louis. *Afghanistan.* Princeton, NJ: Princeton University Press, 1980.

———. "India's Move into Goa." New York: American Universities Field Staff (AUFS), South Asia Series, 6, February 1962.

———. "'Pushtunistan': The Problem and its Larger Implications." Parts 1–3. New York: AUFS, South Asia Series, 5, nos. 2–4, 1961a,b,c.

Dupuy, R. Ernest, and Trevor N. Dupuy. *The Encyclopedia of Military History.* 2d rev. ed. New York: Harper & Row, 1986.

Dupuy, Trevor N. *Elusive Victory: The Arab-Israeli Wars, 1947–1974.* New York: Harper & Row, 1978.

Dupuy, Trevor N., and Paul Martell. *Flawed Victory.* Washington, DC: Hero Books, 1985.

Duroselle, Jean Baptiste. *Le Conflit de Trieste 1943–54.* Bruxelle: Institut de Sociologie de l'Université Libre de Bruxelle, 1966.

Dziewanowski, Marian K. *Poland in the Twentieth Century.* New York: Columbia University Press, 1977.

———. *Joseph Pilsudski: A European Federalist, 1918–1922.* Stanford, CA: Hoover Institution Press, 1969.

———. *The Communist Party of Poland.* Cambridge, MA: Harvard University Press, 1959.

E. B. "The Salazar Regime and Goa." *World Today* 10 (September 1954): 389–97.

Eagleton, Clyde. *International Government.* 3d ed. New York: Ronald Press, 1957.

Eayrs, James, ed. *The Commonwealth and Suez: A Documentary Survey.* London: Oxford University Press, 1964.

Eban, Abba. *Personal Witness: Israel through My Eyes.* New York: G. P. Putnam's Sons, 1992.

———. *An Autobiography.* Tel Aviv: Steimatzky, 1977.

———. *My Country: The Story of Modern Israel.* London: Weidenfeld & Nicolson, 1972.

Ebenstein, William. *Fascist Italy.* New York: Russell & Russell, 1973.

Ebinger, Charles K. *Foreign Intervention in Civil War: The Politics and Diplomacy of the Angolan Conflict.* Boulder, CO: Westview Press, 1984.

Eden, Anthony. *Memoirs: Facing the Dictators.* London: Cassell, 1962.

———. *Memoirs: Full Circle.* London: Cassell, 1960.

Edmondson, Clifton E. *The Heimwehr and Austrian Politics, 1918–1936.* Athens, GA: University of Georgia Press, 1978.

Edmunds, Cecil J. *Kurds, Turks and Arabs: Politics, Travel and Research in North-Eastern Iraq 1919–1925.* London: Oxford University Press, 1957.

van Eekelen, William F. *Indian Foreign Policy and the Border Dispute with China.* The Hague: Martinus Nijhoff, 1964.

Ehrlich, Thomas. *Cyprus 1958–1967.* New York: Oxford University Press, 1974.

Eisenhower, Dwight D. *The White House Years.* Vol. 2, *Waging Peace, 1956–1961.* Garden City, NY: Doubleday, 1965.

———. *The White House Years.* Vol. 1, *Mandate for Change, 1953–1956.* Garden City, NY: Doubleday, 1963.

———. *Crusade in Europe.* Garden City, NY: Doubleday, 1948.

Elliott, David W. P. (ed.). *The Third Indochina Conflict.* Boulder, CO: Westview Press, 1981.

Ely, Paul. *L'Indochine dans la Tourmente.* Paris: Plon, 1964.

Embree, George. *The Soviet Union and the German Question, September 1958-June 1961.* The Hague: Martinus Nijhoff, 1963.

Emerson, Rupert. "Reflections on the Indonesian Case." *World Politics* 1 (October 1948): 59–81.

Emin, A. *Turkey in the World War.* Edited by James Shotwell. New Haven, CT: Yale University Press, 1930.

Emmerson, James T. *The Rhineland Crisis: 7 March 1936, A Study in Multilateral Diplomacy.* London: London School of Economics and Political Science, 1977.

Epstein, H. M., ed. *Revolt in Congo: 1960–64.* New York: Facts on File, 1965.

Epstein, Leon D. *British Politics in the Suez Crisis.* Urbana, IL: University of Illinois Press, 1964.

Erickson, John. *The Road to Berlin.* Boulder, CO: Westview Press, 1983.

———. *The Road to Stalingrad.* New York: Harper & Row, 1975.

van der Esch, Patricia A. M. *Prelude to War: The International Repercussion of the Spanish Civil War.* The Hague: Martinus Nijhoff, 1951.

Espaillat, Arturo R. *Trujillo, The Last Caesar.* Chicago, IL: Regnery, 1963.

Estigarribia, José Felix. *The Epic of the Chaco: Marshal Estigarribia's Memoirs of the Chaco War.* New York: Greenwood Press, 1969.

Eubank, Keith. *Munich.* Norman, OK: University of Oklahoma Press, 1965.

Eudin, Xenia, and Robert C. North. *Soviet Russia and the East 1920–1927: A Documentary Survey.* Stanford, CA: Stanford University Press, 1957.

Evans, Rowland, and Robert Novak. *Nixon in the White House: The Frustration of Power.* New York: Random House, 1971.

———. *Lyndon B. Johnson: The Exercise of Power.* London: Allen & Unwin, 1967.

Evans, Stephen F. *The Slow Rapprochement.* Beverley, U.K.: Eothen Press, 1982.

Evron, Yair. *War and Intervention in Lebanon.* London: Croom Helm, 1987.

Facts on File. *South Vietnam: US-Communist Confrontation in Southeast Asia.* 7 vols. New York: Facts on File, 1973–74.

Fagen, Richard R., and Wayne A. Cornelius Jr., eds. *Political Power in Latin America: Seven Confrontations.* Englewood Cliffs, NJ: Prentice-Hall, 1970.

Fagg, J. E. *Latin America: A General History.* New York: Macmillan, 1967.

Fairbank, John King. *China Perceived.* New York: Vintage, 1976.

———. *The United States and China.* 3d ed. Cambridge, MA: Harvard University Press, 1972.

Fall, Bernard B. *Anatomy of a Crisis: The Laotian Crisis of 1960–61.* Garden City, NY: Doubleday, 1969.

———. *Hell in a Very Small Place: The Siege of Dien Bien Phu.* Philadelphia, PA: Lippincott, 1966.

Farer, Tom J. *War Clouds on the Horn of Africa: The Widening Storm.* 2d rev. ed. New York: Carnegie Endowment for International Peace, 1979.

Farnie, Douglas A. *East and West of Suez: The Suez Canal in History, 1854–1956.* Oxford: Clarendon Press, 1969.

Farnsworth, David N., and James W. McKenney. *U.S.-Panama Relations, 1903–1978: A Study in Linkage Politics.* Boulder, CO: Westview Press, 1983.

Farr, Philip. *Soviet Russia and the Baltic Republics.* London: Russia Today Publication, 1944.

Farrar-Hockley, Anthony. "A Reminiscence of the Chinese People's Volunteers in the Korean War." *China Quarterly* 98 (1984): 287–304.

Feiling, Keith. *Life of Neville Chamberlain.* London: Macmillan, 1946.

Feis, Herbert. *The Atomic Bomb and the End of World War II.* Princeton, NJ: Princeton University Press, 1966.

———. *The Road to Pearl Harbor.* Princeton, NJ: Princeton University Press, 1950.

———. *Seen from E.A.: Three International Episodes.* New York: Knopf, 1947.

Feith, Herbert. *The Decline of Constitutional Democracy in Indonesia.* Ithaca, NY: Cornell University Press, 1962.

Feith, Herbert, and Daniel S. Lev. "The End of the Indonesian Rebellion." *Pacific Affairs* 36 (spring 1963): 32–46.

Fejpoe, François. *Behind the Rape of Hungary.* New York: David McKay, 1957.

Feldman, Herbert. *The End and the Beginning: Pakistan, 1969–1971.* London: Oxford University Press, 1975.

———. *Revolution in Pakistan: A Study of the Martial Law Administration.* London: Oxford University Press, 1967.

Feldman, Shai, and Heda Rechnitz-Kijner. *Deception, Consensus and War: Israel in Lebanon.* Tel Aviv: Tel Aviv University, Jaffee Center for Strategic Studies, Paper No. 27, 1984.

Fenyo, Mario D. *Hitler, Horthy and Hungary: German-Hungarian Relations, 1941–1944.* New Haven, CT: Yale University Press, 1972.

Ferguson, Yale H. "The Dominican Intervention of 1965: Recent Interpretations." *International Organization* 27 (autumn 1973): 517–48.

Feske, Victor H. "The Road to Suez: The British Foreign Office and the Quai D'Orsay, 1951–1957." In *The Diplomats, 1939–1979,* edited by Gordon A. Craig and Francis L. Loewenheim, 167–200. Princeton, NJ: Princeton University Press, 1994.

Fifield, Russell H. *The Diplomacy of South East Asia, 1945–1958.* New York: Harper, 1958.

Filene, Peter Gabriel. *American Views of Soviet Russia, 1917–1965.* Homewood, IL: Dorsey Press, 1968.

Finer, Herman. *Dulles over Suez: The Theory and Practice of His Diplomacy.* Chicago, IL: Quadrangle Books, 1964.

The Finnish Blue Book. *The Development of Finnish-Soviet Relations during the Autumn of 1939.* Philadelphia, PA: Lippincott, 1940.

Finnish Political Science Association. *Essays on Finnish Foreign Policy.* Helsinki, 1969.

Fischer, Beth A. "The Reagan Reversal: America's Soviet Policy, 1981–1985." Ph.D. diss., University of Toronto, 1995.

Fischer, John. *America's Master Plan.* London: Hamilton Press, 1951.

Fischer-Galati, Stephen A. *Twentieth Century Rumania.* New York: Columbia University Press, 1970.

———. *The Socialist Republic of Rumania.* Baltimore, MD: Johns Hopkins University Press, 1969.

Fish, Steven M. "The Berlin Blockade Crisis of 1948–1949." Chap. 10 in *Avoiding War: Problems of Crisis Management,* edited by Alexander L. George. Boulder, CO: Westview Press, 1991.

Fisher, Margaret W., Leo E. Rose, and Robert A. Huttenback. *Himalayan Battleground: Sino-Indian Rivalry in Ladakh.* London: Pall Mall Press, 1963.

Fitzsimmons, Matthew A. *Empire by Treaty: Britain and the Middle East in the Twentieth Century.* Notre Dame, IN: University of Notre Dame Press, 1964.

Flanagan, E. M. *Battle for Panama: Inside Operation JUST CAUSE.* Washington, DC: Brassey's, 1993.

Flapan, Simha. *The Birth of Israel: Myths and Realities.* New York: Pantheon Books, 1987.

Fletcher, Arnold. *Afghanistan: Highway of Conquest.* Ithaca, NY: Cornell University Press, 1966.

Fluharty, Vernon L. *Dance of the Millions: Military Rule and Social Revolution in Colombia, 1930–1956.* Pittsburgh, PA: University of Pittsburgh Press, 1957.

Foley, Charles, and W. I. Scobie. *The Struggle for Cyprus.* Stanford, CA: Hoover Institution Press, 1975.

Foltz, William J. "Libya's Military Power." In *The Green and the Black: Qadhafi's Policies in Africa,* edited by René Lemarchand, 52–69. Bloomington, IN: Indiana University Press, 1988.

———. *From French West Africa to the Mali Federation.* New Haven, CT: Yale University Press, 1965.

Fontaine, Roger Warren. *On Negotiating with Cuba.* Washington, DC: American Enterprise Institute for Public Policy Research, 1975.

Foot, Rosemary. *A Substitute for Victory: The Politics of Peace Making at the Korean Armistice Talks.* Ithaca, NY: Cornell University Press, 1991.

———. "Nuclear Coercion and the Ending of the Korean Conflict." *International Security* 13 (winter 1988–89): 92–112.

———. *The Wrong War: American Policy and the Dimensions of the Korean Conflict, 1950–1953.* Ithaca, NY: Cornell University Press, 1985.

Forbes, Nevill, Arnold J. Toynbee, David Mitrany, and D. G. Hogarth. *The Balkans: A History of Bulgaria, Serbia, Greece, Rumania, Turkey.* Oxford: Clarendon Press, 1915.

Ford, Gerald. *A Time to Heal.* New York: Harper & Row, 1979.

Fraenkel, Peter. "Conflict in the Sahara as Spain Withdraws." *The Middle East* 17 (March 1976): 6–9.

Franck, Dorotheo S. "Pathanistan—Disputed Disposition of a Tribal Land." *Middle East Journal* 6 (winter 1952): 49–68.

Franck, Thomas M. "The Stealing of the Sahara." *American Journal of International Law* 70 (October 1976): 694–721.

Fraser, N. M., K. W. Hipel, J. Jaworsky, and R. Zuijan. "A Conflict Analysis of the Armenian-Azerbaijani Dispute." *Journal of Conflict Resolution* 34, no. 4 (1990): 652–67.

Fraser-Tyler, William K. *Afghanistan: A Study of Political Developments in Central and Southern Asia.* 2d ed. Princeton, NJ: Princeton University Press, 1967.

Freedman, Lawrence. *Britain and the Falklands War.* Oxford: Basil Blackwell, 1988.

———. "The War of the Falklands Islands, 1982." *Foreign Affairs* 61 (fall 1982): 196–210.

Freedman, Lawrence, and Virginia Gamba-Stonehouse. *Signals of War: The Falklands Conflict of 1982.* London: Faber & Faber, 1990.

Freedman, Lawrence, and Efraim Karsh. *The Gulf Conflict.* Princeton, NJ: Princeton University Press, 1993.

Freedman, Robert O. *Soviet Policy toward the Middle East since 1970.* New York: Praeger, 1975.

Fuchser, Larry William. *Neville Chamberlain and Appeasement.* New York: Norton, 1982.

Furniss, Edgar S. Jr. "The Inter-American System and Recent Caribbean Disputes." *International Organization* 4 (November 1950): 585–97.

Gafencu, Grigore. *Prelude to the Russian Campaign.* London: Frederick Muller, 1945.

Galbraith, Francis J. "ASEAN Today: Feeling the Heat." *Asian Affairs* 8 (September–October 1980): 31–40.

Galbraith, John K. *Ambassador's Journal: A Personal Account of the Kennedy Years.* Boston, MA: Houghton Mifflin, 1969.

Galich, Manuel. *Guatemala.* La Habana: Casa de las Américas, 1968.

Galindez, Jesús de. *The Era of Trujillo.* Tucson, AZ: University of Arizona Press, 1973.

Gallery, Daniel V. *The Pueblo Incident.* Garden City, NY: Doubleday, 1970.

Gamba, Virginia. *The Falklands/Malvinas War: A Model for North-South Crisis Prevention.* Boston, MA: Allen & Unwin, 1987.

Gandhi, Indira. *India and Bangladesh: Selected Speeches and Statements, March to December 1971.* New Delhi: Orient Longman, 1972.

Ganguly, Sumit. *The Origins of War in South Asia: Indo-Pakistani Conflicts since 1947.* Boulder, CO: Westview Press, 1986.

Gappert, Gary, and G. Thomas, eds. "The Congo, Africa and America." Syracuse: Maxwell Graduate School of Citizenship and Public Affairs: The Program of East African Studies, Occasional Paper No. 15, 1965.

Gardner, Lloyd C. *Pay Any Price: Lyndon Johnson and the Wars for Vietnam.* Chicago, IL: Ivan R. Dee, 1995.

Garfinkle, Adam M. "U.S. Decision-Making in the Jordan Crisis: Correcting the Record." *Political Science Quarterly* 100, no. 1 (1985): 117–38.

Garratt, Geoffrey T. *Mussolini's Roman Empire.* Harmondsworth, U.K.: Penguin, 1938.

Garrett, Banning, and Bonnie Glaser. "Looking across the Yalu: Chinese Assessments of North Korea." *Asian Survey* 35, no. 6 (1995): 528–545.

Garrett, James L. "The Beagle Channel Dispute: Confrontation and Negotiation in the Southern Cone." *Journal of Inter-American Studies and World Affairs* 27 (fall 1985): 81–109.

Garthoff, Raymond L. "Russian Foreign Ministry Documents on the Cuban Missile Crisis." CWIHP. *Bulletin* 5 (spring 1995): 58, 63–77.

———. "Berlin 1961: The Record Corrected." *Foreign Policy* 84 (fall 1991): 142–56.

———. *Reflections on the Cuban Missile Crisis.* Rev. ed. Washington, DC: Brookings Institution, 1989.

———. *Détente and Confrontation: American-Soviet Relations from Nixon to Reagan.* Washington, DC: Brookings Institution, 1985.

———. "Handling the Cienfuegos Crisis." *International Security* 8 (summer 1983): 46–66.

de Gaulle, Charles. *Memoirs of Hope.* London: Weidenfeld & Nicolson, 1971.

———. *Mémoires de Guerre.* Paris: Librairie Plon, 1956.

Gause, F. Gregory III. *Saudi-Yemeni Relations: Domestic Structures and Foreign Influ ence.* New York: Columbia University Press, 1990.

Gedye, George E. L. *Betrayal in Central Europe: Austria and Czechoslovakia, The Fallen Bastions.* New York: Harper, 1939.

Gehase, Thomas. *The Story of Lithuania.* New York: Stanford House, 1946.

Gehl, Jürgen. *Austria, Germany and the Anschluss, 1931–1938.* London: Oxford University Press, 1963.

Geist, Benjamin. *Hungary 1956: Crisis Decision-Making in a Socialist State.* Jerusalem: ICB, 1995.

Gelb, Leslie H., with Richard K. Betts. *The Irony of Vietnam: The System Worked.* Washington, DC: Brookings Institution, 1979.

Gelb, Norman. *The Berlin Wall: Kennedy, Khrushchev, and a Showdown in the Heart of Europe.* New York: Dorset Press, 1986.

Gelber, Harry G. "Strategic Arms Limitation and the Sino-Soviet Relationship." *Asian Survey* 10 (April 1970): 265–89.

George, Alexander L. "The Cuban Missile Crisis." Chap. 11 in *Avoiding War: Problems of Crisis Management,* edited by Alexander L. George. Boulder, CO: Westview Press, 1991.

———. "Missed Opportunities for Crisis Prevention: The War of Attrition and Angola." Chap. 9 in *Managing U.S.-Soviet Rivalry: Problems of Crisis Prevention,* edited by Alexander L. George. Boulder, CO: Westview Press, 1983.

George, Alexander L., and Richard Smoke. *Deterrence in American Foreign Policy: Theory and Practice.* New York: Columbia University Press, 1974.

Gerard-Libois, Jules W. *Katanga Secession.* Translated by Rebecca Young. Madison, WI: University of Wisconsin Press, 1966.

Gerard-Libois, Jules W., and Jean van Lierde, eds. *Congo 1964: Political Documents of a Developing Nation.* Princeton, NJ: Princeton University Press, 1966.

Gerbrandy, P. S. *Indonesia.* London: Hutchinson, 1950.

Gerteiny, Alfred G. *Mauritania.* London: Pall Mall Press, 1967.

Gerutis, Albertas, ed. *Lithuania: Seven Hundred Years.* 2d rev. ed. New York: Manyland Books, 1969.

Geyelin, Philip. *Lyndon B. Johnson and the World.* New York: Praeger, 1966.

Ghardnay, R. G. *The Dilemma of the Horn of Africa.* New Delhi: Sterling Publications, 1979.

Giap, Vo Nguyen. *Dien Bien Phu.* Hanoi: Foreign Languages Publishing House, 1962.

Gibbons, William C. *The U.S. Government and the Vietnam War: Executive and Legislative Roles and Relationships.* Vols. 1–4. Princeton, NJ: Princeton University Press, 1986–95.

Gibbs, David N. *The Political Economy of Third World Intervention: Mines, Money and U.S. Policy in the Congo Crisis.* Chicago, IL: University of Chicago Press, 1994.

Gibney, Frank. *Frozen Revolution; Poland: A Study in Communist Decay.* New York: Farrar, Straus, 1959.

Gilbert, Felix. *Hitler Directs His War: The Secret Records of His Daily Military Conferences.* New York: Oxford University Press, 1950.

Gilks, Anne. *The Breakdown of the Sino-Vietnamese Alliance, 1970–1979.* Berkeley, CA: Institute of East Asian Studies, Center for Chinese Studies, University of California, Berkeley, 1992.

Gillin, John, and K. H. Silvert. "Ambiguities in Guatemala." *Foreign Affairs* 34 (April 1956): 469–82.

Gilmore, C. William. *The Grenada Intervention (Analysis and Documentation).* London: Mansell Publishing, 1984.

Glantz, David M., and Jonathan M. House. *When Titans Clashed: How the Red Army Stopped Hitler.* Lawrence, KS: University Press of Kansas, 1995.

Glassman, Jon D. *Arms for the Arabs: The Soviet Union and War in the Middle East.* Baltimore, MD: Johns Hopkins University Press, 1975.

Gleijeses, Piero. *The Dominican Crisis: The 1965 Constitutionalist Revolt and American Intervention.* Translated by Lawrence Lipson. Baltimore, MD: Johns Hopkins University Press, 1978.

Glenny, Misha. *The Fall of Yugoslavia: The Third Balkan War.* London: Penguin Books, 1992.

Glubb, Lieutenant-General Sir John Bagot. *A Soldier with the Arabs.* London: Hodder & Stoughton, 1957.

Gluchowski, L. W. "Poland, 1956: Khrushchev, Gomulka, and the 'Polish October'." *CWIHP. Bulletin* 5 (spring 1995): 1, 38–49.

Goichon, A.-M. *L'Eau, Problème Vital de la Région du Jourdain.* Bruxelles: Publication du Centre pour l'Etude des Problèmes du Monde Musulman Contemporain, 1964.

Goitein, Shlomo D.F. *Jews and Arabs, Their Contacts through the Ages.* New York: Schocken, 1965.

Golan, Aviezer. *Sinai Campaign 29/10/56–5/11/56* (in Hebrew). Tel Aviv: Israel Defense Forces, Department of Instruction and Information, 1958.

Golan, Galia. "Soviet Decisionmaking in the Yom Kippur War." In *Soviet Decisionmaking for National Security,* edited by Jiri Valenta and William Potter, 185–217. London: George Allen & Unwin, 1984.

———. *Yom Kippur and After: The Soviet Union and the Middle East Crisis.* Cambridge: Cambridge University Press, 1977.

———. *Reform Rule in Czechoslovakia: The Dubček Era 1968–1969.* Cambridge: Cambridge University Press, 1973.

———. *The Czechoslovak Reform Movement: Communism in Crisis, 1962–1968.* Cambridge: Cambridge University Press, 1971.

Golan, Matti. *The Secret Conversations of Henry Kissinger: Step-by-Step Diplomacy in the Middle East.* New York: Bantam Books, 1976.

Goldenberg, Boris. *The Cuban Revolution and Latin America.* London: Allen & Unwin, 1965.

Goldstein, Martin E. *American Policy toward Laos.* Rutherford, NJ: Fairleigh Dickinson University Press, 1973.

Goncharov, Sergei N., John W. Lewis, and Xue Litai. *Uncertain Partners: Stalin, Mao, and the Korean War.* Stanford, CA: Stanford University Press, 1993.

González, Edward. "Cuba, the Soviet Union, and Africa." In *Communism in Africa,* edited by David E. Albright, 145–67. Bloomington, IN: Indiana University Press, 1980.

———. "The United States and Castro: Breaking the Deadlock." *Foreign Affairs* 50 (July 1972): 722–37.

Good, Robert C. *UDI: The International Politics of the Rhodesian Rebellion.* Princeton, NJ: Princeton University Press, 1973.

Goodrich, Leland M. *Korea: A Study of U.S. Policy in the United Nations.* New York: Council on Foreign Relations, 1956.

Goodspeed, Stephen S. *The Nature and Function of International Organization.* 2d ed. New York: Oxford University Press, 1967.

Gopal, Ram. *Indo-Pakistan War and Peace 1965.* Lucknow: Tej Kuman Press, 1967.

Gopal, Sarvepalli. *Jawaharlal Nehru: A Biography,* Vol. 2, *1947–56.* London: Jonathan Cape, 1979.

Gordenker, Leon. *The United Nations and the Peaceful Unification of Korea: The Politics of Field Operations, 1947–1950.* The Hague: Martinus Nijhoff, 1959.

Gordon, Bernard K., and Kathryn Young. "The Khmer Republic: That Was the Cambodia That Was." *Asian Survey* 11 (January 1971): 26–40.

———. "Cambodia: Following the Leader?" *Asian Survey* 10 (February 1970): 169–76.

Gordon, Dennis, and Margaret M. Munro. "The External Dimension of Civil Insurrection: Internal Organization and the Nicaraguan Revolution." *Journal of Inter-American Studies and World Affairs* 24, no. 1 (1982): 59–80.

Gordon, Murry, ed. *Conflict in the Persian Gulf.* New York: Facts on File, 1981.

Gorman, Robert F. *Political Conflict in the Horn of Africa.* New York: Praeger, 1981.

Goulden, Joseph C. *Truth Is the First Casualty: The Gulf of Tonkin Affair—Illusion and Reality.* Chicago, IL: Rand McNally, 1969.

Graham, Dominick, and Shelford Bidwell. *Tug of War: The Battle for Italy, 1943–1945.* New York: St. Martin's Press, 1986.

Grahame, Iain. *Amin and Uganda: A Personal Memoir.* London: Granada, 1980.

Grant, Bruce, ed. *Indonesia.* Melbourne: Melbourne University Press, 1964.

Grant, Donald. "Guatemala and U.S. Foreign Policy." *Journal of International Affairs* 9, no. 1 (1955): 64–72.

Granville, Johanna. "Imre Nagy, Hesitant Revolutionary." CWIHP. *Bulletin* 5 (spring 1995): 23, 27–28.

Grattan, Hartley C. *The Southwest Pacific since 1900.* Ann Arbor, MI: University of Michigan Press, 1963.

Gravel, Senator Mike. *The Pentagon Papers.* Senator Gravel Edition. 5 vols. Boston, MA: Beacon Press, 1971–72.

Graves, Philip P. *Briton and Turk.* London and Melbourne: Hutchinson & Co., 1941.

Green, Leslie C. "Rescue at Entebbe—Legal Aspects." *Israel Yearbook on Human Rights* 6 (1976): 312–29.

Greene, L. C. "Indonesia, the U.N. and Malaysia." *Journal of Southeast Asian History* 6 (September 1975): 71–86.

Gretton, John. "The Western Sahara in the International Arena." *World Today* 36 (September 1980): 343–50.

Grew, Joseph C. *Turbulent Era—A Diplomatic Record of Forty Years: 1905–1945.* London: Hammond, 1953.

Grey, Ian. *The First Fifty Years: Soviet Russia 1917–1967.* London: Hodder & Stoughton, 1967.

Grieg, Ian. *The Communist Challenge to Africa: An Analysis of Contemporary Soviet, Chinese and Cuban Policies.* Richmond, Surrey, U.K.: Foreign Affairs Publishing Company, 1977.

Gromyko, Andrei. *Memoirs.* Garden City, NY: Doubleday, 1989.

Gross, Leo. "The Dispute between Greece and Turkey Concerning the Continental Shelf in the Aegean." *American Journal of International Law* 71 (January 1977): 31–59.

Grosser, Alfred. *The Federal Republic of Germany: A Concise History.* New York: Praeger, 1964.

Grummon, Stephen R. "The Iran-Iraq War: Islam Embattled." In *The Washington Papers.* No. 92. Westport, CT: Praeger 1982.

Guang, Zhang Shu. *Mao's Military Romanticism: China and the Korean War, 1950–1953.* Lawrence, KS: University Press of Kansas, 1995.

———. "In the Shadow of Mao: Zhou Enlai and New China's Diplomacy." In *The Diplomats, 1939–1979,* edited by Gordon A. Craig and Francis L. Loewenheim, 337–70. Princeton, NJ: Princeton University Press, 1994.

———. *Deterrence and Strategic Culture: Chinese-American Confrontations 1949–1958.* Ithaca, NY: Cornell University Press, 1992.

Gukiina, Peter M. *Uganda: A Case Study in African Political Development.* Notre Dame, IN: University of Notre Dame Press, 1972.

Gupta, Sisir. *Kashmir: A Study in India-Pakistan Relations.* Bombay: Asia Publishing House, 1966.

Gurtov, Melvin. *The United States against the Third World: Anti-Nationalism and Intervention.* New York: Praeger, 1974.

———. *The First Vietnam Crisis: Chinese Communist Strategy and United States Involvement.* New York: Columbia University Press, 1967.

Gurtov, Melvin, and Byong-Moo Hwang. *China under Threat: The Politics of Strategy and Diplomacy.* Baltimore, MD: Johns Hopkins University Press, 1980.

Guttman, Roy. "Nicaragua: America's Diplomatic Charade." *Foreign Policy* 56 (fall 1984): 3–23.

Gwyne, R. N. "Conflict in South America." *Geographical Magazine* 51, no. 3 (1979): 398–402.

Hadawi, Sami. *Palestine in the United Nations.* New York: Arab Information Center, 1964.

Hadju, Tibor. *The Hungarian Soviet Republic.* Budapest: Akademai Niado, 1979.

Hagerty, Devin T. "Nuclear Deterrence in South Asia: The 1990 Indo-Pakistan Crisis." *International Security* 20, no. 3 (1995–96): 79–114.

Haig, Alexander M. Jr. *Caveat: Realism, Reagan, and Foreign Policy.* New York: Macmillan, 1984.

Haile Selassie I. *My Life and Ethiopia's Progress, 1892–1937.* London: Oxford University Press, 1976.

Halberstam, David. *The Best and the Brightest.* New York: Random House, 1972.

Hale, William, and Ali Ihsan Bagiz, eds. *Four Centuries of Turco-British Relations.* Beverley, U.K.: Eothen Press, 1984.

Haley, P. Edward. *Qaddafi and the United States since 1969.* New York: Praeger, 1984.

Hall, David K. "Naval Diplomacy in West African Waters." In *Diplomacy of Power: Soviet Armed Forces as a Political Instrument,* edited by Stephen S. Kaplan, 539–67. Washington, DC: Brookings Institution, 1981.

———. "The Laotian War of 1962 and the Indo-Pakistani War of 1971," In *Force without War: U.S. Armed Forces as a Political Instrument,* edited by Barry M. Blechman and Stephen S. Kaplan, 135–221. Washington, DC: Brookings Institution, 1978.

Hall, Richard. *The High Price of Principles: Kaunda and the White South.* Harmondsworth, U.K.: Penguin, 1973.

Halle, Louis J. *The Cold War as History.* New York: Harper & Row, 1967.

Hallett, Robin. *Africa since 1875: A Modern History.* Ann Arbor, MI: University of Michigan Press, 1974.

Halper, Thomas. *Foreign Policy Crises: Appearance and Reality in Decision Making.* Columbus, OH: Charles Merrill, 1971.

Halperin, Maurice. *The Rise and Decline of Fidel Castro: An Essay in Contemporary History.* Berkeley, CA: University of California Press, 1972.

Halperin, Morton H. *The 1958 Taiwan Straits Crisis: A Documented History.* Santa Monica, CA: Rand, 1966.

Halperin, Morton H., and Tang Tsou. "United States Policy toward the Offshore Islands." *Public Policy* 15 (1966): 119–38.

Hamilton, C. W. *Americans and Oil in the Middle East.* Houston, TX: Gulf Publishing, 1962.

Hammer, Ellen J. *The Struggle for Indochina: 1940–1954.* Stanford, CA: Stanford University Press, 1966.

Hammond, Thomas T. *Red Flag over Afghanistan: The Communist Coup, The Soviet Invasion, and the Consequences.* Boulder, CO: Westview Press, 1984.

Hammond, Thomas T., and R. Barry Farrell, eds. *The Anatomy of Communist Takeovers.* New Haven, CT: Yale University Press, 1975.

Hane, Mikiso. *Japan: A Historical Survey.* New York: Scribner, 1972.

Harris, George S. *Troubled Alliance: Turkish-American Problems in Historical Perspective, 1945–1972.* Washington, DC: American Enterprise Institute for Public Policy Research, 1972.

Harrison, Hope M. "The Bargaining Power of Weaker Allies in Bipolarity and Crisis: Soviet-East German Relations, 1953–1961." Ph.D. diss., Columbia University, 1993a.

———. "Ulbricht and the Concrete 'Rose': New Archival Evidence on the Dynamics of Soviet-East German Relations and the Berlin Crisis, 1958–1961." Washington, DC: Woodrow Wilson International Center for Scholars. CWIHP. Working Paper No. 5, 1993b.

Hart, Jeffrey A. *The Anglo-Icelandic Cod War of 1972–1973: A Case Study of a Fishery Dispute.* Berkeley, CA: Institute of International Studies, University of California, Berkeley, 1976.

Hassouna, Hussein A. *The League of Arab States and Regional Disputes.* Dobbs Ferry, NY: Oceana Publications, 1975.

Hastings, Max. *The Korean War.* New York: Simon and Schuster, 1987.

Hastings, Max, and Simon Jenkins. *The Battle for the Falklands.* London: Michael Joseph, 1983.

Head, Richard G., Frisco W. Short, and Robert C. McFarlane. *Crisis Resolution: Presiden-*

tial Decison-Making in the Mayaguez and Korean Confrontations. Boulder, CO: Westview Press, 1978.

Heikal, Mohamed. *The Sphinx and the Commissar: The Rise and Fall of Soviet Influence in the Middle East.* New York: Harper and Row, 1978.

———. *The Road to Ramadan.* London: Collins, 1975.

———. *The Cairo Documents.* Garden City, NY: Doubleday, 1973.

Heinrichs, Waldo. *Threshold of War: Franklin D. Roosevelt and American Entry into World War II.* New York: Oxford University Press, 1988.

Heller, Peter B. "The Syrian Factor in the Lebanese Civil War." *Journal of South Asian and Middle Eastern Studies* 4 (fall 1980): 56–76.

Hellmann-Rajanayagam, Dagmar. *The Tamil Tigers. Armed Struggle for Identity.* Stuttgart: Franz Steiner Verlag, 1994.

Helmreich, Jonathan. *Belgium and Europe: A Study in Small Power Diplomacy.* The Hague: Mouton, 1976.

Henderson, Gregory. *Korea: The Politics of the Vortex.* Cambridge, MA: Harvard University Press, 1968.

Henderson, Sir Neville. *Failure of a Mission: Berlin 1937–1939.* London: Hodder & Stoughton, 1940.

Henderson, William. *West New Guinea: The Dispute and Its Settlement.* South Orange, NJ: Seton Hall University Press, 1973.

Herring, George C. *LBJ and Vietnam.* Austin, TX: University of Texas Press, 1994.

———. *America's Longest War: The United States and Vietnam, 1950–1975.* 2d ed. New York: McGraw-Hill, 1986.

Herring, George C., and Richard H. Immerman. "Eisenhower, Dulles, and Dien Bien Phu: 'The Day We Didn't Go to War' Revisited." *Journal of American History* 71 (September 1984): 343–63.

Herring, Herbert C. *A History of Latin America, from the Beginnings to the Present.* 3d ed. New York: Knopf, 1968.

Hersh, Seymour M. "In the Nuclear Edge." *New Yorker* 29 March 1993, 56–73.

———. *The Price of Power: Kissinger in the Nixon White House.* New York: Simon & Schuster, 1983.

Hershberg, Jim. "Anatomy of a Controversy: Anatoly F. Dobrynin's Meetings with Robert F. Kennedy, Saturday, 27 October 1962." CWIHP. *Bulletin* 5 (spring 1995): 75, 77–80.

Herzog, Chaim. *The Arab-Israeli Wars.* New York: Random House, 1982.

———. *The War of Atonement.* London: Weidenfeld & Nicolson, 1975.

Hess, Gary. "The Iranian Crisis of 1945–1946 and the Cold War." *Political Science Quarterly* 90 (March 1974): 451–75.

Hewlett, Richard G., and Oscar E. Anderson Jr. *The New World: A History of the United States Atomic Energy Commission.* Rev. ed. Vol. 1, 1939–1946. Berkeley, CA: University of California Press, 1990.

Hicks, Albert C. *Blood in the Streets: The Life and Rule of Trujillo.* New York: Creative Age Press, 1968.

Higgins, Rosalyn. *United Nations Peacekeeping 1946–1967: Documents and Commentary.* Vol. 2, *Asia.* RIIA. London: Oxford University Press, 1970.

———. *United Nations Peacekeeping 1946–1967: Documents and Commentary.* Vol. 1, *The Middle East.* RIIA. London: Oxford University Press, 1969.

Hilsman, Roger. *To Move a Nation: The Politics of Foreign Policy in the Administration of John F. Kennedy.* Garden City, NY: Doubleday, 1967.

Hinton, Harold C. *East Asia and the Western Pacific.* The World Today Series. Washington, DC: Stryker-Post Publications, 1987.

———. *The Sino-Soviet Confrontation: Implications for the Future.* New York: Crane, Russak, 1976.

———. "The US and the Sino-Soviet Confrontation." *Orbis* 10 (spring 1975): 25–46.

———. *The Bear at the Gate: Chinese Policy-Making under Soviet Pressure.* Washington, DC: American Enterprise Institute for Public Policy Research, 1971.

———. *Communist China in World Politics.* Boston, MA: Houghton Mifflin, 1966.

Hoare, M. *Congo Mercenary.* London: Robert Hale, 1967.

Hodges, Tony. *Western Sahara: Roots of a Desert War.* Westport, CT: Lawrence Hill, 1983.

———. "The Struggle for Angola." *Round Table* 262 (April 1976): 173–84.

Hodson, Henry V. *The Great Divide: Britain, India, Pakistan.* New York: Oxford University Press, 1985.

Hoffmann, Steven A. *India and the China Crisis.* Berkeley, CA: University of California Press, 1990.

Hofstadter, Dan, ed. *Egypt and Nasser.* New York: Facts on File, 1973.

Hogan, Michael J. *The Marshall Plan: America, Britain, and the Reconstruction of Western Europe, 1947–52.* Cambridge: Cambridge University Press, 1987.

Holden, David, and Richard Johns. *The House of Saud.* London: Pan Books, 1981.

Hollen, Christopher V. "The Tilt Policy Revisited: Nixon-Kissinger Geopolitics and South Asia." *Asian Survey* 20 (April 1980): 339–61.

Holloway, David. *Stalin and the Bomb: The Soviet Union and Atomic Energy 1939–1956.* New Haven, CT: Yale University Press, 1994.

Holly, Daniel. "Le Conflit du Honduras et du Salvador de 1969." *Etudes Internationales* 10 (March 1979): 19–51.

Hoopes, Townsend. *The Devil and John Foster Dulles.* Boston, MA: Little, Brown, 1973.

———. *The Limits of Intervention.* New York: David McKay, 1969.

Hopkins, Jack W., ed. *Latin America and Caribbean Contemporary Record, 1983–1984.* Vol. 3. New York: Holmes & Meier, 1985.

———. *Latin America and Caribbean Contemporary Record, 1982–1983.* Vol. 2. New York: Holmes & Meier, 1984.

———. *Latin America and Caribbean Contemporary Record, 1981–1982.* Vol. 1. New York: Holmes & Meier, 1983.

Horelick, Arnold L. "The Cuban Missile Crisis: An Analysis of Soviet Calculations and Behavior." *World Politics* 16 (April 1964): 363–89.

Horelick, Arnold L., and Myron Rush. *Strategic Power and Soviet Foreign Policy.* Chicago, IL: University of Chicago Press, 1965.

von Horn, Major General Carl. *Soldiering for Peace.* New York: David McKay, 1966.

Horn, R. C. "Changing Soviet Policies and Sino-Soviet Competition in Southeast Asia." *Orbis* 17 (summer 1973): 493–526.

Horne, Alistair. *Harold Macmillan.* Vol. 1, *1894–1956.* New York: Viking Press, 1989a.

———. *Harold Macmillan.* Vol. 2, *1957–1986.* New York: Viking Press, 1989b.

Horthy, Admiral Nicholas. *Memoirs.* New York: Robert Speller, 1957.

Hoskins, Halford L. "The Guardianship of the Suez Canal: A View of Anglo-Egyptian Relations." *Middle East Journal* 4 (April 1950): 143–54.

Hoskyns, Catherine. *The OAU and the Congo Crisis, 1964–65: Documents.* Dar-es-Salaam: Oxford University Press, 1969a.

————, ed. *Case Studies in African Diplomacy.* Vol. 2, *The Ethiopia-Somalia-Kenya Dispute, 1960–67, Documents.* Dar-es-Salaam: Oxford University Press, 1969b.

————. *The Congo since Independence: January 1960–December 1961.* London: Oxford University Press, 1965.

Hosmer, Stephen T., and Thomas W. Wolfe. *Soviet Policy and Practice toward Third World Conflicts.* Lexington, MA: Lexington Books, 1983.

Hosoya, Chihiro. "Miscalculations in Deterrent Policy: Japanese-US Relations, 1938–1941." *Journal of Peace Research* 5 (1968): 97–115.

Hourani, Albert H. *Syria and Lebanon: A Political Essay.* London: Oxford University Press, 1946.

Hovi, Olavi. *The Baltic Area in British Policy, 1918–1921.* Vol. 1. Helsinki: The Finnish Historical Society, 1980.

Howard, Harry N. *Turkey, the Straits and US Policy.* Baltimore, MD: Johns Hopkins University Press, 1974.

Howe, Jonathan T. *Multicrises: Seapower and Global Politics in the Missile Age.* Cambridge, MA: MIT Press, 1971.

Howland, Charles. *Survey of American Foreign Relations: Publications for the Council on Foreign Relations.* New Haven, CT: Yale University Press, 1929.

Howley, Frank. *Berlin Command.* New York: Putnam's, 1950.

Hsieh, Alice Langley. *Communist China's Strategy in the Nuclear Era.* Englewood Cliffs, NJ: Prentice-Hall, 1962.

Huang, Chi, Woosang Kim, and Samuel S. G. Wu. "Conflict and Cooperation across the Taiwan Strait, 1951–78." *Issues and Studies* 28, no. 6 (1992): 16–35.

Hul, Galen. "Internationalizing the Shaba Conflict." *Africa Report* 22 (July–August 1977): 4–9.

Hull, Cordell. *The Memoirs of Cordell Hull.* 2 vols. New York: Macmillan, 1948.

Hung, Nguyen Manh. "The Sino-Vietnamese Conflict: Power Play among Communist Neighbors." *Asian Survey* 19 (November 1979): 1037–52.

Hunt, Michael. "Beijing and the Korean Crisis, June 1950-June 1951." *Political Science Quarterly* 107, no. 3 (1992): 453–478.

Hunter, S. T. "The Nagorno-Karabakh Conflict: Indigenous and External Causes." In *The Transcaucasus in Transition: Nation Building and Conflict,* edited by S. T. Hunter. Washington, DC: The Center for Strategic and International Studies, 1994.

Hurewitz, Jacob C. *The Struggle for Palestine.* New York: Norton, 1950.

Hussain, Arif. *Pakistan: Its Ideology and Foreign Policy.* London: Frank Cass, 1966.

Hussein, Ibn Talal, King of Jordan. *My "War" with Israel as told and with additional material by V. Vance and P. Lauer.* New York: Morrow, 1969.

————. *Uneasy Lies the Head: An Autobiography.* London: Heinemann, 1962.

Ickes, Harold L. *The Secret Diary of Harold L. Ickes.* Vol. 2, *The Inside Struggle, 1936–39.* New York: Simon & Schuster, 1974.

Ike, Nobutake. *Japan's Decision for War, Records of the 1941 Policy Conferences.* Stanford, CA: Stanford University Press, 1967.

Ikuhiko, Hata. "The Japanese-Soviet Confrontation, 1935–1939." Translated by Alvin D. Coox. In *Deterrence Diplomacy: Japan, Germany, and the USSR, 1935–1940,* edited by James W. Morley, 129–78. New York: Columbia University Press, 1976.

Immerman, Richard H. "Between the Unattainable and the Unacceptable: Eisenhower and Dien Bien Phu." In *Reevaluating Eisenhower: American Foreign Policy in the 1950s,* edited by R. A. Melanson and D. Mayers, 120–54. Urbana, IL: University of Illinois Press, 1987.

Ince, Basil A. "Venezuela-Guyana Boundary Dispute in the UN." *Caribbean Studies* 9 (January 1970): 5–26.

Ingrams, H. *The Yemen Imams: Rulers and Revolutions.* London: John Murray, 1963.

Insight Team of the *Sunday Times* of London. *War in the Falklands: The Full Story.* New York: Harper & Row, 1982.

———. *The Yom Kippur War.* London: André Deutsch, 1974.

Insor, D. *Thailand: A Political, Social and Economic Analysis.* London: Allen & Unwin, 1963.

Institute for the Study of Conflict. *Annual of Power and Conflict 1981–82.* London, 1982.

———. *Annual of Power and Conflict 1980–81.* London, 1981.

Ionescu, Ghita. *Communism in Rumania, 1944–1962.* London: Oxford University Press, 1964.

Iqbal, Sheikh Mohammed. *Emergence of Saudi Arabia.* Srinagar, India: Saudiyah Publishers, 1977.

Ireland, Gordon. *Boundaries, Possessions, and Conflicts in Central and North America and the Caribbean.* New York: Octagon Books, [1938] 1971.

———. *Boundaries, Possessions, and Conflicts in South America.* Cambridge, MA: Harvard University Press, 1938.

Iriye, Akira. *Power and Culture: The Japanese-American War, 1941–1945.* Cambridge, MA: Harvard University Press, 1981.

Isaacson, Walter. *Kissinger: A Biography.* New York: Simon & Schuster, 1992.

Ismael, Tareq Y. *Iraq and Iran: Roots of Conflict.* Syracuse, NY: Syracuse University Press, 1982.

———. *Government and Politics of the Contemporary Middle East.* Homewood, IL: Dorsey Press, 1970.

Jackson, Karl D. "Cambodia 1978: War, Pillage and Purge in Democratic Kampuchea." *Asian Survey* 19 (January 1979): 72–84.

———. "Cambodia 1977: Gone to Pot." *Asian Survey* 18 (January 1978): 76–90.

Jackson, Robert. *South Asian Crisis: India, Pakistan, and Bangladesh, A Political and Historical Analysis of the 1971 War.* New York: Praeger, 1975.

———. *At War with the Bolsheviks: The Allied Intervention into Russia, 1917–1920.* London: Tom Stacey, 1972.

Jacobsen, C. G. "Strategic Considerations Affecting Soviet Policy toward China and Japan." *Orbis* 17 (winter 1974): 1189–1214.

Jain, Jagdish P. *China, Pakistan and Bangladesh.* New Delhi: Radiant, 1974a.

———. *Soviet Policy towards Pakistan and Bangladesh.* New Delhi: Radiant, 1974b.

Jakobson, Max. *Finnish Neutrality: A Study of Finnish Foreign Policy since the Second World War.* New York: Praeger, 1968.

———. *The Diplomacy of the Winter War: An Account of the Russo-Finnish War, 1939–1940.* Cambridge, MA: Harvard University Press, 1961.

James, Harold, and Denis S. Small. *The Undeclared War: The Story of the Indonesian Confrontation.* London: L. Cooper, 1971.

Jansen, G. H. "The Problem of the Jordan Waters." *World Today* 20 (February 1964): 60–68.

Jencks, Harlan W. "Lessons of a 'Lesson': China-Vietnam, 1979." In *The Lessons of Recent Wars in the Third World, Vol. I: Approaches and Case Studies,* edited by

Robert E. Harkavy and Stephanie G. Neuman, 139–60. Lexington, MA: Lexington Books, 1985.

―――. "China's Punitive War on Vietnam: A Military Assessment." *Asian Survey* 19 (August 1979): 801–15.

Jessup, Philip C. "Park Avenue Diplomacy—Ending the Berlin Blockade." *Political Science Quarterly* 87 (1972): 377–400.

―――. "The Berlin Blockade and the Use of the United Nations." *Foreign Affairs* 50 (October 1971): 163–73.

Jian, Chen. "China's Road to the Korean War." CWIHP. *Bulletin* 6–7 (winter 1995–96): 41, 85–86.

―――. *China's Road to the Korean War: The Making of the Sino-American Confrontation.* New York: Columbia University Press, 1994.

―――. "The Sino-Soviet Alliance and China's Entry into the Korean War." Washington, DC: Woodrow Wilson International Center for Scholars. CWIHP. Working Paper No. 1, 1992.

Jie, Chen. "China's Spratly Policy: With Special Reference to the Philippines and Malaysia." *Asian Survey* 34 (October 1994): 893–903.

Johnson, Haynes et al. *The Bay of Pigs: The Invasion of Cuba by Brigade 2506.* London: Hutchinson, 1964.

Johnson, Lyndon B. *The Vantage Point: Perspectives of the Presidency 1963–1969.* New York: Holt, Rinehart & Winston, 1971.

Johnson, Paul. *The Suez War.* London: Macgibbon & Kee, 1957.

Johnson, Seagun. "Burkina-Mali War: Is Nigeria Still a Regional Power?" *India Quarterly* 42, no. 3 (1986): 294–308.

Johnstone, William C. *Burma's Foreign Policy.* Cambridge, MA: Harvard University Press, 1963.

Jones, Christopher D. "Autonomy and Intervention: The CPSU and the Struggle for the Czechoslovak Communist Party, 1968." *Orbis* 19 (1975): 591–625.

Jones, F. C. *Japan's New Order in East Asia: Its Rise and Fall 1937–45.* London: Oxford University Press, 1954.

Jones, Howard P. *Indonesia: The Possible Dream.* New York: Harcourt, Brace & Jovanovich, 1971.

Jonsson, Hannes. *Friends in Conflict: The Anglo-Icelandic Cod Wars and the Law of the Sea.* London: Hurst, 1982.

Jordan, William J. *Panama Odyssey.* Austin, TX: University of Texas Press, 1984.

Joyner, C. C., ed. *The Persian Gulf War.* New York: Greenwood Press, 1990.

Juhász, Gyula. *Hungarian Foreign Policy, 1919–1945.* Budapest: Akadémiai Kiadó, 1979.

Jukes, Geoffrey. *Hitler's Stalingrad Decisions.* Berkeley, CA: University of California Press, 1985.

Kadi, Leila. *Arab Summit Conferences and the Palestine Problem.* Beirut: PLO Research Center, 1966.

Kahin, George McT. *Intervention: How America Became Involved in Vietnam.* New York: Knopf, 1986.

―――. *Nationalism and Revolution in Indonesia.* Ithaca, NY: Cornell University Press, 1952.

―――― et al. *Major Governments of Asia.* Ithaca, NY: Cornell University Press, 1963.

Kahin, George McT., and John W. Lewis. *The United States in Vietnam.* New York: Dial Press, 1967.

Kain, Ronald S. "Bolivia's Claustrophobia." *Foreign Affairs* 16 (July 1938): 704–13.

Kalb, Marvin, and Bernard Kalb. *Kissinger.* Boston, MA: Little, Brown, 1974.

Kalicki, J. H. *The Pattern of Sino-American Crises: Political-Military Interactions in the 1950s.* Cambridge: Cambridge University Press, 1975.

Kallgren, Joyce K. "China 1979: The New Long March." *Asian Survey* 19 (January 1979): 1–19.

Kamm, Henry. "The Silent Suffering of East Timor." *New York Times Magazine* 6 (15 February 1981): 35.

Kaplan, Robert D. *Balkan Ghosts: A Journey through History.* New York: St. Martin's Press, 1993.

Kaplan, Stephen S. et al. *Diplomacy of Power: Soviet Armed Forces as a Political Instrument.* Washington, DC: Brookings Institution, 1981.

Karnow, Stanley. *Vietnam: A History.* New York: Penguin Books, 1984.

Karpat, Kemal H. *Turkey's Foreign Policy in Transition: 1950–1974.* Leiden: L. J. Brill, 1975.

Karsh, Efraim, ed. *The Iran-Iraq War: Impact and Implications.* New York: St. Martin's Press, 1989.

———. "The Iran-Iraq War: The Military Implications." London: IISS. Adelphi Paper No. 220, 1987.

Kase, Tshikazu. *Journey to the Missouri.* Hamden, CT: Archon Books, 1969.

Kaslas, Bronis J. *The Baltic Nations.* Pittston, PA: Euramerica Press, 1976.

Katz, Stephen R. "Issues Arising in the Icelandic Fisheries Case." *International and Comparative Law Quarterly* 22 (1973): 83–108.

Kaul, Brij Mohan. *The Untold Story.* Bombay: Allied Publishers, 1967.

Kavic, Lorne J. *India's Quest for Security: Defense Policies, 1947–1965.* Berkeley, CA: University of California Press, 1967.

Kay, H. *Salazar and Modern Portugal.* London: Eyre & Spottiswoode, 1970.

Kayali, N. *Syria: A Political Study (1920–1950).* Ann Arbor, MI: University Microfilms International, 1976.

Kearns, Doris. *Lyndon Johnson and the American Dream.* New York: Harper & Row, 1976.

Keegan, John, ed. *World Armies.* 2d ed. Detroit, MI: Gale Research, 1983.

Keesing's. *Pakistan from 1947 to the Creation of Bangladesh.* New York: Scribner's, 1973.

Kelley, Michael P. *A State in Disarray: Conditions of Chad's Survival.* Boulder, CO: Westview Press, 1986.

Kelley, Philip, and Jack Child, eds. *Geopolitics of the Southern Cone and Antarctica.* Boulder, CO: Lynne Rienner, 1988.

Kelly, Michael. "Annals of Diplomacy: The Negotiator," *New Yorker,* 6 November 1995.

Kennan, George F. *Memoirs, 1925–1950.* Boston, MA: Little, Brown, 1967.

———. *Russia and the West under Lenin and Stalin.* Boston, MA: Little, Brown, 1960.

Kennedy, John F. *The Burden and the Glory.* New York: Harper & Row, 1964.

———. The Cuban Crisis (President Kennedy's Address, 22 October 1962). US Information Service, 1962.

Kennedy, Robert F. *Thirteen Days—A Memoir of the Cuban Missile Crisis.* New York: Norton, 1969.

Kent, Marian, ed. *The Great Powers and the End of the Ottoman Empire.* London: Allen & Unwin, 1984.

Kerr, Malcolm H. "The Lebanese Civil War." In *The International Regulation of Civil Wars,* edited by Evan Luard, 65–90. London: Thames and Hudson, 1972.
———. *The Arab Cold War 1958–70: A Study of Ideology in Politics.* London: Oxford University Press, 1971.
Kershaw, Roger. "'Unlimited Sovereignty' in Cambodia: The View from Bangkok." *World Today* 35 (March 1979): 101–10.
Kertesz, Stephen D. *Diplomacy in a Whirlwind: Hungary between Nazi Germany and Soviet Russia.* Notre Dame, IN: University of Notre Dame Press, 1953.
———. "The Methods of Communist Conquest: Hungary 1944–1947." *World Politics* 3 (October 1950): 20–54.
Khadduri, Majid. *The Gulf War: The Origins and Implications of the Iraq-Iran Conflict.* New York: Oxford University Press, 1988.
———. *Republican Iraq: A Study in Iraqi Politics since the Revolution of 1958.* RIIA. London: Oxford University Press, 1969.
———. *Independent Iraq, 1932–1958: A Study in Iraqi Politics.* 2d ed. London: Oxford University Press, 1960.
Khalidi, Ahmed S. "The Military Balance 1967–73." In *Middle East Crucible: Studies on the Arab-Israeli War of October 1973,* edited by Naseer H. Aruri, 21–63. Wilmette, IL: Medina University Press International, 1975.
Khalidi, Rashid. *Under Siege: PLO Decisionmaking during the 1982 War.* New York: Columbia University Press, 1986.
Khalidi, Walid. *Conflict and Violence in Lebanon.* Cambridge, MA: Harvard Studies in International Affairs, No. 38, Harvard Center for International Affairs, 1979.
al-Khalil, Samir. *Republic of Fear: The Politics of Modern Iraq.* Berkeley, CA: University of California Press, 1989.
Khong, Yuen Foong. *Analogies at War: Korea, Munich, Dien Bien Phu and the Vietnam Decisions of 1965.* Princeton, NJ: Princeton University Press, 1992.
Khouri, Fred J. *The Arab-Israeli Dilemma.* 3d ed. Syracuse, NY: Syracuse University Press, 1985.
———. "The U.S., the U.N. and the Jordan River Issue." *Middle East Forum* 40 (May 1964): 20–24.
Khrushchev, Nikita. *Khrushchev Remembers.* Edited by Strobe Talbott. Boston, MA: Little, Brown, 1970.
Kilic, A. *Turkey and the World.* Washington, DC: Public Affairs Press, 1959.
Kim, Chum Kon. "The Lessons of the Korean War." In *Witnesses on the Korean War,* edited by Sung Chul Yang and Jong Yil Rah, 202–15 (in Korean). Seoul, Korea: Yejn, 1991.
Kim Il-Sung. *For the Independent Peaceful Reunification of the Country.* Pyongyang, Korea: Foreign Languages Publishing House, 1976.
Kim, Samuel S. "North Korea in 1995: The Crucible of 'Our Style Socialism'." *Asian Survey* 36 (January 1996): 61–72.
———. "North Korea in 1994: Brinkmanship, Breakdown, and Breakthrough." *Asian Survey* 35 (January 1995): 13–27.
Kimche, David, and Dan Bawly. *The Sandstorm: The Arab-Israeli War of 1967.* London: Secker & Warburg, 1968.
Kimche, Jon. "Yemen: Nasser's Vietnam." *Midstream* 12, no. 4 (1966): 34–44.
King, Ralph. "The Iran-Iraq War: The Political Implications." London: IISS. Adelphi Paper No. 219, 1987.

Kinross, Lord. *Ataturk: A Biography of Mustafa Kemal, Father of Modern Turkey.* New York: William Morrow, 1965.

———. *Ataturk: The Rebirth of a Nation.* London: Weidenfeld & Nicolson, 1964.

Kiraly, Bela K. et al., eds. *The First War between Socialist States: The Hungarian Revolution of 1956 and Its Impact.* New York: Brooklyn College Press, distributed by Columbia University Press, 1984.

Kirby, D., ed. *Finland and Russia 1801–1920: From Autonomy to Independence; A Selection of Documents.* London: Macmillan, 1975.

Kirkbride, Wayne A. *DMZ: A Story of the Panmunjom Axe Murder.* Elizabeth, NJ: Hollym International Corp., 1984.

Kirkpatrick, Ivone A. *Mussolini: Study of a Demagogue.* London: Odhams Books, 1964.

Kissinger, Henry. *Diplomacy.* New York: Simon & Schuster, 1994.

———. *Years of Upheaval.* Boston, MA: Little, Brown, 1982.

———. *The White House Years.* Boston, MA: Little, Brown, 1979.

Kitchen, Helen, ed. *Africa: From Mystery to Maize.* Lexington, MA: D. C. Heath, 1976.

———. *Footnotes to the Congo Story: An African Report Anthology.* New York: Walker, 1965.

Klein, H. S. *Parties and Political Change in Bolivia, 1880–1952.* Cambridge: Cambridge University Press, 1969.

Kline, Harvey F. *Colombia: Portrait of Unity and Diversity.* Boulder, CO: Westview Press, 1983.

Klinghoffer, Arthur J. *The Angolan War: A Study of Soviet Policy in the Third World.* Boulder, CO: Westview Press, 1980.

Knapp, Wilfrid F. *A History of War and Peace, 1939–1965.* London: Oxford University Press, 1967.

Knox, MacGregor. *Mussolini Unleashed, 1939–1941: Politics and Strategy in Fascist Italy's Last War.* Cambridge: Cambridge University Press, 1982.

Kodikara, Sheldon U. "The Continuing Crisis in Sri Lanka: The JVP, the Indian Troops and Tamil Politics." *Asian Survey* 29 (July 1989): 716–24.

Koh, Byung Chul. *The Foreign Policy of North Korea.* New York: Praeger, 1969a.

———. "The Pueblo Incident in Perspective." *Asian Survey* 9 (April 1969b): 264–80.

Kohn, Hans. "The Unification of Arabia." *Foreign Affairs* 13 (October 1934): 91–103.

Koliopoulos, J. S. *Greece and the British Connection, 1935–1941.* Oxford: Clarendon Press, 1977.

Kolko, Gabriel M. *Anatomy of a War: Vietnam, the United States, and the Modern Historical Experience.* New York: Pantheon Books, 1985.

Kolko, Joyce, and Gabriel M. Kolko. *The Limits of Power: The World and US Foreign Policy, 1945–1954.* New York: Harper & Row, 1972.

Korbel, Joseph. *Twentieth Century Czechoslovakia: The Meaning of Its History.* New York: Columbia University Press, 1977.

———. *Poland between East and West: Soviet and German Diplomacy toward Poland, 1919–1933.* Princeton, NJ: Princeton University Press, 1963.

———. *The Communist Subversion of Czechoslovakia, 1938–1948: The Failure of Coexistence.* Princeton, NJ: Princeton University Press, 1959.

———. *Danger in Kashmir.* Princeton, NJ: Princeton University Press, 1954.

Korbonski, A. *Politics of Socialist Agriculture in Poland, 1945–1960.* New York: Columbia University Press, 1965.

Kossmann, Ernst. *The Low Countries 1780–1940.* Oxford: Clarendon Press, 1978.

Kosut, Hal, ed. *Cyprus, 1946–68.* New York: Facts on File, 1970.

———, ed. *Indonesia: The Sukarno Years.* New York: Facts on File, 1967.

Kousoulas, Dmitrios G. *The Price of Freedom: Greece in World Affairs.* Syracuse, NY: Syracuse University Press, 1953.

Kovrig, Bennet. *The Hungarian People's Republic.* Baltimore, MD: Johns Hopkins University Press, 1970.

Kramer, Mark. "Poland, 1980–81: Soviet Policy during the Polish Crisis." CWIHP. *Bulletin* 5 (spring 1995a): 1, 116–26.

———. "Declassified Soviet Documents on the Polish Crisis." CWIHP. *Bulletin* 5 (spring 1995b): 116–17, 129–39.

———. "The SED Politburo and the Polish Crisis." CWIHP. *Bulletin* 5 (spring 1995c): 121, 127–28.

———. "The Prague Spring and the Soviet Invasion of Czechoslovakia: New Interpretations." CWIHP. *Bulletin* 3 (fall 1993): 2–13, 54–55.

———. "New Sources on the 1968 Soviet Invasion of Czechoslovakia." CWIHP. *Bulletin* 2 (fall, 1992): 1, 4–13.

Kramer, Martin. "Tragedy in Mecca." *Orbis* 32, no. 2 (1988): 231–47.

Krieg, William L. *Ecuadorean-Peruvian Rivalry in the Upper Amazon.* 2d ed. Bethesda, MD: William L. Krieg, 1987.

van der Kroef, Justus M. "Cambodia: A Third Alternative." *Asian Affairs* 2 (November–December 1979): 105–16.

———. "Cambodia: From 'Democratic Kampuchea' to 'People's Republic.'" *Asian Survey* 19 (August 1979): 731–50.

———. "The West New Guinea Settlement: Its Origins and Implications." *Orbis* 7 (spring 1963): 120–49.

———. "The Indonesian Revolution in Retrospect." *World Politics* 3, no. 3 (1951): 369–98.

Krohn, Lisa H. *Readings in Belizean History.* 2d ed. Belize City: St. John's College, 1987.

Kulski, Wladyslaw W. *De Gaulle and the World: The Foreign Policy of the Fifth French Republic.* Syracuse, NY: Syracuse University Press, 1966.

Kuniholm, Bruce R. *The Origins of the Cold War in the Near East.* Princeton, NJ: Princeton University Press, 1980.

Kushner, David. "Conflict and Accommodation in Turkish-Syrian Relations." In *Syria under Assad: Domestic Constraints and Regional Risks,* edited by Moshe Maoz and Avner Yaniv. London: Croom Helm, 1986.

Kutakov, Leonid N. *Japanese Foreign Policy on the Eve of the Pacific War, A Soviet View.* Tallahassee, FL: The Diplomatic Press, 1972.

Kyemba, Henry. *A State of Blood: The Inside Story of Idi-Amin.* New York: Ace Books, 1977.

Kyle, Keith. *Suez.* New York: St. Martin's Press, 1991.

Lacaze, Yvon. *France and Munich: A Study in Decision-Making in International Affairs.* New York: Columbia University Press, 1995.

Lacey, Robert. *The Kingdom.* New York: Avon Books, 1981.

Lacouture, Jean. *De Gaulle: The Ruler 1945–1970.* New York: W. W. Norton, 1992.

———. *Nasser: A Biography.* New York: Knopf, 1973.

Lacouture, Jean, and Philippe Devillers. *End of a War: Indochina 1954.* Translated by Alexander Lieven and Adam Roberts. New York: Praeger, 1969.

La Feber, Walter. *The Panama Canal: The Crisis in Historical Perspective.* Updated and rev. ed. New York: Oxford University Press, 1989.

———. *America, Russia and the Cold War, 1945–1975.* 3d ed. New York: John Wiley, 1976.

Laffan, R. G. D. *Survey of International Affairs 1938.* Vol. 2. RIIA. London: Oxford University Press, 1951.

Laffan, R. G. D., and Veronica M. Toynbee. "The Crisis over Czechoslovakia, October 1938 to 15 March 1939." In *Survey of International Affairs 1938,* vol. 3, RIIA, edited by R. G. D. Laffan et al., 1–288. London: Oxford University Press, 1953.

Lahav, J. "The Hungarian Communist Party's Path to Power, 1944–1948." (in Hebrew). Ph.D diss., Hebrew University of Jerusalem, 1976.

Laitin, David D., and Said S. Samatar. *Somalia: Nation in Search of a State.* Boulder, CO: Westview Press, 1987.

———. "The War in Ogaden: Implications for Siyaad's Role in Somali History." *Journal of Modern African Studies* 17 (March 1979): 95–116.

Lall, Arthur. *The United Nations and the Middle East Crisis, 1967.* 2d ed. New York: Columbia University Press, 1970.

Lamb, Alistair. *Crisis in Kashmir, 1947–1966.* London: Routledge & Kegan Paul, 1966.

———. *The India-China Border.* London: Oxford University Press, 1964.

Langer, Paul F., and Joseph J. Zasloff. *North Vietnam and the Pathet Lao: Partners in the Struggle for Laos.* Cambridge, MA: Harvard University Press, 1970.

Langer, William L., ed. *Encyclopedia of World History.* 5th ed. 2 vols. New York: Harry N. Abrams, 1974.

Langer, William L., and S. Everett Gleason. *The Undeclared War: 1940–1941.* New York: Harper, 1953.

Langley, Lester D., ed. *The United States, Cuba and the Cold War: American Failure or Communist Conspiracy.* Lexington, MA: D. C. Heath, 1970.

———. *The Cuban Policy of the U.S.: A Brief History.* New York: John Wiley, 1968.

Laniel, Joseph. *Le Drame Indochinois.* Paris: Plon, 1957.

Lapidoth, Ruth. *The Red Sea and the Gulf of Aden.* The Hague: Martinus Nijhoff, 1982.

Laqueur, Walter Z. *The Road to War, 1967: The Origins of the Arab-Israeli Conflict.* London: Weidenfeld & Nicolson, 1968.

Larrabee, Stephen. "Moscow, Angola and the Dialectics of Detente." *World Today* 32 (May 1975): 173–82.

Larson, David L., ed. *"The Cuban Missile Crisis" of 1962: Selected Documents and Chronology.* Boston, MA: Houghton Mifflin, 1963.

Larson, Deborah W. *Origins of Containment.* Princeton, NJ: Princeton University Press, 1985.

Lasky, Melvin J., ed. *The Hungarian Revolution: The Story of an October Uprising in Documents, Dispatches, Eyewitness Accounts, Worldwide Reactions.* London: Secker & Warburg, 1957.

Latourette, Kenneth S. *The American Record in the Far East, 1945–1951.* New York: Macmillan, 1952.

Laurens, Franklin D. *France and the Italo-Ethiopian Crisis, 1935–1936.* The Hague: Mouton, 1967.

Laval, Pierre. *The Unpublished Diary of Pierre Laval.* London: Falcon Press, 1948.

Lawless, Robert. "The Indonesian Takeover of East Timor." *Asian Survey* 16 (October 1976): 948–64.

Lawson, Eugene K. *The Sino-Vietnamese Conflict.* New York: Praeger, 1984.

Lebar, Frank M. et al., eds. *Laos: Its People, Its Society, Its Culture.* New Haven, CT: Human Relations Area Files Press, 1960.

Lebow, R. Ned. "Miscalculation in the South Atlantic: The Origins of the Falklands War." In *Psychology and Deterrence,* edited by Robert Jervis, R. Ned Lebow, and Janice G. Stein. Baltimore, MD: The Johns Hopkins University Press, 1985.

Lebow, R. Ned, and Janice G. Stein. *We All Lost the Cold War.* Princeton, NJ: Princeton University Press, 1994.

Leckie, Robert. *Conflict: The History of the Korean War.* New York: Putnam, 1962.

Lee, Bradford A. *Britain and the Sino-Japanese War 1937–39.* Stanford, CA: Stanford University Press, 1973.

Lee, Byung Joo. "The Chinese Intervention into the Korean War and Its Impact" (in Korean). *Korean Journal of International Relations* (Special Issue) (June 1990): 233–53.

Lee, Chae-Jin. *Communist China's Policy toward Laos: A Case Study, 1954–1967.* Center for East Asian Studies. Lawrence, KS: University Press of Kansas, 1970.

Lee, Chong-sik, and Hyuk-Sang Sohn. "South Korea in 1994: A Year of Trial." *Asian Survey* 35 (January 1995): 28–36.

Lefever, Ernest W. *Uncertain Mandate: Politics of the UN Congo Operation.* Baltimore, MD: Johns Hopkins University Press, 1967.

———. *Crisis in Congo: A United Nations Force in Action.* Washington, DC: Brookings Institution, 1965.

Leffler, Melvyn P. *A Preponderance of Power: National Security, The Truman Administration and the Cold War.* Stanford, CA: Stanford University Press, 1992.

———. "Strategy, Diplomacy, and the Cold War: The United States, Turkey and NATO, 1945–1952." *Journal of American History* 71 (March 1985): 807–25.

Legum, Colin. "Angola and the Horn of Africa." In *Diplomacy of Power: Soviet Armed Forces as a Political Instrument,* edited by Stephen S. Kaplan, 573–605. Washington, DC: Brookings Institution, 1981.

———. "The Soviet Union, China and the West in Southern Africa." *Foreign Affairs* 54 (July 1976): 745–62.

———. "National Liberation in Southern Africa." *Problems of Communism* 24 (January–February 1975): 1–20.

Legum, Colin, and Tony Hodges. *After Angola: The War over Southern Africa.* New York: Holmes & Meier, 1976.

Legum, Colin, and B. Lee. *Continuing Conflict in the Horn of Africa.* New York: Africana Publishing Co., 1979.

Leifer, Michael. *Indonesia's Foreign Policy.* London: Allen & Unwin, 1983.

———. "Post Mortem on the Third Indo-China War." *World Today* 35 (June 1979): 249–59.

———. "Indonesia and the Incorporation of East Timor." *World Today* 32 (September 1976): 347–54.

———. *Cambodia and Neutrality.* Canberra: Australian National University Department of International Relations, 1962.

———. "Cambodia and Her Neighbors." *Pacific Affairs* 34 (winter 1961–62): 361–74.

Leighton, Marian. "Vietnam and the Sino-Soviet Rivalry." *Asian Affairs* 6 (September–October 1978a): 1–31.

———. "Perspectives on the Vietnam-Cambodia Border Conflict." *Asian Survey* 18 (May 1978b): 448–57.

Leitenberg, Milton. "The Stranded USSR Submarine in Sweden and the Question of a Nordic Nuclear-Free Zone." *Cooperation and Conflict* 17, no. 1 (1982): 17–28.

Lellouche, Pierre, and Dominique Moisi. "French Policy in Africa: A Lonely Battle against Destabilization." *International Security* 3, no. 4 (1979): 108–133.

Lemarchand, René. "The Case of Chad." In *The Green and the Black: Qadhafi's Policies in Africa,* edited by René Lemarchand, 106–24. Bloomington, IN: Indiana University Press, 1988.

———. "The Crisis in Chad." In *African Crisis Areas and U.S. Foreign Policy,* edited by Gerald J. Bender, James S. Coleman, and Richard L. Sklar, 239–56. Berkeley, CA: University of California Press, 1985.

———, ed. *America's Policy in Southern Africa: The Stakes and the Stance.* 2d ed. Washington, DC: University Press of America, 1981.

———. *Rwanda and Burundi.* New York: Praeger, 1970.

Lenczowski, George. *Iran under the Pahlavis.* Stanford, CA: Hoover Institution Press, 1978.

———. *The Middle East in World Affairs.* 3d ed. Ithaca, NY: Cornell University Press, 1962.

———. *Russia and the West in Iran, 1918–1948: A Study in Big Power Rivalry.* Ithaca, NY: Cornell University Press, 1949.

Leng, Shao C., and Hundgah Chiu, eds. *Law in Chinese Foreign Policy: Communist China: A Selected Problem of International Law.* Dobbs Ferry, NY: Oceana Publications, 1972.

Lentner, Howard H. "The Pueblo Affair: Anatomy of a Crisis." *Military Review* 44 (1969): 55–66.

Leogrande, William M. *Cuba's Policy in Africa, 1959–1980.* Berkeley, CA: Institute of International Studies, University of California, Berkeley, 1980.

———. "The Revolution in Nicaragua: Another Cuba?" *Foreign Affairs* 58 (fall 1979): 28–50.

Leslie, Robert F., ed. *The History of Poland since 1863.* Cambridge: Cambridge University Press, 1980.

Lev, Daniel S. *The Transition to Guided Democracy, 1957–59.* Ithaca, NY: Cornell University Press, 1966.

Levine, David C., ed. "The Border Issue: China and the Soviet Union, March–October 1969." *Studies in Comparative Communism* 2 (July–October 1969): 121–382.

Lewis, Bernard. *The Emergence of Modern Turkey.* London: Oxford University Press, 1961.

Lewis, Flora. *The Polish Volcano: A Case History of Hope.* London: Secker & Warburg, 1959.

Lewis, Gordon K. *Grenada: The Jewel Despoiled.* Baltimore, MD: Johns Hopkins University Press, 1987.

Lewis, I. M. *A Modern History of Somalia: Nation and State in the Horn of Africa.* London: Longman, 1980.

———. "Pan-Africanism and Pan-Somalism." *Journal of Modern African Studies* 1, no. 2 (1963): 147–61.

Lewis, William H. "Ethiopia-Somalia (1977–1978)." In *The Lessons of Recent Wars in the Third World,* edited by Robert E. Harkavy and Stephanie G. Neuman. Vol. 1, 99–116. Lexington, MA: Lexington Books, 1985a.

———. "War in the Western Sahara." In *The Lessons of Recent Wars in the Third World,* edited by Robert E. Harkavy and Stephanie G. Neuman. Vol. 1, 117–37. Lexington, MA: Lexington Books, 1985b.

Lewy, Guenter. *American in Vietnam.* New York: Oxford University Press, 1978.

Liddell-Hart, Basil H. *History of the Second World War.* London: Cassell, 1970.

———, ed. *The Rommel Papers.* London: Collins, 1953.

Lie, Trygve. *In the Cause of Peace.* New York: Macmillan, 1954.

de Lima, F. X. *Intervention in International Law.* Den Haag: Pax Nederland, 1971.

Lindsay, J. W. "The War over the Chaco." *International Affairs* (London) 14 (March–April 1935): 231–40.

Ling, Dwight L. *Tunisia: From Protectorate to Republic.* Bloomington, IN: Indiana University Press, 1967.

Liss, Sheldon B. *The Canal: Aspects of United States–Panamanian Relations.* Notre Dame, IN: University of Notre Dame Press, 1967.

Little, Tom. *South Arabia: Arena of Conflict.* London: Pall Mall Press, 1968.

Litwak, R. *Sources of Inter-State Conflict.* Aldershot, Hampshire, U.K.: Gower for IISS, 1981.

Liu, Xuecheng. *The Sino-Indian Border Dispute and Sino-Indian Relations.* Lanham, MD: University Press of America, 1994.

Lloyd, Selwyn. *Suez 1956: A Personal Account.* New York: Mayflower Books, 1978.

Löfgren, Stig. "Soviet Submarines against Sweden." *Strategic Review* 12 (1984): 36–42.

Logio, George. *Bulgaria, Past and Present.* Manchester: Sherratt & Hughes, 1936.

Lomax, Bill. *Hungary 1956.* New York: St. Martin's Press, 1976.

Longrigg, Stephen H. *Syria and Lebanon under French Mandate.* London: Oxford University Press, 1958.

———. *Iraq: 1900 to 1950: A Political, Social and Economic History.* Beirut: Librairie du Liban, 1953.

Lorch, Netanel. *History of the War of Independence* (in Hebrew). Tel Aviv: Massada, 1966.

Louis, W. Roger, and Roger Owen, eds. *Suez 1956: The Crisis and Its Consequences.* Oxford: Clarendon Press, 1989.

Louis, W. Roger, Roger Owen, and Robert W. Stookey, eds. *The End of the Palestine Mandate.* London: I. B. Tauris and Co., 1986.

Love, Kenneth. *Suez: The Twice Fought War.* New York: McGraw-Hill, 1969.

Low, D. A. "Uganda Unhinged." *International Affairs* 49 (April 1973): 214–28.

Lowe, Cedric J., and F. Marzari. *Italian Foreign Policy: 1870–1940.* London: Routledge & Kegan Paul, 1975.

Lowe, Peter. *The Origins of the Korean War.* New York: Longman, 1986.

———. *Great Britain and the Origins of the Pacific War: A Study of British Policy in East Asia 1937–1941.* Oxford: Clarendon Press, 1977.

Lowenthal, Abraham F. *The Dominican Intervention.* Cambridge, MA: Harvard University Press, 1972.

———. "The Dominican Intervention in Retrospect." *Public Policy* 18 (1969): 133–48.

Lowenthal, Richard. "Russia and China: Controlled Conflict." *Foreign Affairs* 49 (April 1971): 507–18.

Lowi, Miriam R. *Water and Power: The Politics of a Scarce Resource in the Jordan River Basin.* Cambridge: Cambridge University Press, 1993.

de Luca, Anthony R. "Soviet-American Politics and the Turkish Straits." *Political Science Quarterly* 97 (fall 1977): 503–24.

Lytle, Mark. *The Origins of the Iranian-American Alliance.* New York: Holmes & Meier, 1987.

Macartney, Carlile A. *October Fifteenth: A History of Modern Hungary, 1929–1945.* 2 vols. Edinburgh: Edinburgh University Press, 1956–57.

Macartney, Carlile A. et. al. *Survey of International Affairs 1925.* Vol. 2. RIIA. London: Oxford University Press, 1928.

Macartney, Maxwell H. H., and Paul Cremona. *Italy's Foreign and Colonial Policy 1914–1937.* London: Oxford University Press, 1938.

MacDonald, R. St. John. "The Organization of American States in Action." *University of Toronto Law Journal* 15 (spring 1964): 424–26.

MacDonald, Robert W. *The League of Arab States: A Study in the Dynamics of Regional Organization.* Princeton, NJ: Princeton University Press, 1965.

MacFarquhar, Roderick. *Sino-American Relations 1949–71.* New York: Praeger, 1972.

Mack, Andrew. "The Nuclear Crisis on the Korean Peninsula." *Asian Survey* 33 (April 1993): 339–59.

Mack Smith, Denis. (see Smith, Denis Mack)

Mackie, J. A. C. *Konfrontasi: The Indonesia-Malaysia Dispute, 1963–1966.* New York: Oxford University Press, 1974.

Mackintosh, James M. *Strategy and Tactics of Soviet Foreign Policy.* London: Oxford University Press, 1962.

Maclear, Michael. *The Ten Thousand Day War: Vietnam, 1945–1975.* Toronto: Methuen, 1981.

Macmillan, Harold. *At the End of the Day 1961–1963.* New York: Harper & Row, 1973.

———. *Pointing the Way 1959–1961.* New York: Harper & Row, 1972.

———. *Riding the Storm 1956–1959.* New York: Harper & Row, 1971.

MacNair, Harley F., and Donald F. Lach. *Modern Far Eastern International Relations.* 2d ed. New York: Van Nostrand, 1955.

Magas, Branca. *The Destruction of Yugoslavia: Tracking the Break-up 1980–92.* London: Verso, 1993.

Maggs, W. W. "Armenia and Azerbaijan: Looking toward the Middle East." *Current History* (January 1993): 6–11.

Mahaim, E. *Le Secours de Chomage en Belgique Pendant l'Occupation Allemande.* Paris: Les Presses Universitaires de France, 1926.

Mahjub, Mohammed Ahmed. *Democracy on Trial: Reflections on Arab and African Politics.* London: André Deutsch, 1974.

Makinda, Samuel M. "Conflict and the Superpowers in the Horn of Africa." *Third World Quarterly* 4 (January 1982): 93–103.

Malik, Iftikhar H. "Kashmir Dispute: A Stalemate or Solution?" *Journal of South Asian and Middle Eastern Studies* 16 (summer 1993): 55–72.

Malik, J. Mohan. "The Kashmir Dispute: India and Pakistan in Conflict." *Current Affairs Bulletin* (November 1990): 15–20.

Mamatey, Victor S., and Randomir Luza. *A History of the Czechoslovak Republic, 1918–1948.* Princeton, NJ: Princeton University Press, 1973.

Mangold, Peter. "Shaba I and Shaba II." *Survival* 21 (May–June 1979): 107–10.

Mann, Thomas C. "The Dominican Crisis: Correcting Some Misconceptions." *Department of State Bulletin* 53 (1965): 730–38.

Mansourov, Alexandre Y. "Stalin, Mao, Kim, and China's Decision to Enter the Korean War, September 16–October 15, 1950: New Evidence from the Russian Archives." CWIHP. *Bulletin* 6–7 (winter 1995–96): 94–107.

Maoz, Zeev. "The Decision to Raid Entebbe: Decision Analysis Applied to Crisis Behavior." *Journal of Conflict Resolution* 25 (December 1981): 677–707.

Maprayil, Cyriac. *Britain and Afghanistan in Historical Perspective.* London: Cosmic Books, 1983.

al-Marayati, Abid A. "The Question of Kuwait." *Foreign Affairs Reports* (New Delhi) 15 (July 1966): 91–97.

———. *A Diplomatic History of Modern Iraq.* New York: Speller & Roberts, 1961.

Marcum, John A. *The Angolan Revolution.* Vol. 2, *Exile Politics and Guerrilla Warfare, 1962–1976.* Cambridge, MA: MIT Press, 1978.

———. "Lessons of Angola." *Foreign Affairs* 54 (April 1976): 407–25.

Mariam, Mesfin Wolde. "The Background of the Ethio-Somalian Boundary Dispute." *Journal of Modern African Studies* 2, no. 2 (1964): 189–219.

Markakis, John. *National and Class Conflict in the Horn of Africa.* Cambridge: Cambridge University Press, 1987.

Markides, Kyriacos C. *The Rise and Fall of the Cyprus Republic.* New Haven, CT: Yale University Press, 1977.

Marks, Thomas A. "Spanish Sahara—Background to Conflict." *African Affairs* 75 (January 1976): 3–13.

Marlowe, John. *Anglo-Egyptian Relations, 1800–1953.* London: Cresset, 1954.

Marmullaku, Ramadan. *Albania and the Albanians.* Translated by Margot Milosavljevic and Bosko Milosavljevic. Hamden, CT: Anchor Books, 1975.

Marshall, A. "Portugal: A Determined Empire." *World Today* 17 (March 1961): 95–101.

Martin, D. *General Amin.* London: Faber & Faber, 1974.

Martin, John Bartlow. *Overtaken by Events: The Dominican Crisis from Trujillo to the Civil War.* Garden City, NY: Doubleday, 1966.

Maude, George. *The Finnish Dilemma: Neutrality in the Shadow of Power.* London: Oxford University Press, 1976.

Maung, Maung. *Burma and General Ne Win.* Bombay: Asia Publishing House, 1969.

Maxon, Yale Candee. *Control of Japanese Foreign Policy: A Study of Civil-Military Rivalry, 1930–1945.* Berkeley, CA: University of California Press, 1957.

Maxwell, Neville. "Why the Russians Lifted the Blockade at Bear Island." *Foreign Affairs* 57 (fall 1978): 138–45.

———. "The Chinese Account of the 1969 Fighting at Chenpao." *China Quarterly* 56 (October–December 1973): 730–39.

———. *India's China War.* Garden City, NY: Doubleday, 1970.

Mayall, James. "The Battle for the Horn: Somali Irredentism and International Diplomacy." *World Today* 34 (September 1978): 336–45.

Mazrui, Ali A. *African International Relations: The Diplomacy of Dependency and Change.* London: Heinemann, 1977.

McCain, William D. *The United States and the Republic of Panama.* Durham, NC: Duke University Press, 1937.

McClellan, David S. *Dean Acheson: The State Department Years.* New York: Dodd, Mead, 1976.

McClelland, Charles A. "Access to Berlin: The Quantity and Variety of Events, 1948–1963." In *Quantitative International Politics: Insight and Evidence,* edited by J. D. Singer, 159–86. New York: Free Press, 1968.

McCullough, David. *Truman.* New York: Simon & Schuster, 1992.

McDougall, Walter A. *France's Rhineland Diplomacy 1914–1924.* Princeton, NJ: Princeton University Press, 1978.

McNamara, Robert S. *In Retrospect: The Tragedy and Lessons of Vietnam.* New York: Times Books, 1995.

McNeil, William H. *Greece: American Aid in Action, 1947–1956.* New York: Twentieth Century Fund, 1957.

Mecham, J. Lloyd. *The United States and Inter-American Security, 1889–1960.* Austin, TX: University of Texas Press, 1961.

Mehdi, Muhammad. "The Arab Summit." *Middle East Forum* 40 (May 1964): 25–28.

Meir, Golda. *My Life.* Jerusalem: Steimatzky, 1975.

Melady, Thomas P. *Burundi: The Tragic Years.* Maryknoll, NY: Orbis, 1974.

Mendel, D. *The Politics of Formosan Nationalism.* Berkeley, CA: University of California Press, 1970.

Menon, P. N. "The Anglo-Guatemalan Territorial Dispute over the Colony of Belize." *Journal of Latin American Studies* 11 (November 1979): 343–71.

Menon, Rajan. *Soviet Power and the Third World.* New Haven, CT: Yale University Press, 1986.

Menon, V. P. *The Story of the Integration of the Indian States.* London: Longman, Green, 1956.

Meo, Leila. "The War in Lebanon." In *Ethnic Conflict in International Relations,* edited by Astri Suhrke and Lela G. Noble, 93–126. New York: Praeger, 1977.

Meray, Tibor. *Thirteen Days That Shook the Kremlin.* London: Thames & Hudson, 1959.

Mercer, John. *Spanish Sahara.* London: Allen & Unwin, 1976a.

———. "Confrontation in the Western Sahara." *World Today* 32 (June 1976b): 230–39.

———. "The Cycle of Invasion and Unification in the Western Sahara." *African Affairs* 75 (October 1976c): 498–510.

Merrill, John. "North Korea in 1993: In the Eye of the Storm." *Asian Survey* 34 (January 1994): 10–18.

Merritt, Richard L. "A Transformed Crisis: The Berlin Wall." In *Modern European Governments,* edited by Roy Macridis. Englewood Cliffs, NJ: Prentice-Hall, 1968.

Meyer, Karl E., and Tad Szulc. *The Cuban Invasion: The Chronicle of a Disaster.* New York: Praeger, 1962.

Mezerik, A. G., ed. "Cuba and the United States: Bay of Pigs, October Crisis, UN-OAS Action." *International Review Service* 79 (1962): 7–17.

Middle East Research Center (MERC). *British and French Action in Egypt August–November 1956.* Cairo: 1956.

Middlemas, Keith. *Diplomacy of Illusion: The British Government and Germany, 1937–39.* London: Weidenfeld & Nicolson, 1972.

Mikolajczyk, Stanislaw. *The Pattern of Soviet Domination.* London: Low, Marston, 1948.

Miller, Judith, and Laurie Mylroie. *Saddam Hussein and the Crisis in the Gulf.* New York: Times Books, 1990.

Miller, Linda B. *World Order and Local Disorder.* Princeton, NJ: Princeton University Press, 1967.

Millis, Walter, ed. *The Forrestal Diaries.* New York: Viking Press, 1951.

Minor, Kent J. "U.S.-Panamanian Relations 1958–1973." Ph.D. diss., Case Western Reserve University, 1974.

Misra, K. P. *The Role of the UN in the Indo-Pakistan Conflict, 1971.* New Delhi, Vikas, 1973.

Mitchell, Bruce. "Politics, Fish and International Resource Management: The British-Icelandic Cod War." *Geographical Review* 66 (April 1976): 127–38.

Mitrany, David. *The Effects of the War on Southeastern Europe.* Carnegie Endowment for International Peace. Edited by James Shotwell. New York: Howard Fertig, 1933.

Mlynar, Z. *Nightfrost in Prague: The End of Humane Socialism.* New York: Karz, 1980.

Molesworth, G. *Afghanistan 1919: An Account of Operations in the Third Afghan War.* New York: Asia Publishing House, 1962.

Molnar, Miklos. *Victoire d'une Défaite. Budapest, 1956.* Paris: Librairie Fayard, 1968.

Monroe, Elizabeth, and A. H. Farrar-Hockley. *The Arab-Israel War, October 1973— Background and Events.* London: IISS. Adelphi Paper No. 111, winter 1974–75.

Moore, C. H. "One-Partyism in Mauritania." *Journal of Modern African Studies* 3 (October 1965): 409–20.

Moose, George E. "French Military Policy in Africa." In *Arms and the African: Military Influences on Africa's International Relations,* edited by William J. Foltz and Henry S. Bienen, 59–97. New Haven, CT: Yale University Press, 1985.

Moreno, José A. *Barrios in Arms: Revolution in Santo Domingo.* Pittsburgh, PA: University of Pittsburgh Press, 1970.

Morley, James W. *Japan's Foreign Policy, 1868–1941: A Research Guide.* New York: Columbia University Press, 1974.

Morris, Benny. *The Birth of the Palestinian Refugee Problem, 1947–1949.* Cambridge: Cambridge University Press, 1987.

Morrison, Herbert. *An Autobiography.* London: Odhams Press, 1960.

Morton, Louis. "Japan's Decision for War (1941)." In *Command Decisions,* edited by Kent Roberts Greenfield. New York: Harcourt, Brace, 1959.

Morton, William. *Tanaka Giichi and Japan's China Policy.* New York: St. Martin's Press, 1980.

Mouradian, C. "The Mountainous Karabagh Question: Inter-Ethnic Conflict or Decolonization Crisis?" *Armenian Review* 43 (summer–autumn 1990): 2–3.

Moussa, Farag. *Les Négociations Anglo-Egyptiennes de 1950–1 sur Suez et le Soudan.* Genève: E. Droz, 1955.

Mozingo, David. *Chinese Policy toward Indonesia, 1949–1967.* Ithaca, NY: Cornell University Press, 1976.

Muhammad, Chaudhri. *The Emergence of Pakistan.* New York: Columbia University Press, 1967.

Muni, S. D. *Pangs of Proximity: India and Sri Lanka's Ethnic Crisis.* New Delhi: Sage, 1993.

Munro, Dana G. *The United States and the Caribbean Republics, 1921–1923.* Princeton, NJ: Princeton University Press, 1974.

———. *Intervention and Dollar Diplomacy in the Caribbean, 1900–1921.* Princeton, NJ: Princeton University Press, 1964.

Murphy, Edward R. *Second in Command: The Uncensored Account of the Capture of the Spy Ship Pueblo.* New York: Holt, Rinehart & Winston, 1971.

Murphy, Robert. *Diplomat among Warriors.* London: Collins, 1964.

Mussolini, Benito. *Memoirs, 1942–1943.* London: Weidenfeld & Nicolson, 1949.

Nagy, Feren. *The Struggle behind the Iron Curtain.* New York: Macmillan, 1948.

Nakdimon, Shlomo. *Tammuz in Flames* (in Hebrew). Jerusalem: Edanim/Yediot Aharonot, 1993.

Nanita, Abelardo R. *Trujillo.* Impresora Dominicana: Cuidad Trujillo, 1951.

Napper, Larry C. "The African Terrain and U.S.-Soviet Conflict in Angola and Rhodesia: Some Implications for Crisis Prevention." Chap. 8 in *Managing U.S.-Soviet Rivalry: Problems of Crisis Prevention,* edited by Alexander L. George. Boulder, CO: Westview Press, 1983a.

———. "The Ogaden War: Some Implications for Crisis Prevention." Chap. 10 in *Managing U.S.-Soviet Rivalry: Problems of Crisis Prevention,* edited by Alexander L. George. Boulder, CO: Westview Press, 1983b.

Natkevicius, Ladas. *Aspect Politique et Juridique du Different Polono-Lithuanien.* Paris: Librairie de Jurisprudence Ancienne et Moderne, 1930.

Navarre, General Henri. *Agonie de l'Indochine.* Paris: Plon, 1956.

Neff, Donald. *Warriors for Jerusalem: The Six Days That Changed the Middle East.* New York: Linden Press, 1984.

Nehru, Jawaharlal. *Kashmir 1947–1956. Excerpts from Prime Minister Nehru's Speeches.* New Delhi: Information Service of India, 1956.

Nelson, Harold D. *Libya: A Country Study.* 3d ed. Washington, DC: Foreign Area Studies, USGPO, 1979.

Nelson, Harold D. et al. *Area Handbook for Guinea.* 2d ed. Washington, DC: Foreign Area Studies, USGPO, 1975.

Nere, Jacques. *The Foreign Policy of France from 1914 to 1945.* London: Routledge & Kegan Paul, 1975.

Neuberger, Ralph B. "Involvement, Invasion and Withdrawal: Qadhdhafi's Libya and Chad 1969–1981." Tel Aviv: Tel Aviv University Shiloah Center for Middle East and African Studies, Occasional Papers, vol. 83, 1982.

Neuchterlein, Donald E. *Thailand and the Struggle for Southeast Asia.* Ithaca, NY: Cornell University Press, 1965.

Neustadt, Richard E. *Alliance Politics.* New York: Columbia University Press, 1970.

Nevakivi, Jukka. *The Appeal That Was Never Made.* Montreal and Kingston: McGill-Queen's University Press, 1976.

Newell, Nancy P., and Richard S. Newell. *The Struggle for Afghanistan.* Ithaca, NY: Cornell University Press, 1981.

Newman, Robert P. *Truman and the Hiroshima Cult.* East Lansing, MI: Michigan State University Press, 1995.

Nichterlein, Sue. "The Struggle for East Timor: Prelude to Invasion." *Journal of Contemporary Asia* 7, no. 4 (1977): 486–96.

Nimrod, Yoram. "Conflict over the Jordan—Last Stage." *New Outlook* (Tel Aviv) 8 (September 1965): 5–18.

———. "The Jordan's Angry Waters." *New Outlook* 8 (July–August 1965): 19–33.

———. "The Unquiet Waters." *New Outlook* 8 (June 1965): 38–51.

Nixon, Richard M. *RN: The Memoirs of Richard Nixon.* New York: Grosset & Dunlop, 1978.

Nkrumah, Kwame. *Challenge of the Congo.* New York: International Publishers, 1967.

Northedge, Frederick S. *Descent from Power: British Foreign Policy, 1945–1973.* London: Allen & Unwin, 1974.

Novak, Bogdan C. *Trieste, the Ethnic, Political and Ideological Struggle.* Chicago, IL: University of Chicago Press, 1970.

Nutting, Anthony. *No End of a Lesson: The Story of Suez.* London: Constable, 1967.

———. *I Saw for Myself: The Aftermath of Suez.* London: Hollins Carter, 1958.

Nyerere, Julius K. "America and Southern Africa." *Foreign Affairs* 55 (July 1977): 671–84.

Nyrop, Richard F., and Donald M. Seekins. *Afghanistan: A Country Study.* 5th ed. Washington, DC: Foreign Area Studies, USGPO, 1986.

———, ed. *Syria: A Country Study.* Washington, DC: Foreign Area Studies, USGPO, 1971.

Oakley, Stewart. *The Story of Sweden.* London: Faber & Faber, 1966.

O'Ballance, Edgar. *The Cyanide War: Tamil Insurrection in Sri Lanka, 1973–88.* Washington, DC: Brassey's (UK), 1989.

———. *The Gulf War.* London: Brassey's, 1988.

———. "Underwater Hide-and-Seek." *Military Review* 64 (1984): 64–74.

———. "The Iran-Iraq War." *Marine Corps Gazette* (February 1982): 44–49.

———. *The Third Arab-Israeli War.* London: Faber & Faber, 1972.

———. *The War in the Yemen.* Hamden, CT: Archon Books, 1971.

———. *Korea: 1950–1953.* London: Faber & Faber, 1969.

———. *The Greek Civil War, 1944–49.* New York: Praeger, 1966.

———. *The Indo-China War, 1945–1954: A Study in Guerrilla Warfare.* London: Faber & Faber, 1964.

———. *The Arab-Israeli War, 1948.* New York: Praeger, 1957.

Oberdorfer, Don. *The Turn: From the Cold War to a New Era.* New York: Poseidon Press, 1991.

———. *Tet!* Garden City, NY: Doubleday, 1971.

Ofer, Yehuda. *Operation Thunder, The Entebbe Raid. The Israelis' Own Story.* London: Penguin, 1976.

Ogata, Sadako N. *Defiance in Manchuria: The Making of Japanese Foreign Policy, 1931–1932.* Berkeley, CA: University of California Press, 1964.

Okumu, Washington A. J. *Lumumba's Congo: Roots of Conflict.* New York: Ivan Obolensky, 1963.

Oliver, Robert T. *Verdict in Korea.* State College, PA: Bald Eagle Press, 1952.

Oliver, Roland A., and Michael Crowder, eds. *The Cambridge Encyclopedia of Africa.* Cambridge: Cambridge University Press, 1981.

———. *A Short History of Africa.* 4th ed. Middlesex, U.K.: Penguin African Library, 1972.

Olsson, Sven-Olof. *German Coal and Swedish Fuel, 1939–45.* Gothenburg: Institute of Economic History, Gothenburg University, 1975.

Omara-Otunnu, Amii. *Politics and the Military in Uganda, 1890–1985.* New York: St. Martin's Press, 1987.

O'Neill, Bard E. *Armed Struggle in Palestine: A Political-Military Analysis.* Boulder, CO: Westview Press, 1978.

Osborne, Harold. *Bolivia: A Land Divided.* 3d ed. London: Oxford University Press, 1965.

Ostermann, Christian F. "New Documents on the East German Uprising of 1953." *CWIHP. Bulletin* 5 (spring 1995): 10–21, 57.

———. "The United States, The East German Uprising of 1953, and the Limits of Rollback." Washington, DC: Woodrow Wilson International Center for Scholars. CWIHP. Working Paper No. 11, December 1994.

Ottaway, Marina. *Soviet and American Influence in the Horn of Africa.* New York: Praeger, 1982.

Owen, David. *Balkan Odyssey.* New York: Harcourt, Brace, 1995.

Owen, R. P. "The Rebellion in Dhofar: A Threat to Western Interests in the Gulf." *World Today* 29 (June 1973): 266–72.

Owens, R. J. *Peru.* London: Oxford University Press, 1964.

Pachter, Henry M. *Collision Course: The Cuban Missile Crisis and Co-existence.* London: Pall Mall Press, 1963.

Page, Stanley W. *The Formation of the Baltic States.* New York: Howard Fertig, 1970.

Paige, Glenn D. *The Korean Decision.* New York: Free Press, 1968.

Palit, D. K. *The Lightning Campaign.* Salisbury, U.K.: Compton, 1972.

Palmer, Alan W. *A Dictionary of Modern History.* Harmondsworth, U.K.: Penguin, 1973.

Panikkar, K. M. *In Two Chinas: Memoirs of a Diplomat.* London: Allen & Unwin, 1955.

Pano, Nicholas. *The People's Republic of Albania.* Baltimore, MD: Johns Hopkins University Press, 1968.

Papandreou, Andreas. *Democracy at Gunpoint: The Greek Front.* Garden City, NY: Doubleday, 1970.

von Papen, Franz. *Memoirs.* London: André Deutsch, 1952.

Papp, Daniel S. "The Angolan Civil War and Namibia: The Role of External Intervention." In *Making War and Waging Peace: Foreign Intervention in Africa,* edited by David R. Smock, 161–96. Washington, DC: United States Institute of Peace Press, 1993.

Parkinson, F. *Latin America, the Cold War and World Powers, 1945–1973.* Beverly Hills, CA: Sage, 1974.

Parrish, Scott D., and Mikhail M. Narinsky. "New Evidence on the Soviet Rejection of the Marshall Plan, 1947: Two Reports." Washington, DC: Woodrow Wilson International Center for Scholars. CWIHP. Working Paper No. 9, 1994.

Parsons, Sir Anthony. "From Southern Rhodesia to Zimbabwe, 1965–1980." *International Relations* 9 (November 1988): 353–61.

Pastor, Peter. *Hungary between Wilson and Lenin.* New York: Columbia University Press, 1976.

Paterson, Thomas G. *Soviet-American Confrontation: Postwar Reconstruction and the Origins of the Cold War.* Baltimore, MD: Johns Hopkins University Press, 1973.

Patrick, Richard A. "Political Geography and the Cyprus Conflict: 1963–1971." Waterloo, Ontario: Department of Geography, Faculty of Environmental Studies, University of Waterloo, 1976.

Pattee, Richard. *La Republica Dominica.* Madrid: Ediciones Cultura Hispánica, 1967.

Patterson, George N. *Peking versus Delhi.* New York: Praeger, 1964.

Paul, David W. "Soviet Foreign Policy and the Invasion of Czechoslovakia: A Theory and a Case Study." *International Studies Quarterly* 15 (June 1971): 159–202.

Paust, J. J. "The Seizure and Recovery of the Mayaguez." *Yale Law Journal* 85 (May 1976): 774–806.

Pavel, Pavel. *Why Rumania Failed.* London: Alliance Press, 1944.

Payne, Anthony, Paul Sutton, and Tony Thorndike. *Grenada: Revolution and Invasion.* New York: St. Martin's Press, 1984.

Payne, P. S. Robert. *The Civil War in Spain, 1936–1939.* London: Secker & Warburg, 1963.

Payne, Stanley G. *Franco's Spain.* London: Routledge & Kegan Paul, 1967.

Pelling, Henry. *Britain and the Marshall Plan*. New York: St. Martin's Press, 1988.

Penrose, Edith T. *Iraq: International Relations and National Development*. London: E. Benn, 1978.

Peres, Shimon. *David's Sling*. London: Weidenfeld and Nicolson, 1970.

Perham, Margery F. *The Government of Ethiopia*. 2d ed. London: Faber & Faber, 1969.

Perlmutter, Amos, Michael Handel, and Uri Bar-Joseph. *Two Minutes over Baghdad*. London: Corgi, 1982.

Perman, D. *The Shaping of the Czechoslovakian State*. Leiden, Netherlands: E. J. Brill, 1962.

Peterson, John E. *Yemen: The Search for a Modern State*. Baltimore, MD: Johns Hopkins University Press, 1982.

————. "Conflict in the Yemens and Superpower Involvement. Washington, DC: Center for Contemporary Arab Studies, Georgetown University, 1981.

Petrow, Richard. *The Bitter Years: The Invasion and Occupation of Denmark and Norway, April 1940–May 1945*. New York: William Morrow, 1974.

Pettman, Jan. *Zambia: Security and Conflict*. New York: St. Martin's Press, 1974.

Pike, Douglas. "The USSR and Vietnam: Into the Swamp." *Asian Survey* 19 (December 1979): 1159–70.

————. "Vietnam in 1977: More of the Same." *Asian Survey* 18 (January 1978): 68–75.

Pike, Frederick B. "Guatemala, the United States and Communism in the Americas." *Review of Politics* 17 (April 1955): 232–61.

Pineau, Christian. *Mille Neuf Cent Cinquante Six: Suez*. Paris: Robert Laffont, 1976.

Pipes, Daniel. "A Border Adrift: Origins of the Conflict." *The Washington Papers*. No. 92. Westport: CT: Praeger, 1982.

Plank, John, ed. *Cuba and the United States: Long-Range Perspectives*. Washington, DC: Brookings Institution, 1967.

Playfair, Ian S. O. *The Mediterranean and the Middle East*. 2 vols. London: HMSO, 1954.

Pochando, Bernardo. *Resumon de Historia Patua*. Ste. Domingo, Dominican Republic, 1974.

Pogue, Forrest C. *George C. Marshall: Statesman, 1945–1959*. New York: Viking Penguin, 1987.

Pollak, Allen, and Anne Sinai, eds. *The Syrian Arab Republic: A Handbook*. New York: American Academic Association for Peace in the Middle East, 1976.

Polo, Stefanag, and Arben Pato. *The History of Albania*. London: Routledge & Kegan Paul, 1981.

Polonsky, Antony. *Politics in Independent Poland 1921–1939. The Crisis of Constitutional Government*. Oxford: Clarendon Press, 1972.

Poole, Peter A. "Thai-Cambodian Relations: The Problem of the Border." *Asian Affairs* 5 (May–June 1978): 286–95.

————. "Cambodia 1975: The GRUNK Regime." *Asian Survey* 16 (January 1976): 23–30.

Popovici, Andrei. "The Political Status of Bessarabia. Washington, DC: School of Foreign Service, Georgetown University, 1931.

Porter, Bruce D. *The USSR in Third World Conflicts: Soviet Arms and Diplomacy in Local Wars, 1945–1980*. Cambridge: Cambridge University Press, 1984.

Poullada, Leon. *Reform and Rebellion in Afghanistan 1919–1929: King Amanullah's Failure to Modernize a Tribal Society*. Ithaca, NY: Cornell University Press, 1973.

Pounds, Norman J. G. *Poland between East and West*. Princeton, NJ: Van Nostrand, 1964.

Powell, Colin L., with Joseph E. Persico. *My American Journey.* New York: Random House, 1995.

Powell, R. "China's Conflict with Russia: War or Polemic?" *Pacific Community* 5 (October 1973): 28–41.

Prange, Gordon W. *Pearl Harbor: The Verdict of History.* New York: McGraw-Hill, 1986.

———. *At Dawn We Slept: The Untold Story of Pearl Harbor.* New York: McGraw-Hill, 1981.

Preston, Paul. *Franco: A Biography.* New York: Basic Books, 1994.

———. *The Spanish Civil War 1936–1939.* London: Weidenfeld & Nicolson, 1986.

Primakov, Evgueni. "The Fourth Arab-Israeli War." *World Marxist Review* 16 (December 1973): 52–60.

Princen, Thomas. "Mediation by a Transnational Organization: The Case of the Vatican." In *Mediation in International Relations: Multiple Approaches to Conflict Management,* edited by Jacob Bercovitch and Jeffrey Z. Rubin, 149–75. New York: St. Martin's Press, 1992a.

———. *Intermediaries in International Conflict.* Princeton, NJ: Princeton University Press, 1992b.

———. "International Mediation—The View from the Vatican: Lessons from Mediating the Beagle Channel Dispute." *Negotiation Journal* 3 (October 1987): 347–66.

Pry, Peter. *Israel's Nuclear Arsenal.* Boulder, CO: Westview Press, 1984.

Psomiades, Harry J. *The Eastern Question: The Last Phase.* Thessaloniki, Greece: Institute for Balkan Studies, 1968.

Public Relations Association of (South) Korea. "Who Started the War: The Truth about the Korean Conflict." Seoul, June 1973.

Quandt, William B. *Peace Process: American Diplomacy and the Arab-Israeli Conflict since 1967.* Washington, DC: Brookings Institution; and Berkeley, CA: University of California Press, 1993.

———. "Lebanon, 1958, and Jordan, 1970." In *Force without War: U.S. Armed Forces as a Political Instrument,* edited by Barry M. Blechman and Stephen S. Kaplan., 222–88. Washington, DC: Brookings Institution, 1978.

———. *Decade of Decisions: American Policy toward the Arab-Israeli Conflict, 1967–1976.* Berkeley, CA: University of California Press, 1977.

Quandt, William B., Fuad Jabber, and Anne Mosley Lesch. *The Politics of Palestinian Nationalism.* Berkeley, CA: University of California Press, 1973.

Qubain, Fahem Issa. *Crisis in Lebanon.* Washington, DC: Middle East Institute, 1961.

Quester, George H. "Missiles in Cuba, 1970." *Foreign Affairs* 49 (April 1971): 493–506.

Qureshi, S. M. M. "Pakhtunistan: The Frontier Dispute between Afghanistan and Pakistan." *Pacific Affairs* 39, nos. 1–2 (1966): 99–114.

Rabin, Yitzhak. *The Rabin Memoirs.* Boston, MA: Little, Brown, 1979.

Rabinovich, Itamar. *The Road Not Taken: Early Arab-Israeli Negotiations.* New York: Oxford University Press, 1991.

———. *The War for Lebanon, 1970–1985.* Ithaca, NY: Cornell University Press, 1985.

Radford, Arthur W., and Stephen Jurika Jr. *From Pearl Harbor to Vietnam: The Memoirs of Admiral Arthur W. Radford.* Stanford, CA: Hoover Institution Press, 1980.

Rafael, Gideon. "May 1967—A Personal Report" (in Hebrew). *Ma'ariv* (Tel Aviv) 18 (21 April 1972).

Rahman, Sheikh Mujibur. *Bangladesh, My Bangladesh: Selected Speeches and Statements, October 28, 1970 to March 26, 1971.* New Delhi: Orient Longman, 1972.

Rainer, Janos M. "The Yeltsin Dossier: Soviet Documents on Hungary, 1956." CWIHP. *Bulletin* 5 (spring 1995): 22–27, 29–36.

Ramazani, Rouhollah K. *Revolutionary Iran: Challenge and Response in the Middle East.* Baltimore, MD: Johns Hopkins University Press, 1986.

———. *Iran's Foreign Policy, 1941–1973: A Study of Foreign Policy in Modernizing Nations.* Charlottesville, VA: University Press of Virginia, 1975.

———. *The Persian Gulf: Iran's Role.* Charlottesville, VA: University Press of Virginia, 1972.

———. *The Foreign Policy of Iran 1500–1941: A Developing Nation in World Affairs.* Charlottesville, VA: University Press of Virginia, 1964.

Ramchandani, R. R. "Conflicts in the Horn of Africa and Western Sahara." *IDSA Journal* 9 (April–June 1977): 449–73.

Randle, Robert R. *Geneva 1954: The Settlement of the Indo-China War.* Princeton, NJ: Princeton University Press, 1969.

Randolph, R. Sean. *The United States and Thailand: Alliance Dynamics, 1950–1985.* Berkeley, CA: University of California Press, 1986.

Rao, R. P. *Portuguese Rule in Goa, 1510–1961.* London: Asia Publishing House, 1963.

Rao, V. P. "Ethnic Conflict in Sri Lanka: India's Role and Perceptions." *Asian Survey* 28 (April 1988): 419–36.

von Rauch, George. *The Baltic States.* London: C. Hurst, 1970.

Razvi, Mujtaba. *The Frontiers of Pakistan.* Karachi, Pakistan: National Publishing House, 1971.

Reagan, Ronald. *An American Life.* New York: Simon & Schuster, 1990.

Reed, D. *One Hundred Eleven Days in Stanleyville.* New York: Harper & Row, 1965.

Rees, David. *Korea: The Limited War.* London: Macmillan, 1964.

Reinhardt, Jon M. *Foreign Policy and National Integration: The Case of Indonesia.* New Haven, CT: Yale University Press, 1971.

Rezun, Miran. *The Soviet Union and Iran: Soviet Policy in Iran from the Beginnings of the Pahlavi Dynasty until the Soviet Invasion in 1941.* Institut Universitaire des Hautes Etudes Internationales. Geneve: Sijthoff & Noordhoff International Publishers, 1981.

Rhee, T. C. "Sino-Soviet Military Conflict and the Global Balance of Power." *World Today* 26 (January 1970): 29–37.

Rhodes, Richard. *The Making of the Atomic Bomb.* New York: Simon & Schuster, 1986.

Riad, Mahmud. *The Struggle for Peace in the Middle East.* London: Quartet Books, 1981.

Richardson, James L. *Crisis Diplomacy: The Great Powers since the Mid-Nineteenth Century.* Cambridge: Cambridge University Press, 1994.

Richter, James G. *Khrushchev's Double Bind: International Pressures and Domestic Co-alition Politics.* Baltimore, MD: Johns Hopkins University Press, 1994.

Ridgway, Matthew B. *The War in Korea.* London: Cresset Press, 1967.

von Riekhoff, Harald. *German-Polish Relations, 1928–1933.* Baltimore, MD: Johns Hopkins University Press, 1971.

Riga, Lilliana. "The Yugoslav Crisis and the Unified Model." M.A. paper, McGill University, Montreal, 1992.

Ristic, Dragista N. *The Yugoslavian Revolution of 1940.* University Park, PA: Pennsylvania State University Press, 1961.

Riviere, Claude. *Guinea: The Mobilization of a People.* Ithaca, NY: Cornell University Press, 1977.

Rizvi, Hasan Askari. *Internal Strife and External Intervention: India's Role in the Civil War in East Pakistan (Bangladesh).* Lahore, Pakistan: Progressive Publishers, 1981.

Robbins, Keith. *Munich 1938.* London: Cassell, 1968.

Roberts, Bryan. "The Social Structure of Guatemala: The Internal Dynamics of U.S. Influence." In *Patterns of Foreign Influence in the Caribbean,* edited by Emanuel de Kadt. London: Oxford University Press, 1972.

Roberts, Chalmers M. "The Day We Didn't Go to War." *The Reporter* (New York) (11 September 1954): 14.

Robertson, Esmonde M. *Mussolini as Empire-Builder: Europe and Africa, 1932–36.* New York: Macmillan, 1977.

Robertson, Terence. *Crisis: The Inside Story of the Suez Conspiracy.* London: Hutchinson, 1964.

Robinson, Richard D. *The First Turkish Republic: A Case Study in National Development.* Cambridge, MA: Harvard University Press, 1963.

Robinson, Thomas W. "The Sino-Soviet Border Conflict." In *Diplomacy of Power: Soviet Armed Forces as a Political Instrument,* edited by Stephen S. Kaplan, 265–313. Washington, DC: Brookings Institution, 1981.

———. "The Sino-Soviet Dispute: Background, Development and the March 1969 Clashes." *American Political Science Review* 66 (December 1972): 1175–1202.

Robol, T. R. "Notes: Jurisdiction—Limits of Consent—The Aegean Sea Continental Shelf Case." *Harvard International Law Journal* 18 (summer 1977): 649–75.

Rogers, James. "The Process of Inflation in France 1914–1927." In *Social and Economic Studies of Post-war France,* edited by Carlton J. H. Hayes. New York: Columbia University Press, 1934.

Roi, August. *Nazi-Soviet Conspiracy and the Baltic States.* London: Boreas Publishing, 1948.

Roos, Hans. *A History of Modern Poland.* London: Eyre & Spottiswoode, 1966.

Rosenthal, Mario. *Guatemala.* New York: Twayne Publishers, 1962.

Rosner, Gabriella. *The United Nations Emergency Force.* New York: Columbia University Press, 1963.

Ross, Edward W. "Chinese Conflict Management." *Military Review* (January 1980): 13–25.

Ross, Robert S. *The Indochina Tangle: China's Vietnam Policy, 1975–1979.* New York: Columbia University Press, 1988.

Rossow, Robert J. "The Battle of Azerbaijan, 1946." *Middle East Journal* 10 (winter 1956): 17–32.

Rostow, Walt W. *The Diffusion of Power: An Essay in Recent History.* New York: Macmillan, 1972.

Rotberg, Robert I., with Christopher K. Clague. *Haiti: The Politics of Squalor.* Boston, MA: Houghton Mifflin, 1971.

Roucek, Joseph. *Contemporary Roumania and Her Problems.* New York: Arno Press & New York Times, 1971.

Rowland, John. *A History of Sino-Indian Relations.* Princeton, NJ: Van Nostrand, 1967.

Royal Institute of International Affairs (RIIA). *Great Britain and Egypt, 1914–1951.* London: Oxford University Press, 1952.

———. *Chronology of the Second World War.* London: RIIA, 1947.

Rubinoff, Arthur G. *India's Use of Force in Goa.* Bombay: Popular Prakashan, 1971.

Rubinstein, Alvin Z. *Red Star on the Nile.* Princeton, NJ: Princeton University Press, 1977.

Rudolph, James D., ed. *Nicaragua: A Country Study.* 2d ed. Washington, DC: Foreign Area Studies, USGPO, 1982.

Ruf, Werner Klaus. "The Bizerte Crisis: A Bourguibist Attempt to Resolve Tunisia's Border Problem." *Middle East Journal* 25 (spring 1971): 201–11.

Rush, Myron, ed. *The International Situation and Soviet Foreign Policy. Key Reports by Soviet Leaders from the Revolution to the Present.* Columbus, OH: Charles E. Merrill, 1970.

Rushkoff, Bennet C. "Eisenhower, Dulles, and the Quemoy-Matsu Crisis, 1954–55." *Political Science Quarterly* 96 (August 1981): 465–80.

Rusk, Dean. *As I Saw It.* Edited by Daniel Papp. New York: Bantam, 1990.

Rutland, B. "Democracy and Nationalism in Armenia." *Europe-Asia Studies* 46, no. 5 (1994): 839–61.

Sabaliunas, Leonas. *Lithuania in Crisis: Nationalism to Communism 1939–1940.* Bloomington, IN: Indiana University Press, 1972.

el-Sadat, Anwar. *In Search of Identity.* London: Collins, 1978.

———. *Revolt on the Nile.* Translated by Thomas Graham. London: Wingate, 1957.

Safran, Nadav. *Saudi Arabia: The Ceaseless Quest for Security.* Ithaca, NY: Cornell University Press, 1988.

———. *From War to War: The Arab-Israeli Confrontation, 1948–1967.* New York: Pegasus, 1969.

Sagan, Scott D. "Nuclear Alerts and Crisis Management." *International Security* 9 (1985): 99–139.

———. "Lessons of the Yom Kippur Alert." *Foreign Policy* 36 (fall 1979): 160–77.

Salazar, Oliveira. "Goa and the Indian Union: The Portuguese View." *Foreign Affairs* 34 (April 1956): 418–31.

Saliba, Samir N. *The Jordan River Dispute.* The Hague: Martinus Nijhoff, 1968.

Salih, Khalil Ibrahim. *Cyprus: The Impact of Diverse Nationalism on a State.* University, AL: University of Alabama Press, 1978.

Sandler, M. D. "Critique of the 'Seizure and Recovery of the Mayaguez' " and reply by the author (J. J. Paust). *Yale Law Journal* 86 (November 1976): 203–13.

Sansom, Sir George. "Japan's Fatal Blunder." *International Affairs* (London) 24 (October 1948): 543–54.

Sauvy, Alfred et al. *Histoire Economique de la France entre les Deux Guerres.* Paris: Librairie Fayard, 1972.

Schaefer, Ludwig F., ed. *The Ethiopian Crisis: Touchstone of Appeasement.* Boston, MA: D. C. Heath, 1961.

Schandler, Herbert Y. *The Unmaking of a President: Lyndon Johnson and Vietnam.* Princeton, NJ: Princeton University Press, 1977.

Schatzberg, Michael C. "Military Intervention and the Myth of Collective Security: The Case of Zaire." *Journal of Modern African Studies* 27 (June 1989): 315–40.

Schick, Jack M. *The Berlin Crisis, 1958–1962.* Philadelphia, PA: University of Pennsylvania Press, 1971.

Schiff, Zeev. "The Green Light." *Foreign Policy* 50 (1983): 73–85.

Schiff, Zeev, and Eitan Haber, eds. *Israel, Army and Defence, A Dictionary.* Tel Aviv: Zmora, Bitah, Nodim, 1976.

———. "The Full Story of the Encirclement That Ended the Yom Kippur War" (in Hebrew). Tel Aviv: *Ha'aretz,* 14 September 1975.

Schiff, Zeev, and Ehud Yaari. *Israel's Lebanon War.* New York: Simon & Schuster, 1984.

Schlesinger, Arthur M. Jr. *Robert Kennedy and His Times.* Boston, MA: Houghton Mifflin, 1978.

———. *The Dynamics of World Power: A Documentary History of US Foreign Policy, 1945–73.* New York: Chelsea House, 1973.

———. *A Thousand Days: John F. Kennedy in the White House.* Boston, MA: Houghton Mifflin, 1965.

Schmidt, Dana Adam. *Yemen: The Unknown War.* London: Bodley Head, 1968.

Schneider, Ronald M. *Communism in Guatemala, 1944–1954.* New York: Praeger, 1959.

Schoenbaum, Thomas. *Waging Peace and War: Dean Rusk in the Truman, Kennedy and Johnson Years.* New York: Simon & Schuster, 1988.

Schoenfeld, H. F. Arthur. "Soviet Imperialism in Hungary." *Foreign Affairs* 26 (April 1948): 554–66.

Schofield, Richard. *Kuwait and Iraq: Historical Claims and Territorial Disputes.* London: RIIA, 1991.

Schonfield, Hugh Joseph. *The Suez Canal in Peace and War, 1869–1969.* Coral Gables, FL: University of Miami Press, 1969.

———. *The Suez Canal in World Affairs.* London: Constellation, 1952.

Schroeder, Paul W. *The Axis Alliance and Japanese-American Relations.* Ithaca, NY: Cornell University Press, 1958.

Schroter, Heinz. *Stalingrad.* London: Michael Joseph, 1958.

Schueftan, Dan. "Nasser's 1967 Policy Reconsidered." *Jerusalem Quarterly* 3 (1977): 124–44.

Schuman, Frederick L. *Night over Europe: The Diplomacy of Nemesis, 1939–1940.* London: Robert Hale, 1941.

———. *Europe on the Eve: The Crises of Diplomacy, 1933–1939.* New York: Knopf, 1939.

Schurmann, Franz, and Orville Schell, eds. *The China Reader.* 4 vols. New York: Random House, 1967–74.

Schurz, William L. "The Chaco Dispute between Bolivia and Paraguay." *Foreign Affairs* 7 (July 1929): 650–55.

Schwab, Peter. "Cold War on the Horn of Africa." *African Affairs* 77 (January 1978): 6–22.

Schwarzkopf, H. Norman. *It Doesn't Take a Hero.* New York: Linda Grey/Bantam Books, 1992.

Sciolino, Elaine. *The Outlaw State: Saddam Hussein's Quest for Power and the Gulf Crisis.* New York: Wiley, 1991.

Scott, Franklin. *Sweden: The Nation's History.* Minneapolis, MI: University of Minnesota Press, 1977.

Scranton, Margaret E. "Panama." In *Intervention into the 1990s: U.S. Foreign Policy in the Third World,* 2d ed. edited by Peter J. Schraeder, 343–60. Boulder, CO: Lynne Rienner, 1992.

———. *The Noriega Years: U.S.-Panamanian Relations, 1981–1990.* Boulder, CO: Lynne Rienner, 1991.

Seale, Patrick. *The Struggle for Syria: A Study of Post War Arab Politics, 1945–1958.* London: Oxford University Press, 1965.

Seaton, Albert. *The Russo-German War, 1941–45.* New York: Praeger, 1970.

Segal, David. "The Iran-Iraq War: A Military Analysis." *Foreign Affairs* 66 (summer 1988): 946–63.

Segal, Gerald. *Defending China.* New York: Oxford University Press, 1985.

Selassie, Bereket H. "The American Dilemma on the Horn." *Journal of Modern African Studies* 22, no. 3 (1984): 249–72.

Sen Gupta, Jyoti. *Bangladesh in Blood and Tears.* Calcutta, India: Naya Prakash, 1981.

———. *History of the Freedom Movement in Bangla Desh, 1943–1973.* Calcutta, India: Naya Prakash, 1974.

Seton-Watson, Hugh. *The East-European Revolution.* London: Methuen, 1956.

Shapira, Yoram. "The 1954 Guatemala Crisis." *Jerusalem Journal of International Relations* 2–3 (winter-spring 1978): 81–116.

Shapiro, Leonard. "Communists in Collision." *Studies in Comparative Communism* 2 (July–October 1969): 121–30.

Shapley, Deborah. *Promise and Power: The Life and Times of Robert McNamara.* Boston, MA: Little, Brown, 1993.

Shaw, Stanford J., and E. K. Shaw. *History of the Ottoman Empire and Modern Turkey, 1808–1975.* Vol. 2. Cambridge: Cambridge University Press, 1977.

Shawcross, William. *Sideshow: Kissinger, Nixon and the Destruction of Cambodia.* New York: Simon & Schuster, 1979.

———. *Dubček.* New York: Simon & Schuster, 1970.

Shazli, Saad-al-Din. *The Crossing of Suez: The October War.* London: The Third World Centre for Research and Publishing, 1980.

Sheik-Abdi, Abdi. "Somali Nationalism: Its Origins and Future." *Journal of Modern African Studies* 15 (December 1977): 657–66.

Sherwin, Martin J. *A World Destroyed: The Atomic Bomb and the Grand Alliance.* New York: Knopf, 1975.

Shigemitsu, M. *Japan and Her Destiny: My Struggle for Peace.* New York: E. D. Dutton, 1958.

Shimoni, Yaacov. *Political Dictionary of the Arab World.* London: Macmillan, 1987.

Shirer, William L. *The Nightmare Years, 1930–1940.* New York: Bantam Books, 1985.

———. *Collapse of the Third Republic: An Inquiry into the Fall of France in 1940.* New York: Simon & Schuster, 1969.

———. *The Rise and Fall of the Third Reich.* London: Pan Books, 1964.

Shlaim, Avi. *Collusion across the Jordan.* London: Oxford University Press, 1988.

———. *The United States and the Berlin Blockade, 1948–1949: A Study in Crisis Decision-Making.* Berkeley, CA: University of California Press, 1983.

Shuckburgh, Evelyn. *Descent to Suez: Diaries 1951–56.* London: Weidenfeld & Nicolson, 1986.

Shulman, Marshall. *Stalin's Foreign Policy Reappraised.* Cambridge, MA: Belknap Press, 1963.

Shultz, George P. *Turmoil and Triumph: My Years as Secretary of State.* New York: Scribner's, 1993.

Shwadran, Benjamin. *The Middle East, Oil and the Great Powers.* New York: John Wiley, 1973.

———. "The Kuwait Incident." *Middle Eastern Affairs* 13 (January 1962): 2–13, and 13 (February 1962): 43–53.

———. *Jordan: A State of Tension.* New York: Council for Middle East Affairs, 1959.

Sick, Gary. *October Surprise: America's Hostages in Iran and the Election of Ronald Reagan.* New York: Random House, 1991.

————. *All Fall Down: America's Tragic Encounter with Iran.* New York: Viking Penguin, 1985.

Sifty, Micah L., and Christopher Cerf, eds. *The Gulf War Reader: History, Documents, Opinions.* New York: Times Books, 1991.

Sihanouk, Prince Norodom. "The Future of Cambodia." *Foreign Affairs* 49 (October 1970): 1–10.

Sik, Endre. *The History of Black Africa.* Budapest: Akademia Kiado, 1970.

Silber, Laura, and Allan Little. *Yugoslavia: Death of a Nation.* New York: T.V. Books, 1995.

Silbert, Kalman H. "A Study in Government: Guatemala." New Orleans, LA: Central American Research Institute of Tulane University, Publication 21, 1954.

Silcock, T. H. *Thailand: Social and Economic Studies in Development.* Canberra, Australia: ANU Press, 1967.

de Silva, C. R. "The Sinhalese-Tamil Rift in Sri Lanka." In *South Asia: Problems of National Integration,* edited by A. J. Wilson and Denis Dalton, 155–74. London: C. Hurst, 1982.

de Silva, K. M. *Regional Powers and Small State Security: India and Sri Lanka, 1977–1990.* Baltimore, MD: Johns Hopkins University Press, for Woodrow Wilson Center Press, 1995.

Simmonds, John D. *China's World: The Foreign Policy of a Developing State.* New York: Columbia University Press, 1970.

Simmons, Robert R. "The *Pueblo,* EC-121, and *Mayaguez* Incidents." Chap. 14 in *The Use of the Armed Forces as a Political Instrument,* edited by Barry M. Blechman and Stephen S. Kaplan. Washington, DC: Brookings Institution, 1976 (Mimeo).

————. *The Strained Alliance: Peking, P'yongyang, Moscow and the Politics of the Korean Civil War.* New York: Free Press, 1975.

Simon, Sheldon W. *War and Politics in Cambodia.* Durham, NC: Duke University Press, 1974.

————. "China, the Soviet Union and the Subcontinental Balance." *Asian Survey* 13 (July 1973): 647–58.

Singer, Marshall R. "Sri Lanka's Tamil-Sinhalese Ethnic Conflict: Alternative Solutions." *Asian Survey* 32 (1992): 712–22.

————. "New Realities in Sri Lankan Politics." *Asian Survey* 30 (1990): 409–25.

Sisson, Richard, and Leo E. Rose. *War and Secession: Pakistan, India, and the Creation of Bangladesh.* Berkeley, CA: University of California Press, 1990.

Skilling, H. Gordon. *Czechoslovakia's Interrupted Revolution.* Princeton, NJ: Princeton University Press, 1976.

Sklar, Richard L. "Zambia's Response to the Rhodesian Unilateral Declaration of Independence." In *Politics in Zambia,* edited by William Tordoff. Manchester, U.K.: Manchester University Press, 1974.

Slater, Jerome N. "The Dominican Republic, 1961–66." In *Force without War: U.S. Armed Forces as a Political Instrument,* edited by Barry M. Blechman and Stephen S. Kaplan, 289–342. Washington, DC: Brookings Institution, 1978.

————. *Intervention and Negotiation: The United States and the Dominican Revolution.* New York: Harper & Row, 1970.

————. "The Limits of Legitimization in International Organizations: The Organization of American States and the Dominican Crisis." *International Organization* 23 (winter 1969): 48–72.

———. *The OAS and United States Foreign Policy.* Columbus, OH: Ohio State University Press, 1967.

Slusser, Robert M. "The Berlin Crises of 1958–59 and 1961." In *Force without War: U.S. Armed Forces as a Political Instrument,* edited by Barry M. Blechman and Stephen S. Kaplan, 343–439. Washington, DC: Brookings Institution, 1978.

———. *The Berlin Crisis of 1961: Soviet-American Relations and the Struggle for Power in the Kremlin, June–November 1961.* Baltimore, MD: Johns Hopkins University Press, 1973.

Smelser, Ronald. *The Sudeten Problem 1933–1938: Volkstumpolitik and the Formulation of Nazi Foreign Policy.* Middletown, CT: Wesleyan University Press, 1975.

Smith, C. Jay Jr. *Finland and the Russian Revolution 1917–1922.* Athens, GA: University of Georgia Press, 1958.

Smith, Denis Mack. *Mussolini.* New York: Random House, 1982.

———. *Mussolini's Roman Empire.* New York: Viking Press, 1976.

Smith, George Ivan. *Ghosts of Kampala.* New York: St. Martin's Press, 1980.

Smith, Jean Edward, ed. *The Papers of General Lucius D. Clay: Germany 1945–1949.* Bloomington, IN: Indiana University Press, 1974.

———. *The Defense of Berlin.* Baltimore, MD: Johns Hopkins University Press, 1963.

Smith, Michael Llewellyn. *Ionian Vision: Greece in Asia Minor, 1919–1922.* New York: St. Martin's Press, 1973.

Smolansky, Oles M. *The Soviet Union and the Arab East under Khrushchev.* Lewisburg, PA: Bucknell University Press, 1974.

Snell, John L. *Illusion and Necessity: The Diplomacy of Global War 1939–1945.* Boston, MA: Houghton Mifflin, 1963.

Snyder, Frank G. *One Party Government in Mali: Transition toward Control.* New Haven, CT: Yale University Press, 1965.

Snyder, Scott. "A Framework for Achieving Reconciliation on the Korean Peninsula: Beyond the Geneva Agreement." *Asian Survey* 35, no. 8 (1995): 699–710.

Sofer, Sasson. *Begin: An Anatomy of Leadership.* Oxford: Basil Blackwell, 1988.

Sonvel, Salahi R. *Turkish Diplomacy, 1918–1923: Mustafa Kemal and the Turkish National Movement.* Beverly Hills, CA: Sage, 1975.

Sorensen, Theodore C. *Kennedy.* New York: Harper & Row, 1965.

Sowden, John K. *The German Question, 1945–1973: Continuity in Change.* New York: St. Martin's Press, 1975.

Spaak, Paul Henri. *The Continuing Battle: Memoirs of a European, 1936–1966.* Boston, MA: Little, Brown, 1971.

Spain, James W. *The Pathan Borderland.* The Hague: Mouton, 1963.

Spanier, John W. *The Truman-MacArthur Controversy and the Korean War.* Cambridge, MA: Belknap Press, 1959.

Speer, Albert. *Inside the Third Reich: Memoirs.* New York: Macmillan, 1970.

Spekke, Arnold. *History of Latvia: An Outline.* Stockholm: M. Goppers, 1951.

Spencer, John H. "Ethiopia, the Horn of Africa and U.S. Policy." Cambridge, MA: Institute for Foreign Policy Analysis, 1977.

Spiegel, Steven L. *The Other Arab-Israeli Conflict: Making America's Middle East Policy from Truman to Reagan.* Chicago, IL: University of Chicago Press, 1985.

Spiegel, Steven L., and Kenneth N. Waltz, eds. *Conflict in World Politics.* Cambridge, MA: Winthrop, 1971.

Spinner, Thomas J. Jr. *A Political and Social History of Guyana, 1945–1983*. Boulder, CO: Westview Press, 1984.

Spurr, Russell. *Enter the Dragon: China's Undeclared War against the U.S. in Korea, 1950–1951*. New York: New Market, 1988.

St. John, Robert. *The Boss: The Story of Gamal Abdel Nasser*. New York: McGraw-Hill, 1960.

Stavrakis, Peter J. *Moscow and Greek Communism, 1944–1949*. Ithaca, NY: Cornell University Press, 1989.

Stebbins, Richard P., ed. *The United States in World Affairs, 1965*. New York: Council on Foreign Relations, by Harper & Row, 1966.

Stedman, Stephen J. *Peacemaking in Civil War: International Mediation in Zimbabwe, 1974–1980*. Boulder, CO: Lynne Rienner, 1991.

Stein, Janice G. "Deterrence and Compellance in the Gulf, 1990–91." *International Security* 17 (fall 1992): 147–79.

———. "The Arab-Israeli War of 1967: Inadvertent War through Miscalculated Escalation." In *Avoiding War: Problems of Crisis Management*, edited by Alexander L. George, 126–59. Boulder, CO: Westview Press, 1991.

———. "Extended Deterrence in the Middle East: American Strategy Reconsidered." *World Politics* 39 (April 1987): 326–52.

Stein, Janice G., and Raymond Tanter. *Rational Decision-Making: Israel's Security Choices, 1967*. Columbus, OH: Ohio State University Press, 1980.

Steinberg, Blema S. *Shame and Humiliation: Presidential Decision-Making on Vietnam*. Montreal and Kingston: McGill-Queen's University Press, 1996.

Stephens, Robert. *Nasser*. New York: Simon & Schuster, 1971.

Stern, Eric. "Information Management and the Whiskey on the Rocks Crisis." *Cooperation and Conflict* 27 (1992): 45–96.

Stern, Eric, and Bengt Sundelius. "The U 137 Incident: A Narrative Description." *Krishantering U 137-KRISEN*. Stockholm, 1994. Mimeographed.

———. "Managing Asymmetrical Crisis: Sweden, the USSR, and the U-137." *International Studies Quarterly* 36 (June 1992): 213–39.

Stevens, Christopher. "The Soviet Union in Angola." *African Affairs* 75 (April 1976): 137–51.

Stevens, Georgiana. *Jordan River Partition*. Hoover Institution Studies, No. 6. Stanford, CA: 1965.

Stevenson, Charles A. *The End of Nowhere: American Policy toward Laos since 1954*. Boston, MA: Beacon Press, 1972.

Stevenson, William. *90 Minutes at Entebbe*. New York: Bantam Books, 1976.

Stewart, Rhea. *Fire in Afghanistan, 1914–1929: Faith, Hope and the British Empire*. Garden City, NY: Doubleday, 1973.

Stickney, Edith. *Southern Albania or Northern Epirus in European International Affairs, 1912–1923*. Stanford, CA.: Stanford University Press, 1926.

Stimson, Henry L. *American Policy in Nicaragua*. New York: Scribners, 1927.

Stockwell, John. *In Search of Enemies: A CIA Story*. New York: Norton, 1978.

Stolper, Thomas E. *China, Taiwan, and the Offshore Islands*. Armonk, NY: M. E. Sharpe, 1985.

Stone, Isidor F. *The Hidden History of the Korean War*. New York: Monthly Review Press, 1952.

Stookey, Robert W. *South Yemen: A Marxist Republic in Arabia.* Boulder, CO: Westview Press, 1982.

Stuart, Graham H. *Latin America and the United States.* Englewood Cliffs, NJ: Prentice-Hall, 1975.

Stueck, William W. *The Korean War: An International History.* Princeton, NJ: Princeton University Press, 1995.

Sulzberger, Cyrus L. *The Coldest War: Russia's Game in China.* New York: Harcourt, Brace & Jovanovich, 1974.

Sundhaussen, Ulf. *The Road to Power: Indonesian Military Politics, 1945–1965.* Kuala Lumpur, Malaysia: Oxford University Press, 1982.

Suny, R. G., "Nationalism and Democracy: The Case of Karabagh." In *Looking toward Ararat,* edited by R. G. Suny. Bloomington, IN: Indiana University Press, 1993.

Svabe, Arveds. *The Story of Latvia and Her Neighbors: A Historical Survey.* Edinburgh: Scottish League for European Freedom, 1947.

Swire, Joseph. *Albania—The Rise of a Kingdom.* New York: Arno Press & New York Times, [1929] 1971.

Sykes, Brigadier-General Percy. *Persia.* Oxford: Clarendon Press, 1922.

Sykes, Christopher. *Crossroads to Israel, 1917–1948.* Bloomington, IN: Indiana University Press, 1973.

Szilassy, Sandor. *Revolutionary Hungary.* Astor Park, FL.: Danubian Press, 1971.

Szulc, Tad. *Then and Now: How the World Has Changed since WWII.* New York: William Morrow, 1990.

———. *Czechoslovakia since World War II.* New York: Viking Press, 1971a.

———, ed. *The United States and the Caribbean.* Englewood Cliffs, NJ: Prentice-Hall, 1971b.

———. *Dominican Diary.* New York: Delacorte Press, 1965.

———. *The Winds of Revolution: Latin America Today and Tomorrow.* New York: Praeger, 1963.

Tahir-Kheli, Sharin, and Shaheen Ayubi. *The Iran-Iraq War: New Weapons, Old Conflicts.* New York: Praeger, 1983.

Talon, U. *Diarios de la guerra del Congo.* Madrid: Sedmay, 1976.

Tamkov, Metin. *The Warrior Diplomats: Guardians of the National Security and Modernization of Turkey.* Salt Lake City, UT: University of Utah Press, 1976.

Tanner, Vaino A. *The Winter War: Finland against Russia, 1939–1940.* Stanford, CA: Stanford University Press, 1957.

Tanter, Raymond. *Who's at the Helm? Lessons of Lebanon.* Boulder, CO: Westview Press, 1990.

———. *Modelling and Managing International Conflicts: The Berlin Crises.* Beverly Hills, CA: Sage, 1974.

Tarulis, Albert N. *Soviet Policy toward the Baltic States, 1918–1940.* Notre Dame, IN: University of Notre Dame Press, 1959.

Tatu, Michel. "Intervention in Eastern Europe." In *Diplomacy of Power: Soviet Armed Forces as a Political Instrument,* edited by Stephen S. Kaplan, 205–64. Washington, DC: Brookings Institution, 1981.

Taubman, William. *Stalin's American Policy: From Entente to Detente to Cold War.* New York: Norton & Norton, 1982.

Taylor, A. J. P. *Origins of the Second World War.* New York: Atheneum, 1968.

———. *English History, 1914–1945.* Oxford: Clarendon Press, 1966.

Taylor, A. M. *Indonesian Independence and the United Nations.* London: Stevens, 1960.

Taylor, Edmund. *The Fall of the Dynasties: The Collapse of the Old Order, 1905–1922.* Edited by John Gunther. Garden City, NY: Doubleday, 1963.

Taylor, Philip B. Jr. "The Guatemalan Affair: A Critique of United States Foreign Policy." *American Political Science Review* 50 (September 1956): 787–806.

Taylor, Telford. *Munich: The Price of Peace.* Garden City, NY: Doubleday, 1979.

Temperley, Harold, ed. *A History of the Peace Conference of Paris.* Vol. 6. RIIA. London: Oxford University Press, 1969.

Tessler, Mark. *A History of the Israeli-Palestinian Conflict.* Bloomington, IN: Indiana University Press, 1994.

Thatcher, Margaret. *The Downing Street Years.* New York: HarperCollins, 1993.

Thee, Marek. *Notes of a Witness: Laos and the Second Indochina War.* New York: Random House, 1973.

Thien, Ton That. "New Confrontations in Southeast Asia." *Asian Affairs* 6 (November–December 1978): 88–96.

Thomas, Alfred B. *Latin America: A History.* New York: Macmillan, 1956.

Thomas, Hugh S. *The Suez Affair.* Rev. ed. London: Penguin, 1970.

———. *The Spanish Civil War.* New York: Harper & Row, 1961.

Thomas, Stephen. "Beyond the Wall." *Survey: Journal of Soviet and East European Studies* 42 (June 1962): 96–106.

Thompson, Virginia M., and Richard Adloff. *Conflict in Chad.* Berkeley, CA: University of California Institute of International Studies, 1981.

———. *The Western Sahara: Background to Conflict.* Totowa, NJ: Barnes and Noble, 1980.

Thompson, W. Scott. *Ghana's Foreign Policy, 1957–1966.* Princeton, NJ: Princeton University Press, 1969.

Thorndike, Tony. *Grenada: Politics, Economics, and Society.* Boulder, CO: Lynne Rienner, 1985.

———. "The Grenada Crisis." *World Today* 39 (December 1983): 468–76.

Thorndyke, A. E. "Belize among Her Neighbors: An Analysis of the Guatemala-Belize Dispute." *Caribbean Review* 7 (April–June 1978): 13–19.

Thorne, Christopher. *Allies of a Kind: The United States, Britain, and the War against Japan, 1941–1945.* London: Oxford University Press, 1978.

———. *The Limits of Foreign Policy: The West, the League and the Far Eastern Crisis of 1931–1933.* London: H. Hamilton, 1972.

———. *The Approach of War: 1938–1939.* London: Macmillan, 1967.

Thornton, Richard C. *China: The Struggle for Power: 1917–1972.* Bloomington, IN: Indiana University Press, 1973.

Thornton, Thomas P. "The Indo-Pakistani Conflict: Soviet Mediation at Tashkent, 1966." In *International Mediation in Theory and Practice,* edited by Saadia Touval and I. William Zartman, 141–71. Boulder, CO: Westview Press, 1985.

Tibawi, Abdul L. *A Modern History of Syria Including Lebanon and Palestine.* London: Macmillan, 1969.

Toland, John. *The Rising Sun: The Decline and Fall of the Japanese Empire, 1936–1945.* New York: Random House, 1970.

Tomasek, Robert D. "The Haitian-Dominican Republic Controversy of 1963 and the Organization of American States." *Orbis* 12 (1968–69): 294–313.

Tondel, Lyman M. Jr., ed. *The Legal Aspects of the United Nations Action in the Congo.* Dobbs Ferry, NY: Oceana, 1963.

Toriello Garrido, Guillermo. *La Batalla de Guatemala.* Santiago de Chile: Editorial Universitaria, 1955.

Torres, H. *Pierre Laval.* London: Gollancz, 1941.

Torrey, Gordon H. *Syrian Politics and the Military, 1945–1958.* Columbus, OH: Ohio State University Press, 1964.

Touval, Saadia. *The Boundary Politics of Independent Africa.* Cambridge, MA: Harvard University Press, 1972.

———. "Somalia, Ethiopia and Kenya." In *Conflict in World Politics,* edited by Steven L. Spiegel and Kenneth N. Waltz. Cambridge, MA: Winthrop, 1971.

———. *Somalia Nationalism: International Politics and the Drive for Unity in the Horn of Africa.* Cambridge, MA: Harvard University Press, 1963.

Toye, Hugh. *Laos: Buffer State or Battleground.* London: Oxford University Press, 1968.

Toynbee, Arnold J. *Survey of International Affairs, 1929.* RIIA. London: Oxford University Press, 1930.

———. *Survey of International Affairs, 1928.* RIIA. London: Oxford University Press, 1929a.

———. *Survey of International Affairs, 1927.* RIIA. London: Oxford University Press, 1929b.

———. *Survey of International Affairs, 1925: The Islamic World since the Peace Settlement.* RIIA. London: Oxford University Press, 1927a.

———. *Turkey.* New York: Scribners, 1927b.

———. *Survey of International Affairs, 1920–23.* RIIA. London: Oxford University Press, 1927c.

———. *Survey of International Affairs, 1924.* RIIA. London: Oxford University Press, 1926.

Toynbee, Veronica M. "Relations between Germany and Poland, January 1938 to March 1939." In *Survey of International Affairs, 1938,* vol. 3, edited by R. G. D. Laffan et al., 289–342. RIIA. London: Oxford University Press, 1953a.

———. "Relations between Poland and Lithuania, 1937–9." In *Survey of International Affairs 1938,* vol. 3, edited by R. G. D. Laffan et al., 342–90. RIIA. London: Oxford University Press, 1953b.

Trachtenberg, Marc. "The Berlin Crisis." In *History and Strategy,* 169–234. Princeton, NJ: Princeton University Press, 1991.

Tretiak, Daniel. "China's Vietnam War and its Consequences." *China Quarterly* 80 (December 1979): 740–67.

Troen, Selwyn I., and Moshe Shemesh, eds. *The Suez-Sinai Crisis 1956: Retrospective and Reappraisal.* London: Frank Cass, 1990.

Truman, Harry S. *Years of Trial and Hope. Memoirs by Harry Truman,* vol. 2. Garden City, NY: Doubleday, 1956.

———. *Year of Decisions: 1945. Memoirs by Harry Truman,* vol. 1. Garden City, NY: Doubleday, 1955.

Tshombe, Moise. "My Fifteen Months in Government." Plano, TX: University of Plano, 1967.

Tsou, Tang. *America's Failure in China, 1941–50.* Chicago, IL: University of Chicago Press, 1963.

———. *The Embroilment over Quemoy: Mao, Chiang and Dulles.* Salt Lake City, UT: Utah University Press, 1958.

Twaddle, Michael. "The Ousting of Idi Amin." *Round Table* 275 (July 1979): 216–21.

Ulam, Adam B. *Expansion and Coexistence: A History of Soviet Foreign Policy, 1917–73.* 2d ed. New York: Praeger, 1974.

———. *The Rivals—America and Russia since World War II.* New York: Viking Press, 1971.

———. *Titoism and the Cominform.* Cambridge, MA: Harvard University Press, 1952.

Ullman, Harlan K. "Profound or Perfunctory: Observations on the South Atlantic Conflict." In *The Lessons of Recent Wars in the Third World,* edited by Robert E. Harkavy and Stephanie G. Neuman. Vol. 1, *Approaches and Case Studies,* 239–59. Lexington, MA: Lexington Books, 1985.

Ullman, Richard H. *Anglo-Soviet Relations, 1917–1921: The Anglo-Soviet Accord.* Vol. 3. Princeton, NJ: Princeton University Press, 1972.

———. *Britain and the Russian Civil War.* Princeton, NJ: Princeton University Press, 1968.

United Nations. *Report of the Special Committee on the Problem of Hungary.* General Assembly Official Records (GAOR), Eleventh Session, Supp. 18 (A/3592), 1957.

Upton, Anthony F. *Finland in Crisis, 1940–41: A Study in Small-Power Politics.* London: Faber & Faber, 1964.

Valenta, Jiri. "The Soviet-Cuban Alliance in Africa and the Caribbean." *World Today* 37 (February 1981): 45–53.

———. "Soviet Decision-Making on the Intervention in Angola." In *Communism in Africa,* edited by David E. Albright, 93–117. Bloomington, IN: Indiana University Press, 1980.

———. *Soviet Intervention in Czechoslovakia 1968: Anatomy of a Decision.* Baltimore, MD: Johns Hopkins University Press, 1979a.

———. "Bureaucratic Politics Paradigm and the Soviet Invasion of Czechoslovakia." *Political Science Quarterly* 94 (spring 1979b): 55–76.

Valenta, Jiri, and V. Valenta. "Leninism in Grenada." In *Grenada and Soviet/Cuban Policy: Internal Crisis and US/OECS Intervention,* edited by Jiri Valenta and Herbert J. Ellison. Boulder, CO: Westview Press, 1986.

Váli, Ferencz. *Strife and Revolt in Hungary: Nationalism versus Communism.* Cambridge, MA: Harvard University Press, 1961.

Vance, Cyrus. *Hard Choices: Critical Years in America's Foreign Policy.* New York: Simon & Schuster, 1983.

Vandenbosch, Amry. *Dutch Foreign Policy since 1815: A Study in Small Power Politics.* The Hague: Martinus Nijhoff, 1959.

Vanezis, P. N. *Cyprus: The Unfinished Agony.* London: Abelard-Schuman, 1977.

Vanniasingham, Somasundaram. *Sri Lanka, the Conflict Within.* New Delhi: Lancer, 1988.

Varon, Amnon. "The Spratly Islands Embroilment: A Test Case in Post-Cold War Southeast Asia." Bundoora, Australia: La Trobe Politics Working Paper No. 3, July 1994.

Vatikiotis, Panayiotis J. *The Modern History of Egypt.* London: Weidenfeld & Nicolson, 1979.

Vayrynen, Raimo. "Conflicts of Interest in Territorial Waters: Iceland, Ecuador and the Straits of Malacca." *Instant Research on Peace and Violence* 3, no. 3 (1973): 123–48.

Veliz, Claudio. *Latin America and the Caribbean: A Handbook.* New York: Praeger, 1968.

Vella, Walter. *The Impact of the West on Government in Thailand.* Berkeley, CA: University of California Press, 1955.

Vere-Hodge, Edward. "Turkish Foreign Policy, 1918–1948." Université de Genève, Institut Universitaire des Hautes Etudes Internationales, 1950.

Vertzberger, Yaacov Y. I. *Risk Taking and Decisionmaking: Foreign Military Intervention Decisions.* Stanford, CA: Stanford University Press, 1997.

———. *Misperceptions in Foreign Policymaking: The Sino-Indian Conflict, 1959–1962.* Boulder, CO: Westview Press, 1984.

———. "Afghanistan in China's Policy." *Problems of Communism* 31, no. 3 (1982): 1–23.

van der Veur, Paul W. "The United Nations in West Irian: A Critique." *International Organization* 18 (winter 1964): 53–73.

Vichit-Vadakan, Juree. "Thailand in 1984: Year of Administering Rumors." *Asian Survey* 25 (February 1985): 232–40.

Villari, Luigi. *Italian Foreign Policy under Mussolini.* New York: Devin-Adair, 1956.

Vinacke, Harold. *History of the Far East in Modern Times.* 6th ed. New York: Appleton-Century-Crofts, 1959.

Vital, David. *The Inequality of States: A Study of the Small Power in International Relations.* Oxford: Clarendon Press, 1967.

Viviani, Nancy. "Australians and the Timor Issue." *Australian Outlook* 30, no. 2 (1976): 197–226.

Vloyantes, John P. *Silk Glove Hegemony: Finnish-Soviet Relations, 1944–1974: A Case Study of the Theory of the Soft Sphere of Influence.* Kent, OH: Kent State University Press, 1975.

Vocke, Harold. *The Lebanese War.* London: Hurst, 1978.

Volgyes, Iran, ed. *Hungary in Revolution, 1918–19.* Lincoln, NE: University of Nebraska Press, 1971.

Volkan, Vamik D. *Cyprus: War and Adaptation: A Psychoanalytic History of Two Ethnic Groups in Conflict.* Charlottesville, VA: University Press of Virginia, 1979.

Vondracek, Felix. *The Foreign Policy of Czechoslovakia 1918–1935.* New York: Columbia University Press, 1937.

Wainhouse, David W., in association with Bernhard G. Bechhoefer. *International Peace Observation: A History and Forecast.* Baltimore, MD: Johns Hopkins University Press, 1966.

Waldeck, Rosie (Goldschmidt). *Athene Place Bucharest: Hitler's New Order Comes to Rumania.* London: Constable, 1943.

Wallensteen, Peter, and Margareta Sollenberg. "After the Cold War: Emerging Patterns of Armed Conflict, 1989–94." *Journal of Peace Research* 32, no. 3 (1995): 345–60.

Walters, Francis P. *A History of the League of Nations.* London: Oxford University Press, 1952.

Warner, Albert L. "How the Korea Decision Was Made." *Harper's,* 202, 1951, 99–106.

Warner, Geoffrey. *Pierre Laval and the Eclipse of France.* New York: Macmillan, 1969.

Warren, Harris G. *Paraguay: An Informal History.* Norman, OK: University of Oklahoma Press, 1949.

Watson, B. W., and P. G. Tsouras, eds. *Operation JUST CAUSE: The U.S. Intervention in Panama.* Boulder, CO: Westview Press, 1990.

Watt, Alan S. *The Evolution of Australian Foreign Policy, 1938–1965.* Cambridge: Cambridge University Press, 1967.

Watt, Donald C. *How War Came: The Immediate Origins of the Second World War.* New York: Pantheon Books, 1989.

———. *Survey of International Affairs, 1961.* RIIA. London: Oxford University Press, 1965.

———. *Britain and the Suez Canal.* RIIA. London: Oxford University Press, 1957.

Weathersby, Kathryn. "New Russian Documents on the Korean War." CWIHP. *Bulletin* 6–7 (winter 1995–96): 30–40, 42–84.

———. "Korea, 1949–50: To Attack, or Not to Attack? Stalin, Kim Il Sung, and the Prelude to War." CWIHP. *Bulletin* 5 (spring 1995): 1–9.

———. "New Findings on the Korean War." CWIHP. *Bulletin* 3 (fall 1993a): 1, 14–18.

———. "Soviet Aims in Korea and the Origins of the Korean War, 1945–1950: New Evidence from Russian Archives." CWIHP. Working Paper No. 8 (November 1993b).

Weeks, John, and Andrew Zimbalist. "The Failure of Intervention in the Backyard." *Third World Quarterly* 11 (1989): 1–27.

Weigley, R. F. *Eisenhower's Lieutenants: The Campaign of France and Germany, 1944–1945.* London: Sidgwick & Jackson, 1981.

Weil, Thomas et al. *Area Handbook for Panama.* Washington, DC: USGPO, 1972.

Weinberg, Gerhard L. *A World at Arms: A Global History of World War II.* Cambridge: Cambridge University Press, 1994.

———. "Munich after 50 Years." *Foreign Affairs* 67 (1988): 165–78.

———. *The Foreign Policy of Hitler's Germany.* Vol. 1, *A Diplomatic Revolution in Europe, 1933–1936;* vol. 2, *Starting World War II, 1937–1939.* Chicago, IL: University of Chicago Press, 1970, 1980.

———. *Germany and the Soviet Union, 1939–1941.* Leyden, Netherlands: E. J. Brill, 1954.

Weintraub, Stanley. *Long Day's Journey into War: December 7, 1941.* New York: Penguin, 1991.

Weissman, Steve, and Herbert Krosney. *The Islamic Bomb: The Nuclear Threat to Israel and the Middle East.* New York: Times Books, 1981.

Weizmann, Chaim. *Trial and Error.* New York: Harper & Bros., 1949.

Weller, Marc, ed. *Regional Peacekeeping and International Enforcement: The Liberian Case.* New York: Cambridge University Press, 1994.

Welles, Benjamin. *Spain: The Gentle Anarch.* London: Pall Mall Press, 1965.

Wenner, Manfred W. *Modern Yemen: 1918–1966.* Baltimore, MD: Johns Hopkins University Press, 1967.

Werth, Alexander, ed. *The Twilight of France, 1933–1940.* New York: Howard Fertig, 1966.

———. *Russia at War, 1941–1945.* London: Pan Books, 1964.

West, Rebecca. *Black Lamb and Grey Falcon: A Journey through Yugoslavia.* New York: Viking Press, 1941.

Westwood, John. *Endurance and Endeavour: Russian History, 1812–1971.* London: Oxford University Press, 1973.

Wheeler-Bennett, Sir John. *Munich: Prologue to Tragedy.* New York: Viking Press, 1948.

Whetten, Lawrence L. *The Canal War: Four-Power Conflict in the Middle East.* Cambridge, MA: MIT Press, 1974.

Whitaker, Arthur P. *Spain and the Defense of the West: Ally and Liability.* New York: Harper, 1961.

———. "Guatemala, OAS and US." *Foreign Policy Bulletin* 33 (1 September 1954): 4–6.

Whiting, Allen S. "The U.S.-China War in Korea." In *Avoiding War: Problems of Crisis Management,* edited by Alexander L. George, 103–25. Boulder, CO: Westview Press, 1991.

———. *The Chinese Calculus of Deterrence.* Ann Arbor, MI: University of Michigan Press, 1975a.

————. "Quemoy 1958: Mao's Miscalculations." *China Quarterly* 62 (June 1975b): 263–70.

————. *China Crosses the Yalu: The Decision to Enter the Korean War.* Stanford, CA: Stanford University Press, 1960.

Wiarda, Howard J. *Dictatorship and Development: The Methods of Control in Trujillo's Dominican Republic.* Gainesville, FL: Center for Latin American Studies, University of Florida Press, 1970.

————. *The Dominican Republic: Nation in Transition.* New York: Praeger, 1969.

Widstrand, Carl G., ed. "African Boundary Problems." Uppsala: The Scandinavian Institute of African Studies, 1969.

Wiener, Sharon. "Turkish Foreign Policy Decision-Making on the Cyprus Issue: A Comparative Analysis of Three Crises." Ph.D. diss., Duke University. Ann Arbor, MI: University Microfilms, 1980.

Wigney, Pierre. "Belgium and the Congo." *International Affairs* 37 (July 1961): 273–84.

Wild, Berko. "The Organization of African Unity and the Algeria-Moroccan Border Conflict." *International Organization* 20 (winter 1966): 18–36.

Wilgus, A. Curtis, ed. *The Caribbean: Contemporary International Relations.* Gainesville, FL: University of Florida Press, 1963.

Willis, F. Roy. *France, Germany and the New Europe, 1945–1967.* Rev. and enl. ed. London: Oxford University Press, 1968.

Wilson, A. Jeyaratnam. *The Break-Up of Sri Lanka: The Sinhalese-Tamil Conflict.* Honolulu, HI: University of Hawaii Press, 1988.

Wilson, Andrew. "The Aegean Dispute." London: IISS. Adelphi Paper No. 155, winter 1979–80.

Wilson, Harold. *Final Term: The Labour Government, 1974–1976.* London: Weidenfeld & Nicolson, 1979.

————. *The Labour Government: A Personal Record 1964–1970.* London: Weidenfeld & Nicolson, 1971.

Wilson, Larman C. "The Monroe Doctrine, Cold War Anachronism: Cuba and the Dominican Republic." *Journal of Politics* 1 (May 1966): 322–46.

Windchy, Eugene G. *Tonkin Gulf.* Garden City, NY: Doubleday, 1971.

Windsor, Philip. "Yugoslavia, 1951, and Czechoslovakia, 1968." In *Force without War: U.S. Armed Forces as a Political Instrument,* edited by Barry M. Blechman and Stephen S. Kaplan, 440–512. Washington, DC: Brookings Institution, 1978.

————. *City on Leave: A History of Berlin, 1945–1962.* New York: Praeger, 1963.

Windsor, Philip, and Adam Roberts. *Czechoslovakia 1968: Reform and Resistance.* New York: Columbia University Press, 1969.

Wirtz, James J. *The Tet Offensive: Intelligence Failure in War.* Ithaca, NY: Cornell University Press, 1993.

Wise, David, and Thomas B. Ross. *The Invisible Government.* New York: Random House, 1964.

Wiseman, Henry, and Alastair M. Taylor. *From Rhodesia to Zimbabwe: The Politics of Transition.* New York: Pergamon Press, 1981.

Wiskemann, Elizabeth. *The Rome-Berlin Axis: A Study of the Relations between Hitler and Mussolini.* London: Collins, 1966.

Wittner, Laurence S. *American Intervention in Greece, 1943–1949.* New York: Columbia University Press, 1982.

Wohlstetter, Albert, and Roberta Wohlstetter. "Controlling the Risks in Cuba." London: IISS. Adelphi Paper No. 17, April 1965.

Wohlstetter, Roberta. *Pearl Harbor, Warning and Decision.* Stanford, CA: Stanford University Press, 1962.

Wolfe, Thomas W. *Soviet Power and Europe, 1945–1970.* Baltimore, MD: Johns Hopkins University Press, 1970.

Wood, Bryce. *The United States and Latin American Wars, 1932–1942.* New York: Columbia University Press, 1966.

———. *The Making of the Good Neighbor Policy.* New York: Columbia University Press, 1961.

Woodhouse, Christopher M. *The Struggle for Greece, 1940–1945.* London: Hart-Davis, McGibbon, 1976.

———. *A Short History of Modern Greece.* New York: Praeger, 1968.

Woodman, Dorothy. *Himalayan Frontiers.* New York: Praeger, 1969.

Woodward, Bob. *The Commanders.* New York: Simon & Schuster, 1991.

Woodward, Sir Llewellyn. *British Foreign Policy in the Second World War.* 2 vols. London: HMSO, 1962.

Woodward, Susan L. *Balkan Tragedy: Chaos and Dissolution after the Cold War.* Washington, DC: Brookings Institution, 1995.

Wright, Quincy. "The Goa Incident." *American Journal of International Law* 56 (July 1962): 617–32.

Wu, Ai-Ch'en. *China and the Soviet Union: A Study of Sino-Soviet Relations.* London: Methuen, 1950.

Wyden, Peter. *Wall: The Inside Story of Divided Berlin.* New York: Simon & Schuster, 1989.

———. *Bay of Pigs.* New York: Simon & Schuster, 1979.

Xiaobing, Li, Chen Jian, and David L. Wilson. "Mao Zedong's Handling of the Taiwan Straits Crisis of 1958: Chinese Recollections and Documents." CWIHP. *Bulletin* 6–7 (winter 1995–96): 208–26.

Xydis, Stephen G. *Greece and the Great Powers, 1944–1947.* Thessaloniki, Greece: Institute for Balkan Studies, 1963.

Yaacobi, Gad. *Government* (in Hebrew). Tel Aviv: Am Oved, 1980.

Yahuda, Michael B. "China's New Outlook: The End of Isolationism." *World Today* 35 (May 1979): 180–89.

———. *China's Role in World Affairs.* London: Croom Helm, 1978.

Yaniv, Avner. *Dilemmas of Security: Politics, Strategy, and the Israeli Experience in Lebanon.* London: Oxford University Press, 1987.

Ydigoras, Fuentes M. *My War with Communism, as told to Mario Rosenthal.* Englewood Cliffs, NJ: Prentice-Hall, 1963.

Yoo, Tae-Ho. *The Korean War and the United Nations: A Legal and Diplomatic Historical Study.* Louvain: Desbarax, 1965.

Young, John W. *France, the Cold War and the Western Alliance, 1944–49: French Foreign Policy and Post-War Europe.* Leicester, U.K.: Leicester University Press, 1990.

Young, Kenneth W. *Stanley Baldwin.* London: Weidenfeld & Nicolson, 1976.

Young, Marilyn. *The Vietnam Wars 1945–1990.* New York: HarperCollins, 1991.

Young, Oran R. *The Politics of Force: Bargaining during International Crises.* Princeton, NJ: Princeton University Press, 1968.

Yufan, Hao, and Zhai Zhihai. "China's Decision to Enter the Korean War: History Revisited." *China Quarterly* 121 (March 1990): 94–115.

Zabih, Sepehr. *The Communist Movement in Iran*. Berkeley, CA: University of California Press, 1966.

Zagoria, Donald S., and Janet D. Zagoria. "Crises on the Korean Peninsula." In *Diplomacy of Power: Soviet Armed Forces as a Political Instrument,* edited by Stephen S. Kaplan, 357–411. Washington, DC: Brookings Institution, 1981.

Zammit, J. Ann. *The Belize Issue*. London: Latin American Bureau, 1978.

Zartman, I. William. *Ripe for Resolution: Conflict and Intervention in Africa*. Rev. ed. New York: Oxford University Press, 1989.

———. *International Relations in the New Africa*. Englewood Cliffs, NJ: Prentice-Hall, 1966.

———. *Problems of New Power: Morocco*. New York: Atherton, 1964.

———. "A Disputed Frontier Is Settled." *Africa Report* 8 (August 1963): 13–14.

Zayyid, Mahmud Y. *Egypt: Struggle for Independence*. Beirut: Khayats Press, 1965.

Ziadeh, Nicobi A. *Syria and Lebanon*. London: E. Benn, 1957.

Ziemke, Earl F. *Moscow to Stalingrad: Decision in the East*. Washington, DC: USGPO, 1987.

———. *Stalingrad to Berlin: The German Defeat in the East*. Washington, DC: USGPO, 1968.

———. *The German Northern Theater of Operations, 1940–1945*. Washington, DC: USGPO, 1960.

Zimmerman, William. "The Korean and Vietnam Wars." In *Diplomacy of Power: Soviet Armed Forces as a Political Instrument,* edited by Stephen S. Kaplan, 314–56. Washington, DC: Brookings Institution, 1981.

Zimmern, Alfred. *The League of Nations and the Rule of Law 1918–1935*. London: Macmillan, 1936.

———. "The League's Handling of the Italo-Abyssinian Dispute." *International Affairs* (London) 14 (November–December 1935): 751–68.

Zinkin, Taya. "The Background to Indo-Pakistani Relations." *International Relations* 9 (May 1987): 31–38.

Ziring, Lawrence. *Pakistan, The Enigma of Political Development*. Boulder, CO: Westview Press, 1980.

Zook, David H. *The Conduct of the Chaco War*. New York: Bookman Associates, 1960.

Zubok, Vladislav M. "Khrushchev's Nuclear Promise to Beijing during the 1958 Crisis." *CWIHP. Bulletin* 6–7 (winter 1995–96): 219, 226–27.

———. "'Dismayed by the Actions of the Soviet Union': Mikoyan's Talks with Fidel Castro and the Cuban Leadership, November 1962." *CWIHP. Bulletin* 5 (spring 1995): 59, 89–109.

———. "Khrushchev and the Berlin Crisis (1958–1962)." Washington, DC: Woodrow Wilson International Center for Scholars. *CWIHP*. Working Paper No. 6, 1993.

Name Index

Note: The designation indicated for many of the names in this index—president, foreign minister, general, etc.—refers to their position/status at the time of the crisis in which the person was involved.

A. H. H., 603, 910
Abacha, S., Nigerian general, military ruler, 482, 492
Abdolali, N., 803, 896
ʿAbd-ul-ʿAziz ibn ʾAbd-ul-Rahman ("Ibn Saʿud"), Najd ruler, 629, 630, 633
Abdulghani, J., 305, 309, 910
Abdullah, Jordanian king, 270, 910
Abel, E., 353, 910
Abidi, A., 270, 910
Abir, M., 330, 910
Abu Nidal (al-Banna, S), leader of the Palestinian Al-Fatah Revolutionary Command, 472
Acheson, D., U.S. secretary of state, 213, 214, 339, 341, 343, 353, 368, 380, 430, 603, 910
Ackerman, A., 58
Acosta, J., Costa Rican president, 133
Acyle, A., Chadian foreign minister, 90
Adamec, L., 148, 537, 910
Adams, M., 277, 910
Adams, N., 187, 191, 910
Adams, T., 369, 910
Adamthwaite, A., 429, 910
Adan, A., 289, 910
Adkin, M., 529, 910
Adloff, R., 85, 121, 967
Adomeit, H., 32, 343, 351, 867, 887, 910
Adoula, C., Congolese premier, 435
Agrell, W., 613, 910
Agung, I., 205, 210, 910
Agwani, M., 640, 910
Ahidjo, A., Cameroonian president, 461
Ahlström, C., 895, 906
Ahmad, Yemeni Imam, 324

Ait-Ahmad, H., Algerian rebel leader, 438
Ajomo, A., 291, 911
Albrecht-Carrié, R., 590, 911
Albright, D., 933, 969
Alcalá Zamora, N., Spanish president, 262
Alexander, H., British field marshal, 250
Alexander, G., 337, 911
Alexander, R., 345, 911
Alexander, Y., 280, 911
Alexander, Yugoslav king, 587–89, 614
Ali, C. M., Pakistani prime minister, 149
Alker, H., 901, 907
Allan, P., 37, 887
Allen, R., 553, 911
Allison, G., 31, 37, 353, 887, 911
Allyn, B., 353, 911
Alperovitz, G., 423, 911
Amanullah, Afghan king, 536
Ambrose, S., 348, 911
ʿAmer, ʾAbd-ul-Hakim, Egyptian field marshal, 641
Amer, R., 202, 358, 455, 529, 532, 895, 906, 911
Ameringer, C., 134, 911
Amin, H., Afghan deputy prime minister, 356, 357
Amin, I., Ugandan president, 290, 448, 449, 450, 453, 454, 455
Amoo, S., 91, 911
Amstutz, B., 358, 911
An, T.-S., 202, 555, 911
Anbari, A. al-, Iraqi UN permanent representative, 320
Anderson, D., 182, 911
Anderson, E., 351, 911

Sa'id, N. al-, Iraqi prime minister, 277, 638
Said, A., 779, 899
Saito, H., Japanese ambassador to the U.S., 540
Salazar, A. de O., Portuguese premier, 68, 550, 960
Salek, M., Mauritanian military ruler, 123–24
Saliba, S., 280, 960
Salih, K., 368, 960
Sallal, A. al-, Yemeni president, 324, 326, 327, 328
Sallato, H. C., Chilean foreign minister, 521
Samatar, S., 440, 945
Sampson, N., Cypriot president, 370
Sandino, A., Nicaraguan revolutionary general, 142
Sandler, M., 202, 960
Sandys, D., British commonwealth secretary, 367
Sanjurjo, J., Spanish rebel general, 262
Sankara, T., Upper Voltan/Burkino Fasan president, 473
Sansom, G., 423, 960
Santos, J. E. dos, Angolan president, 79, 81, 83
Saperstein, A., 38, 899
Sapin, B., 31, 900
Sardesai, D., 559, 920
Sarit, Thai field marshal, military ruler, 186
Sa'ud ibn 'Abd-ul-'Aziz, King of Sa'udi Arabia, 638
Sauvy, A., 242, 960
Savimbi, J., Angolan UNITA movement leader, 82, 83
Sawyer, A., Liberian interim government head, 486
Sayrs, L., 839, 899
Schaefer, L., 427, 960
Schandler, H., 191, 960
Schatzberg, M., 73, 960
Schechterman, B., 780, 899
Schell, O., 154, 383, 961
Schick, J., 351, 960
Schiff, Z., 279, 290, 297, 914, 960

Schleicher, J., xix
Schlesinger, A., 187, 351, 354, 445, 961
Schmidt, D., 325, 961
Schneider, R., 345, 961
Schöber, J., Austrian chancellor, 581
Schoenbaum, T., 191, 214, 271, 282, 339, 343, 351, 354, 512, 961
Schoenfeld, A., 338, 961
Schofield, R., 318, 961
Schonfield, H., 430, 961
Schraeder, P., 961
Schroeder, P., 407, 961
Schroter, H., 409, 961
Schueftan, D., 282, 961
Schulenberg, F. von der, German ambassador to the Soviet Union, 389
Schuman, F., 24, 230, 231, 235, 244, 249, 264, 395, 396, 398, 427, 589, 590, 591, 592, 594, 595, 597, 899, 961
Schurmann, F., 154, 383, 961
Schurz, W., 499, 961
Schuschnigg, K., Austrian chancellor, 591–92
Schwab, P., 100, 961
Schwarzkopf, N., U.S. general, 318, 961
Schwebach, V., 803, 897
Sciolino, E., 318, 961
Scobie, British general, 600
Scobie, W., 369, 929
Scott, F., 579, 961
Scranton, M., 532, 961
Seale, P., 273, 346, 961
Seaton, A., 409, 961
Seekins, D., 358, 954
Segal, D., 305, 961
Segal, G., 160, 216, 385, 387, 552, 962
Segna, T., Georgian prime minister, 569
Selassie, B., 440, 962
Sella, A., xix
Selter, K., Estonian foreign minister, 391, 596
Senghor, L., Senegalese president, 436, 459
Sen Gupta, J., 174, 962
Seton-Watson, H., 338, 339, 962
Seyss-Inquart, A., Austrian chancellor, 591, 592

Subject Index

Note: Crisis case numbers are listed in parentheses after each crisis title when it appears as a main entry. In addition to the Subject Index, readers are advised to make full use of the Master Table of Crises, 1918–1994, pp. 659–737.

WSLF
Ogaden I (282), 99–100
Todghere Incident (373), 102

Yemen, 41
background to Yemen protracted con-
flict, 324
involvement in other crises, 320, 636
Sa'udi/Yemen War (44), 632–33, 672t
UN Observer Mission, 326
Yemen/Egypt Joint Defense Pact, 325
Yemen War I (195), 324–25, 700t
Yemen War II (209), 325–26, 704t
Yemen War III (212), 326–27, 704t
Yemen War IV (219), 327–29, 706t
Yemen protracted conflict, 324–31. *See
also* North Yemen; South Yemen;
Yemen
Yemen War I (195), 700t
summary, 324–25
Yemen War II (209), 704t
summary, 325–26
Yemen War III (212), 704t
summary, 326–27
Yemen War IV (219), 706t
summary, 327–29
Yugoslavia, xviii, 24, 27, 42, 779. *See
also* Italy/Albania/Yugoslavia pro-
tracted conflict
Albanian Frontier (23), 245–46, 670t
Assassination of King Alexander (46),
587–89, 672t
Austria Putsch (45), 586–87, 672t
Austrian Separatists (22), 581–82, 668t
background to Italy/Albania/Yugoslavia
protracted conflict, 245
Balkan Invasions (83), 400–402, 682t
Hegemony over Albania (34), 246–47,
670t
involvement in other crises, 70, 201,
213, 214, 242, 282, 336, 337, 426,
584, 585, 595, 607, 617–24, 635
Karl's Return to Hungary (21), 579–
81, 668t
Remilitarization of Rhineland (51),
242–44, 674t
Soviet Bloc/Yugoslavia (131), 602–3,
690t

Trieste I (104), 249–51, 684t
Trieste II (142), 251–52, 692t
Yugoslavia I: Croatia, Slovenia (397),
613–17, 736t
Yugoslavia I: Croatia, Slovenia (397),
736t
summary, 613–17
UN Resolution, 616, 617, 713
Yugoslavia II: Bosnia (403), 736t
summary, 617–24
Dayton Accord, 624
Geneva Conference, 621–22
Statement of Basic Principles, 624
UN Protection Force (UNPROFOR),
619, 620, 621, 622, 623, 624
UN Resolution 757, 620
Union of Three Republics, 622
Vance-Owen Peace Plan, 621, 622, 623

Zaire. *See also* Congo
Foreign Intervention in Zaire (399),
489–90, 736t
involvement in other crises, 91, 93, 95,
126, 485, 486
Shaba I (277), 72–73, 716t
Shaba II (292), 75–76, 718t
War in Angola (260), 69–72, 714t
Zambia, 45t
Air Rhodesia Incident (293), 113–14,
718t
Caprivi Strip (244), 447, 710t
involvement in other crises, 75, 81,
102–3, 107, 108, 109, 113, 440,
446, 454, 471, 479
Raids on ZIPRA (300), 114–15, 720t
Rhodesia Raid (283), 111–12, 716t
Rhodesia Settlement (307), 115–17,
720t
Rhodesia's UDI (218), 104–6, 706t
South Africa Cross-Border Raid (365),
477–78, 730t
War in Angola (260), 69–72, 714t
Zambia Raid (250), 106–7, 712t
Zambia Raid (250), 712t
summary, 106–7
ZANLA, 104
Chimoio-Tembue Raids (286), 112–13
Mapai Seizure (278), 110–11